AutoCAD 2025 For Beginners

CADFolks

For Resource files, visit:

https://autocadforbeginners.weebly.com

For Technical Support, contact us at:
online.books999@gmail.com

Table of Contents

Introduction

Computer-Aided Design (CAD) is a process that utilizes computers for designing and drafting components. This process involves creating designs and drawings for products or systems.

AutoCAD, developed and sold by Autodesk Inc., is a CAD software that allows users to create both two-dimensional (2D) and three-dimensional (3D) models of products. These models can be sent to other computer programs for further analysis and testing. Additionally, these computer models can be converted into numerical data, which manufacturing equipment like machining centers, lathes, mills, or rapid prototyping machines can use to produce the product.

First released in 1982, AutoCAD was among the early CAD software programs. Since its introduction, it has grown to be the leading CAD product in the industry, making it the most commonly used CAD software. Many other systems have adopted the commands and ideas that AutoCAD introduced. For students, learning AutoCAD provides a significant benefit over learning other CAD software, due to its widespread adoption and influence.

Scope of this Book

The '**AutoCAD 2025 for Beginners**' book is a practical guide for users to learn AutoCAD. It's designed for students and engineers who wish to use AutoCAD 2025 for creating designs and drawings, or anyone who uses technical drawings in their work. The book covers the following topics:

- Chapter 1, 'Introduction to AutoCAD 2025', provides an overview of AutoCAD, its user interface, and the terminology used.

- Chapter 2, 'Drawing Basics', introduces the fundamental drawing tools in AutoCAD. You'll create simple drawings using these tools.

- Chapter 3, 'Drawing Aids', discusses the drawing settings that assist you in creating drawings.

- Chapter 4, 'Editing Tools', covers the tools needed to modify drawing objects or create new ones from existing ones.

- Chapter 5, 'Multi View Drawings', guides you on how to create multi-view drawings using standard projection techniques.

- Chapter 6, 'Dimensions and Annotations', instructs you on how to apply dimensions and annotations to a drawing.

- Chapter 7, 'Parametric Tools', shows you how to create parametric drawings. These are drawings made using logical operations and parameters that control the shape and size of a drawing.

- Chapter 8, 'Section Views', teaches you how to create section views of a component. A section view shows the inside of a component when it's cut open.

- Chapter 9, 'Blocks, Attributes, and Xrefs', instructs you on how to create Blocks, Attributes, and Xrefs. Blocks are groups of objects in a drawing that can be reused. Attributes are notes or values associated with an object. Xrefs are drawing files attached to another drawing.

- Chapter 10, 'Layouts and Annotative Objects', guides you on how to create layouts and annotative objects. Layouts are the digital counterparts of physical drawing sheets. Annotative objects are dimensions and notes that change their sizes according to the drawing scale.

- Chapter 11, 'Templates and Plotting', instructs you on how to create drawing templates and plot drawings.

- Chapter 12, '3D Modeling Basics', introduces the basic tools to create 3D models.

- Chapter 13, 'Solid Editing Tools', covers the tools needed to edit solid models and create new ones from existing ones.

- Chapter 14, 'Creating Architectural Drawings', introduces you to architectural design in AutoCAD. You'll design a floor plan, staircase, elevations, roof plan, and details of roofs and walls.

Chapter 1: Introduction to AutoCAD 2025

In this chapter, you will learn about:

- **AutoCAD user interface**
- **Customizing user interface**
- **Important AutoCAD commands**

Introduction

AutoCAD is a legendary software in the world of Computer Aided Designing (CAD). It has completed 42 years by 2024. If you are a new user of this software, then the time you spend on learning this software will be a wise investment. If you have used previous versions of AutoCAD, you will be able to learn the new enhancements. I welcome you to learn AutoCAD using this book through step-by-step examples to learn various commands and techniques.

System requirements

The following are system requirements for running AutoCAD smoothly on your system.

- 64-bit Microsoft® Windows® 11 and Windows 10 version 1809 or above.
- CPU Type:
    - Basic: 2.5 to 2.9 gigahertz (GHz)
    - Recommended: 3+ GHz processor (base), 4+ GHz (turbo)
- 8 GB of RAM (32 GB Recommended).
- Resolution 1920 x 1080 or higher recommended with True Color.
- Resolutions up to 3840 x 2160 supported on Windows 10, 64 bit systems (with capable display card) for High Resolution & 4K Displays.
- 10 GB of free space for installation.
- Google Chrome Browser.
- .NET Framework Version 8

Starting AutoCAD 2025

To start **AutoCAD 2025**, double-click the **AutoCAD 2025** icon on your Desktop (or) click **Start > All apps > AutoCAD 2025 > AutoCAD 2025**.

AutoCAD user interface

When you double-click the AutoCAD 2025 icon on the desktop, the AutoCAD 2025 Start screen appears. On the Start Screen, click the **New** button to open a new drawing file. The drawing file consists of a graphics window, ribbon, menu bar, toolbars, command line, and other screen components, depending on the workspace that you have selected.

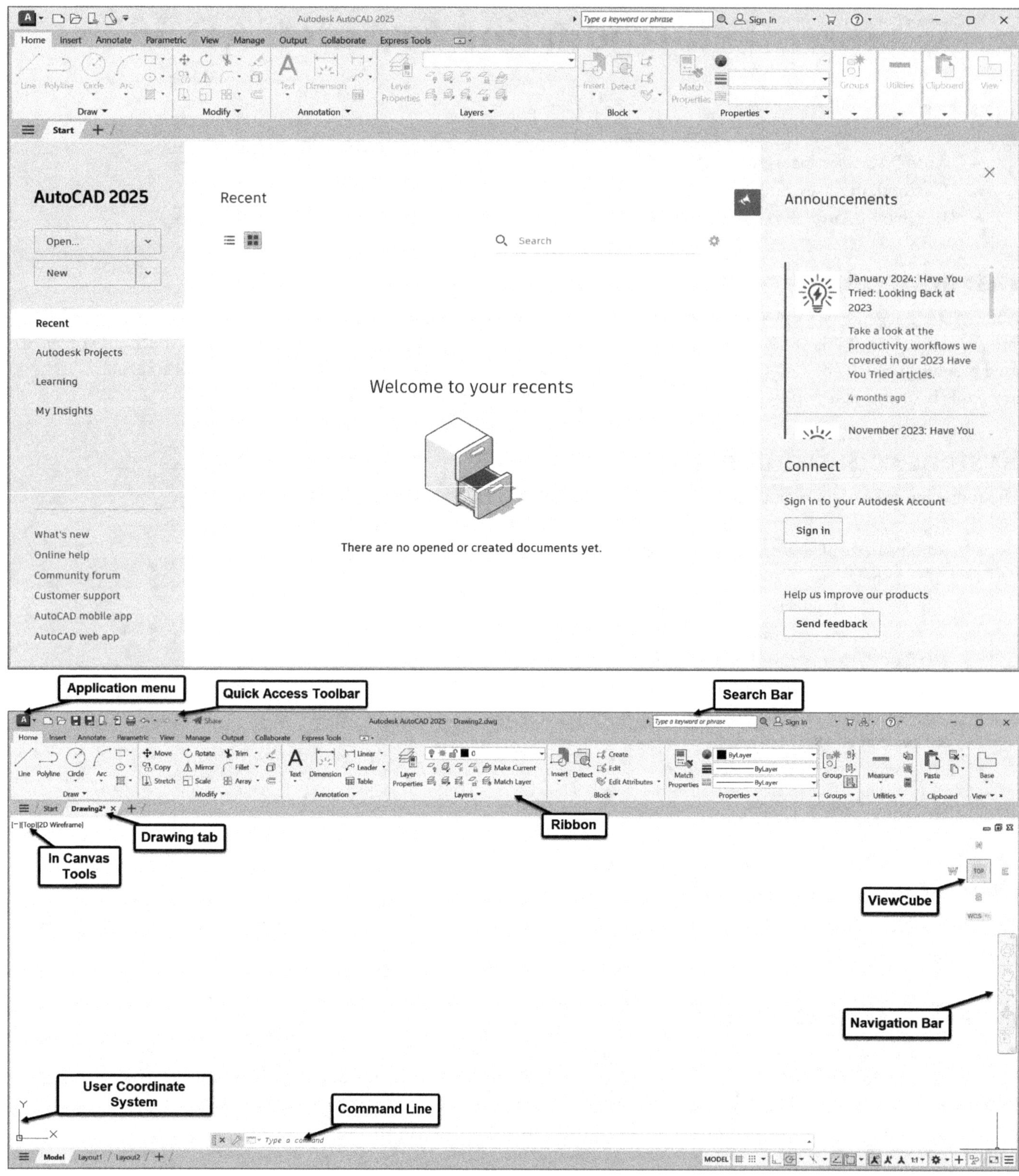

Application menu
Quick Access Toolbar
Search Bar
Ribbon
Drawing tab
In Canvas Tools
ViewCube
Navigation Bar
User Coordinate System
Command Line

Changing the Color theme

AutoCAD 2025 is available in two different color themes: **Dark** and **Light**. You can change the Color theme by using the **Options** dialog. Click the right mouse button and select **Options** from the shortcut menu. On the **Options** dialog, click the **Display** tab and select an option from the **Color theme** drop-down.

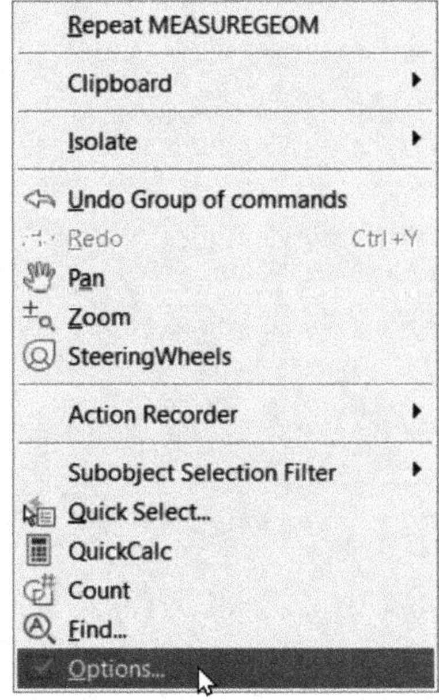

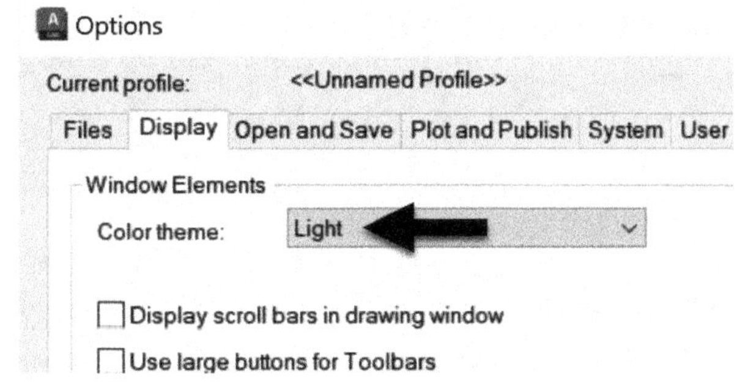

Workspaces in AutoCAD

There are three workspaces available in AutoCAD: **Drafting & Annotation**, **3D Basics**, and **3D Modeling**. By default, the **Drafting & Annotation** workspace is activated. You can create 2D drawings in this workspace. You can also enable other workspaces by using the **Workspace** drop-down on the top-left corner or the **Workspace Switching** menu on the lower-right corner of the window.

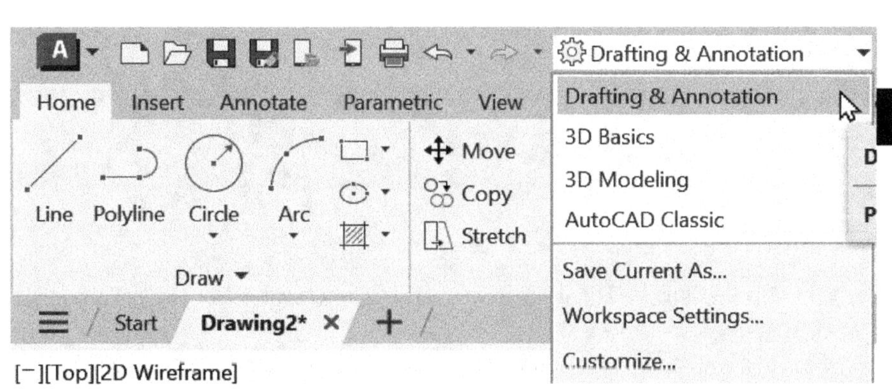

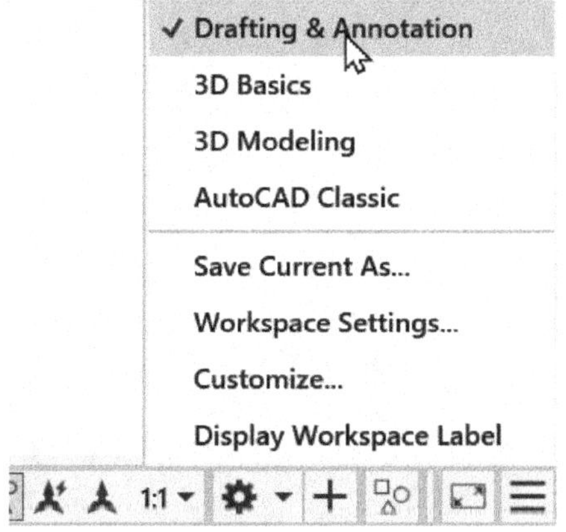

Tip: *If the **Workspace** drop-down is not displayed at the top left corner, then click the down arrow next to Quick Access Toolbar. Next, select **Workspace** from the drop-down; the **Workspace** drop-down will be visible on the Quick Access Toolbar.*

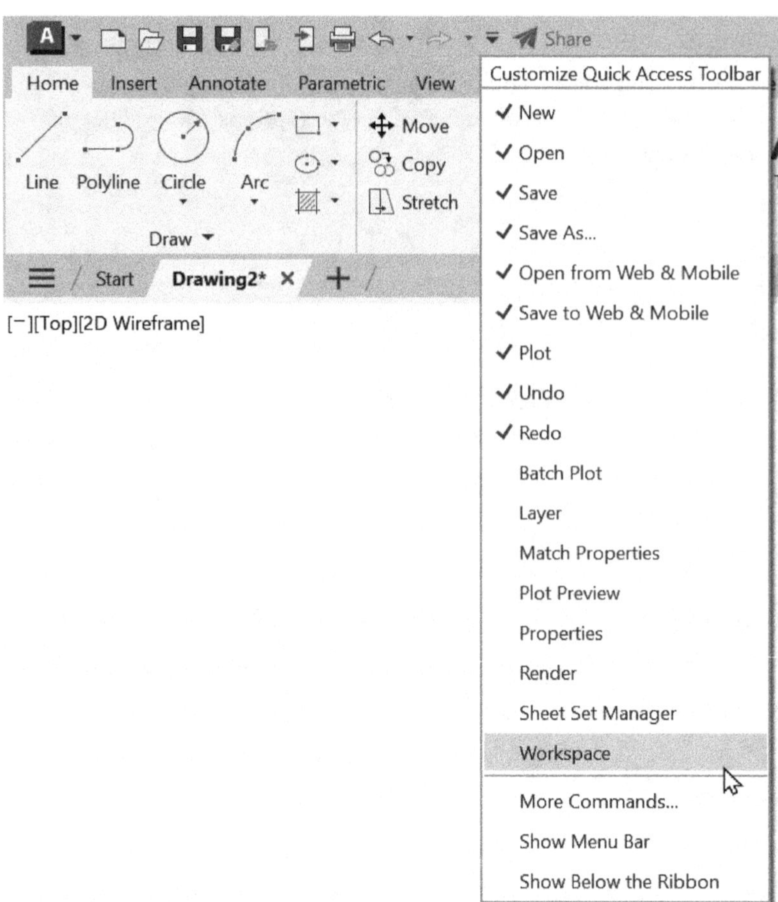

Drafting & Annotation Workspace

This workspace has all the tools to create a 2D drawing. It has a ribbon located at the top of the screen. The ribbon is arranged in a hierarchy of tabs, panels, and tools. Panels such as **Draw**, **Modify**, and **Layers** consist of tools that are grouped based on their usage. Panels, in turn, are grouped into various tabs. For example, the panels, such as **Draw**, **Modify**, and **Layers**, are located in the **Home** tab.

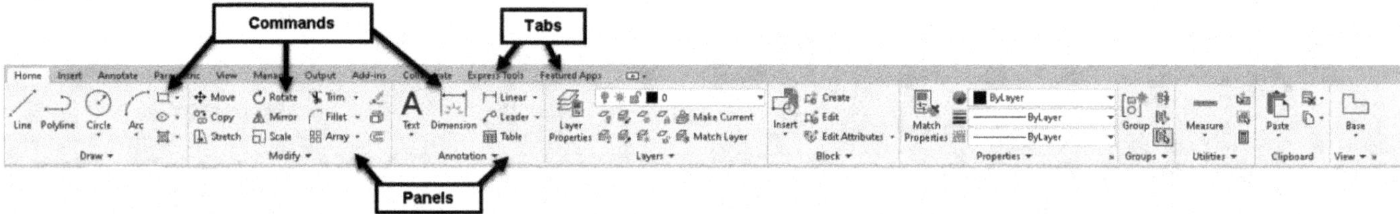

3D Basics and 3D Modeling Workspaces

These workspaces are used to create 3D models. You will learn more about these workspaces in Chapter 12. The other components of the user Interface are discussed next.

Application Menu

The **Application Menu** appears when you click on the icon located at the top left corner of the window. The **Application Menu** consists of a list of options such as **New**, **Open**, **Save**, and **Print** on the left side. Place the pointer on any one of the options on the left side; a list of additional options is displayed on the right side. You can see a list of recently opened documents or a list of currently opened documents by clicking the **Recent Documents** and **Open Documents** buttons, respectively. The Search Bar is used to search for any command. You can type any keyword in the search bar and find a list of commands related to it. In addition to that, there are two buttons, **Options** and **Exit Autodesk AutoCAD 2025** located at the bottom of the **Application Menu**. You can use the **Options** button to open the **Options** dialog. In this dialog, you can specify various settings related to display, printing, and user preferences.

Quick Access Toolbar

The Quick Access Toolbar is located at the top left corner of the window and helps you to access commands quickly. It consists of commonly used commands such as **New**, **Save**, **Open**, **Save As**, **Open from Web & Mobile**, and **Save to Web & Mobile**.

File tabs

The File tabs are located underneath the ribbon at the top of the screen. These tabs help you work with different drawing files.

Switching Between Files

- To switch to a different file, click on its tab.
- To open a new file, click the "+" button.

Each open file has its own tab. The tab for the file you are currently working on is a lighter gray, while tabs for other open files are darker gray.

When you move your mouse over a tab:

- The location of the file on your computer appears below the tab.
- You will see the "model space" (the main drawing area) and any "layouts" (different views of your drawing) below that.
- A blue frame around the model space shows that it is the active view.

Switching to a Layout View

Move your mouse to the right side of the tab area. The layouts will appear in the main part of the screen. Click on a layout to switch to that view.

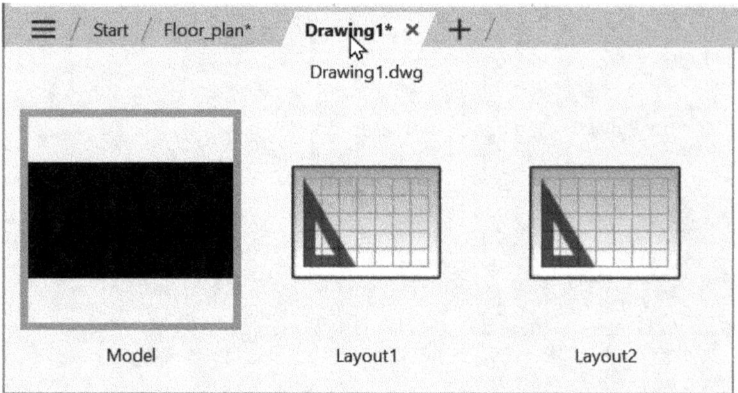

You have the flexibility to hide or display the **File** tabs and **Layout** tabs. To do this, navigate to the **View** tab, locate the **Interface** panel, and click on the respective buttons to switch them off.

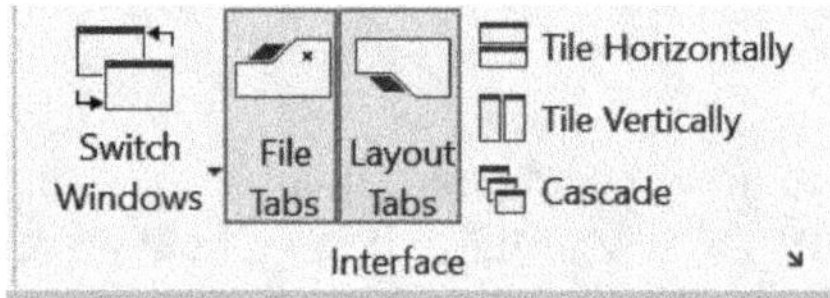

You can use the **File tab menu** located on the left side of the Drawing File tabs to switch between the file tabs, open, save, or close a drawing file tab.

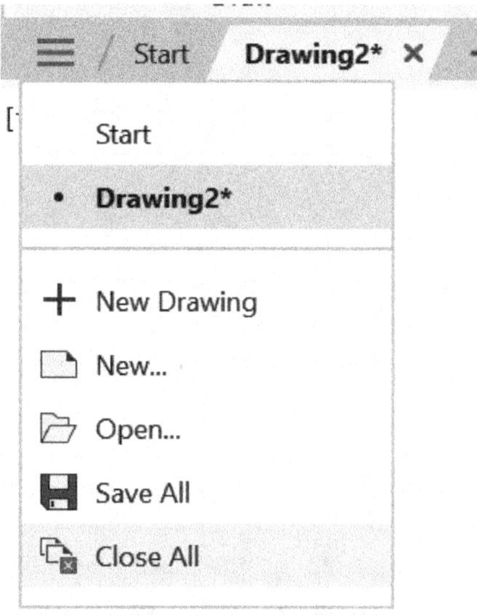

Graphics Window

The Graphics window is the blank space located below the file tabs. You can draw objects and create 3D graphics in the graphics window. The top left corner of the graphics window has **In-Canvas Controls**. Using these controls, you can set the orientation and display style of the model.

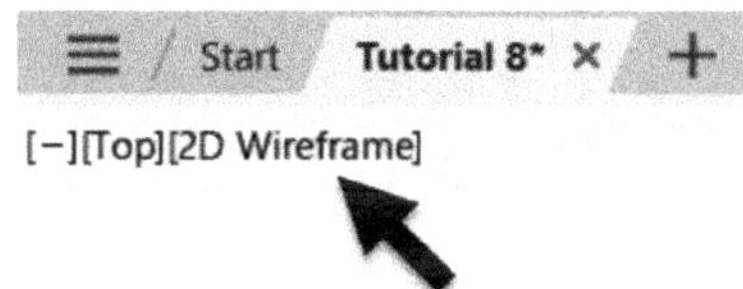

ViewCube

The ViewCube allows you to navigate in the 3D Modeling and 2D drafting environments. Using the ViewCube, you can set the orientation of the model. For example, you can select the top face of the ViewCube to set the orientation to Top. You can click the corner points to set the view to Isometric.

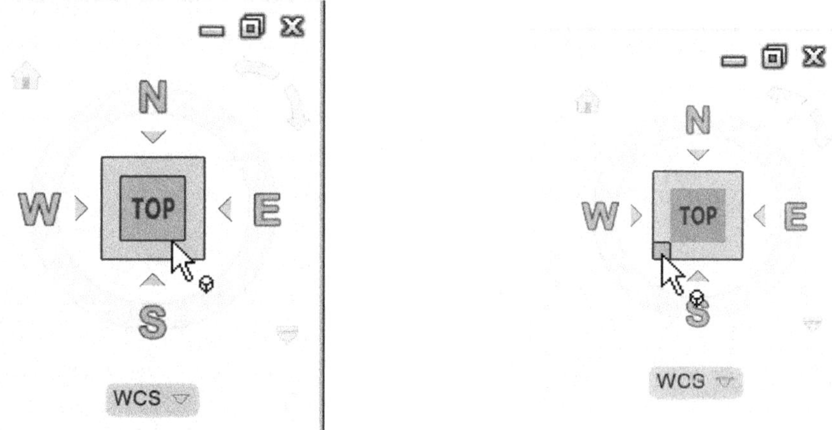

Navigation Bar

The Navigation Bar contains navigation tools such as **Steering wheel**, **Pan**, **Zoom**, **Orbit**, and **Show Motion**.

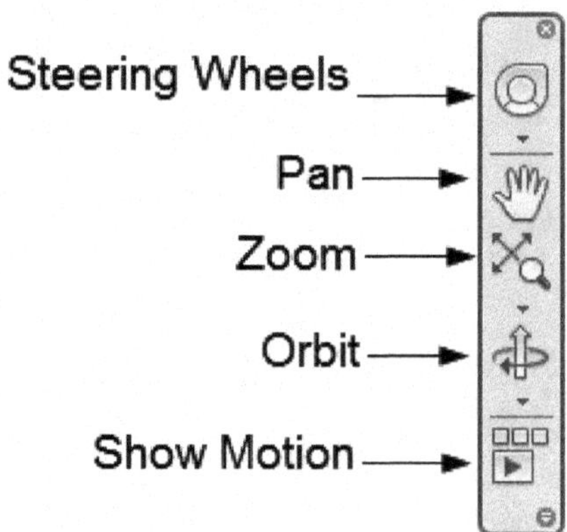

Command line

The command line is located below the graphics window. It is effortless to execute a command using the command line. You can just type the first letter of a command, and it lists all the commands starting with that letter. It helps you to activate commands very quickly and increases your productivity.

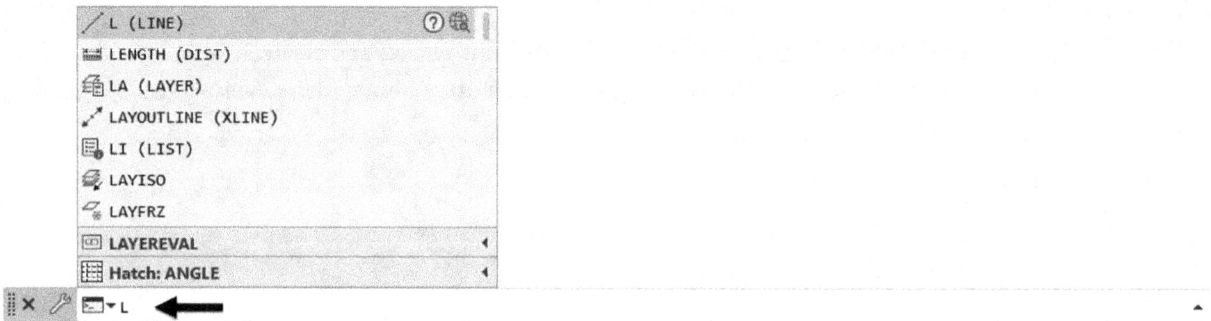

Also, the command line shows the current state of the drawing. It shows various prompts while working with any command. These prompts are a series of steps needed to execute a command successfully. For example, when you activate the LINE command, the command line displays a prompt, "Specify the first point." You need to click in the graphics window to specify the first point of the line. After defining the first point, the prompt, "Specify next point or [Undo]:" appears. Now, you need to determine the next end of the line. It is recommended that you should always have a look at the command line to know the next step while executing a command.

If the Command line is missing, you can use the shortcut Ctrl+9 (CMD+3 in AutoCAD for Mac) to toggle it on.

Furthermore, for adjusting the Command window's size and position:

Vertical Resizing: You can increase or decrease the vertical size of the Command window by dragging the splitter bar, located at the top edge of the window when docked at the bottom, and at the bottom edge when docked at the top. Make sure that a minimum of two lines of text are visible in the Command Window to make it easy to read.

Horizontal Resizing: To resize the window horizontally, simply drag the right or left edge of the Command window.

Moving the Command Window: Press and hold the left mouse button on the two vertical bars on the left of the window, then drag it to your desired location.

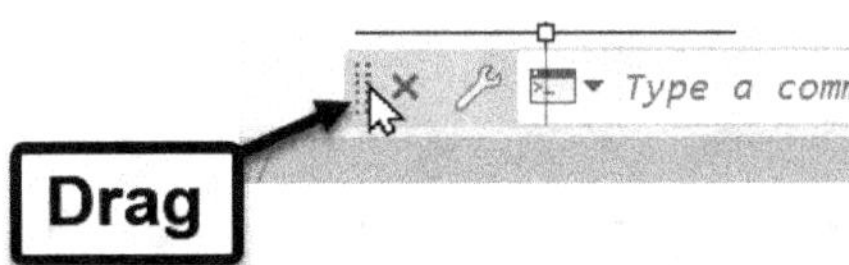

Floating or Docked: The Command window can either be floating or docked. To dock it, click and drag the window to your preferred location until it locks in place.

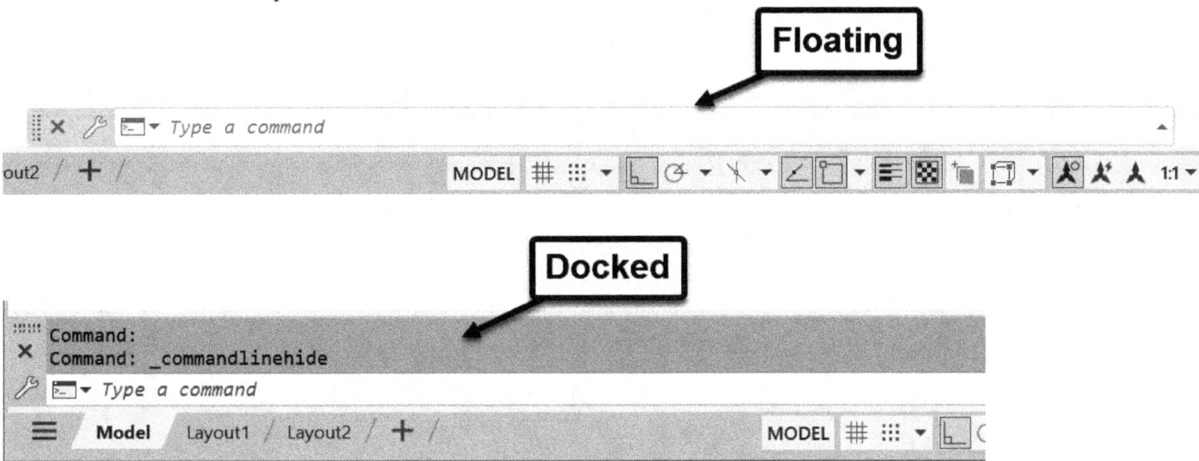

Transparency: If the Command window is floating, you can adjust its transparency. Click on the Customize icon, select Transparency, and set the Transparency Level in the dialog box that appears.

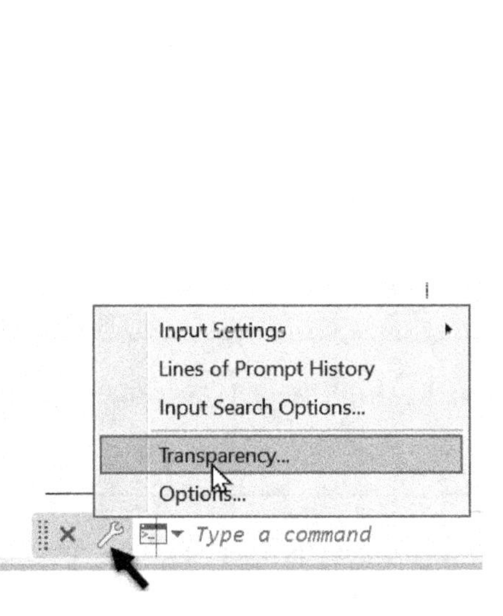

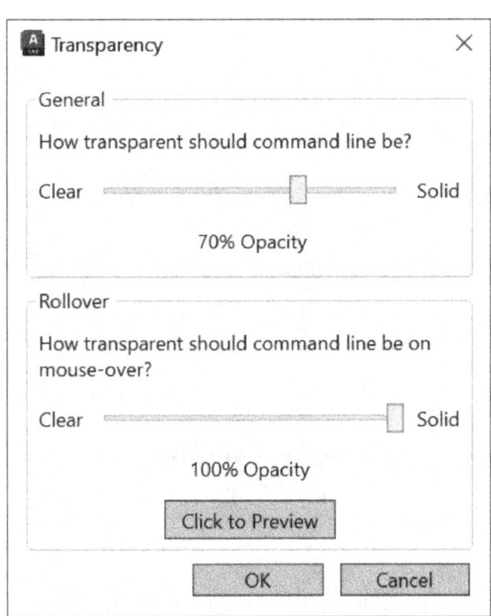

Status Bar

Status Bar is located at the bottom of the AutoCAD window. It contains many buttons which help you to create a drawing very easily. You can turn ON or OFF these buttons just by clicking on them. Some buttons are hidden by default. You can display more buttons on the status bar by clicking the **Customization** button at the bottom right corner and selecting the options from the menu. The buttons available on the status bar are briefly discussed in the following section.

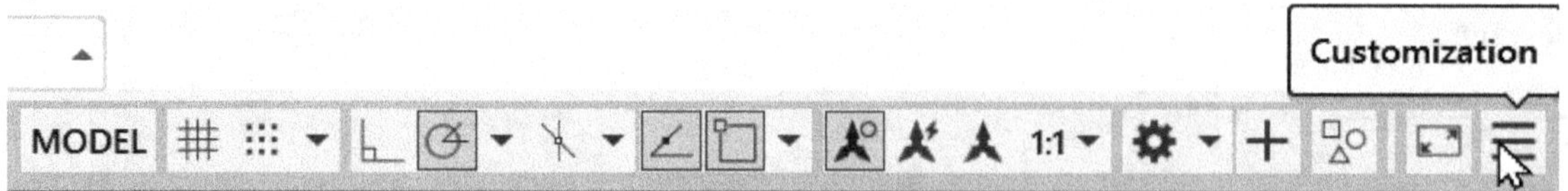

Button	Description
6505.7547, 178.4229, 0.0000 **Coordinates**	It displays the drawing coordinates when you move the pointer in the graphics window. You can turn OFF this button by clicking on it. If this button is not displayed, you can show it by using the **Customization** menu.
Infer Constraints	This icon automatically creates constraints when you draw objects in the graphics window. Constraints are logical operations that control the shape of a drawing. You can turn it ON or OFF by clicking on it.
Snap mode (F9)	The Snap mode aligns pointer only with the Grid points. When you turn ON this button, the pointer will be able to select only the Grid points.
GRIDMODE (F7)	It turns the Grid display ON or OFF. You can set the spacing between the grid lines by clicking the down arrow next to the Snap Mode button and selecting the **Snap Settings** option. You can use the grid lines along with the Snap Mode to draw objects quickly and accurately.
ORTHOMODE (F8)	It turns the Ortho Mode ON or OFF. When the Ortho Mode is ON, only horizontal or vertical lines can be drawn.
Polar Tracking (F10)	This icon turns ON or OFF the Polar Tracking. When the Polar Tracking is turned ON, you can draw lines quickly at regular angular increments, such as

5, 10, 15, 23, 30, 45, or 90 degrees. You will notice that a trace line is displayed when the pointer is at a particular angular increment. You can set the angular increment by clicking the down arrow next to this button and selecting the required angle.

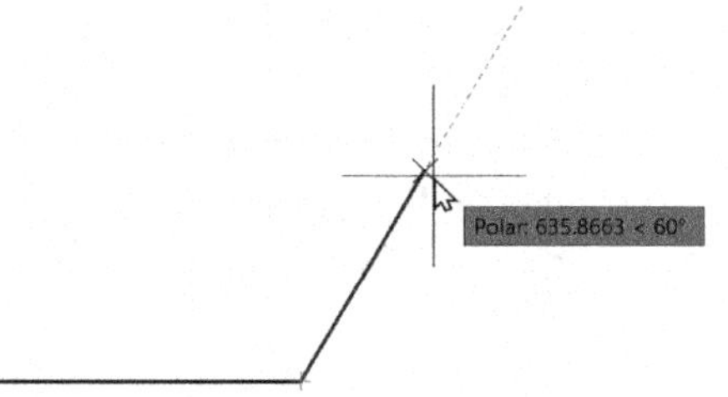

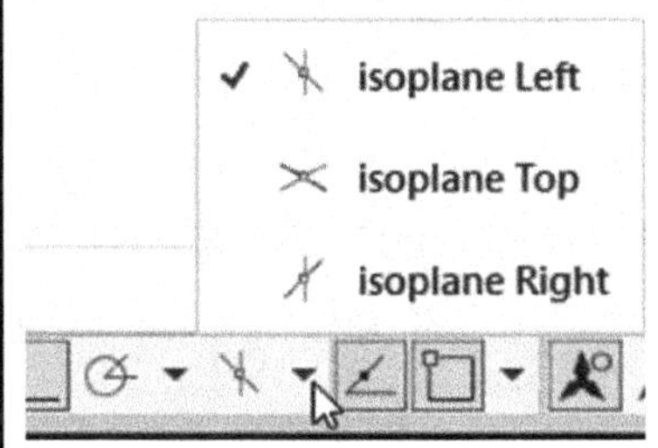

Isometric Drafting

This icon is used to switch between planes while drawing isometric views. The grid lines are also displayed if the Grid Mode is turned ON. The orientation of the grid lines changes based on the selected isoplane option.

Object Snap (F3)

This icon turns ON or OFF the Object Snap mode. When this mode is turned ON, you can easily select the key points of objects such as endpoints, midpoint, and center point. You can find it very useful while specifying exact points. Right-click on the Object Snap icon to display a flyout. On this flyout, you can view the list of all the object snaps. Select the required object snaps from this flyout to activate them. All the active object snaps have a check mark next to them. After activating the required object snaps, the pointer snaps to the activated object snaps based on its location.

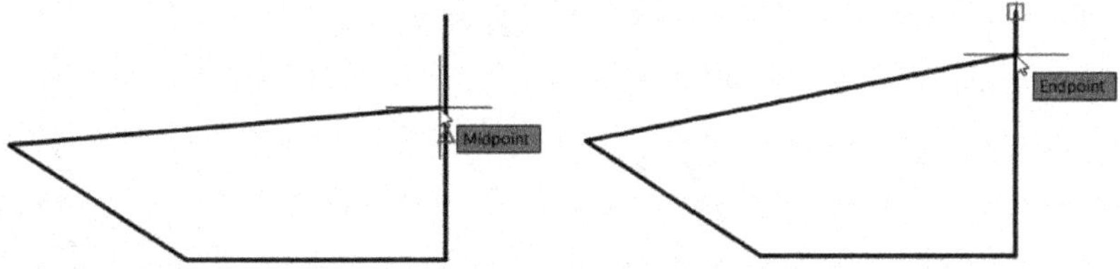

3D Object Snap (F4)

This icon turns ON or OFF the 3D Object Snap. The 3D Object Snap is used to select the key points of 3D objects.

 **Object Snap Tracking (F11)**

This icon is used to turn ON or OFF the Object Snap Tracking mode. When this mode is turned ON, you can easily select points by tracking the movement of the cursor along a line, arc, or other object. This helps you to specify complex points without creating dummy objects. You can use the Object Snap Tracking mode works in combination with the Object Snap mode to specify new points at a specific distance or angle from an existing object. In addition to these, the Object Snap Tracking mode displays the tracking lines when the cursor is aligned with any object or part of the drawing. The alignment angle can be 0, 90, 180, or 270 degrees.

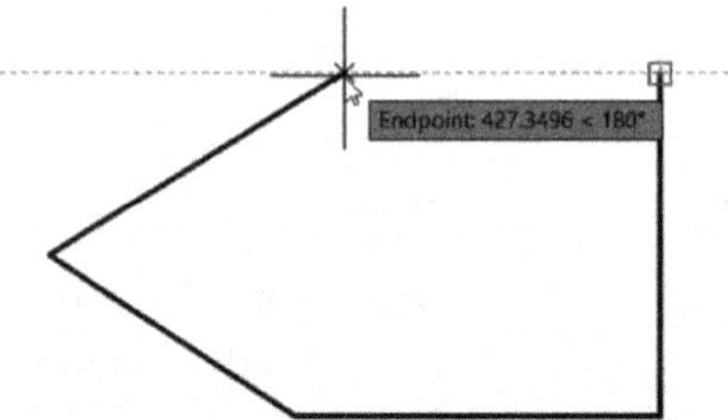

Dynamic UCS (F6)

This icon turns ON/OFF the Dynamic UCS. When the Dynamic UCS is turned ON, you can draw and create objects on any face of a 3D Model, dynamically.

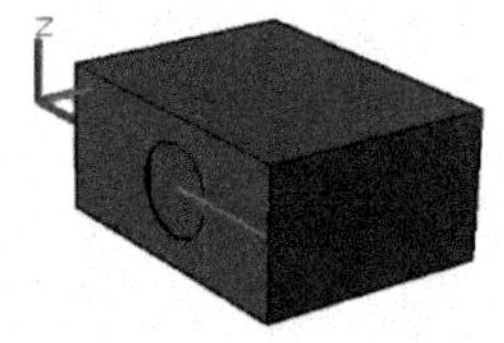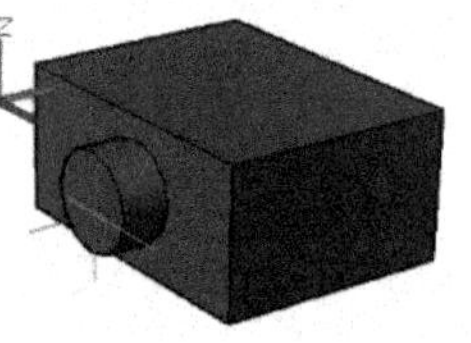

Dynamic Input (F12)

This icon turns ON or OFF the Dynamic Input mode. When this mode is turned ON, a dynamic input box is attached to the pointer along with a prompt. You can directly enter a value in the dynamic input box. You can use Dynamic Input in place of the command line.

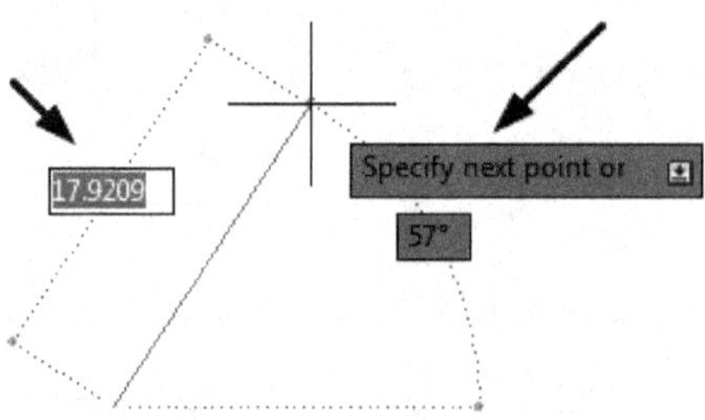

<table>
<tr><td>

Show/Hide Lineweight

</td><td>

This icon turns ON or OFF the lineweight. Line weight is the thickness of objects. You can set the thickness of objects by specifying the lineweight. If the Lineweight is turned OFF, the objects are displayed with the default thickness.

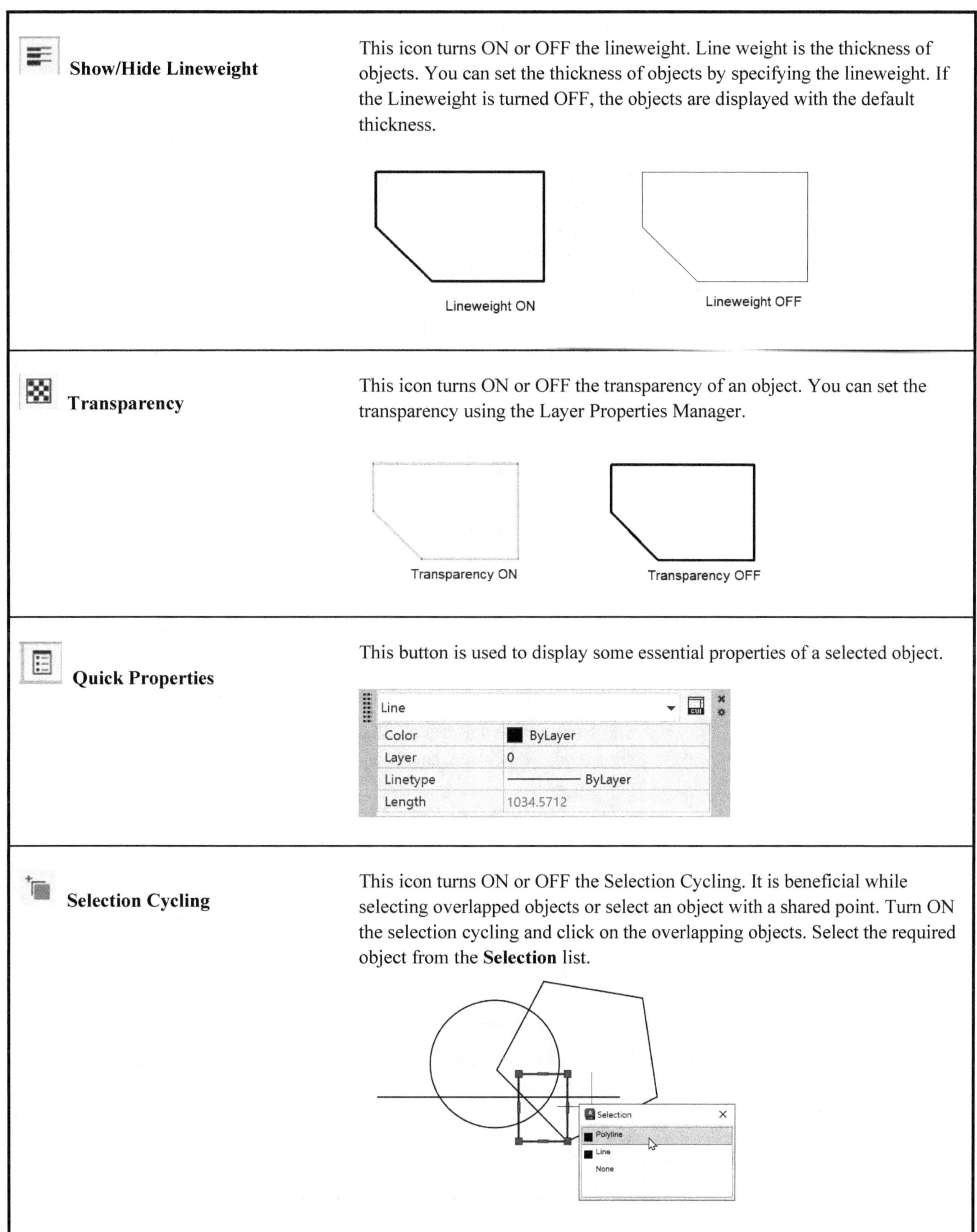

</td></tr>
<tr><td>

Transparency

</td><td>

This icon turns ON or OFF the transparency of an object. You can set the transparency using the Layer Properties Manager.

</td></tr>
<tr><td>

Quick Properties

</td><td>

This button is used to display some essential properties of a selected object.

</td></tr>
<tr><td>

Selection Cycling

</td><td>

This icon turns ON or OFF the Selection Cycling. It is beneficial while selecting overlapped objects or select an object with a shared point. Turn ON the selection cycling and click on the overlapping objects. Select the required object from the **Selection** list.

</td></tr>
</table>

	If you cannot find this icon, simply click on the **Customization** button at the right-hand side of the Status bar, represented by three horizontal dashes. By clicking it, you will reveal all the hidden buttons, including Selection Cycling. From there, select it and enable this useful feature.
Selection Filtering	This drop-down allows the filtering of the objects (Vertices, edges, faces, a solid history, or drawing view components) that can be selected from the graphics window. Select an option from the drop-down and click on the **Selection Filter** icon to activate the selected filters.
Annotation Monitor	This icon turns the Annotation Monitor ON or OFF. The Annotation Monitor checks whether the annotations are attached to their respective objects. When an annotation is not connected to any object, it displays an error message.
Model or Paper Space	This icon switches between the Model space and Paper space. Model space is used to create drawings, and Paper space is used to print drawings.
Annotation Scale	This icon controls the size of annotative objects. Annotative objects are dimensions, texts, notes, and other objects which can be sized as per the drawing scale.
Annotation Visibility	This icon displays annotative objects that are not created in the current scale.
AutoScale	This icon resizes the annotative objects as per the new drawing scale.

Workspace Switching	This icon changes the workspace.
UNITS	This drop-down allows you to set the units of the current drawing.
Hardware Acceleration On/Off	This icon increases or decreases the graphics speed. Right click on this icon and select **Graphics Performance** to display the **Graphics Performance** dialog. On this dialog, you can turn ON/OFF the Hardware acceleration. Click **OK** to close the dialog.
Isolate Objects	This icon hides or isolates objects in a drawing. If you hide an object, it will be hidden, and all the other objects in the drawing will be visible. If you isolate an object, the other objects in the drawing will be hidden, and the selected object will be visible.

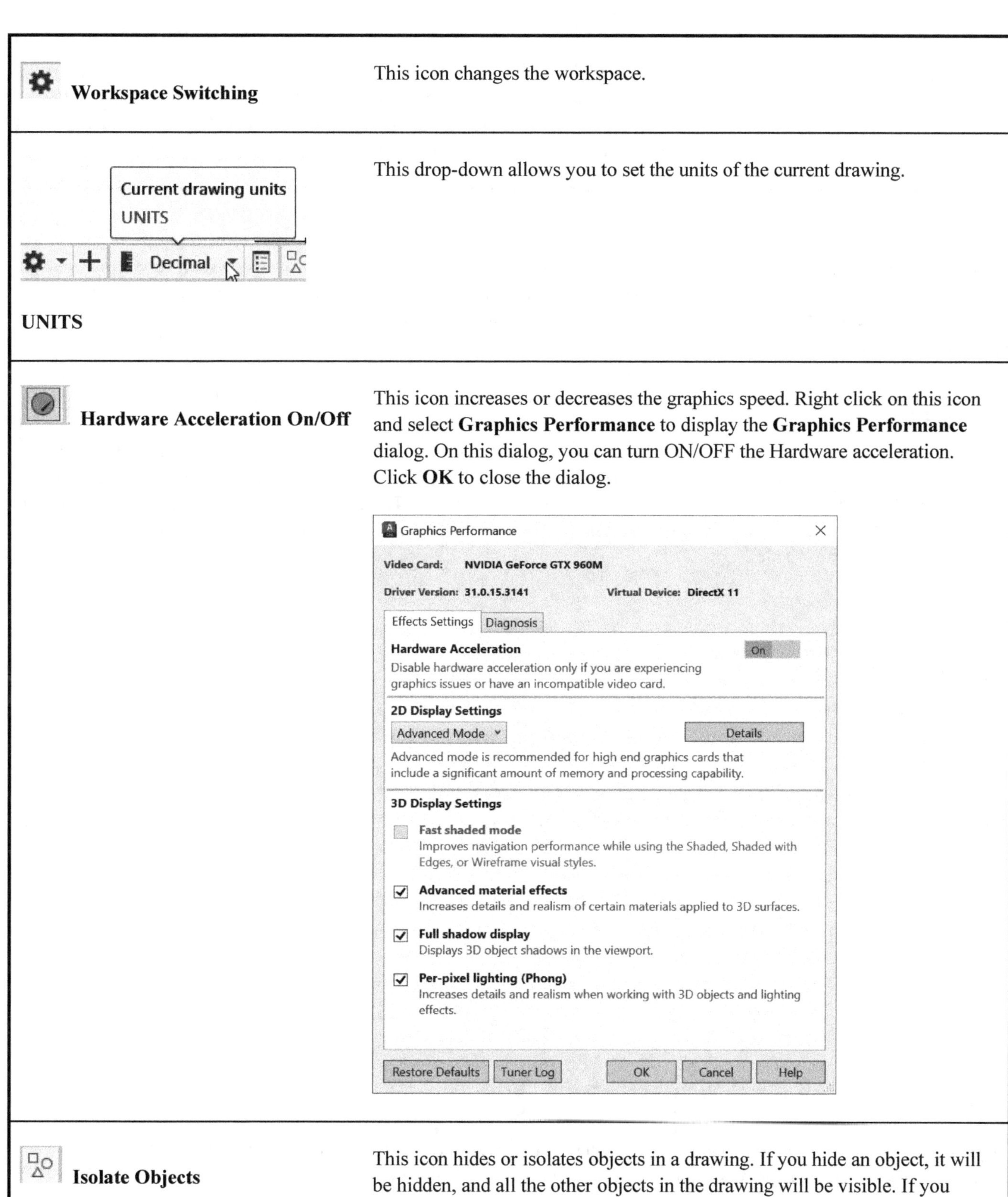

 **Lock UI** — This icon locks the toolbars, panel, tool palettes, and other User Interface elements at their current position. Click the down arrow next to this icon to view the options (**Floating Toolbars/Panels**, **Docked Toolbars/Panels**, **Floating Windows**, and **Docked Windows**) to lock the user interface.

System Variables

System variables control the behavior of various functions and commands in AutoCAD. Usually, system variables have two or more values. You can control a system variable value from the command line. For example, the MIRRTEXT system variable controls the direction of text when you mirror it. The 0 value retains the text direction when you mirror it. Whereas, the 1 value reverses the text direction when you mirror it.

In AutoCAD, you can also control the system variables by using the **System Variable Monitor** dialog. Type SYSVARMONITOR in the command line and press Enter to open this dialog. A list of system variables, which are monitored by default, appears on the dialog. You can know the function of a system variable by clicking the **Help** ❓ icon located next to it. You can change a system variable value in the **Preferred** column of the dialog. The **Status** column shows a yellow triangle if you have changed the default value of a system variable. The **Enable balloon notification** option shows a balloon on the status bar if you have changed any system variable value. You can click the **Reset All** button to restore the default values of system variables.

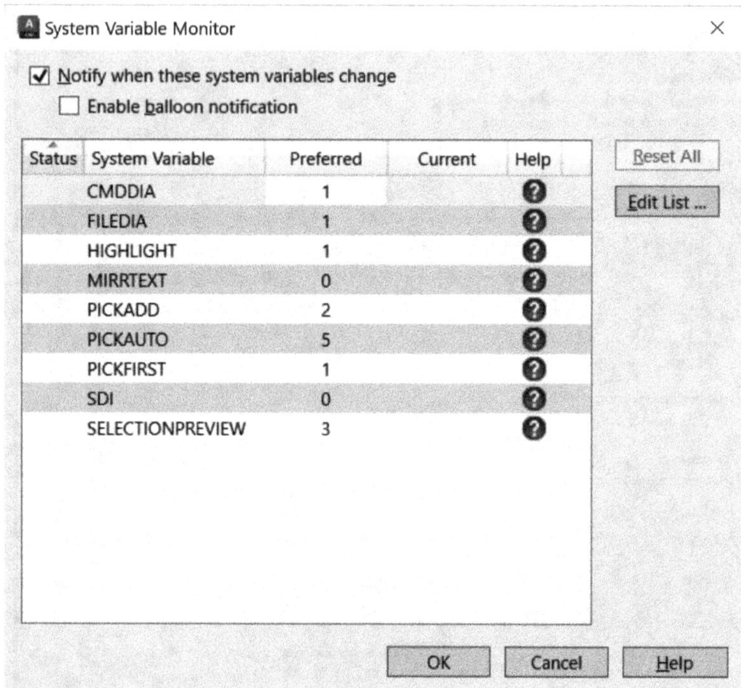

You can monitor more system variables by clicking the **Edit List** button. Next, on the **Edit System Variable List** dialog, select a system variable from the **Available system variables** list, and click the **Add** (>>) button. You can also remove system variables from the Monitored system variables list by selecting them and clicking the **Remove** (<<) button. Click **OK** on both the dialogs after changing the values.

In AutoCAD, the **System Variable Monitor** icon appears on the Status bar when you change the value of any one of the system variables. Right click on this icon to display a menu. The options on this menu are **Configure System Variable Monitor**, **Reset System Variables**, and **Display Notification**. The **Configure System Variable Monitor** option displays the **System Variable Monitor** dialog, whereas the **Reset System Variables** option resets the system variables to default values. The **Display Notification** option displays a balloon when there is a change in the value of any system variable.

Menu Bar

Menu Bar is not shown by default. However, you can view the Menu Bar by clicking on the down-arrow located on the right side of the Quick Access Toolbar and selecting the **Show Menu Bar** option. The Menu Bar is located at the top of the window just below the title bar. It contains various menus such as File, Edit, View, Insert, Format, Tools, Draw, Dimensions, Modify, and so on. Clicking on any of the words on the Menu Bar displays a menu. The menu contains various tools and options. There are also sub-options available on the list. These sub-options are displayed if you click on an option with an arrow. If you click on an option with (…), a dialog will appear.

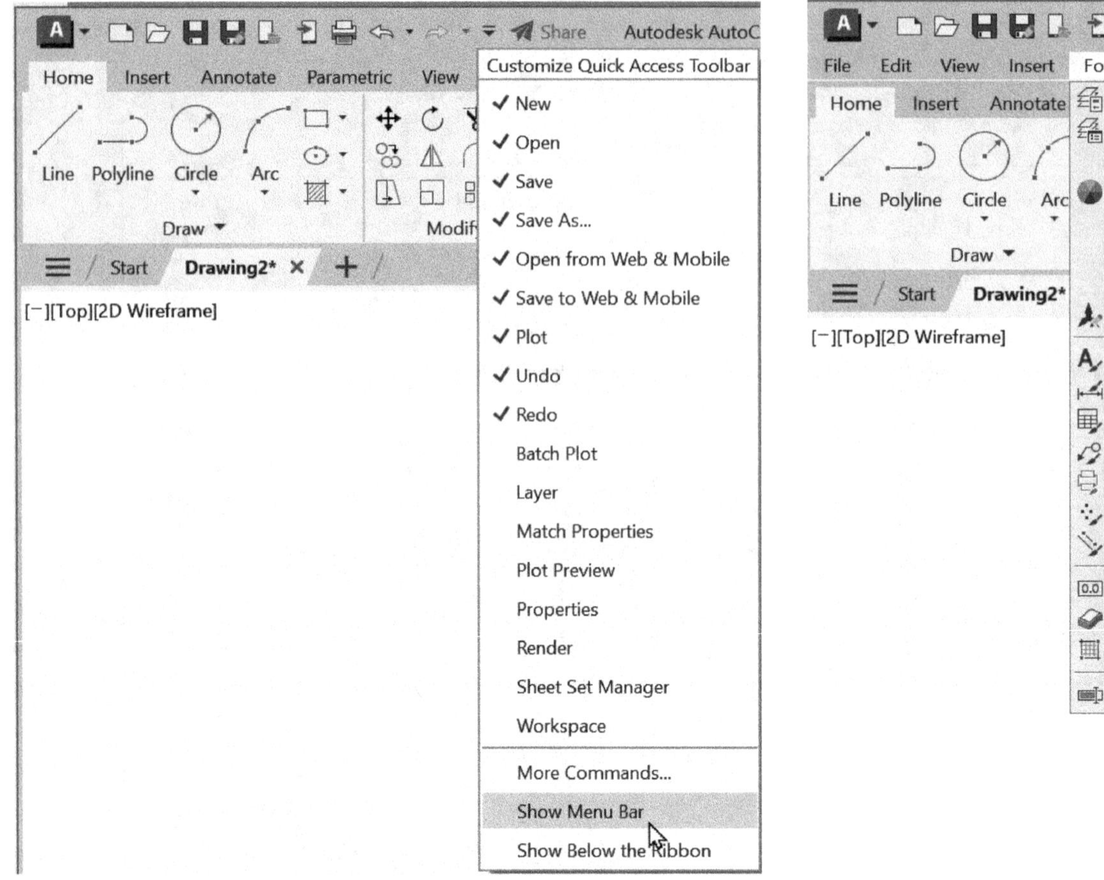

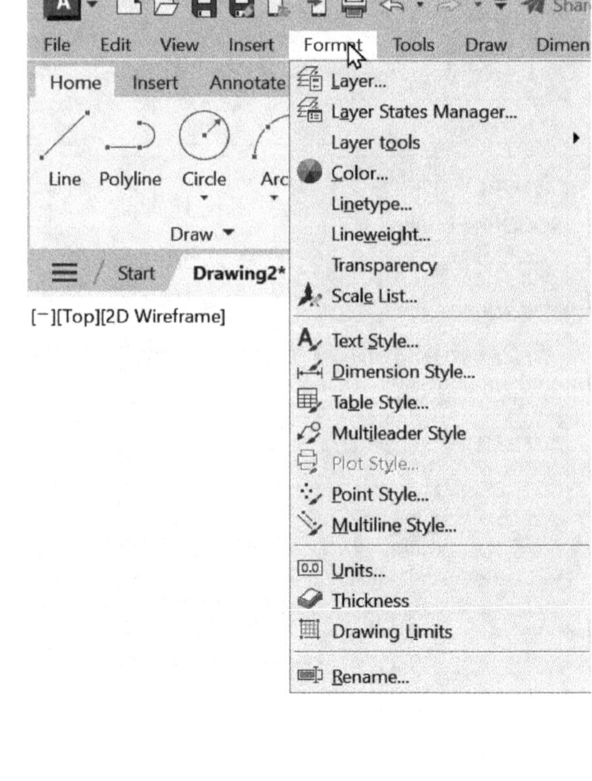

Changing the display of the Ribbon

You can change the presentation of the ribbon by clicking the arrow button located at the top of it. The ribbon can be displayed in three different modes, as shown below.

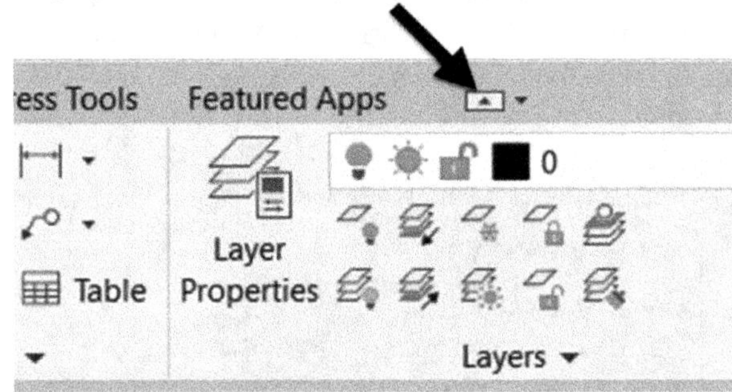

Minimized to Panel Buttons

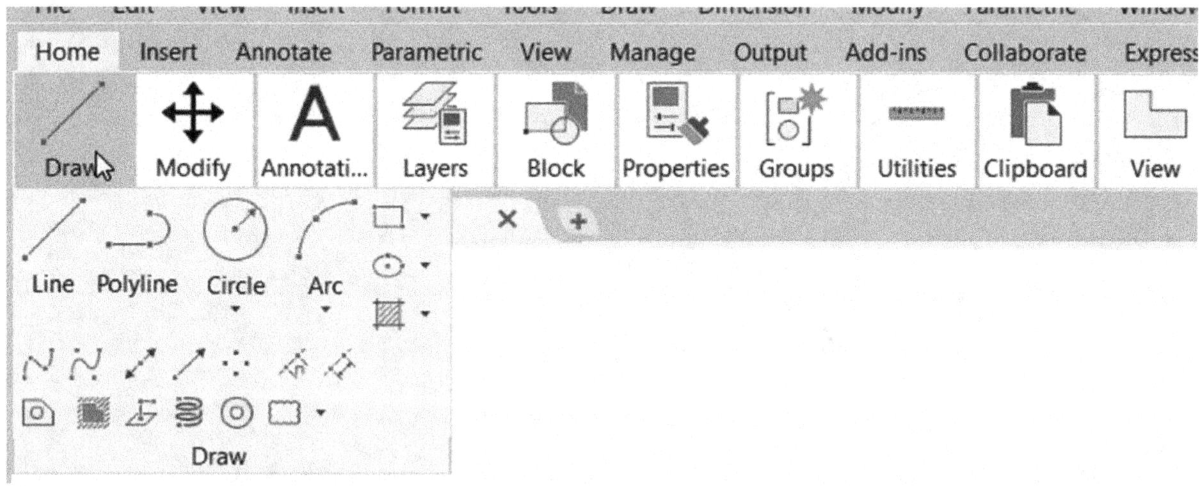

Minimized to Panel Titles

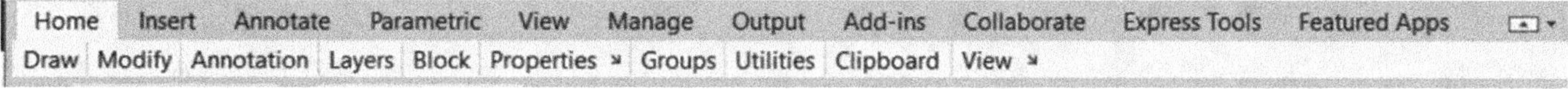

Minimized to Tabs

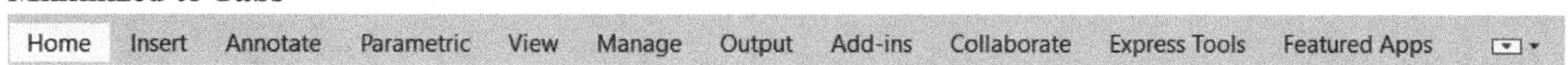

You can use the GALLERYVIEW system variable to hide or show galleries on the ribbon. Enter the GALLERYVIEW system variable in the command line and set the system variable value. The system variable value 1 displays a gallery for dimension styles, blocks, table styles, and mleader styles. The value 0 hides the gallery view.

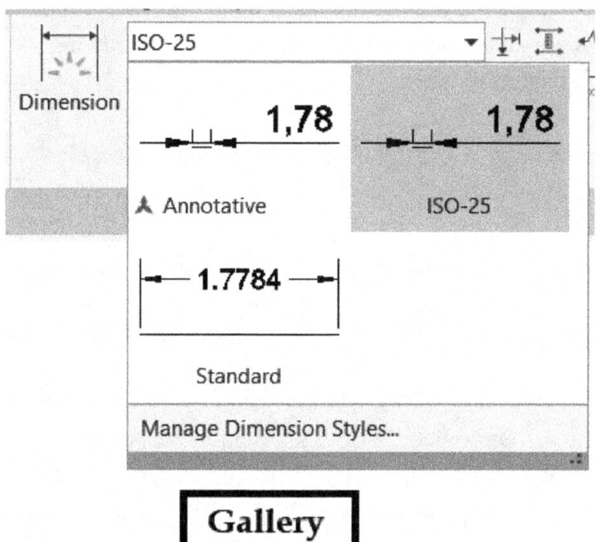

Gallery

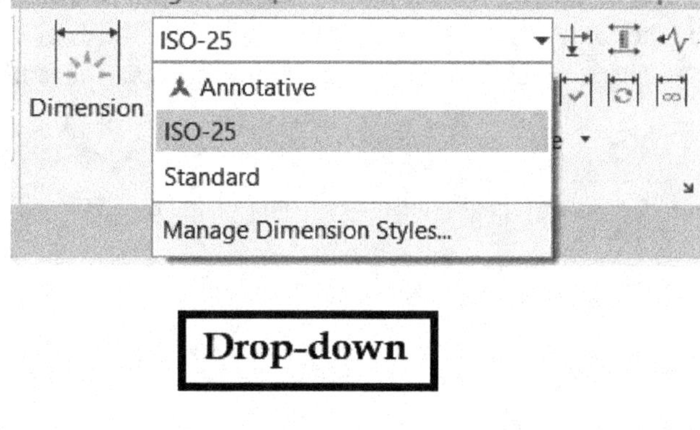

Drop-down

Dialogs and Palettes

Dialogs and Palettes are part of the AutoCAD user interface. Using a dialog or a palette, you can easily specify many settings and options at a time. Examples of dialogs and palettes are as shown below.

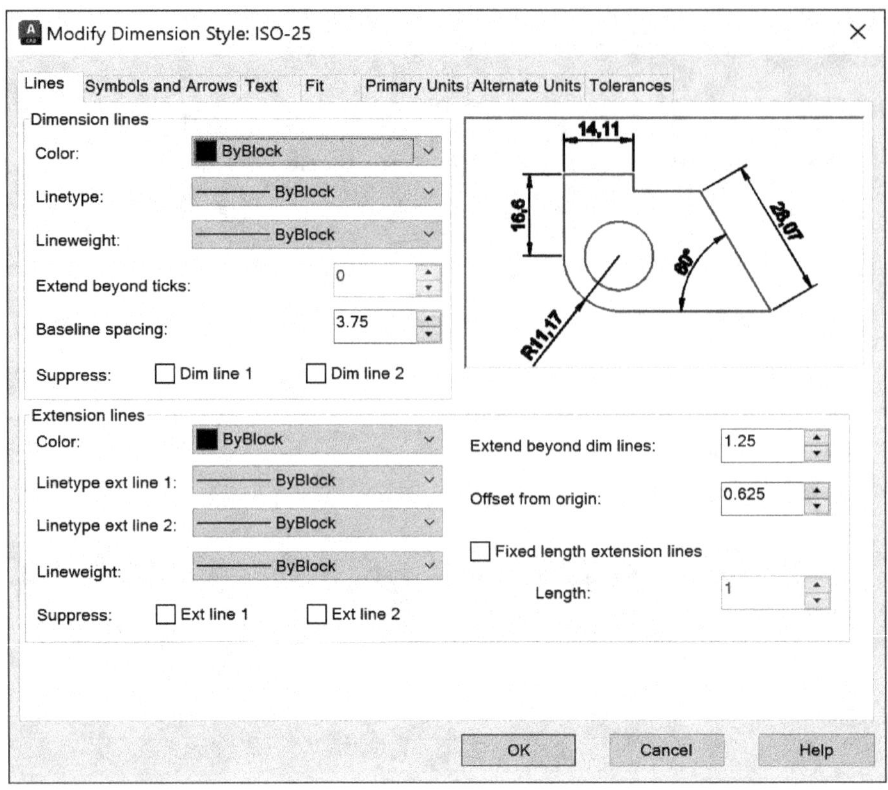

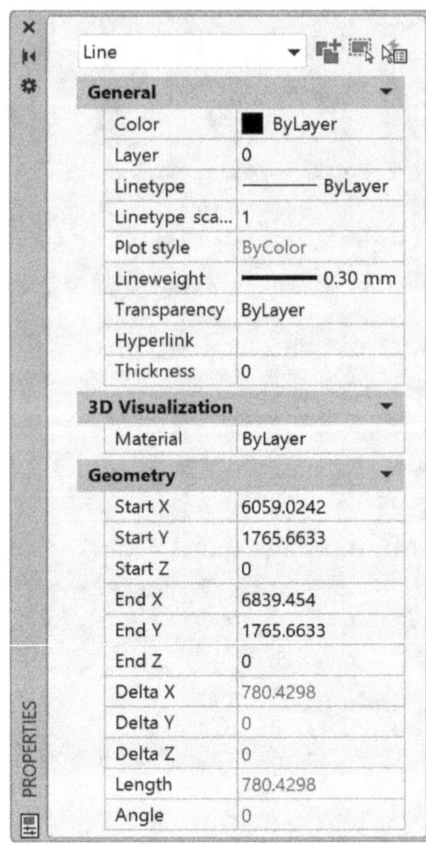

Tool Palettes

Tool Palettes provide you with another way of selecting tools and placing objects. You can display Tool Palettes by clicking **View > Palettes > Tool Palettes** on the ribbon. A Tool Palette is similar to a palette except that it has many palettes grouped in the form of tabs. You can select tools from the Tool Palettes as well as drag and place objects (blocks) into the drawing. You can also create a new Tool Palette and add frequently used tools and objects to it.

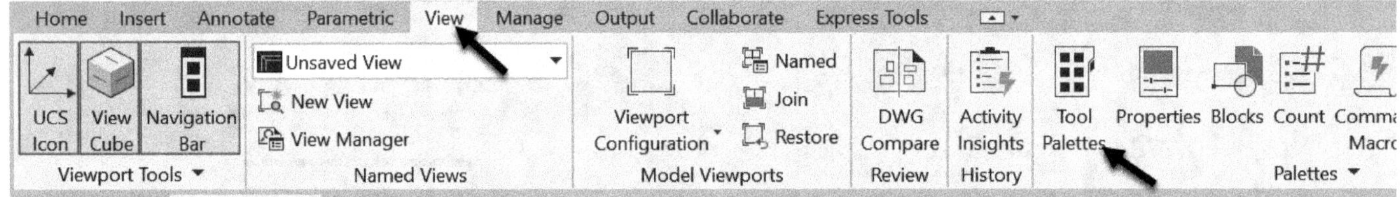

Shortcut Menus

Shortcut Menus appear when you right-click in the graphics window. AutoCAD provides various shortcut menus to help you access tools and options very easily and quickly. There are multiple types of shortcut menus available in AutoCAD. Some of them are discussed next.

Right-click Menu

This shortcut menu appears whenever you right-click in the graphics window without activating any command or selecting an object.

Select and Right-click menu

This shortcut menu appears when you select an object from the graphics window and right-click. It consists of editing and selection options.

Command Mode shortcut menu

This shortcut menu appears when you activate a command and right-click. It shows options depending upon the active command. The shortcut menu below shows the options related to the RECTANGLE command.

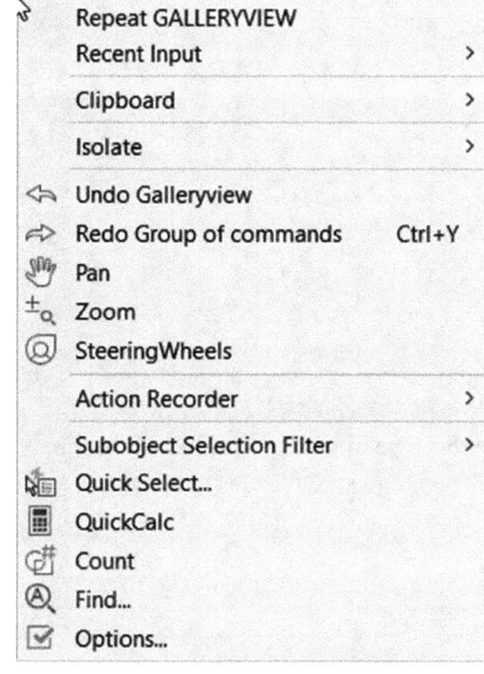
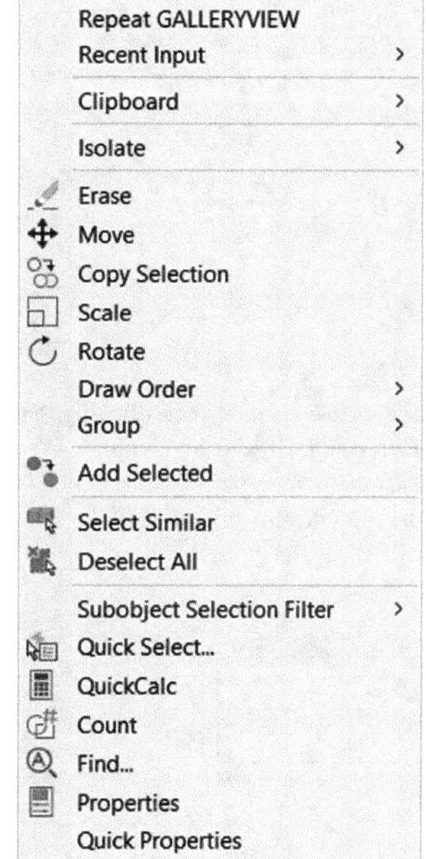
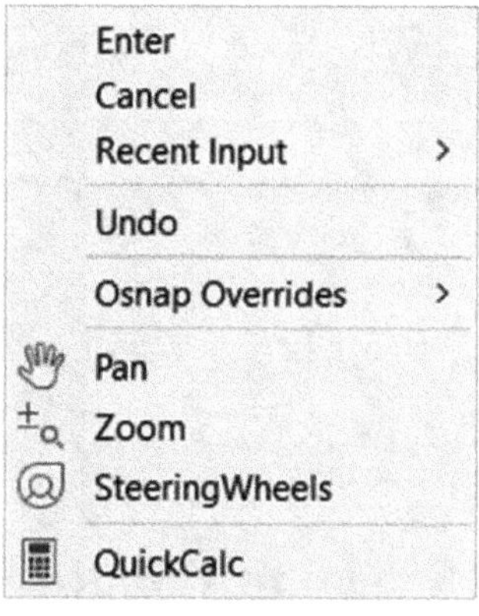

Grip shortcut menu

This shortcut menu is displayed when you select a grip of an object, move the pointer and right-click. It shows various operations that can be performed using grips.

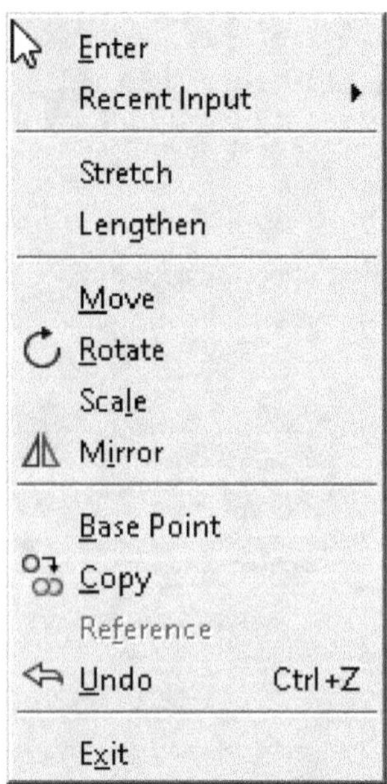

Selection Window

A selection window is used to select multiple elements of a drawing. You can select various elements by using two types of selection windows. The first type is a rectangular selection window. You can create this type of selection window by defining its two diagonal corners. When you set the first corner of the selection window on the left and second corner on the right side, the elements which fall entirely under the selection window will be selected.

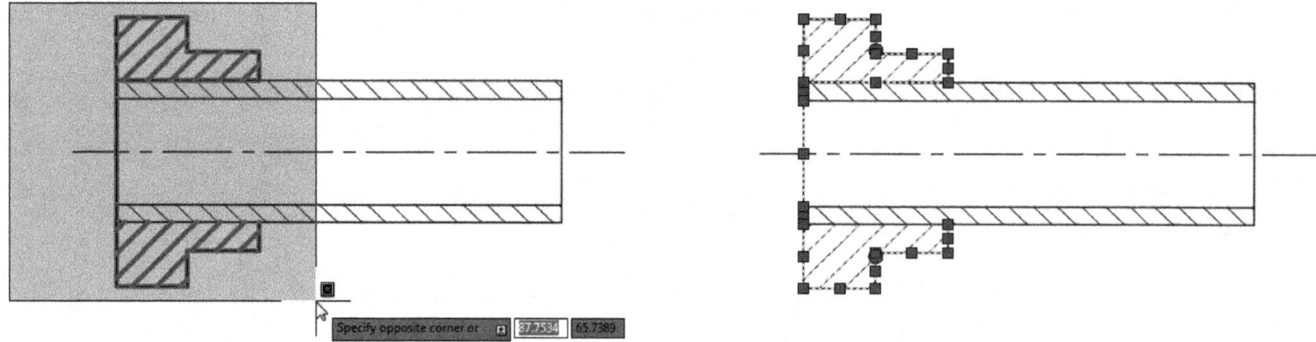

However, if you define the first corner on the right side and the second corner on the left side, the elements, which fall entirely or partially under the selection window, will be selected.

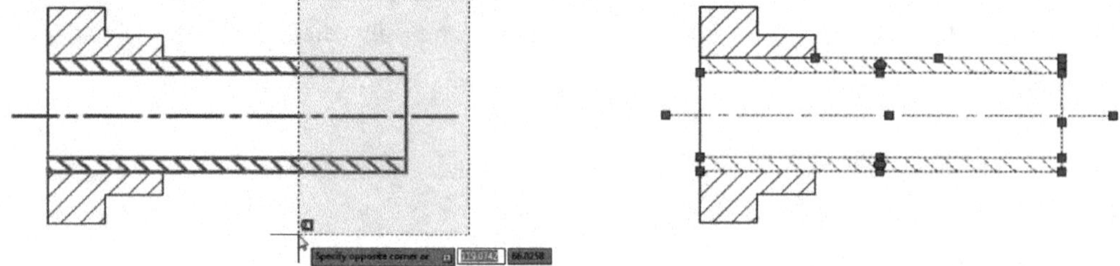

The second type of selection window is Lasso. Lasso is an irregular shape created by holding the left mouse button and dragging the pointer across the elements to select. If you drag the pointer from left to right, the elements falling entirely under the lasso will be selected.

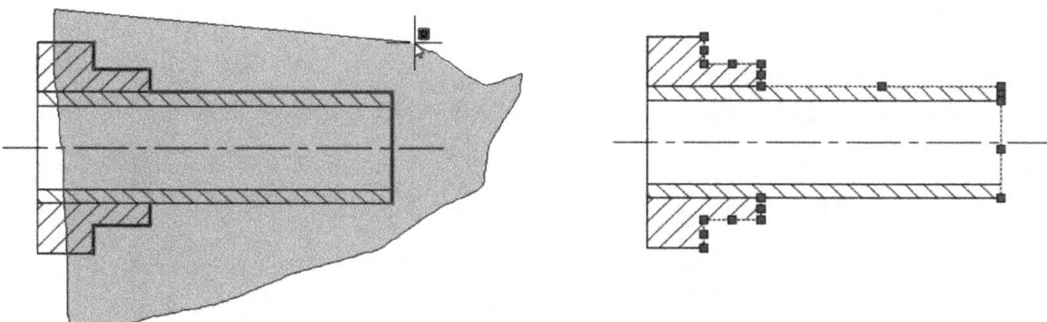

If you drag the pointer from right to left, the elements which fall wholly or partially under the lasso will be selected.

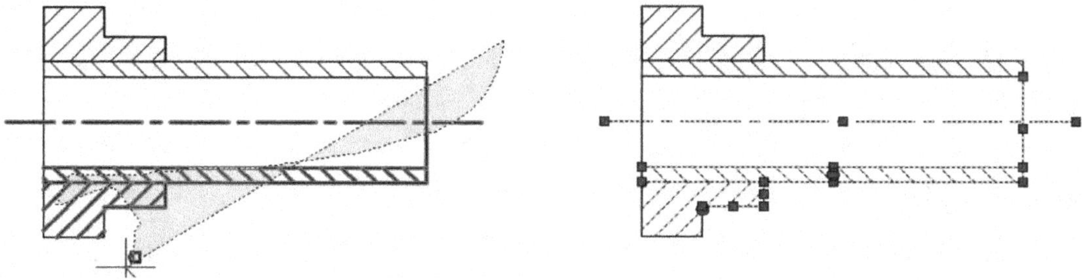

In AutoCAD, you can specify the first corner of the selection window at one portion of a large drawing. Next, zoom and pan to the rest of the drawing, and then specify the second corner of the selection window. By doing so, you can select the portion of the drawing, which is currently not visible on the screen.

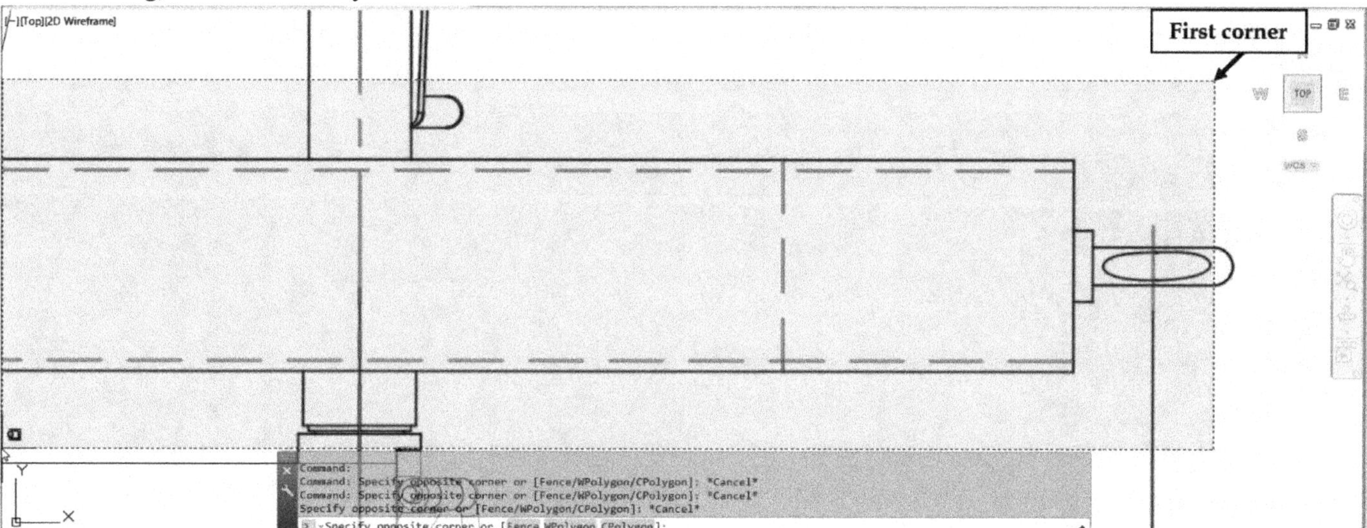

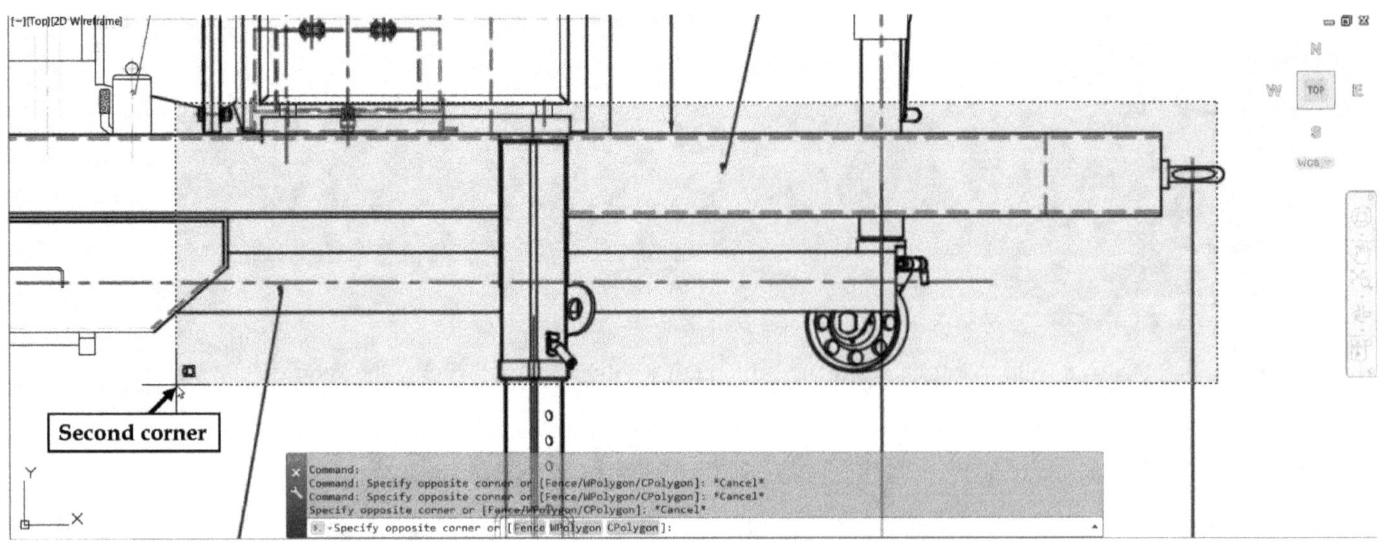

Starting a new drawing

You can start an AutoCAD document by using the **New** drop-down available on the Start screen or by using the **Select template** dialog.

New drop-down on the Initial Screen

To start a new drawing, select the New option from the New drop-down available at the left side of the **Start** screen. You can also select the acadiso.dwt template from the **New** drop-down to start a new drawing in the ISO format.

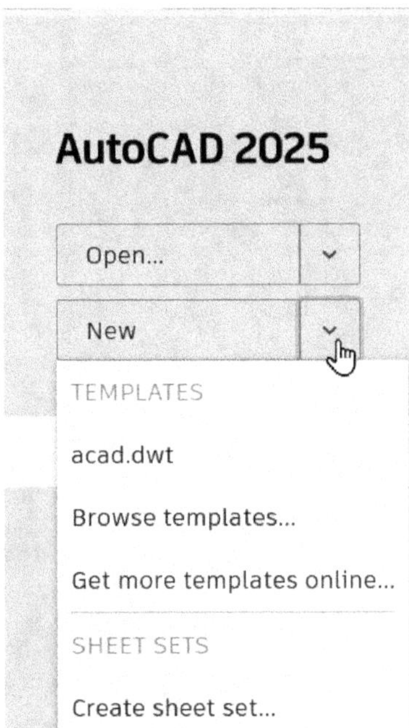

The Select Template dialog

- To start a new drawing using the **Select Template** dialog, click the **New** button on the Quick Access Toolbar (or) Application Menu. You can also select the **Browse Templates** option from the **New** drop-down available on the **Start** screen.

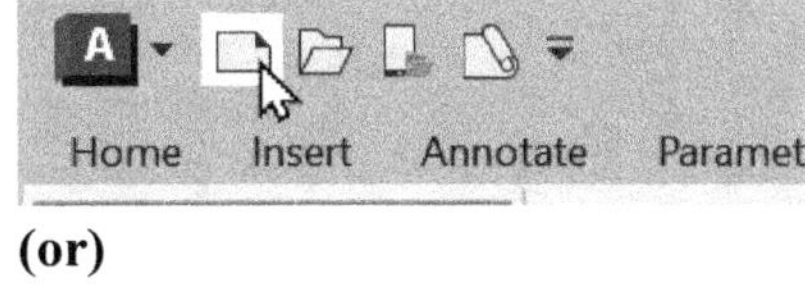

(or)

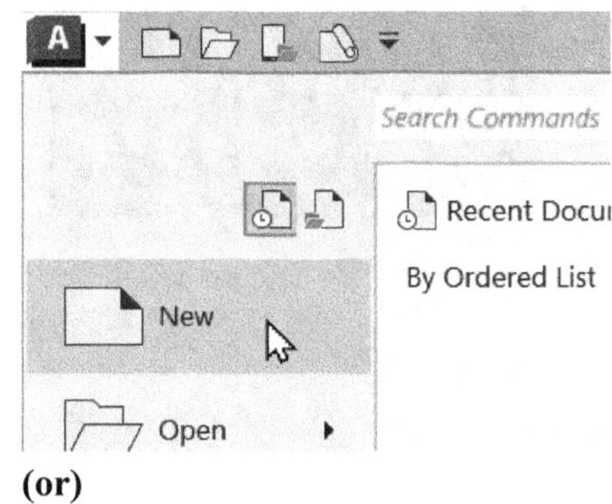

(or)

On the **Select Template** dialog, select the **acad.dwt** (inch units) or **acadiso.dwt** (metric units) template for creating a 2D drawing. Select the **acad3D.dwt** or **acadiso3D.dwt** template for creating 3D models.

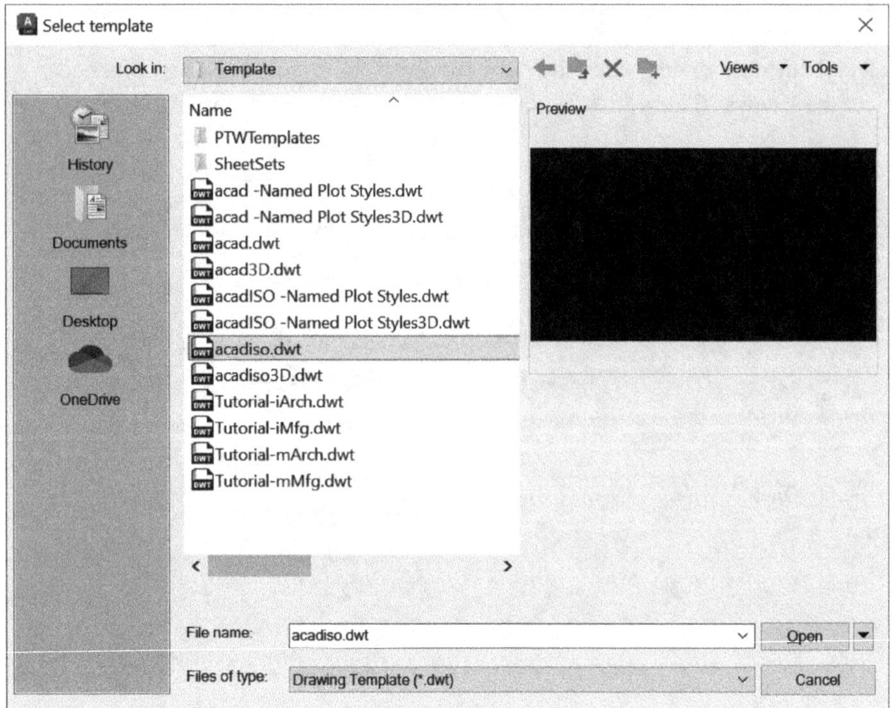

Saving a new drawing to Web & Mobile

You can save a drawing to AutoCAD Web & Mobile using the Save to AutoCAD Web & Mobile application. This application helps you view and make changes to the drawing from AutoCAD Web and AutoCAD Mobile application. The drawings edited in AutoCAD Web and AutoCAD Mobile can be opened in AutoCAD.

- Click the **Save to AutoCAD Web & Mobile** icon on the Quick Access Toolbar; the **Install Save to AutoCAD Web & Mobile** dialog appears.

- Check the **I have read and agree to the App Store End Use License Agreement** option.
- Click the **Install** button; the **Save to AutoCAD Web & Mobile** application is installed in the background.
- On the **Save in AutoCAD Web & Mobile** dialog, type in the **File name** box and then click the **Save** button.

To open the file saved in AutoCAD Web and Mobiles applications, click the **Open from Web & Mobile** icon on the Quick Access Toolbar. Next, select the files from the **Open from Web & Mobile** dialog, and then click **Open**.

Help

Press F1 or type a keyword in the search bar located at the top right corner of the window to get help for any topic. On the Autodesk AutoCAD 2025 –Help window, click the **Find** option next to the topic; an animated arrow appears on the window showing the tool location.

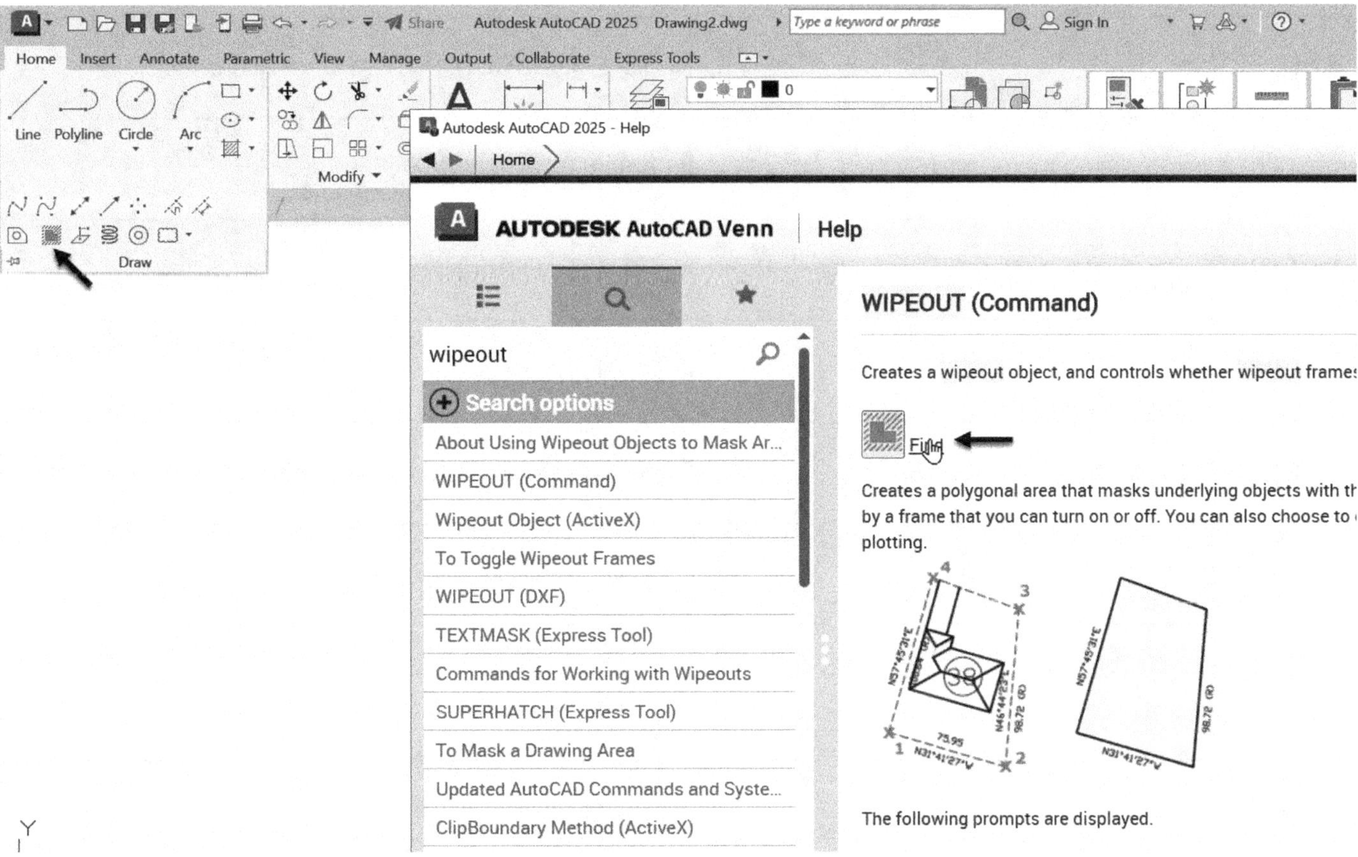

Command List

Various commands in AutoCAD are given in the table below:

Command	Alias	Description
APPLOAD		This command activates the **Load/Unload Applications** dialog.
ADCENTER	**DC**	Opens the **DESIGNCENTER** palette.
ALIGN	**AL**	It is used to align objects with other objects.
ARC	**A**	It is used to create an arc.

AREA		This command displays the area of a selected closed object.
ARRAY	**AR**	Creates Rectangular, Path, or Polar 2D arrays.
ASE		Displays the **DBCONNECT MANAGER** palette.
ATTDEF	**ATT**	It displays the **Attribute Definition** dialog.
ATTEDIT	**ATE**	It is used to edit Attributes.
AUDIT		It is used to check and fix errors.
AUTOCONSTRAIN		It is used to apply constraints automatically.
AUTOPUBLISH		It is used to create a DWF file.
BACTION	**AC**	It is used to add an action to a dynamic block. This command is available in Block Editor.
BLOCK		It is used to create a block.
BMAKE	**B**	It is used to create a block.
BMPOUT		It is used to create a Raster image out of the drawing.
BOUNDARY	**BO**	It is used to create a hatch boundary.
BREAK	**BR**	It is used to break an object.
CAL		It is used to calculate mathematical expressions.
CHAMFER	**CHA**	It is used to create chamfers.

CHPROP		This command changes the properties of a selected object.
CIRCLE	**C**	It is used to create a circle.
COLOR	**COL**	This command displays the **Select Color** dialog.
COPYTOLAYER		It is used to copy objects from one layer to another.
COPY	**CO**	It is used to copy objects inside a drawing.
COPYCLIP		It is used to copy objects from one drawing to another.
CUSTOMIZE		It is used to customize the tool palettes.
DDEDIT	**ED**	It is used to edit a note or annotation.
DIMSTYLE	**D**	It is used to create or modify a dimension style.
DDMODIFY		Displays the Properties palette.
DELCONSTRAINT		It is used to delete constraints.
OSNAP	**OS**	It is used to set the **Object Snap** settings.
DDPTYPE		It is used to set the point style and size.
VIEW	**V**	It is used to save views by names.
DGNEXPORT		It is used to export the drawing to Microstation (DGN) format.
DGNIMPORT		It is used to import a Microstation (DGN) format file.

DIMCONSTRAINT	**DCON**	It is used to apply dimensional constraints to objects.
DIMLINEAR	**DLI**	It is used to create a linear dimension.
DIMALIGNED	**DAL**	It is used to create an aligned dimension.
DIMARC	**DAR**	It is used to dimension the arc length.
DIMRADIUS	**DIMRAD**	It is used to create a radial dimension.
DIMJOGGED	**JOG**	It is used to create a jogged dimension.
DIMDIAMETER	**DIMDIA**	It is used to create a diameter dimension.
DIMANGULAR	**DAN**	It is used to create an angular dimension.
DIMORDINATE	**DOR**	It is used to create an ordinate dimension.
DIMCONTINUE	**DIMCONT**	It is used to create continuous dimensions from an existing one.
DIMBASELINE	**DIMBASE**	It is used to create baseline dimensions.
DIMINSPECT		It is used to create an inspection dimension.
-DIMSTYLE		Update a dimension according to the current dimension style.
DIMSPACE		It is used to adjust the space between dimensions.
DIMBREAK		It is used to break the extension line of a dimension when it intersects with another dimension.

DIMOVERRIDE		It is used to override the system variables of a selected dimension.
DIMCENTER		It is used to create a center mark of a circle.
DIMEDIT	**DIMED**	It is used to edit a dimension.
DIMTEDIT	**DIMTED**	It is used to edit the dimension text.
DIMDISASSOCIATE		This command disassociates a dimension from the object.
DIST	**DI**	It is used to measure the distance between two points.
DISTANTLIGHT		It is used to create a distant light.
DIVIDE	**DIV**	Places evenly spaced objects on a line segment
DONUT	**DO**	It is used to create a donut.
DVIEW		It is used to get the aerial view of a drawing.
DXBIN		It is used to open a DXB file.
DXFIN		It is used to open a DXF file.
DXFOUT		It is used to save a file in the DXF format.
ELLIPSE	**EL**	It is used to create an ellipse.
ERASE	**E**	It is used to erase objects.
EXIT		It is used to close AutoCAD.

EXPLODE	**X**	It is used to explode or ungroup objects.
EXPLORER		This command displays the Windows Explorer.
EXPORT	**EXP**	It is used to export data.
EXTEND	**EX**	It is used to extend an object up to another.
FILLET	**F**	It is used to create a fillet at the corner.
FILTER		It is used to set object selection filters.
GEOMCONSTRAINT	**GCON**	It is used to apply geometric constraints.
GRADIENT		It is used to apply the gradient to a closed area.
GROUP	**G**	It is used to group objects.
HATCH	**H**	It is used to apply hatch to a closed area.
HATCHEDIT	**HE**	It is used to edit hatch.
HELP		Display the Help window.
HIDE	**HI**	This command changes the Visual Style to Hidden.
ID		This command displays the coordinate values of a selected point.
IMAGE, IMAGEATTACH	**IM**	It is used to attach an Image reference.

IMAGEADJUST	**IAD**	It is used to adjust images.
IMAGECLIP		It is used to crop an image.
IMPORT	**IMP**	It is used to import other forms of CAD data.
INSERT	**I**	It is used to insert a block.
INSERTOBJ		It is used to insert an object into the drawing.
ISOPLANE	**CTRL+E**	It is used to set the current isometric plane.
JOIN	**J**	It is used to join the endpoints of two linear or curved objects.
LAYCUR		The Layer of the selected objects will be made current.
LAYER	**LA**	It is used to create a new layer and modify its properties.
LAYFRZ		It is used to freeze the layer of a selected object.
LAYISO		This command isolates the layer of a selected object.
LAYOUT		It is used to modify layouts.
LAYOFF		It is used to turn off the layer of a selected object.
LAYON		It is used to turn ON all the layers.
LAYOUTWIZARD		This command displays the Create Layout dialog.
LENGTHEN	**LEN**	It is used to increase the length of an object.

LIMITS		It is used to set the drawing limits.
LIMMAX		It is used to set the maximum limit of a drawing.
LINE	L	It is used to create a line.
LINETYPE	LT	It is used to set the line type.
LIST	LI	This command lists the properties of a selected object in the text window.
LOAD		This command imports the shapes that can be used by the SHAPE command.
LTSCALE	LTS	It is used to set the linetype scale.
MEASURE	ME	It is used to place points or blocks at regular intervals on an object.
MENU		It is used to load a customization file.
MENULOAD		It is used to load or unload a customizable file.
MIRROR	MI	It is used to create a mirror image of an object.
MLEDIT		It is used to edit a multiline.
MLINE	ML	It is used to create multiple parallel lines.
MLSTYLE		It is used to create and modify a multiline style.
MOVE	M	It is used to move selected objects.

MSLIDE		It is used to create a slide out of a drawing.
MSPACE	**MS**	I used to switch from paper space to model space.
MSTRETCH		It is used to stretch multiple objects at a time.
MTEXT	**MT or T**	It is used to write text in multiple lines.
MVIEW	**MV**	It is used to create and modify viewports.
MVSETUP		It is used to set drawing specifications for printing purposes.
NEW	**CTRL+N**	It is used to open a new file.
NOTEPAD		It is used to edit a file in Notepad.
OFFSET	**O**	This command creates a parallel copy of a selected object at a specified distance.
OOPS		It is used to undo the ERASE command.
OPEN		It is used to open an existing file.
OPTIONS	**OP**	It is used to set various options related to the drawing.
ORTHO		This command turns ON/OFF the Ortho Mode.
OSNAP	**OS**	I am used to the **Object Snap** settings.
PAGESETUP		It is used to specify the printing properties of a layout.
PAN	**P**	It is used to drag a drawing to view its different portions.

PARAMETER	**PAR**	It is used to assign expressions to a dimensional constraint.
PBRUSH		Opens the **Windows Paint** application.
PEDIT	**PE**	It is used to edit polylines.
PLINE	**PL**	It is used to create a polyline. A polyline is a single object which can have continuous lines and arcs.
PLOT	**CTRL+P**	It is used to plot a drawing.
POINT	**PO**	It is used to place a point in the drawing.
POLYGON	**POL**	It is used to create a polygon.
PREVIEW	**PRE**	It is used to preview the plotted drawing.
PROPERTIES	**PR**	Displays the **Properties** palette.
PSOUT		It is used to create a postscript file.
PURGE	**PU**	It is used to remove unwanted data from the drawing.
QDIM		It is used to create a quick dimension.
QSAVE		It is used to save the current drawing.
QUICKCALC	**QC**	This command displays the QuickCalc calculator.
QUIT		It is used to close the current drawing session.
RAY		It is used to create a line that starts from a selected point and extends up to infinity.

RECOVER		It is used to repair and open the damaged files.
RECOVERALL		It is used to repair a damaged file along with the attached external references.
RECTANG		It is used to create a polyline rectangle.
REDEFINE		It is used to restore an AutoCAD command, which has been overridden.
REDRAW	**R**	Refreshes the current viewport.
UNDEFINE		It is used to override an existing command with a new one.
REDO		It is used to cancel the previous UNDO command.
REDRAWALL	**RA**	This command refreshes all the viewports in a drawing.
REGEN	**RE**	This command regenerates the current viewport of a drawing.
REGENALL	**REA**	This command regenerates all the viewports of a drawing.
REGION	**REG**	This command converts the area enclosed by objects into a region.
RENAME	**REN**	It is used to rename blocks, viewports, and dimension styles.
REVCLOUD		It is used to highlight a portion of drawing by creating a cloud around it.
RIBBON		This command displays the ribbon.
RIBBONCLOSE		This command hides the ribbon.

SAVE	**CTRL+S**	This command saves the currently opened drawing.
SAVEAS		This command saves the drawing with another name and location.
SAVEIMG		It is used to save a rendered output file.
SCALE	**SC**	It is used to increase or decrease the size of a drawing.
SCRIPT	**SCR**	It is used to load a script file. A script is used to run various commands sequentially.
SETVAR	**SET**	It is used to list or change a system variable.
SHAPE		It is used to insert a shape into a drawing.
SHELL		It is used to enter MS-DOS commands.
SKETCH		It is used to draw freehand sketches.
SOLID	**SO**	It is used to create filled triangles or quadrilaterals.
SPELL	**SP**	It is used to check the spelling of a text.
SPLINE	**SPL**	It is used to create a spline (curved object).
SPLINEDIT	**SPE**	It is used to edit a spline.
STATUS		It is used to display the details of a drawing, such as limits, model space usage, and layers.
STRETCH	**S**	It is used to stretch objects.

STYLE	**ST**	It is used to create or modify the text style.
TABLET		Allows using a tablet for creating drawings.
TBCONFIG		It is used to customize the user interface.
TEXT		It is used to enter text in the drawing.
THICKNESS	**TH**	It is used to set a thickness value to 2D objects.
TOLERANCE		It is used to apply geometric tolerances to the drawing.
TOOLBAR	**TO**	It is used to customize toolbars.
TRIM	**TR**	It is used to trim unwanted portions of an object.
UCS		It is used to specify the location of the user coordinate system.
UNDO	**CTRL+Z (or) U**	It is used to undo the last operation.
UNITS	**UN**	Set the units of the drawing
VIEW		It is used to save and restore the model space, layout, and preset views.
VPLAYER		It is used to control layer visibility in paper space.
VPORTS		It is used to create multiple viewports in model space of paper space.
VSLIDE		It is used to show an image slide file.
WBLOCK	**W**	It is used to convert a block into a drawing.

WMFIN		It is used to import a Windows Metafile. This file contains the drawing and image data. But only the drawing data is imported.
WIPEOUT		It is used to wipe out a portion of the drawing.
WMFOPTS		It is used to specify the options for importing a Windows Metafile.
WMFOUT		It is used to save objects as Windows Metafile.
XATTACH	XA	It is used to attach a drawing as an external reference.
XLINE	XL	It is used to create construction lines. Construction lines extend to infinity and help in drawing objects.
XREF	XR	It is used to attach a drawing as an external reference.
ZOOM	Z	It is used to Zoom in or out of a drawing.

3D Commands

Command	Shortcut	Description
3DARRAY	3A	It is used to create three-dimensional arrays of an object.
3DALIGN	3AL	It is used to align 3D objects.
3DFACE	3F	It is used to create a three or four-sided 3D surface.
3DMESH		It is used to create a freeform 3D mesh.

Command	Alias	Description
3DCORBIT		It is used to rotate a view in the 3D space with continuous motion.
3DDISTANCE		It is used to control the distance.
3DEDITBAR		It is used to add and edit control vertices on a NURBS surface or spline.
3DFLY		It is used to view the 3D model as if you are flying through.
3DFORBIT		It is used to rotate a view in 3D space freely.
3DMOVE	**3M**	It is used to move the objects in 3D space.
3DORBIT	**3DO**	It is used to rotate the view constrained along the horizontal or vertical axis.
3DORBITCTR		It is used to set the center for rotating the view in 3D space.
3DPAN		It is used to pan the 3D models horizontally or vertically. This is used when working in perspective view.
3DPOLY	**3P**	It is used to create a 3D polyline.
3DPRINT	**3DP**	It is used to print the model in 3D (plastic prototype).
3DROTATE		It is used to rotate 3D objects in 3D space.
3DSCALE	**3S**	It is used to increase or decrease the size of a 3D object along the X, Y, Z directions.
3DSIN		It is used to import a 3ds Max file.
3DDWF		Export the 3D model to a 3D DWF file.

3DWALK	It is used to view the 3D model as if you are walking through it.
ANIPATH	It is used to create an animation when you are navigating through the model.
BOX	It is used to create a 3D box.
CONE	It is used to create a 3D cone.
CONVERTOLDLIGHTS	It is used to convert lights created in previous releases to the current format.
CONVERTOLDMATERIALS	It is used to convert old materials to the new format
CONVTONURBS	It is used to convert a surface to NURBS. You can easily edit a NURBS by using control vertices displayed on it.
CONVTOSOLID	It is used to convert 3D meshes, polylines, and circles to 3D solids.
CONVTOSURFACE	It is used to convert objects to surfaces.
CVADD	It is used to add control vertices to a NURBS surface or spline.
CVREMOVE	It is used to remove control vertices from a NURBS surface or spline.
CVHIDE	It is used to hide the control vertices of a NURBS surface or splines,
CVSHOW	It is used to display the control vertices of a NURBS surface or splines.
CVREBUILD	It is used to rebuild the control vertices of a NURBS surface.

CYLINDER		It is used to create a Cylinder.
EDGESURF		It is used to create a mesh surface from four adjacent edges.
EXTRUDE	**EXT**	It is used to extrude a closed region or polyline.
FILLETEDGE		It is used to blend an edge of a 3D object.
FLATSHOT		It is used to create a 2D representation of a 3D model.
FREEPOINT		It is used to create point light that emits light in all directions.
FREESPOT		It is used to create a spotlight without any target.
HELIX		It is used to create a helical or spiral curve.
INTERFERE		It is used to create a 3D solid at the interference point of the various solid objects.
INTERSECT	**IN**	It is used to create a 3D solid at the intersection portion of solid.
LIGHT		It is used to create a light.
LIGHTLIST		This command displays the lights available in the current 3D model.
LOFT		It is used to create a 3D solid or surface between various cross-sections.
MATERIALS		This command displays the Material Browser.
MATERIALASSIGN		It is used to assign a material to the model.

MATERIALMAP	It is used to control the texture.
MATERIALATTACH	It is used to associate materials with layers.
MESH	It is used to create 3D mesh objects.
MESHREFINE	It is used to refine the mesh of 3D mesh objects.
MESHSMOOTH	It is used to increase the smoothness of mesh objects.
MIRROR3D	It is used to mirror 3D objects in 3D space.
OFFSETEDGE	It is used to create a parallel copy of an edge at a specified distance.
PFACE	It is used to create a 3D Polyface mesh by specifying vertices.
PLAN	This command displays the top view of the 3D model.
PLANESURF	It is used to create a planar surface.
POINTLIGHT	It is used to create point light that emits light in all directions.
PRESSPULL	It is used to extrude or subtract material.
PYRAMID	It is used to create a pyramid.
-RENDER	It is used to specify settings for rendering.
RENDERCROP	It is used to render a rectangular portion of a 3D model.
RENDERENVIRONMENT	It is used to control the visual properties of the rendered image.

RENDEREXPOSURE		It is used to control the lighting of a rendered image.
RENDERONLINE		It is used to render an image in Autodesk 360 (cloud).
RENDERPRESETS		It is used to specify preset values for rendering an image.
RENDERWIN		Displays the render window.
REVOLVE	**REV**	It is used to create a revolved solid.
REVSURF		It is used to create a revolved surface.
RMAT		This command displays the Material Browser.
RPREF	**RPR**	It is used to specify advanced render settings.
SECTION	**SEC**	It is used to create a section plane in a 3D model.
SLICE	**SL**	It is used to slice a 3D model.
SOLPROF		Create a profile from a 3D model in the paper space.
SOLIDEDIT		It is used to edit faces and edges of a 3D solid.
SPACETRANS		It is used to calculate equivalent model space and paper space distance.
SPHERE		It is used to create a sphere.
SPOTLIGHT		It is used to create a spotlight that emits light like a torch.
STLOUT		It is used to export a file to STL format.

SUNPROPERTIES		Displays the Sun properties palette.
SURFBLEND	**BLENDSRF**	It is used to create a continuous blend surface between two surfaces.
SURFEXTEND		It is used to lengthen a surface up to another surface.
SURFEXTRACTCURVE		It is used to create Isoline curves on a surface, solid, or a face in U and V directions.
SURFFILLET		It is used to create a surface fillet between two surfaces.
SURFOFFSET		It is used to create a parallel surface at a specified distance.
SURFNETWORK		It is used to create a surface from various curves in U and V directions.
SURFPATCH		It is used to create a surface using the edges, forming a closed loop.
SURFSCULPT		It is used to create a closed surface by trimming and combining the surfaces that form a region together.
SURFTRIM		It is used to trim portions of a surface at intersections with other surfaces.
SURFUNTRIM		It is used to untrim the trimmed surface.
SWEEP		It is used to create a 3D solid or surface by sweeping a profile along a path.
TABSURF		It is used to create a mesh from a line or curve swept along a straight path

TORUS	**TOR**	It is used to create a torus.
UNION	**UNI**	It is used to combine various solids into one.
VISUALSTYLES		It is used to create and modify visual styles.
VPOINT		It is used to set the viewing direction of the 3D model.
WEDGE	**WE**	It is used to create a wedge shape.
XEDGES		It is used to create a 3D wireframe from a 3D solid.

Chapter 2: Drawing Basics

In this chapter, you will learn to do the following:

- **Draw lines, rectangles, circles, ellipses, arcs, polygons, and polylines**
- **Use the Erase, Undo and Redo tools**
- **Draw entities using the absolute coordinate points**
- **Draw objects using the relative coordinate points**
- **Draw objects using the tracking method**

Drawing Basics

This chapter teaches you to create simple drawings. You will create these drawings using the essential drawing tools. These tools include **Line**, **Circle**, **Polyline**, and **Rectangle**, and they are available in the **Draw** panel of the ribbon, as shown below. You can also activate these tools by typing them in the command line.

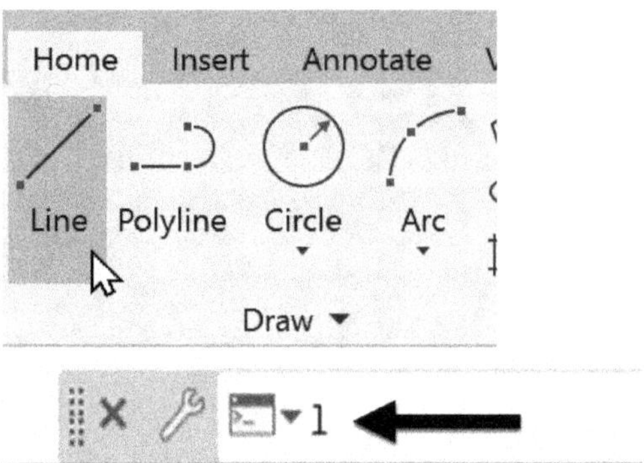

Drawing Lines

You can draw a line by specifying its start point and endpoint using the **Line** tool. However, there are various methods to specify the start and endpoint of a line. These methods are explained in the following examples.

Example 1 (using the Absolute Coordinate System)

In this example, you will create lines by specifying points in the absolute coordinate system. In this system, you specify the points with respect to the origin (0, 0). A point will be defined by entering its X and Y coordinates separated by a comma, as shown in the figure below.

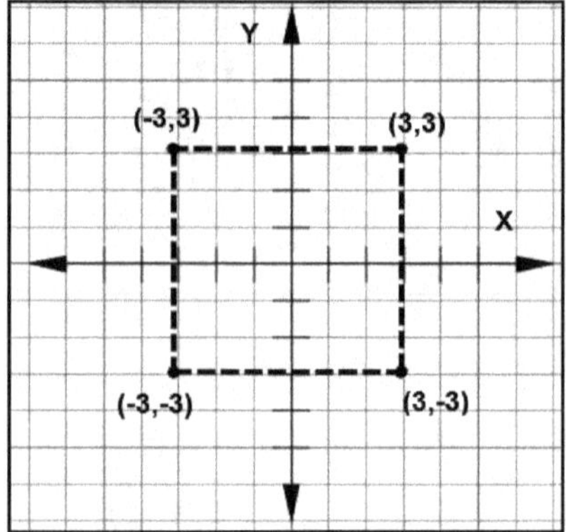

- Start AutoCAD 2025 by clicking the **AutoCAD 2025** icon on your desktop.
- On the Start screen, click **New > Templates > Browse Templates**.
- Double-click on the **acadiso.dwt** template. This starts a new drawing using the ISO template.

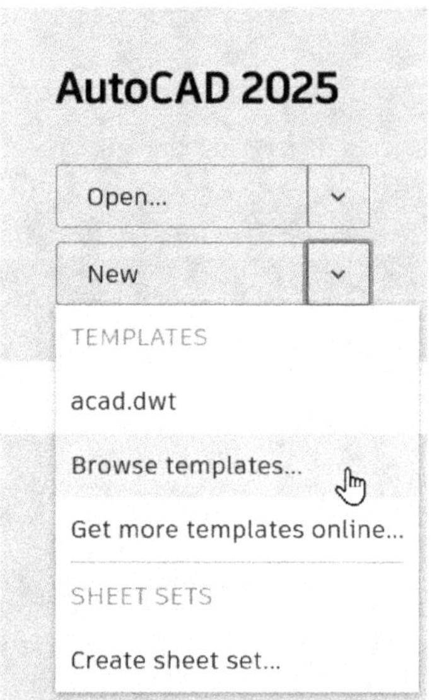

- Click **Zoom > Zoom All** on the **Navigation Bar**; the entire area in the graphics window will be displayed.

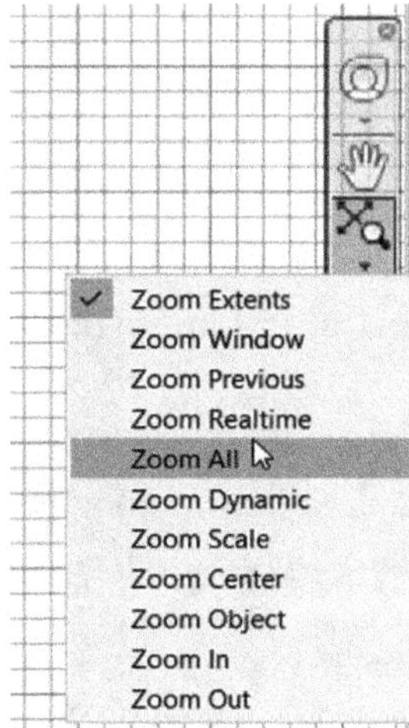

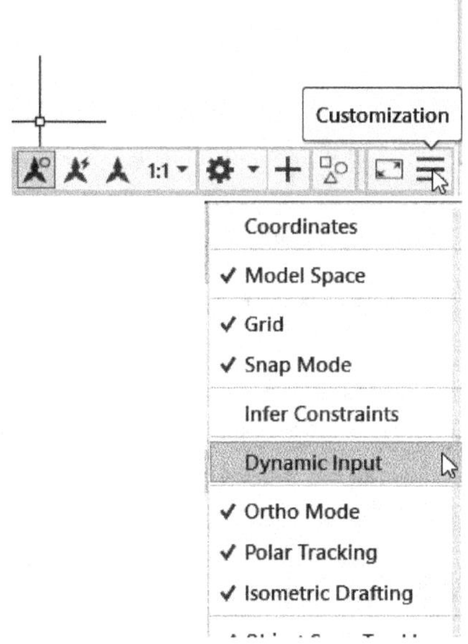

- Turn OFF the **GRIDMODE** by pressing the F7 key.
- Click the **Customization** button on the status bar, and then select **Dynamic Input** from the flyout. This displays the **Dynamic Input** icon on the status bar.

- Turn OFF the **Dynamic Input** icon. You will learn about **Dynamic Input** later in this chapter.

- To draw a line, click **Home > Draw > Line** on the ribbon, or enter **LINE** or **L** in the command line.

- Type **50, 50**, and press ENTER.
- Type **150, 50**, and press ENTER.
- Type **150,100** and press ENTER.
- Type **50,100** and press ENTER.
- Select the **Close** option from the command line. It creates a rectangle, as shown below.

(50,100)   **(150,100)**

(50,50)   **(150,50)**

- Click **Save** on the **Quick Access Toolbar**.

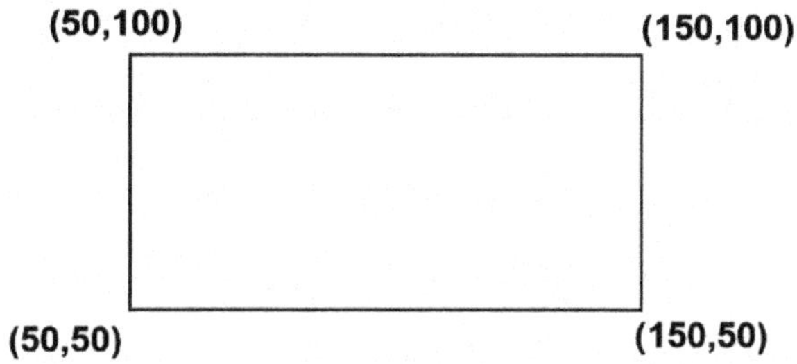

- Browse to a location on your computer.
- Type **Line-example1.dwg** in the **File name** box.
- Click **Save**.
- Close the file by closing the file tab, as shown.

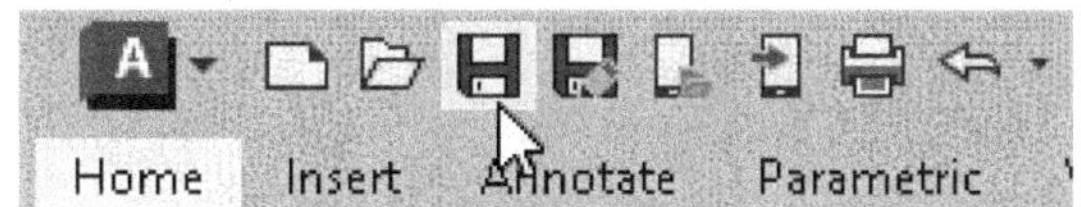

Example 2 (using the Relative Coordinate system)

In this example, you will draw lines by defining its endpoints in the relative coordinate system. In the relative coordinate system, you define the location of a point with respect to the previous point. For this purpose, the symbol, '@' is used before the point coordinates. This symbol means that the coordinate values are defined in relation to the previous point.

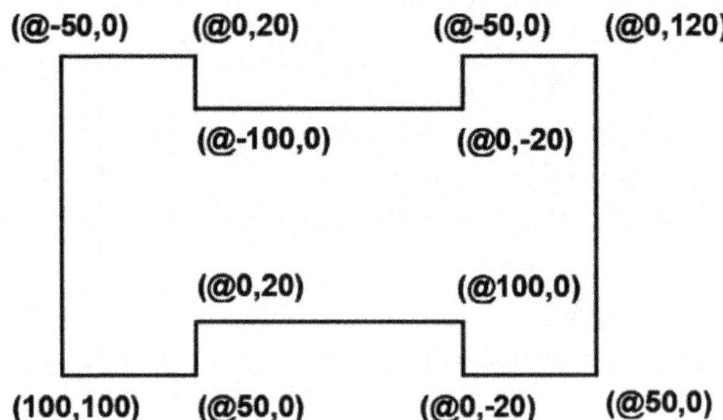

- Click **New** on the **Quick Access Toolbar**.

- Select the **acadISO-Named Plot Styles** template.
- Click **Open**.
- Type-in **Z** in the command line
- Press ENTER to activate the **ZOOM** command.
- Click the **All** option in the command line. It displays the entire area in the graphics window.
- Turn OFF the **Grid** icon on the status bar.

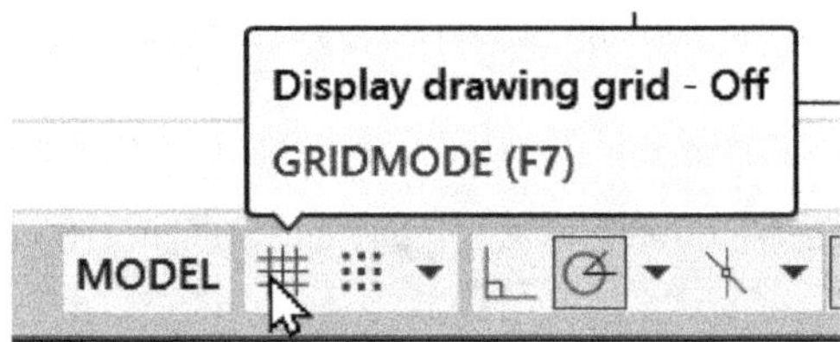

- Turn OFF the **Dynamic Input** mode, if active.
- Click **Home > Draw > Line** on the ribbon, or enter **LINE** or **L** in the command line.
- Type **100,100** and press ENTER. It defines the first point of the line.
- Type **@50,0** and press ENTER.
- Type **@0,20** and press ENTER.
- Type **@100,0** and press ENTER.
- Type **@0,-20**, and press ENTER.
- Type **@50,0** and press ENTER.
- Type **@0,120** and press ENTER.
- Type **@-50,0** and press ENTER.
- Type **@0,-20**, and press ENTER.
- Type **@-100,0** and press ENTER.
- Type **@0,20** and press ENTER.

- Type **@-50,0** and press ENTER.
- Select the **Close** option from the command line.
- Save the file as **Line-example2.dwg**.
- Close the file.

Example 3 (using the Polar Coordinate system)

In the polar coordinate system, you define the location of a point by entering two values: distance from the previous point and angle from the zero degrees. You enter the distance value along with the @ symbol and angle value with the < symbol. You have to make a note that AutoCAD measures the angle in the anti-clockwise direction.

Drawing Task

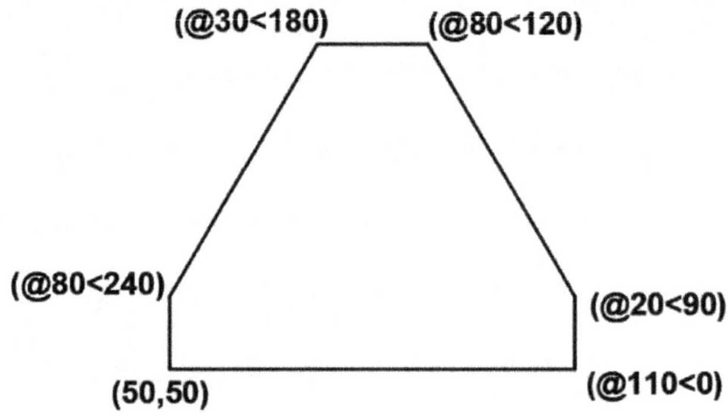

- Open a new file using the **acadISO-Named Plot Styles.dwt** template.
- Click **Zoom > Zoom All** on the **Navigation Bar**.
- Turn OFF the **Grid** icon on the status bar.
- Turn OFF the **Dynamic Input** mode, if active.
- Click **Home > Draw > Line** on the ribbon, or enter **LINE** or **L** in the command line.
- Type **50,50** and press the **Enter** key.
- Type **@110<0** and press ENTER.
- Type **@20<90** and press ENTER.
- Type **@80<120** and press ENTER.
- Type **@30<180** and press ENTER.
- Type **@80<240** and press ENTER.
- Select the **Close** option from the command line.
- Save the file as **Line-example3.dwg**.
- Close the file.

Example 4 (using the Direct Input method)

In the direct input method, you draw a line by entering its distance and angle values. You use the **Dynamic Input** mode in this method.

Dynamic Input provides a command interface near the cursor in the drawing area. It's a tool that helps you visualize and specify coordinate values and angular values when drawing lines, arcs, circles, etc.

When you enable Dynamic Input, a tooltip appears near the cursor, displaying dynamically updated information relevant to the task you are performing. For instance, when you activate a command, you can specify options and values directly in the tooltip text box.

Dynamic Input compliments the Command window, in speeding up the drawing tasks. It displays the information next to the cursor, allowing you create drawings quickly without looking at the command line.

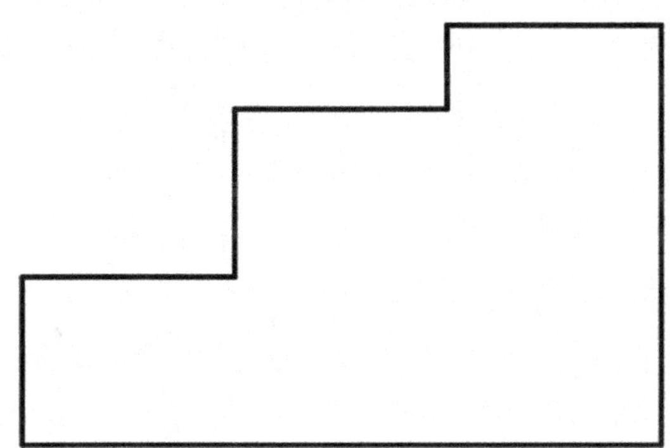

- Open a new file using the **acadISO-Named Plot Styles.dwt** template.
- Turn OFF the **Grid** ⊞ and **Snap Mode** ⣿ icons on the Status Bar.
- Click **Zoom > Zoom All** on the **Navigation Bar**.
- Activate the **Dynamic Input** icon on the Status Bar.

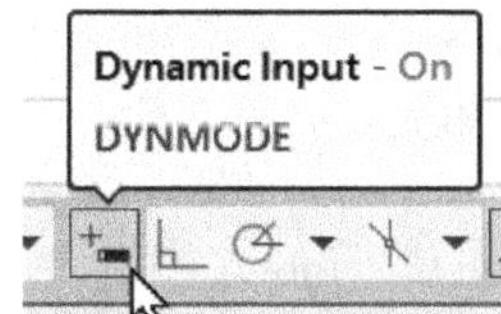

- Click **Home > Draw > Line** on the ribbon, or enter **LINE** or **L** in the command line.
- Define the first point of the line by typing 50,50 and pressing ENTER.

- Move the pointer horizontally toward right and type in 150 in the length box.
- Press the TAB key and type 0 as the angle. Next, press ENTER.

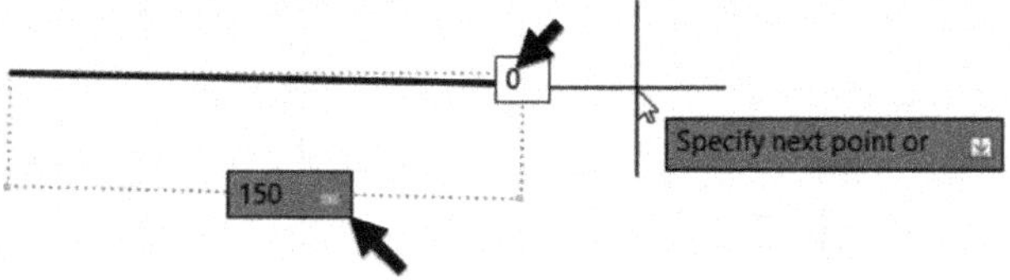

- Move the pointer vertically upwards and type-in 100 as length.
- Press the TAB key and type 90 as the angle — next, press ENTER.
- Move the pointer horizontally toward left and type 50.
- Press the TAB key and type 180 as the angle — next, press ENTER.
- Move the pointer vertically downwards and type 20.
- Press the TAB key and type 90 as the angle — next, press ENTER.
- Move the pointer horizontally toward left and type 50.
- Press the TAB key and type 180 as the angle — next, press ENTER.
- Move the pointer vertically downwards and type 40.
- Press the TAB key and type 90 as the angle — next, press ENTER.
- Move the pointer horizontally toward left and type 50.
- Press the TAB key and type 180 as the angle — next, press ENTER.
- Click the **Close** option in the command line.
- Save and close the file.

Erasing, Undoing and Redoing

- Draw the sketch shown below using the **Line** tool. You can use the Direct Input method to create this sketch. Do not dimension the drawing.

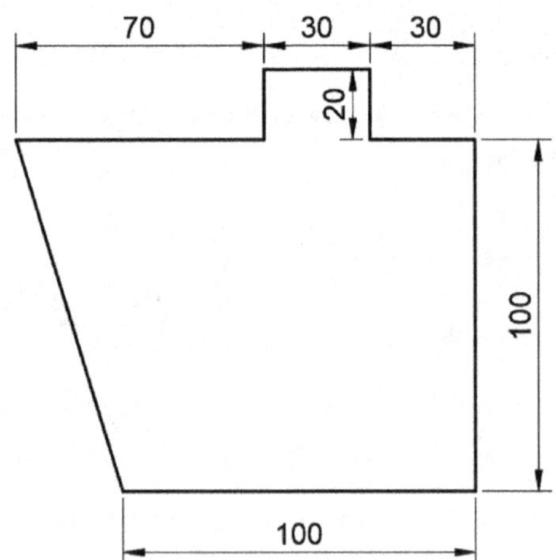

* Click **Home > Modify > Erase** on the ribbon or Enter **ERASE** or **E** in the command line.

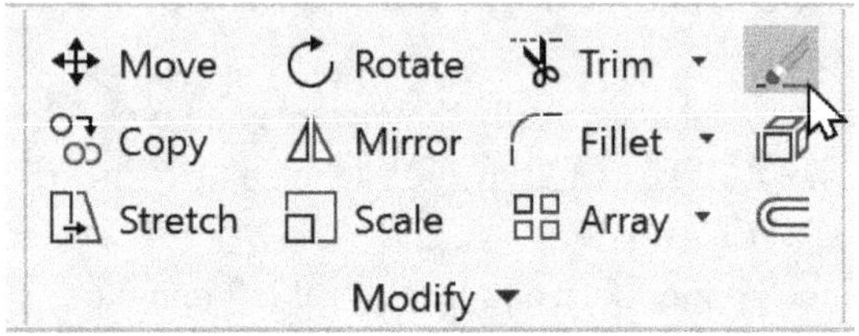

* Select the lines shown below and press ENTER. It erases the lines.

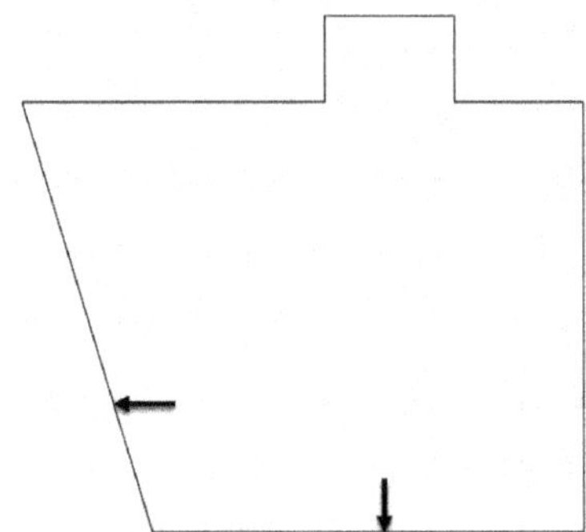

* Click the **Undo** button on the **Quick Access Toolbar**. This action restores the lines.

* Click the **Redo** button on the **Quick Access Toolbar**. This action erases the lines again.

* Type **E** in the command line and press the SPACEBAR; the **ERASE** command will be activated.
* Drag a selection lasso as shown below and press ENTER; the entities will be erased. (Refer to the Selection Window section in Chapter 1 to learn about the selection lasso)

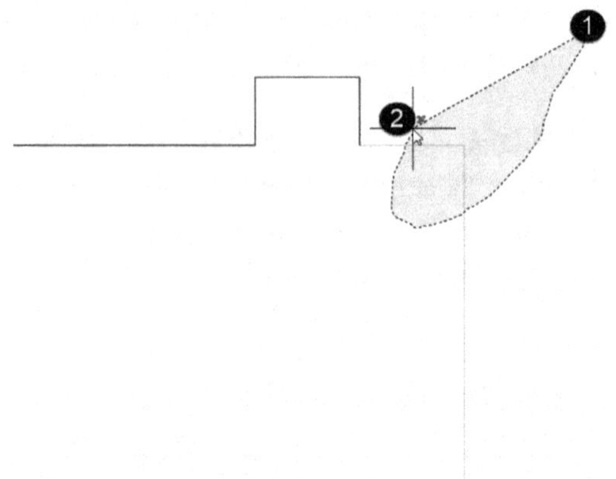

Drawing Circles

The tools in the **Circle** drop-down on the **Draw** panel can be used to draw circles. You can also type-in the **CIRCLE** command in the command line and create circles. There are various methods to create circles. These methods are explained in the following examples.

Example 1(Center, Radius)

In this example, you will create a circle by specifying its center and radius value.

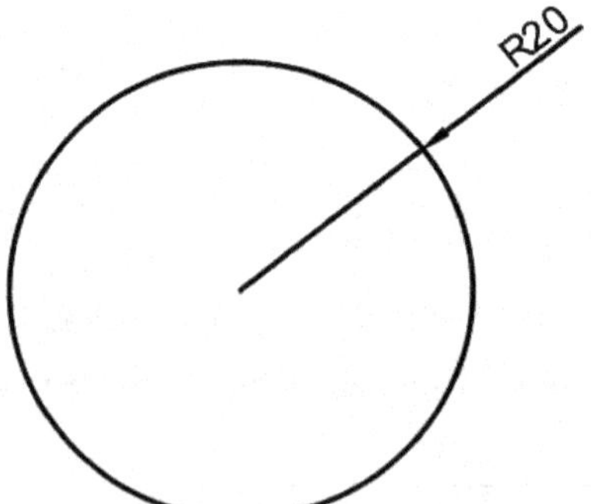

* Click **Home > Draw > Circle** drop-down **> Center, Radius** on the ribbon.
* Click in the graphics window.
* Type 20 as the radius and press ENTER.

Example 2(Center, Diameter)

In this example, you will create a circle by specifying its center and diameter value.

- Click **Home > Draw > Circle > Center, Diameter** 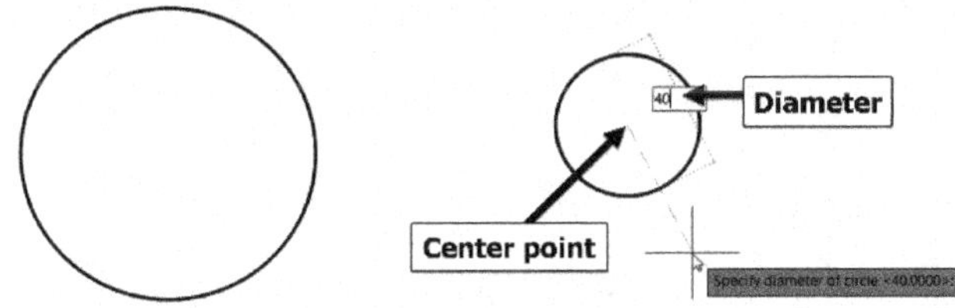 on the ribbon. The message, "Specify center point for circle or [3P/2P/Ttr (tan tan radius)]:" appears in the command line.
- Pick a point in the graphics window, which is approximately horizontal to the previous circle.

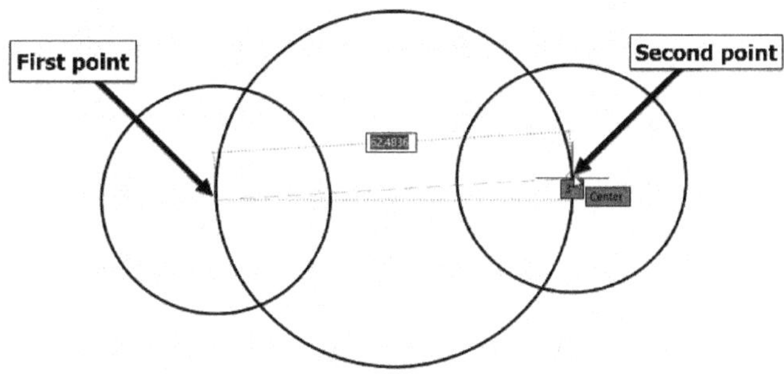

- Type 40 as the diameter and press ENTER; the circle will be created.

Example 3(2-Point)

In this example, you will create a circle by specifying two points. The first point is to specify the location of the circle, and the second defines the diameter.

- Click the down arrow next to the **Object Snap** icon on the status bar. A flyout appears. The options in this flyout are called Object Snaps. You will learn about these Object Snaps later in Chapter 3.
- Activate the **Center** option, if it is not already active.
- Now, you will create a circle by selecting the center points of the previous circles.

- Click **Home > Draw > Circle > 2-Point** on the ribbon. The message, "Specify the first endpoint of circle's diameter:" appears in the command line.
- Select the center point of the left side circle; the message, "Specify the second endpoint of circle's diameter:" appears in the command line.
- Select the center point of the right-side circle; the circle will be created, as shown below.

Example 4(3-Point)

In this example, you will create a circle by specifying three points. The circle will pass through these three points.

- Open a new file.
- Use the **Line** tool and create the drawing shown in the figure below. The coordinate points are also given in the figure.

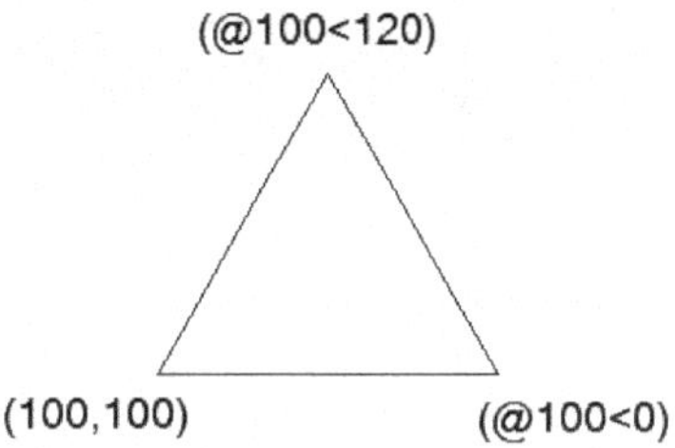

- Click **Home > Draw > Circle > 3-Point** on the ribbon.
- Select the three vertices of the triangle; a circle will be created, passing through the selected points.

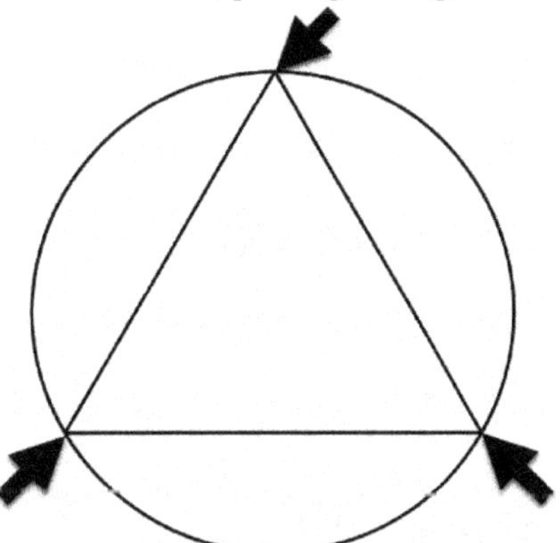

Example 5 (Tan, Tan, Radius)

In this example, you will create a circle by selecting two objects and then specifying the radius of the circle. A circle is created tangent to the selected objects.

- Click **Home > Utilities > Measure > Radius** on the ribbon. The message, "Select arc or circle: "appears in the command line.
- Select the circle passing through the three vertices of the triangle; the radius and diameter values of the circle will be displayed above the command line.

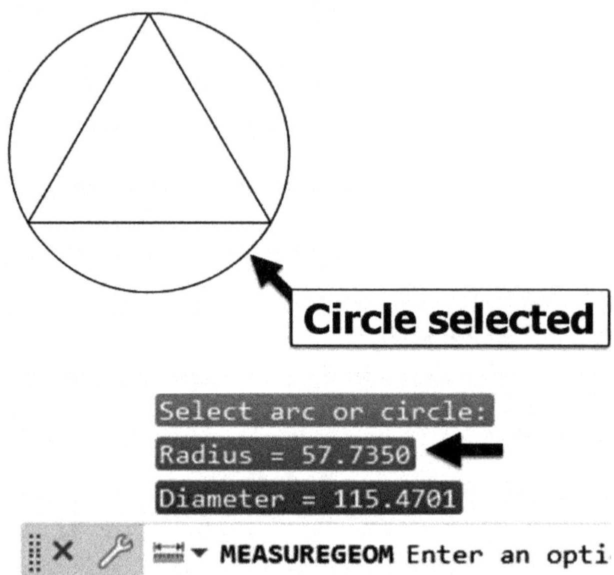

- Select the **eXit** option from the command line.
- Click **Home > Utilities > Quick Calculator** on the ribbon; the **Quick Calculator** appears.

- Type-in **57.7350** in the **Quick Calculator**.

- Click the / button and then the **2** button on the **Number Pad**.

- Click the = button; the value **28.8675** is displayed in the value box.

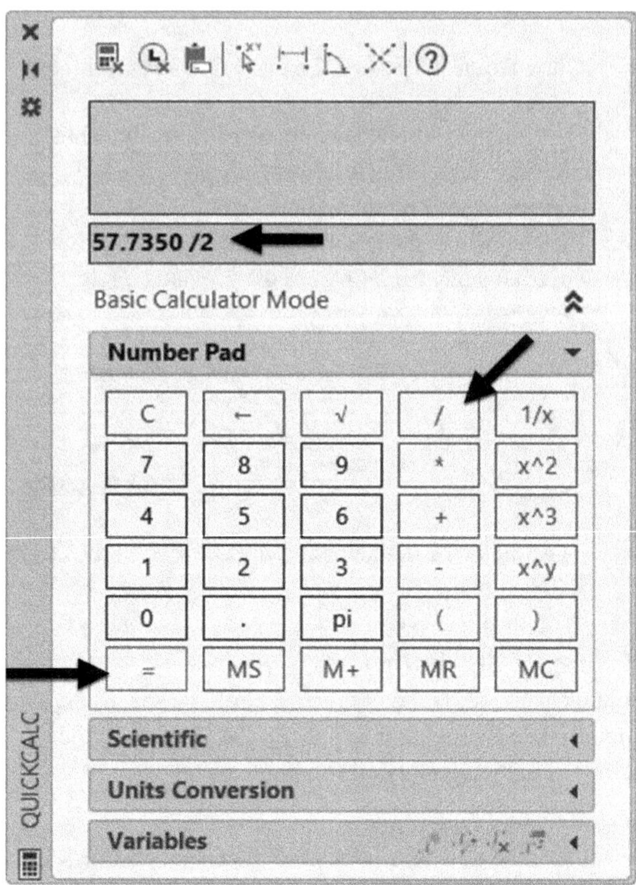

- Click **Home > Draw > Circle > Tan, Tan, Radius** on the ribbon; the message, "Specify point on the object for first tangent of circle:" appears in the command line.
- Select the horizontal line of the triangle; the message, "Specify point on object for second tangent of circle:" appears in the command line.
- Select any one of the inclined lines; the message, "Specify radius of circle," appears in the command line.
- Click the **Paste value to command line** button on the **Quick Calculator**; the value **28.8675** will be pasted in the command line.

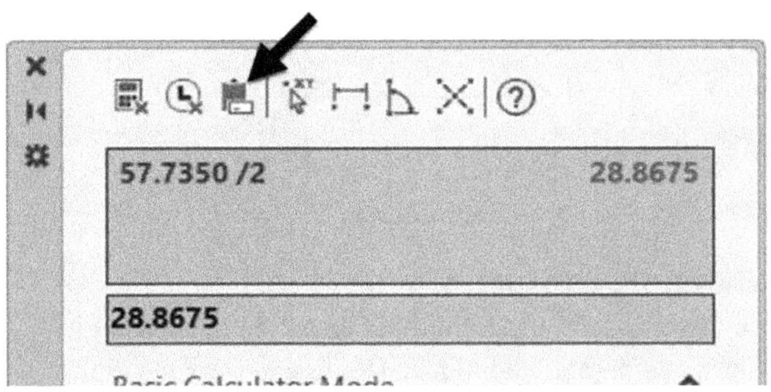

- Press ENTER to specify the radius; the circle will be created, touching all three sides of the triangle.

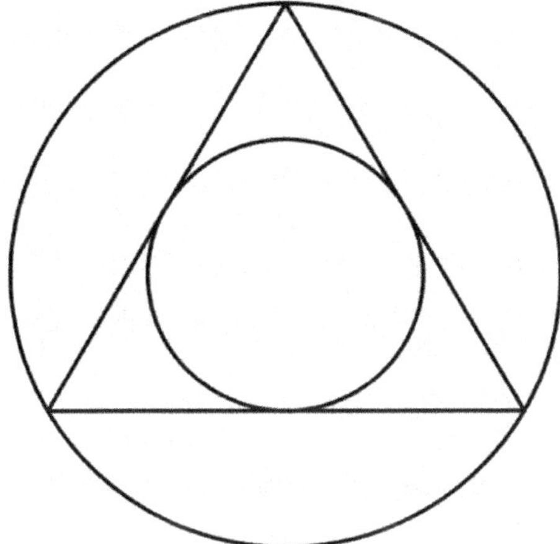

- Save and close the file.

Example 6 (Tan, Tan, Tan)

In this example, you will create a circle by selecting three objects to which it will be tangent.

- Click the **Open** button on the **Quick Access Toolbar**; the **Select File** dialog appears.

- Browse to the location of the **Line-example3.dwg** file and double-click on it; the file will be opened.

- Click **Home > Draw > Circle > Tan, Tan, Tan** on the ribbon.
- Select the bottom horizontal line of the drawing.
- Select the two inclined lines. This creates a circle tangent to the selected lines.

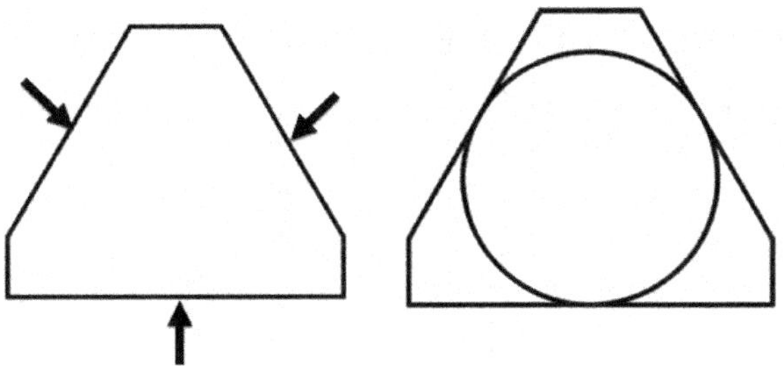

- Save and close the file.

Drawing Arcs

An arc is a portion of a circle. The total angle of an arc will always be less than 360 degrees, whereas the total angle of a circle is 360 degrees. AutoCAD provides you with eleven ways to draw an arc. You can draw arcs in different ways by using the tools available in the **Arcs** drop-down of the **Draw** panel. The usage of these tools will depend on your requirement. Some methods to create arcs are explained in the following examples.

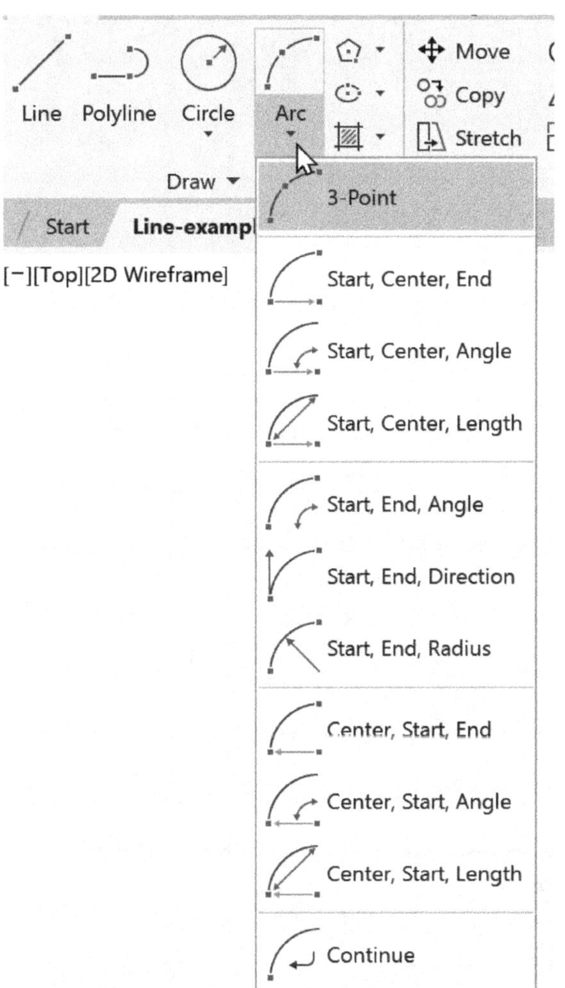

Example 1 (3-Point)

In this example, you will create an arc by specifying three points. The arc will pass through these points.

- Open the **Line-example1.dwg** file.
- Expand the **Draw** panel in the **Home** tab and select the **Multiple Points** tool.

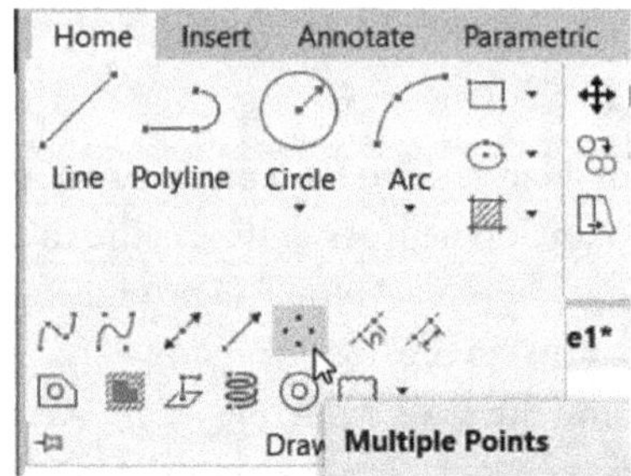

- Type 100,120 in the command line and press ENTER. It places a point above the rectangle.

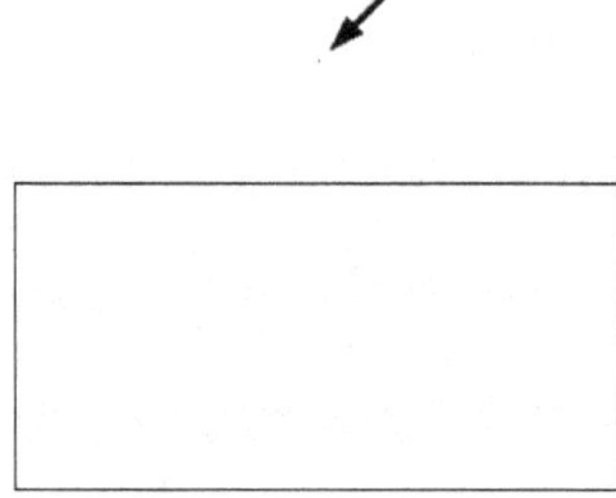

- Press ESC.
- Click the down arrow next to the **Object Snap** icon on the status bar, and then select the **Node** option from the menu.
- Click **Home > Draw > Arc > 3-Point** on the ribbon. The message, "Specify start point of arc or [Center]:" appears in the command line.
- Select the top left corner of the rectangle.
- Select the point located above the rectangle.
- Select the top right corner of the rectangle; the three-point arc will be created.

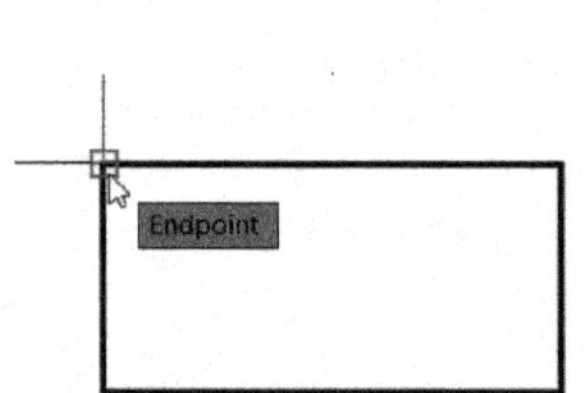

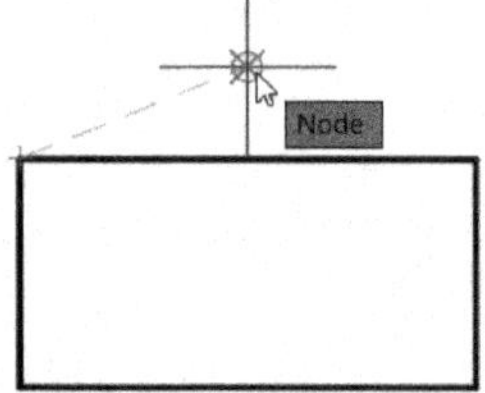

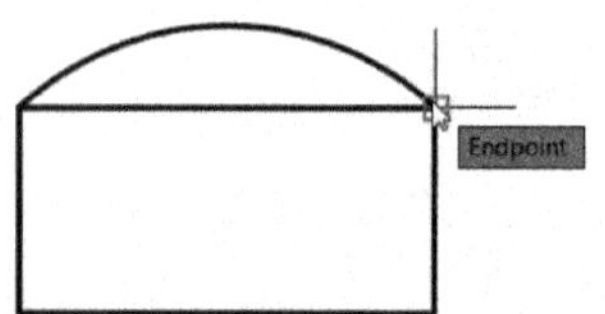

Example 2 (Start, Center, End)

In this example, you will draw an arc by specifying its start, center, and endpoints. The first two points define the radius of the arc, and the third point defines its included angle.

- Click **Home > Draw > Arc > Start, Center, End** on the ribbon. The message, "Specify start point of arc or [Center]:" appears in the command line.
- Pick an arbitrary point in the graphics window to define the start point of an arc. The message, "Specify center point of arc:" appears.
- Pick a point to define the radius of the circle. You can also type in the radius value and press ENTER; the message, "Specify end point of arc or [Angle/chord Length]:" appears.
  You will notice that, as you move the pointer, the included angle of the arc changes. The included angle of the arc is measured in the counter-clockwise direction. Press and hold the Ctrl key if you want to reverse the direction.

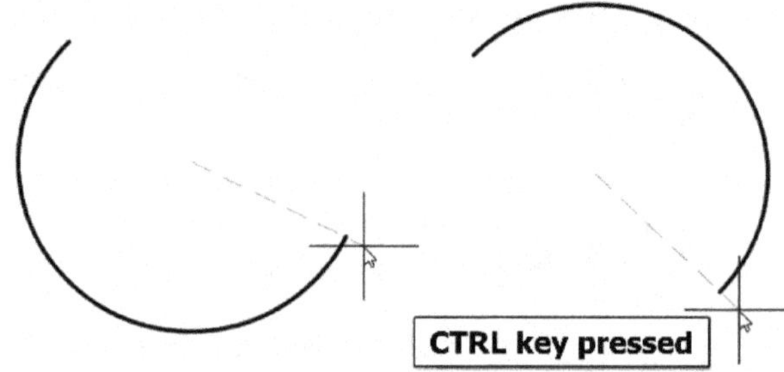

- Pick a point to define the included angle of the arc. You can also type the angle value and press ENTER.

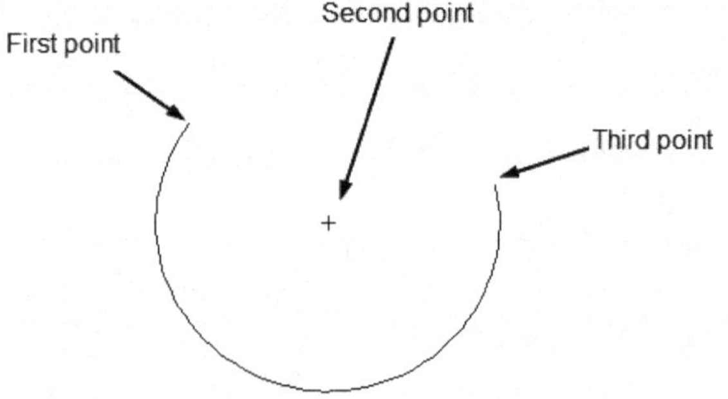

Example 3 (Start, End, Direction)

- Use the **Line** tool and create the drawing shown in the figure below. The dimensions are also given in the figure. (Use any one of the procedures given in the **Drawing Lines** section)

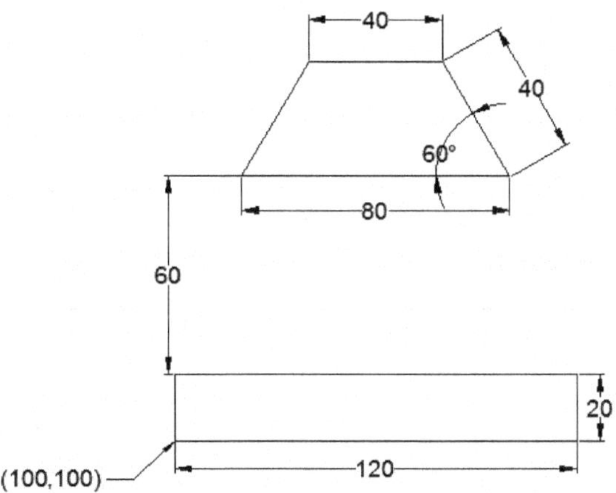

- Click **Home > Draw > Arc > Start, End, Direction** on the ribbon.
- Select the start and end points of the arc, as shown in the figure.

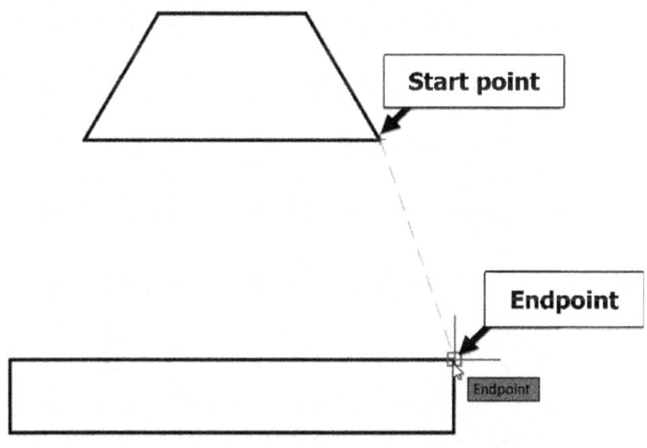

- Activate the **ORTHOMODE** icon on the status bar.
- Move the pointer vertically downward and click to specify the direction.

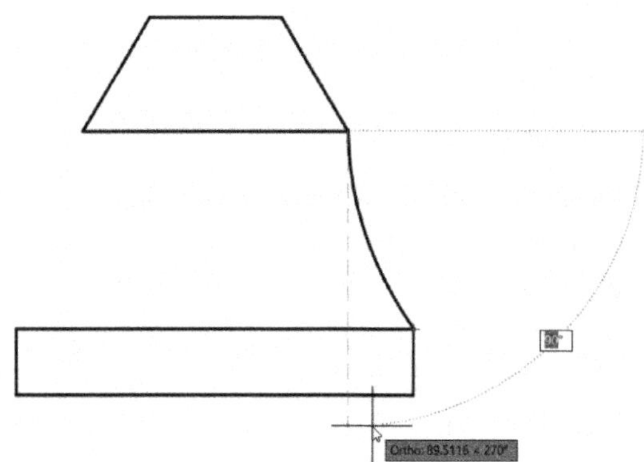

- Likewise, create another arc.

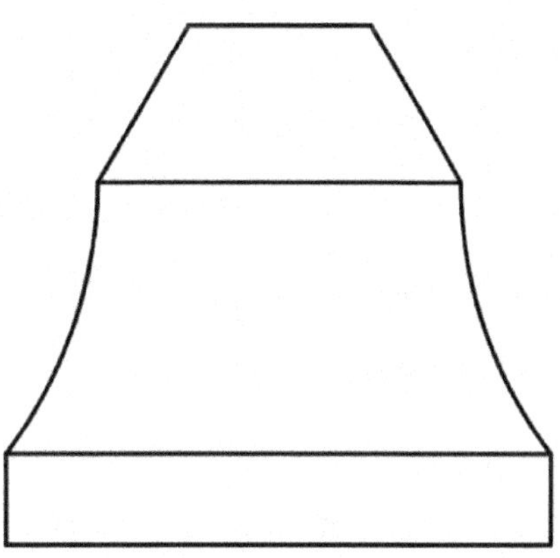

Drawing Polylines

A Polyline is a single object that consists of line segments and arcs. It is more versatile than a line, as you can assign a width to it. In the following example, you will create a closed polyline.

Example 1

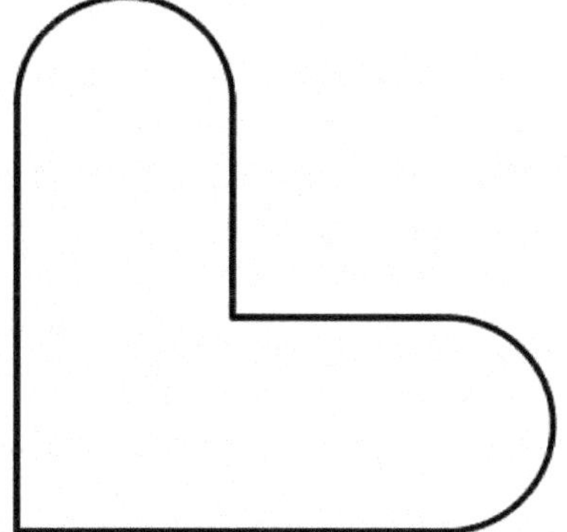

- Activate the **Ortho Mode** on the Status Bar.
- Click **Home > Draw > Polyline** on the ribbon or enter **PLINE** or **PL** in the command line; the message, "Specify start point:" appears in the

command line.

- Select an arbitrary point in the graphics window.
- Move the pointer horizontally toward right and type 100 — next, press ENTER.
- Select the **Arc** option from the command line.
- Move the pointer vertically upward and type **50** — next, press ENTER.
- Select the **Line** option from the command line.
- Move the pointer horizontally toward left and type **50** — next, press ENTER.
- Move the pointer vertically upward and type **50** — next, press ENTER.
- Select the **Arc** option from the command line.
- Move the pointer horizontally toward left and type **50** — next, press ENTER.
- Select the **CLose** option from the command line.

Now, when you click on a line segment from the sketch, the whole sketch will be selected. It is because the polyline created is a single object.

Drawing Rectangles

A rectangle is a four-sided single object. You can create a rectangle by just specifying its two diagonal corners. However, there are various methods to create a rectangle. These methods are explained in the following examples.

Example 1

In this example, you will create a rectangle by specifying its corner points.

- Open a new file.
- Click **Home > Draw > Rectangle** on the ribbon, or enter **RECTANG** or **REC** in the command line; the message, "Specify first corner point or [**Chamfer Elevation Fillet Thickness Width**]:" appears in the command line.
- Pick an arbitrary point in the graphics window; the message "Specify other corner point or [**Area Dimensions Rotation**]:" appears in the command line.
- Move the pointer diagonally toward the right and click to create a rectangle.

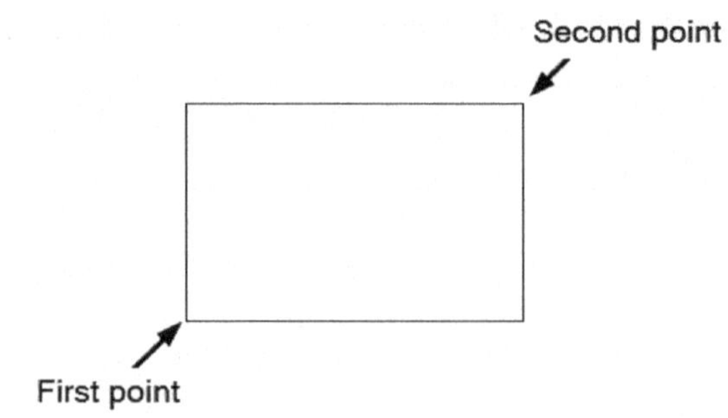

Example 2

In this example, you will create a rectangle by specifying its length and width.

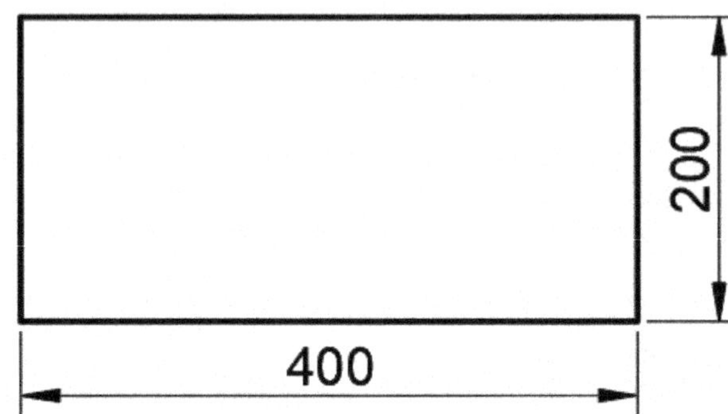

- Click **Home > Draw > Rectangle** on the ribbon, or enter **RECTANG** or **REC** in the command line.
- Specify the first corner of the rectangle by picking an arbitrary point in the graphics window.
- Follow the prompt sequence given next:
  Specify other corner point or [Area Dimensions Rotation]: Select the **Dimensions** option from the command line
  Specify length for rectangles: Type **400** and press ENTER.
  Specify width for rectangles: Type **200** and press ENTER.
  Specify other corner point or [Area Dimensions Rotation]: Move the pointer upward and click to create the rectangle.

Example 3

In this example, you will create a rectangle by specifying its area and width.

- Click **Home > Draw > Rectangle** on the ribbon, or enter **RECTANG** or **REC** in the command line.
- Specify the first corner of the rectangle by picking an arbitrary point.
- Follow the prompt sequence given next:
  Specify other corner point or [Area Dimensions Rotation]: Select the **Area** option from the command line
  Enter area of rectangle in current units: Type **20000** and press ENTER.
  Calculate rectangle dimensions based on [Length Width] <Length>: Select the **Width** option from the command line.
  Enter rectangle width: Type **100** and press ENTER; the length will be calculated automatically.

Example 4

In this example, you will create a rectangle with chamfered corners.

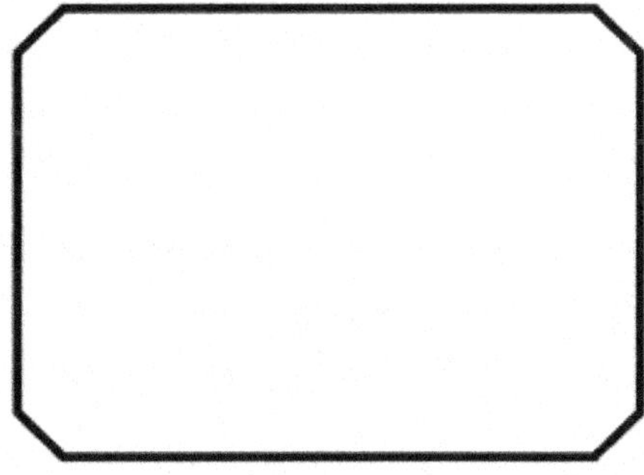

- Click **Home > Draw > Rectangle** on the ribbon, or enter **RECTANG** or **REC** in the command line.
- Follow the prompt sequence given next:
  Specify first corner point or [Chamfer Elevation Fillet Thickness Width]: Select the **Chamfer** option from the command line.
  Specify first chamfer distance for rectangles: Type **20** and press ENTER.
  Specify second chamfer distance for rectangles: Type **20** and press ENTER.

Specify first corner point or [Chamfer Elevation Fillet Thickness Width]: Click at an arbitrary point in the graphics window to specify the first corner.
Specify other corner point or [Area Dimensions Rotation]: Move the pointer diagonally toward the right and click to specify the second corner.

Example 5

In this example, you will create a rectangle with rounded corners.

- Click **Home > Draw > Rectangle** on the ribbon, or enter **RECTANG** or **REC** in the command line.
- Follow the prompt sequence given next:

  Specify first corner point or [Chamfer Elevation Fillet Thickness Width]: Select the **Fillet** option from the command line.
  Specify fillet radius for rectangles: Type **50** and press ENTER.
  Specify first corner point or [Chamfer Elevation Fillet Thickness Width]: Click at an arbitrary point in the graphics window to specify the first corner.
  Specify other corner point or [Area Dimensions Rotation]: Move the pointer diagonally toward the right and click to specify the second corner.

Example 6

In this example, you will create an inclined rectangle.

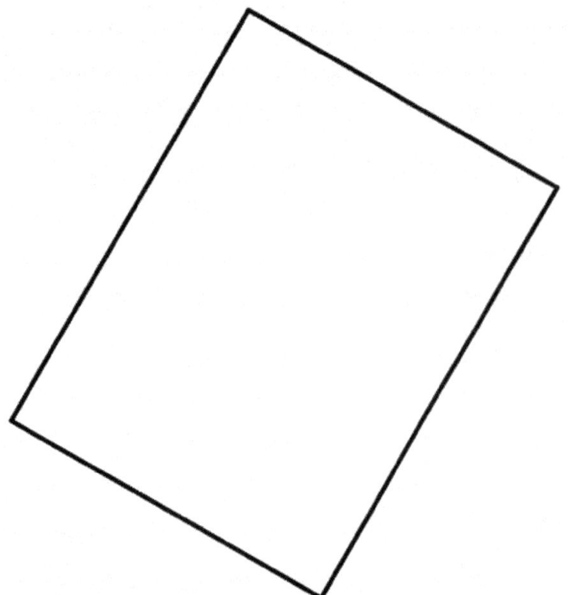

- Click **Home > Draw > Rectangle** on the ribbon, or enter **RECTANG** or **REC** in the command line.
- Select the **Fillet** option from the command line.
- Type 0 and press Enter.
- Specify the first corner of the rectangle by picking an arbitrary point.
- Follow the prompt sequence given next:

  Specify other corner point or [Area/Dimensions/Rotation]: Select the **Rotation** option from the command line.
  Specify rotation angle or [Pick points]: Type **60** and press ENTER.
  Specify other corner point or [Area/Dimensions/Rotation]: Select the **Dimensions** option from the command line.
  Specify length for rectangles: Type 400 and press ENTER.
  Specify width for rectangles: Type 300 and press ENTER.

- Move the pointer toward the right and click to position the rectangle.

Drawing Polygons

A Polygon is a single object having many sides ranging from 3 to 1024. In AutoCAD, you can create regular polygons having sides with equal length. There are two methods to create a polygon. These methods are explained in the following examples.

Example 1

In this example, you will create a polygon by specifying the number of sides and then determining the length of one side.

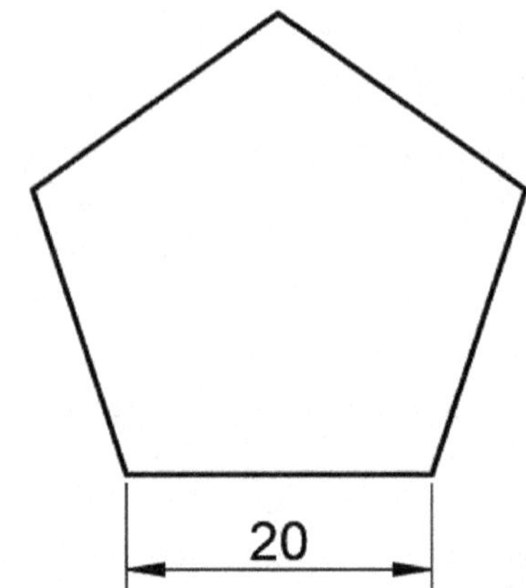

- Click **Home > Draw > Polygon** on the ribbon.

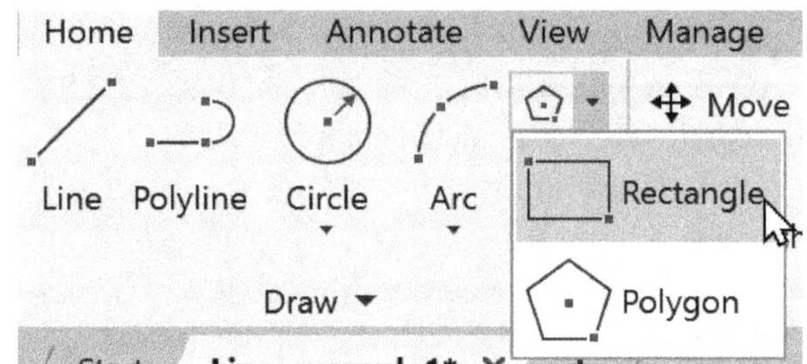

- Follow the prompt sequence given next.

  Enter number of sides <4>: Type **5** and press **ENTER**.
  Specify center of polygon or [Edge]: Select the **Edge** option from the command line.
  Specify first endpoint of edge: Select an arbitrary point.
  Specify second endpoint of edge: Move the pointer horizontally toward the right. Next, type **20**, and press **ENTER**.

Example 2

In this example, you will create a polygon by specifying the number of sides and drawing an imaginary circle (inscribed circle). The polygon will be created with its corners located on the imaginary circle. You can also create a polygon with the circumscribed circle. A circumscribed circle is an imaginary circle which is tangent to all the sides of a polygon.

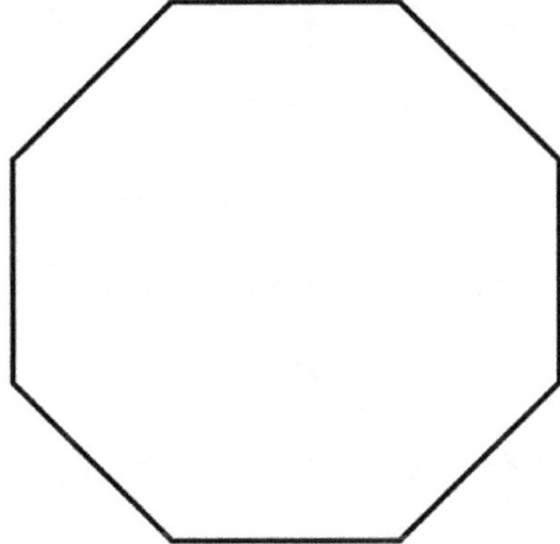

- Type **POL** in the command line and press ENTER; the **POLYGON** command will be activated.
- Follow the prompt sequence given next:

  Enter number of sides <5>: Type **8** and press ENTER.
  Specify center of polygon or [Edge]: Select an arbitrary point
  Enter an option [Inscribed in circle Circumscribed about circle] <C>: Select the **Inscribed in circle** option from the command line.
  Specify radius of circle: Type **20** and press ENTER; a polygon will be created with its corners touching the imaginary circle.

Drawing Splines

A spline is a smooth curve that is defined mathematically and passes through a series of points, known as control points. Splines are used to create complex shapes and curves that would be difficult or impossible to create using straight lines or simple curves.

There are several types of splines used in CAD, including B-splines, Bezier curves, and NURBS (Non-Uniform Rational B-Splines). The Spline command in CAD creates a NURBS curve, which allows for irregular spacing of selected points to achieve sharp corners, for example. A Spline can also be used to create regular shapes such as arcs, circles, and ellipses. Irregular shapes can be combined with regular curves, all in one spline curve definition.

Splines are non-uniform curves, which are used to create irregular shapes. In AutoCAD, you can create splines by using two methods: **Spline Fit** and **Spline CV**. These methods are explained in the following examples:

Example 1: (Spline Fit)

In this example, you will create a spline using the **Spline Fit** method. In this method, you need to specify various points in the graphics window. The spline will be created, passing through the specified points.

- Start a new drawing file.
- Use the **Line** tool and create a sketch similar to the one shown below.

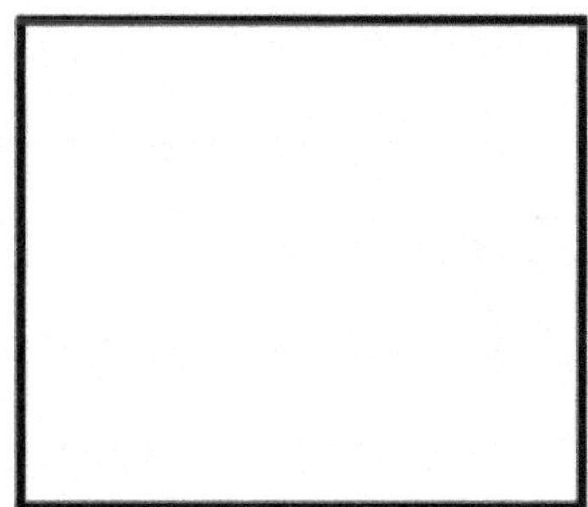

- Expand the **Draw** panel in the **Home** tab and select the **Spline Fit** button; the message, "Specify first point or [Method Knots Object]:" appears in the command line.

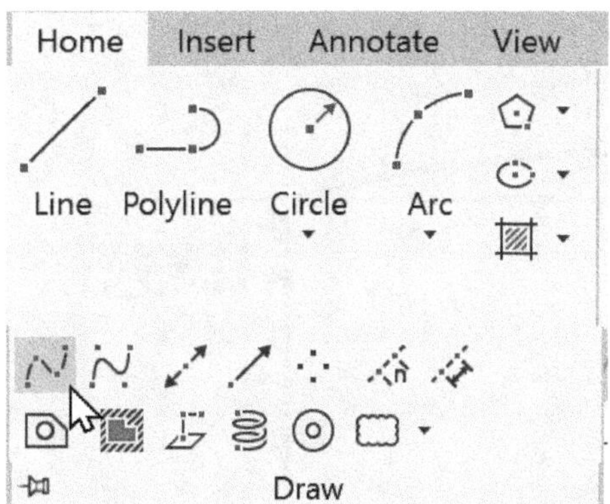

- Select the lower-left corner of the sketch; the message, "Enter next point or [start Tangency toLerance]:" appears in the command line.

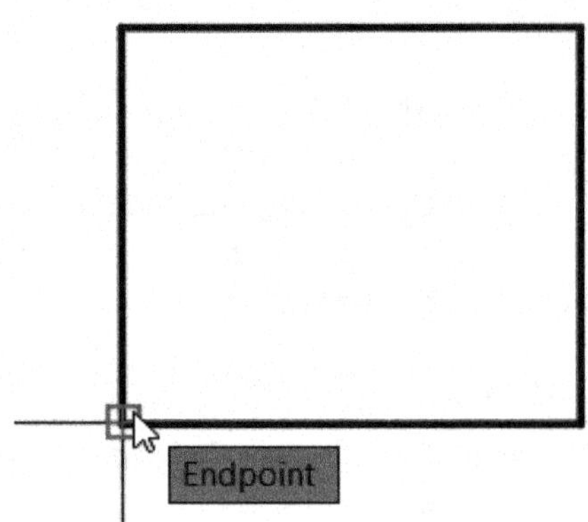

- Select the top-left corner point of the sketch.

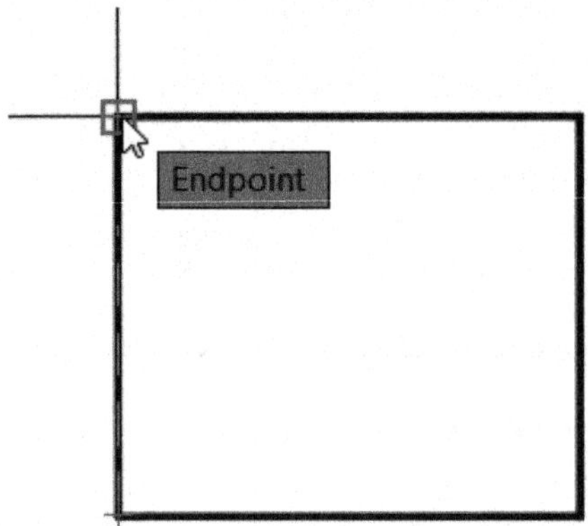

- Similarly, select the top-right and lower-right corners; a spline will be attached to the pointer.
- Press ENTER.

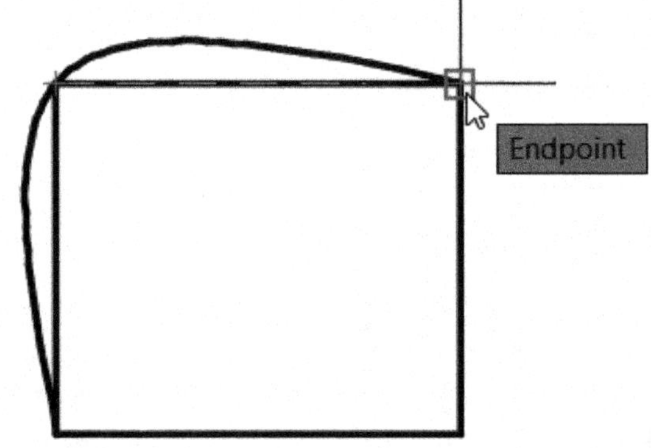

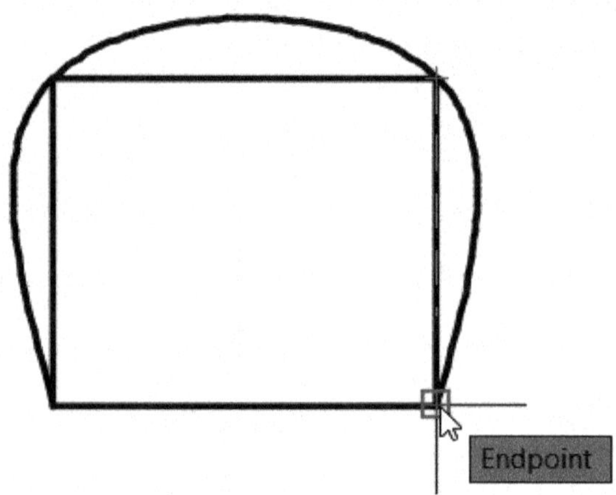

Example 2: (Spline CV)

In this example, you will create a spline by using the **Spline CV** method. In this method, you will specify various points called control vertices. As you specify the control vertices, imaginary lines are created connecting them. The spline will be drawn tangent to these lines.

- Expand the **Draw** panel in the **Home** tab and select the **Spline CV** button.

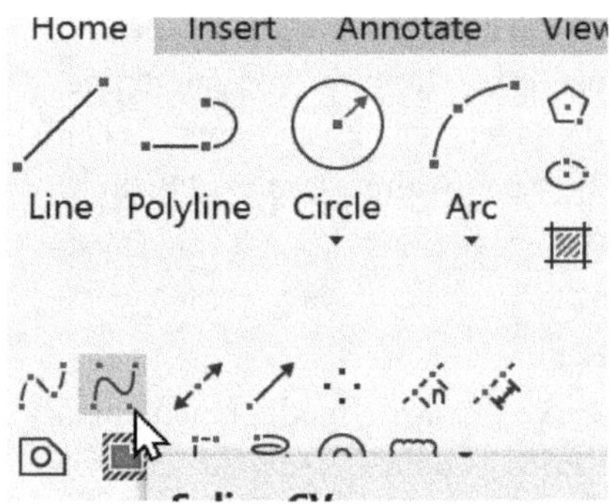

- Select the four corners of the sketch in the same sequence as in the earlier example.

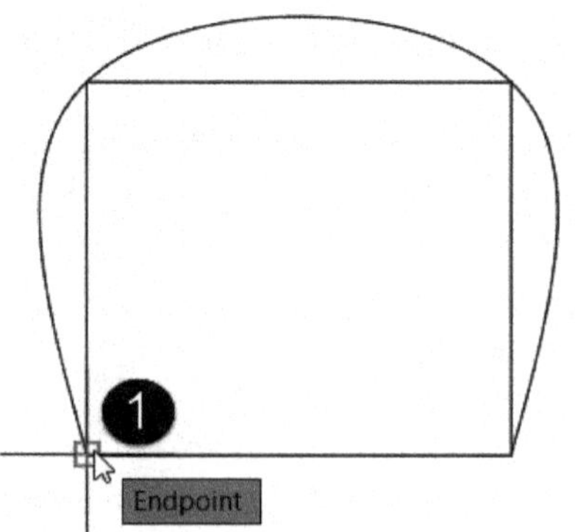

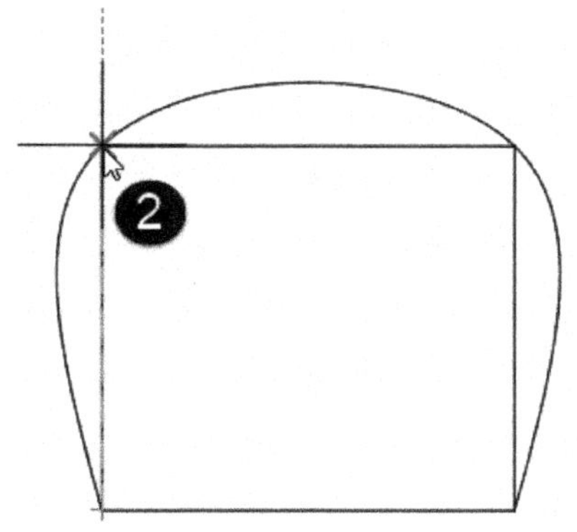

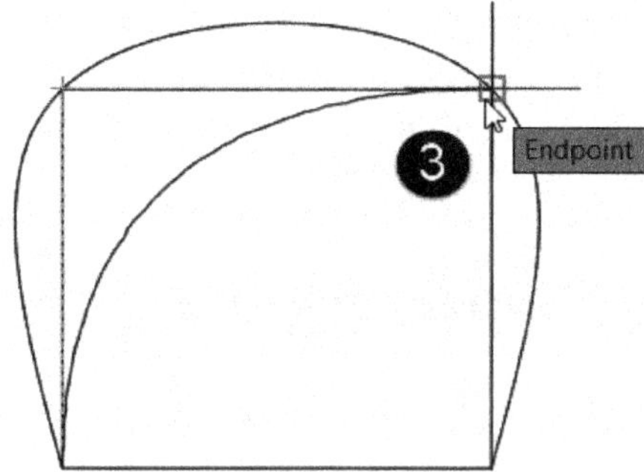

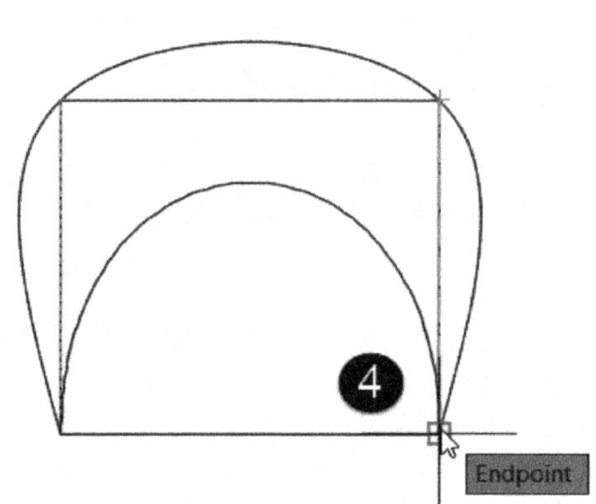

- Press ENTER; a spline with control vertices will be created.

Example 3:

- Create a polyline, as shown.

- Activate the **Spline CV** command.
- Select **Object** from the command line.

- Select the polyline and press Enter; the polyline is converted into a spline.

Drawing Ellipses

An ellipse is two dimensional shape formed when it intersects with a plane at angle. It looks like an elongated circle and has two axes (major and minor). The Major axis is the longest diameter of the ellipse. Whereas, the minor axis is its shortest diameter.

In AutoCAD, you can draw an ellipse in three different ways by using the tools available in the **Ellipse** drop-down of the **Draw** panel. The three different ways to draw ellipses are explained in the following examples.

Example 1 (Center)

In this example, you will draw an ellipse by specifying three points. The first point defines the center of the ellipse. The second and third points define the two axes of the ellipse.

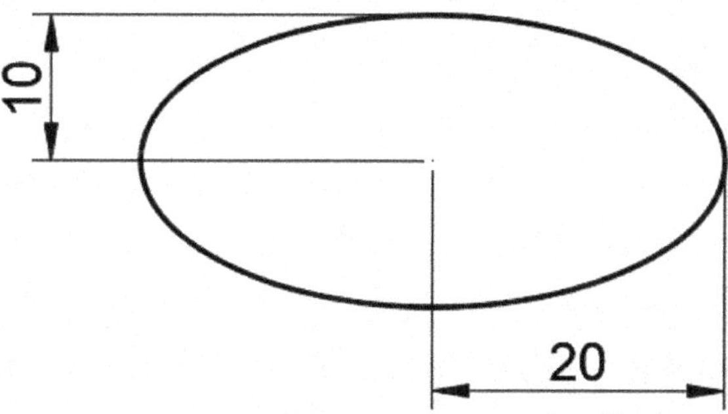

- Click **Home > Draw > Ellipse > Center** on the ribbon; the message, "Specify center of ellipse:" appears in the command line.
- Select an arbitrary point in the graphics window; the message, "Specify endpoint of axis:" appears in the command line.
- Move the pointer horizontally and type 20. Next, press ENTER; the message, "Specify distance to other axis or [Rotation]:" appears in the command line.

- Type 10 and press ENTER; the ellipse will be created.

Example 2 (Axis, End)

In this example, you will draw an ellipse by specifying three points. The first two points define the location and length of the first axis. The third point defines the second axis of the ellipse.

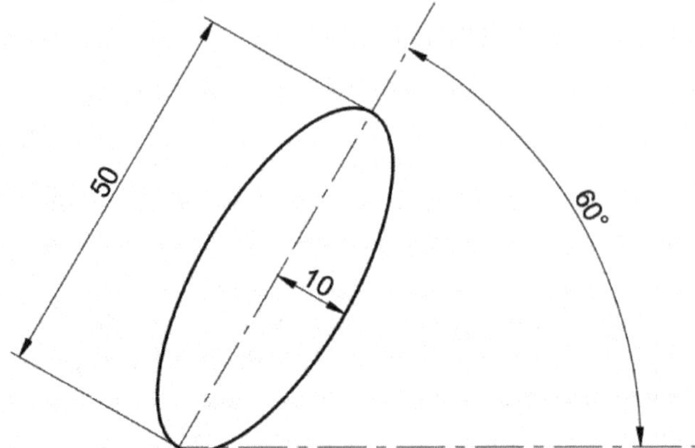

- Activate the **Dynamic Input** icon on the status bar, if it is not active.
- Click **Home > Draw > Ellipse > Axis, End** on the ribbon.
- Select an arbitrary point to specify an axis endpoint.
- Type **50** as the length of the first axis and press TAB.
- Type **120** as angle and press ENTER.
- Type **10** as the radius of the second axis and press ENTER; the ellipse will be created inclined at a 60-degree angle.

Example 3 (Elliptical Arc)

In this example, you will draw an elliptical arc. To draw an elliptical arc, first, you need to define the location and length of the first axis. Next, set the radius of the second axis; an ellipse will be displayed. Next, you need to set the start angle of the elliptical arc. The start angle can be any angle between 0 and 360. After defining the start angle, you need to specify the end angle of the elliptical arc.

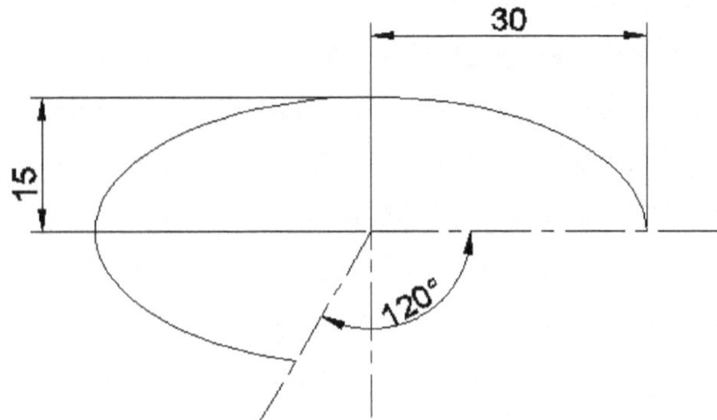

- Turn on the **ORTHOMODE** on the Status bar.

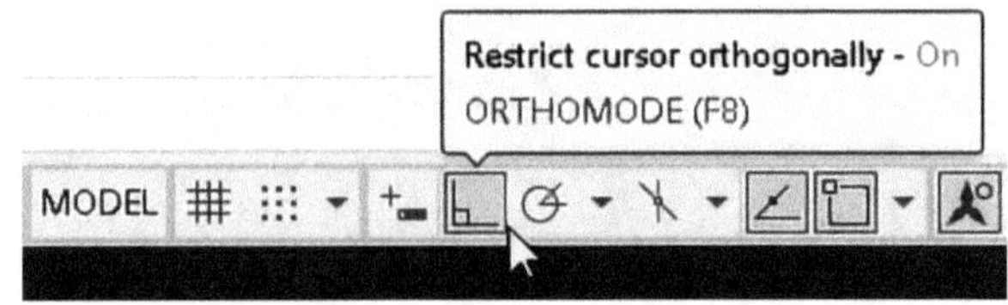

- Click **Home > Draw > Ellipse > Elliptical Arc** on the ribbon.
- Select an arbitrary point to specify an axis endpoint.
- Move the pointer horizontally toward left and type **60**. Next, press ENTER to specify the axis length.
- Move the pointer upward and type 15. Next, press ENTER to specify the length of another axis.
- Type **0** and press ENTER to specify the start angle.
- Type **240** and press ENTER to specify the end angle.

Solid

The **Solid** command creates a two-dimensional triangle or quadrilateral. The area inside the triangle or quadrilateral is filled with a solid color. Type SOLID in the command line and press ENTER. Next, specify the first point. Next, move the pointer and specify the second point. Move the pointer and select the third point; you are prompted to specify the fourth point. Now, you can press ENTER to create a solid triangle or specify the fourth point to create a solid quadrilateral.

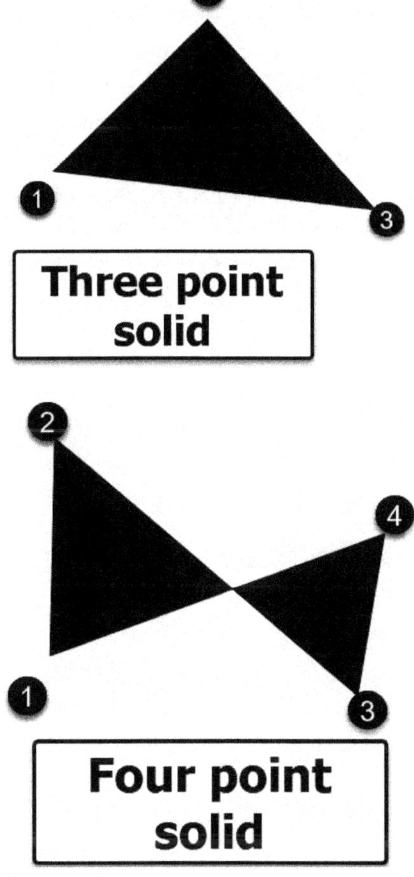

Three point solid

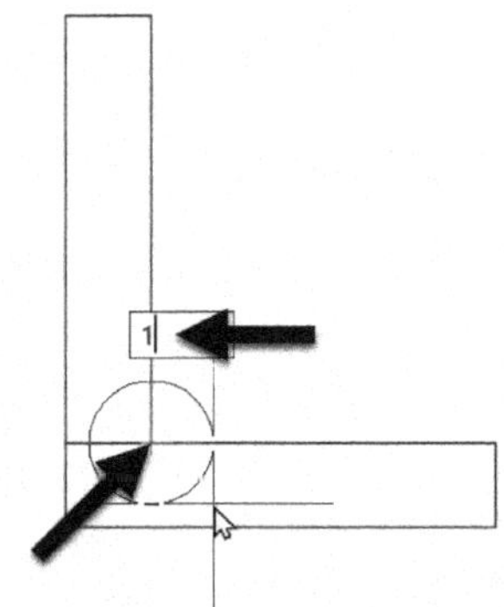

Four point solid

Example

- Download and open the SOLID_example.dwg file.
- Type CIRCLE in the command line and press ENTER.
- Select the corner point, as shown.
- Move the pointer outward, type 1 and press ENTER; a circle is created.

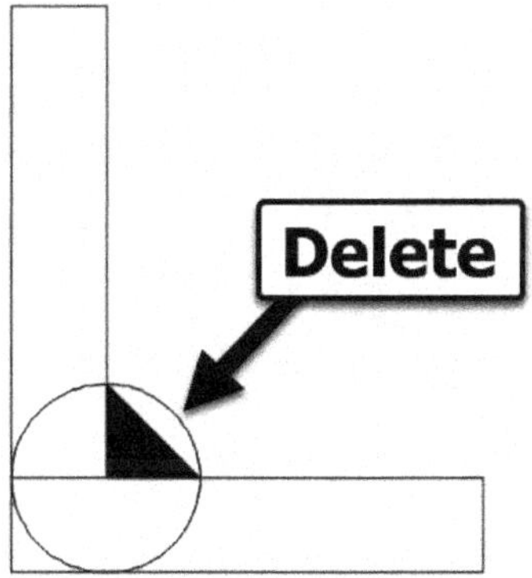

- Type SOLID in the command line and press ENTER.
- Select the left quadrant point of the circle.
- Select the top quadrant point of the circle.
- Select the center point of the circle and press ENTER twice.

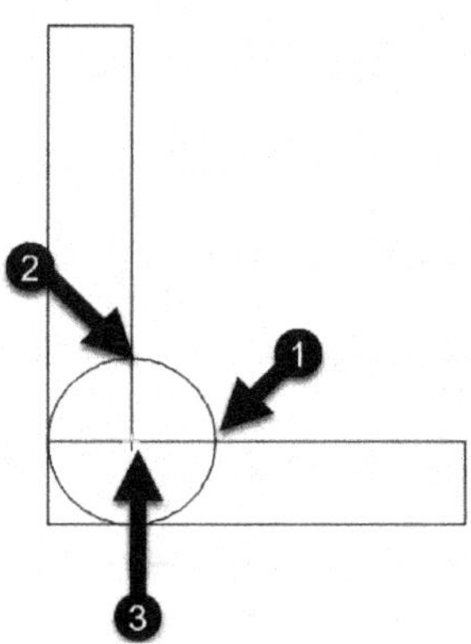

- Select the circle and press DELETE.

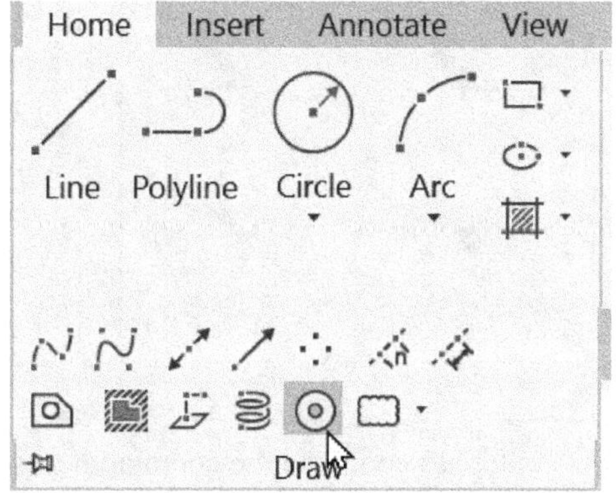

Donut

The **DONUT** command is used to create a closed ring or filled circle with a hollow center. This command is useful in creating designs that require shapes with circular openings or rings. To use the DONUT command, follow these steps:

- Download and open the Donut_example.dwg file.
- Type DONUT into the command line (or) click **Home** tab > **Draw** panel > **Donut** on the ribbon.

- Specify the diameter of the inside edge of the donut by either selecting two points or typing in the desired value.

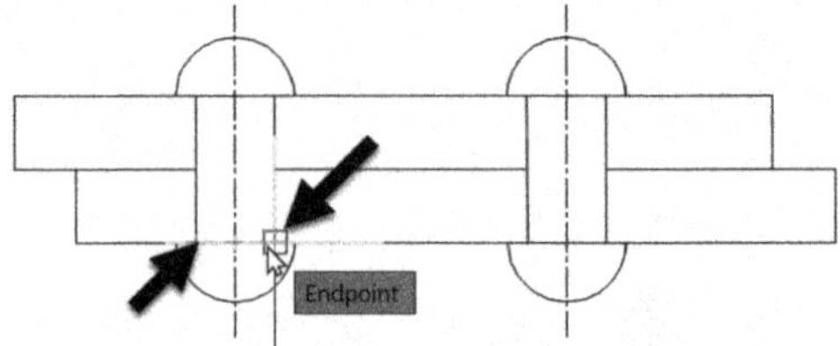

Two points selected to define the inner diameter

- Specify the diameter of the outside edge of the donut by either selecting an existing point or typing in the desired value. The outside diameter must be larger than the inside diameter.

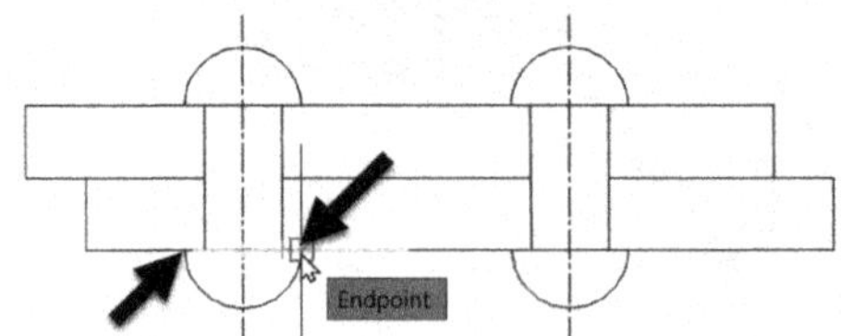

Two points selected to define the outside diameter

- Specify the center point of the donut by either selecting an existing point or typing in the X, Y, and Z coordinates.

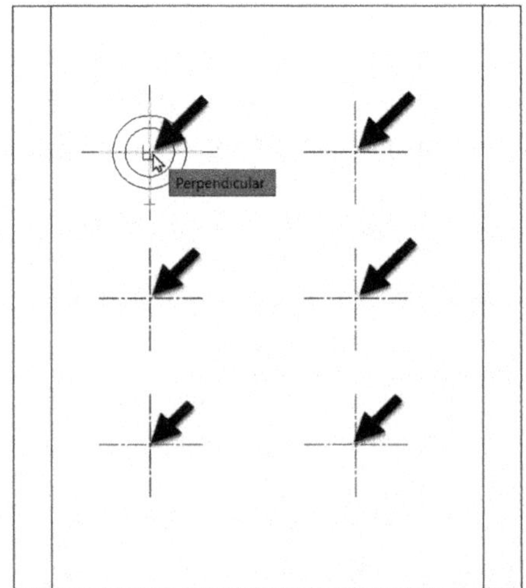

- Press "Enter" to complete the command.

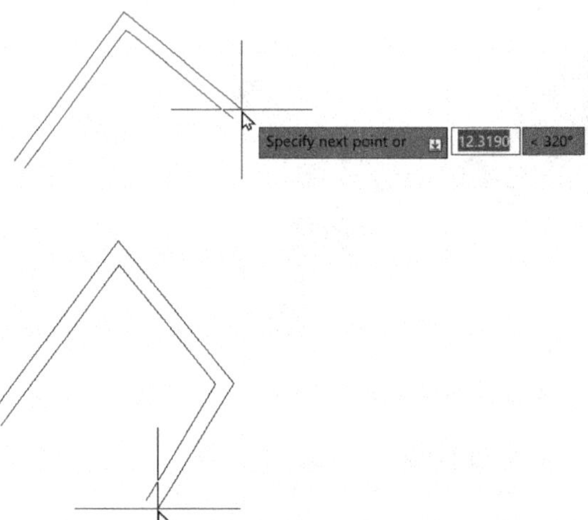The MLINE Command

The **MLINE** command is used to create complex lines and shapes that have multiple segments with different properties such as width, style, and color. This command allows you to create parallel lines, zigzag lines, and other types of shapes with ease. To use the MLINE command, simply type **MLINE** in the command line. Once the command is activated, you can specify the start point of the first segment. Next, specify the endpoint of the first segment. Then, specify the endpoint of the second segment, and so on, until all the required multiline segments have been established.

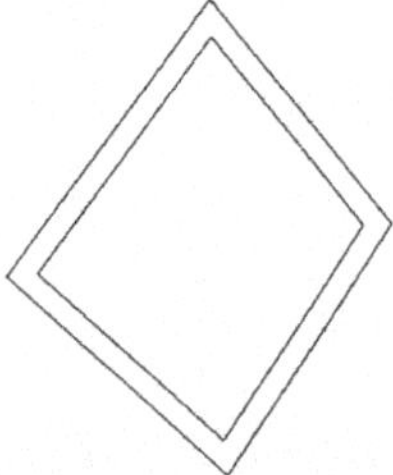

To generate a closed shape, choose the **Close** option from the command line. Alternatively, press ENTER to finalize the creation of the multiline segments.

The command line displays various options when you activate the **MLINE** command. these options are discussed next.

Style

Allows you to select the style of the line segments. You can choose from the default STANDARD style or any other line style that has been created. You can create you own multiline style using the **MLSTYLE** command. To do this, type MLSTYLE in the command line and press ENTER. In the **Multiline Style** dialog box that appears, click on the **New** button to create a new multiline style.

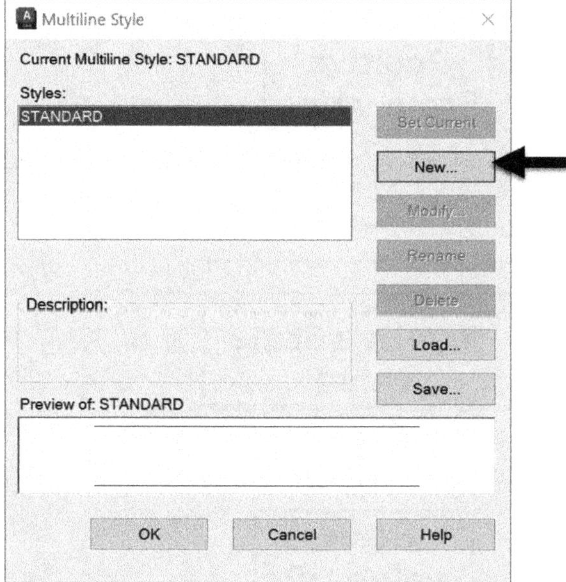

Enter a name for the new multiline style in the **New Style name** box of the **Create New Multiline Style** dialog. Next, click the **Continue** button.

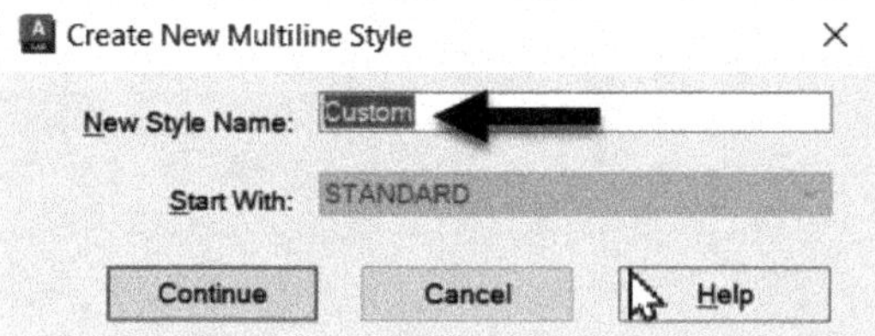

On the **New Multiline Style** dialog, in the **Elements** section, click on the **Add** button to add a new element to the multiline style. Next, select the newly added element and specify a value in the **Offset** box located below the **Elements** section. Next, specify the **Color** and **Linetype** of the newly added element using the **Color** drop-down and **Linetype** button, respectively.

Use the options in the **Caps** section to add caps to the start and end points of the multiline. You can add a Line, Outer arc, or Inner arcs at the start and endpoints of the multline.

To specify a color to be filled inside the area enclosed by the elements of the multiline, utilize the **Fill color** drop-down. If you wish to see lines at the points where two

segments are joined, select the **Display joints** option. Once you have defined all the elements, click **OK** to save the new multiline style.

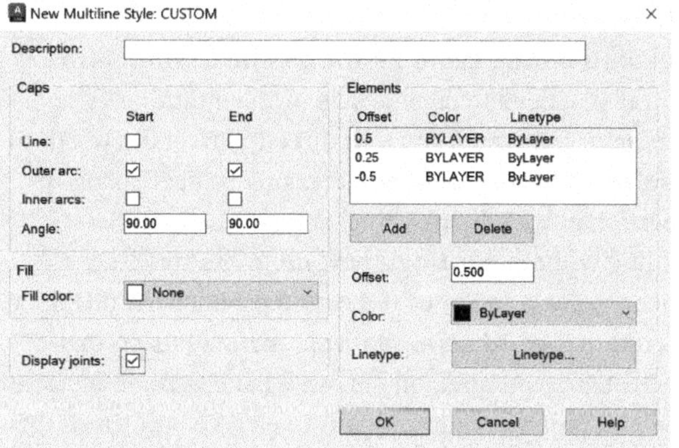

Click **Set Current** on the **Multiline Style** dialog and click to set the newly create multiline style as current. Your newly created multiline style can now be used in the current drawing or saved for use in future drawings.

Justification

The way in which the multiline is drawn between specified points is dependent on the chosen justification. The available justification options include **Top**, **Zero**, or **Bottom**.

When **Top** is selected, the top of the line elements are aligned with the chosen points during the drawing process.

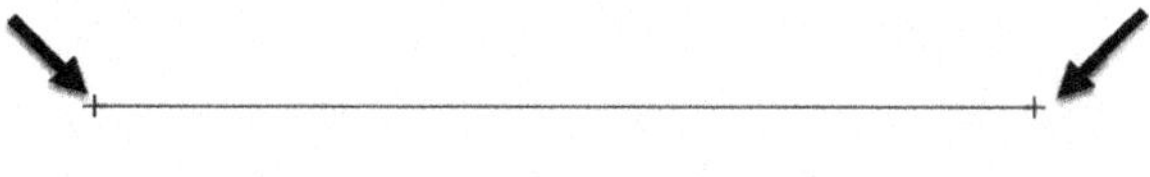

On the other hand, selecting **Zero** will result in the center of the line elements being used as the chosen point.

Selecting **Bottom** will align the bottom line element between the specified points.

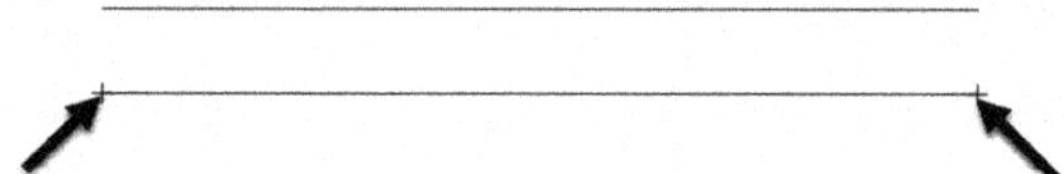

The **Justification** methods are designed for drawing in the positive X direction, from left to right. This means that when using the Bottom justification, the bottom of the multiline will be positioned between specified points when drawn from left to right. However, if you draw the

multiline from right to left, the multiline will be flipped
upside down.

Scale

Specifies the scale factor for the multiline. This option is
useful if you need to change size of the multiline. The
scale factor that you input will directly affect the width of
the defined multiline, either increasing or decreasing it
proportionately. It helps you change the size of the
multiline without creating a new multiline style. For
instance, a scale factor of 0.5 would produce a multiple
line pattern that is half of the width defined using the
MLSTYLE command. On the other hand, a scale factor of
1.5 would create a pattern that is one and a half times the
width, while a scale factor of 4.0 would result in a pattern
four times wider than the multiline width defined using
the MLSTYLE command.

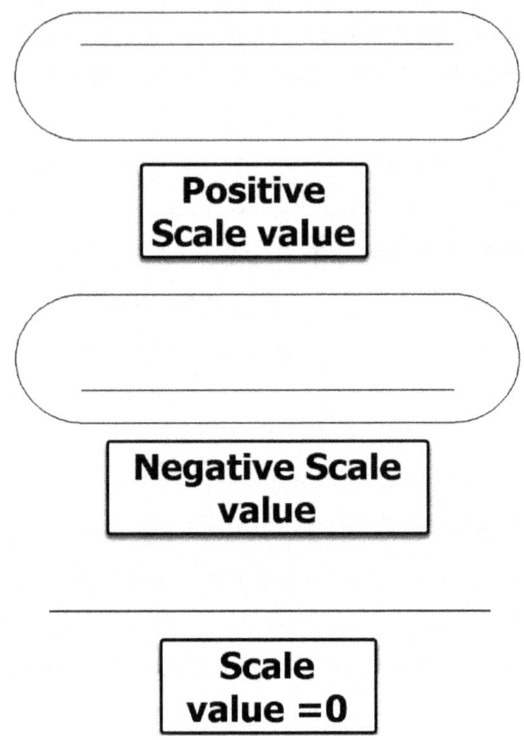

Note that you also have the option to input negative scale
values, which will reverse the order of the multline.
Alternatively, using a value of 0 will collapse the
multiline pattern into a single line.

Exercises

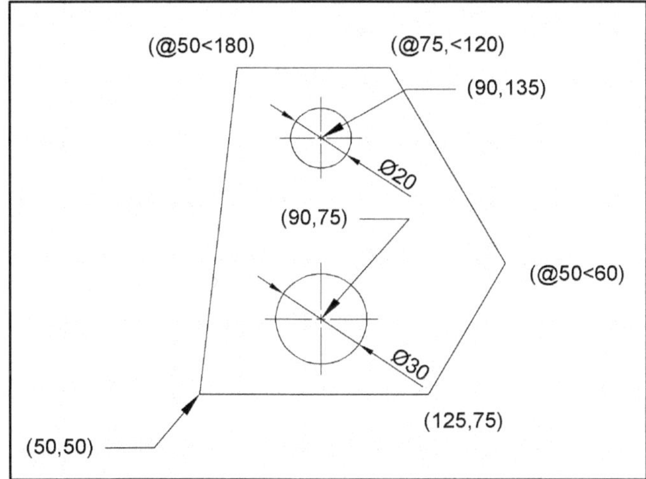

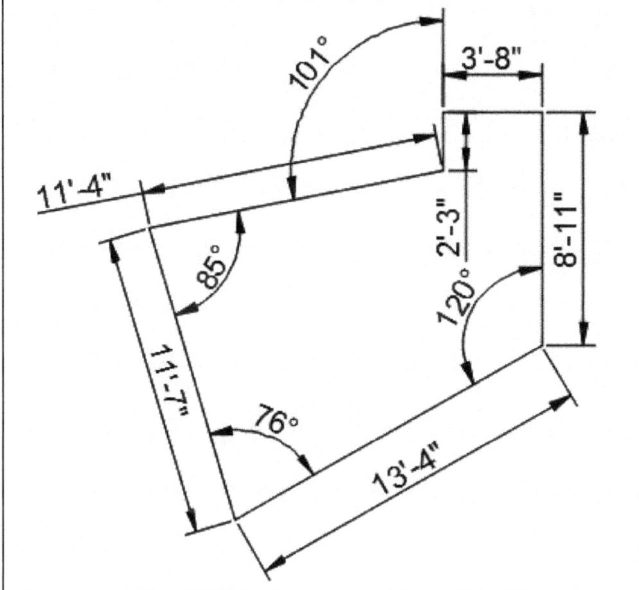

(@50<180)
(@75,<120)
(90,135)
Ø20
(90,75)
(@50<60)
(125,75)
Ø30
(50,50)

101°
3'-8"
11'-4"
2'-3"
8'-11"
85°
120°
11'-7"
76°
13'-4"

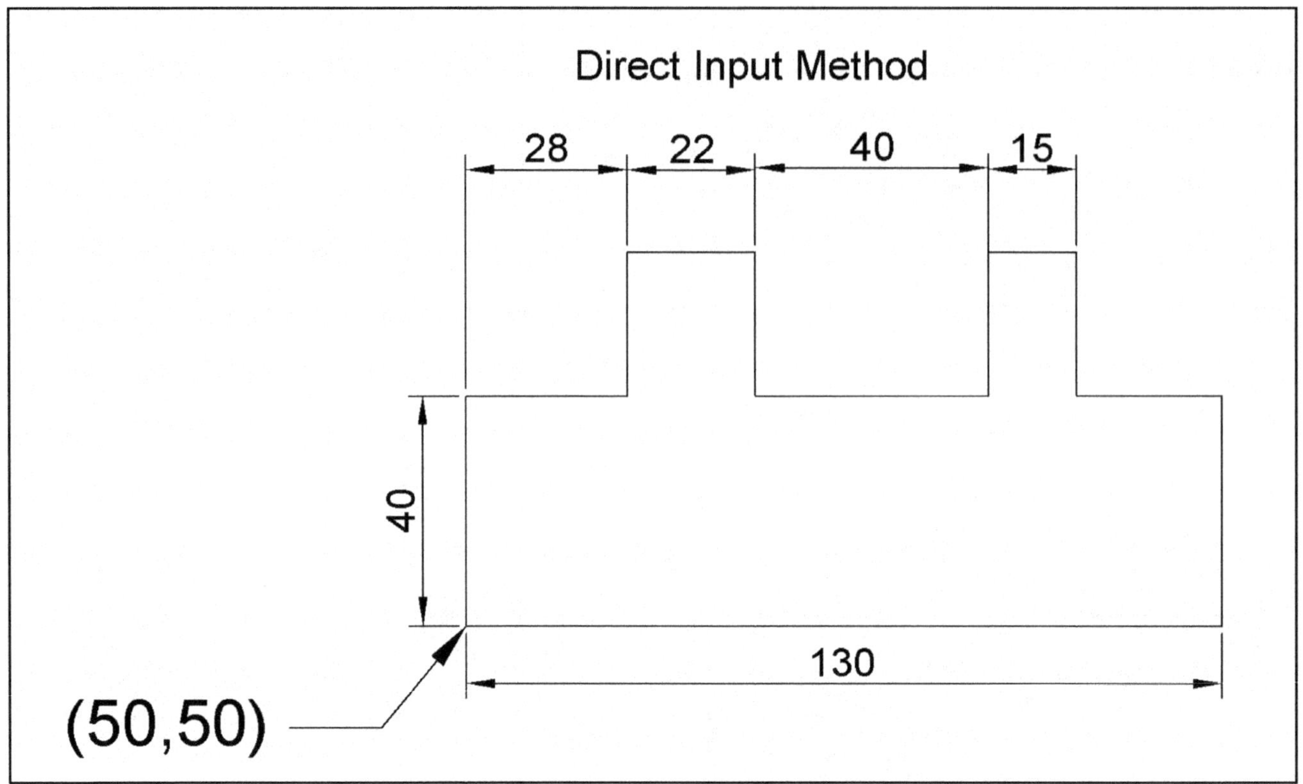

Direct Input Method
28
22
40
15
40
130
(50,50)

Chapter 3: Drawing Aids

In this chapter, you will learn to do the following:

- **Use Grid and Snap**
- **Use Ortho Mode and Polar Tracking**
- **Use Object Snaps and Object Snap Tracking**
- **Create Layers and assign properties to it**
- **Zoom and Pan drawings**

Drawing Aids

In AutoCAD, drawing requires considering two important factors: speed and accuracy. As you progress, you'll understand the significance of these aspects.

While speed is about completing your drawings quickly, accuracy takes precedence. It's more important to produce precise and correct designs rather than rushing through them. Accuracy allows for better collaboration and ensures that others can work effectively with your drawings.

To achieve precise and swift results, it's crucial to define the drawing settings in AutoCAD. Many of these settings can be easily turned on or off from the status bar, conveniently located for quick access. Additionally, by right-clicking on the status bar button, you can access additional drawing settings beyond the default options.

Setting Grid and Snap

Grid is the primary drawing setting. It makes the graphics window appear like a graph paper. You can turn ON the grid display by clicking the **Grid** icon on the status bar or just pressing **F7** on the keyboard.

Snap is used for drawing objects by using the intersection points of the grid lines. When you turn the **Snap Mode** ON, you will be able to select only grid points. In the following example, you will learn to set the grid and snap settings.

Example:

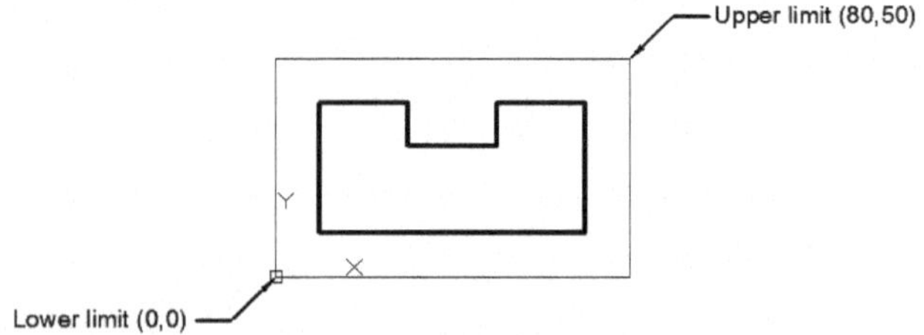

- Click **Application Menu > New**; the **Select Template** dialog appears.
- Select the **acadISO-Named Plot Styles** template. Click **Open**.
- On the Status bar, click the down arrow next to the **Snap Mode** icon and select **Snap Settings**. The **Drafting Settings** dialog appears.
- Click the **Snap and Grid** tab on the dialog.
- Set **Grid X spacing** to **10** and press the TAB key; the **Grid Y spacing** is updated with the same value.
- Set **Major line every** to **10**.

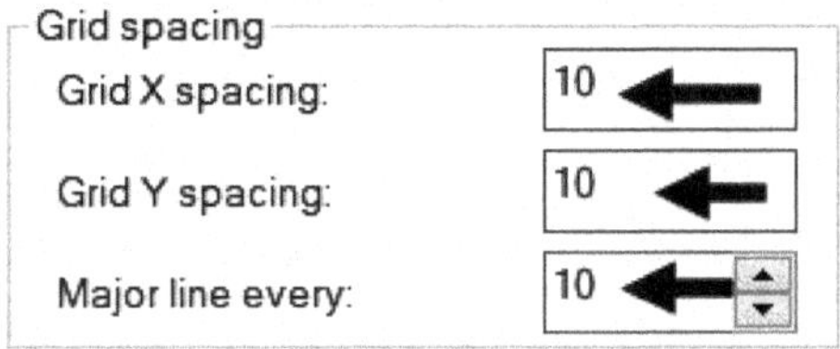

- Select the **Snap On** checkbox.
- Make sure that **Snap X spacing** and **Snap Y spacing** is set to **10**.

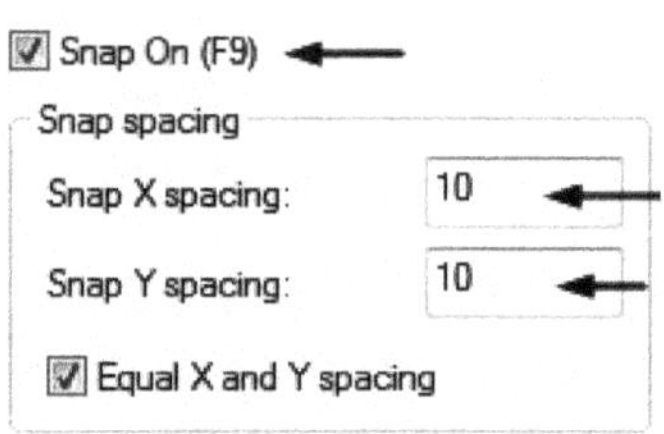

- Make sure that the **Grid snap** option is selected in the **Snap type** group.

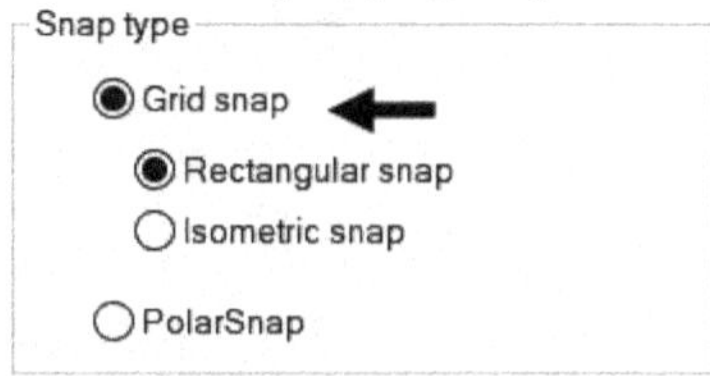

- Select the **Rectangular snap** option under **Grid snap**.

- Click **OK** on the dialog.
- Activate the **Grid** # icon on the Status Bar.

Setting the Limits of a drawing

You can set the limits of a drawing by defining its lower-left and top-right corners. By setting Limits of a drawing, you will determine the size of the drawing area. In AutoCAD, limits are set to some default values. However, you can redefine the limits to change the drawing area as per your requirement.

- Type **Limits** at the command line and press ENTER.

- Type 0,0 and press ENTER to define the lower limit. Now, you need to define the upper limit.
- Type 80,50 and press the ENTER key.
- On the Navigate Bar, click **Zoom > Zoom All**; the graphics window will be zoomed to the limits.

Setting the Lineweight

Line weight is the thickness of the objects that you draw. In AutoCAD, there is a default lineweight assigned to objects. However, you can set a new lineweight. The method to set the lineweight is explained below.

- On the Status bar, click the **Customization** ≡ option, and then select **LineWeight** from the flyout. This shows the **LineWeight** icon on the status bar.
- Activate the **Show/Hide Lineweight** icon located on the status bar.
- Right click on the **Show/Hide Lineweight** icon, and then select **Lineweight Settings**. The **Lineweight Settings** dialog appears.
- On the **Lineweight Settings** dialog, select **0.40** mm from the **Default** drop-down.

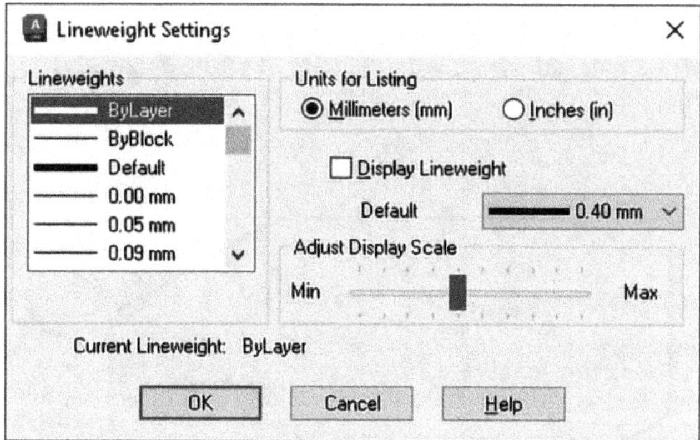

- Click **OK**.
- Type **L** in the command line and press ENTER.
- Type 10,10 and press ENTER to define the first point.
- Move the pointer horizontally toward the right and click on the sixth grid point from the first point.
- Move the pointer vertically upwards and select the third grid point from the second point.
- Move the pointer horizontally toward the left and select the second grid point from the previous point.
- Move the pointer vertically downwards and select the grid point next to the previous point.
- Move the pointer horizontally toward the left and select the second grid point from the previous point.
- Move the pointer vertically upwards and select the grid point next to the previous point.
- Move the pointer horizontally toward the left and select the second grid point from the previous point.
- Right-click and select **Close**.

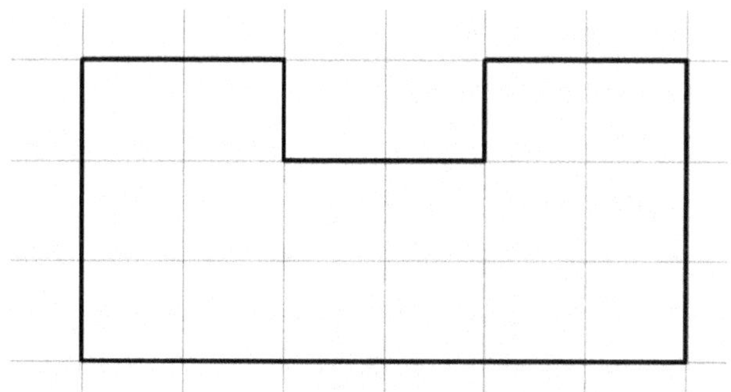

- Save and close the file.

Using Ortho mode and Polar Tracking

Ortho mode is used to draw orthogonal (horizontal or vertical) lines. Polar Tracking is used to constrain the lines to angular increments. In the following example, you will create a drawing with the help of Ortho Mode and Polar Tracking.

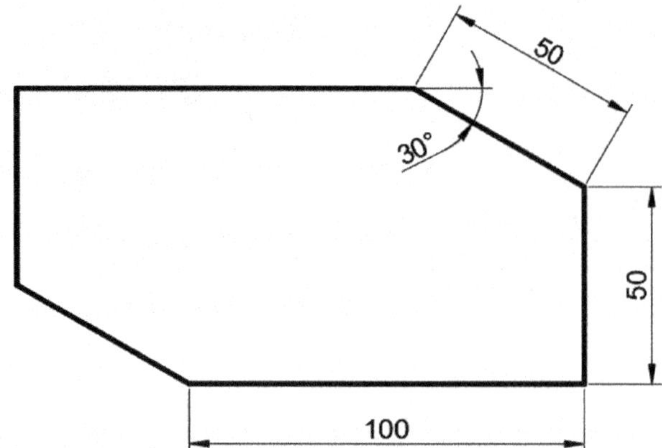

- Open a new AutoCAD file.
- Deactivate the **Grid Mode** and **Snap Mode** icons on the status bar.
- Click the **Ortho Mode** icon on the status bar.
- Click **Zoom All** on the **Navigation Bar**.
- Click the **Line** button on the **Draw** panel.
- Select an arbitrary point to define the starting point.
- Move the pointer toward the right, type 100, and press ENTER; you will notice that a horizontal line is created.
- Move the pointer upwards, type 50, and press ENTER; you will notice that a vertical line is created.
- Click the **Polar Tracking** icon on the status bar.
- Click the down arrow next to the **Polar tracking** icon and select **30** from the menu.

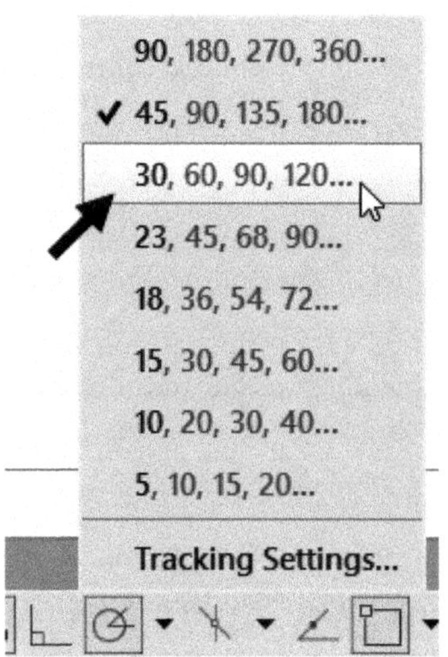

You will notice a track line at 30-degree increments when you rotate the pointer.

- Move the pointer and stop when the tooltip displays <150 angle value.

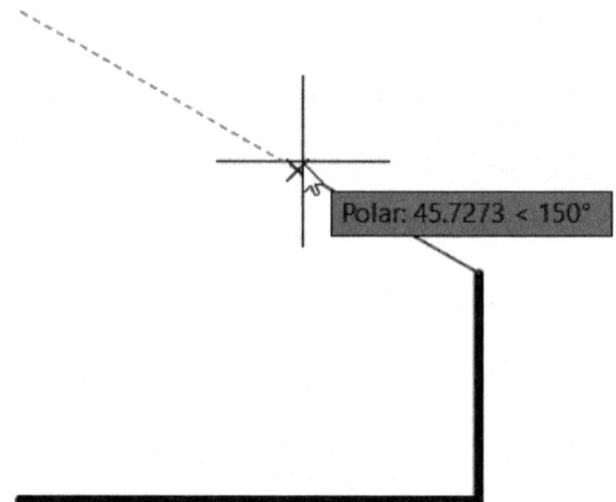

- Type 50 and press ENTER when the tooltip displays <150°.
- Move the pointer toward left.
- Type 100 and press ENTER when the tooltip displays <180°.
- Move the pointer vertically downward.
- Type 50 and press ENTER when the tooltip displays <270°.
- Right-click and select **Close**.

Using Layers

Layers are like a group of transparent sheets that are combined into a complete drawing. The figure below displays a drawing consisting of object lines and dimension lines. In this example, the object lines are created on the 'Object' layer, and dimensions are created on the layer called 'Dimension.' You can easily turn-off the 'Dimension' layer for a more unobstructed view of the object lines.

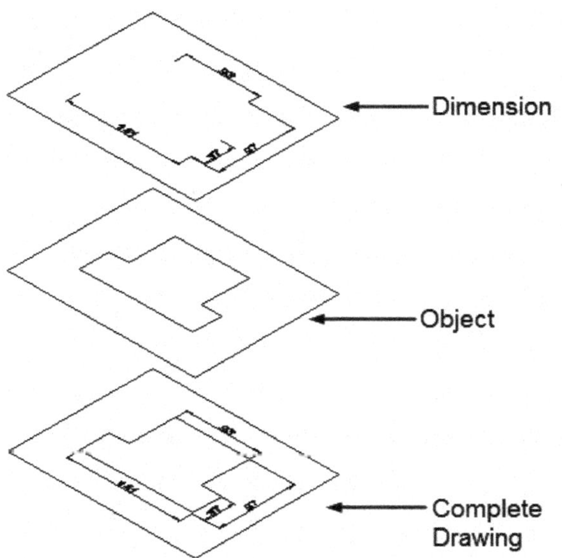

Layer Properties Manager

The **Layer Properties Manager** is used to create and manage layers. To open **Layer Properties Manager**, click **Home > Layers > Layer Properties** on the ribbon or enter **LA** in the command line.

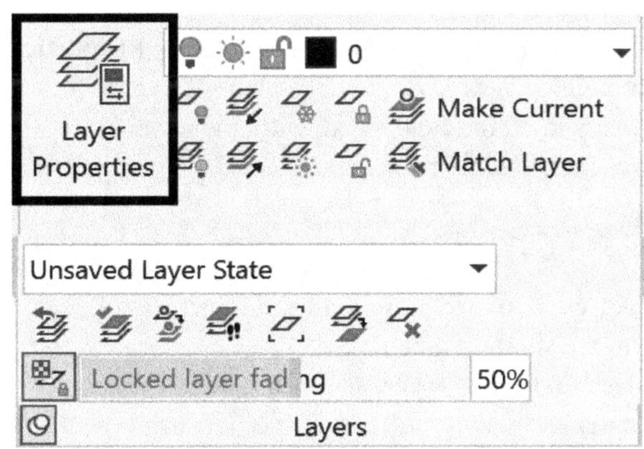

The components of the **Layer Properties Manager** are shown below. The **Tree View** section is used for displaying layer filters, group, or state information. The **List View** section is the main body of the **Layer Properties Manager**. It lists the individual layers that currently exist in the drawing.

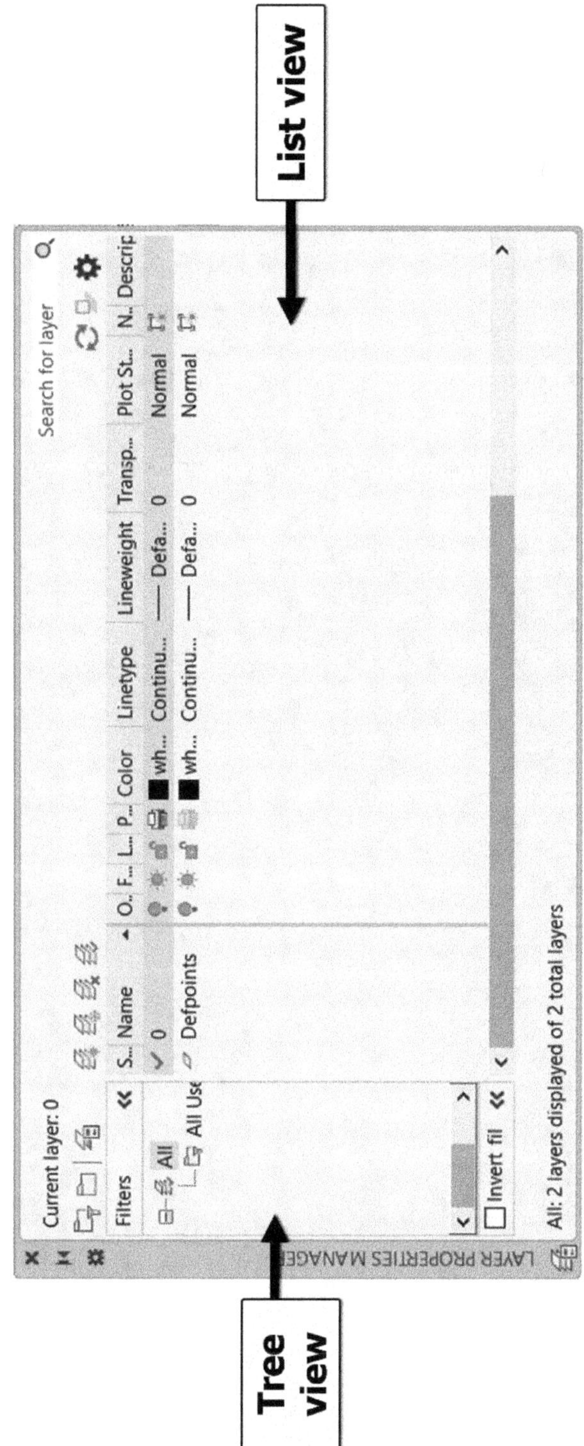

The **List View** section contains various properties. You can set layer properties and perform multiple operations in the **List View** section. A brief explanation of each layer property is given below.

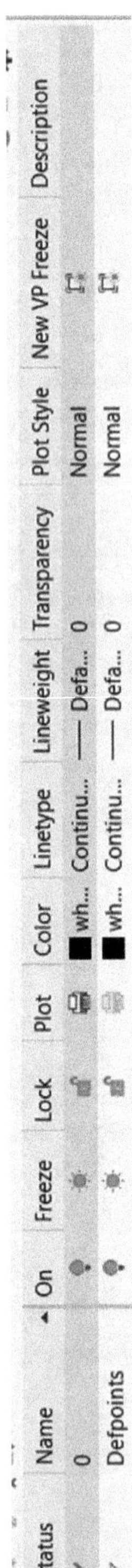

Status – Shows a green check when a layer is set to current.

Name - Shows the name of the layer.

On – It is used to turn on/off the visibility of a layer. When a layer is turned on, it shows a yellow light-bulb. When you turn off a layer, it shows a grey light-bulb.

Freeze/Thaw – It is used to freeze the objects of a layer so that they cannot be modified. Also, the visibility of the object is turned off.

Lock/Unlock- It is used to lock the layer so that the objects on it cannot be modified.

Color – It is used to assign a color to the layer.

Linetype – It is used to assign a linetype to the layer.

Lineweight – It is used to define the lineweight (thickness) of objects on the layer.

Transparency – It is used to define the transparency of the layer. You set a transparency level from 0 to 90 for all objects on a layer.

Plot Style – It is used to override the settings such as color, linetype, and lineweight while plotting a drawing.

Plot – It is used to control which layer will be plotted.

New VP Freeze – It is used to create and freeze a layer in any new viewport.

Description – It is used to enter a detailed description of the layer.

Creating a New Layer

You can create a new layer by using any one of the following methods:

1. Click the **New Layer** button on the **Layer Properties Manager**; a new layer with the name '**Layer1**' appears in **Name** field. Next, enter the name of the layer in the **Name** field.

2. Right-click in the **Name** field and select **New Layer** from the shortcut menu.
3. Select an existing layer, and then type ENTER or comma (,).

Making a layer current

If you want to draw objects on a particular layer, then you have to make it current. You can make a layer current using the methods listed below.

1. Select the layer from the List view and click the **Set Current** button on the **Layer Properties Manager**.

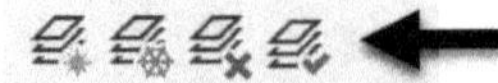

2. Double-click on the **Name** field of the layer.
3. Right-click on the layer and select **Set current**.
4. Select the layer from the **Layer** drop-down of the **Layer** panel.

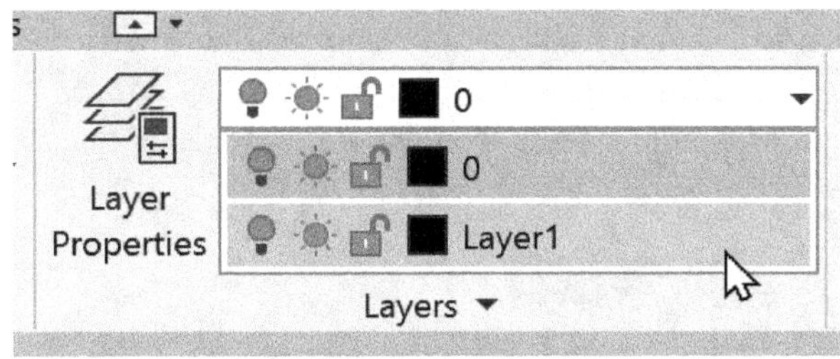

You can also display the **Layer** drop-down on the Quick Access Toolbar. To do this, click the down arrow next to the Quick Access Toolbar and select **Layer** from the menu.

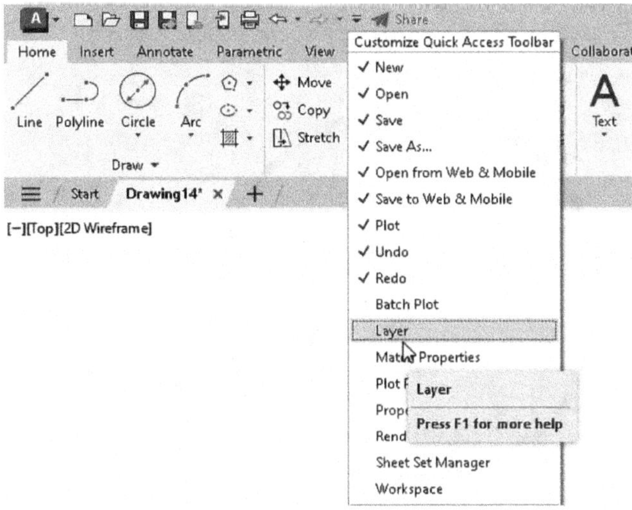

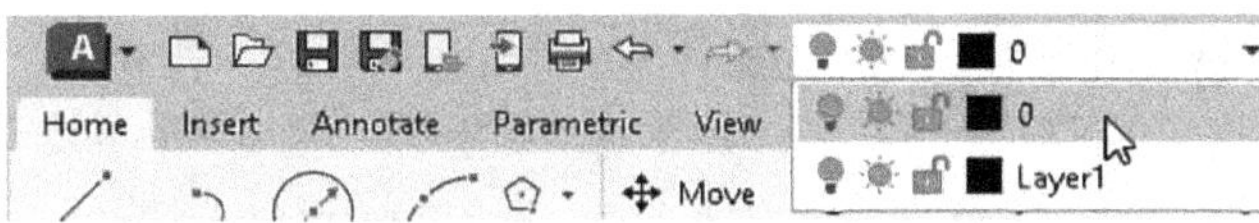

5. Click the **Make Current** button on the **Layers** panel. Next, select an object from the graphics window; the layer related to the selected object will become current.

Deleting a Layer

You can delete a layer by using any one of the following methods:

1. Click the **Delete Layer** button or press ALT+D.

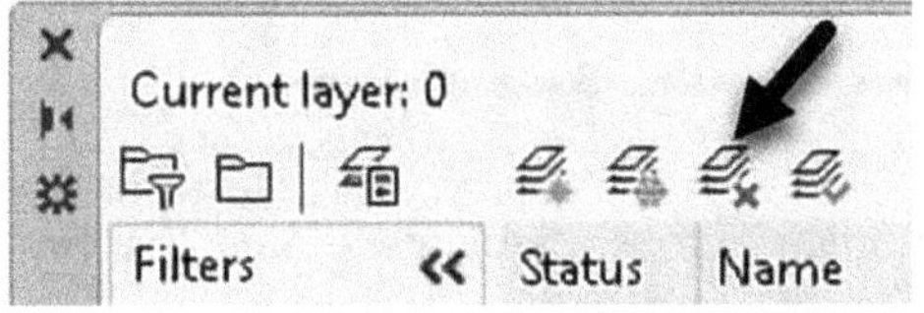

2. Right-click in the **Name** field and select **Delete Layer** from the shortcut menu.

You will learn more about layers in later chapters. You can find an example related to layers in the **Offset** tool section of chapter 4.

Using Object Snaps

Object Snaps are essential settings that improve your performance and accuracy while creating a drawing. They allow you to select key points of objects while creating a drawing. You can activate the required Object Snap by using the **Object snap** shortcut menu. Press and hold the SHIFT key and right-click to display this shortcut menu. Note that the object snaps can be used only when a drawing command is active.

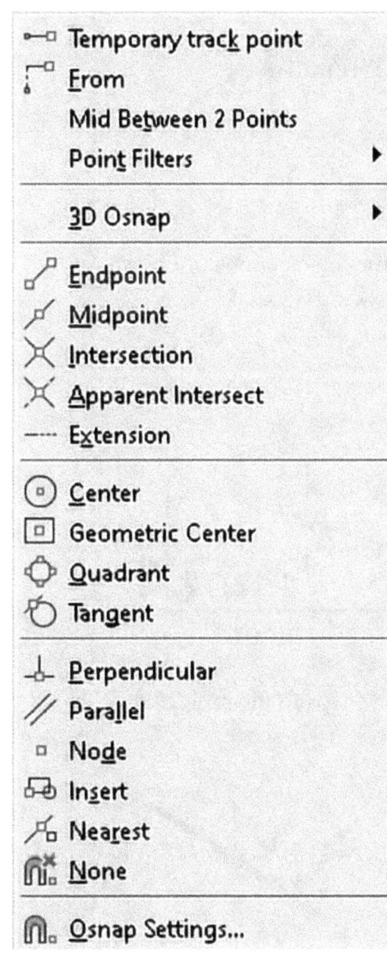

The functions of various Object Snaps are explained next.

Endpoint: Snaps to the endpoints of lines and arcs.

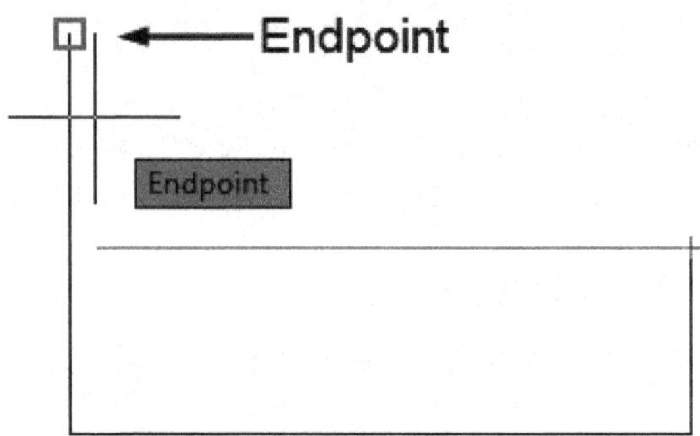

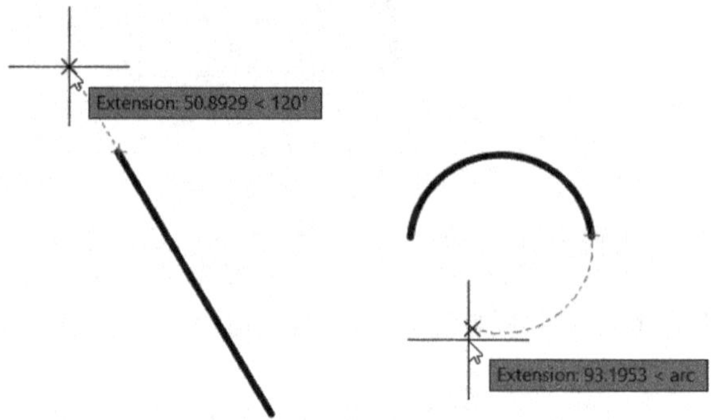

Extension: Creates a temporary extension line when the pointer passes through the endpoints of a line or an arc. You can pick points along the temporary extension lines.

Midpoint: Snaps to the midpoint of a line.

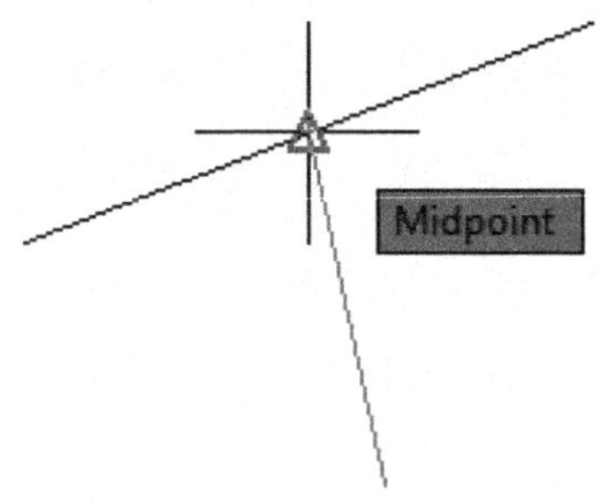

Intersection: Snaps to the intersections of objects.

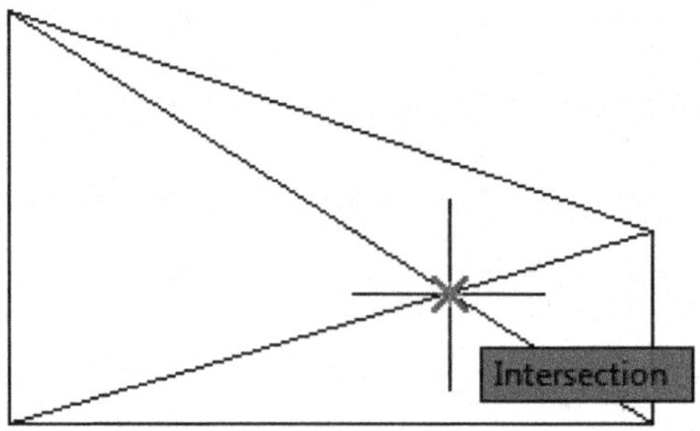

Center: Snaps to the centers of circles and arcs.

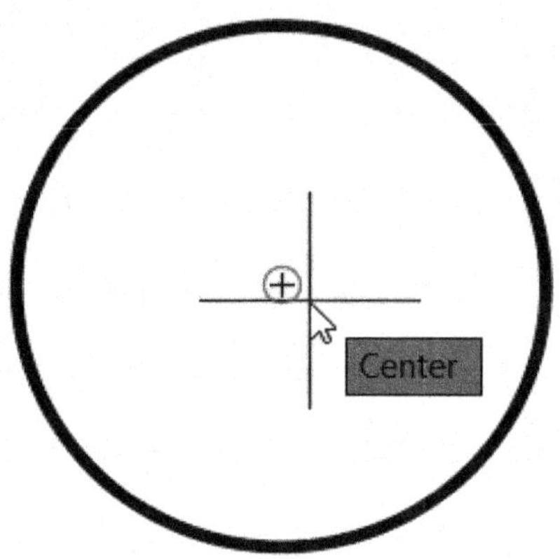

Geometric Center: Snaps to the center point of a closed geometry created by a single object such as polyline, rectangle, or polygon.

Apparent Intersection: Snaps to the projected intersection of two objects in 3D space.

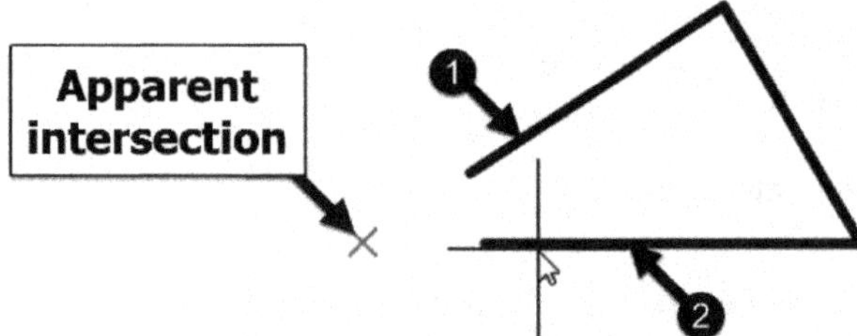

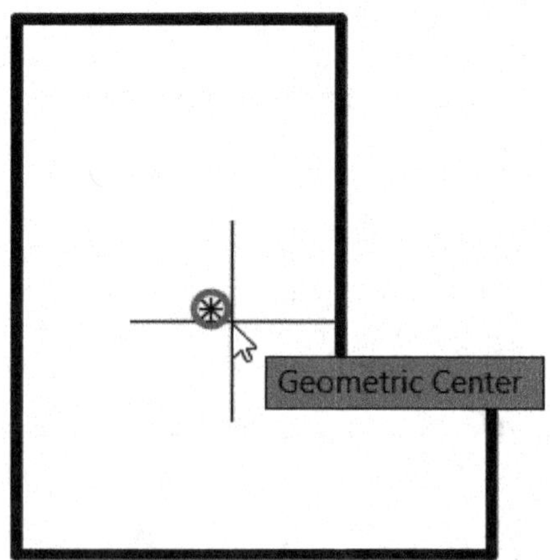

Quadrant: Snaps to four key points located on a circle.

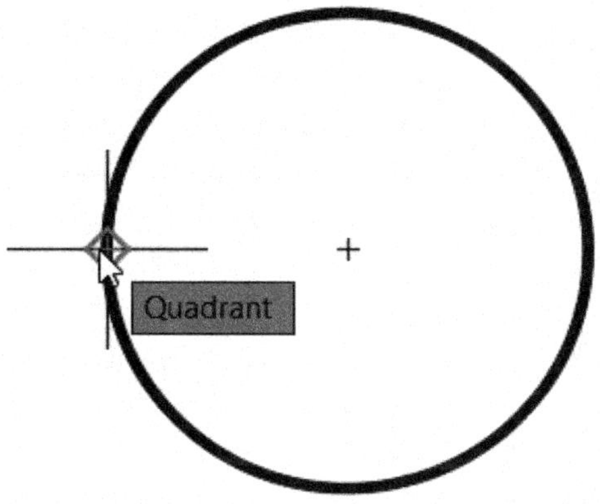

Tangent: Snaps to the tangent points of arcs and circles.

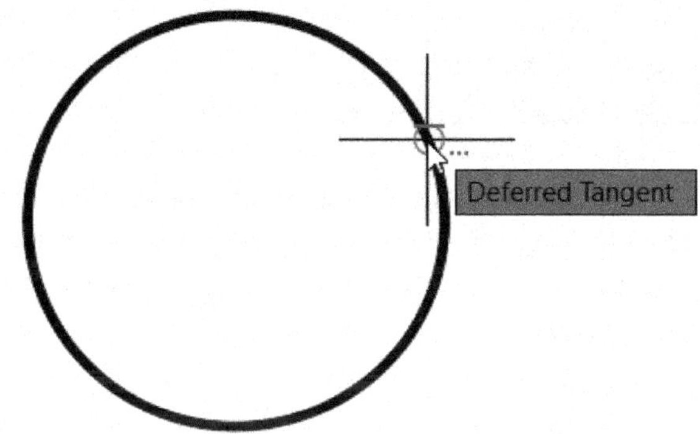

Perpendicular: Snaps to a perpendicular location on an object.

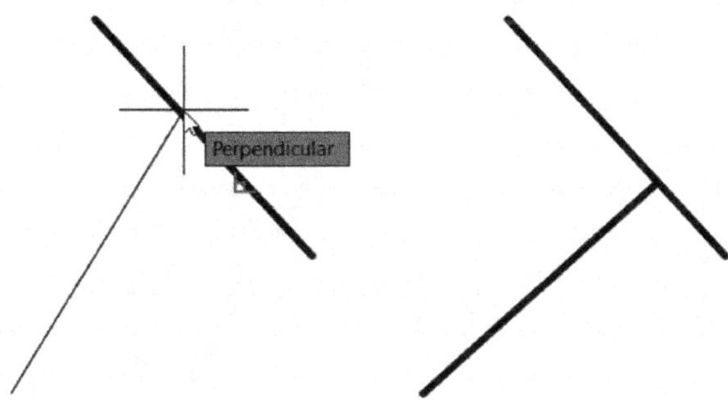

Parallel: It is used to draw an object parallel to another object. Select this option and place the pointer on the first line. Next, move the pointer and notice the track line parallel to the first object. Move along the track line and click to create a line parallel to the first line.

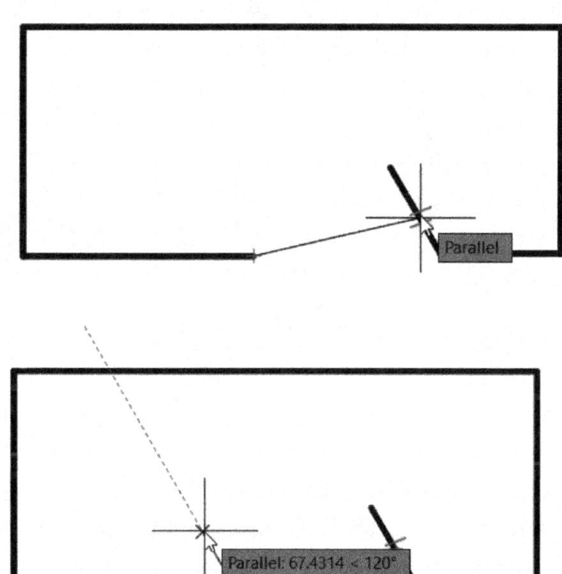

Node: Snaps to points of dimension` lines, text objects, and dimension text.

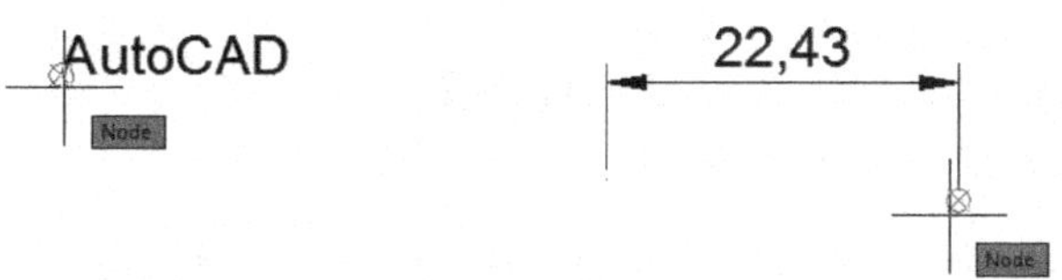

Insert: Snaps to the insertion point of blocks, shapes, and text.

Nearest: Snaps to the nearest point found along with any object.

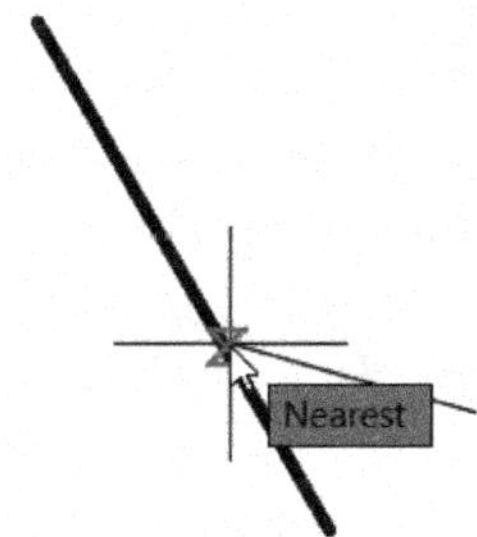

None: Deactivates the Object Snap.

Temporary Track Point: It is used to locate a point by using trace lines from a reference point.

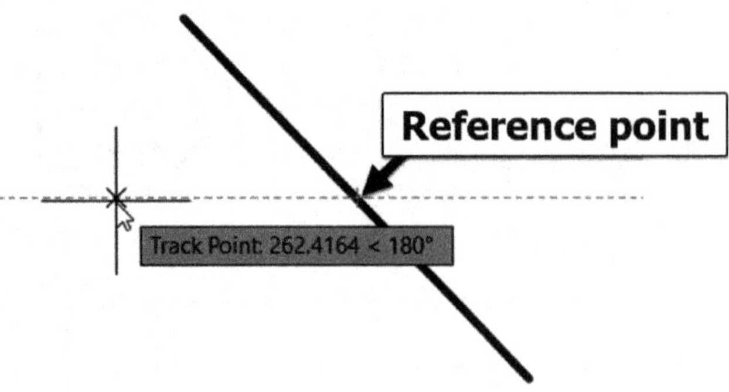

From: Locates a point at a specified distance and direction from a selected reference point.

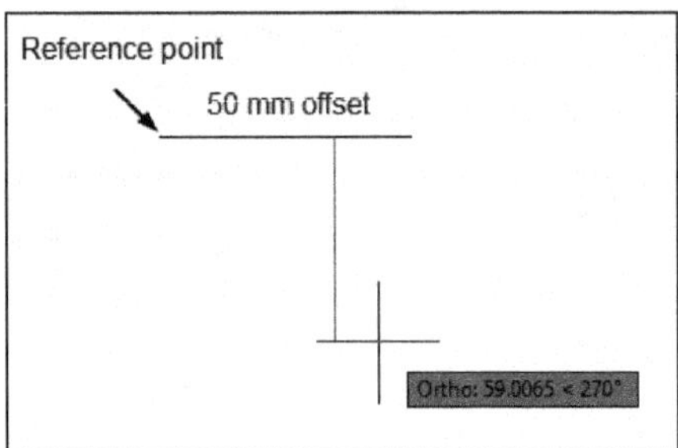

Midpoint Between 2 Points: Snaps to the middle point of two selected points.

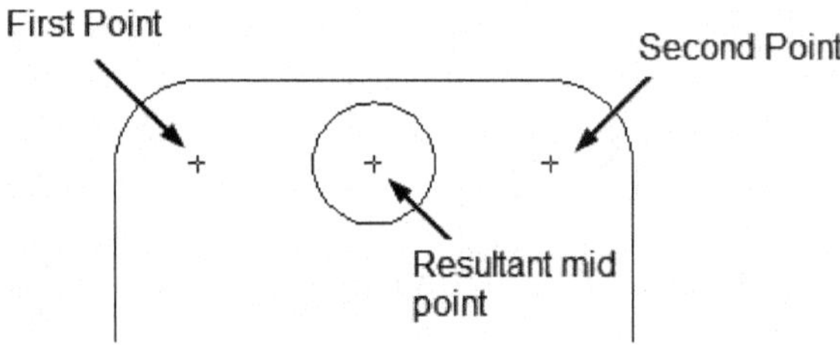

Running Object Snaps

Previously, you have learned to select Object Snaps from the shortcut menu. However, you can make Object Snap modes available continuously instead of picking them every time. You can do this by using the **Running Object Snaps**. To use the Running Object Snaps, click the down arrow next to the **Object Snaps** button on the status bar and select the required object snap from the menu.

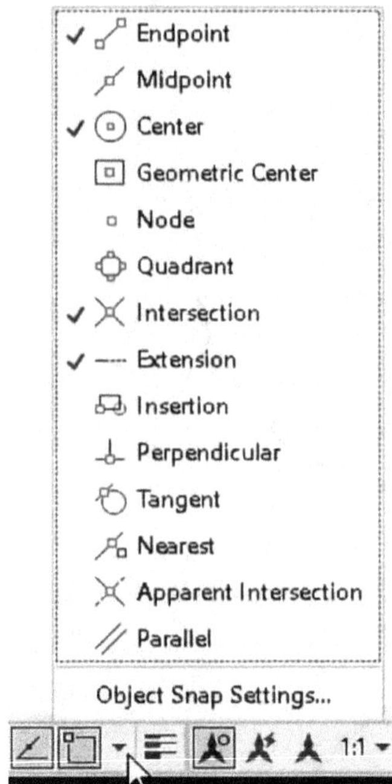

You can also select the **Object Snap Settings** option from the menu to open the **Drafting Settings** dialog. In this dialog, you can choose the required Object Snaps by selecting checkboxes.

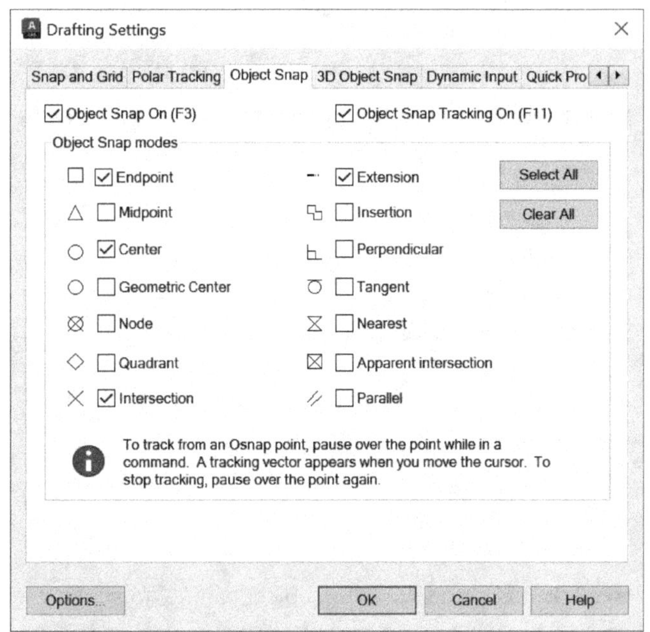

Cycling through Object Snaps

After setting the Running Object Snap settings, AutoCAD displays object snaps depending on the shape of the object. However, you can cycle through the object snaps by pressing the TAB key. In the following example, you will learn to cycle through different object snaps.

Example:

- Click the down arrow next to the **Object Snap** button and select the **Object Snap Settings** option; the **Drafting Settings** dialog appears.
- Click the **Select All** button and click the **OK** button.
- Draw the objects, as shown below.

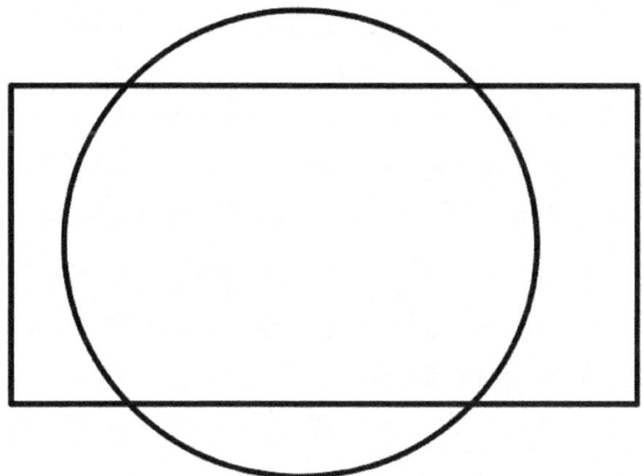

- Click the **Circle** button on the **Draw** panel.
- Place the pointer on the drawing. Press the TAB key; you will notice that the object snaps change.

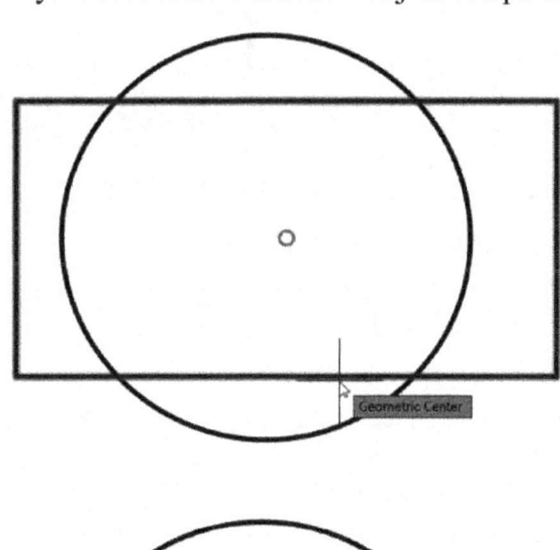

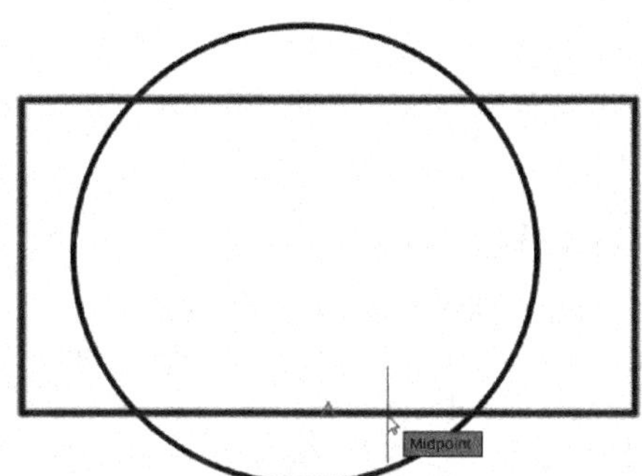

- Click when the **Center** snap is displayed and draw a circle.

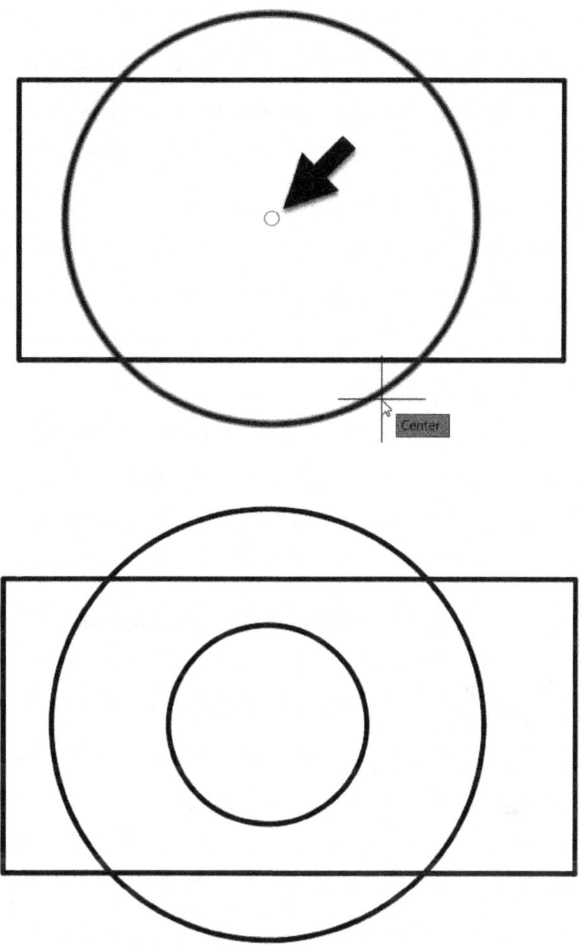

Using Object Snap Tracking

Object Snap tracking is the movement of the pointer along the trace lines originating from the key points of objects. Object Snap Tracking works only when the **Object Snap** mode is turned on. In the following example, you will learn to use Object Snap Tracking for creating objects.

Example:

- Select the **Object Snap Tracking** button from the Status bar.

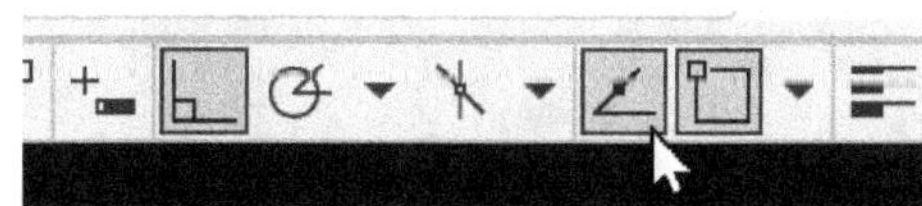

(OR)

- Open the **Drafting Settings** dialog and click the **Object Snap** tab.
- Select the **Object Snap Tracking On** checkbox.

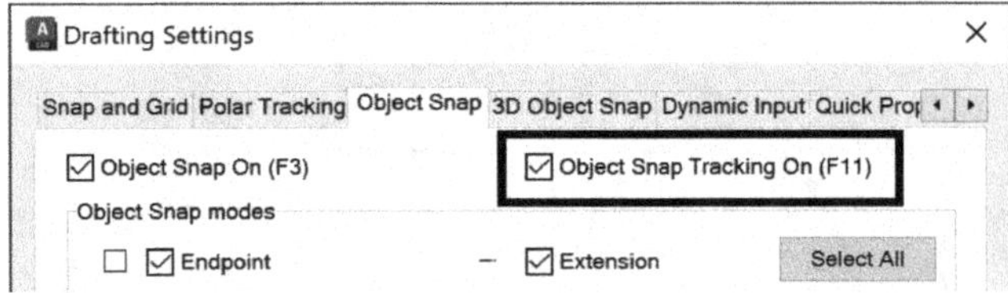

- Click **OK**.
- Use the **Line** tool and draw the objects, as shown below.

- Press the ENTER key twice to start drawing lines from the last point.
- Move the pointer and place it on the endpoint of the lower horizontal line.

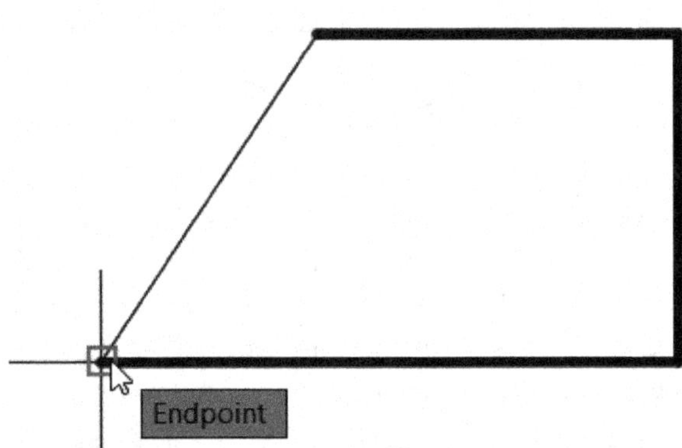

- Move the pointer vertically upward; you will notice the trace line, as shown below.

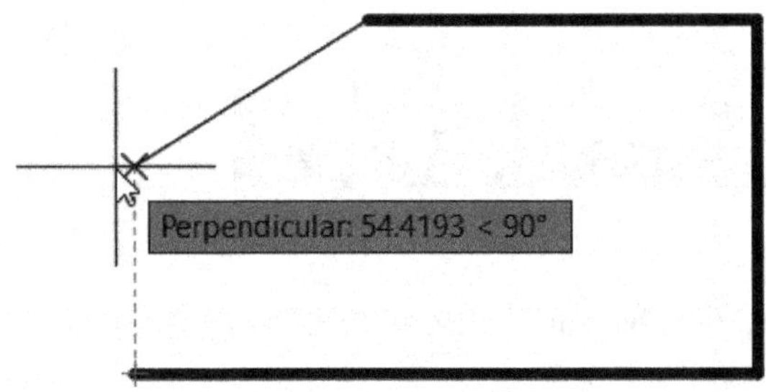

- Click on the trace line to create an inclined line.

- Snap the pointer to the endpoint of the lower horizontal line and click.

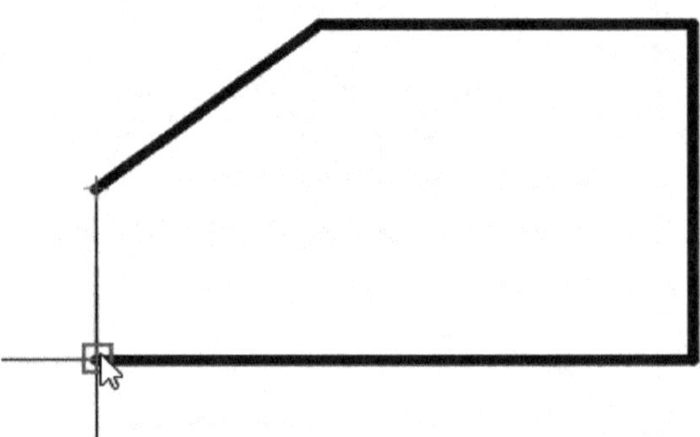

- Right-click and select **Enter**.
- Click the **Circle** button on the **Draw** panel of the ribbon.
- Place the pointer over the lower endpoint of the inclined line and move horizontally; you will notice that a trace line is displayed.
- Place the pointer on the midpoint of the lower horizontal line; a vertical trace line is displayed from the midpoint of the horizontal line, as shown below.

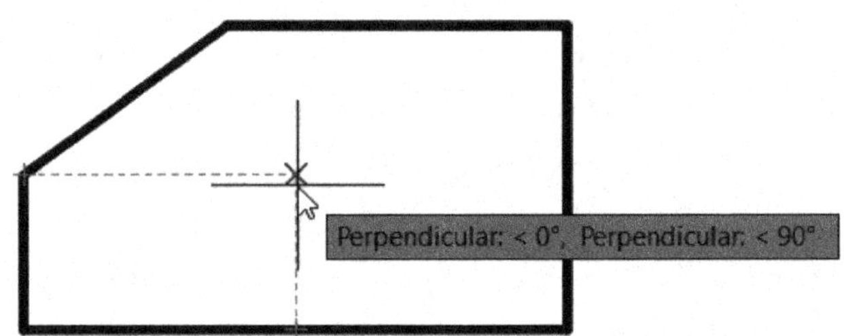

- Click at the point where the horizontal and vertical trace lines intersect. Next, create a circle, as shown below.

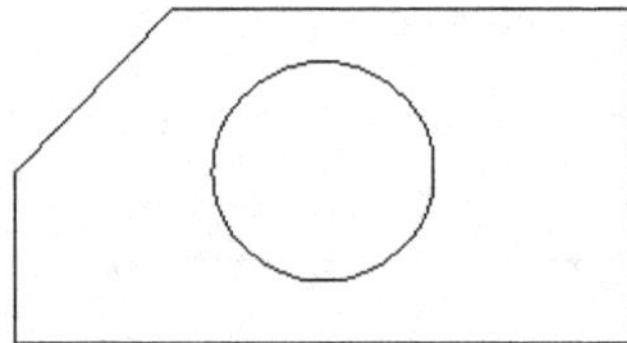

Linetype gap selection

AutoCAD makes it easy to select line types such as centerlines, dashed-dotted lines, hidden, and phantom. Earlier, it was difficult to select these linetypes by clicking in the gaps. Now, you can select them by clicking on the gaps.

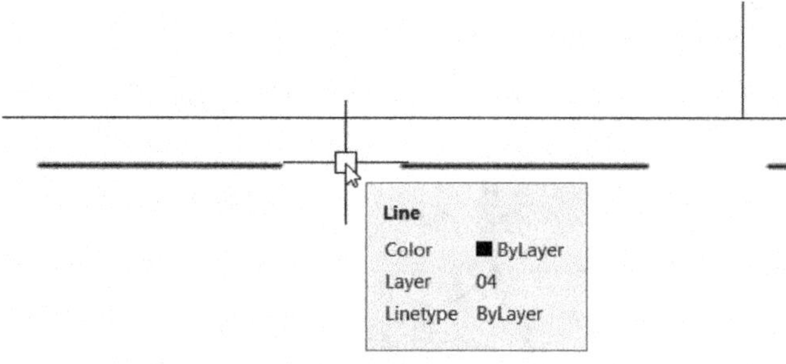

You can also snap to the line at the gaps.

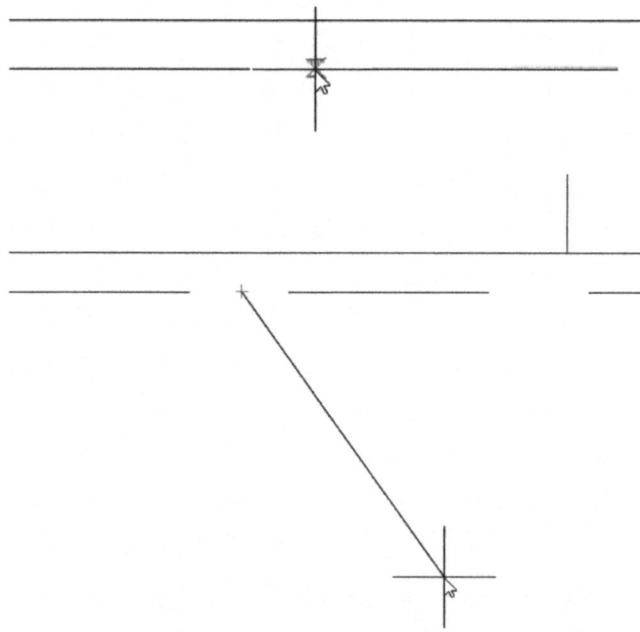

The LTGAPSELECTION system variable, when set to 1, helps you to select the line by clicking in the gaps. You can turn OFF this feature by setting the LTGAPSELECTION system variable to 0.

Using Zoom tools

Using the zoom tools, you can magnify or reduce a drawing. You can use these tools to view the minute details of a very complicated drawing. The Zoom tools can be accessed from the Navigation Bar, Command line, and Menu Bar.

Navigation Bar

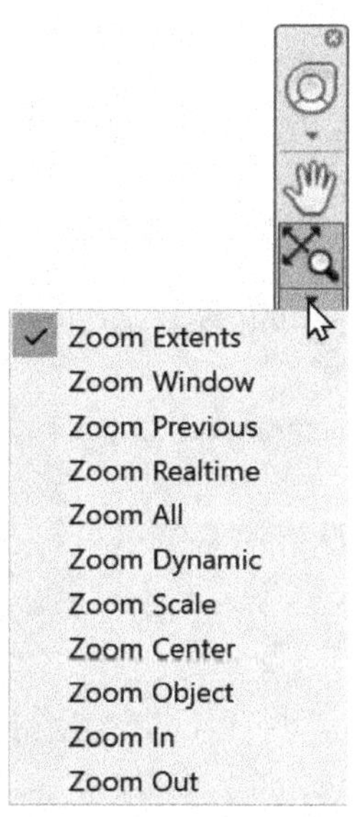

Menu Bar

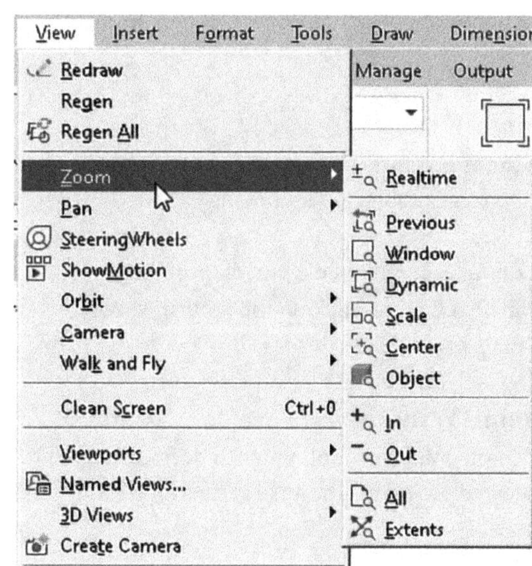

Command line

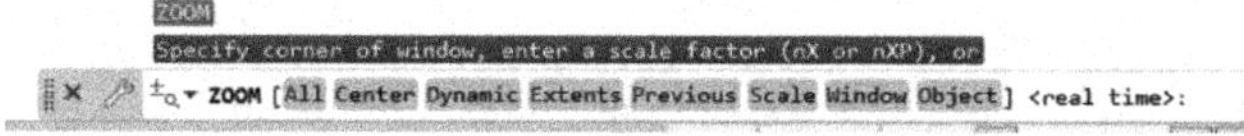

Zooming with the Mouse Wheel

Zooming using the mouse wheel is one of the easiest methods.

- Roll the mouse wheel forward to zoom into a drawing.

- Roll the mouse wheel backward to zoom out of the drawing.
- Press the mouse wheel and drag the mouse to pan the drawing.

The amount of zooming that occurs with every scroll of your mouse wheel is controlled by the ZOOMFACTOR system variable. To adjust this setting, follow these steps:

- Type "ZOOMFACTOR" in the command line and press Enter.
- Enter a value between 3 and 100 to set the zoom factor.

A higher value will result in more significant zoom changes with each scroll, while a lower value will provide finer control over the visibility of intricate details. Remember that this setting is unique to each computer and is saved in its system files, making it a standard setting for all your AutoCAD projects on that specific machine.

Using Zoom Extents

Using the **Zoom Extents** tool, you can zoom to the extents of the largest object in a drawing.

- Click **Zoom Extents** on the Navigation Bar.
- You can also double-click on the mouse wheel to zoom to extents.

Using Zoom-Window

Using the **Zoom-Window** tool, you can define the area to be zoomed by selecting two points representing a rectangle.

- Click **Zoom > Zoom Window** on the Navigation Bar.
- Specify the first point of the zoom window, as shown.
- Move the pointer diagonally toward the right, and then specify the second point, as shown.
  The area inside the window will be zoomed.

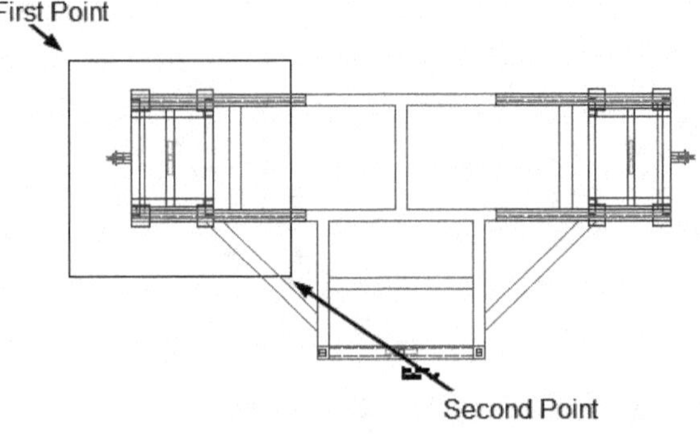

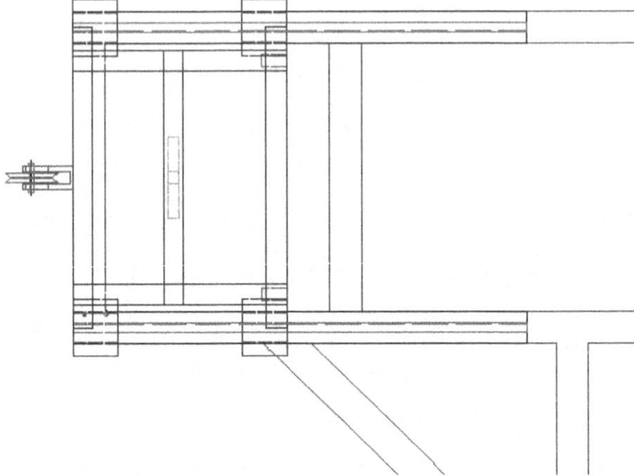

Using Zoom-Previous

After magnifying a small area of the drawing, you can use the **Zoom-Previous** tool to return to the previous display.

- Click **Zoom > Zoom Previous** on the Navigation Bar.

Using Zoom-Realtime

Using the **Zoom-Realtime** tool, you can zoom in or zoom out of a drawing dynamically.

- Click **Zoom > Zoom Realtime** on the **Navigation Bar**; the pointer is changed to a magnifying glass with plus and minus symbols.
- Press and hold the left mouse button and drag the mouse forward to zoom into the drawing.
- Drag the mouse backward to zoom out of the drawing.

Using Zoom-All

The **Zoom All** tool is used to adjust the drawing space to the limits set by using the LIMITS command.

- Click **Zoom > Zoom All** on the **Navigation Bar**; the drawing will be zoomed to its limits.

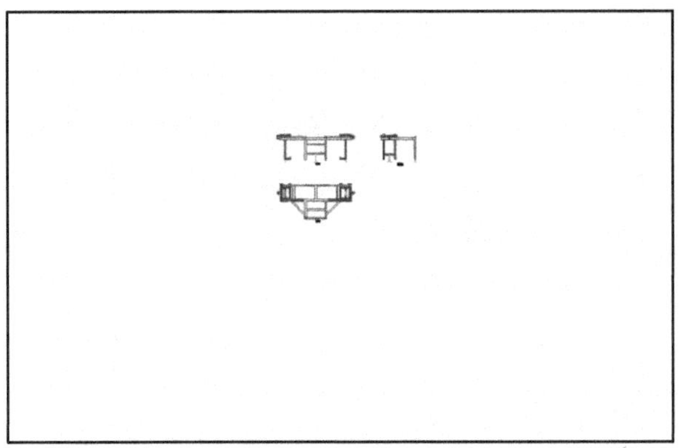

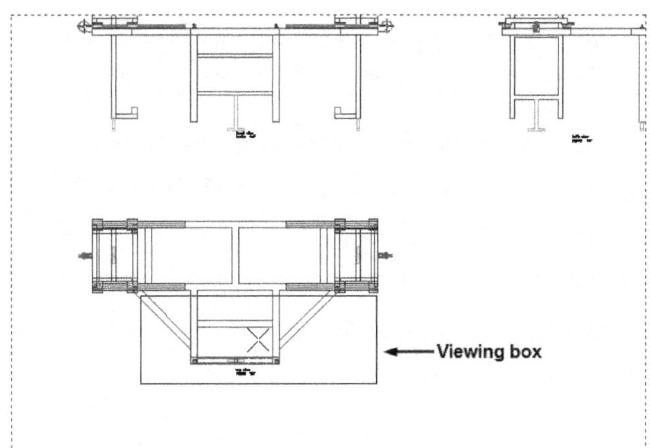

- Click the right mouse button. The area covered by the viewing box is magnified.

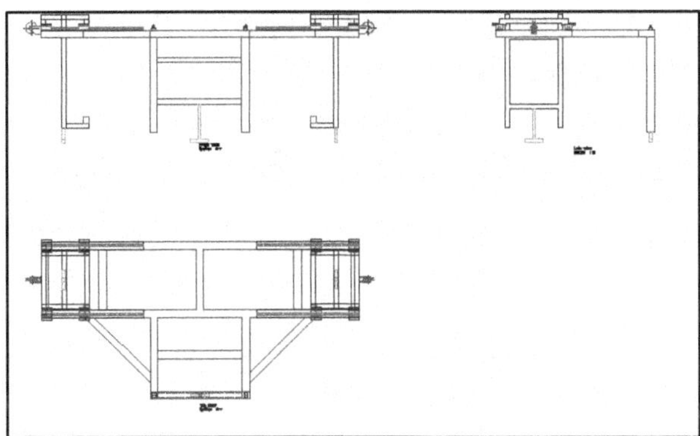

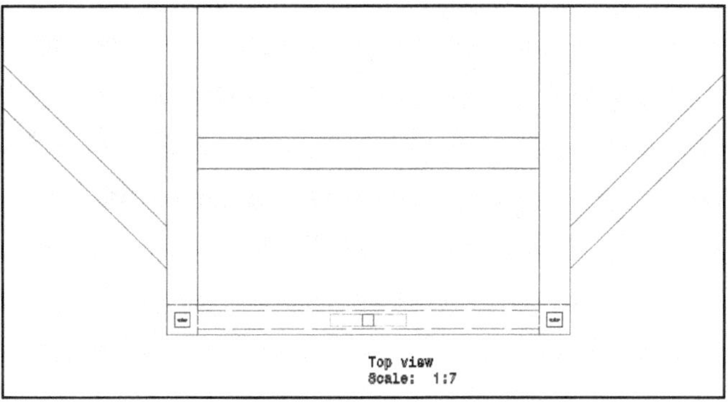

Using Zoom Dynamic

With the **Zoom Dynamic** tool, you can zoom to a particular portion of a drawing by using a viewing box.

- Click **Zoom Dynamic** on the **Navigation Bar**; the drawing will be zoomed to its limits. Also, a viewing box is attached to the pointer.

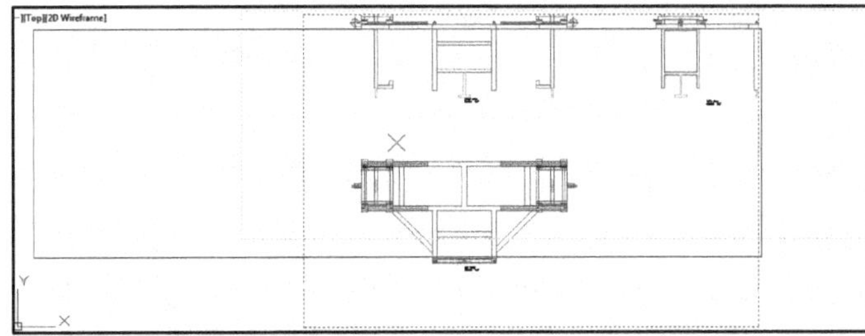

- Click and drag the pointer to define the size of the viewing box.
- Left-click and move the pointer to the area to be zoomed.

Using Zoom-Scale

Using the **Zoom-Scale** tool, you can zoom in or zoom out of a drawing by entering zoom scale factors directly from your keyboard.

- Click the **Zoom > Zoom Scale** on the Navigation Bar. The message, "**Enter a scale factor (nX or nXP),**" appears in the command line.
- Enter the scale factor 0.25 to scale the drawing to 25% of the full view.
- Enter the scale factor 0.25X to scale the drawing to 25% of the current view.
- Enter the scale factor 0.25XP to scale the drawing to 25% of the paper space.

Using Zoom-Center

Using the **Zoom Center** tool, you can zoom to an area of the drawing based on a center point and magnification value.

- Click **Zoom > Zoom Center** on the Navigation Bar; the message, "**Specify Center point**," appears in the command line.
- Select a point in the drawing to which you want to zoom in; the message, "**Enter magnification or height**," appears in the command line.

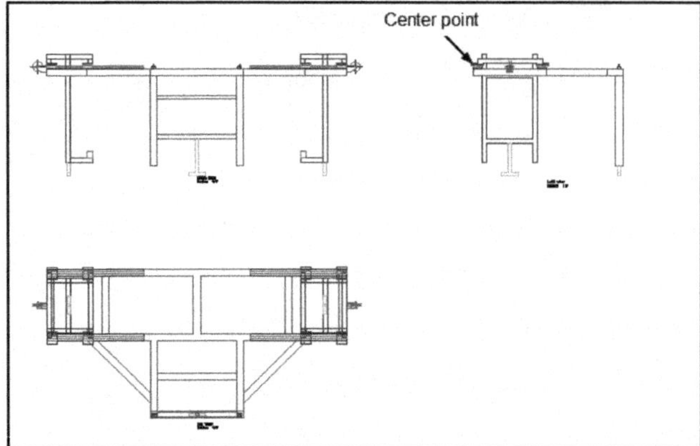

- Enter 10X in the command line to magnify the location of the point by ten times.

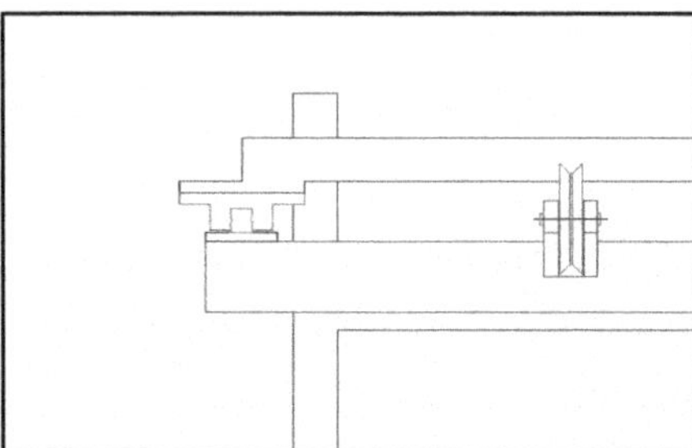

Using Zoom-Object

Using the **Zoom Object** tool, you can magnify a portion of the drawing by selecting one or more objects.

- Click **Zoom > Zoom Object** on the Navigation Bar.
- Select one or more objects from the drawing and press ENTER; the objects will be magnified.

Using Zoom-In

Using the **Zoom In** tool, you can magnify the drawing by a scale factor of 2.

- Click **Zoom > Zoom-In** on the Navigation Bar; the drawing is magnified to double.

Using Zoom-Out

The **Zoom-out** tool is used to de-magnify the display screen by a scale factor of 0.5.

Panning Drawings

After zooming into a drawing, you may want to view an area that is outside the current display. You can do this by using the **Pan** tool.

- Click **Pan** on the Navigation Bar.

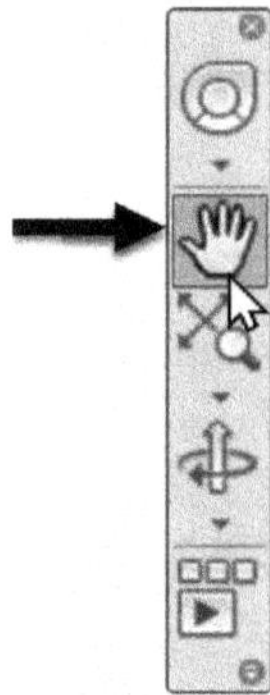

- Press and hold the left mouse button and drag the mouse; a new area of the drawing, which is outside the current view, is displayed.

Exercises

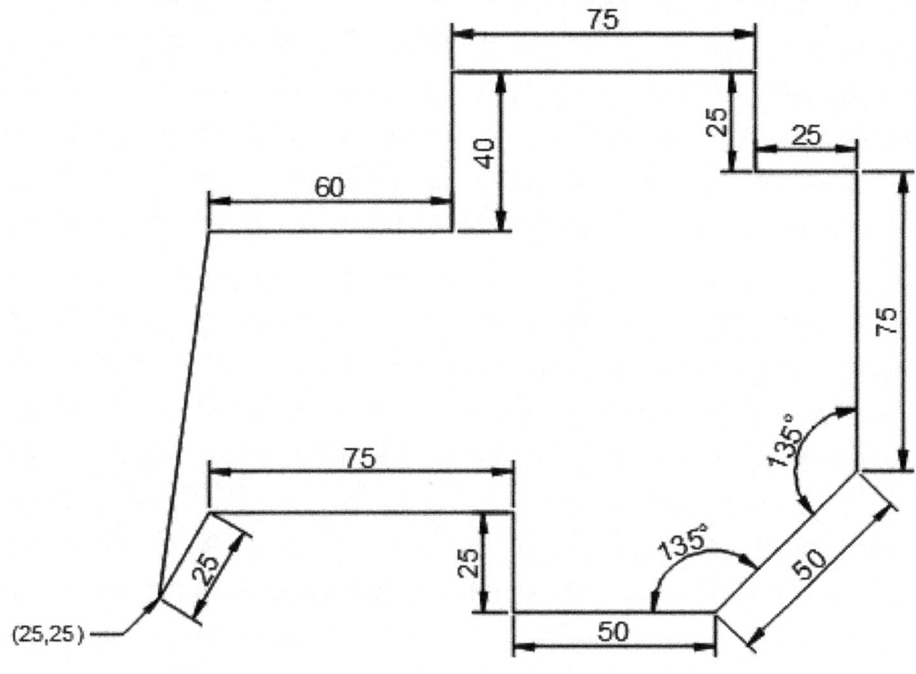

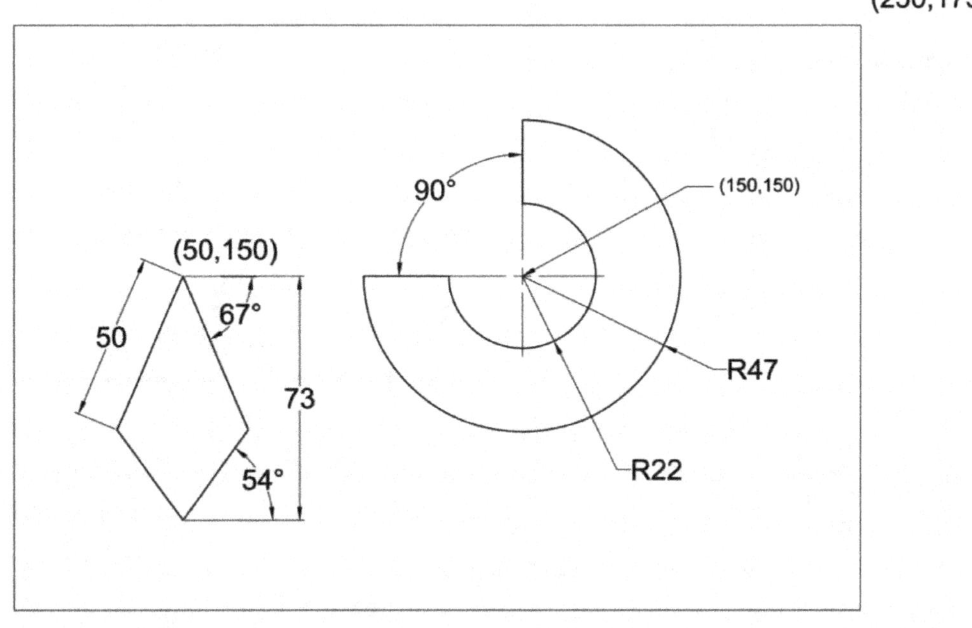

Chapter 4: Editing Tools

In this chapter, you will learn the following tools:

- The **Move** tool
- The **Copy** tool
- The **Rotate** tool
- The **Scale** tool
- The **Trim** tool
- The **Extend** tool
- The **Fillet** tool
- The **Chamfer** tool
- The **Mirror** tool
- The **Explode** tool
- The **Stretch** tool
- The **Polar Array** tool
- The **Offset** tool
- The **Path Array** tool
- The **Rectangular Array** tool

Editing Tools

In previous chapters, you have learned to create some simple drawings using the basic drawing tools. However, to create complex drawings, you may need to perform various editing operations. The tools to perform the editing operations are available in the **Modify** panel on the **Home** ribbon. You can click the down arrow on this panel to find more editing tools. Using these editing tools, you can modify existing objects or use existing objects to create new or similar objects.

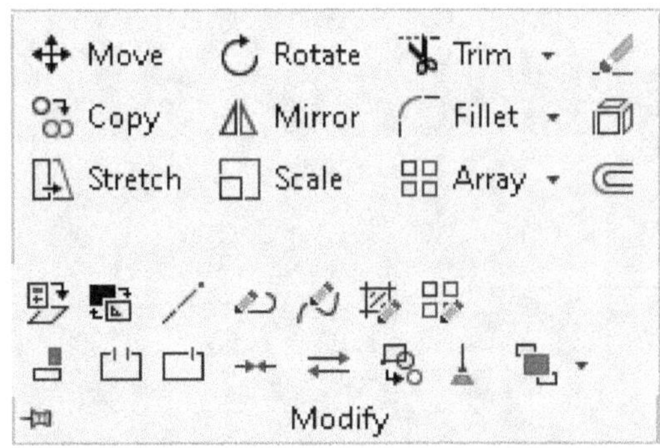

The Move tool

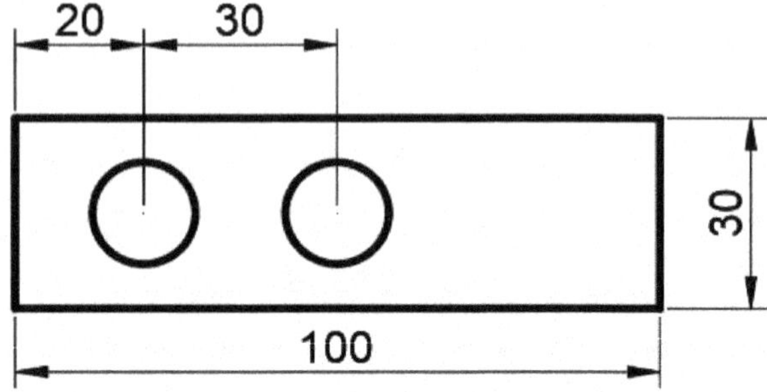

The **Move** tool moves a selected object(s) from one location to a new location without changing its orientation. To move objects, you must activate this tool and select the objects from the graphics window. After selecting the objects, you must define the 'base point' and the 'destination point.'

Example:

- Create the drawing, as shown below.

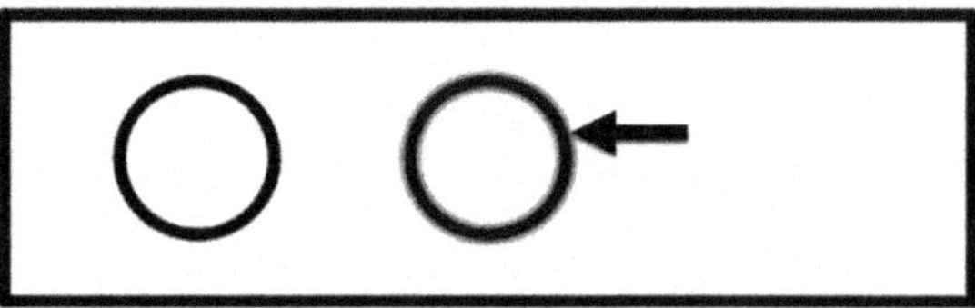

- Click **Home > Modify > Move** on the ribbon or enter **M** in the command line.
- Click on the circle located at the right side, and then right-click to accept the selection.

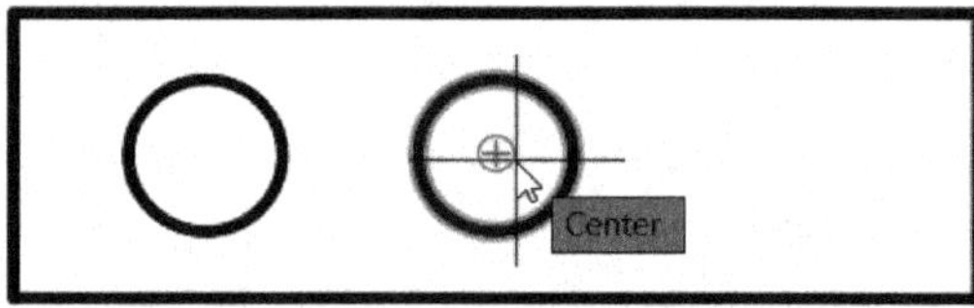

- Select the center of the circle as the base point.

- Make sure that the **Ortho Mode** is activated.
- Move the pointer toward the right, type 30, and then press Enter. It moves the circle to the new location.

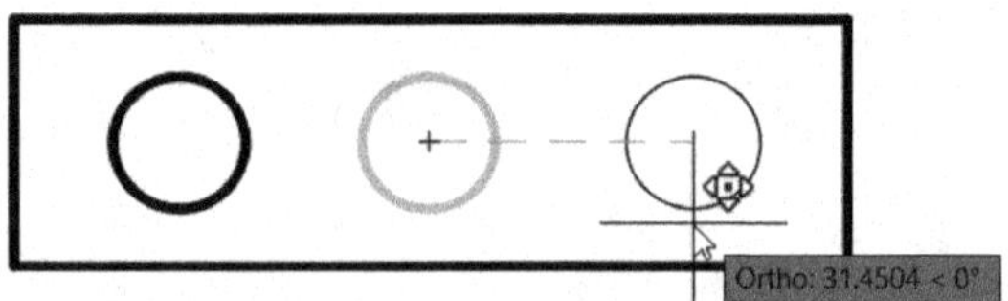

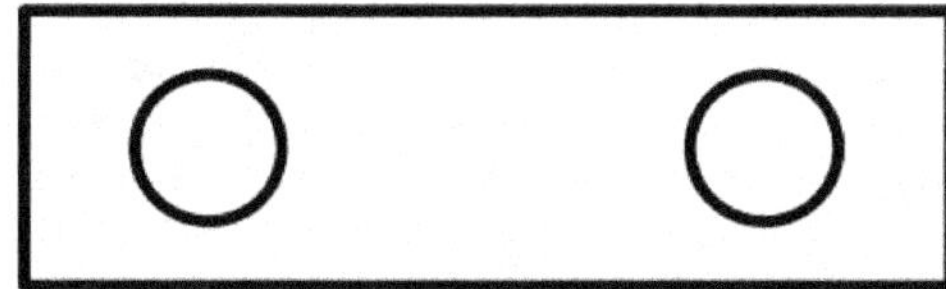

The Copy tool

The **Copy** tool is used to copy objects and place them at a required location. This tool is similar to the **Move** tool, except that the object will remain at its original position, and a copy of it will be placed at the new location.

Example:

- Draw two circles of 40 mm and 70 mm radii, respectively.

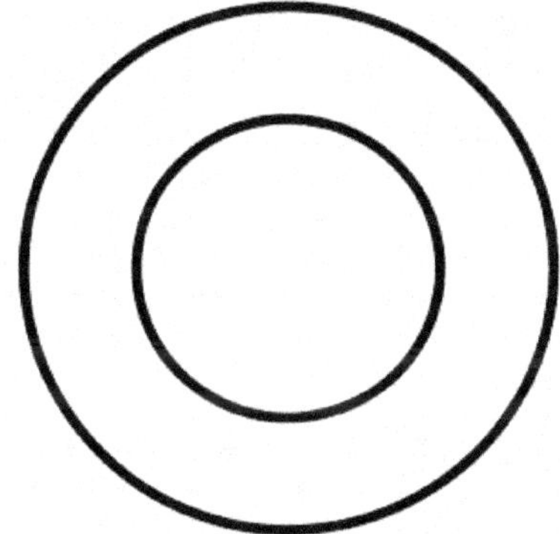

- Click **Home > Modify > Copy** on the ribbon or enter **CO** in the command line.
- Select the two circles and then right-click to accept the selection.

The command line displays two options:

Displacement: This option defines relative distance and direction using the two points that you pick from the graphics window.

mOde: This option controls whether the Copy command repeats automatically after copying the object. The Single option ends the command after creating a single copy of selected objects. The Multiple option repeats the command automatically after creating the first copy of the selected object.

- Select the center of the circle as the base point.

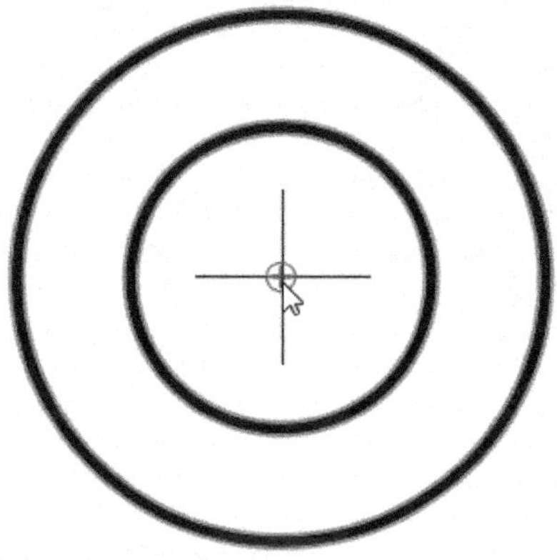

The command line displays the **Array** option.

*Array: This option arranges a specified number of copies in a linear array. The **Fit** option fits the specified number of copies between the selected two points.*

- Make sure that the **Ortho Mode** is active.
- Move the pointer toward the right.
- Type 200 and press ENTER. This action creates a copy of the circles at the new location

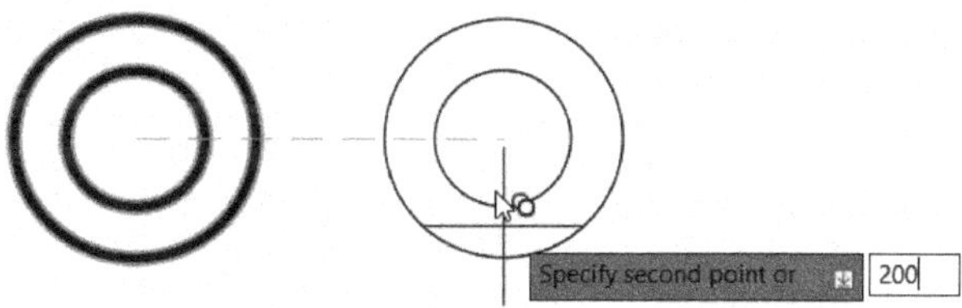

- Select **Exit** from the command line.

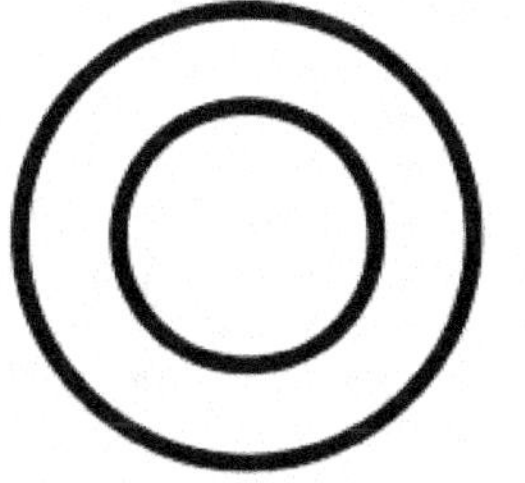
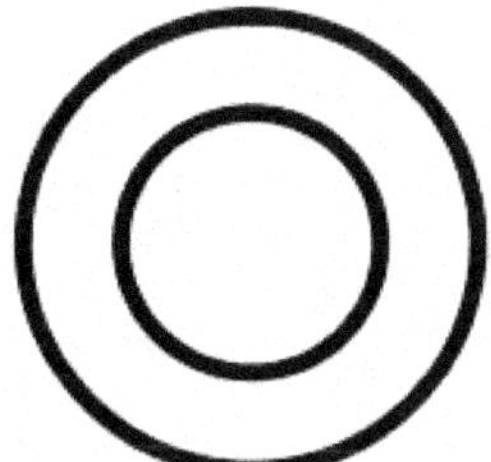

The Rotate tool

The **Rotate** tool rotates an object or a group of objects about a base point. Activate this tool and select the objects from the graphics window. After selecting objects, you must define the 'base point' and the angle of rotation. It rotates the object(s) about the base point.

- Click **Home > Modify > Rotate** on the ribbon or enter **RO** in the command line.
- Select the circles as shown below, and then right-click to accept.

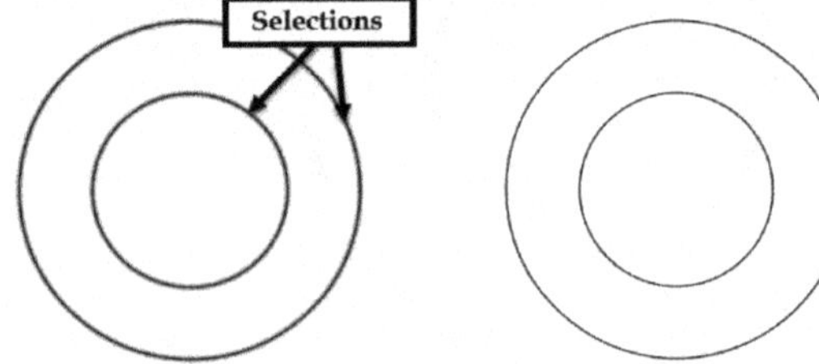

- Select the center of the other circle as the base point.

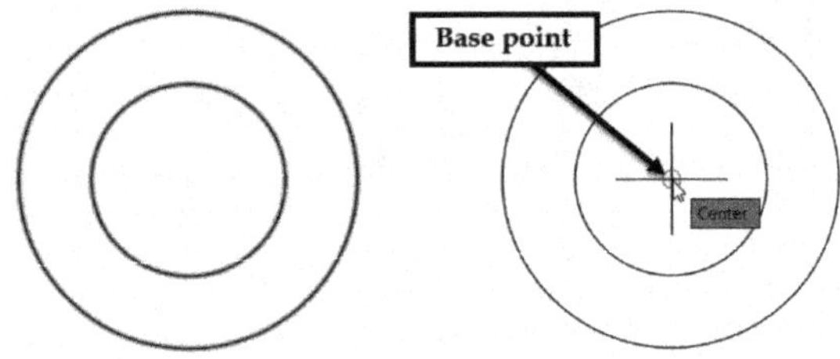

- Select the **Copy** option from the command line.
- Type -90 as the rotation angle and press ENTER; the selected objects are rotated by 90 degrees.

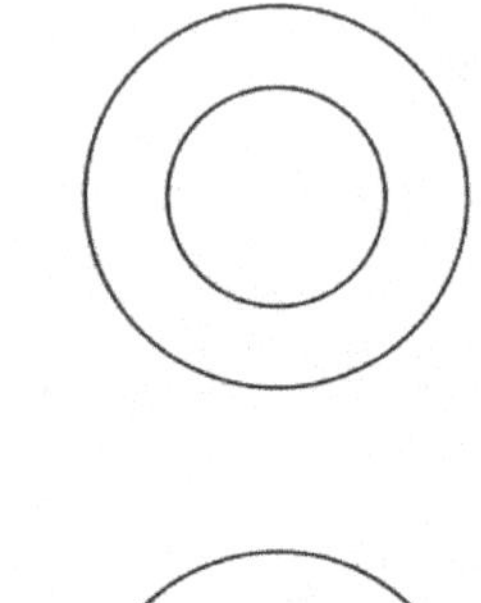

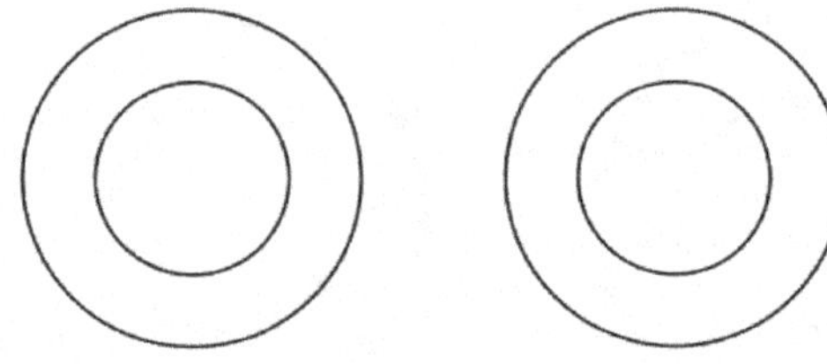

The Scale tool

The **Scale** tool changes the size of objects. It reduces or enlarges the size without changing the shape of an object.

- Click **Home > Modify > Scale** on the ribbon or enter **SC** in the command line.
- Select the circles as shown below and right-click to accept the selection.

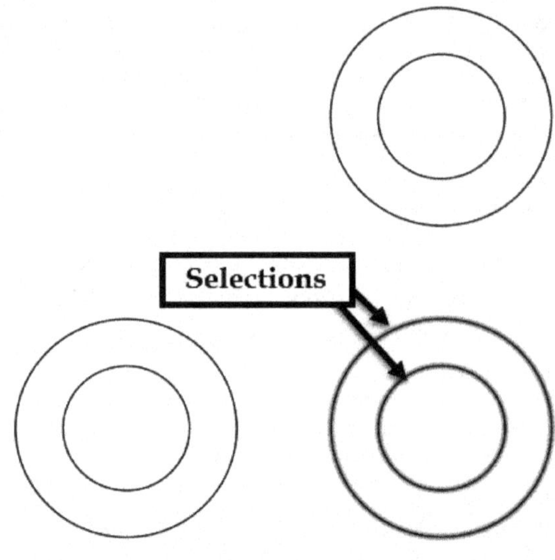

- Select the center point of the selected circles as the base point.
- Type 0.8 as the scale factor and press ENTER.

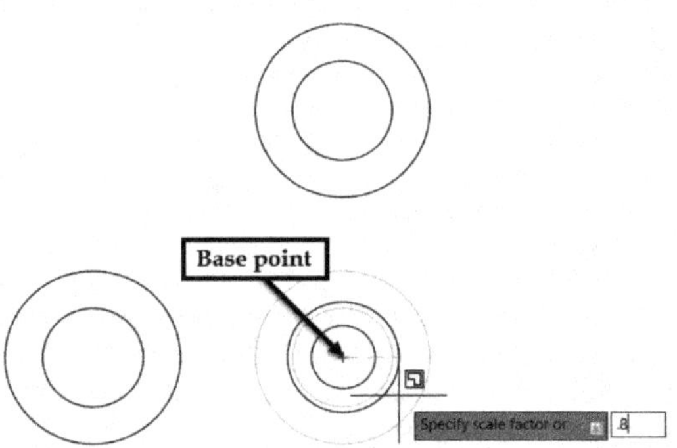

- Likewise, scale the circles located at the top to 0.7.

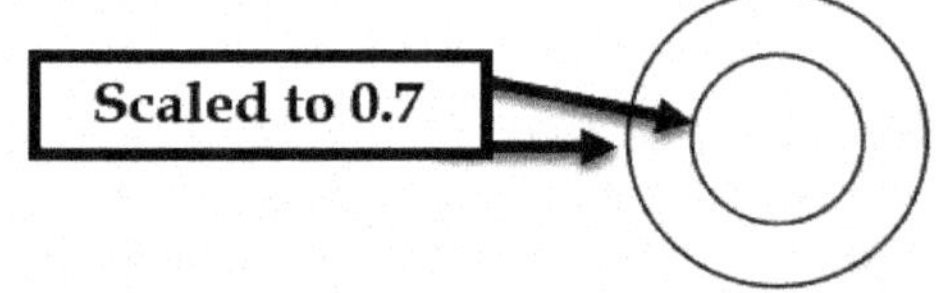

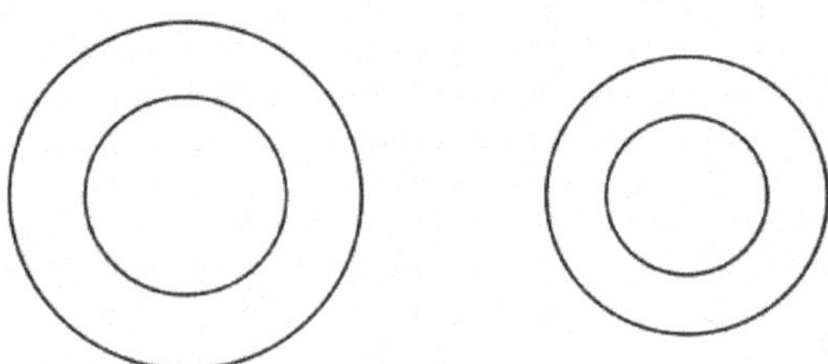

- Click **Home > Draw > Circle > Tan, Tan, Radius** on the ribbon.
- Select the two circles shown below to define the tangent points.

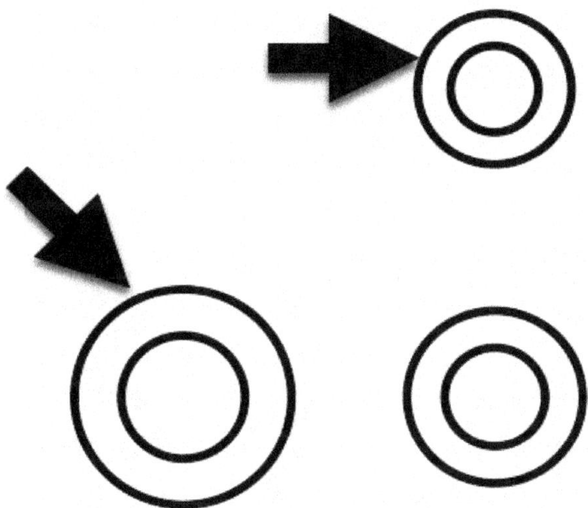

- Type 150 as the radius of the circle and press ENTER.

- Likewise, create other circles of radius 100 and 120.

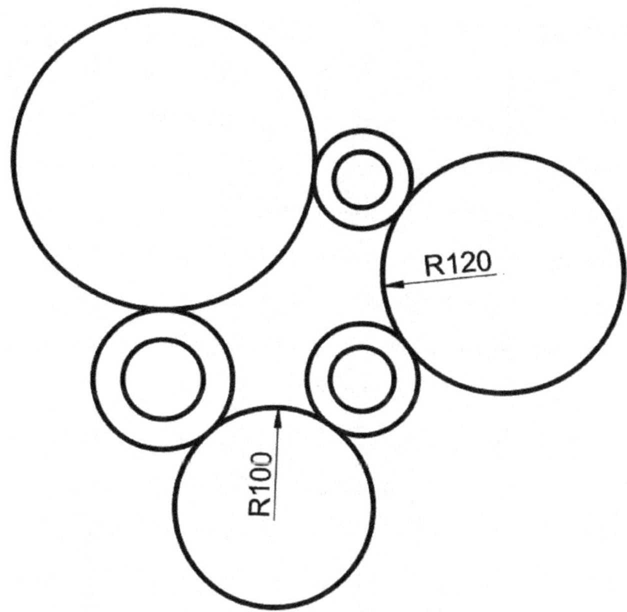

The Cut with Base Point Tool

The **Cut With Base Point** tool allows you to cut and paste the selected objects using a base point. You can paste the cut objects within a drawing or in another drawing.

- Click **Home > Clipboard > Cut** drop-down > **Cut With Base Point** on the ribbon.
- Select the base point of the selection.

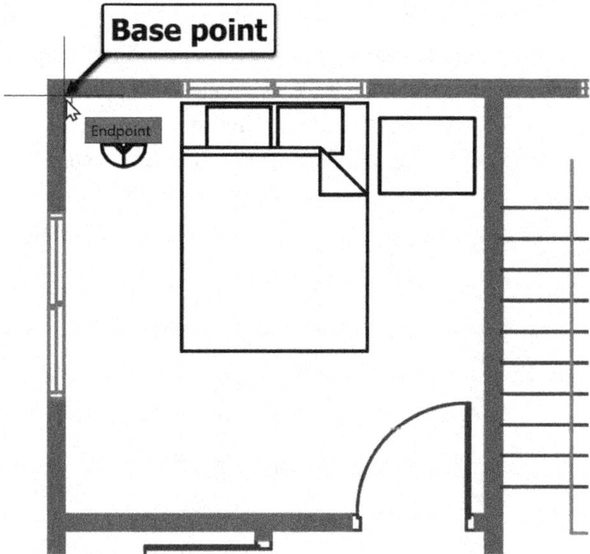

- Create a selection window across all the objects tob be moved. Next, press ENTER.

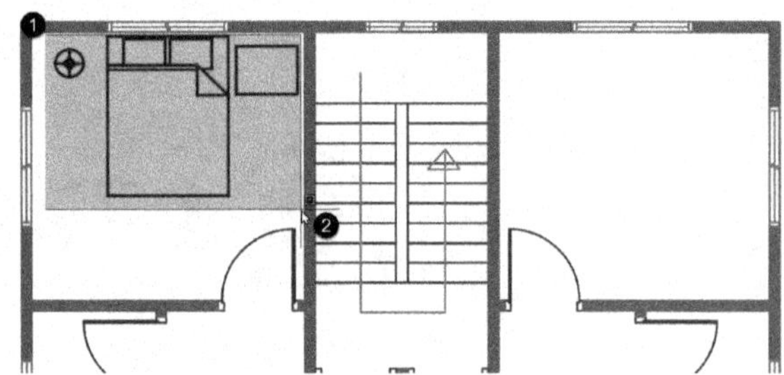

- Click **Home > Clipboard > Paste** on the ribbon.
- Select the destination point.

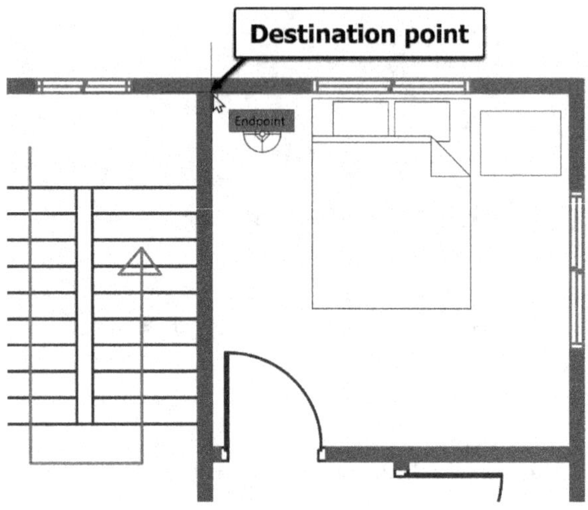

The Trim tool

When an object intersects with another object, you can remove its unwanted portion by using the **Trim** tool. To trim an object, you must first activate the **Trim** tool, and then select the elements to be trimmed. You can also select the elements to trim by dragging the cursor across them.

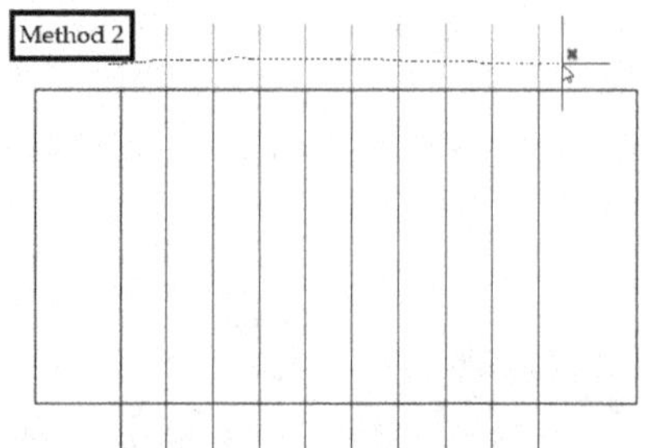

Click and move the pointer across the elements to trimmed. Next, click again to select them.

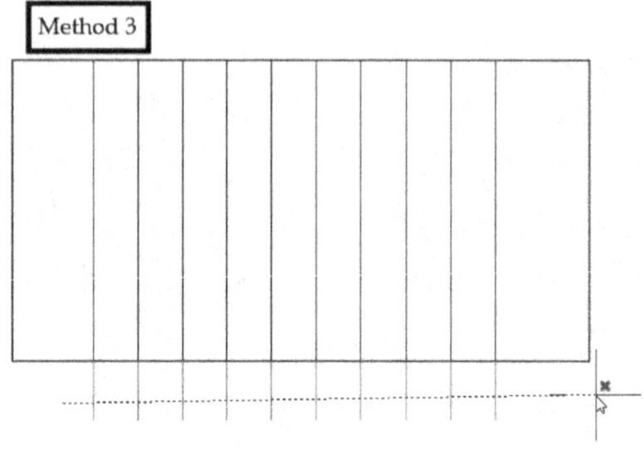

However, if you want to trim the elements using an intersecting object, then select **cuTting edges** option from the command line and select the cutting edges (intersecting objects). Next, press ENTER and select the portions to be removed.

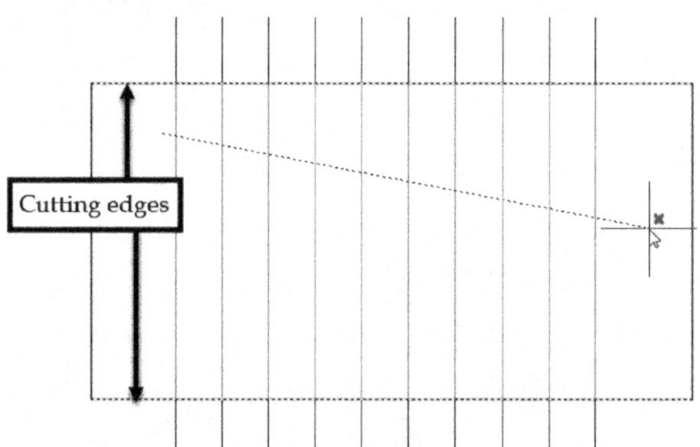

- Click **Home > Modify > Trim** on the ribbon or enter **TR** in the command line.
  Now, you must select the objects to be trimmed.
- Select the large circles one by one; the circles will be trimmed.

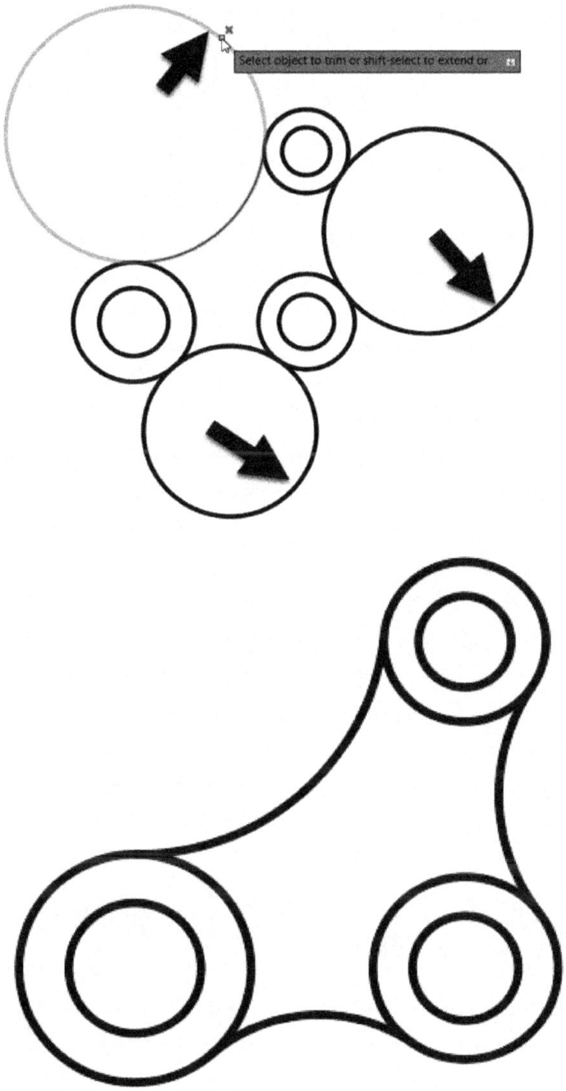

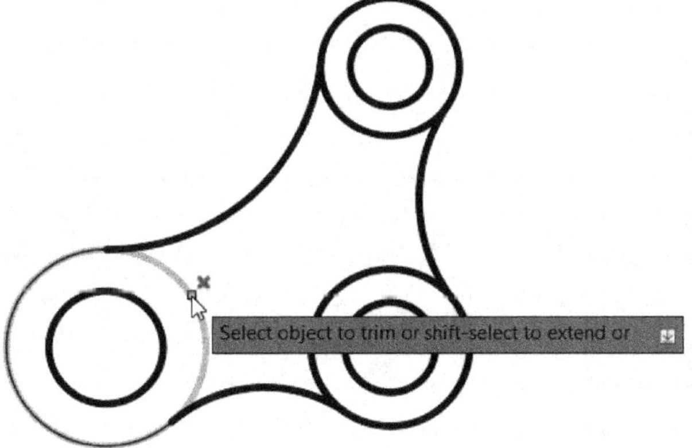

- Likewise, trim the other circles, as shown below.

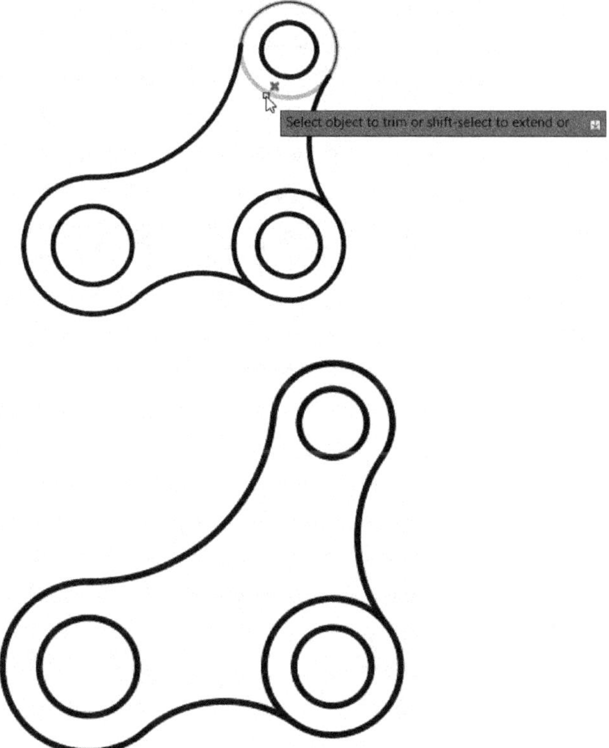

- Save and close the drawing.

The Extend tool

The **Extend** tool is similar to the **Trim** tool, but its use is the opposite of it. This tool is used to extend lines, arcs, and other open entities to connect to other objects.

- Start a new drawing.
- Create a sketch, as shown below, using the **Line** tool.

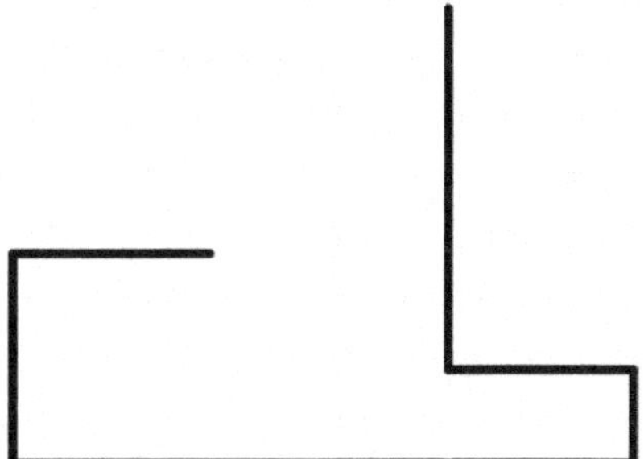

- Click **Home > Modify > Trim > Extend** on the ribbon or enter **EX** in the command line.
- Select the horizontal open line. It will extend the line up to the next element.

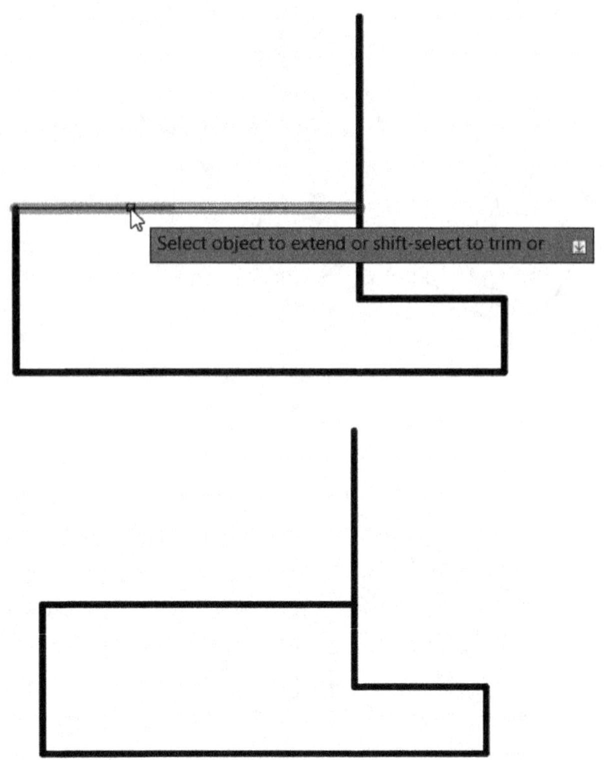

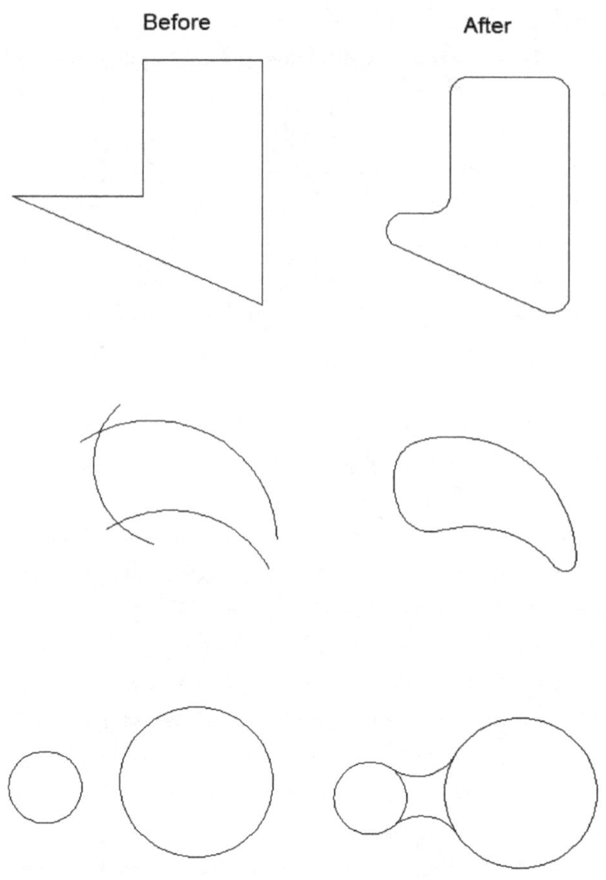

The Fillet tool

The **Fillet** tool converts the sharp corners created by lines, polyline, circles, or arcs into round corners. You must define the radius and select the objects forming a corner. The objects don't need to intersect or overlap for the fillet to work. The following figure shows some examples of rounding the corners.

If you're working with parallel objects, the **Fillet** tool automatically creates a fillet with the right radius.

You can apply fillets to polylines just like you would with lines. If you want to add a fillet to each vertex of a polyline, use the **Polyline** option.

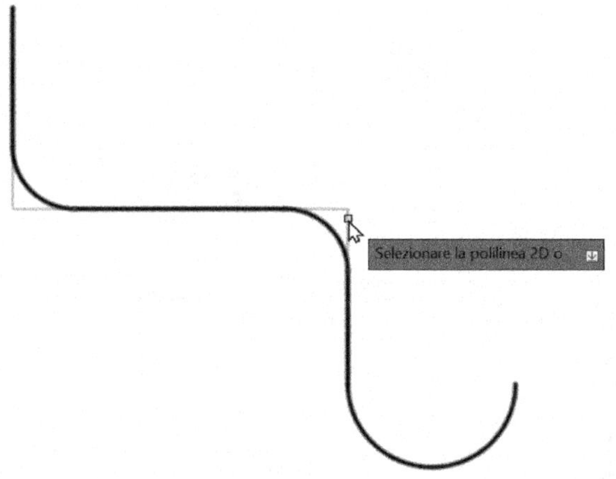

In **Trim** mode, objects are automatically adjusted to meet the fillet's radius.

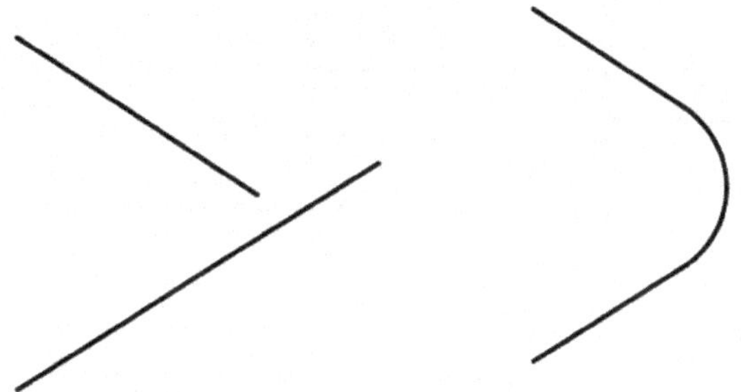

In **Notrim** mode, the fillet is created without modifying the objects. You can switch between these options to control how the **Fillet** tool works.

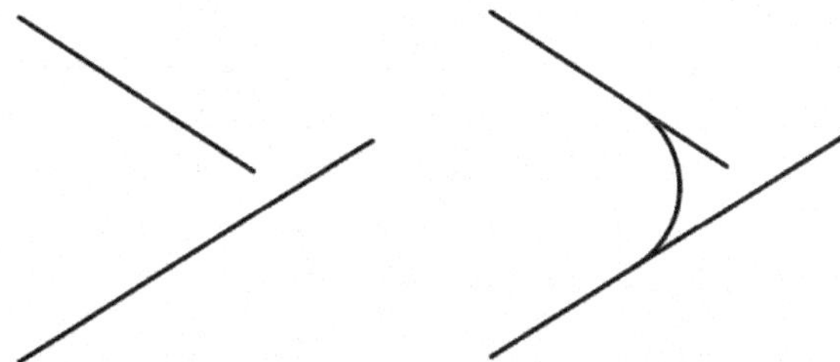

To create multiple fillets consecutively, use the **Multiple** option. If you want to remove the most recent fillet, use the **Undo** option.

If you prefer creating a sharp corner instead of a rounded one, just select the first line, hold the Shift key, and select the second line. This will create a sharp corner automatically.

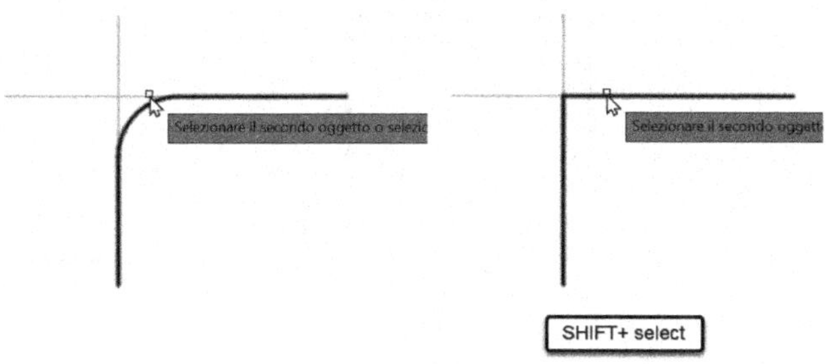

Example

- Start a new drawing.
- Type **Limmax** in the command line and press ENTER.
- Set the maximum limit to 100,100 and press ENTER.
- Click **Zoom All** on the Navigation Bar.
- Click **Home > Draw > Polyline** on the ribbon.
- Define the start point as 20, 50.
- Draw the lines, as shown below.

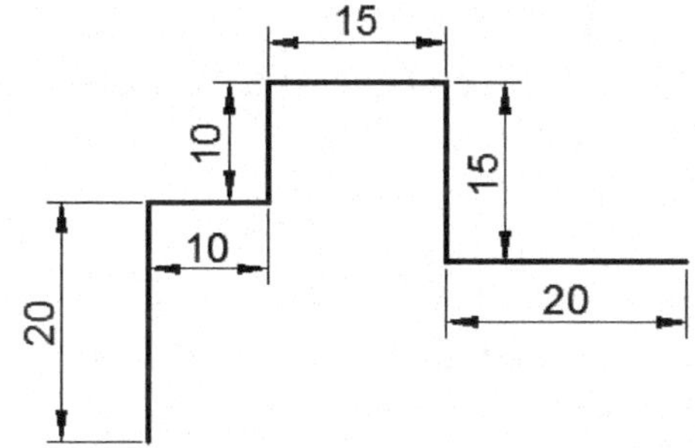

- Right-click and select **Enter**.
- Click **Home > Modify > Fillet** on the ribbon or enter **F** in the command line.
- Select the **Radius** option from the command line.
- Type **5** and press ENTER.
- Select the vertical and horizontal lines, as shown below.

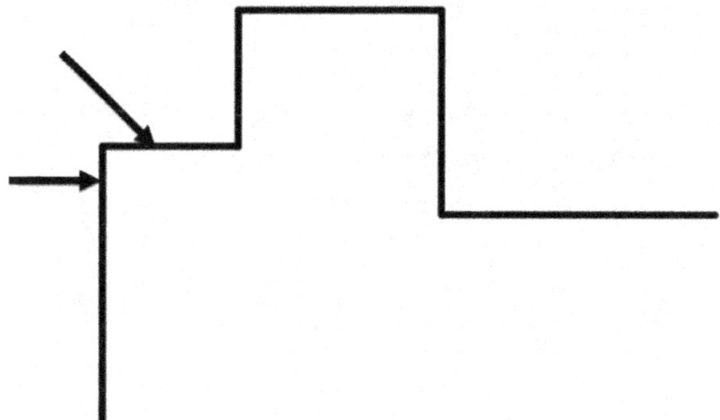

- Notice that a fillet is created.

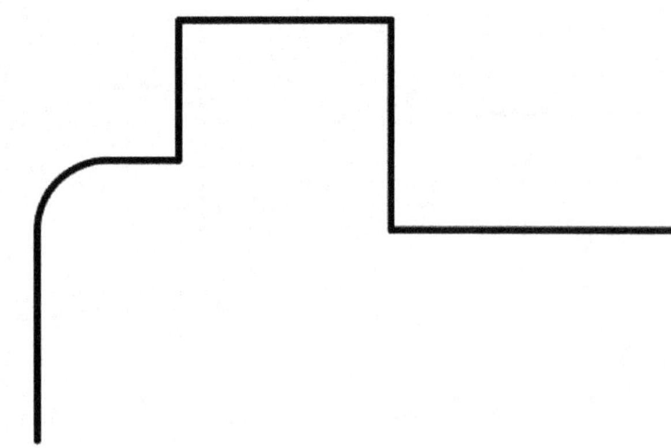

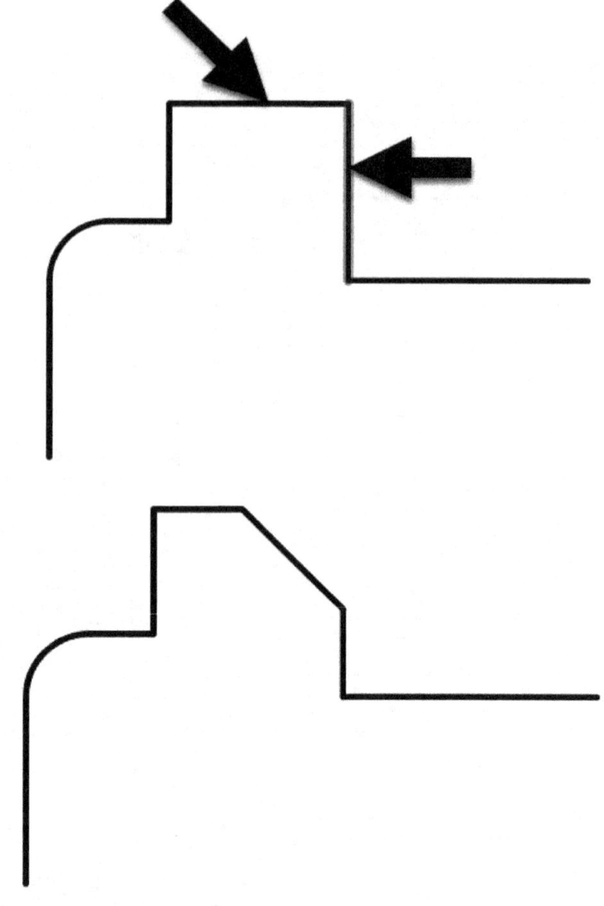

The Chamfer tool

The **Chamfer** tool replaces the sharp corners with an angled line. This tool is similar to the **Fillet** tool, except that an angled line is placed at the corners instead of rounds.

- Click **Home > Modify > Fillet > Chamfer** on the ribbon or enter **CHA** in the command line.
- Follow the prompt sequence given next:

  Select first line or [Undo Polyline Distance Angle Trim mEthod Multiple]: Select the **Distance** option from the command line.

  Define first chamfer distance <0.0000>: Enter **8** as the first chamfer distance and press ENTER.

  Define second chamfer distance <8.0000>: Press ENTER to accept 8 as the second chamfer distance.

  Select first line or [Undo Polyline Distance Angle Trim mEthod Multiple]: Select the vertical line on the right-side.

  Select second line or shift-select to apply corner or [Distance Angle Method]: Select the horizontal line connected to the vertical line.

The Mirror tool

The **Mirror** tool creates a mirror image of objects. You can create symmetrical drawings using this tool. Activate this tool and select the objects to mirror, and then define the 'mirror line' about which the objects will be mirrored. You can define the mirror line by either creating a line or selecting an existing line.

If you want to mirror only in a vertical or horizontal direction, make sure to turn **ORTHOMODE (F8)** on before selecting the second point of the mirror line. This can be particularly useful when you're drawing symmetrical objects, as you only have to draw half of the object and then mirror it.

If you're mirroring text, remember to specify the MIRRTEXT variable. By default, the text will not be reflected if you try to mirror it. If you want the text to be reflected, type MIRRTEXT at the command line and change the value to 1. Keep in mind that dimensions aren't affected by the MIRRTEXT variable and won't be reflected.

- Click **Home > Modify > Mirror** on the ribbon or enter **MI** in the command line.
- Select the drawing by clicking on it, and then press Enter.

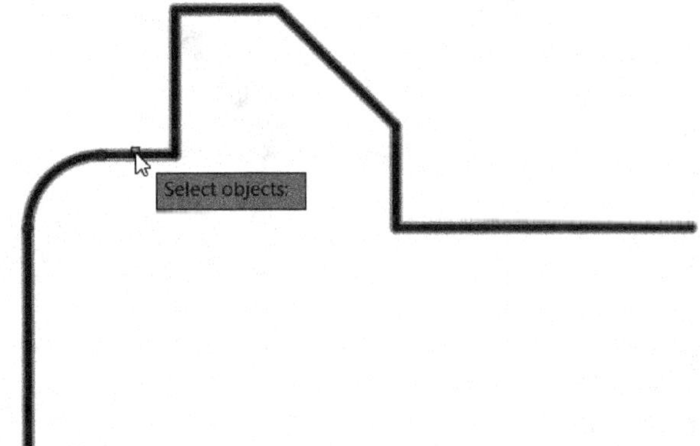

- Select the first point of the mirror line, as shown below.

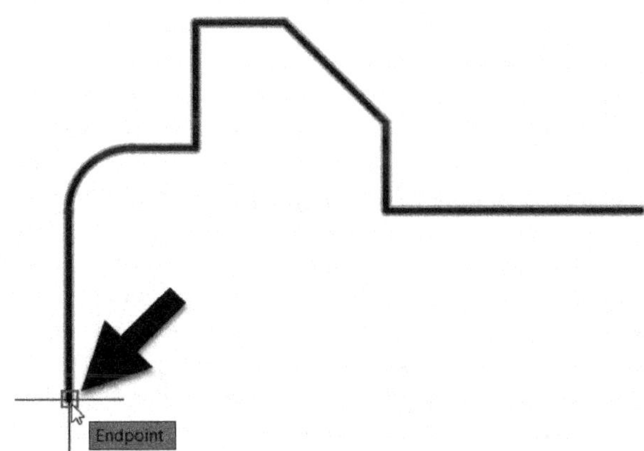

- Make sure that the **Ortho Mode** on the status bar is active.
- Move the pointer toward the right and click.

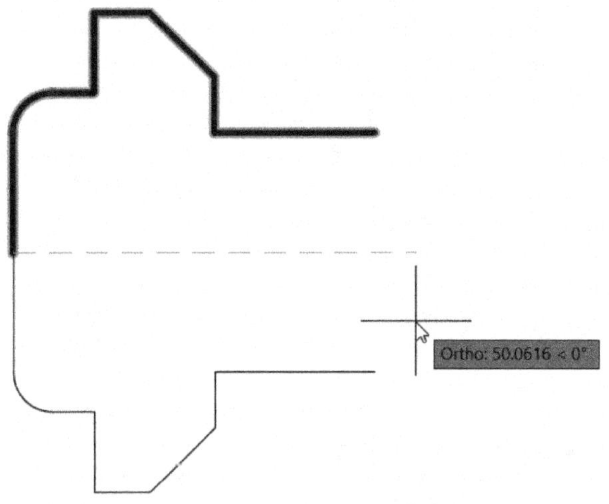

- Select the **No** option from the command line to retain the source objects.

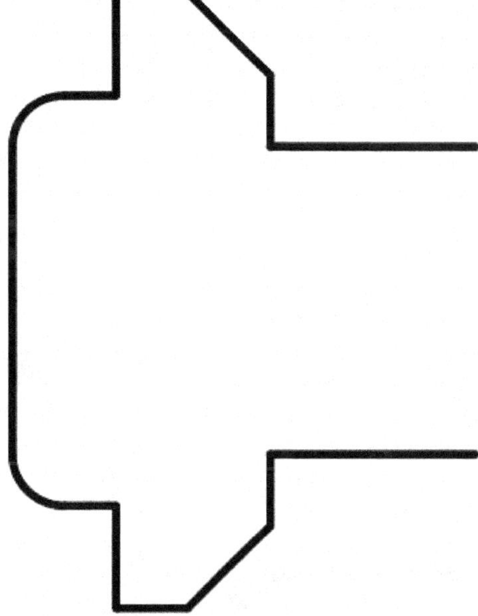

- Click **Home > Draw > Arc > Start, End, Direction** on the ribbon.
- Select the start point of the arc, as shown.
- Select the endpoint of the arc, as shown.

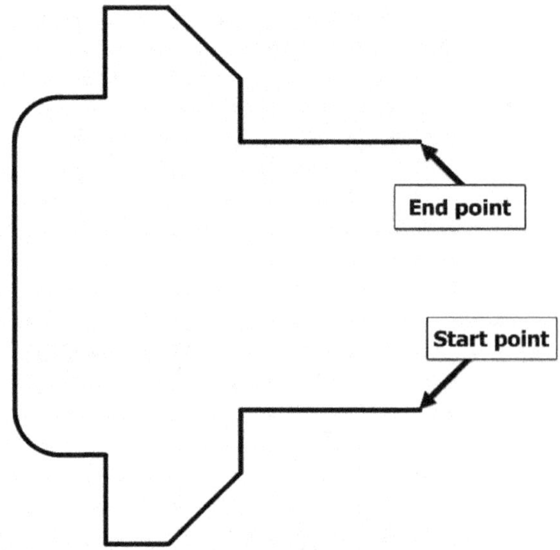

- Make sure that the **Ortho Mode** is active.
- Move the pointer toward the right and click.

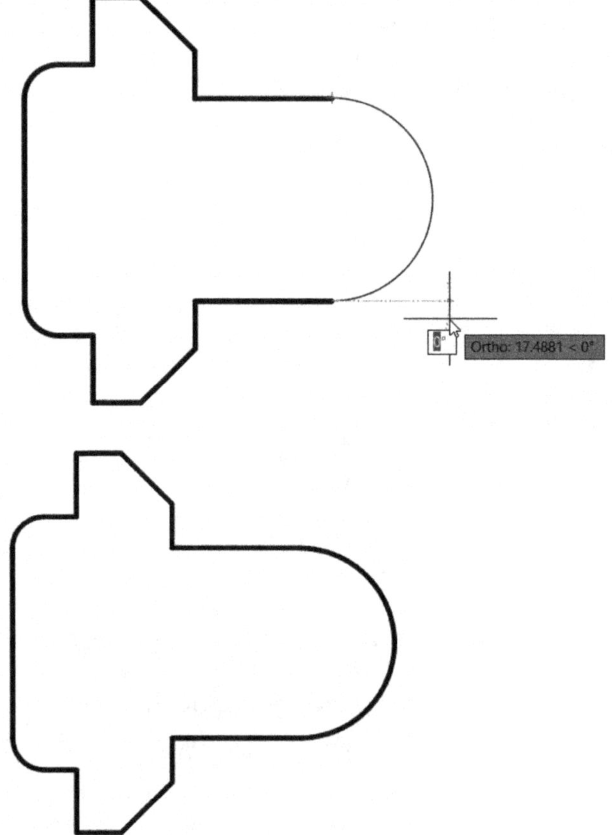

The Explode tool

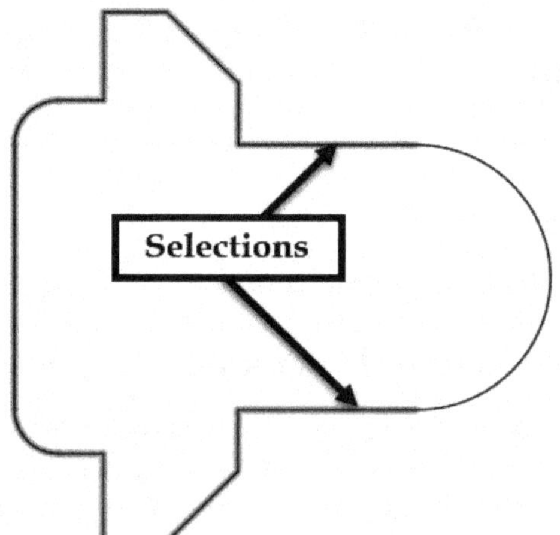The **Explode** tool explodes a group of objects such as polylines, blocks, and hatch patterns, into their individual components or segments. For example, when you create a drawing using the **Polyline** tool, it acts as a single object.

You can explode a polyline or rectangle or any group of objects using the **Explode** tool.

- Click on the portion of the drawing created using the **Polyline** tool; you will notice that the complete polyline is selected as a single object.

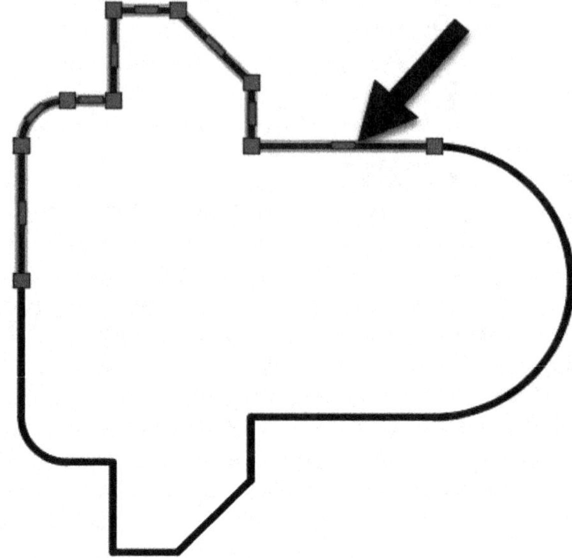

- Click **Home > Modify > Explode** on the ribbon or enter **X** in the command line.
- Select the polylines from the drawing.

- Press ENTER; the polyline is exploded into individual objects.

Now, you can select the individual objects of the polyline.

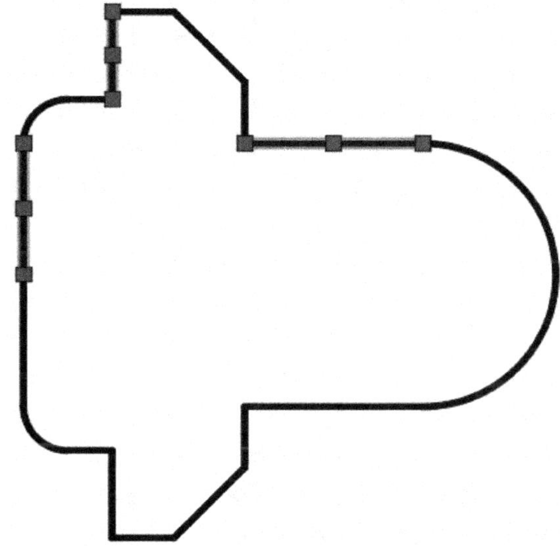

Some key points to remember while exploding an object:

- **Objects:** When you explode an object, its color, linetype, and lineweight might change. So, be prepared for these changes to occur.

- **2D Polylines with Width:** If you select a 2D polyline with a width and explode it, the width will be removed from the resulting lines and arcs. You'll be left with lines and arcs without width attributes.

- **3D Polylines:** When you explode a 3D polyline, it will break down into line segments. Any linetype you assigned to the 3D polyline will be applied to each resulting line segment.

- **Blocks:** When you explode a block, you'll remove one level of grouping at a time. If the block contains a polyline or a nested block, you'll need to explode it further to expose its individual objects. So, be prepared to repeat the process until you reach the individual components.

- **Associative Arrays:** When you explode an associative array, you'll get copies of the original objects. This can be a useful feature for creating multiple instances of a design element.

- **Circles in Nonuniformly Scaled Blocks:** If you have a circle within a nonuniformly scaled block and you explode it, it will turn into an ellipse. This is

because the scaling operation distorts the original circular shape, resulting in an elliptical form.

- **Leaders:** When you explode a leader, it will break down into its individual components, which can include lines, splines, solids, block inserts, multiline text, or tolerance objects. The specific components you'll get depend on the type of leader you're working with.

The Stretch tool

The **Stretch** tool lengthens or shortens drawings or parts of drawings. You can change the shape and size of objects while keeping them connected. Note that you cannot stretch circles, ellipses, and blocks using this tool. Also, you must select the portion of the drawing to be stretched by dragging a selection window or polygon. If objects are fully inside this window or selected alone, they move instead of stretch.

- Click **Home > Modify > Stretch** on the ribbon or enter **STRETCH** in the command line.
- Create a crossing window to select the objects of the drawing.

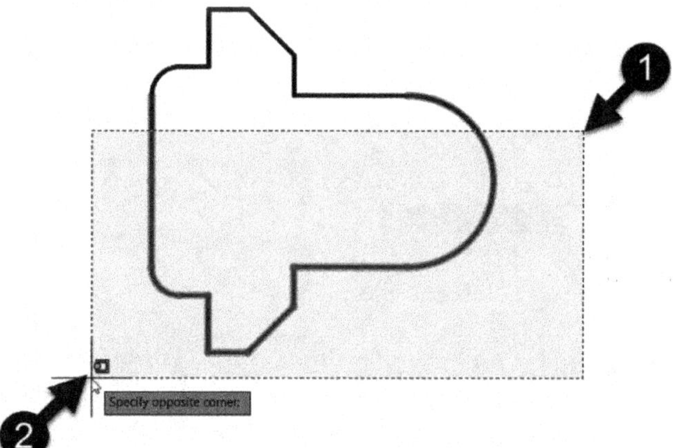

- Press ENTER (or) right-click to accept the selection.
- Select the base point, as shown below.

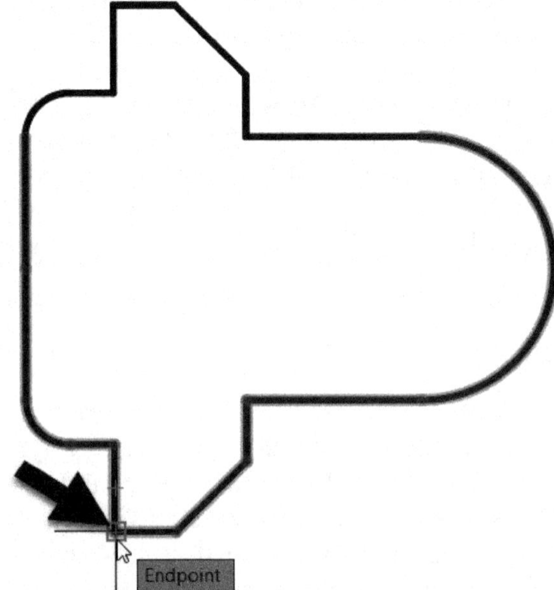

- Move the pointer downward and click; lines and polylines get longer or shorter, and arcs change radius.

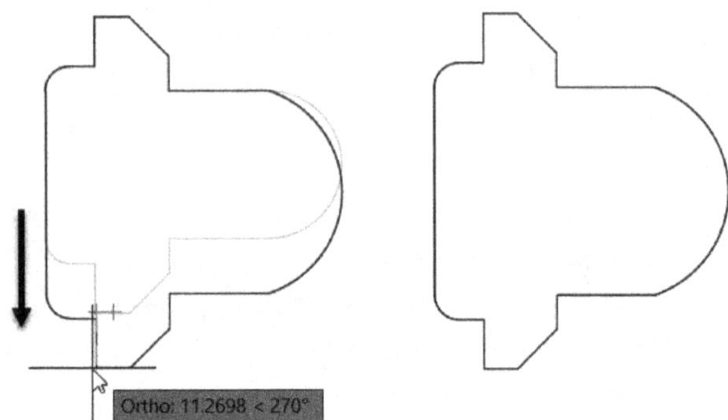

- Save and close the file.

The Polar Array tool

The **Polar Array** tool creates an arrangement of objects around a point in a circular form. The following example shows you to create a polar array.

- Create two concentric circles of 140 and 50 diameters.

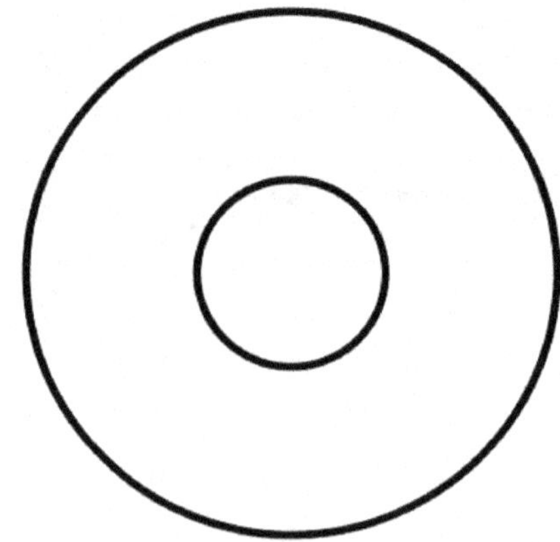

- Type **C** in the command line and press ENTER.
- Press and hold the Shift key, right-click, and select **Quadrant** from the shortcut menu.
- Select the quadrant point of the circle, as shown below.

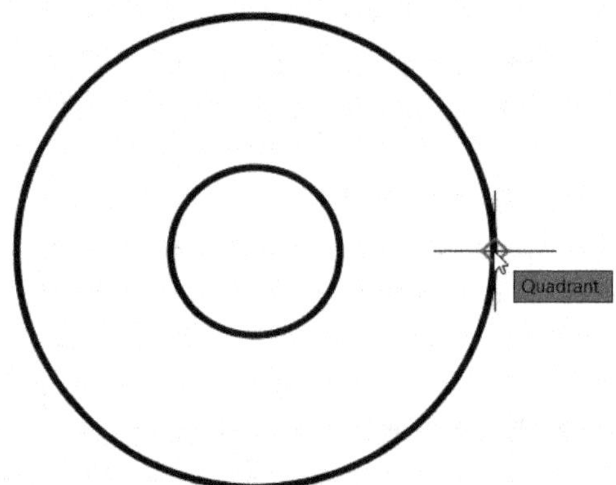

- Type 30 as radius and press ENTER.

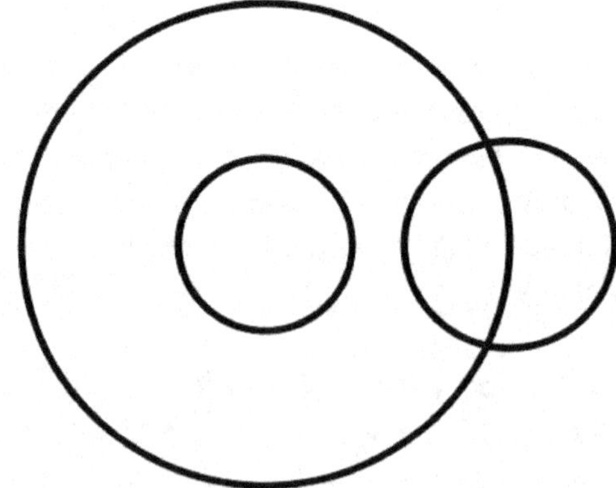

- Click **Home > Modify > Trim** on the ribbon.
- Select the circle on the quadrant as the object to be trimmed.

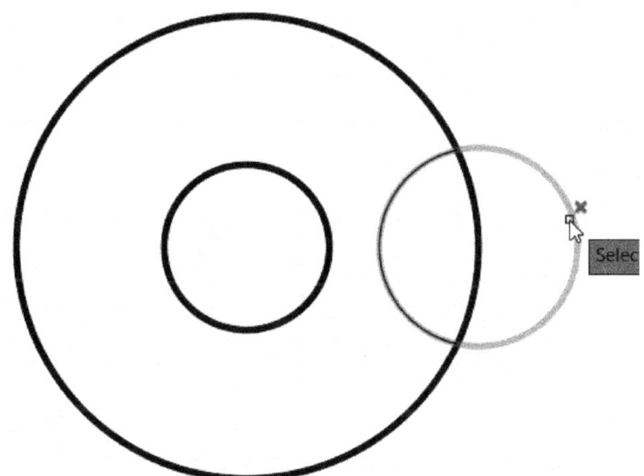

- Press Enter.
- Click **Home > Modify > Array > Polar Array** on the ribbon or **ARRAYPOLAR** in the command line.
- Select the arc created after trimming the circle. Next, right-click to accept the selection.

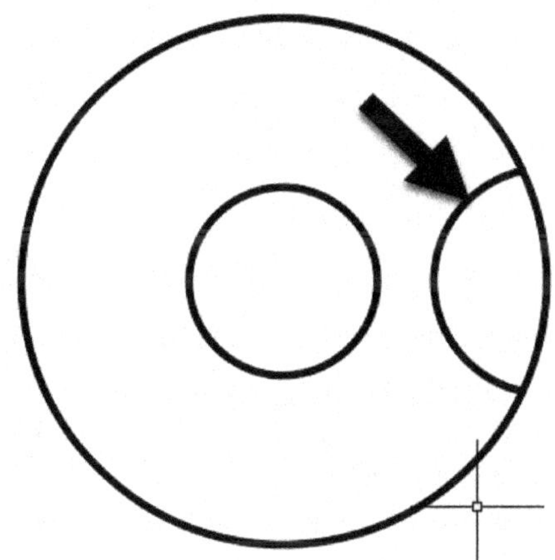

- Make sure that **Object Snap** is activated.
- Select the center of the large circle as the center of the array; the **Array Creation** tab appears in the ribbon.
- In the **Items** panel of the **Array Creation** tab, set the **Items** value to 4.

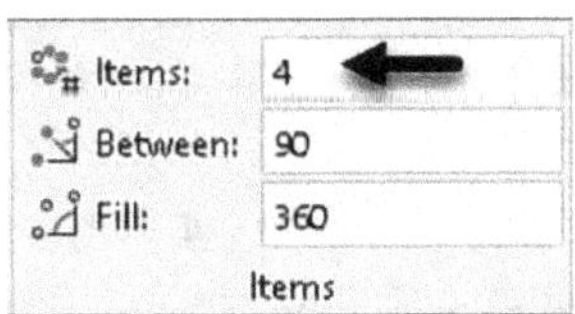

Notice that the **Rotate Items** button is active in the **Properties** panel of the **Array Creation** tab. It rotates the objects of the polar array. If you deactivate this button,

the polar array is created without rotating the objects, as shown in the figure.

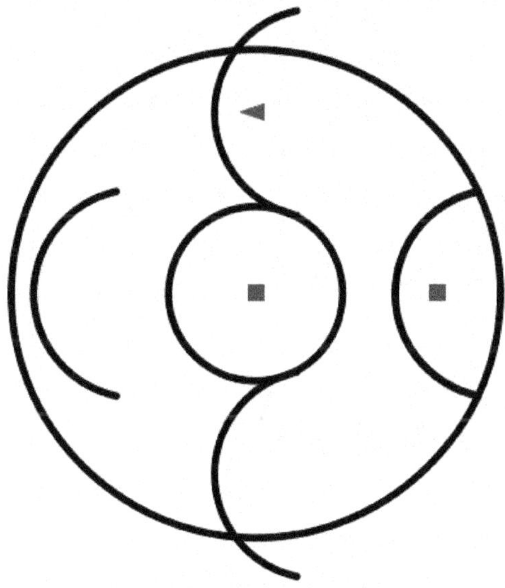

In addition, the **Associative** button is active by default. It ensures that you can edit the array after creating it.

- Make sure that the **Associative** and the **Rotate Items** buttons are active. Next, click the **Close Array** button on the ribbon.

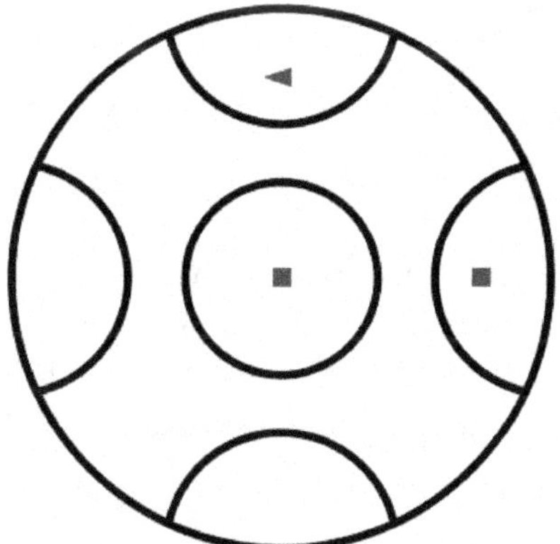

- Click the **Trim** button on the **Modify** panel.
- Trim the unwanted portions, as shown below.

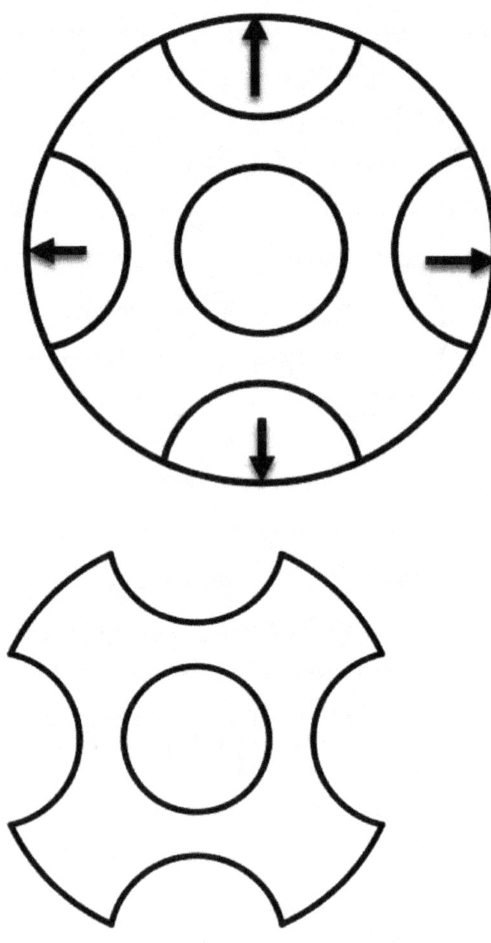

The Offset tool

The **Offset** tool creates parallel copies of lines, polylines, circles, and arcs. To create a parallel copy of an object, first, you must define the offset distance and then select the object. Next, you must define the side in which the parallel copy will be placed.

One thing to remember is that the way OFFSET works depends on the object. For lines, it creates a parallel copy that's equal in length. For arcs or circles, it creates a concentric offset. And for closed polylines or splines, it results in a complete parallel shape.

- Create the drawing shown below using the **Polyline** tool. Do not add dimensions.

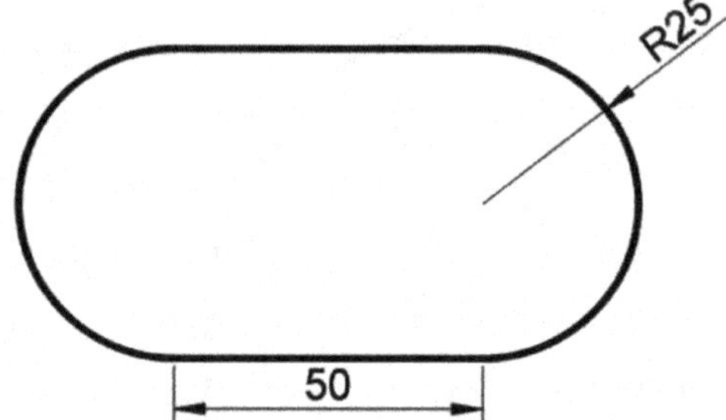

- Click **Home > Modify > Offset** on the ribbon or enter **O** in the command line.
- Type **20** as the offset distance and press ENTER.
- Select the polyline loop.
- Click outside the loop to create a parallel copy.

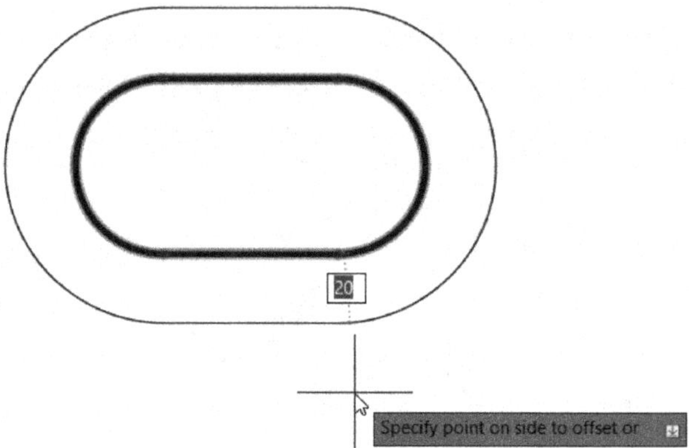

- Select **Exit** from the command line.
- Click **Home > Layers > Layer Properties** on the ribbon (or) type **LA** in the command line; the **Layer Properties Manager** appears.
- Click the **New layer** button on the **Layer Properties Manager**. Enter **Centerline** in the **Name** field.

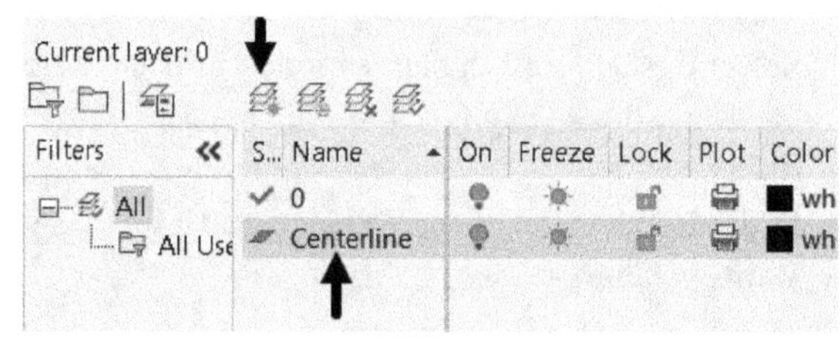

- Click the **Set current** icon. It activates the new layer.
- Click in the **Linetype** field of the current layer; the **Select Linetype** dialog appears.

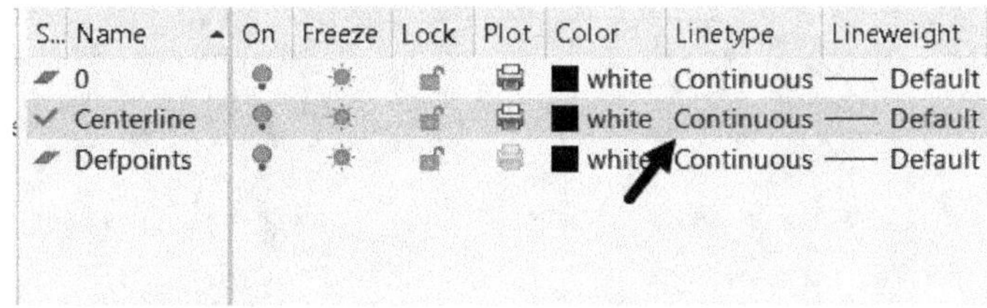

- On the **Select Linetype** dialog, click the **Load** button; the **Load or Reload Linetypes** dialog appears.

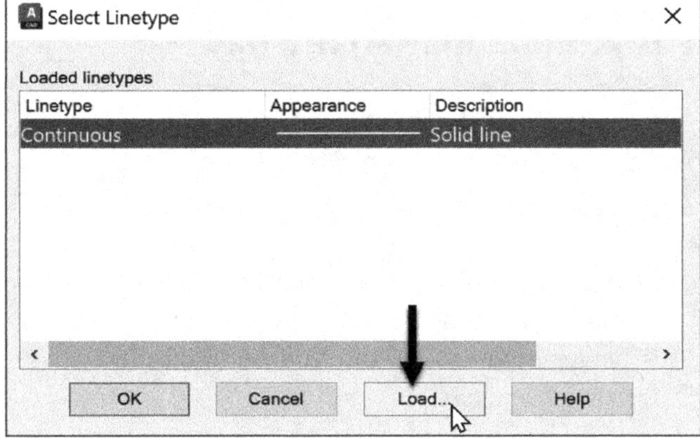

- Select the **CENTER2** Linetype from this dialog. Click **OK**. It adds the linetype to the **Select Linetype** dialog.

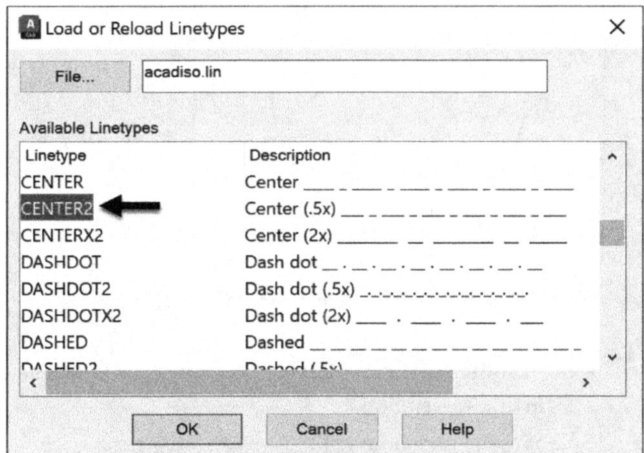

- Select the **CENTER2** linetype from the **Select Linetype** dialog and click **OK**.
- Close the **Layer Properties Manager**.
- Click the **Offset** button on the **Modify** panel.
- Select the **Layer** option from the command line.

- Select the **Current** option from the command line; this ensures that the offset entity will be created with the currently active layer properties. If you select the **Source** option, the offset entity will be created with the properties of the source object.
- Type **10** as the offset distance and press ENTER.
- Select the outer loop of the drawing.
- Move the pointer inwards and click to create the offset entity.
- Select **Exit** from the command line.

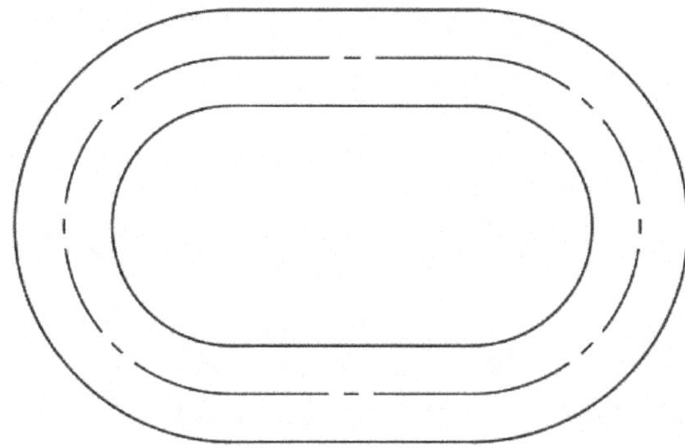

- Click on the **Layer** drop-down on the **Layer** panel of the ribbon.
- Select the **0** layer from the drop-down.

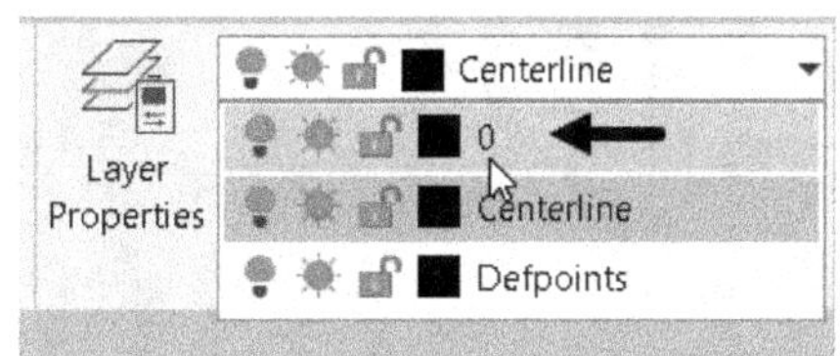

- Create a circle of 6 mm in radius, as shown.

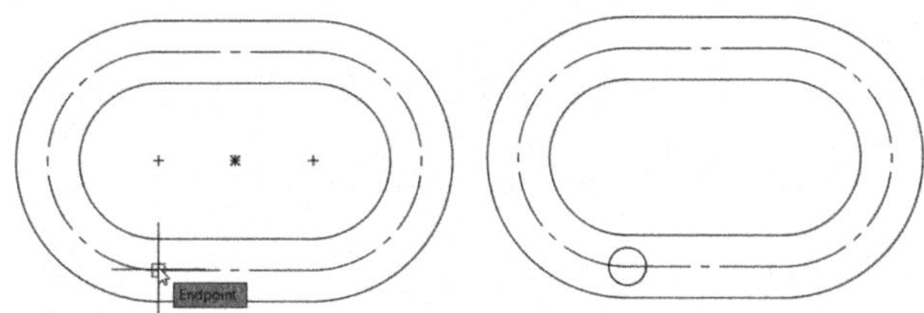

The Path Array tool

The **Path Array** tool creates an array of objects along a path (line, polyline, circle, helix, and spline).

- Click **Home > Modify > Array > Path Array** on the ribbon or enter **ARRAYPATH** in the command line.
- Select the circle and right-click.

- Select the centerline as the path; the preview of the path array appears.

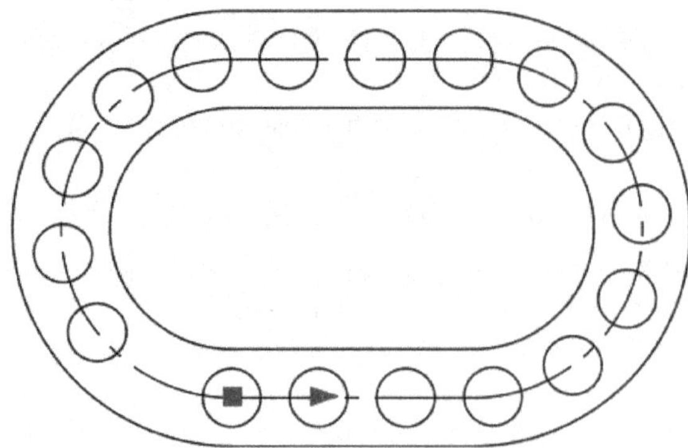

- On the **Array Creation** tab, click **Measure** > **Divide** n on the **Properties** panel. Now, you must enter the number of items in the path array.

If you select the **Measure** method, you must enter the distance between the items in the path array.

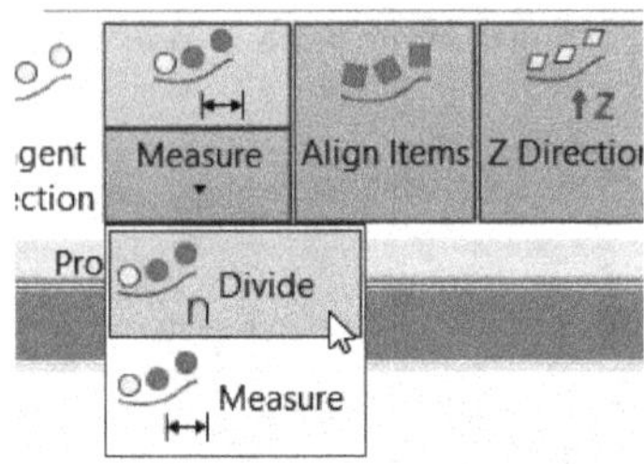

- Set the **Items** count to 12.

Notice that the **Align Items** button is active by default. As a result, the items are aligned with the path. If you deactivate this button, the items will not be aligned with the path.

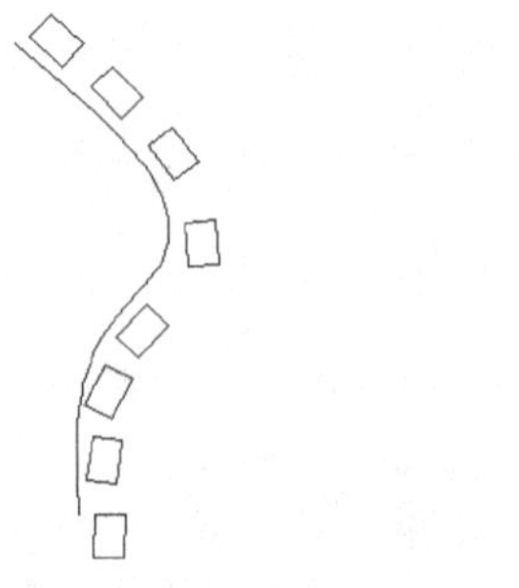

- Click the **Close Array** button.

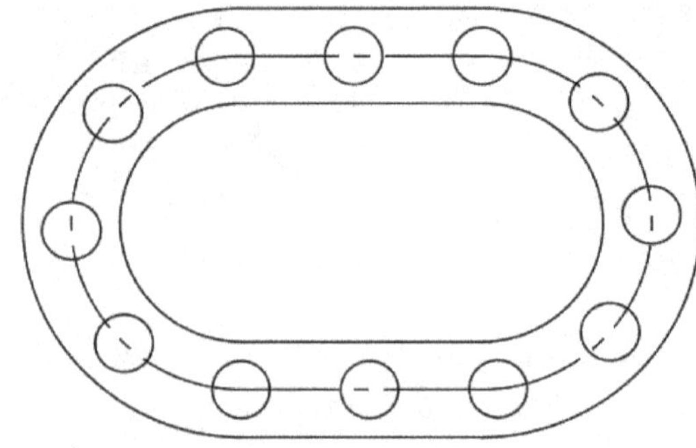

- Save and close the file.

The Rectangular Array tool

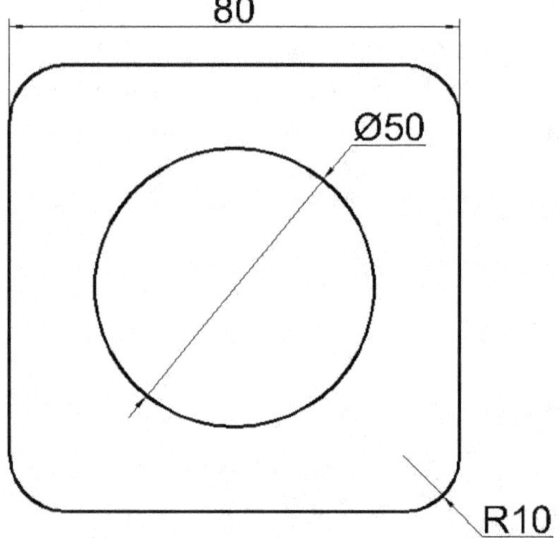

The **Rectangular Array** tool creates an array of objects along with the X and Y directions.

- Open a new AutoCAD file and draw the sketch shown below. Do not add dimensions. (refer to the **Drawing Rectangles** and **Drawing Circles** section in Chapter 2 to know the procedure to draw the rectangle and circle)

- Click **Home** > **Draw** > **Circle** drop-down > **Center, Radius** on the ribbon.
- Select the center point of the lower-left fillet.

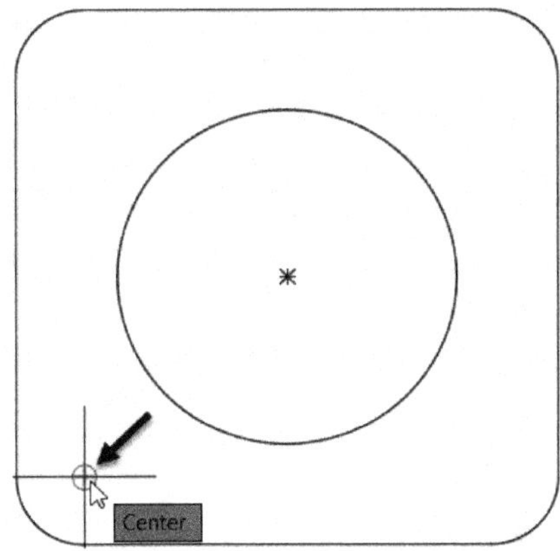

- Type 5 and press Enter.

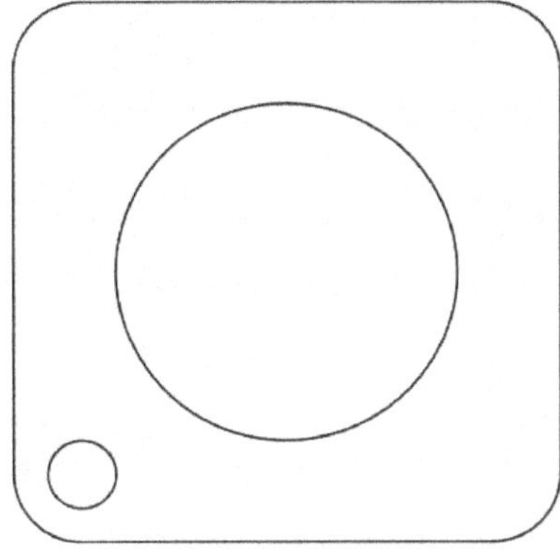

- Click **Home > Modify > Array > Rectangular Array** on the ribbon or enter **ARRAYRECT** in the command line.
- Select the small circle and right-click; a rectangular array with default values appears.

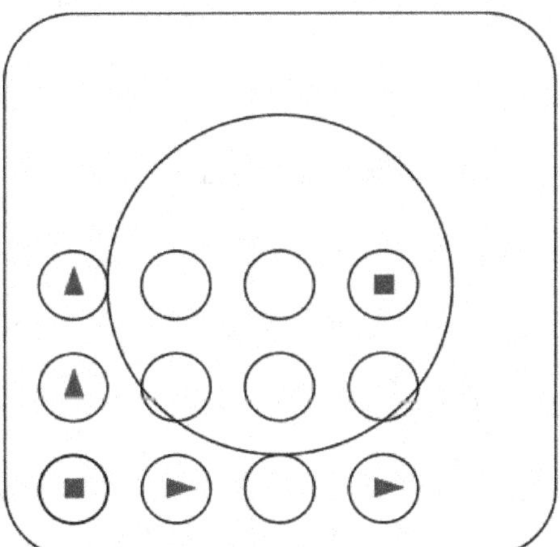

Also, the **Array Creation** tab appears.

- Set the **Columns** count to 2.

- Set the **Rows** count to 2.
- Set the **Between** value in the **Columns** panel to 60.
- Set the **Between** value in the **Rows** panel to 60.

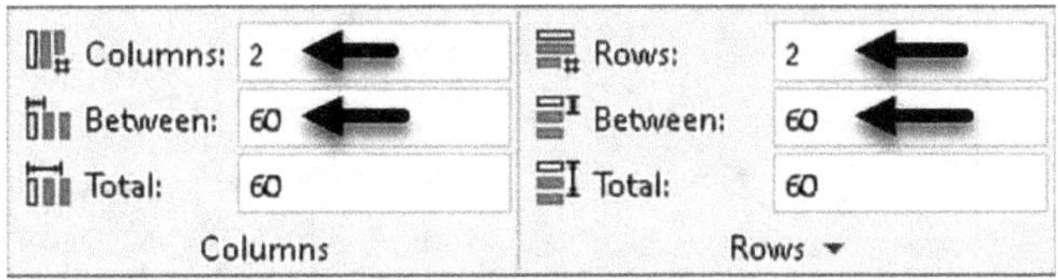

- Click **Close Array** on the ribbon.

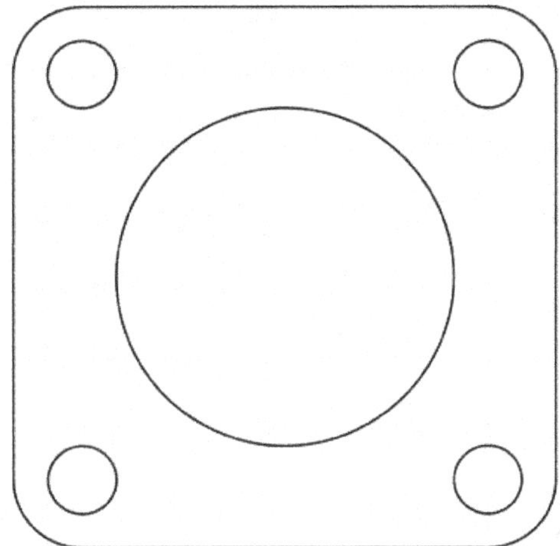

- On the ribbon, click **Home** tab > **Utilities** > **Measure** Drop-down > **Quick**.

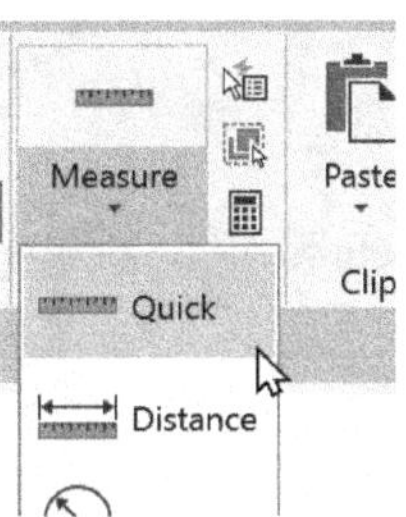

- Place the cursor inside the circle located at the center; the radius of the circle is displayed.

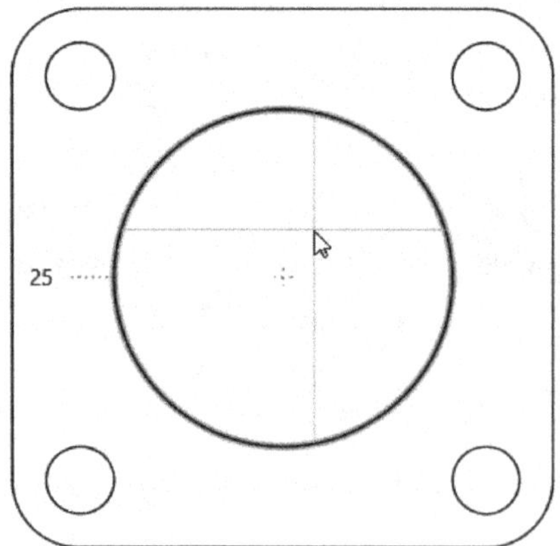

- Place the cursor between the two circles located at the bottom; the measurements of the objects located in four directions of the cursor are displayed.

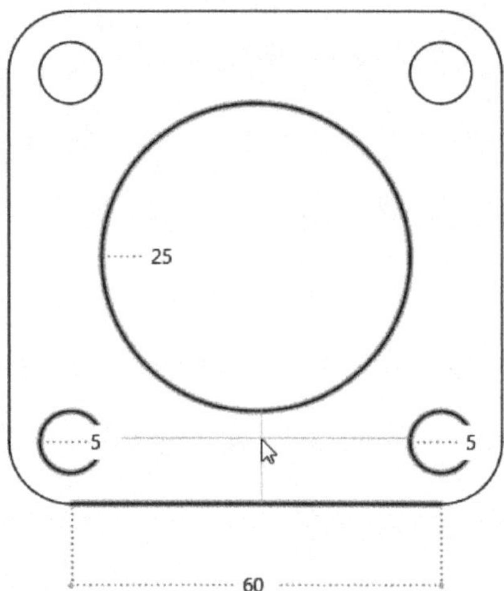

Editing Using Grips

When you select objects from the graphics window, small squares appear on them. These squares are called grips. You can use these grips to stretch, move, rotate, scale and mirror objects, change properties, and perform other editing operations. Grips displayed on selecting different objects are shown below.

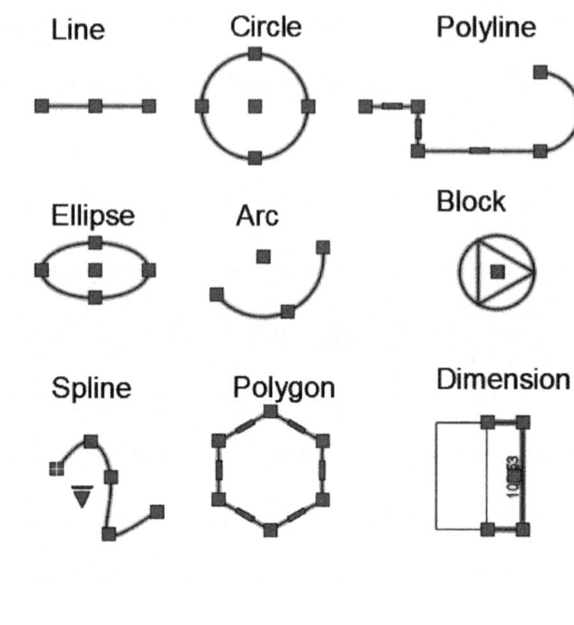

The following table gives you the details of the editing operations that can be performed when you select and drag grips.

Object	Grip	Editing Operation
Circle	Grip on circumference	**Scale**: Select any one of the grips on the circumference and move the pointer to scale a circle.

	Center point grip	**Move**: Select the center grip of the circle and move the pointer.
Arc	Grip on circumference	**Stretch**: Select the grip on the circumference and move the pointer.
	Center point grip	**Move**: Select the center grip of the arc and move the pointer.
Line	Midpoint Grip	**Move**: Select the Midpoint grip and move the pointer.
	Endpoint Grip	**Stretch/Lengthen**: Select an endpoint grip and move the pointer.

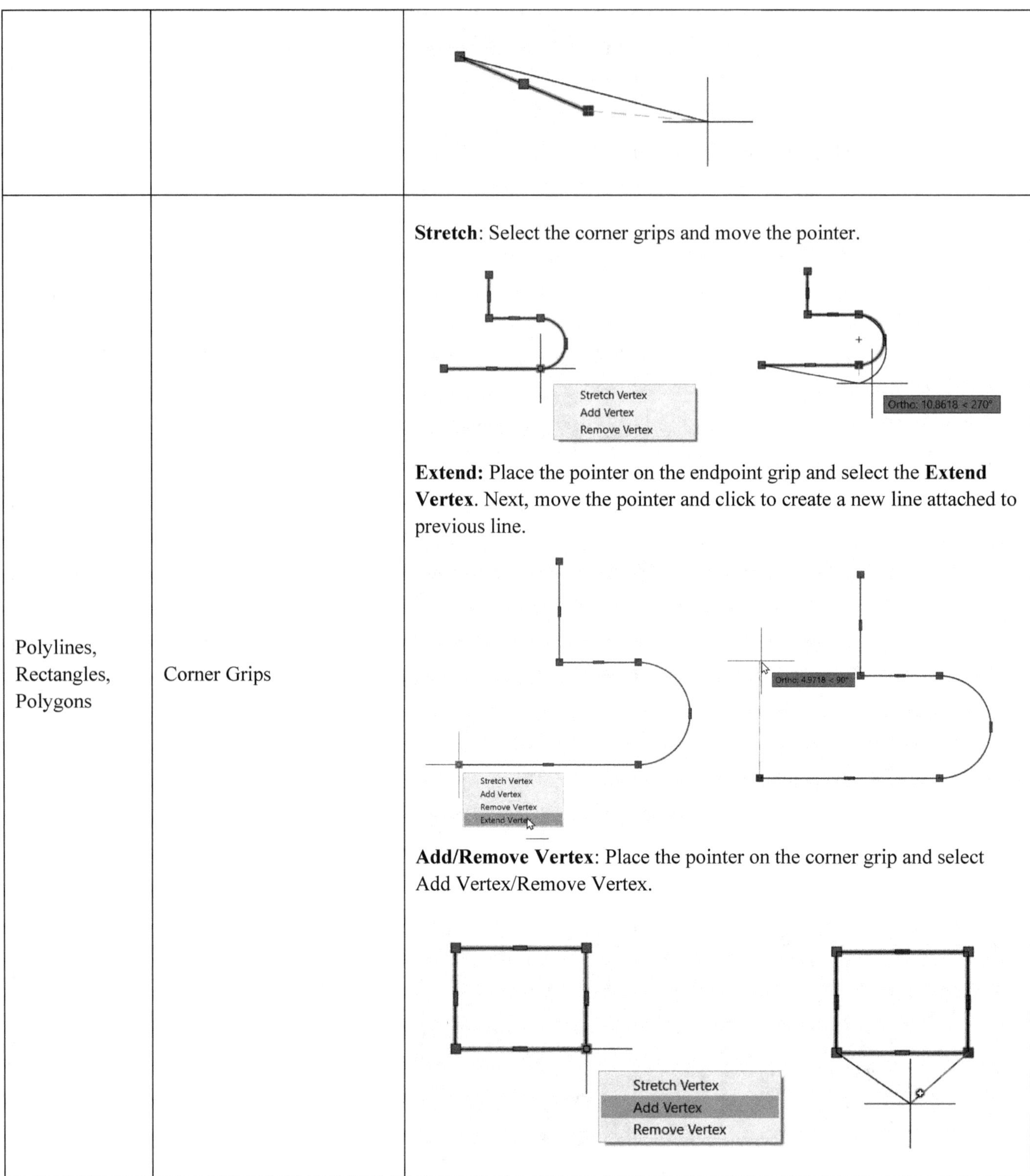

Stretch: Select the corner grips and move the pointer.

Extend: Place the pointer on the endpoint grip and select the **Extend Vertex**. Next, move the pointer and click to create a new line attached to previous line.

Add/Remove Vertex: Place the pointer on the corner grip and select Add Vertex/Remove Vertex.

Polylines, Rectangles, Polygons	Corner Grips	

	Midpoint Grips	**Convert to Arc**: Place the pointer on the midpoint grip and select **Convert to Arc**. **Convert to Line**: Place the pointer on the midpoint grip of a polyline arc and select **Convert to Line**.
Ellipse	Center Grip	**Move**: Select the center grip and move the pointer.
	Grips on circumference	**Stretch**: Select a grip on the circumference and move the pointer.

| Spline | Fit Points | **Stretch**: Select a grip on the spline and move the pointer.

Add/Remove Fit Point: Place the pointer on a fit point and select **Add Fit Point** or **Remove Fit Point**.

 |
| | Control Vertices | **Stretch Vertices**: Select the control vertices of a CV spline and move the pointer.

Add/Remove Vertex: Place the pointer on a control vertex and select **Add Vertex** or **Remove Vertex**.

Refine Vertices: Place the pointer on a control vertex and select **Refine Vertices**. |

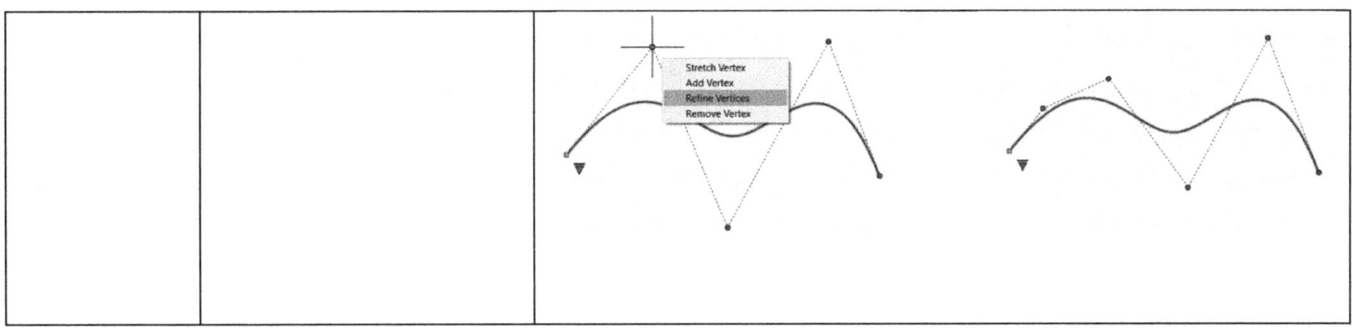

Modifying Rectangular Arrays

You can use grips to edit rectangular arrays dynamically. Various array editing operations using grips are given next.

Moving a Rectangular array

- Create a rectangular array, as shown below.

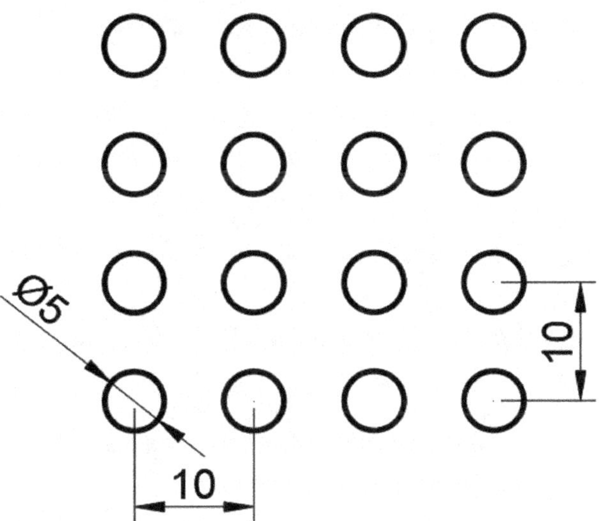

- Select the array; you will notice that grips are displayed on it.
- Select the grip located at the lower-left corner and move the array, as shown below.

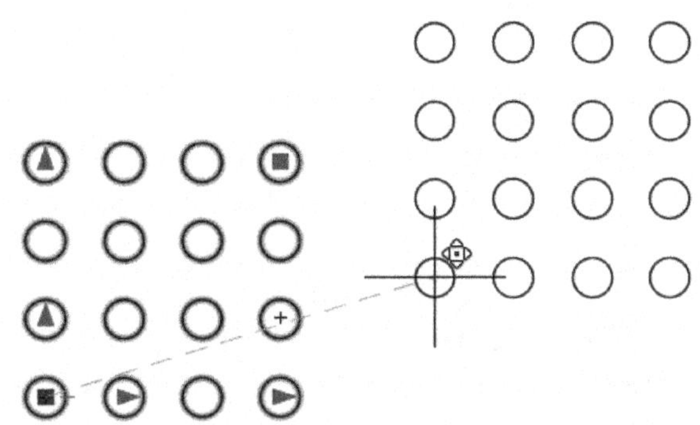

Adding/Removing Level to a Rectangular array

- Place the pointer on the lower left grip of the rectangular array; a shortcut menu appears.
- Select **Level Count** from the shortcut menu; the message, "**Specify number of levels**," appears in the command line.
- Type 3 and press ENTER.
- Click the **Home** button near the ViewCube to view the levels.

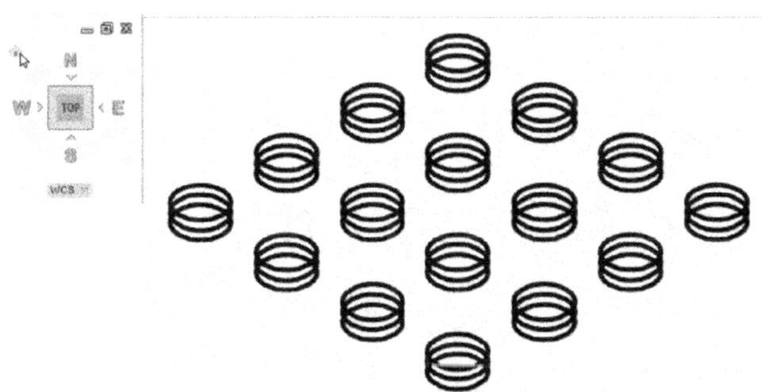

- Change the view to Top view by using the In-Canvas controls.

[−][Custom View][2D Wireframe]

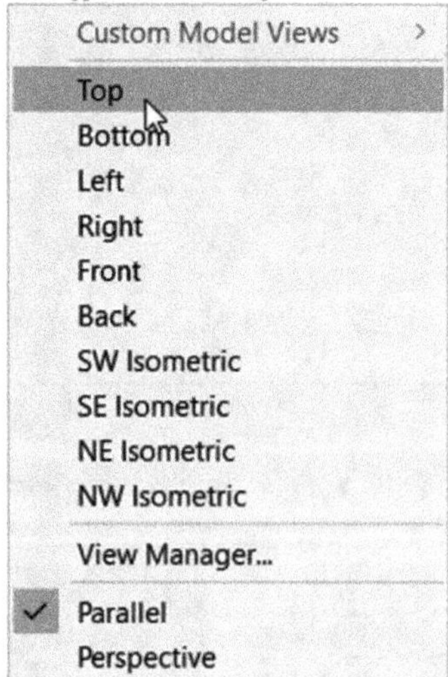

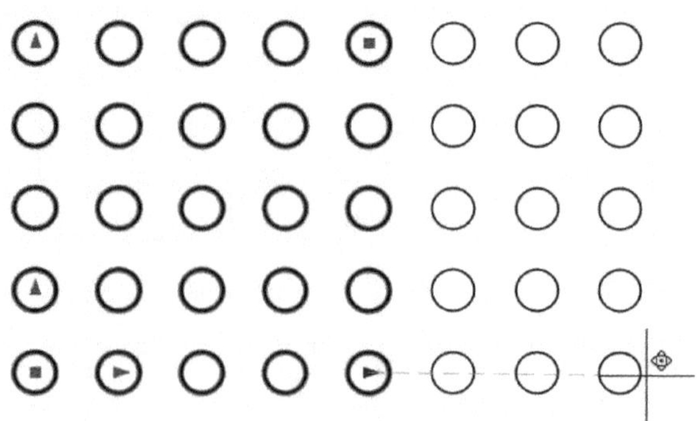

- To change the row count only, click the top left corner grip and drag the pointer. You can also enter the row count in the command line.

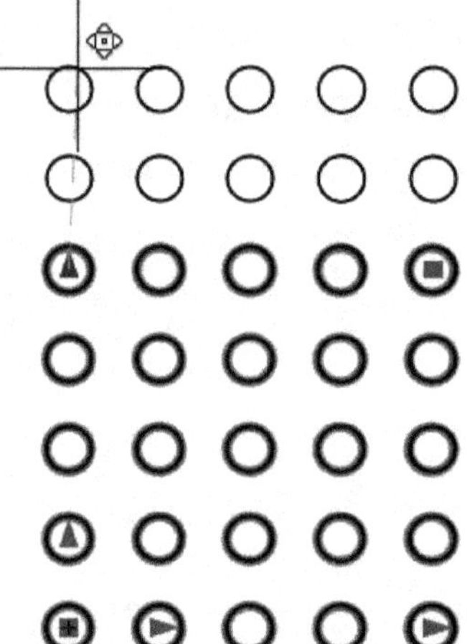

Changing the Column and Row Count

- To change the column and row count, place the pointer on the top right corner grip; a shortcut menu appears.
- Select **Row and Column Count** from the shortcut menu; the message, "**Specify number of rows and columns**," appears in the command line.
- Type **5** in the command line and press ENTER; the number of rows and columns is changed to 5.
- If you only want to change the column count, place the pointer on the lower right corner grip of the array.

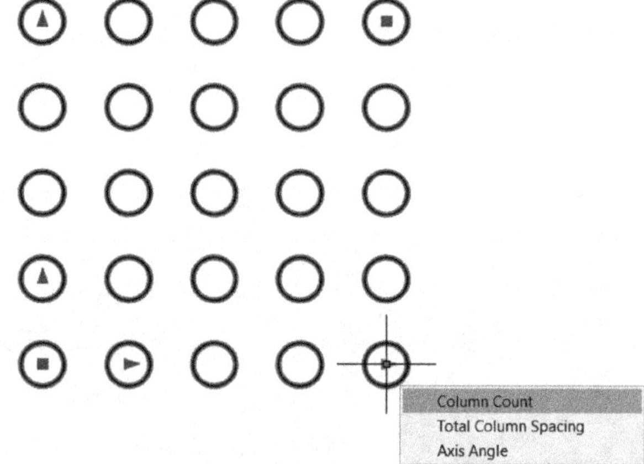

- Select **Colum Count** from the shortcut menu.
- Next, enter the number of columns or drag the pointer and click.

Changing the Column and Row Spacing

- To change the total column and row spacing, place the pointer on the top right corner grip and select **Total Row and Column Spacing** from the shortcut menu.

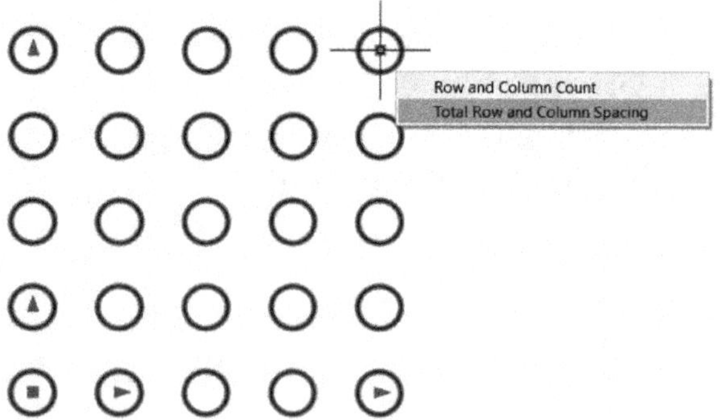

- Type 80 in the command line; the spacing between the columns and rows is adjusted to fit the total length.

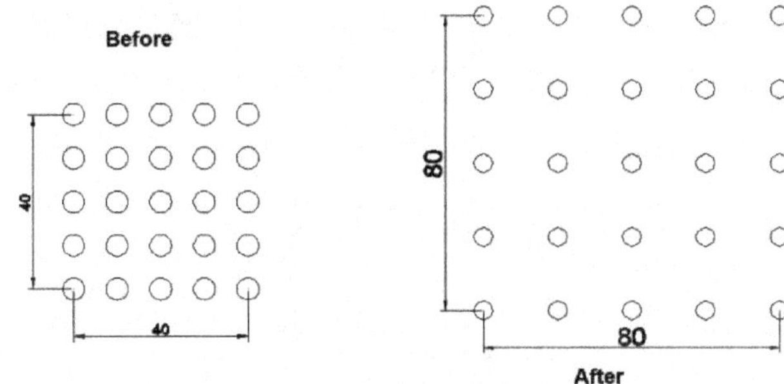

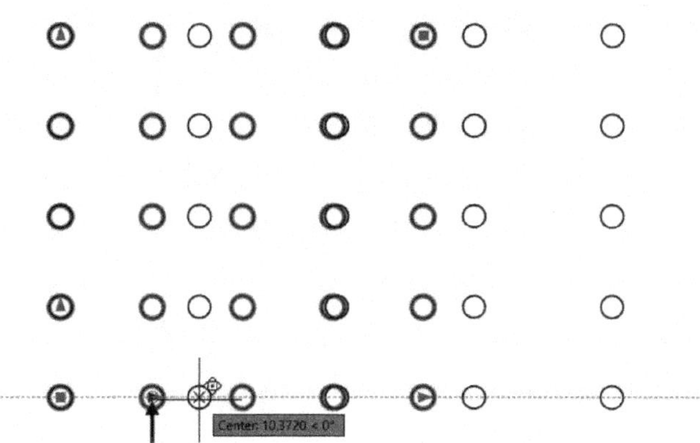

- To change the total column spacing only, place the pointer on the lower right corner grip and select **Total Column Spacing** from the shortcut menu.

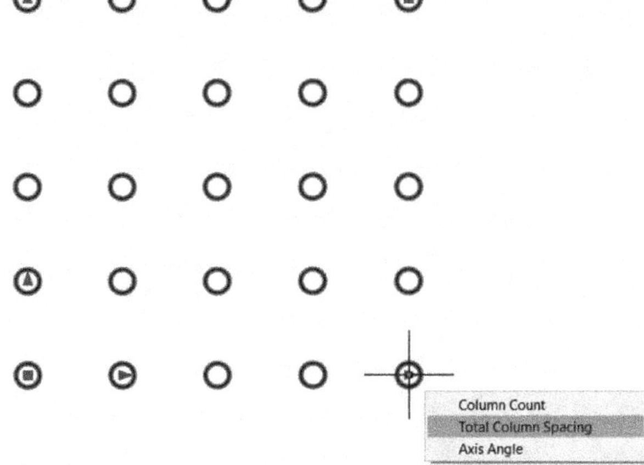

- You can also enter the distance in the command line.
- Likewise, you can change the total row spacing and distance between the individual rows by using the grips shown below.

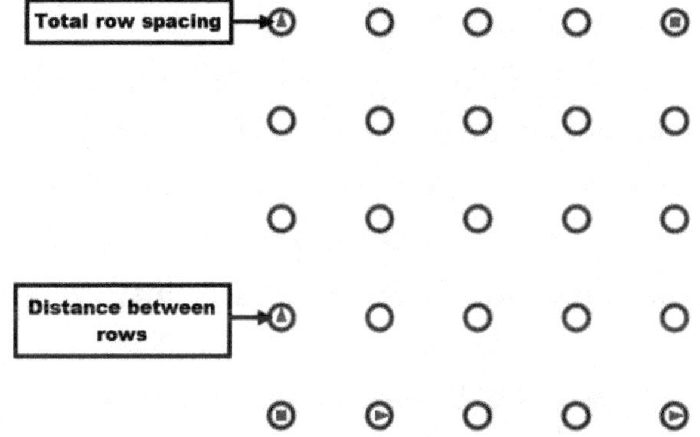

- Next, enter the total column distance or drag the pointer and click.

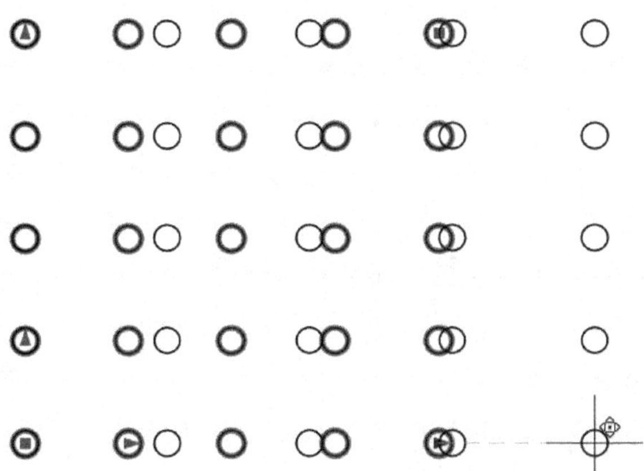

Changing the Axis Angle of the Rectangular Array

- To change the Axis angle of the rows, place the pointer on the lower right corner grip and select the **Axis angle** option from the shortcut menu.
- Type the angle and press ENTER. Note that the angle is calculated from the first column of the array. For example, if you enter 60 as the axis angle, the rows will be inclined by 60 degrees from the first column.

- If you want to change the distance between the individual columns, click the second column grip and drag the pointer.

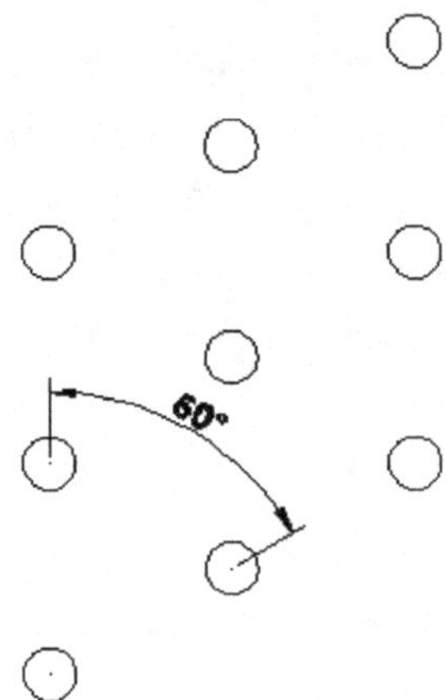

- Likewise, you can change the axis angle of the columns by using the top left corner grip.

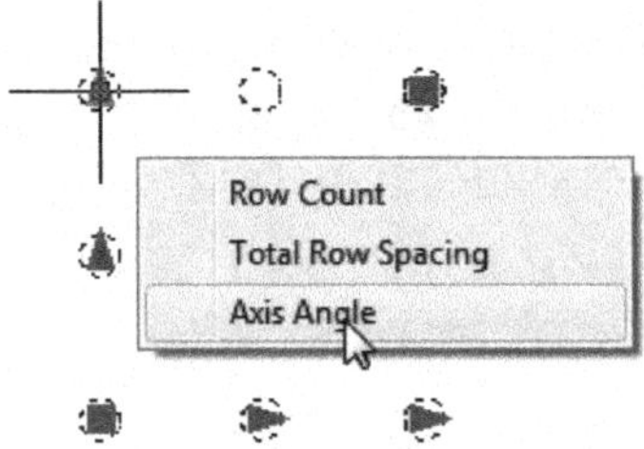

Editing the Source Item of the Rectangular Array

- Create a rectangular array, as shown below.

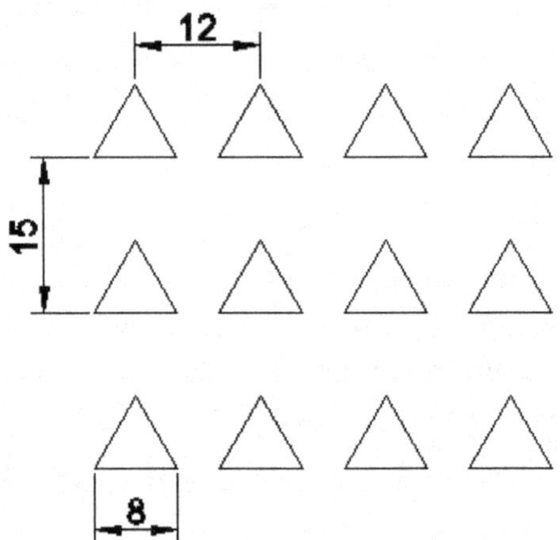

- Click **Close Array** on the **Array Creation** tab.
- Select the rectangular array; the **Array** tab appears in the ribbon.

- Click the **Edit Source** button on the **Options** panel; the message, "**Select item in array**" message appears in the command line.

- Select the lower left triangle of the rectangular array; the **Array Editing State** message box appears.

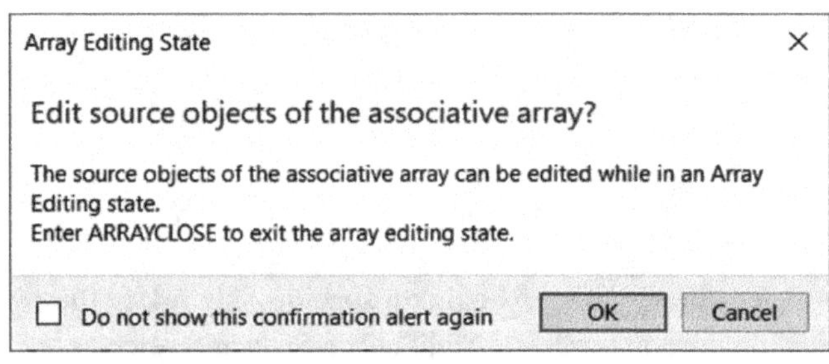

- Click **OK**; the array editing state is activated.
- Draw a circle and trim the unwanted portion, as shown below.

- Click **Save Changes** on the **Edit Array** panel of the **Home** tab of the ribbon.

Modifying Polar Arrays

Similar to editing rectangular arrays, you can also edit a polar array by using grips. Various array editing operations using grips are given next.

Changing the Radius of a Polar array

- Create the polar array, as shown in the figure.

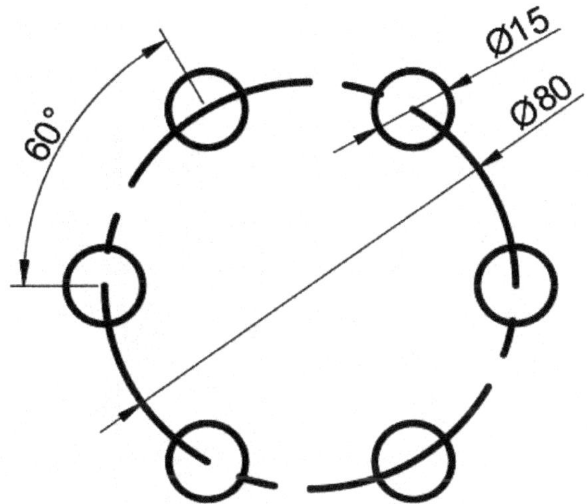

- Select the polar array; grips will be displayed on it.
- Place the pointer on the base grip, as shown in the figure.
- Select **Stretch Radius** from the shortcut menu.

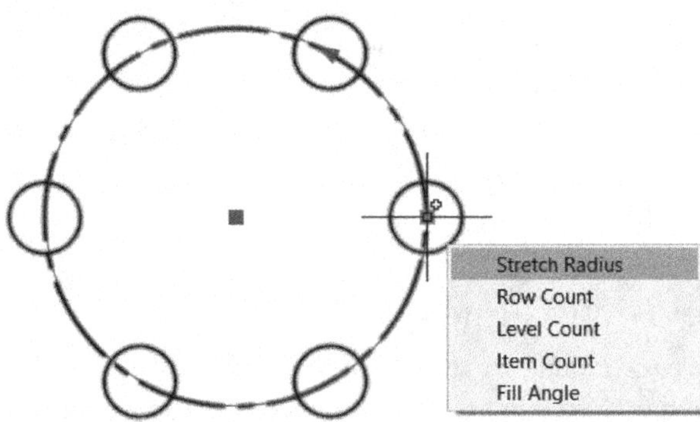

- Move the pointer outward or inward and click. You can also enter a new radius value of the polar array.

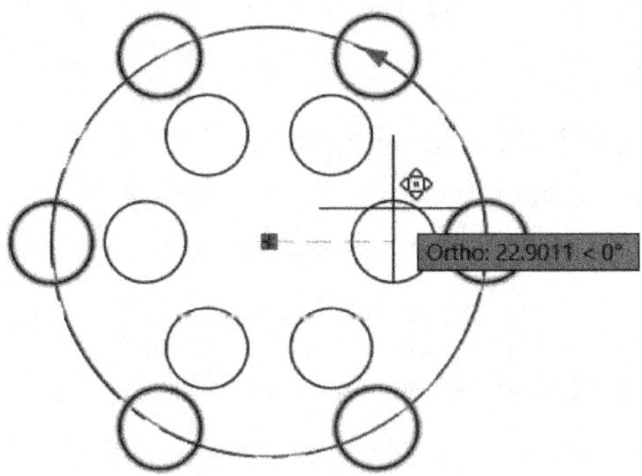

Changing the Row Count of a Polar array

- Place the pointer on the base grip of the array and select **Row Count** from the shortcut menu.

- Move the pointer outward and click. You can also enter the number of rows in the command line.

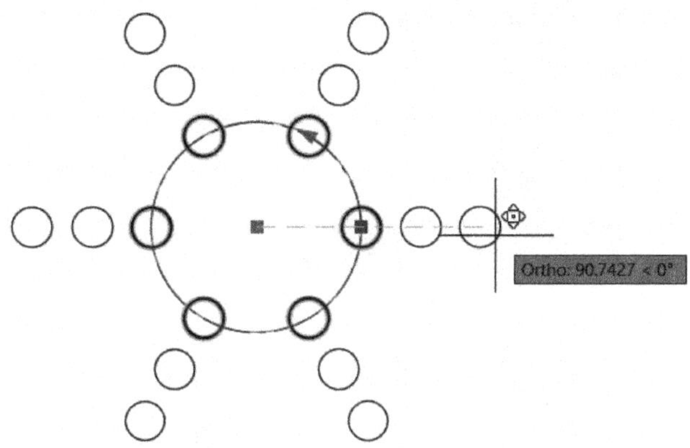

- You can again change the **Row Count** by using the last row grip.

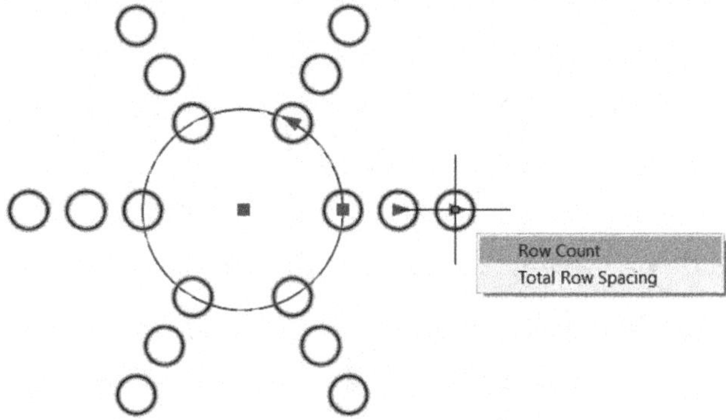

Changing the Row Spacing

- To change the total row spacing, place the pointer on the last row grip and select **Total Row Spacing**.

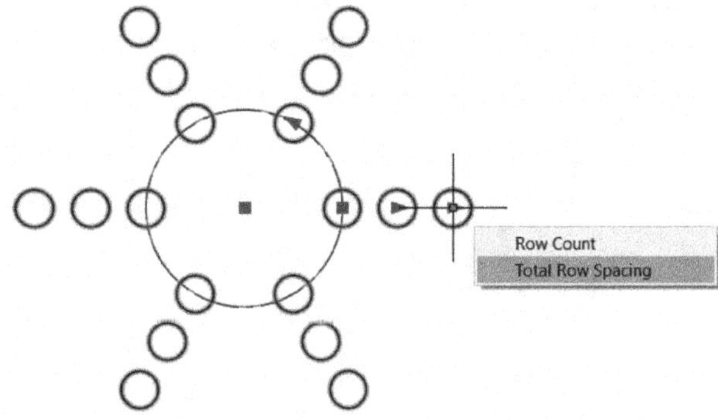

- Next, move the pointer and click. You can also enter the total row spacing value in the command line.

- To change the distance between the individual rows, click the second-row grip and move the pointer outward. You can also enter the distance in the command line.

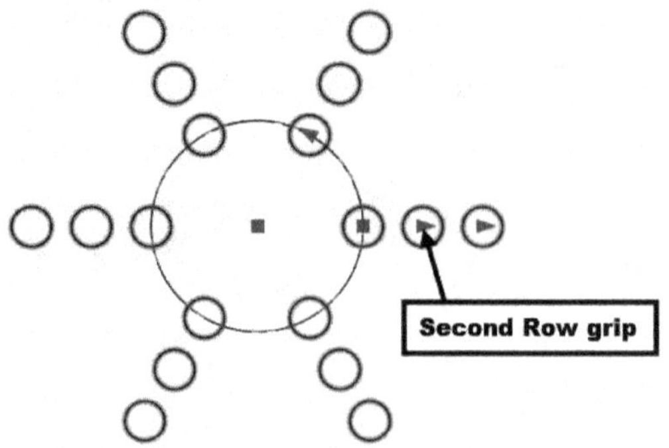

Changing the Angle between the Items

- To change the angle between the items, click the second radial grip, and enter the new angle value.

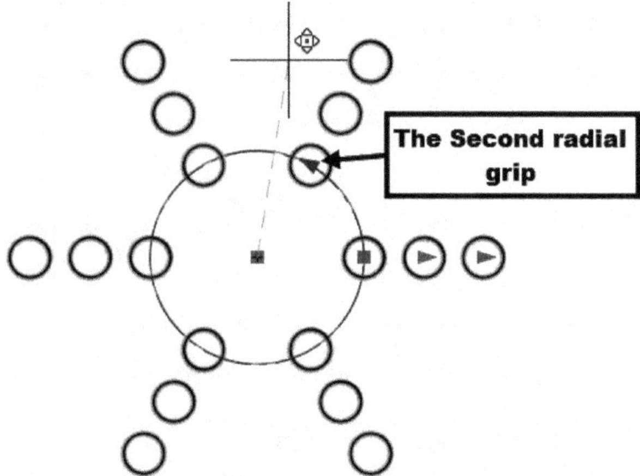

Changing the Fill angle of the array

- The default fill angle of a polar array is 360 degrees. To change the fill angle, place the pointer on the base grip and select **Fill Angle** from the shortcut menu.

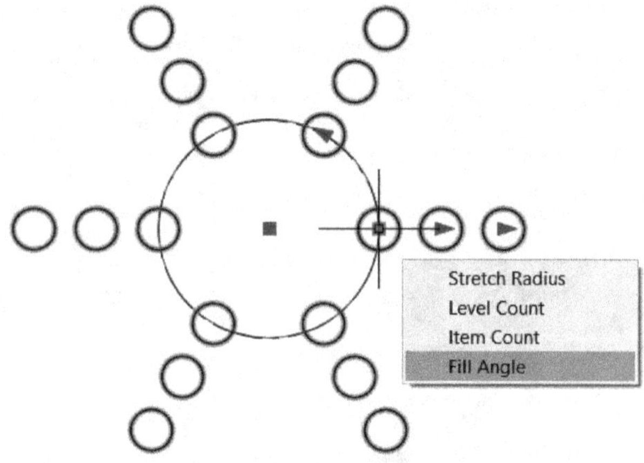

- Enter a new value for the fill angle or drag the pointer and click.

Changing the Item count of a Polar array

- Select the polar array and enter a new item count in the **Items** box of the **Array** ribbon.

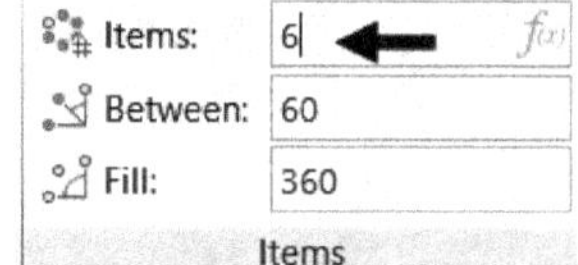

- Click **Close Array** on the ribbon.

Revision Clouds

Revision clouds are used to highlight the areas in a drawing. You can create revision clouds using three different tools.

Example 1:

- Start a new drawing using the acadISO template.
- On the ribbon, click **Annotate > Markup > Revision Cloud > Rectangular** (or) click **Home > Draw > Revision Cloud > Rectangular**.
- Select **Arc Length** from the command line.
- Type 3 and press Enter to specify the approximate arc length.
- Specify the first and second corners of the revision cloud. You can also select the **Object** option and select an object from the graphics window. The selected object will be converted into a revision cloud.

- Select the revision cloud and notice the grips. You can use the midpoint grip to stretch or add new vertices to the revision cloud.

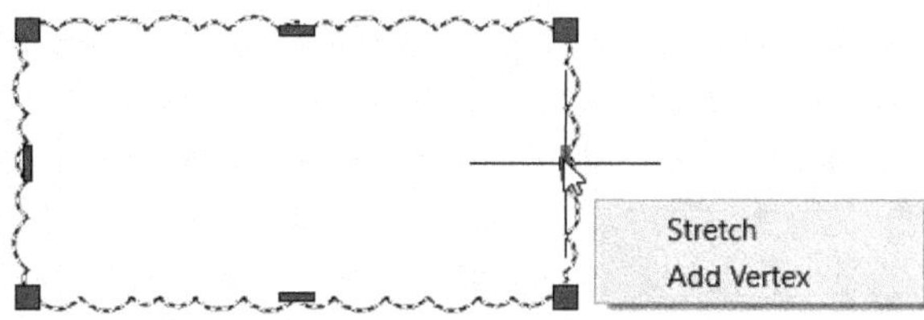

You can use the corner point grip to stretch, add, or remove vertices.

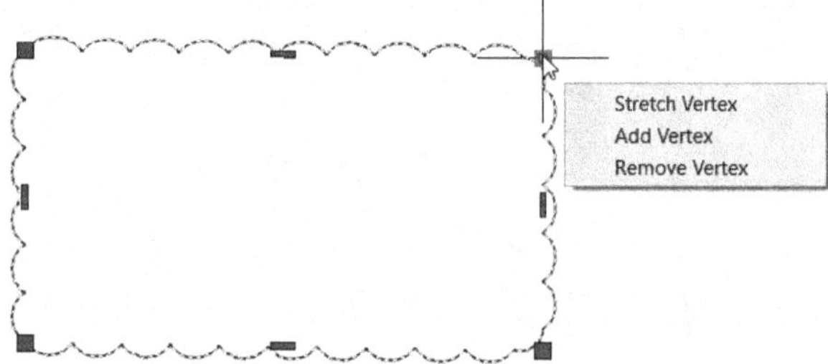

- Select the revision cloud, right-click, and select **Properties**. Notice that object type is displayed at **Revcloud** in the drop-down displayed at the top of the **Properties** palette.

The Properties Palette lets you inspect and alter the properties of chosen objects. Alternatively, open the palette first and then choose the objects. You can easily toggle the palette on and off using Ctrl+1.

When you've selected multiple objects, a drop-down list will appear at the top of the palette. Use this list to pick the object(s) you want to modify.

To adjust an object's layer, linetype, lineweight, or color properties, simply highlight the objects in the drawing and select the properties to alter from the right side of the palette. You'll find these properties in the upper section of the General list.

If you use the ByLayer method for assigning linetype, lineweight, and color properties, you can easily alter an object's linetype, lineweight, and color by simply changing its layer.

- Scroll down to the **Misc** section of the **Properties** palette.
- Click in the **Arc Length** box, type **5**, and press ENTER. The arc length is changed.

Example 2:

- On the ribbon, click **Annotate > Markup > Revision Cloud > Polygonal** (or) click **Home > Draw > Revision Cloud > Polygonal**.
- Select **Style** from the command line.
- Select **Calligraphy** from the command line.
- Specify the corners of the revision cloud and press Enter.

Example 3:

- On the ribbon, click **Annotate > Markup > Revision Cloud > Freehand** (or) click **Home > Draw > Revision Cloud > Freehand**.
- Specify the start point of the revision cloud.
- Move the pointer around the area to be highlighted.
- Move the pointer onto the start point to close the cloud.

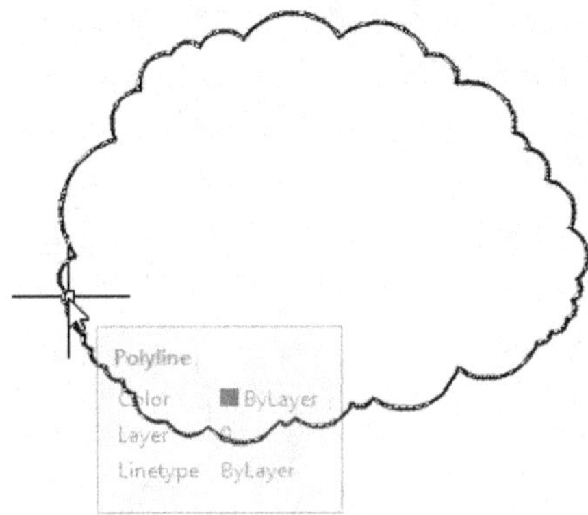

PEDIT

The **PEDIT** command is a powerful tool for modifying polylines. Its various options allow you to perform a wide range of edits, from simple vertex modifications to complex curve conversions.

On the ribbon, click **Home** tab > **Modify** panel > **Edit Polyline** (or) type **PEDIT** command in the command line and press ENTER.

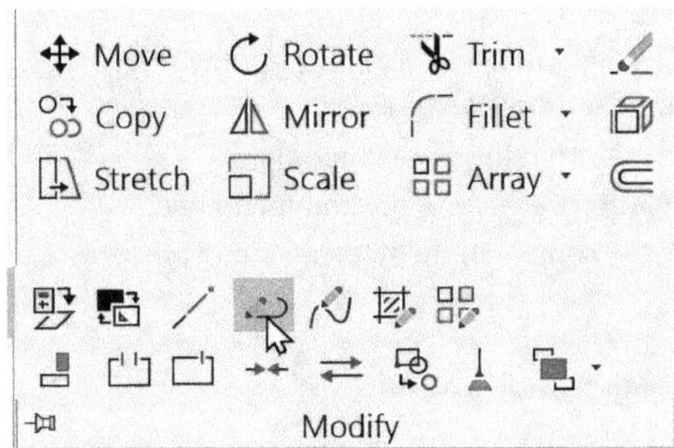

Select a polyline to edit (or) select the **Multiple** option from the command line. With the **Multiple** option, it's possible to edit several polylines at once. The poylines that have been selected don't have to be related or connected in any way, and can be completely separate objects. After selecting the polyline(s), you will see a series of options that allow you to perform different types of edits on the polyline or spline. Here is a detailed explanation of each option:

Close

This option allows you to close an open polyline or spline by connecting the end points. If the polyline or spline is already closed, this option will have no effect.

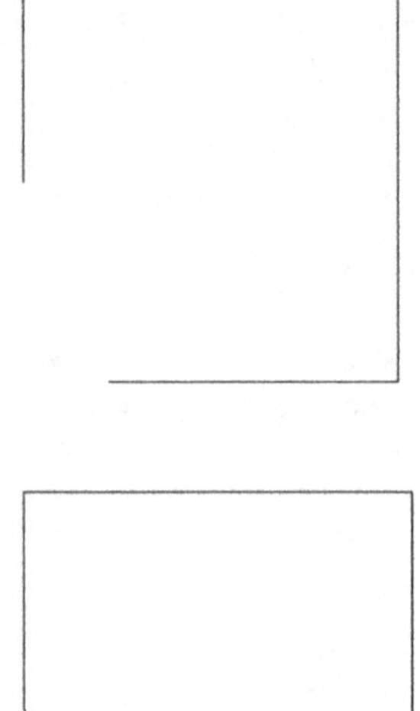

Open

If the **Close** option was used before, selecting the **Open** option will eliminate the closing segment of the polyline.

Join

This option allows you to join two or more open polylines, lines, arcs, or splines into a single entity.

Example 1

- Open a new drawing file and create a horizontal and inclined lines.

- Click **Home > Modify > Edit Polyline** on the ribbon, or enter **PEDIT** in the command line.
- Select the **Multiple** option from the command line.
- Select the two lines and press the **Enter** key.
- Select the **Yes** option from the command line to convert the lines into a polyline.
- Select the **Join** option from the command line.
- Select the **Jointype** option from the command line.
- Select the **Extend** option from the command line. By selecting this option, AutoCAD will join the chosen polylines by either extending or trimming the

segments to the closest endpoints. However, you can also select the **Add** option. It allows you to insert a straight segment connecting the closest endpoints.

- Type-in a value in the command line and press ENTER (or) select two points from the graphics window to specify the Fuzz distance. The endpoints of the line segments will be only if they fall within specified distance.

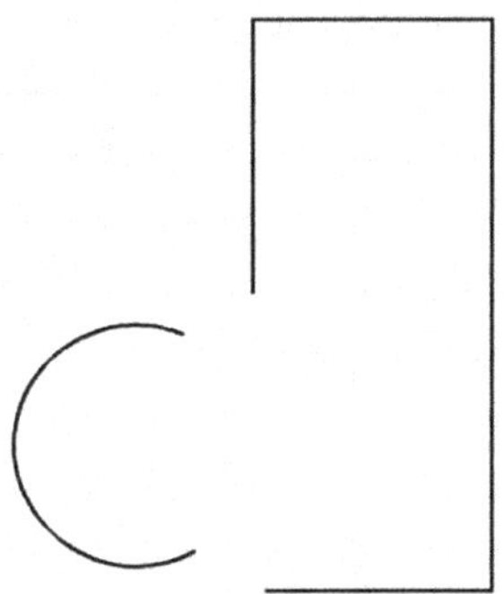

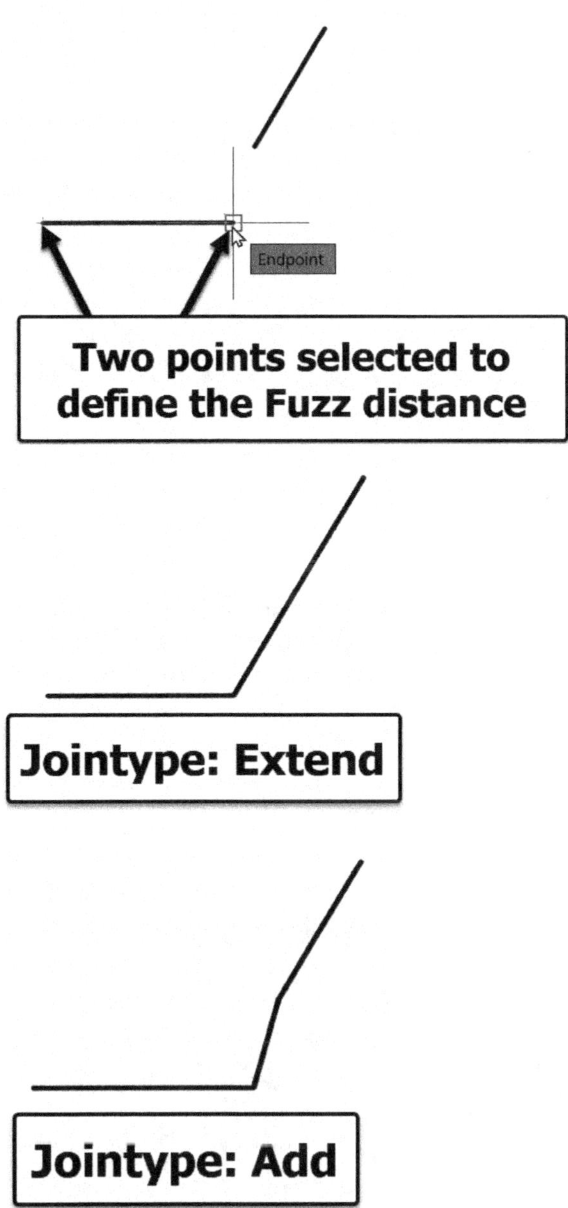

- Click **Home > Modify > Edit Polyline** e.
- Select the **Multiple** option from the command line.
- Create a selection window across all the objects of the drawing and press the **Enter** key.
- Select the **Yes** option from the command line to convert the lines into a polyline.
- Select the **Join** option from the command line.
- Select the **Jointype** option from the command line.
- Select the **Both** option from the command line. By selecting this option, you can join the specified polylines by either extending or trimming them wherever possible.
- Select the end points of the horizontal line, as shown; the fuzz distance is defined. Also, the endpoint that fall within the fuzz distance are joined together.

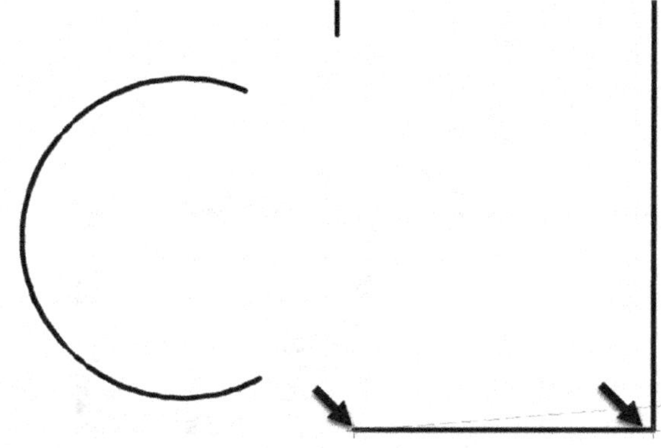

- Press ESC and close the file.

Example 2

- Open a new drawing file and create an arc and four lines, as shown.

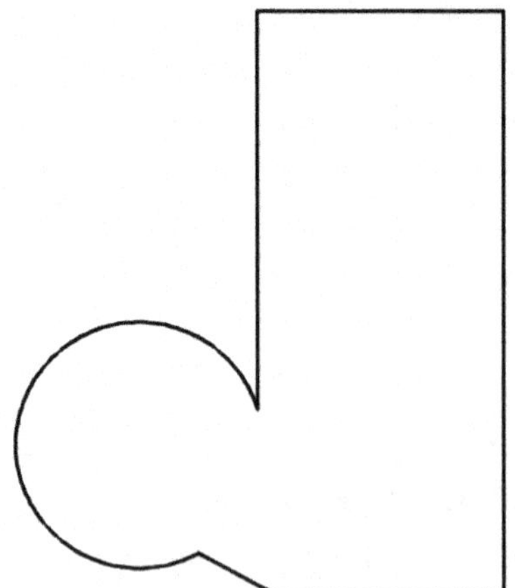

Note that when the two line segments to be joined are near almost parallel lines, a straight segment will be added between the closest endpoints.

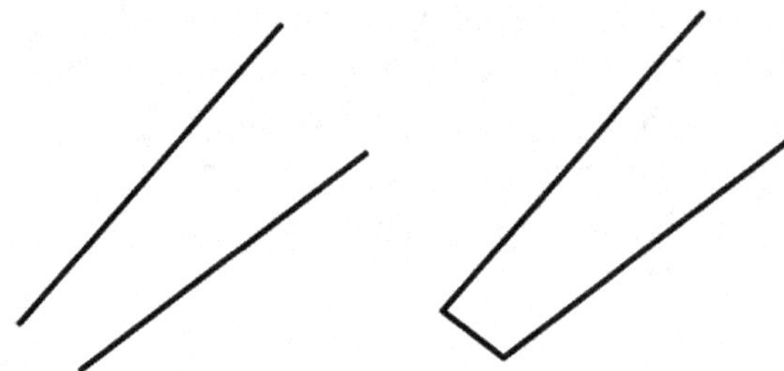

Width

This option allows you to change the width of the polyline by assigning a new consistent width. Select this option and type-in a new width value. Press ENTER to apply the new width.

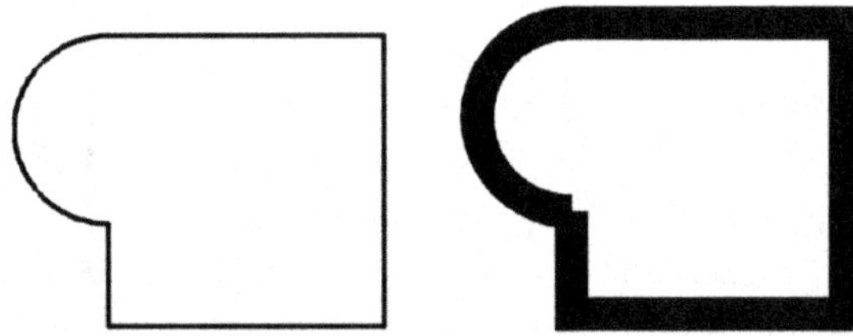

Edit Vertex

This option allows you to move, add, or delete vertices of the polyline or spline. After selecting this option from the command line, a group of sub-options will appear in the command line.

Next

After selecting the **Edit Vertex** option, a marker in the shape of an X is positioned at the initial endpoint. You can use the Next and Previous options to move the marker along the polyline to the desired vertex in sequence.

Break

By selecting this option, you can create a gap between the marked vertex and another vertex. Using the **Next** or **Previous** option, you can select another vertex.

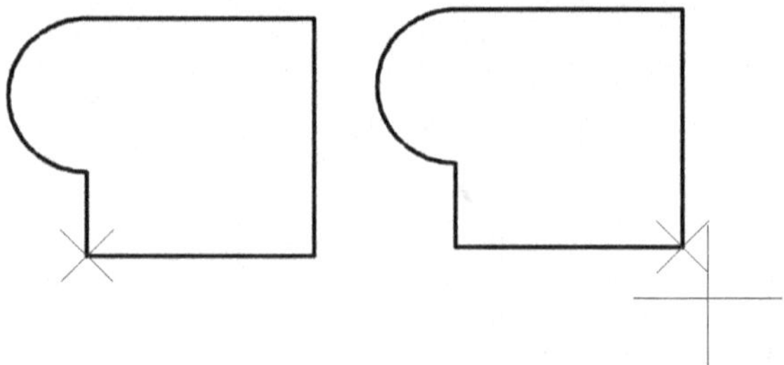

Next, select the **Go** option to create a between two select vertices.

Insert

With the help of the **Insert** option, you have the ability to add a fresh vertex at any point beyond the vertex labeled with the X marker. Select this option and specify the location of the new vertex to inserted.

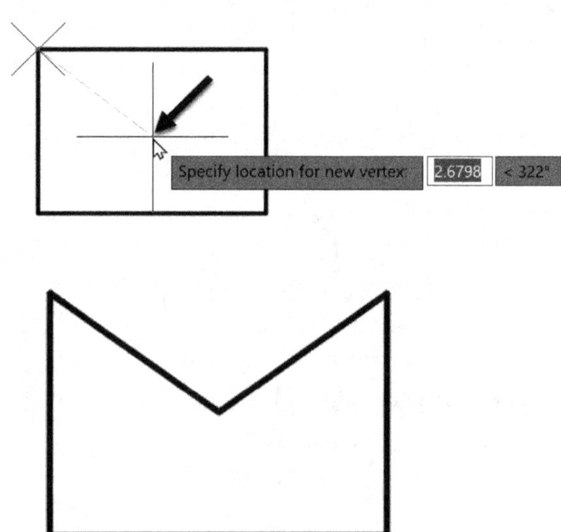

Move

This option allows you move the X marked vertex to a new location. Select this option and specify a location in the graphic window; the X marked vertex is moved to the specified location.

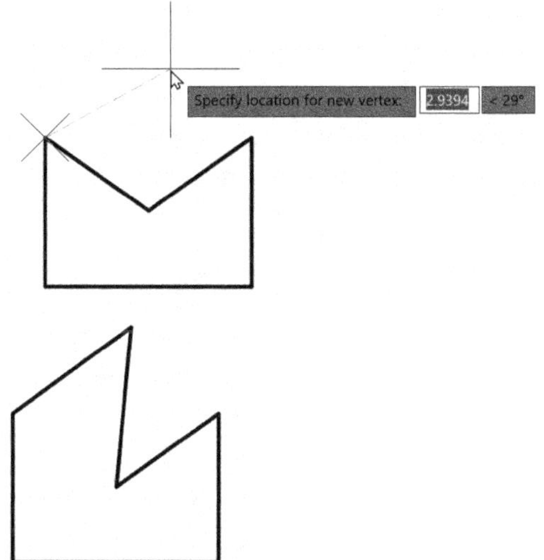

Regen

This is used to regenerate the current viewport to view the changes made to the polyline.

Straighten

This option straightens the Zig-Zag line segments between the X marked vertex and another vertex. You can select another vertex by using the **Next** or **Previous** options.

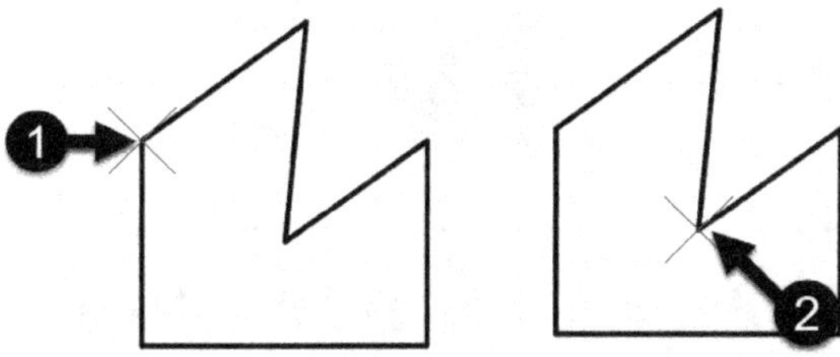

Select the **Go** option after select the two points.

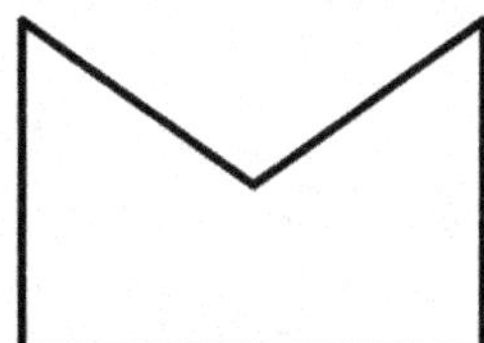

Tangent

With the **Tangent** option, you can specify the tangency direction selected vertex. This option will be useful when a polyline is converted to a curve.

Width

By using this option, you can modify the width of the polyline segment next to the X marked vertex. Select this option and specify the start width of the line segment. Next, specify the end width of the line segment.

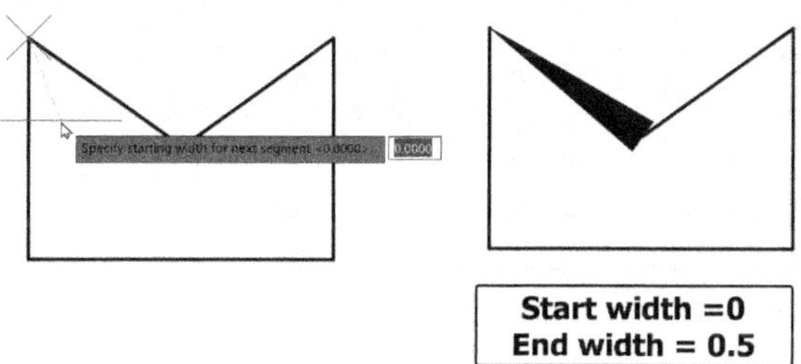

eXit

Select this option to exit the **Edit Vertex** mode.

Note that the **Edit Vertex** option can be quite lengthy, tedious, and difficult if you are a beginner. You can explode the polyline, perform any necessary modifications using the editing tools, and then join the lines and arcs into a single polyline again.

Fit

If you choose this option, the polyline you have will be transformed from straight line segments into arcs. The resulting curve will pass through all the vertices in the polyline. This means that for every pair of vertices in the polyline, there will be two arcs that form the curve.

Note that if the original polyline has steep angles, the resulting curve can be quite unexpected.

Spline

This option can be used to convert a polyline into a B-spline (Bezier spline) curve. A spline is a smooth curve that passes only through the end vertices of the polyline. By using this option, you will be able to create a more precise curve.

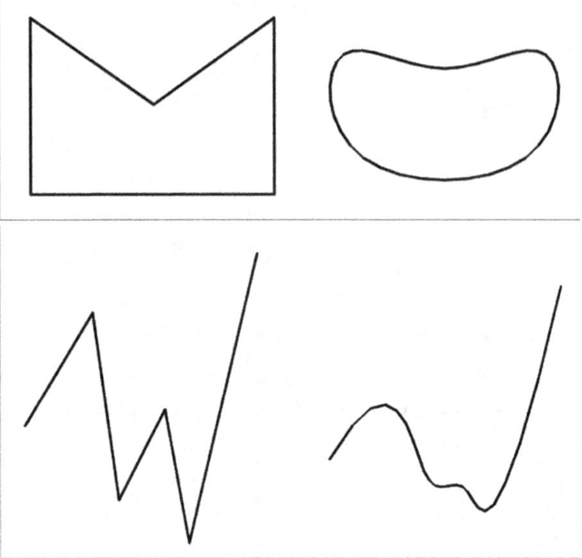

Decurve

When you select this option, it converts the curved lines created by **Spline** or **Fit** options into the original polyline.

Ltype gen

This option determines how non-continuous lines are drawn. Select this option, and then select the **Off** option from the command line; it generated non-continuous lines with dashes that start and stop at each vertex. This means that each line segment will begin and end with a full dashed segment. If you select the **ON** option; it generates a non-continuous line in a consistent pattern, regardless of the vertices. This means that some vertices may have a space instead of a dash.

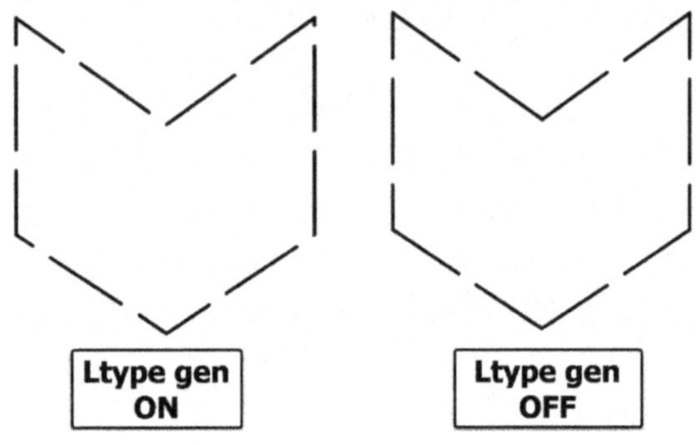

Reverse

Select this option to change the order of the first and last points of a polyline.

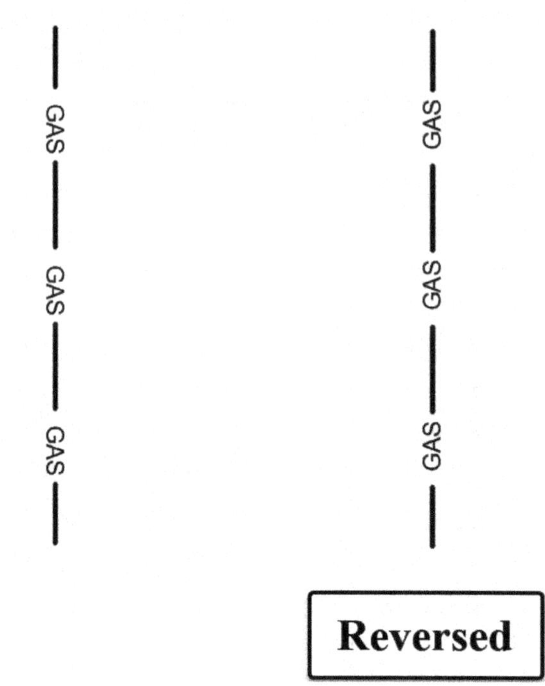

Note that the PLINEREVERSEWIDTHS system variable controls direction in which a polyline's width is displayed. When the value of this variable is set to 0, the polyline's width will not be reversed. However, if the value is changed to 1, the polyline's width will be reversed.

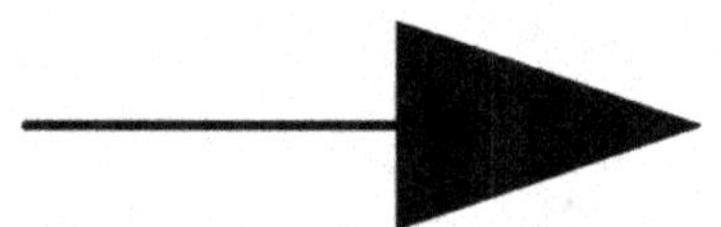

Undo

If you make a mistake when using **Pedit** command, you can use the **Undo** option to reverse the most recent operation you performed.

Example 1

In this example, you will create the drawing shown in the figure.

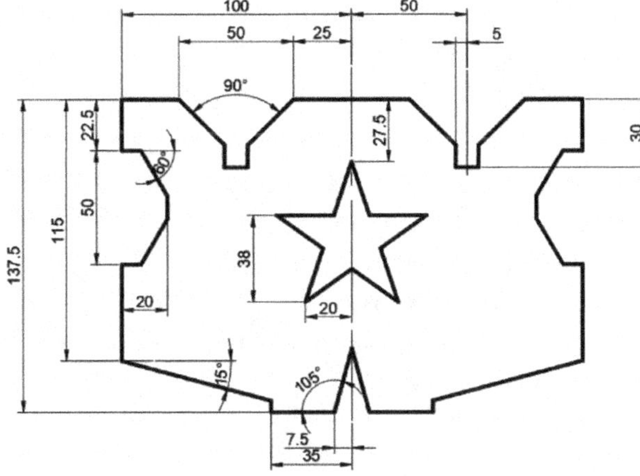

- Start a new drawing file using the acadISO-Named Plot Styles.dwt.
- Type LIMMAX in the command line and press ENTER.
- Type 200,200 and press ENTER.
- Click **Zoom** drop-down > **Zoom All** on the Navigation bar.
- Click the **Line** tool on the **Draw** panel of the **Home** ribbon tab.
- Pick a point in the graphics area.
- Move the pointer toward the right.
- Type 35 and press ENTER.
- Move the pointer upward.
- Type 22.5 and press ENTER.
- Move the pointer toward the right.
- Type 65 and press ENTER.
- Move the pointer upward.
- Type 42.5 and press ENTER.
- Move the pointer toward left.
- Type 20 and press ENTER.
- Move the pointer upward.
- Type 50 and press ENTER.
- Move the pointer toward the right.
- Type 20 and press ENTER.
- Move the pointer upward.

- Type 22.5 and press ENTER.
- Move the pointer toward left.
- Type 45 and press ENTER.
- Move the pointer downward.
- Type 30 and press ENTER.
- Move the pointer toward left.
- Type 10 and press ENTER.
- Move the pointer upward.
- Type 30 and press ENTER.
- Move the pointer toward left.
- Type 45 and press ENTER.
- Move the pointer downward and select the start point of the drawing.

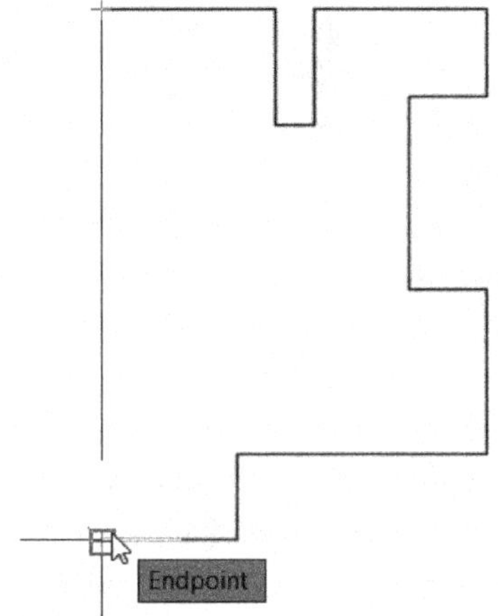

- Click **Fillet** drop-down > **Chamfer** on the **Modify** panel of the **Home** ribbon tab.
- Select **Angle** from the command line.
- Type 20 as the chamfer distance.
- Type 45 as the chamfer angle.
- Select the horizontal and vertical lines, as shown in the figure.

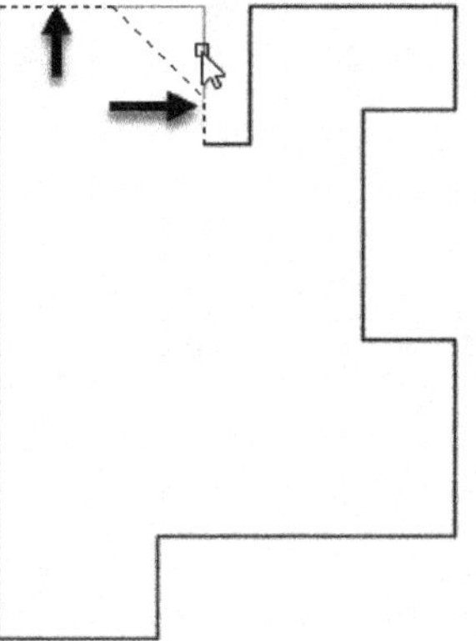

- Press ENTER to activate the **Chamfer** tool.
- Select the horizontal and vertical lines, as shown.

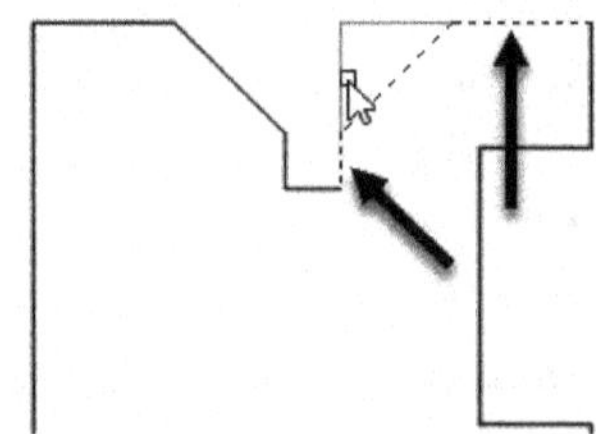

- Press ENTER to activate the **Chamfer** tool.
- Select **Angle** from the command line.
- Type 20 as the chamfer distance.
- Type 30 as the chamfer angle.
- Select the vertical and horizontal lines, as shown in the figure.

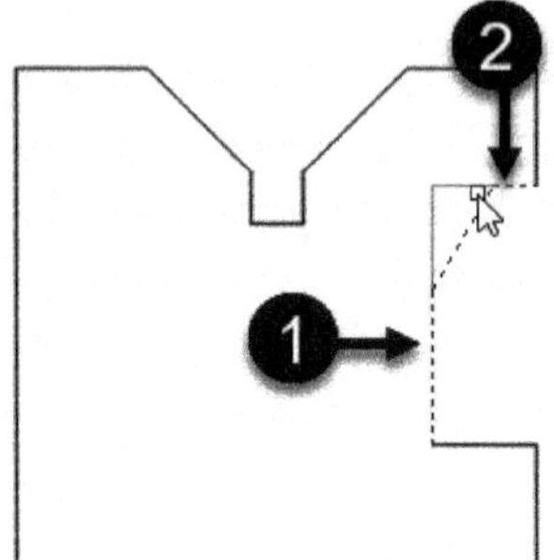

- Press ENTER to activate the **Chamfer** tool.
- Select the vertical and horizontal lines, as shown in the figure.

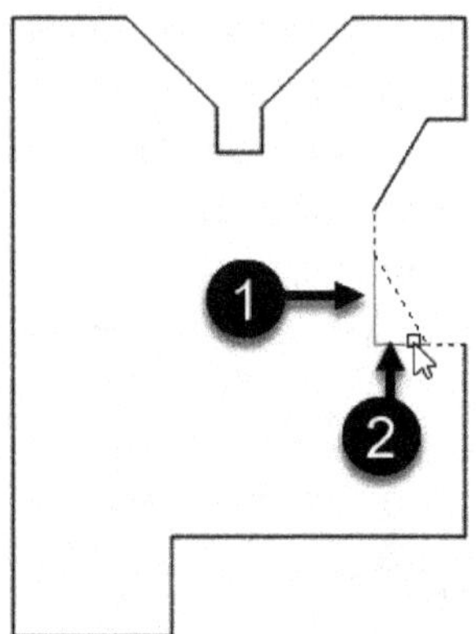

- Press ENTER to activate the **Chamfer** tool.
- Select **Angle** from the command line.
- Type 65 as the chamfer distance.
- Type 15 as the chamfer angle.
- Select the horizontal and vertical lines, as shown in the figure.

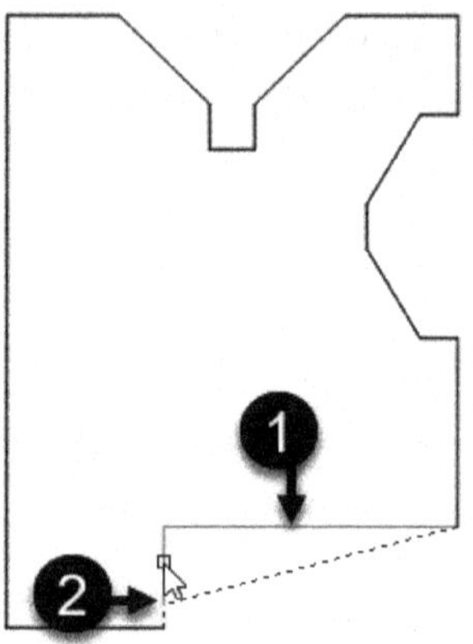

- Press ENTER to activate the **Chamfer** tool.
- Select **Angle** from the command line.
- Type 7.5 as the chamfer distance.
- Type 75 as the chamfer angle.
- Select the horizontal and vertical lines, as shown in the figure.

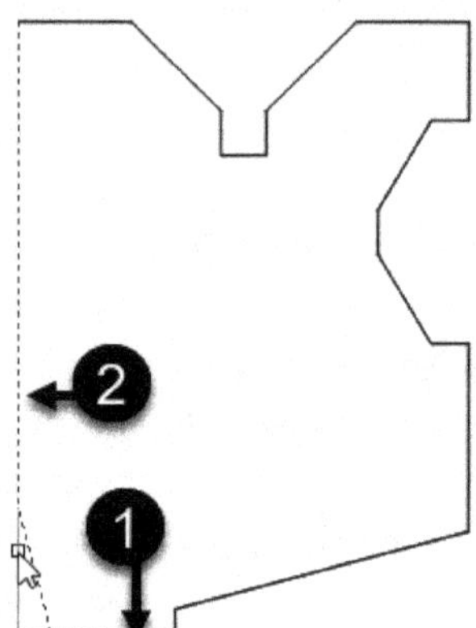

- Select the left vertical line and press Delete.

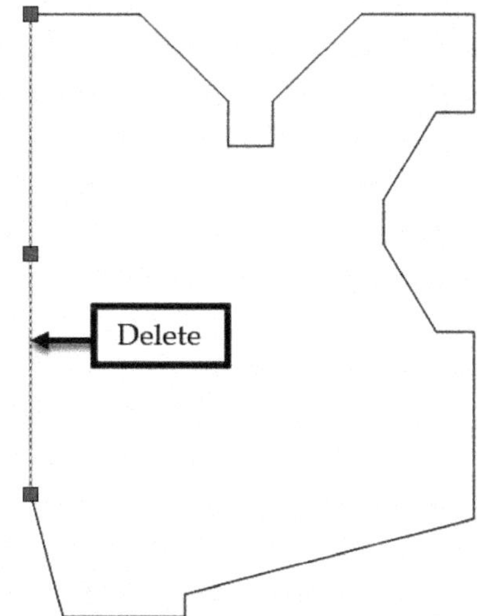

- Create a selection window across all the objects.

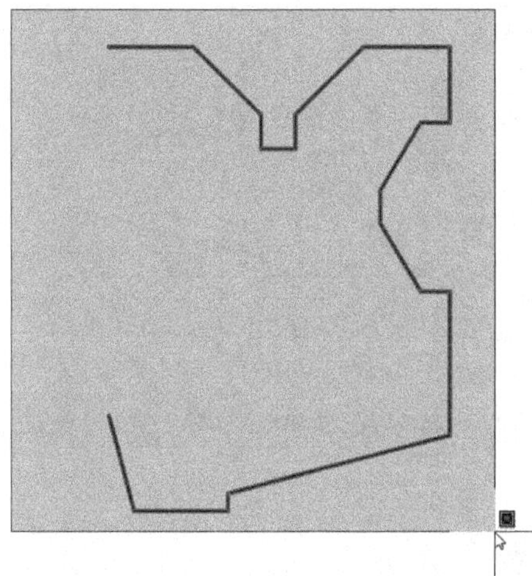

- Click **Mirror** on the **Modify** panel of the **Home** ribbon tab.
- Select the points, as shown. The mirror line is defined.

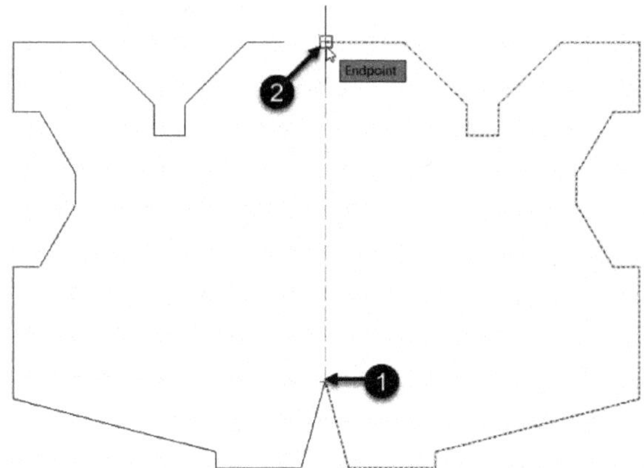

- Select **No** from the command line. The selected objects are mirrored about the mirror line.

- Click **Rectangle** drop-down > **Polygon** on the **Draw** panel of the **Home** ribbon tab.
- Type 5 and press ENTER.
- Select the **Edge** option from the command line.
- Click in the empty area.
- Move the pointer toward the right.

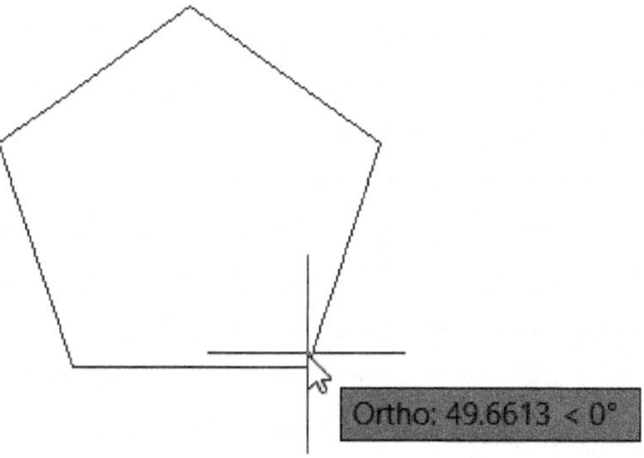

- Type **40** and press ENTER.
- Select the polygon and click the **Move** icon on the **Modify** panel of the **Home** ribbon tab.
- Select the vertex point of the polygon, as shown.

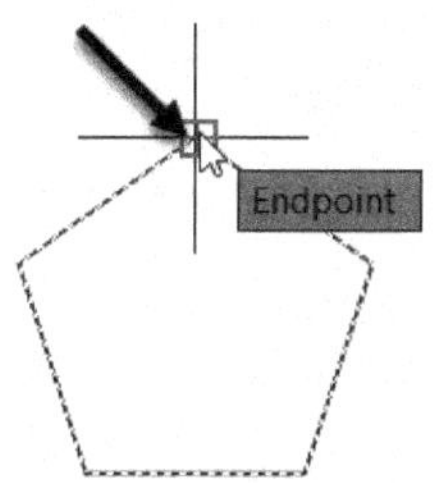

- Move the pointer and select the endpoint of the line, as shown.

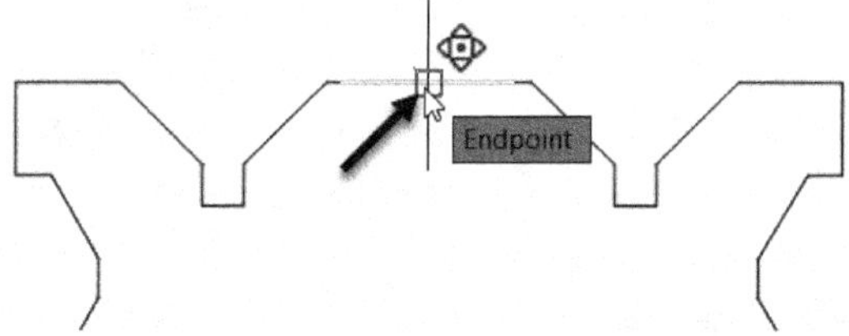

- Select the polygon and click the **Move** icon on the **Modify** panel of the **Home** ribbon tab.

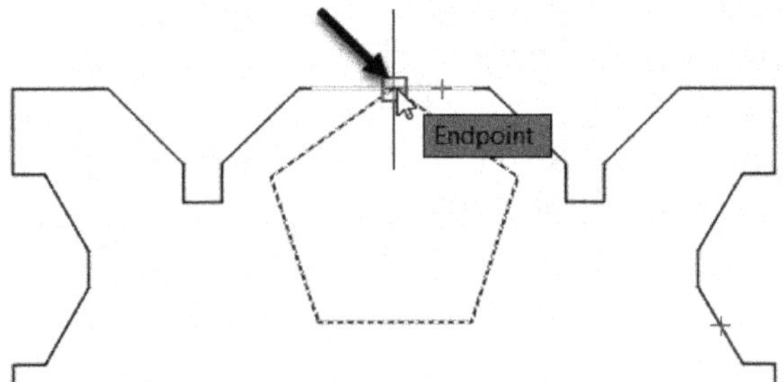

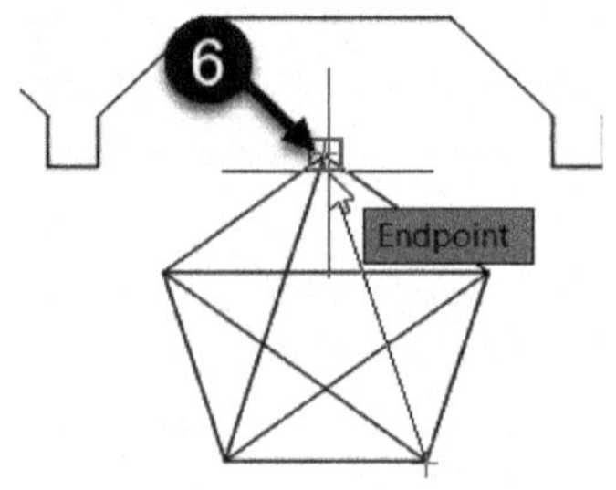

- Select the vertex point of the polygon, as shown.
- Move the pointer downward.
- Type 27.5 and press ENTER.

- Press ESC.
- Select the polygon and press Delete.

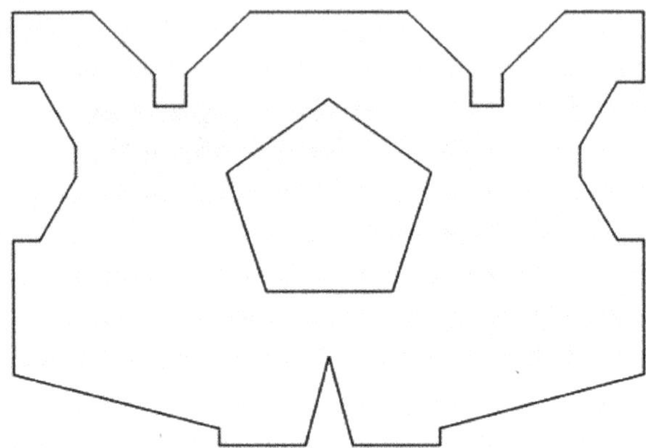

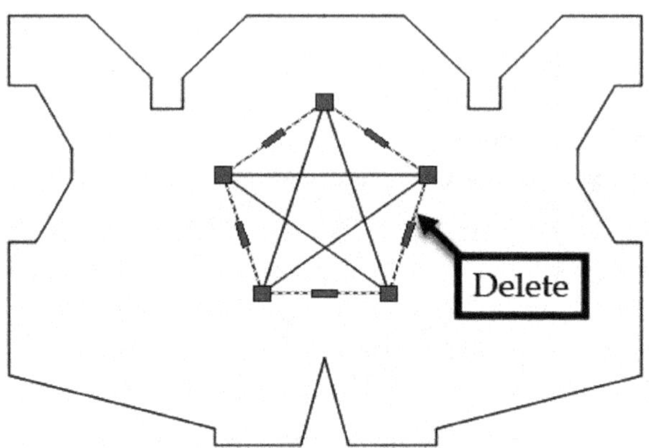

- Click the **Line** icon on the **Draw** panel of the **Home** ribbon tab.
- Deactivate the ORTHOMODE icon on the status bar.
- Select the vertices of the polygon, as shown.

- Click the **Trim** icon on the **Modify** panel of the **Home** ribbon tab.
- Select the inner lines of the star, as shown.

- Save and close the drawing file.

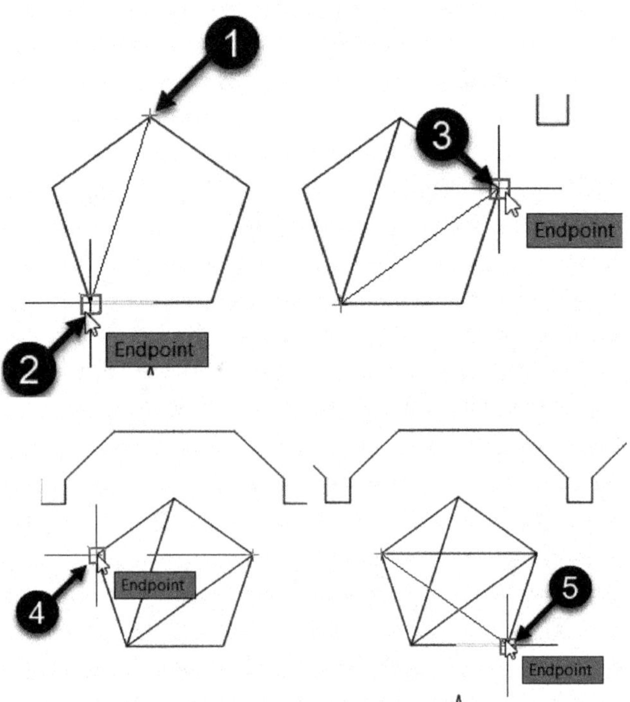

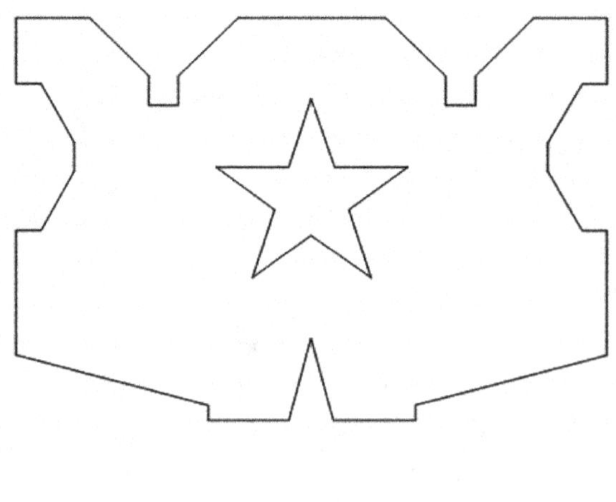

Exercises

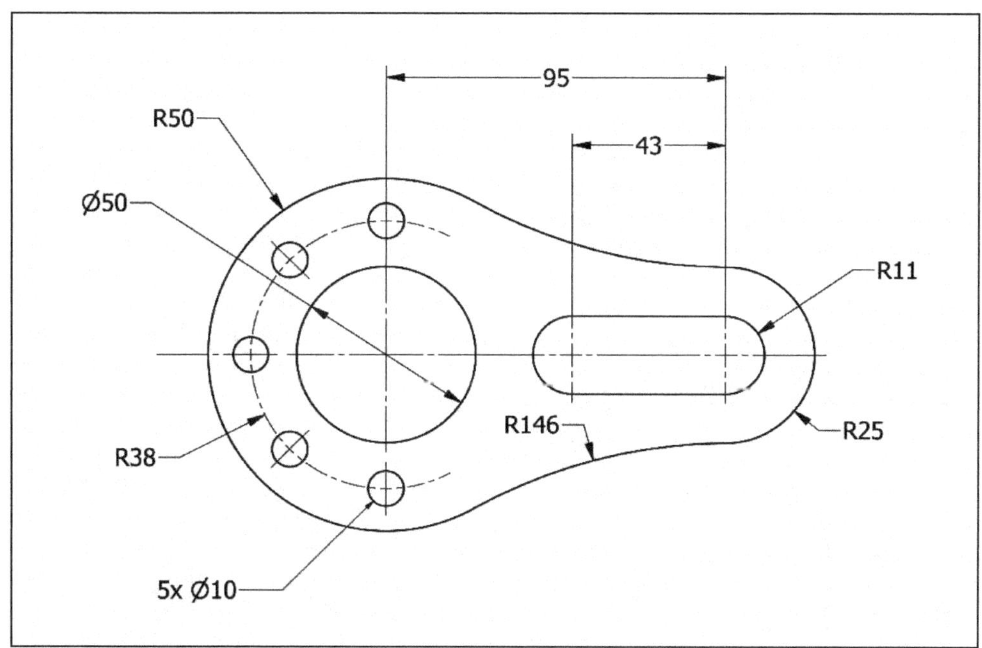

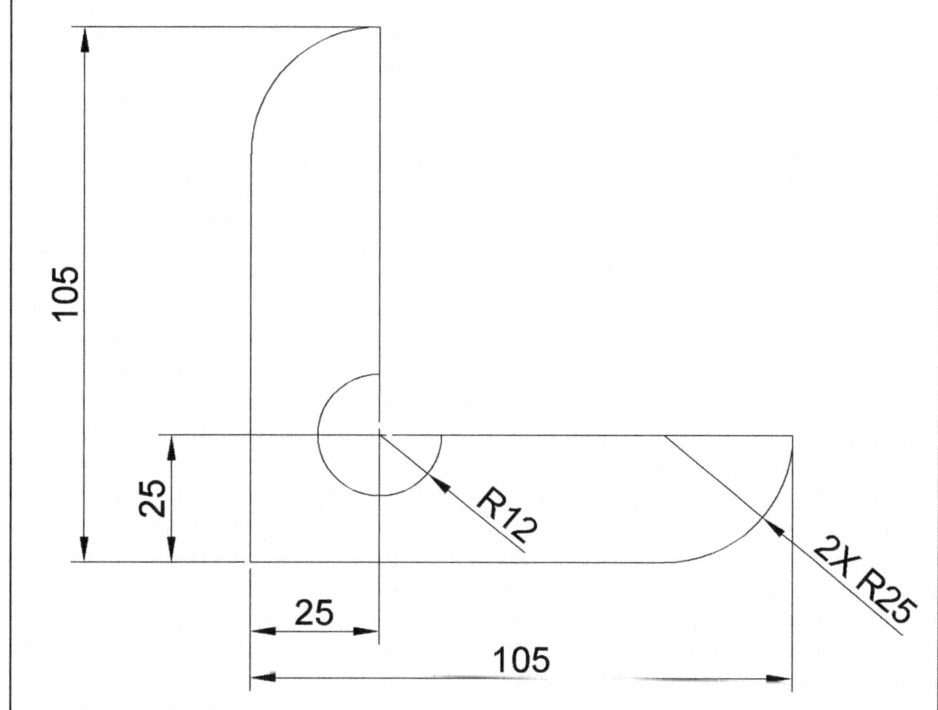

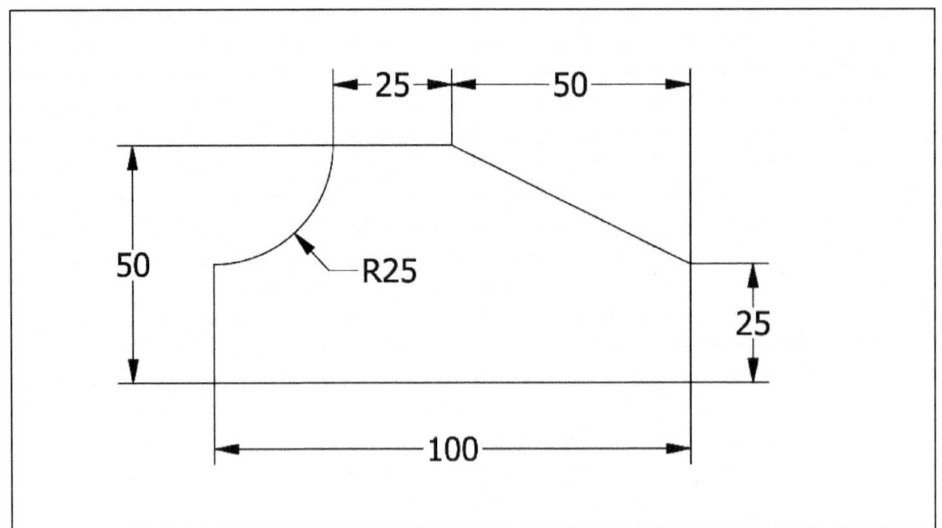

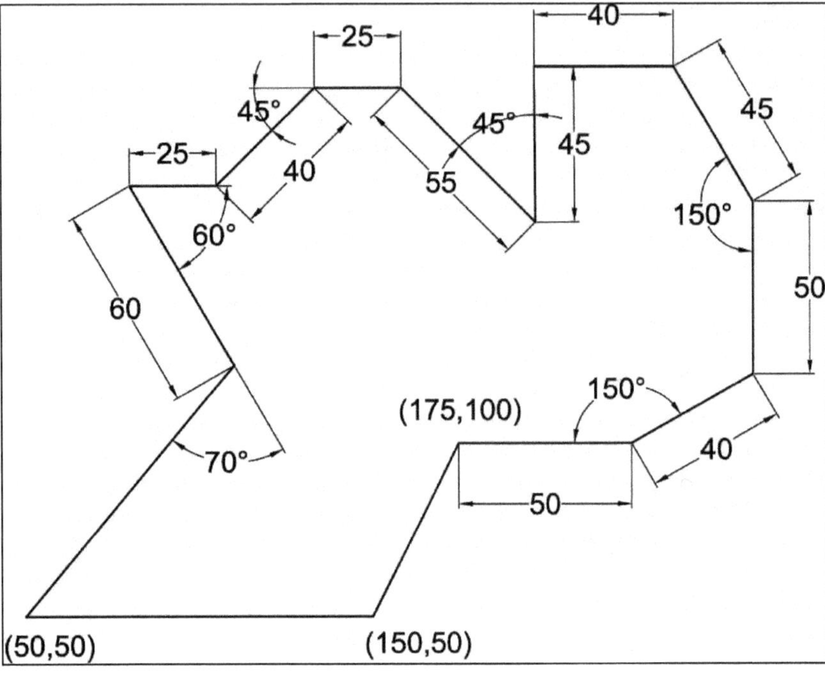

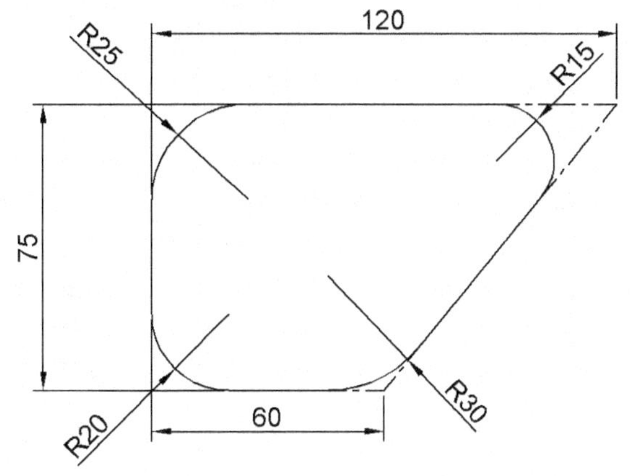

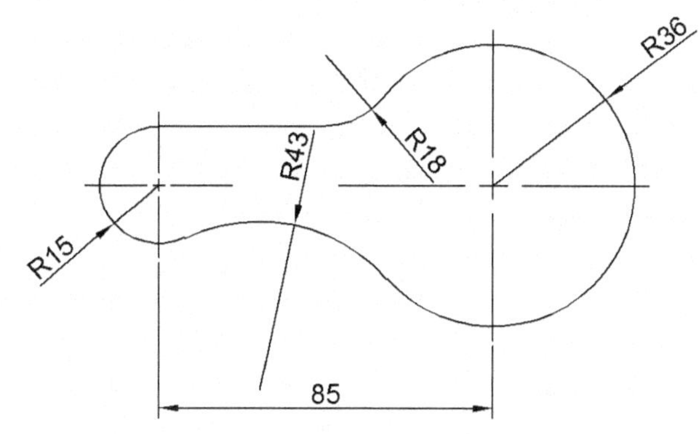

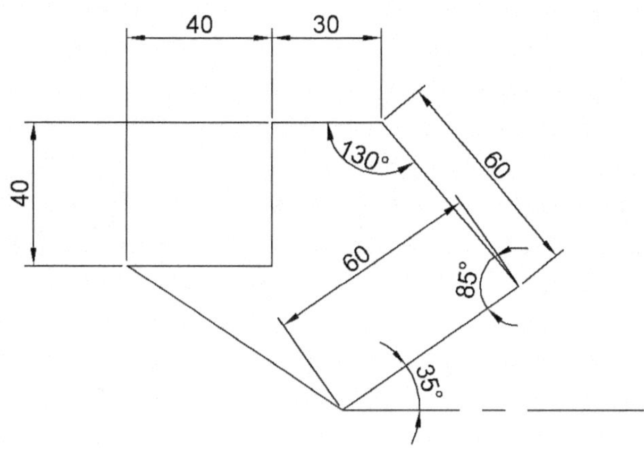

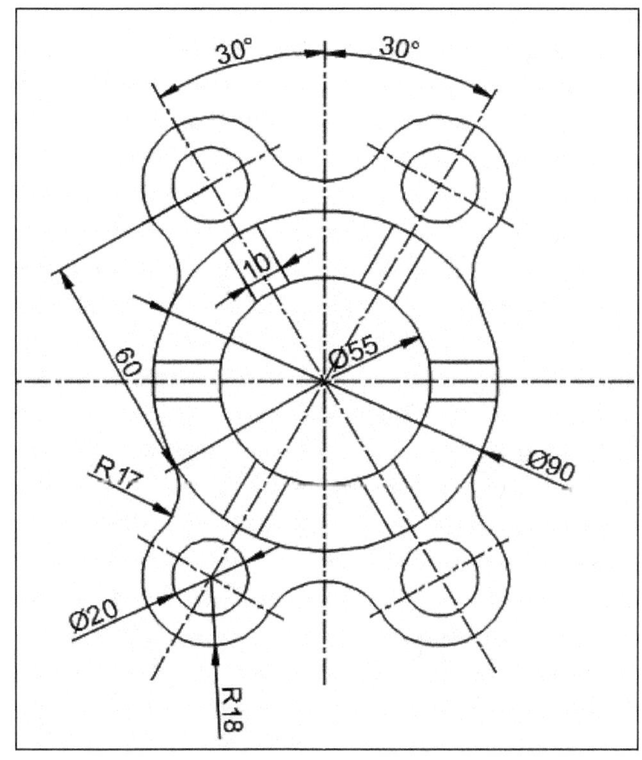

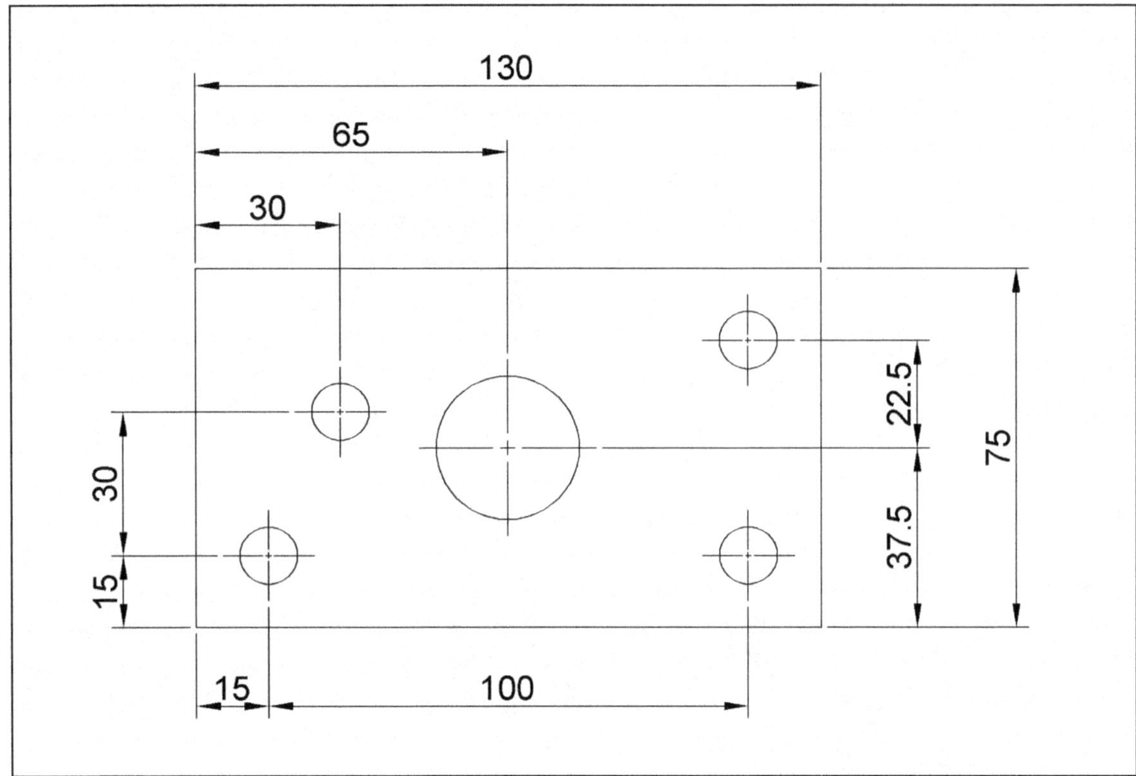

130
65
30
22.5
75
37.5
30
15
15
100

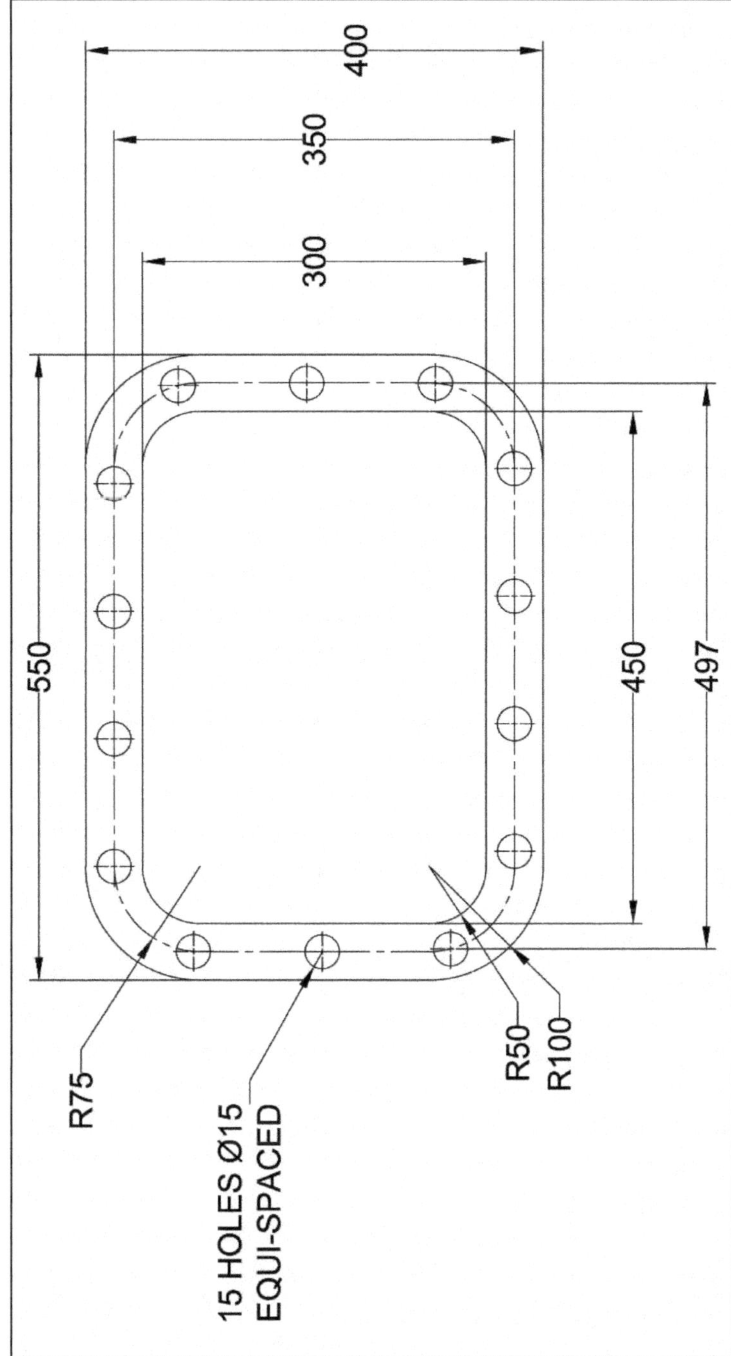

400
350
300
550
450
497
R75
15 HOLES Ø15 EQUI-SPACED
R50
R100

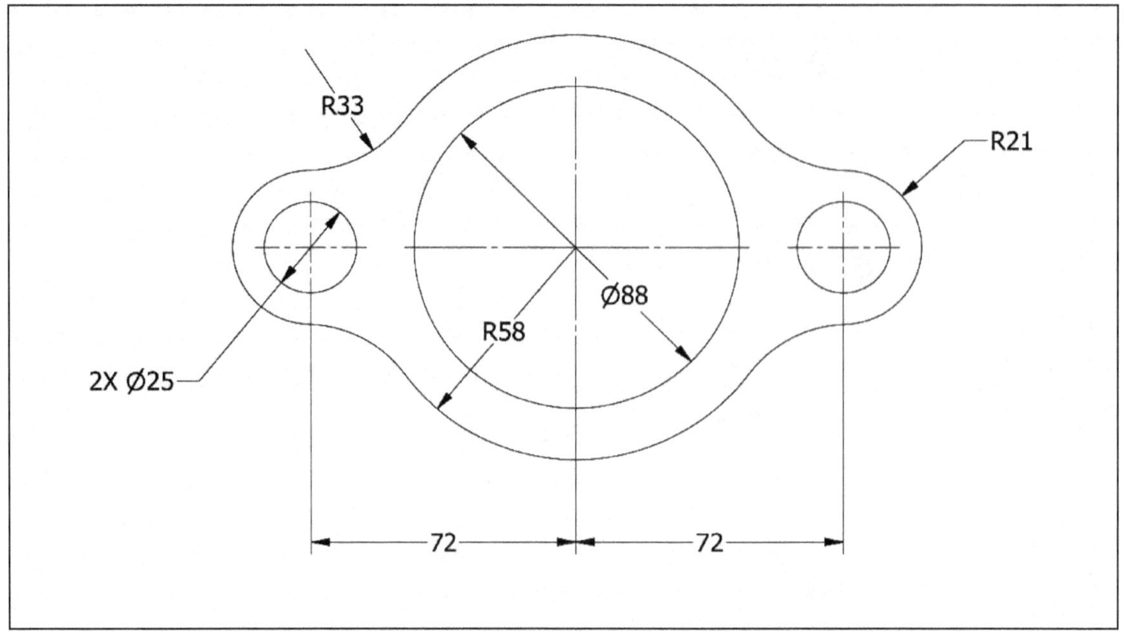

R33
R21
Ø88
R58
2X Ø25
72
72

R100
R125
R40
R75
30°
30°
Ø40
R12
65
140

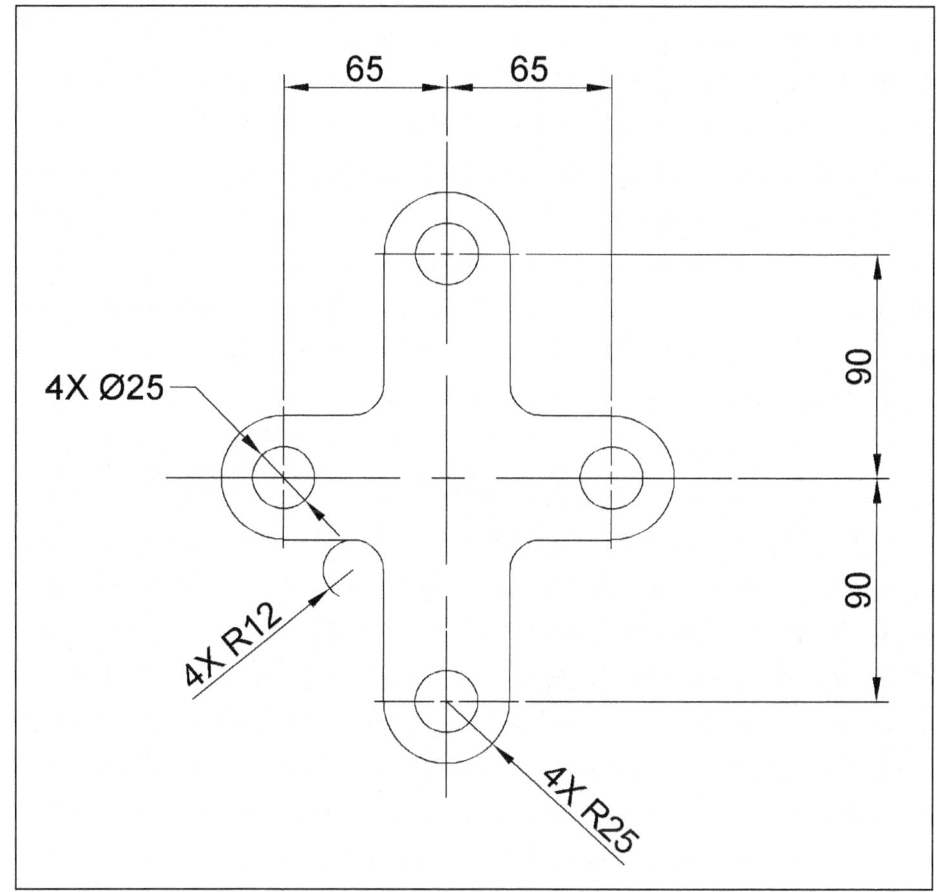

65
65
90
90
4X Ø25
4X R12
4X R25

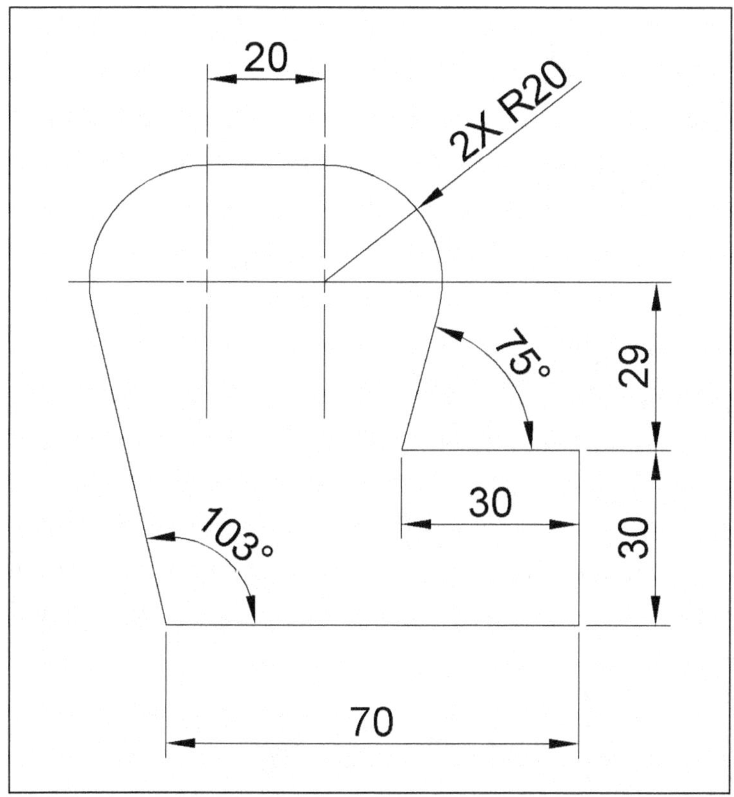

20
2X R20
75°
29
30
103°
30
70

Chapter 5: Multi View Drawings

In this chapter, you will learn to create:

- **Orthographic Views**
- **Auxiliary Views**
- **Named Views**

Multi-view Drawings

To manufacture a component, you must create its engineering drawing. The engineering drawing consists of various views of the object, showing its true shape and size so that it can be dimensioned. It can be achieved by creating the orthographic views of the object. In the first section of this chapter, you will learn to create orthographic views of an object. The second section introduces you to auxiliary views. The auxiliary views clearly describe the features of a component, which are located on an inclined plane or surface.

Creating Orthographic Views

Orthographic Views are standard representations of an object on a sheet. These views are created by projecting an object onto three different planes (top, front, and side planes). You can project an object by using two different methods: **First Angle Projection** and **Third Angle Projection**. The following figure shows the orthographic views that will be created when an object is projected using the **First Angle Projection** method.

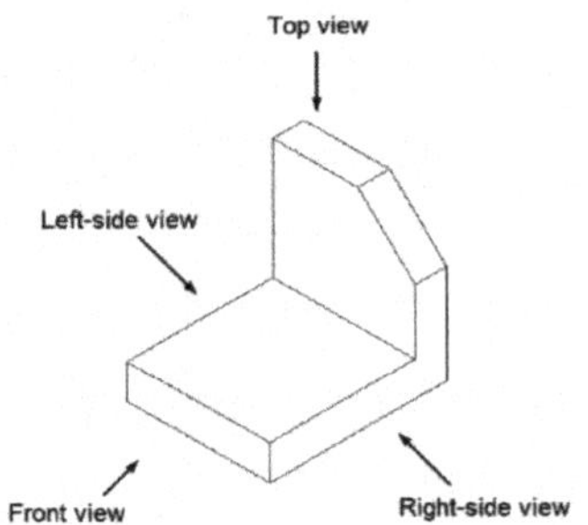

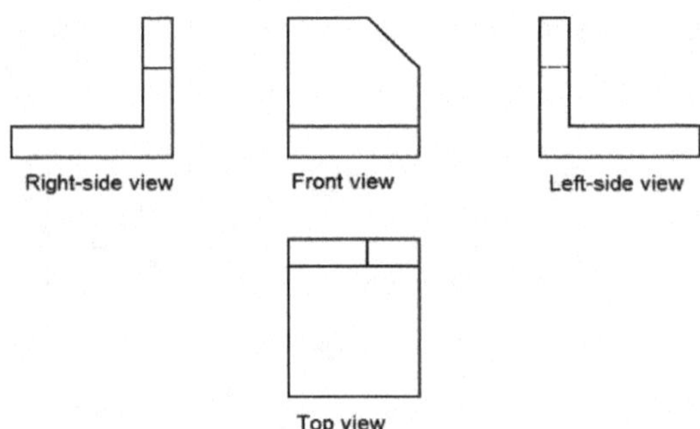

The following figure shows the orthographic views that will be created when an object is projected using the **Third Angle Projection** method.

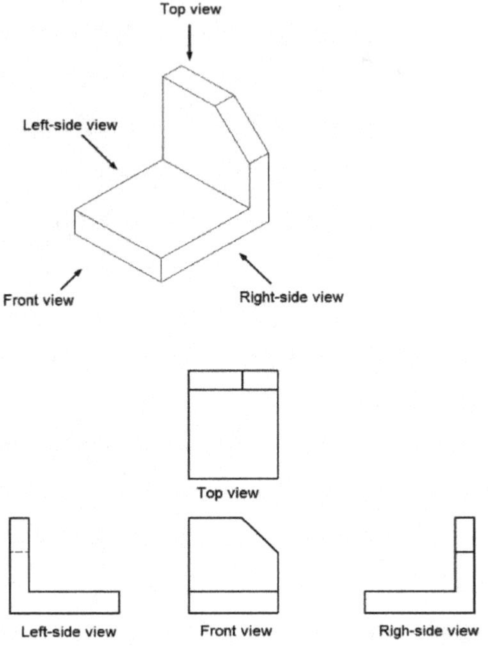

Example:

In this example, you will create the orthographic views of the part shown below. The views will be created by using the **Third Angle Projection** method.

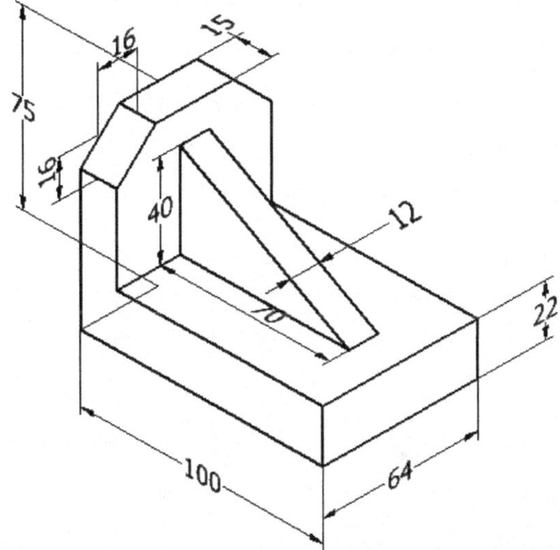

- Open a new drawing using the **acadISO –Named Plot Styles.dwt** template.

- Click the **Layer Properties** button on the **Layers** panel; the **Layer Properties Manager** appears.

- Click the **New Layer** button on the **Layer Properties Manager** to create new layers.

- Create two new layers with the following properties.

Layer Name	Lineweight	Linetype
Construction	0.00 mm	Continuous
Object	0.30 mm	Continuous

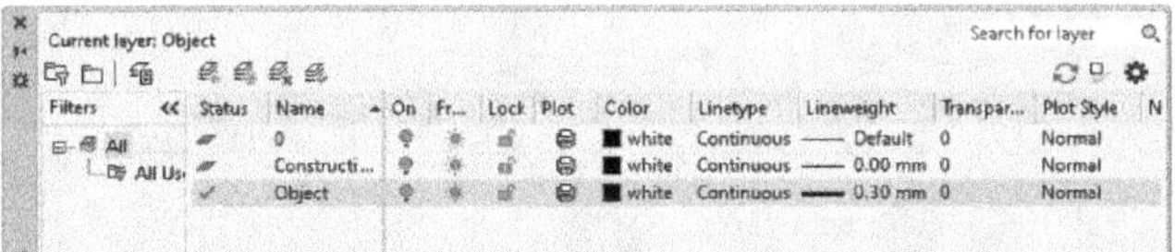

- Right-click on the **Construction** layer and select **Set current**.

- Close the **Layer Properties Manager**.

- Activate the **Ortho Mode** icon on the status bar.

- Click **Zoom > Zoom All** on the Navigation Bar. Next, you need to draw construction lines. They are used as references to create actual drawings. You will create these construction lines on the **Construction** layer so that you can hide them when required.

- Click **Home > Draw > Construction** line on the ribbon or enter **XLINE** in the command line.

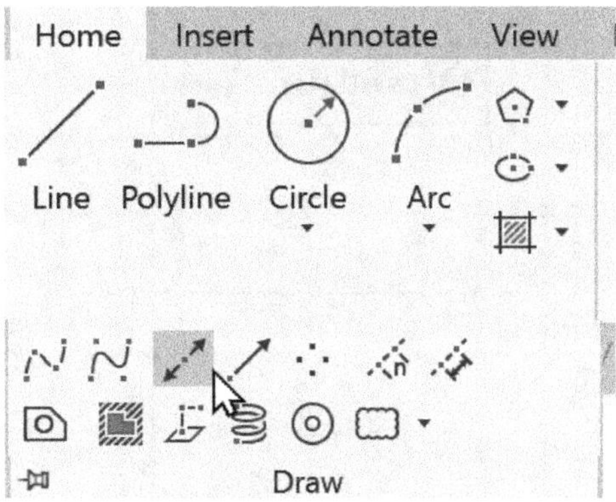

- Click anywhere in the lower-left corner of the graphics window.

- Move the pointer upward and click to create a vertical construction line.

- Move the pointer toward the right and click to create a horizontal construction line.

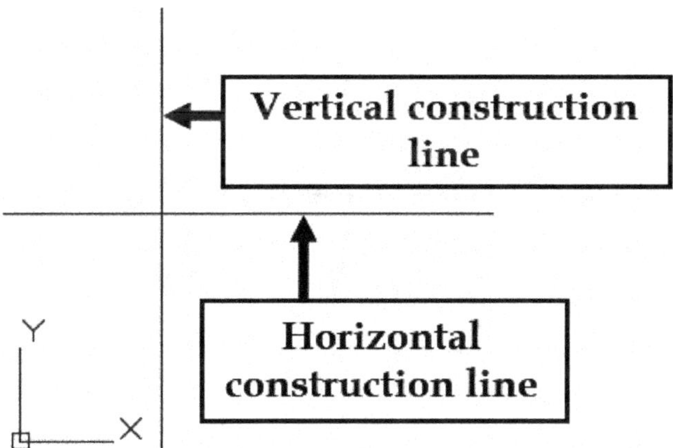

- Press ENTER to exit the tool.
- Click the **Offset** button on the **Modify** panel.
- Type 100 as the offset distance and press ENTER.
- Select the vertical construction line.
- Move the pointer toward the right and click to create an offset line.

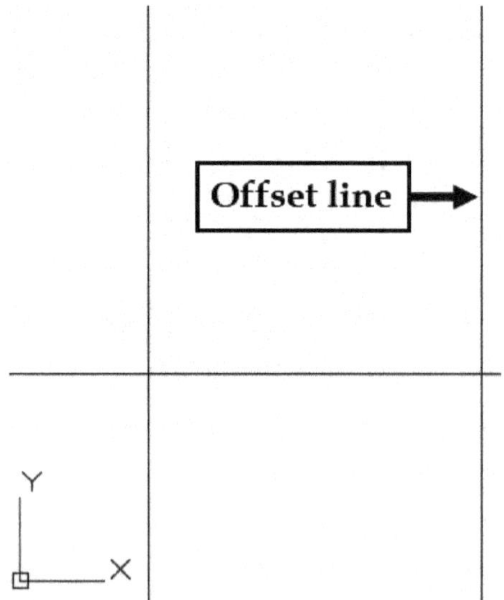

- Right-click and select **Enter** to exit the **Offset** tool.
- Press the SPACEBAR on the keyboard to start the **Offset** tool again.
- Type 75 as the offset distance and press ENTER.
- Select the horizontal construction line.
- Move the pointer above and click to create the offset line.

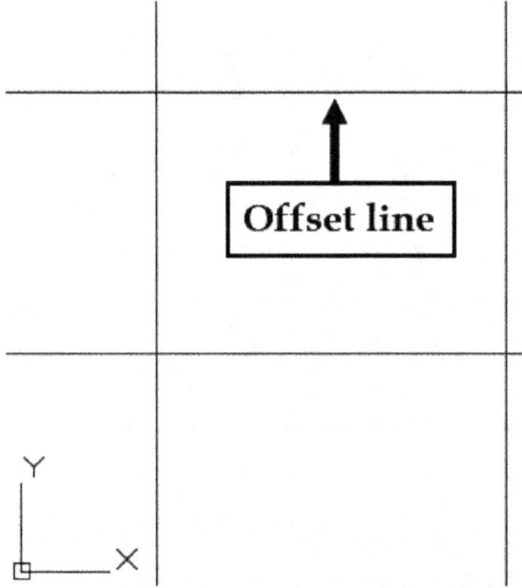

- Press ENTER to exit the **Offset** tool.
- Likewise, create other offset lines, as shown below. The offset dimensions are displayed in the image. Do not add dimensions to the lines.

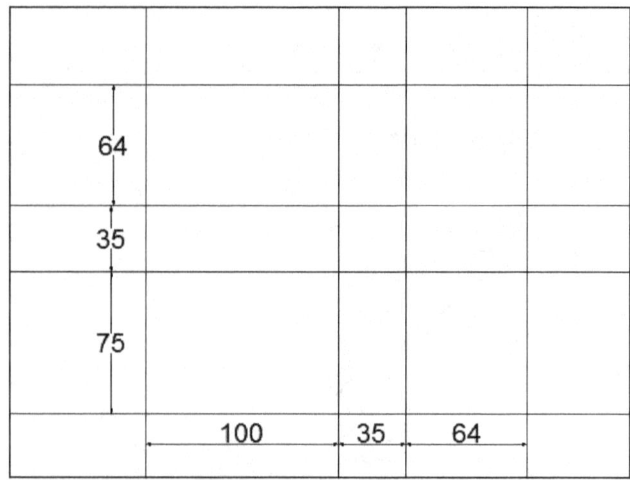

- Activate the **Object** layer.

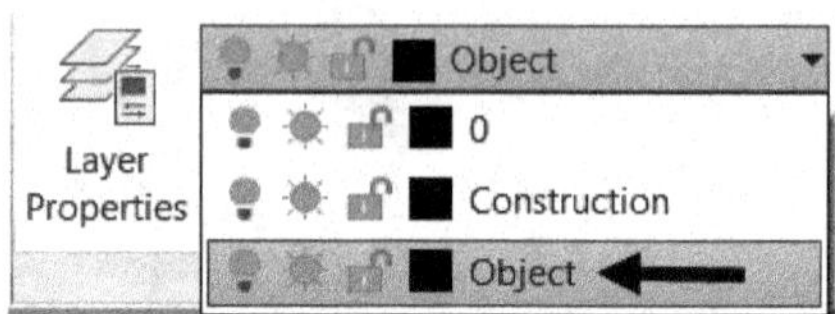

Now, you must create the object lines.

- Activate the **Show/Hide Lineweight** button on the status bar.
- Click the **Line** button on the **Draw** panel.
- Select the intersection points of the construction lines, as shown.

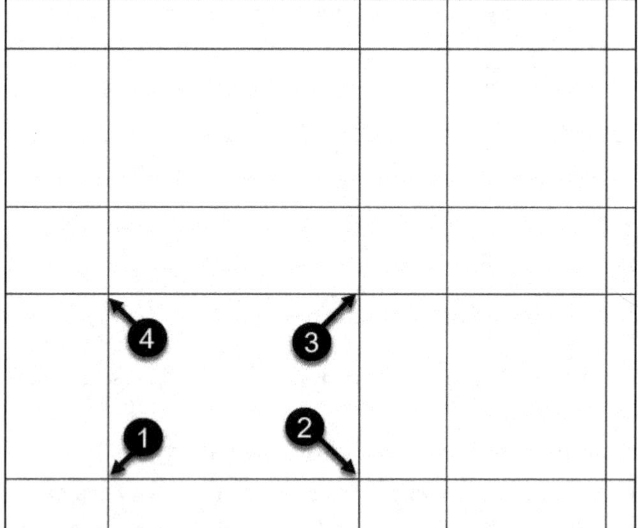

- Select the **Close** option from the command line to create the outline of the front view.

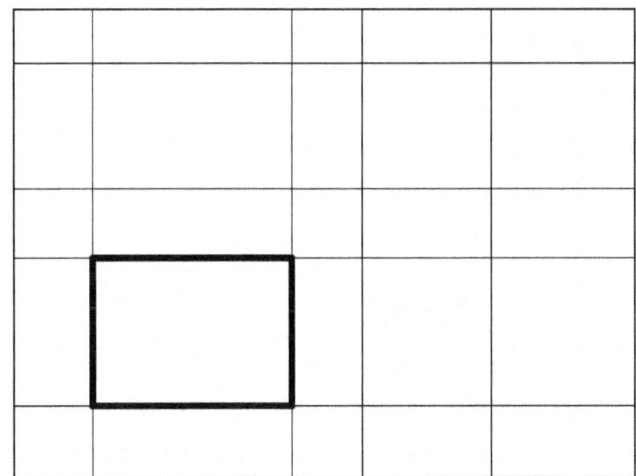

- Likewise, create the outlines of the top and side views.

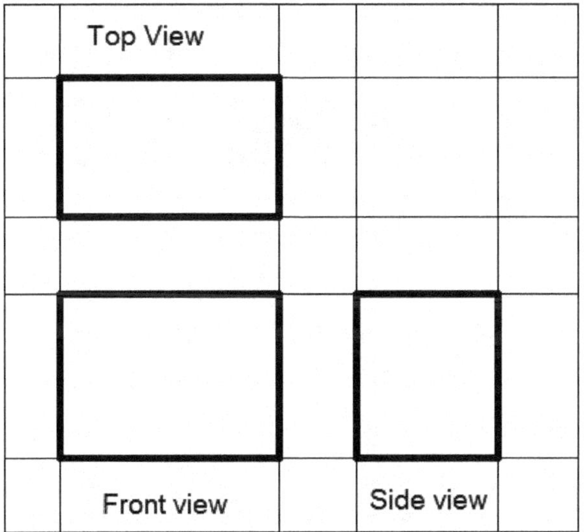

Next, you must turn off the **Construction** layer.

- Click on the **Layer** drop-down in the **Layers** panel.
- Click the light-bulb of the **Construction** layer; the layer will be turned off.

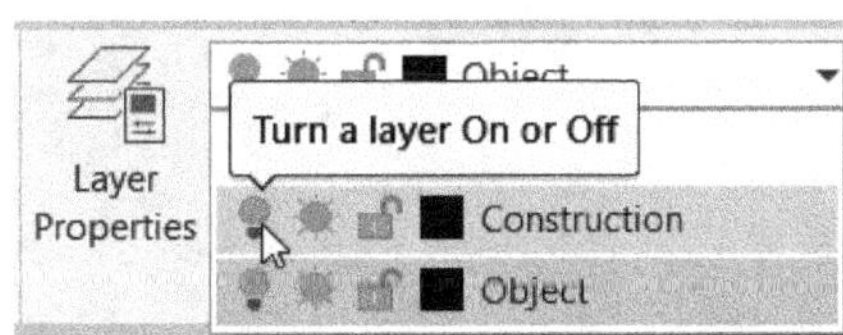

- Use the **Offset** tool and create two parallel lines on the front view, as shown below.

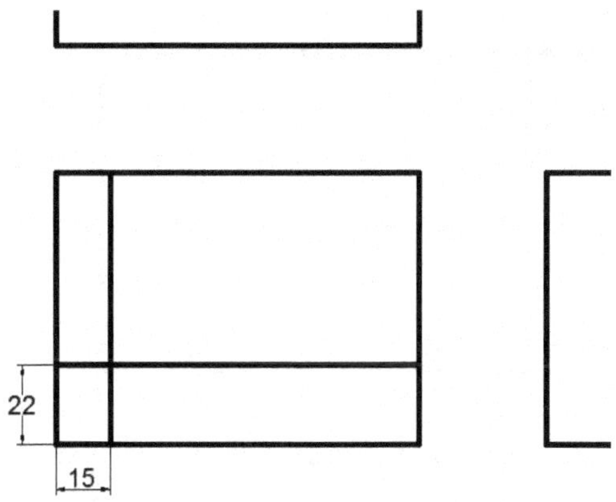

- Use the **Trim** tool and trim the unwanted lines of the front view, as shown below.

- Use the **Offset** tool to create the parallel line, as shown below.

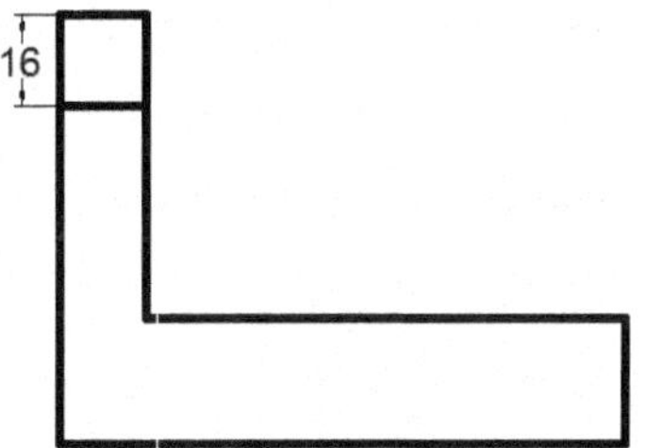

- Use the **Offset** tool and create offset lines in the Top view, as shown below.

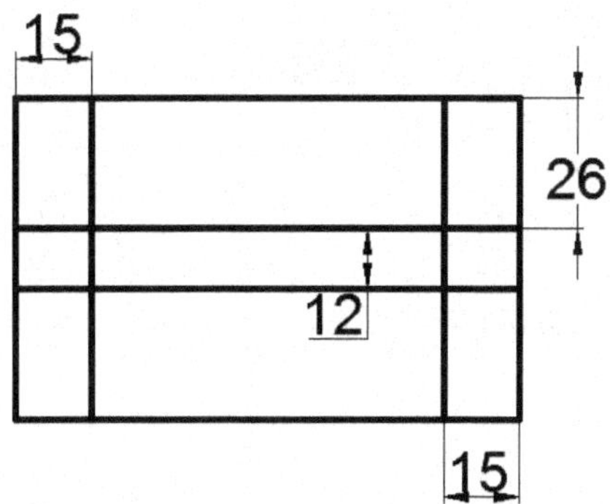

- Use the **Trim** tool and trim unwanted objects.

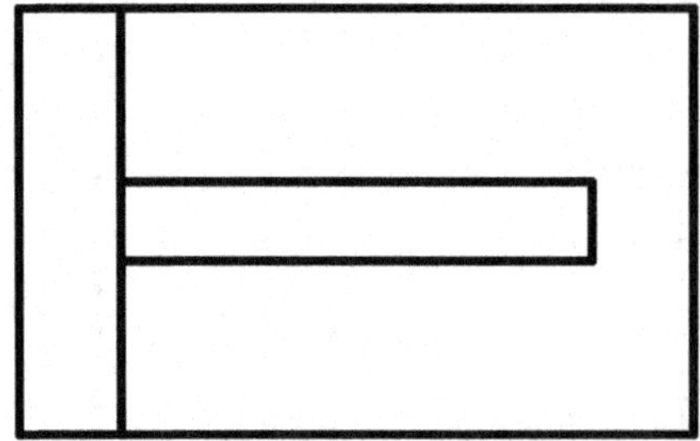

- Create other offset lines and trim the unwanted portions, as shown below.

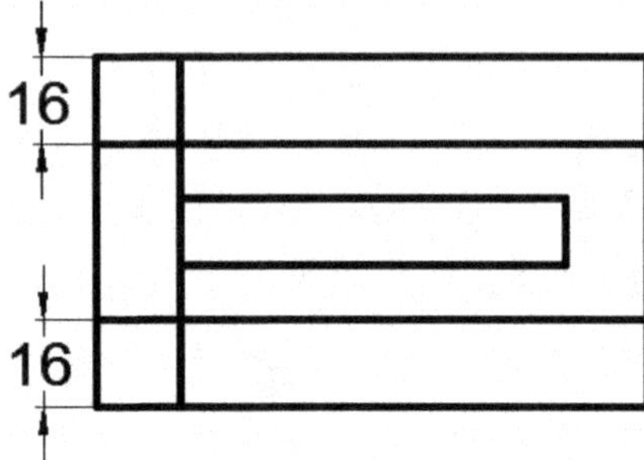

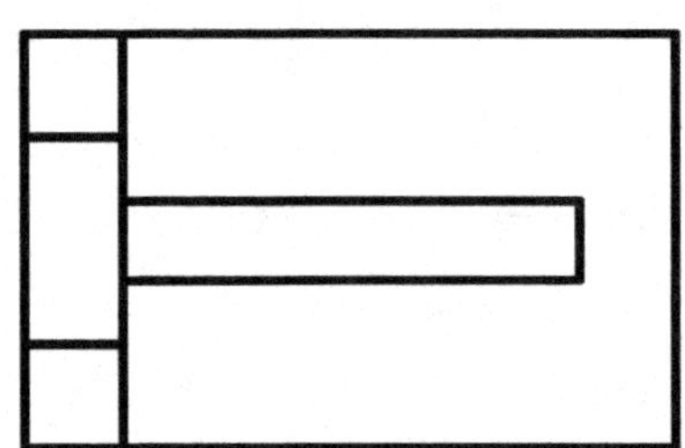

- Deactivate the **Ortho Mode** icon on the status bar.
- Click the **Line** button on the **Draw** panel.
- Press and hold the SHIFT key and right-click. Select the **From** option.

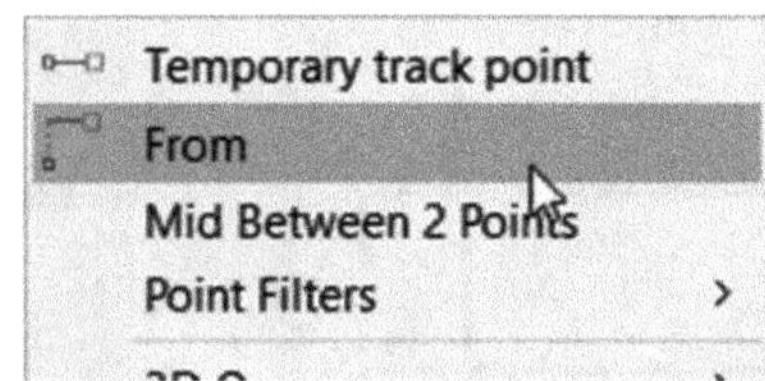

- Select the endpoint of the line in the front view, as shown below.

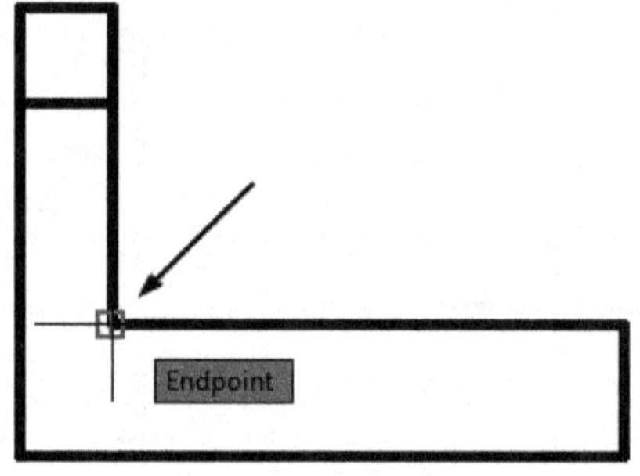

- Move the pointer on the vertical line and enter **40** in the command line; the first point of the line is specified at a point 40 mm away from the endpoint. Also, a rubber band line will be attached to the pointer.

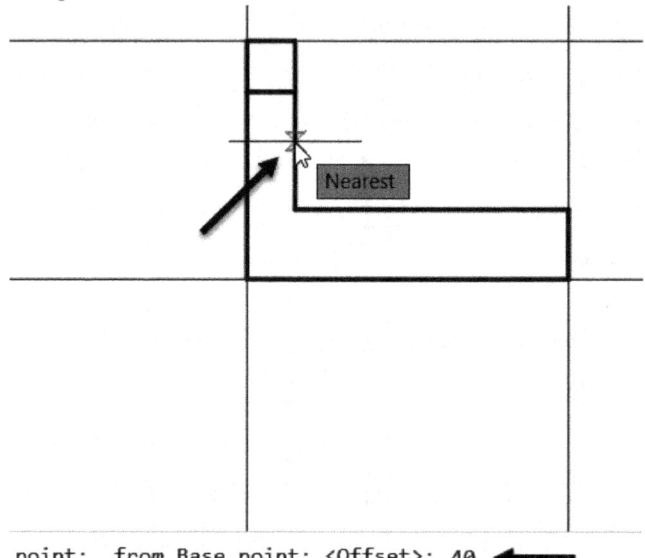

- Move the pointer onto the endpoint on the top view, as shown below.

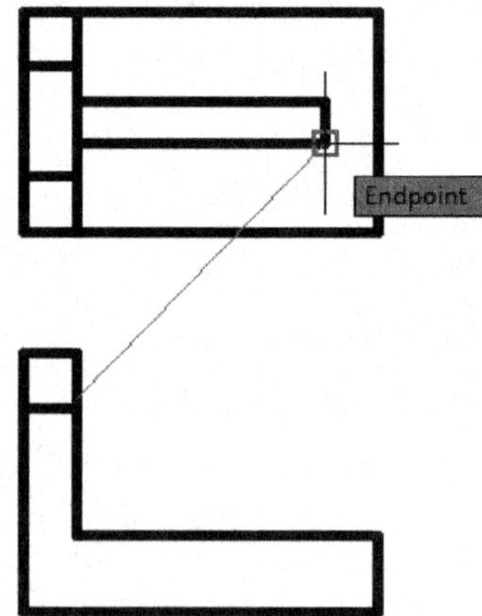

- Move the pointer vertically downward; you will notice the track lines.

- Move the pointer near the horizontal line of the front view and click at the intersection point, as shown below. Press ENTER to exit the tool.

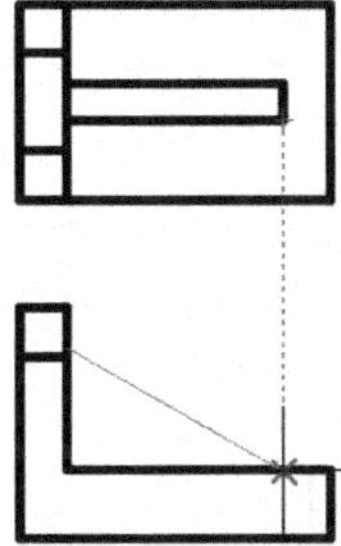

Next, you must create the right-side view. To do this, you must draw a 45-degree miter line and project the measurements of the top view onto the side view.

- Click on the **Layer** drop-down in the **Layers** panel.
- Click the light-bulb icon of the **Construction** layer; the **Construction** layer is turned on.
- Select the **Construction** layer from the **Layer** drop-down to set it as the current layer.
- Draw an inclined line by connecting the intersection points of the construction lines, as shown below.

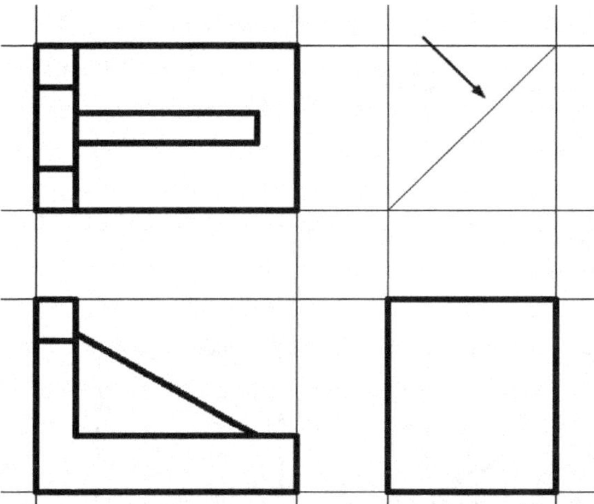

- Click the **Construction Line** button on the **Draw** panel.
- Select the **Hor** option from the command line and select the points on the top and front views, as shown below.

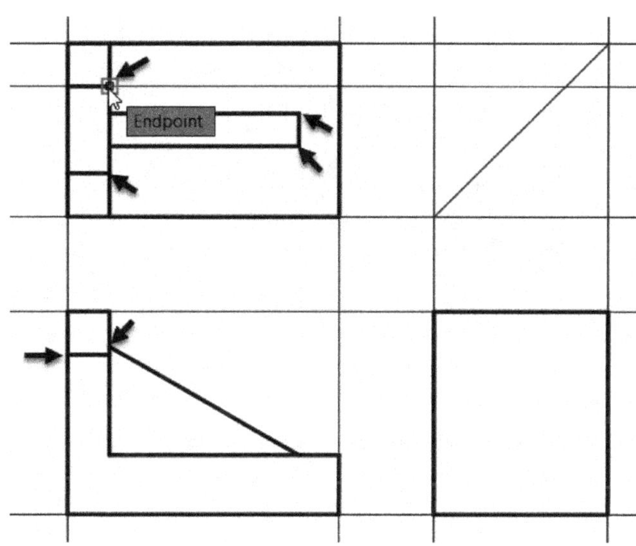

The projection lines are created, as shown below.

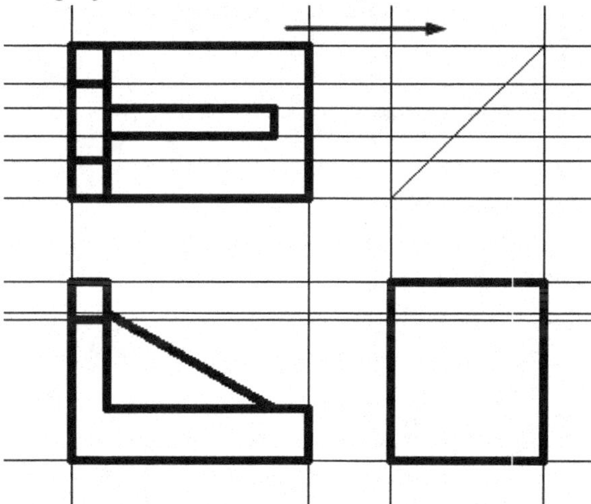

- Right-click to exit the **Construction Line** tool.
- Press ENTER and select the **Ver** option from the command line.
- Create vertical projection lines, as shown below.

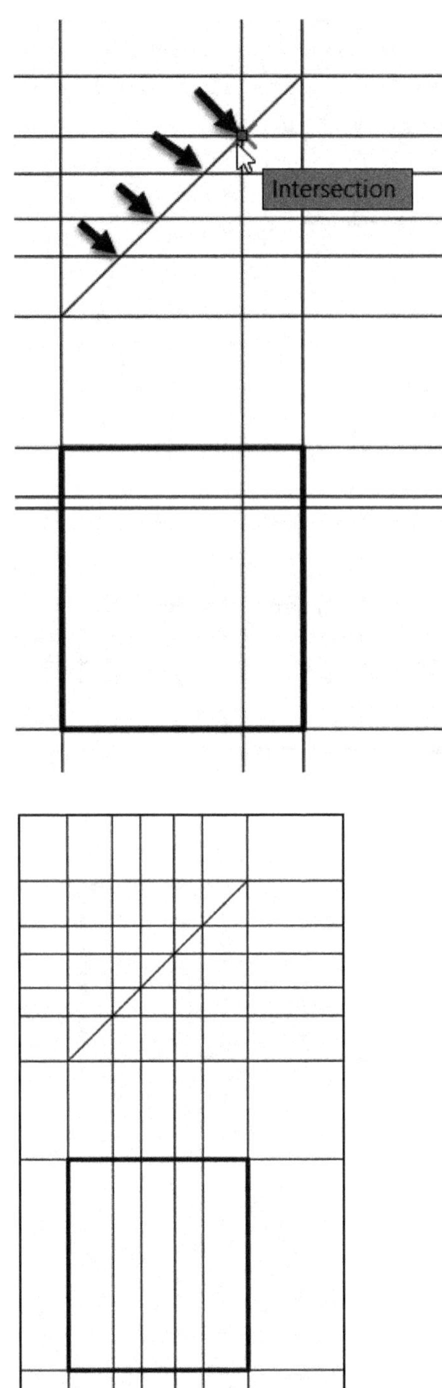

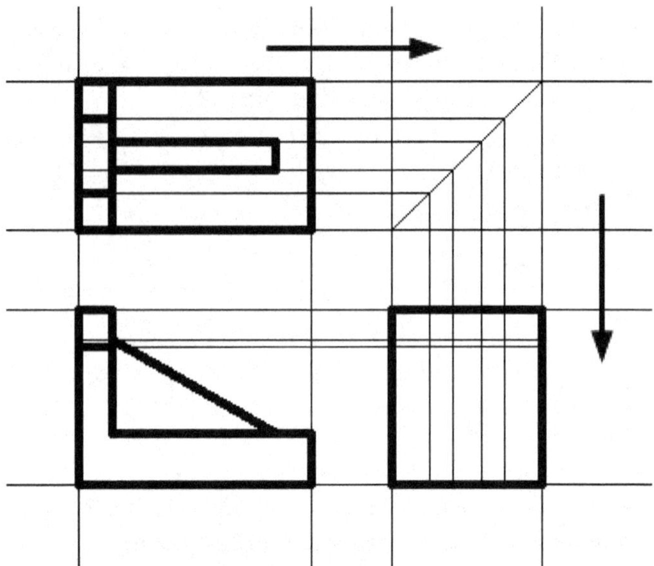

- Use the **Trim** tool and trim the extended portions of the construction lines.

- Set the **Object** layer as current.
- Click the **Offset** button on the **Modify** panel.
- Select the **Through** option from the command line.
- Select the lower horizontal line of the side view.

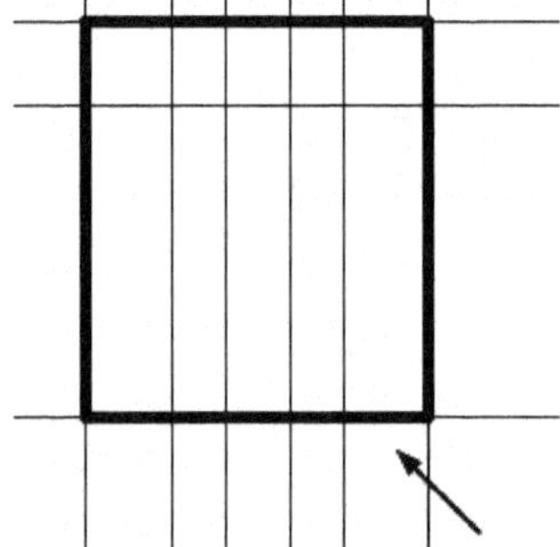

- Select the endpoint on the front view, as shown below.

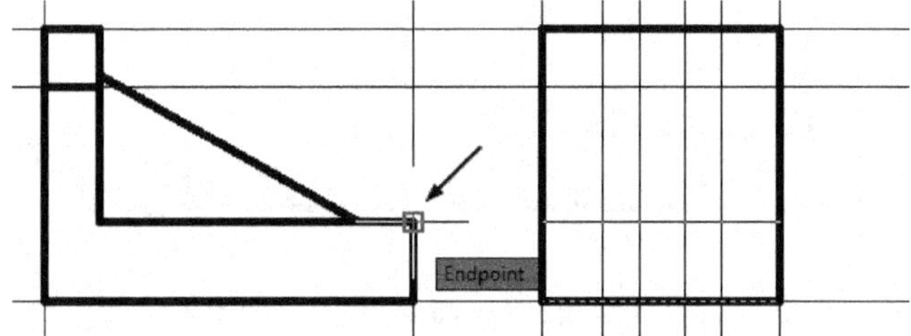

- Click **Exit** in the command line.
- Use the **Line** tool and create the objects in the side view, as shown below.

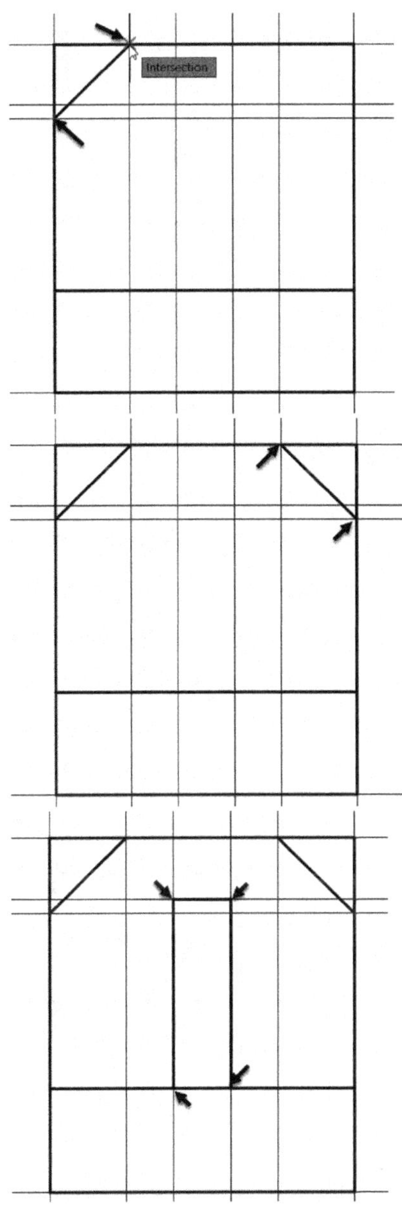

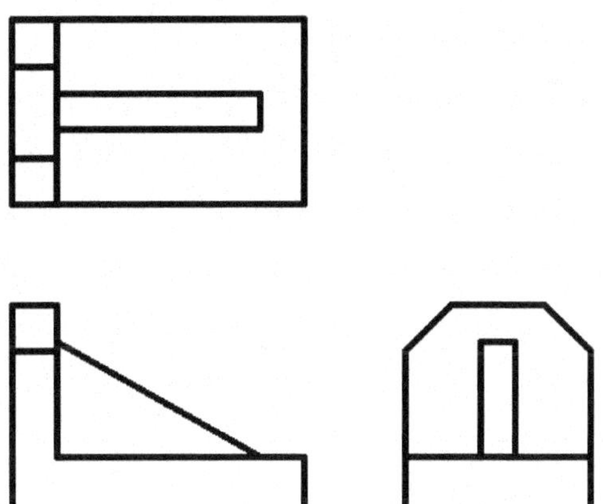

- Save the file as **ortho_views.dwg**. Close the file.

Creating Auxiliary Views

Most of the components are represented by using orthographic views (front, top and side views). But many components have features located on inclined faces. You cannot get the true shape and size for these features by using the orthographic views. To see an accurate size and shape of the inclined features, you must create an auxiliary view. An auxiliary view is created by projecting the component onto a plane other than horizontal, front, or side planes. The following figure shows a component with an inclined face. When you create orthographic views of the component, you will not be able to get the true shape of the hole on the inclined face.

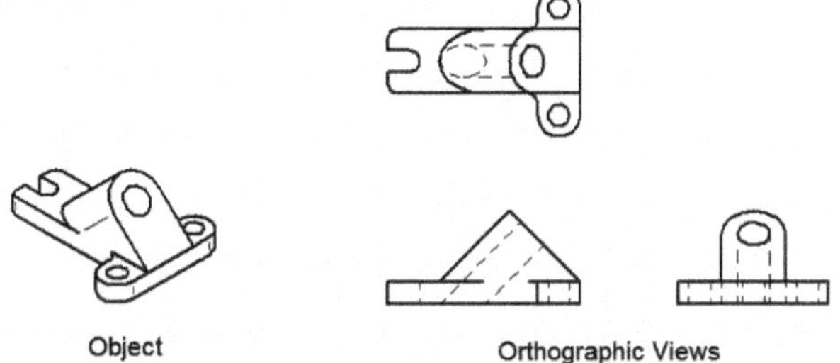

To get the actual shape of the hole, you must create an auxiliary view of the object, as shown below.

- Turn off the **Construction** layer by clicking on the light-bulb of the **Construction** layer.
- Trim the unwanted portions on the right-side view.

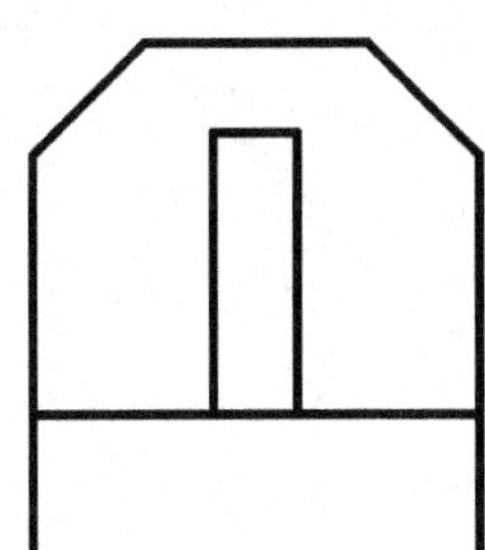

The drawing after creating all the views is shown below.

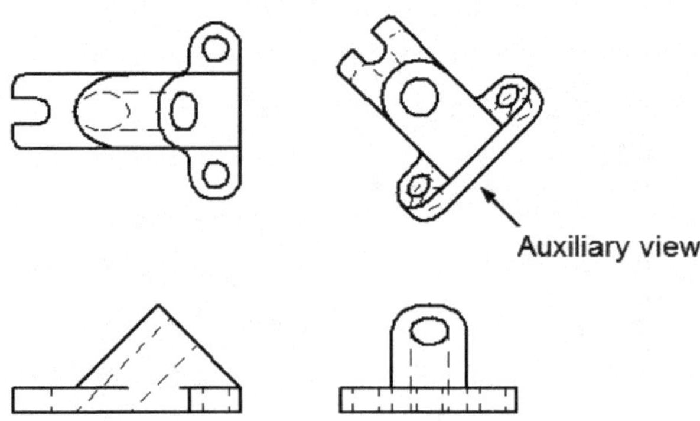

Example:

In this example, you will create an auxiliary view of the object shown below.

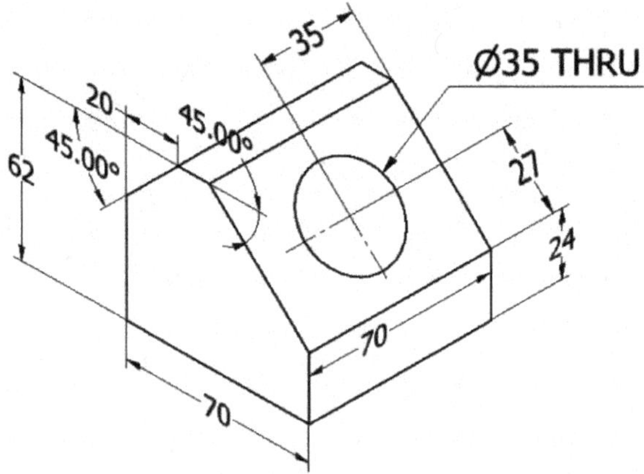

- Open a new AutoCAD file.
- Create four new layers with the following properties.

Layer Name	Lineweight	Linetype
Construction	0.00 mm	Continuous
Object	0.50 mm	Continuous
Hidden	0.30 mm	HIDDEN
Centerline	0.30 mm	CENTER

- Select the **Construction** layer from the **Layer** drop-down in the **Layers** panel.
- Create a rectangle at the lower-left corner of the graphics window, as shown in the figure.

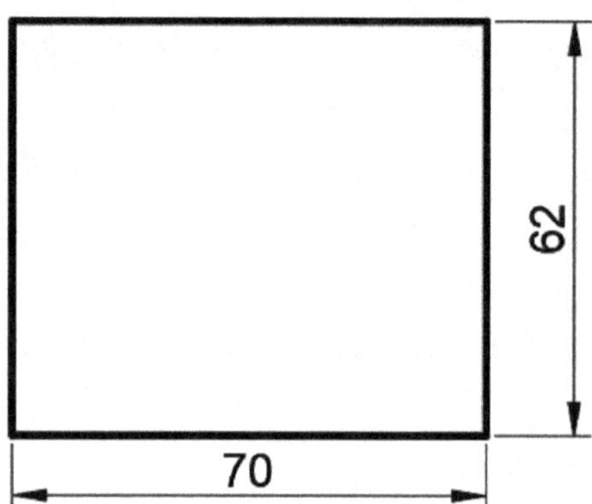

- Select the rectangle and click the **Copy** button on the **Modify** panel.
- Select the lower-left corner of the rectangle as the base point.
- Make sure that the **Ortho mode** is activated.
- Move the pointer upward and type **25** in the command line — next, press ENTER.
- Press ESC to exit the **Copy** tool.

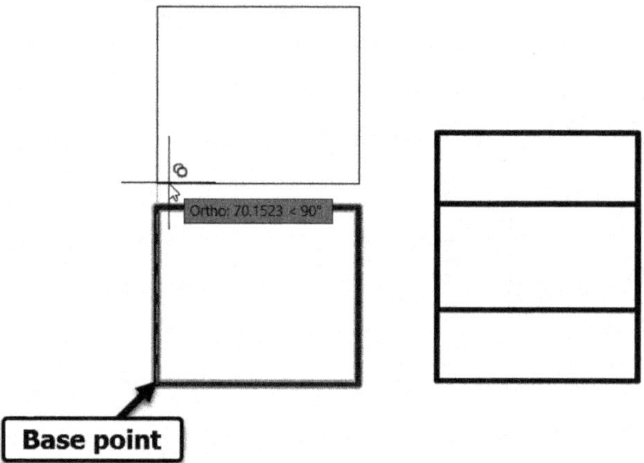

- Click the **Rotate** button on the **Modify** panel and select the copied rectangle. Press ENTER to accept.
- Select the lower right corner of the copied rectangle as the base point.
- Type 45 as the angle and press ENTER.

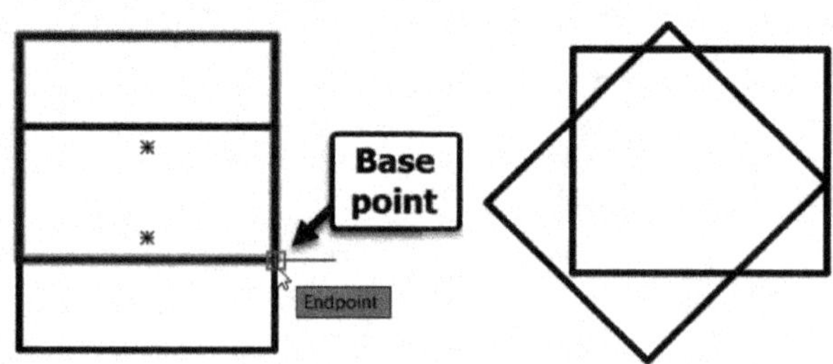

- Click the **Object Snap Tracking** icon on the Status Bar.

- Click the down arrow next to the **Object Snap** icon, and then select **Endpoint** from the list.
- Activate the **Rectangle** command.
- Place the pointer on the top left corner of the existing rectangle.
- Move the pointer vertically upward, and then notice a vertical tracking line from the top left corner of the rectangle.
- Move the pointer along the tracking line up to an approximate distance of 60 mm.

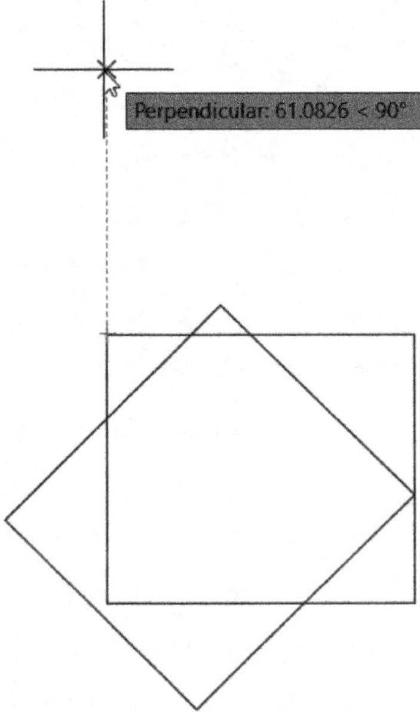

- Click to specify the first corner of the rectangle.
- Select **Dimensions** from the command line.
- Type 70 and press Enter to specify the length of the rectangle.
- Again, type 70 and press Enter to specify the width of the rectangle.
- Move the pointer up and click to position the rectangle.

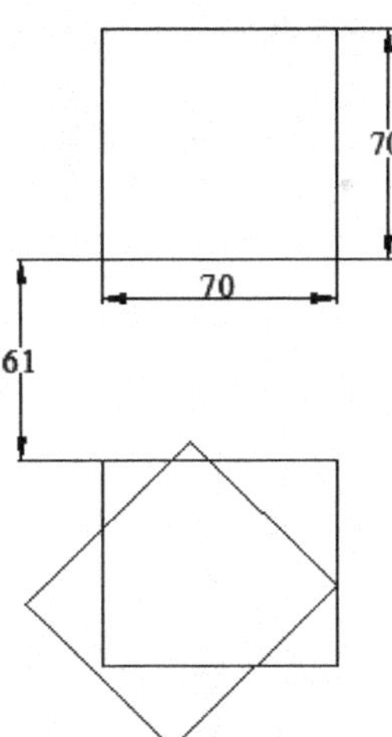

The rectangle located at the top is considered as top view and the below one as the front view.

- Click the **Explode** button on the **Modify** panel and select the newly created rectangle. Next, right-click to explode the rectangle.
- Activate the **Offset** tool and select the **Through** option from the command line.
- Select the left vertical line of the top rectangle.
- Select any one of the through points, as shown; the selected vertical line is offset through the selected point.
- Again, select the left vertical line.
- Move the pointer, and then select the remaining through point.

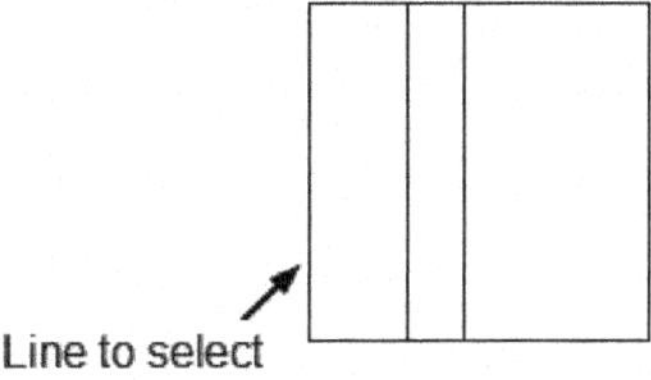

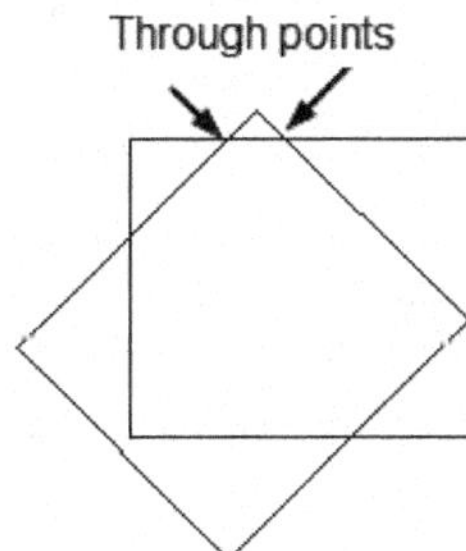

- Press Esc to deactivate the **Offset** tool.
- Select the **Object** layer from the **Layer** drop-down in the **Layers** panel.

- Activate the **Show/Hide Lineweight** button on the status bar.
- Activate the **Line** tool and select the intersection points on the front view, as shown.

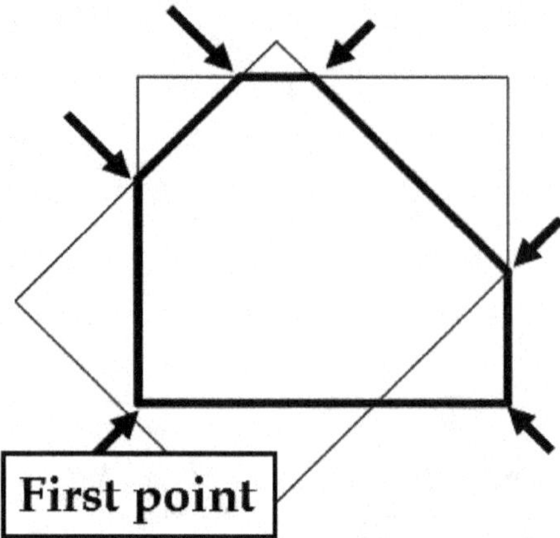

- Likewise, create the object lines in the top view, as shown below.

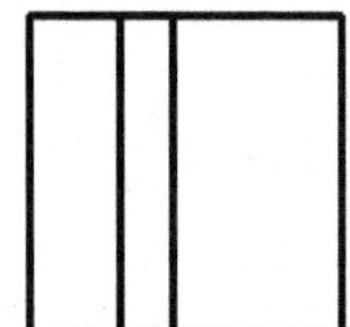

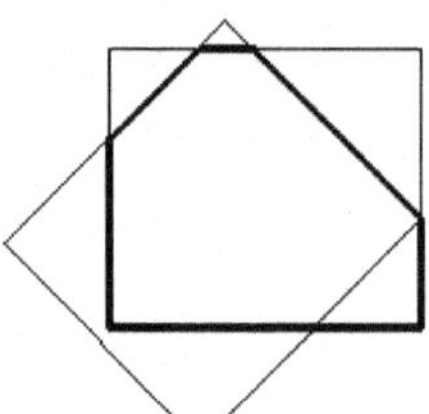

- Select the **Construction** layer from the **Layers** panel.
- Click the **Construction Line** button on the **Draw** panel.
- Select the **Offset** option from the command line. Next, select the **Through** option.
- Select the inclined line on the front view. Next, select the intersection point, as shown below.

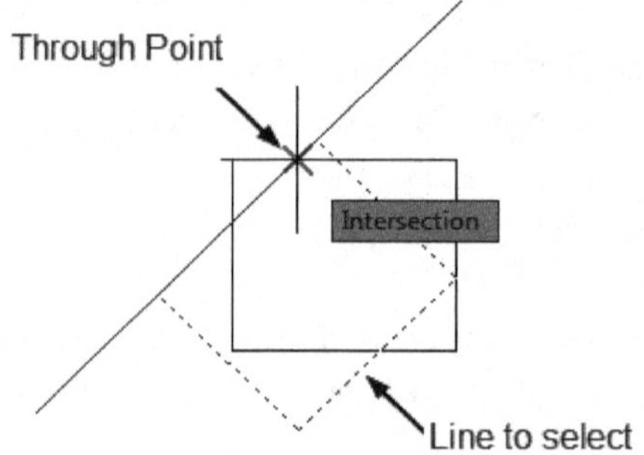

- Likewise, create other construction lines, as shown below.

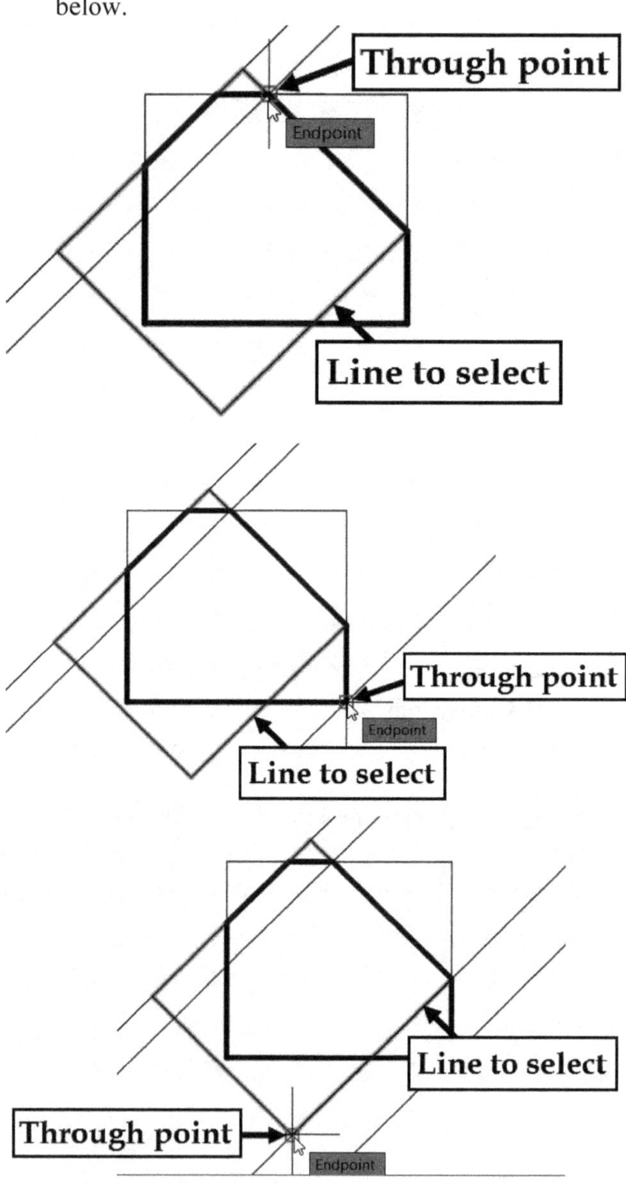

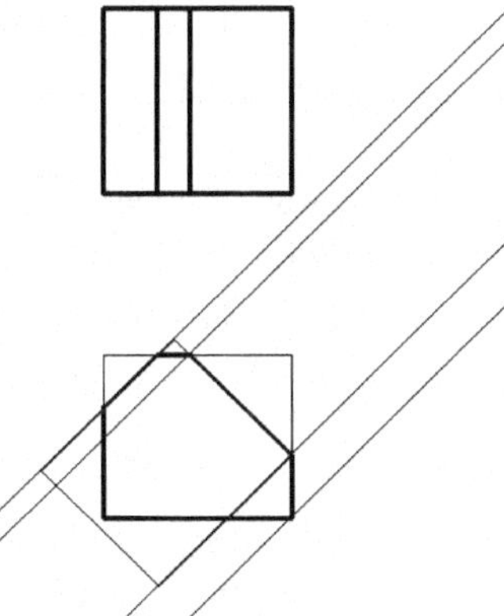

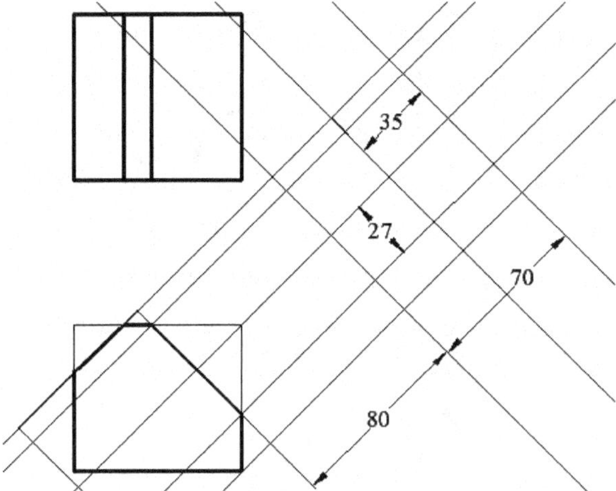

- Press Esc to deactivate the **Construction Line** command.
- Activate the **Construction Line** command and select **Offset** from the command line.
- Type 80 and press ENTER.
- Select the inclined line of the front view, as shown.
- Move the pointer toward the right and click to create the construction line.

- Set the **Object** layer as the current layer. Next, create the object lines using the intersection points between the construction lines.
- Use the **Circle** tool and create a circle of 35 mm in diameter.

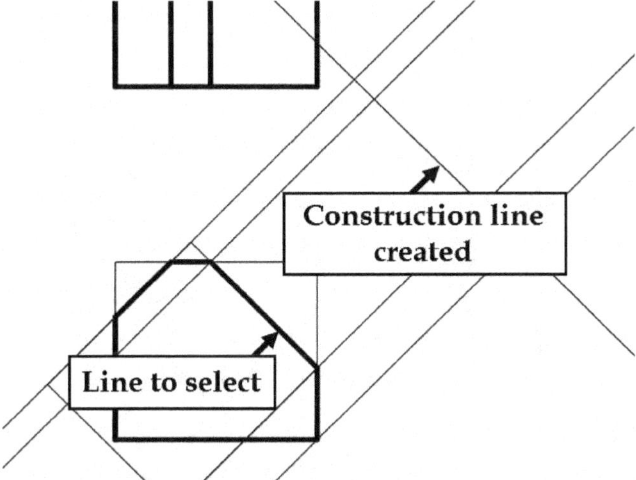

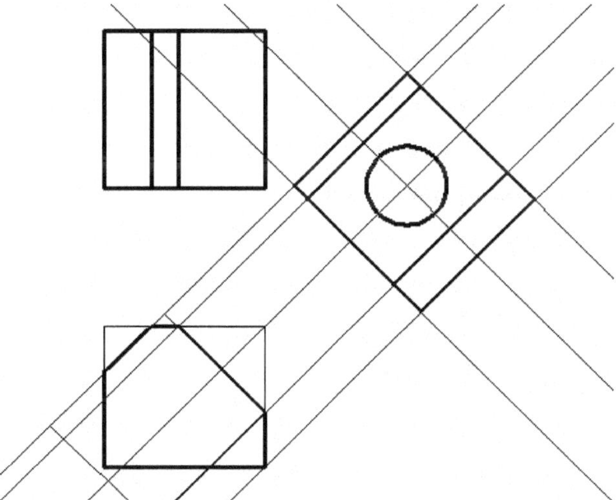

- Create other construction lines, as shown. The offset dimensions are given in the figure.

- Set the **Construction** layer as the current layer.
- Create projection lines from the circle.

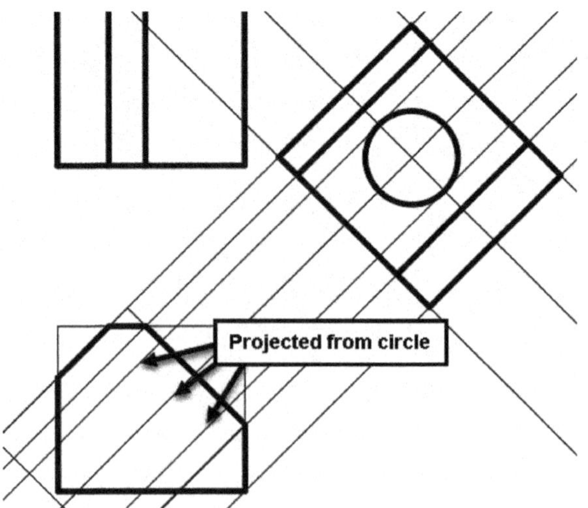

- Set the **Hidden** layer as the current layer,
- Create the hidden lines, as shown.

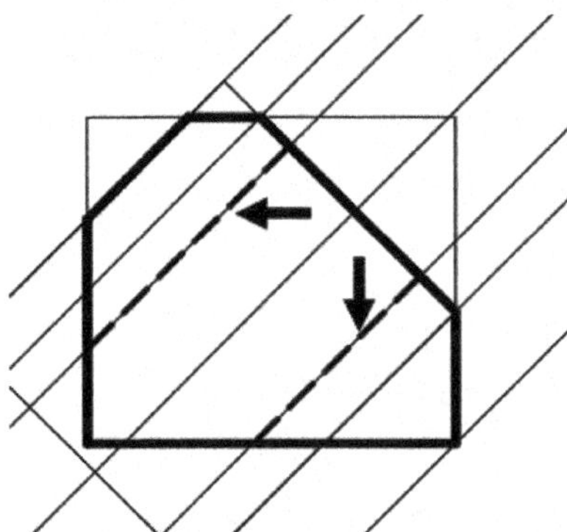

- Set the **Centerline** layer as the current layer.
- Activate the **Line** tool.
- Create the centerlines, as shown.

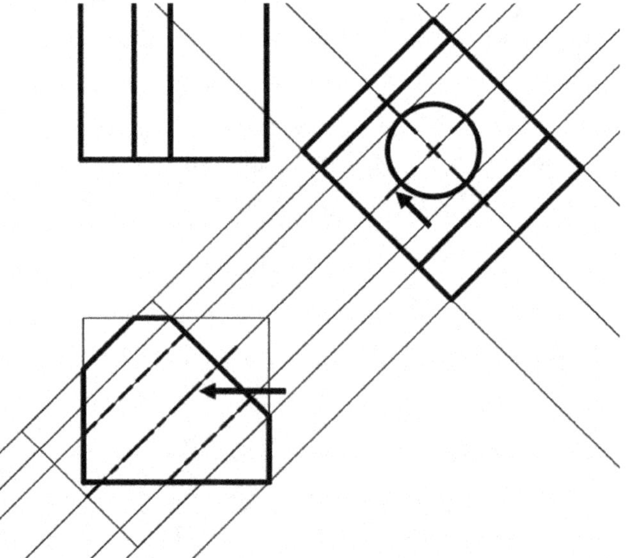

- Set the **Construction** layer as the current layer.
- On the ribbon, click **Home > Draw > Ray** .

A ray is a basic geometric construction tool that consists of a fixed starting point and a line segment extending infinitely in one direction from that point. Unlike a construction line, a ray has one defined endpoint but no termination on the other side.

To make a ray, you specify the origin point and the angle defining the direction the infinite line portion travels. Rays are useful tools in technical drawing for establishing precise orientations, positioning objects, and creating angular layout guides and references.

Multiple rays can be generated at once through a single command. You can convert a ray into line segments using editing tools such as Trim or Break.

- Select the intersection point of the centerline and object line, as shown.
- Move the pointer upward and click to create a ray.

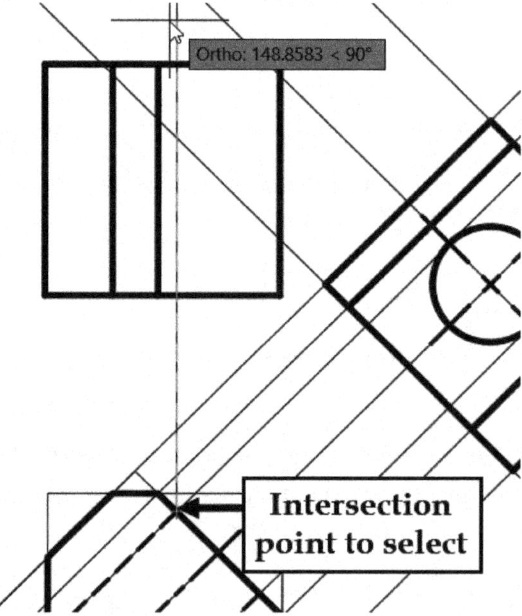

- Press ENTER twice.
- Likewise, create two more rays, as shown.

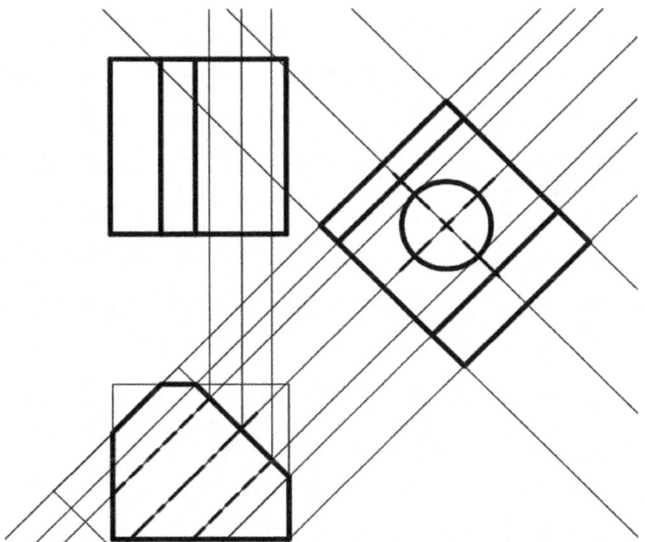

- Create a horizontal construction line passing through the midpoint of the top view, as shown.

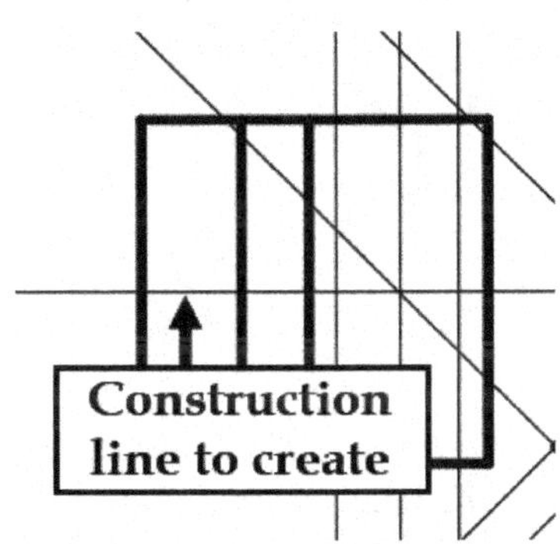

- Set the **Object** layer as the current layer,
- On the ribbon, click **Home > Draw > Ellipse drop-down > Axis, End**.
- Specify the first and second points, as shown.

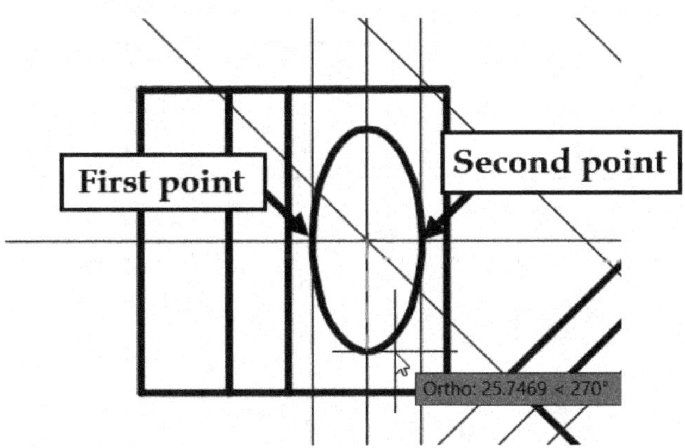

- Move the pointer downward, type-in 17.5, and then press ENTER.

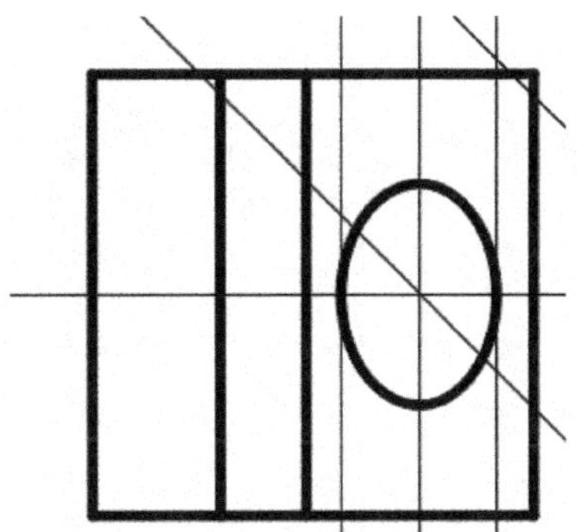

- Set the **Centerline** layer as a current layer,
- Create the remaining centerlines.
- The drawing after hiding the **Construction** layer is shown next.
- Save the file as auxiliary_views.dwg.

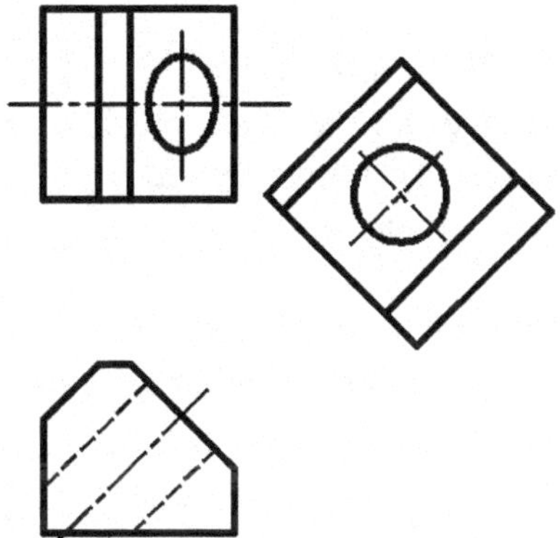

Creating Named views

While working with a drawing, you may need to perform numerous zoom and pan operations to view key portions of a drawing. Instead of doing this, you can save these portions with a name. Then, restore the named view and start working on them.

- Open the **ortho_views.dwg** file (The drawing file created in the Orthographic Views section of this chapter).
- Click the **View** tab on the ribbon.
- To create a named view, click **View > Named Views > View Manager** on the ribbon; the **View Manager** dialog appears.

The **View Manager** allows you to create, save, and restore custom views of your drawing. This dialog box enables you to efficiently navigate and manage your design, saving you time and effort.

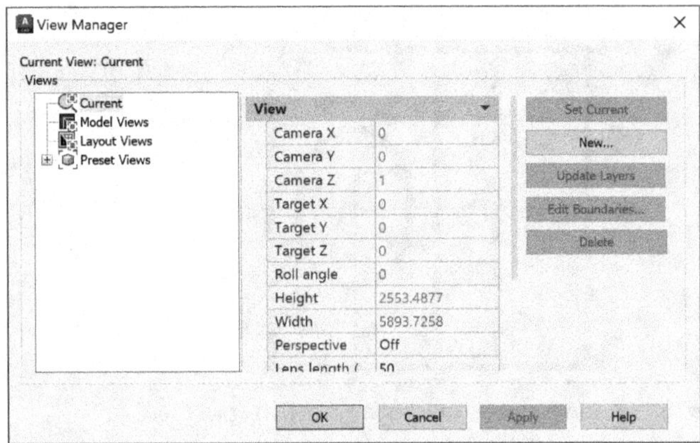

- Click the **New** button on the **View Manager** dialog; the **New View/Shot Properties** dialog appears.

On this dialog box, you can specify options for your new named view, including a view name, category, and description. You can also define the area of the drawing that will be displayed when the view is restored by selecting the **Boundary** section.

- Select the **Define Window** option from the **Boundary** section of the **New View/Shot Properties** dialog.
- Create a window on the front view, as shown below.

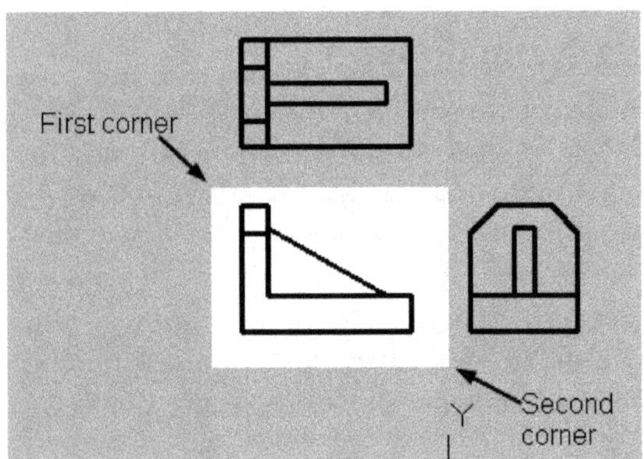

- Press ENTER to accept.
- Enter **Front** in the **View name** box.

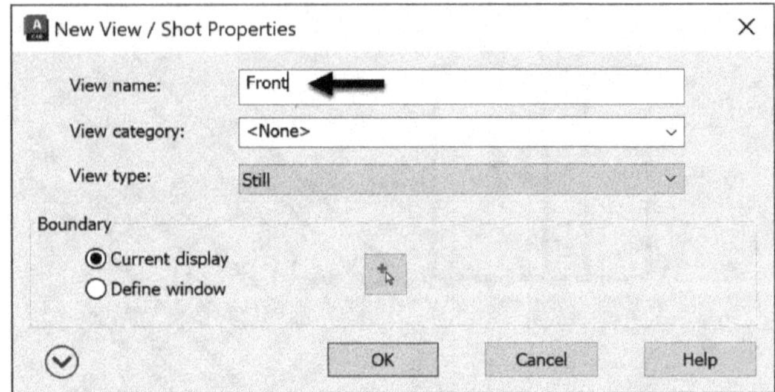

- Click **OK** on the **New View/Shot Properties** dialog.
- Likewise, create the named views for the top and right views of the drawing.

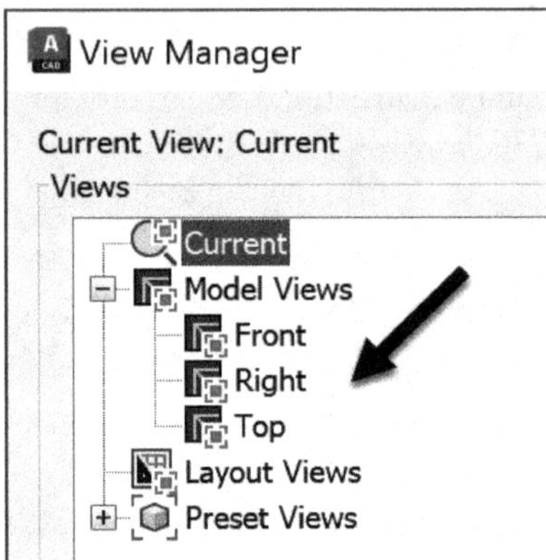

- To set the **Top** view to current, select it from the **Views** tree and click the **Set Current** button on the dialog. Next, click **OK** on the **View Manager** dialog; the **Top** view will be zoomed and fitted to the screen.

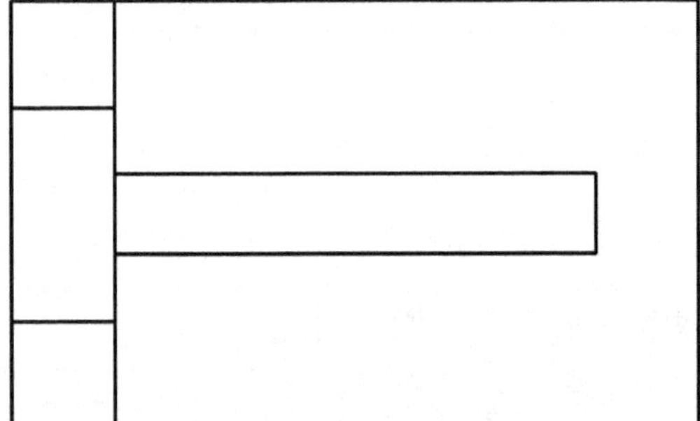

- Save and close the file.

Exercises

Exercise 1

Create the orthographic views of the object shown below.

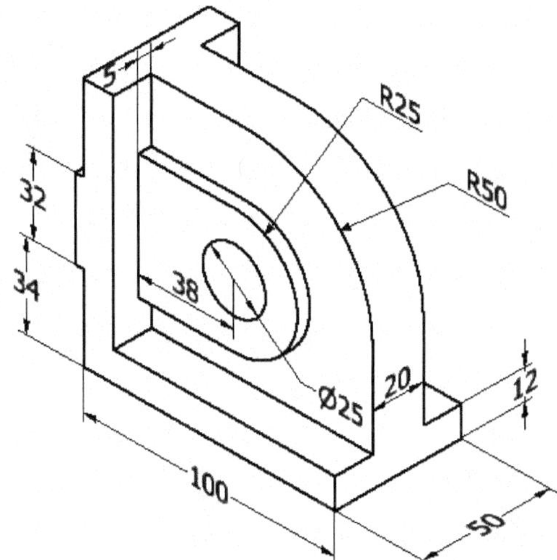

5
R25
R50
32
34
38
Ø25
20
12
100
50

Exercise 2

Create the orthographic views of the object shown below.

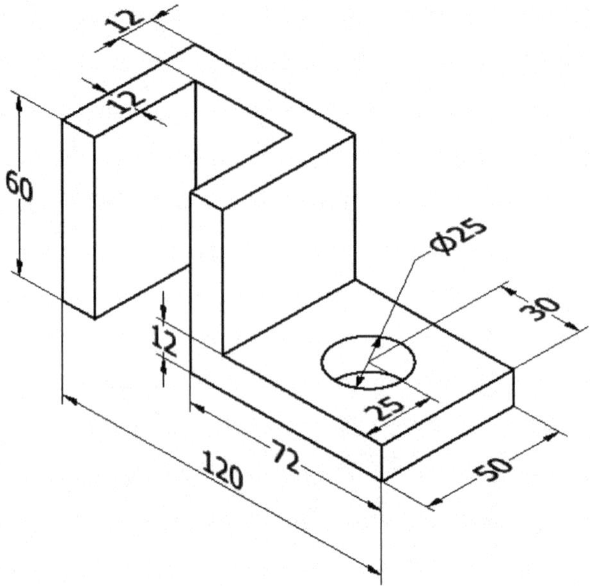

Exercise 3

Create the orthographic and auxiliary views of the object shown below.

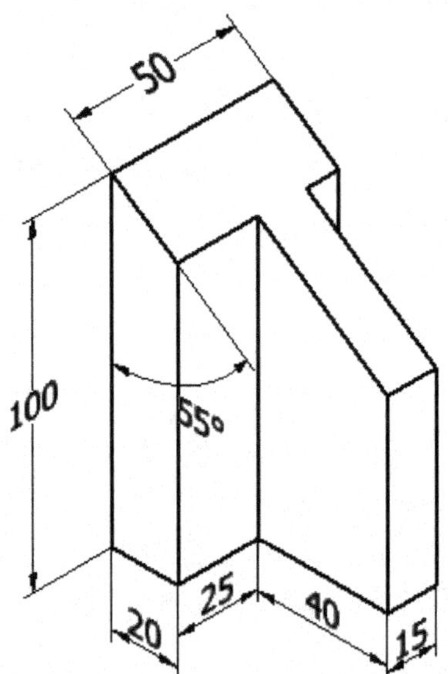

Exercise 4

Create the orthographic and auxiliary views of the object shown below.

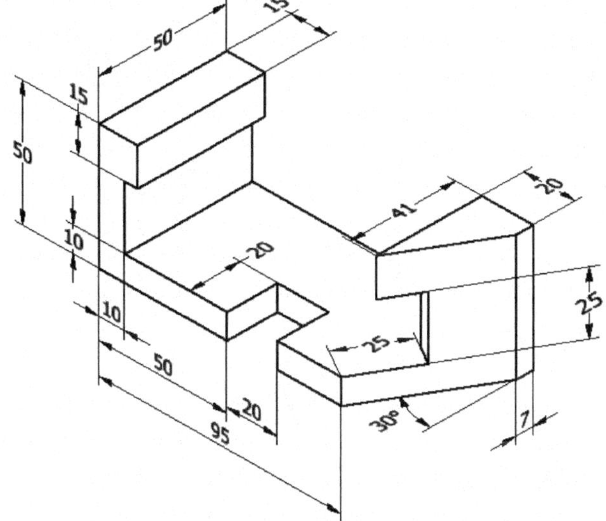

Chapter 6: Dimensions and Annotations

In this chapter, you will learn to do the following:

- **Create Dimensions**
- **Create Dimension Style**
- **Add Leaders**
- **Create Centerlines**
- **Add Dimensional Tolerances**
- **Add Geometric Tolerances**
- **Edit Dimensions**

Dimensioning

In previous chapters, you have learned to draw shapes of various objects and create drawings. However, while creating a drawing, you also need to provide the size information. You can provide the size information by adding dimensions to the drawings. In this chapter, you will learn how to create various types of dimensions. You will also learn about some standard ways and best practices of dimensioning.

Creating Dimensions

In AutoCAD, there are many tools available for creating dimensions. You can access these tools from the Ribbon, Command line, and Menu Bar.

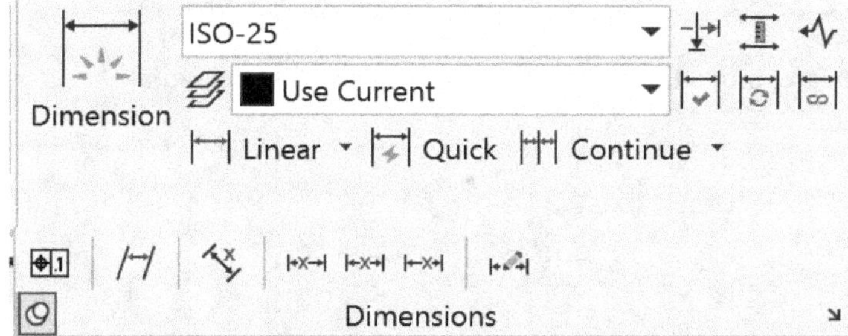

The following table gives you the functions of various dimensioning tools.

Tool	Shortcut	Function
Dimension	DIM	This tool creates a dimension based on the selected geometry.

- Create a rectangle, circle, arc, and two intersecting lines, as shown in the previous figure.
- Click **Annotate > Dimensions > Dimension** on the ribbon.
- Select a line, move the pointer, and click to create the linear dimension.

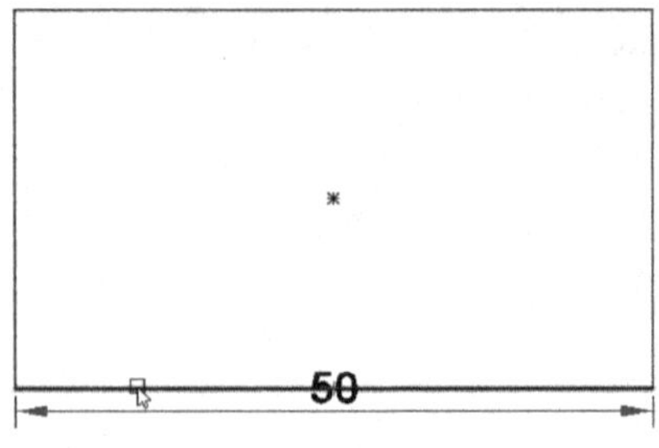
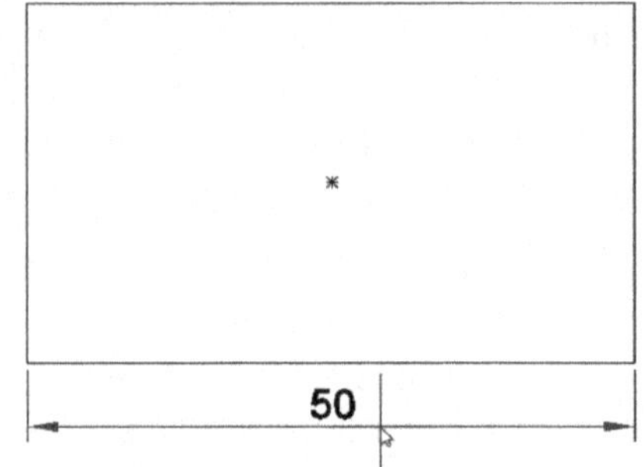

- Select a circle, move the pointer, and click to position the diameter dimension.

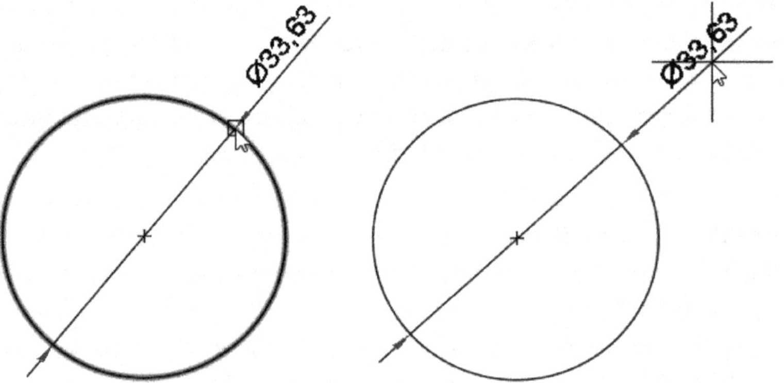

- Select an arc, move the pointer, and click to position the radial dimension.

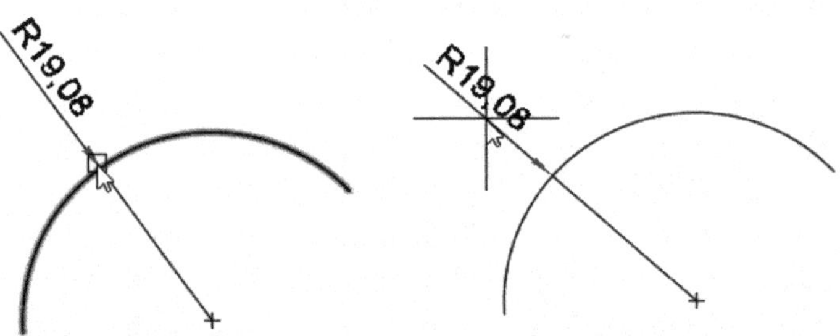

- Place the pointer on the arc, type L, and press Enter. Select the arc, move the pointer, and click to position the arc length dimension.

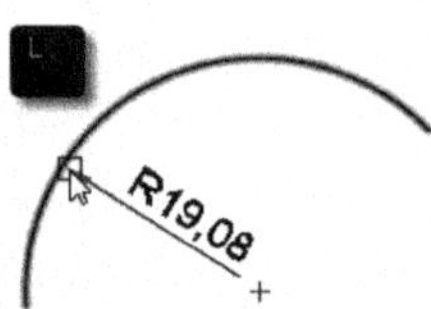
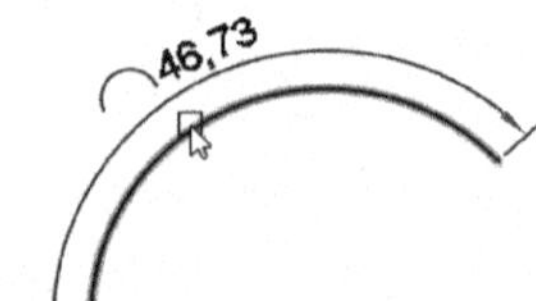
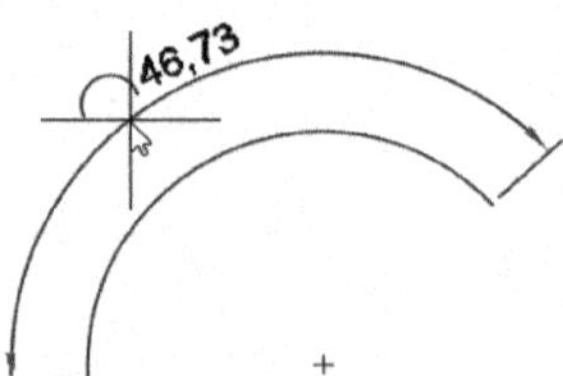

- Place the pointer on the arc, type A, and press Enter. Select the arc, move the pointer, and click to position the angle of the arc.

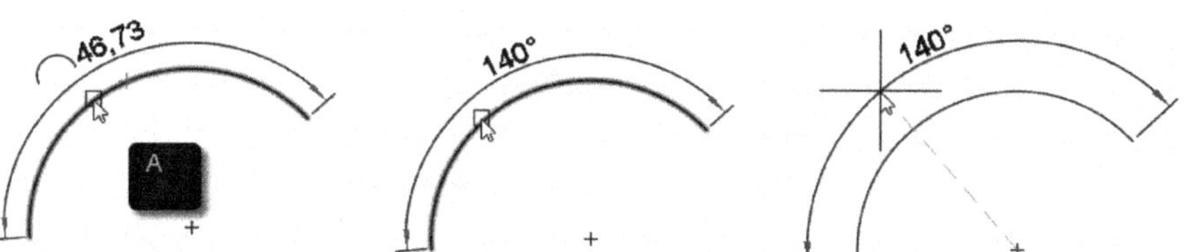

- Select two non-parallel lines and position the angular dimension between them.

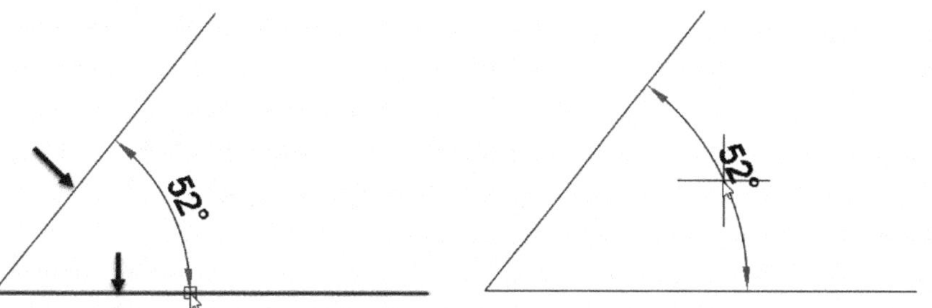

Likewise, you can create other types of dimensions using the **Dimension** tool.

Linear	DLI	This tool creates horizontal and vertical dimensions.

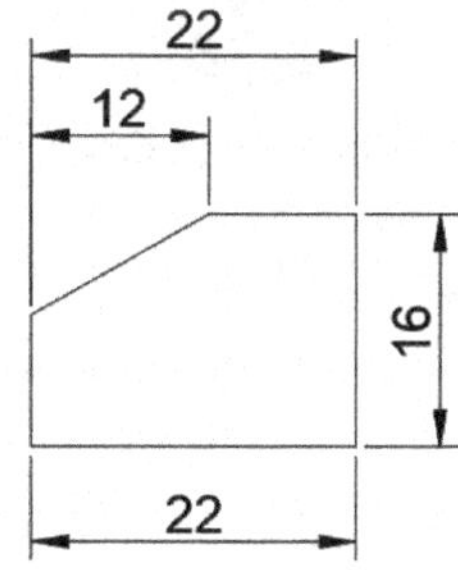

- Click **Annotate > Dimensions > Dimension** drop-down **> Linear** on the ribbon.
- Select the first and second points of the dimension.
- Move the pointer in the horizontal direction to create a vertical dimension (or) move in the vertical direction to create a horizontal dimension.

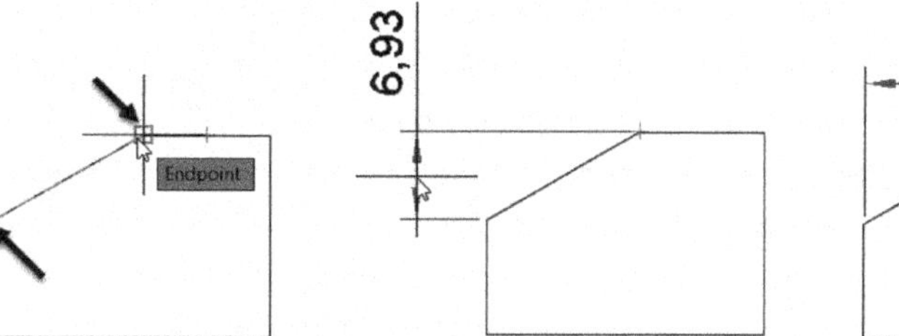

- Click to position the dimension.

| **Aligned** | DAL | This tool creates a linear dimension parallel to the object. |

- Click **Annotate > Dimensions > Dimension** drop-down > **Aligned** on the ribbon.
- Select the first and second points of the dimension line.

(or) press Enter and select the line.

- Move the pointer and click to position the dimension.

| **Arc Length** | DAR | It dimensions the total or partial length of an arc. |

- Click **Annotate > Dimensions > Dimension** drop-down > **Arc Length** on the ribbon.
- Select an arc from the drawing.
- If you want to dimension only a partial length of an arc, select **Partial** option from the command line. Next, select the two points on the arc.
- Move the pointer and click to position the dimension.

| **Continue** | DCO | It creates a linear dimension from the second extension line of the previous dimension. |

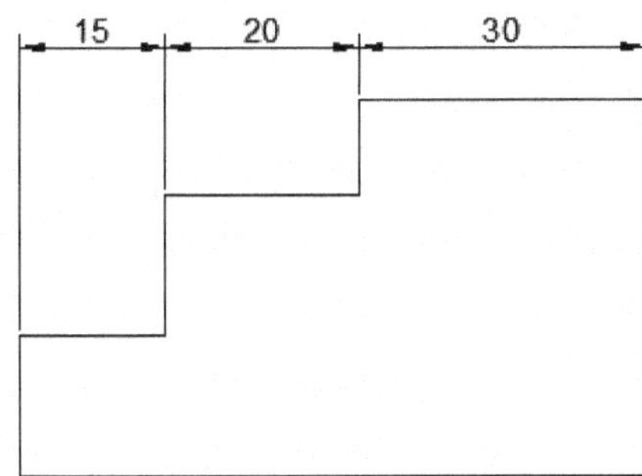

- Create a linear dimension by selecting the first and second points.

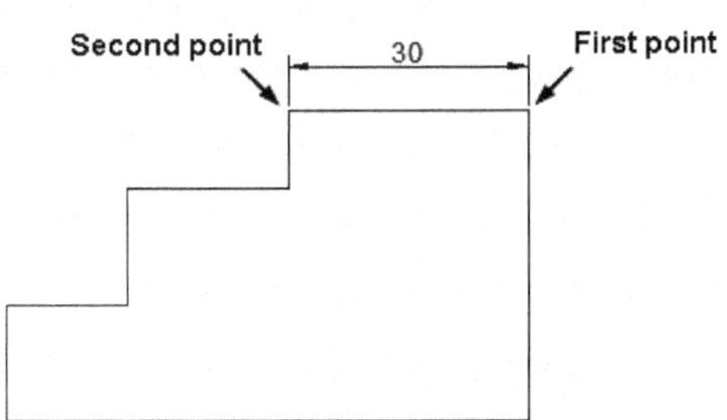

- Click **Annotate > Dimensions > Continue** on the ribbon; a chain dimension is attached to the pointer.

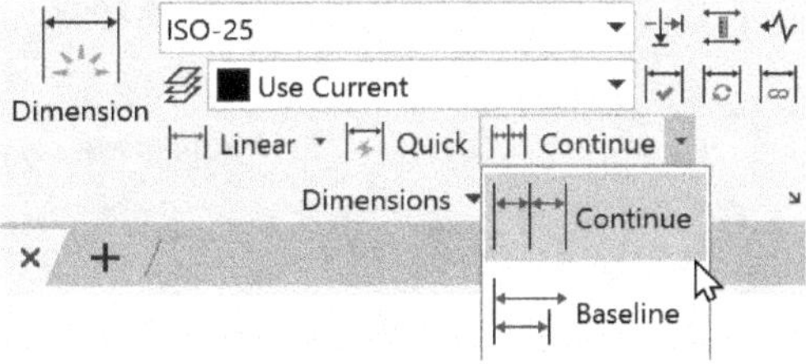

- Select the third and fourth points of the chain dimension.

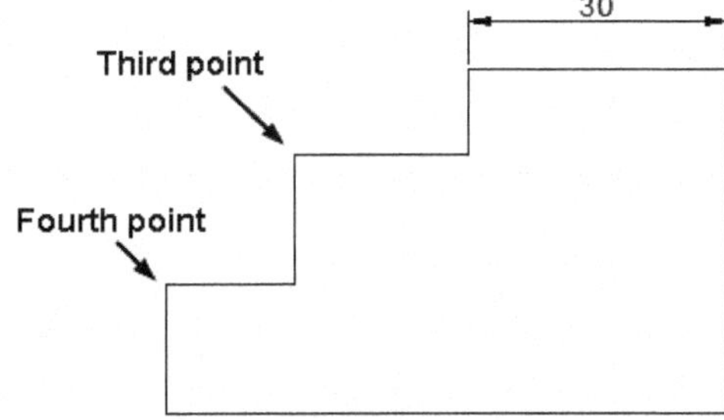

- Position the chain dimension. Next, right-click and select **Enter**.

Baseline	DBA	It creates dimensions by using the previously created dimension, as shown below.

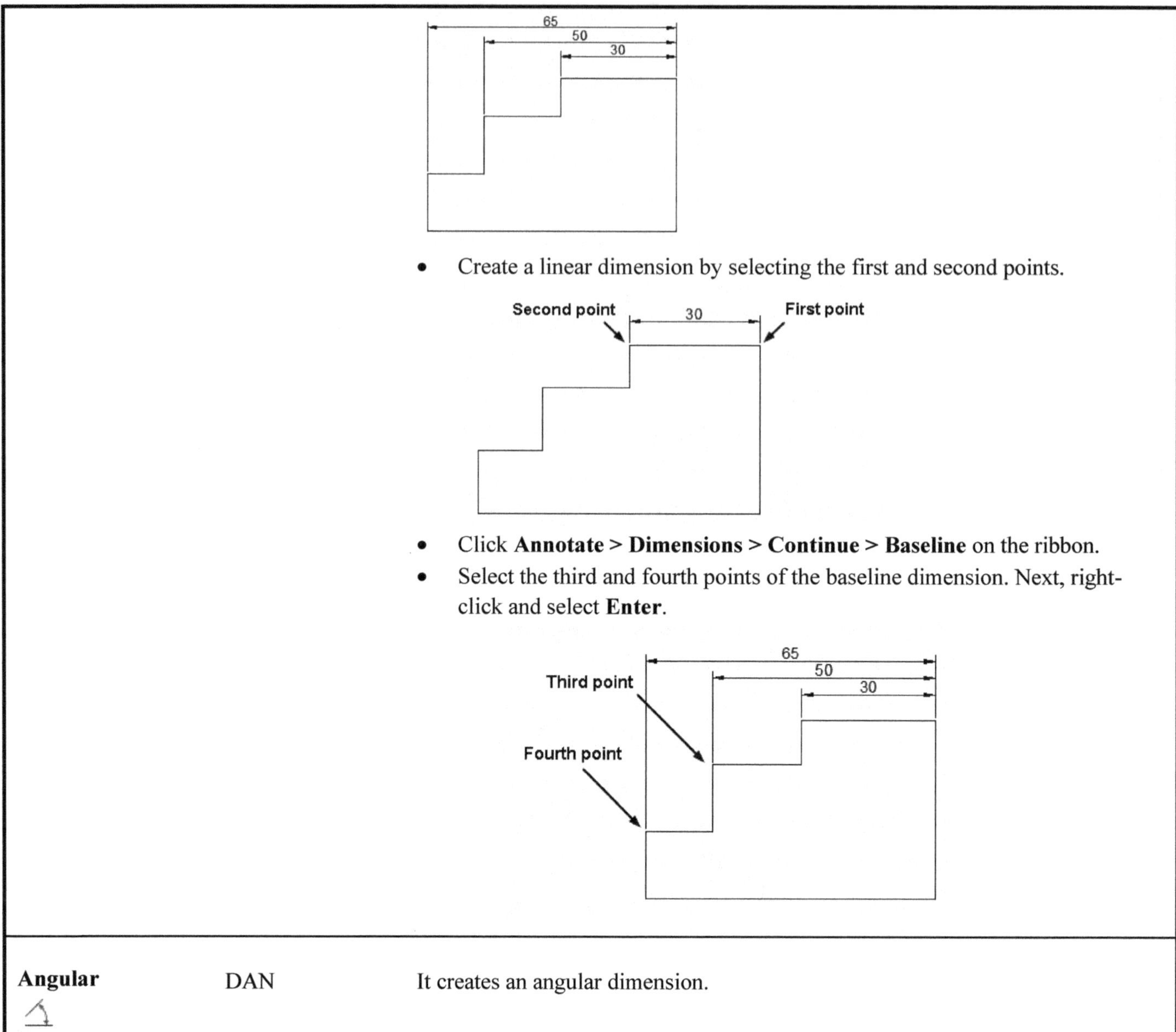

- Create a linear dimension by selecting the first and second points.

- Click **Annotate > Dimensions > Continue > Baseline** on the ribbon.
- Select the third and fourth points of the baseline dimension. Next, right-click and select **Enter**.

Angular	DAN	It creates an angular dimension.

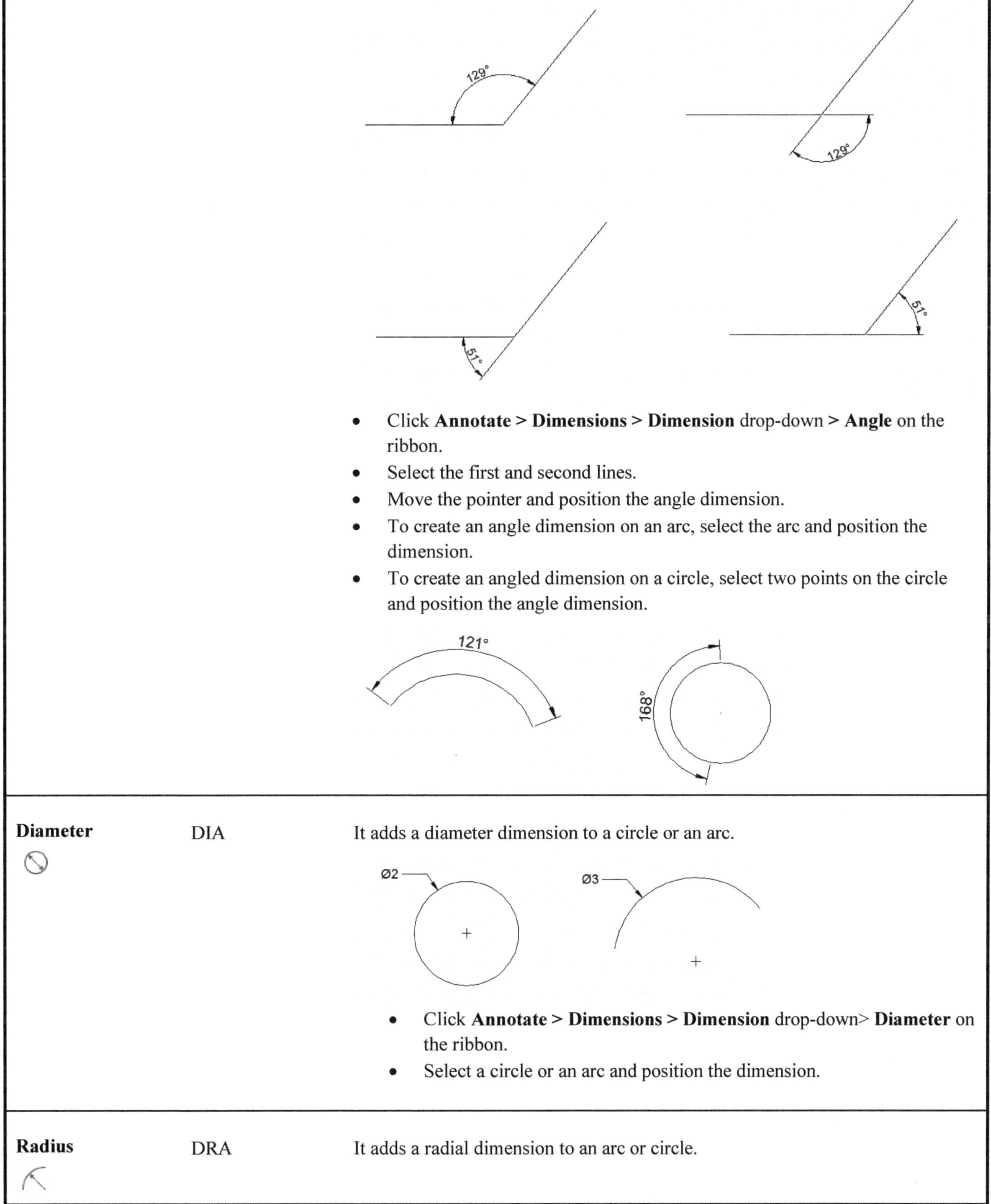

- Click **Annotate > Dimensions > Dimension** drop-down **> Angle** on the ribbon.
- Select the first and second lines.
- Move the pointer and position the angle dimension.
- To create an angle dimension on an arc, select the arc and position the dimension.
- To create an angled dimension on a circle, select two points on the circle and position the angle dimension.

| **Diameter** | DIA | It adds a diameter dimension to a circle or an arc. |

- Click **Annotate > Dimensions > Dimension** drop-down**> Diameter** on the ribbon.
- Select a circle or an arc and position the dimension.

| **Radius** | DRA | It adds a radial dimension to an arc or circle. |

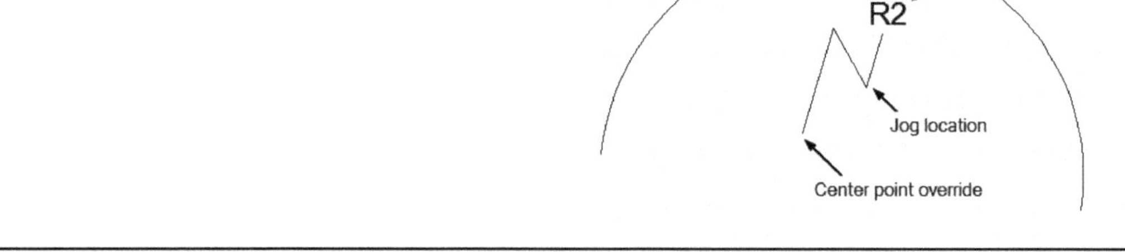

Jogged 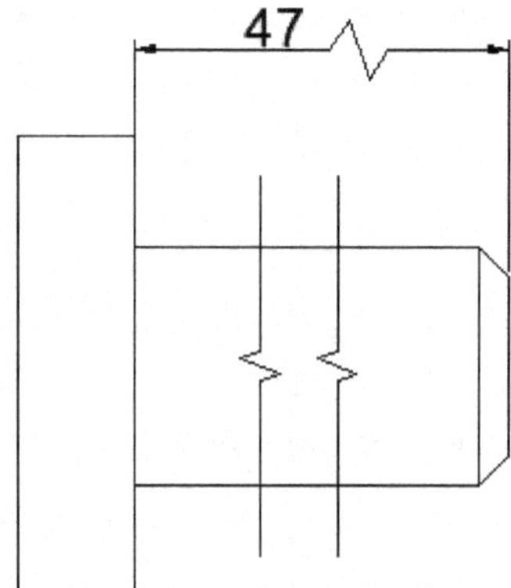	DJO	It creates jogged dimensions. A jogged dimension is created when it is not possible to show the center of an arc or circle.

- Click **Annotate > Dimensions > Dimension** drop-down > **Jogged** on the ribbon.
- Select an arc or circle.
- Select a new center point override.
- Locate the dimension and the jog location.

Dimension, Dimjogline   DJL   It creates a jogged linear dimension.

- Click **Annotate > Dimensions > Dimension, Dimjogline** on the ribbon.

		• Select the linear dimension to add a jog. • Define the location of the jog on the dimension.
Center Mark ⊕	CENTERMARK	It adds a center mark to a circle or an arc. • Click **Annotate > Centerlines > Center Mark** on the ribbon. • Select an arc or a circle; the center mark will be positioned at its center.
Centerline ===	CENTERLINE	It creates a centreline between two lines. The centreline has the associative property. It changes with the position of the lines • Click **Annotate > Centerlines > Centerline** on the ribbon. • Select two lines that are parallel or non-parallel to each other; a centreline is created between them. • Change the position of the lines; the centreline also changes.
Ordinate ⊢ˣʸ	DOR	It creates ordinate dimensions based on the current position of the User Coordinate System (UCS).

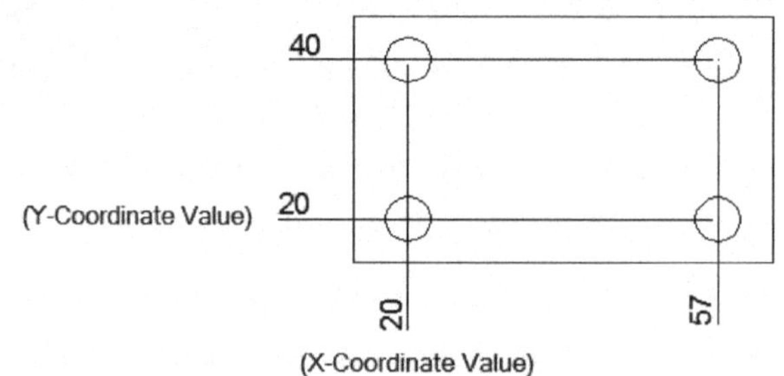

- Click **Annotate > Dimensions > Dimension** drop-down > **Ordinate** on the ribbon.
- Select the point of the object.
- Move the pointer in the vertical direction and click to position the X-Coordinate value.
- Select the point of the object.
- Move the pointer in the horizontal direction and click to position the Y-Coordinate value.

Quick

QDIM

It dimensions one or more objects at the same time.

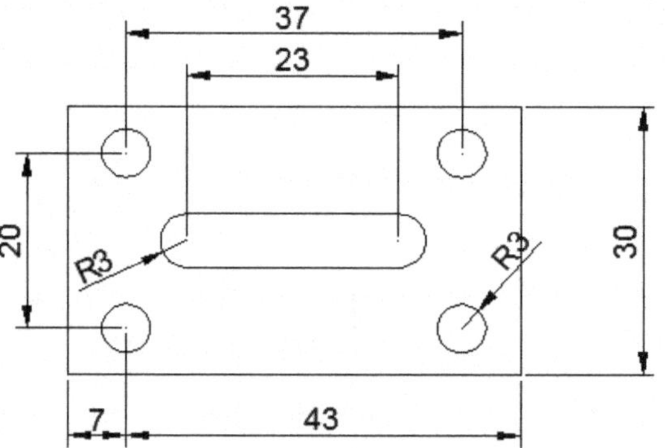

- Click **Annotate > Dimensions > Quick** on the ribbon.
- Select one or more objects from a drawing.
- Right-click and position the dimensions.

Adjust Space

DIMSPACE

In the following figure, the drawing on the left side has congested dimensions, whereas the right side drawing has dimensions with ample space between them. You can use the **Adjust Space** tool to adjust the space between the dimensions.

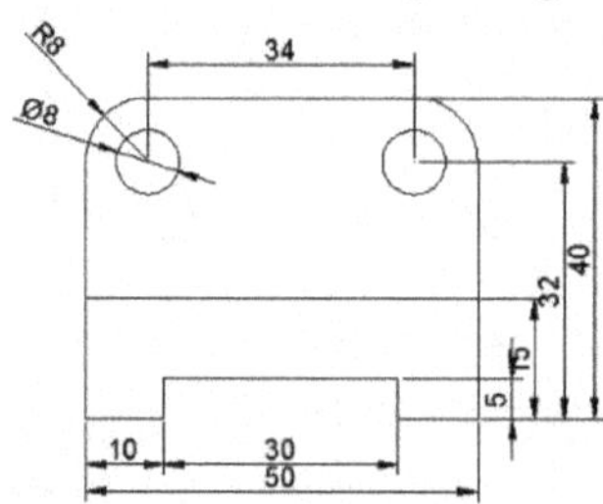

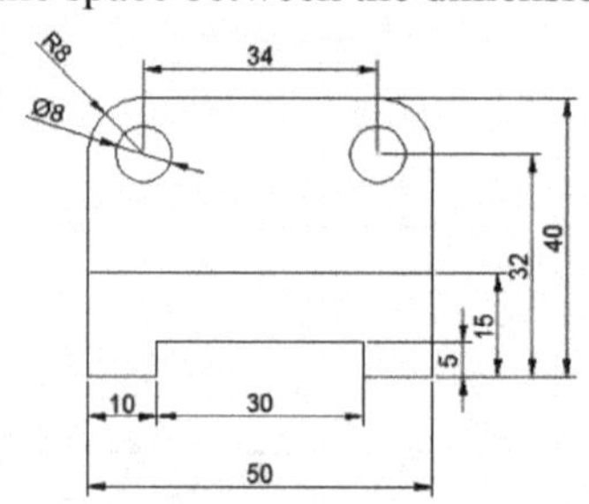

		• Click **Annotate > Dimensions > Adjust Space** on the ribbon. • Select the base dimension from which the other dimensions are to be adjusted. • Select the dimensions to adjust. • Right-click to accept. • Enter the value of the spacing between the dimensions or select the **Auto** option; the dimensions will be adjusted with respect to the base dimension.
Break 	DIMBREAK	It adds breaks to a dimension, extension, and leader lines. • Click **Annotate > Dimensions > Break** on the ribbon. • Select the dimension to add a break. • Select the dimension or object intersecting the dimension selected in the previous step. It breaks the dimension by the intersecting object. • Right-click to exit the tool.
Inspect 	DIMINSPECT	It creates an inspection dimension. The inspection dimension describes how frequently the dimension should be checked during the inspection process to ensure the quality of the component. • Click **Annotate > Dimensions > Inspect** on the ribbon; the **Inspection Dimension** dialog appears.

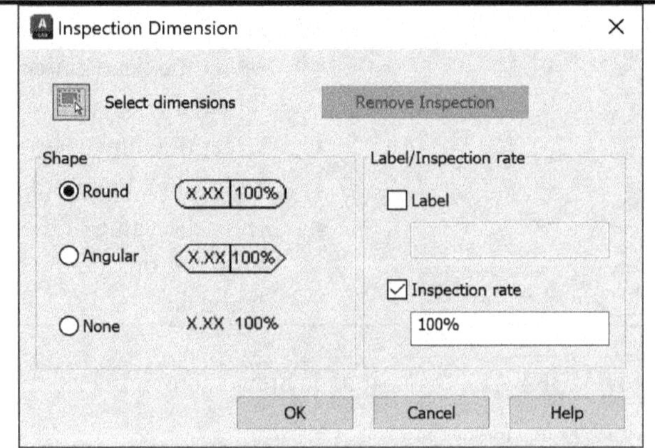

- Click the **Select dimensions** button on the dialog and select the dimension to apply the inspection rate.
- Right-click to accept.
- Select the shape of the inspection from the **Shape** section.
- Enter the **Inspection rate**. 100% means that the value will be checked every time during the inspection process. 50% means half the time.
- If required, select the **Label** checkbox and enter the inspection label.
- Click **OK**.

Example:

In this example, you will create the drawing, as shown in the figure, and add dimensions to it.

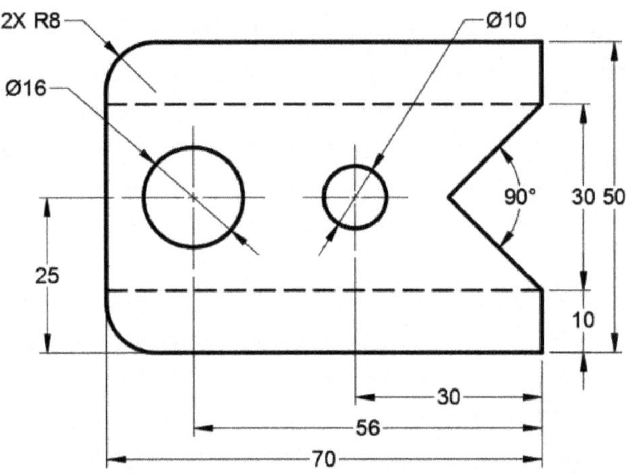

- Create four new layers with the following settings.

Layer	Lineweight	Linetype
Construction	0.00 mm	Continuous
Object	0.50 mm	Continuous
Hidden	0.30 mm	HIDDEN2
Dimensions	0.30 mm	Continuous

- Type LIMMAX and press ENTER.
- Type 100, 100, and press ENTER to set the maximum limit of the drawing.
- Click **Zoom All** on the **Navigation Bar**.
- Create the drawing on the **Object** and **Hidden** layers.

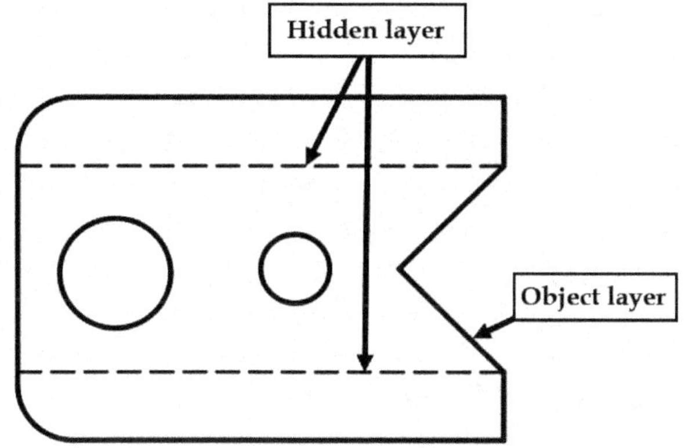

- Select the **Dimensions** layer from the **Layer** drop-down in the **Dimensions** panel.

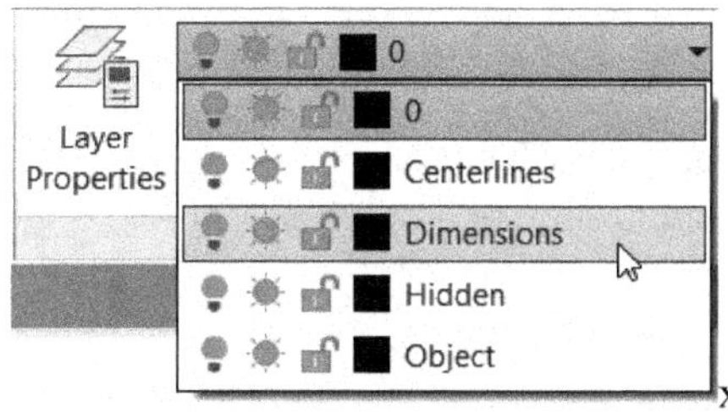

Creating a Dimension Style

The appearance of the dimensions depends on the dimension style that you use. You can create a new dimension style using the **Dimension Style Manager** dialog. In this dialog, you can specify various settings related to the appearance and behaviour of dimensions. The following example helps you to create a dimension style.

- Expand the **Annotation** panel on the **Home** ribbon tab and click **Dimension Style**.

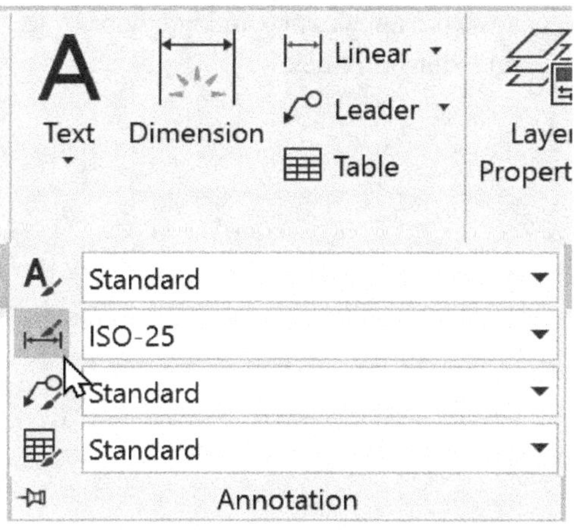

The **Dimension Style Manager** dialog appears.

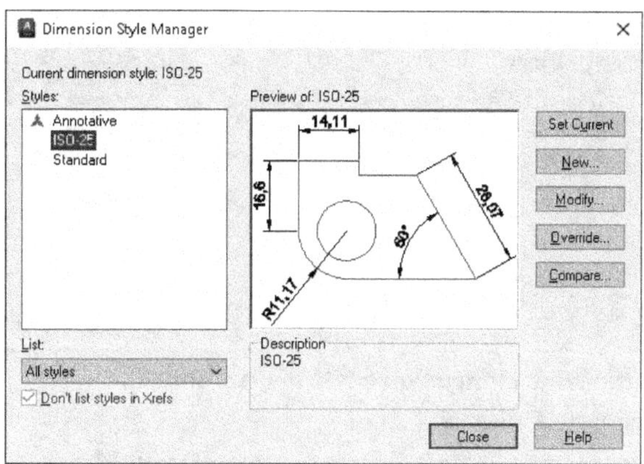

The basic nomenclature of dimensions is given below.

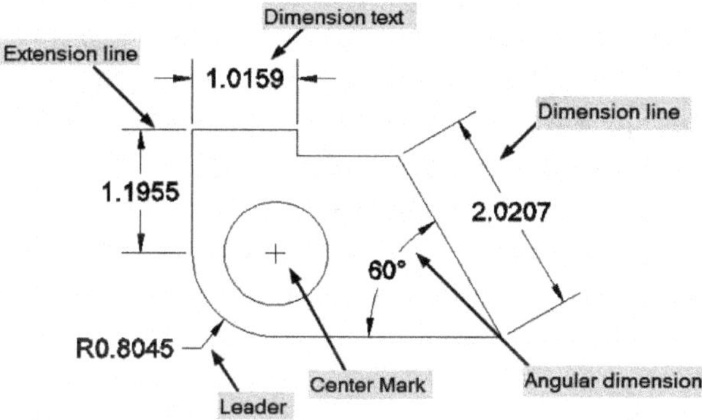

By default, the **ISO-25** or the **Standard** dimension style is active. If the default dimension style does not suit the dimensioning requirement, you can create a new dimension style and modify the nomenclature of the dimensions.

- To create a new dimension style, click the **New** button on the **Dimension Style Manager** dialog; the **Create New Dimension Style** dialog appears.
- In the **Create New Dimension Style** dialog, enter **Mechanical** in the **New Style Name**.
- Select **ISO-25** from the **Start With** drop-down and click **Continue**.

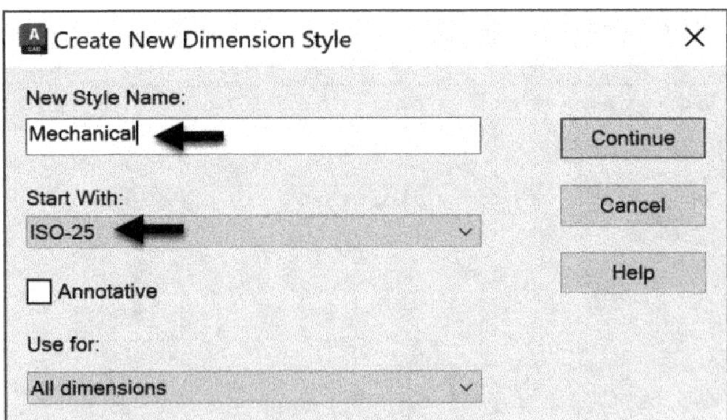

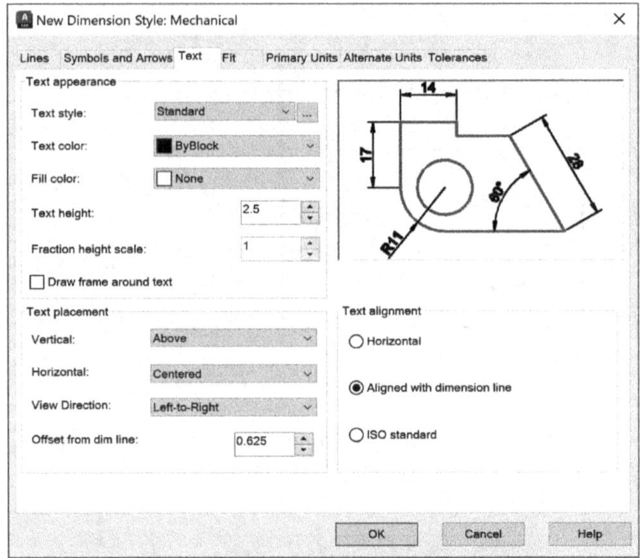

- In the **New Dimension Style** dialog, click the **Primary Units** tab.
- Ensure that the **Unit Format** is set to **Decimal**.
- Set **Precision** to **0**.
- Select **Decimal separator** > '**.**'(**Period**).

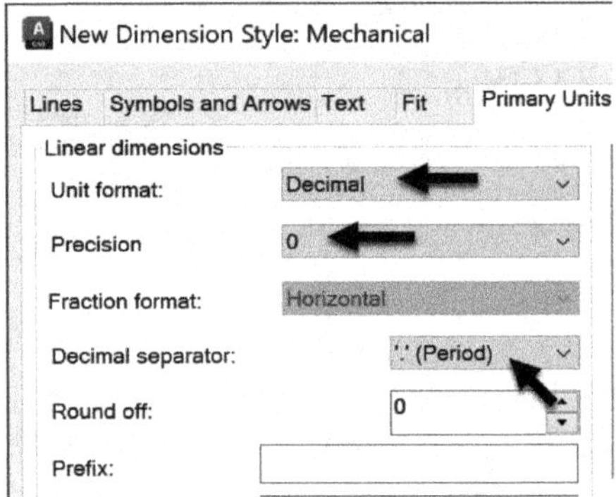

Study the other options in the **Primary Units** tab. Most of them are self-explanatory.
- Click the **Text** tab.
- Ensure that the **Text height** is set **2.5**.
- In the **Text placement** section, set the **Vertical** and **Horizontal** values to **Centered**.
- Select **Text alignment** > **Horizontal**.

Study the other options in the **Text** tab. These options let you change the appearance of the dimension text.

- Click the **Lines** tab on the dialog.
- In this tab, notice the two options in the **Extension lines** section: **Extend beyond dim lines** and **Offset from origin**.

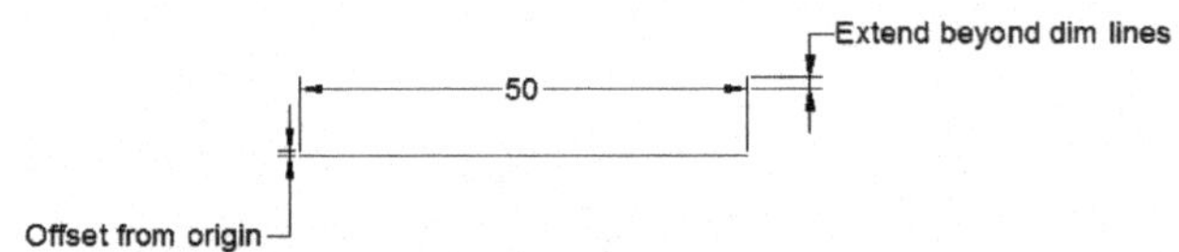

- Set **Extend beyond dim lines** and **Offset from origin** to **1.25**.
- Set the **Baseline spacing** in the **Dimension lines** section to **5**.

Study the different options in this tab. The options in this tab are used to change the appearance and behavior of the dimension lines and extension lines.

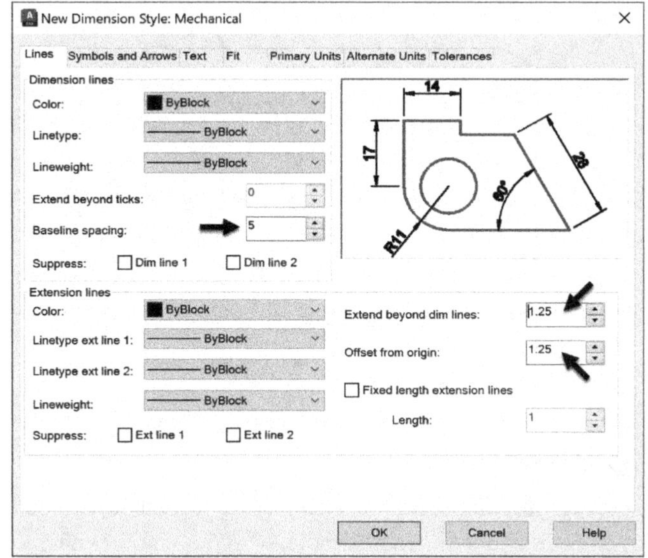

- Click the **Symbols and Arrows** tab, and then set **Arrow size** and **Center Marks** to 3.
- Select the **Line** option in the **Center marks** section.

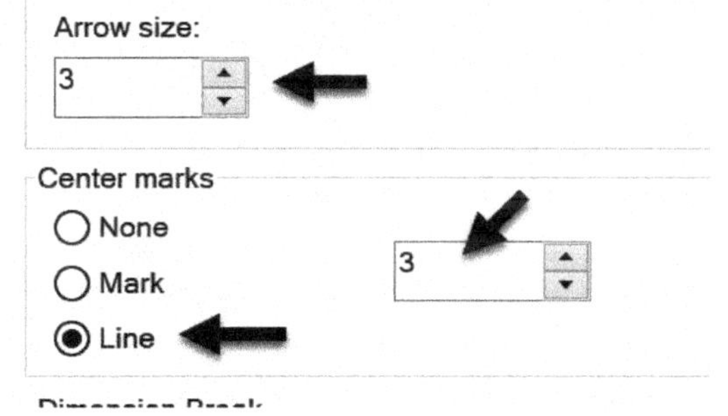

Notice the different options in this tab. The options in this tab are used to change the appearance of the arrows and symbols. Also, you can set the appearance of the center marks and centerlines of circles and arcs.

- Click **OK** to accept the settings.
- Click **Set Current** on the **Dimension Style Manager** dialog; the **Mechanical** dimension style will be set as current.
- Click **Close** to close the dialog.
- On the **Annotate** tab of the ribbon, click **Centerlines > Center Mark** .
- Select the circles from the drawing to apply the center mark to them.

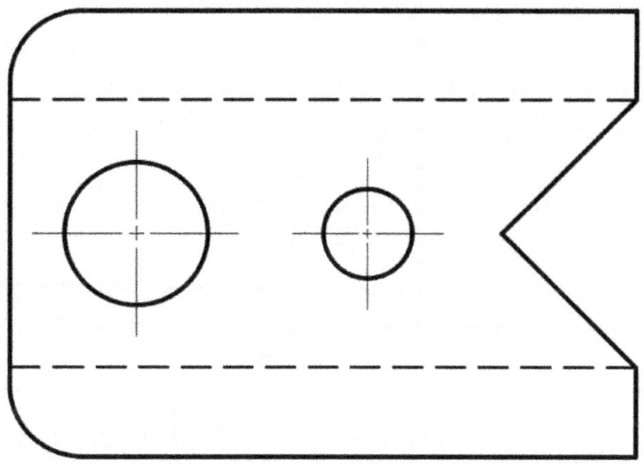

- On the ribbon, click **Annotate > Dimensions > Dimension**  .
- Make sure that the **Object Snap** icon is turned on the status bar.
- Select the lower right corner of the drawing.
- Select the endpoint of the center mark of the small circle; the dimension is attached to the pointer.
- Move the pointer vertically downwards and position the dimension, as shown below.

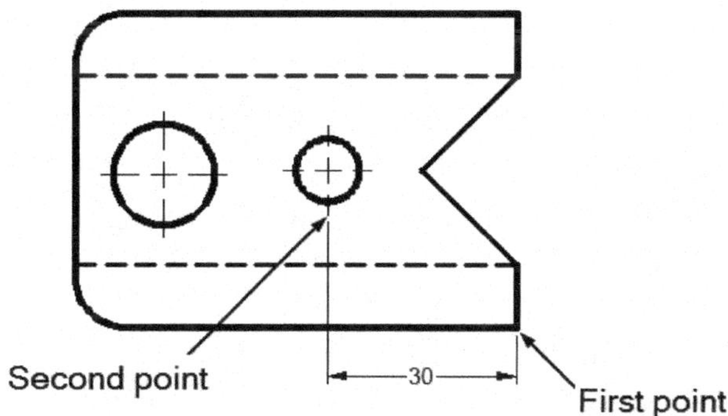

- Select the **Baseline** option from the command line.
- Select the right extension line of the linear dimension; a dimension is attached to the pointer.
- Select the endpoint of the center mark of the large circle; another dimension is attached to the pointer.
- Select the lower-left corner of the drawing.
- Press ENTER twice.

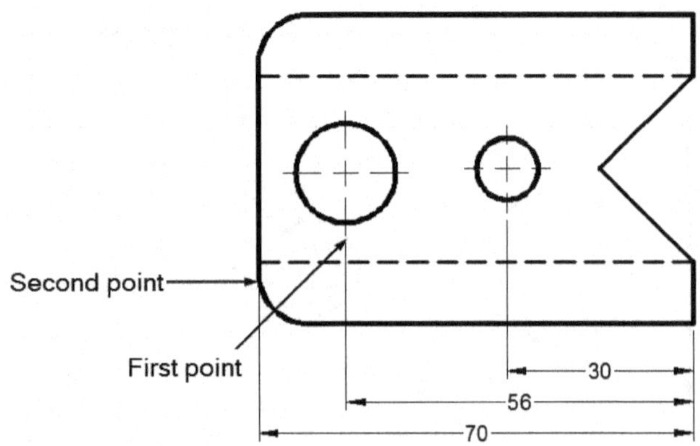

- Select the **Angular** option from the command line.
- Select the two angled lines of the drawing and position the angle dimension.

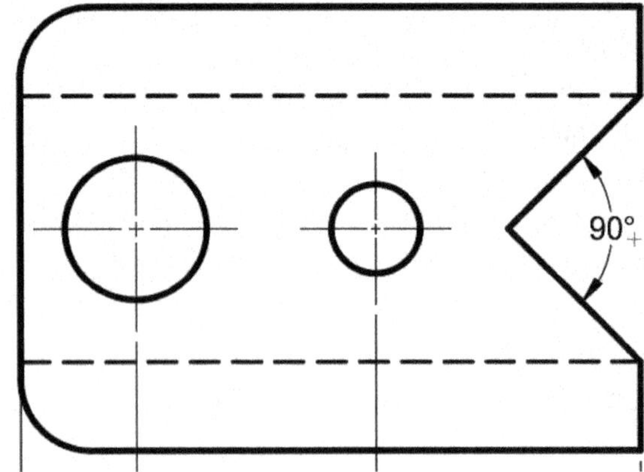

- Select the large circle and position the diameter dimension.
- Likewise, select the small circle and position the dimension.
- Press ENTER twice.
- Select the fillet located at the top left corner.
- Right-click and select **Radius**; the radial dimension is attached to the pointer.
- Select **Mtext** from the command line and type **2X** and press SPACEBAR.
- Click in the graphics window to update the dimension text.
- Next, position the radial dimension approximately at 45 degrees.
- Likewise, apply the other dimensions, as shown.
- Save and close the drawing.

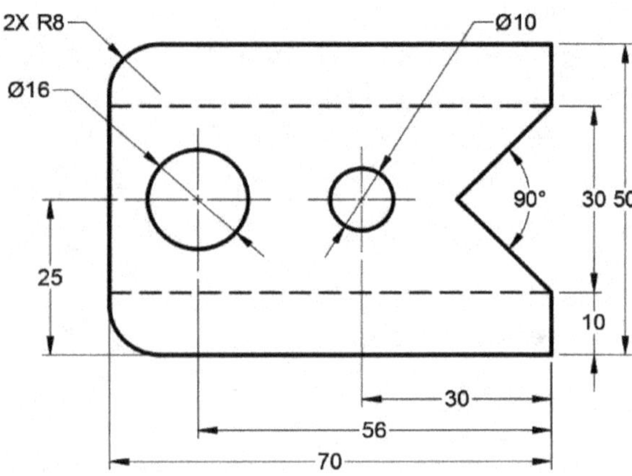

Adding Leaders

A leader is a thin solid line terminating with an arrowhead at one end and a dimension, note, or symbol at the other end. In the following example, you will learn to create a leader style and then create a leader.

Example 1:

- Draw a square of 24 mm side length.
- Create a circle of 10.11 mm diameter at the center of the square.

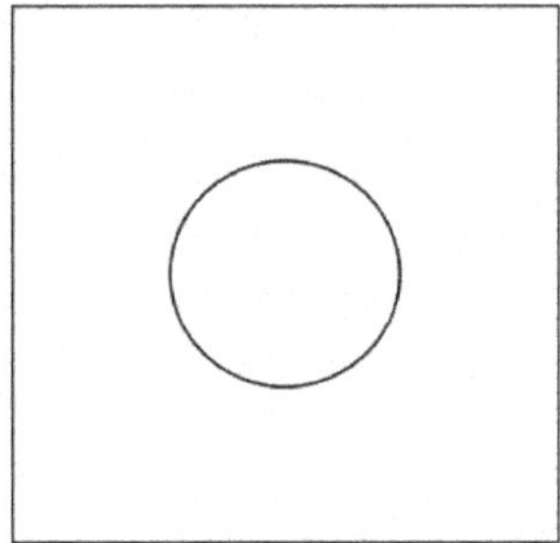

- Click **Home > Draw > Arc > Center, Start, Angle** on the ribbon.
- Select the center point of the circle.
- Move the pointer horizontally toward the right.
- Type 6 as the radius and press ENTER.
- Move the pointer vertically downward and click.

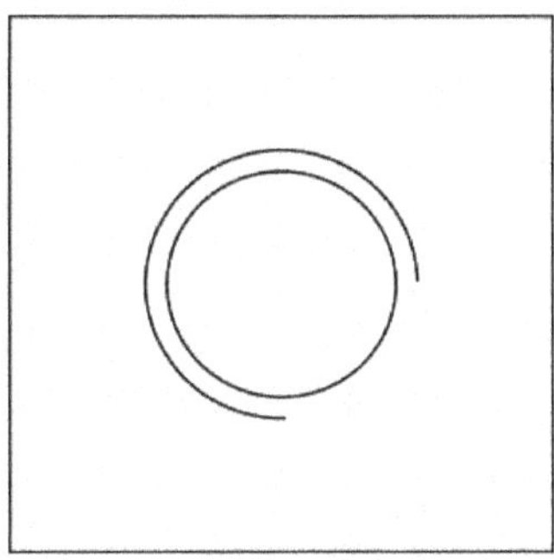

- On the **Home** tab of the ribbon, expand **Annotation** panel and click the **Multileader Style** icon; the **Multileader Style Manager** appears.

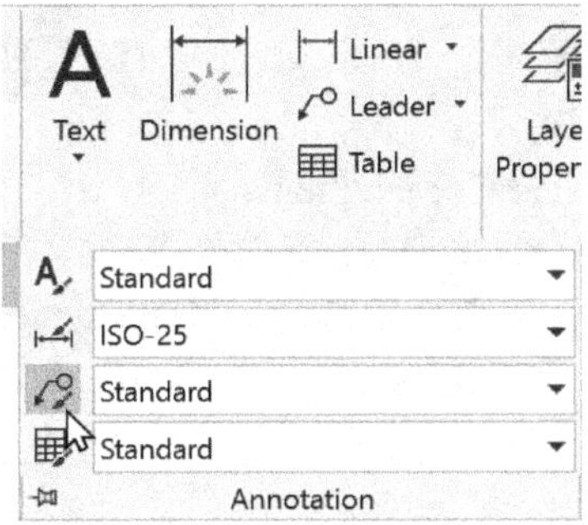

- In the **Multileader Style Manager** dialog, click the **New** button; the **Create New Multileader Style** dialog appears.

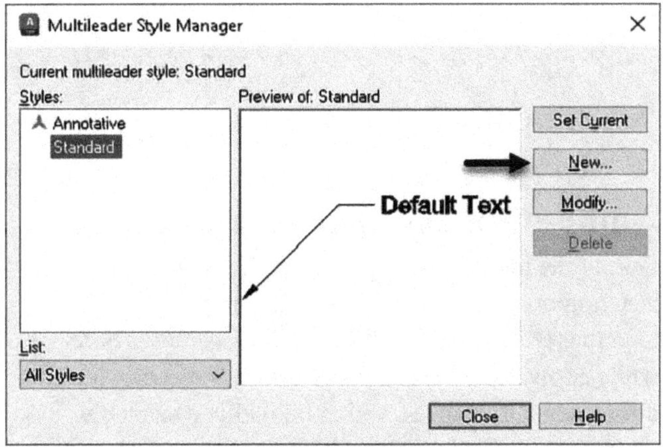

- In the **Create New Multileader Style** dialog, enter **Hole callout** in the **New style name** box and select **Standard** from the **Start with** drop-down.

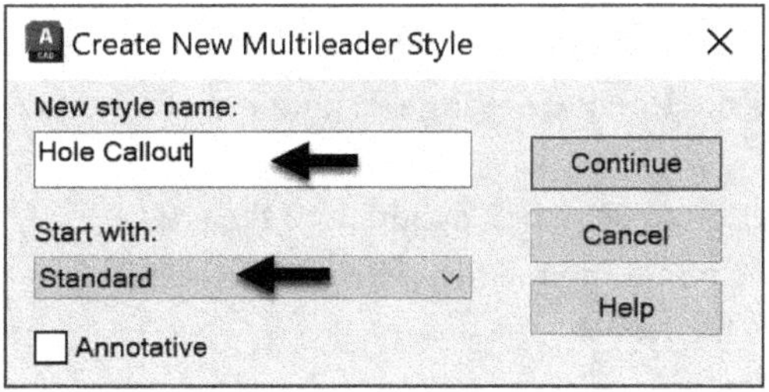

- Click **Continue**; the **Modify Multileader Style** dialog appears.
- Click the **Leader Format** tab and set the **Arrowhead Size** to **2.5**.

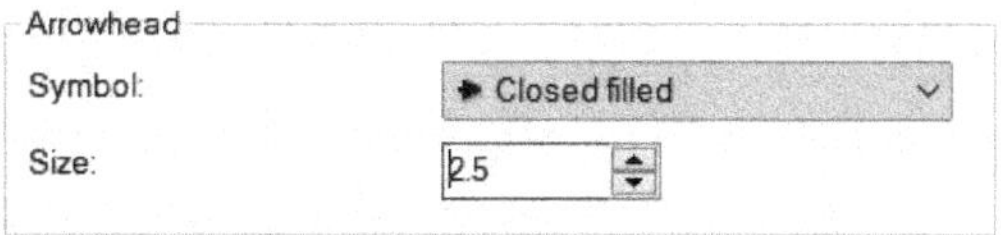

Also, notice the other options in this tab. They are used to set the appearance of the multileader lines and the arrowhead.

- Click the **Leader Structure** tab and set the **Landing distance** to **5**.

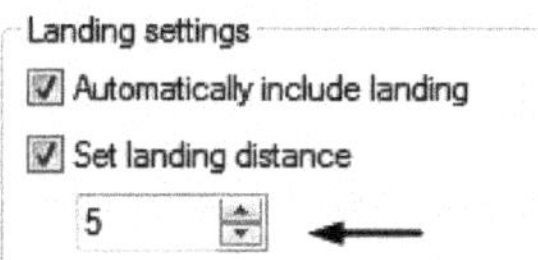

- Click the **Content** tab and set the **Text height** to **2.5**.

The other options in this tab are used to define the appearance of the text or block that will be attached at the end of the leader line.

- Click **OK** on the **Modify Multileader Style** dialog.
- Click **Set Current** on the **Multileader Style Manager** dialog.
- Click **Close** to close the dialog.
- Click **Annotate > Leaders > Multileader** on the ribbon.

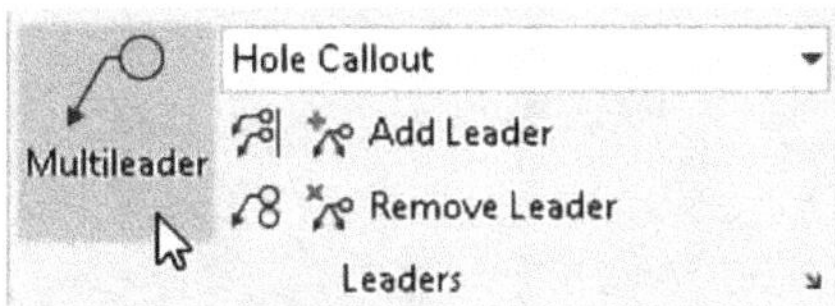

- Click the down arrow next to the **Polar tracking**

button on the status bar and select **45** from the menu.

- Activate the **Polar tracking** button on the status bar.
- Select a point in the first quadrant of the arc.
- Move the pointer in the top-right direction and click to create the leader.

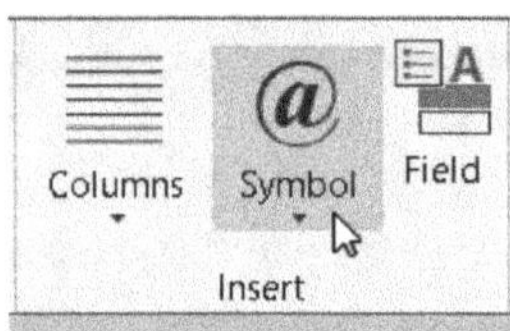

- Type **M12x1.75 – 6H 16** in the text editor.
  Next, you must insert the depth symbol before 16.
- Position the pointer before 16 and click the **Symbol** button on the **Insert** panel of the **Text Editor** ribbon; a menu appears.

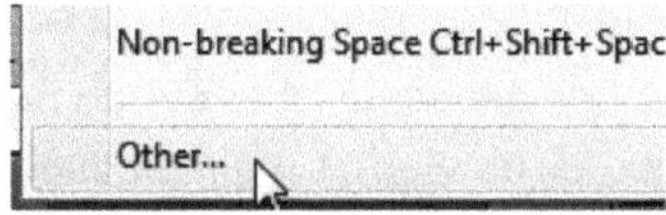

- Click **Other** on the menu; the **Character Map** dialog appears.

- In the **Character Map** dialog, select **GDT** from the **Font** drop-down.
- Select the Depth symbol from the fonts table.

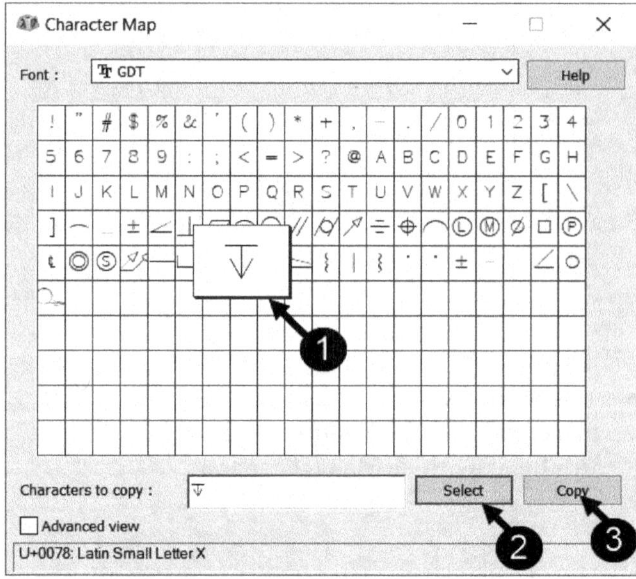

- Click **Select** and **Copy** buttons.
- Close the **Character Map** dialog.
- Right-click and select **Paste**; the depth symbol is pasted in the text editor.
- Adjust the spacing so that the complete text is in one line.
- Click in the graphics window.

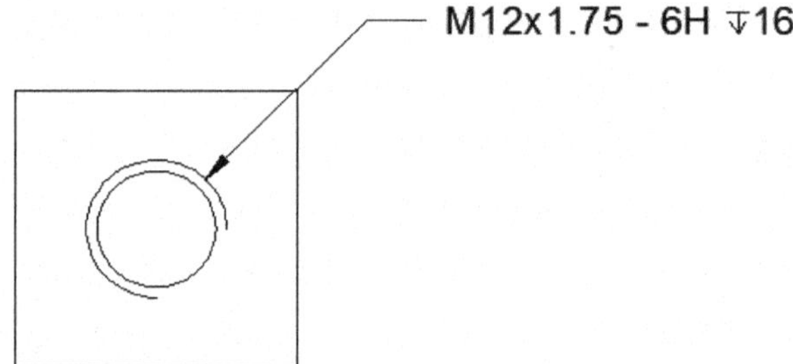

Adding Dimensional Tolerances

During the manufacturing process, the accuracy of a part is an important factor. However, it is impossible to manufacture a part with the exact dimensions. Therefore, while applying dimensions to a drawing, we provide some dimensional tolerances, which lie within acceptable limits. The following example shows you to add dimension tolerances in AutoCAD.

Example:

- Create the drawing, as shown below. Do not add dimensions to it.

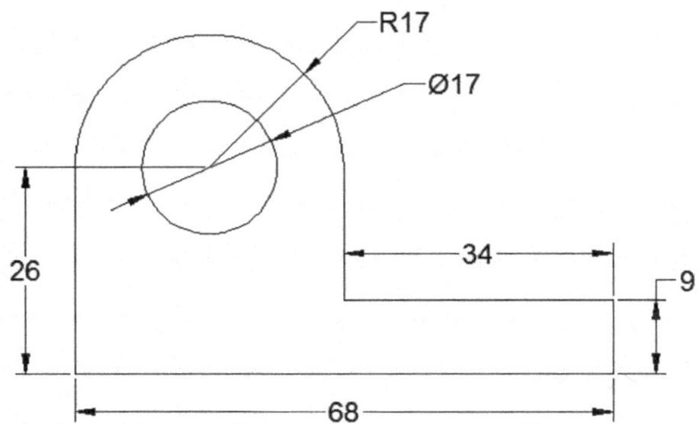

- Create a new dimension style with the name **Tolerances**.
- In the **New Dimension Styles** dialog, click the **Tolerances** tab.
- In the **Tolerances** tab, set the **Method** as **Deviation**.
- Set **Precision** as **0.00**.
- Set the **Upper Value** and **Lower Value** to **0.05**.
- Set the **Vertical position** as **Middle**.
- Specify the following settings in the **Primary Units**, **Text**, and **Symbols and Arrows** tab:

> The **Primary Units** tab:
> *Unit format: Decimal*
> *Precision: 0.00*
> *Decimal Separator: '.' Period*
>
> The **Text** tab:
> *Text Height: 2.5*
> *Text placement:*
> > *Vertical: Centered*
> > *Horizontal: Centered*
> *Text alignment: Horizontal*
>
> The **Symbols and Arrows** tab:
> *Arrow Size: 2.5*
> *Center Marks: Line*

- Click **OK** on the **New Dimension Styles** dialog.
- Click **Set Current** and **Close** on the **Dimension Style Manager** dialog.
- Apply dimensions to the drawing.

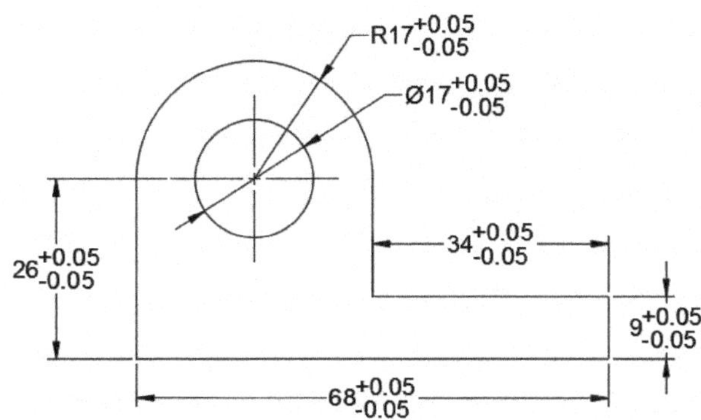

Geometric Dimensioning and Tolerancing

Earlier, you have learned how to apply tolerance to the size (dimensions) of a component. However, the dimensional tolerances are not sufficient for manufacturing a component. You must give tolerance values to its shape, orientation, and position as well. The following figure shows a note which is used to explain the tolerance value given to the shape of the object.

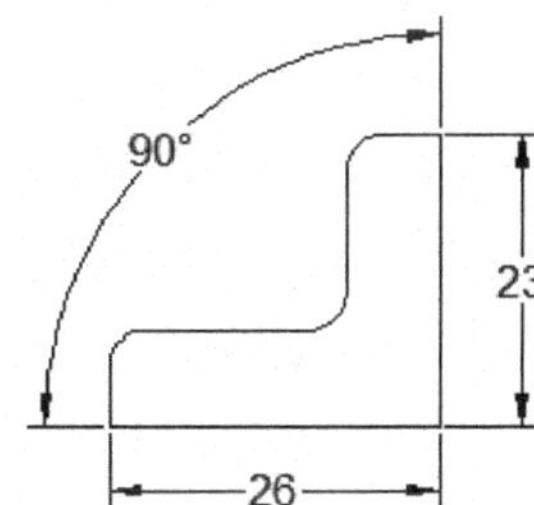

Providing a note in a drawing may be confusing. To avoid this, we use Geometric Dimensioning and Tolerancing (GD&T) symbols to specify the tolerance values to shape, orientation, and position of a component. The following figure shows the same example represented by using the GD&T symbols. In this figure, the vertical face to which the tolerance frame is connected must be within two parallel planes 0.08 apart and perpendicular to the datum reference (horizontal plane).

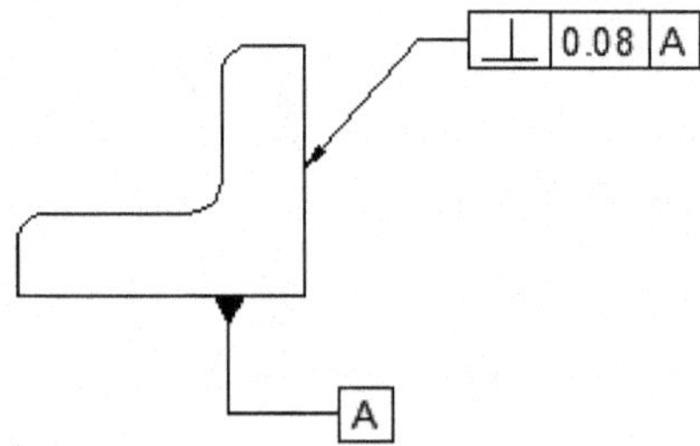

The Geometric Tolerancing symbols that can be used to interpret the geometric conditions are given in the table below.

Purpose		Symbol
To represent the shape of a single feature.	Straightness	—
	Flatness	▱
	Cylindricity	⌭
	Circularity	○
	Profile of a surface	⌓
	Profile of a line	⌒
To represent the orientation of a feature with respect to another feature.	Parallelism	//
	Perpendicularity	⊥
	Angularity	∠
To represent the position of a feature with respect to another feature.	Position	⌖

	Concentricity and coaxiality	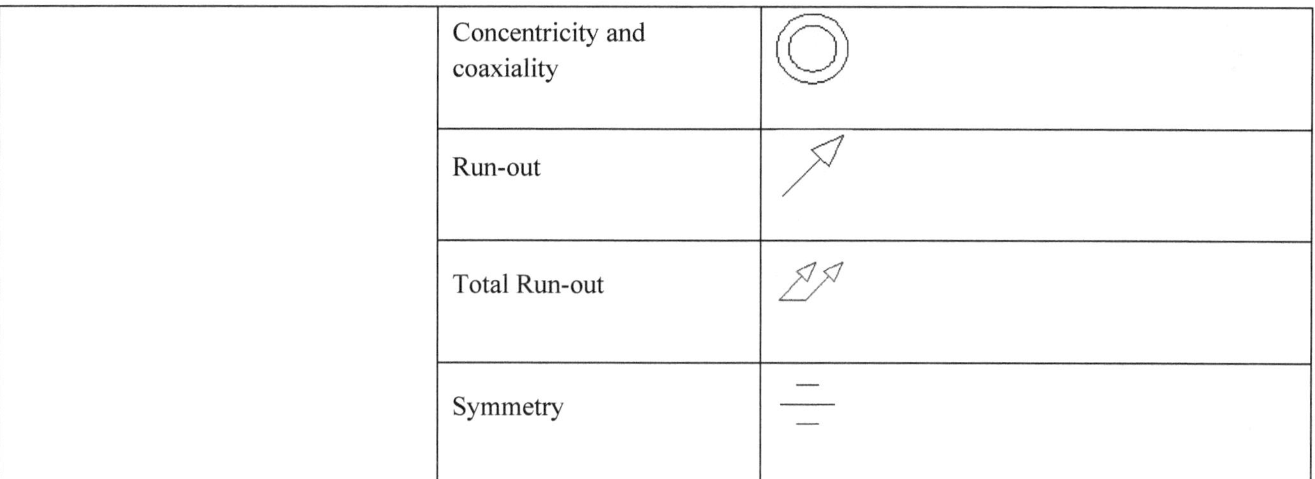
	Run-out	
	Total Run-out	
	Symmetry	

Example 1:

In this example, you will apply geometric tolerances to the drawing shown below.

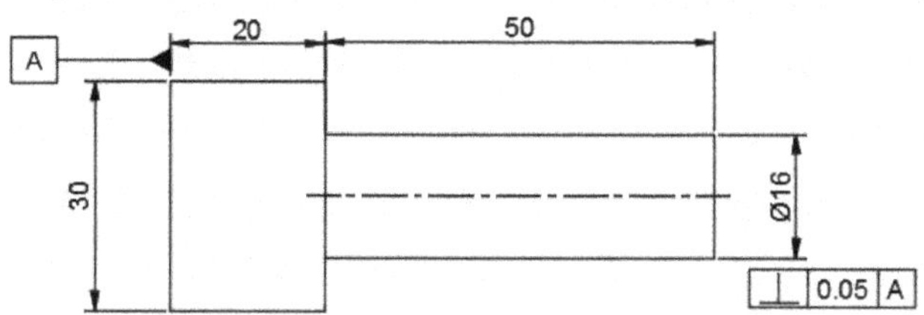

- Create the drawing, as shown below.

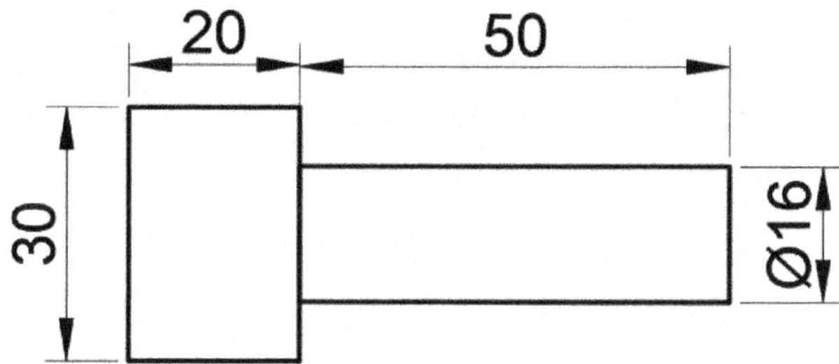

- Click **Annotate > Dimensions > Tolerance** on the ribbon; the **Geometric Tolerance** dialog appears.

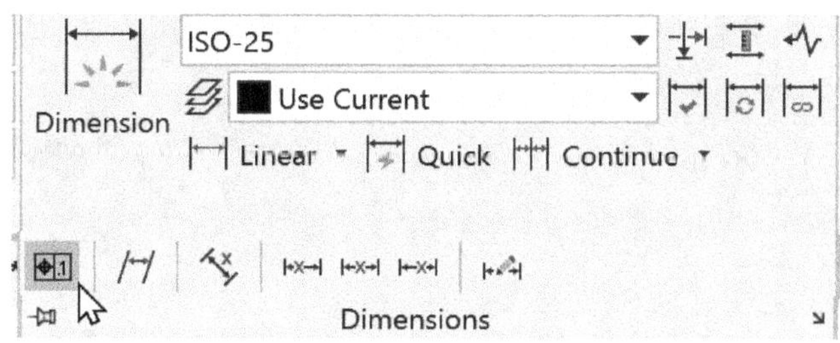

- In the **Geometric Tolerance** dialog, click the upper box of the **Sym** group. The **Symbol** dialog appears.

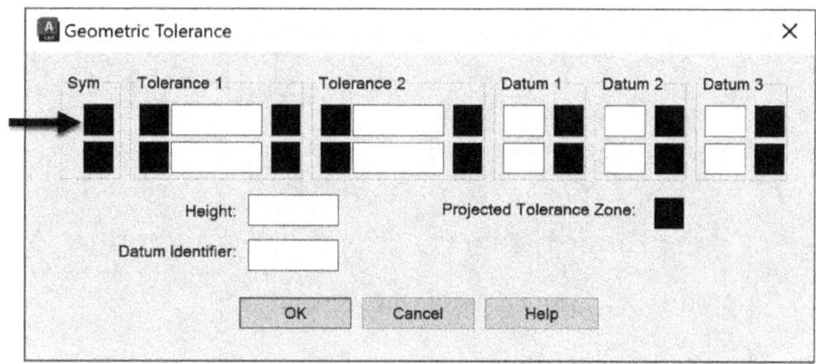

- In the **Symbol** dialog, click the **Perpendicularity** symbol. The symbol appears in the **Sym** group.

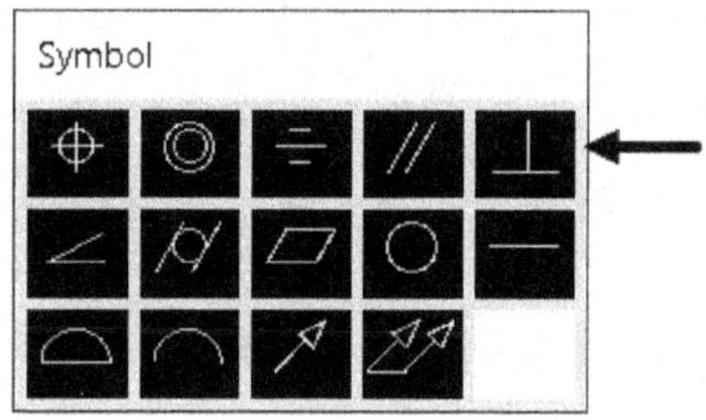

- Click in the top left box in the **Tolerance 1** group. The diameter symbol appears in the box.
- Enter **.05** in the box next to the diameter symbol.

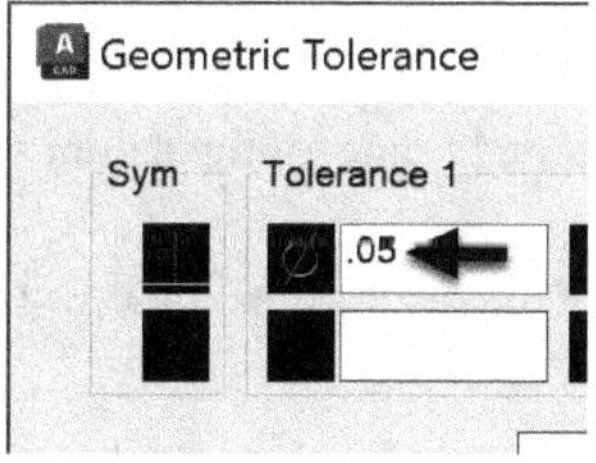

- Enter **A** in the upper box of the **Datum 1** group.

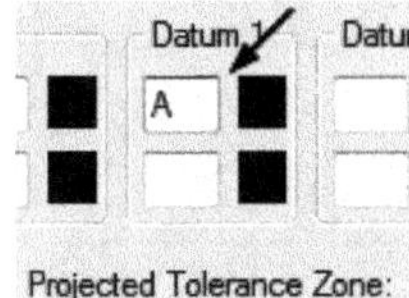

- Click **OK** and position the **Feature Control frame**, as shown below.

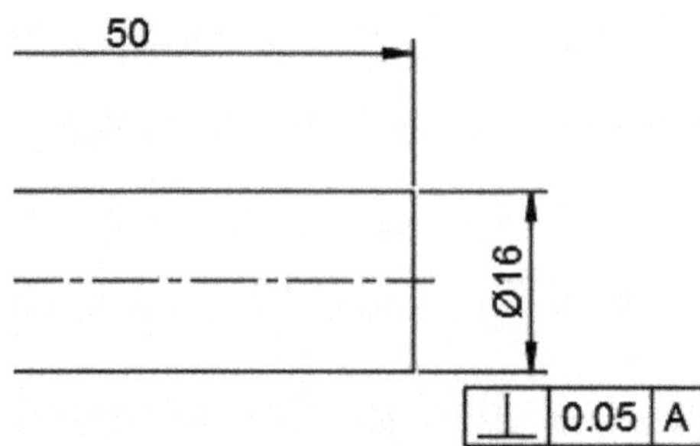

Next, you must add the datum reference.

- On the **Home** ribbon tab, expand the **Annotation** panel and click **Multileader Style** .
- Click the **New** button.
- On the **Create New Multileader Style** dialog, type **Tolerance** in the **New Style name** box, and click **Continue**.
- Click the **Leader Format** tab and select **Arrowhead > Symbol > Datum triangle filled**.
- Set the **Size** to 2.5.
- On the **Leader Structure** tab, set **Maximum leader points** to **2**.
- Click the **Content** tab and select **Multileader type > Block**.
- Select **Source block > Box**.
- Set the **Scale** value to 0.75.
- Click **OK**, **Set Current**, and **Close**.
- On the **Home** ribbon tab, click **Annotation > Leader** .
- Specify the first and second points of the datum reference, as shown.
- On the **Edit Attributes** dialog, type **A** in the **Enter tag number** box.
- Click **OK**.

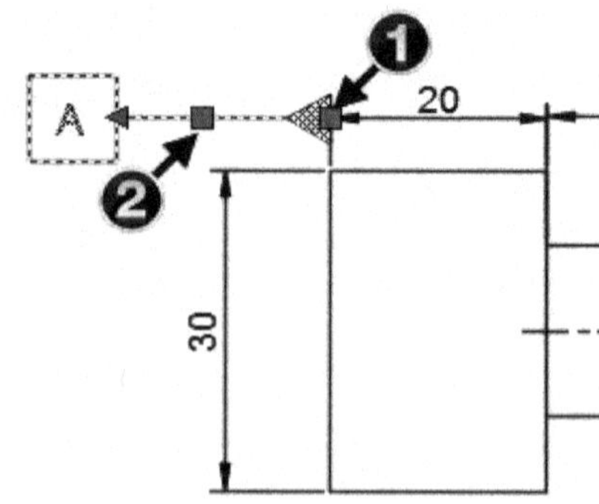

Editing Dimensions by Stretching

In AutoCAD, the dimensions are associated with the drawing. If you modify a drawing, the dimensions will be modified automatically. In the following example, you will stretch the drawing to modify the dimensions.

Example:

- Create the drawing, as shown below, and apply dimensions to it.

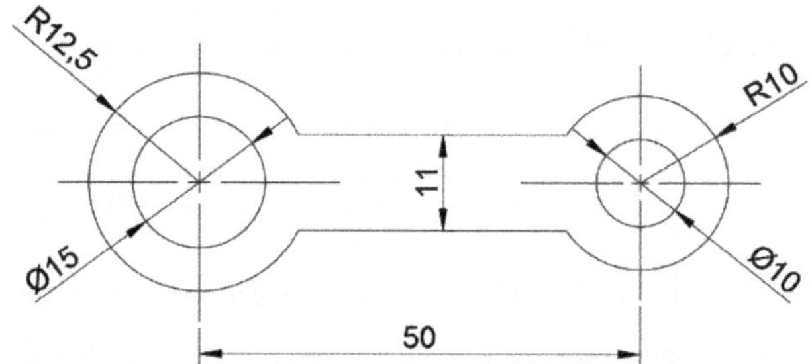

- Click **Home > Modify > Stretch** on the ribbon.
- Drag a window and select the right-side circles and the horizontal lines.

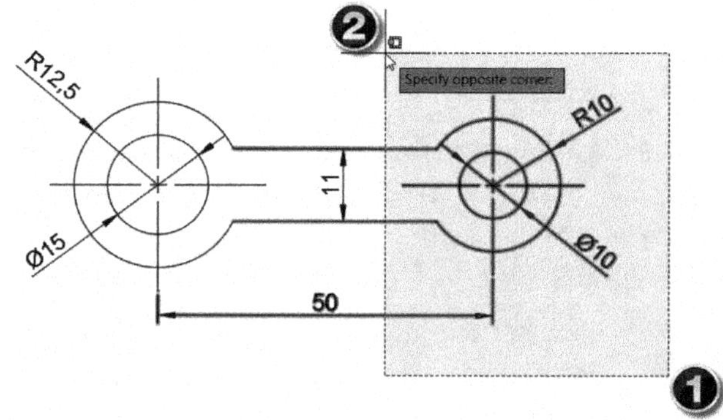

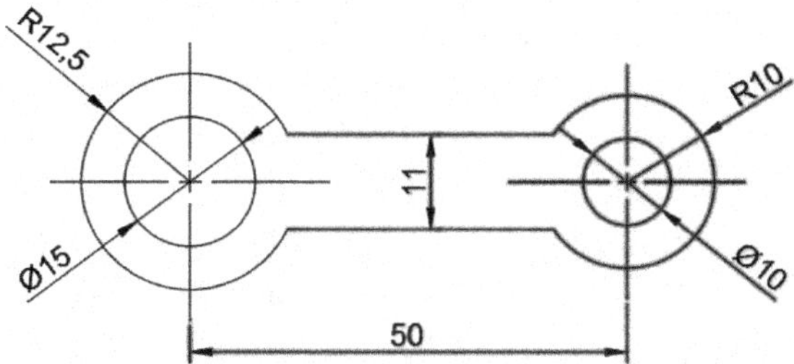

- Right-click and select the center point of the right-side circles.
- Move the pointer to stretch the drawing; you will notice that the horizontal dimension also changes.
- Type **30** and press ENTER; the horizontal dimension is updated to 80.

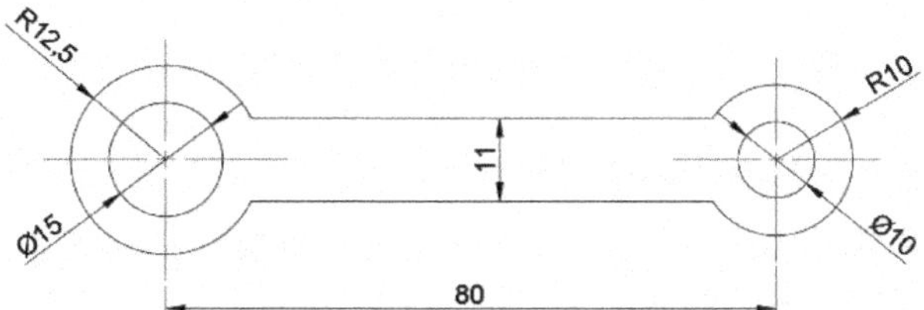

Modifying Dimensions by Trimming and Extending

In earlier chapters, you have learned to modify drawings by trimming and extending objects. In the same way, you can modify dimensions by trimming and extending. The following example shows you to modify dimensions by this method.

Example:

- Create a drawing, as shown below, and add dimensions to it.

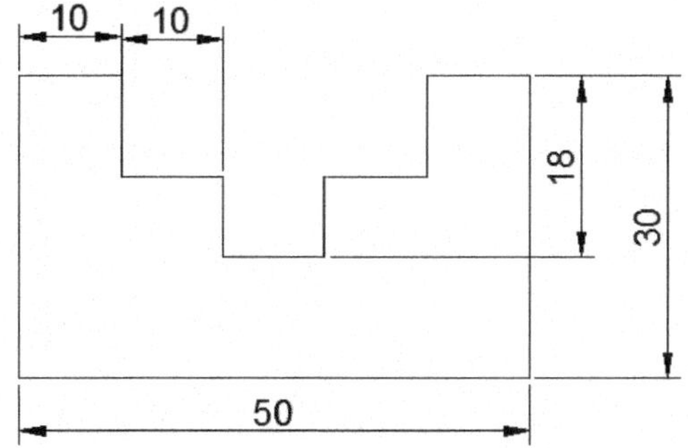

- Click **Home > Modify > Trim** on the ribbon.
- Select the **cuTting edges** option from the command line and press ENTER.

- Select the horizontal edge, as shown in the figure, to define the cutting edge.
- Right-click to accept.

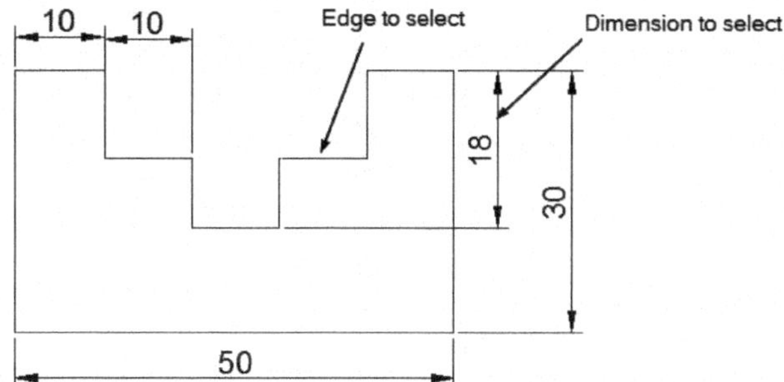

- Select the vertical dimension with the value 18. It trims the dimension up to the selected edge.

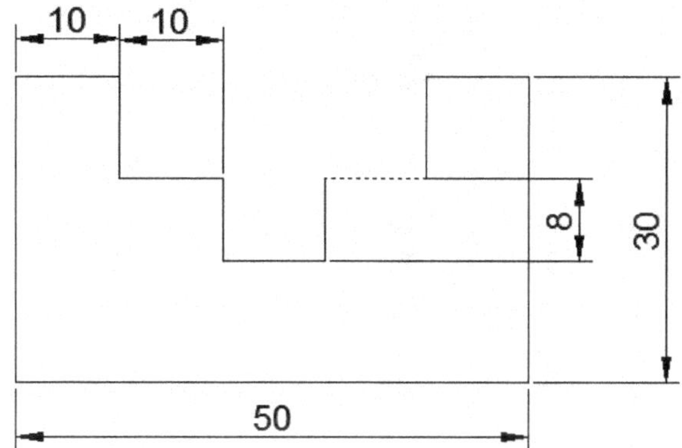

- Press ESC.
- Click **Home > Modify > Trim > Extend** on the ribbon.
- Select **Boundary edges** option from the command line and press ENTER.
- Select the vertical edge as the boundary, as shown below. Next, right-click to accept.

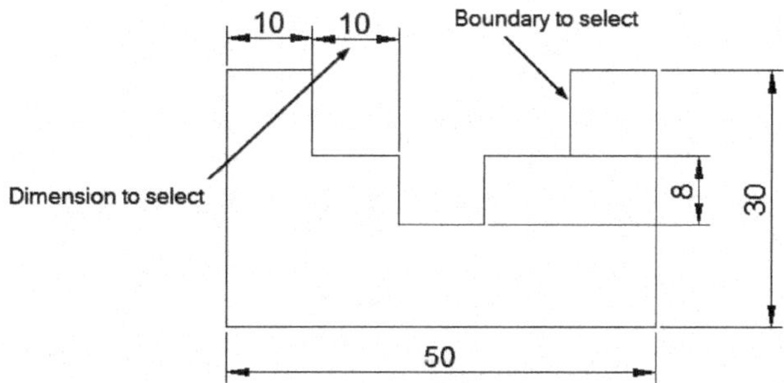

- Select the horizontal dimension with the value 10. It will extend the dimension up to the selected boundary.
- Press Esc.

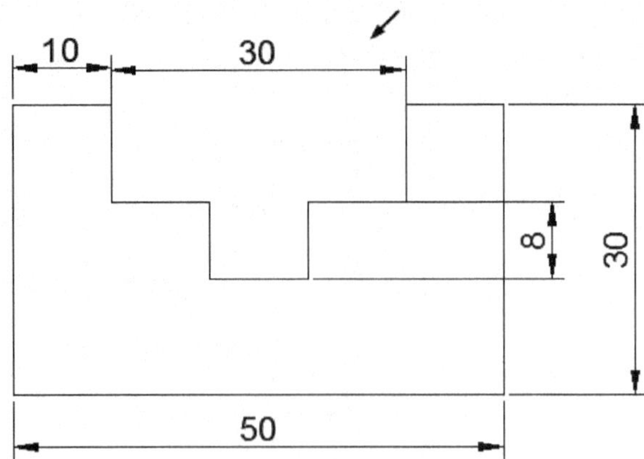

Using the DIMEDIT command

The **DIMEDIT** command can be used to modify dimensions. Using this command, you can add text to a dimension, rotate the dimension text and extension lines, or reset the position of the dimension text.

Example 1: (Adding Text to the dimension)

- Type **DED** in the command line and press ENTER.
- Select the **New** option from the command line; a text box appears.
- Enter **TYP** in the text box and press the SPACEBAR.

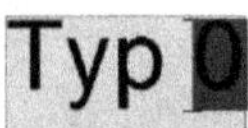

- Left-click and select the dimension with value 10.

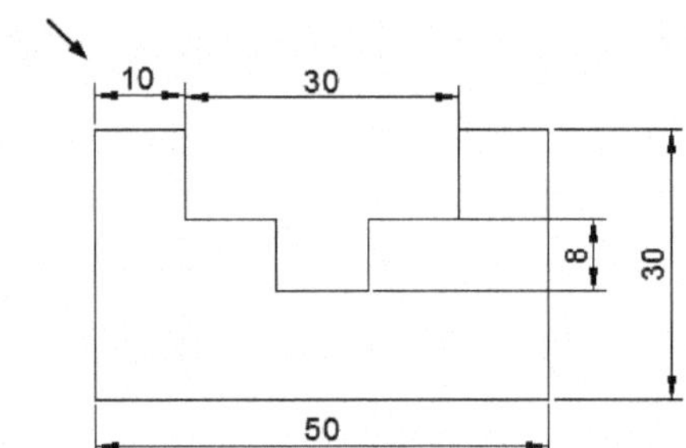

- Press ENTER; the dimension text will be changed.

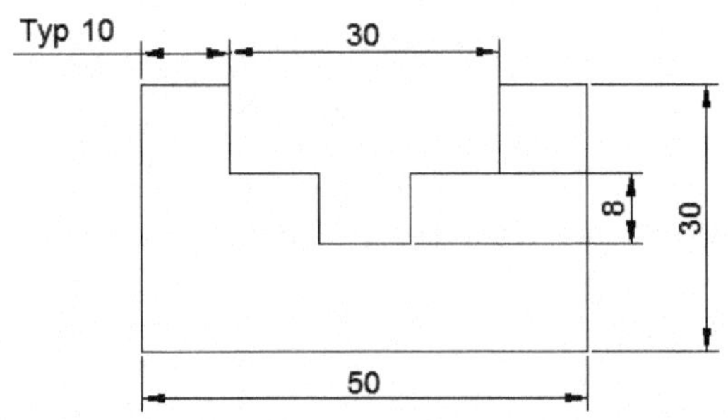

Example 2: (Rotating the dimension text)

- Enter **DED** in the command line and select the **Rotate** option; the message, "Specify angle for dimension text," appears in the command line.
- Type **30** and press ENTER.
- Select the dimension with the value 50 and right-click. The angle of the dimension text is changed to 30 degrees. Note that the angle is measured from the horizontal axis (X-axis).

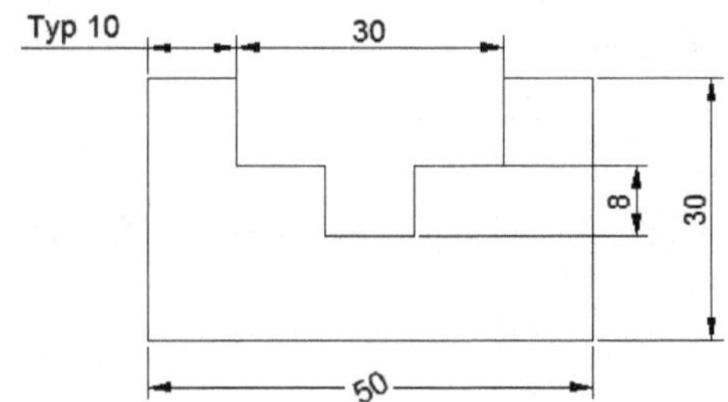

Using the Update tool

The **Update** tool is used to update a dimension with the currently active dimension style. For example, if you have created a new dimension style, you can apply it to an already existing dimension using the **Update** tool. The following example shows you to update a dimension.

- Type **D** in the command line and press ENTER; the **Dimension Style Manager** dialog appears.
- In the **Dimension Style Manager** dialog, select **Standard** from the **Styles** list and click **Modify**.
- In the **Modify Dimension Style** dialog, click the **Text** tab, and then set the **Text height** to **2.5**.
- Click the **Text Style** button; the **Text Style** dialog appears.

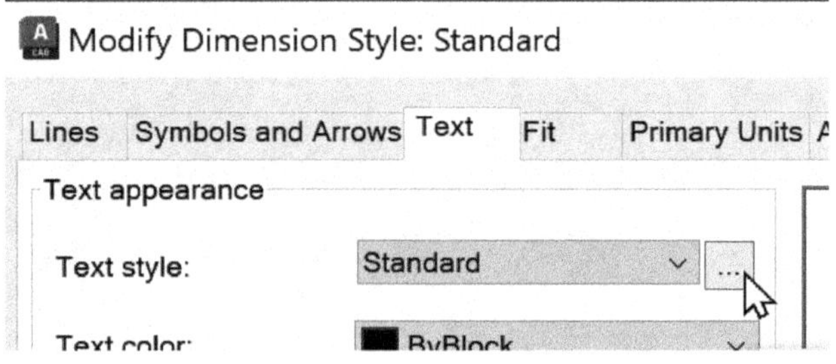

- In the **Text Style** dialog, change the **Font Style** to **Italic**.
- Click **Apply** and close the **Text Style** dialog.
- Click **OK** on the **Modify Dimension Style** dialog.

- Click **Close** on the **Dimension Style Manager** dialog.
- In the **Dimensions** panel, set the dimension style to **Standard**.

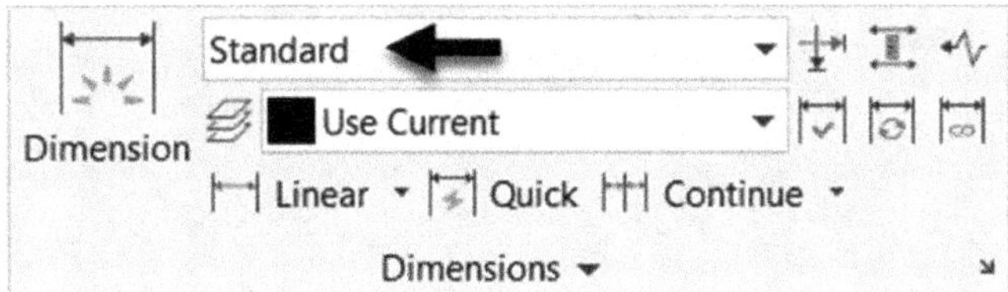

- Click the **Update** button on the **Dimensions** panel.

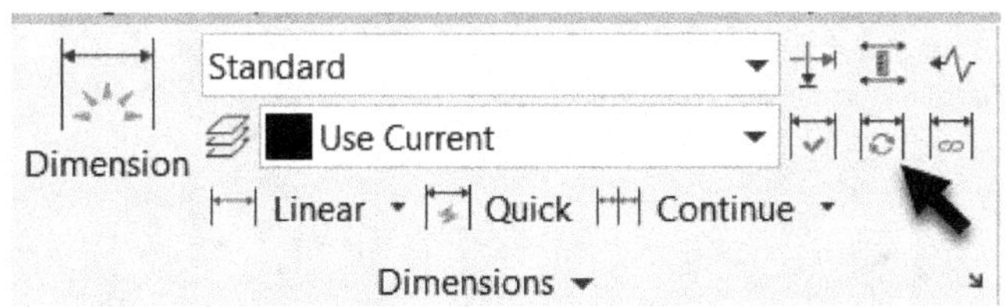

- Select the horizontal dimension with the value 30. Next, right-click; the dimension will be updated with the current dimension style.

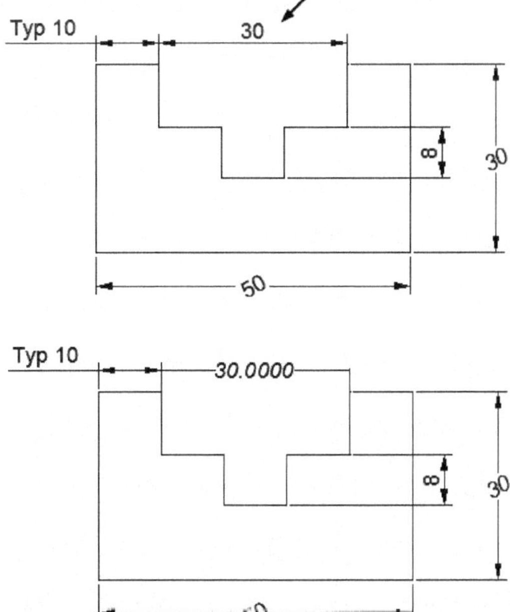

Using the Oblique tool

The **Oblique** tool is used to incline the extension lines of a dimension. This tool is very useful while dimensioning the isometric drawings. It can also be used in 2D drawings when the dimensions overlap with each other.

Example:

In this example, you will create an isometric drawing and add dimensions to it. Next, you will use the **Oblique** tool to change the angle of the dimension lines.

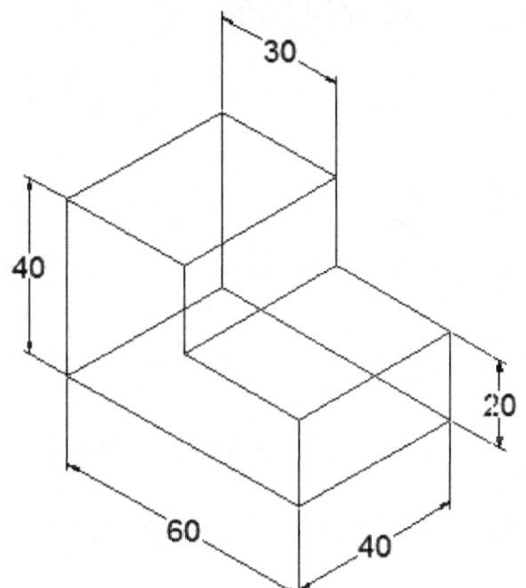

- Type-in **DS** in the command line, and then press Enter.
- On the **Drafting Settings** dialog, click the **Snap and Grid** tab.
- In the **Drafting Settings** dialog, set **Snap type** to **Isometric snap** and click **OK**.

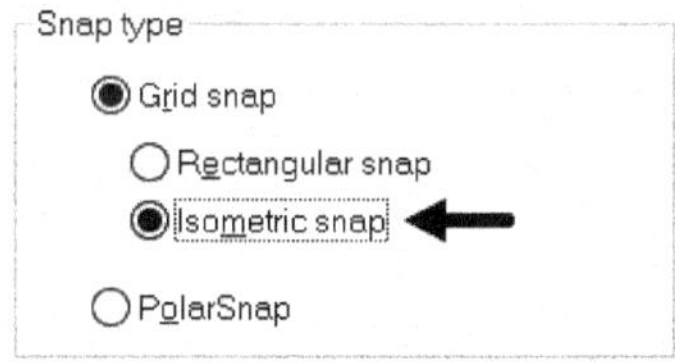

- Turn on the **Snap Mode** and the **Ortho Mode**. Also, turn on the **Dynamic Input**.
- Click **Zoom All** on the Navigation Bar.
- Type **L** in the command line and press ENTER.
- Click at a random point and move the pointer vertically.
- Type 40 in the command line and press ENTER; a vertical line will be created.
- Move the pointer toward the right; you will notice that an inclined line is attached to the pointer.

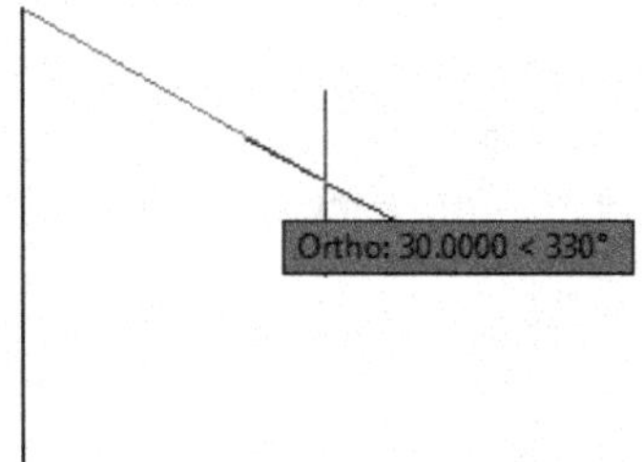

- Type 30 and press ENTER; an inclined line is drawn.
- Move the pointer downward.
- Type 20 and press ENTER.

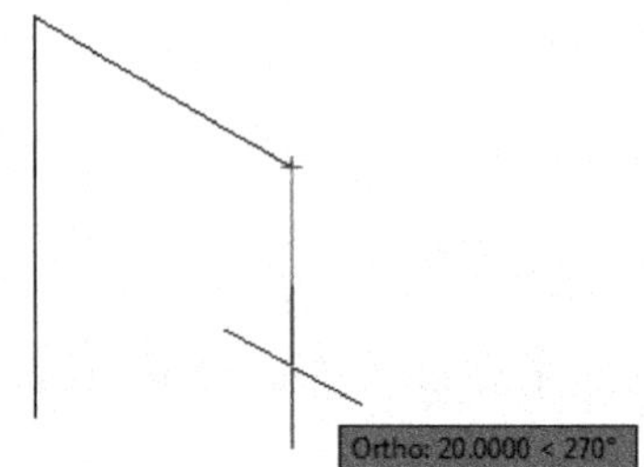

- Move the pointer toward the right.
- Type 30 and press ENTER.
- Move the pointer downward, type 20, and then press ENTER.
- Move the pointer toward the left and click on the start point of the sketch.
- Right-click select **Enter**.

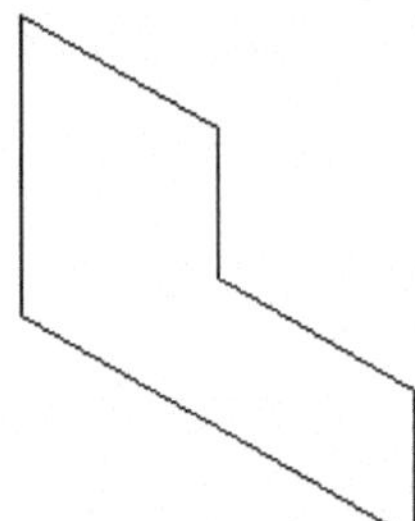

- Turn off the **Ortho Mode**.
- Click the down-arrow next to the **Polar Tracking (F10)** icon on the Status bar, and then select **30** from the flyout.
- Create a selection window and select all the objects of the sketch.
- Right-click and select **Copy-Selection** from the shortcut menu.
- Select the lower-left corner point as the base point.

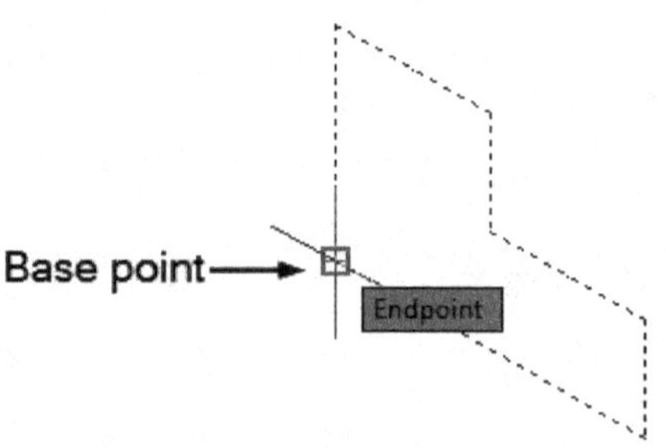

- Move the pointer in the direction perpendicular to the drawing; the track line is displayed.
- Move the pointer along the track line.

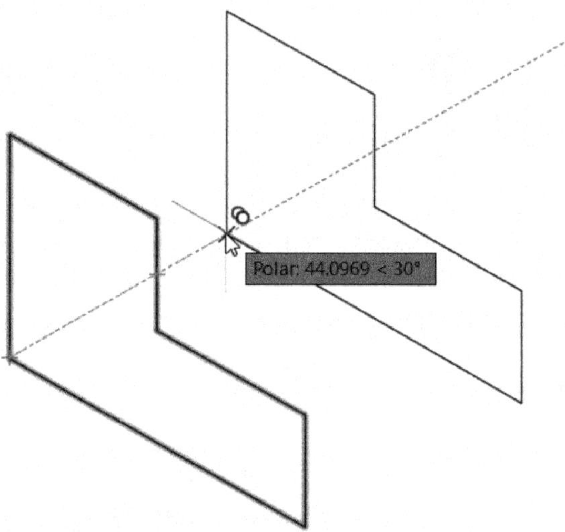

- Type 40 and press ENTER.
- Right-click and select **Enter**.

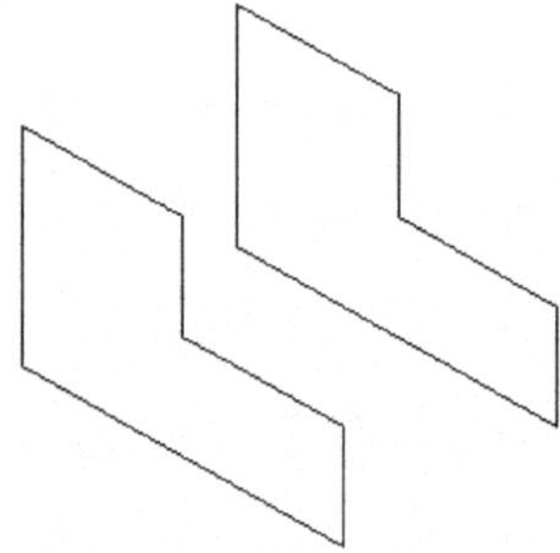

- Use the **Line** tool and connect the endpoints of the two sketches.

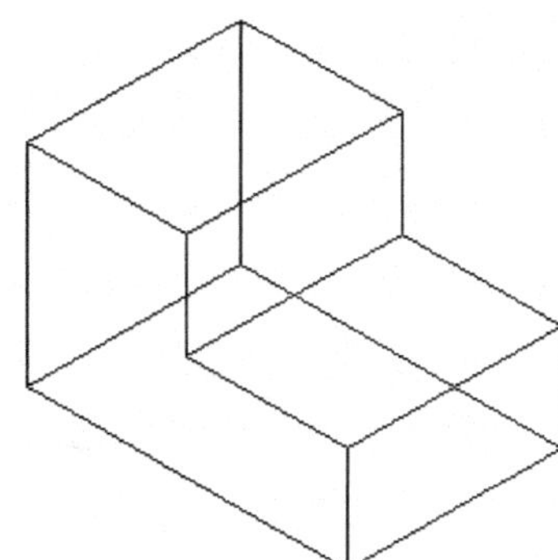

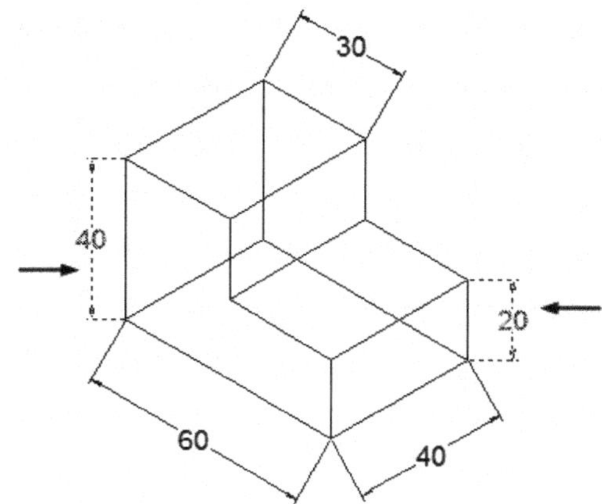

- Deactivate the ISODRAFT ⟋ and the Snap Mode icons on the Status bar.
- Use the dimensioning tools and apply dimensions to the sketch.

- Type 150 as the oblique angle and press ENTER; the dimensions are oblique, as shown below.

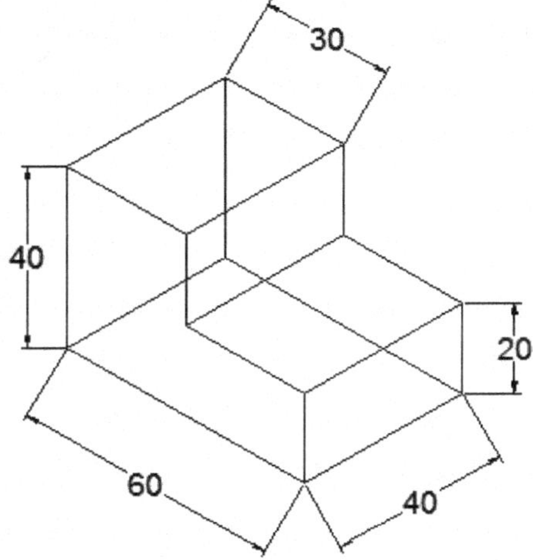

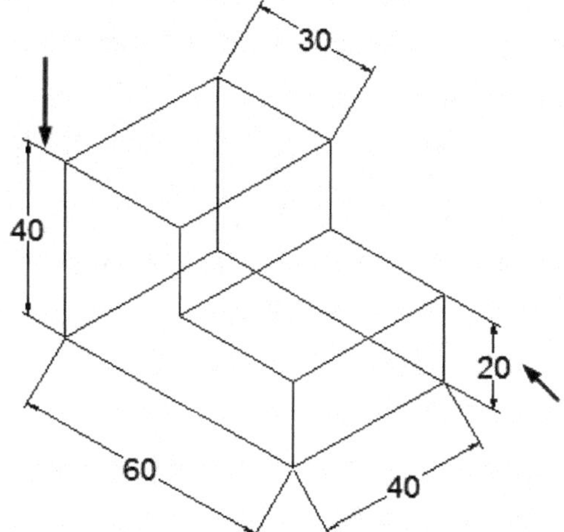

- Expand the **Dimensions** panel on the **Annotate** ribbon tab and click the **Oblique** button.

- Again, click the **Oblique** tool on the **Dimensions** panel and select the aligned dimensions. Next, right-click to accept.

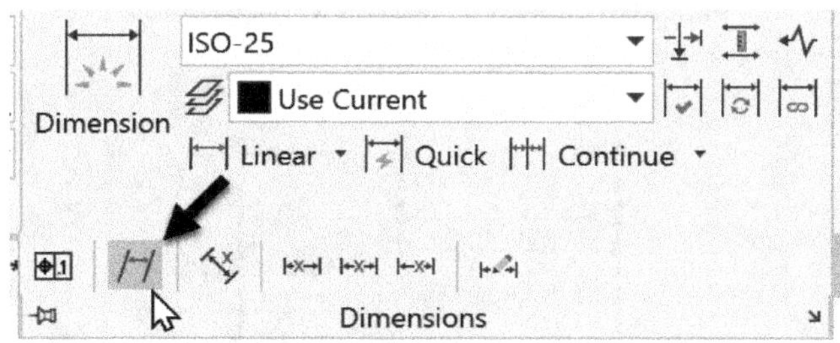

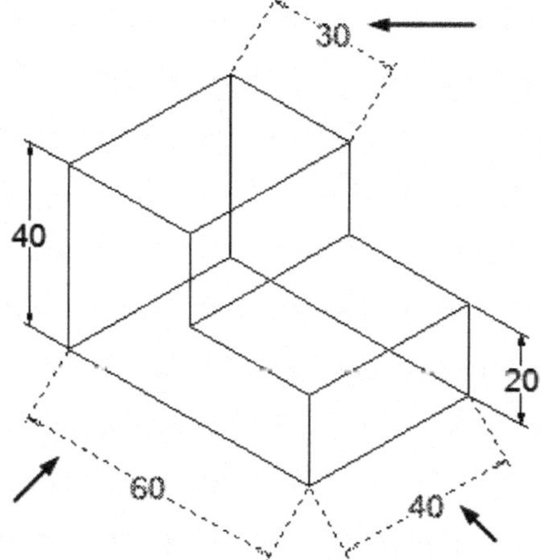

- Select the vertical dimensions and right-click to accept; the message, "**Enter obliquing angle**," appears in the command line.

- Type 90 as the oblique angle and press ENTER; the dimensions will be oblique, as shown below.

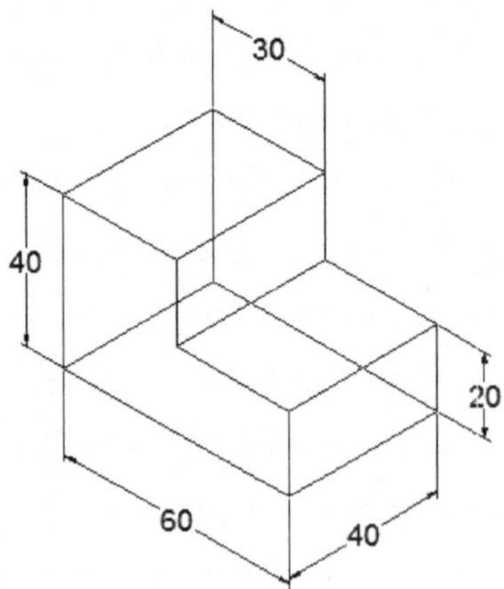

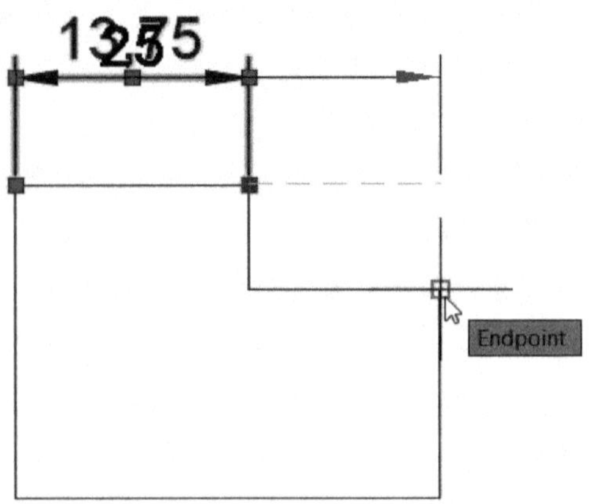

Editing Dimensions using Grips

In Chapter 4, you have learned to edit objects using grips. In the same way, you can edit dimensions using grips. The editing operations using grips are discussed next.

Example 1: (Stretching the Dimension)

- Select the dimension to display grips on it.
- Select the endpoint grip of the dimension.
- Next, move the pointer and select a new point; the dimension value will be updated automatically.

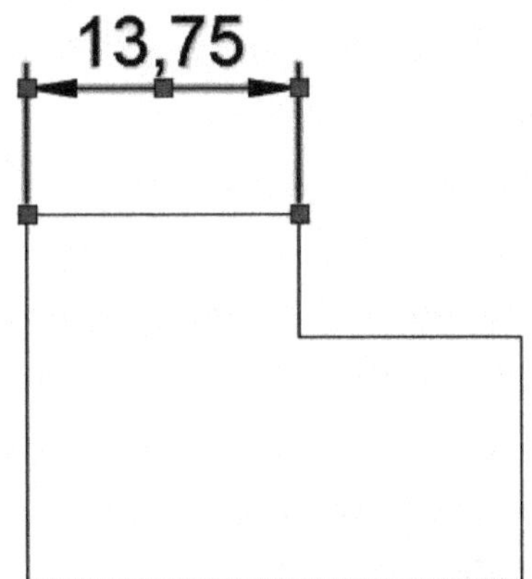

- You can also stretch the angular or radial dimensions.

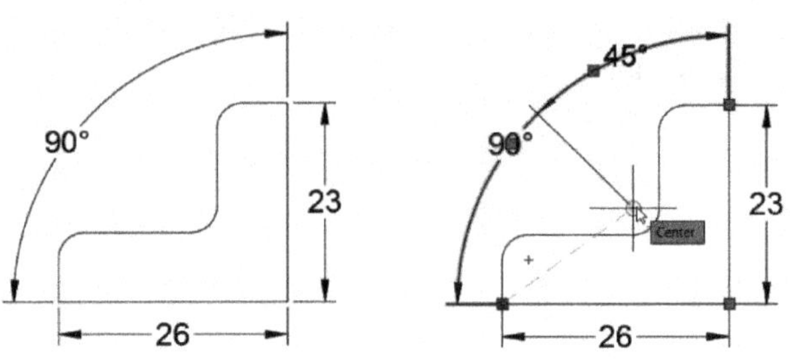

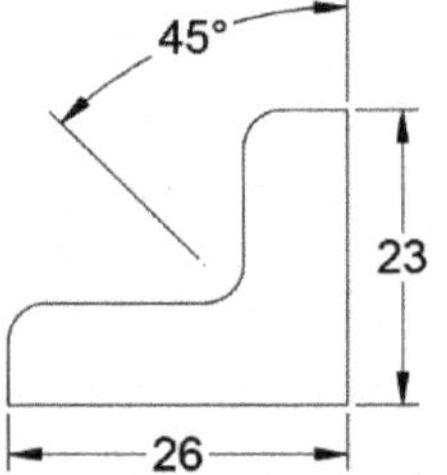

Example 2: (Moving the Dimension)

- To move a linear dimension, select the middle grip and move the pointer.

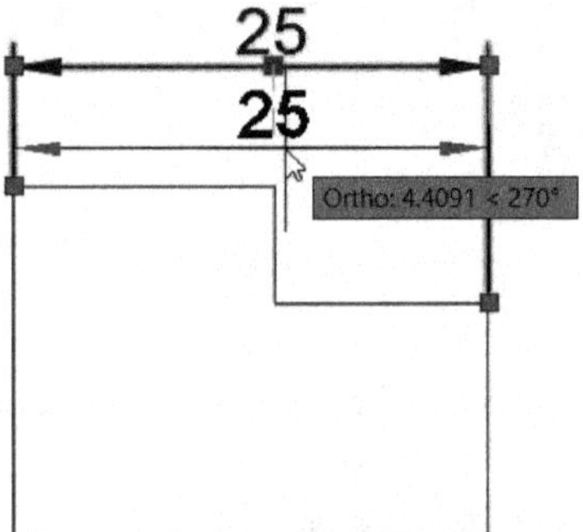

- Likewise, you can move the angular and radial dimensions.

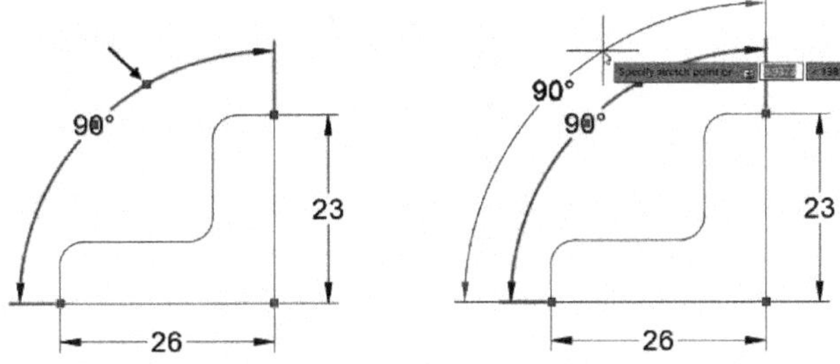

Example 3: (Modifying the Dimension text)

- Select the dimension and position the pointer on the middle grip; a shortcut menu appears as shown below.

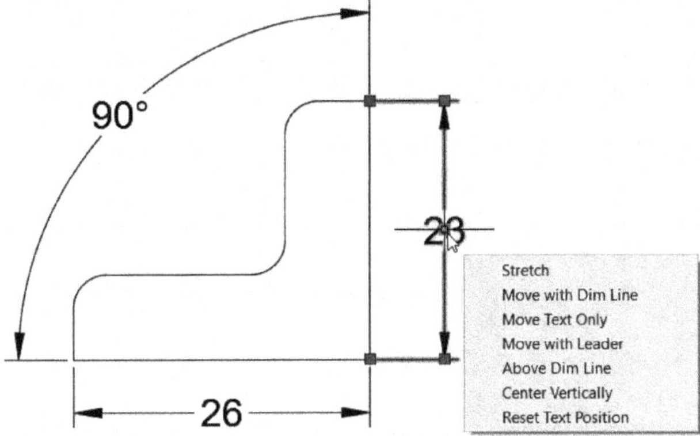

The options in the menu are self-explanatory. You can perform the required operation by selecting the corresponding option.

- Likewise, position the pointer on the endpoint of the dimension line and select the required option from the menu.

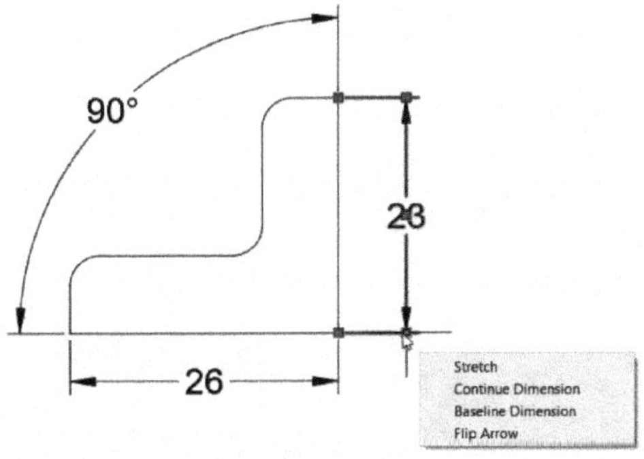

Modifying Dimensions using the Properties palette

Using the **Properties** palette, you can modify the dimensional properties such as text, arrow size, precision, linetype, and lineweight. The **Properties** palette comes in handy when you want to modify the properties of a particular dimension only.

Example:

- Create the drawing shown in the figure and apply dimensions to it.

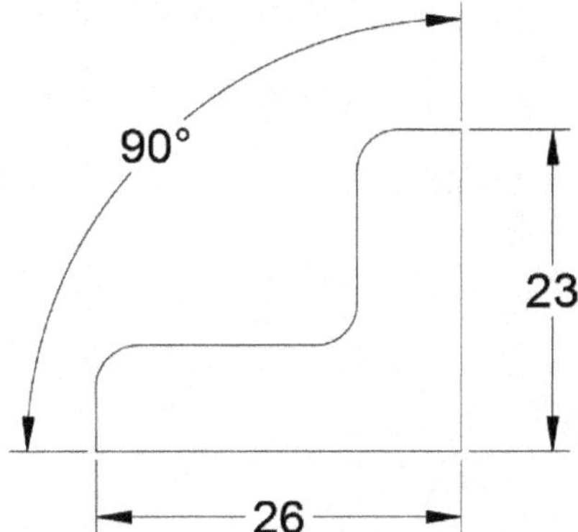

- Select the vertical dimension and right-click.
- Select **Properties** from the shortcut menu; the **Properties** palette appears.
- In the **Properties** palette, under the **Lines & Arrows** section, set the **Arrow size** to **2**.

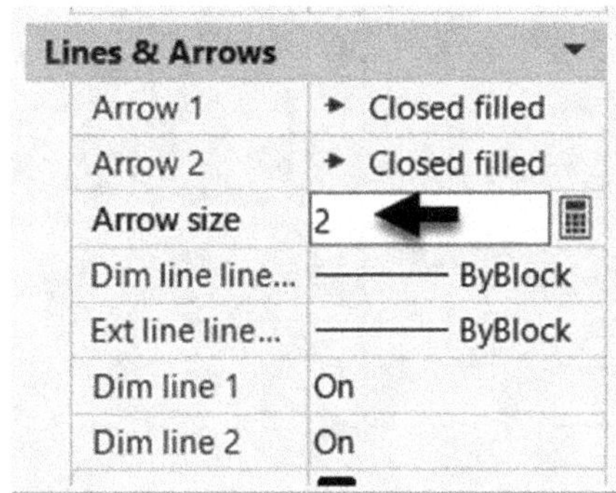

- Under the **General** section, set **Color** to **Blue**.

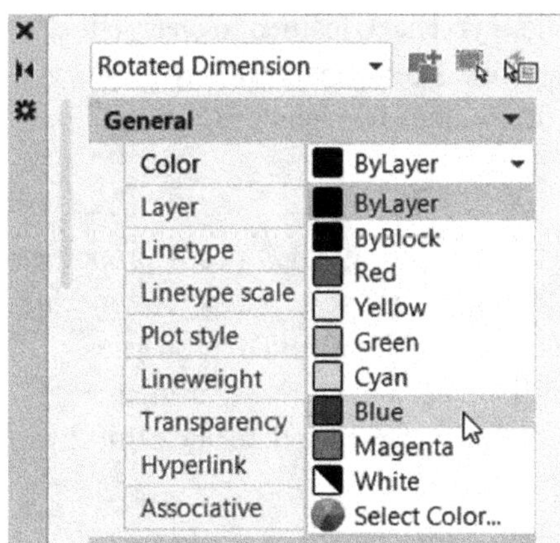

- In the **Properties** palette, under the **Lines & Arrows** section, set the **Ext line offset** value to **1.25**.
- Scroll down to the **Text** section and set **Text height** to **2**.

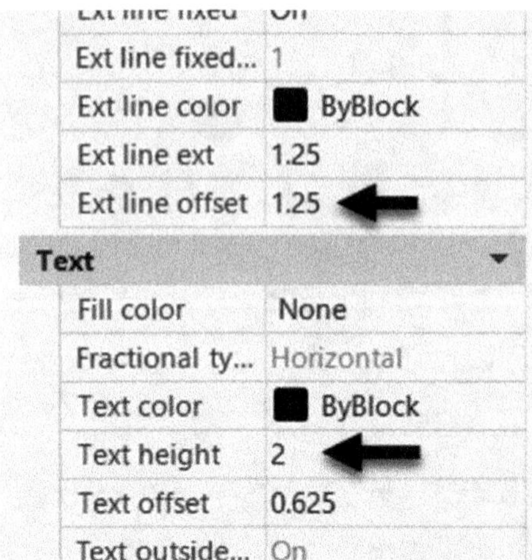

- Close the **Properties** palette; you will notice that the properties of the dimension are updated as per the changes made.

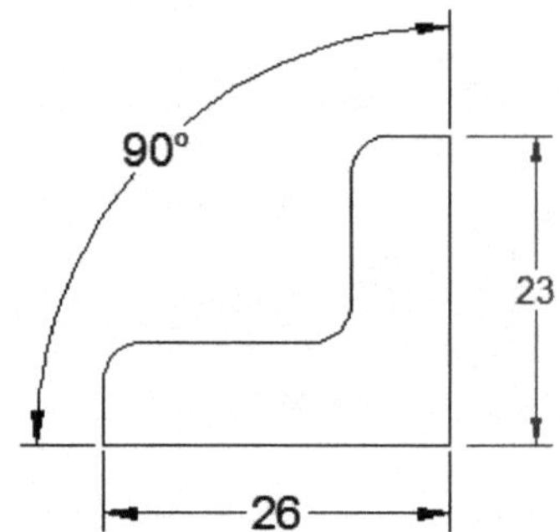

Matching Properties of Dimensions or Objects

In the previous section, you have learned to change the properties of a dimension. Now, you can apply these properties to other dimensions by using the **Match Properties** tool.

The **Match Properties** tool allows you to copy properties from one object to another. It is useful when you working with multiple objects that require identical properties, such as layer, color, linetype, and more. By using the **Match Properties** tool, you can save time and effort by

avoiding the need to modify each object individually, which can be a tedious and error-prone process.

- Click **Home > Properties > Match Properties** on the ribbon or type **MA** and press ENTER; the message, "Select source object," appears in the command line.

- Select the vertical dimension from the drawing; the message, "Select destination object(s) or [Settings]:" appears in the command line.

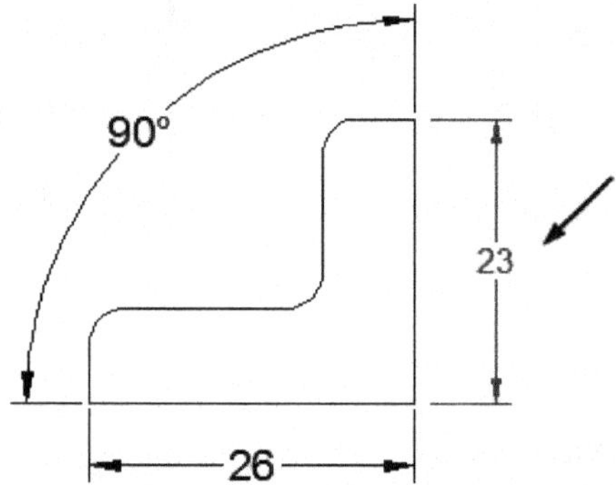

- Select the **Settings** option from the command line; the **Property Settings** dialog appears.

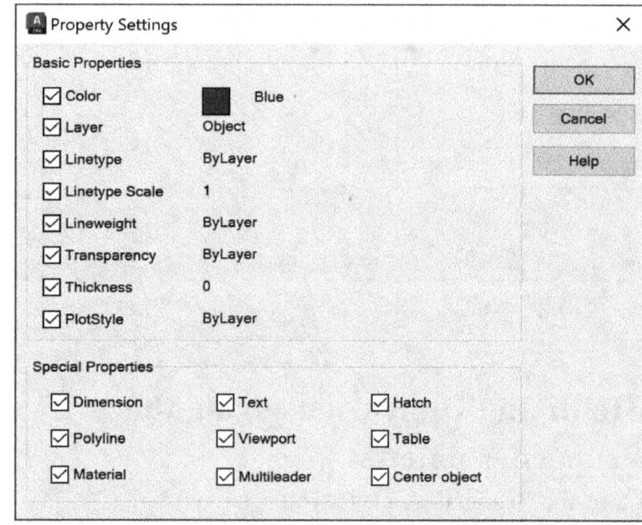

In this dialog, you can select the settings that can be applied to the destination dimensions or objects. By default, all the options are selected in this dialog.

- Click **OK** on the **Property Settings** dialog. Next, you must select the destination objects.
- Select the other dimensions from the drawing; the properties of the source dimension are applied to other dimensions.

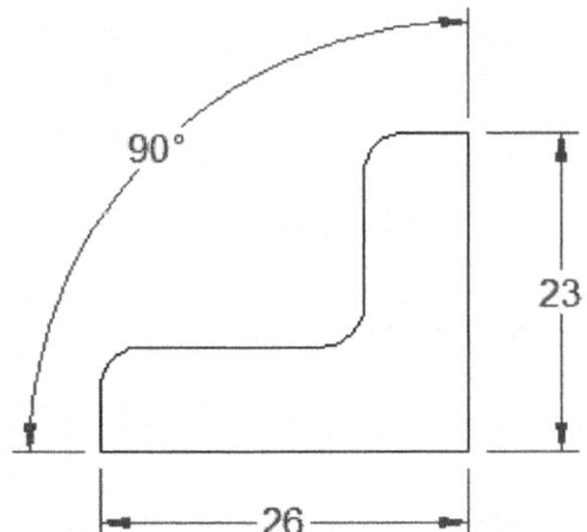

- Right-click and select **Enter**.

Exercises

Exercise 1

Create the drawing shown below and create hole callouts for different types of holes. Assume missing dimensions.

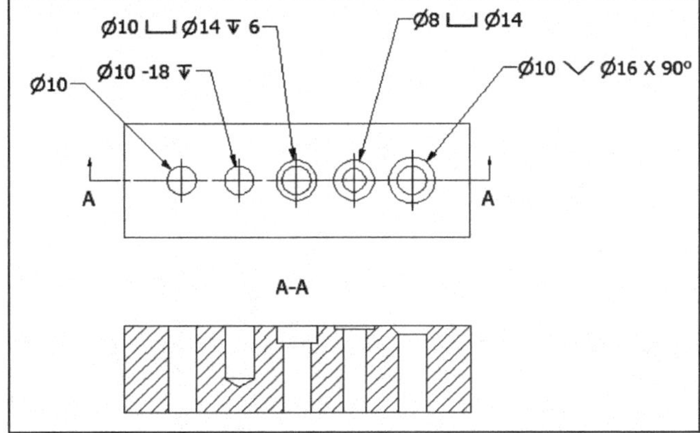

Exercise 4

Create the drawing shown below.

Exercise 2

Create the following drawings and apply dimensions and annotations. The Grid Spacing X= 10 and Grid Spacing Y=10.

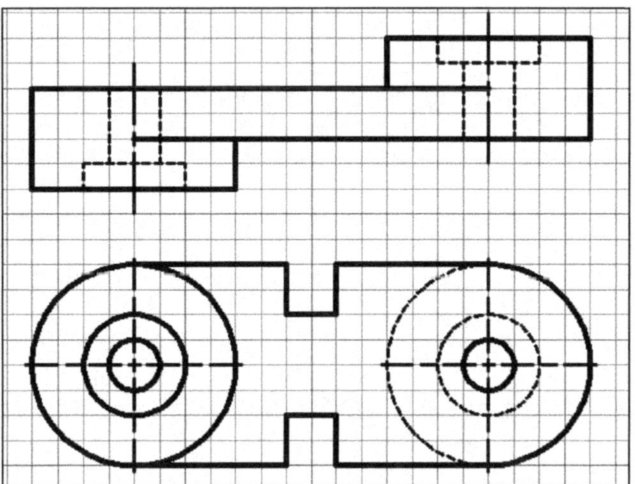

Exercise 3

Create the drawing shown below. The Grid spacing is 10 mm. After creating the drawing, apply dimensional tolerances to it. The tolerance specifications are given below.

Method: Limits
Precision: 0.00
Upper Value: 0.05
Lower Value: 0.05

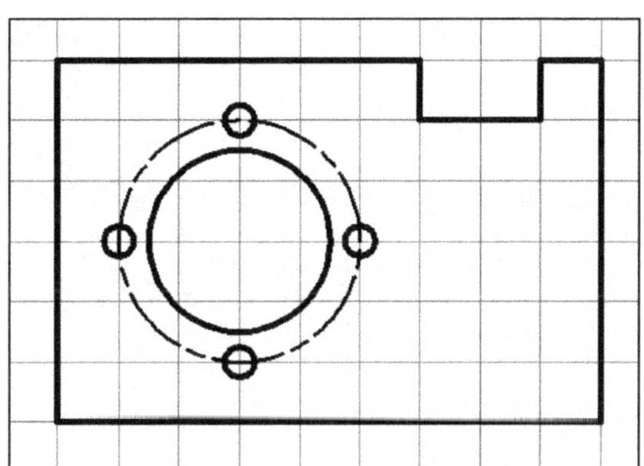

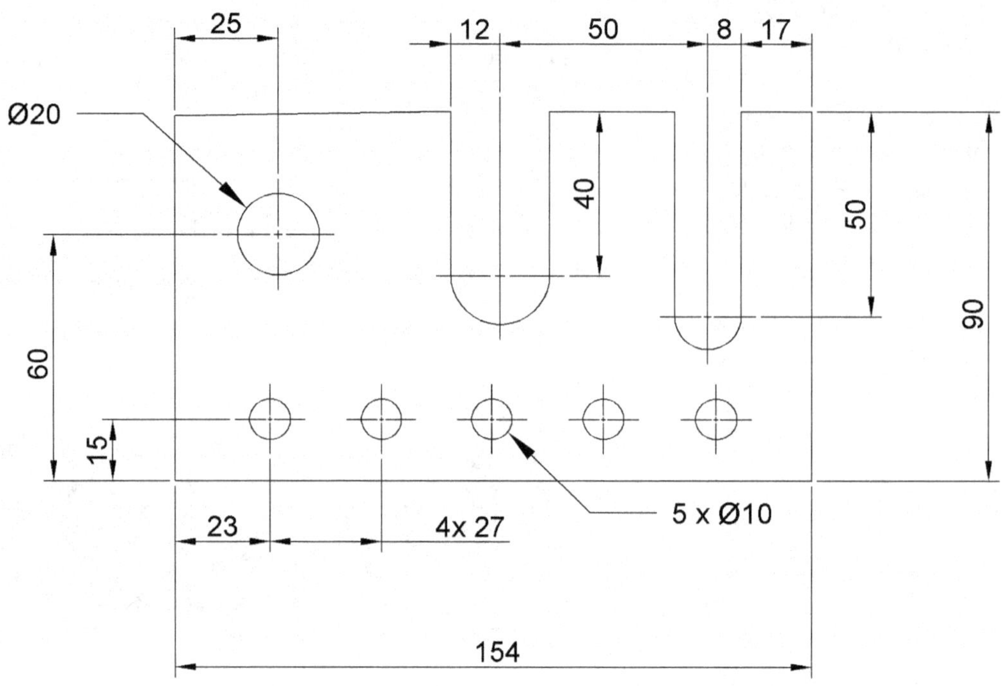

Exercise 5

Create the drawing shown below.

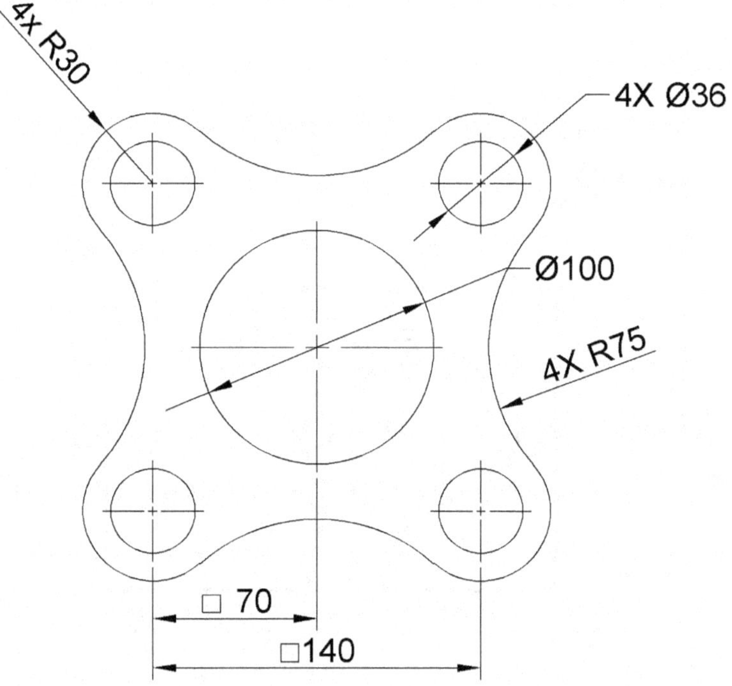

Chapter 7: Parametric Tools

In this chapter, you will learn to do the following:

- **Apply Geometric and Dimensional Constraints**
- **Create Equations using the Parameter Manager**
- **Create Inferred Constraints**

Parametric Tools

Parametric tools are one of the main advancements in Computer-Aided Design. Using the parametric tools, you can define the shape and size of a drawing by applying relations and dimensions between the objects. You can also use equations in place of dimensions. Changing one parameter of an equation would change the entire shape and size of the drawing. It makes it easy to modify the design.

The parametric tools can be accessed from the Ribbon, Command line, and Menu Bar.

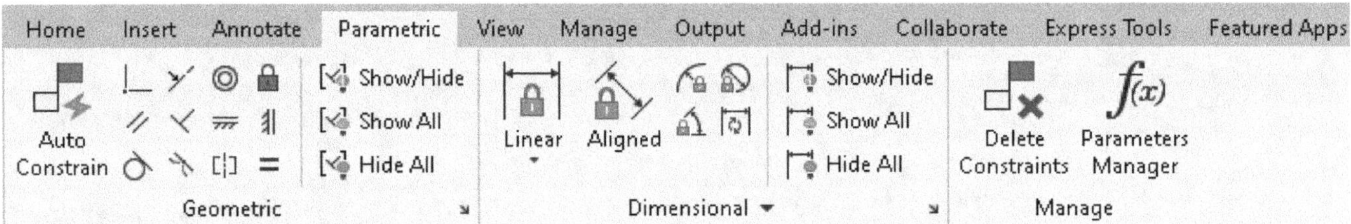

Geometric Constraints

Geometric Constraints are used to control the shape of a drawing by applying geometric relationships between the objects. For example, you can apply the **Tangent** constraint to make a line tangent to a circle. You can use the **Equal** constraint to make two lines equal in length.

The following table shows various geometric constraints and their functions.

Constraint	Function
Coincident	It is used to constrain a point to lie on another point or an object. • Click **Parametric > Geometric > Coincident** on the ribbon. • Select a point on a line or arc. • Select a point on another object; the two points will coincide with each other. 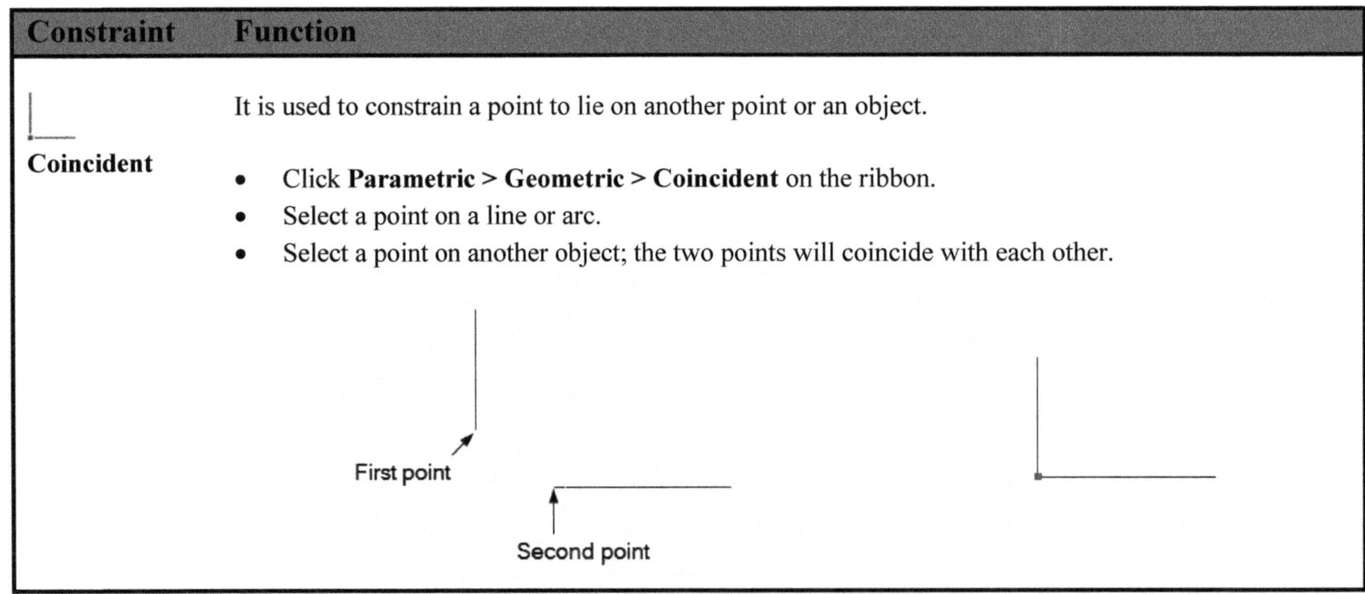

 **Collinear**

It is used to constrain a line along another line. The lines are not required to touch each other.

- Click **Parametric > Geometric > Collinear** on the ribbon.
- Select the first line and the second line; the second line will be made collinear with the first line.

 **Concentric**

It is used to make the center points of arcs, circles, or ellipses coincident.

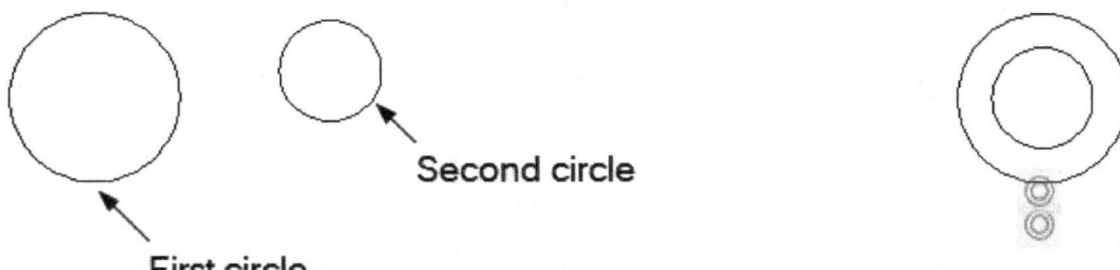

- Click **Parametric > Geometric > Concentric** on the ribbon.
- Select a circle or arc from the drawing.
- Select another circle or arc; the second circle will be concentric with the first circle.

Equal

It is used to make two objects equal. For example, if you select two circles, the diameter of the two circles will become equal. If you select two lines, the length of the two lines will be equal.

- Click **Parametric > Geometric > Equal** on the ribbon.
- Select two objects from the drawing; the second object will be made equal to the first object.

Horizontal

It is used to make a line horizontal. You can also make two points lie along the horizontal axis.

- Click **Parametric > Geometric > Horizontal** on the ribbon.
- Select a line to make it horizontal.
- If you want to make points horizontal, select the **2Points** option from the command line and select the two points.

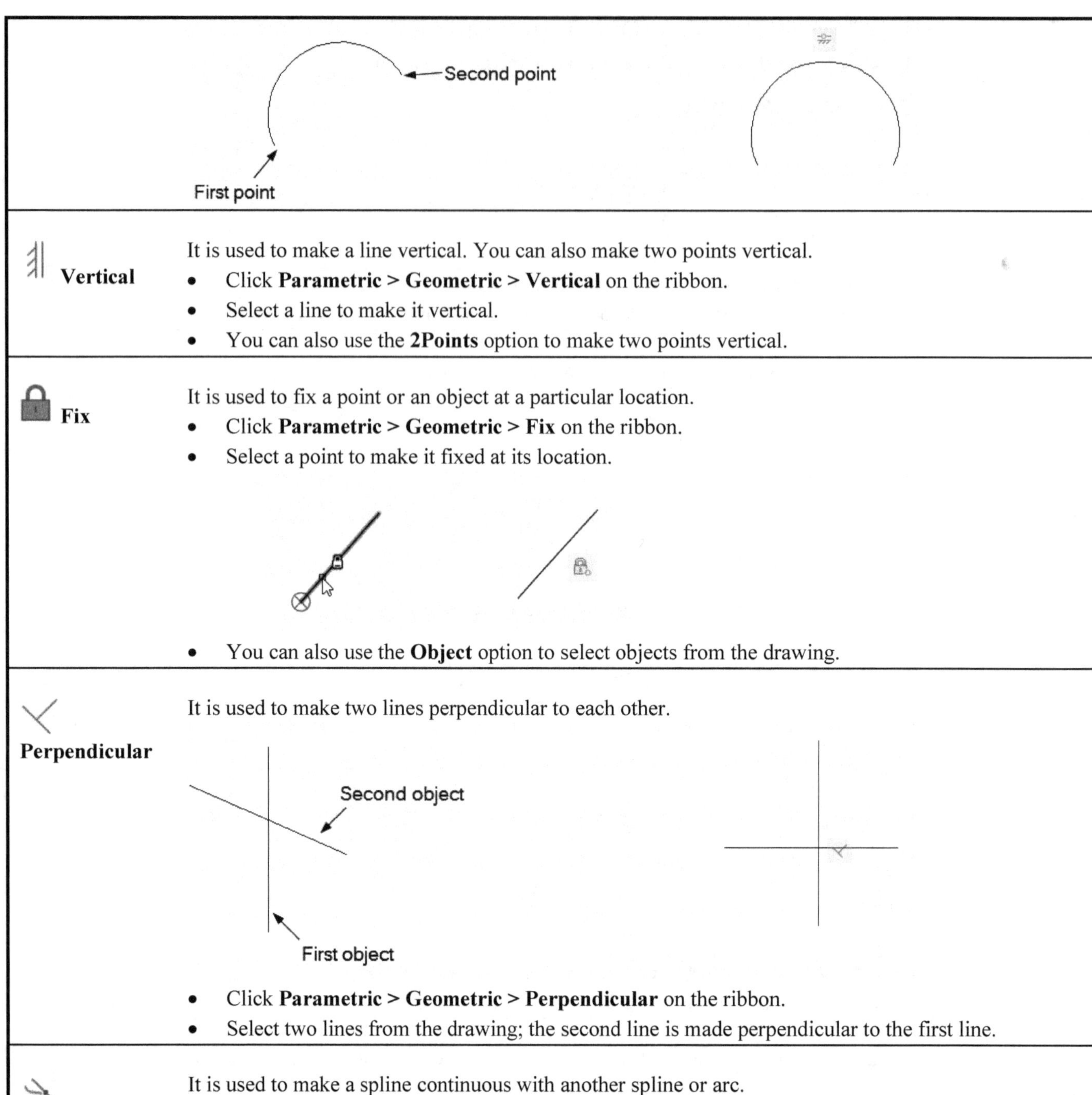

	Vertical	It is used to make a line vertical. You can also make two points vertical. • Click **Parametric > Geometric > Vertical** on the ribbon. • Select a line to make it vertical. • You can also use the **2Points** option to make two points vertical.

	Fix	It is used to fix a point or an object at a particular location. • Click **Parametric > Geometric > Fix** on the ribbon. • Select a point to make it fixed at its location. • You can also use the **Object** option to select objects from the drawing.

	Perpendicular	It is used to make two lines perpendicular to each other. • Click **Parametric > Geometric > Perpendicular** on the ribbon. • Select two lines from the drawing; the second line is made perpendicular to the first line.

	Smooth	It is used to make a spline continuous with another spline or arc.

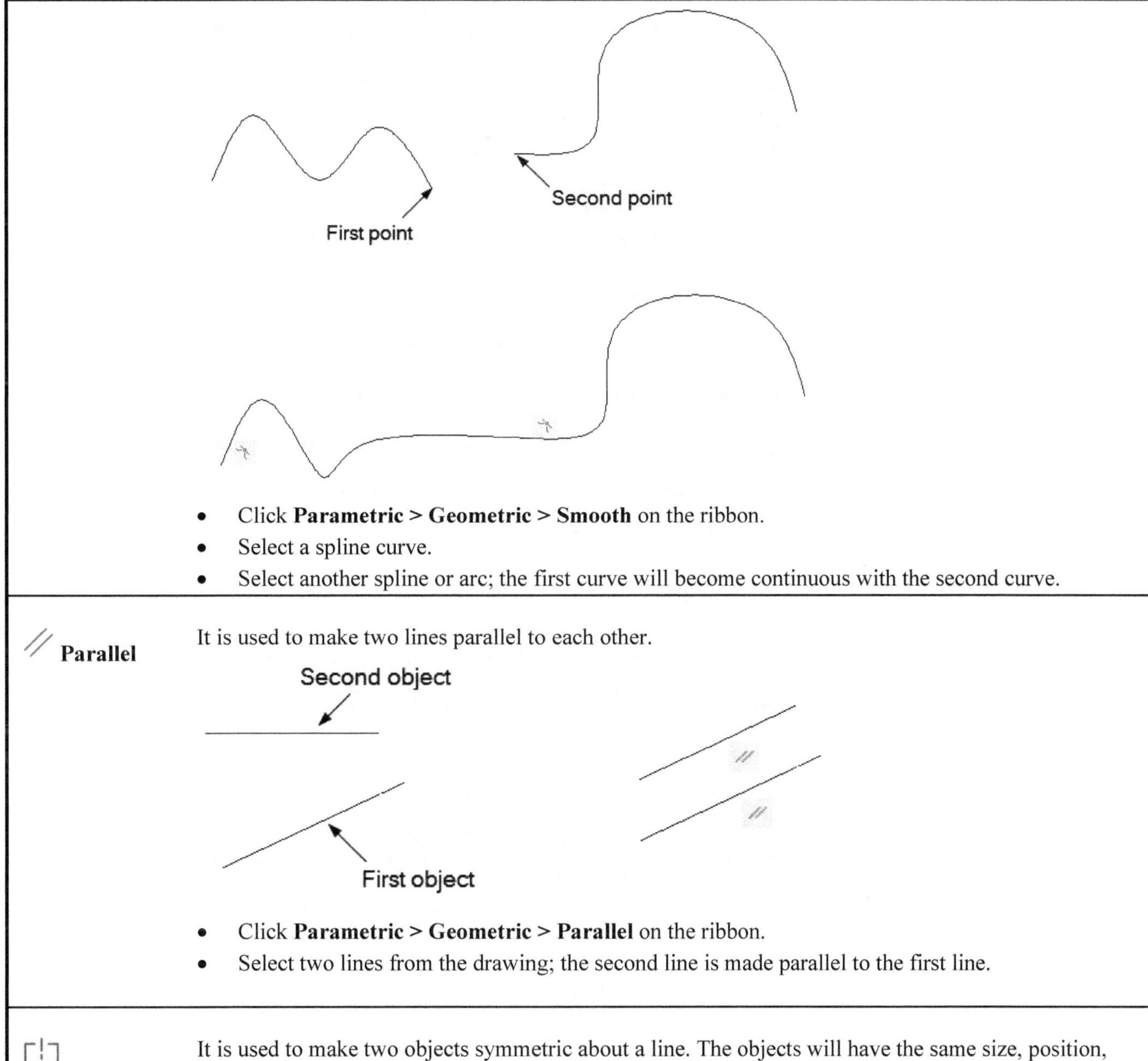

- Click **Parametric > Geometric > Smooth** on the ribbon.
- Select a spline curve.
- Select another spline or arc; the first curve will become continuous with the second curve.

Parallel

It is used to make two lines parallel to each other.

- Click **Parametric > Geometric > Parallel** on the ribbon.
- Select two lines from the drawing; the second line is made parallel to the first line.

Symmetric

It is used to make two objects symmetric about a line. The objects will have the same size, position, and orientation about a line.

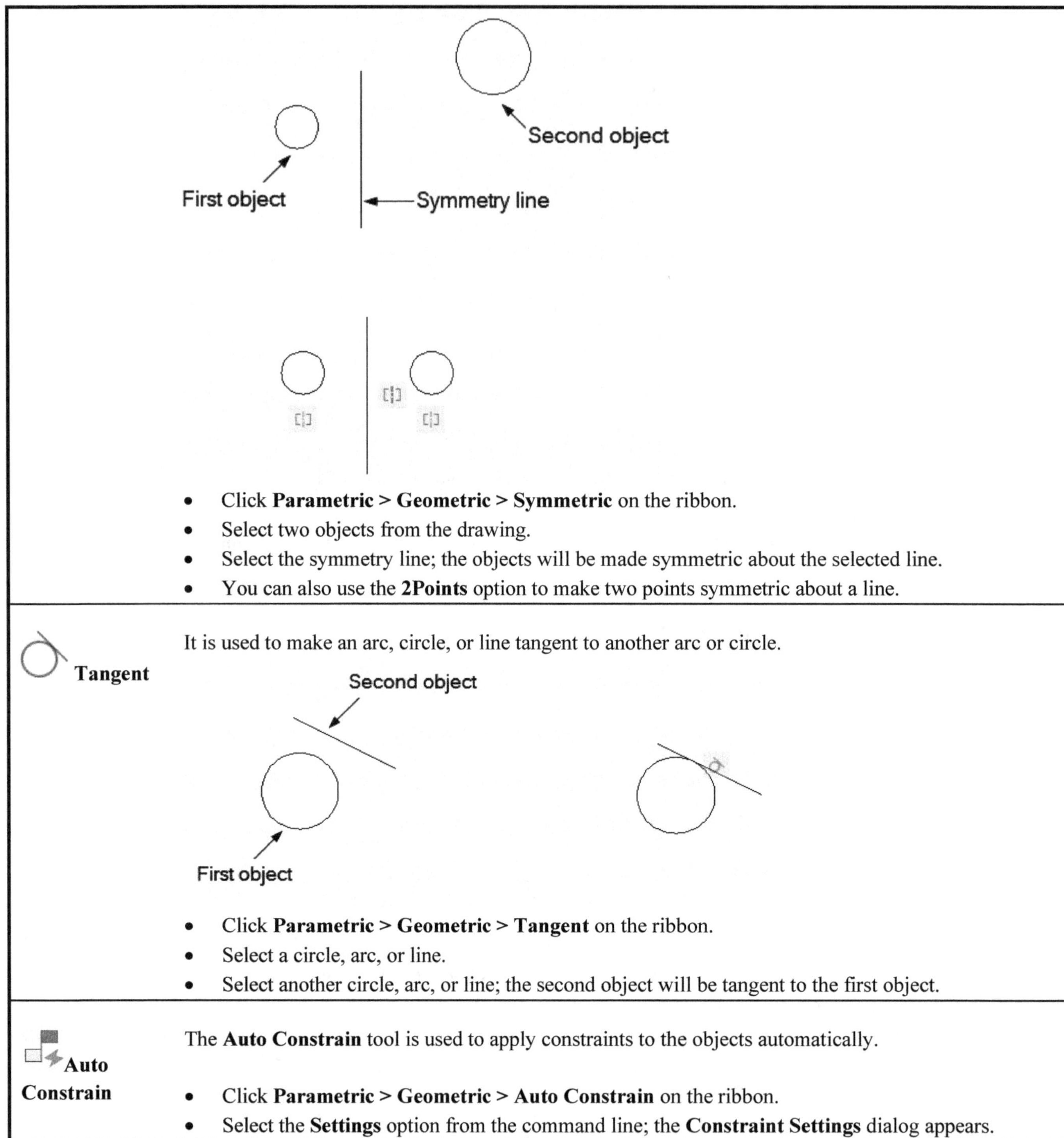

- Click **Parametric > Geometric > Symmetric** on the ribbon.
- Select two objects from the drawing.
- Select the symmetry line; the objects will be made symmetric about the selected line.
- You can also use the **2Points** option to make two points symmetric about a line.

Tangent

It is used to make an arc, circle, or line tangent to another arc or circle.

- Click **Parametric > Geometric > Tangent** on the ribbon.
- Select a circle, arc, or line.
- Select another circle, arc, or line; the second object will be tangent to the first object.

Auto Constrain

The **Auto Constrain** tool is used to apply constraints to the objects automatically.

- Click **Parametric > Geometric > Auto Constrain** on the ribbon.
- Select the **Settings** option from the command line; the **Constraint Settings** dialog appears.

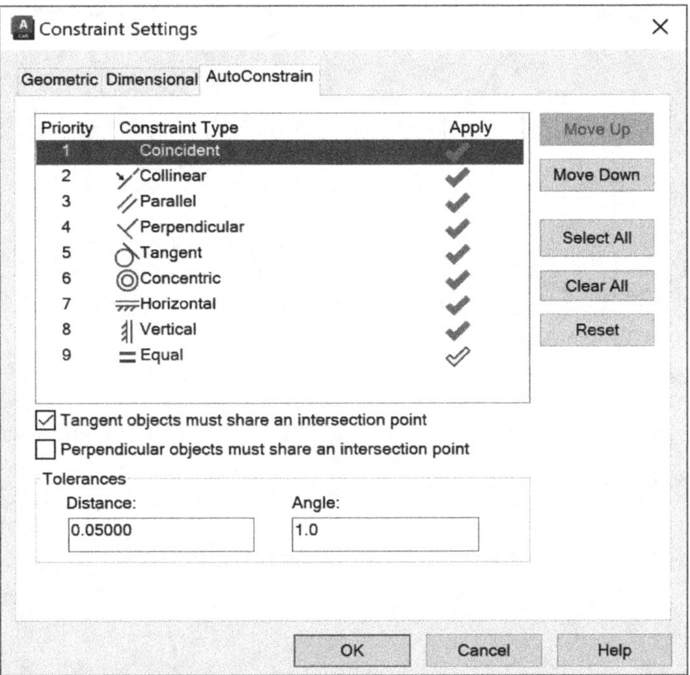

- In this dialog, select the constraints that you want to apply. You can also select the **Tangent objects must share an intersection point**, and **Perpendicular objects must share an intersection point** option.
- Click **OK**.
- Select multiple objects by clicking on them or by dragging a selection window.
- Right-click and select **Enter**; geometric constraints are applied to the objects based on their geometric condition.

Example:

In this example, you will create the following drawing by using the drawing and parametric tools.

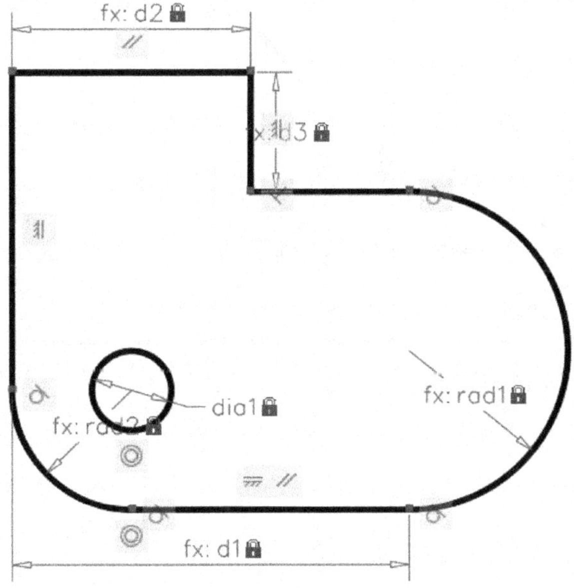

- Open a new AutoCAD file.

- Create two circles and a line, as shown in the figure.

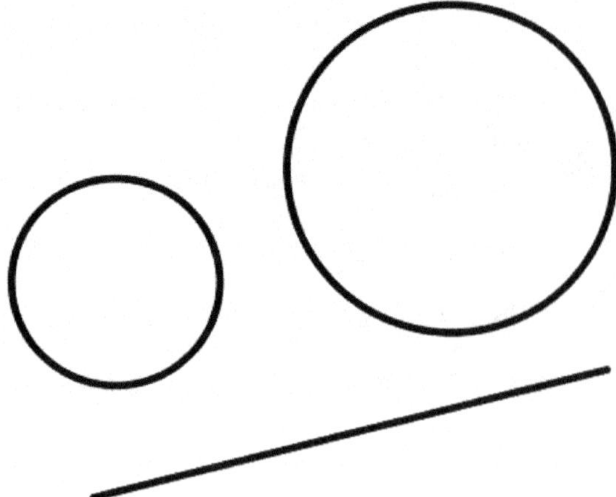

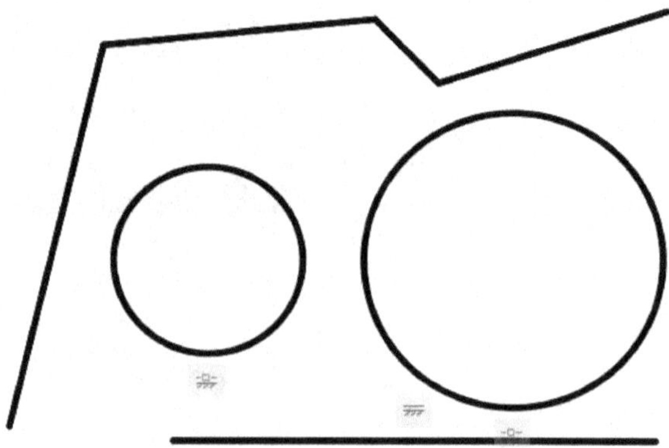

- Click **Parametric > Geometric > Horizontal** on the ribbon.
- Select the line to make it horizontal.

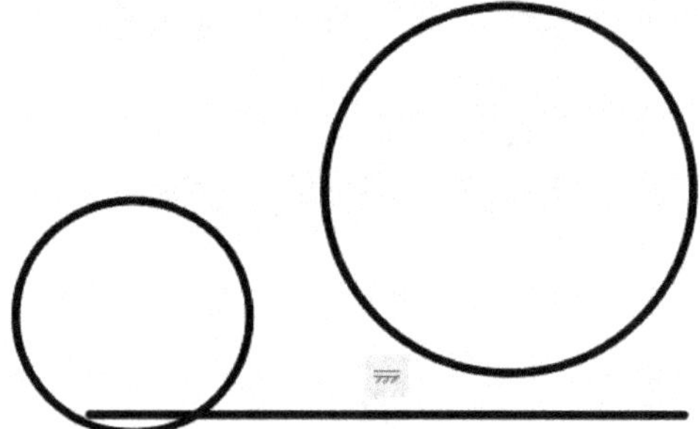

- Press the SPACEBAR and select the **2Points** option from the command line.
- Select the large circle and the small circle; the center points of the two circles will be horizontal.

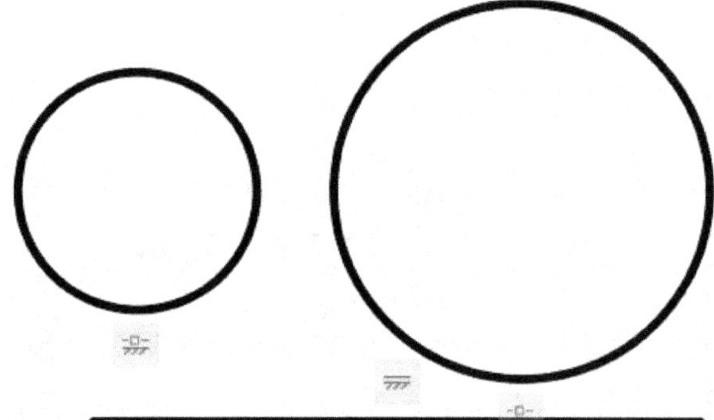

- Create four lines, as shown below.

- Click the **Coincident** ⌐ button on the **Geometric** panel and select the two endpoints of the lines as shown below; the endpoints will be made coincident.

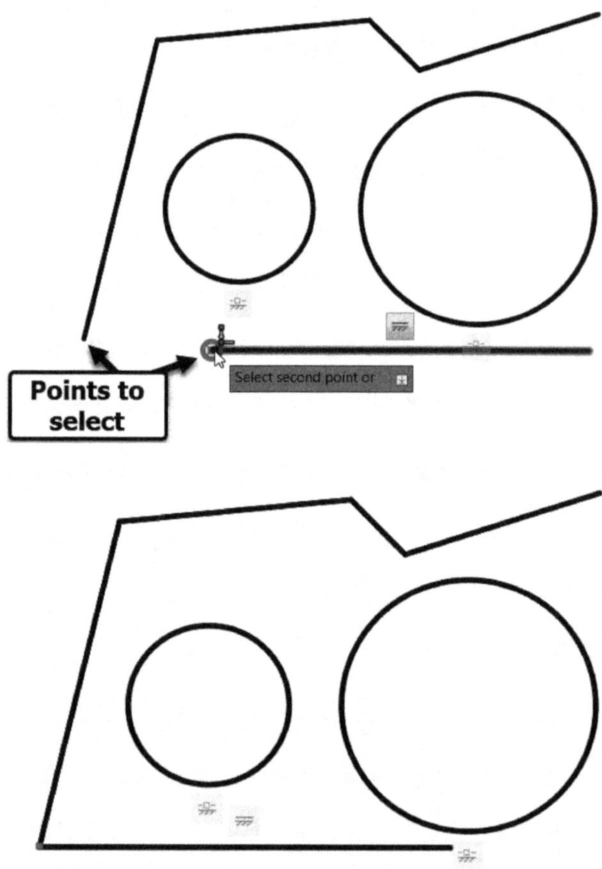

- Click the **Auto Constrain** button on the **Geometric** panel and select the four lines, as shown below.

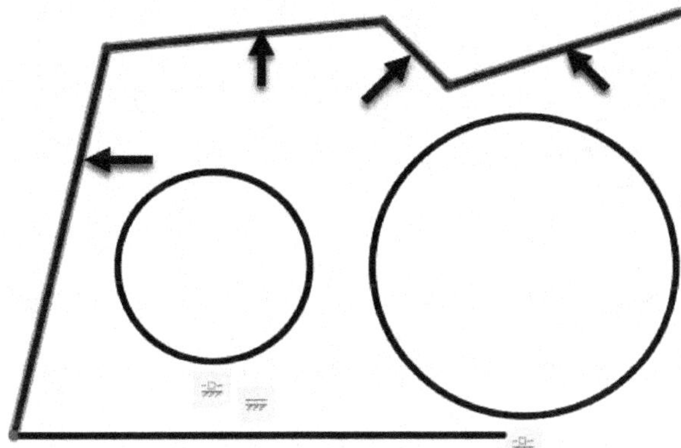

- Right-click and select **Enter**; constraints are applied to the selected objects, automatically.

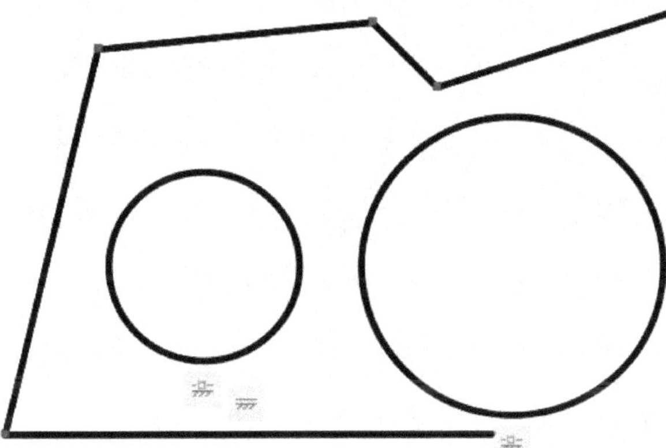

- Click the **Vertical** ⫴ button on the **Geometric** panel and select the line as shown below; the line will become vertical.

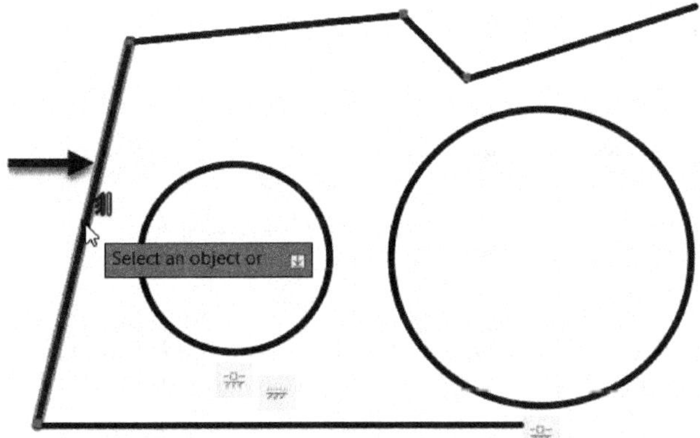

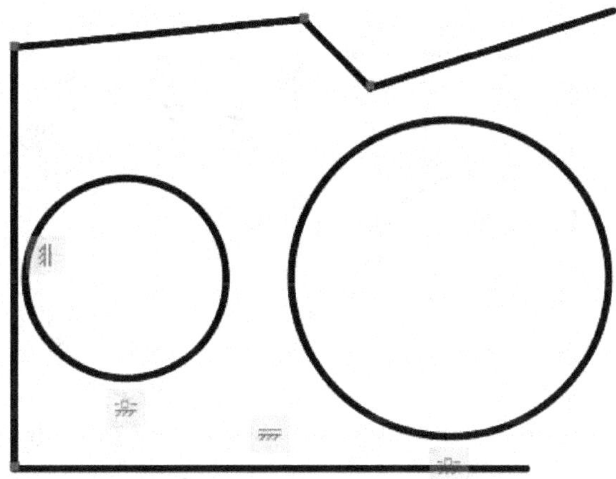

- Use the **Parallel** ∥ tool and make the two lines parallel to each other, as shown below.

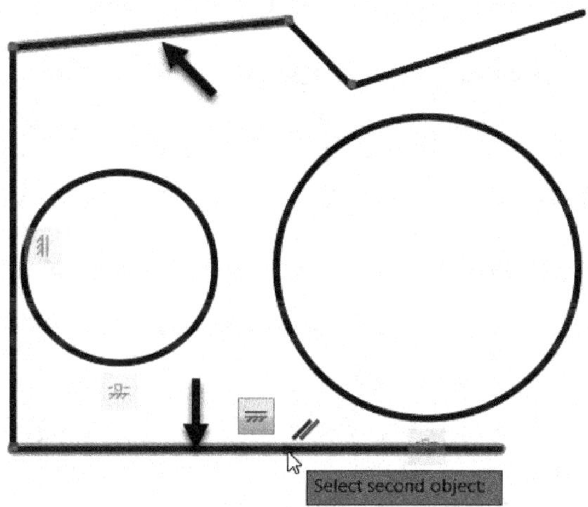

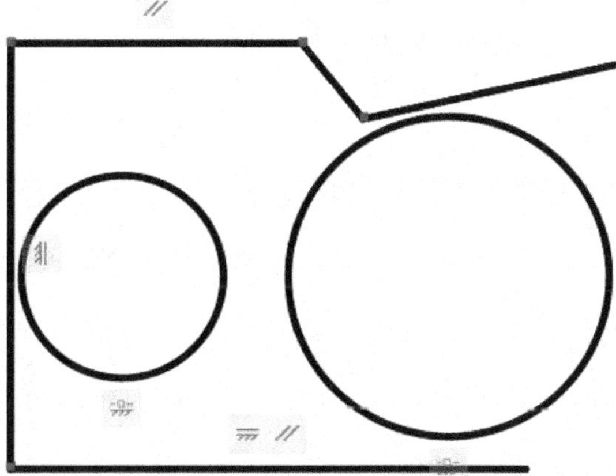

- Use the **Tangent** ◯ tool and make the two lines tangent to the large circle, as shown below.

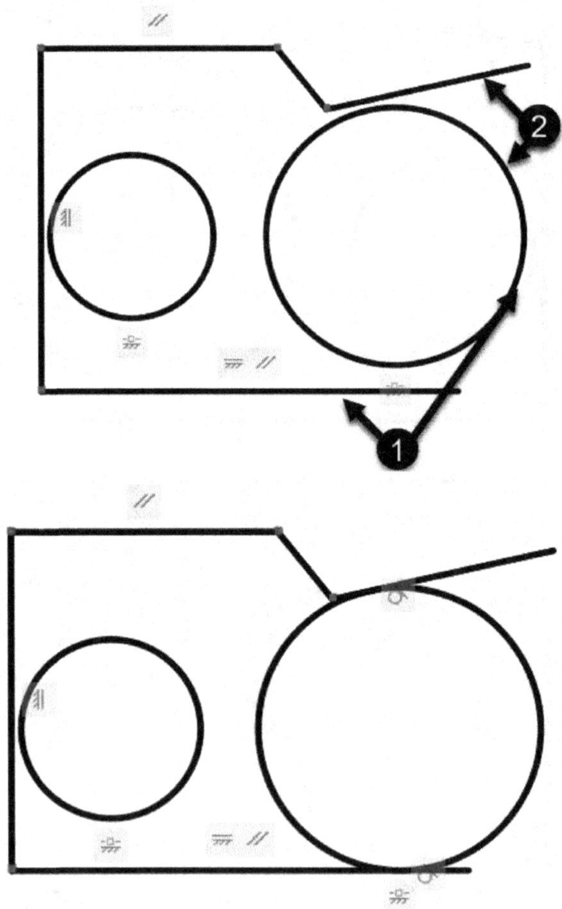

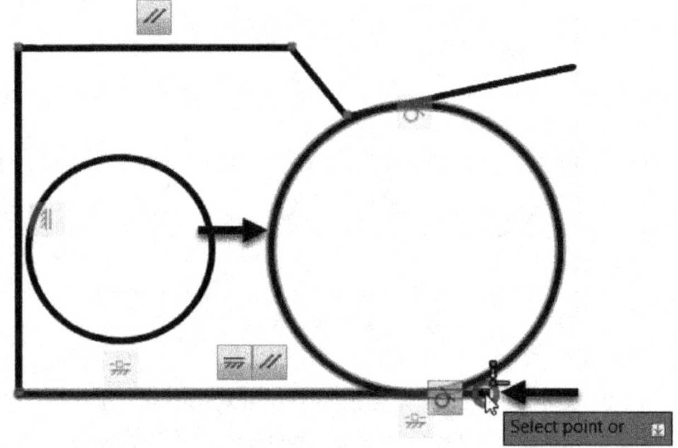

- Click the **Coincident** ⌐ button on the **Geometric** panel.
- Select the **Object** option from the command line and select the large circle.
- Select the endpoint of the lower horizontal line to make it coincident with the circle.

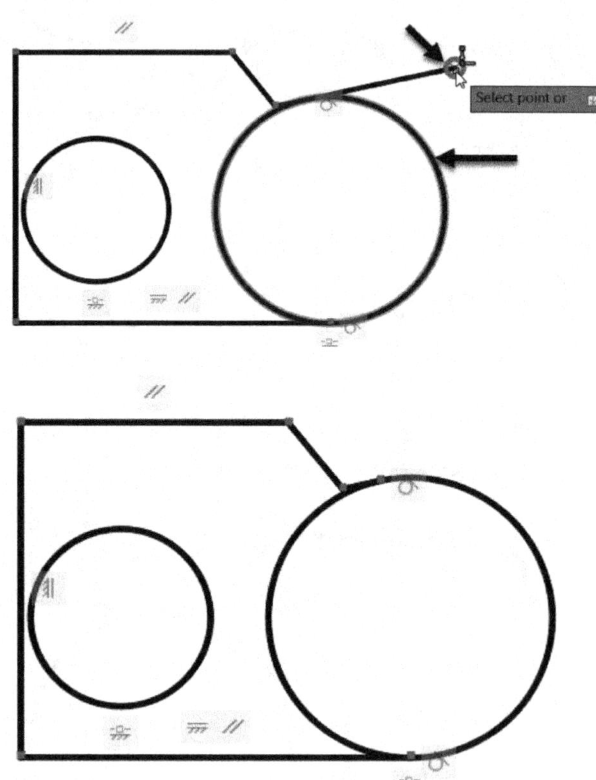

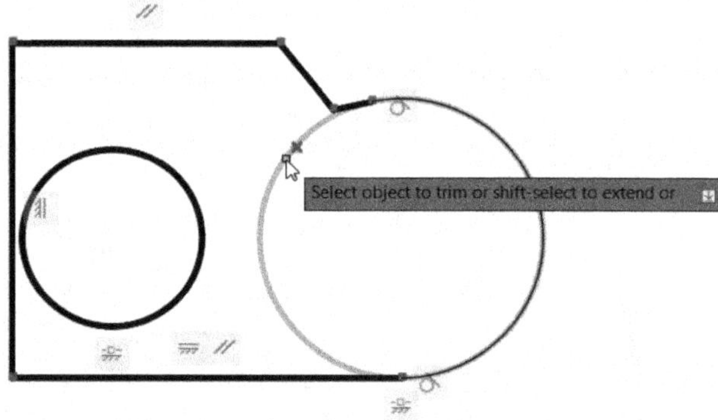

- Likewise, apply the **Coincident** constraint between the large circle and the upper horizontal line.

- Use the **Trim** tool and trim the unwanted portion of the circle.

Follow the next three steps if the **Tangent** and **Coincident** constraints are deleted.

- Click the **Auto Constrain** button on the **Geometric** panel.
- Drag a window around the arc and lines, as shown.
- Right-click and select **Enter**; the **Tangent** and **Coincident** constraints are applied between the arc and the horizontal lines.

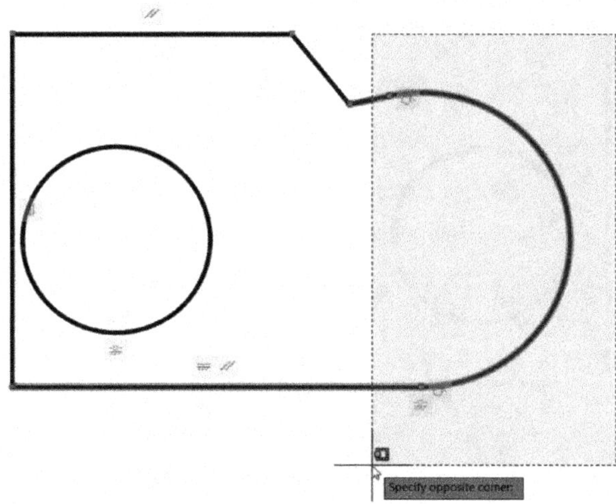

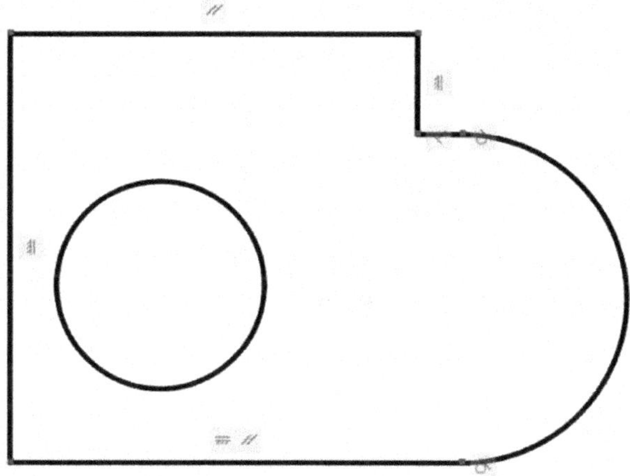

- Click the **Perpendicular** button on the **Geometric** panel.
- Select the two lines, as shown.

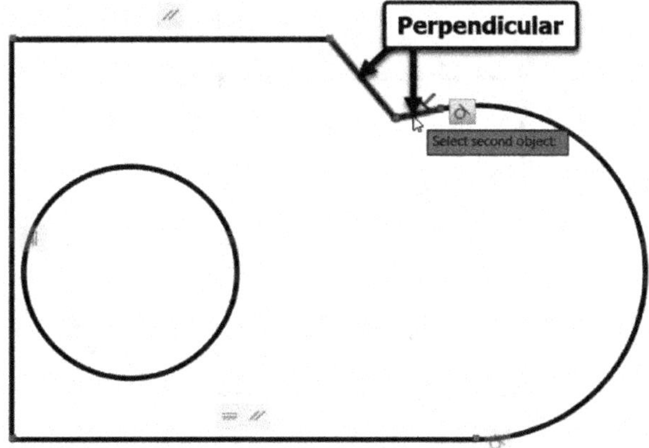

- Click the **Vertical** button on the **Geometric** panel.
- Select the line, as shown.

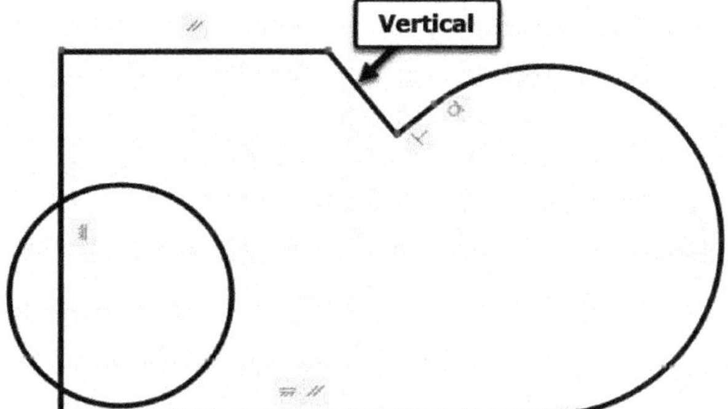

Dimensional Constraints

Dimensional constraints are applied to a drawing after applying the Geometric constraints. They are used to control the size and position of the objects in a drawing. You can apply the dimensional constraints using the tools available in the **Dimensional** panel of the **Parametric** ribbon.

- Click the inclined arrow on the **Dimensional** panel; the **Constraint Settings** dialog appears.

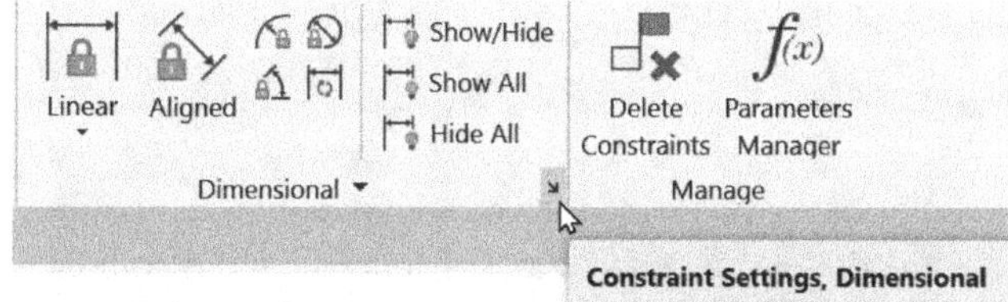

- On the **Constraint Settings** dialog, set **Dimension name format** to **Name**.

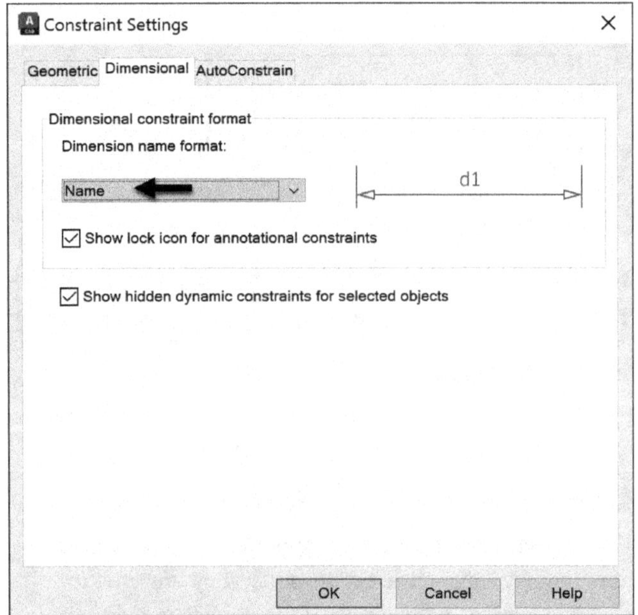

- Click the **OK** button.
- Click **Parametric > Dimensional > Linear** on the ribbon.

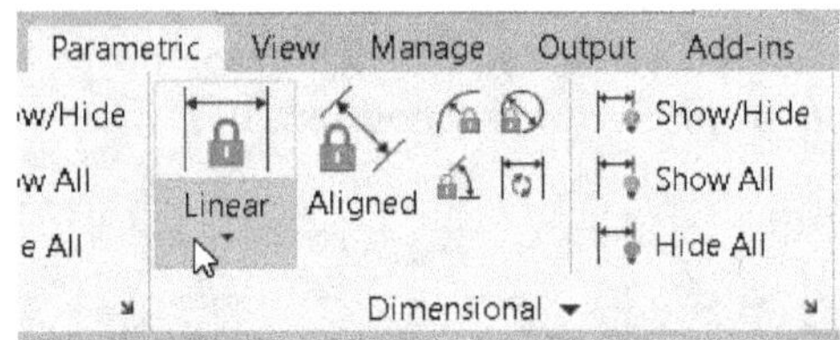

- Select the two endpoints of the lower horizontal line; the dimensional constraint is attached to the pointer.

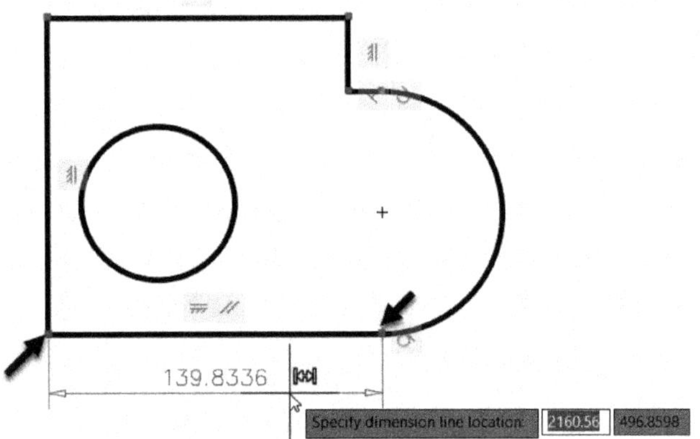

- Place the dimension constraint and left-click.

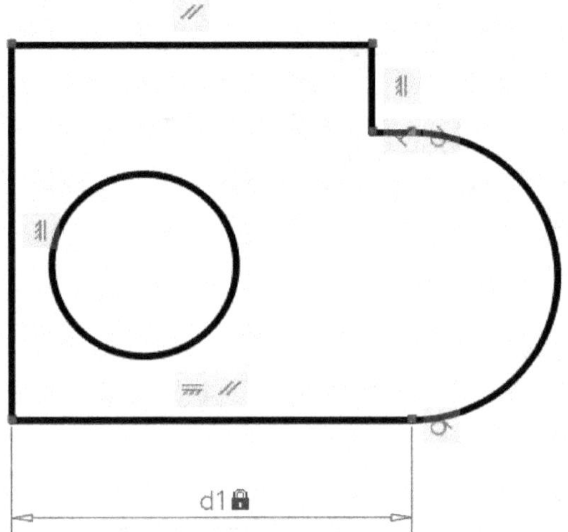

- Similarly, apply linear dimensions to other lines, as shown below.

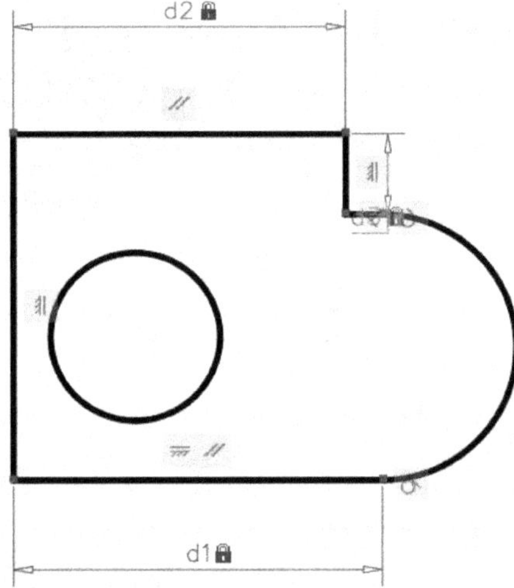

You will notice that when you try to apply the dimensional constraint to the horizontal line connected to the arc, the **Dimensional Constraints** message box appears. It shows that the dimension will over-constrain the geometry. In an over-constrained geometry, there are conflicting dimensions or relations or both. Click the **Cancel** button on the **Dimensional Constraints** message box.

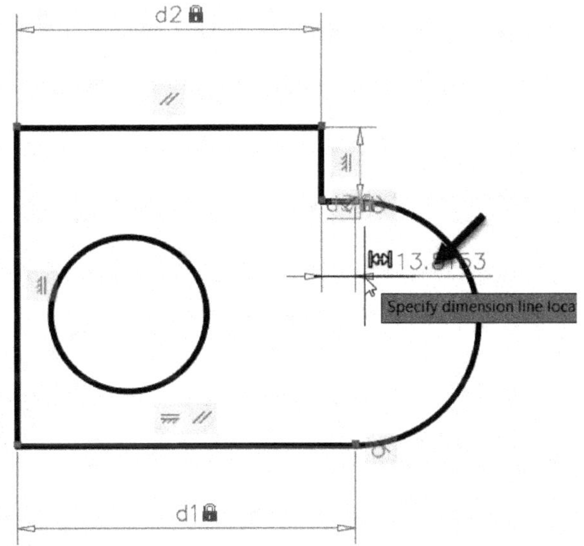

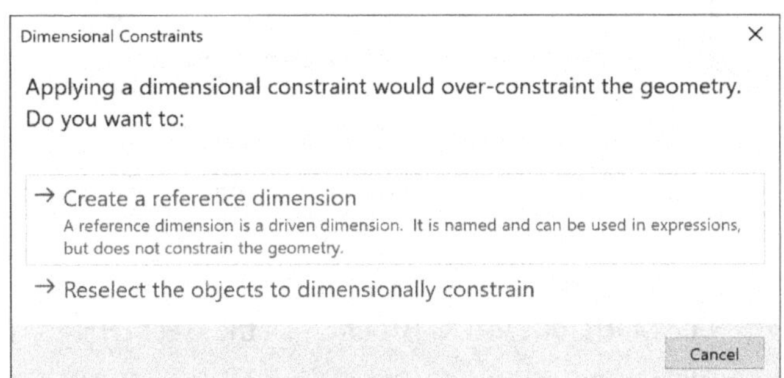

- Click the **Diameter** button on the **Dimensional** panel and apply the diameter dimension to the circle located on the left side.

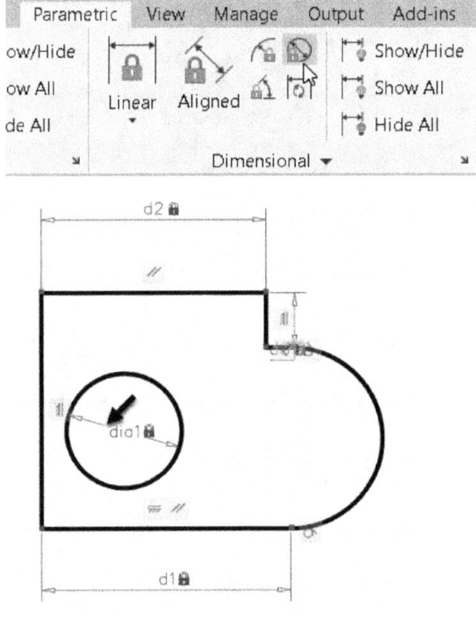

- Click the **Radius** button on the **Dimensional** panel and apply the radial dimension to the arc.

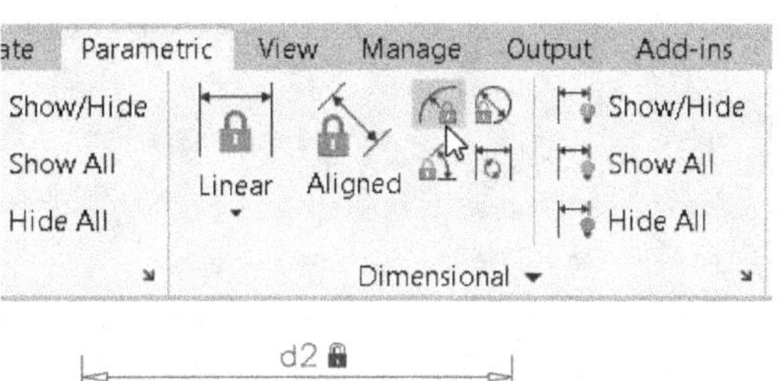

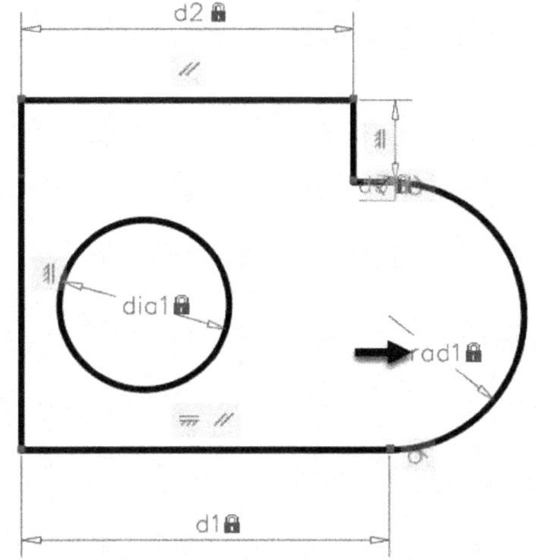

Creating equations using the Parameters Manager

Equations are relations between the dimensional constraints. Look at the drawing given below. In this drawing, all the dimensions are controlled by the diameter of the hole. In AutoCAD, you can create this type of relations between dimensions very easily using the **Parameters Manager** palette.

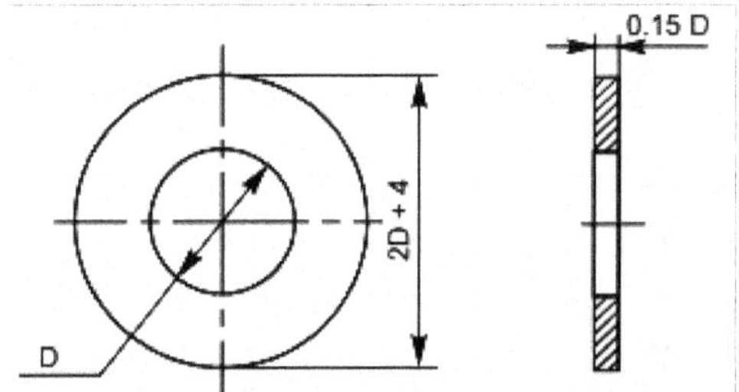

- Click the **Parameters Manager** button on the **Manage** panel of the **Parameters** tab; the **Parameters Manager** palette appears.

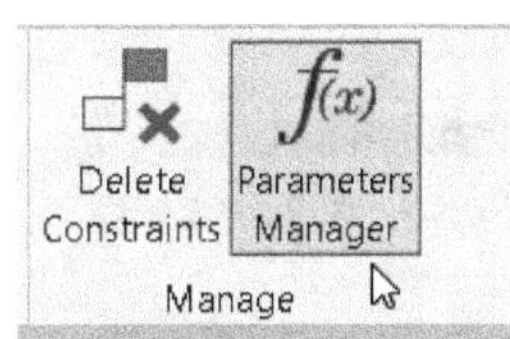

- Double-click in the box next to the **dia1** and enter **50**.

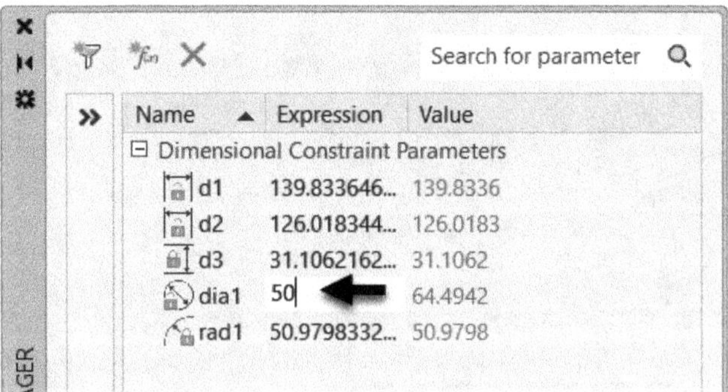

- Likewise, change the values of the other dimensions, as shown below.

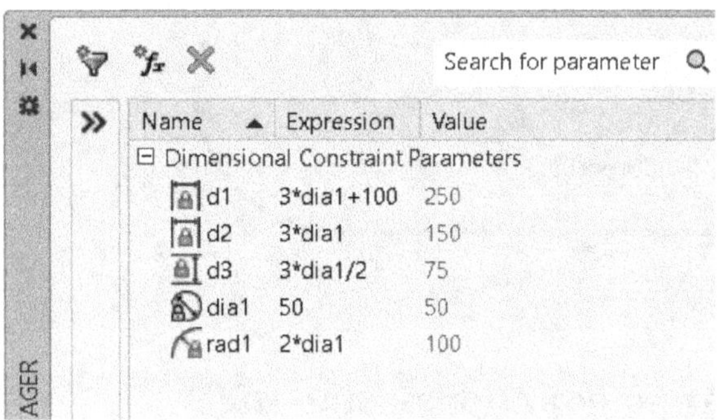

You will notice that the circle is placed outside the loop.

- Click **Zoom All** on the **Navigation Bar** to view the circle.

Creating Inferred Constraints

The **Infer Constraints** button helps you to create constraints automatically. With this button active on the status bar, you can automatically create constraints while drawing a sketch.

- On the status bar, click the **Customization** button and select **Infer Constraints** from the flyout. It adds the **Infer Constraints** button to the status bar.
- Activate the **Infer Constraints** button on the status bar.

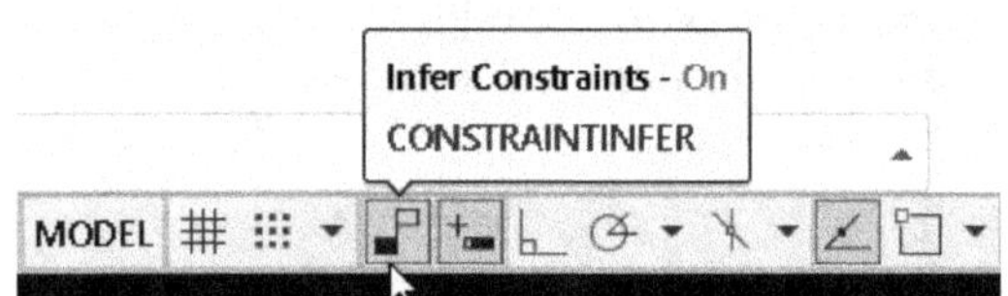

- Click the **Fillet** button on the **Modify** panel of the **Home** ribbon.

- Select the **Radius** option from the command line and enter **50** as the radius.
- Create a fillet at the lower-left corner of the sketch.

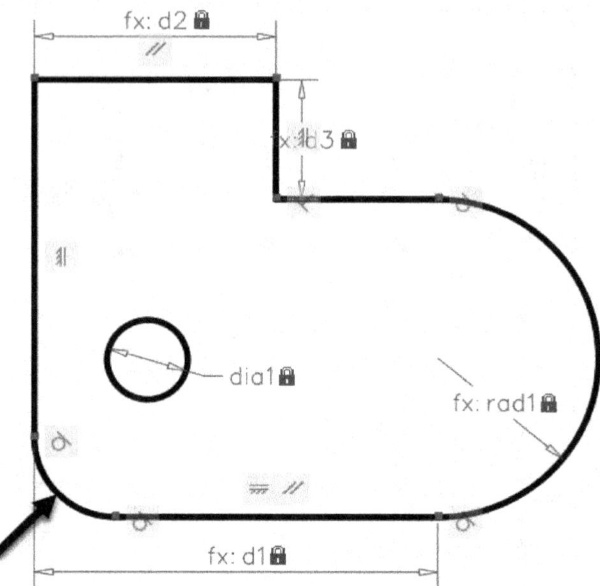

You will notice that the **Tangent** and **Coincident** constraints are applied automatically.

- Click the **Concentric** button on the **Geometric** panel.
- Select the circle located outside the loop and the fillet; they both will be concentric.

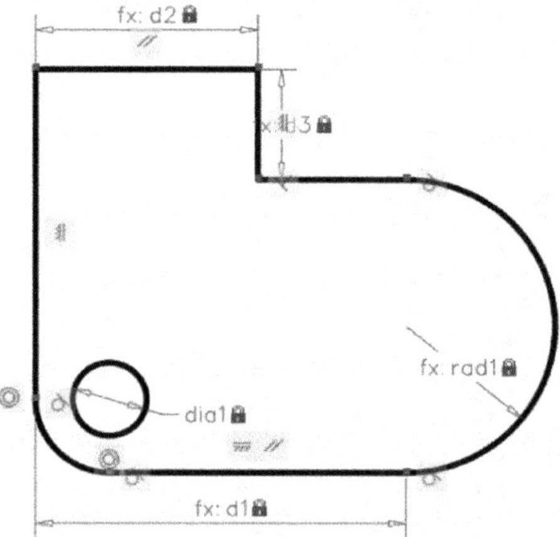

- Use the **Radius** tool from the **Dimensional** panel and apply the dimensional radius constraint to the fillet.
- Open the **Parameters Manager** palette and modify the **rad2** value to **3/2*dia1**.

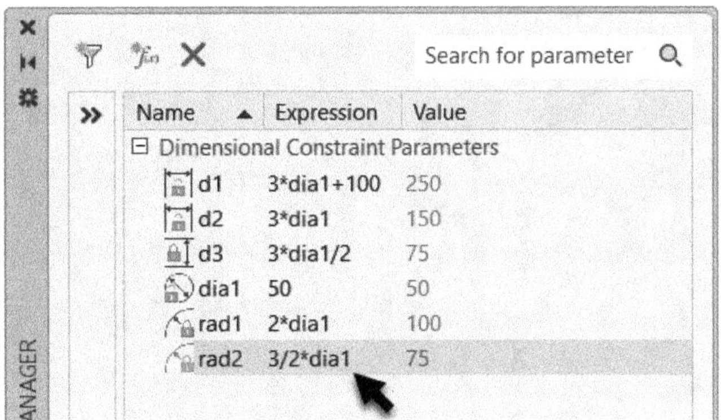

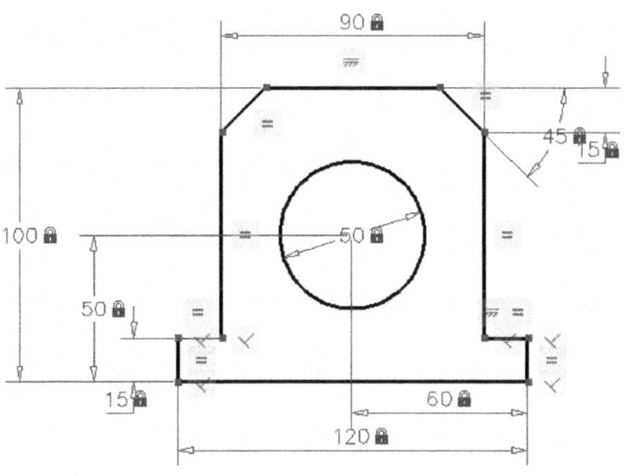

- To hide all the **Geometric Constraints**, click the **Hide All** button on the **Geometric** panel.
- Similarly, click **Hide All** on the **Dimensional** panel to hide all the dimensional constraints.

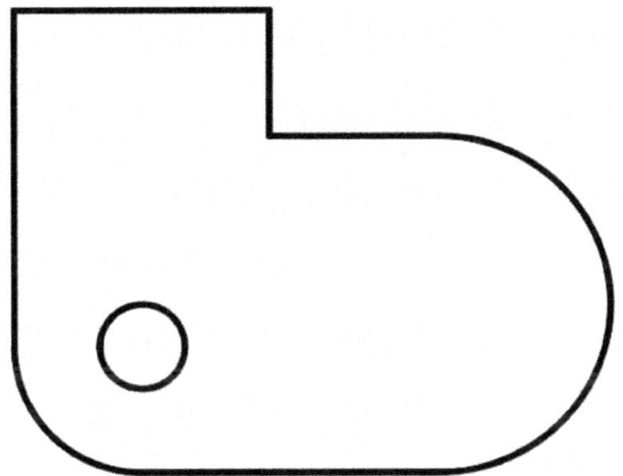

- To modify the size of the drawing, change the value of **dia1** in the **Parameters Manager** window; you will notice that all the values will be changed automatically.
- Save and close the file.

Exercises

Exercise 1

In this exercise, you need to create the drawing shown in the figure and apply geometric and dimensional constraints to it.

Exercise 2

In this exercise, you need to create the drawing as shown below and apply geometric and dimensional constraints to it. Also, create relations between dimensions in the **Parameters Manager**.

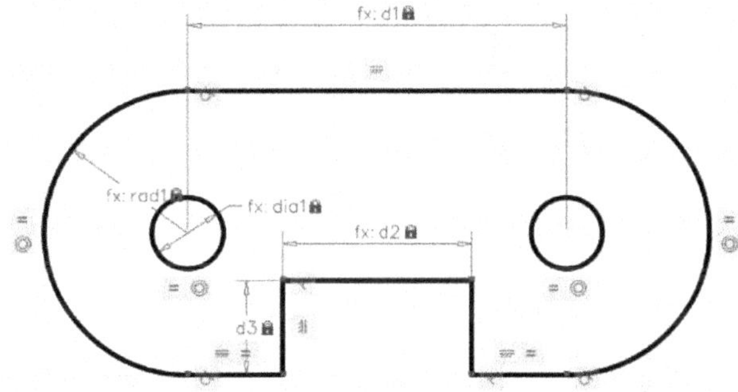

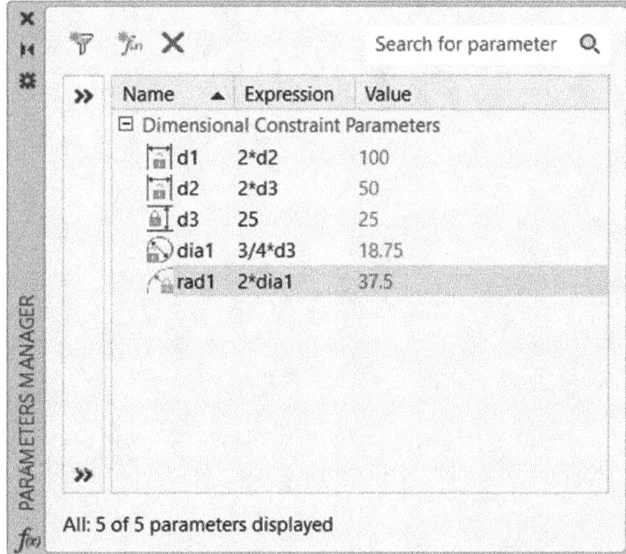

Chapter 8: Section Views

In this chapter, you will learn to:

- **Create Section Views**
- **Set Hatch Properties**
- **Use Island Detection tools**
- **Create text in Hatching**
- **Edit Hatching**

Section Views

In this chapter, you will learn to create section views. You can create section views to display the interior portion of a component that cannot be shown clearly using hidden lines. It can be done by cutting the component using an imaginary plane. In a section view, section lines, or cross-hatch lines are added to indicate the surfaces that are cut by the imaginary cutting plane. In AutoCAD, you can add these section lines or cross-hatch lines using the **Hatch** tool.

The Hatch tool

The **Hatch** tool is used to generate hatch lines by clicking inside a closed area. When you click inside a closed area, a temporarily closed boundary will be created using the PLINE command. The closed boundary will be filled with hatch lines, and then it will be deleted.

Example 1:

In this example, you will apply hatch lines to the drawing, as shown in the figure below.

- Open a new AutoCAD file.
- Create four layers with the following properties.

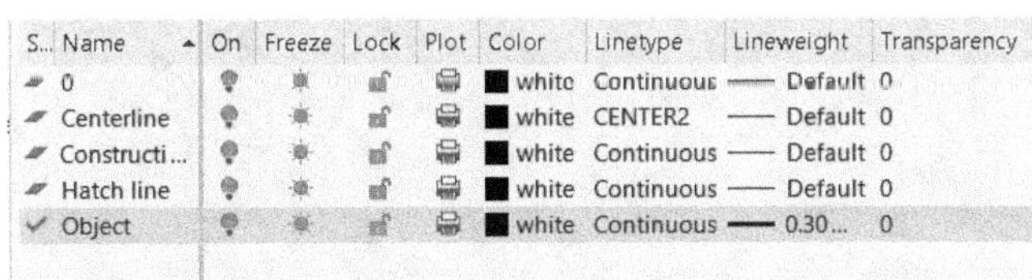

S... Name	On	Freeze	Lock	Plot	Color	Linetype	Lineweight	Transparency
0					white	Continuous	Default	0
Centerline					white	CENTER2	Default	0
Constructi...					white	Continuous	Default	0
Hatch line					white	Continuous	Default	0
Object					white	Continuous	0.30...	0

- Create the drawing, as shown below. Do not apply dimensions.

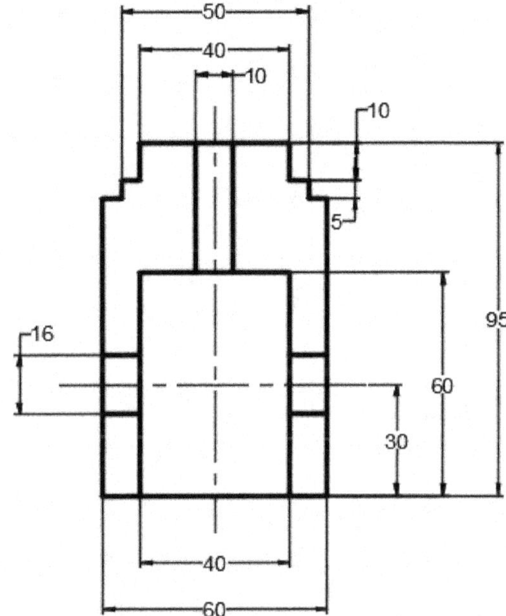

- Select the **Hatch lines** layer from the **Layer** drop-down of the **Layers** panel.
- Click **Home > Draw > Hatch** on the ribbon or enter **H** in the command line; the **Hatch Creation** tab appears in the ribbon.

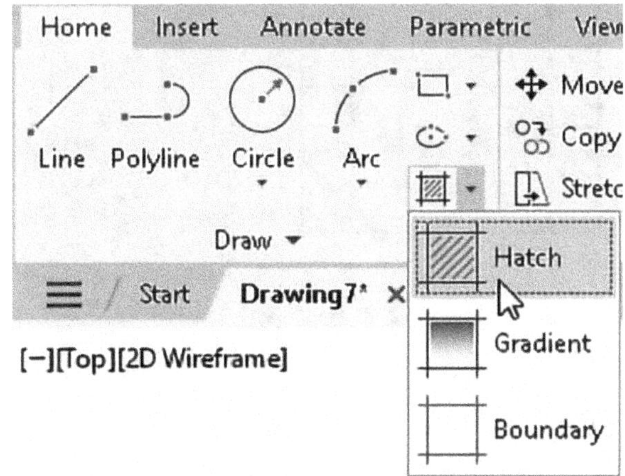

- Select **ANSI31** from the **Pattern** panel of the **Hatch Creation** ribbon tab.

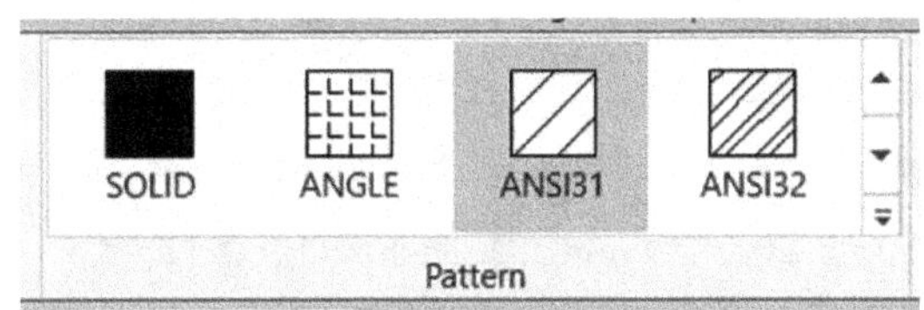

- Click on the four regions of the drawing, as shown below.

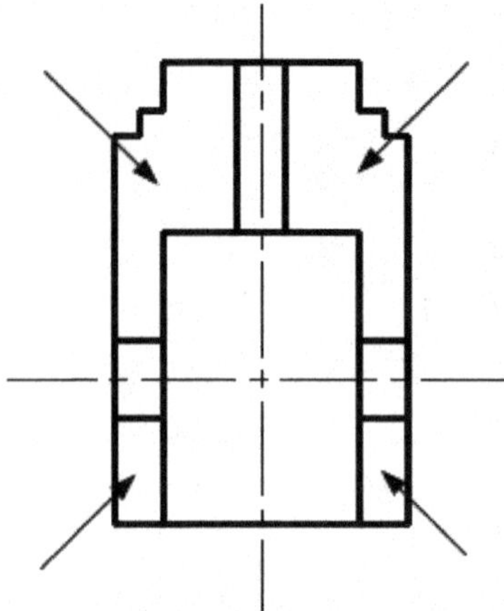

- Click the **Close Hatch Creation** button on the ribbon.

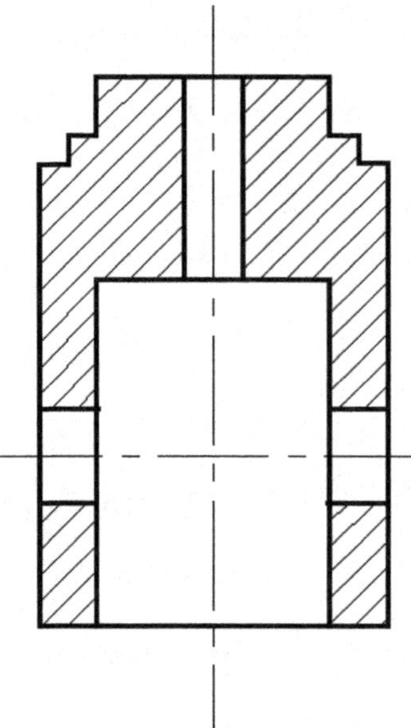

Example 2:

In this example, you will create the front and section views of a crank.

- Create five layers with the following settings:

Layer	Lineweight	Linetype
Construction	0.00 mm	Continuous
Object	0.30 mm	Continuous
Centerline	0.00 mm	CENTER
Hatch lines	0.00 mm	Continuous

Cutting Plane	0.30 mm	PHANTOM

- Activate the **Construction** layer and create construction lines, as shown.

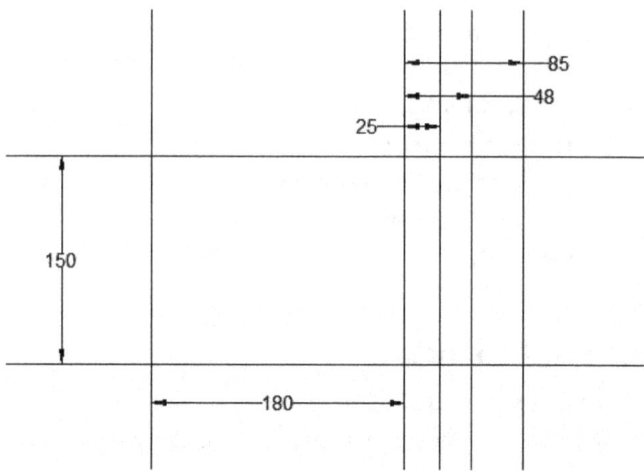

- Set the **Object** layer as current and create circles, as shown below.

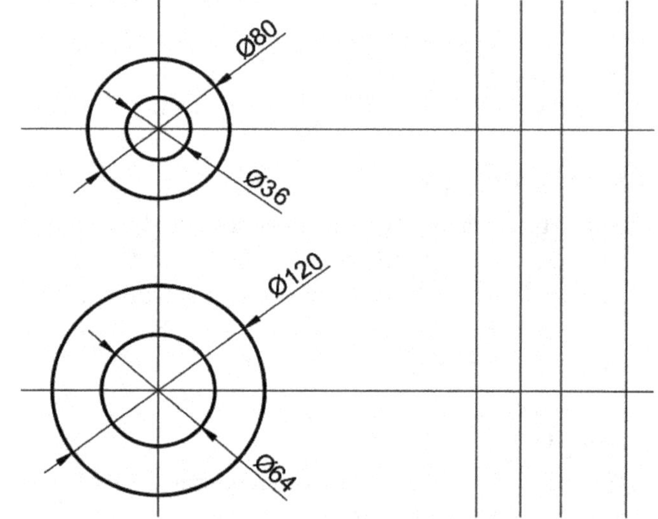

- Switch to the **Construction** layer and create construction lines, as shown.

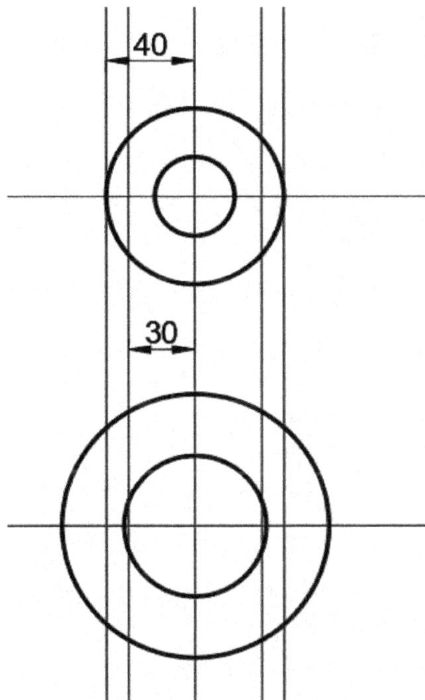

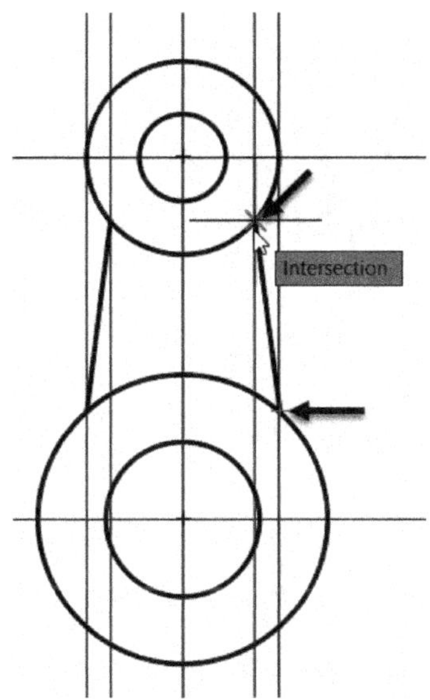

- Switch to the **Object** layer and create two lines, as shown.

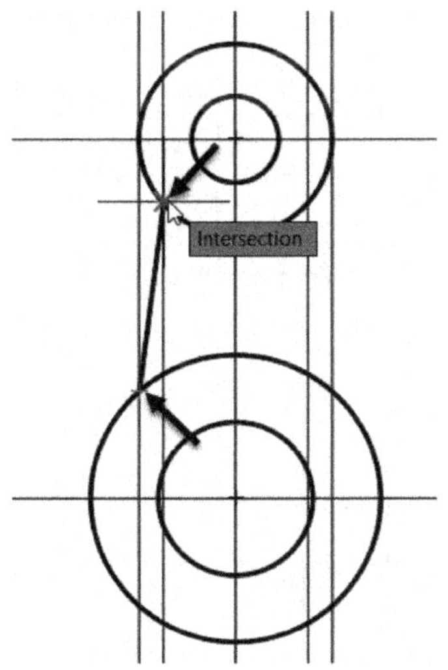

- Create the fillets at the corners, as shown.

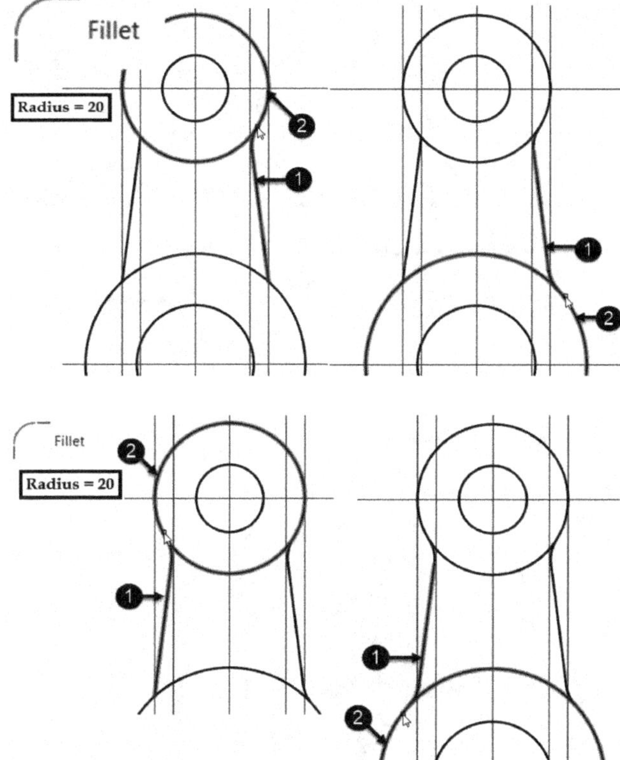

- Create a 16X38 rectangle, as shown.

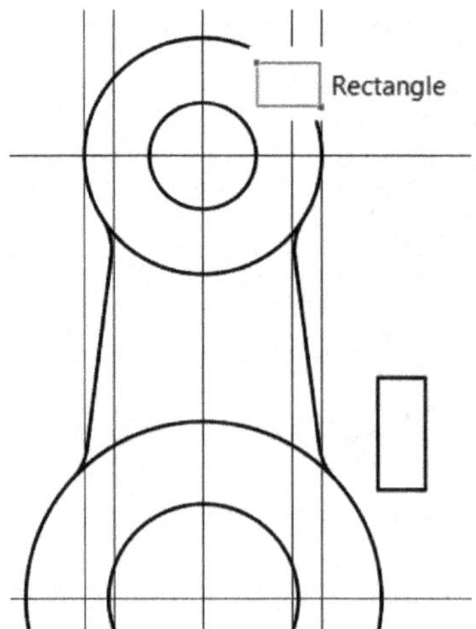

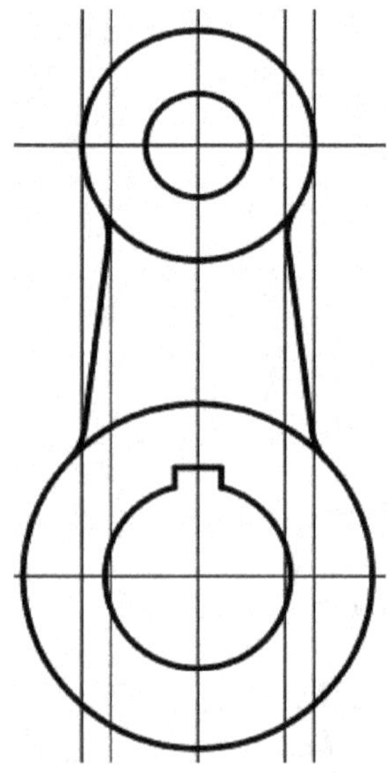

- Move the rectangle and place it at the centerpoint of the bottom circle, as shown.

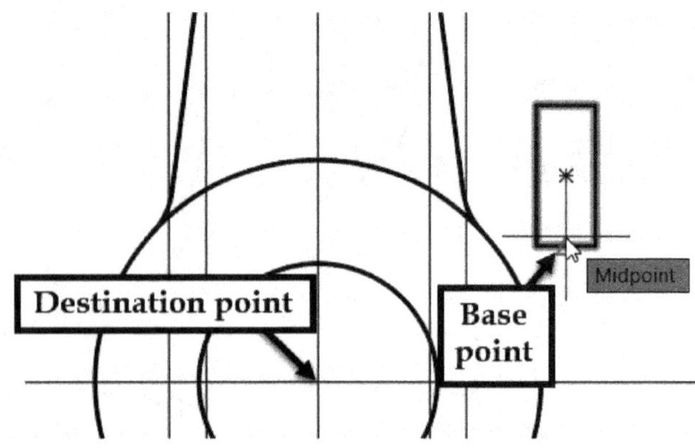

- On your own, create the objects of the section view, as shown below. (For any help, refer to the **Multi view Drawings** section of Chapter 5)

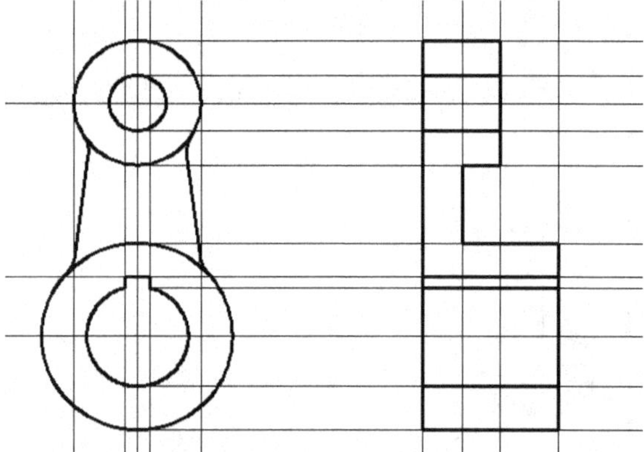

- Trim the unwanted entities of the rectangle, as shown.

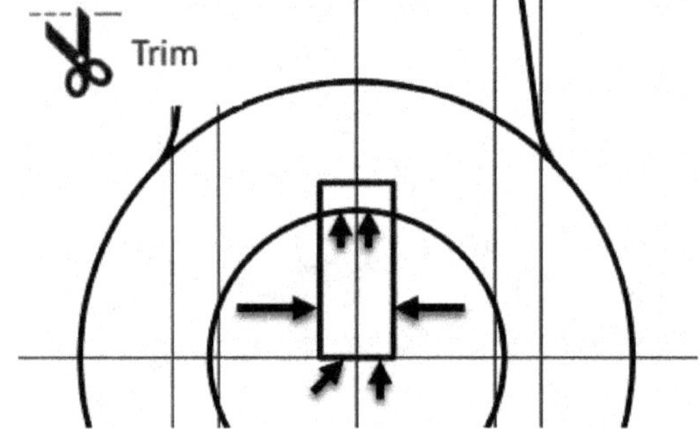

- Hide the **Construction** layer.
- Set the **Centerlines** layer as current and create center marks and centrelines.

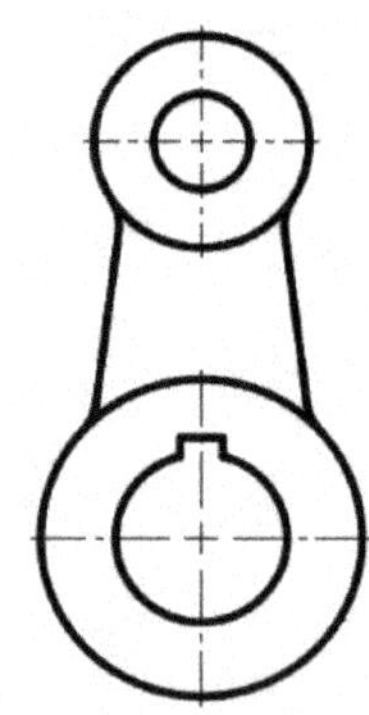
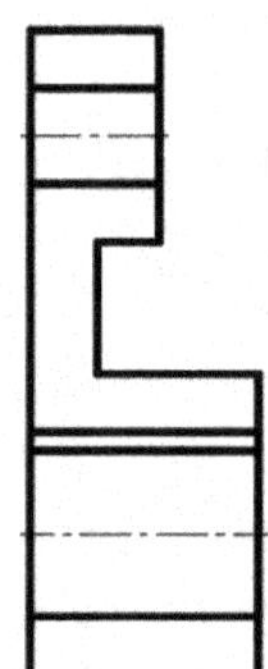

- Set the **Cutting Plane** layer as current.
- Activate the **Ortho Mode** icon on the Status bar, if not already active.
- Click the **Polyline** button on the **Draw** panel and pick a point below the front view, as shown.

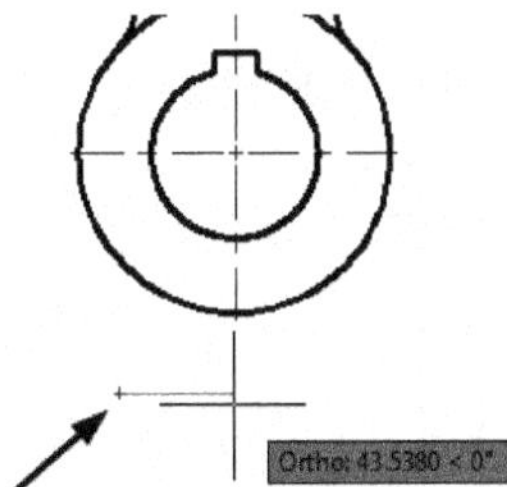

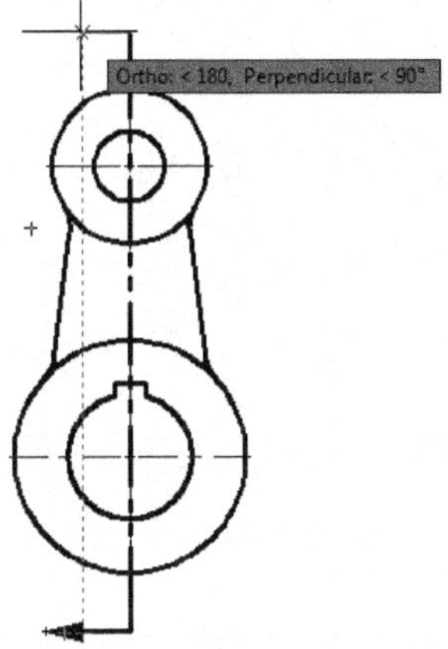

- Select the **Width** option from the command line.
- Type 0 as the starting width and press ENTER.
- Type 10 as the ending width and press ENTER.
- Move the pointer horizontally toward the right and enter 20.
- Again, select the **Width** option from the command line.
- Set the starting and ending width to 0.
- Move the pointer horizontally and click when trace lines are displayed, as shown below.

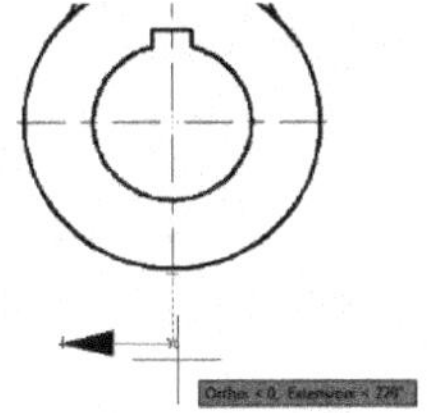

- Move the pointer vertically up and click.
- Move the pointer to the endpoint of the lower horizontal line.

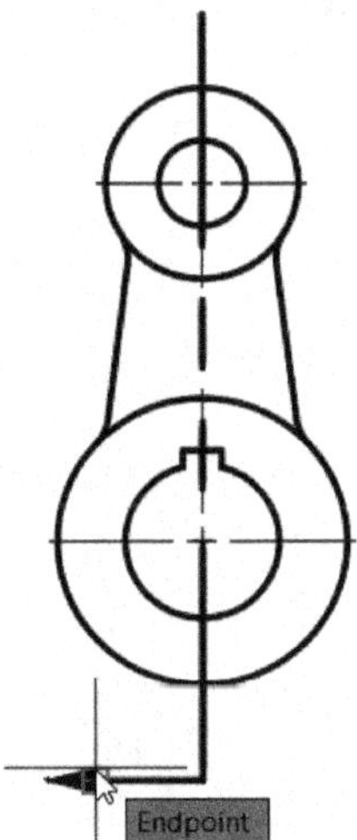

- Move the pointer upward.
- Move the pointer toward the left and click when trace lines are displayed from the endpoint of the lower horizontal line.

- Click the **Width** option in the command line.
- Type 10 and press Enter.
- Type 0 and press Enter.
- Move the pointer toward the left, type 20, and then press Enter.

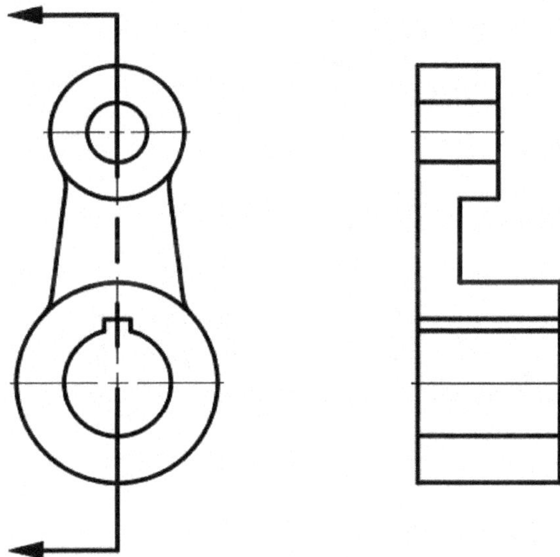

- Press Esc to deactivate the **Polyline** tool.
- Activate the **Hatch lines** layer.
- Type **H** in the command line and press ENTER.
- Select the **seTtings** option from the command line; the **Hatch and Gradient** dialog appears.
- Click in the **Swatch** box under the **Type and pattern** group; the **Hatch Pattern Palette** dialog appears.

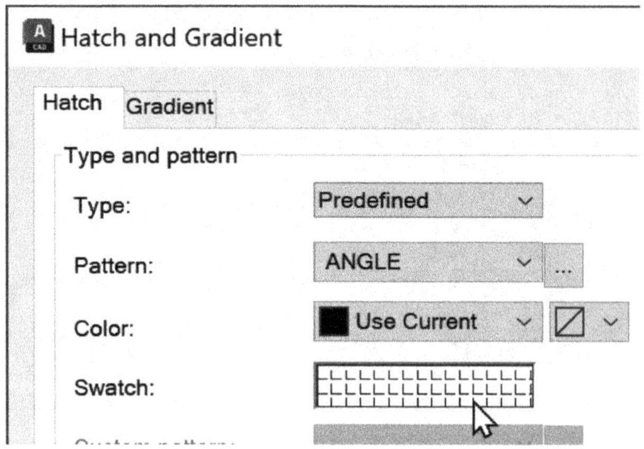

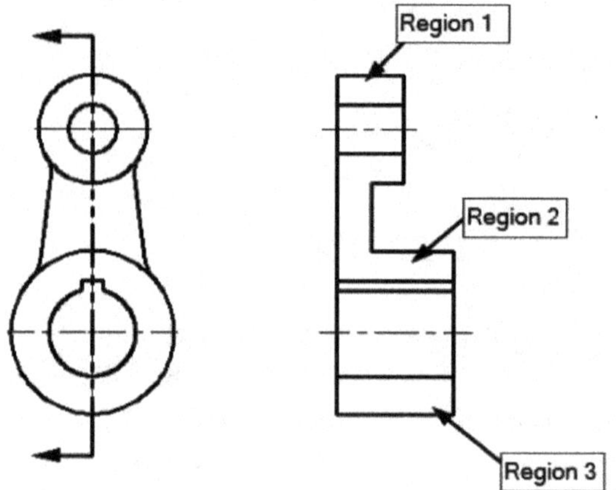

- Click the **ANSI** tab, select **ANSI31** from the dialog, and then click **OK**.
- Set the **Scale** value to **2**.

- Press ENTER to create hatch lines.

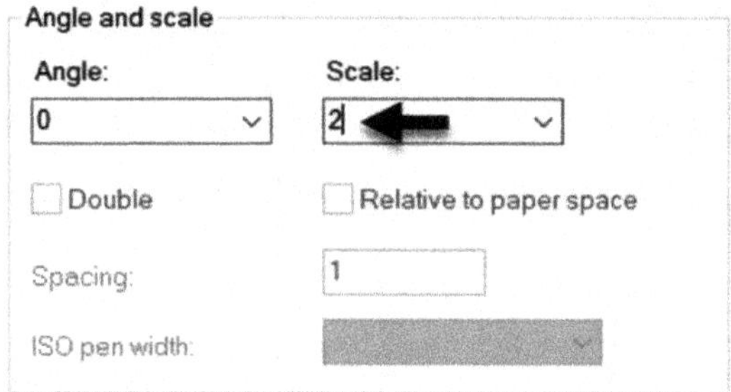

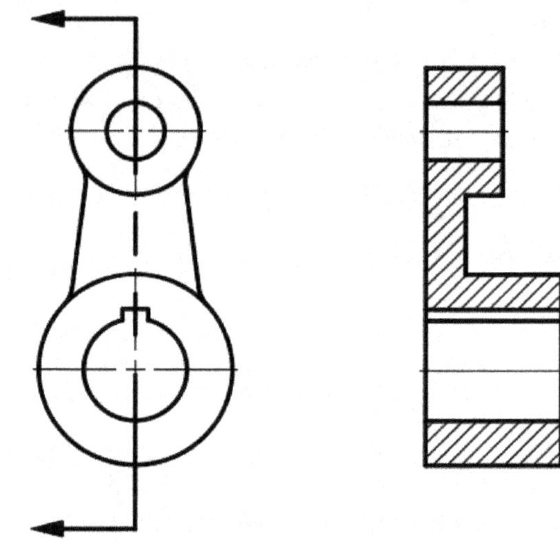

- Click the **Add Pick Points** button from the **Boundaries** group and click in Region 1, Region 2, and Region 3.

- Save the drawing as **Crank.dwg** and close.

Setting the Properties of Hatch lines

You can set the properties of the hatch lines such as angle, scale, and transparency in the **Properties** panel of the **Hatch Creation** ribbon.

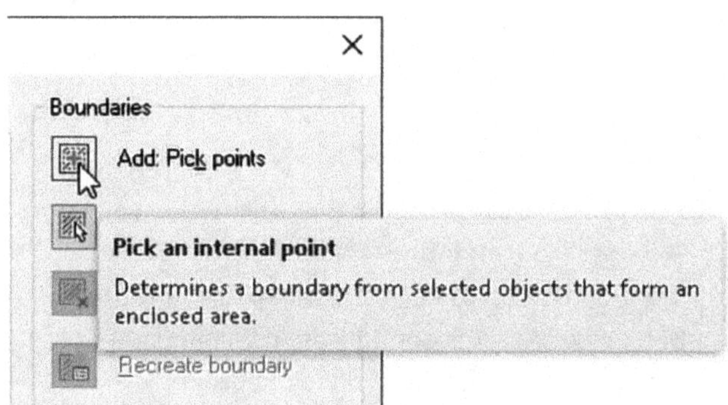

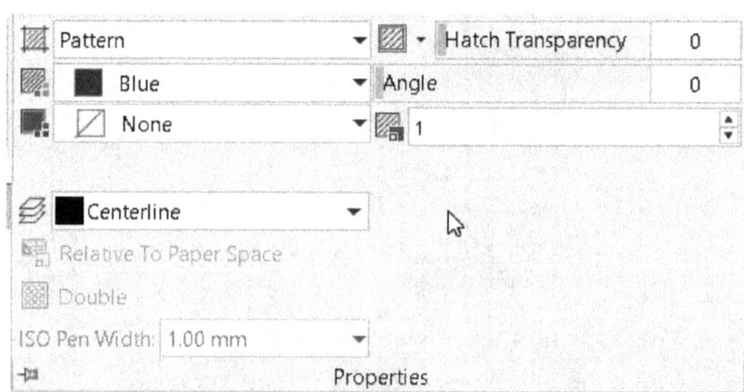

Example:

- Create four layers with the following settings.

Layer	Lineweight	Linetype
Construction	0.00 mm	Continuous
Object	0.30 mm	Continuous
Centerline	0.00 mm	CENTER2
Hatch lines	0.00 mm	Continuous

- Create the following drawing in different layers. Do not apply dimensions.

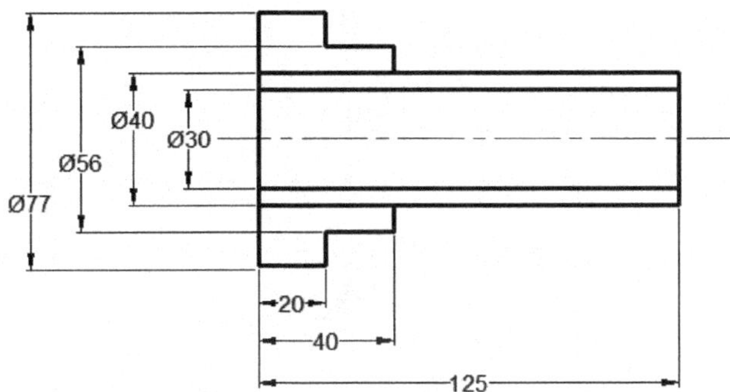

- Type **H** and press ENTER; the **Hatch Creation** tab appears in the ribbon.
- Select the **Pattern** option from the **Hatch Type** drop-down in the **Properties** panel.

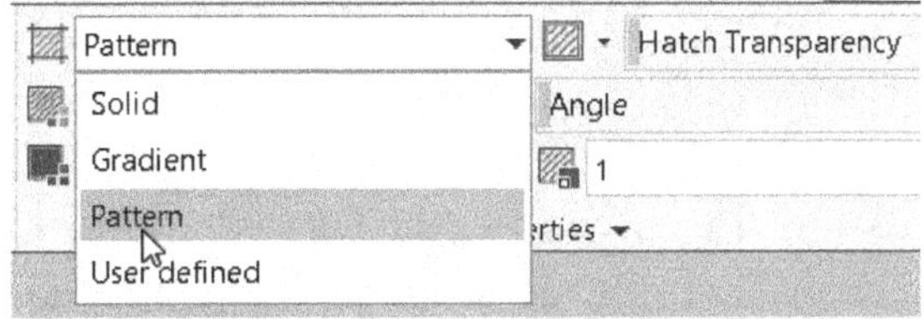

You can also select a different hatch type, such as Solid, Gradient, and User-defined.

- Select **ANSI31** from the **Pattern** panel.
- Select **Blue** from the **Hatch Color** drop-down.

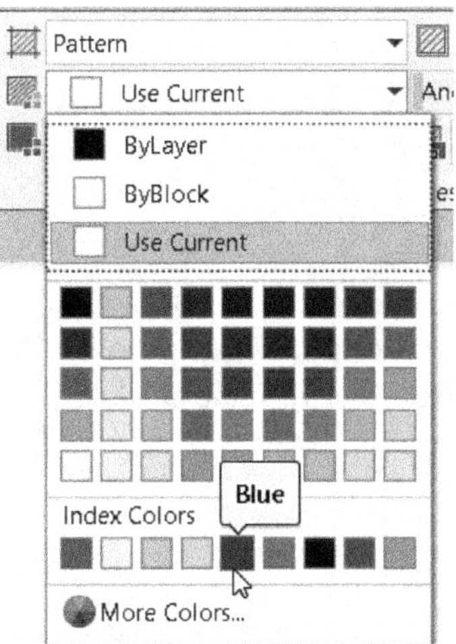

- Expand the **Properties** panel and set the **Hatch Layer Override** to **Hatch lines**.

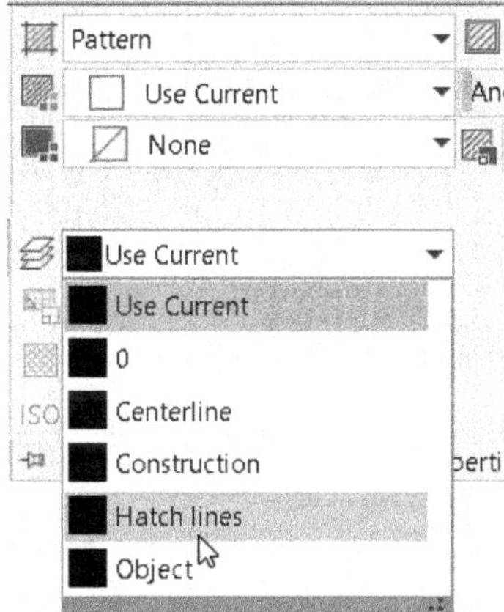

- Click the **Pick Points** button from the **Boundaries** panel.

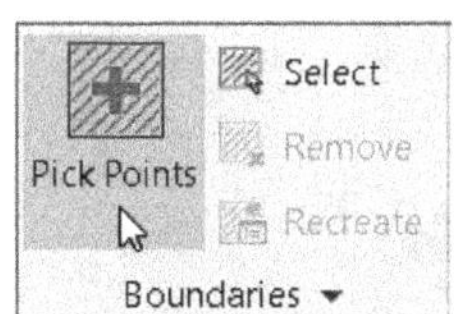

- Pick points in the outer areas of the drawing, as shown below.

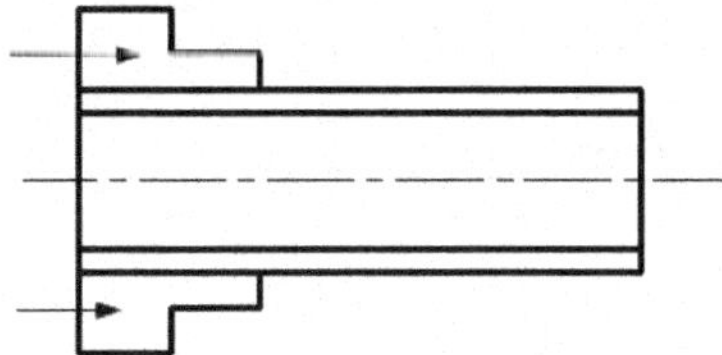

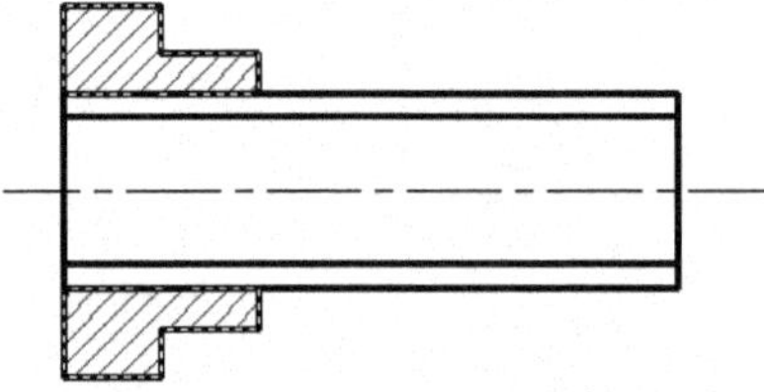

* Adjust the **Hatch Pattern Scale** to **1.5**; you will notice that the distance between the hatch lines changes.

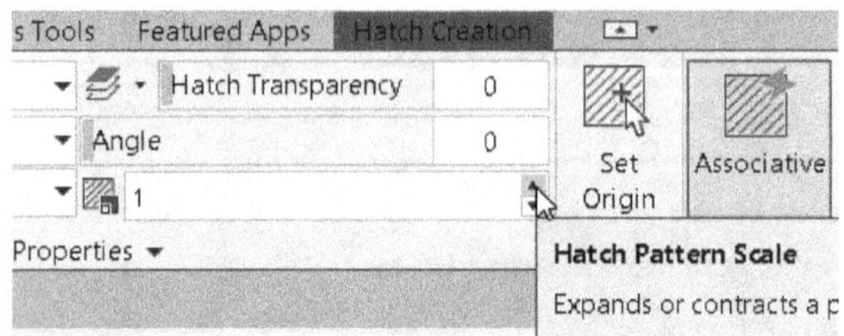

* Click the **Close Hatch Creation** button on the **Close** panel.

* Press the SPACEBAR to activate the **HATCH** command again.
* Change the **Hatch Angle** value to **90** in the **Properties** panel.

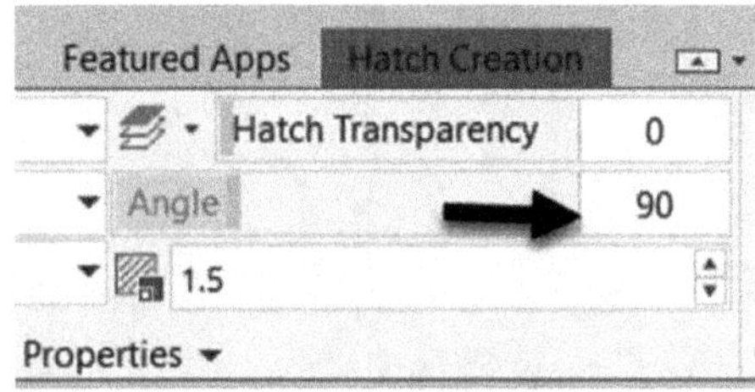

* Pick points in the area, as shown below.

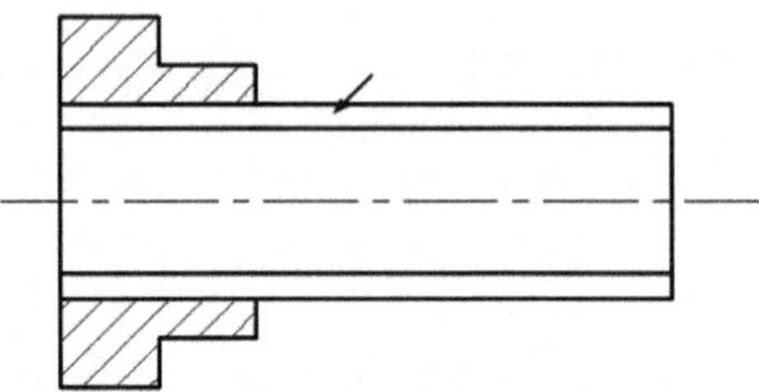

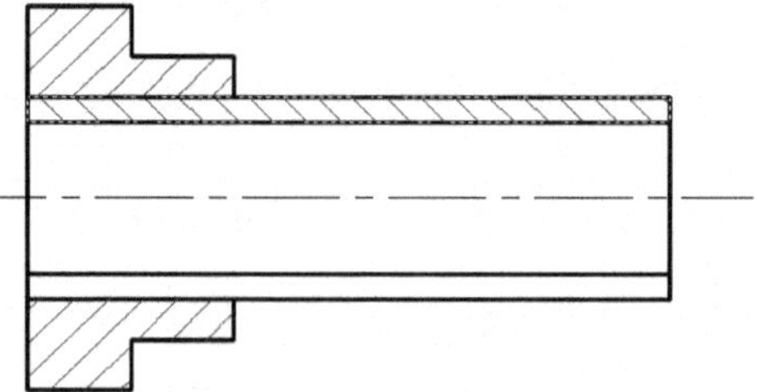

On zooming into the hatch lines, you may notice that they are not aligned properly. It is because the **Use Current Origin** button activated in the **Origin** panel. As a result, the origin of the drawing will act as the origin of the hatch pattern. However, you can change the origin of the hatch pattern.

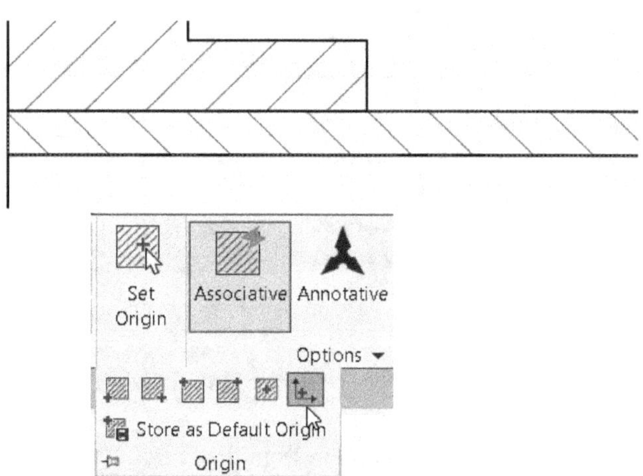

* Click **Set Origin** button on the **Origin** panel.
* Set the origin point, as shown below.

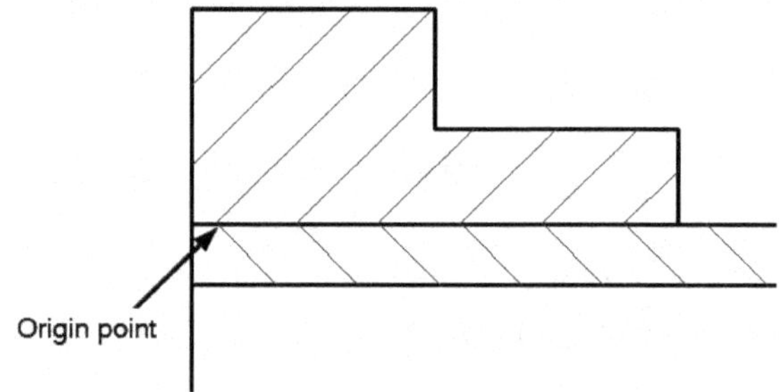

* Click **Close Hatch Creation**.
* Activate the **Hatch** tool and click **Match Properties > Use source hatch origin** on the **Options** panel.

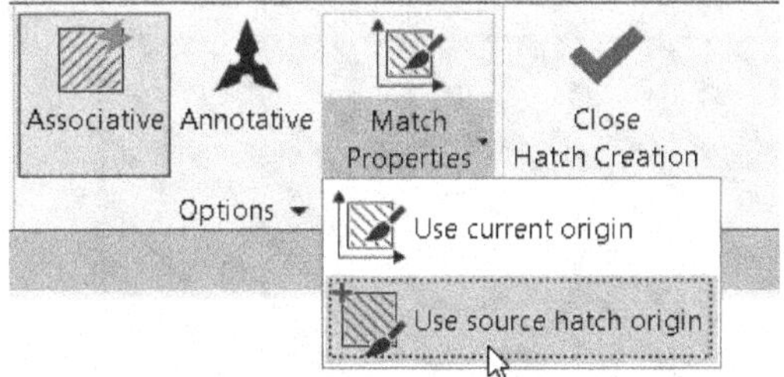

The **Match Properties** tools are used to create new hatch lines by using the properties of an existing one. The **Use source hatch origin** tool will create new hatching using the origin of the source.

* Select the source hatching, as shown in the figure.
* Pick a point in the empty area, as shown below.

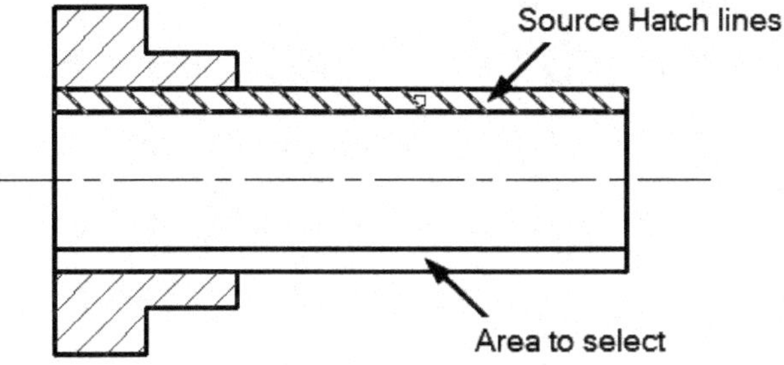

New hatch lines are created using the properties and origin of the source hatching.

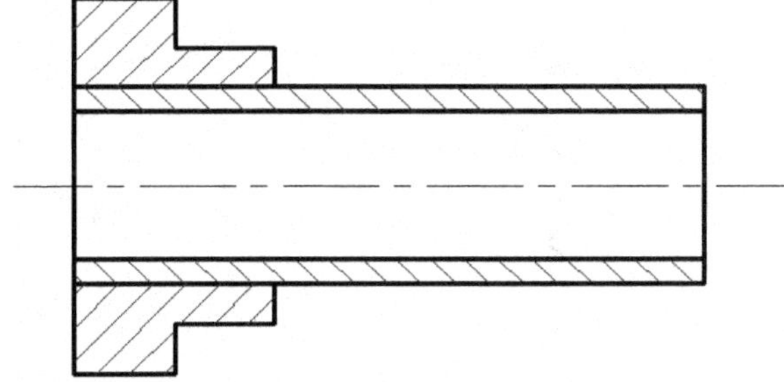

* Save and close the file.

Island Detection tools

While creating hatch lines, the island detection tools help you to detect the internal areas of a drawing.

Example:

* Create the drawing, as shown below. Do not apply dimensions.

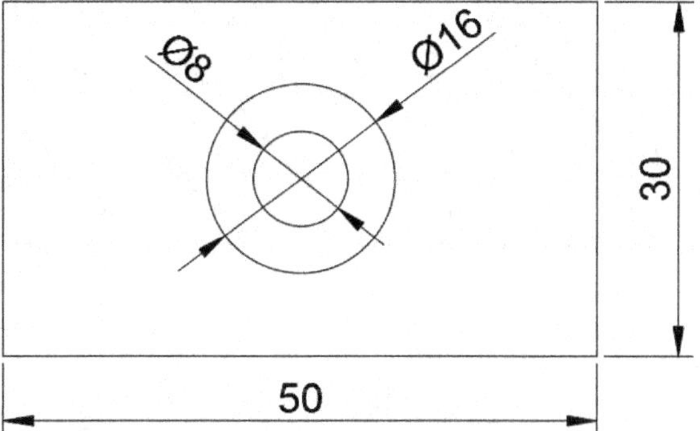

* Click **Home > Draw > Hatch** on the ribbon.
* Select **ANSI31** from the **Pattern** panel.
* Expand the **Options** panel and select the **Normal Island Detection** tool.

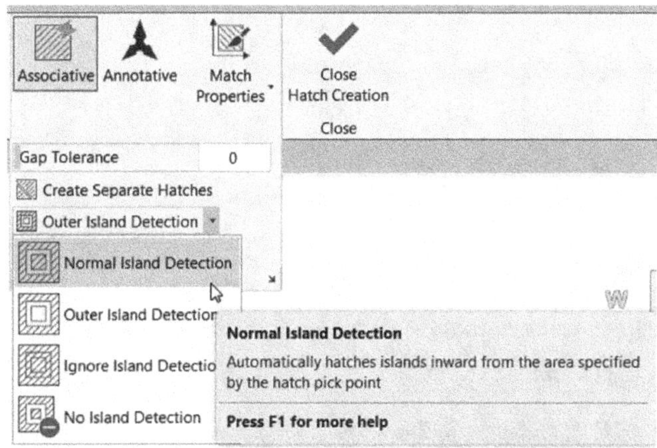

* Pick a point in the area outside the large circle; you will notice that the area inside the small circle is detected automatically. Also, hatch lines are created inside the small circle.

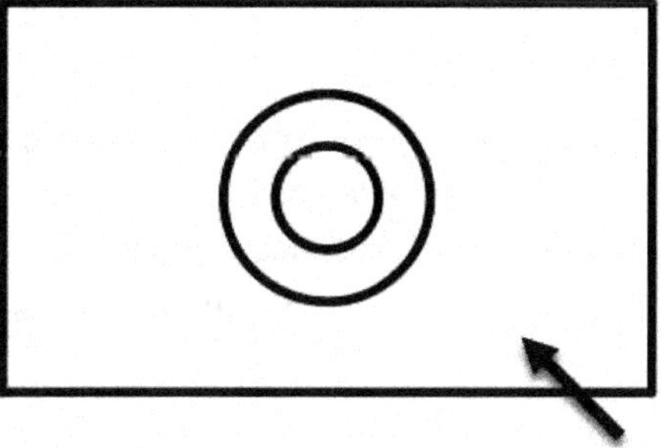

* Press **Enter**.

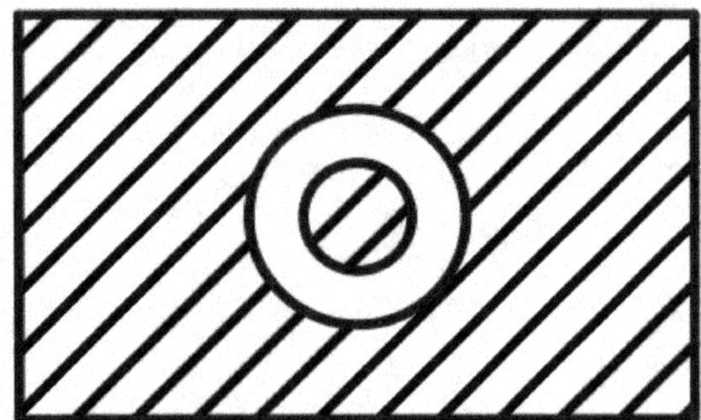

- Click **Undo** on the **Quick Access Toolbar**.

- Activate the **Hatch** tool and select **ANSI31** from the **Pattern** panel.
- Expand the **Options** panel and select the **Outer Island Detection** option.

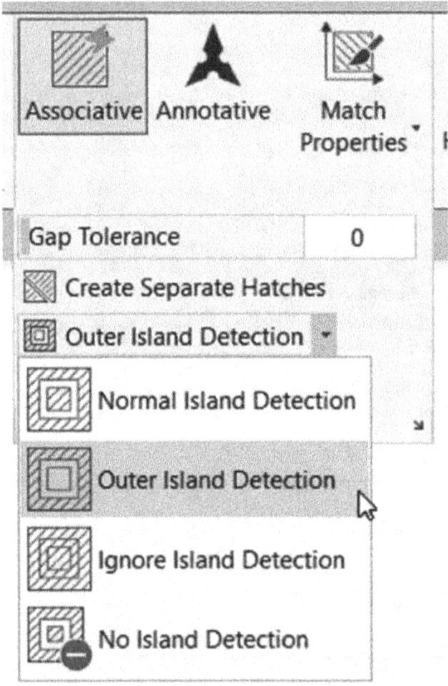

- Pick a point in the area outside the large circle and press ENTER; you will notice that hatch lines are created only outside the large circle. The **Outer Island Detection** tool will enable you to create hatch lines only in the outermost level of the drawing.

- Repeat the process using the **Ignore Island Detection** tool. You will notice that the internal loops are ignored while creating the hatch lines.

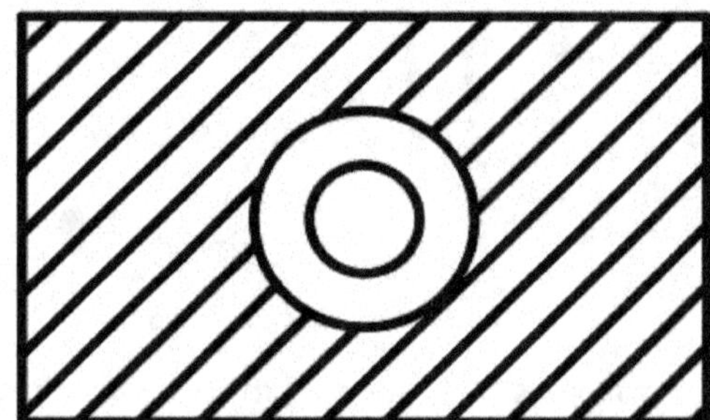

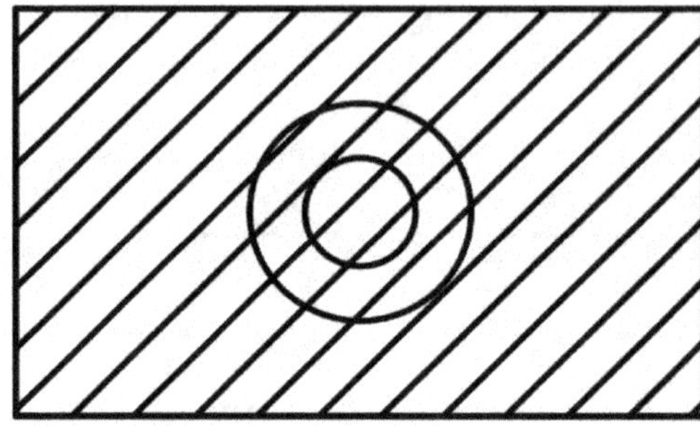

Text in Hatching

You can create hatching without passing through the text and dimensions.

- Create a drawing, as shown in the figure.

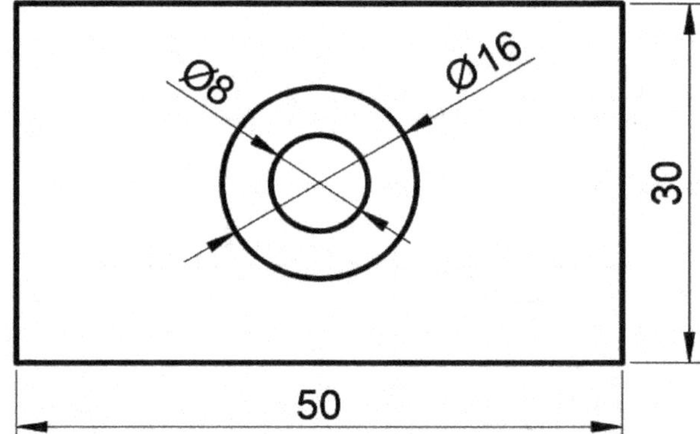

- Click **Home > Annotation > Multiline Text** on the ribbon.

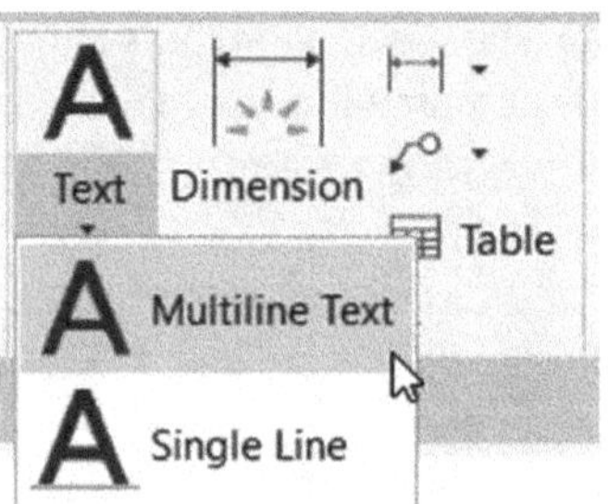

- Specify the first and second corners of the text editor, as shown below.

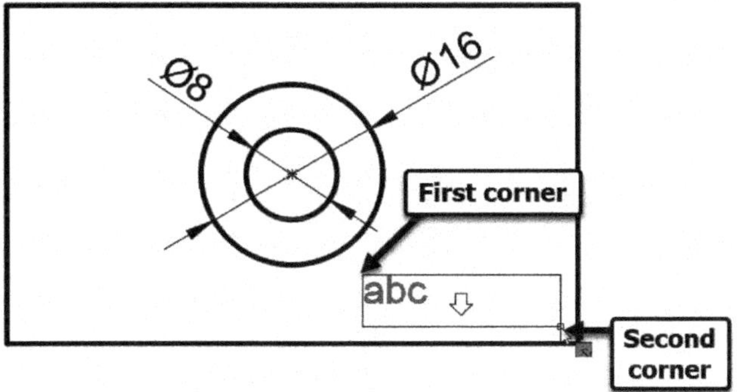

- Select **Arial** from the **Font** drop-down of the **Formatting** panel.

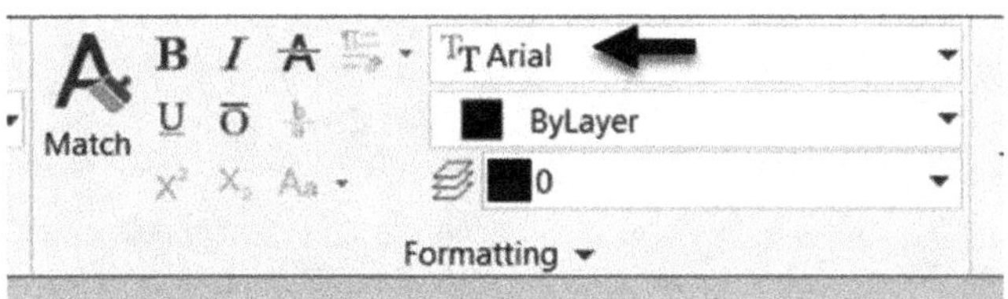

- Ensure that **Text Height** is set to **2.5**.

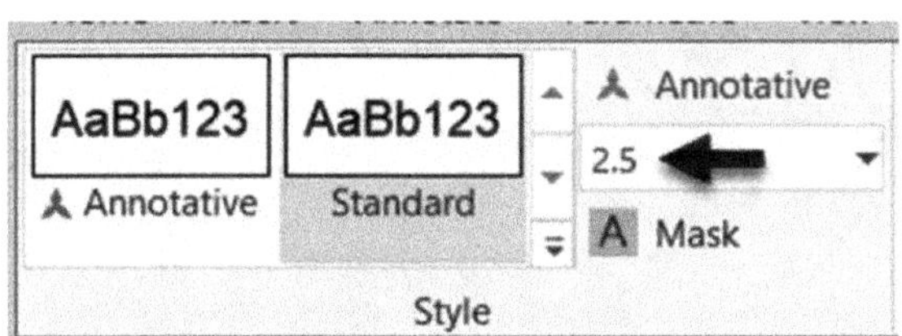

- Type **AutoCAD** in the text editor. Left-click in the space of the graphics window.

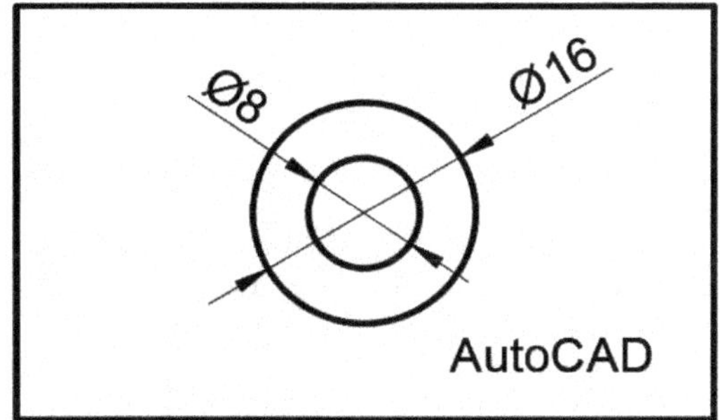

- Activate the **Hatch** tool and select the **Normal Island Detection** option from the **Options** panel.
- Pick a point in the area covered by the outside boundary and press ENTER; hatch lines are created. You will notice that hatch lines do not pass through the text and dimension.

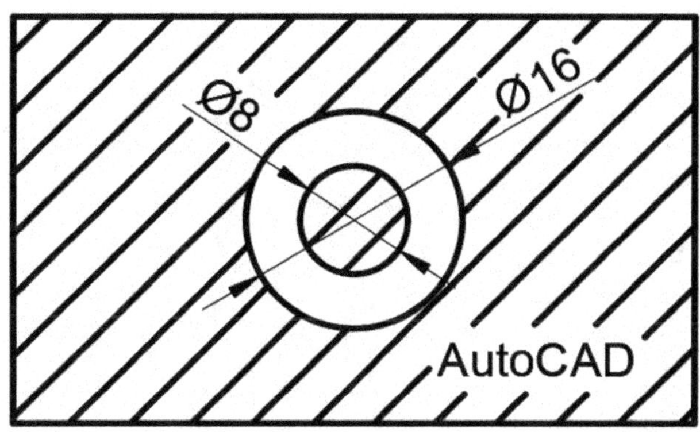

Editing Hatch lines

You can edit a hatch by using the **Edit Hatch** tool or simply selecting the hatch.

- To edit a hatch using the **Edit Hatch** tool, expand the **Modify** panel of the **Home** ribbon and select the **Edit Hatch** tool.

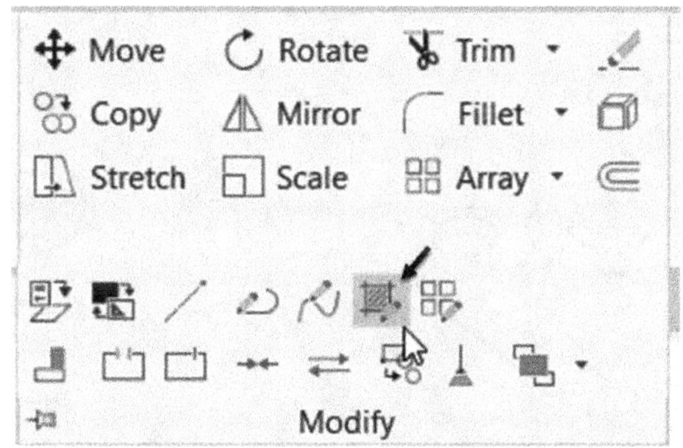

- Select the hatch from the drawing, the **Hatch Edit** dialog appears. The options in this dialog are the same as that available in the **Hatch Creation** ribbon. Expand this dialog by clicking the **More Options** button located at the bottom right corner.

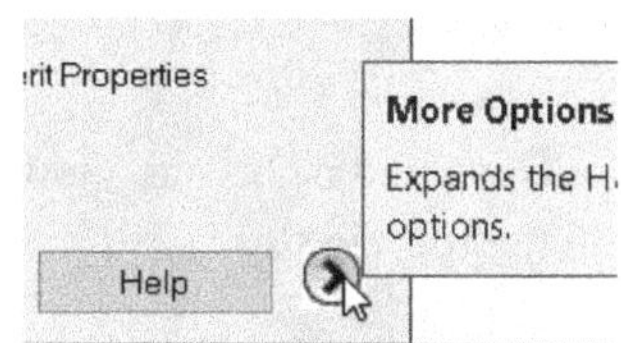

The expanded dialog will display more options, as shown below. The options in this dialog are the same as that available in the **Hatch Creation** tab.

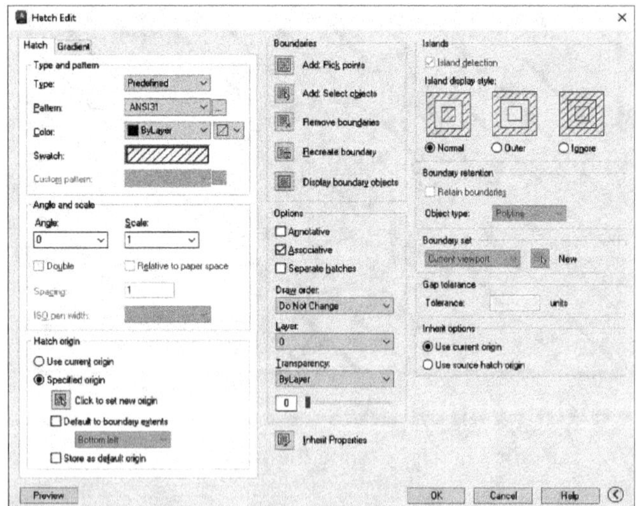

- Edit the options in the **Hatch Edit** dialog and click the **OK** button; the hatch pattern will be modified.

Exercises

Exercise 1

Create the half-section view of the object shown below.

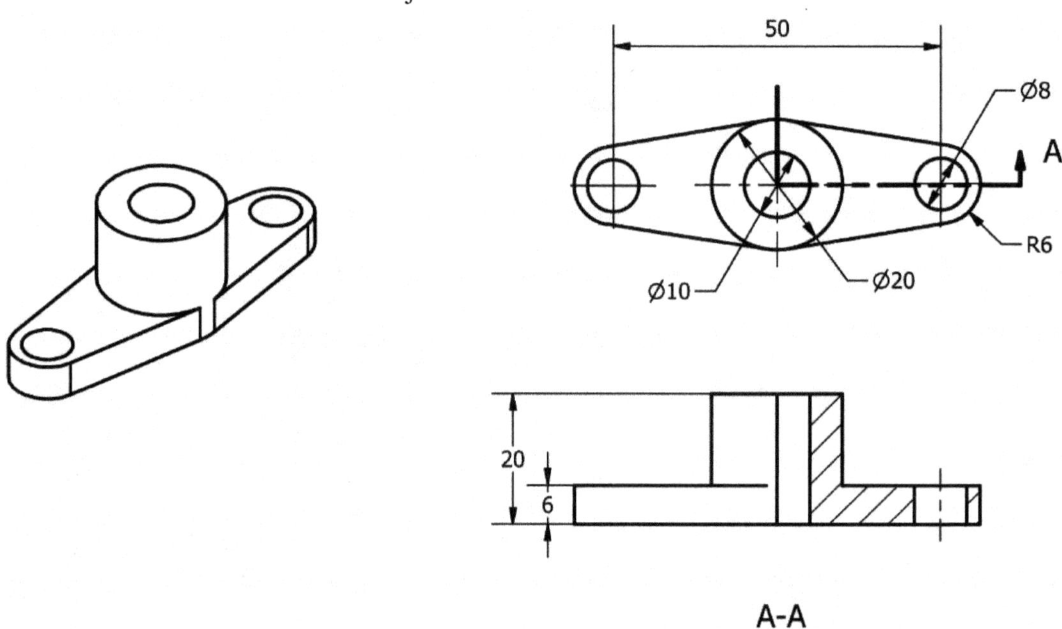

Exercise 2

In this exercise, the top, front, and right-side views of an object are given. Replace the front view with a section view. The section plane is given in the top view.

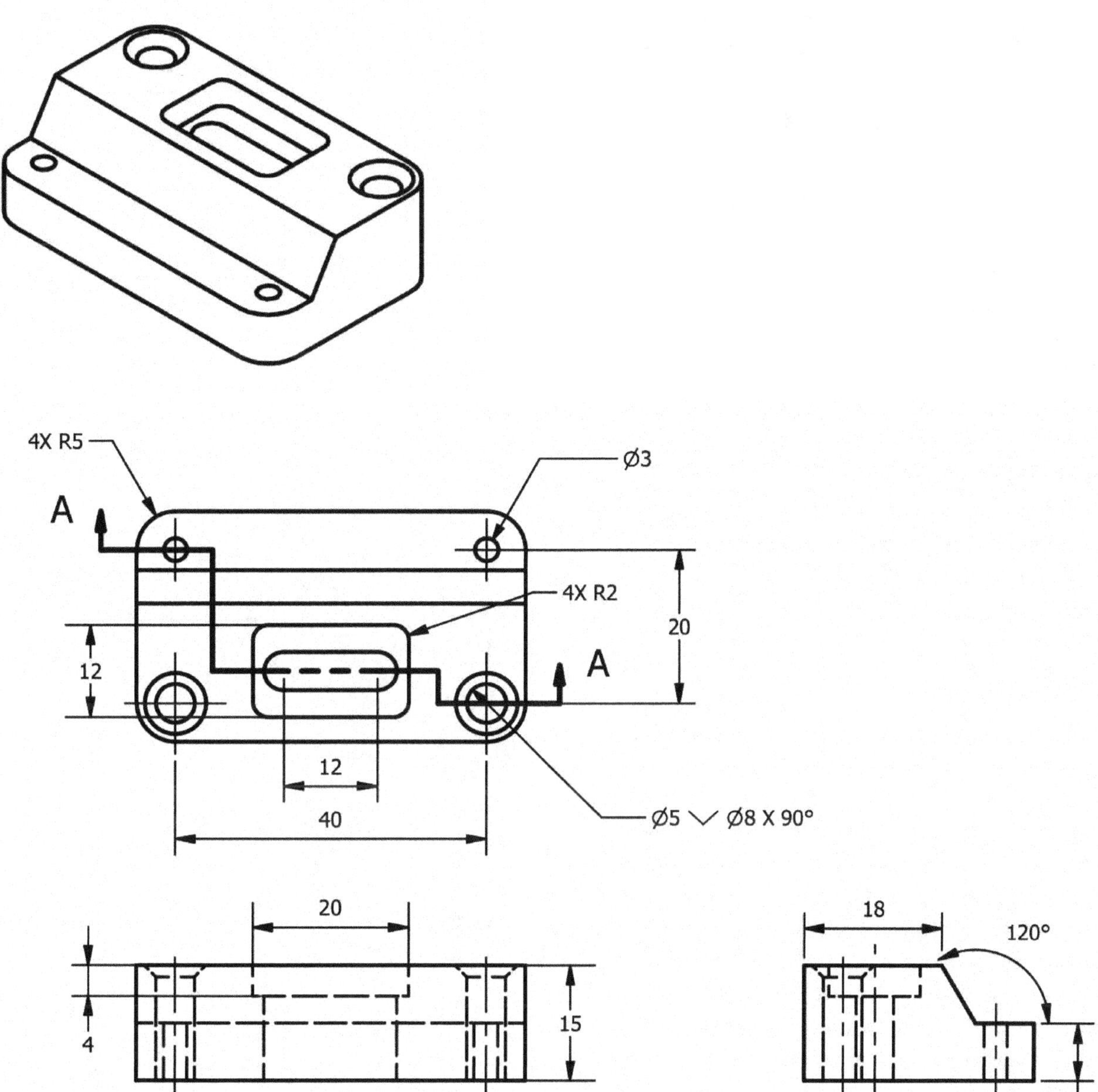

4X R5
Ø3
A
4X R2
20
12
A
12
40
Ø5 ⌵ Ø8 X 90°
20
15
4
18
120°
7.5

Chapter 9: Blocks, Attributes, and Xrefs

In this chapter, you will learn to do the following:

- **Create and insert Blocks**
- **Create Annotative Blocks**
- **Explode and purge Blocks**
- **Use the Divide tool**
- **Use the DesignCenter and Tool Palettes to insert Blocks**
- **Insert Multiple Blocks**
- **Edit Blocks**
- **Create Blocks using the Write Block tool**
- **Define and insert Attributes**
- **Work with Xrefs**

Introduction

In this chapter, you will learn to create and insert Blocks and Attributes in a drawing. You will also learn to attach external references to a drawing. The first part of this chapter deals with Blocks. A Block is a group of objects combined and saved together. You can later insert it in drawings. The second part of this chapter deals with Attributes. An Attribute is an intelligent text attached to a block. It can be any information related to the block such as description, part name, and value, and so on. The third part of the chapter deals with the Xrefs (external references). External references are drawing files, images, PDF files attached to a drawing.

Creating Blocks

To create a block, first, you need to create shapes using the drawing tools and use the BLOCK command to convert all the objects into a single object. The following example shows the procedure to create a block.

Example 1

- Create the drawing, as shown below. Do not apply dimensions. Assume the missing dimensions.

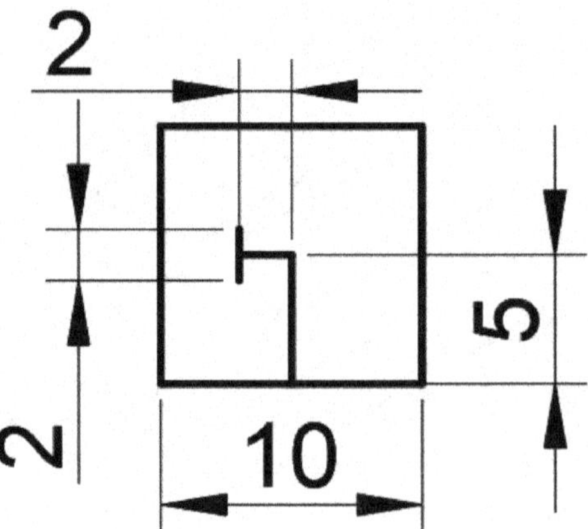

- Click **Insert > Block Definition > Create Block** on the ribbon; the **Block Definition** dialog appears.

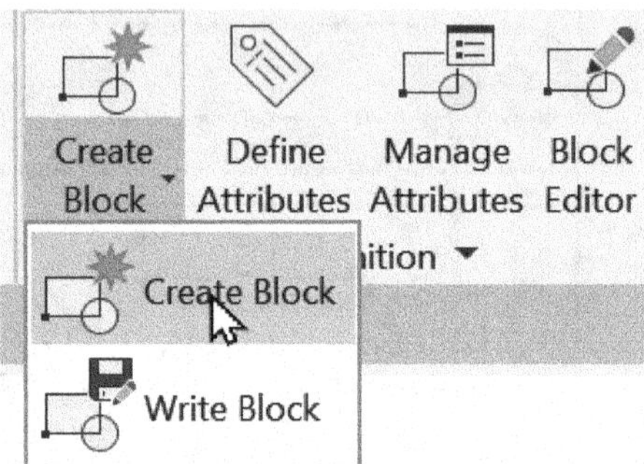

- Enter **Target** in the **Name** field.

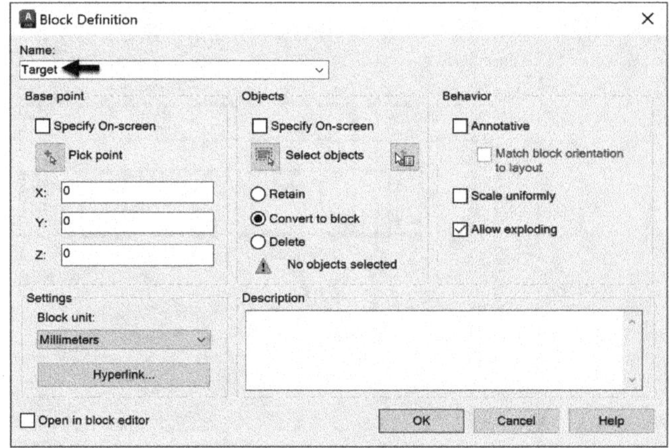

- Click the **Select Objects** button on the dialog. Drag a window and select all the objects of the drawing.
- Right-click to accept; the dialog appears again. You can choose to retain or delete the objects after defining the block. The **Retain** option under the **Objects** section retains the objects in the graphics window after defining the block. The **Convert to Block** option deletes the objects and displays the

block in place of them. The **Delete** option completely deletes the objects from the graphics window.

- Select the **Delete** option under the **Objects** section.
- Click the **Pick point** button on the dialog.
- Select the midpoint of the left vertical line. The selected point will be the insertion point when you insert this block into a drawing.

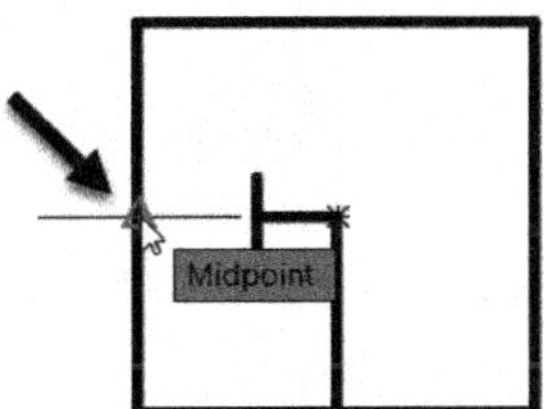

You can also add a description to the block in the **Description** box. In addition to that, you can set the behavior of the block such as scalability, annotative, and explode ability using the options in the **Behavior** section. The options in the **Settings** area can be used to set the units of the block and link a website or other files with the block.

- Uncheck the **Scale uniformly** option (for this example).
- Uncheck the **Open in block editor** option, if selected.
- Click **OK** on the dialog; the block will be created and saved in the database.

Inserting Blocks

After creating a block, you can insert it at the desired location inside the drawing using the INSERT command. The procedures to insert blocks are explained in the following examples.

Example 1

- Click **Insert > Block > Insert > Target** on the ribbon.

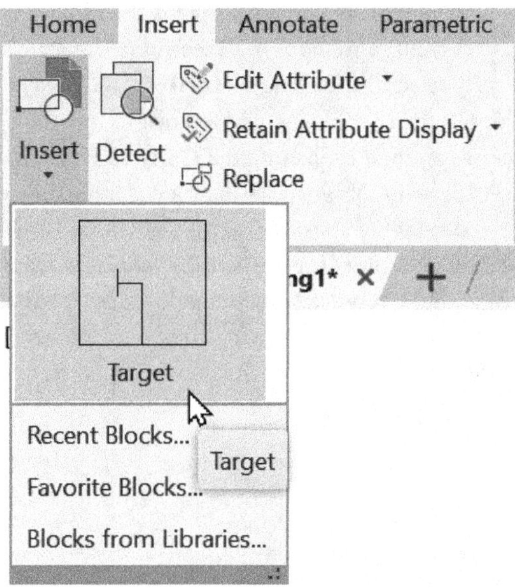

- Pick a point in the graphics window to place the block.

Example 2 (Scaling the block)

- On the ribbon, click **Insert > Block > Insert > Recent Blocks**; the **BLOCKS** palette appears.

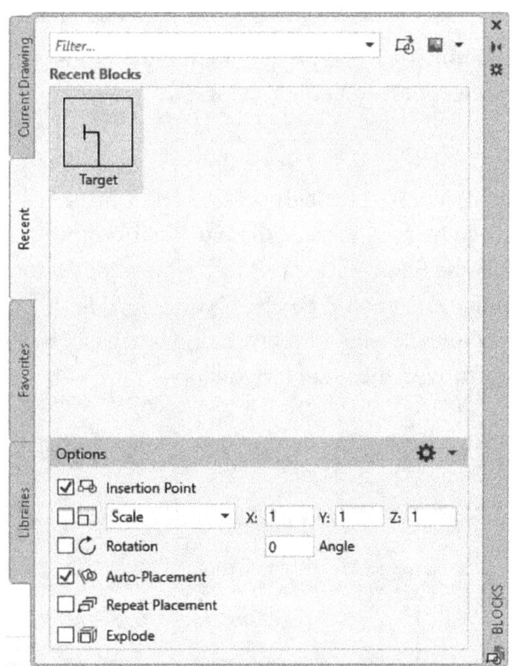

The BLOCKS palette can be used to access a large number of blocks. There are four tabs on this palette: **Current Drawing**, **Recent**, **Favorites**, and **Libraries**. The **Current Drawing** tab displays the blocks available in the current drawing. The **Recent** tab displays the recently used blocks. The **Favorites** tab displays your favorite blocks. You can add a block to this tab by right-clicking on it and selecting the **Copy to Favorites** option. The **Libraries** tab displays the blocks available in the selected drawing files. To do this, click the **Libraries** tab, and then click the **Open Block Libraries** button. Next, browse to the required location and select the drawing file; the blocks in the drawing file are displayed on the palette. Note that you can also insert an entire drawing file as a block.

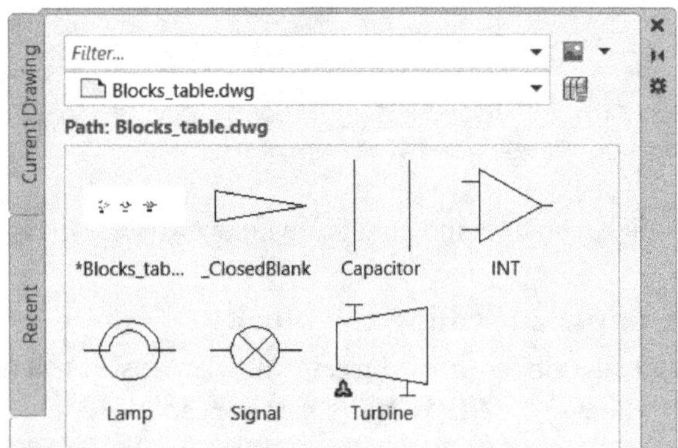

If you want to select another drawing file, then click the **Browse block libraries** icon next to the **File** drop-down. Next, select the required drawing file.

You can use the options in the **Scale** drop-down available in the **Options** section to scale the block. The **Uniform Scale** option can be used to scale the block uniformly. You can select the **Scale** option to specify the scale factor separately in the X, Y, and Z boxes. If you select the checkbox next to the **Scale** drop-down, the block can be scaled dynamically in the graphics window.

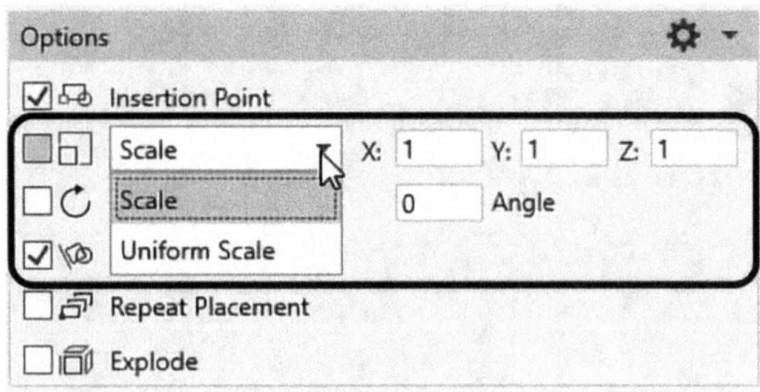

- Make sure that the **Insertion Point** option is checked.

- Select the checkbox next to the **Scale** drop-down.
- Select the **Scale** option from the **Scale** drop-down.
- Select the **Target** block from the **Recent Blocks** section; the block is attached to the pointer.
- Pick a point in the graphics window; the message, "Enter X scale factor, specify opposite corner, or [Corner/XYZ]:" appears in the command line. Also, as you move the pointer, the block automatically scales.
- Type 3 and press ENTER; the message, "Enter Y scale factor <use X scale factor>:" appears.
- Type 2 as the Y scale factor and press ENTER; the block will be scaled, as shown below.

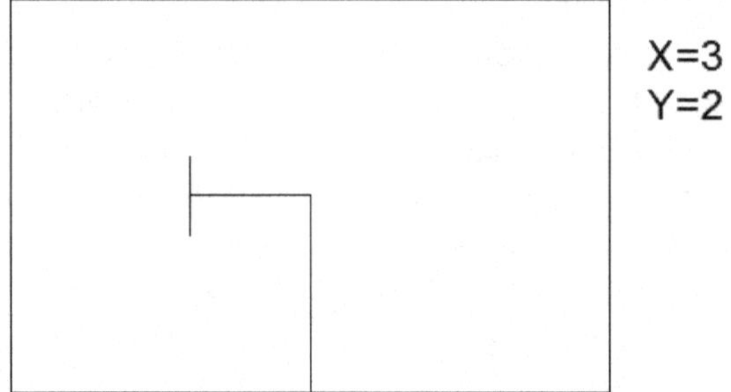

Example 3 (Rotating the block)
- Click **Home > Block > Insert > Recent Blocks** on the ribbon; the **BLOCKS** palette appears.
- Clear the checkbox next to the **Scale** drop-down.
- Select the **Uniform scale** option from the **Scale** drop-down.

The **Rotation** option can be used to rotate the block. You can enter the rotation angle in the **Angle** box. You can dynamically rotate the block by selecting the checkbox next to the **Rotation** option.

- Select the checkbox next to the **Rotation** option.
- Select the **Target** block from the **Recent Blocks** section; the block is attached to the pointer.
- Pick a point in the graphics window; the message, "Specify rotation angle <0>:" appears in the command line. As you rotate the pointer, the block also rotates. You can dynamically rotate the block and pick a point to orient the block at an angle or type a value and press ENTER to specify the angle.
- Type **45** and press **ENTER**; the block will be rotated by **45** degrees.

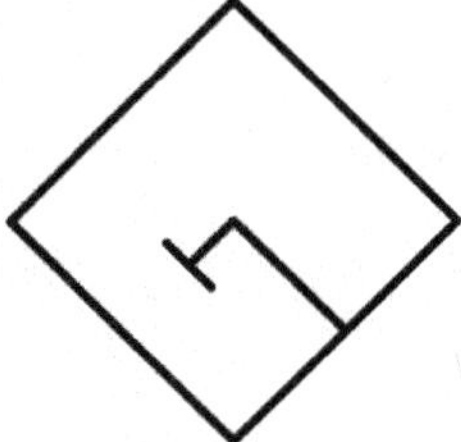

- Save and close the drawing file.

Example 4 (Using the Auto-Placement option)

The Auto-Placement option provides you recommendations for Insertion Point, taking into account previous instances of the block within the drawing.

- Create the drawing, as shown below.
- Click **Insert > Block Definition > Create Block** on the ribbon; the **Block Definition** dialog appears.
- Create a selection window across the elements of the drawing.
- Enter **Auto_placement** in the **Name** field.
- Click the Pick Point button in the Base point section and select the bottom-right corner of the drawing, shown.

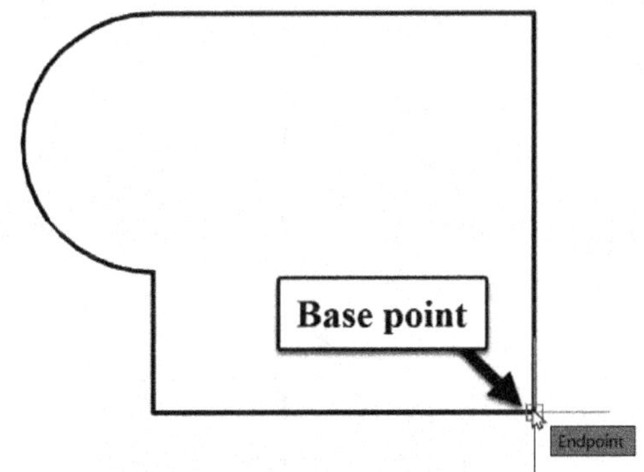

- Leave the other default settings and click **OK**.
- Create a square.
- Create a rectangular array of the square, as shown.

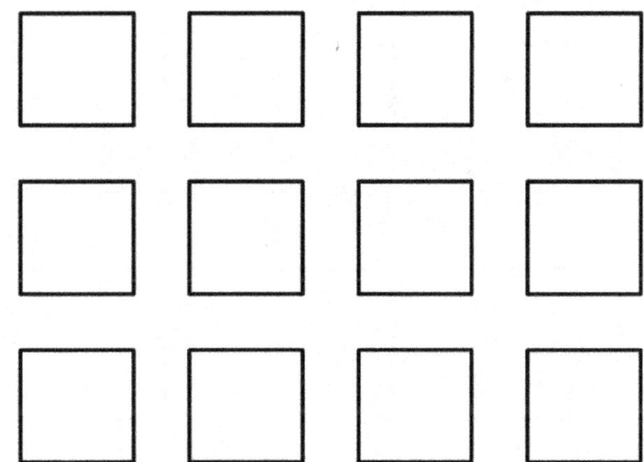

- Click **Home > Block > Insert > Recent Blocks** on the ribbon; the **BLOCKS** palette appears.
- On the BLOCKS palette, check the **Auto-placement** option.
- Select the **Auto_placement** block from **Recent Blocks** section.
- Select the lower-right corner of the square, as shown.

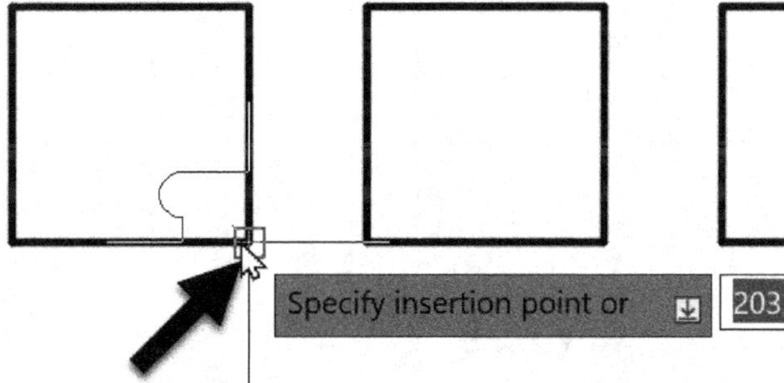

- Deactivate the **Object Snap** icon on the Status bar.
- Select the Auto_placement block from the BLOCKS palette.
- Move the pointer near to the placement point of the previous block placement; the block attached to the pointer is snaped to the previous placement point.
- Click to place the block.

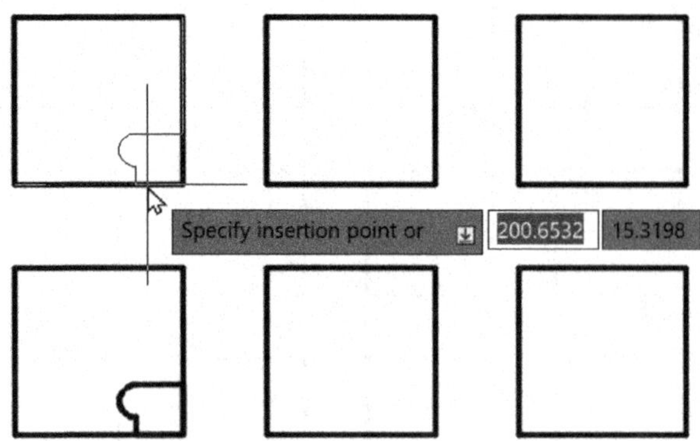

- Likewise, place the other blocks using the **Auto-placement** option.

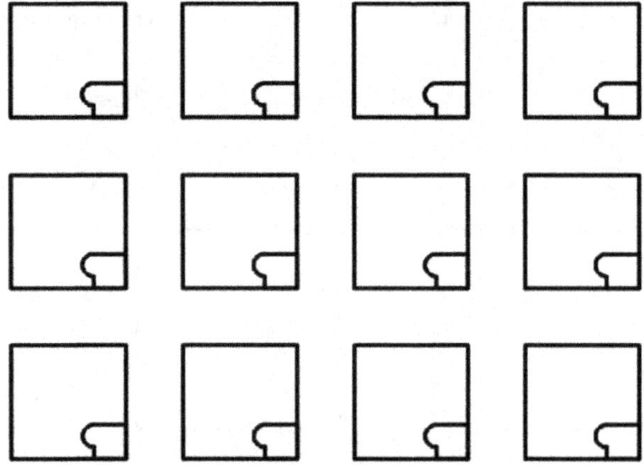

Replacing Blocks

The **Replace Block** command allows you replace a block with another block inside a drawing. It retains the original block's insertion point, scale, and rotation.

- Download the Replace_block.dwg and open it.

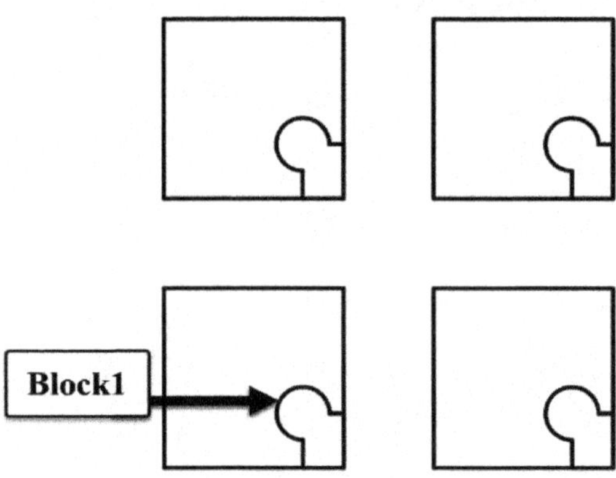

- Type BLOCKREPLACE on the command line and press ENTER (or) click **Express Tools > Blocks > Replace Block with Another Block** on the ribbon.

- In the **BLOCKREPLACE** dialog box, select the block you want to replace from the list of blocks in the drawing. You can also click the Pick button and select the block to be replaced directly from the graphics window.
- Click **OK**.
- Select the block you want to replace it with from the list of blocks available in the drawing.
- Click **OK**; the command line displays "Purge unreferenced items when finished? <Y>:"
- Type **N** and press ENTER. The original block is replaced with the new one.

Redefining Blocks

AutoCAD allows you to redefine an already-created block.

- Download the Redefining Blocks.dwg file from the companion website.
- Open the downloaded drawing file.

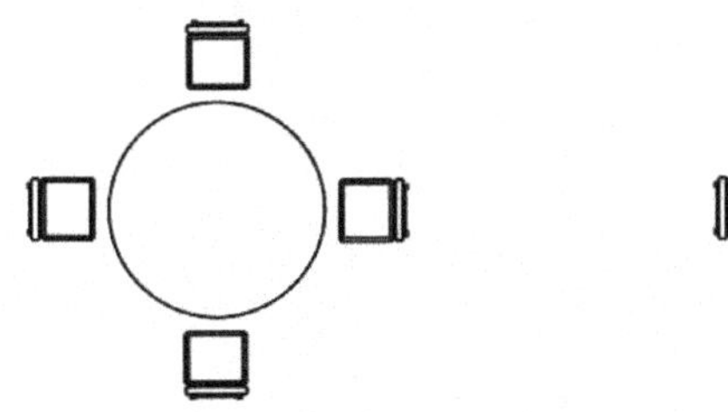 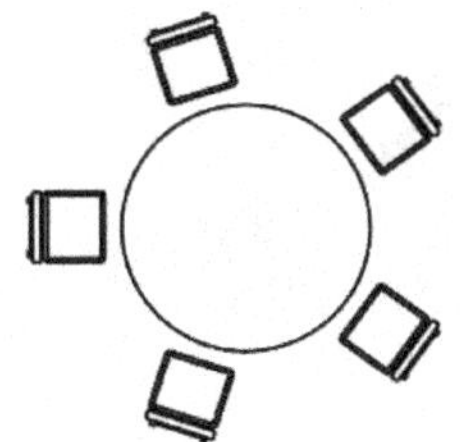

- On the ribbon, click **Insert > Block Definition > Create Block**.
- Click the **Select Objects** button on the **Block Definition** dialog.
- Create a selection window across the objects located on the left side, as shown.

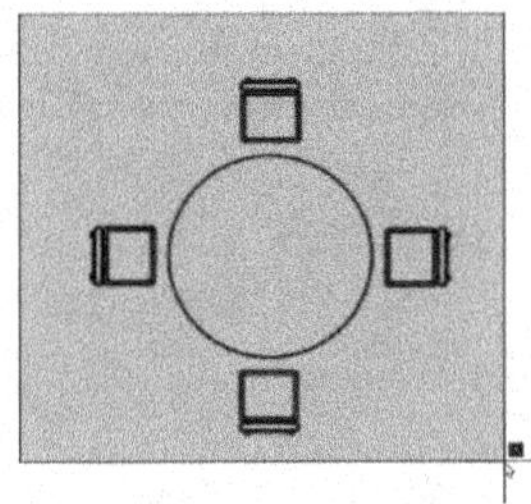 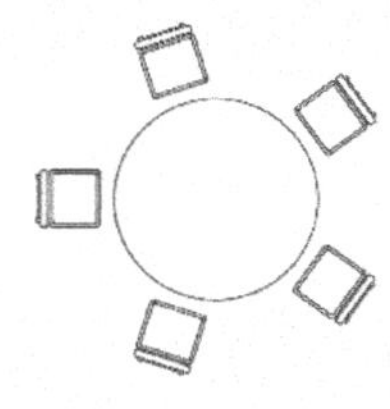

- Press Enter to accept the selection.
- On the **Block Definition** dialog, click the **Pick Point** button in the **Base point** section.
- Select the center point of the circle to define the base point of the block.

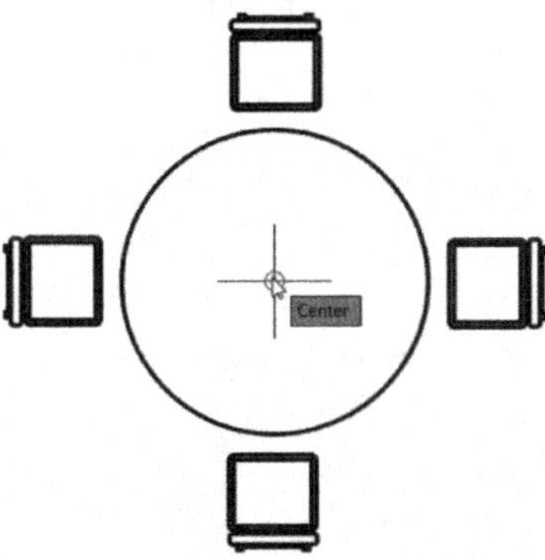

- Type **Dining Table** in the **Name** box.
- Select the **Retain** option in the **Objects** section.
- Click **OK** on the **Block Definition** dialog; the block is created.
- Click **Insert > Block > Insert > Dining Table**.
- Click in the graphics window to insert the block.

Now, you need to redefine the Dining Table block with the objects located on the right side.

- On the ribbon, click **Insert > Block Definition > Create Block**.
- Click on the down-arrow located next to the **Name** box.
- Select **Dining Table** from the list.
- Click the **Select Objects** button on the **Block Definition** dialog.
- Create a selection across the objects located on the right side.

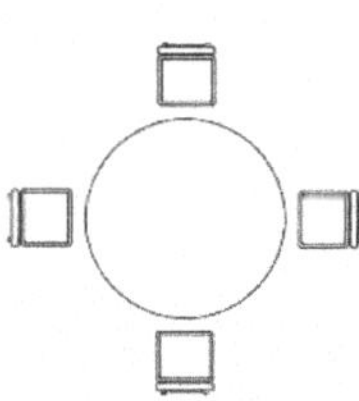 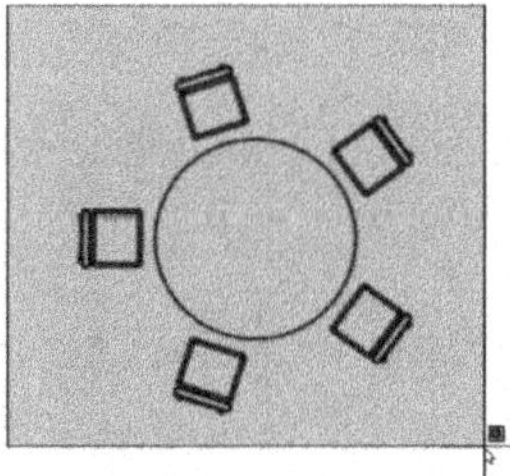

- Press Enter to accept the selection.
- On the **Block Definition** dialog, click the **Pick Point** button in the **Base point** section.
- Select the center point of the circle to define the base point of the block.

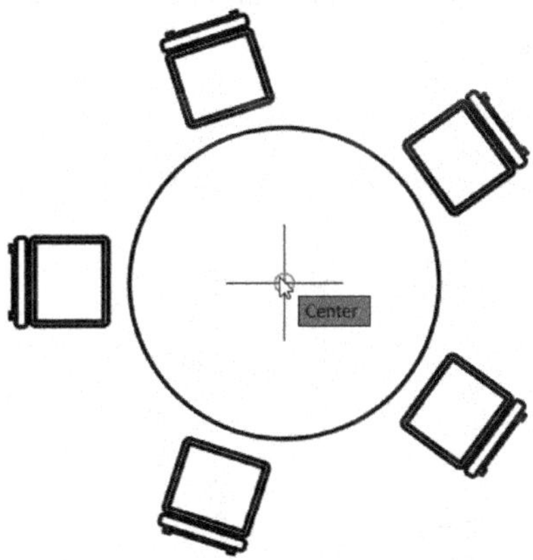

- Click **OK** on the **Block Definition** dialog; the **Block – Redefine Block** message box appears.
- Click the **Redefine Block** option; the block is redefined and updated in the graphics window.

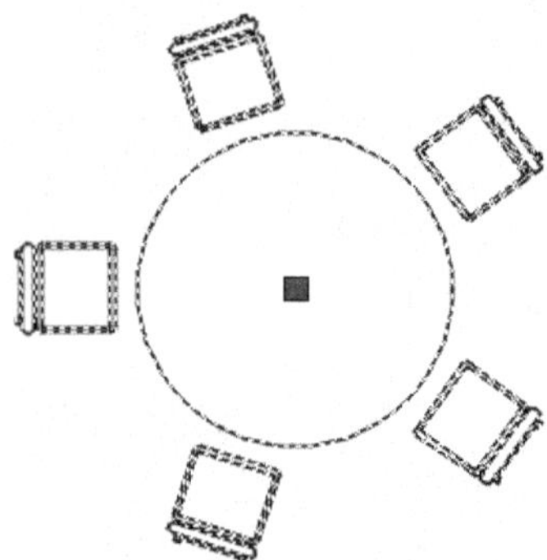

- Close the Drawing file without saving.

Creating Annotative Blocks

Annotative blocks possess annotative properties. They will be scaled automatically depending upon the scale of the drawing sheet. The procedure to create and insert annotative blocks is explained in the following example.

Example:

- Create the drawing shown in the figure. Assume the missing dimensions.

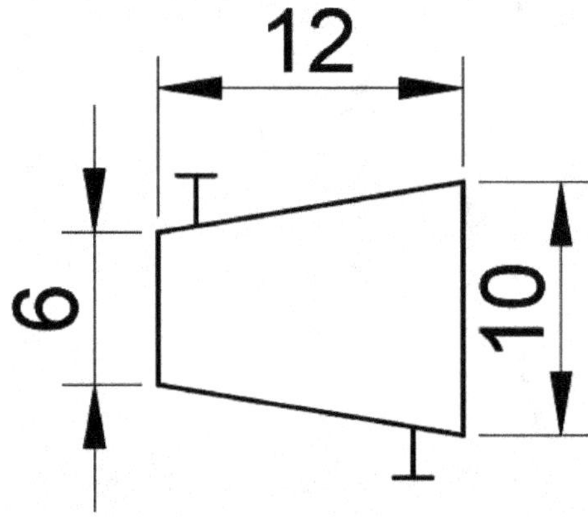

- Click **Insert > Block Definition > Create Block** on the ribbon; the **Block Definition** dialog appears.
- Enter **Turbine Driver** in the **Name** field.
- Click the **Select Objects** button on the dialog. Create a window and select all the objects of the drawing. Right-click to accept the selection.
- Select the **Delete** option under the **Objects** section.
- Click the **Pick Point** button and select the midpoint of the left vertical line.

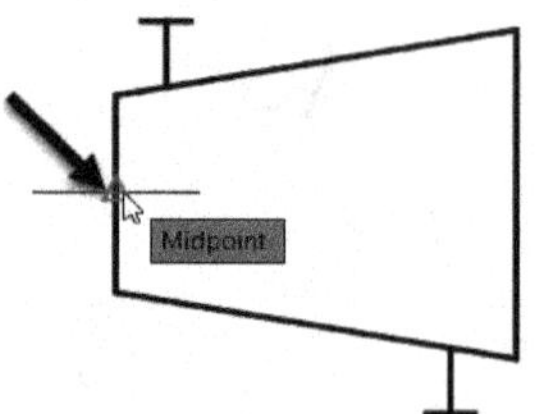

- Check the **Annotative** option under the **Behavior** section. Click the **OK** button on the dialog.
- Activate the **Automatically Add Scale to Annotative Objects** button located on the right side of the Status Bar.

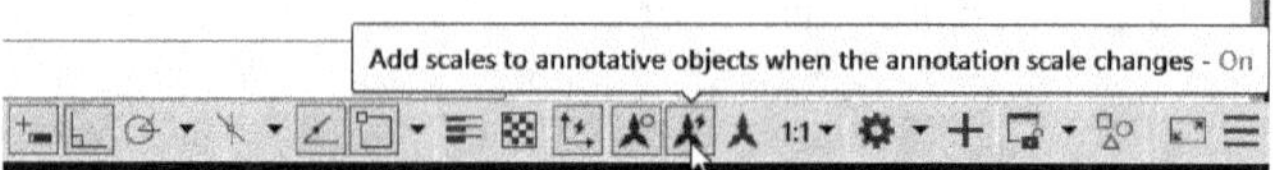

- Set the **Annotation Scale** to **1:10**.

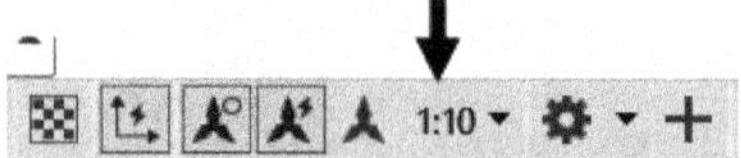

- Click **Insert > Block > Insert > Turbine Driver**.
- Pick a point in the graphics window; the block will be inserted with the scale factor 1:10.
- Click **Zoom All** on the **Navigation Bar** to view the block.
- Change the **Annotation Scale** to **1:2**; you will notice that the block is automatically scaled to **1:2**.

Exploding Blocks

When you insert a block into a drawing, it will be considered as a single object, even though it consists of numerous individual objects. At many times, you may require to break a block into its parts. Use the **Explode** tool to break a block into its individual objects.

- To explode a block, click **Home > Modify > Explode** on the ribbon or type EXPLODE in the command line and press ENTER.
- Select the block and press ENTER; the block will be broken into individual objects. You can select the individual objects by clicking on them. (Refer to the **Explode Tool** section of Chapter 4).

Using the Purge tool

You can remove the unused blocks and other unwanted drawing items from the database using the **Purge** tool.

This tool also allows you to find non-purgeable items from the current drawing.

- To activate the **Purge** tool, click **Manage > Cleanup > Purge** on the ribbon; the **Purge** dialog appears.

- Click the **Find Non-Purgeable Items** button on the dialog to view the items that cannot be purged. The items that are currently displayed in the drawing cannot be purged. Also, the items such as styles, layers, and linetypes that are currently used in the drawing cannot be purged. You can expand the node under the All items tree to view the individual items that cannot be purged. Next, select the item to view the possible reasons not to purge in the **Possible reasons** section.

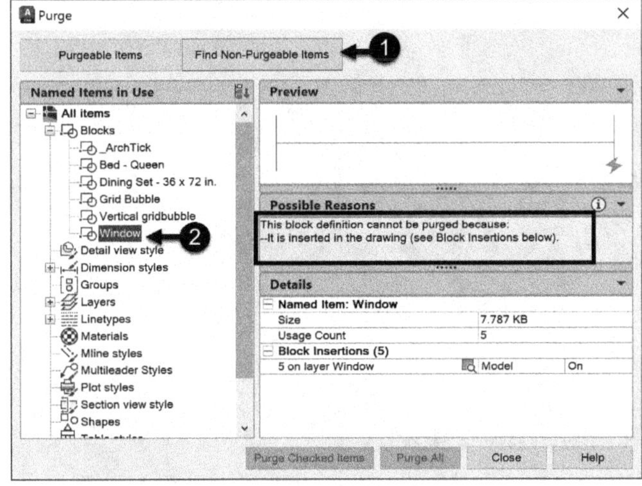

- Click the **Purgeable Items** button to view the items in the drawing that can be purged.
- To remove unwanted blocks from the database, expand the **Blocks** tree, and select the blocks.

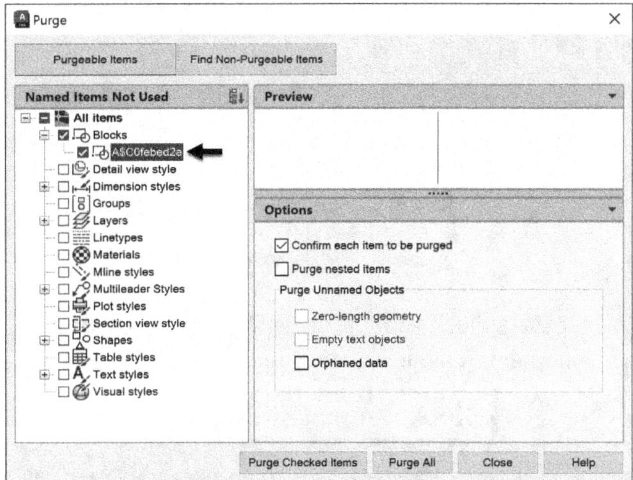

- Click the **Purge Checked Items** button on the dialog; the **Purge – Confirm Purge** message box appears.
- Click **Purge this item** to delete the item from the database.

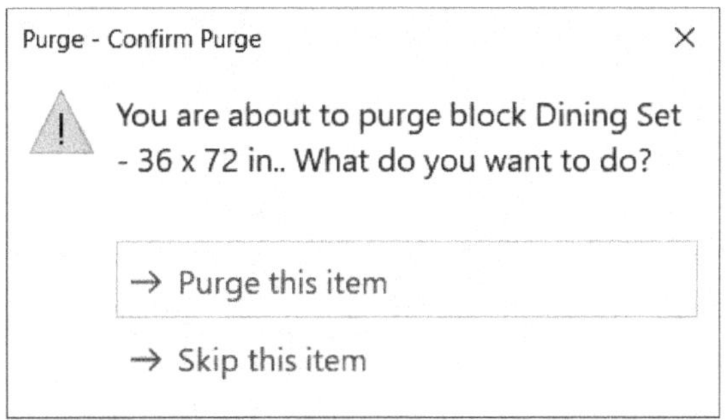

- Click **Close** on the **Purge** dialog.

Using the Divide tool

The **Divide** tool allows you to divide a line, arc, or polyline into a specified number of equal segments. It is useful for creating evenly spaced points or divisions along a line or curve. You can also create evenly spaced Point objects such as blocks along the selected object using this tool. These Point objects are not actually breaking the object into parts—it remains as one object. The following example shows you to divide a line using the **Divide** tool.

Example:
- Create the object, as shown in the figure.

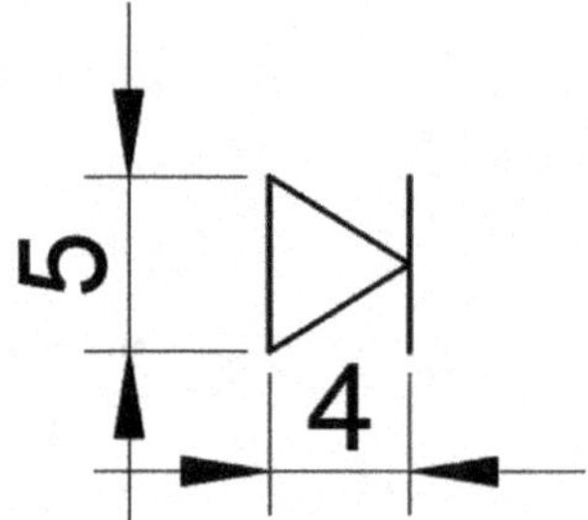

- Create a block with the name **Diode**. Specify the midpoint of the left vertical line as the base point.

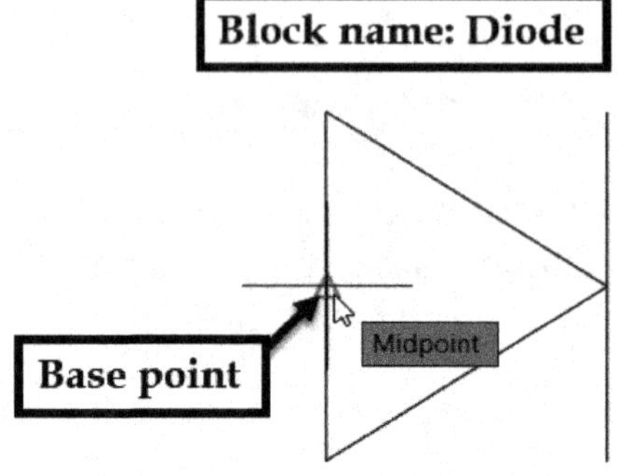

- Create a line of 50 mm length and 45 degrees inclination.

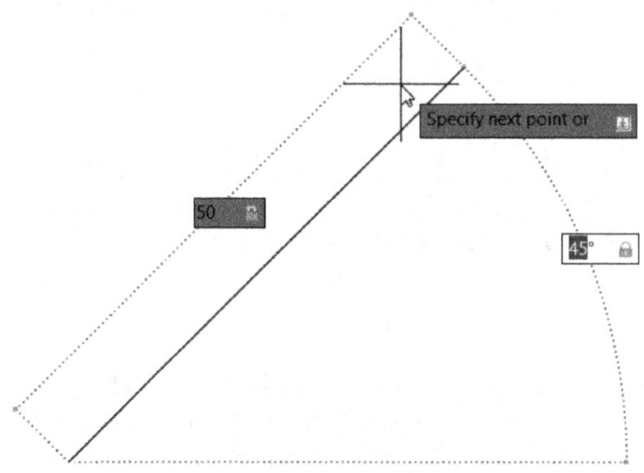

- Expand the **Draw** panel in the **Home** tab and click **Divide**.

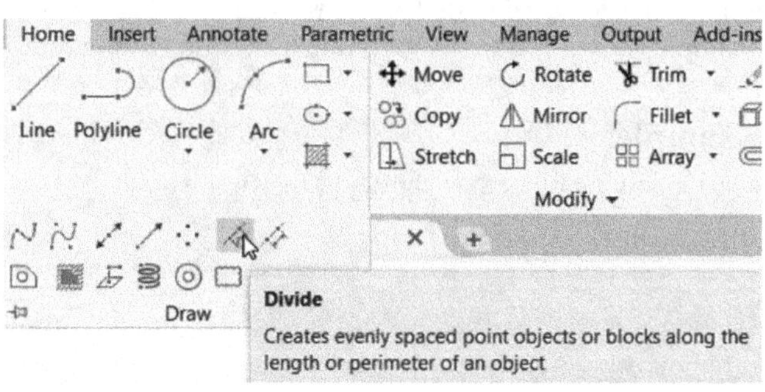

- Select the line segment; the message, "Enter the number of segments or [Block]:" appears.
- Select the **Block** option from the command line; the message, "Enter name of block to insert," appears.
- Type **Diode** and press ENTER; the message, "Align block with object? [Yes/No] <Y>:" appears.
- Select the **Yes** option; the message, "Enter the number of segments:" appears.
- Type **5** and press ENTER; the line segment will be divided into five segments, and four instances of blocks will be placed.

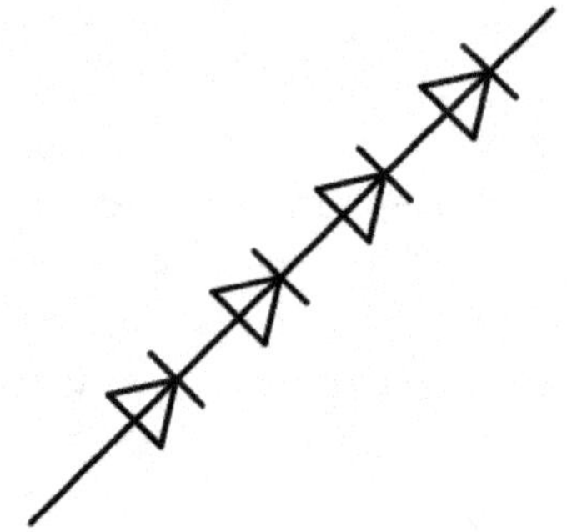

- Trim the unwanted portions, as shown below.

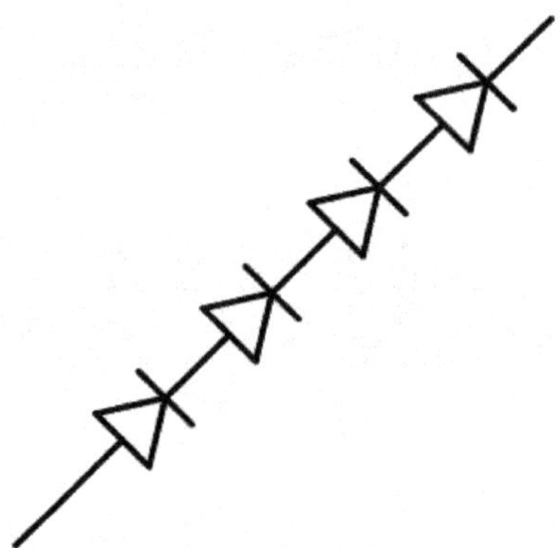

Renaming Blocks

You can rename blocks at any time. The procedure to rename blocks is discussed next.

- On the Quick Access Toolbar, click the down arrow located on the right side.
- Select **Show Menu Bar** from the drop-down.
- On the Menu bar, click **Format > Rename** or type **RENAME** in the command line and press ENTER; the **Rename** dialog appears.
- In the **Rename** dialog, select **Blocks** from the **Named Objects** list.
- Select the block to be named from the **Items** list and enter a new name in the **Rename To** box.

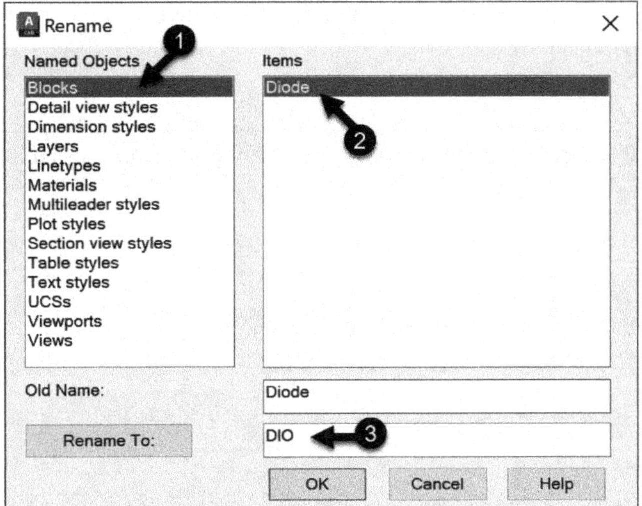

• Click **OK**; the block will be renamed.

Inserting Blocks in a Table

You can insert blocks in a table and fit inside the table cells. Note that you cannot insert Annotative blocks in a table. The following example shows you to insert a block in a table.

Example:

• Create three blocks, as shown below. You can also download them from the companion website.

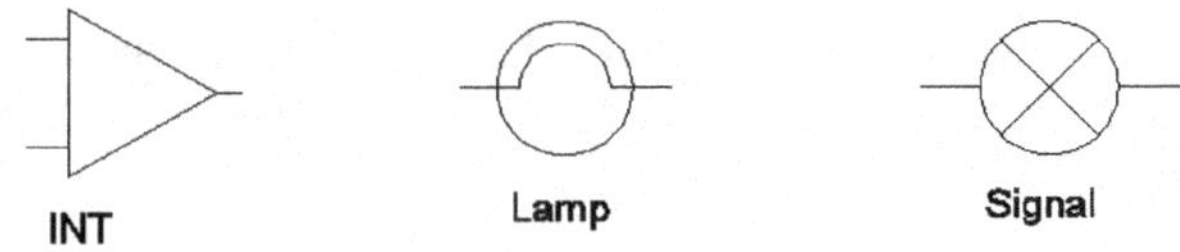

• On the ribbon, click **Annotate > Tables > Table**.

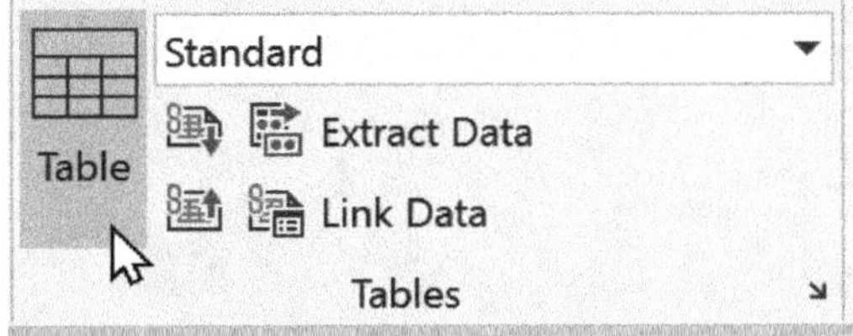

• On the **Insert table** dialog, specify the values, as shown below.

> **Columns:2**
> **Column width: 60**
> **Data rows:3**
> **Row height:2**

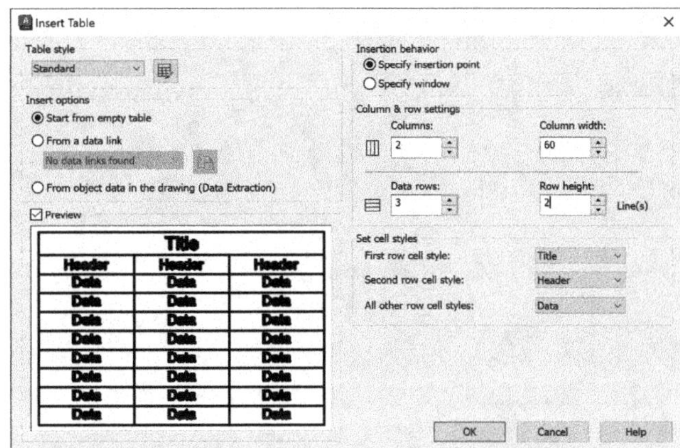

• Click **OK** and define the insertion point of the table.
• Type-in text in the table cells (double-click in the cells and type), as shown below.

Electronic/Electrical Symbols	
Symbol	Name
	INT
	Lamp
	Signal

• Select the first cell in the **Symbol** row and right-click.
• Select **Insert > Block** from the shortcut menu; the **Insert a Block in a Table Cell** dialog appears.

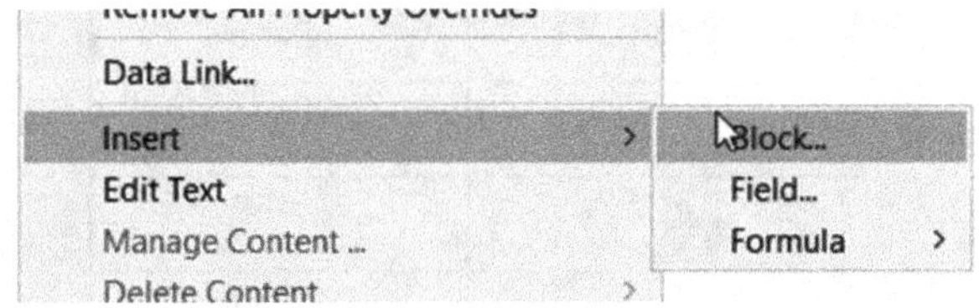

• In the **Insert a Block in a Table Cell** dialog, select **INT** from the **Name** drop-down.
• Set **Overall cell alignment** to **Middle Center**.

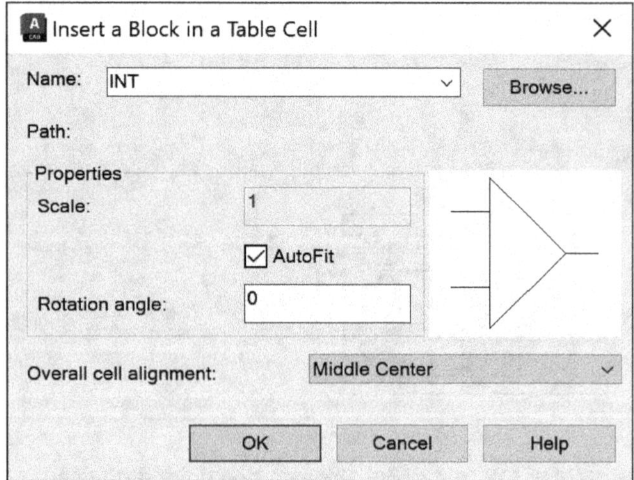

you can copy and paste content, such as layer definitions, between drawings.

You can display the DesignCenter by clicking **View > Palettes > DesignCenter** on the ribbon (or) entering **DC** in the command line.

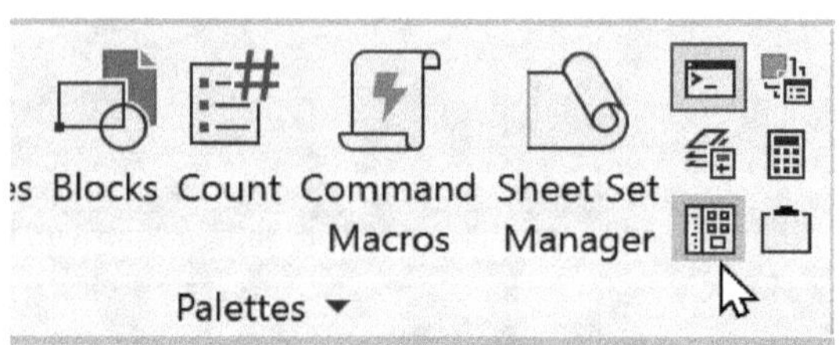

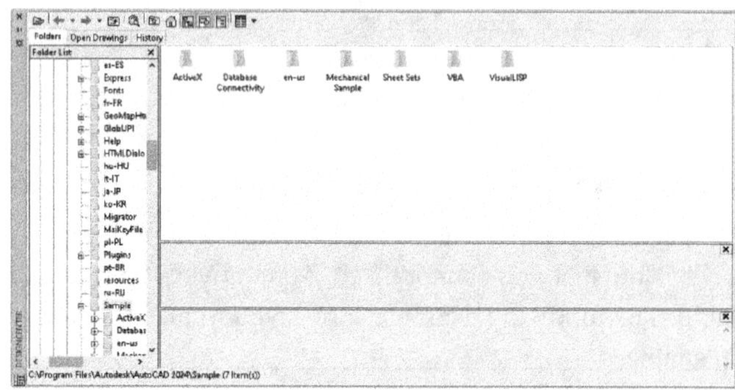

To resize, dock, or hide the DesignCenter palette in AutoCAD, follow these steps:

Resizing:

- Click **OK**; the **INT** symbol will be placed in the selected cell.

Electronic/Electrical Symbols	
Symbol	Name
	INT
	Lamp
	Signal

- Likewise, insert the other symbols in the corresponding cells.

Electronic/Electrical Symbols	
Symbol	Name
	INT
	Lamp
	Signal

Using the DesignCenter

DesignCenter is one of the additional means by which you can effectively navigate and insert blocks and drawings located anywhere accessible to your workstation. Using the DesignCenter, you can insert blocks created in one drawing into another drawing using drag-and-drop. In addition to that, you can view and manage dimension styles, layers, layouts, linetypes, table styles, textstyles, xrefs, raster images, and URLs (Web site addresses) using the DesignCenter. If you have multiple drawings open,

Resizing:
- To change the width and height, place your pointer on one of the borders (not the title bar) until a double arrow appears, then drag to the desired size.
- To resize both height and width, place your pointer on the lower corner (where the bevel appears) and drag.

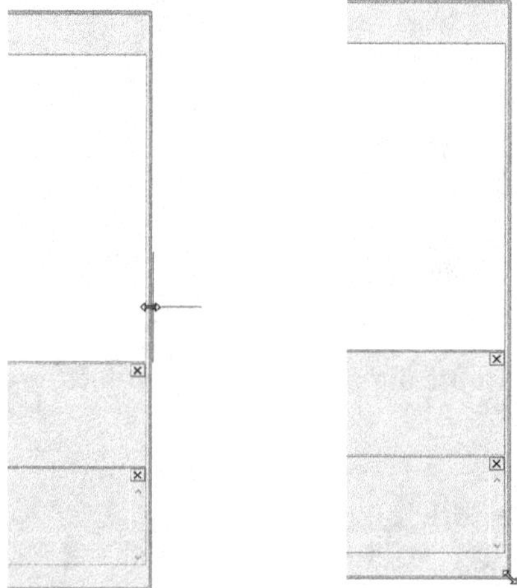

Increase/Decrease the Tree View area:

- Move the bar between the Content Area and the Tree View area by clicking and dragging it.

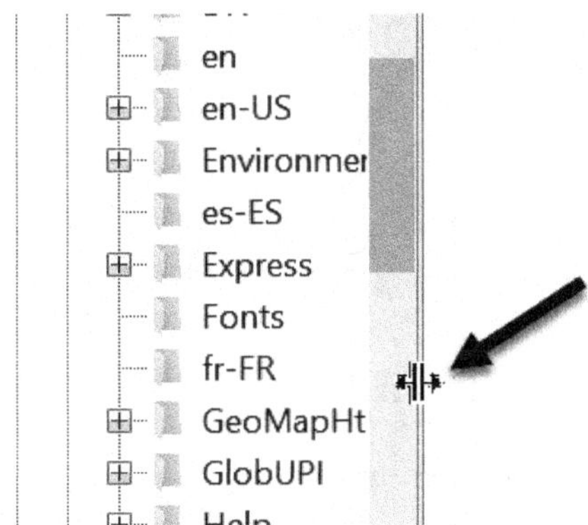

Docking:

- Dock DesignCenter by clicking the title bar, then dragging it to either edge of the drawing window.

Hiding:

- To hide the DesignCenter palette, use the Auto-hide option. Click on the Properties button at the bottom of the title bar to display the Properties menu. When Auto-hide is on, the palette is normally hidden (only the title bar is visible), and it appears when you bring the pointer to the title bar.

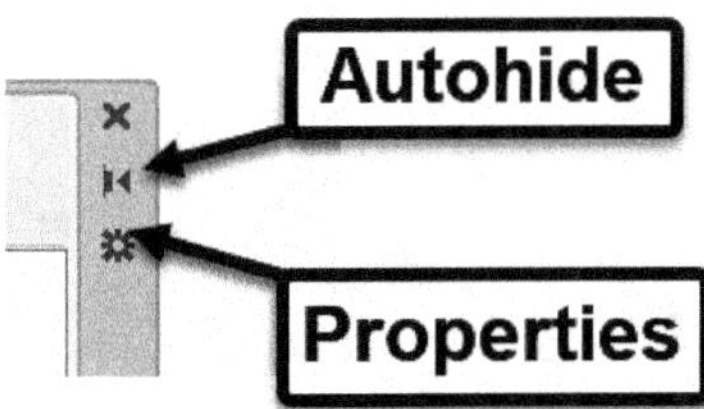

The following example shows you to use DesignCenter to insert blocks.

Example:

- Open a new drawing file.
- Create the following symbols and convert them into blocks. You can also download them from the companion website.

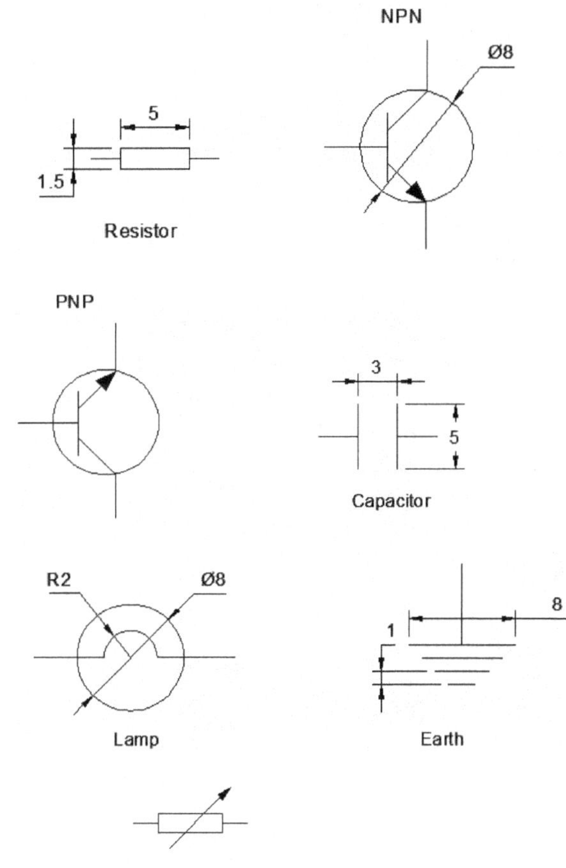

- Save the file as **Electronic Symbols.dwg**. Close the file.
- Open a new drawing file.
- Set the maximum limit of the drawing to 100,100.
- Click **Zoom All** on the Navigation Bar.
- Click **View > Palettes > DesignCenter** on the ribbon; the **DesignCenter** palette appears.
- In the **DesignCenter** palette, browse to the location of the **Electronic Symbols.dwg** file using the **Folder List**.
- Select the file and double-click on the **Blocks** icon; all the blocks present in the file will be displayed.
- Drag and place the blocks in the graphics window.

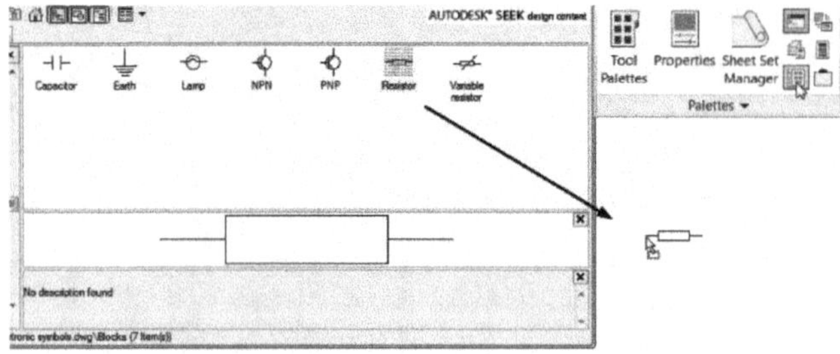

You can also insert blocks by activating the **Insert** dialog. To do this, right-click on the block in the Design Center, and then select **Insert Block**; the **Insert** dialog appears. Click **OK** on the **Insert** dialog; the selected block is attached to the pointer. Next, click in the graphics window to insert the block.

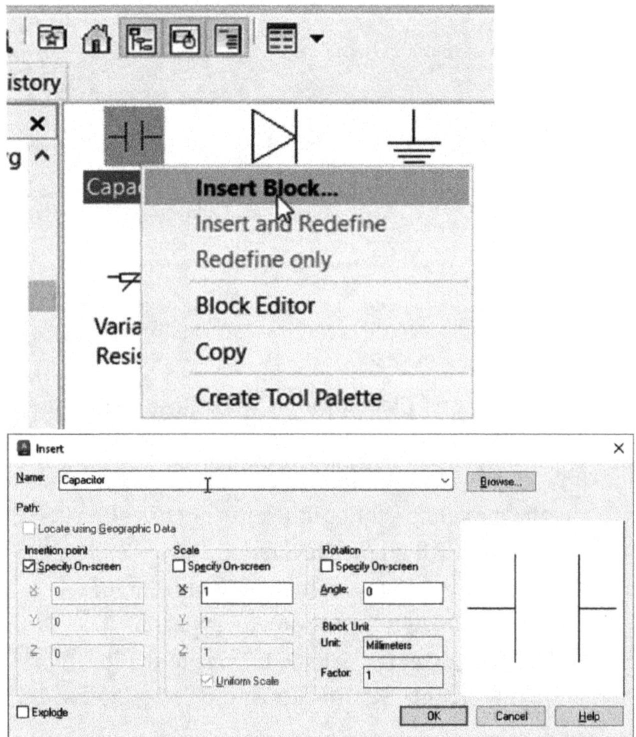

- Use the **Move** and **Rotate** tools and arrange the blocks, as shown below.

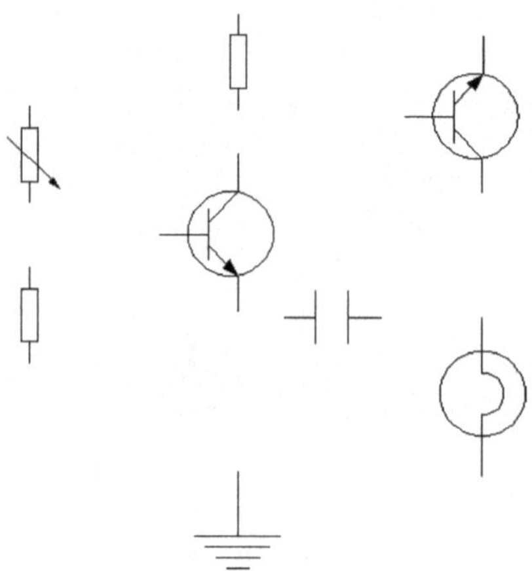

- Close the **DesignCenter** palette.

- Use the **Line** tool and complete the drawing, as shown below.

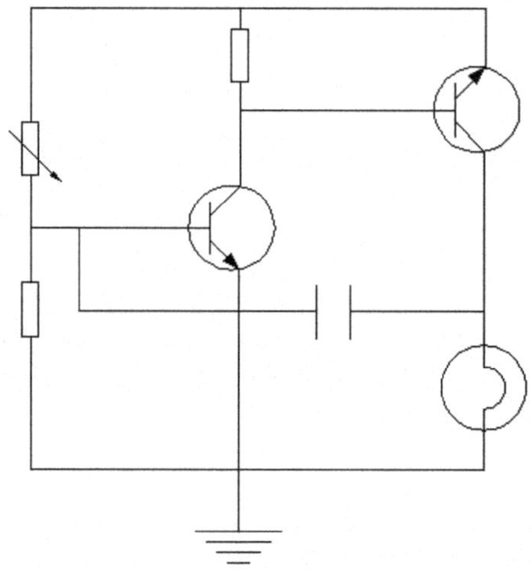

Using Tool Palettes

You can arrange blocks, dimensions, hatch patterns, and other frequently used tools in Tool Palettes. Similar to the **DesignCenter** palette, you can drag and place various features from Tool Palettes into the drawing. Tool palettes offer several advantages, including the ability to set scale, rotation, and layer properties for each tool individually. You can display the Tool Palettes by clicking **View > Palettes > Tool Palettes** on the ribbon or entering **TOOLPALETTES** in the command line.

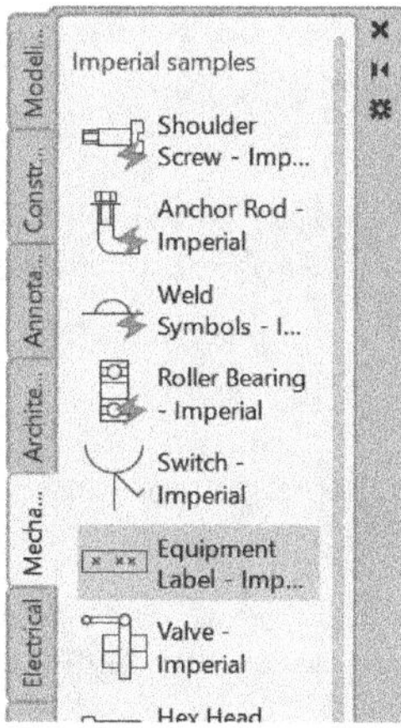

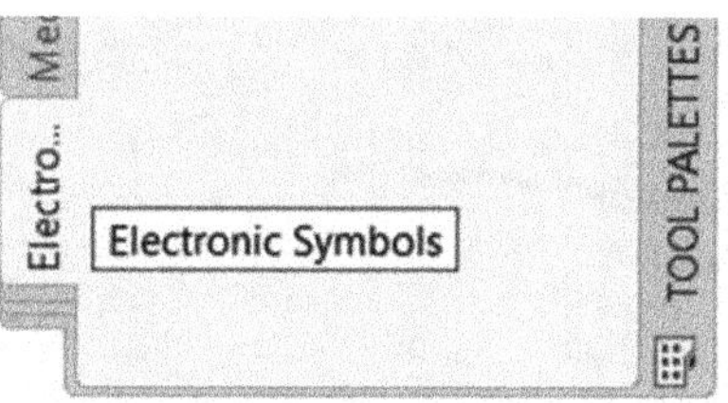

You can also create a new tool palette using the **Customize** dialog.

- Right-click on Tool Palettes and select **Customize Palettes**; the **Customize** dialog appears.
- In the **Customize** dialog, right-click in the **Palettes** list and select **New Palette**.

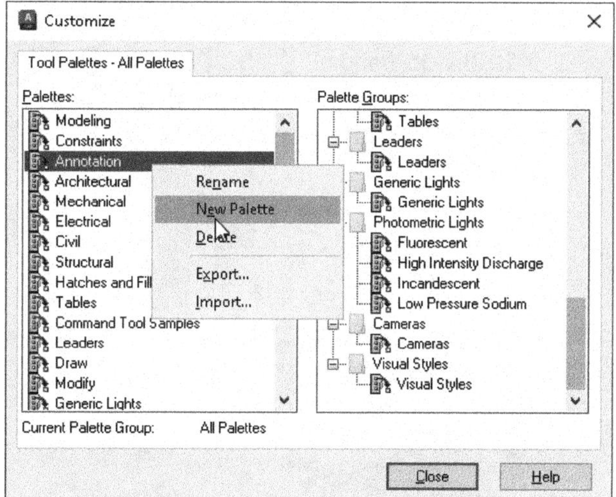

- Enter the name of the palette and click the **Close** button.

Adding Blocks to a Tool Palette

- Open the **DesignCenter** palette and select the **Electronic Symbols.dwg** file from the **Folders** list; the blocks available in the selected file appear.
- Drag the blocks from the **DesignCenter** and place them in the Tool Palette.

There are many palettes arranged in the Tool Palettes window. You can display more palettes by clicking the lower-left corner of the Tool Palettes and selecting the required palettes.

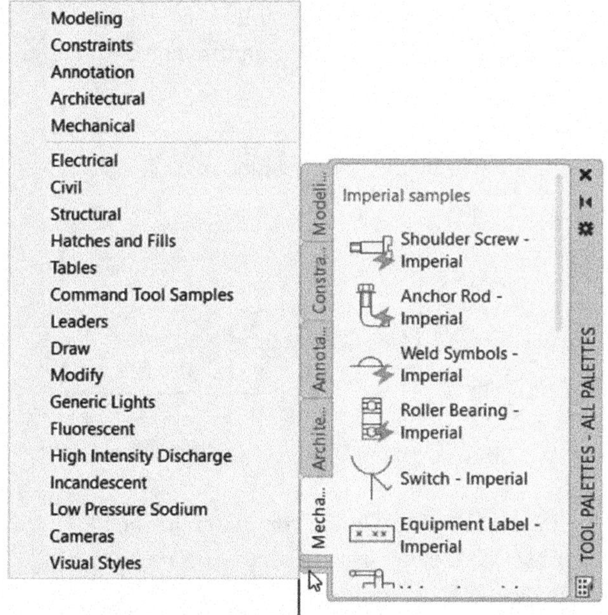

There are many blocks available in the **Architectural**, **Mechanical**, **Electrical**, **Civil**, and **Structural** palettes. You can drag and place blocks from these palettes. You can also right-click on a block and perform various operations using the shortcut menu displayed, as shown in the figure.

Creating a New Tool Palette

- Right-click on the Tool Palette and select **New Palette** from the shortcut menu; a new palette is added to Tool Palettes.
- Enter **Electronic Symbols** as the name.

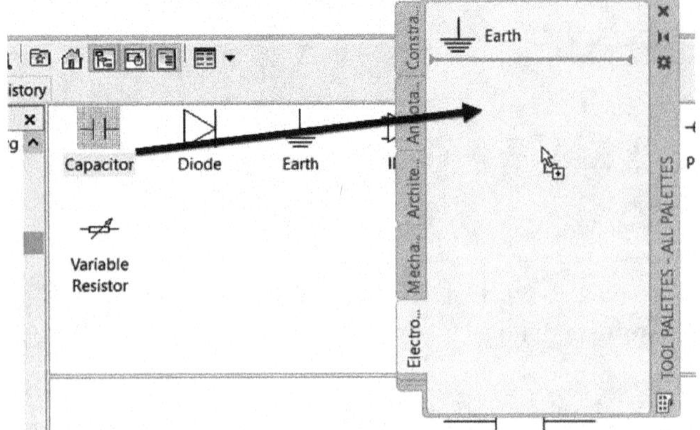

You can also create a new tool palette from a drawing consisting of blocks.

- In the **DesignCenter** palette, select the **Electronic symbols.dwg** file from **Folder List**.
- Select the **Blocks** option.
- Right-click and select **Create Tool Palette**; a new palette will be created from the drawing file.

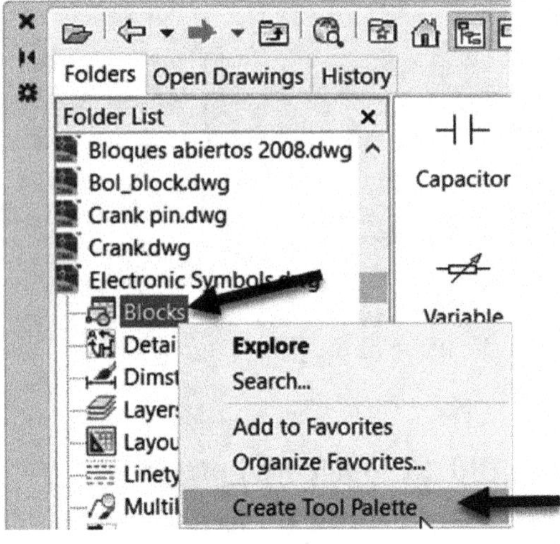

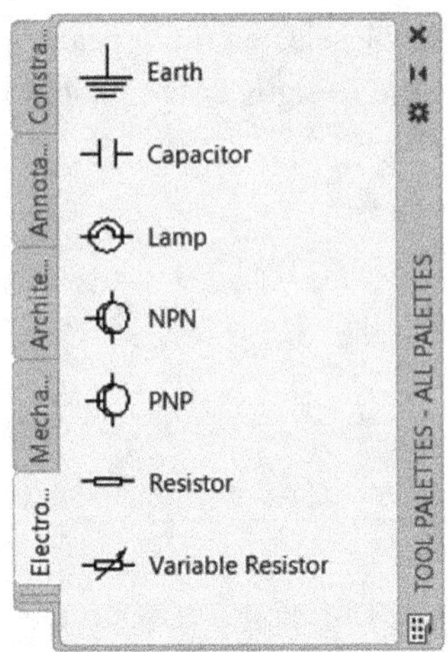

In the Tool Palette, you can group blocks depending on their function.

- Right-click on the **Tool Palette** and select **Add Separator**; a separator will be added.
- Right-click and select **Add Text**. Enter the name of the group.

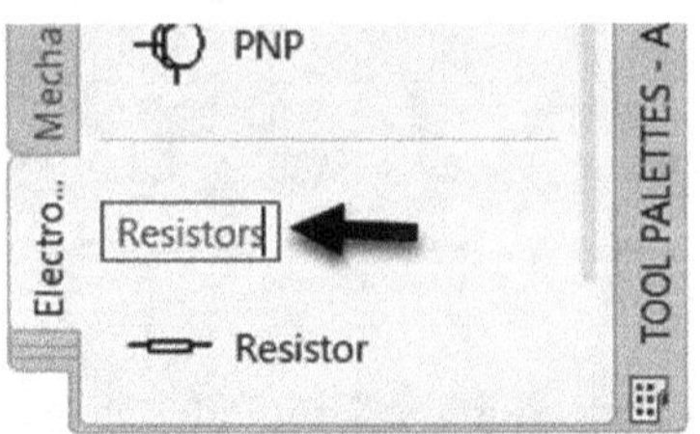

Inserting Multiple Blocks

You can insert multiple instances of a block at a time by using the **MINSERT** command. This command is similar to the **ARRAY** command. The following example explains the procedure to insert multiple blocks at a time.

Example:

- Create two blocks, as shown below.

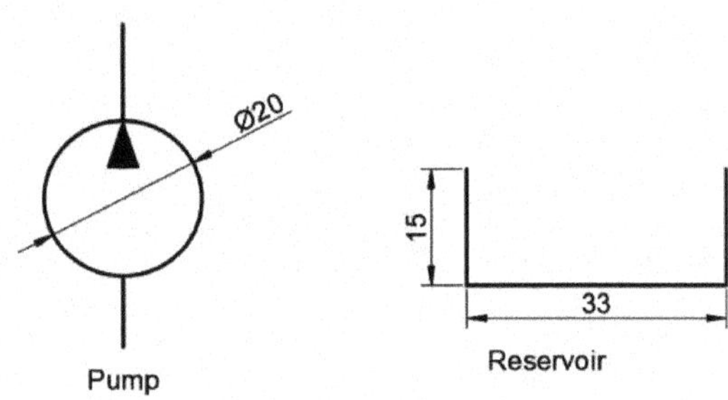

- Type **MINSERT** in the command line and press ENTER; the message, "Enter block name or [?]:" appears.
- Type **Pump** and press ENTER; the Pump is attached to the pointer.
- Pick a point in the graphics window.
- Enter 1 as the scale factor.
- Enter 0 as the rotation angle; the message, "Enter number of rows (---) <1>:" appears.
- Enter 1 as the row value; the message, "Enter number of columns (|||) <1>:" appears.
- Enter 4 as the column value; the message, "Specify distance between columns (|||):" appears.
- Type 60 and press ENTER; the pumps will be inserted as shown below.

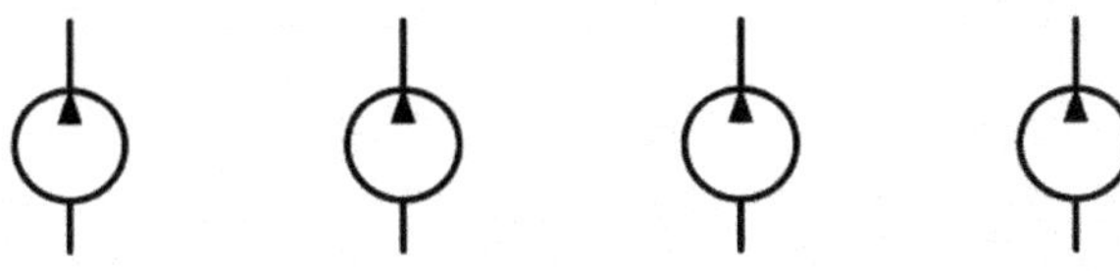

- Likewise, insert the reservoirs and create lines, as shown below.

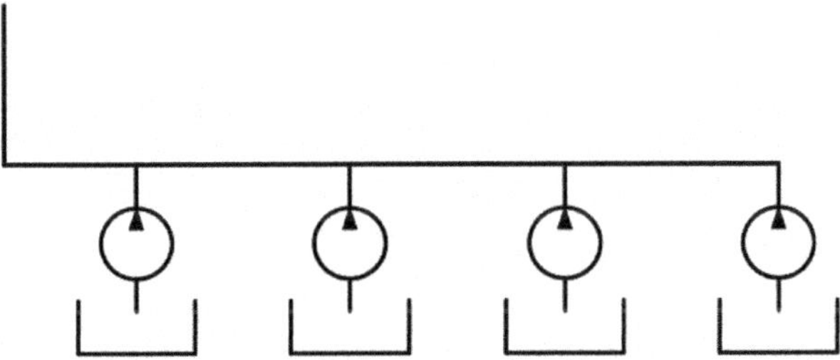

Editing Blocks

During the design process, you may need to edit blocks. You can easily edit a block using the **Block Editor** window. As you edit a block, all the instances of it will be automatically updated. The procedure to edit a block is discussed next.

- Click **Insert > Block Definition > Block Editor** on the ribbon; the **Edit Block Definition** dialog appears.

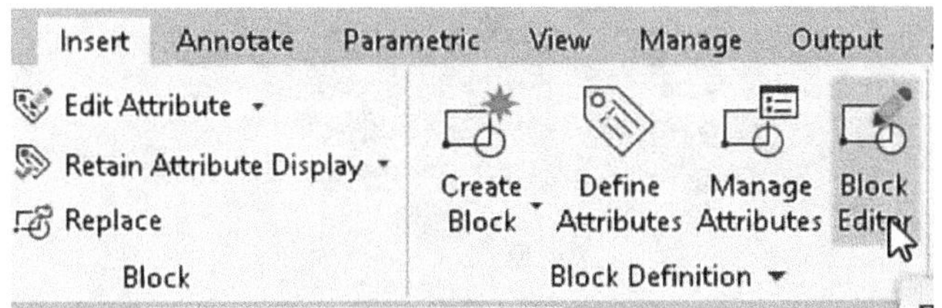

- In the **Edit Block Definition** dialog, select **Pump** from the list and click **OK**; the **Block Editor** window appears.

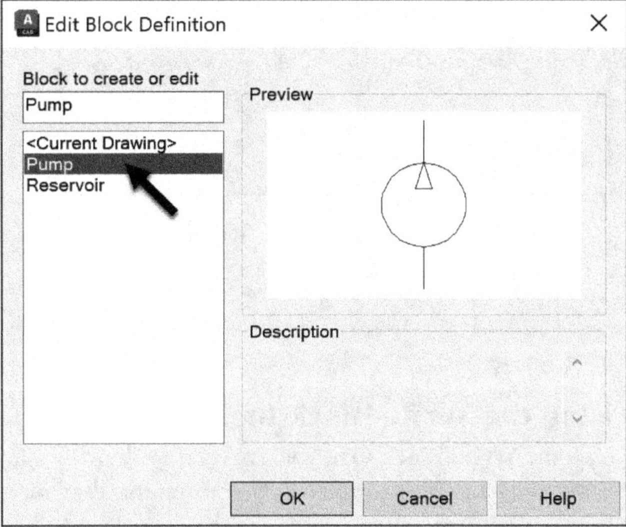

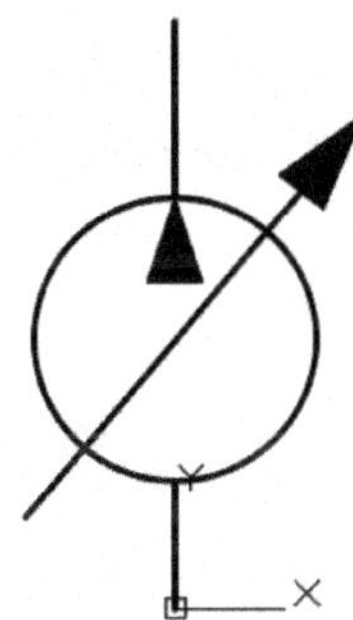

- Click **Home > Draw > Polyline** on the ribbon and draw a polyline, as shown below.

- Click **Close Block Editor** on the **Close** panel.

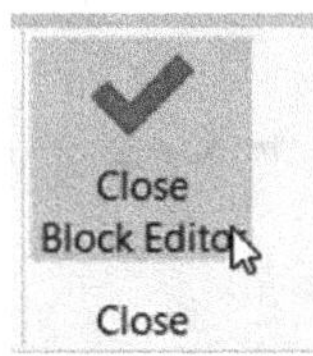

- In the **Block – Changes Not Saved** dialog, click **Save the changes to Pump**.

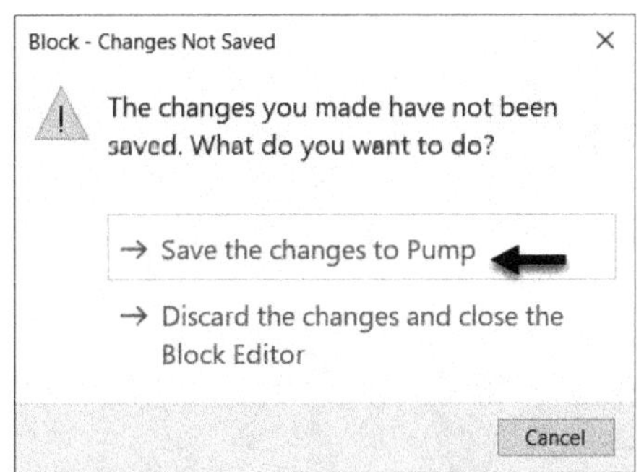

All the instances of the block will be updated automatically.

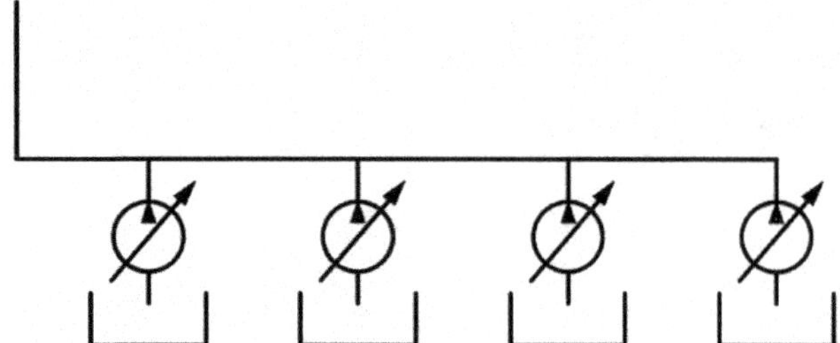

Using the Write Block tool

Using the **Write Block** tool, you can create a drawing file from a block or objects. You can later insert this drawing file as a block into another drawing. The procedure to create a drawing file using blocks is discussed in the following example.

Example:

* Start a new drawing file and create two blocks, as shown below. You can also download them from the companion website.

Gate Valve

Orifice

* Insert the blocks and create the drawing, as shown below.

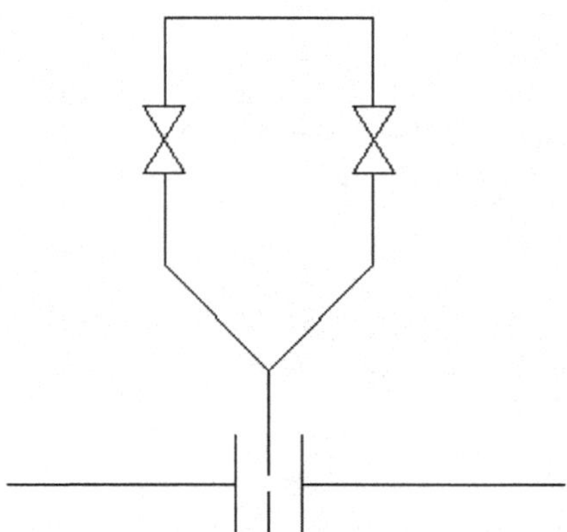

* Expand the **Block Definition** panel and select the **Set Base point** button.

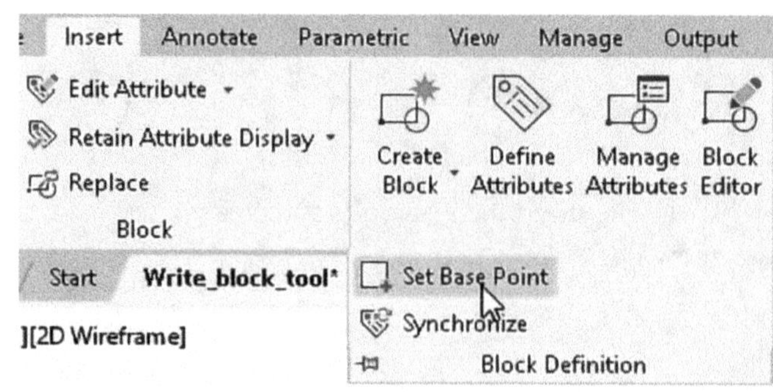

* Select the endpoint of the lower horizontal line, as shown.

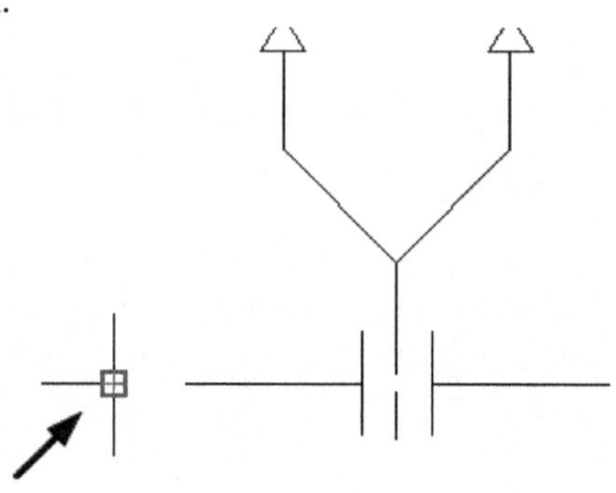

* Click **Insert > Block Definition > Write Block** on the ribbon; the **Write Block** dialog appears.

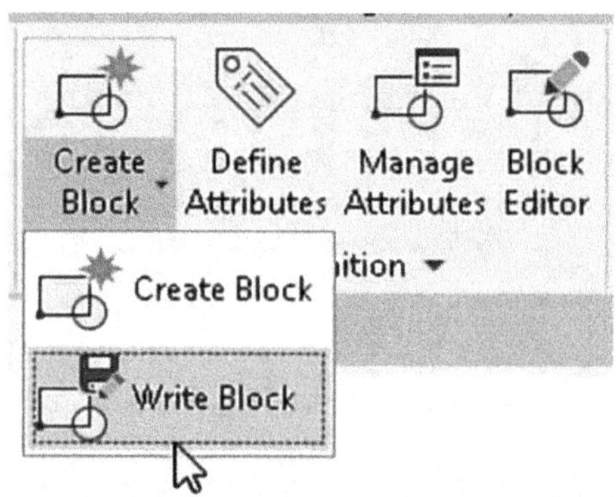

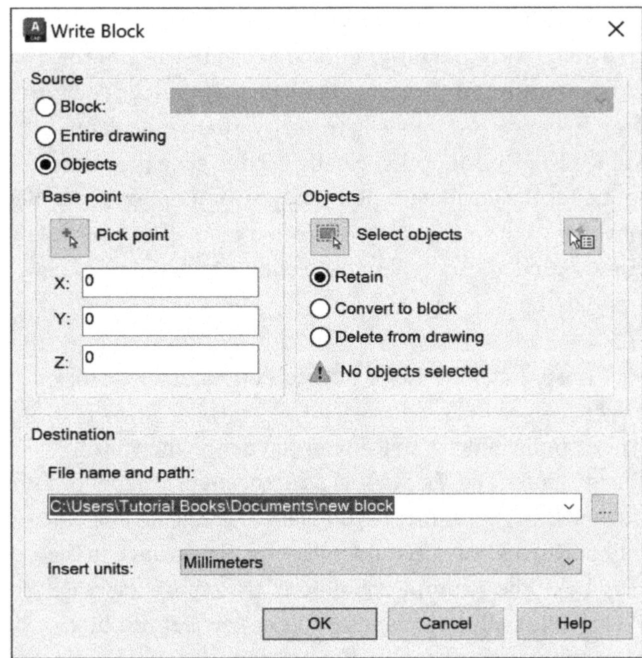

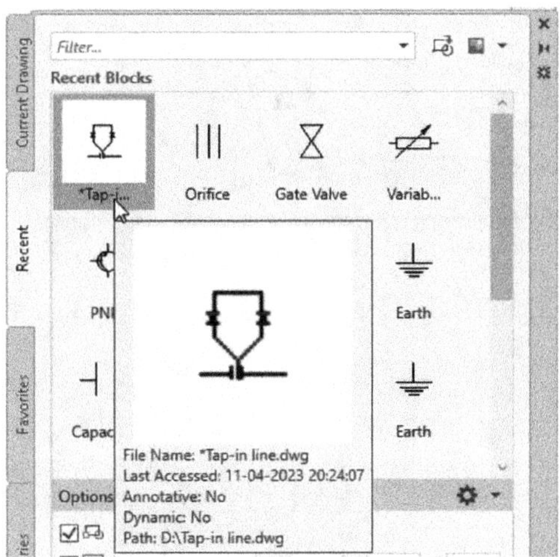

- Pick a point in the graphics window to insert the block.

Defining Attributes

An attribute is a line of text attached to a block. It may contain any type of information related to a block. For example, the following image shows a Compressor symbol with an equipment tag. The procedure to create an attribute is discussed in the following example.

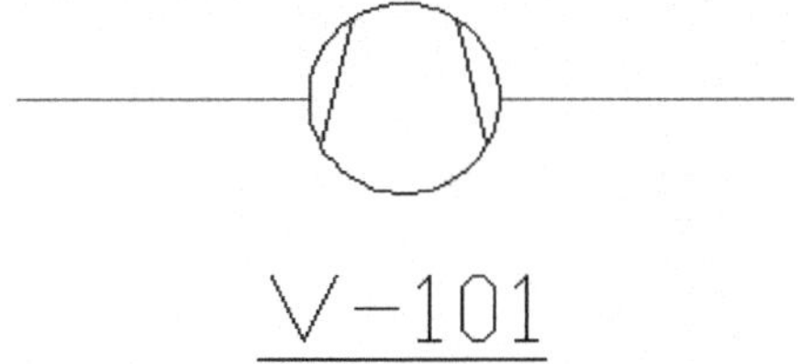

In the **Write Block** dialog, you can select three different types of sources (Block, entire drawing, or objects) to create a block. If you select the **Block** option, you can select blocks present in the drawing from the drop-down.

- Select the **Entire drawing** option.
- Specify the location of the file and name it as **Tap-in line**.

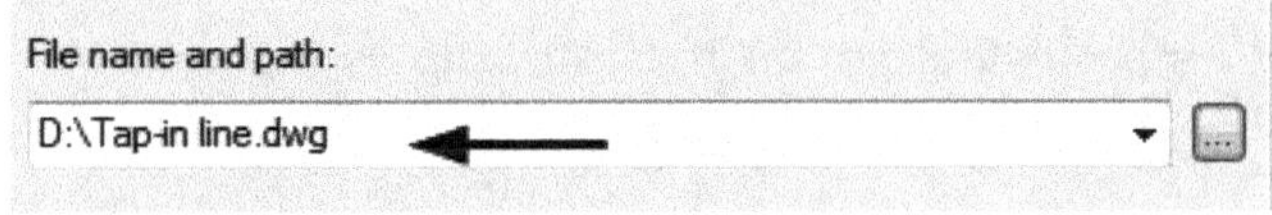

- Click the **OK** button.
- Close the drawing file.
- Open a new drawing file, and then type **I** in the command line and press ENTER; the **BLOCKS** palette appears.
- Click the **Recent** tab and select the **Tap-in Line** file from the **Recent Blocks** section.

Example 1:

- Open a new drawing file.
- Create the symbols, as shown below.

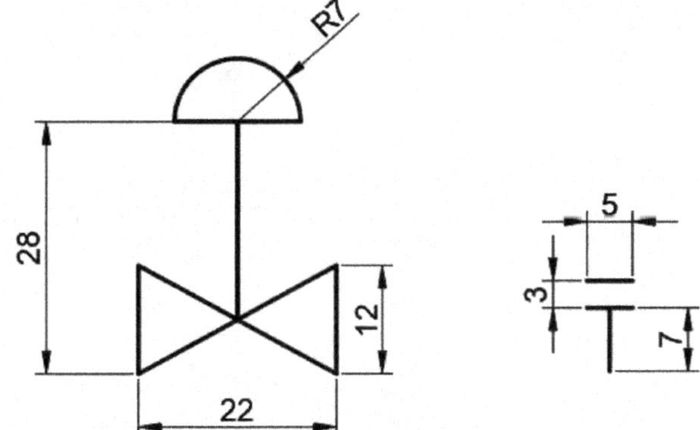

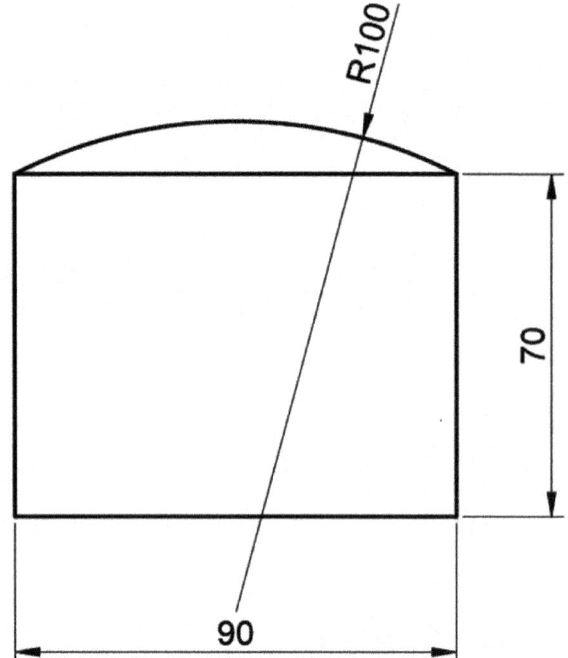

- Click **Insert > Block Definition > Define Attributes** on the ribbon; the **Attribute Definition** dialog appears.

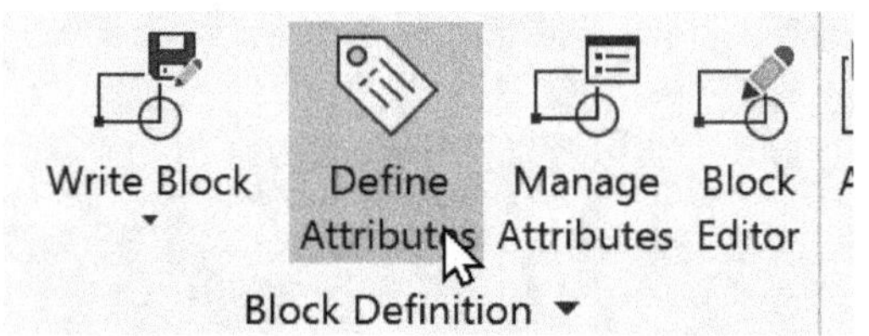

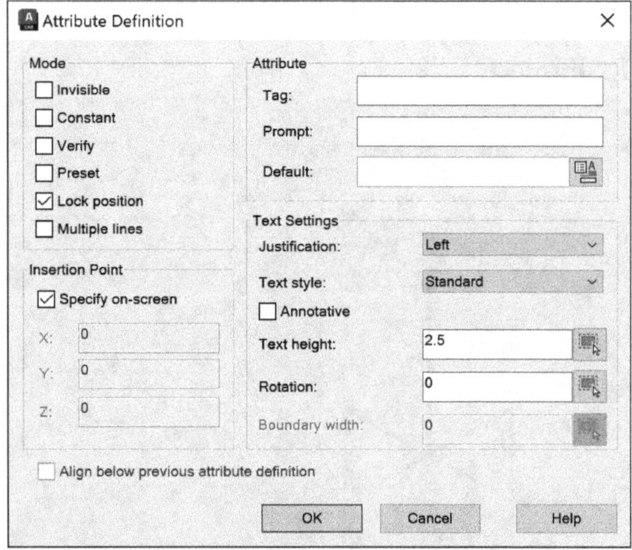

The options in the **Mode** group of the **Attribute Definition** dialog define the display mode of the attribute.

If you check the **Invisible** option, the attribute will be invisible. The **Constant** option makes the value of the attribute constant. You cannot change the value. The **Verify** option prompts you to verify after you enter a value. The **Preset** option can be used to set a predefined value for the attribute. The **Lock position** option fixes the position of the attribute to a selected point. The **Multiple lines** option allows typing the attribute value in single or multiple lines.

- Ensure that the **Lock position** option is selected.

The options in the **Attribute** group define the values of the attribute. The **Tag** box is used to enter the label of the attribute. For example, if you want to create an attribute called RESISTANCE, you must type **Resistance** in the **Tag** box. The **Prompt** box defines the prompt message that appears after placing the block. The **Default** box defines the default value of the attribute.

- In the **Attribute Definition** dialog, enter **Valvetag** in the **Tag** box.

The **Text Settings** options define the display properties of the text, such as style, and height. Observe the other options in this dialog. Most of them are self-explanatory.

- Enter **5** in the **Text height** box.
- Set the **Justification** to **Middle** and click **OK.**
- Specify the location of the attribute, as shown below.

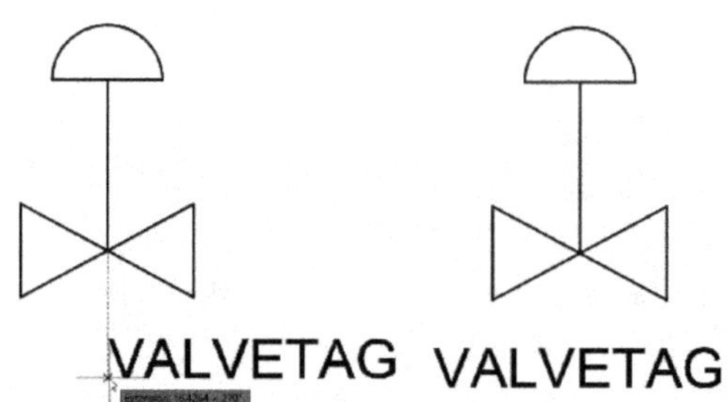

- Click the **Create Block** button on the **Block Definition** panel; the **Block Definition** dialog appears.
- On the dialog, click the **Select objects** button.
- Drag a window and select the control valve symbol and attribute — next, press ENTER.
- Select the **Delete** option from the **Objects** group.

- Click the **Pick Point** button under the **Base point** group and select the point, as shown below.

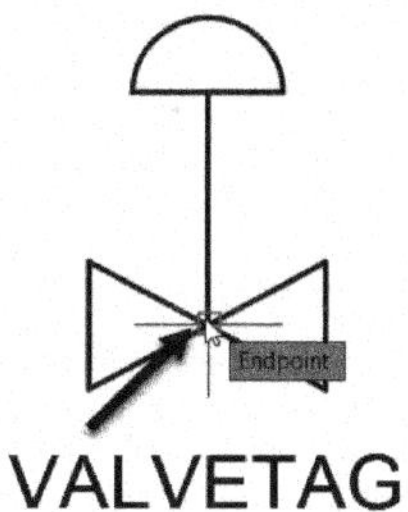

- Enter **Control Valve** in the **Name** box and click **OK**.
- Likewise, create the **Equipmenttag** attribute and place it inside the tank symbol.
- Create a block and name it as **Tank**.

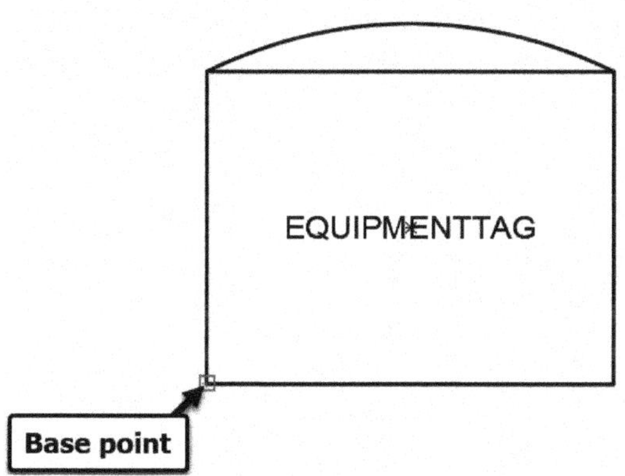

- Also, create a block of the nozzle symbol and name it **Nozzle**.

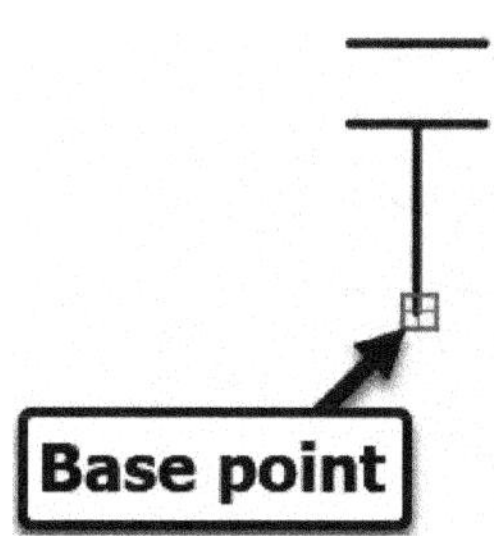

Inserting Attributed Blocks

You can use the INSERT command to insert the attributed blocks into a drawing. The procedure to insert attributed blocks is discussed next.

- On the ribbon, click **Insert > Block > Insert > Tank**.

- Click in the graphics window to define the insertion point. The **Edit Attributes** dialog appears.
- Enter **TK-001** in the **EQUIPMENTTAG** field and click **OK**; the block will be placed along with the attribute.

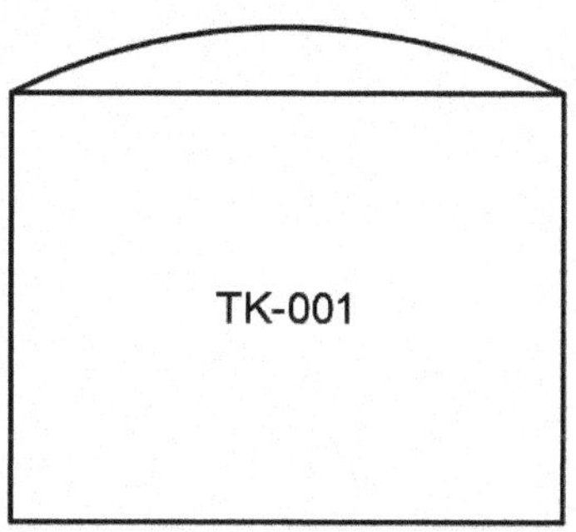

- Likewise, place the control valves, as shown below.

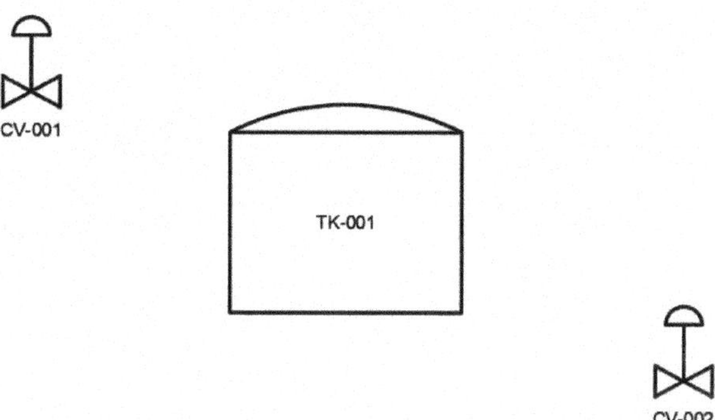

- Place and rotate the nozzles on the tank, as shown below.

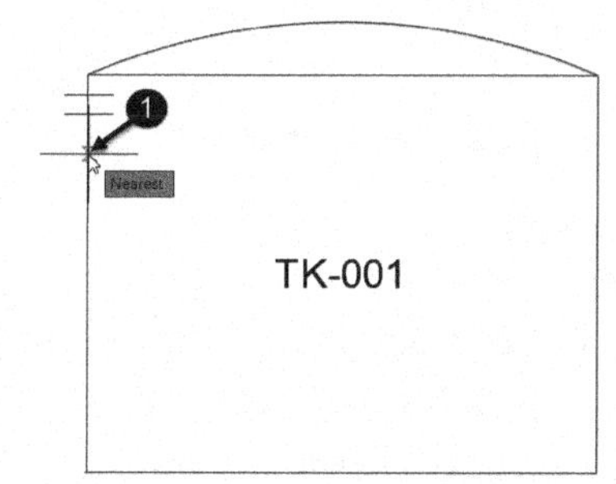

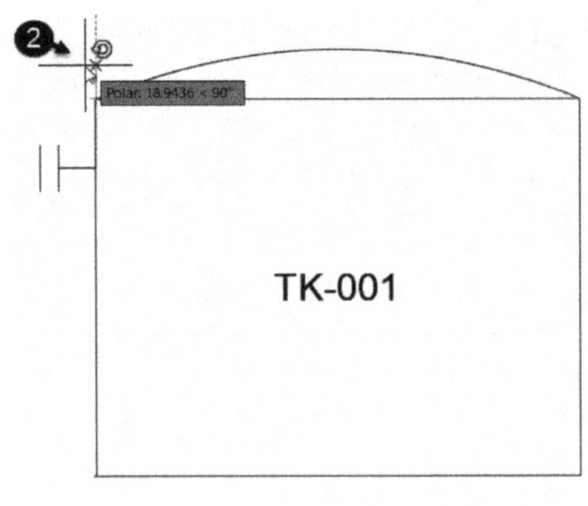

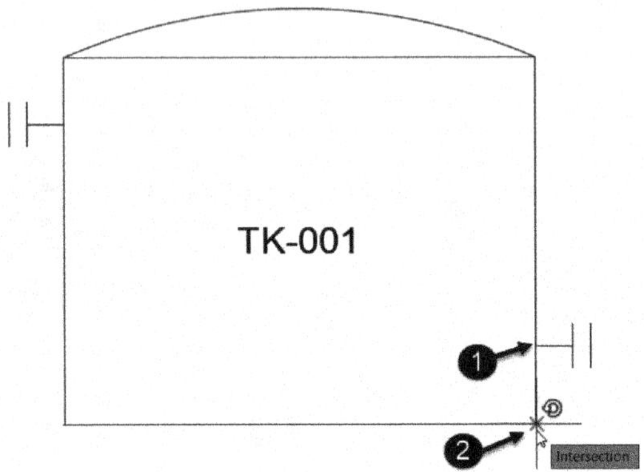

- Use the **Polyline** tool and connect the control valves and tank.

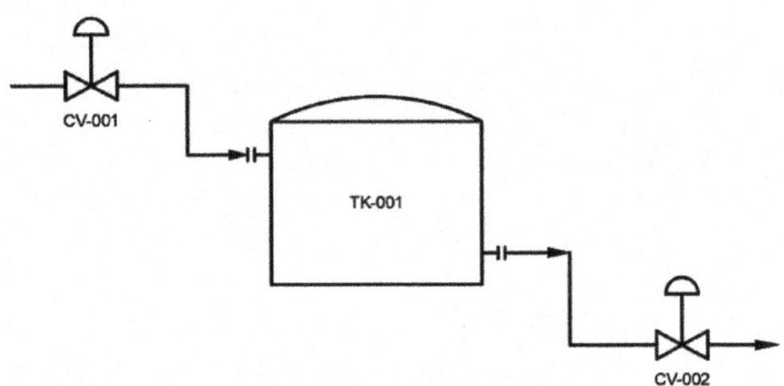

Working with External references

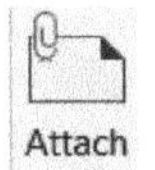

In AutoCAD, you can attach a drawing file, image, or pdf file to another drawing. These attachments are called External References (Xrefs). They are dynamic in nature and update when changes are made to them. In the following example, you will learn to attach drawing files to a drawing.

Example 1:

- Create the drawing shown below.

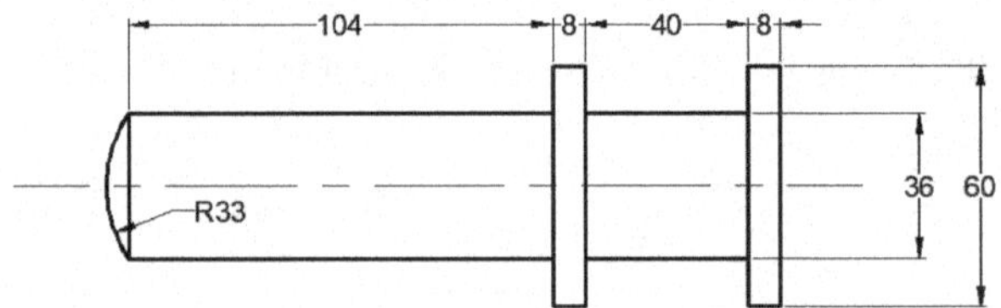

- Type **BASE** in the command line and press ENTER.
- Select the midpoint of the vertical line as the base point, as shown.

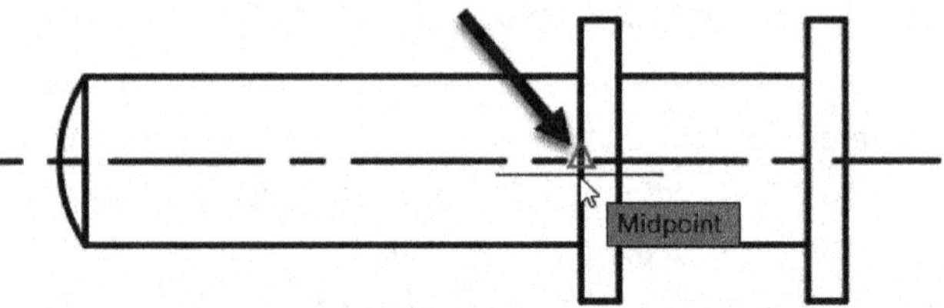

- Save the drawing as **Crank pin.dwg**
- Create another drawing as shown below (For help, refer to the **Multi View Drawings** section in Chapter 5).

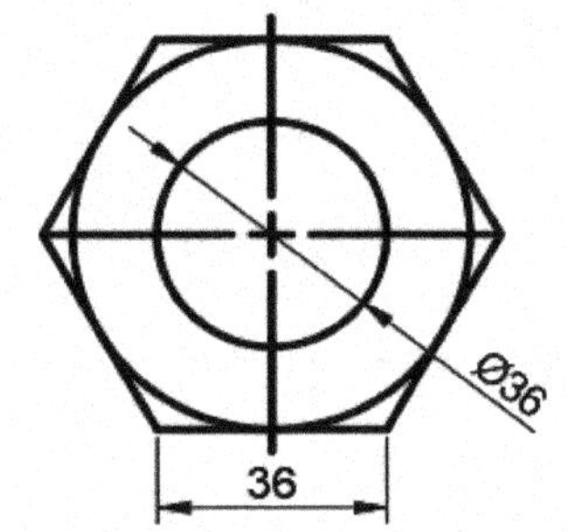

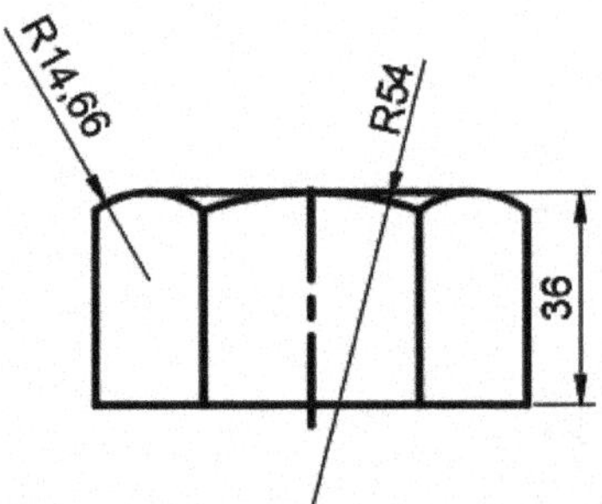

- Use the **Set Base Point** tool and specify the base point, as shown below.

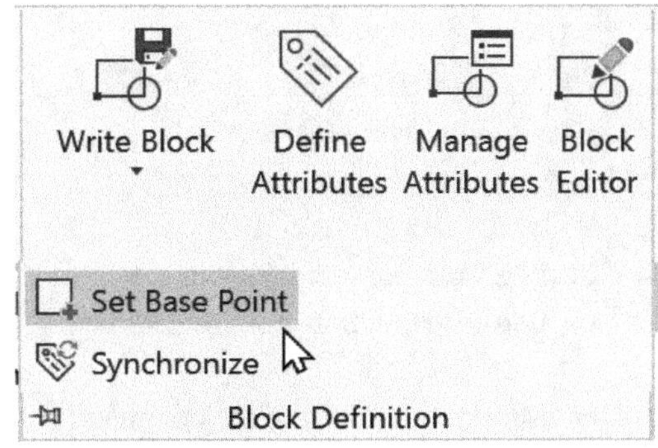

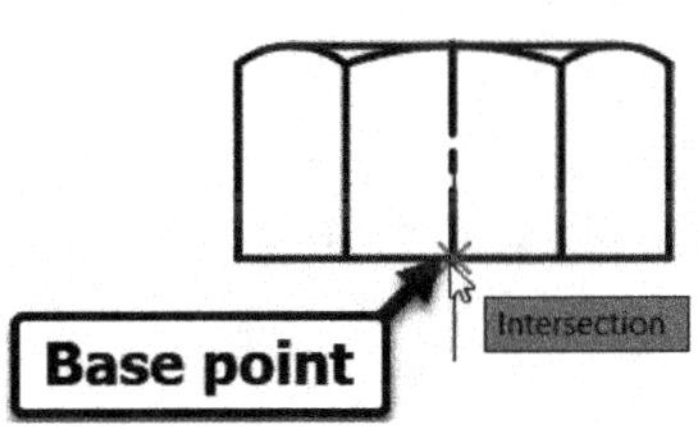

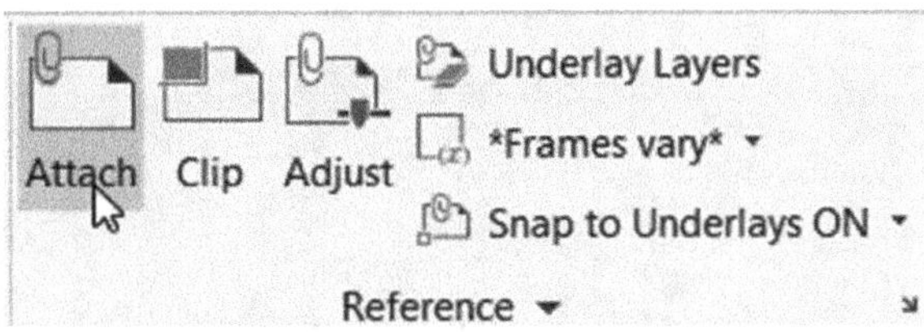

- Save the drawing as **Nut.dwg** and close it.
- Open the **Crank.dwg** file created in Chapter 8.
- Click **Insert > Reference > Attach** on the ribbon; the **Select Reference file** dialog appears.

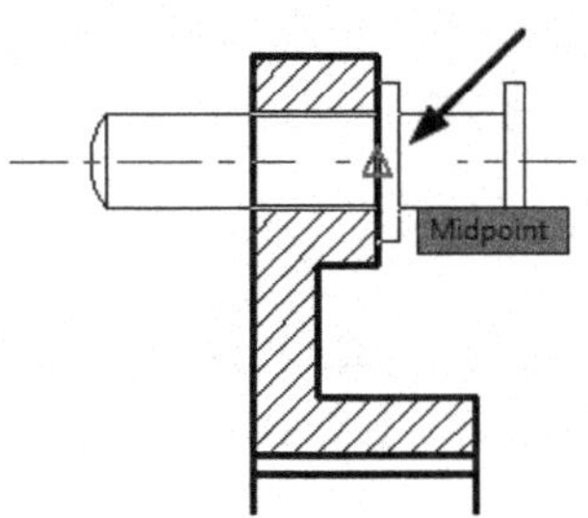

- Browse to the location of the **Crankpin.dwg** and double-click on it; the **Attach External Reference** dialog appears.

Some of the options available in this dialog are similar to that in the **Insert** dialog. The options include the insertion point, scale, and rotation angle of the external reference.

- Accept the default settings in this dialog and click **OK**; the crankpin will be attached to the pointer.
- Select the point on the hatched view, as shown below.

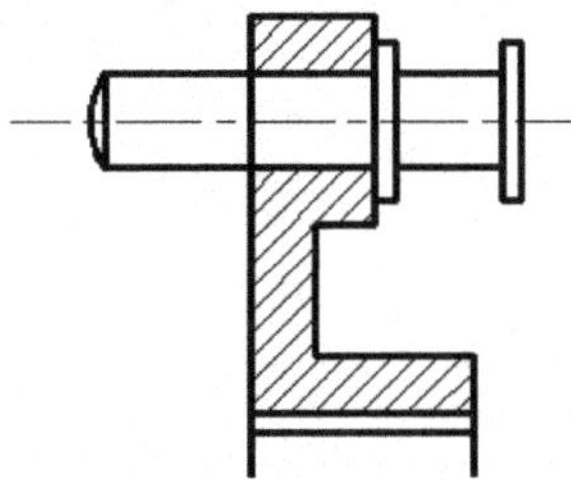

- On the ribbon, click **View** tab > **Palettes** panel > **External References Palette**.

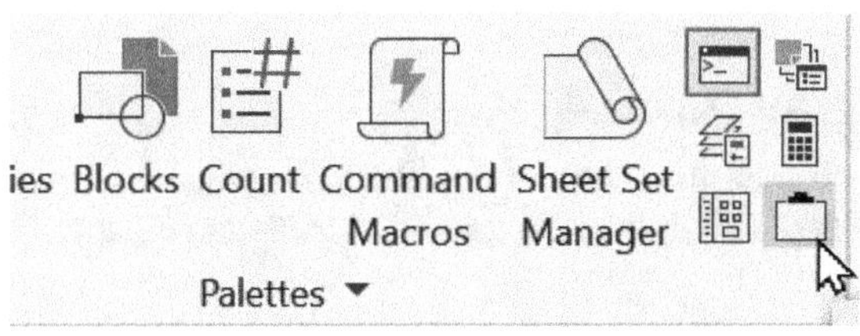

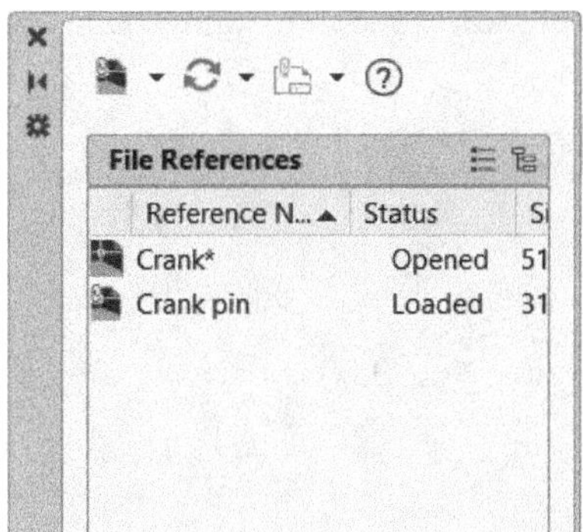

- In the **External References** palette, open the **Attach** drop-down and select the **Attach DWG** option; the **Select References file** dialog appears.

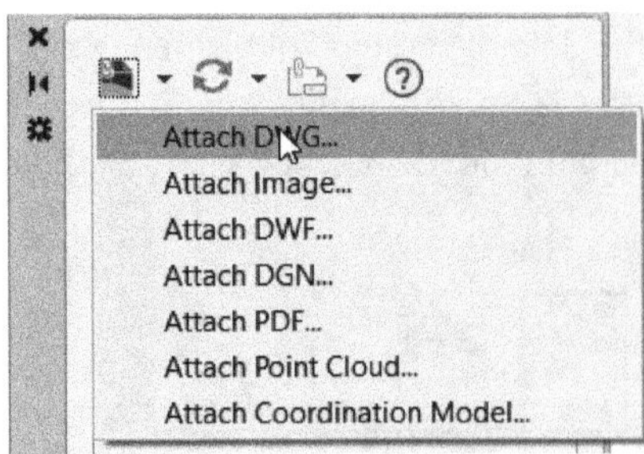

- Browse to the location of the **Nut.dwg** and double-click on it; the **Attach External Reference** dialog appears.
- In the **Attach External Reference** dialog, enter **90** in the **Angle** box under the **Rotation** group and click **OK**.
- Select the insertion point on the section view, as shown below.

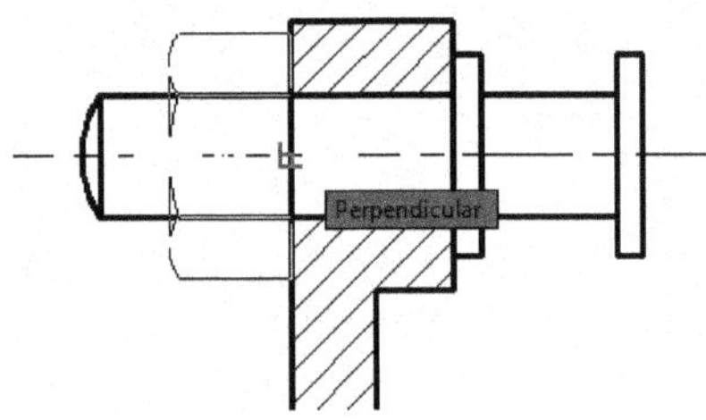

Fading an Xref

You can change the fading of Xref by using the Xref fading slider available in the expanded **Reference** panel.

- Expand the **Reference** panel of the **Insert** ribbon and use the **Xref fading** slider to adjust the fading.

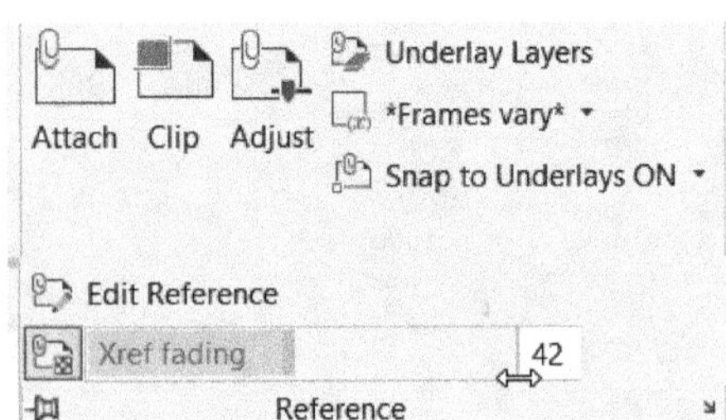

Clipping External References

You can hide the unwanted portion of an external reference by using the **Clip** tool.

- Click **Insert > Reference > Clip** on the ribbon; the message, "Select Object to clip," appears in the command line.

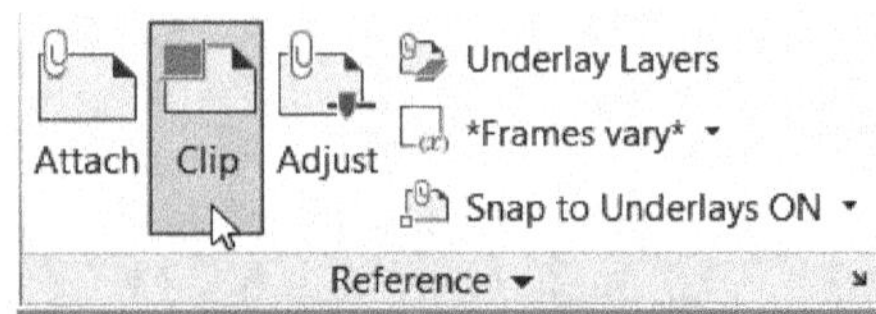

- Select the **Nut.dwg** from the graphics window.
- Select the **New boundary** option from the command line.
- Select the **Rectangular** option from the command line.
- Draw a rectangle as shown below; only the front view of the nut is visible, and the top view is hidden. Also, the clipping frame is visible.

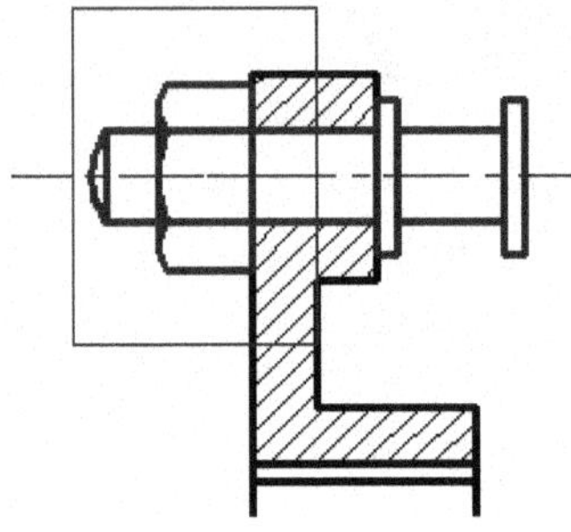

- To hide the clipping frame, type XCLIPFRAME in the command line
- Type 0 and press ENTER.
- You can also hide the frame by clicking **Modify > Object > External reference > Frame** on the Menu Bar.

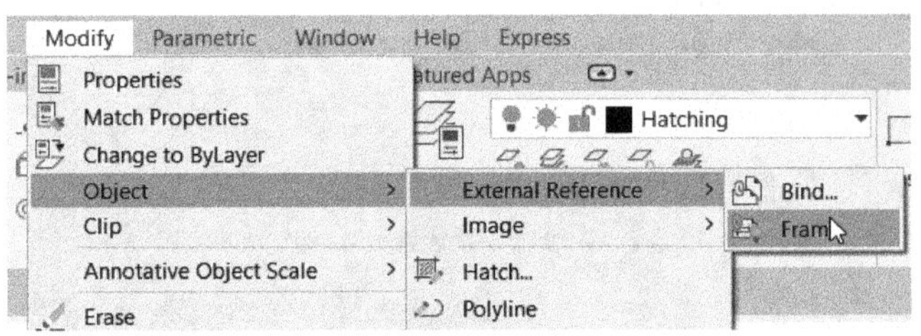

- Attach another instance of the **Nut.dwg** file.
- Use the **Rotate** and **Move** tools to position the top view, as shown below.

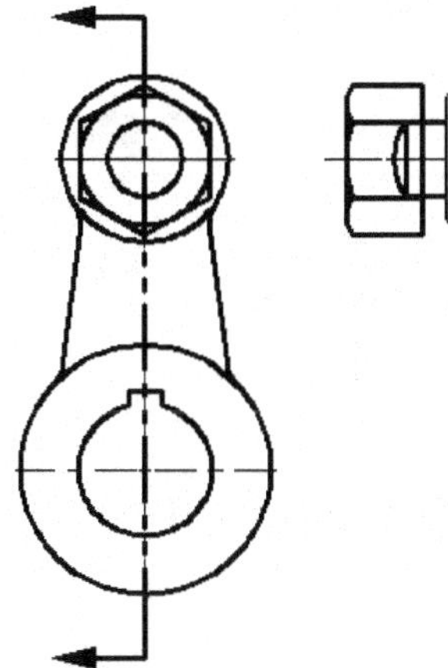

- Use the **Clip** tool and clip the Xref.

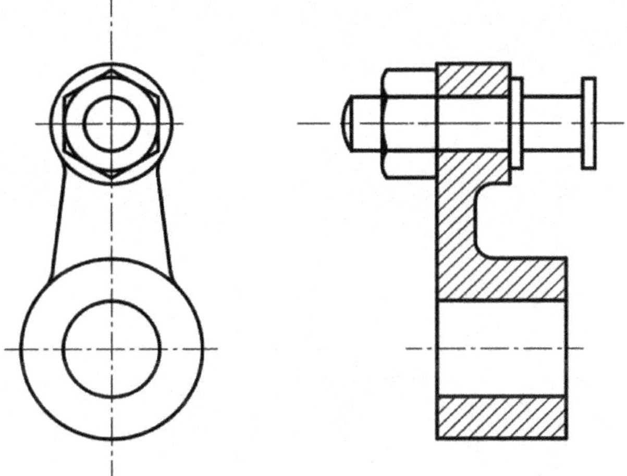

Editing the External References

AutoCAD allows you to edit the external references in the file to which they are attached. You can also edit them by opening their drawing file. The procedure to edit an external reference is discussed next.

- To edit an external reference, expand the **Reference** panel and click the **Edit Reference** button.

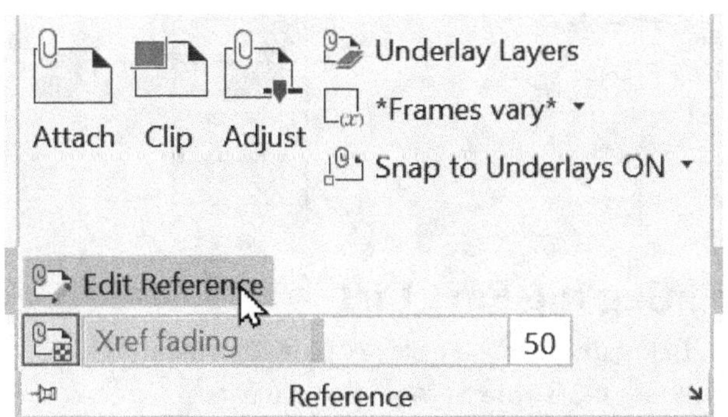

- Select **Nut** from the drawing; the **Reference Edit** dialog appears
- Click **OK** to get into the reference editing mode.
- In the drawing, the centerlines of the nut are overlapping on the centerlines of the crank. Delete the centerlines and center marks of the nut.
- Click **Save Changes** on the **Edit Reference** panel of the **Insert** tab; the **AutoCAD** message box appears.

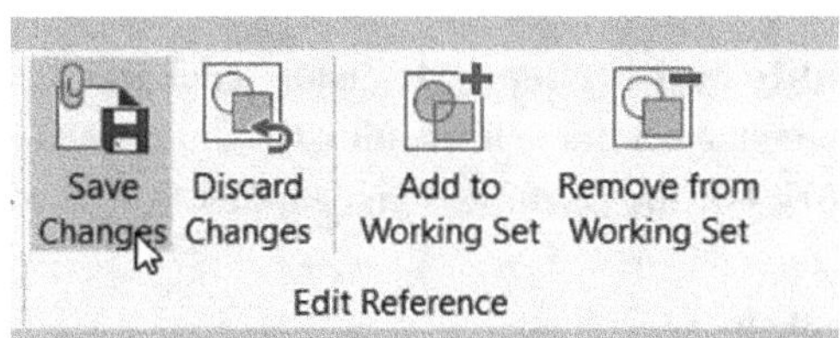

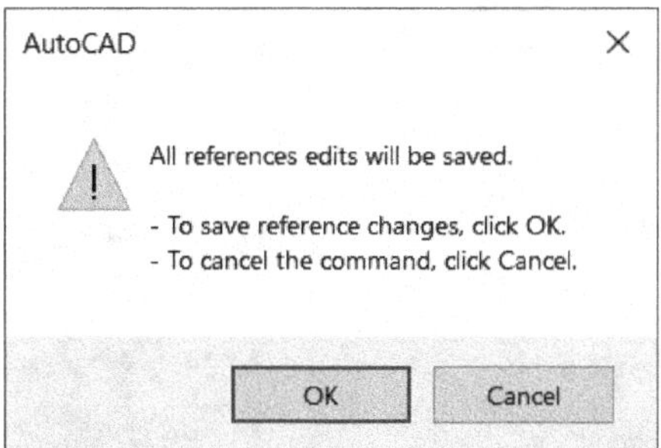

- Click **OK**.

Adding Balloons

- Click **Annotate > Leaders > Multileader Style Manager** (inclined arrow) button on the ribbon; the **Multileader Style Manager** dialog appears.

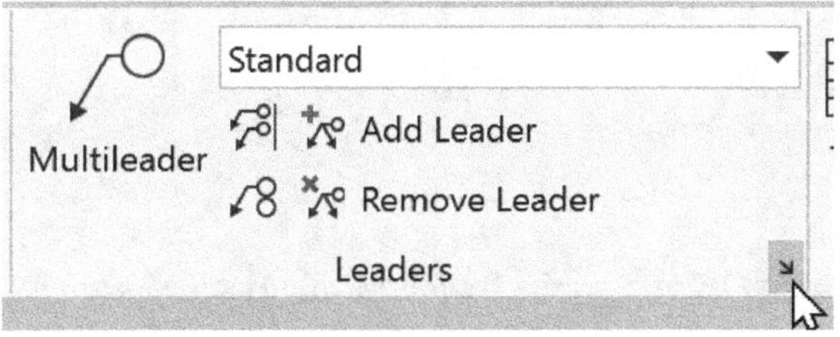

- Click the **New** button on the dialog.
- In the **Create New Multileader Style** dialog, enter **Balloon Callout** in the **New Style name** box and click **Continue**.

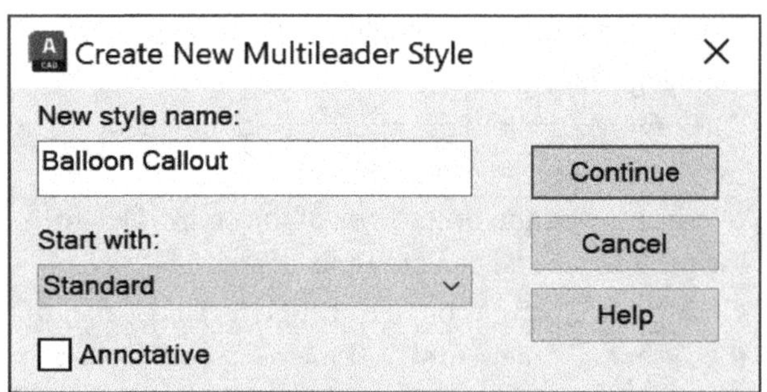

- In the **Modify Multileader Style** dialog, click the **Content** tab, and set the **Multileader type** to **Block**.
- Under **Block Options**, set the **Source block** to **Circle**.
- Set the **Scale** to **3**.

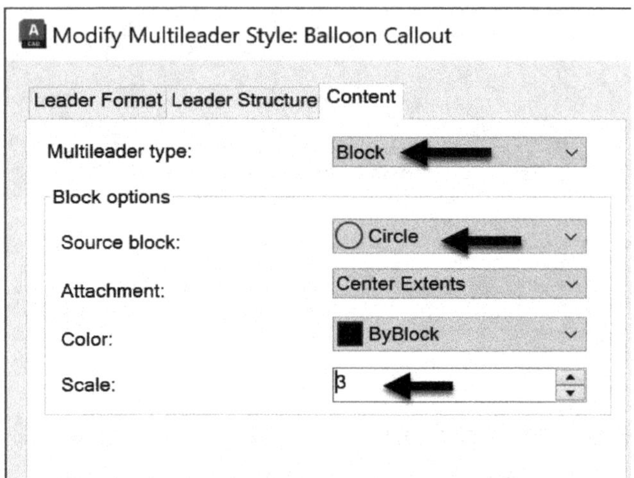

- Click the **Leader Format** tab and set the Arrowhead **Size** to 8.

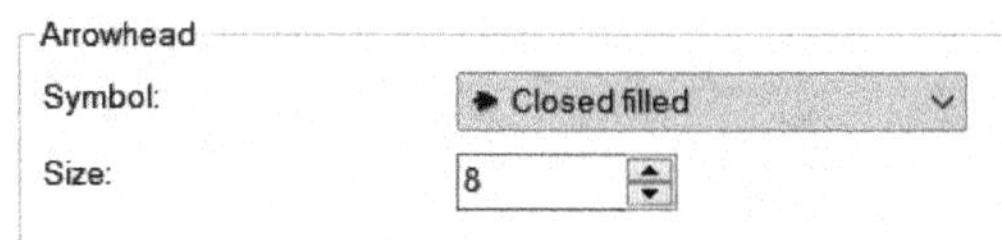

- Click **OK** and set the **Balloon Callout** style as current.
- Click **Close**.
- Click **Annotate > Leaders > Multileader** on the ribbon.
- Click the down arrow next to the **Polar Tracking** icon on the status bar and select **45** from the menu. Activate the **Polar Tracking**.
- Select a point on the section view of the crank.
- Move the pointer along the polar trace lines and click; the **Edit Attributes** dialog appears.

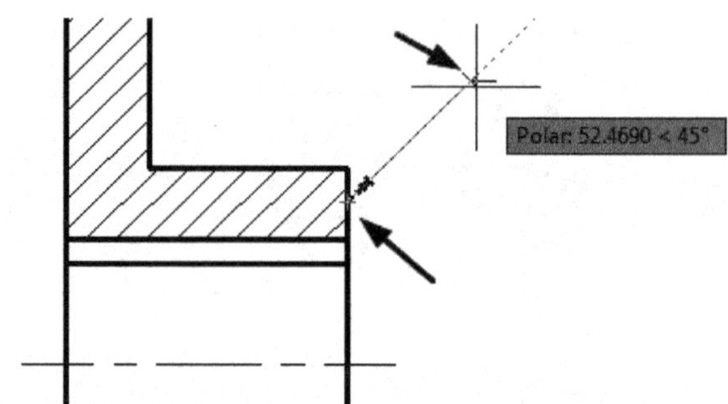

- In the **Edit Attributes** dialog, enter 1 in the **Enter tag number** field.

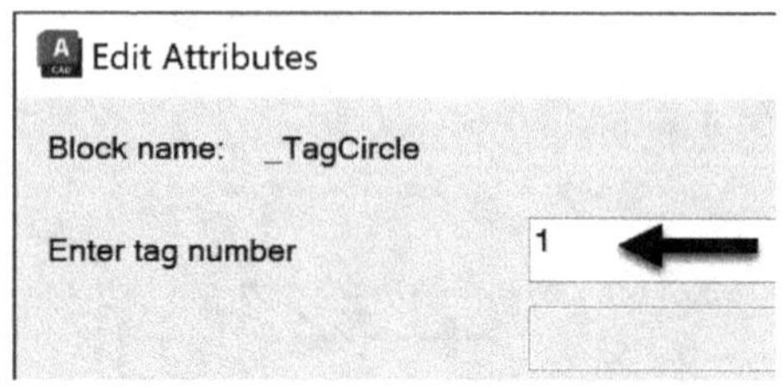

- Click **OK**; the balloon will be created.

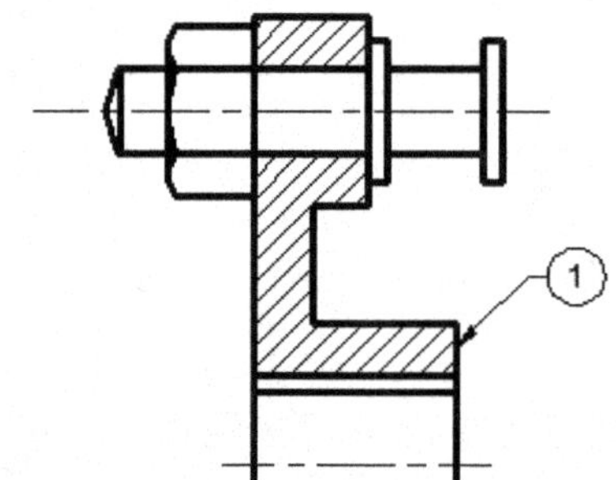

- Likewise, create other balloons.

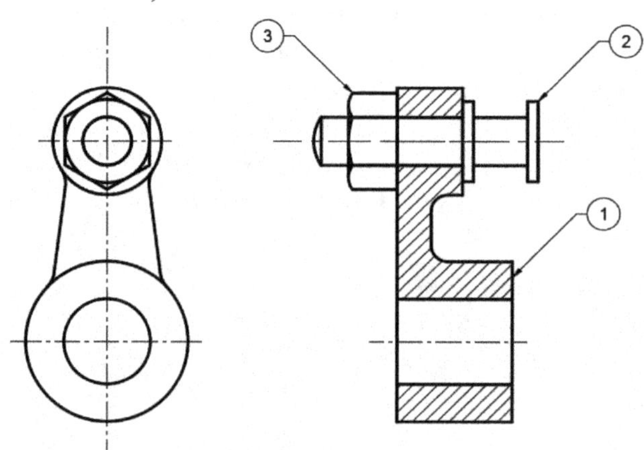

Creating the Part List

- Click **Annotate > Tables > Table Style** on the ribbon; the **Table Style** dialog appears.

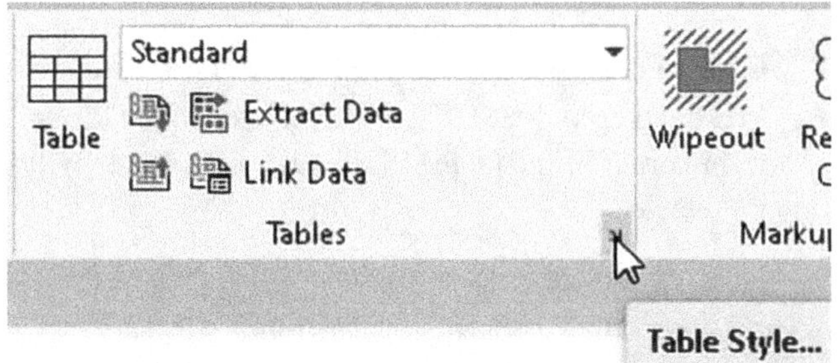

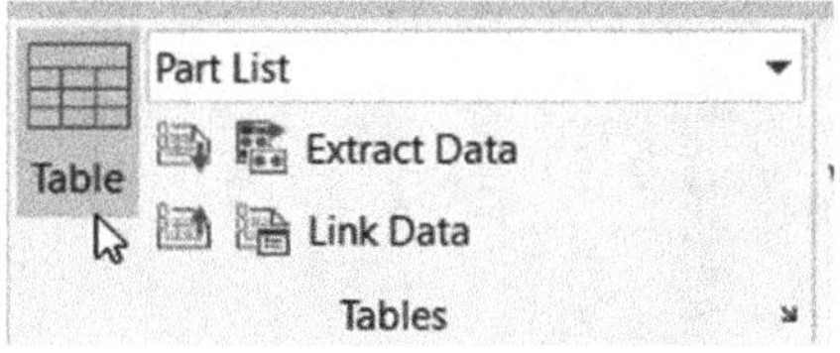

- Ensure that the **Table style** is set to **Part List**.

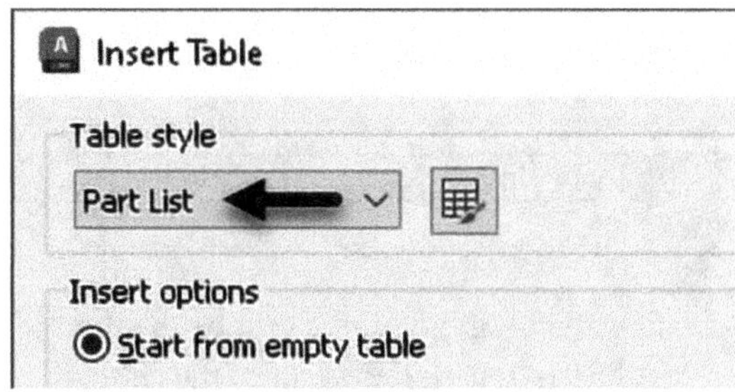

- In the **Table Style** dialog, click the **New** button; the **Create New Table Style** dialog appears,
- In the **Create New Table Style** dialog, enter **Part List** in the **Name** box. Click **Continue**; the **New Table Style** dialog appears.
- Click the **Text** tab and set the **Text height** to **10**.

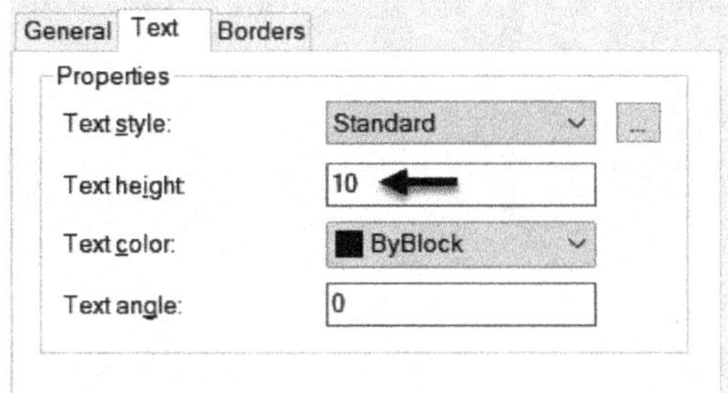

- Select the **Header** option from the **Cell Styles** drop-down and set the **Text height** to **10**.

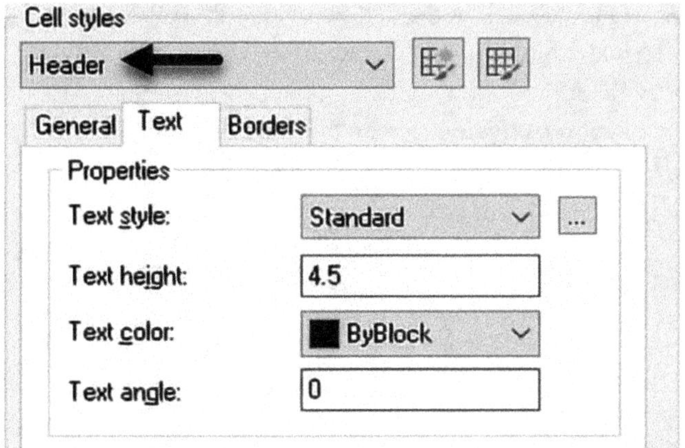

- Under the **Set cell Styles** group, set the **First row cell style** to **Header**.
- Set the **Second row cell style** and **All other row cell styles** to **Data**.

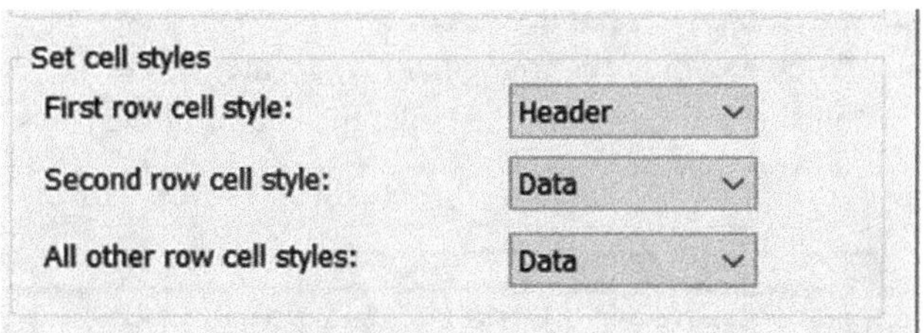

- Set the number of **Columns** to **4** and **Column width** to **65**.
- Set the **Data rows** and **Row height** to 1 and 1, respectively.
- Click **OK** and place the table at the lower right corner of the graphics window.
- Enter **PART No., NAME, MATERIAL, QTY** in the first row of the **Part list** table. Use the **TAB** key to navigate between the cells.

Part No.	Name	Material	Qty

- Click the **Close Text Editor** button on the ribbon.

- Click **OK**.
- In the **Table Style** dialog, select the **Part List** style and click **Set current**.
- Close the dialog.
- Click the **Table** button on the **Tables** panel; the **Insert table** dialog appears.

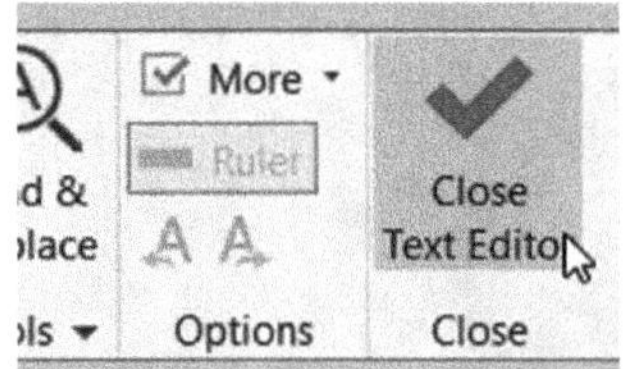

- Click on any one of the edges of the table; you will notice that grips are displayed on it. You can edit the table using these grips.

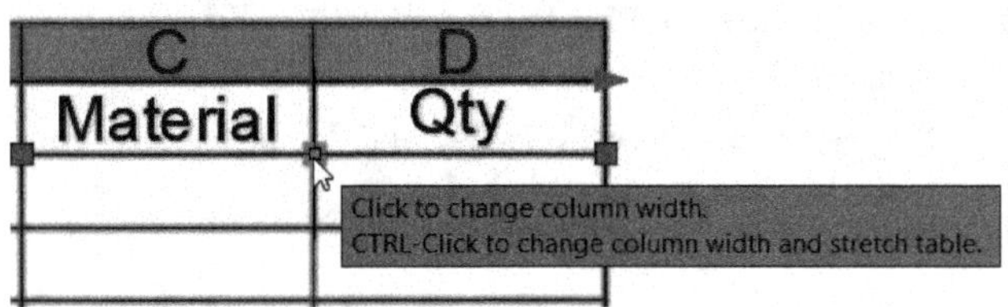

- Click and drag the square grip below the MATERIAL cell; the width of the cell will be changed.

- Click and drag the triangular grip located at the bottom left corner of the table; the height of the rows will be increased uniformly.

- Click on the second cell of the first column; the **Table Cell** ribbon appears. You can use this ribbon to modify the properties of the table cell.
- Click the **Insert Below** button on the **Rows** panel; a new row will be added to the cell.

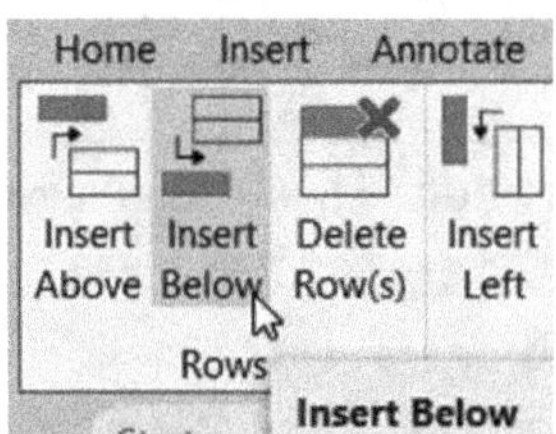

Exercise

- Click in the top left corner cell of the table.
- Press and hold the SHIFT key and click in the lower right corner of the table; all the cells in the table will be selected.

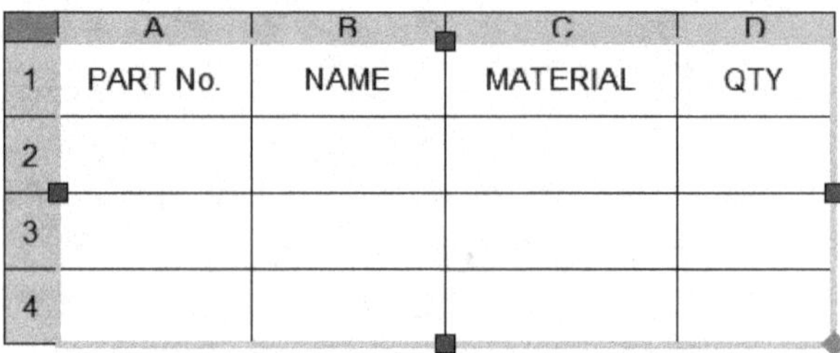

- In the **Table Cell** ribbon, click **Cell Styles > Alignment** drop-down > **Middle Center**; the data in all the cells will appear in the middle center of the cells.

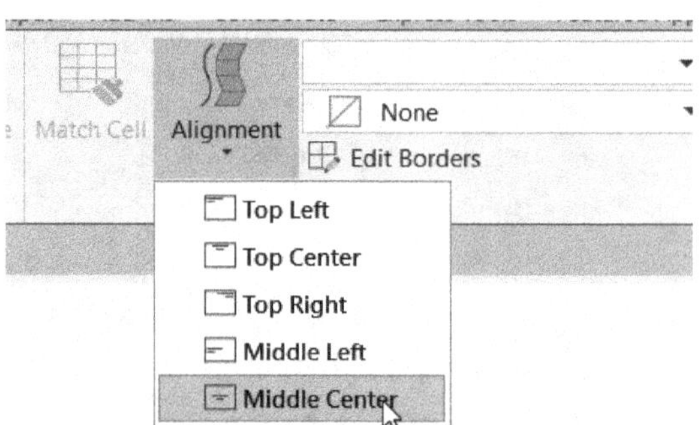

- Double-click in the cell below the **PART No.**; the text editor will be activated.
- Enter the following data in the cells. Use the TAB key to navigate between the cells.

PART No.	NAME	MATERIAL	QTY
1	Crank	Forged Steel	1
2	Crank pin	45C	1
3	Nut	MS	1

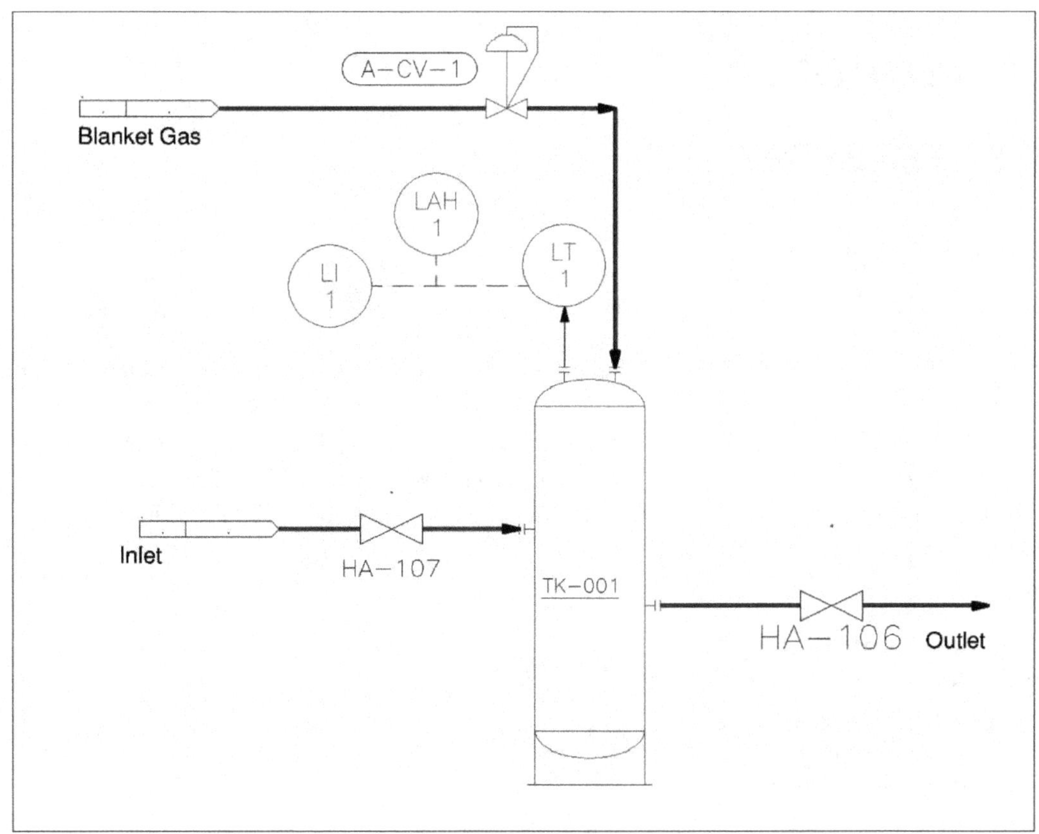

A-CV-1
Blanket Gas
LAH
1
LI
1
LT
1
Inlet
HA-107
TK-001
HA-106
Outlet

Chapter 10: Layouts & Annotative Objects

In this chapter, you will learn to do the following:

- **Create Layouts**
- **Specify the Paper space settings**
- **Create Viewports in Paper space**
- **Change Layer properties in Viewports**
- **Create a Title Block on the layout**
- **Use Annotative objects in Viewports**

Drawing Layouts

There are two workspaces in AutoCAD: The Model space and the Paper space. In the Model space, you create 2D drawings and 3D models. You can even plot drawings from the model space. However, it is difficult to plot drawings at a scale or if a drawing consists of multiple views arranged at different scales. For this purpose, we use Layouts or paper space. In Layouts or paper space, you can work on notes and annotations and perform the plotting or publishing operations. In Layouts, you can arrange a single view or multiple views of a drawing or multiple drawing by using Viewports. These viewports display drawings at specific scales on layouts. They are mainly rectangular in shape, but you can also create circular and polygonal viewports. In this chapter, you will learn about viewports and various annotative objects.

Working with Layouts

Layouts represent the conventional drawing sheet. They are created to plot a drawing on a paper or in electronic form. A drawing can have multiple layouts to print in different sheet formats. By default, there are two layouts available: Layout 1 and Layout 2. You can also create new layouts by clicking the plus (+) symbol next to the layout. Next, select **New layout** from the shortcut menu. In the following example, you will create two layouts, one representing the ISO A1 (841 X 594) sheet and another representing the ISO A4 (210 X 297) sheet.

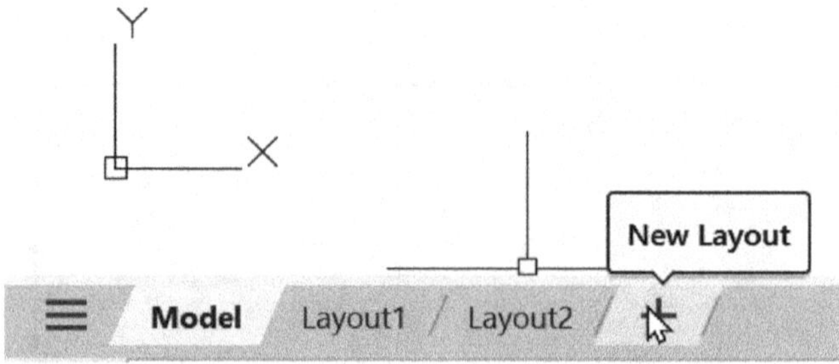

You can use the **Layout tab menu** located on the left side of the **Model** tab to create a new layout, define the page settings of the model tab or layouts, select all layouts, publish the selected layouts, and dock the model and layout tabs above the status bar or inline with it.

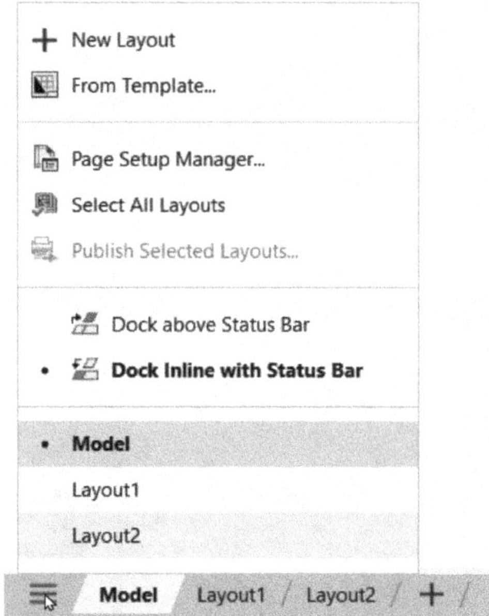

Example:
- Open a new drawing file.
- Create layers with the following settings:

Layer	Linetype	Lineweight
Construction	Continuous	0.25mm
Object Lines	Continuous	0.6 mm
Hidden Lines	Hidden	0.3 mm
Center Lines	CENTER	0.25 mm

Dimensions	Continuous	0.25 mm
Title Block	Continuous	1.2 mm
Viewport	Continuous	0.25 mm

- Create the drawing, as shown next. Do not add dimensions.

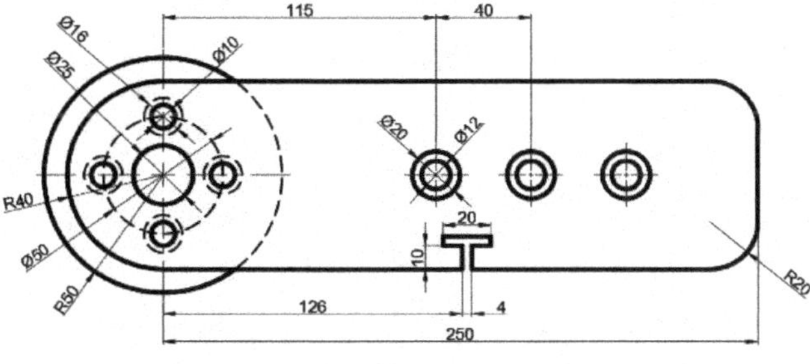

- Click the **Layout 1** tab at the bottom of the graphics window.

You will notice that a white paper is displayed with the viewport created automatically. The components of a layout are shown in the figure below.

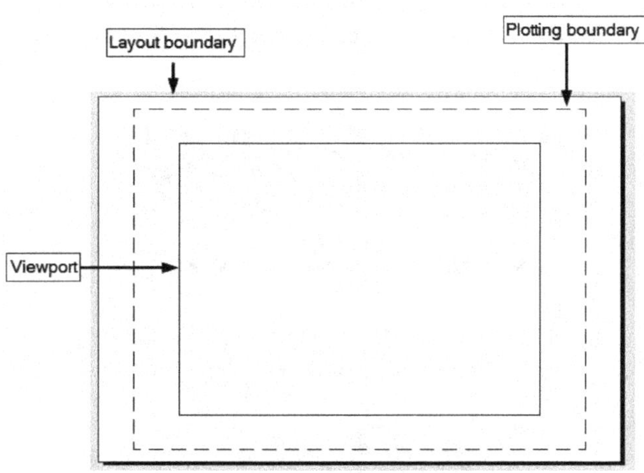

- Click **Output > Plot > Page Setup Manager** on the ribbon; the **Page Setup Manager** dialog appears.

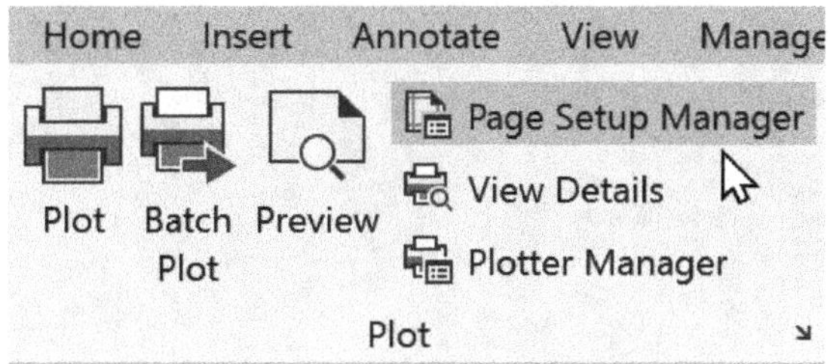

- In the **Page Setup Manager** dialog, click the **Modify** button; the **Page Setup –Layout1** dialog appears.

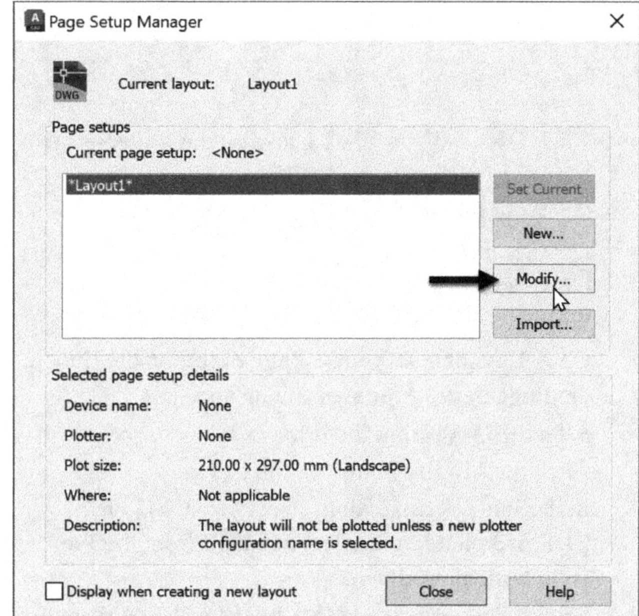

- In the **Page Setup** dialog, select **DWG to PDF.pc3** from the **Name** drop-down under the **Printer/Plotter** group.
- Set the **Plot Style table** to **acad.stb**.
- Set the **Paper size** to **ISO A1 (841.00 x 594.00 MM)**. Set the **Plot scale** to **1:1**.

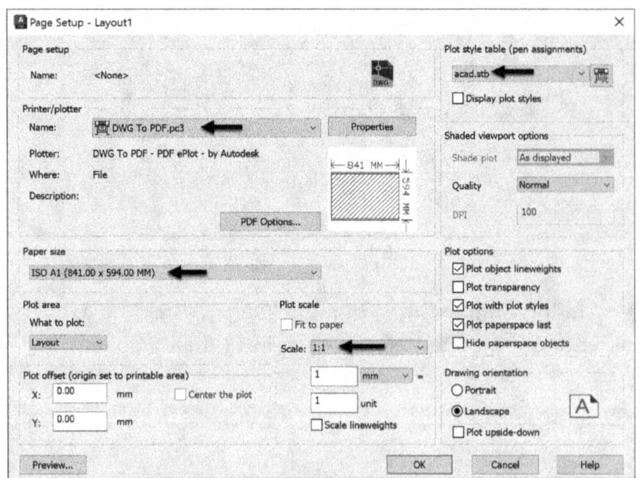

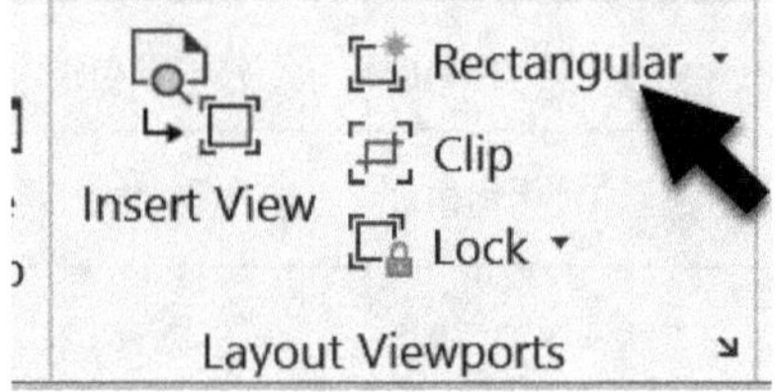

- Click **OK**, and then click **Close** on the **Page Setup Manager** dialog.
- Click the **Layout2** tab below the graphics window.
- Double-click on the **Layout1** tab and enter **ISO A1**; the **Layout1** is renamed.
- Similarly, rename the **Layout2** to **ISO A4**.
- Click **Layout > Layout > Page Setup** on the ribbon; the **Page Setup Manager** dialog appears.
- Select **ISO A4** from the list.
- Click the **Modify** button on the dialog.
- In the **Page Setup** dialog, select the **DWG to PDF.pc3** plotter and select **acad.stb** from the **Plot style table** drop-down.
- Set the **Paper size** to **ISO A4 (210 x 297 MM)** and **Scale** to **1:1.**
- Set **Drawing Orientation** as **Portrait** and click **OK**; you will notice that the size of the Layout is changed to A4 size.
- Close the **Page Setup Manager** dialog.

Creating Viewports in the Paper space

The viewports that exist in the paper space are called floating viewports. It is because you can position them anywhere in the layout and modify their shape and size with respect to the layout.

Creating a Viewport in the ISO A4 layout

- Open the **ISO A4** layout, if not already open.
- Select the default viewport that exists in the **ISO A4** layout.
- Press the DELETE key; the viewport will be deleted.
- Click **Layout > Layout Viewports > Rectangular** on the ribbon.

- Create the rectangular viewport by picking the first and second corner points, as shown in the figure.

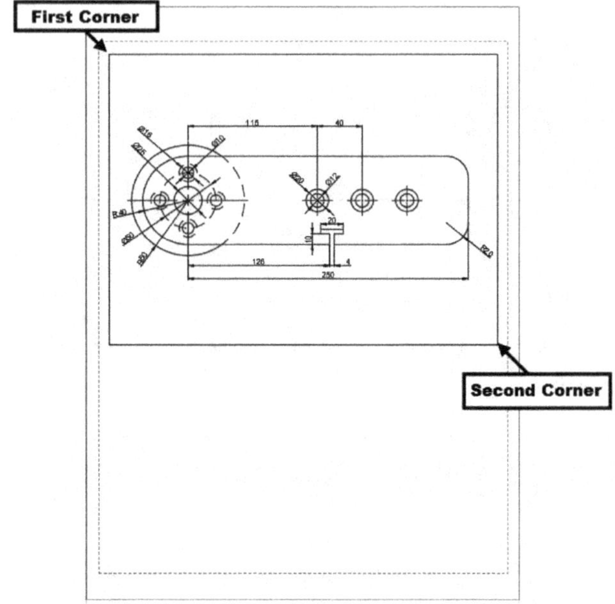

- Click the **PAPER** button on the status bar; the model space inside the viewport will be activated. Also, the viewport frame will become thicker when you are in model space.

- Click the **Viewport Scale** button and select **1:2** from the menu; the drawing will be zoomed out.

- Use the **Pan** tool and position the drawing in the center of the viewport.

- After fitting the drawing inside the viewport, you can lock the position by clicking the **Lock/Unlock Viewport** button on the status bar.

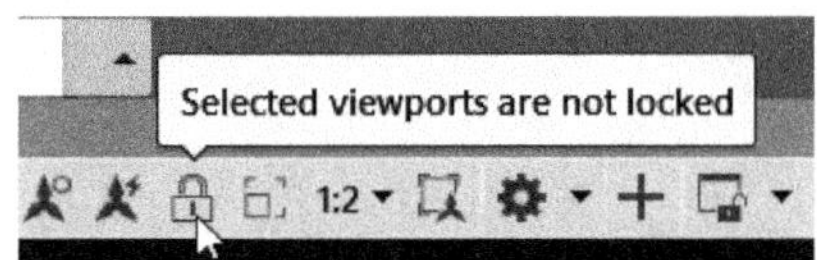

After locking the viewport, you cannot change the scale or position of the drawing.

- Click the **MODEL** button on the status bar to switch back to paper space.

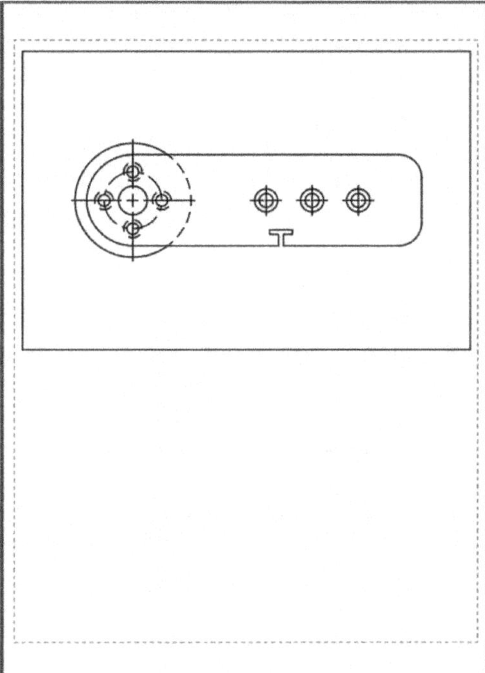

Creating Viewports in the ISO A1 layout

- Click the **ISO A1** tab below the graphics window.
- Select the viewport frame and modify the viewport using the grips, as shown below.

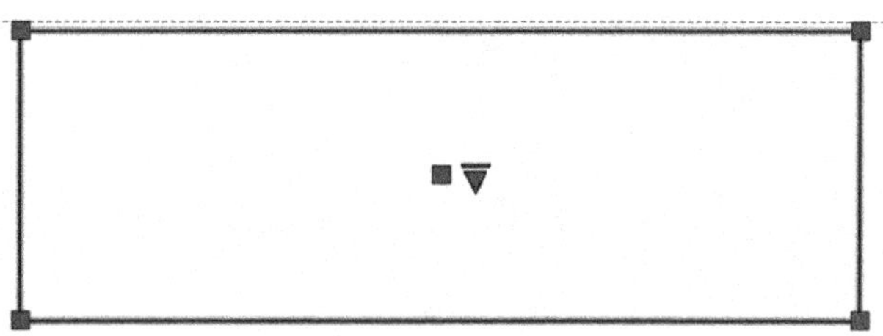

- Double-click inside the viewport to switch to the model space.
- Use the **Zoom** and **Pan** tools and drag the drawing to the center of the viewport.
- Click the **Viewport Scale** button and select **2:1** from the menu.
- Use the **Pan** tool and position the drawing, as shown in the figure.
- Click the **Lock/Unlock Viewport** button on the status bar.
- Double-click outside the viewport to switch to the paper space.
- Use the **Circle** tool and create a 180 mm diameter circle on the layout, as shown below.

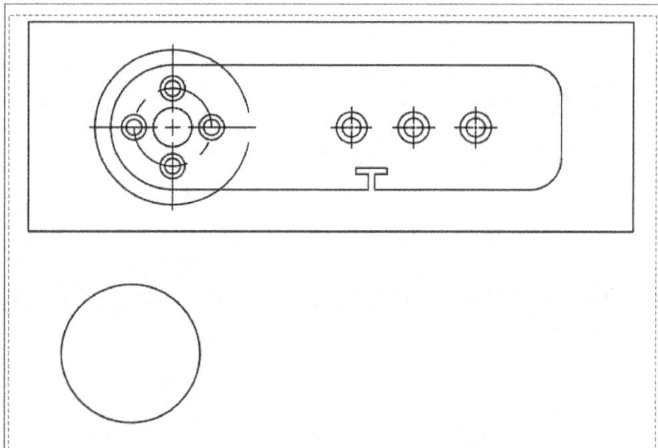

- Click **Layout > Layout Viewports > Viewport drop-down > Object** on the ribbon.

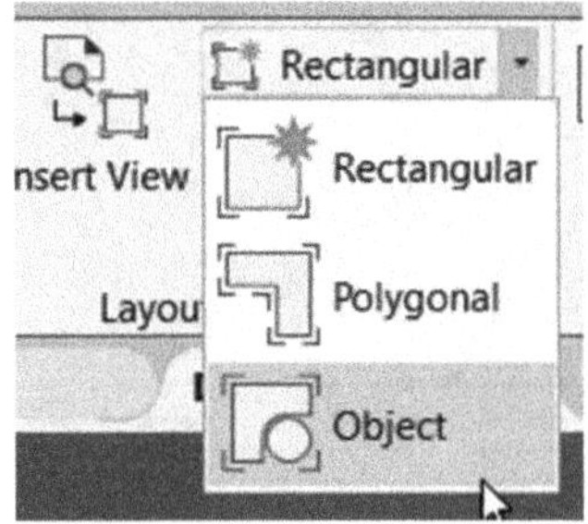

- Select the circle from the layout; it will be converted into a viewport.

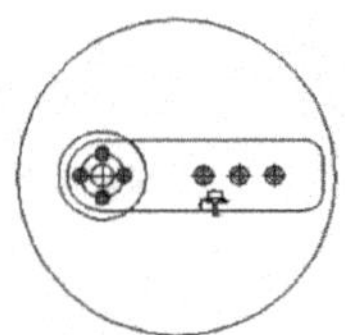

- Double-click in the circular viewport to switch to the model space.
- Click the **Viewport Scale** button on the status bar and select **4:1** from the menu; the drawing will be zoomed in to its center.
- Use the **Pan** tool and adjust the drawing, as shown below.

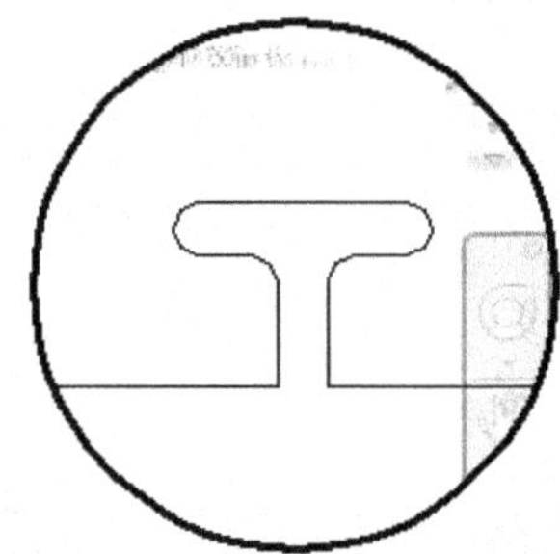

- Click the **Lock** button on the **Layout Viewports** panel.

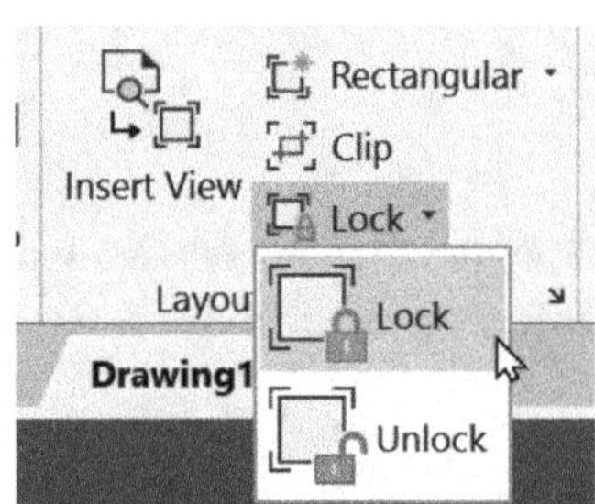

- Select the circular viewport and press ENTER; the drawing inside the viewport will be locked. Now, you cannot zoom or pan the drawing.

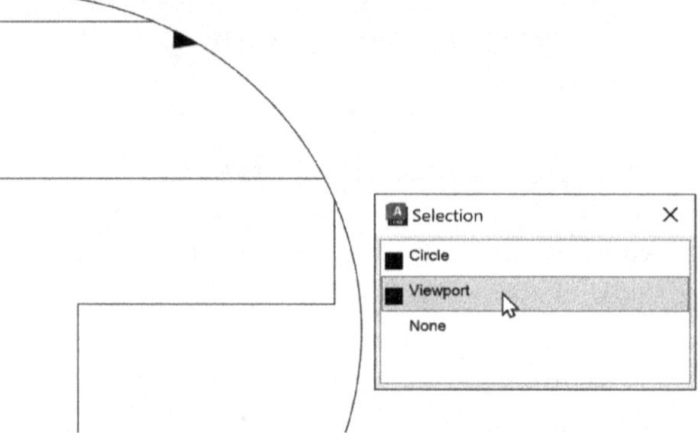

- Click **Output > Plot > Preview** on the ribbon; the plot preview will be displayed. You will notice that the viewport frames are also displayed in the preview.

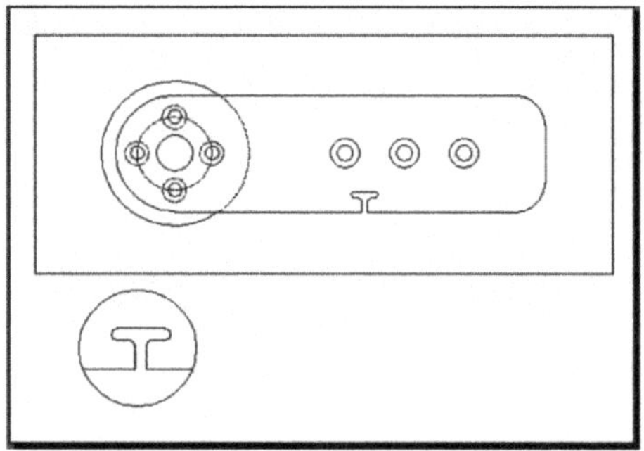

- Press ESC to close the preview window.

To hide viewport frames while plotting a drawing, follow the steps given below.

- Type **LA** in the command line to open the **Layer Properties Manager**.
- In the **Layer Properties Manager**, create a new layer called **Hide Viewports** and make it current.
- Deactivate the plotter symbol 🖶 under the **Plot** column of the **Hide Viewports** layer; the object on this layer will not be plotted.
- Close the **Layer Properties Manager**.
- Click the **Home** tab on the ribbon and expand the **Layers** panel.
- Click the **Change to Current Layer** button on the **Layers** panel.

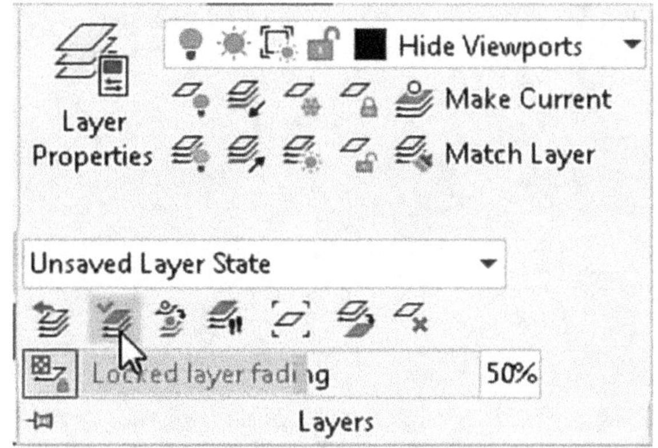

- Select the viewports in the **ISO A1** layout and press ENTER; the viewport frames will become unplottable. To check this, click the **Preview** button on the **Plot** panel of the **Output** ribbon tab; the plot preview will be displayed as shown below.

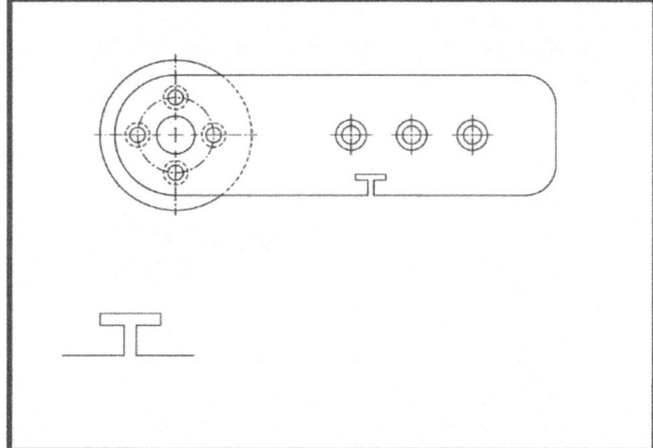

- Close the preview window.

Changing the Layer Properties in Viewports

The layer properties in viewports are not related to the layer properties in model space. You can change the layer properties in viewports without any effect in the model space.

- Double-click inside the larger viewport to activate the model space.
- Type **LA** in the command line to open the **Layer Properties Manager**.

- In the **Layer Properties Manager**, click the icon in the **VP Freeze** column of the **Hidden lines** layer; the hidden lines will disappear in the viewport, as shown below.

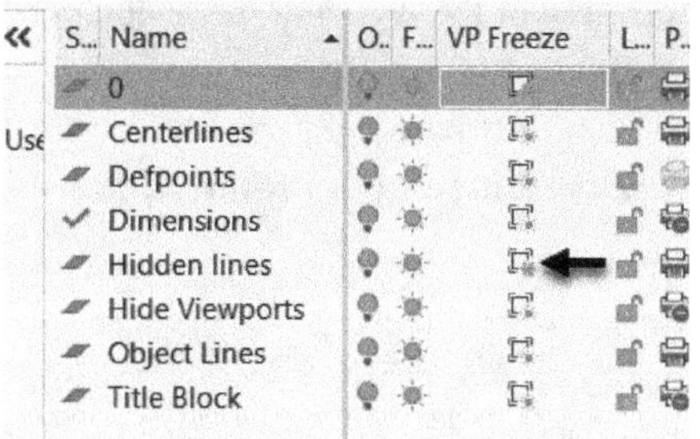

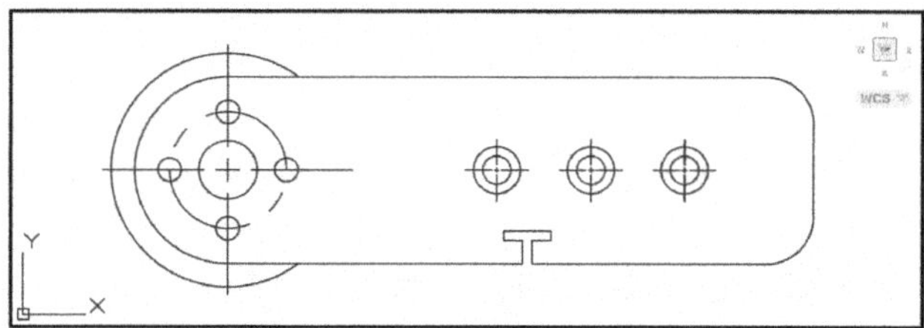

- Double-click outside the viewport to switch to paper space.
- Click the **Model** tab below the graphics window; you will notice that the hidden lines are retained in the model space.

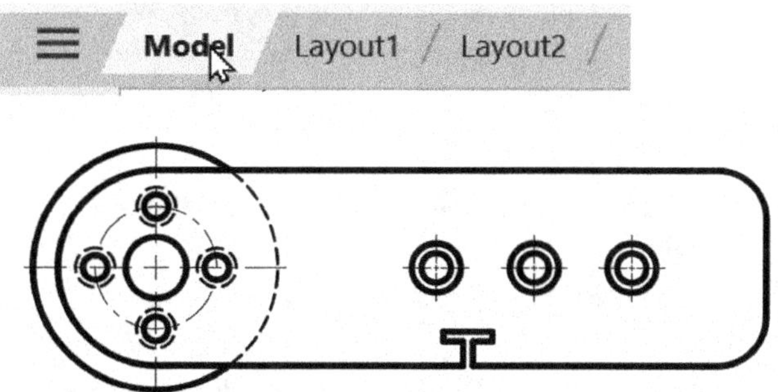

Creating the Title Block on the Layout

You can draw objects on layouts to create a title block, borders, and viewports. However, it is not recommended to draw the actual drawing on layouts. You can also create dimensions on layouts.

Example1:
- Click the **ISO A1** layout tab.
- Set the **Title Block** layer as current.
- Click the **Rectangle** button on the **Draw** panel.

- Pick a point at the lower right corner of the layout.
- Select the **Dimensions** option from the command line.
- Specify the length of the rectangle as **820** and width as **550**.
- Click in the upper area of the layout; a rectangular border will be created.
- Create a title block at the lower right corner, as shown below (**Use the Line** and **Multiline Text** tools).

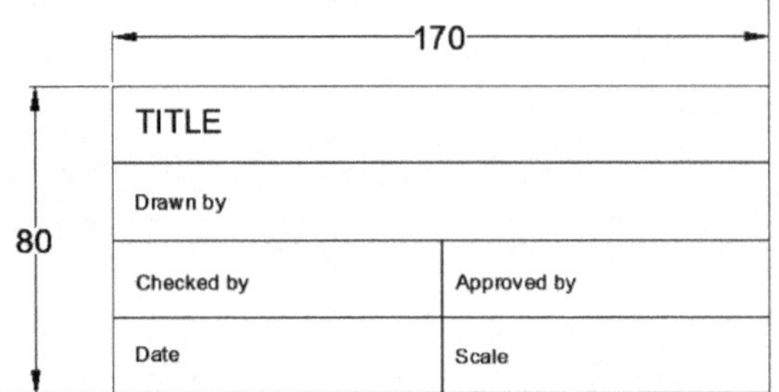

- Create attributes and place them inside the title, as shown below (refer to *Chapter 9: Blocks, Attributes, and Xrefs* to learn how to create attributes).

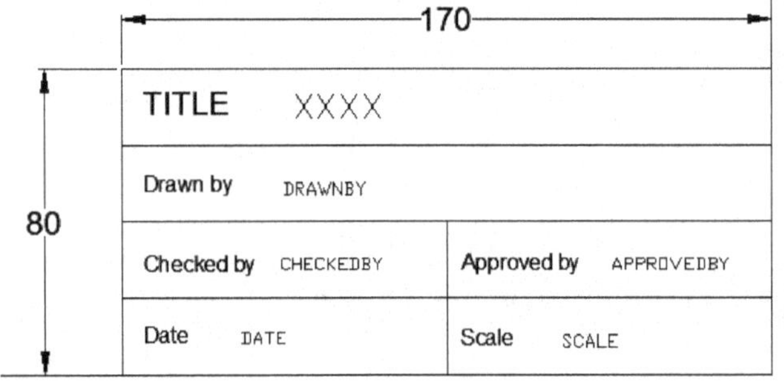

- Use the **Create Block** tool and convert it into a block.
- Use the **Insert** tool and insert it at the lower right corner of the layout.
- Save the drawing file as **Viewports-Example.dwg**.

Working with Annotative Dimensions

In AutoCAD, you create drawings at their actual size. However, when you scale a drawing to fit inside a viewport, the size of the dimensions will not be appropriately scaled. For example, in the following figure, the first viewport is scaled to 1:2, and the second viewport

is scaled to 1:1. The dimensions in the first viewport appear much smaller.

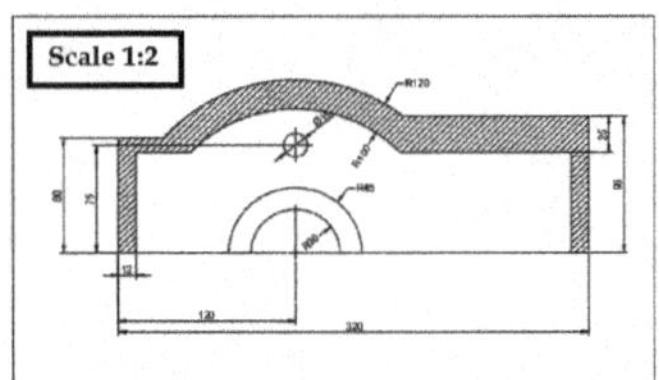

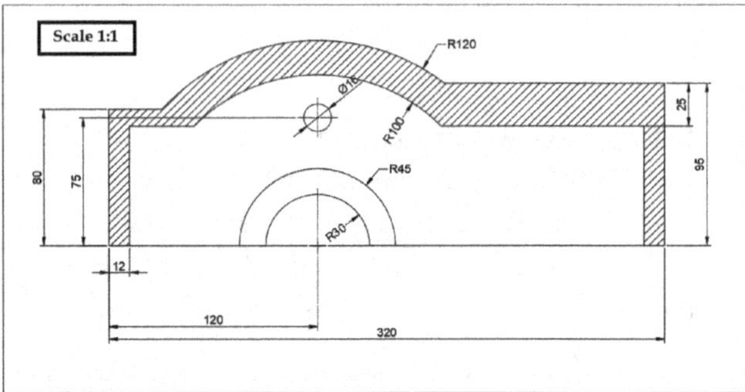

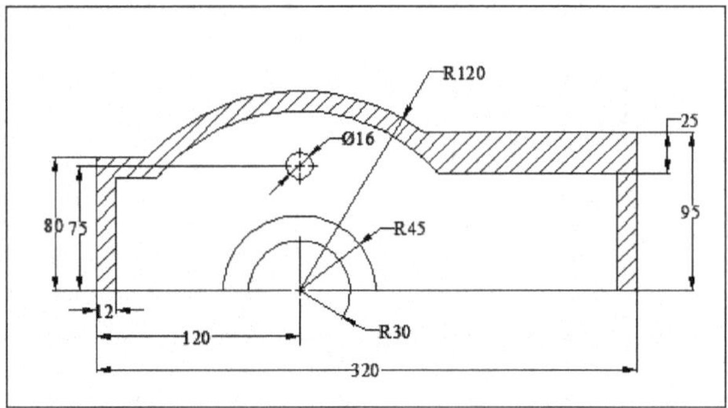

You can fix this problem by applying the Annotative property to dimensions.

- Open the **Viewports-Example.dwg**, if not already opened.
- Set the **Dimensions** layer as current.
- Type **D** in the command line and press ENTER.
- In the **Dimension Style Manager**, click the **New** button.
- In the **Create New Dimension Style** dialog, enter **New style name** as **Dim_Anno** and select the **Annotative** checkbox. Click **Continue**.

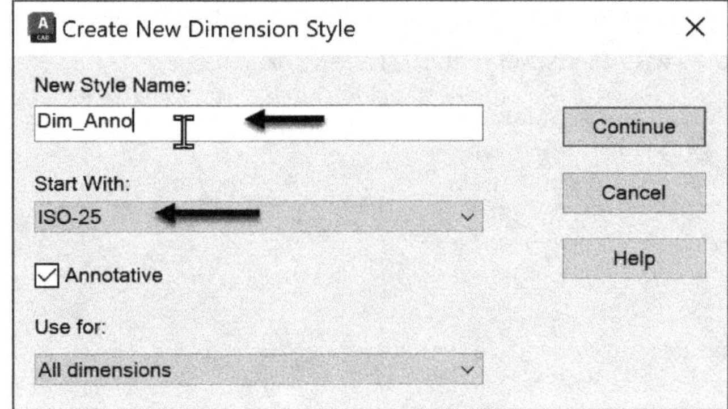

- Set the following settings in the **New Dimension Style** dialog.

  Lines tab: Offset from origin 1.25
  Symbols and Arrows tab: Arrow size 2.5, Center Marks-Line.
  Text tab: Text height – 2.5, Text placement - Vertical-Centered, Text alignment - Horizontal
  Primary Units tab: Units Format – Decimal, Precision – 0, Decimal separator – '.' period

- In the **Fit** tab, ensure that the **Annotative** checkbox is selected.

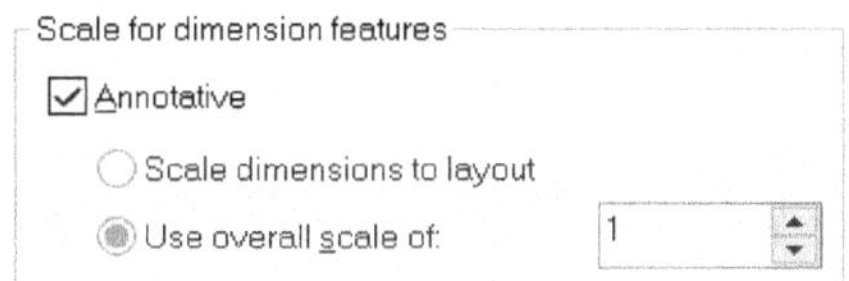

- Click **OK** on the **New Dimension Style** dialog; you will notice that the **Dim_Anno** style is listed in the **Dimension Style Manager**. Also, the annotation symbol is displayed next to it. It indicates that all dimensions created using this style will have annotative property. Click on the **Close** button.

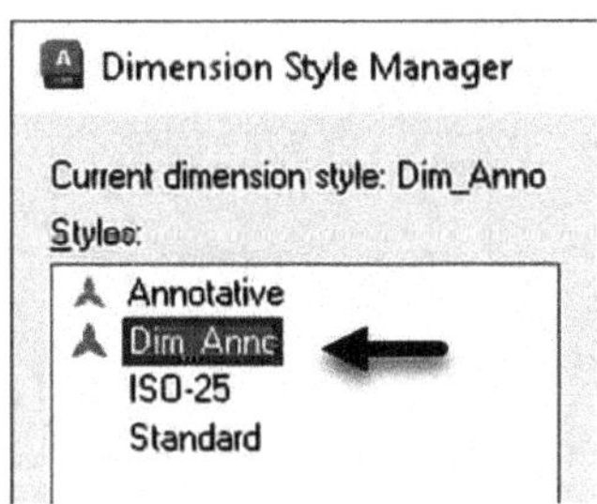

- Activate the **Dimension** tool and set the Annotation Scale to **1:1**. Click **OK**.

- Create a linear dimension, as shown below.

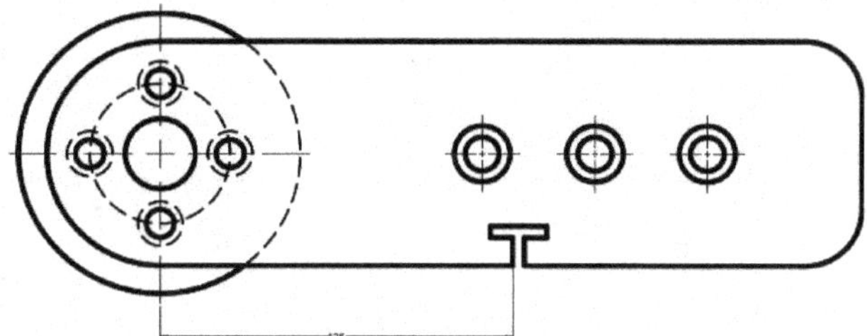

- Activate **Automatically add scales to annotative objects when the annotation scale changes** on the status bar.

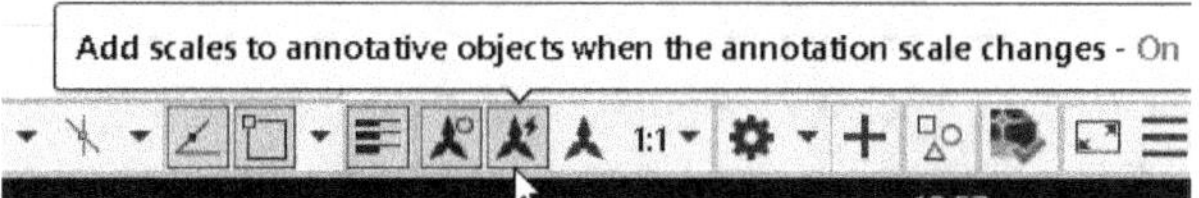

- Set the **Annotation Scale** to **1:2**; the size of the dimension will automatically increase by two times.

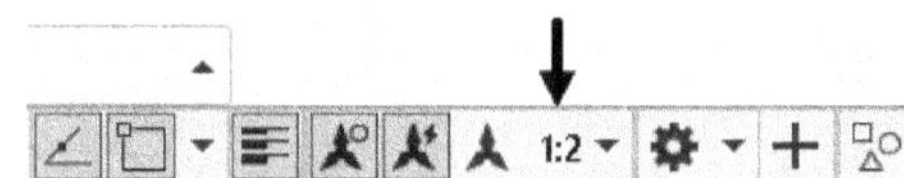

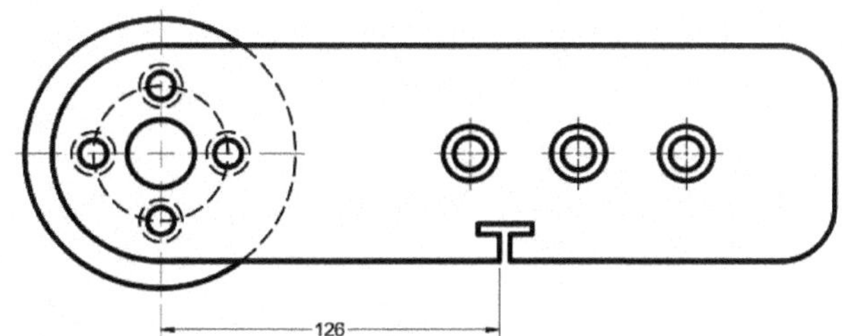

Example 2:

- Ensure that the **Annotation Scale** is set to **1:2** and create another linear dimension, as shown in the figure.

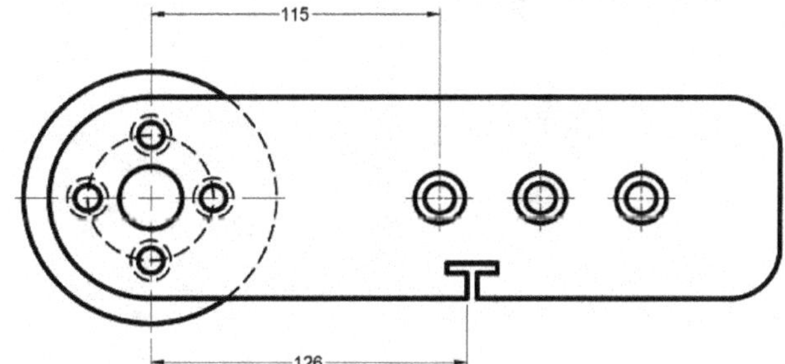

- Click the **ISO A4** layout in which the viewport scale is set to 1:2; you will notice that the dimensions are scaled with respect to the viewport.

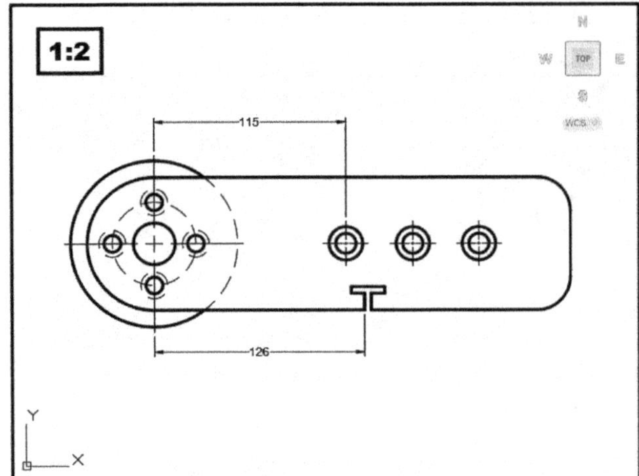

- Click the **ISO A1** layout; you will notice that the dimensions are not displayed in the 2:1 viewport. To display dimensions in the 2:1 viewport, you need to add 2:1 scale to dimensions.

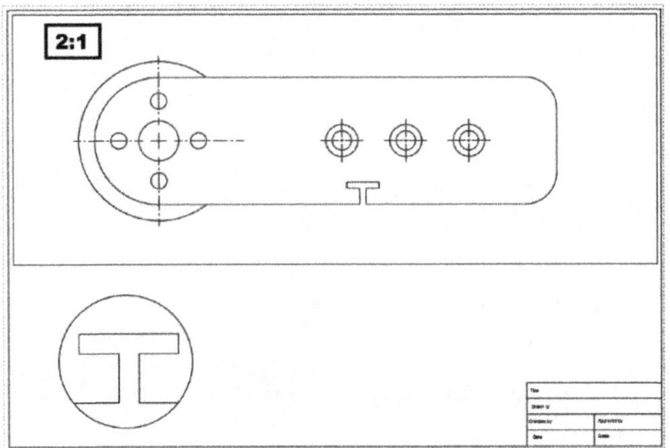

- Click the **Model** tab below the graphics window to switch to the model space.
- Click **Annotate > Annotation Scaling > Add/Delete Scales** on the ribbon.

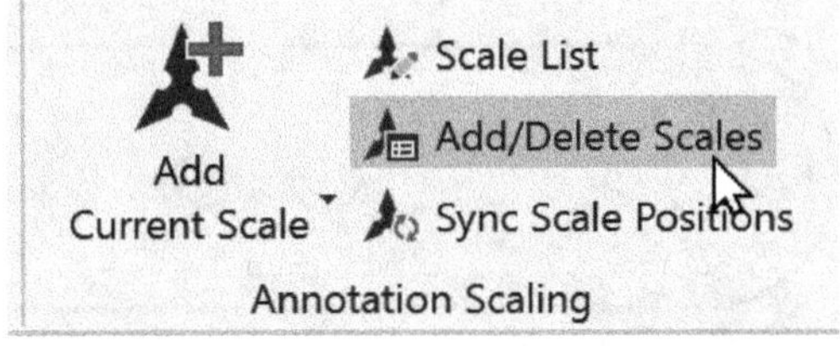

- Select the dimensions from the graphics window and right-click; the **Annotation Object Scale** dialog appears. In this dialog, the **Object Scale List** shows the scales applied to the selected dimensions. You

need to add a 2:1 scale to the dimensions so that they will be visible in the 2:1 viewport.

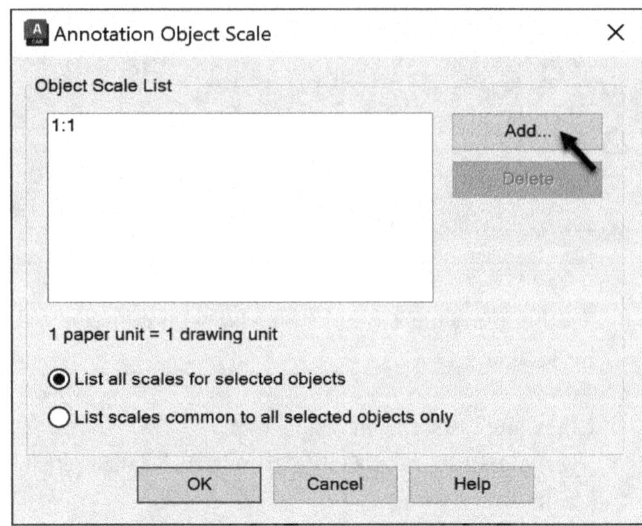

- To add a new scale to the dimensions, click the **Add** button; the **Add Scales to Object** dialog appears.
- Select the **2:1** scale from the list and click **OK**; the scale will be added to the **Object Scale list**.
- Click **OK** on the **Annotation Object Scale** dialog.
- Click the **ISO A1** layout; the dimensions are displayed in both 2:1 and 1:2 viewports.

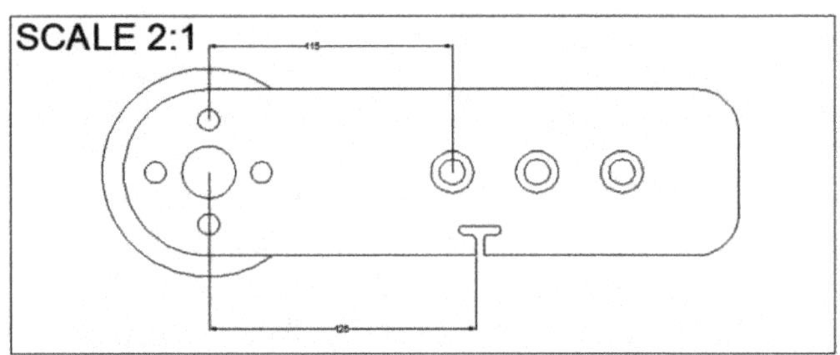

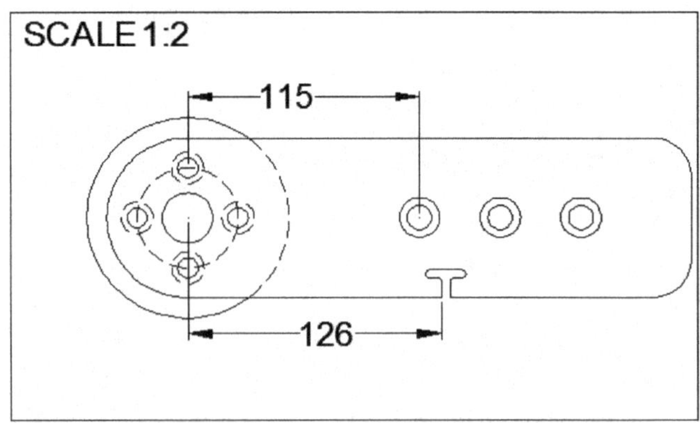

- Similarly, create other dimensions, as shown below. Add 2:1 and 1:2 scales to dimensions and check the drawing in two different layouts.

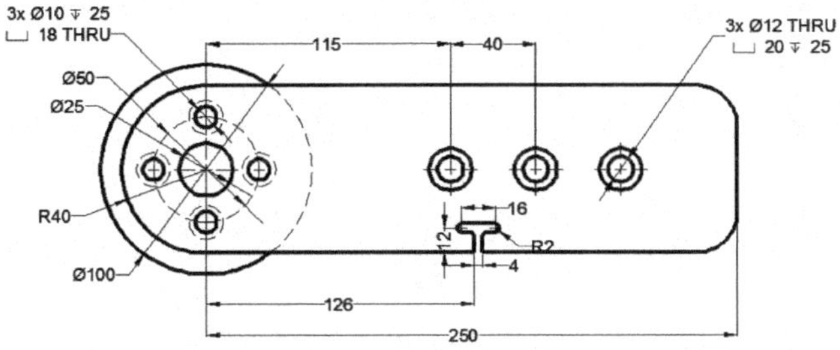

Scaling Hatches relative to Viewports

While working in layouts, you may also need to scale the hatch with respect to the viewport scale. The following figure shows a drawing in two different viewports 1:2 and 1:1. The hatch in the left viewport is smaller than that in the right-side viewport. You can correct this problem by using the **Relative to Paper Space** option.

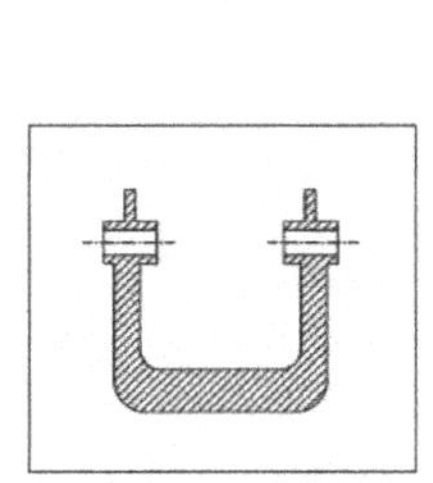
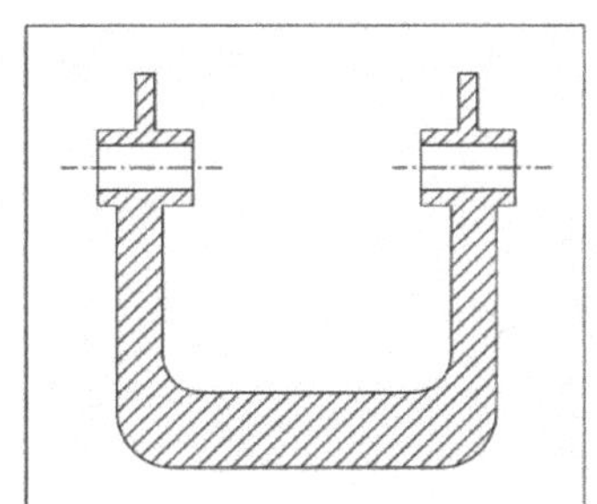

- Double-click inside a viewport; the model space will be activated.
- Select the hatch patterns from the drawing; the **Hatch Editor** tab appears.
- In the **Hatch Editor** tab, expand the **Properties** panel and select the **Relative to Paper Space** button.

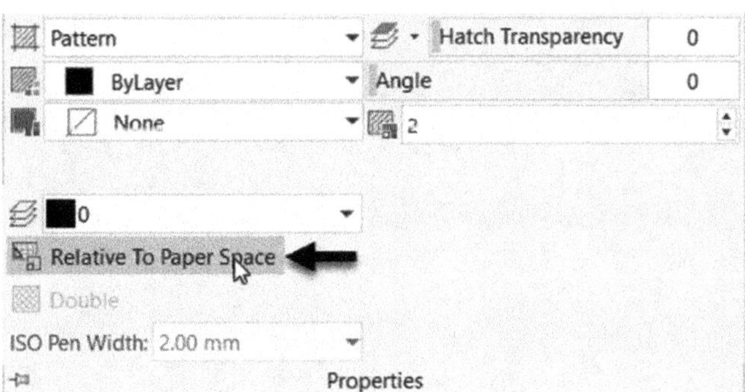

- Click the **Close Hatch Editor** button; you will notice that the hatch will be scaled with respect to the viewport scale. Double-click outside the viewport to switch to the paper space.

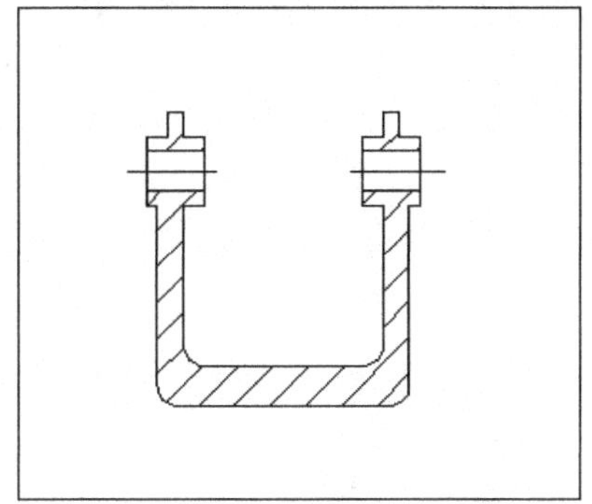

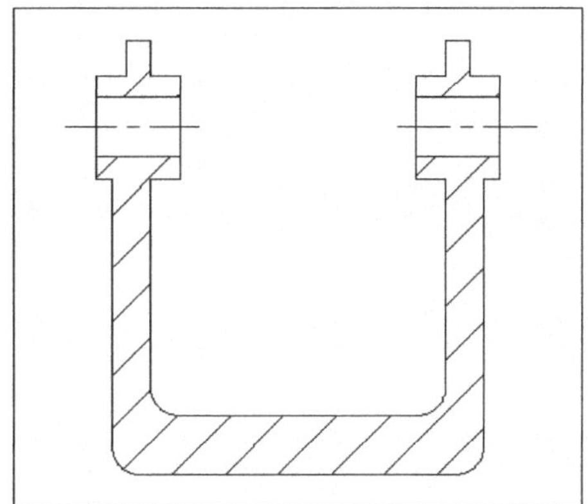

Working with Annotative Text

Annotative property can also be assigned to text. The annotative text will be scaled with respect to the viewport scale.

- Open the **Viewports-Example.dwg**, if not already opened.
- Click **Annotate > Text > Text Style** on the ribbon; the **Text Style** dialog appears.

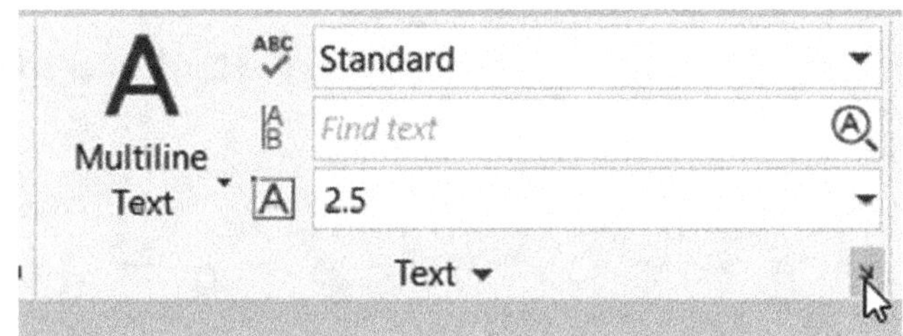

- Click the **New** button on the **Text Style** dialog; the **New Text Style** dialog appears.
- Enter **Text_Anno** as the **Style name** and click **OK**.

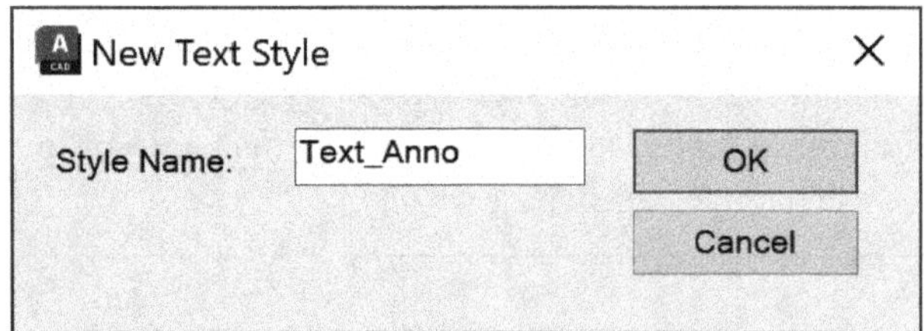

- Select the **Text_Anno** style from the **Styles** list.
- Set **Font Name** to **Arial** and select the **Annotative** checkbox.
- Set **Paper Text Height** to **2.5** and **Width Factor** to **1**.
- Click **Apply** and **Close**.
- Select **1:1** from the **Viewport Scale** menu at the status bar.
- Click **Annotate > Text > Multiline Text** on the ribbon.
- Specify the first corner of the text editor by picking an arbitrary point.
- Select the **Justify** option from the command line; the command line displays:

- Select the **MC** option from the command line.
- Move the pointer toward the right and specify the second corner of the text editor.
- Type **All dimensions are in mm** and click the **Close Text Editor** button on the **Close** panel.

- Move the text and place it at the bottom left corner of the drawing, as shown below. You can also add a frame to the text. Right-click on it and select **Properties**. On the **Properties** palette, under the **Text** section, set **Text Frame** to **Yes**.

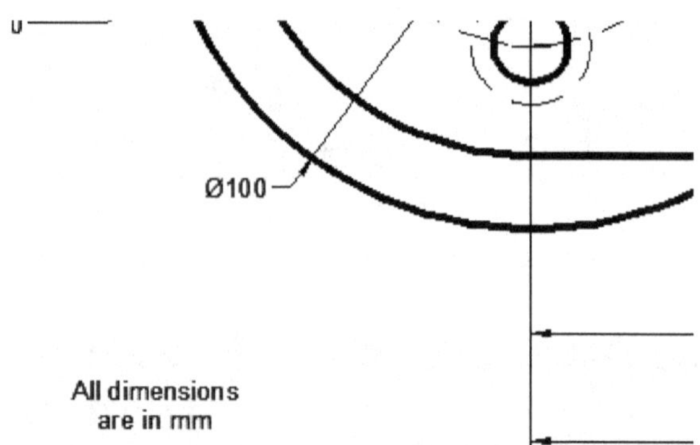

- View the drawing in the **ISO A4** layout; you will notice that the text is not displayed. It is because the text is set to a 1:2 scale.
- On the status bar, click the **Show annotation objects** button.

The text is visible in the ISO A4 layout.

- Save the drawing as **Layout Example.dwg** and close.

Exercises

Exercise 1

Create the drawing, as shown below. After creating the drawing, perform the following tasks:
- Create a layout of the A3 size and then create a viewport.
- Set the viewport scale to 1:2.
- Set the scale of the dimensions and hatch lines with respect to the viewport.

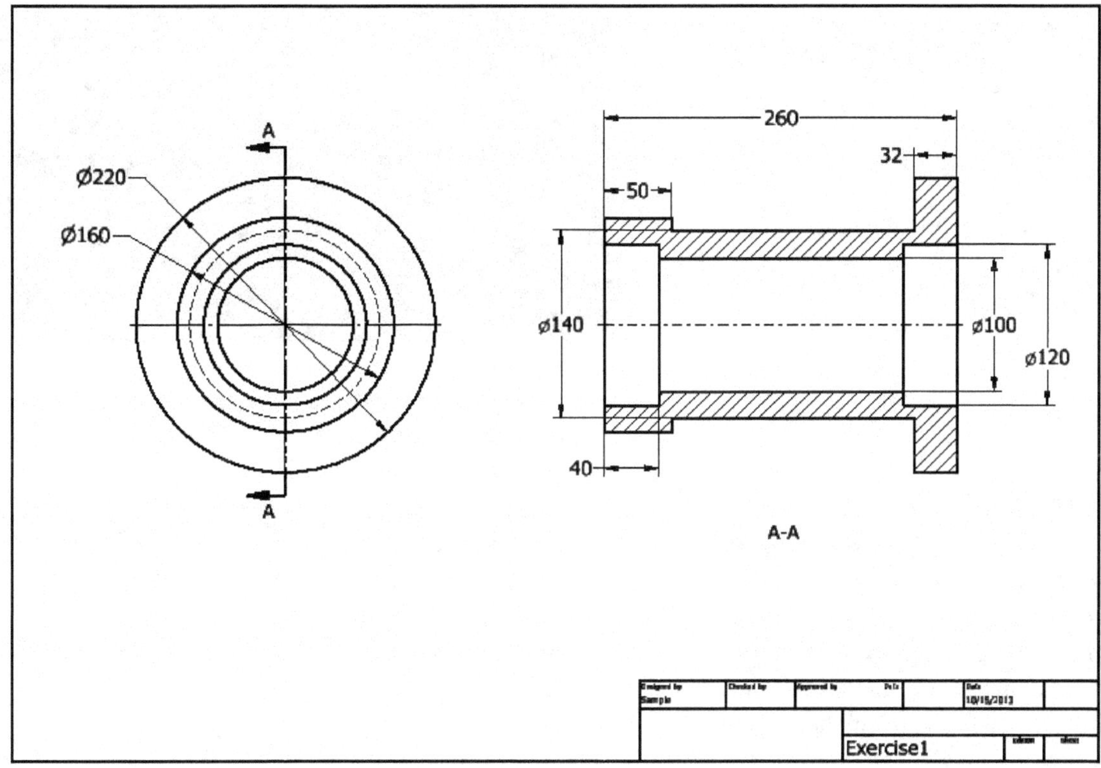

A
Ø220
Ø160
A
260
32
50
ø140
ø100
ø120
40
A-A
Designed by
Sample
Checked by
Approved by
Date
10/15/2013
Exercise1

Chapter 11: Templates and Plotting

In this chapter, you will learn to do the following:

- **Configure Plotters**
- **Create Plot Style Tables**
- **Use Plot styles**
- **Create Templates**
- **Plot/Print the drawing**

Plotting Drawings

Plotting is the process of producing a physical copy of the drawing using a printer or plotter. The printer may be directly connected to an AutoCAD workstation or on the network of workstations. Although the process of plotting is straightforward, it is essential to know how to establish communication between AutoCAD and the plotter. In this chapter, you will learn to connect a plotter with AutoCAD, define plotting style, and produce professional prints of drawings. You will also learn to print and publish drawings in digital format.

Configuring Plotters

It is assumed that you have connected the plotter to your workstation and installed the drivers related to it. Even after doing so, you need to set a connection between the plotter and AutoCAD. You can establish this connection by using the Add-plotter wizard. The following example explains the procedure to connect a plotter to AutoCAD.

Example:

- Start AutoCAD 2025 and open a new drawing file.
- Click **Application Menu > Print > Manage Plotters** or type PLOTTERMANAGER in the command line; the **Plotters** folder will be opened, as shown below. All the configured plotters are displayed in this folder.

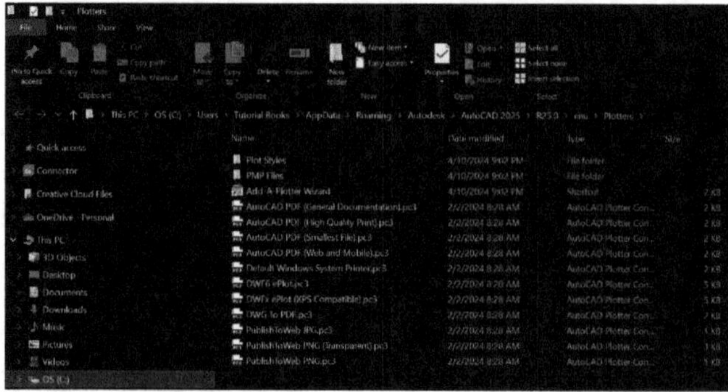

- In the **Plotters** folder, double-click on the **Add-A-Plotter Wizard** icon; the **Add Plotter – Introduction** page appears.
- Click the **Next** button; the **Add Plotter – Begin** page appears. On this page, three options allow you to set up a plotter: **My Computer**, **Network Plotter Server**, and **System Printer**. These options are explained in the dialog itself, as shown below.

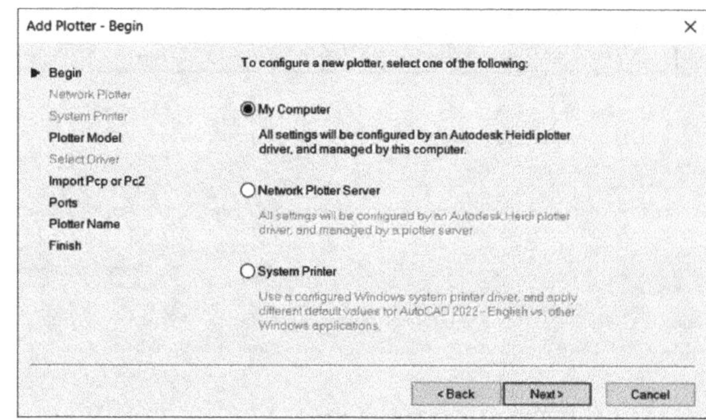

- Select the **System Printer** option and click **Next**; the **System Printer** page appears. A list of printers installed on your workstation is displayed.

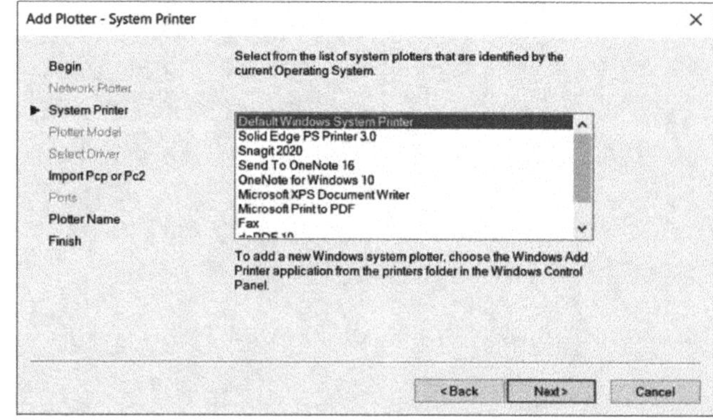

- From the list, select the required printer (**Adobe PDF**

in this case) and click **Next**; the **Import** page appears.

- Click the **Next** button; the **Plotter Name** page appears.

- Type name of the plotter in the **Plotter Name** box and click **Next**; the **Finish** page appears. You can edit the configuration of the plotter by using the **Edit Plotter Configuration** button.

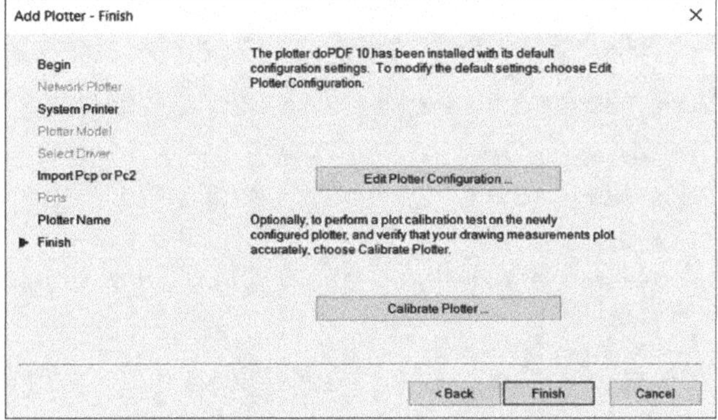

If you click the **Edit Plotter Configuration** button, the **Plotter Configuration Editor** dialog appears. In this dialog, you can modify the default settings of the plotter. The **Calibrate Plotter** button is used to test the plotter.

- Click the **Finish** button; a new plotter will be added to the **Plotters** folder.

Creating Plot Style Tables

Plot styles determine the final look of the plotted drawing. They are used to override the layer properties such as color, linetype, and lineweight when the drawing is printed. After configuring a plotter, you need to create a plot style. There are two types of plot styles: **Color-dependent** and **Named** plot style. **Color-dependent** plot styles are assigned based on the object color, whereas the **Named** plot styles are assigned based on layer or by an object.

- On the **Application Menu**, click **Print > Manage Plot styles** or type STYLESMANAGER in the command line; the **Plot Styles** folder appears.

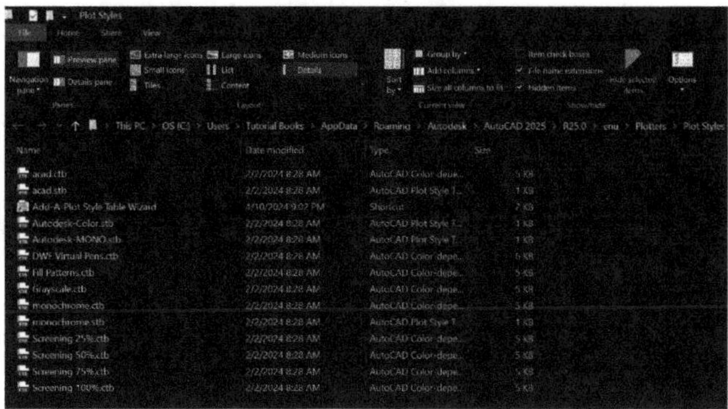

- Double-click on the **Add-A-Plot Style Table Wizard** icon; the **Add Plot Style Table** dialog appears. Read the information on this dialog and click **Next**.

- Select the **Start from Scratch** option and click **Next**.

- Select the **Named Plot Style Table** option and click **Next**.

- Enter **Sample** in the **File name** box and click **Next**; the **Finish** page appears.

- Click the **Plot Style Table Editor** button; the **Plot Style Table Editor** dialog appears.

- Click the **Add Style** button available at the bottom left of the dialog; a new style named **Style 1** is added.

- Enter **PS1** in the **Name** box.

- Select **Black** from the **Color** drop-down.

- Set the **Screening** value to 70. The screening factor will fade objects in the printed output. A 20% screening factor will result in more fading of objects than a 50% screening factor.

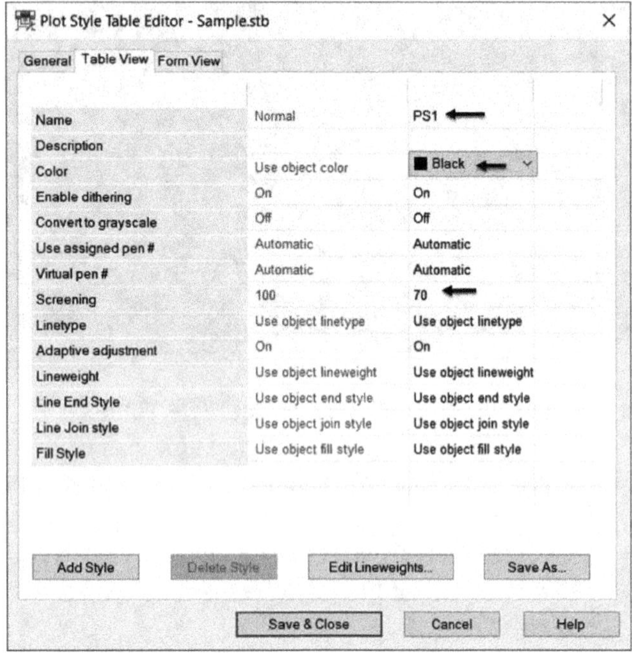

- Click **Save & Close** on the **Plot Style Table Editor** dialog.
- Click **Finish** to close the **Add Plot Style Table** dialog; the **Sample** plot style will be added to the **Plot Styles** folder.

Using Plot Styles

In AutoCAD, the Color-Dependent Plot style is used by default. To use the newly created plot style, you need to specify a setting in the **Options** dialog.

- Right-click in the graphics window and select **Options**; the **Options** dialog appears.
- Select the **Plot and Publish** tab in the **Options** dialog and click the **Plot Style Table Settings** button; the **Plots Style Table settings** dialog appears.

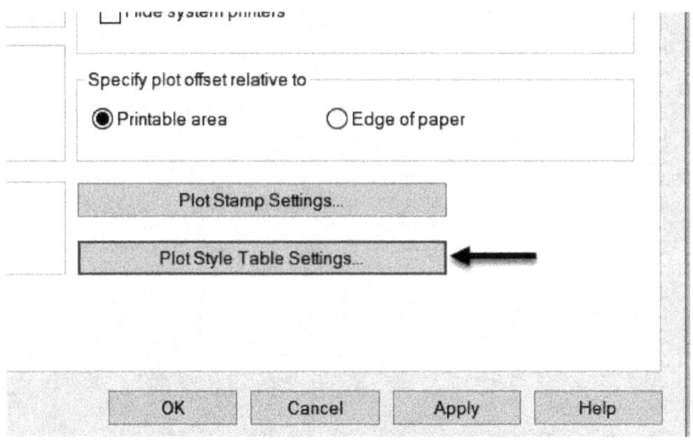

- Select the **Use named plot styles** option from the dialog.
- Select **Sample.stb** from the **Default plot style table** drop-down.
- Select **PS1** from the **Default plot style for layer 0** drop-down.
- Set the **Default plot style for objects** to **ByLayer**.

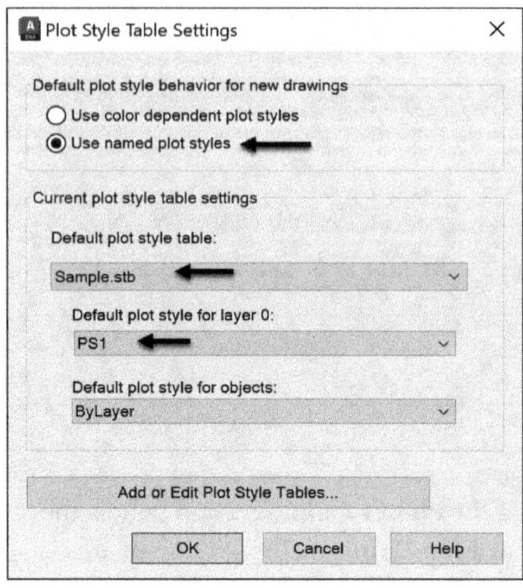

- Click **OK** twice to close both the dialogs.
- Close the drawing file by clicking the **Close** button located at the top-right corner.

- Click **NO** on the **AutoCAD** alert message.
- Click the **New** button on the **Quick Access Toolbar**; the **Select Template** dialog appears.
- Select **Open > Open with no Template – Metric** from the bottom right corner of the dialog; a drawing file will be opened.

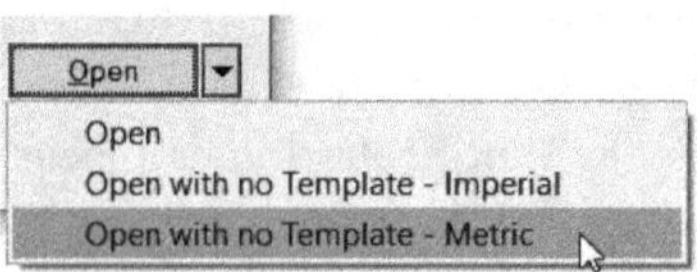

- Open the **Layers Properties Manager** and create the layers shown in the table below:

Layer	Linetype	Lineweight	Plot Style
Construction	Continuous	0.25	PS1
Object	Continuous	0.7 mm	PS1
Hidden Lines	Hidden	0.3 mm	PS1
Center Lines	CENTER	0.25 mm	PS1
Dimensions	Continuous	0.25 mm	PS1
Section Lines	Continuous	0.5 mm	PS1
Cutting Plane	Phantom	0.6mm	PS1
Title Block	Continuous	1mm	PS1
Viewport	Continuous	0.25 mm	PS1
Text	Continuous	0.25	PS1
Title block text	Continuous	0.25	PS1

- Click the **Layout 1** tab to activate the paper space.
- Click **Output > Plot > Page setup Manager** on the ribbon; the **Page Setup Manager** dialog appears.
- Click **Modify** on the **Page Setup** Manager; the **Page Setup** dialog appears.
- Under the **Printer/plotter** group, select the plotter that you have configured to your workstation.
- Set the **Paper Size** to **A3** and **Drawing orientation** to **Landscape**.
- Click **OK** and **Close** to exit both the dialogs.
- Draw a title block in the paper space, as shown below.

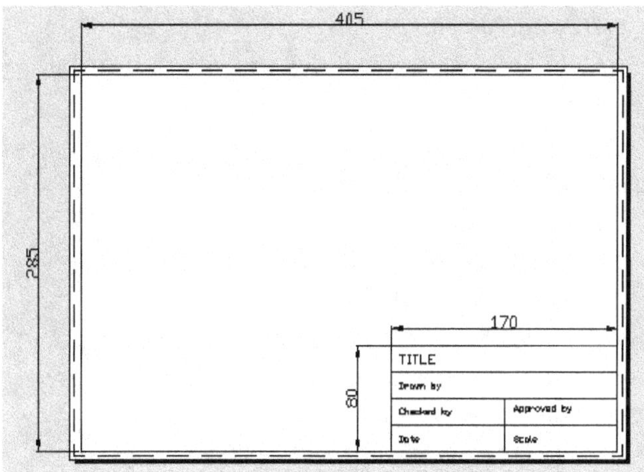

- Create a viewport inside the title block (refer to the **Creating Viewports in the Paper space** section discussed earlier in this chapter).

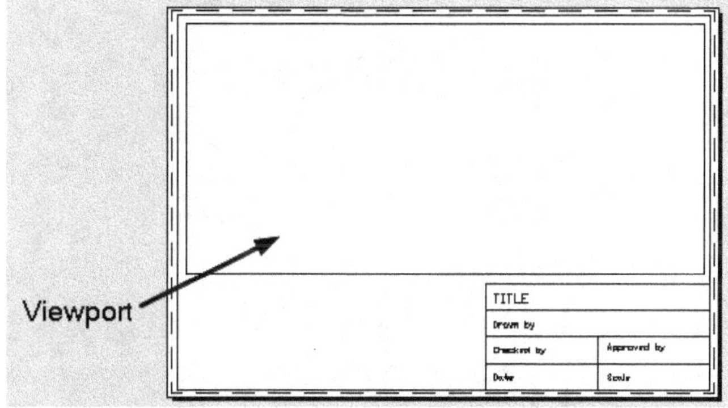

Creating Templates

After specifying the required settings in a drawing file, you can save those settings for future use. You can do so by creating a template. Template files have settings such as units, limits, and layers already created, which will increase your productivity. In previous sections, you have configured various settings, such as layers, colors, linetypes, and plotting settings. Now, you will create a template file containing all of these settings and the title block that you have created.

- On the **Quick Access toolbar**, click the **Save** button; the **Save Drawing As** dialog appears.
- In the **Save Drawing As** dialog, set **Files of type** to **AutoCAD Drawing Template (*.dwt).**
- Enter **ISOA3** in the **File name** box and click **Save**.
- In the **Template Options** dialog, enter **ISO-A3 Horizontal layout with title block** in the

Description box.

- Click **OK** to close the dialog and save the template file.

Plotting/Printing the drawing

- Click the **New** button.
- Double-click on **ISOA3**. A new drawing will be started with the selected template.
- Open the **Layer Properties Manager**; you will notice that the layers saved in the template file are loaded automatically.
- Close the **Layer Properties Manager**.
- Create a drawing, as shown below. You can also download the drawing from the companion website.

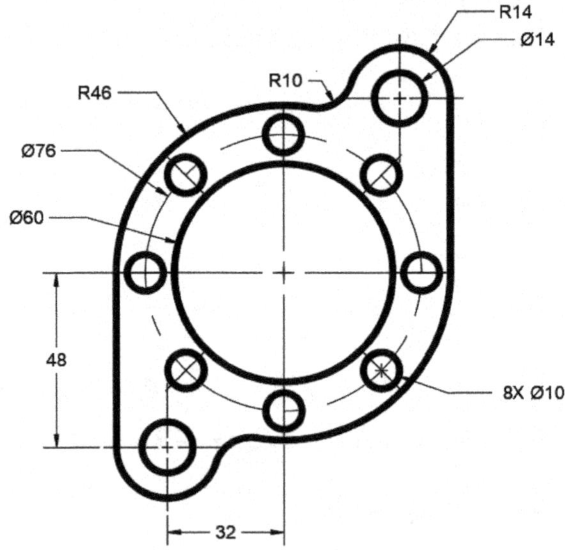

- Click the **Layout 1** tab to activate the paper space.
- Double-click inside the viewport to activate the model space.
- Set the **Viewport Scale** to 1:1 on the status bar.
- Use the **Pan** tool and position the drawing at the center of the viewport.
- Double-click outside the viewport to activate the paper space.
- Hide the viewport frame by freezing the **Viewport** layer.

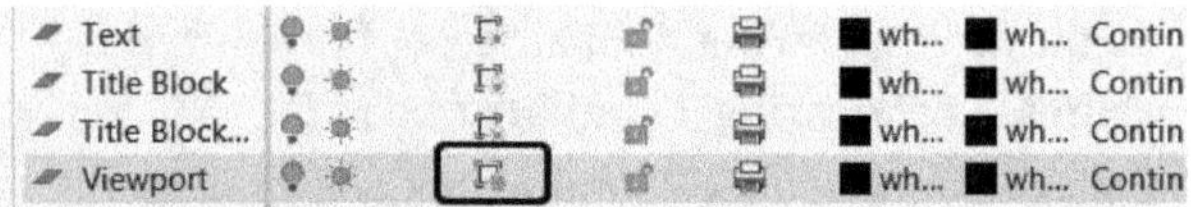

- Click the **Plot** button on the **Quick Access Toolbar**; the **Plot** dialog appears.

- Make sure that the options in this dialog are the same as that you specified while creating the template.
- Click the **Preview** button located at the bottom left corner; the preview window appears.
- Click the **Zoom Original** button to fit the drawing to the window.

- Examine the print preview for the desired output and click the **Plot** button; the drawing will be plotted.

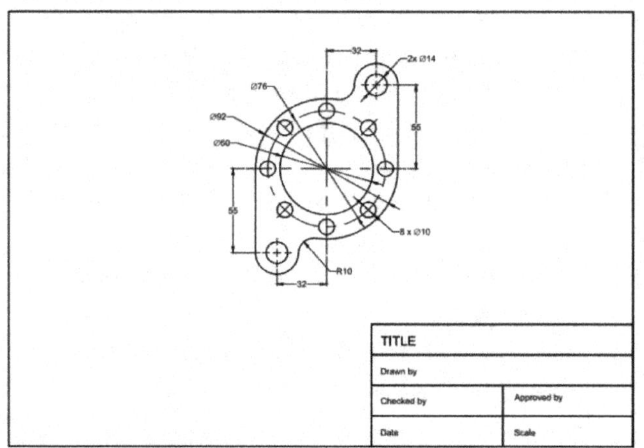

- Save and close the drawing file.

Exporting to PDF

The PDF and DWF files are one of the commonly used file formats to exchange drawings between designers and clients. AutoCAD makes it easy to export the drawing to the PDF or DWF formats.

- On the ribbon, click **Output > Export to DWF/PDF > Export to PDF Options**.

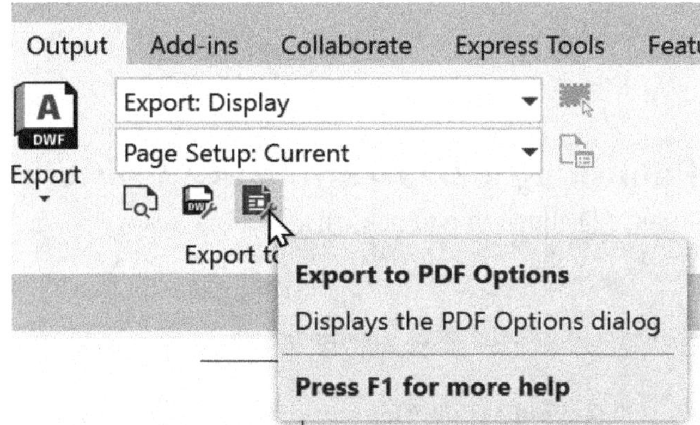

- On the **Export to PDF Options** dialog, set the Vector quality, Raster image quality, line merge control, and Data options.

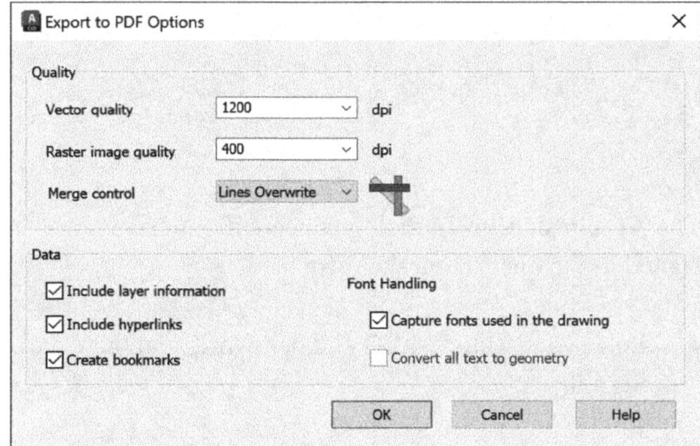

The options in the **Data** section help you to include layer information, hyperlinks, and create bookmarks. Also, you can capture fonts used in the drawing.

- Click **OK**.
- On the ribbon, click **Output > Export DWF/PDF > Export > PDF** .
- On the **Save As PDF** dialog, select a **PDF Preset** to specify the PDF quality.

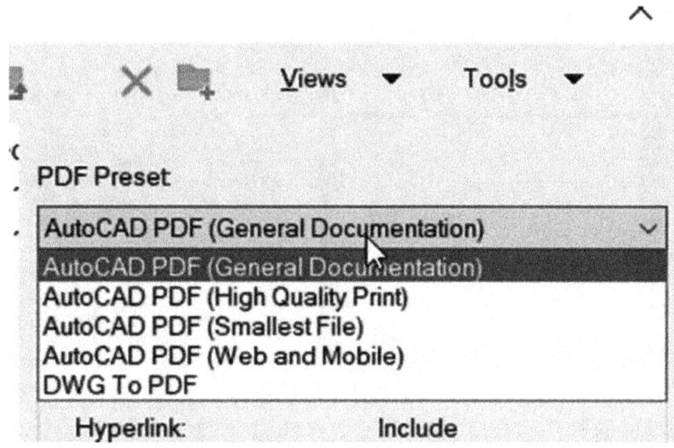

- Examine the options in the **Output Controls** section, Export, and Page Setup.
- Specify the location of the PDF file and click **Save**. A bubble appears on the status bar after exporting the PDF file.
- Open the PDF file in a PDF viewer and notice the layers, bookmarks, hyperlinks in the drawing. Also, you can find any text in the drawing using the text search option in the PDF viewer.

Importing a PDF

AutoCAD allows you to import a PDF into a drawing file.

- On the ribbon, click **Insert > Import > PDF Import**.
- On the **Select PDF File** dialog, browse to the location of the PDF file.
- Select the PDF file, and a preview appears in the **Preview** area of the **Select PDF File** dialog.
- Click **Open**; the **Import PDF** dialog appears.
- On the **Import PDF** dialog, specify the **Scale** factor.
- Under the **PDF data to import** section, check the **TrueType text** option.
- Under the **Layers** section, check the **Use PDF Layers** option.

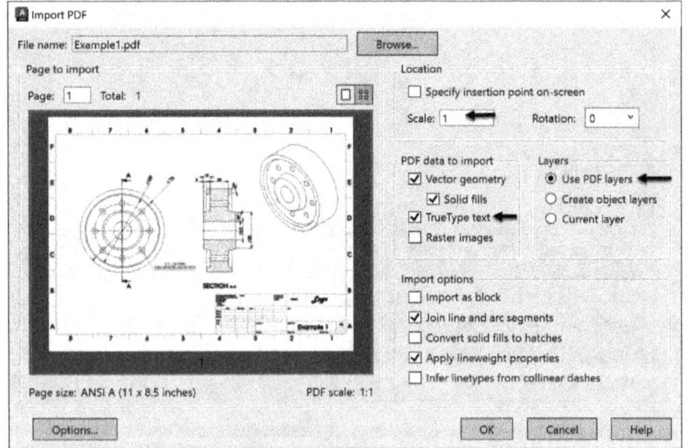

- Click **OK** to insert the PDF into the drawing.

Combining the Text of the Imported PDF

After importing the PDF into an AutoCAD drawing, the text of the PDF is converted into single-line text objects. However, you can combine them into a multi-line text using the **Combine Text** command.

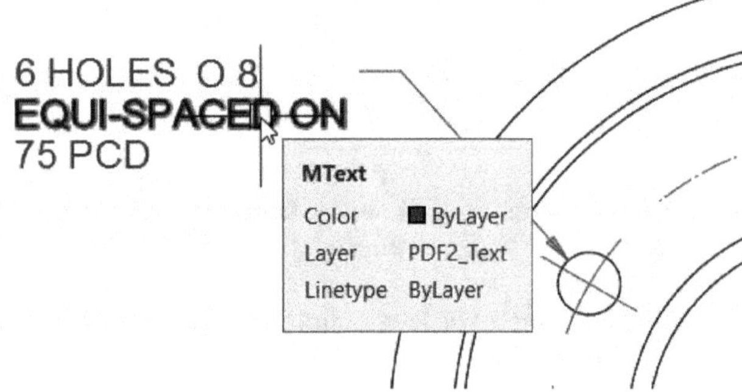

- On the ribbon, click **Insert > Import > Combine Text** 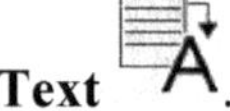.
- Select the fragments of the text to combine them.
- Press Enter.

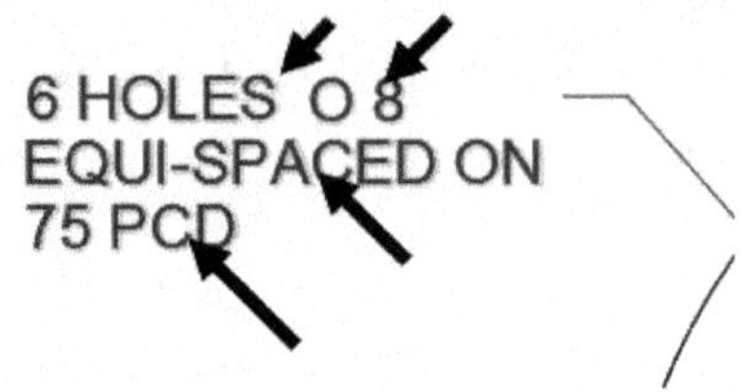

- Click on the text and notice that the text is converted into a multi-line text.

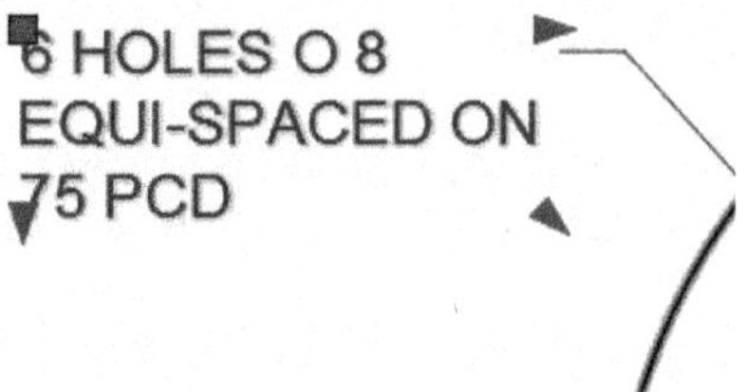

Publishing a 2D Drawing to a Browser

AutoCAD allows you to publish a drawing to a web browser so that you can view it without any application installed on your device. To publish drawing to a web browser, follow the steps given next:

- Click **Application Menu > Publish > Share View**.

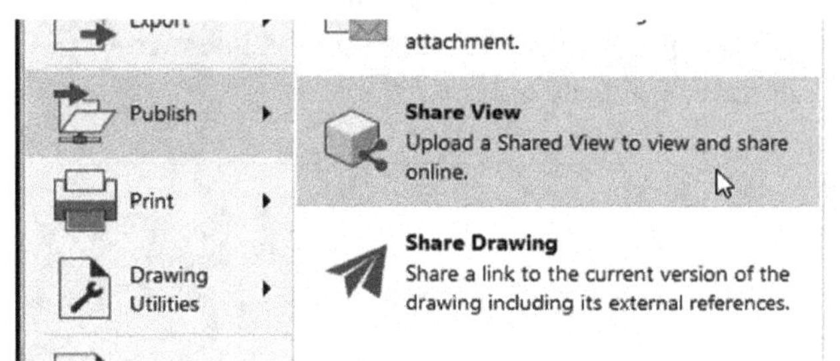

The **Autodesk Sign In** dialog appears if you have not signed in to your Autodesk Account.

- Enter your Autodesk ID and password, and then click **Sign in**.

The **Share View** dialog appears.
- Enter the name of the drawing in the **Name** box.
- Select the appropriate option from the **View to share** section.

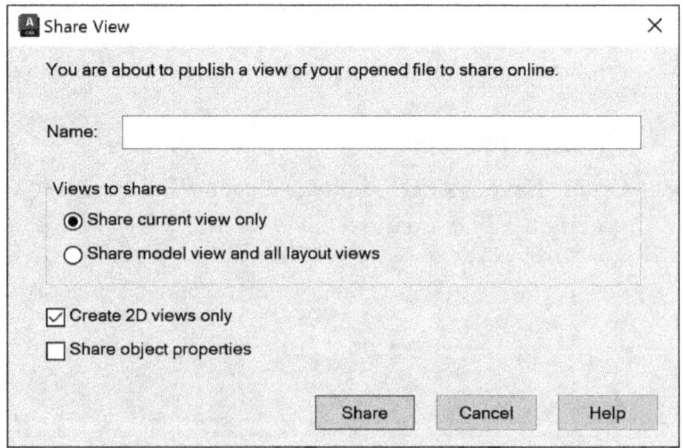

- Click **Share** and **Proceed** to share the views online.
- To view the shared drawing, click the **View in Browser line** displayed at the bottom right corner of the application window; the drawing view will open in the internet browser.

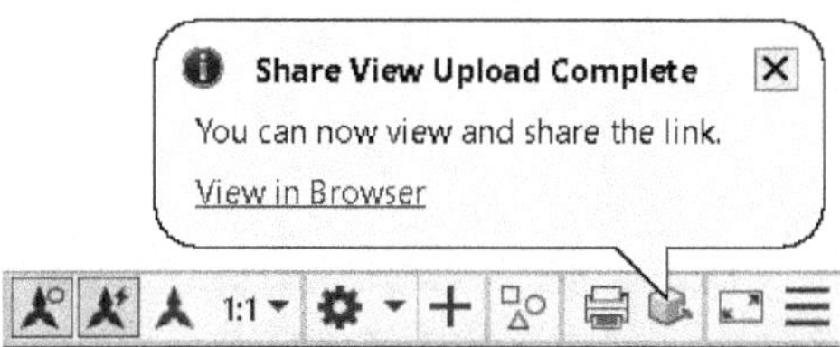

- To add comments to the shared views, click **Collaborate > Share > Shared Views** on the ribbon.
- On the **Shared Views** palette, click the **Refresh** icon to display the shared views.
- Select the shared view from the palette and click **Add Comment**.

Share Drawings

The **Share** command helps you to create a link to copy the drawing. You can view and edit the share drawing in the AutoCAD web app. The shared drawing has all the external references and image attachments. Click the **Share** icon on the Quick Access Toolbar. Next, select the **View only** or **Edit and save copy** option. Click the **Copy Link** button to copy the drawing.

Compare Drawings

The **DWG Compare** command compares two revisions of a drawing or two different drawings.

- Download the DWG_compare1 and DWG_compare2 drawing files from the companion website.
- Open the DWG_compare1 drawing.

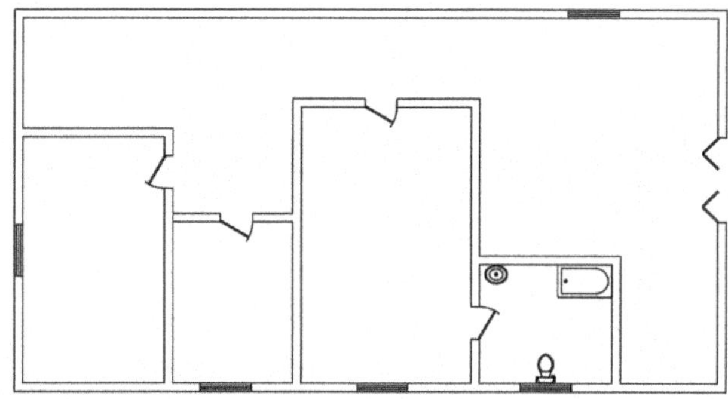

- On the ribbon, click the **Collaborate > Compare > DWG Compare** .
- Browse to the location of the DWG_compare2 file and double click on it; The differences between the two drawings are highlighted by a revision cloud. Also, the DWG Compare toolbar is displayed below the ribbon.

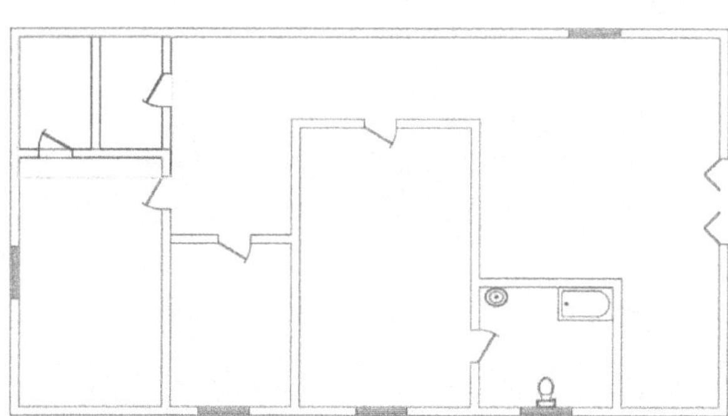

You can click the **On or off** icon to turn ON or OFF the comparisons.

Use the **Next** and **Previous** icons to zoom to different results.

On the **DWG Compare** toolbar, click the **Settings** drop-down to specify the color settings, revision cloud settings, and objects to be filtered.

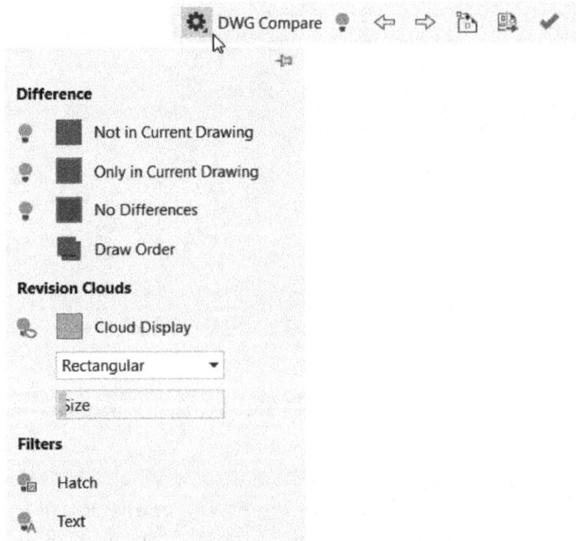

- Select the **Polygonal** option from the drop-down in the **Revision Clouds** section.
- Click and drag the **Margin** dragger to change the margin between the revision cloud and highlighted objects.

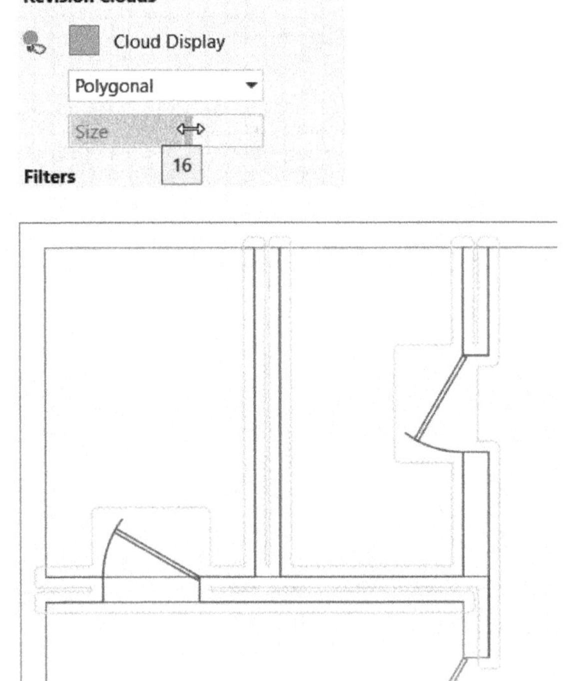

- Click the **Import Objects** icon on the **DWG Compare** toolbar.

- Select the objects highlighted in red color.

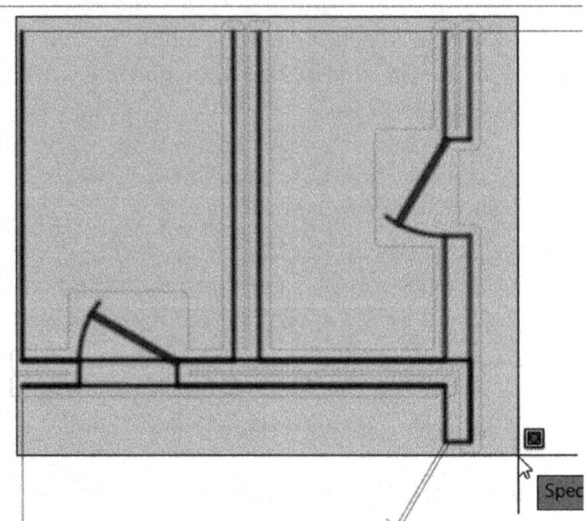

- Press Enter; the selected objects are imported into the current drawing.

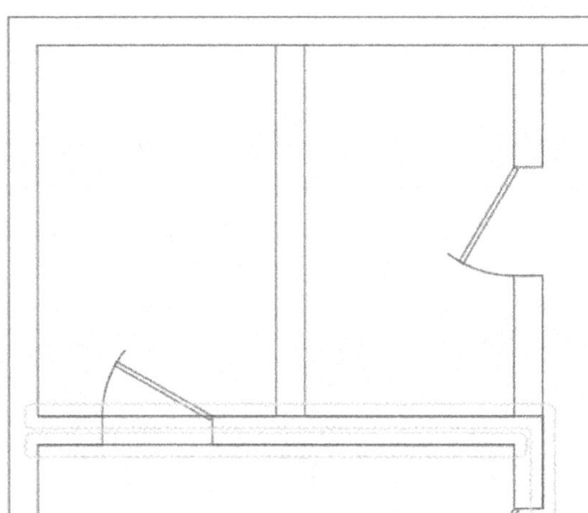

Notice that there is a revision cloud still displayed around the objects highlighted in green. These objects exist only in the current drawing.

- Select the objects highlighted in green color and press Delete on your keyboard; the revision clouds disappear.

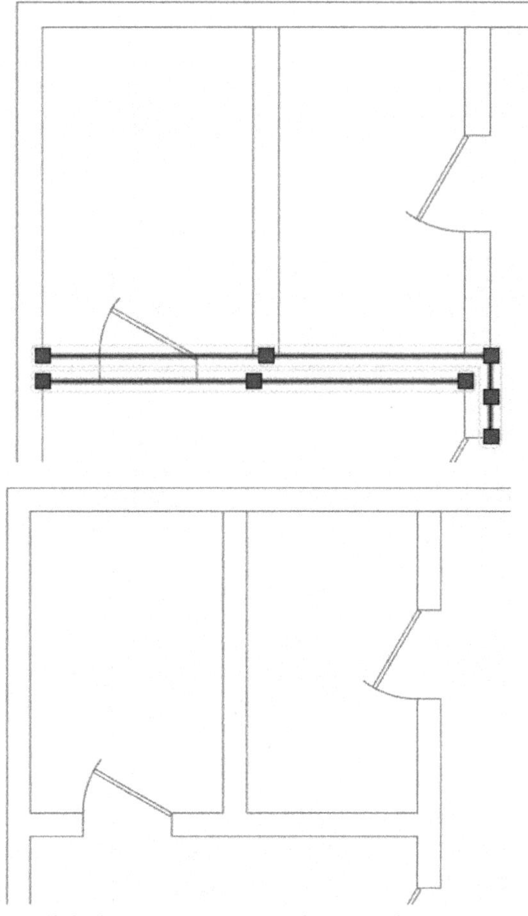

- Click the **Exit Compare** icon on the **DWG Compare** toolbar.
- Close the DWG_compare1 file without saving.

Exporting the Compared results to a new drawing

- Open the DWG_compare1 drawing.

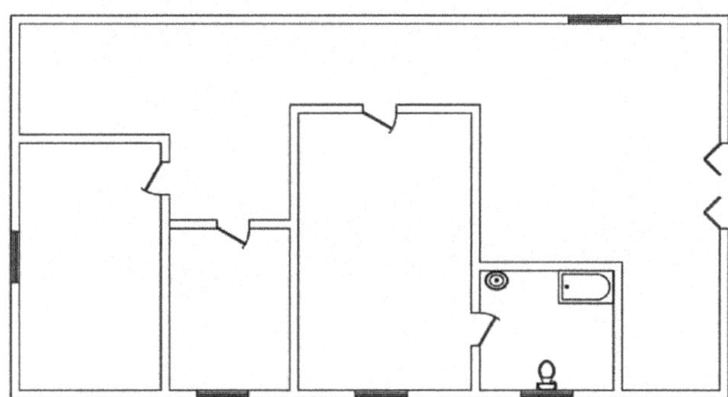

- On the ribbon, click **Collaborate > Compare > DWG Compare** .

- Browse to the location of the DWG_compare2 file and double click on it; The differences between the two drawings are highlighted by a revision cloud. Also, the DWG Compare toolbar is displayed below the ribbon.
- Click the **Export Snapshot** icon on the **DWG Compare** toolbar.

- Specify the location of the export file and click **Save**; the exported file is opened in another tab.
- Click **Continue** on the **Compare – Export a Comparison Snapshot** message box.

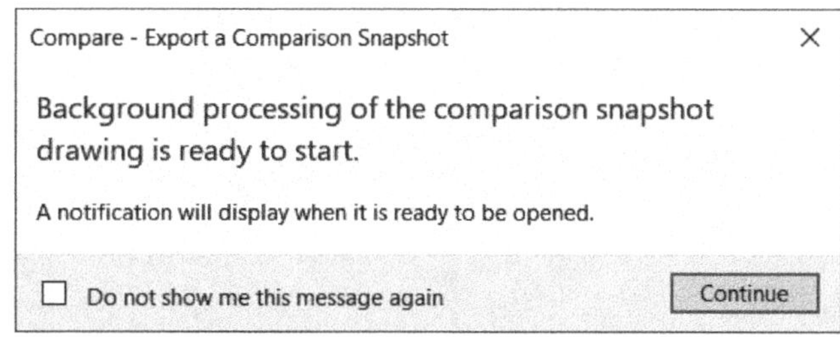

- Click **Open Drawing** on the **Snapshot Processing Complete** bubble.

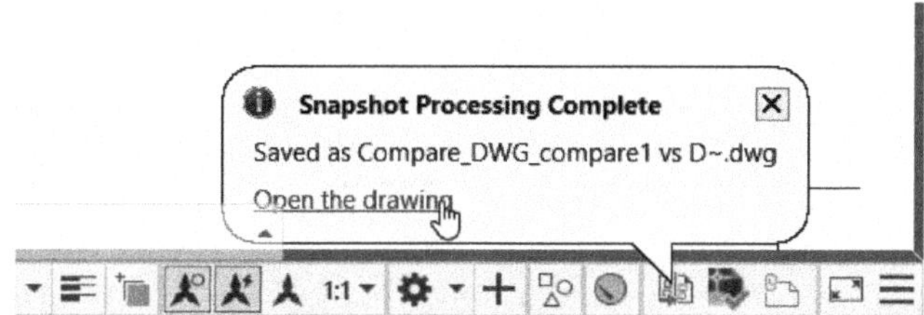

You can examine the DWG compare results using the **DWG Compare Snapshot** toolbar.

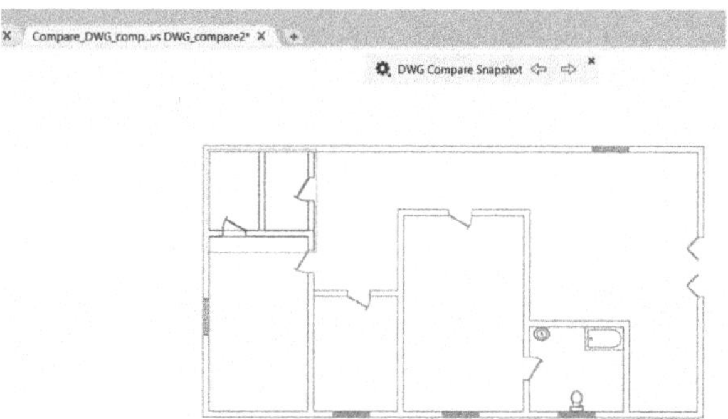

- Close all the files.

Exercise

Create and plot the drawing, as shown in the figure.

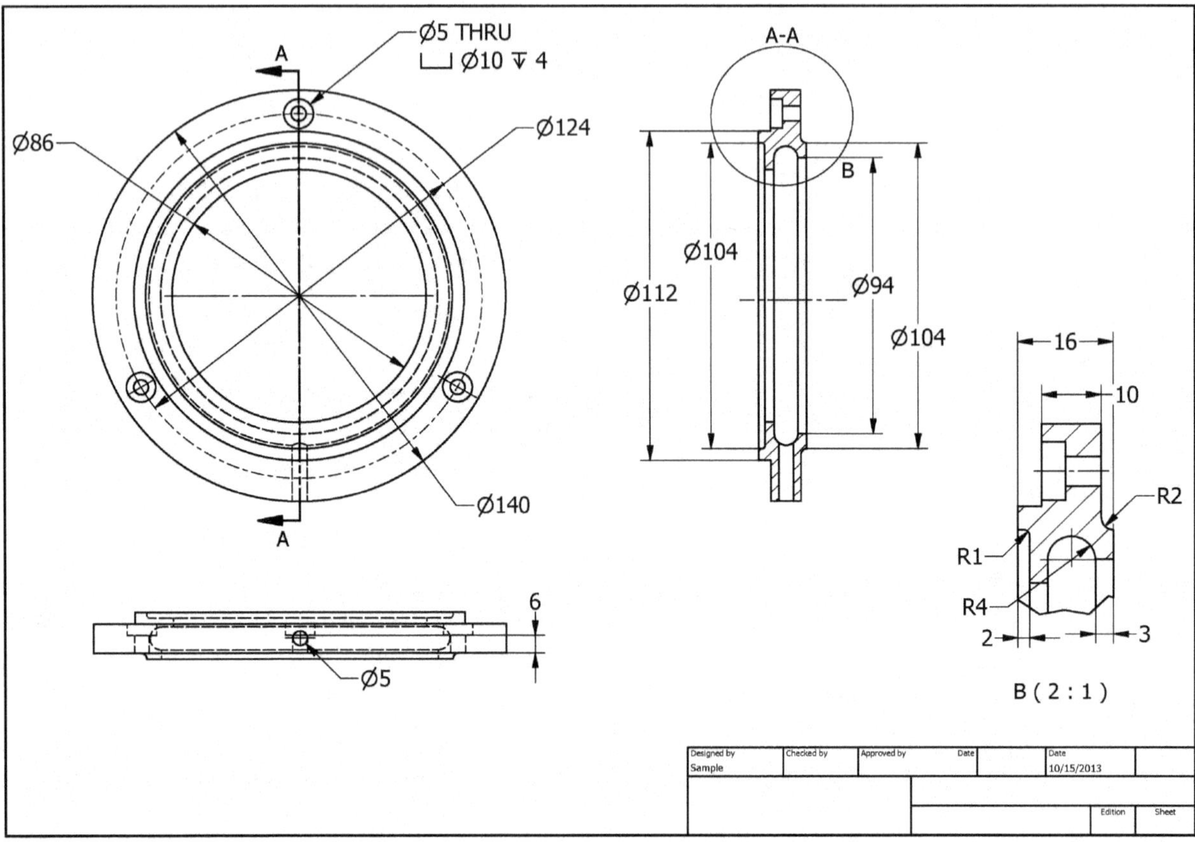

Chapter 12: 3D Modeling Basics

In this chapter, you will learn to do the following:

- **Create boxes, cylinders, wedges, cones, pyramids, spheres, and torus**
- **Create User Coordinate Systems**
- **Work with Dynamic UCS**
- **Change the View Style of objects**
- **Create Viewports in model space**
- **Create walls using the Polysolid tool**
- **Change the view orientation**
- **Create extruded, revolved, swept, lofted, and press-pulled objects**
- **Perform Boolean operations**
- **Align objects**
- **Create spiral and helical curves**

Introduction

In AutoCAD, you can create three types of 3D models: surfaces, solids, and meshes. Solids are used to create 3D models of engineering components and assemblies, and surfaces are used to create complex shapes such as plastic parts and meshes that are used for games and movies. Solids are three-dimensional models of actual objects that possess physical properties such as mass properties, the center of gravity, surface area, and moments of inertia. Surfaces are construction features without any thickness. They do not possess any physical properties. Meshes are similar to solids without mass and volume properties. In this chapter, you will learn the basics of 3D modeling, such as creating, navigating, and visualizing solid models.

3D Modeling Workspaces in AutoCAD

In AutoCAD, there are separate workspaces created to work on 3D models. In these workspaces, the tools are organized into ribbon tabs, menus, toolbars, and palettes to perform a specific task in 3D modeling. You can activate these workspaces by using the **Workspace** drop-down located on the **Quick Access Toolbar**, or by using the **Workspace Switching** menu on the status bar. You can also start an AutoCAD session directly in the 3D Modeling workspace using the **acad3D.dwt**, **acadiso3D.dwt**, **acad -Named Plot Styles3D**, or **acadISO-Named Plot Styles3D** templates.

*Tip: If the **Workspace** drop-down is not displayed at the top left corner, then click the down arrow next to the Quick Access Toolbar. Next, select **Workspace** from the drop-down; the **Workspace** drop-down will be visible on the Quick Access Toolbar.*

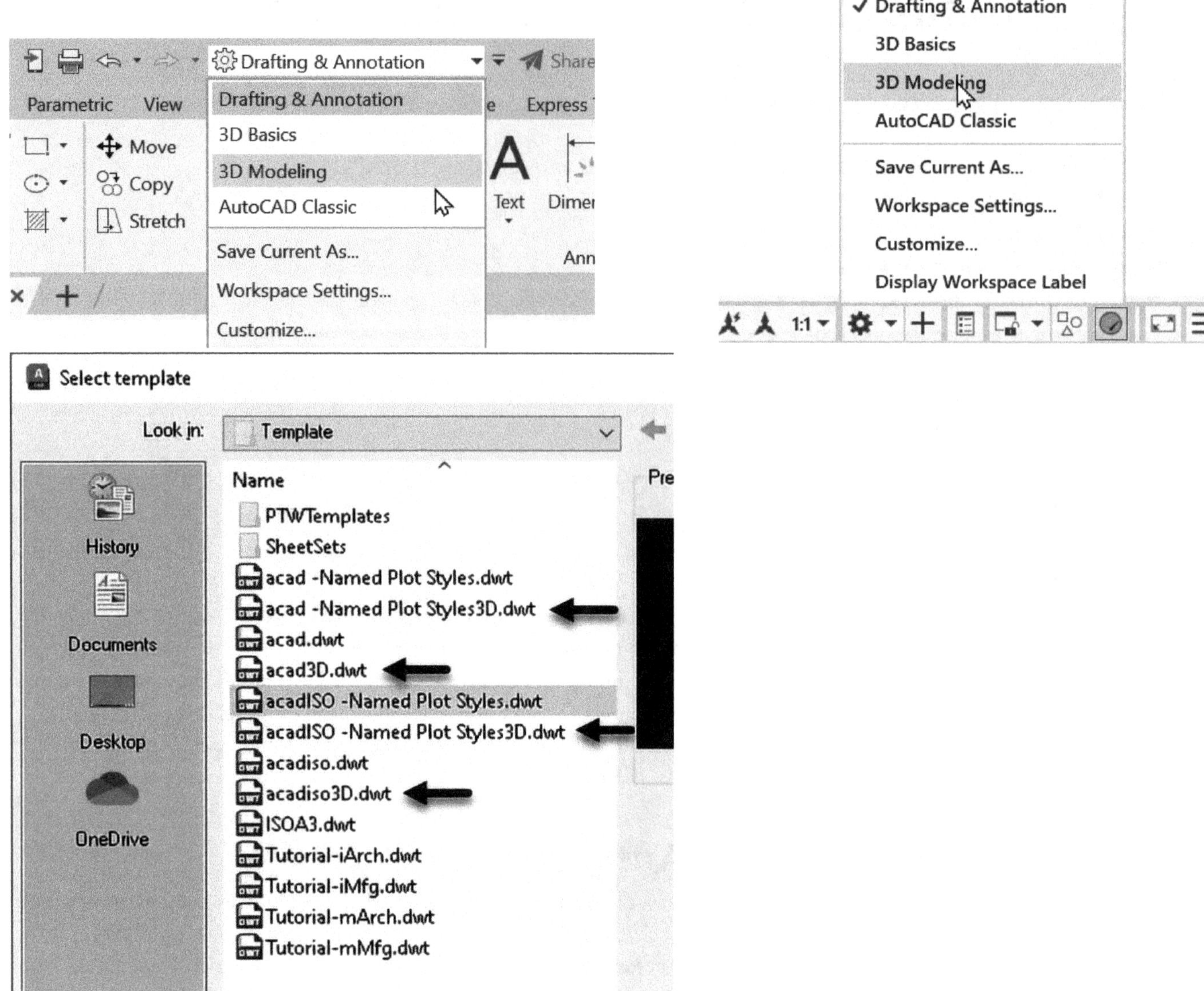

There are two workspaces of 3D modeling: **3D Basics** and **3D Modeling**. The **3D Basics** workspace has commonly used tools, whereas the **3D Modeling** workspace includes all the tools required for creating 3D models.

The 3D Modeling Workspace

Activating the **3D Modeling** workspace either by using the template or from the **Workspace** drop-down displays the screen as shown below. It contains the ribbon and tools related to 3D modeling. By default, the **Home** tab is activated in the ribbon. From this tab, you can access the tools for creating and editing solids and meshes, modifying the model display, working with coordinate systems, and sectioning 3D models.

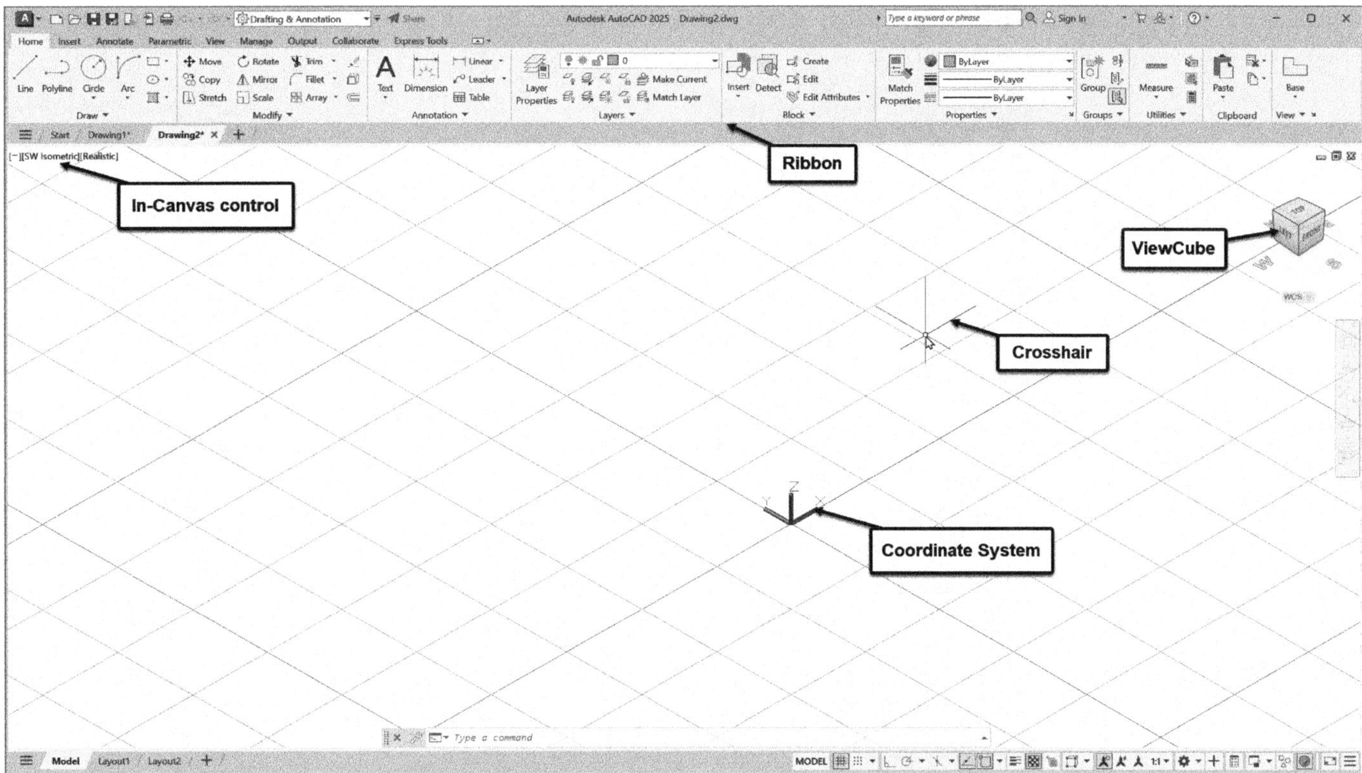

There are some additional tabs, such as **Solid**, **Surface**, **Mesh**, and **Render**. The **Solid** tab contains tools to create solid models; the **Surface** and **Mesh** tabs are used to create surface models and complex shapes; the **Visualize** tab is used for creating realistic images of solid and surface models.

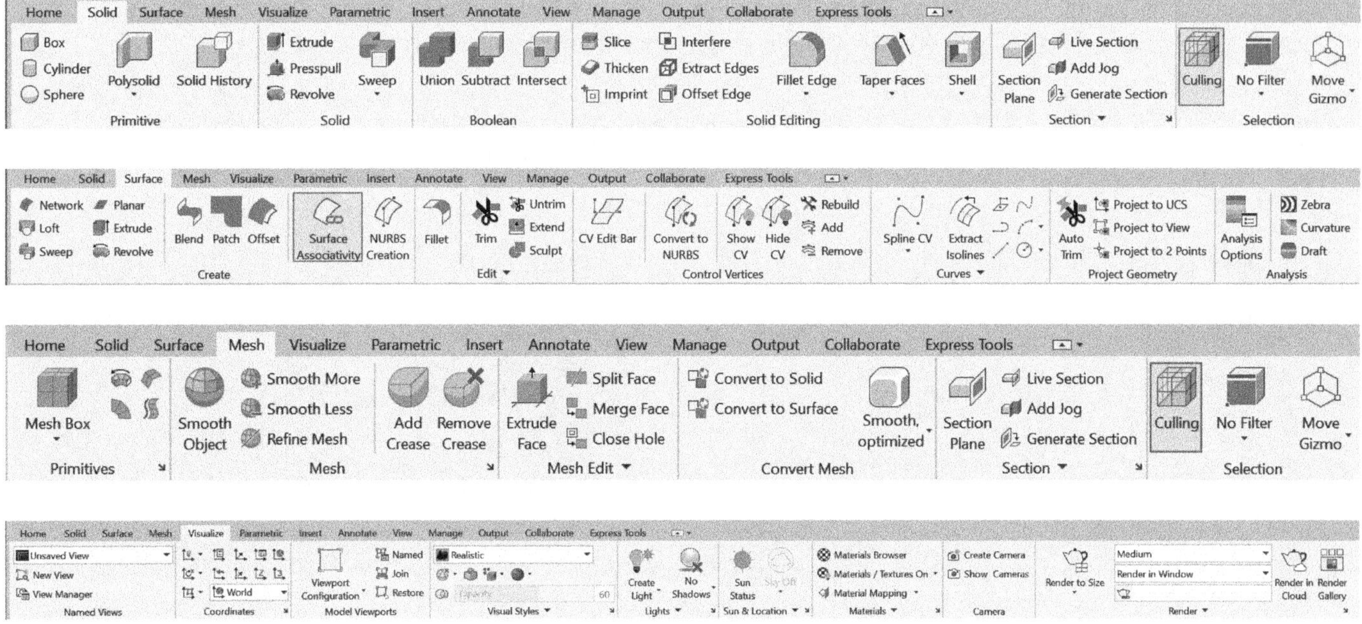

The **ViewCube** can be used to modify the view of the model quickly and easily. It is located at the top right corner of the graphics window. Using the **ViewCube**, you can switch between the standard and isometric views, rotate the model, switch to the **Home** view of the model, and create a new user coordinate system. You can also change the way the ViewCube functions by using the **ViewCube Settings** dialog. Right-click on the ViewCube, and then select the **ViewCube Settings** option; the **ViewCube Settings** dialog will be opened.

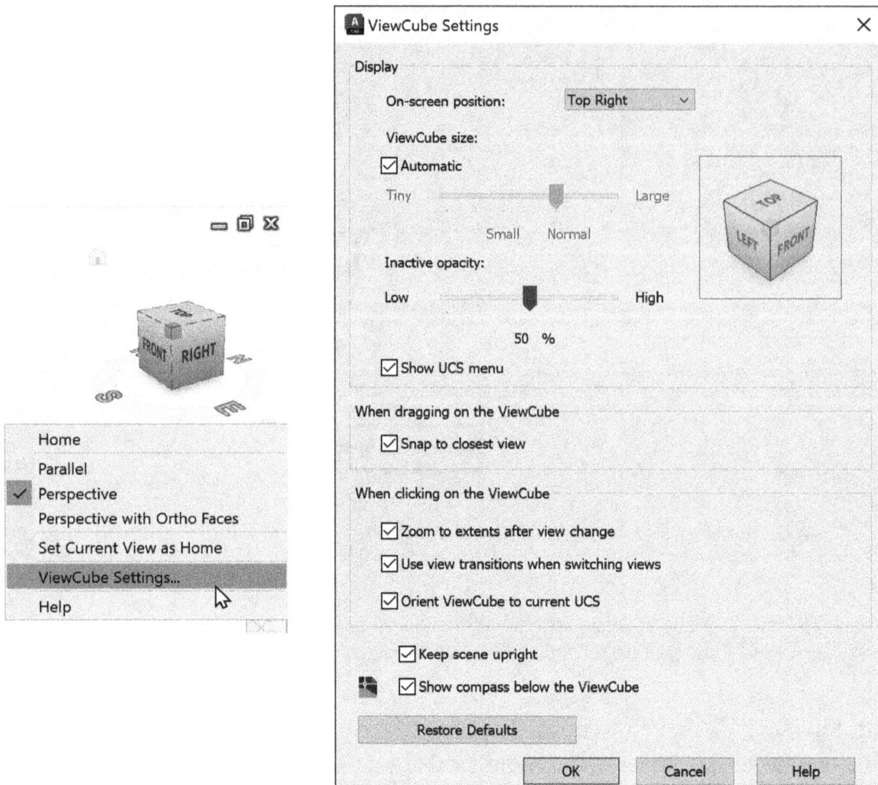

You can also modify the model view by using the In-canvas controls. In addition to that, you can also change the view style of the model and control the display of other tools in the graphics window using the In-canvas controls.

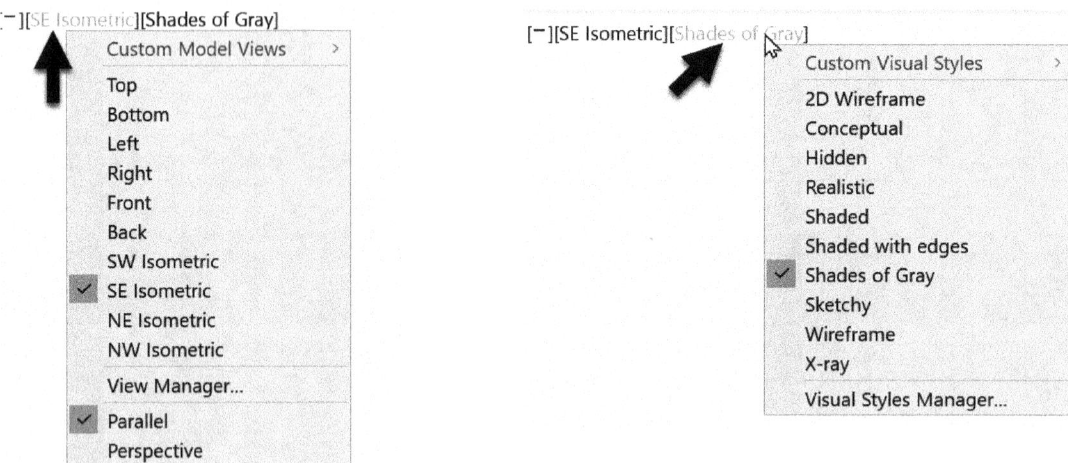

Now, you will create 3D models using the tools available in AutoCAD.

The Box tool

The **Box** tool is used to create boxes having six rectangular or square faces. It is the most commonly used tool, as many 3D objects are made of boxes.

- Click the **AutoCAD 2025** icon on your desktop.
- On the Quick Access Toolbar, click the **New** icon.
- On the **Select Template** dialog, click **acadiso3D**, and then click **Open**. A new file will be started in the **3D Modeling** workspace.
- Click **Home > Modeling > Box** on the ribbon or type **BOX** in the command line; the message, "Specify the first corner," appears in the command line.

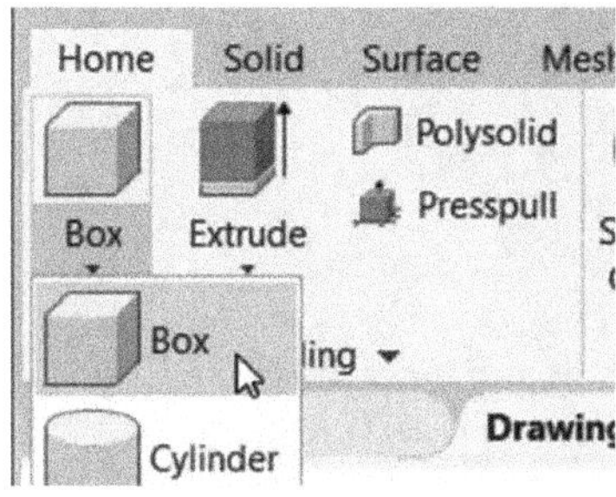

- Pick an arbitrary point in the graphics window; the message, "Specify the other corner," appears in the command line.
- Ensure that the **Dynamic Input** icon is active on the status bar. You will notice the two value boxes to specify the length and width of the box.
- Type 100 in the length box and press the TAB key.
- Type 70 in the width box and press ENTER.
- Move the pointer upward, type 60 as height, and press ENTER; the box will be created as shown.
- Click **Zoom > Zoom All** on the Navigation Bar.
- On the In-canvas controls, click **View Style Controls > Shades of Grey**.
- Right click on the **Home** icon above the ViewCube and select **Parallel**.

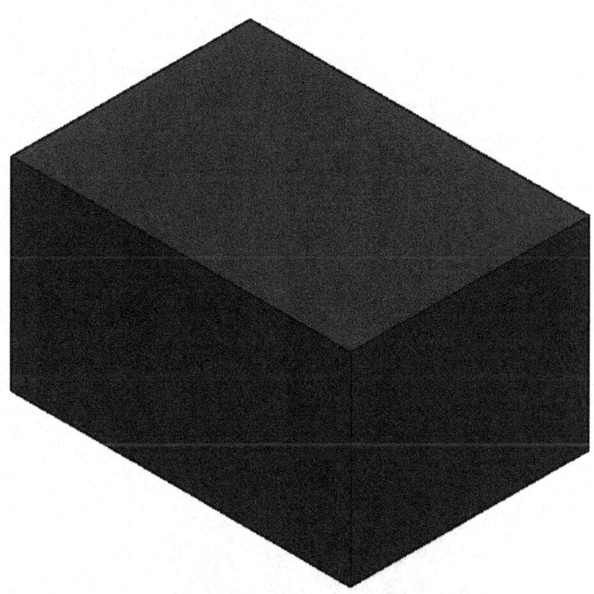

Creating the User Coordinate System

User Coordinate Systems assist you while creating 3D models. They are used to create construction planes on which you can add additional features to the model. Various methods to create User coordinate systems are discussed next.

Example1:

- On the status bar, click the **Customization** button and select **Dynamic UCS** from the menu. Also, select **3D Object Snap** from the menu.
- Deactivate the **Dynamic UCS** icon on the status bar. You will learn about this option later in this chapter.

- Click **Home > Coordinates > UCS** on the ribbon; the UCS is attached to the pointer, and the message, "Specify the origin of UCS," appears.

- Activate the **3D Object Snap** icon on the status bar.

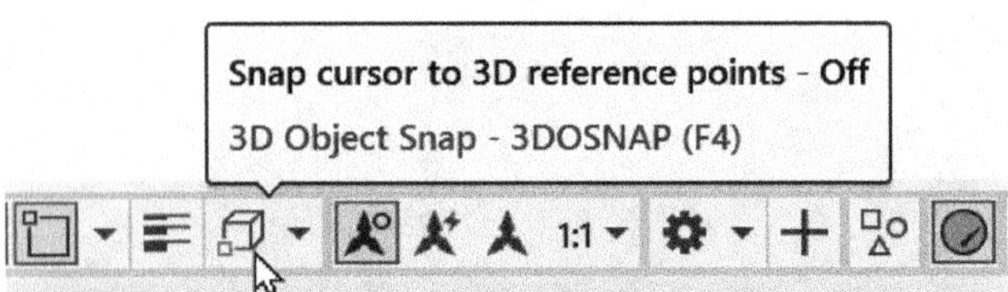

- Select the vertex point on the top left corner of the box as shown below; the message, "Specify point on X-axis or <accept>:" appears in the command line.

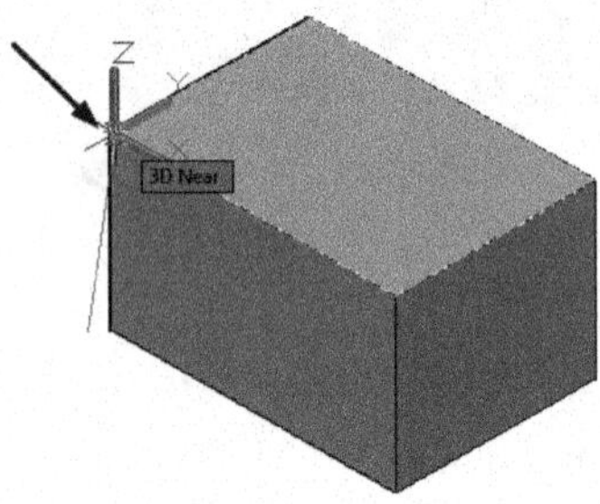

- Press ENTER to accept the orientation of the UCS, as shown below.

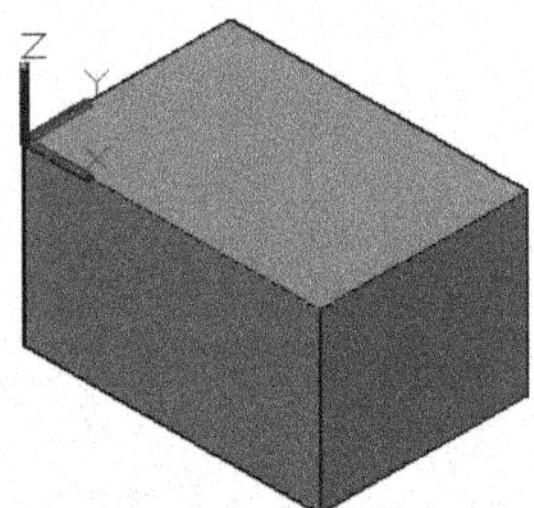

Creating a Wedge

When you slice a box diagonally, it results in a wedge. A wedge has five faces, three rectangular and two triangular.

- Click **Home > Modeling > Primitives** drop-down > **Wedge** on the ribbon or type **WE** in the command line and press ENTER; the message, "Specify first corner or [Center]" appears in the command line.
- Select the endpoint of the top face of the box, as shown in the figure; the message, "Specify other corner or [Cube Length]:" appears in the command line.
- On the Status bar, click the down arrow next to the **3D Object Snap** icon, and select **Midpoint on edge**.
- Select the midpoint of the front edge of the box, as

shown below.

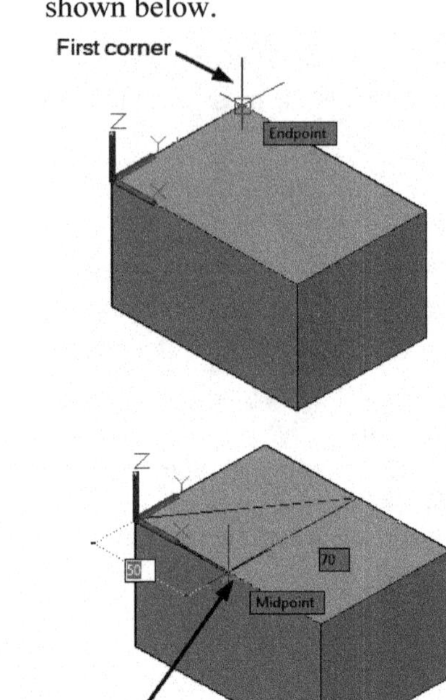

- Move the pointer upward and enter 40 as the height; the wedge will be created, as shown below.

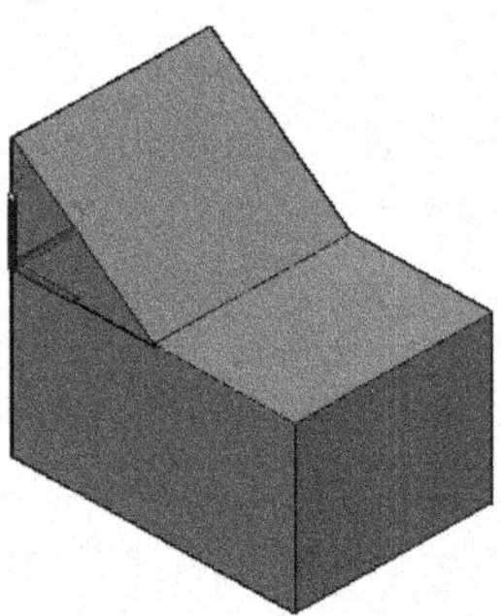

Example2: (Creating UCS by selecting 3-points)

You can create a UCS by selecting three points. The first point will be the origin of the UCS, the second point will define the X-axis, and the third point defines the Y-axis.

- Click **Home > Coordinates > 3 Point** on the ribbon; the UCS is attached to the pointer and the message, "Specify new origin point <0,0,0>:" appears.

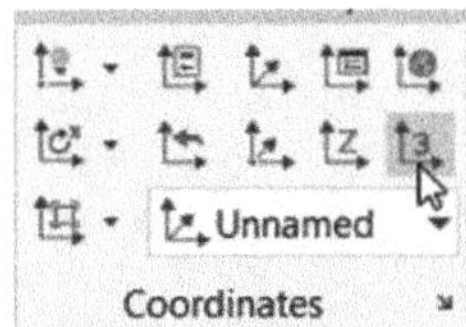

- Select the lower endpoint of the wedge, as shown in the figure.

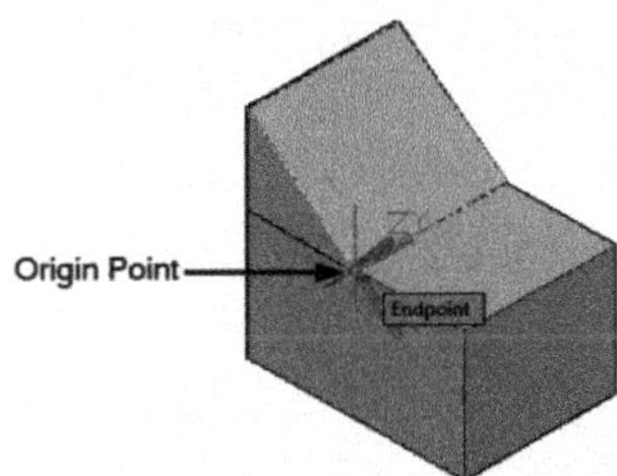

- Move the pointer toward the right.
- Select the other endpoint of the bottom edge of the wedge, as shown in the figure.

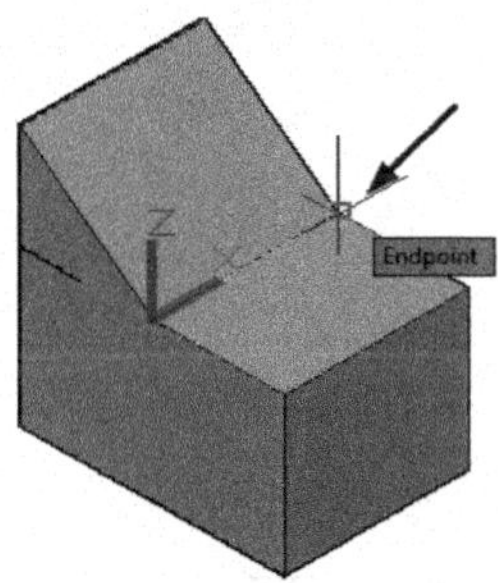

- Move the pointer along the diagonal edge of the wedge
- Select the endpoint on the top edge, as shown. The UCS will be created and aligned to the inclined face of the wedge.

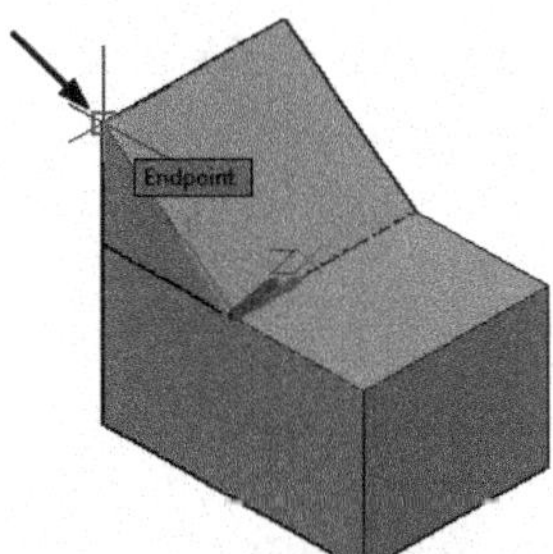

Creating a Cylinder

Cylinders are commonly used features after boxes. In AutoCAD, you can create cylinders easily by using the **Cylinder** tool. You can create a circular or elliptical cylinder by using this tool.

- Click **Home > View > View Styles** drop-down > **Wireframe** on the ribbon; the view style of the model will be changed to the wireframe style.

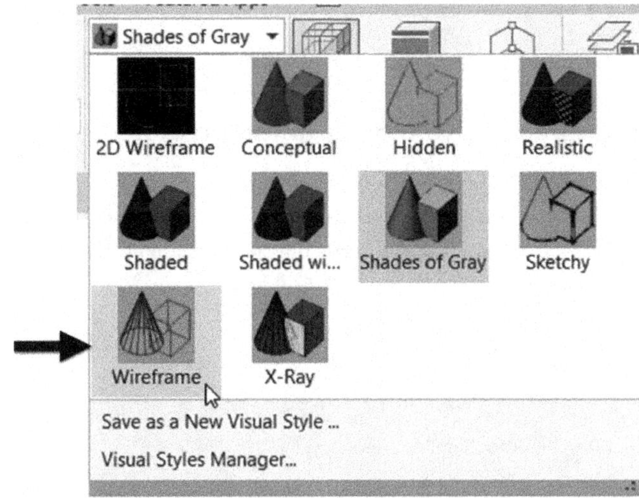

- On the Status bar, click the down arrow next to the **3D Object Snap** icon and select the **Center of face** option, if not already selected.
- Click **Home > Modeling > Primitives drop-down > Cylinder** on the ribbon or type **CYL** in the command line.
- Snap to the center point of the inclined face, and then click to select it; the center point of the cylinder is specified on the inclined face of the wedge.

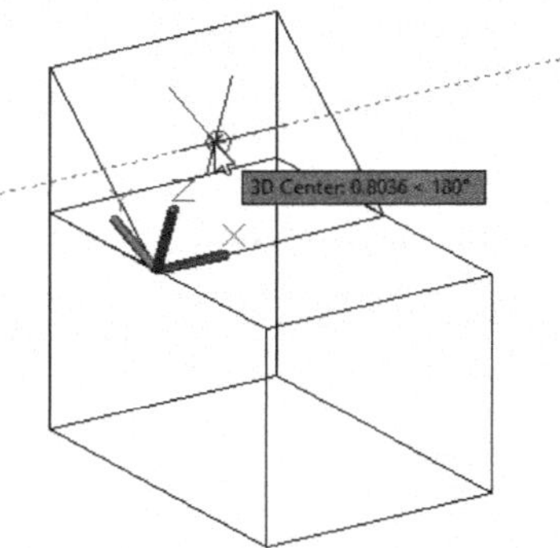

- Type 20 as the base radius and press ENTER.
- Move the pointer upward; you will notice that the pointer moves along the Z-axis of the UCS.
- Type 25 as height and press ENTER; the cylinder will be created as shown below.

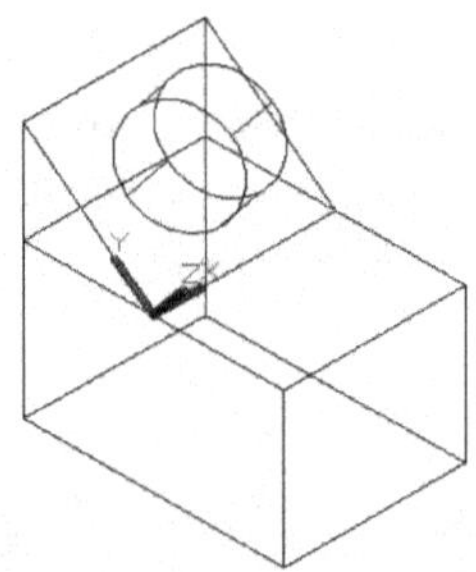

Example 3: (Returning to the previous position of the UCS)

- Click **Home > Coordinates > UCS, Previous** on the ribbon; the UCS will return to its previous position.

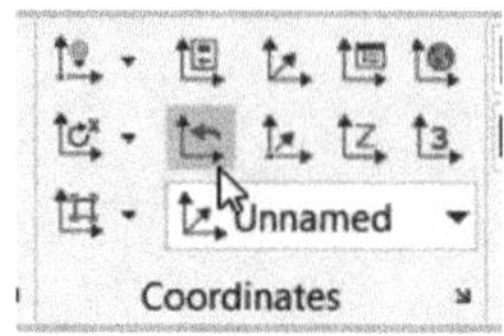

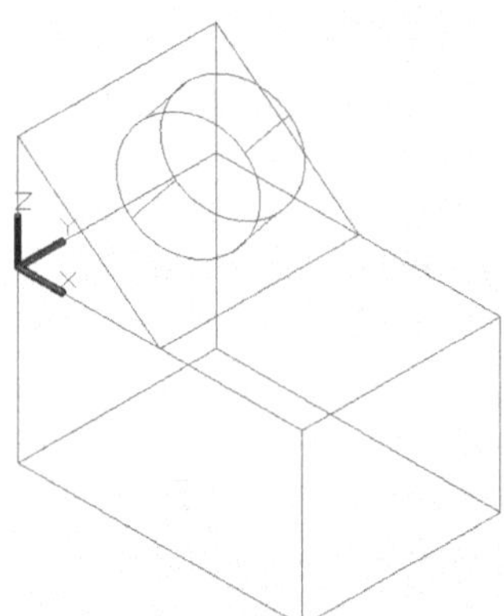

Example 4: (Creating a UCS by specifying its origin)

- Click **Home > Coordinates > Origin** on the ribbon; the UCS will be attached to the pointer.

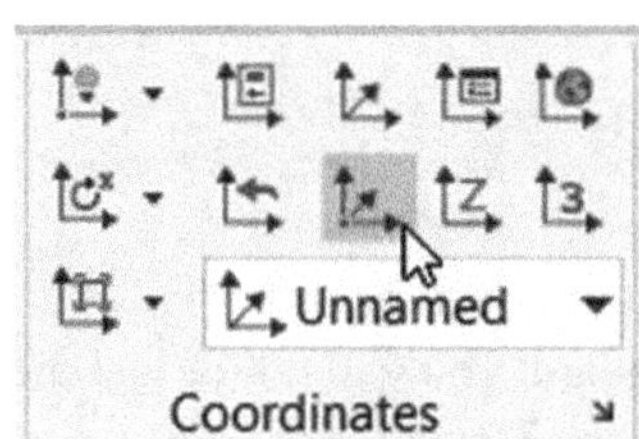

- Select the lower-left corner point of the box; the UCS will be placed at that point. Note that the orientation will not change.

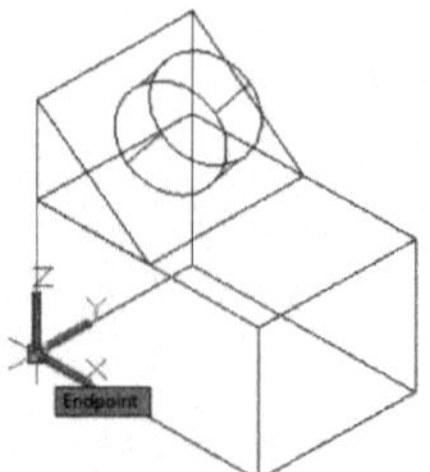

Example 5: (Rotating the UCS about X, Y, and Z axes)

You can rotate a UCS about X, Y, or Z axes by using the drop-down available in the **Coordinates** panel, as shown below.

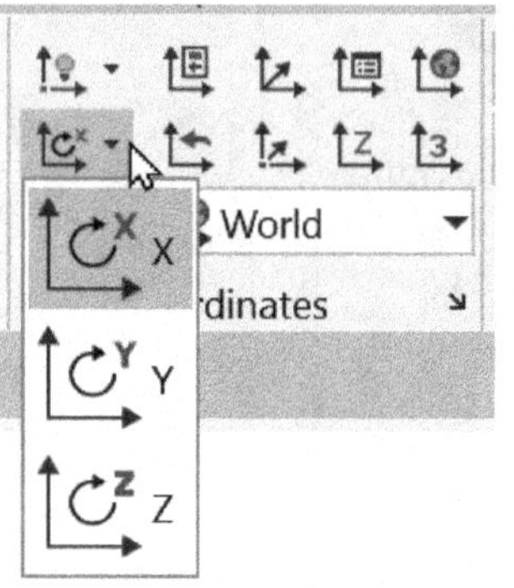

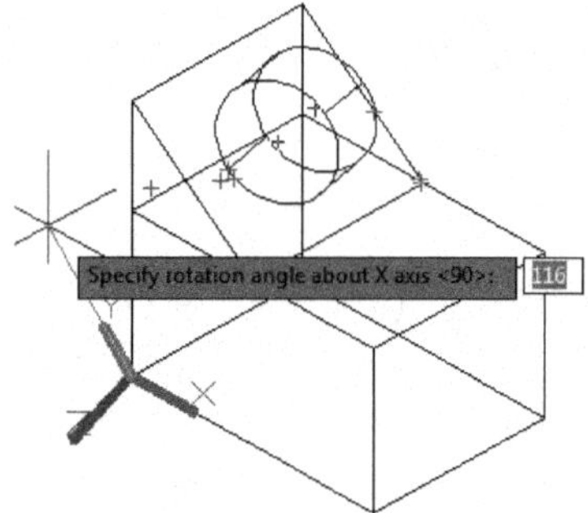

- Click the **X** option from the drop-down shown in the above figure; the message, "Specify rotation angle about X axis <90>:" appears in the command line. Also, a rubber band line originating from the Y axis is attached to the pointer.
- Rotate the pointer and pick a point to specify the rotation angle. You can also type in the rotation angle in the dynamic input or command line.
- Similarly, you can rotate the UCS about the Y and Z axes using the respective options from the drop-down.

Example 6: (Creating the UCS by specifying the Z-axis)

Using the **Z-Axis Vector** tool, you can create a UCS by specifying its Z-axis.

- Click **Home > Coordinates > Z-Axis Vector** on the ribbon.
- Select the bottom right endpoint as the origin; the message, "Specify point on positive portion of Z-axis:" appears in the command line. Also, a rubber band line originating from the Z-axis is attached to the pointer. Now, as you move the pointer, you will notice that the Z-axis also moves.

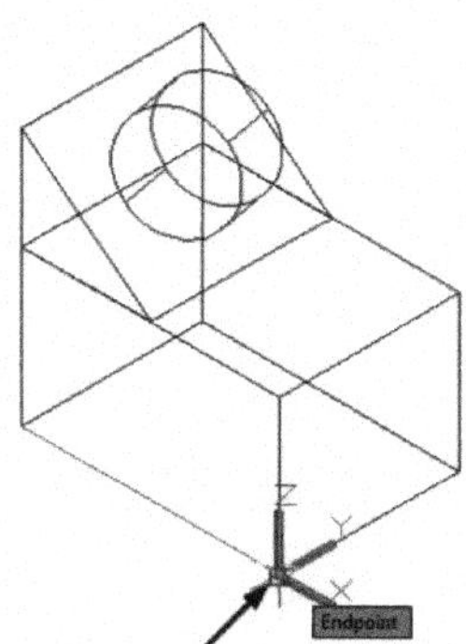

- Move the pointer and select the left endpoint of the bottom edge, as shown below; the Z-axis will be aligned to the bottom edge.

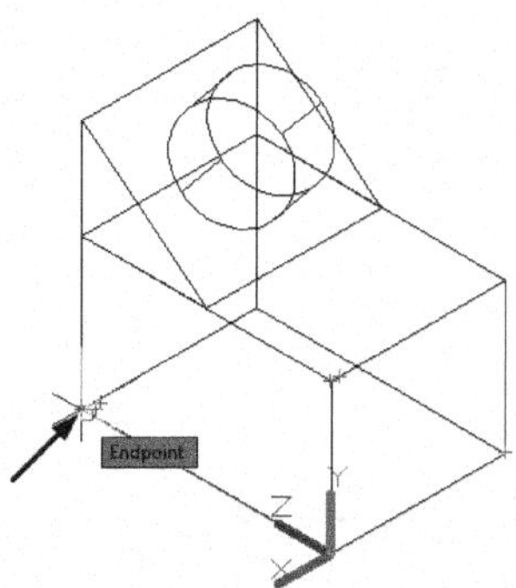

Example 7: (Creating UCS parallel to the screen)

Using the **View** tool in the **Coordinates** panel, you can create a UCS which is parallel to the screen.

- Click **Home > Coordinates > View** on the ribbon; the XY plane of the UCS will become parallel to the screen. The UCS origin will not change. This option is useful if you want to use the current view and add a title block or any other

annotation.

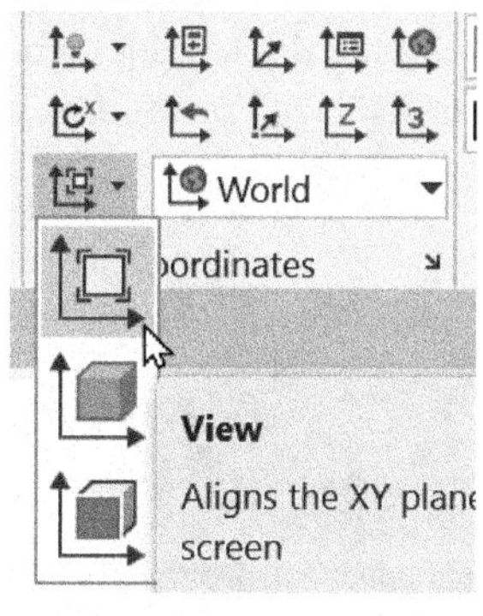

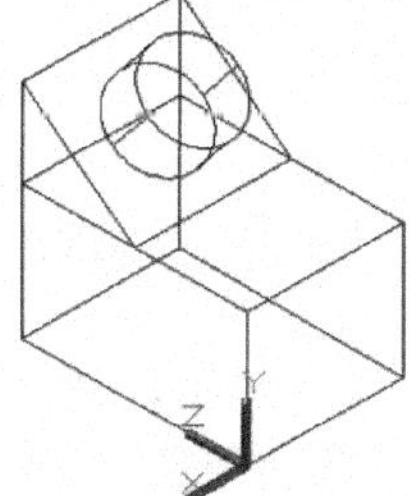
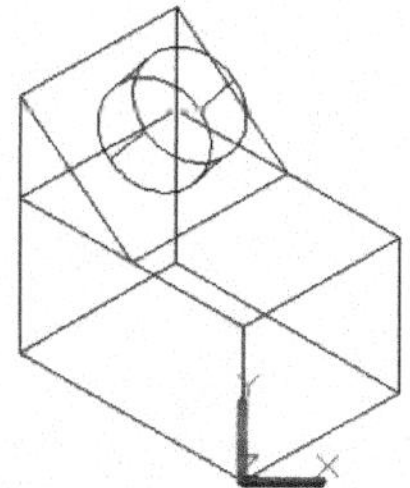

Example 8: (Creating UCS aligned to an object)

You can create a UCS aligned to an object. The origin of the UCS will be aligned to the nearest endpoint of the object.

- Click **Home > Coordinates > View > Object** on the ribbon; the message, "Select object to align UCS:" appears in the command line.
- Select the cylindrical object from the model; the UCS will be aligned to it.

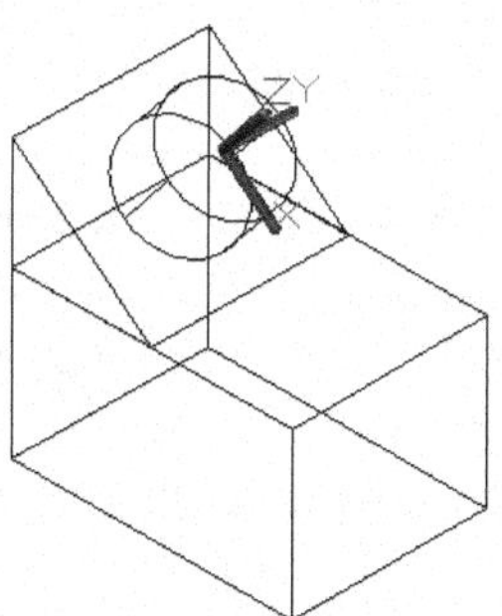

Example 9: (Creating UCS aligned to a face)

You can align a UCS to a planar or curved face of a model using the **Face** tool.

- Click **Home > Coordinates >View** drop-down > **Face** on the ribbon; the message, "Select face of solid, surface, or mesh:" appears in the command

line.
- Move the pointer over the faces of the model; you will notice that the UCS is displayed on the faces.

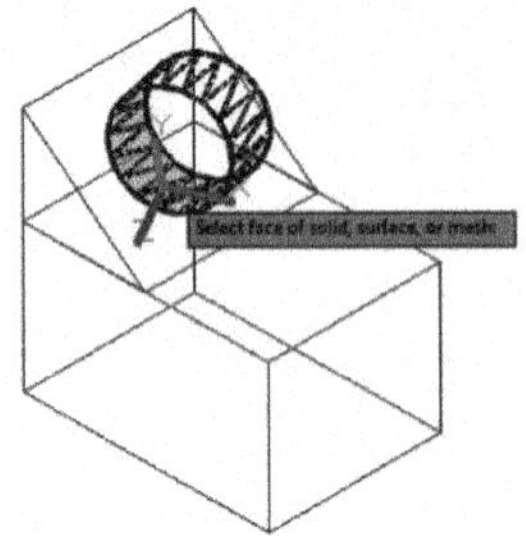
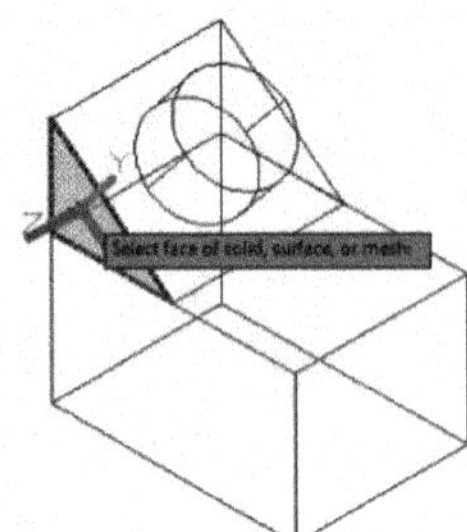

- Select the top face of the box; the message, "Enter an option [Next Xflip Yflip] <accept>:" appears in the command line.
  If you select the **Next** option, the adjacent face will be highlighted. The **Xflip** option is used to rotate the UCS 180 degrees about the X axis. The **Yflip** option is used to rotate the UCS 180 degrees about the Y axis.
- Press ENTER to accept; the UCS will be aligned to the selected face.

Using Dynamic User Coordinate System

In the previous section, you have learned to create various types of static user coordinate systems. They are active until you define another user coordinate system. You can also create dynamic user coordinate systems. A Dynamic User Coordinate System is a temporary UCS that appears automatically when you place your pointer over the face of a 3D solid object. Note that the Dynamic User Coordinate system appears only when you use tools that create objects directly (For example, drawing tools and primitive tools). To create a Dynamic UCS, you need to activate the **Dynamic UCS** option on the status bar.

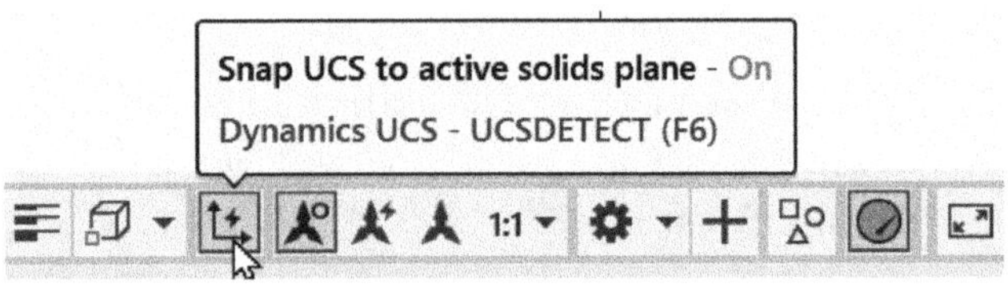

- Click the **Cylinder** button on the **Modeling** panel.
- Ensure that the **Dynamic UCS** button is active on the status bar.

- Move the pointer over the faces of the model; they will be highlighted.
- Click on the front face of the box and create the cylinder, as shown below.

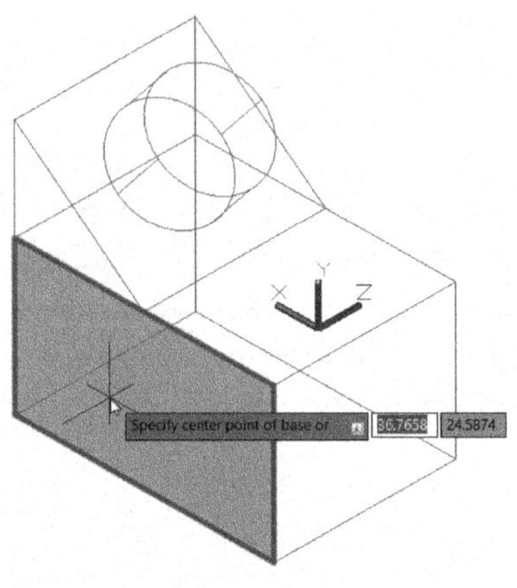

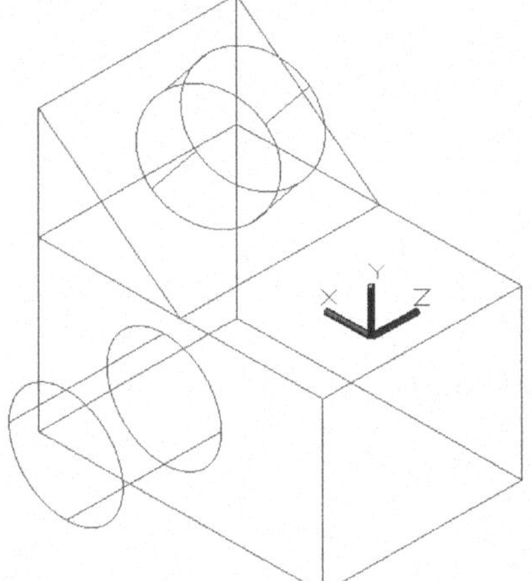

Model Space Viewports for 3D Modeling

While creating 3D models, it is useful to have a look at your model from several different orientations at the same time. For this purpose, you need to create different viewports in model space. You can create multiple viewports in model space using the **Viewport Configuration** drop-down available in the **Model Viewports** panel of the **Visualize** tab. It can also be done by using the **Viewports** dialog. To load this dialog, click **Visualize > Model Viewports > Named**; the **Viewports** dialog appears. In the dialog, select the **New Viewports** tab and then select **Four: Equal** from the **Standard viewports** list. Next, select **3D** from the **Setup** drop-down. Click the **OK** button; four tiled viewports are displayed on the screen. You can notice that each viewport has a different view and a different UCS. Click inside any viewport to activate it and perform any operation. To return to the single viewport, click the **Restore Viewports** 🔲 button on the **Model Viewports** panel; the currently active viewport will fill the screen area.

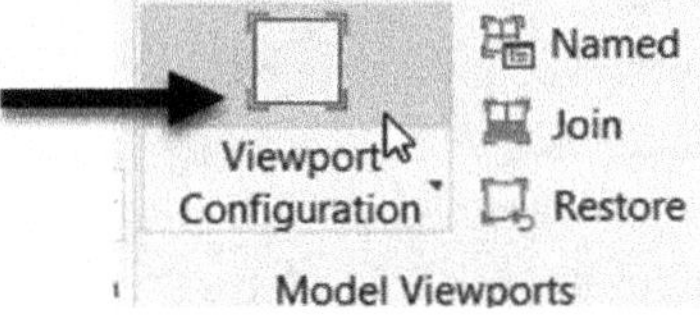

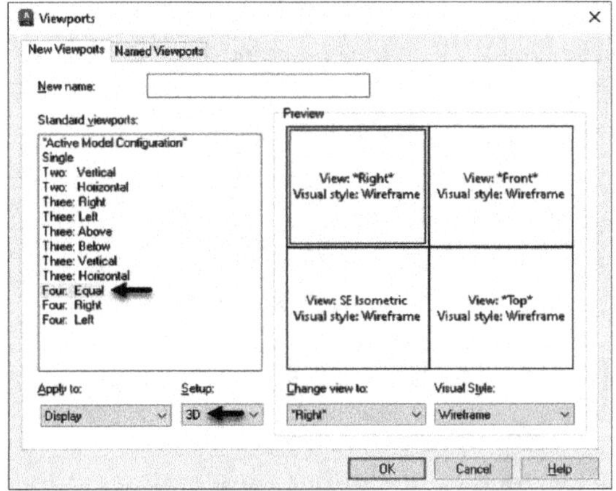

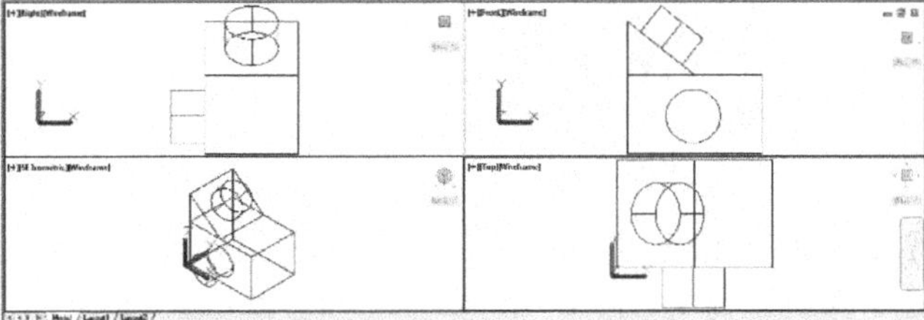

Creating Other Primitive Shapes

In AutoCAD, there is a set of tools to create basic geometric shapes. In earlier sections, you have learned to create boxes, wedges, and cylinders. Now, you will learn to create other primitive shapes.

Creating Cones

Creating a cone is similar to creating a cylinder. It has a similar shape compared to a cylinder, but it is tapered on one side.

Example 1:

- To create a cone, click **Home > Modeling > Primitives drop-down > Cone** 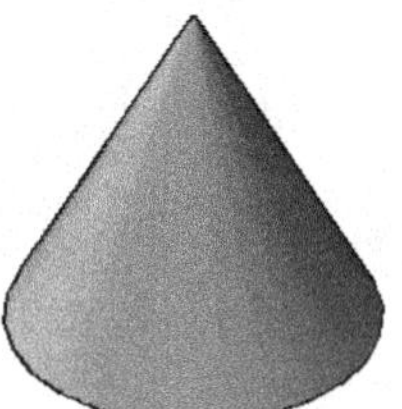 on the ribbon; the message, "Specify center point of base or [3P/2P/Ttr/Elliptical]:" appears in the command line.
- Pick an arbitrary point from the graphics window; the message, "Specify base radius or [Diameter]:" appears.
- Type a radius value in the command line and press ENTER. You can also select the **Diameter** option to specify the diameter of the base.
- Move the pointer in the vertical direction and pick a point to specify the height of the cone. You can also type in the height value in the command line and press ENTER; the cone will be created.

Example 2:

- Type **CONE** in the command line and press ENTER.
- Select the **Elliptical** option from the command line; the message, "Specify endpoint of first axis or [Center]:" appears in the command line.
- Pick a point to specify the endpoint of the first axis.
- Move the pointer and click to specify the other endpoint of the first axis. You can also type in the length of the first axis and press ENTER; the message, "Specify endpoint of second axis:" appears.
- Pick a point or type-in the radius value to specify the second axis.
- Move the pointer upward and pick a point to specify the height. You can also enter the value of height in the command line or the **Dynamic Input** box.

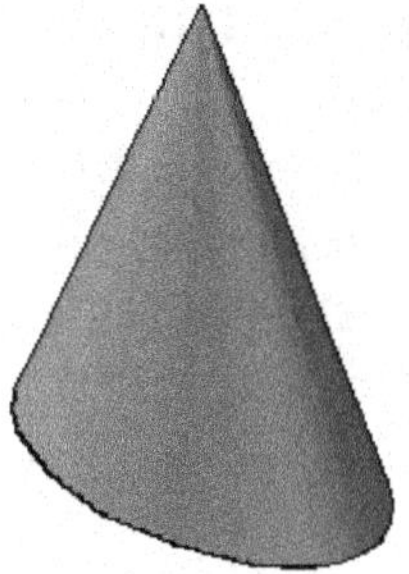

Example 3:

- Click **Solid > Primitive > Primitive drop-down > Cone** on the ribbon.
- Select the center point and specify the base radius as 20; the message, "Specify height or [2Point/Axis endpoint/Top radius]," appears in the command line.
- Select the **Top radius** option from the command line; the message, "Specify top radius:" appears.
- Type 10 as the top radius value and press ENTER.
- Move the pointer upward and enter 40 as the height.

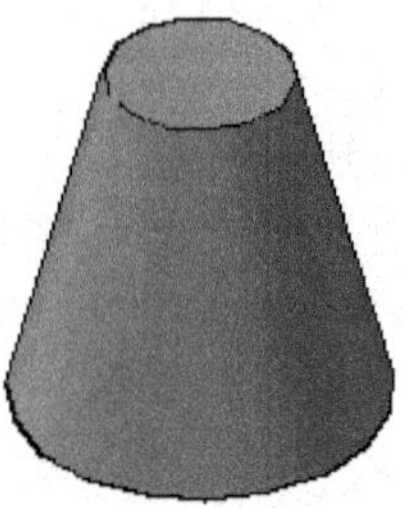

Creating a Sphere

- Click **Home > Modeling > Primitives drop-down > Sphere**  on the ribbon.
- Specify the center point of the sphere.
- Move the pointer outward and enter the radius value. You can also select the **Diameter** option to specify the diameter of the sphere.

Creating a Torus

Torus is a donut-shaped solid primitive. To create a torus, you need to specify the center of the torus, radius or diameter of the torus, and radius or diameter of the tube.

- Click **Home > Modeling > Primitives drop-down >Torus** on the ribbon or type **TOR** in the command line and press ENTER.
- Specify the center point of the torus.
- Move the pointer outward and enter the radius of the torus. You can also select the **Diameter** option to specify the diameter of the torus.
- Type the tube radius and press ENTER; the torus will be created.

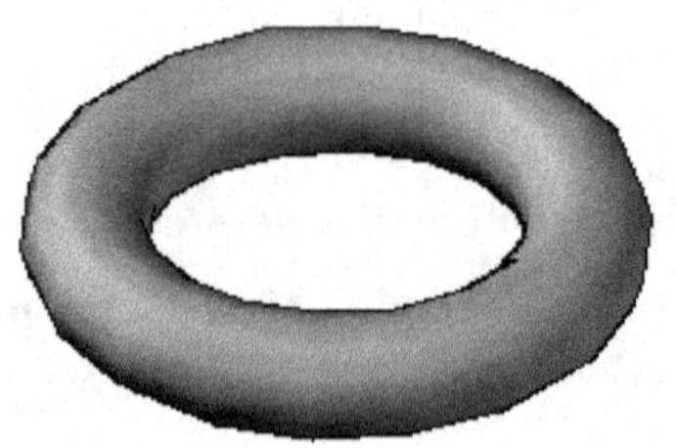

Creating a Pyramid

Pyramids are similar to cones except that the base of the pyramid is not circular in shape.

- To create a pyramid, click **Home > Modeling > Primitives drop-down > Pyramid** on the ribbon or type **PYR** in the command line and press ENTER.
- Specify the center point of the base. The base of the pyramid is a polygon. The method to create a polygon is already discussed in Chapter 2.
- After creating the base, move the pointer in a vertical direction and pick a point to specify the height of the pyramid. You can also type the value of the height and press ENTER; the pyramid will be created.

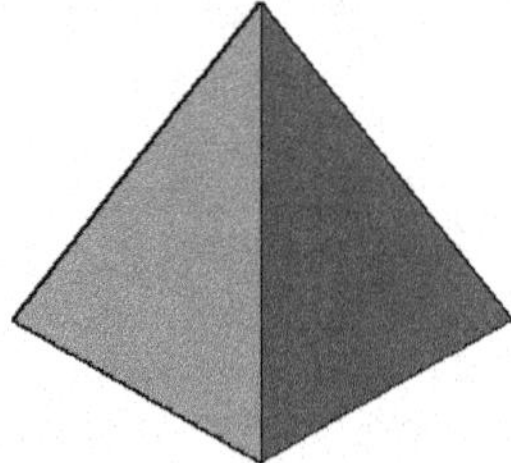

The other options displayed in the command line while creating the pyramid are the same as in the **Cone** tool.

Using the Polysolid tool

The **Polysolid** tool is used to create a 3D wall. It can also be used to convert a line, polyline, arc, or a circle to a wall. The **Polysolid** tool is similar to the **Polyline** tool except that you create a rectangular-shaped wall that has a pre-defined height and width.

- Click **Home > Modeling > Polysolid** on the ribbon; the message, "Specify start point or [Object/Height/Width/Justify] <Object>:" appears in the command line.
- Activate the **Ortho Mode** on the status bar.
- Pick an arbitrary point in the graphics window and

move the pointer in the X-direction.

- Type 200 in the command line and press ENTER; a 3D wall of 200 length is created.
- Select the **Arc** option from the command line and move the pointer in the Y-direction.
- Type 100 as the arc diameter and press ENTER.
- Select the **Line** option from the command line and move the pointer in the –X-direction.
- Type 100, and press ENTER.
- Move the pointer in the Y-direction and enter 150 as the wall length.
- Move the pointer in –X-direction and enter 100 as the wall length.
- Select the **Close** option from the command line; the wall will be closed.

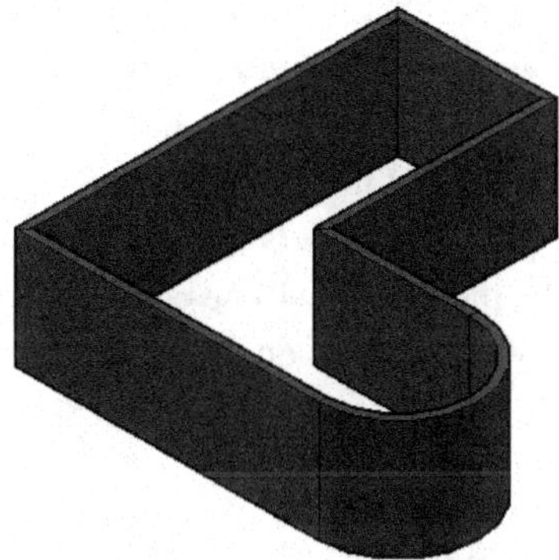

Using the Extrude tool

 The **Extrude** tool is used to add a third dime nsion (height) to an existing 2D shape. If you extrude a closed shape such as circle and closed polylines, a solid is created. If you extrude an open sketch such as lines and arcs, a surface is created.

Example 1:
- Start a new AutoCAD file in the **3D Modeling** workspace.
- Click **Home > View > 3D Navigation > Front** on the ribbon; the front view will become parallel to the screen.

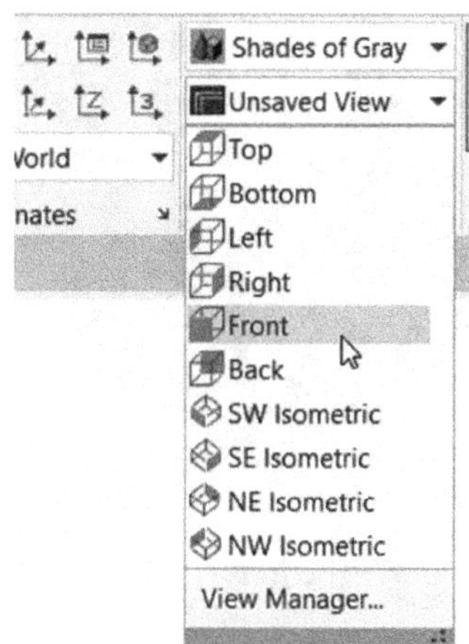

- Click **Home > Draw > Polyline** on the ribbon and create the sketch, as shown below.

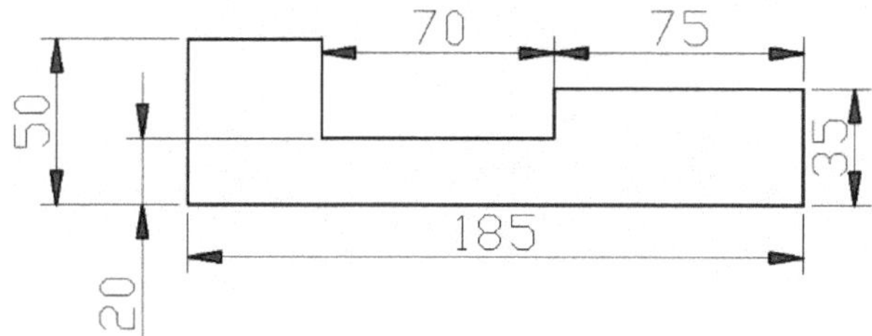

- Select **SE Isometric** from the **In-canvas controls**; the view orientation will be changed to Southeast Isometric.

- Click **Home > Modeling > Extrude.**
- Select the polyline sketch and press Enter.
- Move the pointer toward the right.
- Type **100** in the command line or **Dynamic Input** box and press ENTER; the polyline sketch will be extruded.

Example 2:

- Open a new AutoCAD file in the **3D Modeling** Workspace.
- Click **Home > View > 3D Navigation > Top** on the ribbon; the view will become parallel to the screen.

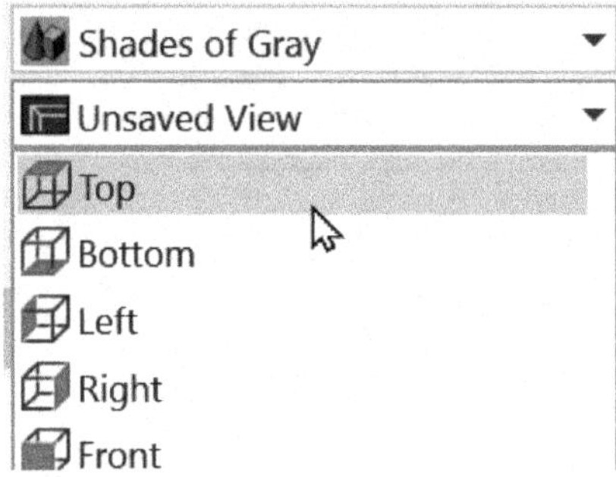

- Click **Home > Draw > Line** on the ribbon and create the sketch, as shown below.

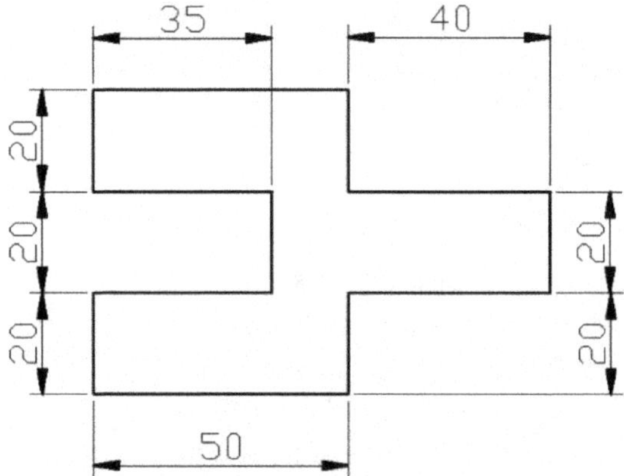

- Click **Home > View > 3D Navigation > SE Isometric** on the ribbon; the view orientation will be changed to southeast Isometric.
- Expand the **Draw** panel of the **Home** tab and click the **Region** button.

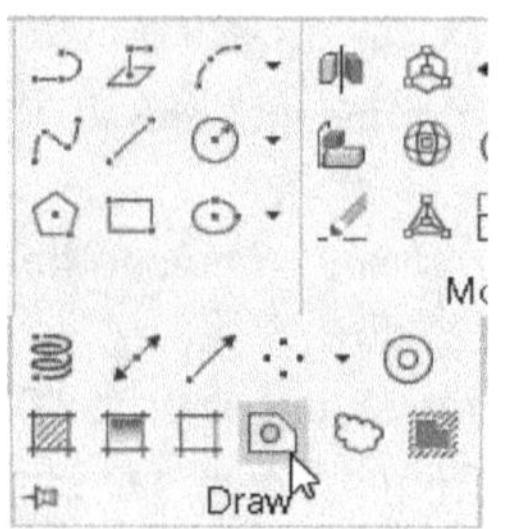

With the help of the Region tool, you can convert one or more objects that form a closed shape into a single object called a Region. Regions have special properties that allow you to combine them with other Regions using Boolean operations like Union, Subtract, and Intersect to form a composite Region. Additionally, Regions are considered planar surfaces, defined by their edges, with no edges existing within the Region perimeter. You can even use Regions with surface modeling.

- Press and hold the left mouse button. Next, drag a window across all the objects of the sketch.
- Press ENTER; the sketch will be converted into a region. Now, you can extrude the region to create a solid. If you try to extrude the lines without creating a region, it will result in a surface.

Remember, when you convert your objects to a Region, the original objects will be deleted unless you set the system variable DELOBJ to 0. Also, if your original objects were hatched, hatch associativity will be lost. To restore associativity, you'll need to rehatch the Region.

- Click **Solid > Solid > Extrude** on the ribbon. 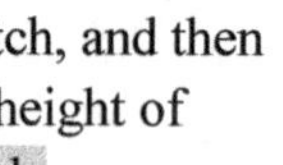
- Select the region created from the sketch, and then press ENTER; the message, "Specify height of extrusion or [Direction Path Taper angle Expression]:" appears in the command line.
- Select the **Taper angle** option from the command line.
- Type 5 as the taper angle and press ENTER.
- Move the pointer upward, type 40 in the command line and press ENTER; the extruded solid will be

created with a taper.

Example 3:

- Type **EXT** in the command line and press ENTER.
- Press and hold the CTRL key and select the top face of the model.
- Press ENTER and move the pointer upward.
- Type 25 as the extrusion height and press ENTER; the extruded solid will be created.

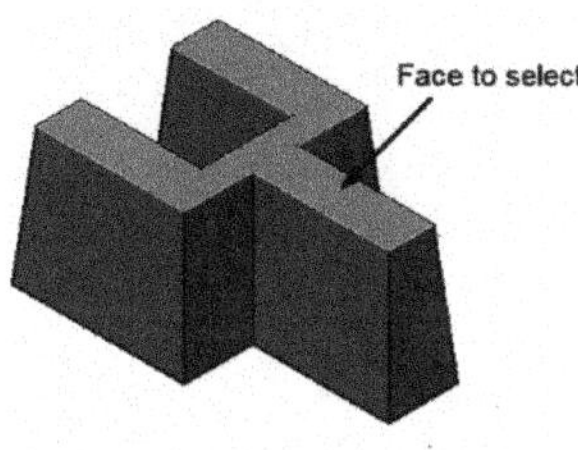

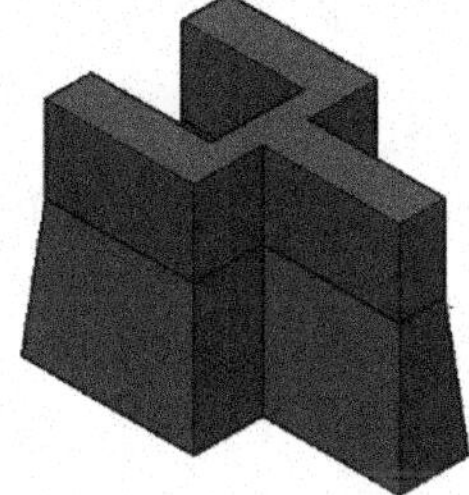

Using the Revolve tool

The **Revolve** tool is used to revolve an open or closed 2D sketch about a selected axis. If you revolve a closed profile such as a polyline sketch, polygon, circle, or a sketch region, a solid object is created. An open profile results in a surface. The sketch is deleted after revolving it. If you want to retain the sketch, you need to set the **DELOBJ** system variable to 0.

- Open a new file in the **3D Modeling** workspace.
- Set the view orientation to front and create the sketch using the **Line** tool. Do not add dimensions.

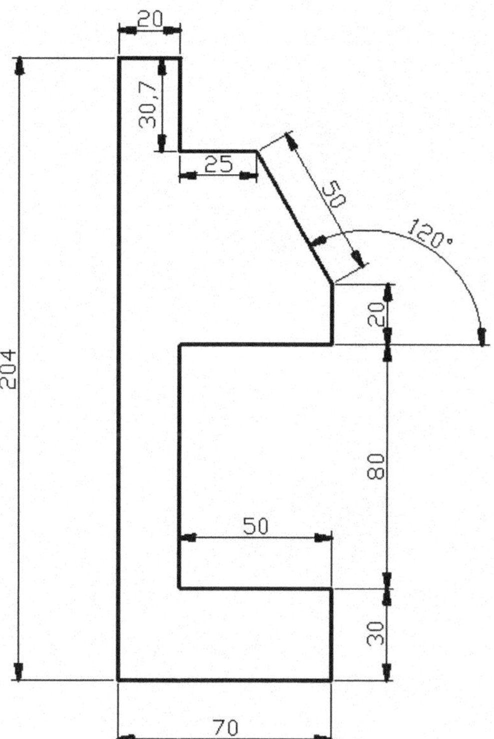

- Convert the sketch into the region using the **Region** tool.

- Create a vertical line at a distance of 10 mm from the left vertical edge of the region.

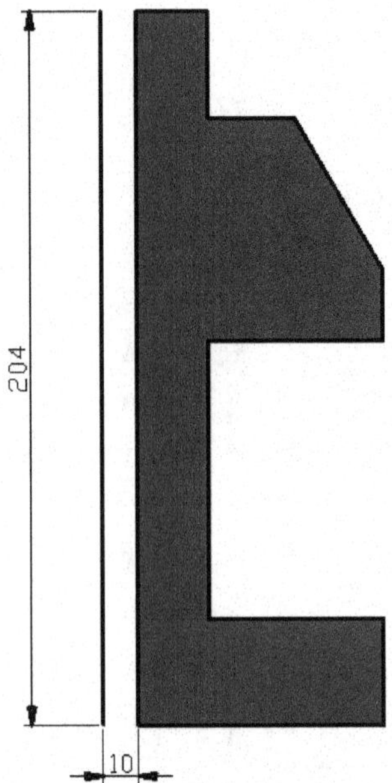

- Click **Solid > Solid > Revolve** on the ribbon or type REV in the command line.
- Select the sketch region and press ENTER; the message, "Specify axis start point or define axis by [Object/X/Y/Z] <Object>:" appears in the command line.
- Select the **Object** option from the command line and select the vertical line created at an offset; the message, "Specify angle of revolution or [STart angle/Reverse/EXpression] <360>:" appears.

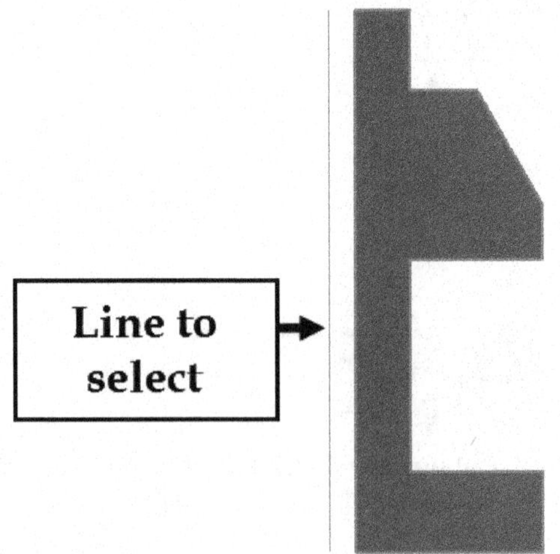

- Press ENTER to specify 360 as the revolution angle.

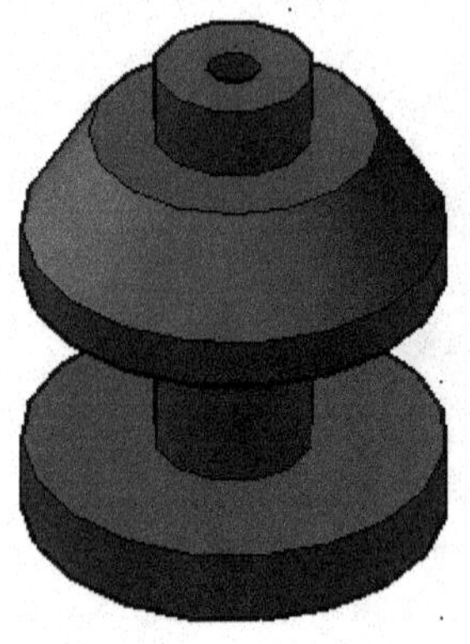

Using the Sweep tool

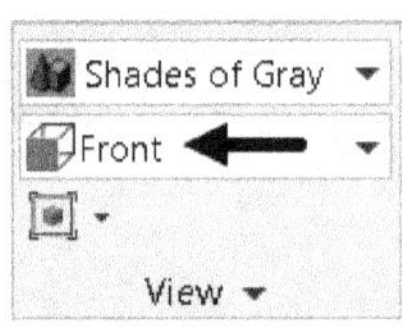

The **Sweep** tool is used to create a new solid or surface by sweeping a closed or open planar profile along an open or closed 2D or 3D path. The procedure to create a solid by using the **Sweep** tool is discussed next.

Example:

- Open a new file in the **3D Modeling** workspace.
- Set the view orientation to **Front**.

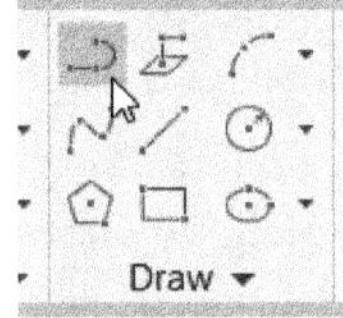

- Activate the **Polyline** tool.

- Deactivate the **ORTHOMODE** icon on the Status bar, if already active.
- Turn ON the Dynamic Input icon on the Status bar.
- Specify the start point of the polyline.
- Move the pointer vertically downward.
- Type 38 and press the TAB key.
- Type 270, and press ENTER.

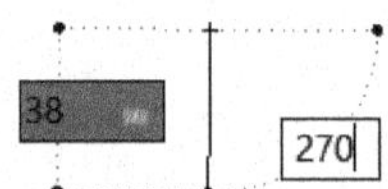

- Move the pointer toward the bottom-left corner.

- Type 83 and press the TAB.
- Type 229, and press ENTER.

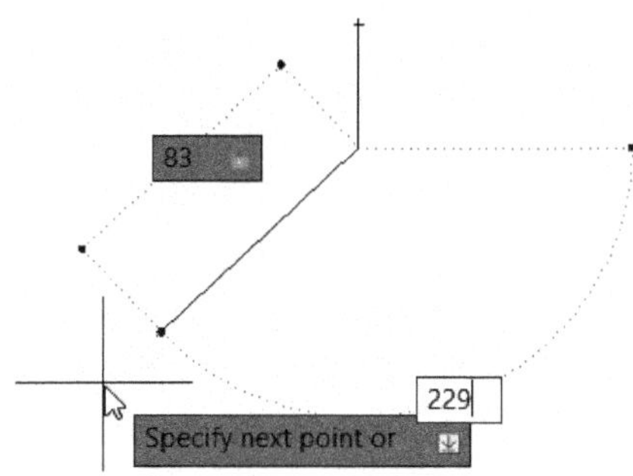

- Move the pointer downward.
- Type 66 and press the TAB key.
- Type 270, and press ENTER.

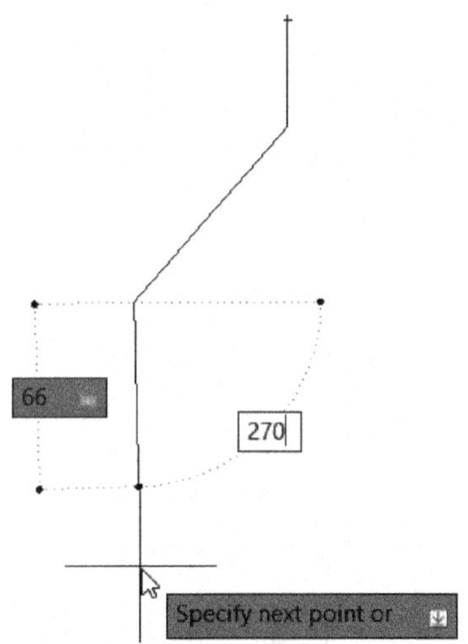

- Select the **Arc** option from the command line.
- Move the pointer toward right.
- Type 108 and press TAB.
- Type 0 and press ENTER.

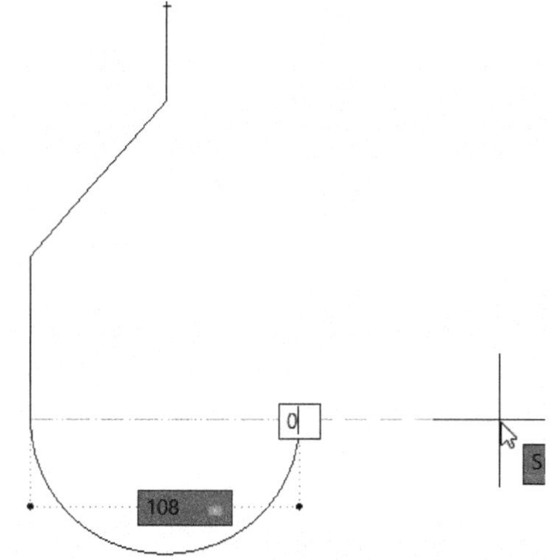

- Press Esc to deactivate the **Polyline** tool.
- Use the **Fillet** tool and apply fillets of 25 mm radius.

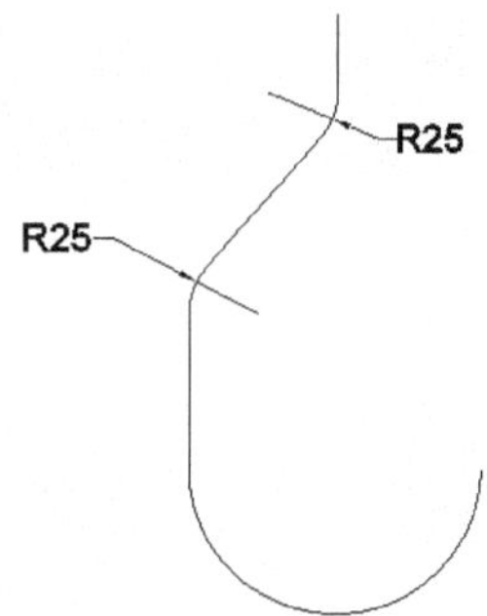

- Change the view orientation to SE Isometric.
- Click **Home > Coordinates > Z-Axis Vector** on the ribbon.
- Select the endpoint of the top vertical line as the UCS origin.
- Move the pointer downward and select the endpoint of the vertical line; the Z-axis is aligned to the vertical line.

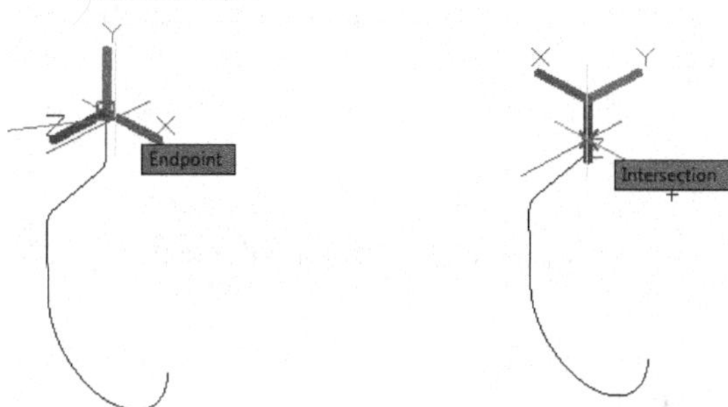

- Click the **Circle** button on the **Draw** panel.
- Select the endpoint of the vertical line to specify the center point of the circle. Specify 5 mm as the radius

of the circle.

- Click the **UCS, World** button on the **Coordinates** panel; the User Coordinate System will be set to World Coordinate System (0,0,0).

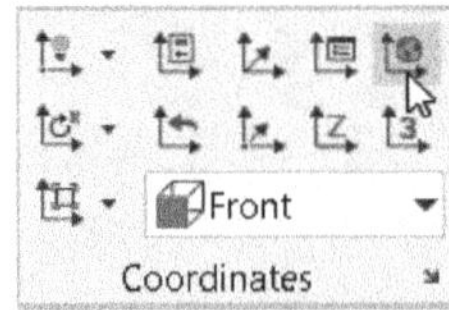

- Click **Home** > **Modeling** > **Solids** drop-down > **Sweep** on the ribbon.

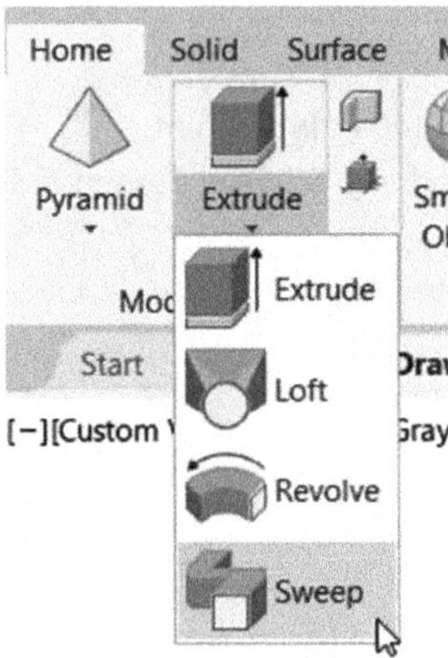

- Select the circle as the profile and press ENTER; the message, "Select sweep path or [Alignment/Base point/Scale/Twist]:" appears in the command line.

The **Alignment** option aligns the profile perpendicular to the direction of the sweep path. By default, the profile is aligned to the path.

The **Base point** specifies the base point of the profile. By default, the center of the profile is used as the base point. You can select any other point on the profile to define the base point.

The **Scale** option scales the profile along the path.

The **Twist** option twists the profile as it is swept along the length of the path.

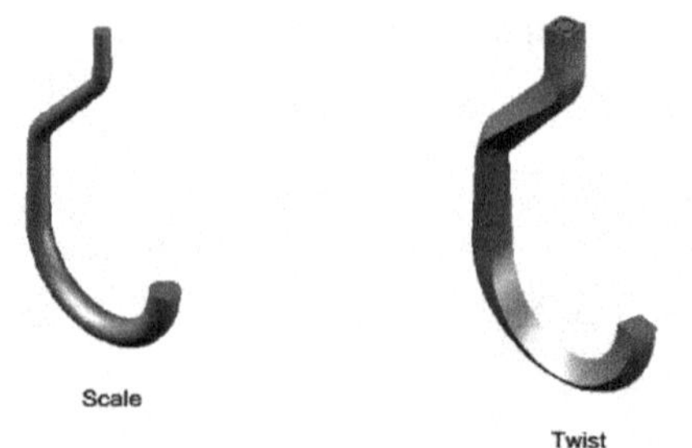

- Select the path to create the swept solid object.

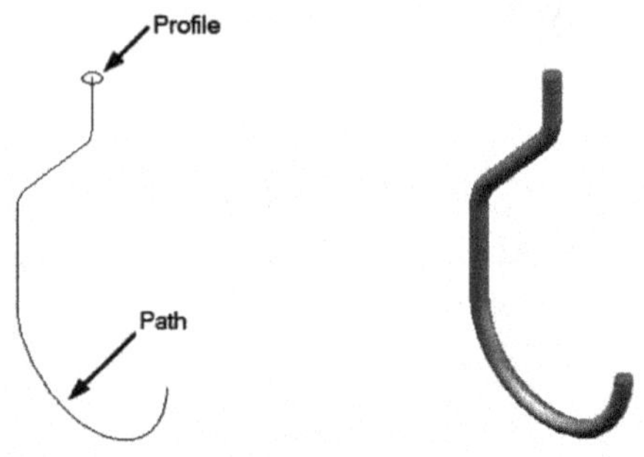

Using the Loft tool

Using the **Loft** tool, you can create a solid or surface by selecting a series of cross-sections. The selected cross-sections will define the shape of the lofted solid.

Example 1:

- Deactivate the **Dynamic Input** icon on the status bar.
- Type CIRCLE in the command line and press ENTER.
- Type 0,0,0 in the command line and press ENTER.
- Type 25 as the radius value and press ENTER.
- Type CIRCLE in the command line.
- Type 0,0,70 in the command line and press ENTER.
- Type 50 as the radius value and press ENTER.
- Type CIRCLE in the command line.
- Type 0,0,140 in the command line and press ENTER.
- Type 25 as the radius value and press ENTER.

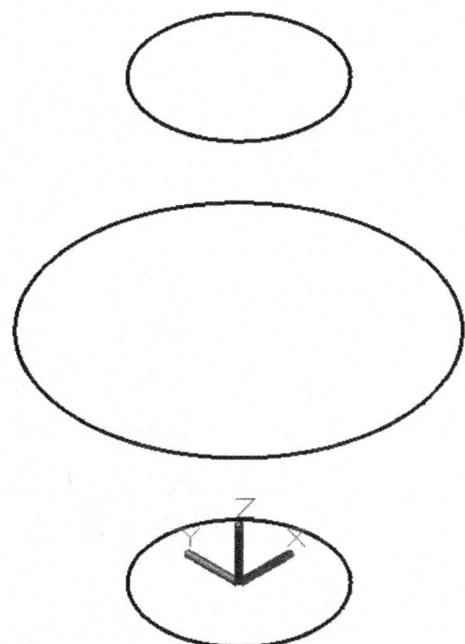

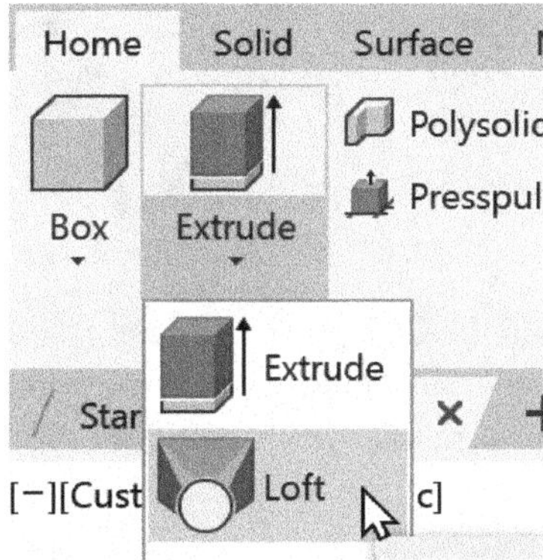

- Click **Home > Modeling > Solids drop-down > Loft** on the ribbon (or) type **LOFT** in the command line and press ENTER.

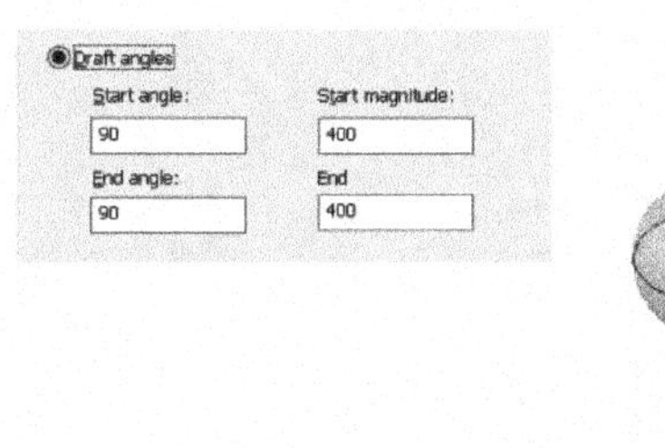

- Select the first, second, and third cross-sections one by one; the preview of the lofted solid appears.
- Press ENTER to accept the selection; the message, "Enter an option [Guides/Path/Cross sections only/Settings] <Cross sections only>:" appears in the command line.
- Select the **Settings** option from the command line; the **Loft Settings** dialog appears. In this dialog, the **Smooth Fit** option creates a smooth connection between the cross-sections. If you select the **Ruled** option, the lofted solid or surface has sharp edges.

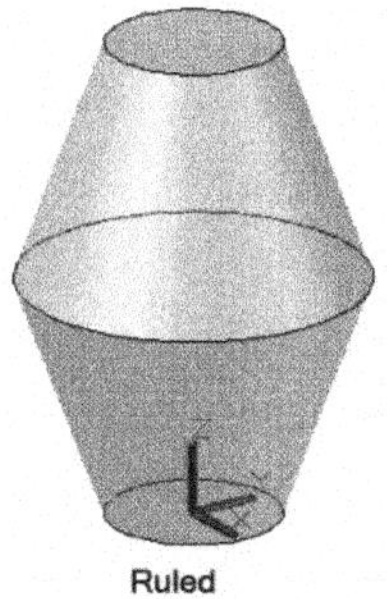
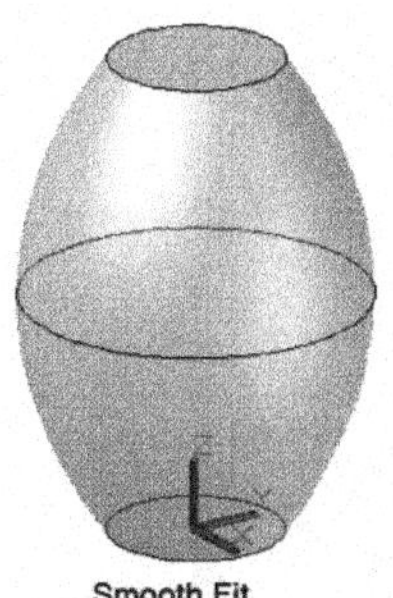

The **Normal to** option creates a solid or surface normal to the cross-section. You can select the loft solid or surface to be normal to **All cross sections**, or **Start Cross Section** or **End Cross Section** or **Start and End Cross Sections**.

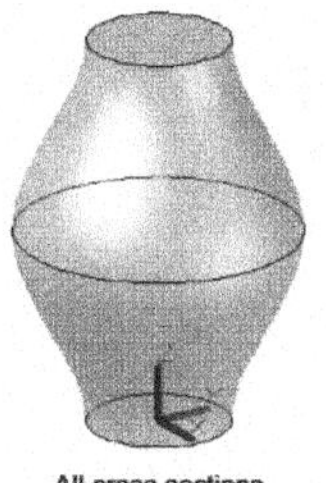
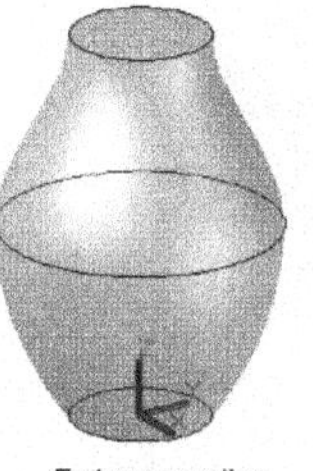
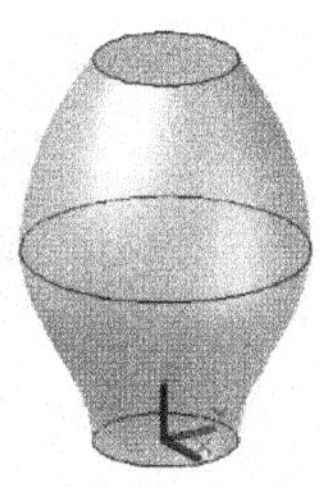

The **Draft angles** option defines the draft angle and magnitude at start and end cross-sections. The draft angle is the beginning direction of the loft surface. If you set the draft angle to 90 degrees, the loft surface starts vertically from the cross-section, and the 0-draft angle starts loft surface horizontally. The Magnitude is the relative distance up to which the loft surface will follow the draft angle before it bends.

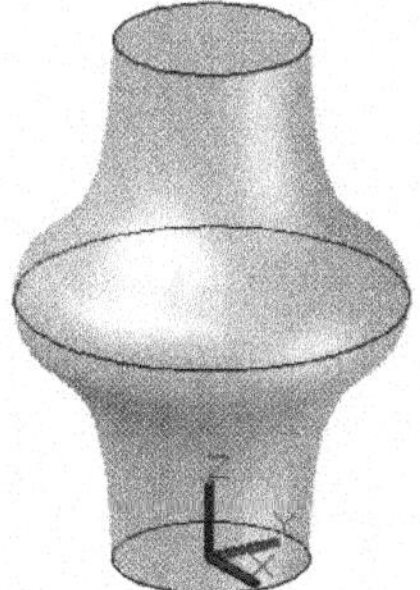

The **Close surface or solid** option connects the start and end section of the lofted object.

- Select the **Normal to** option and select **All cross sections**. Click **OK**; the loft solid will be created, as shown below.

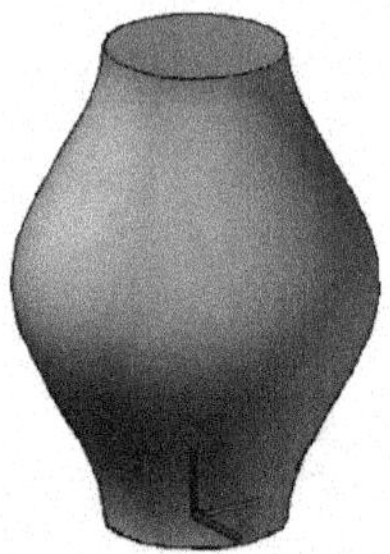

Using the Presspull tool

The **Presspull** tool is used to create and modify solid models with greater ease and speed. It can be used to accomplish two types of operations: extruding closed 2D shapes and add or remove material from a solid object based on whether you "pull" or "push" the extrusion.

- Start a new file.
- Create two layers called **Sketch** and **Solid**. Make the **Sketch** layer as current.
- Set the view orientation to **Right** and draw the sketch, as shown below.

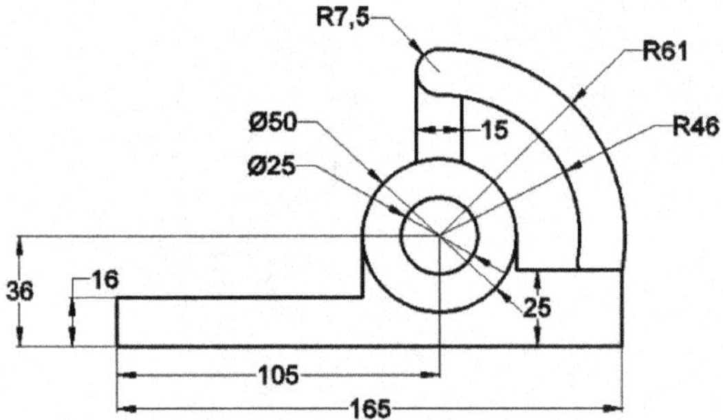

- Change the view orientation to SE Isometric.
- Ensure that the **Dynamic Input** icon is activated on the status bar.

- Set the **Solid** layer are current.
- Click **Home > Modeling > Presspull** on the ribbon.
- Click inside the bottom region of the sketch and move the pointer backward. Type 60 in the Dynamic input box and press ENTER; the extruded feature will be created.

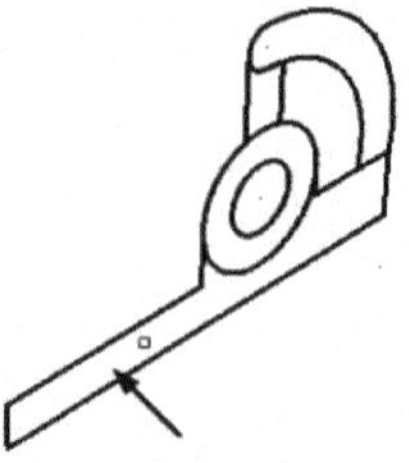
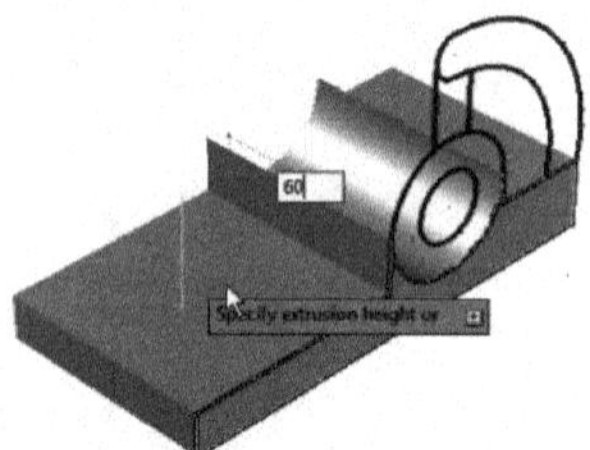

- Click on the region enclosed by the larger circle and extrude it up to 64 mm distance.

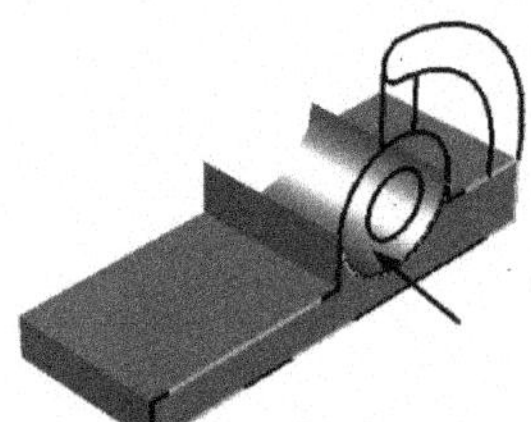
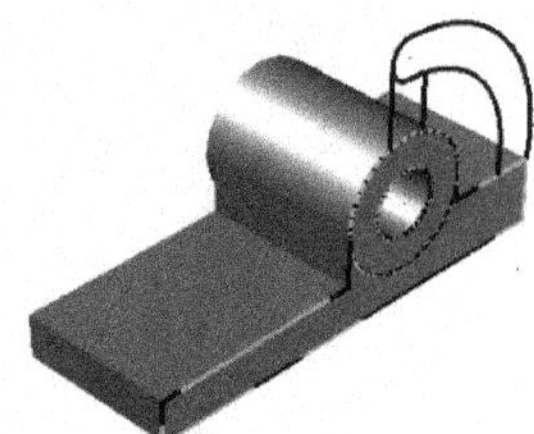

- Press and hold the CTRL key and select the front face of the cylindrical object. Move the pointer forward. Type 4 in the dynamic input box and press ENTER.

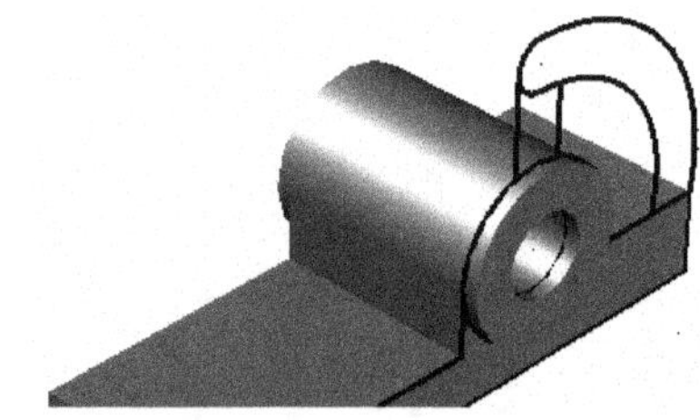

- Click in the curved slot region and move the pointer backward; the message, "Specify extrusion height or [Multiple]:" appears in the command line.
- Select the **Multiple** option from the command line and click in the region enclosed by the two vertical lines.

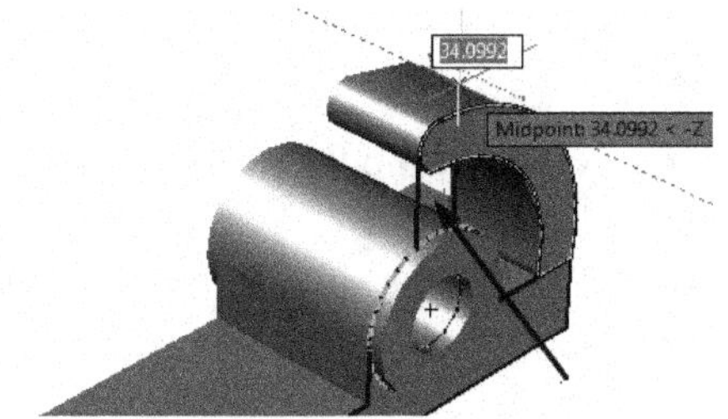

- Right-click and move the pointer backward. Type **12** in the dynamic input box and press ENTER.

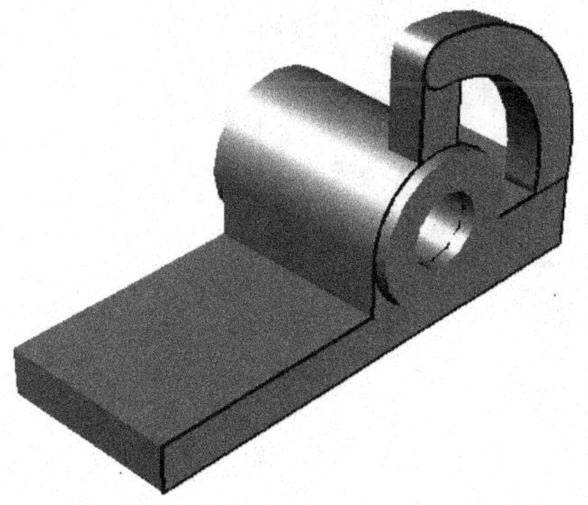

- Activate the **Presspull** tool.
- Press and hold the CTRL key and select the front face of the slot and move the pointer forward — type 4 in the dynamic input box and press ENTER.
- Set the **Sketch** layer as current.
- Activate the **Dynamic UCS** icon on the status bar.
- Click the **Circle** button on the **Draw** panel of the **Home** ribbon tab.
- Press and hold the SHIFT key. Right-click and select the **Center** option from the shortcut menu.
- Select the center point of the slot end cap and create a circle of 4 mm radius.

- Click **Home > Modify > Array** drop-down > **Path Array** on the ribbon.
- Select the circle created in the previous step and press ENTER.

- Select the arc as the path curve; the preview of the path array is displayed.

- In the **Array Creation** tab, set the **Between** value to 25 in the **Items** panel; the item count is automatically adjusted.
- Click the **Close Array** button on the ribbon; the polar array is created.

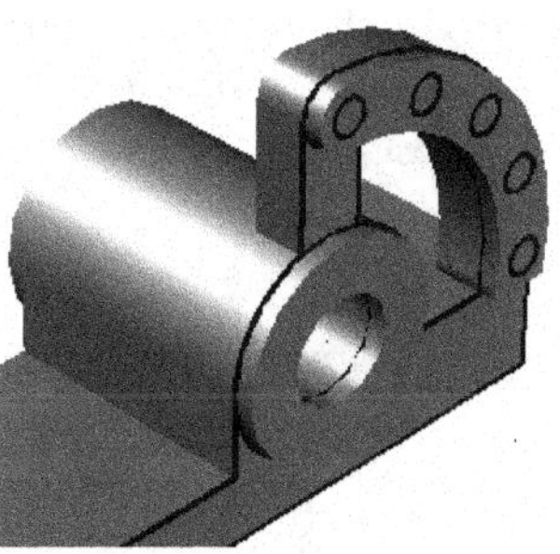

- Set the **Solid** layer as current.
- Activate the **Presspull** command.
- Click in any one of the circles and select the **Multiple** option from the command line.
- Click inside the rest of the circles of the polar array. Right-click to accept.
- Move the pointer backward and click; the holes will be created, as shown in the figure.
- Turn Off the **Sketch** layer; the sketches will be hidden.

- Click the **Orbit** button on the **Navigation Bar**.
- Press and drag the left mouse button to rotate the model.

Performing the Boolean Operations

Boolean operations are performed to add two or more solids together, subtract a single solid or group of solids from another, or form a common portion when two solids are combined. You must have at least two solids to perform a Boolean operation. There are three tools available to perform Boolean Operations- **Union Subtract** and **Intersect**. These tools are discussed next.

The Union tool

The **Union** tool joins two or more solids together into a single solid. For example, when you try to select the complete model, its individual objects are selected. But, after performing the Union operation, all the solid objects are combined and act as one object.

- To perform the Union operation, click **Solid > Boolean > Union** on the ribbon.

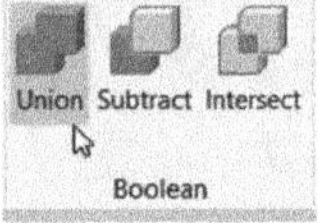

- Click the left mouse button and create a selection window across the model; all the objects of the model will be selected.
- Press ENTER; all the solid objects of the model will be combined.

  Now, when you select an individual object, the complete model will be selected.

The Subtract tool

The **Subtract** tool is used to subtract one or more solid objects from another object.

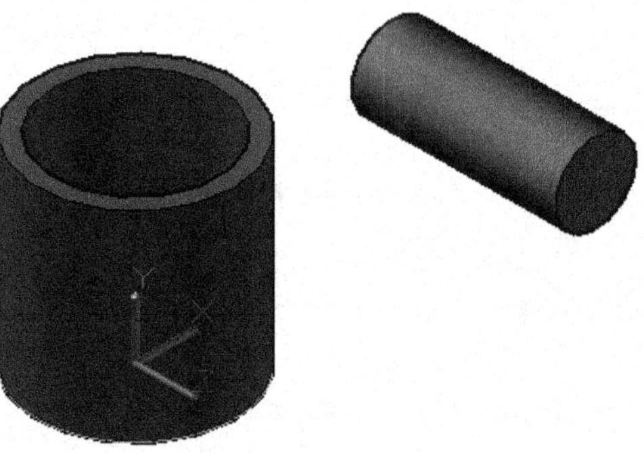

- Open a new 3D drawing file.
- Change the view orientation to Top.

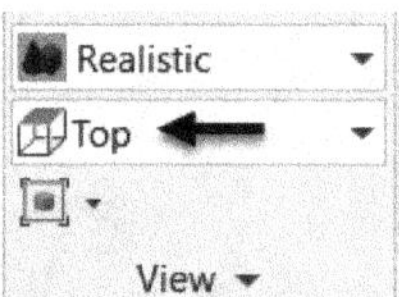

- Create two concentric circles of 240 and 200 mm in diameter.

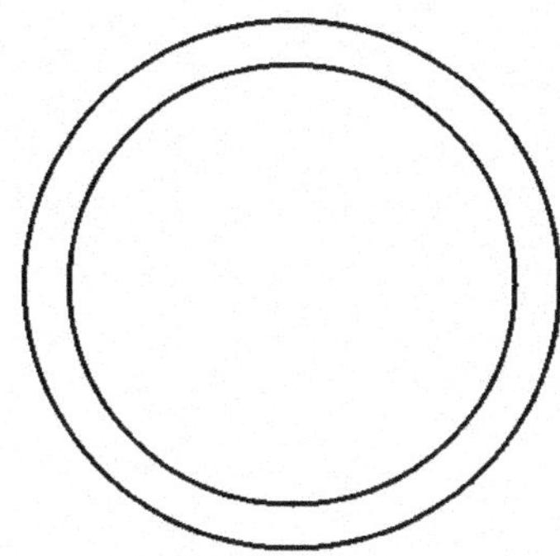

- Change the view orientation to SE Isometric.

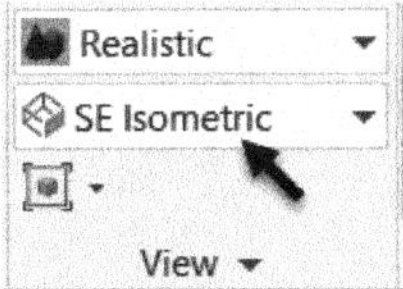

- Activate the **Presspull** tool.
- Click inside the region between the large and small circles.

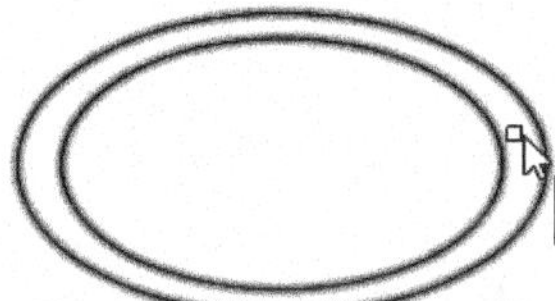

- Move the pointer upward, type 250, and then press Enter.

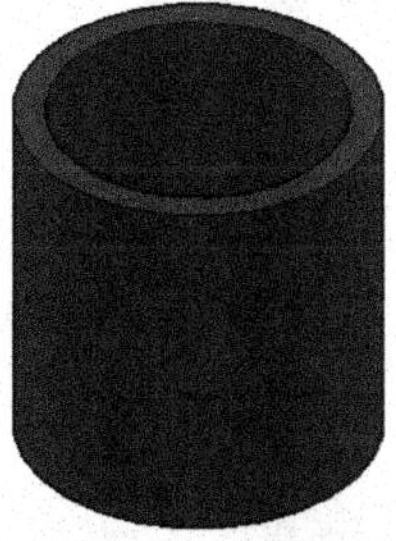

- Press Esc to deactivate the **Presspull** tool.
- Set the view orientation to **Right**.

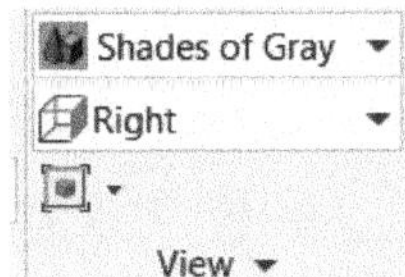

- Click **Home > Modeling > Primitive** drop-down > **Cylinder** on the ribbon.
- Select an arbitrary point in the graphics window.

- Move the pointer outward, type 50, and then press Enter.
- Type 240 and press ENTER.
- Change the view orientation to **SE Isometric**.

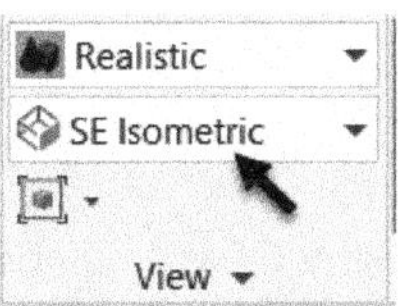

- Expand the **Modify** panel and click the **Align** button.

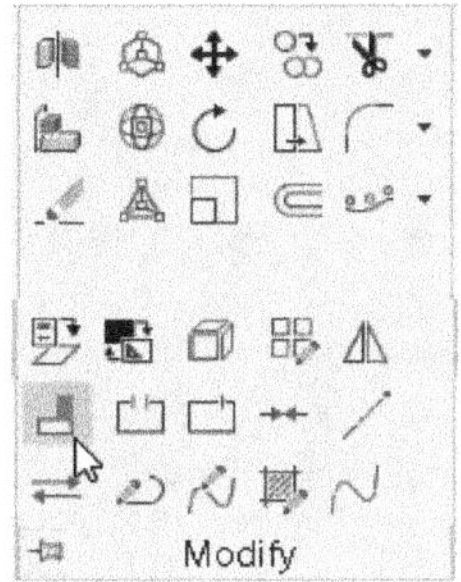

- Select the horizontal cylinder and press ENTER; the message, "Specify first source point:" appears in the command line.
- Press and hold the SHIFT key. Right-click and select the **Center** option.
- Select the center point of the front face of the horizontal cylinder; the message, "Specify first destination point:" appears in the command line.

- Press and hold the SHIFT key. Right-click and select the **Quadrant** option.
- Select the quadrant point of the outer circle on the top face of the hollow cylinder.

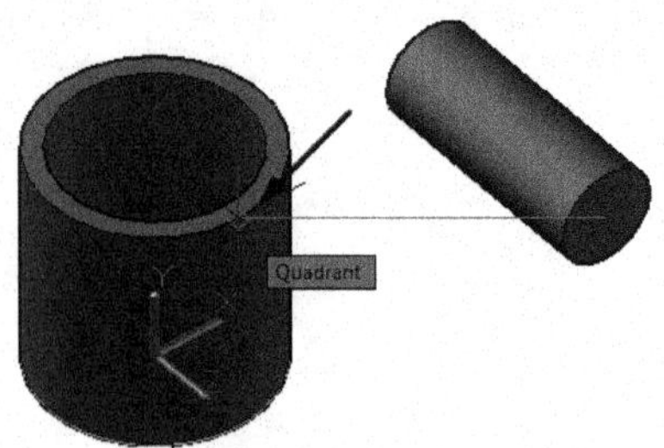

- Press ENTER; the horizontal cylinder will be aligned with the hollow cylinder.

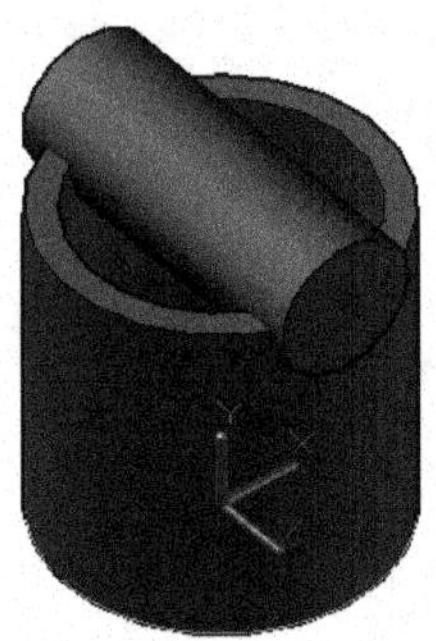

- Click **Solid > Boolean > Subtract** on the ribbon; the message, "Select objects," appears in the command line.
- Select the hollow cylinder and press ENTER; the message, "Select objects," appears in the command line.
- Select the horizontal cylinder and press ENTER; it will be subtracted from the hollow cylinder, as shown next.

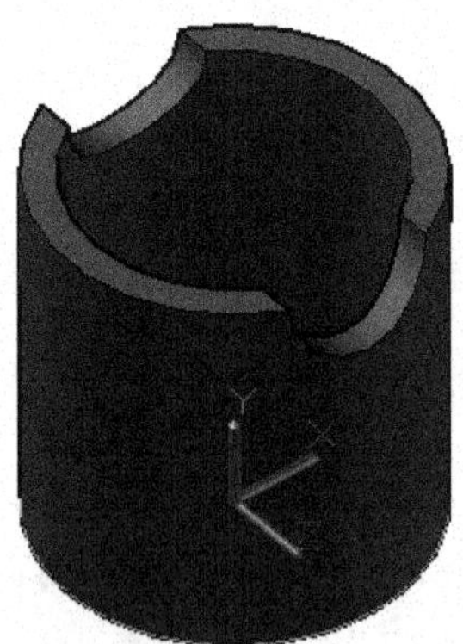

The Intersect tool

The **Intersect** tool is used to create a composite solid by finding common volume shared by the selected objects.

- Start a new file.

- Set the view orientation to **Front** and create the sketch, as shown below.

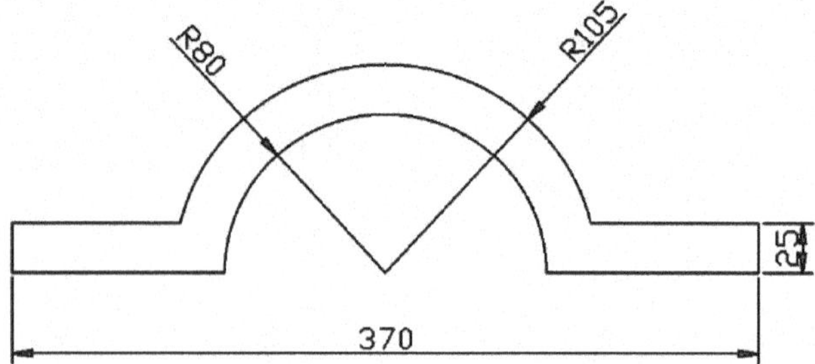

- Change the view orientation to **SE Isometric**.

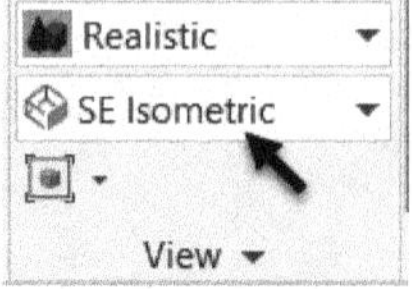

- Use the **Presspull** tool and extrude the sketch up to 150 mm distance.

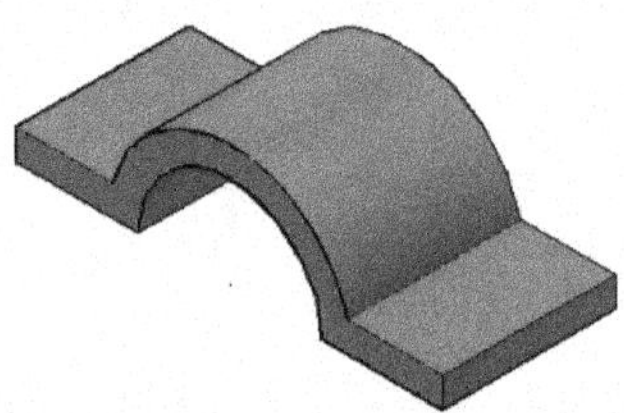

- Set the view orientation to Top.

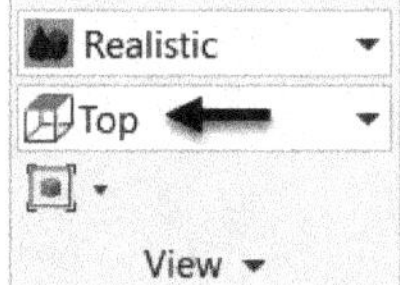

- Activate the **Circle** tool and create three circles, as shown.

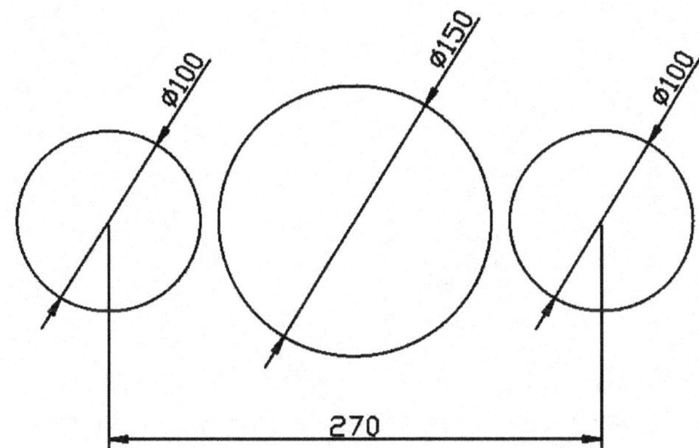

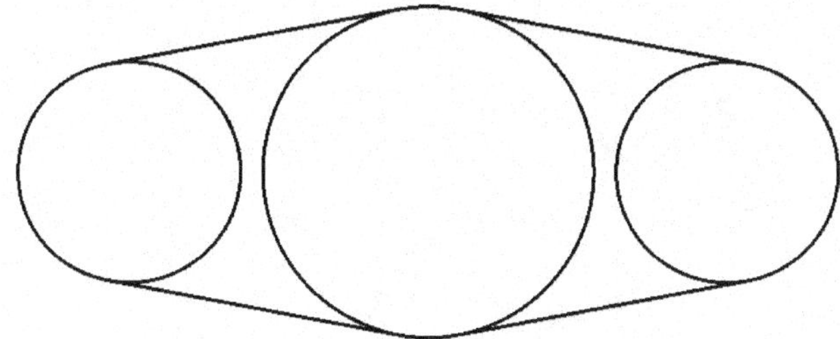

- Click **Home > Draw > Line** on the ribbon.
- Press and hold the SHIFT key, and then right-click.
- Select the **Tangent** option.
- Select the small circle by clicking at the location, as shown.

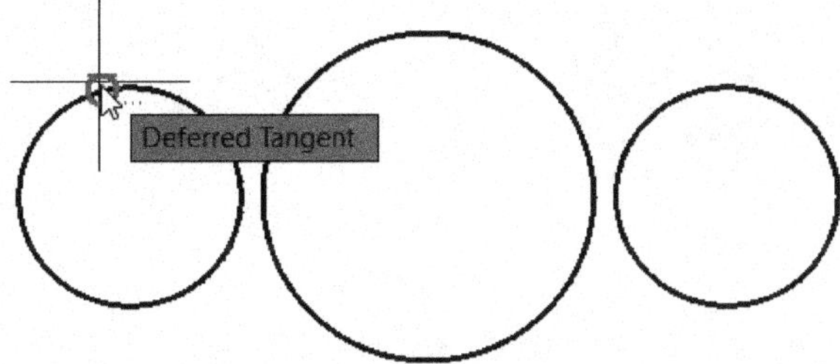

- Click **Home > Modify > Trim** on the ribbon.
- Select the entities to trim, as shown.

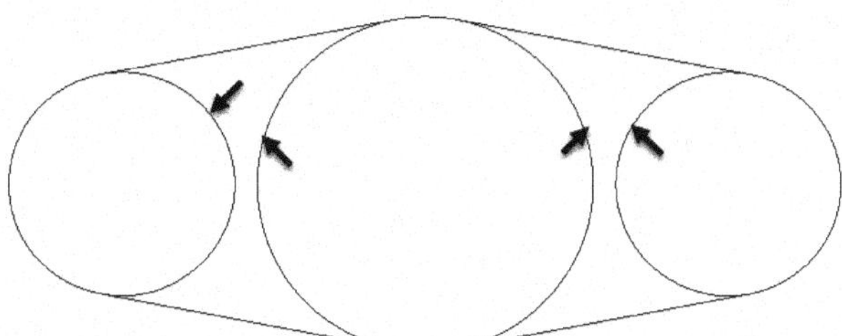

- Press and hold the SHIFT key, and then right-click.
- Select the **Tangent** option.
- Select the large circle by clicking at the location, as shown.

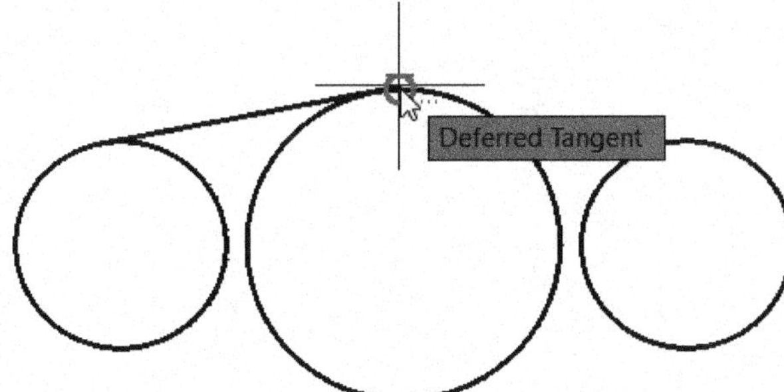

- Press Esc.

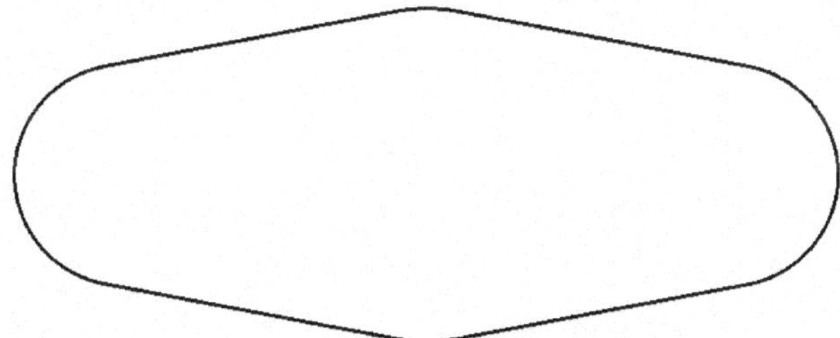

- Right-click and select **Enter**.
- Likewise, create three more lines tangent to the circles, as shown.

- Change the view orientation to SE Isometric.

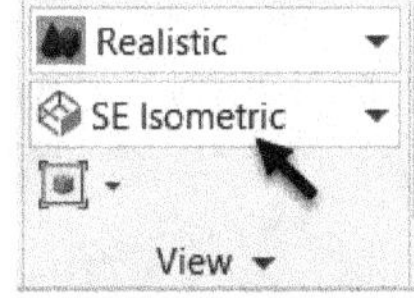

- Use the **Presspull** tool and extrude the sketch up to 200 mm height, as shown below.

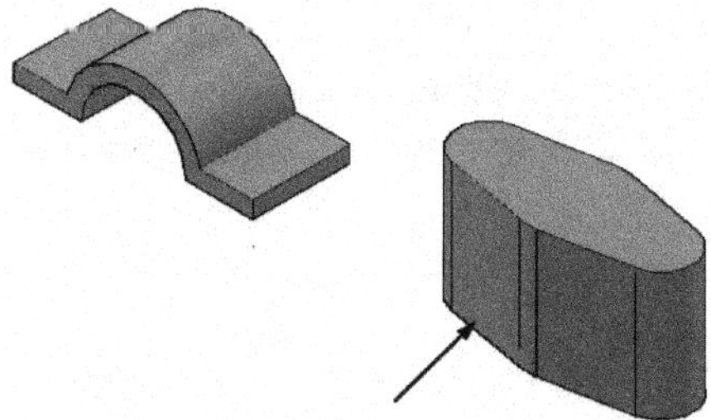

- Change the View style to **Wireframe**.

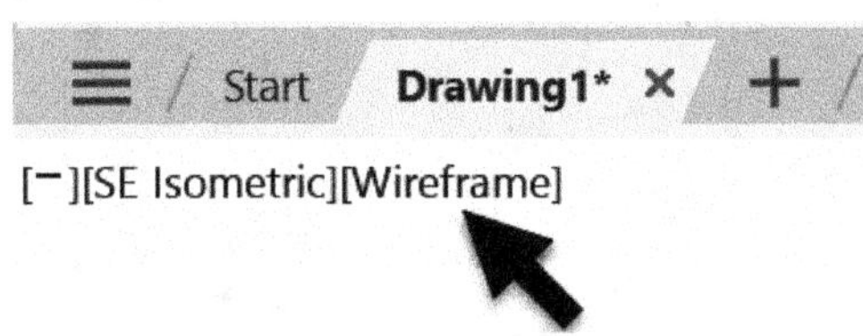

- Deactivate the **3D Object Snap** option on the status bar.
- Type **DS** in the command line and press ENTER; the **Drafting Settings** dialog appears.
- Click the **Object Snap** tab and **Clear All** the **Object Snap** modes.
- Now, select the **Quadrant** and **Midpoint** options and click **OK**.

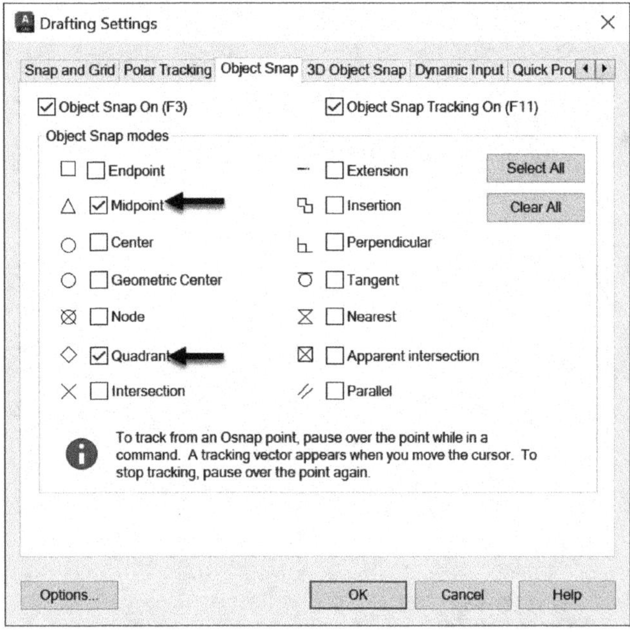

- Type **AL** in the command line and press ENTER.
- Select the second extrusion and press ENTER; the message, "Specify first source point:" appears.
- Select the point on the source object as shown below; the message, "Specify first destination point:" appears.
- Select the point on the destination object as shown below; the message, "Specify second source point:" appears.

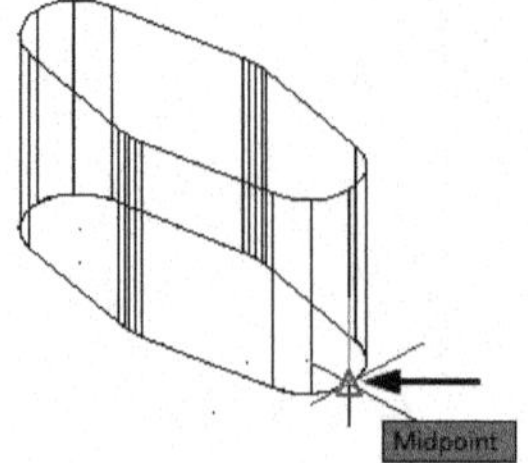
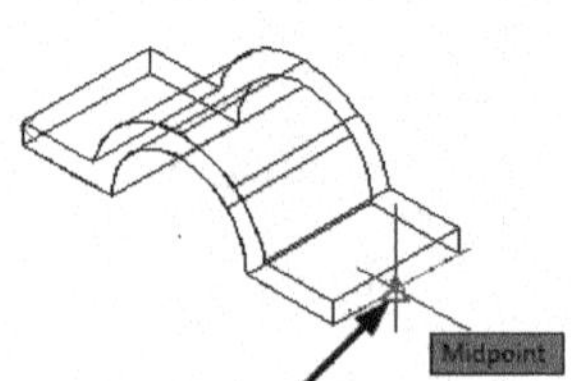

- Select another point on the source object, as shown below; the message, "Specify second destination point:" appears.
- Select another point on the destination object, as shown below; the message, "Specify third source point or <continue>:" appears.

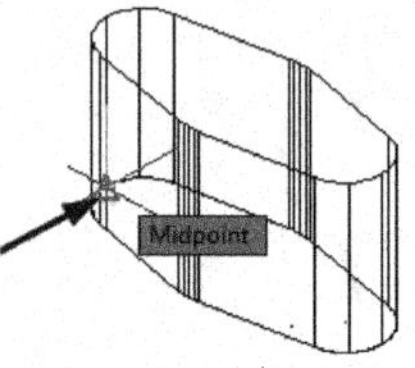
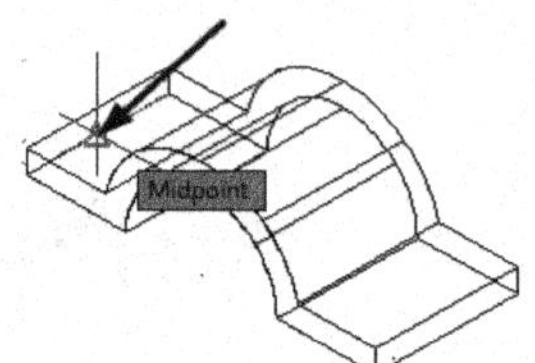

- Press ENTER to continue; the message, "Scale objects based on alignment points? [Yes/No] <N>:" appears.
- Select the **NO** option; the two objects will be aligned.
- Change the **View style** to **Shades of Gray**.

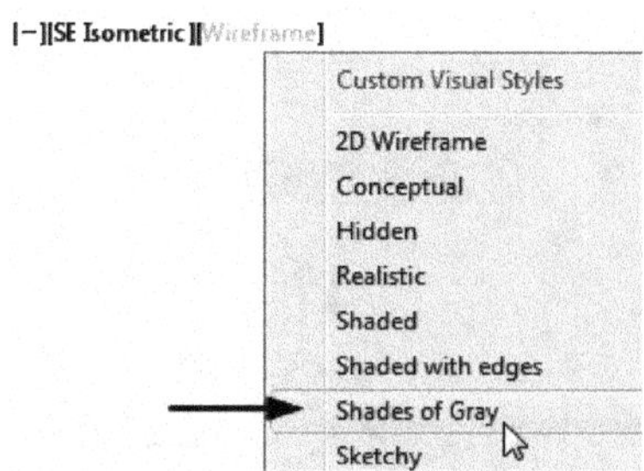

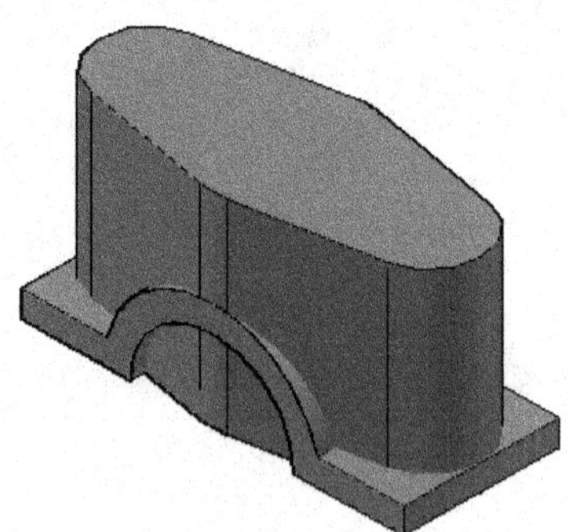

- Click **Solid > Boolean > Intersect** on the ribbon.
- Select the two objects and press ENTER; the intersection object will be created as shown below.

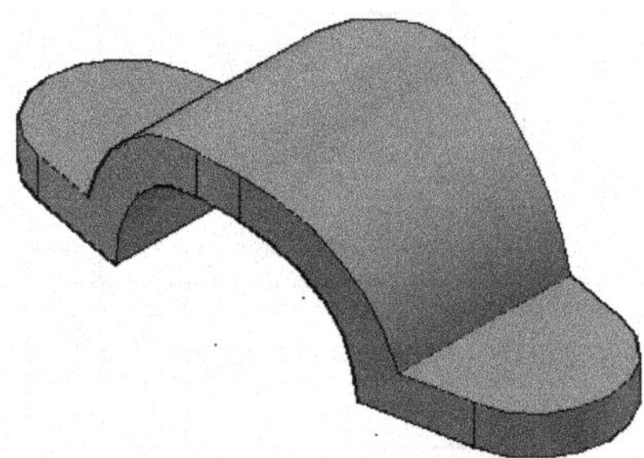

Using the Helix tool

The **Helix** tool is used to create a spiral or helix object. You can use this helix object as a path for a swept solid object.

Example 1:

- Start a new file.
- Expand the **Draw** panel in the **Home** tab and click the **Helix** button.

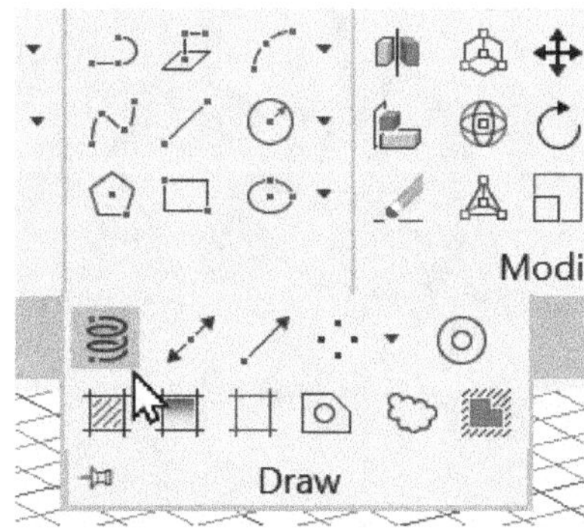

- Type 0,0 as the center point of the helix and press ENTER; the message, "Specify base radius or [Diameter]:" appears in the command line.
- Type 50 and press ENTER; the message, "Specify top radius or [Diameter] <50.0000>:" appears.
- Type 0 and press ENTER; the message, "Specify helix height or [Axis endpoint/Turns/turn Height/tWist] <1.0000>:" appears.
- Select the **Turns** option from the command line.
- Type 8 as the number of turns and press ENTER; the message, "Specify helix height or [Axis endpoint/Turns/turn Height/tWist] <1.0000>:" appears.

- Type 0 as the height and press ENTER; the spiral curve will be created as shown in the figure.

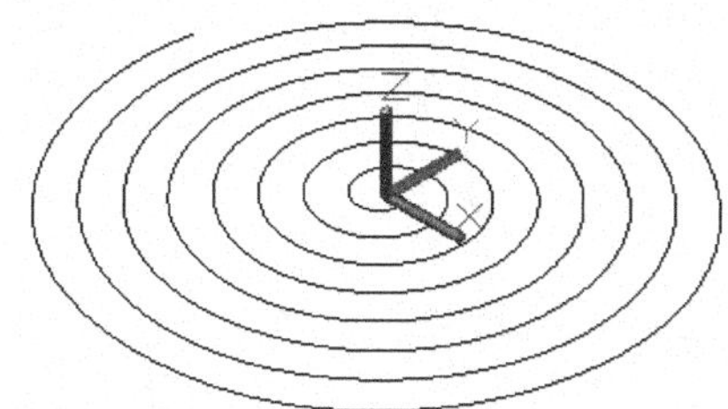

Example 2:

- Start a new file.

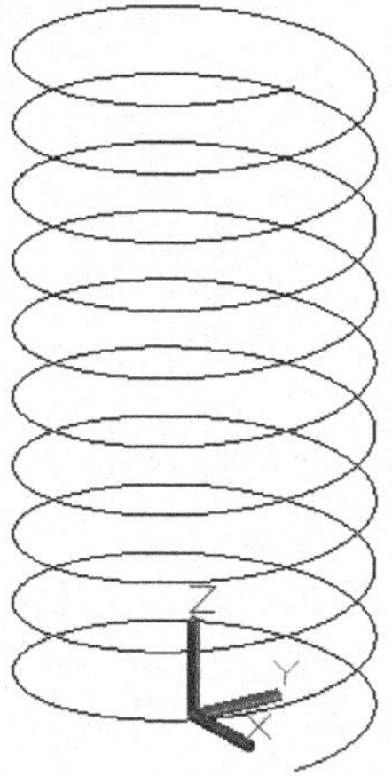

- Type HELIX in the command line and press ENTER.
- Type 0, 0 as the center point of the helix.
- Type 50 as the base radius and press ENTER.
- Press ENTER to accept 50 as the top radius.
- Select the **turn Height** option from the command line.
- Type 20 as the turn height (pitch) and press ENTER.
- Type 200 as the total height of the helix and press ENTER; the helix will be created as shown in the figure.

Exercises

Create 3D models using the drawing views and dimensions.

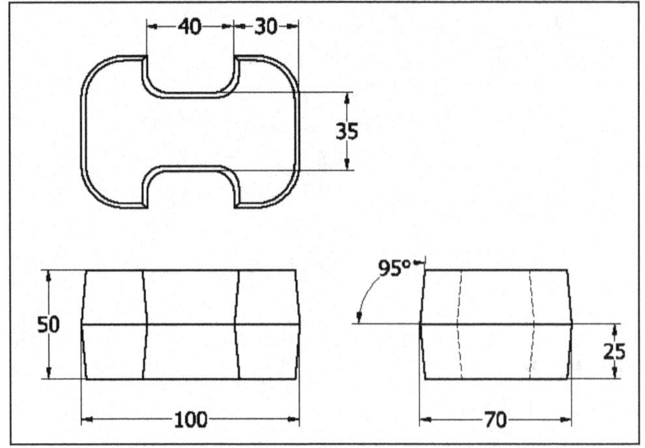

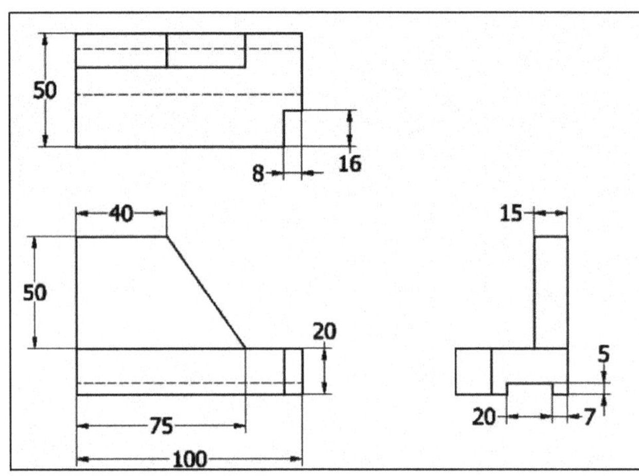

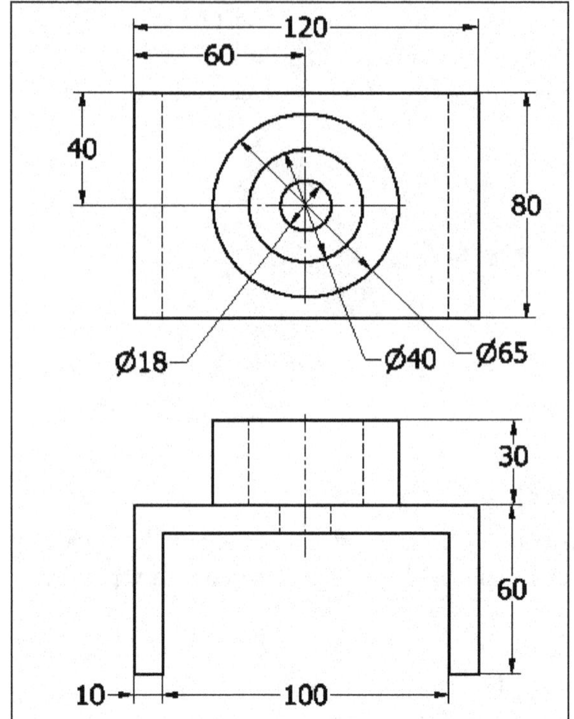

Chapter 13: Solid Editing & generating 2D views

In this chapter, you will learn to do the following:

- **Move objects in 3D space**
- **Create 3D Arrays**
- **Mirror objects in 3D space**
- **Fillet edges**
- **Taper faces of a solid object**
- **Offset faces**
- **Rotate objects**
- **Create 3D Polylines**
- **Shell objects**
- **Chamfer edges**
- **Create Live sections**
- **Generate 2D views of a 3D model**
- **Create section and detailed views**

Introduction

In the previous chapter, you have learned to create simple solid objects. Now, you will learn to use the solid editing tools to create complex models. You will also learn to generate orthographic views of 3D models.

Using the Move tool

The **Move** tool that you used in 2D drawings can also be used in 3D modeling. You can change the position of an object using the **Move** tool. The application of this tool in 3D modeling is discussed next.

Example:

- Start a new file in the **3D Modeling** workspace.
- Select **Front** from the **Restore View** drop-down of the **View** panel.
- Create the sketch on the front view and presspull it up to 100 mm distance.

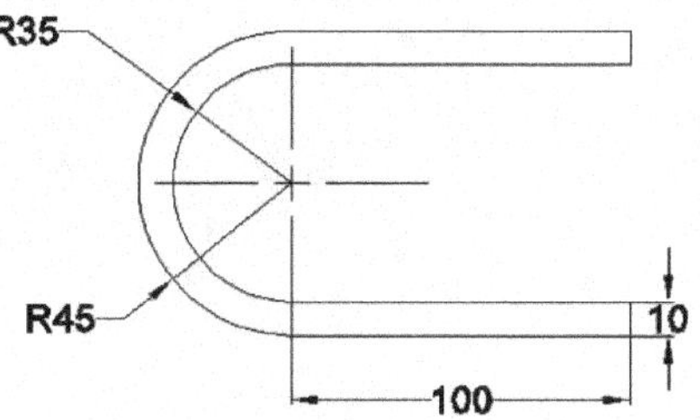

- Select **Top** from the **Restore View** drop-down of the **View** panel.
- Create a cylinder of 20 mm diameter and 20 mm in height.
- Change the view orientation to SE Isometric.

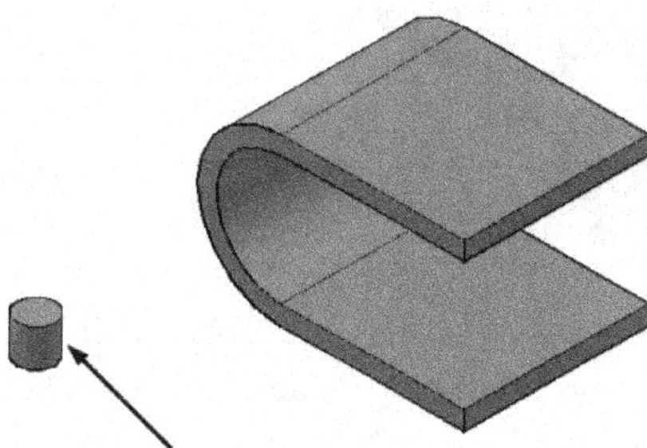

- Type **M** in the command line and press ENTER; the **Move** tool is activated.
- Select the cylinder and press ENTER.
- Select the center point of the cylinder to define the base point.

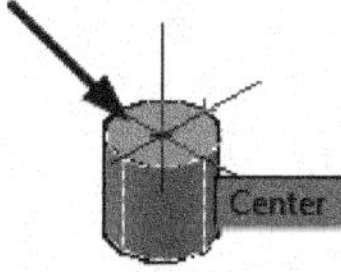

- Select the endpoint of the base object, as shown; the cylinder will be aligned to it.

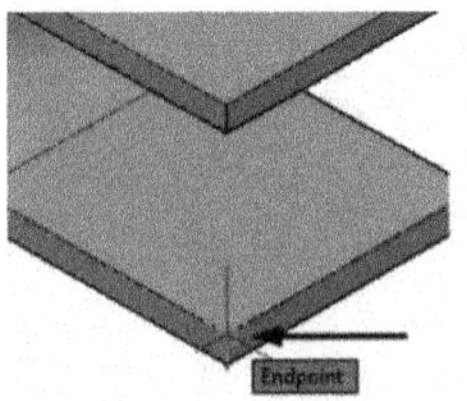
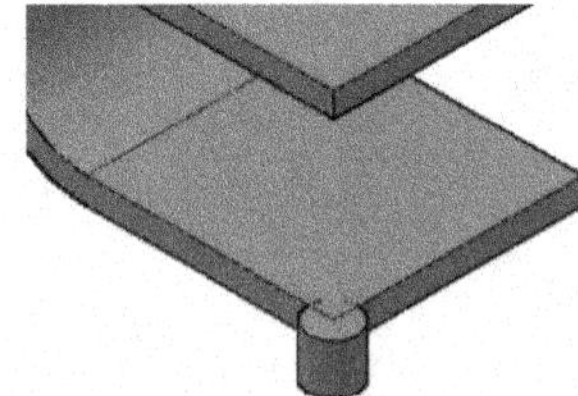

Using the 3D Move tool

The **3D Move** tool is similar to the **Move** tool. You can use this tool to move objects in 3D space. By default, the **3D Move** tool is activated, and the **Move gizmo** is displayed when you select an object. You can use the **Move gizmo** to move the object along a particular axis.

- Select the cylinder to display the **Move gizmo** tool.
- Select the X-axis (Red arrow) of the gizmo and move the pointer backward.

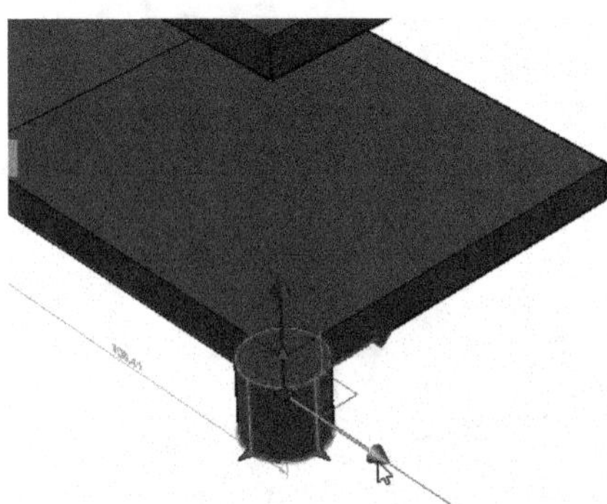

- Type 20 and press ENTER; the cylinder will be moved through a 20 mm distance along the X-axis.

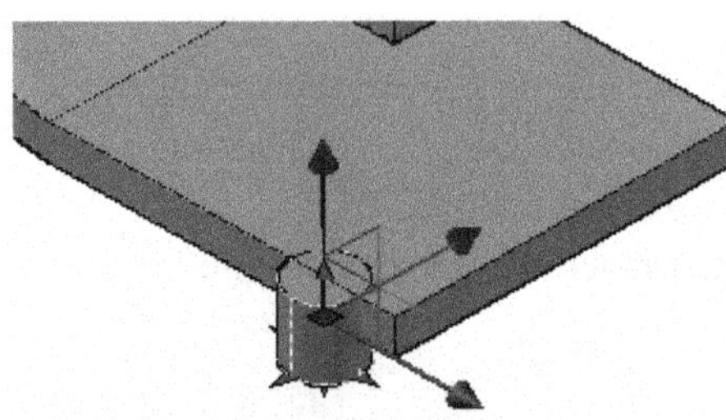

- Select the Y-axis (Green arrow) of the gizmo and move the pointer toward the right.
- Type 20 and press ENTER; the cylinder will be moved, as shown below.

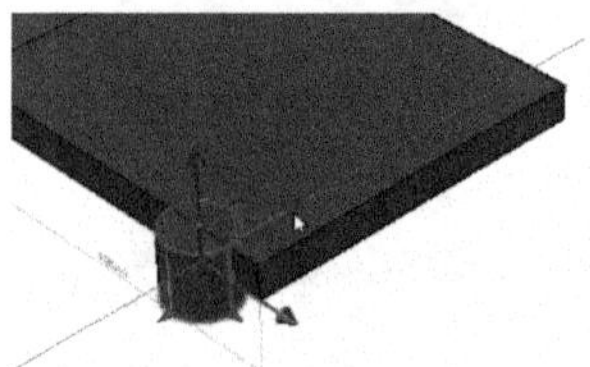
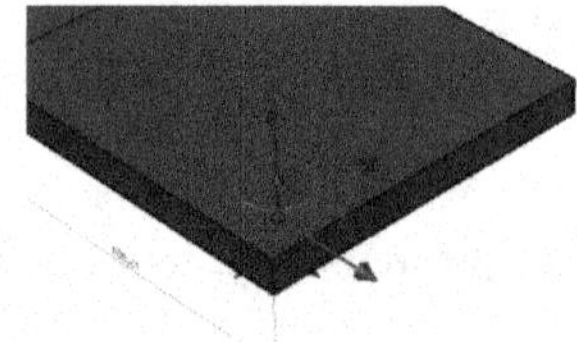

Using the Array tool

The **Array** tool is used to create Rectangular, path, and polar arrays. You can create a rectangular array by specifying the item count and distance along the X, Y, and Z directions.

Example 1 (Rectangular Array)

- Type **ARRAY** in the command line and press ENTER.
- Select the cylinder from the model and press ENTER; the message, "Enter array type [Rectangular Path POlar] <Path>:" appears in the command line.
- Select the **Rectangular** option from the command line.
- On the **Array Creation** tab, type 2 in the **Columns**, **Rows**, and **Levels** boxes, respectively.
- Type -40, 60, 80 in the **Between** boxes of the **Columns**, **Rows**, and **Levels** panels, respectively.
- Deactivate the **Associative** icon on the **Array Creation** tab.
- Click **Close Array** on the **Array Creation** tab.

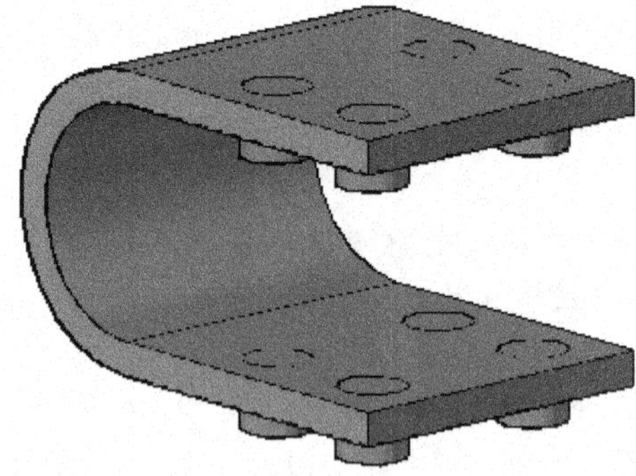

- Type **SU** in the command line and press ENTER; the **Subtract** tool will be activated.
- Select the base object and press ENTER; the

message, "Select solids, surfaces, and regions to subtract" appears.

- Select all the cylinders and press ENTER; holes will be created on the model.

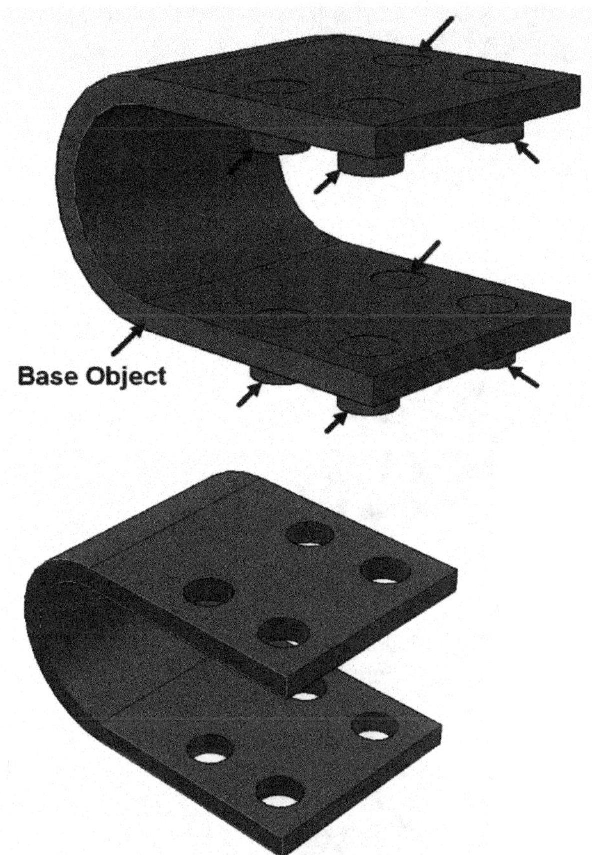

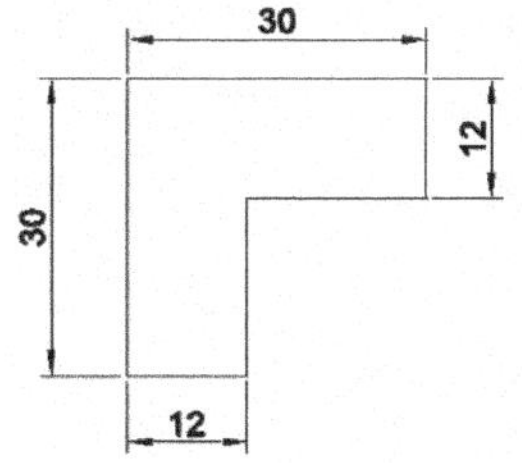

- Select **Front** from the **Restore View** drop-down in the **View** panel. Draw the sketch as shown below and extrude it up to 12 mm using the **Presspull** tool.
- Change the view orientation to SE Isometric.

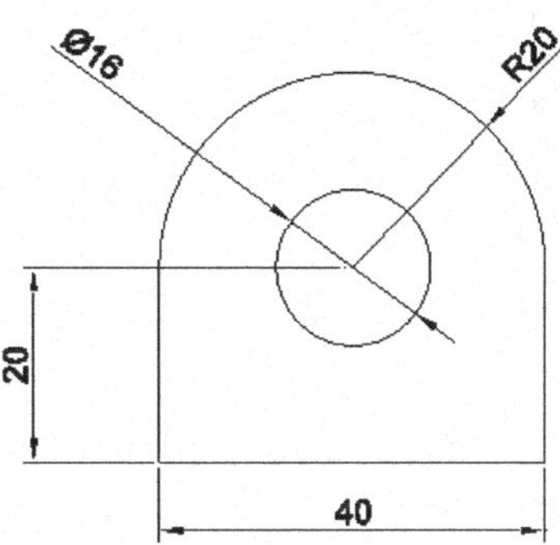

Using the 3D Align tool

The **3D Align** tool aligns one solid with another. It translates and rotates the object to align with the destination object. You need to select three points on the source object and destination object to align them together. An example of the **3D Align** tool is given next.

Example 2:

- Start AutoCAD in the **3D Modeling** workspace.
- Select **Front** from the **Restore View** drop-down in the **View** panel. Create a solid object, as shown below. The extrusion distance is 40 mm.

- Deactivate the **3D Object Snap** button on the status bar.
- Type **DS** in the command line and press ENTER; the **Drafting Settings** dialog appears.
- Click the **Object Snap** tab and **Clear All** the **Object Snap** modes.
- Now, select the **Endpoint** option and click **OK**.

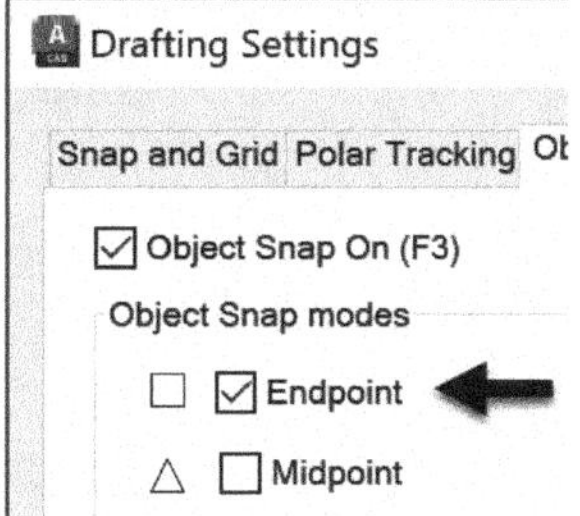

- Click **Home > Modify > 3D Align** on the ribbon.

- Select the second solid object from the graphics window and press ENTER; the message, "Specify base point or [Copy]:" appears in the command line.

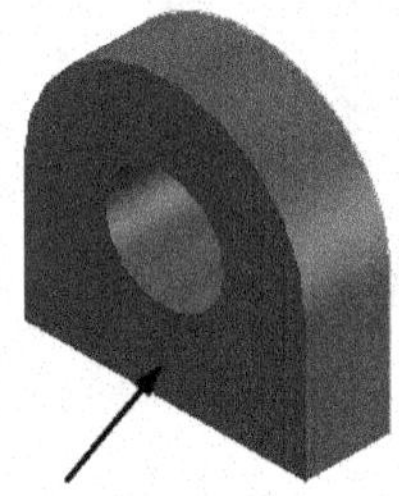

- Select the **Copy** option from the command line.
- Select three endpoints on the source object, as shown below.

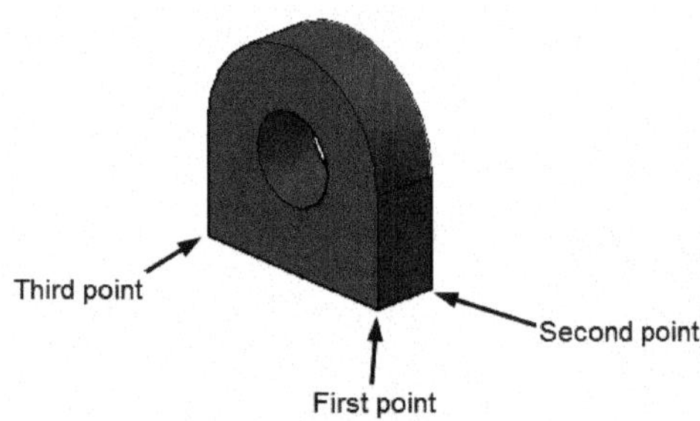

- Select three endpoints on the destination object as shown below; a copy of the source object will be aligned to the destination object.

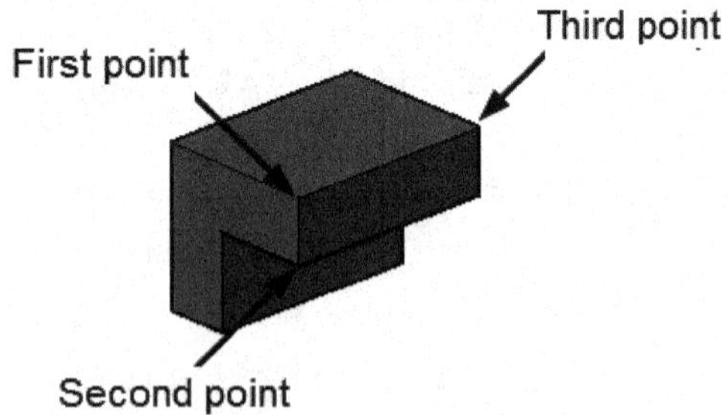

- Activate the **Ortho Mode** button on the status bar.
- Type **3DALIGN** in the command line and press ENTER.
- Select the second solid object. Press ENTER to accept the selection.

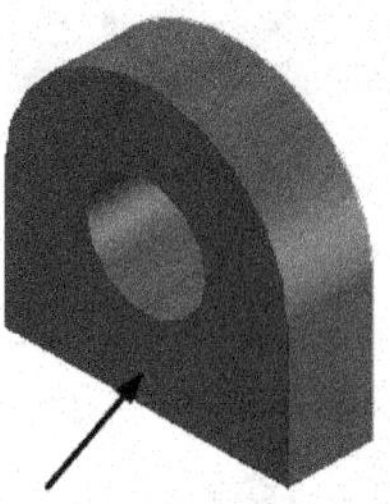

- Select the base point on the object as shown in the figure; the message, "Specify second point or [Continue] <C>:" appears in the command line.

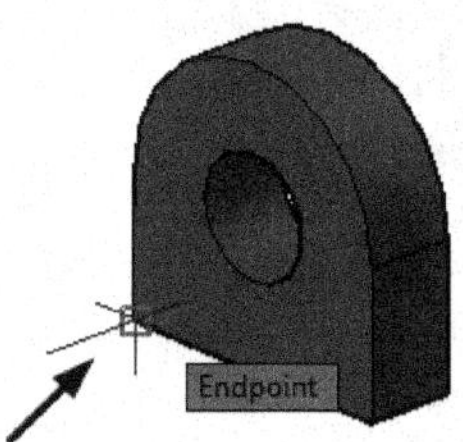

- Select the **Continue** option from the command line; the message, "Specify first destination point:" appears in the command line.
- Select the endpoint on the destination object, as shown below.

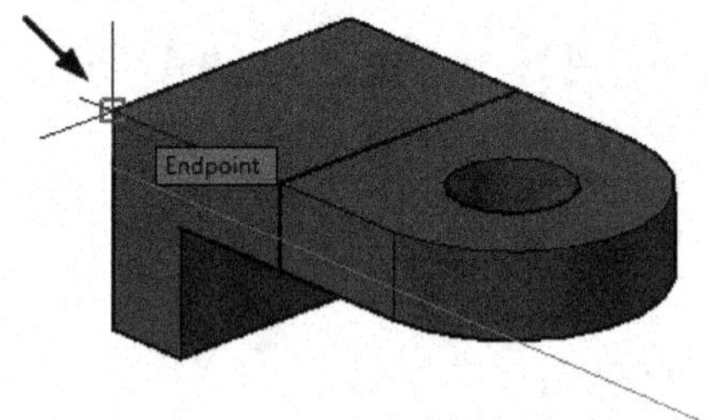

- Move the pointer along the X-direction and select the endpoint as shown in the figure; the message, "Specify third destination point or [eXit] <X>:"

appears in the command line.

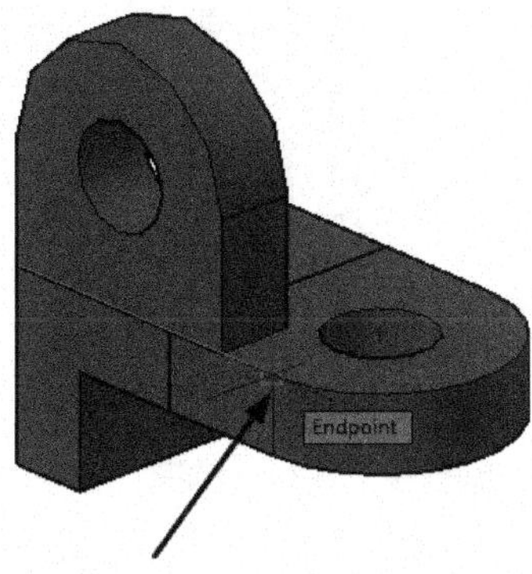

- Select the **eXit** option from the command line; the source object will be aligned, as shown below.

Using the 3D Mirror tool

The **3D Mirror** tool is similar to the **Mirror** tool. Using the **Mirror** tool, you can create a mirrored replica of an object in a 2D drawing. The objects are mirrored about an axis lying on a plane. But, with the **3D Mirror** tool, you need to define a plane about which the object will be mirrored. The **3D Mirror** tool provides many options to define the mirror plane.

- Click **Home > Modify > 3D Mirror** on the ribbon.

- Select the object to be mirrored from the model and press ENTER; the message, "Specify first point of mirror plane (3 points)," appears above the command line.

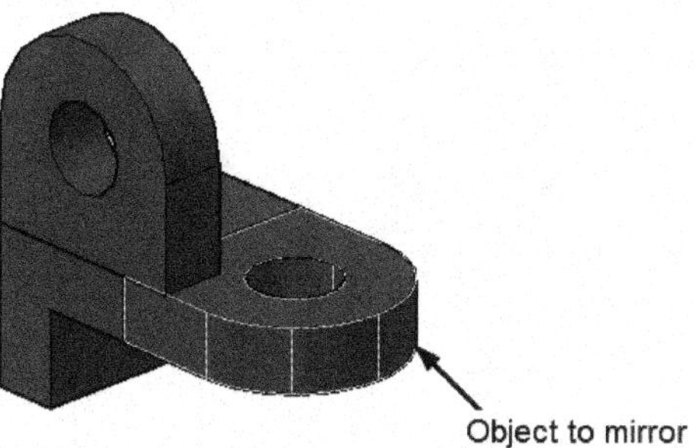

The **3points** option is selected by default to create the mirror plane. You need to specify three points to create a mirror plane. The mirror plane will pass through the selected points.

- Select the first and second points of the mirror plane, as shown below.

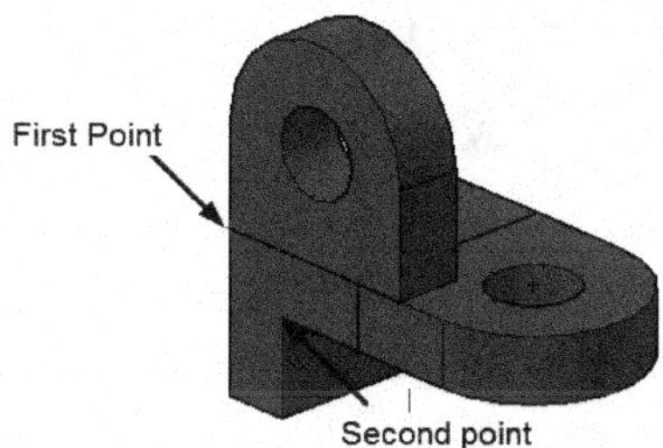

- Click the **Orbit** button on the **Navigation Bar** and rotate the model, as shown below.

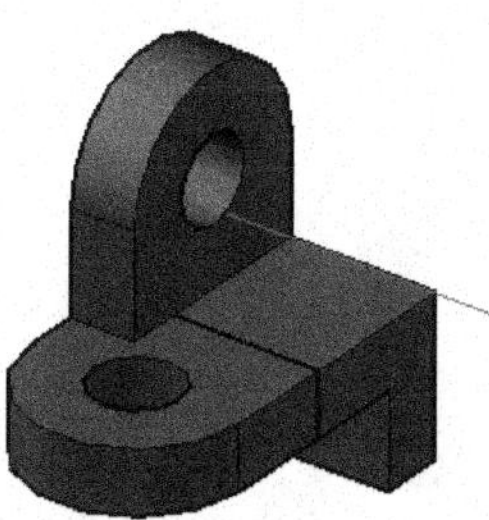

- Right-click and select **Exit** from the shortcut menu.
- Select the third point to define the mirror plane; the message, "Delete source objects? [Yes No] <N>:" appears in the command line.

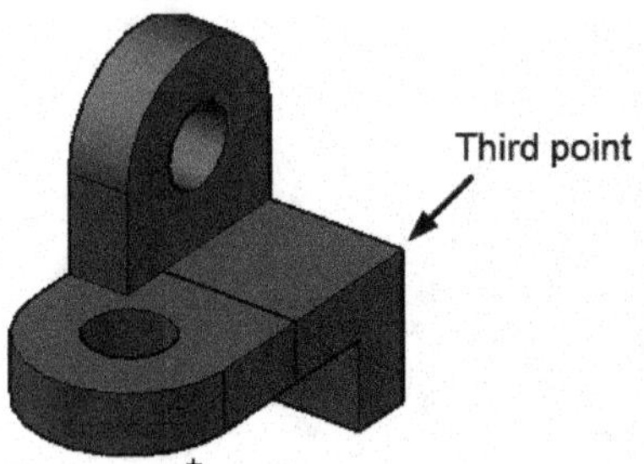

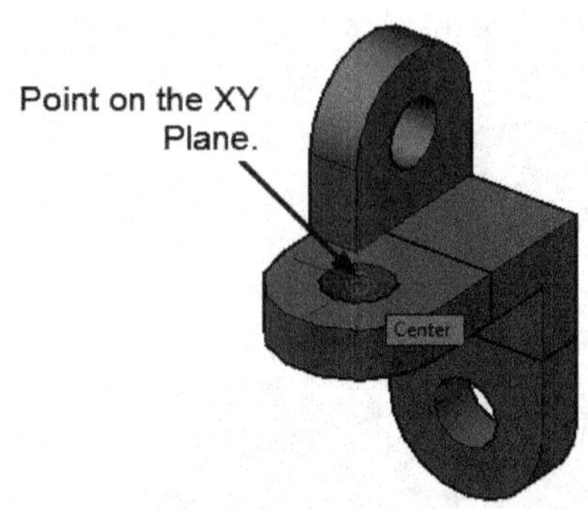

- Select the **No** option from the command line; the object will be mirrored.

- Select the **No** option; the object will be mirrored, as shown below.

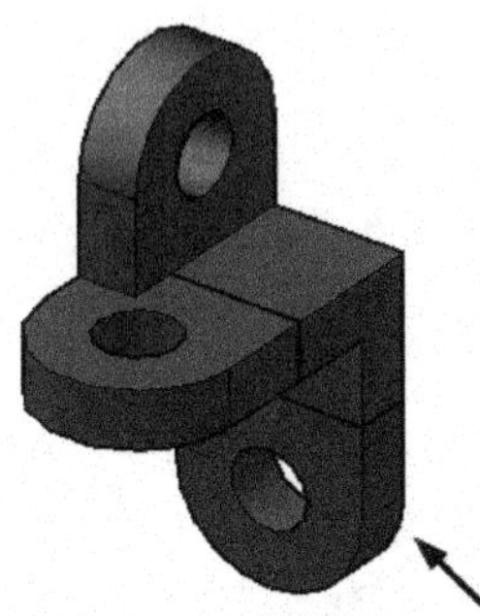

- Click the down arrow next to the **Object Snap** icon on the status bar and select **Center**.
- Type **3DMIRROR** in the command line and press ENTER.
- Select the object to be the mirror from the model and press ENTER.

- Click the **Union** button on the **Solid Editing** panel and select all the objects of the model.
- Press ENTER; the objects will be combined into a single object.
- Change the view to SE Isometric.

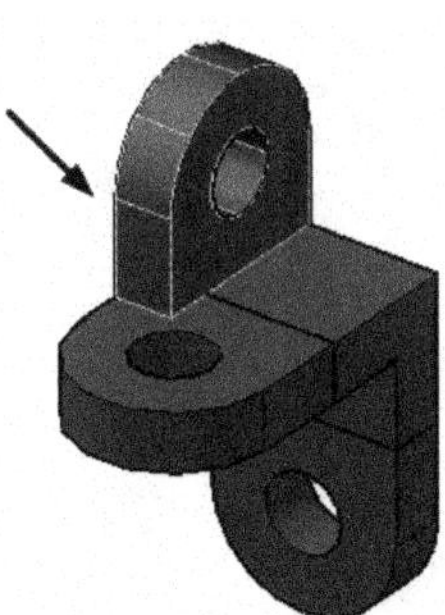

- Select the **XY** option from the command line; the message, "Specify point on XY plane <0,0,0>:" appears in the command line.

    The **XY** option creates a plane parallel to the XY plane. You need to specify a point at which the plane parallel to the XY plane will be created.

- Select the center point of the horizontal hole to define the mirror plane; the message, "Delete source objects? [Yes No] <N>:" appears in the command line.

Using the Fillet Edge tool

The **Fillet Edge** tool is used to create rounds (convex corners) or fillets (concave corners) on solid objects, just as in 2D drawings.

- Click **Solid > Solid Editing > Fillet Edge** on the ribbon (or) type **FILLETEDGE** in the command line and press ENTER; the message, "Select an edge or [Chain Loop Radius]:"

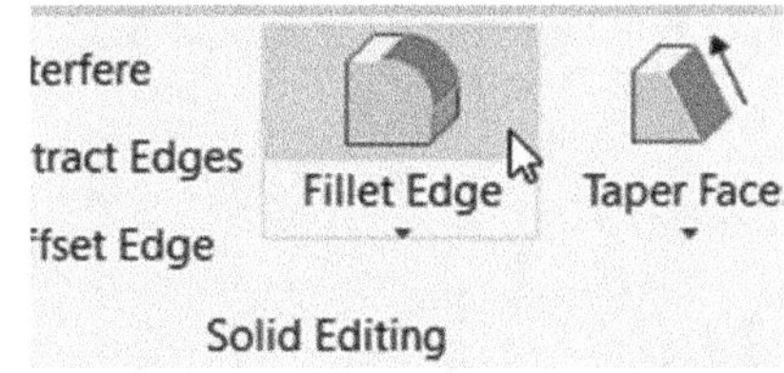

- Select the **Chain** option from the command line; the message, "Select an edge chain or [Edge Radius]:" appears.
- Select the edges from the model, as shown below; you will notice that a chain of edges is selected.

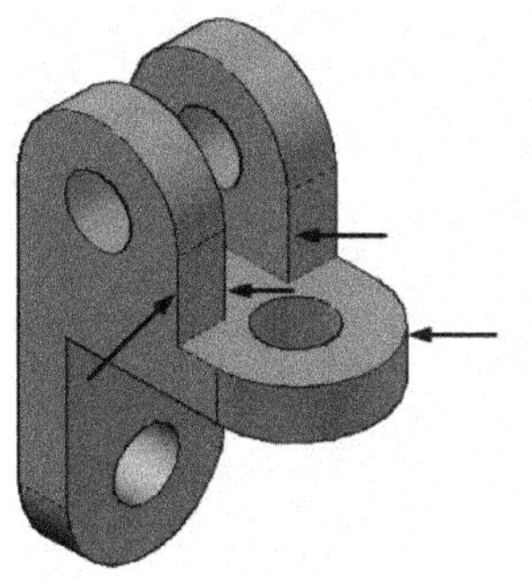

- Select the **Radius** option from the command line; the message, "Enter fillet radius or [Expression] <1.0000>:" appears.
- Type 2 in the command line and press ENTER.
- Press ENTER; the message, "Press Enter to accept the fillet or [Radius]:" appears. Also, a grip displayed on the fillets. You can use this grip to change the fillet radius dynamically.

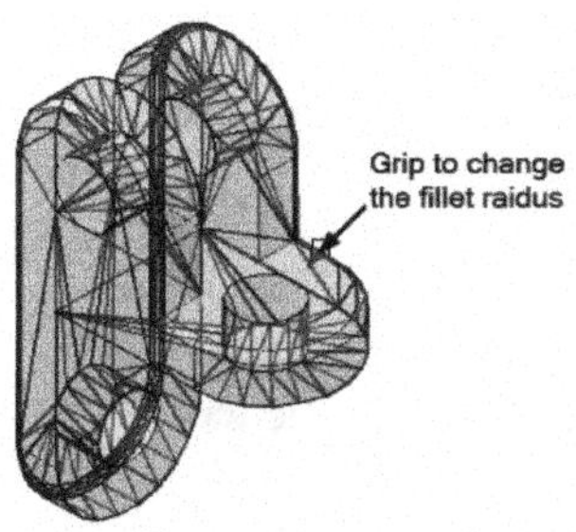

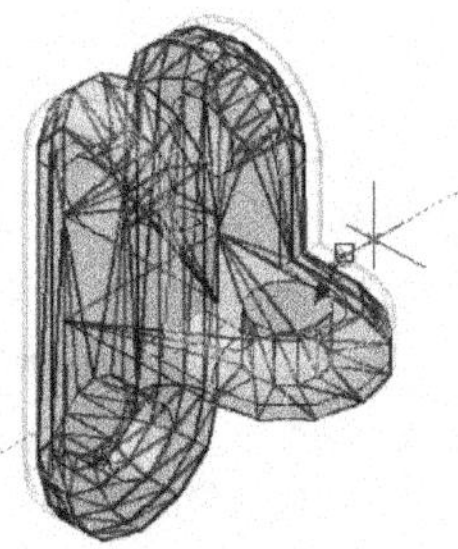

- Press ENTER to create rounds, as shown in the figure.

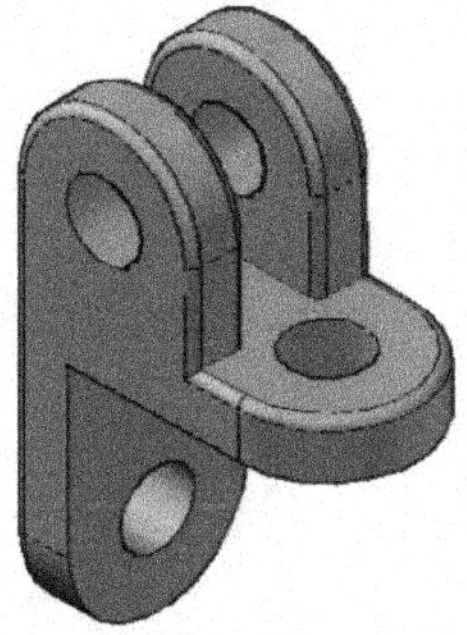

- Click the **Fillet Edge** button on the **Solid Editing** panel.
- Select the **Loop** option from the command line.
- Select the edge from the model, as shown in the figure; the edges on the front face of the model are highlighted. Also, the message, "Enter an option [Accept Next] <Accept>:" appears in the command line.

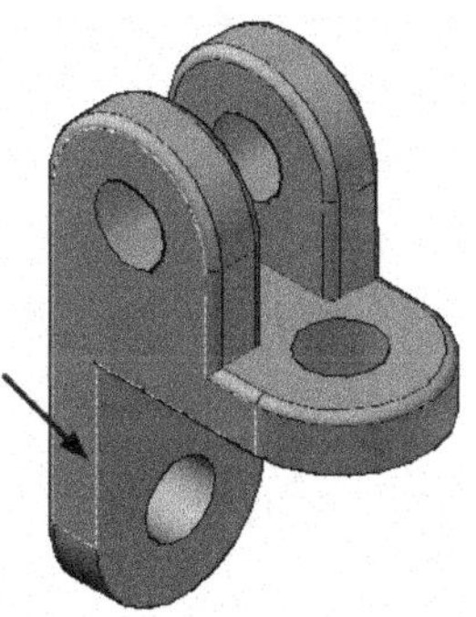

- Select the **Next** option from the command line; the edges on the side face will be highlighted.
- Select the **Accept** button; rounds and fillets are displayed on the side face.

- Likewise, select the round edge, as shown in the figure, and select the **Next** option from the command line; the edges on the bottom face of the model will be highlighted.

- Click the **Orbit** button on the **Navigation Bar** and rotate the model.
- Select the **Accept** option to view rounds and fillets on the bottom face.
- Select the **Radius** option and type 2. Press ENTER to accept.
- Press ENTER twice to create rounds, as shown in the figure.

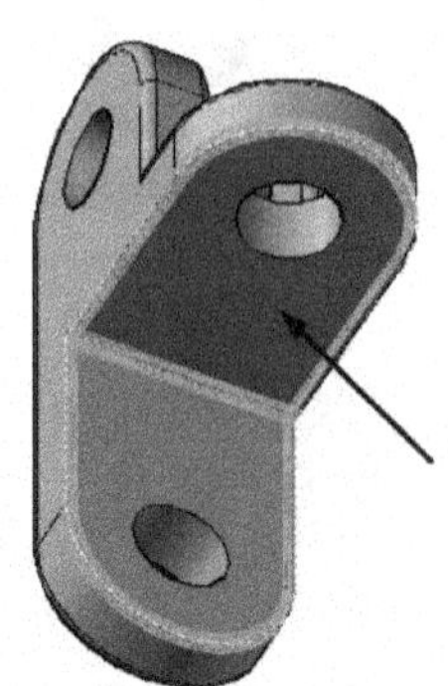

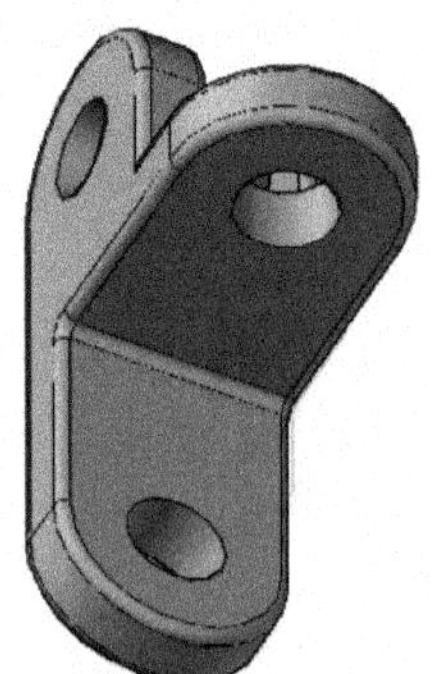

- Similarly, create fillets on the remaining edges by using the **Chain** option.

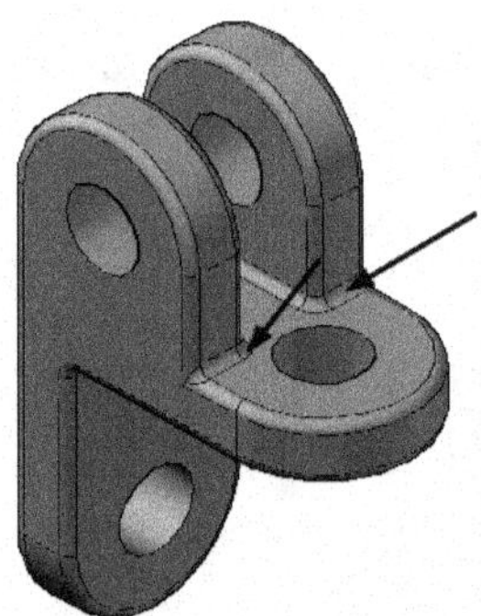

- Save and close the file.

Using the Taper Faces tool

The **Taper Faces** tool is used to taper faces. You can use this tool to change the angle of planar or curved faces.

Example 3:

In this example, you will create a cylinder and taper the outer face.

- Start a new AutoCAD file.
- Set the **Workspace** to **3D Modeling**.
- Select **Front** from the **Restore View** drop-down on the **Views** panel.
- Create a hollow cylinder with an inner and outer diameter as 140 and 150, respectively. The cylinder height is 50.

- Click **Solid > Solid Editing > Taper Faces** on the ribbon.

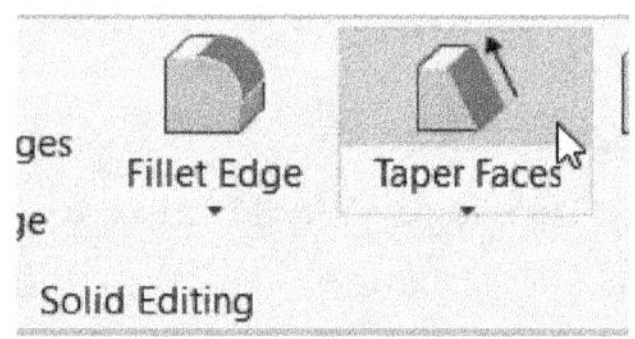

- Select the outer cylindrical face and press ENTER to accept; the message, "Specify the base point:" appears in the command line.
- Press and hold the SHIFT key and right-click to display the shortcut menu. Select the **Center** option from the shortcut menu.
- Move the pointer over the circular edge on the front face; the center point of the circular edge will be highlighted.
- Select the center point of the circular edge.
- Move the pointer along the Z-direction in the direction, as shown in the figure.
- Click to specify the axis of the taper; the message, "Specify the taper angle:" appears in the command line.

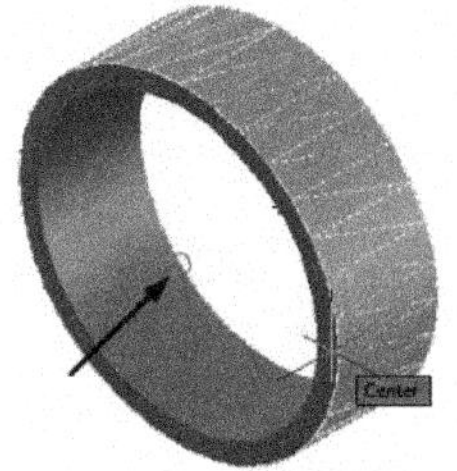
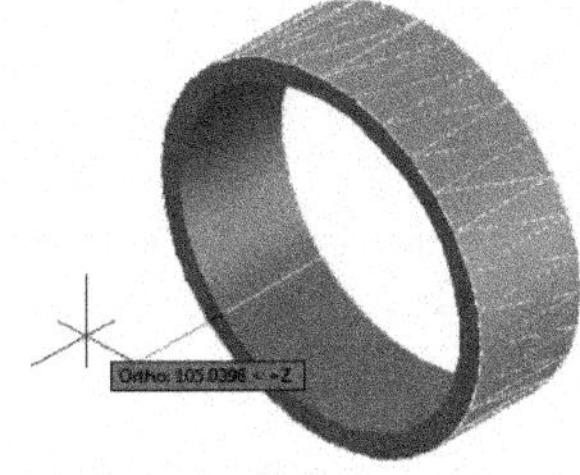

- Type 10 as the taper angle and press ENTER; the outer cylindrical face will be tapered as shown in the figure.

- Press Esc

Using the Offset Faces tool

The **Offset Faces** tool is used to move the faces of a 3D object in the perpendicular direction.

- On the ribbon, click **Solid > Selection > Selection Filter** drop-down > **Face**.

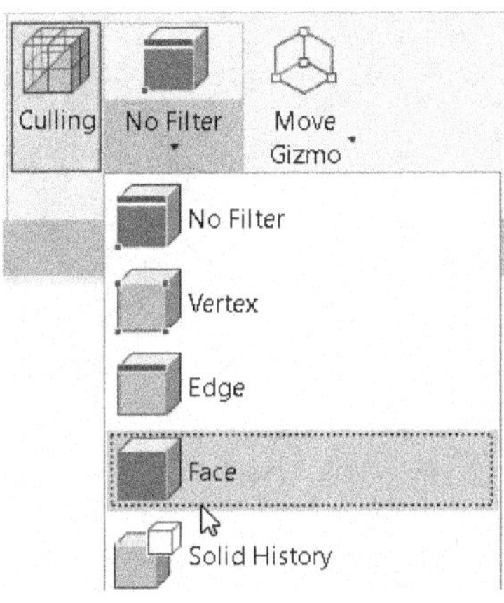

- Click **Solid > Solid Editing > Faces** drop-down > **Offset Faces** on the ribbon.

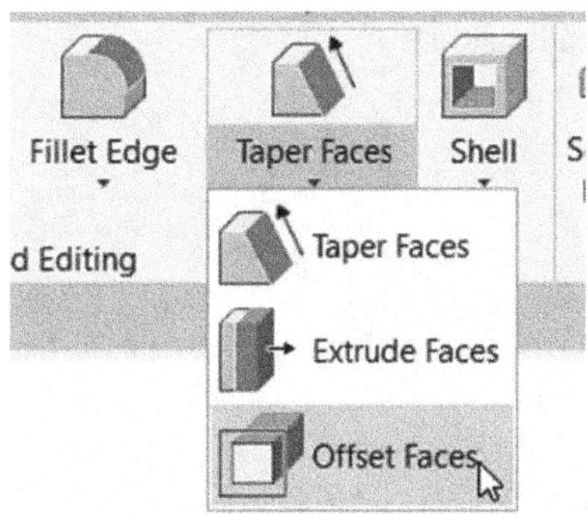

- Select the front face of the model and press ENTER; the message, "Specify the offset distance:" appears in the command line.

  Note: By mistake, if you have selected the side faces, then click the Remove option in the command line. Next, click on the side faces, and then press ENTER to remove them from the selection.

- Type -20 in the command line and press ENTER; the face will be offset.

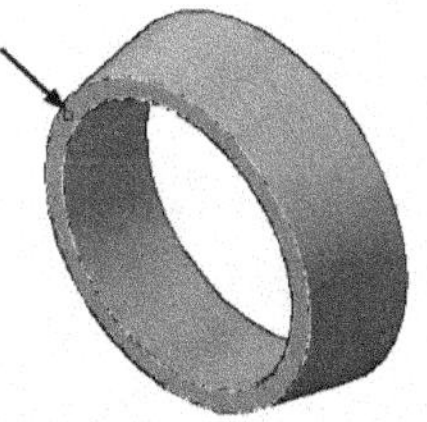

- Press Esc.
- On the ribbon, click **Solid > Selection > Selection Filter** drop-down > **No Filter**.
- Create a cylinder of 40 mm diameter and 30 mm length at the center of the hollow cylinder.

- Create a truncated cone with the following dimensions.

  Base radius: 8 mm

Top radius: 5 mm
Height: 65mm

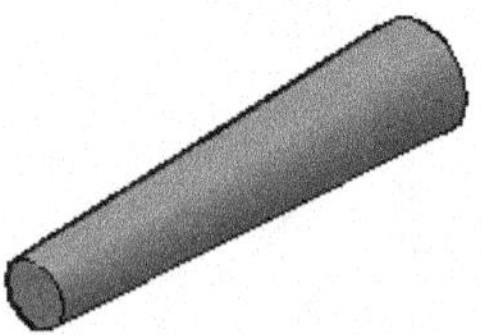

Using the 3D Rotate tool

The **3D Rotate** tool is used to rotate objects about an axis. You can define the axis of rotation by using the **Rotate Gizmo** tool. The **Rotate Gizmo** tool will be displayed when you activate the **3D Rotate** tool and select an object.

- Click **Home > Modify > 3D Rotate** on the ribbon.

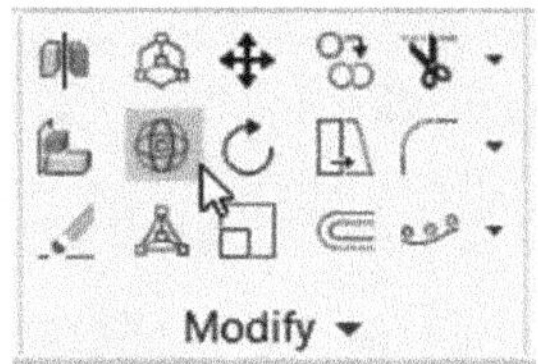

- Select the truncated cone and press ENTER; the **Rotate Gizmo** tool will be displayed.
- Select the center point of the front face as the base point; the **Rotate Gizmo** tool will be moved to the selected point.

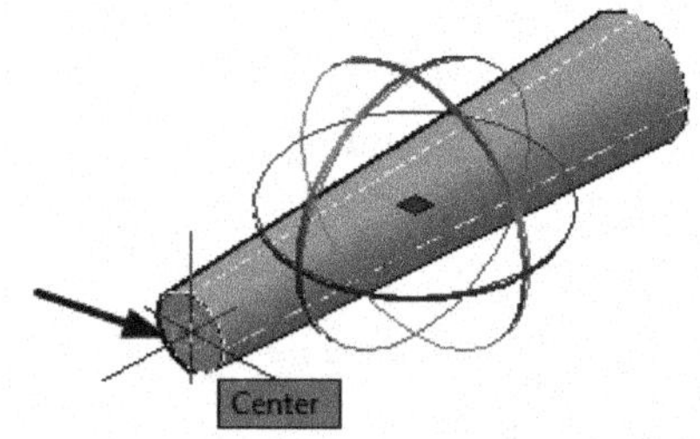

- Select the Z axis (Blue ring) of the **Rotate Gizmo**; an axis line is displayed along the Z-axis.
- Type **270** as the rotation angle and press ENTER; the cone will be rotated by 270 degrees.

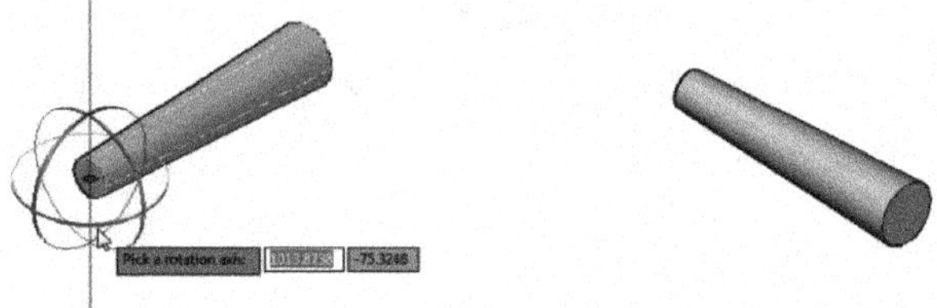

- On the status bar, click the down arrow next to the **Object Snap** icon, and then select the **Quadrant** option, if not already selected.
- Click the **Move** button on the **Modify** panel and select the cone. Press ENTER to accept.
- Select the base point and the destination point, as shown below; the cone will be placed at the destination point.

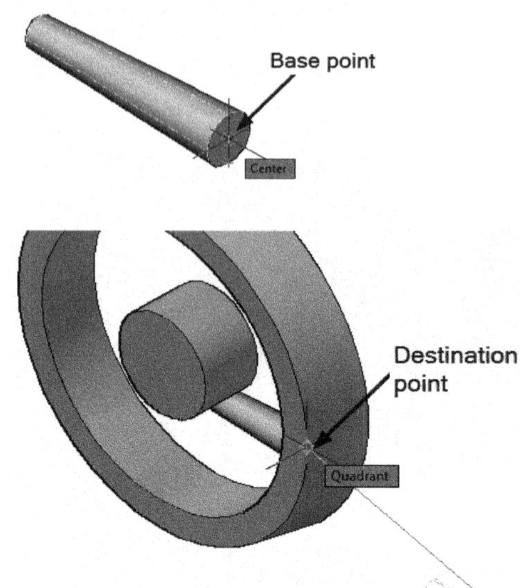

- Select the cone; the **Move Gizmo** tool will be displayed on it.
- Select the Y-axis (Green arrow) of the **Move Gizmo** tool and move the pointer toward the right.
- Type 22 in the command line and press ENTER; the cone will be moved through 22 mm.

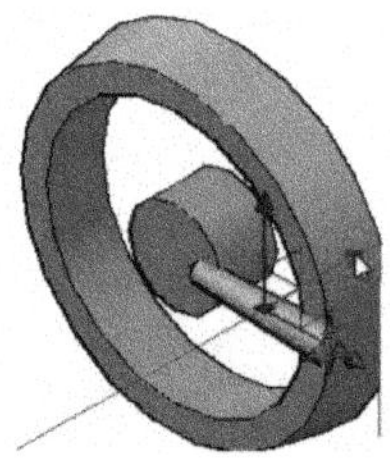
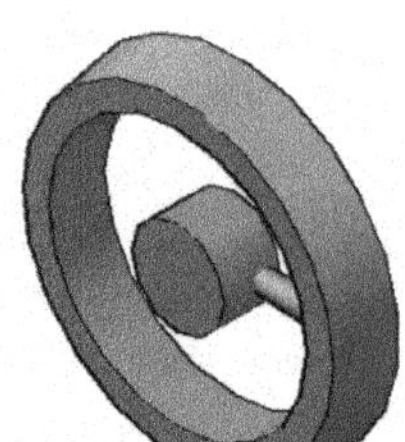

Using the 3D Polyline tool

The **3D Polyline** tool is similar to the **Polyline** tool, except that you can create a polyline by specifying coordinate points in three dimensions. Also, you can only create straight lines using this tool.

- Change the **Visual Style** of the model to **Wireframe**.
- Click **Home > Draw > 3D Polyline** on the ribbon.

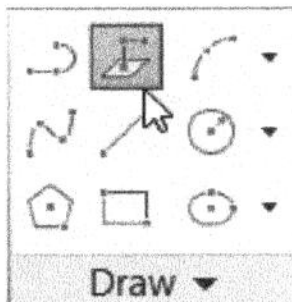

- Select the center point on the front face of the cylindrical object.
- Move the pointer toward the right and select the center point on the back face of the cylindrical object.

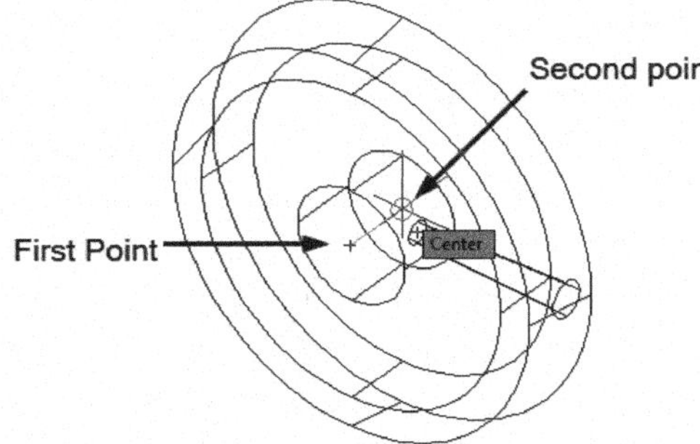

- Press ENTER; the 3D polyline will be created.

Creating a 3D Polar Array

You can create a 3D polar array by using the **Polar** option of the **3DARRAY** command. This option is similar to the **2D Polar Array** tool. The only difference between these two tools is that you need to specify an axis of rotation in 3D polar array, whereas in 2D Polar array, you need to specify an axis point. The axis of rotation in a 3D polar array can be specified by selecting two points. It allows you to create a 3D polar array about an axis in the 3D workspace.

- Type **3A** in the command line and press ENTER.
- Select the truncated cone from the model and press ENTER.
- Select the **Polar** option from the command line; the message, "Enter the number of items in the array:" appears.
- Type 6 in the command line and press ENTER; the message, "Specify the angle to fill (+=ccw, -=cw) <360>:" appears in the command line.

    Type + and press ENTER to create the polar array in counter-clockwise direction and type – to create it in the clockwise direction.
- Press ENTER to accept 360 as the fill angle; the message, "Rotate arrayed objects? [Yes No] <Y>:" appears in the command line.

- Select the **Yes** option from the command line; the message, "Specify center point of array:" appears.
- Select the first and second points of the axis, as shown in the figure; the polar array will be created.

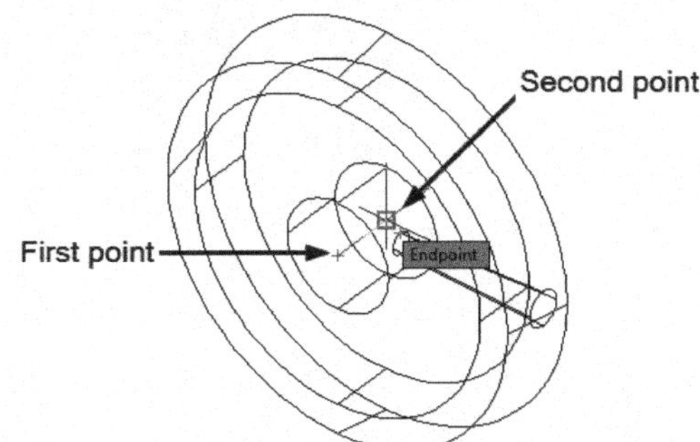

- Change the **Visual Style** to **Shades of Grey**.
- Perform the **Union** operation to combine all the objects.

Using the Shell tool

The **Shell** tool converts a solid object into a thin-walled hollow object. You need to first select the object to be shelled, and then select the faces to be removed and enter the thickness of the walls.

- Click **Solid > Solid Editing > Shell** on the ribbon.
- Select the solid model; the message, "Remove faces or [Undo Add ALL]:" appears.
- Select the front face of the cylindrical object.
- Click the **Orbit** icon on the Navigation Bar.
- Press and hold the left mouse button and drag; the model will be rotated.
- Right-click and select **Exit**.
- Select the back face of the cylindrical object.

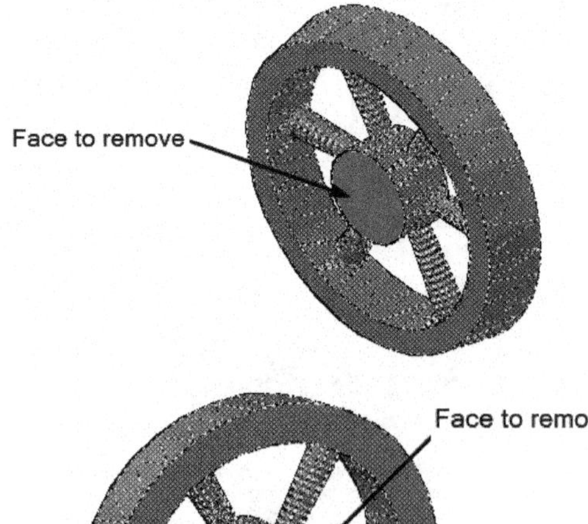

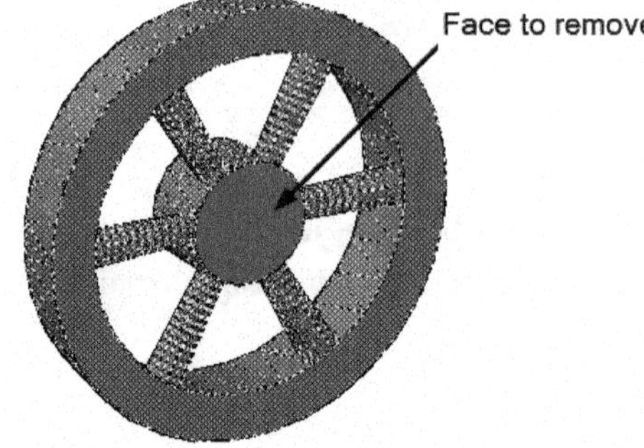

- Press ENTER; the message, "Enter the shell offset distance:" appears.
- Type 10 in the command line and press ENTER; the cylindrical object will be shelled.
- Select the **eXit** option from the command line.

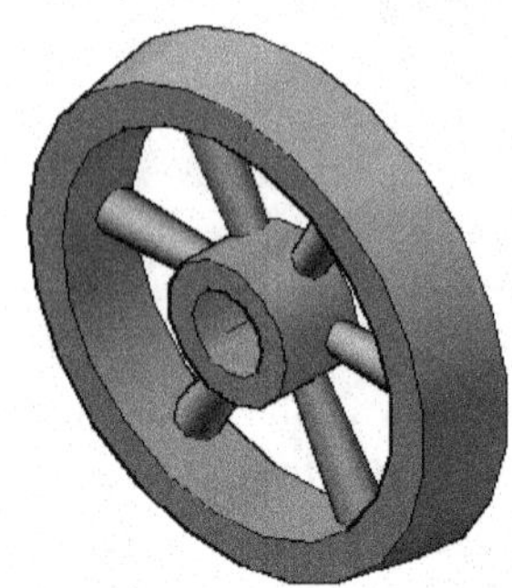

Using the Chamfer Edge tool

The **Chamfer Edge** tool is used to bevel sharp edges of a solid object. When you chamfer an edge, a wedge is created automatically, and the Boolean operation is performed to subtract it from the solid object.

- Click **Solid > Solid Editing > Chamfer Edge** on the ribbon.

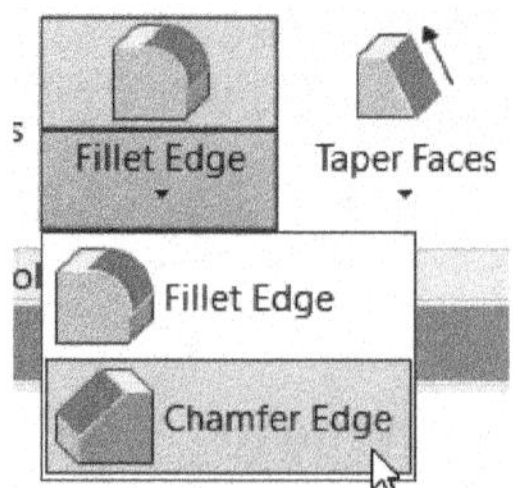

- Select the outer circular edge of the cylindrical object.
- Select the **Distance** option from the command line; the message, "Specify Distance1 or [Expression] <1.0000>:" appears.
- Type 4 in the command line and press ENTER; you will notice that the preview of the chamfer changes. Also, the message, "Specify Distance2 or [Expression] <1.0000>:" appears in the command line.
- Type 2 in the command line and press ENTER.
- Press ENTER twice to create the chamfer, as shown in the figure.

Using the Section Plane tool

The **Section Plane** tool creates a translucent cutting plane passing through a solid object to show the inside portion of it. This tool is handy when the inside portion of the solid is not visible. You can move this cutting plane dynamically to view the inside portion at different locations of the solid.

- To create a section plane, click **Solid > Section > Section Plane** on the ribbon; the message, "Select face or any point to locate section line or [Draw section Orthographic]:" appears.
- Select the **Orthographic** option from the command line.
- Select **Right**.

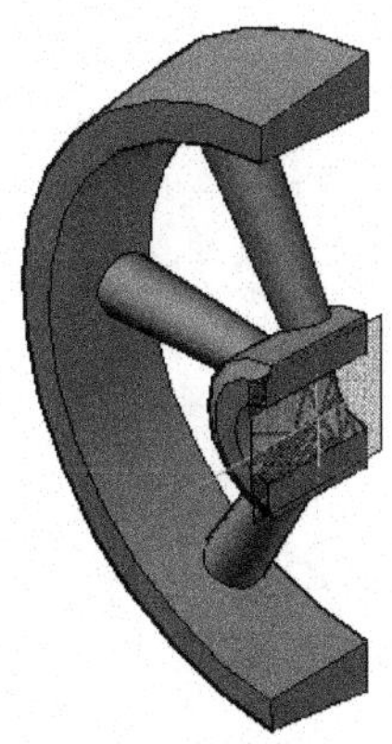

Using the Live Section tool

The **Live Section** tool is used to make a side of the section plane invisible or visible. When you create a section plane by selecting a plane, one side of the section plane will be invisible automatically. However, when you create a section plane by selecting points, you need to use the **Live Section** tool to make one side invisible. Click **Solid > Section > Live Section** on the ribbon. Next, select the section plane; one side of the section plane will be hidden or unhidden, as shown in the figure.

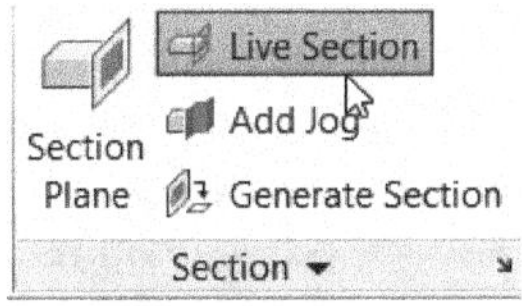

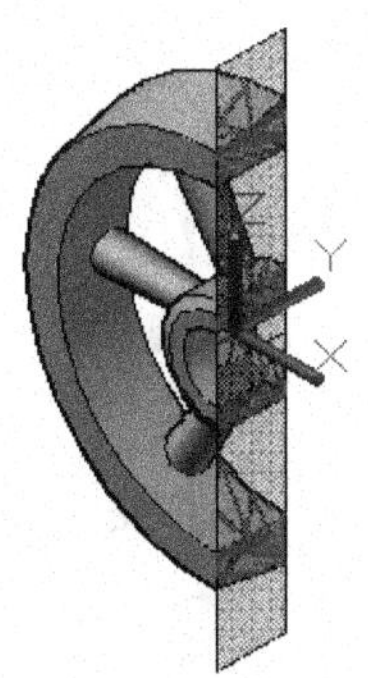

- Save the file as **Example 3**.

Creating Drawing Views

In Chapter 5, you have learned to create multi-view drawings using the standard projection techniques. Now, you will learn to generate views of a 3D model automatically.

Setting the Drafting Standard

Before you start generating the drawing views of the 3D model, you need to specify the drafting standard. It defines the way the views will be generated. To specify the drafting standard, click **Home > View > Drafting Standard (inclined arrow)** on the ribbon; the **Drafting Standard** dialog appears.

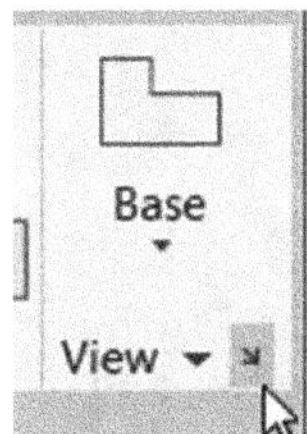

- In the **Drafting Standard** dialog, set the **Projection type** to **Third angle.**

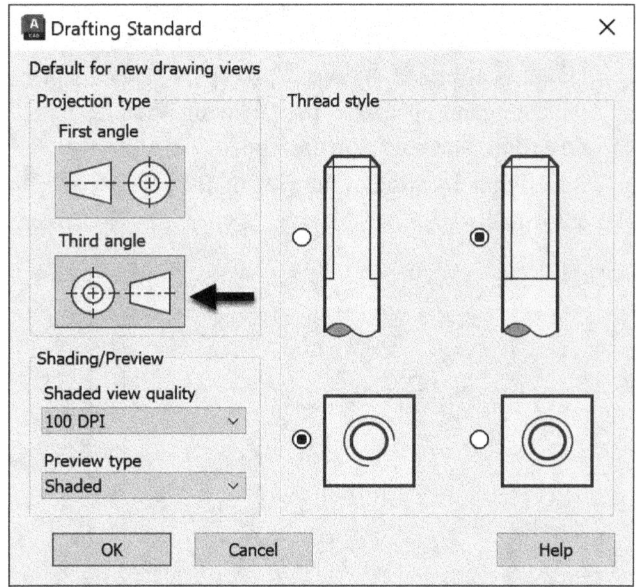

- Examine the other options in the dialog, as they are self-explanatory.
- Click the **OK** button.

Creating a Base View

The base view will be the first view of the drawing. It can be any view (front, top, right, left, bottom, or back view) of the model. But commonly, the front or top views of the model are generated first.

- Open the **Example 3.dwg,** if it is not already opened.

- To generate the base view of the model, click **Home > View > Base > From Model Space** on the ribbon; the message, "Select objects or [Entire model] <Entire model>:" appears in the command line.

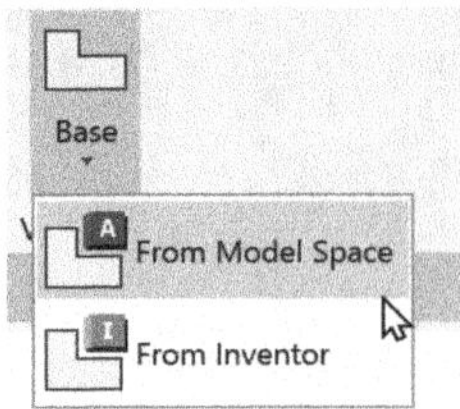

- Select the **Entire model** option from the command line; the model in the model space will be selected and the message, "Enter new or existing layout name to make current or [?] <Layout1>:" appears in the command line.
- Press ENTER to select **Layout 1**; the base view will be attached to the pointer and the message, "Specify location of base view or [Type sElect Orientation Hidden lines Scale Visibility] <Type>:" appears in the command line. Also, the **Drawing View Creation** tab appears in the ribbon.
- Specify the location of the view in the paper space, as shown below.

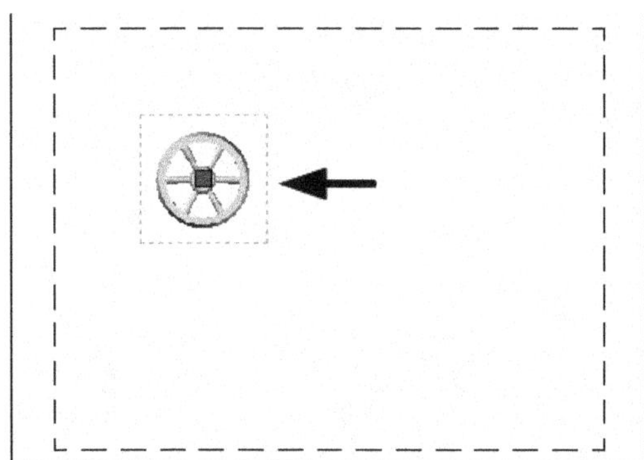

- In the **Drawing View Creation** tab, set the **Orientation** to **Front**.
- Select the **Visible Lines** option from the **Hidden Lines** drop-down.

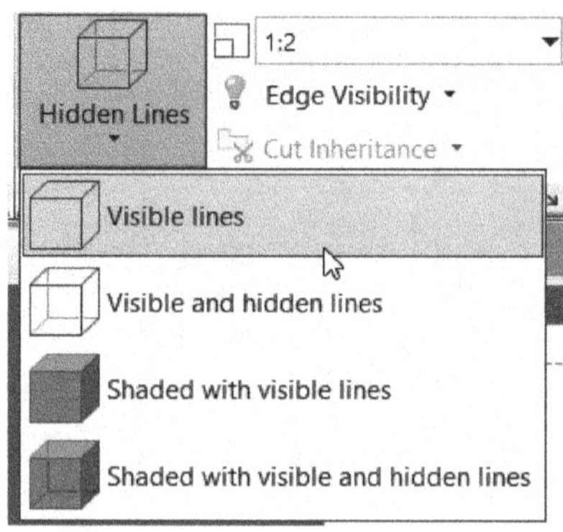

- Set the **Scale** in the **Appearance** panel to **1:4**.
- Click the **OK** button on the **Create** panel to create the base view; a projected view will be attached to the pointer, and you will be asked to specify its location. You will learn to create projected views in the next section.
- Press ENTER to exit the command.

Creating a Projected View

A projected view can be created from an existing view. It can be an orthographic view or isometric view generated by projecting from a base view or any other existing view.

- To create a projected view, click **Layout > Create View > Projected** on the ribbon, and then select the base view from **Layout 1**; the projected view will be attached to the pointer.

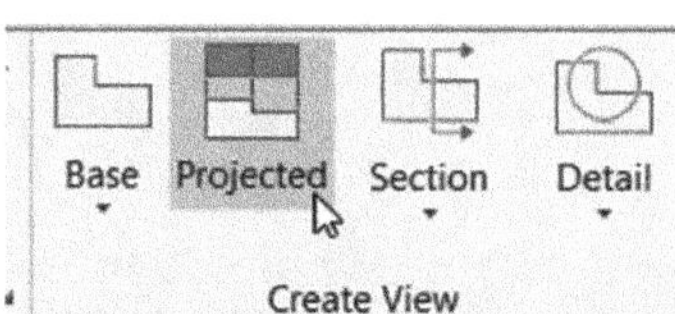

- Move the pointer downward and specify the location of the projected view, as shown below.

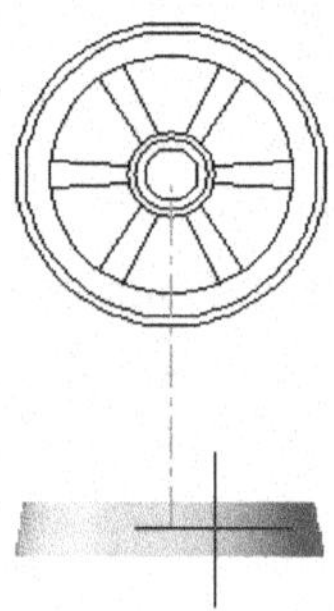

- Move the pointer diagonally toward the top-right corner and place the isometric view, as shown below.

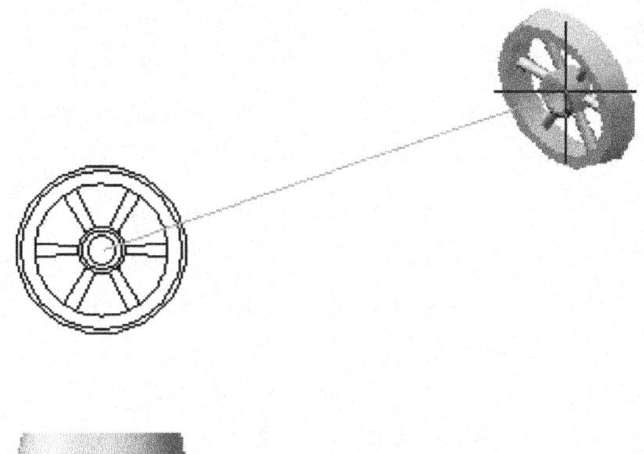

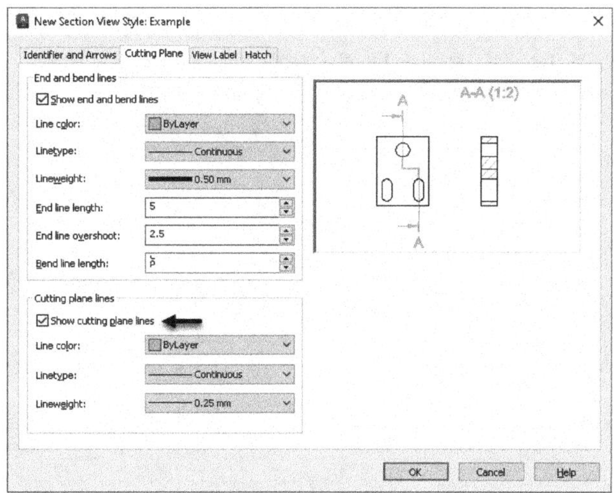

- Select the **eXit** option from the command line to exit the command.

Creating Section Views

In Chapter 8, you have learned to create section views manually. Now, you will learn to generate section views automatically from a 3D model. You can create different types of section views using the tools available in the **Section** drop-down in the **Create Views** panel.

Creating the Section View Style

Section View Style defines the display of the section view and the cutting plane. To create a section view style, click **Layout > Styles and Standards > Section View Style** on the ribbon; the **Section View Style Manager** dialog appears. Click the **New** button in the **Section View Style Manager** dialog; the **Create New Section View Style** dialog appears. Type **Example** in the **New Style Name** box and click **Continue**; the **New Section View Style** dialog appears. In this dialog, click the **Cutting Plane** tab and select the **Show cutting plane lines** option.

Click the **Hatch** tab and set the **Hatch Scale** to **0.5** and click **OK**. Click the **Set current** button on the **Section View Style Manager** dialog and click **Close**.

Creating a Full Section View

To create a full section view, click **Layout > Create Views > Section > Full** on the ribbon. Next, select the base view from the layout. After selecting the base view, you need to specify the start and endpoints of the cutting plane. Select the start point of the cutting plane, as shown below. Move the pointer vertically upward and specify the endpoint of the cutting plane.

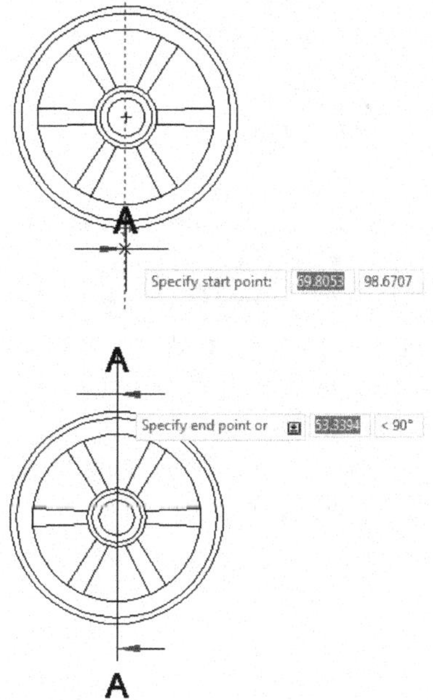

Move the pointer toward the right and click to specify the location of the section view. Select the **eXit** option to create the section view.

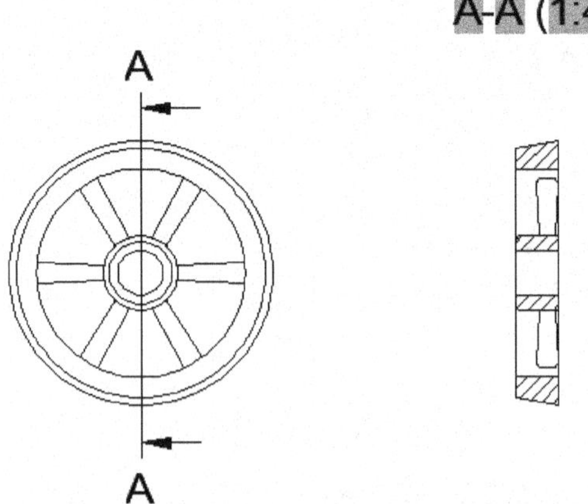

Creating a Detailed View

A detailed view is created to enlarge and view small portions of a drawing.

- To create a detailed view, click **Layout > Create Views > Detail > Circular** on the ribbon; the message, "Select parent view," appears in the command line.

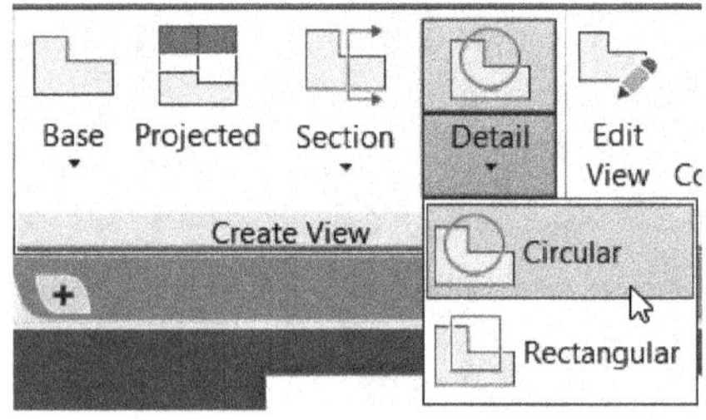

- Select the section view from the layout; the message, "Specify center point or [Hidden lines Scale Visibility Boundary model Edge Annotation] <Boundary>:" appears in the command line.
- Select a point on the section view, as shown below; the message, "Specify size of boundary or [Rectangular Undo]:" appears in the command line.
- Draw a circle similar to the one shown below.

- Next, place the detailed view on the lower right corner of the layout.
- Select the **Smooth with border** button on the **Model Edge** panel of the **Detail View Creation** tab.

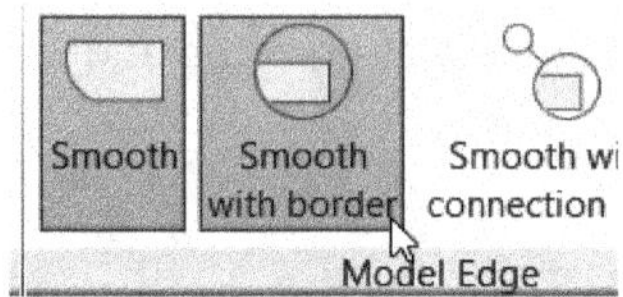

- Press Enter; the detail view will be created.

Exercises

Create 3D models using the drawing views and dimensions.

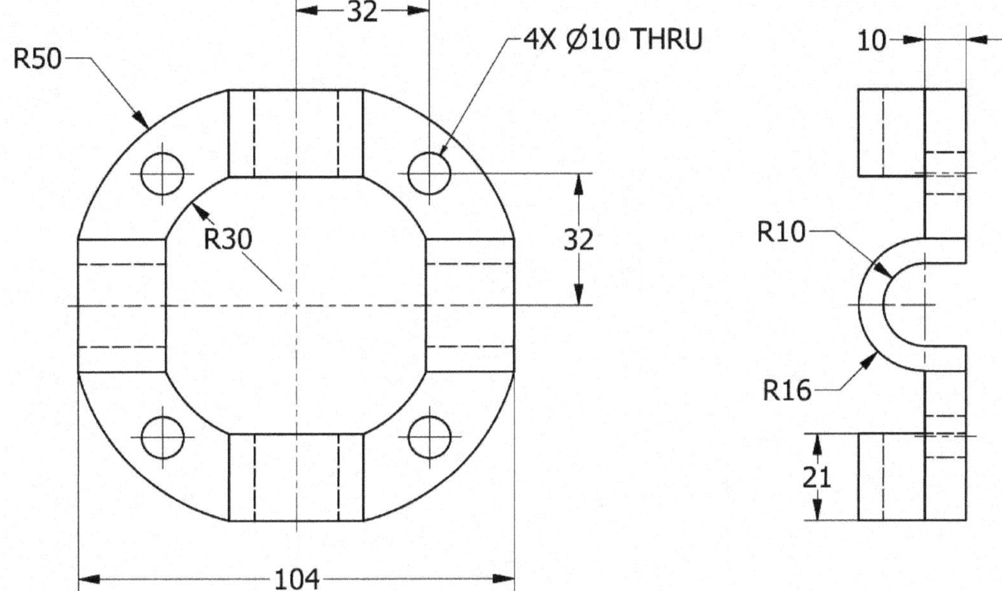

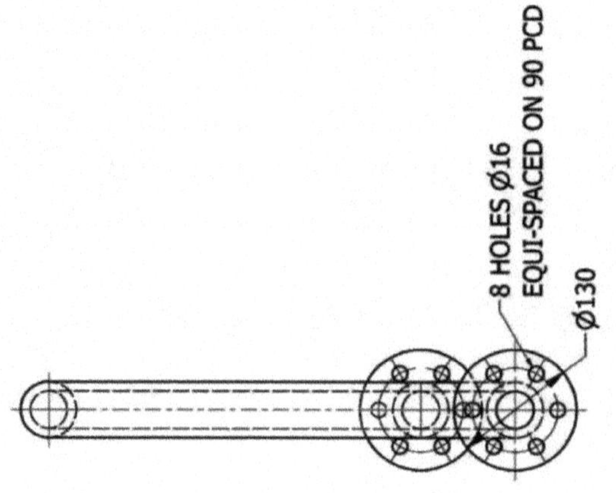
8 HOLES Ø16
EQUI-SPACED ON 90 PCD
Ø130

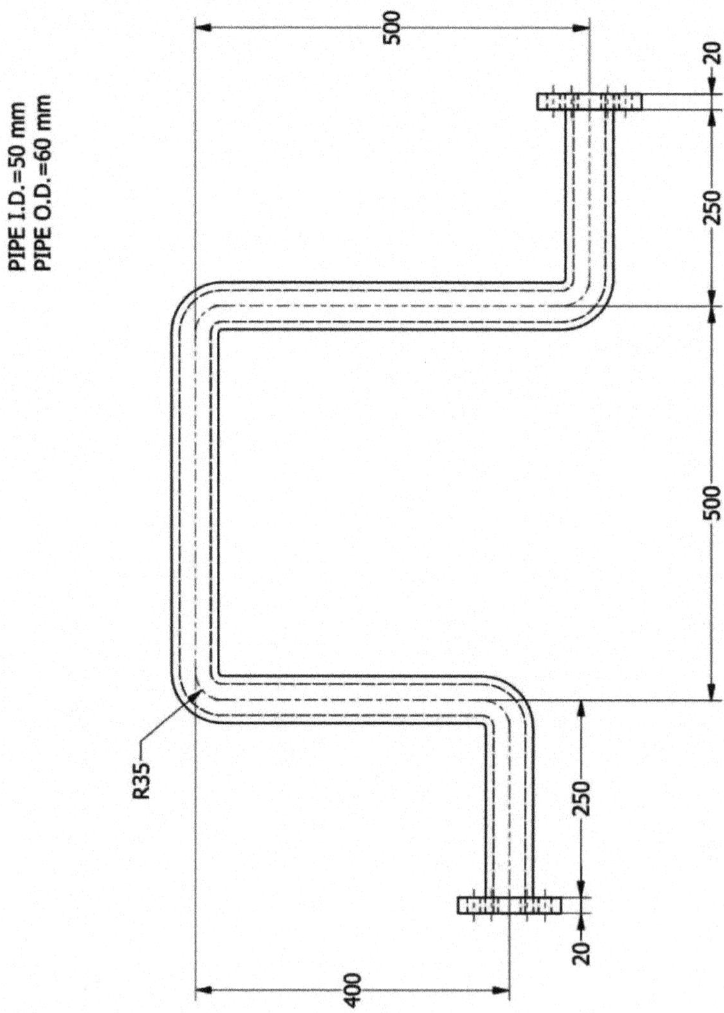
PIPE I.D.=50 mm
PIPE O.D.=60 mm
500
20
250
500
R35
250
20
400

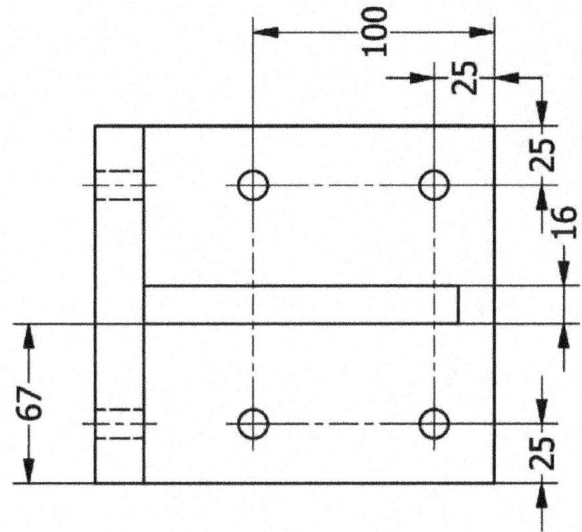

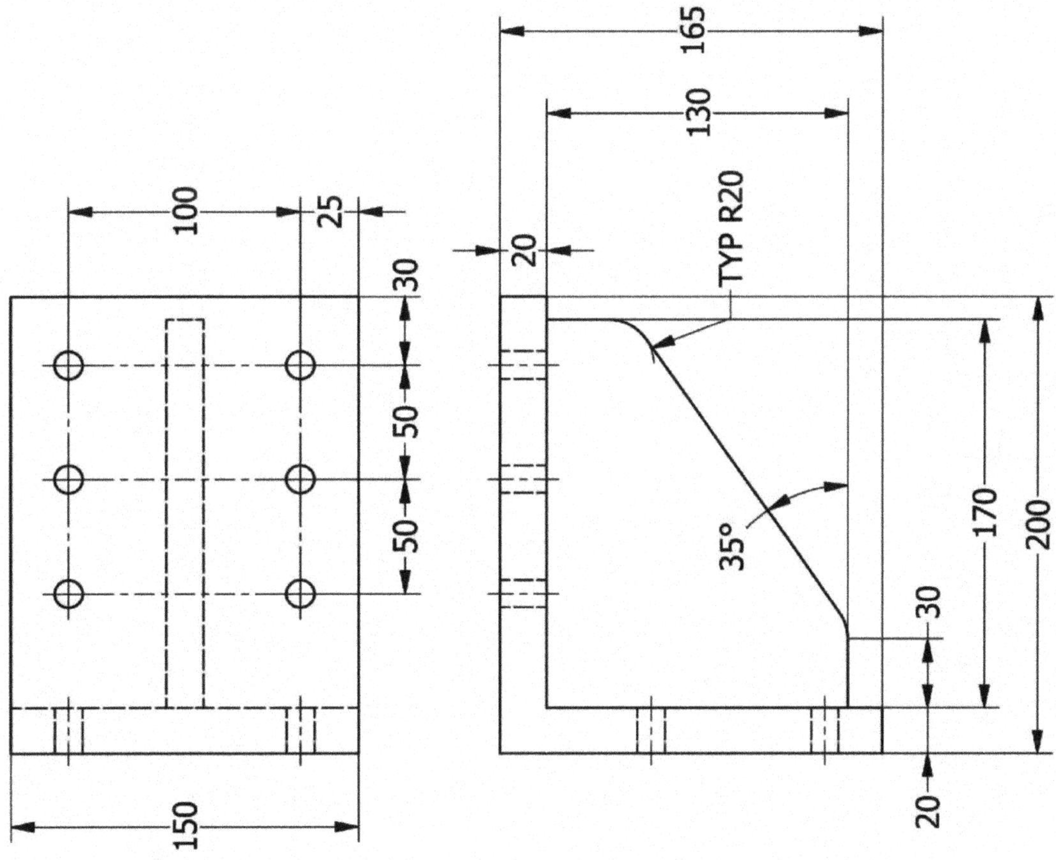

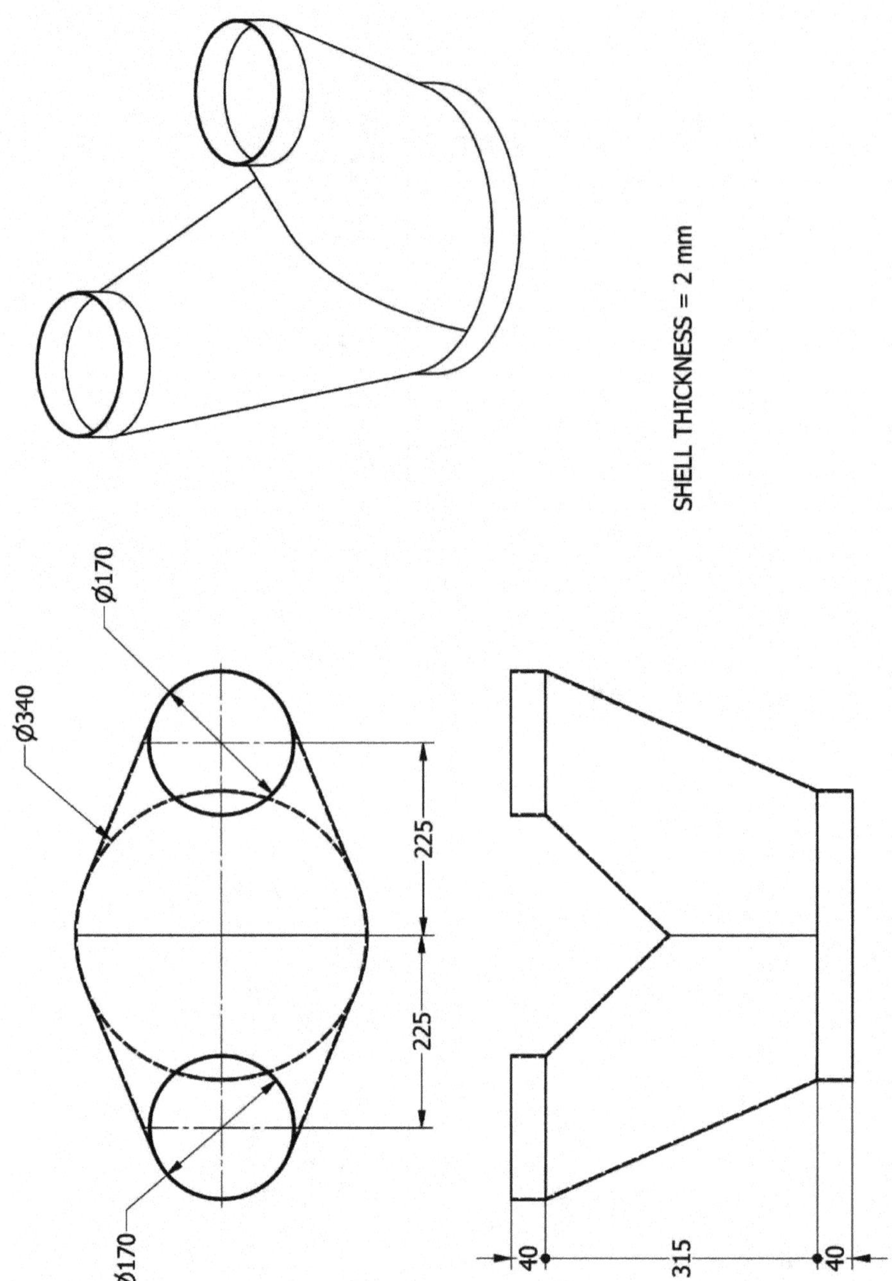

SHELL THICKNESS = 2 mm
Ø170
Ø340
Ø170
225
225
40
315
40

Chapter 14: Creating Architectural Drawings

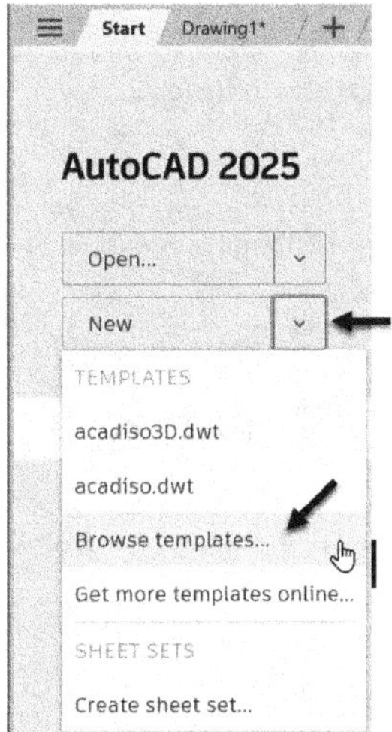

In this chapter, you will learn to do the following:

- **Defining Settings for Architectural Drawings**
- **Creating Inner Walls**
- **Creating Openings and Doors**
- **Creating Kitchen Fixtures**
- **Creating Bathroom Fixtures**
- **Adding Furniture using Blocks**
- **Adding Windows**
- **Arranging Objects of the drawing in Layers**
- **Creating Grid Lines**
- **Adding Dimensions**
- **Create Stair Details**
- **Elevation View**
- **Roof Plan**
- **Wall and Roof details**

Example 1

In this example, you will learn to create an architectural drawing.

Creating Outer Walls

- Start **AutoCAD 2025** and click **New > Browse Templates**.

- Select the **acad** template from the **Select Template** dialog and click the **Open** button.
- Set the **Workspace** to **Drafting & Annotation**.

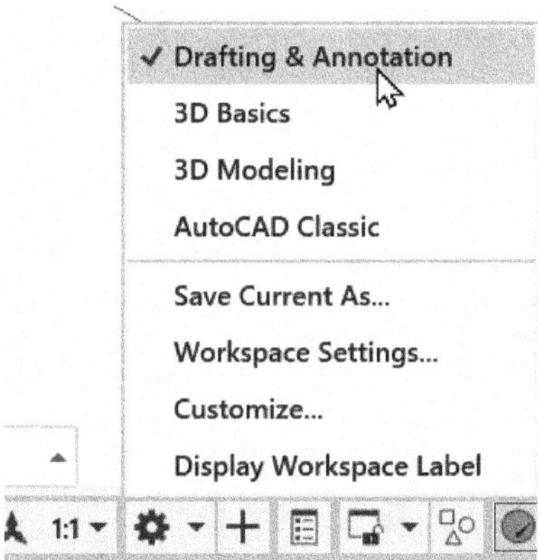

- Type **UN** in the command line and press Enter.
- On the **Drawing Units** dialog, select **Type > Architectural**.
- Select **Precision > 0-01/16**.
- Set the **Insertion Scale** to **Inches** and click **OK**.
- Type **LIMITS** in the command line and press Enter.
- Press Enter to accept 0, 0 as the lower limit.
- Type 100', 80' in the command line, and press Enter. The program sets the upper limit of the drawing.
- Turn OFF the grid.

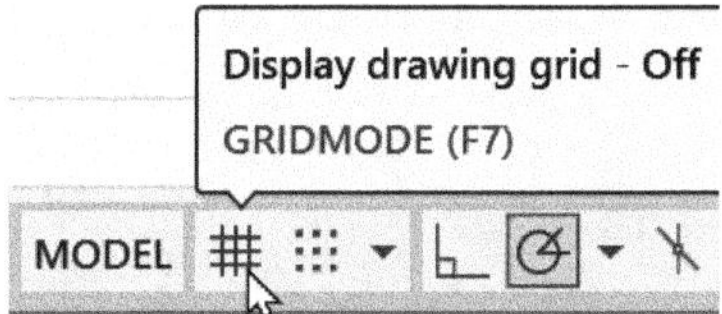

- Select **Zoom > Zoom All** on the Navigation Bar.
- On the Status bar, turn ON the **Ortho Mode** icon.

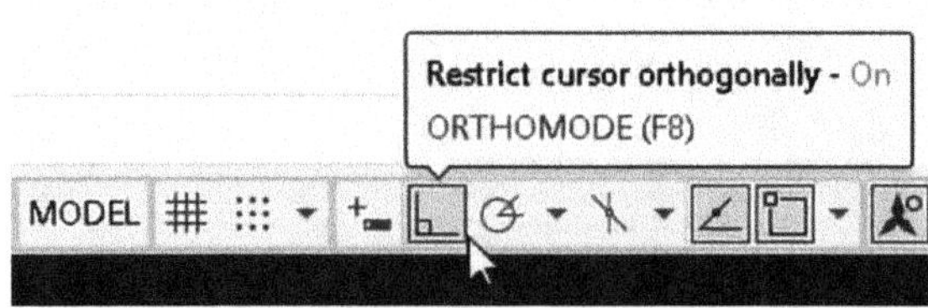

- On the ribbon, click **Home > Draw > Line**, and then select an arbitrary point. It defines the start point of the line.
- Move the pointer toward right horizontally and type-in 412 — press Enter.
- Move the pointer vertically and type-in 338 — press Enter.
- Move the pointer onto the starting point of the drawing, and then move it upwards. You will notice that a dotted line appears.

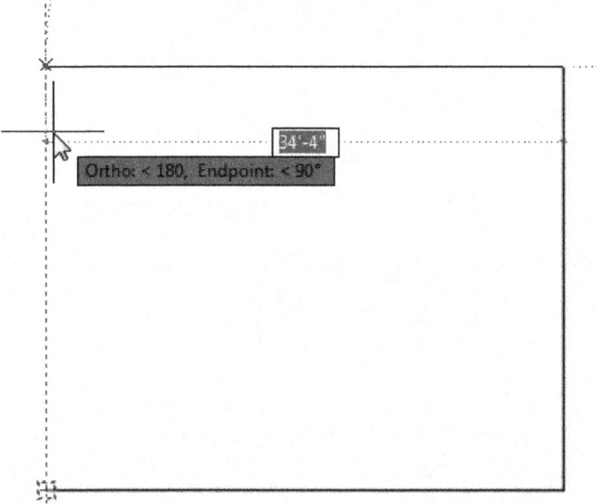

- Click to create a horizontal line. You will notice that the two horizontal lines are of the same length.
- Click the right mouse button and select **Close**.

- On the ribbon, click **Home > Modify > Offset**.
- Type-in 6 as offset distance and press Enter.
- Select the left vertical line of the drawing.
- Move the pointer inside the drawing and click to create an offset line.
- Likewise, offset the other lines, as shown below.

- On the Navigation Bar, click **Zoom > Zoom Window**.

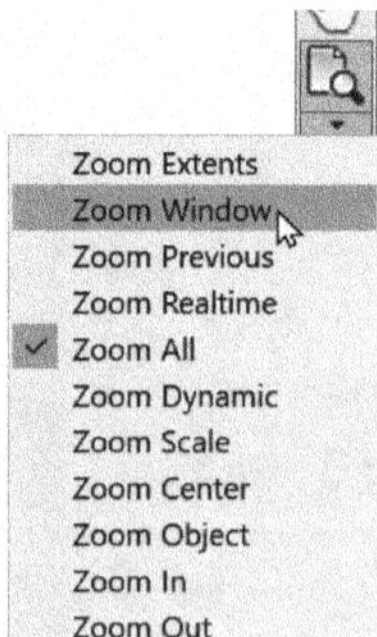

- Create a window on the top left corner of the drawing. The corner portion will be zoomed in.

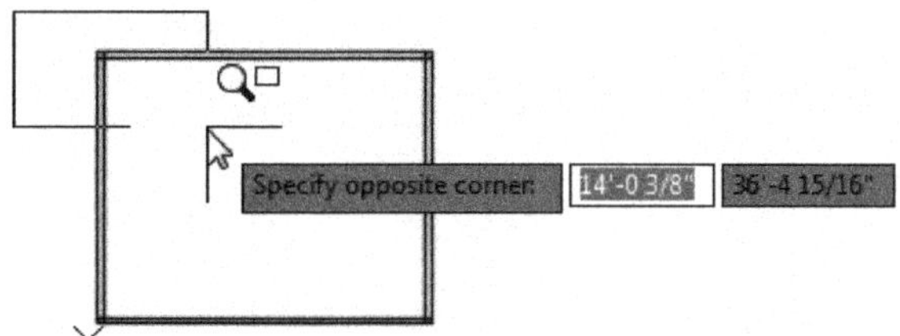

- On the ribbon, click **Home > Modify > Fillet** .
- Select the **Radius** option on the command line, and then type in 0 — press Enter.
- Select the inner offset lines, as shown below.

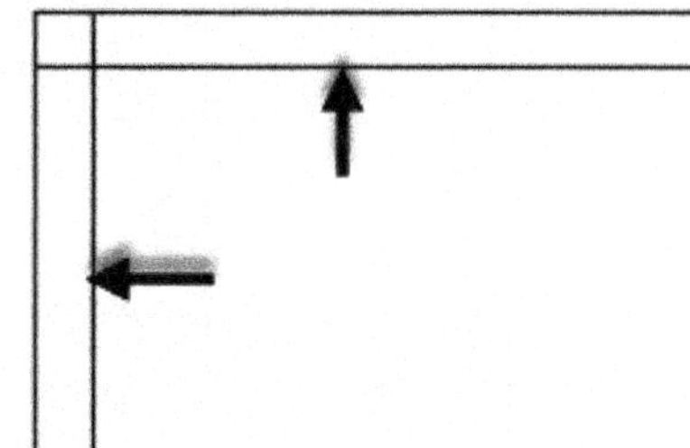

- Likewise, fillet the other corners.

- Save the drawing. Make sure that you save the drawing after each section.

Creating Inner Walls

- Activate the **Offset** command and type in **130** in the command line, and then press Enter.
- Select the inner line of the right side wall and click inside the drawing.
- Press Esc.

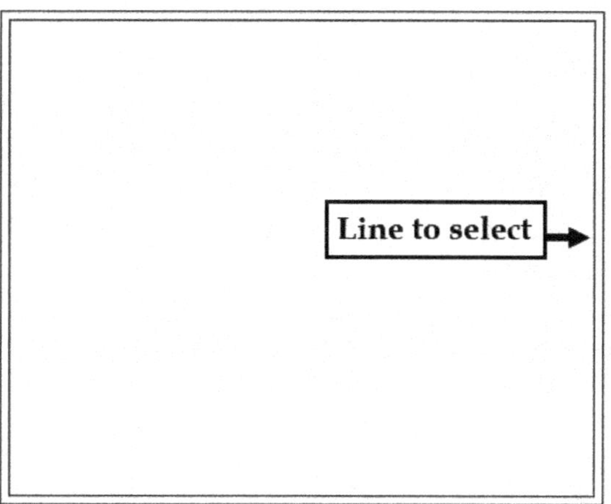

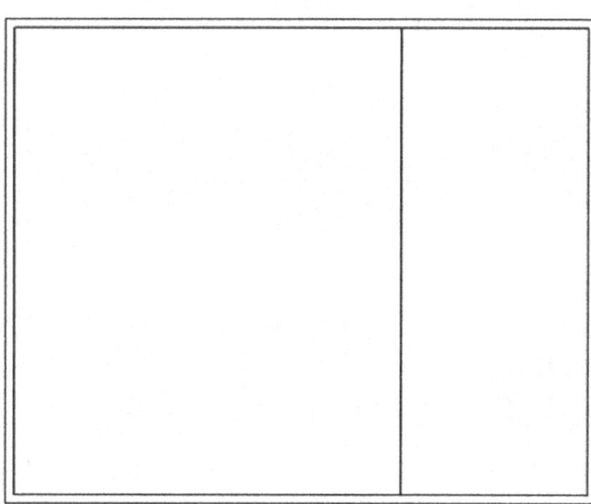

- Select the new offset line. You will notice that three grips are displayed on the line.
- Click the right mouse button and select **Copy Selection**.

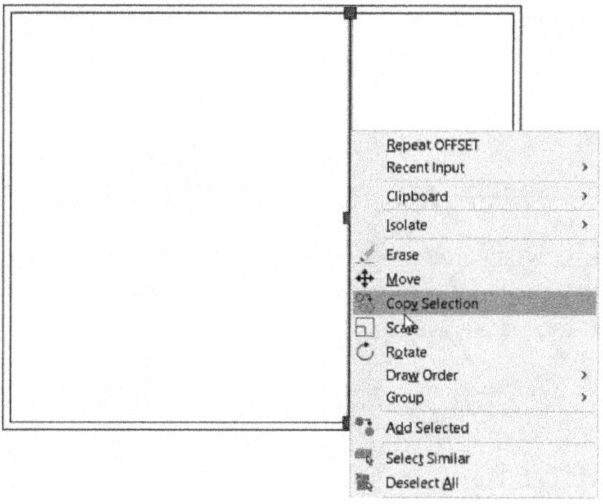

- Select the endpoint of the selected line as a base point.
- Move the pointer toward the left and type in 4, and then press Enter. A new line is created, and another line is attached to the pointer.
- Move the pointer toward the left and type in 118, and then press Enter.

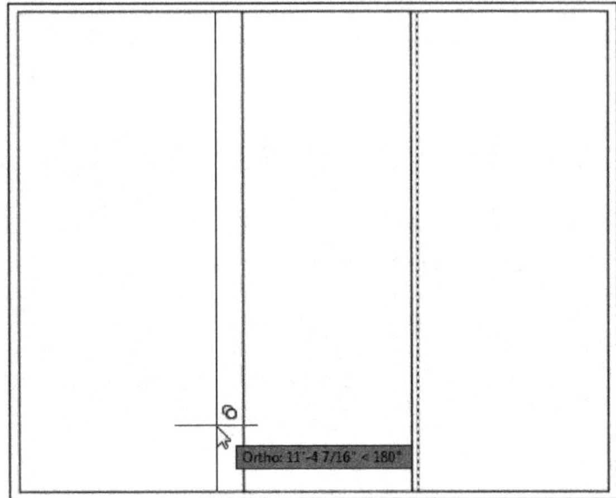

- Move the pointer toward the left and type in 122, and then press Enter.
- Press Esc to come out of the **Copy** command.

- Likewise, create horizontal offset lines, as shown below.

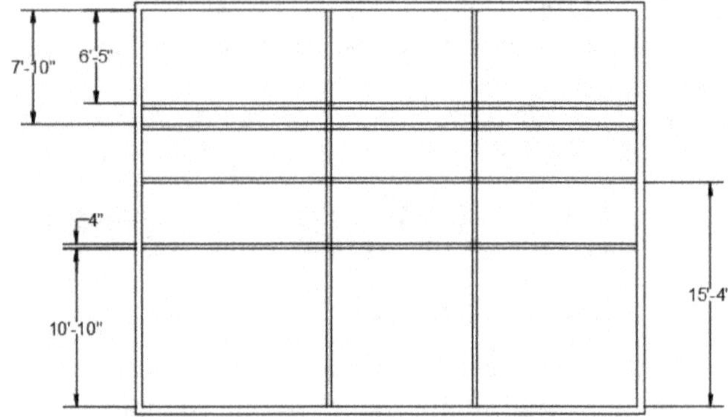

- On the ribbon, click **Home > Modify > Trim**.
- Click on the lines at the locations shown below.

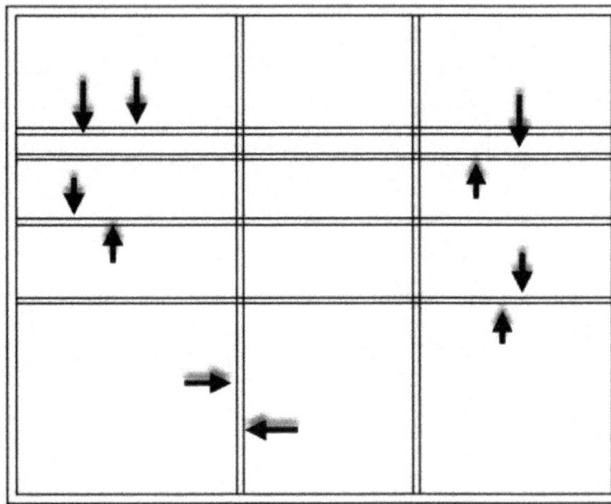

- Specify the fence points across the horizontal lines, as shown below.

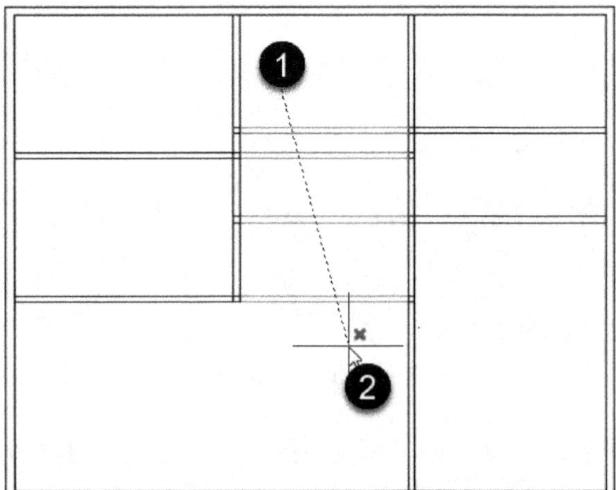

- Select the **Crossing** option from the command line and create the selection window, as shown.

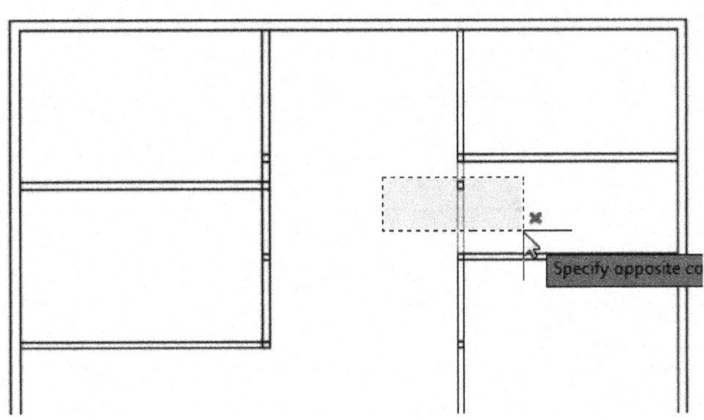

- Select the **Crossing** option from the command line and create the selection window, as shown.

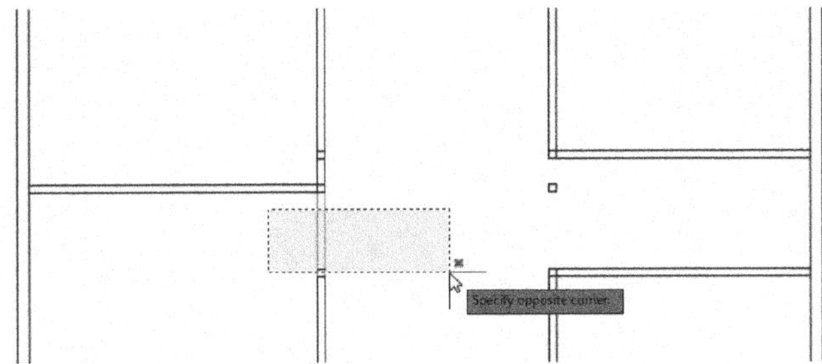

- Zoom to the top portion of the drawing by placing the pointer in the top portion and rotating the mouse scroll in the forward direction.
- Select the portion of the horizontal line that lies between the lines of the inner wall. The selected portions will be trimmed.

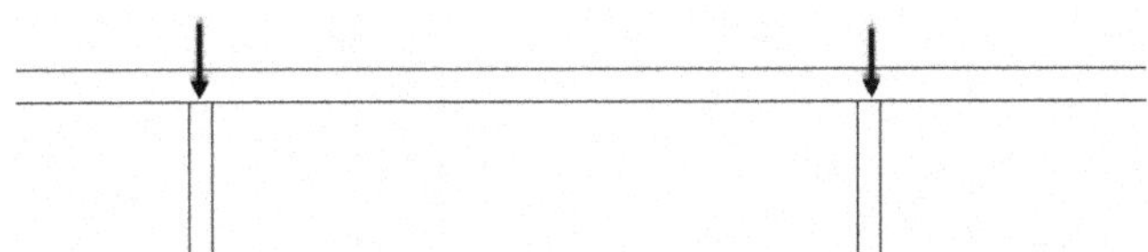

- Press and hold the mouse scroll wheel and drag downwards until the lower portion of the drawing is visible.
- Trim the unwanted portion, as shown below.

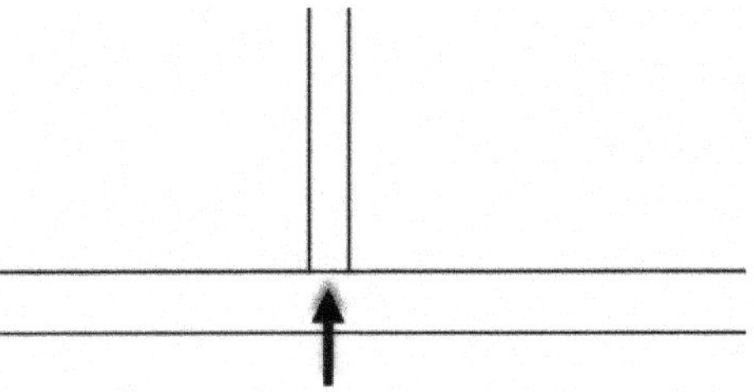

- Trim the unwanted portions, as shown below.

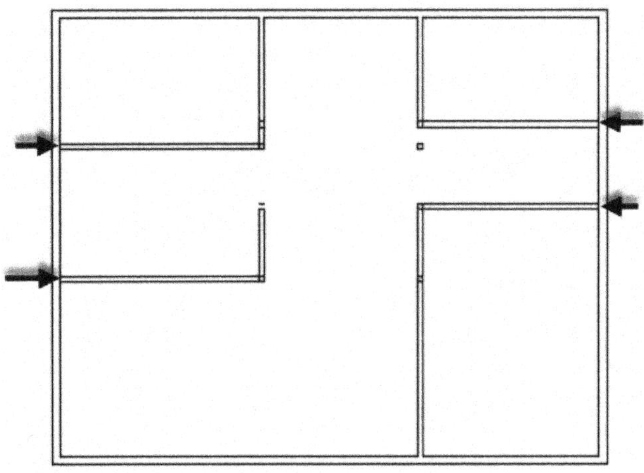

- Trim the unwanted portions at the corners.

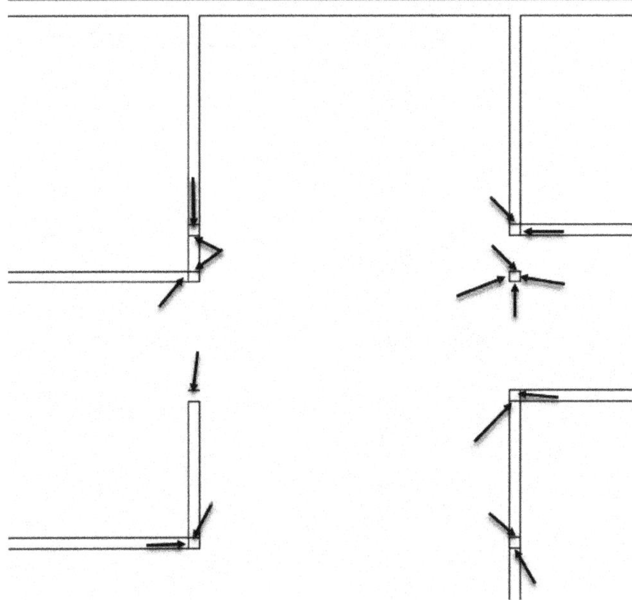

- Press Esc to deactivate the **Trim** command.

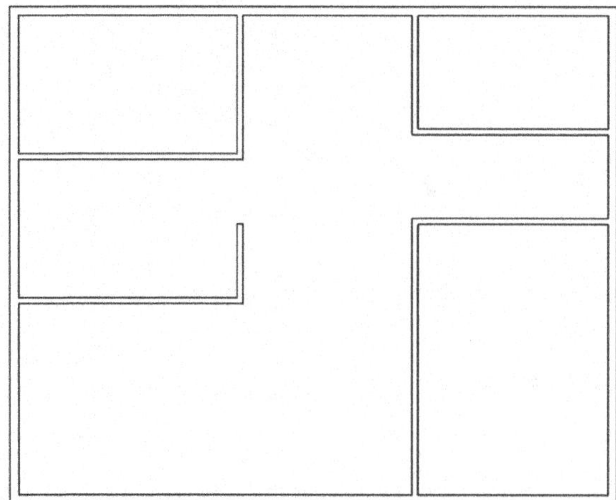

Creating Openings and Doors

- Activate the **Line** command and select the corner of the inner wall, as shown below.
- Move the pointer downward and select the other corner point.

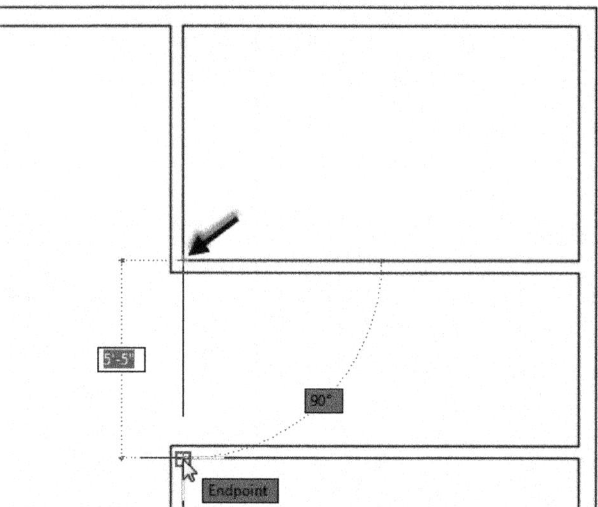

- Deactivate the **Line** command and select the new line.
- Select the middle point of the new line and move the pointer toward the right.
- Type-in 6 and press Enter.

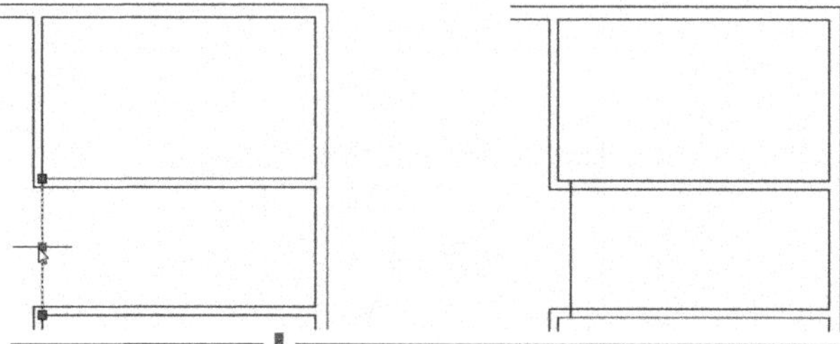

- Activate the **Offset** command and specify 32 as the offset distance.
- Select the new line and move rightwards, and then click.

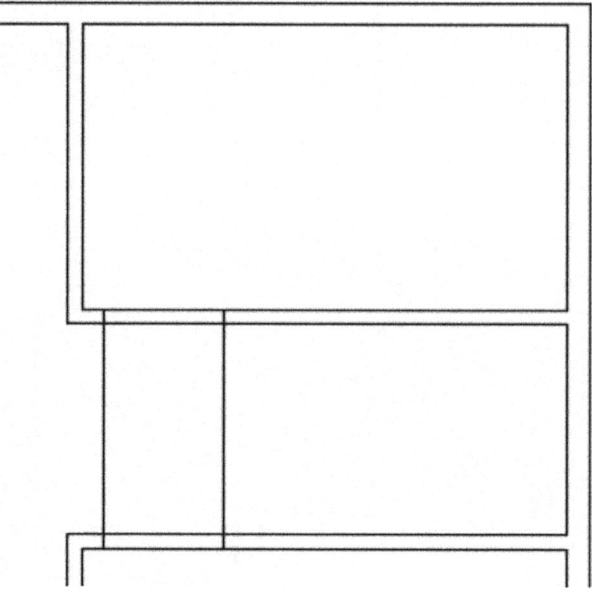

- Activate the **Trim** command and trim the unwanted portions.

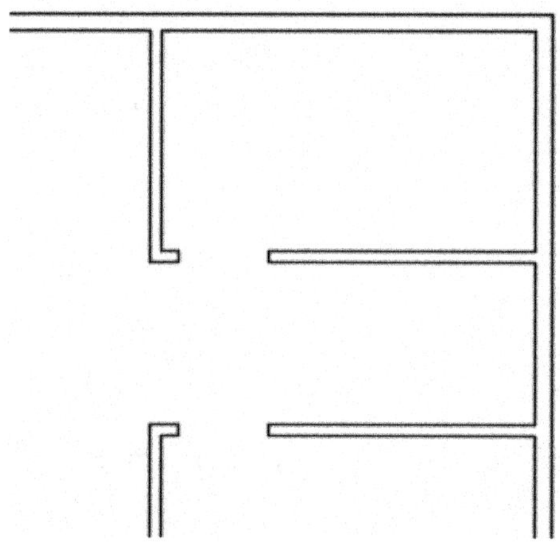

- Likewise, create other openings, as shown below (use the method described in the earlier step).

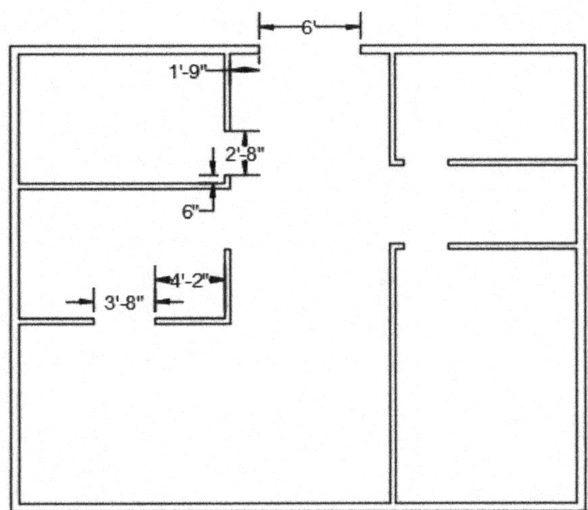

- On the ribbon, click **Home > Draw > Rectangle**.
- Select the endpoint of the opening, as shown below.

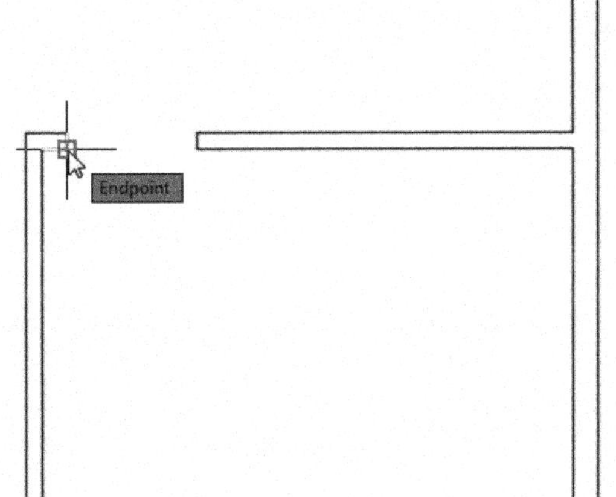

- Select **Dimensions** from the command line.
- Type-in 1 and press Enter. It defines the length of the rectangle.
- Type-in 32 and press Enter. It defines the width of the rectangle.
- Move the pointer down and click to create the door. Now, you need to create the door swing.

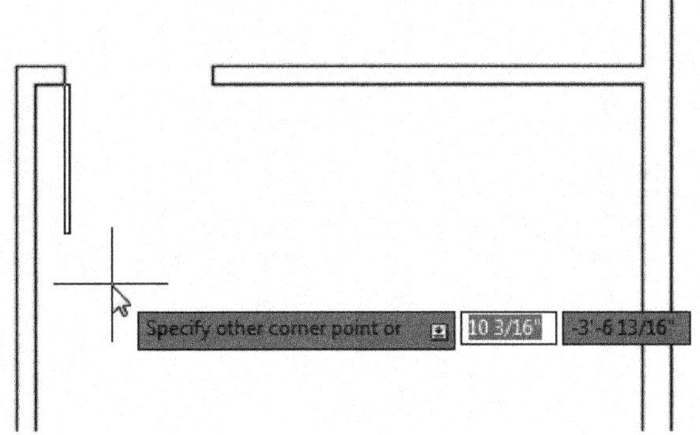

- On the ribbon, click **Home > Draw > Arc** drop-down > **Start Center End**.

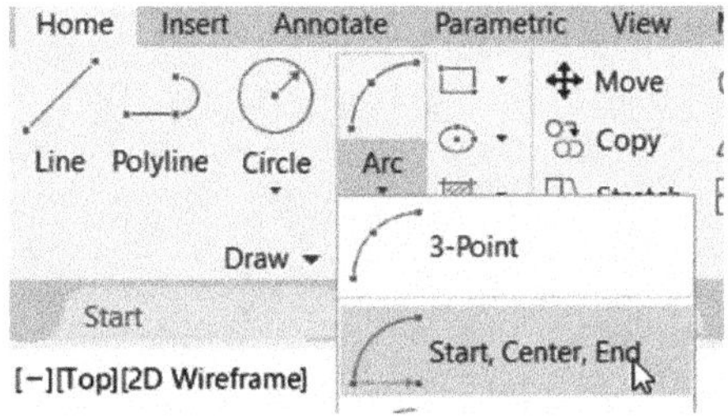

- Select the start, center, and end of the arc in the sequence shown below.

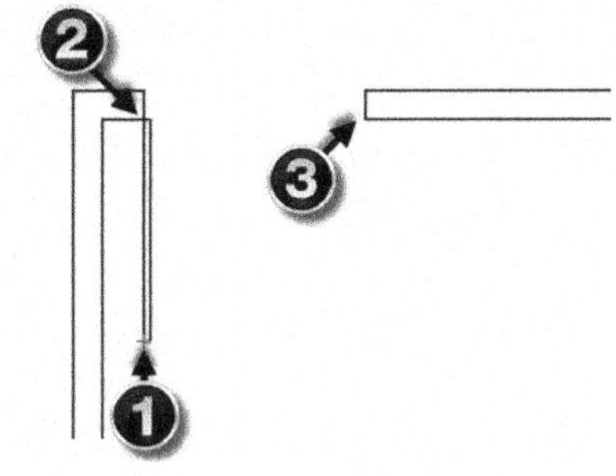

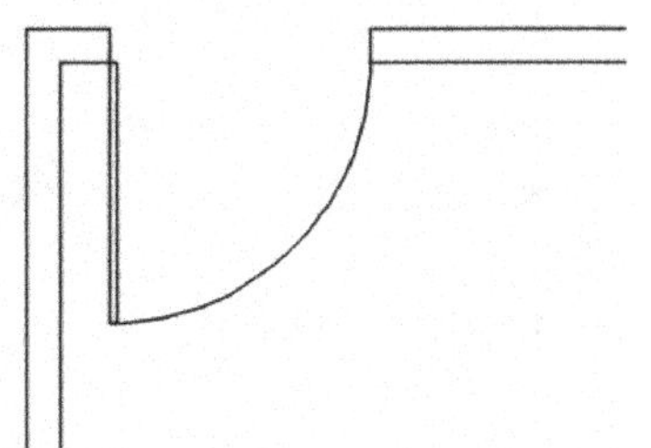

- Select the door and door swing.
- Click the right mouse button and select **Copy Selection**.
- Select the corner point of the rectangle as the base point.

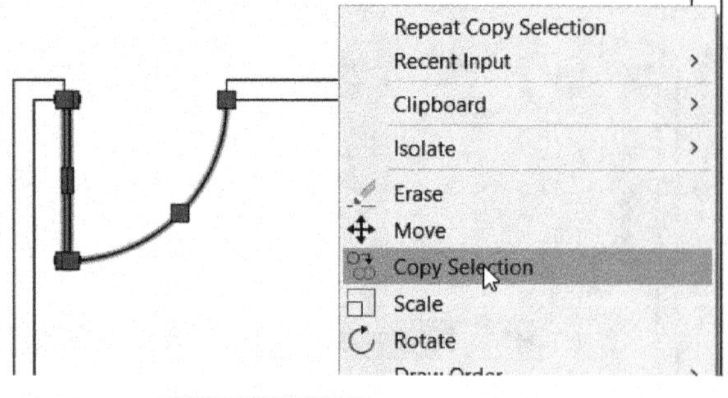

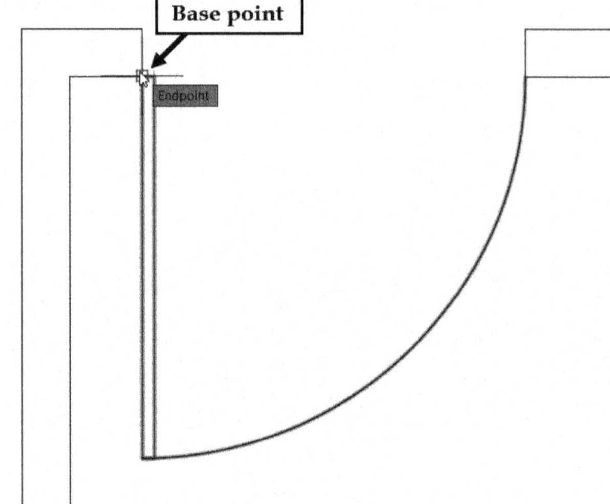

- Select the corner points of openings, as shown below.

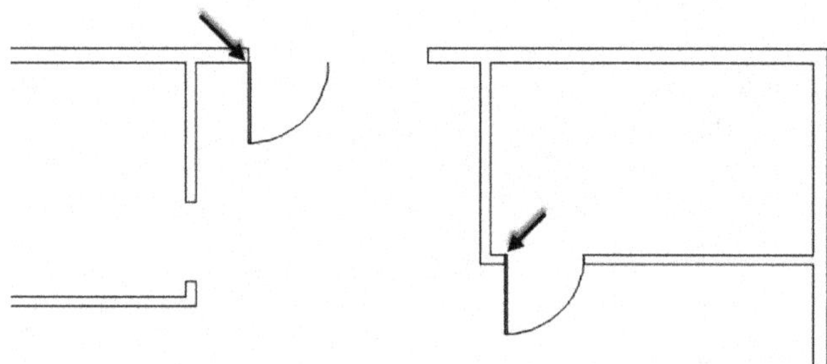

- Press Esc to deactivate the **Copy** command.
- Click the down arrow next to the **Object Snap** icon on the status bar.
- Make sure that the **Midpoint** option is selected.
- On the ribbon, click **Home > Modify > Mirror**, and then select the door and swing of the bathroom, as shown. Press Enter to accept the selection.

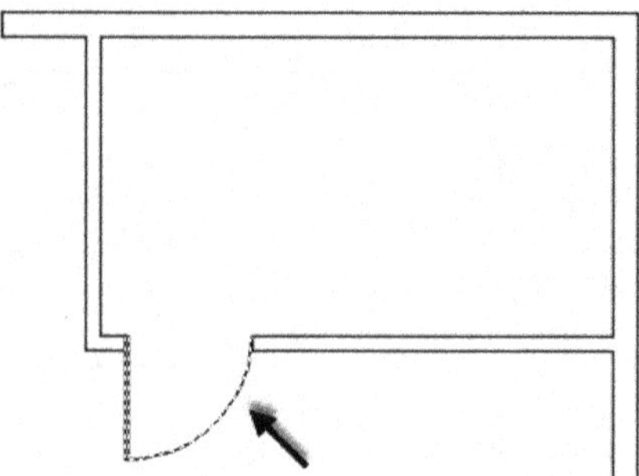

- Define the mirror line by selecting the points, as shown below.

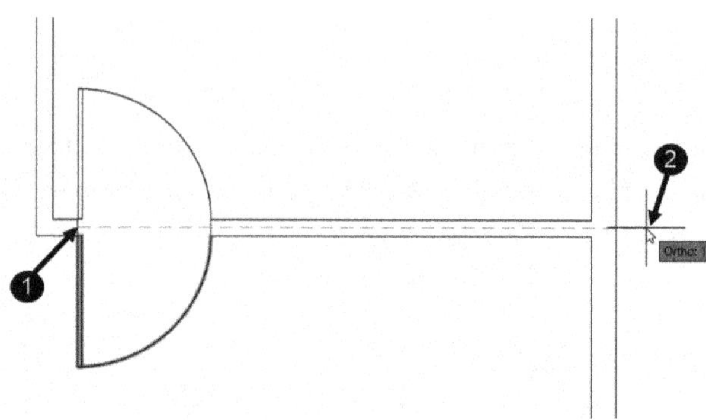

- Select **Yes** from the command line. It deletes the original object.
- On the ribbon, click **Home > Modify > Scale**, and then select the door & swing at the main entrance — press Enter.
- Select the base point, as shown below.

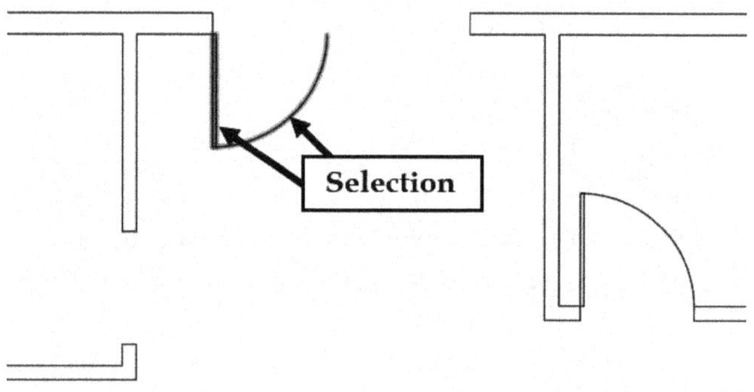

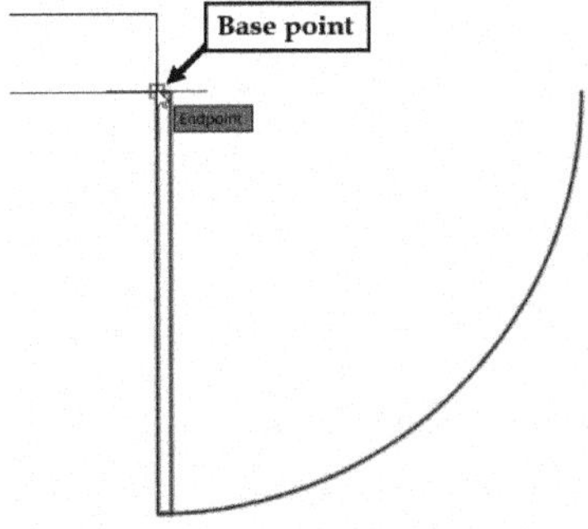

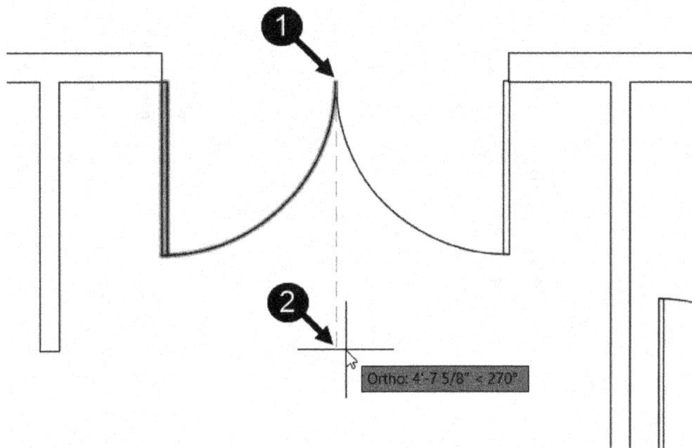

- Select the **Reference** option from the command line.
- Select the two endpoints, as shown below. It defines the reference length of the objects. Now, you need to define the length up to which you want to scale the objects.
- Type-in 36 and press Enter. The objects will be scaled.

- Select **No** from the command line. It keeps the original object.
- Copy the door & swing of the bathroom and place it at the opening, as shown below.
- Press Esc.

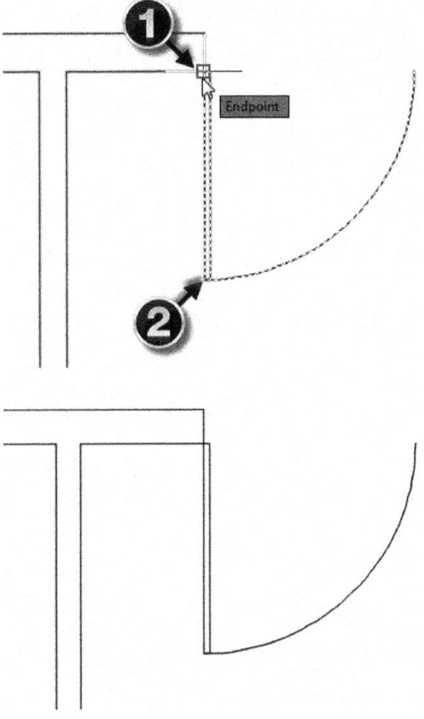

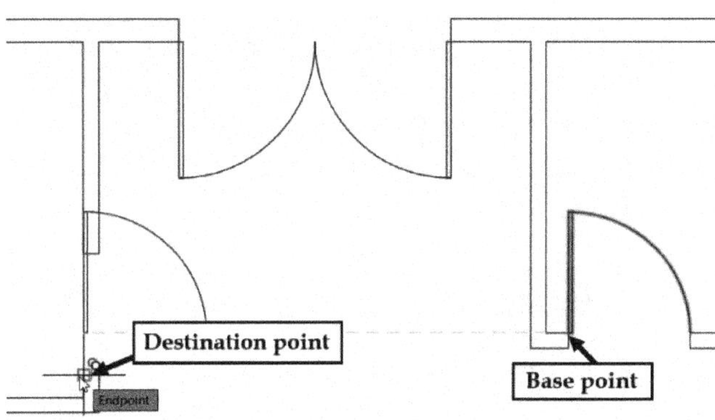

- On the ribbon, click **Home > Modify > Rotate**, and then select the copied object. Next, press Enter.
- Select the base point, as shown.

- Activate the **Mirror** command and select the door & swing at the entrance. Press Enter to accept the selection.
- Define the mirror line by selecting the points, as shown below.

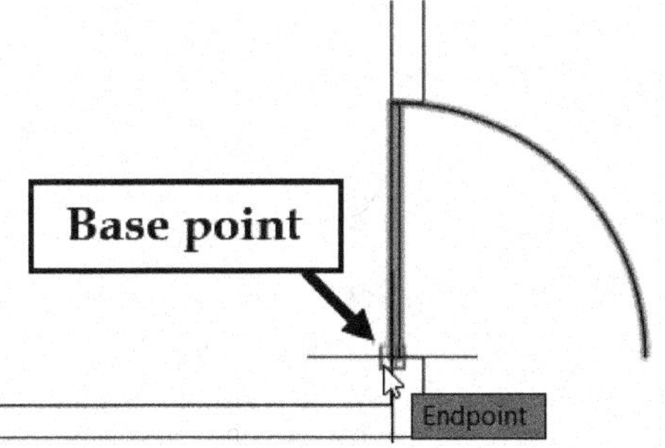

- Move the pointer vertically upward, and then click.

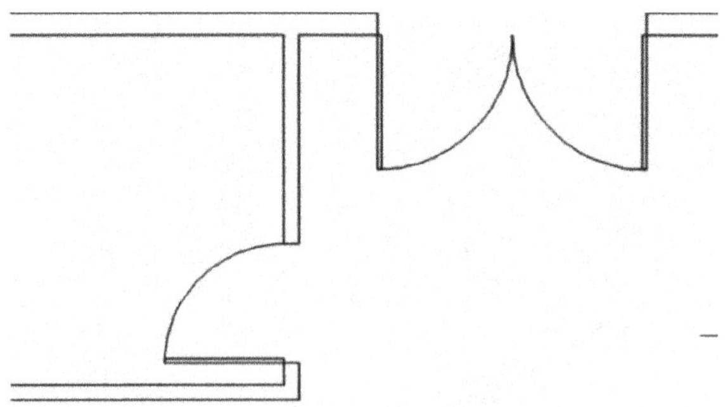

- Create an opening on the rear side of the plan, as shown below.

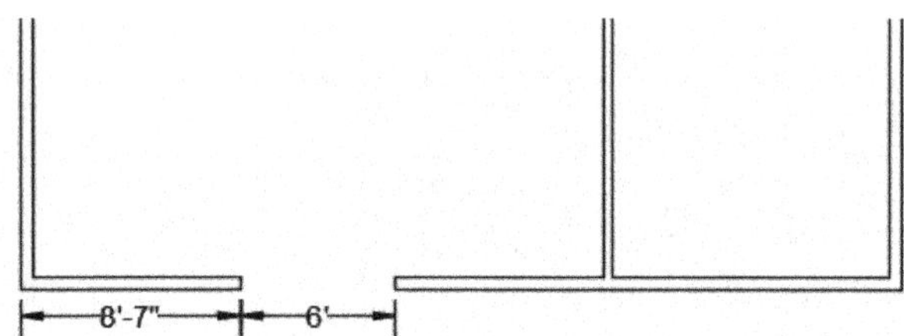

Now, you will create a sliding door in the opening.

- Activate the **Rectangle** command and select the corner point of the opening, as shown below.

- Select the **Dimensions** option from the command line.
- Specify 37 and 2 as the length and width of the rectangle, respectively.
- Move the pointer upward and click to create the rectangle.

- Type **M** in the command line and press Enter. Select the rectangle, and then press Enter.
- Select its lower-left corner point to define the base point. Move the pointer upward and type-in 1 in the command line, and then press Enter.

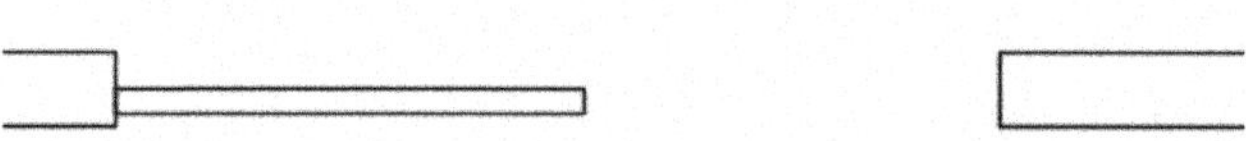

- On the ribbon, click **Home > Modify > Explode**, and select the rectangle. Press Enter to explode the

rectangle.

- Activate the **Offset** command and specify 2 as the offset distance.
- Offset the left and right vertical lines of the rectangle.

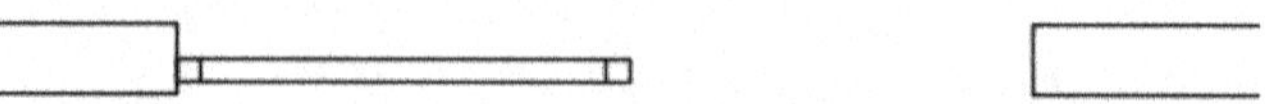

- Press **Esc** to deactivate the **Offset** command.
- Activate the **Line** command and select the midpoints of the offset lines. It creates a line connecting the offset lines. It creates one part of the sliding door.

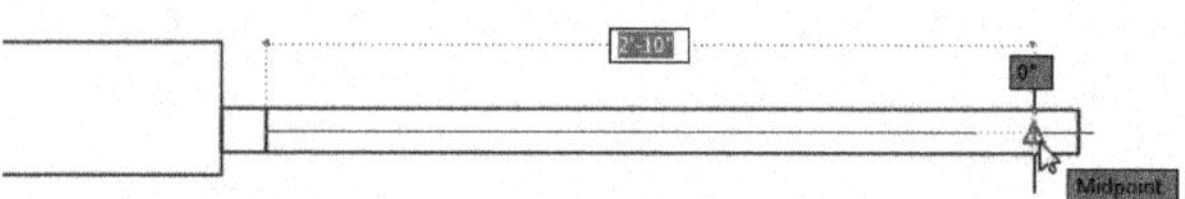

- Press **Esc** to deactivate the **Line** command.
- Type-in **CO** in the command line and press Enter.
- Drag a selection window covering all the elements of the sliding door. Press Enter.

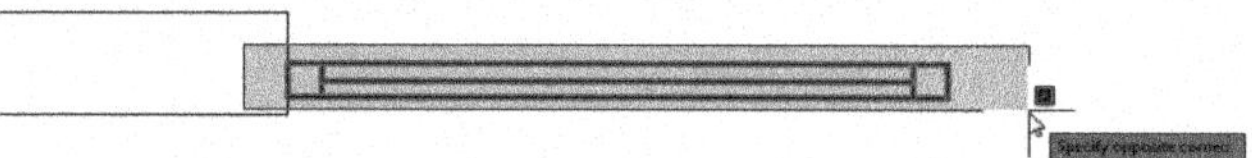

- Select the lower-left corner of the sliding door as the base point.
- Move the pointer and select the endpoint of the offset line, as shown.

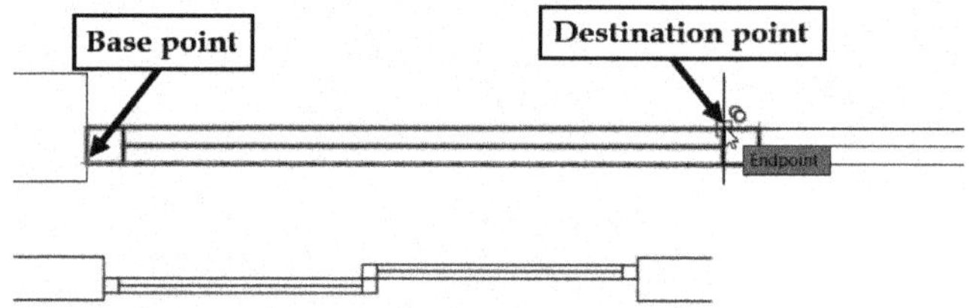

- Press **Esc** to deactivate the **Copy** command.

Now, you need to draw thresholds on the door openings.

- Zoom to the front door area using the **Zoom Window** tool.

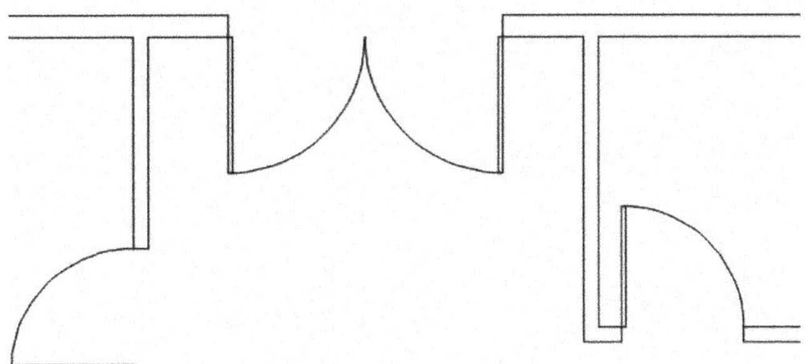

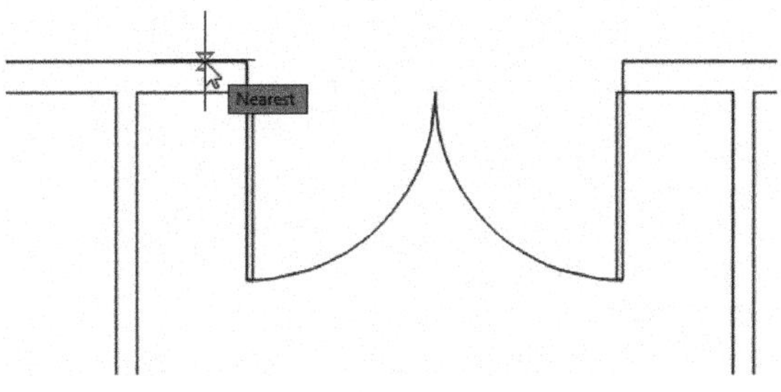

- On the status bar, click the down arrow next to the **Object Snap** button and make sure that **Endpoint**, **Nearest,** and **Perpendicular** options are selected.

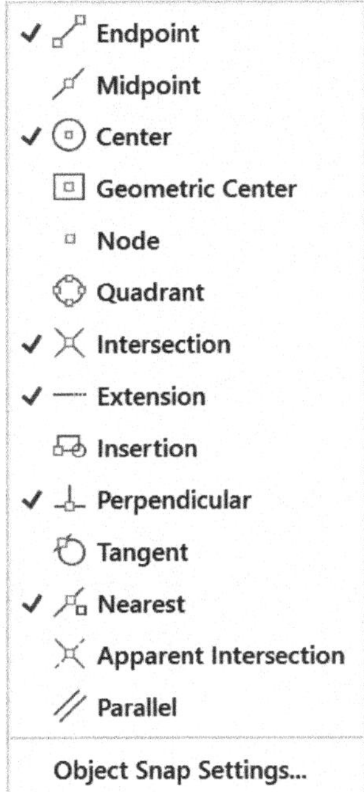

- Type-in **L** in the command line and press Enter.
- Press and hold the **Shift** key and click the right mouse button.
- Select **From** from the shortcut menu and click the endpoint of the door opening, as shown below.
- Move the pointer on the horizontal line and type in 3, and then press Enter. It defines the start point of the line at 3 distance from the endpoint.

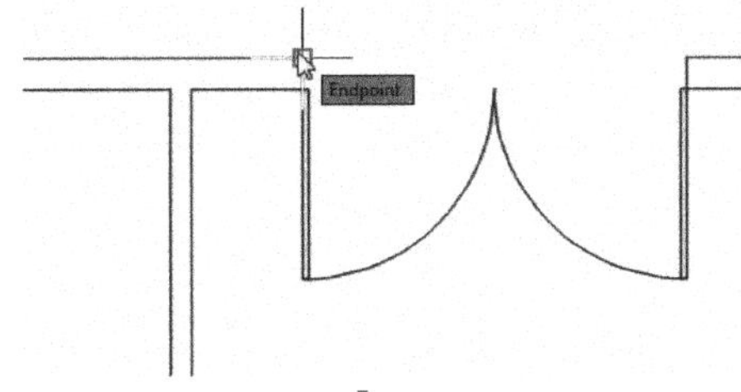

- Move the pointer up and type-in 2, and then press Enter.
- Move the pointer toward the right and type in 78, and then press Enter.
- Move the pointer downward and type in 2, and then press Enter. It creates a threshold.

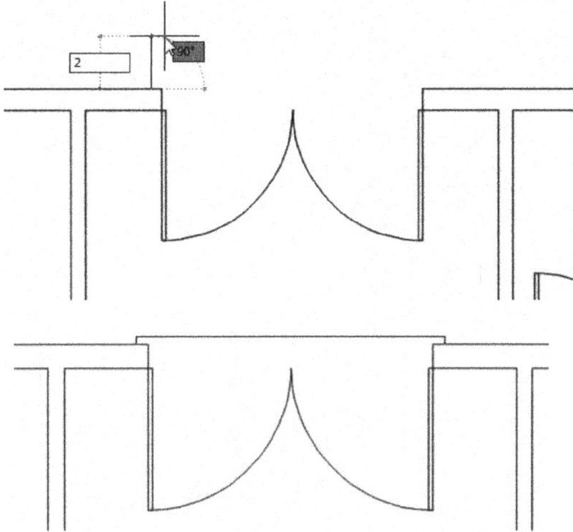

- Press Esc to deactivate the **Line** command.
- Likewise, create a threshold on the sliding glass door.

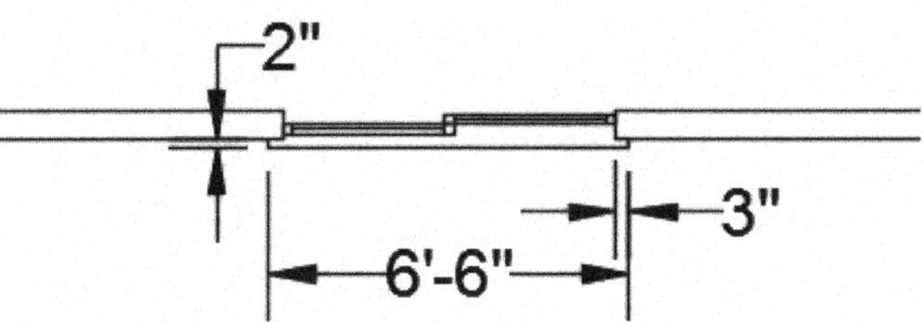

Creating Kitchen Fixtures

- Zoom to the kitchen area by using the **Zoom Window** tool.

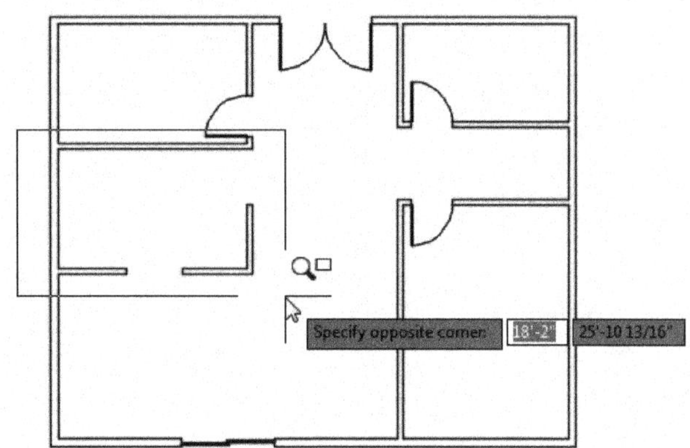

- Activate the **Offset** command and specify 26 as the offset distance.
- Offset the lines shown below.

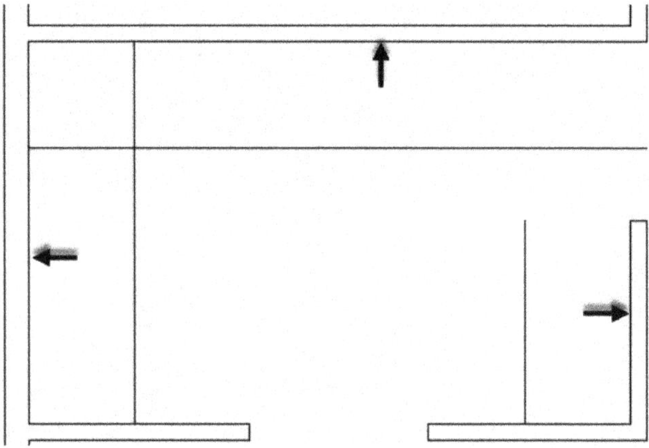

- Trim the unwanted portions.

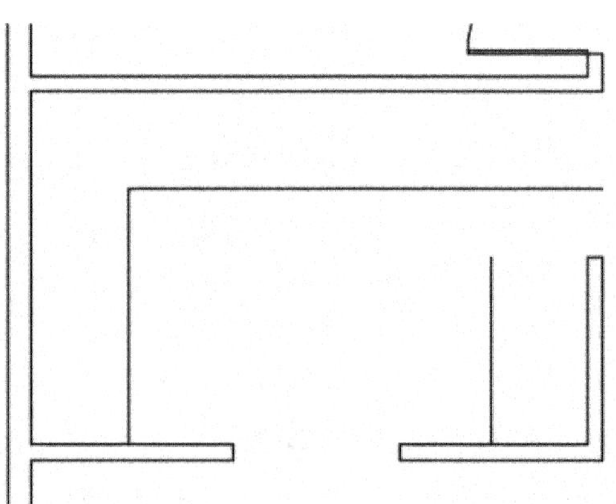

- Create another offset line at 54 distance, and then trim the unwanted elements.

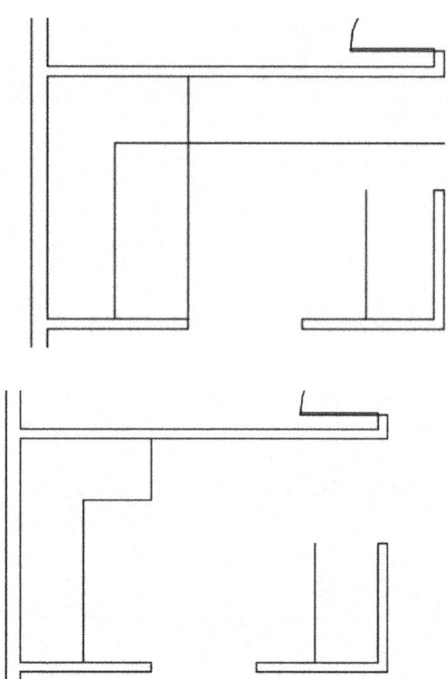

- Create another line, as shown below.

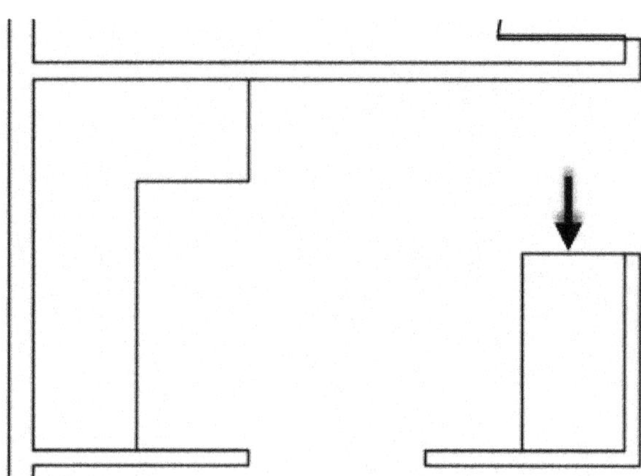

Now, you have finished drawing the counters. You need to draw a refrigerator, stove and sink.

- Type-in **REC** in the command line and press Enter. It activates the **Rectangle** command.
- Select the corner point of the counter.
- Select the **Dimensions** option from the command line.
- Specify 28 as length and width of the rectangle. Move the pointer toward the right and click to create the rectangle.

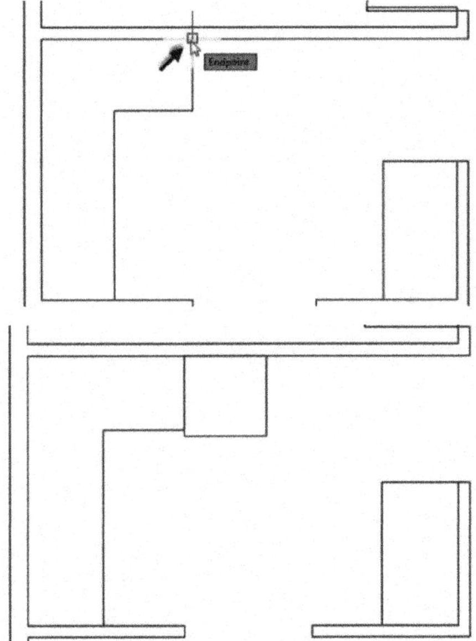

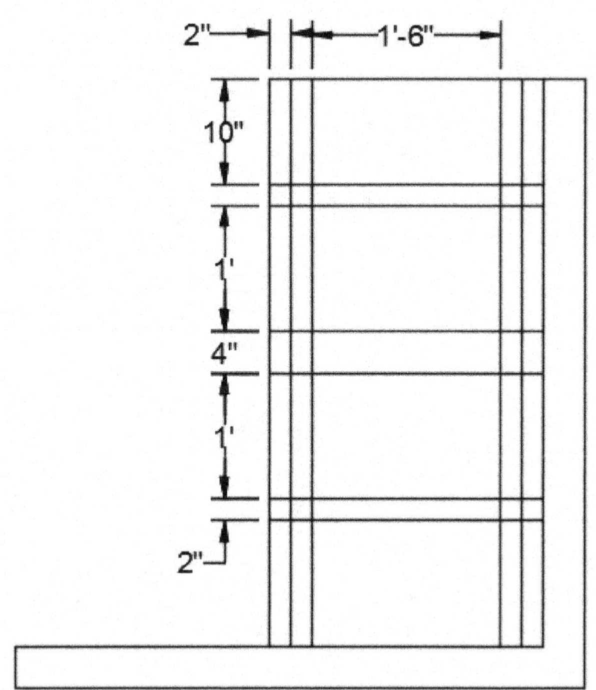

- Use the **Move** command to move the rectangle 2 inches rightwards and downwards.

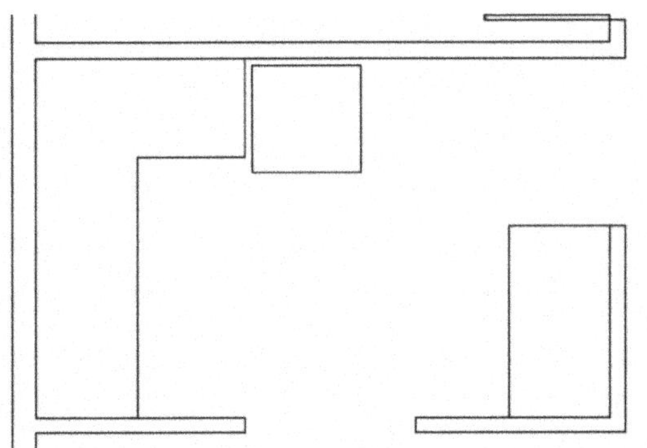

- Trim the unwanted elements, as shown below.

- Create the outline of the stove using the **Offset** and **Trim** commands.

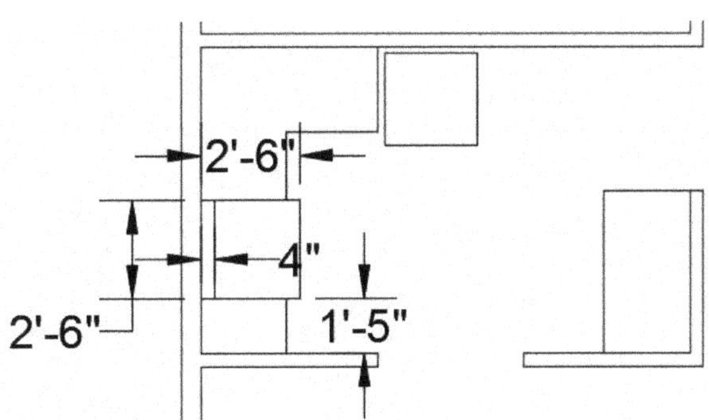

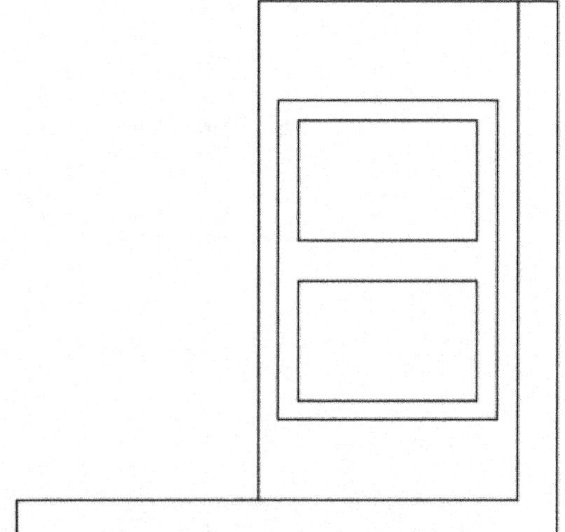

- Fillet the corners, as shown below.

Now, you need to create the sink.

- Use the **Offset** command and create offset lines, as shown below.

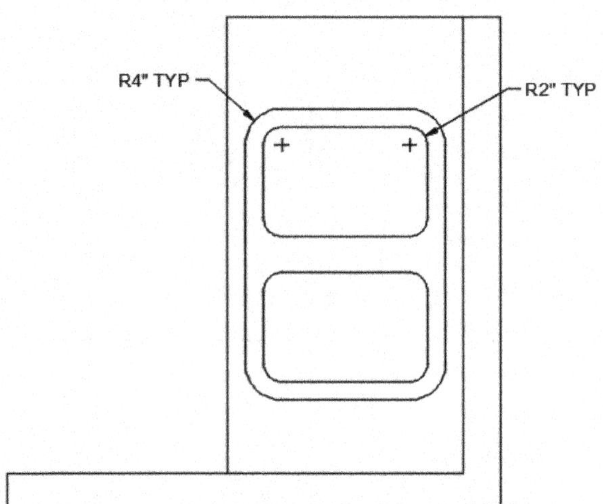

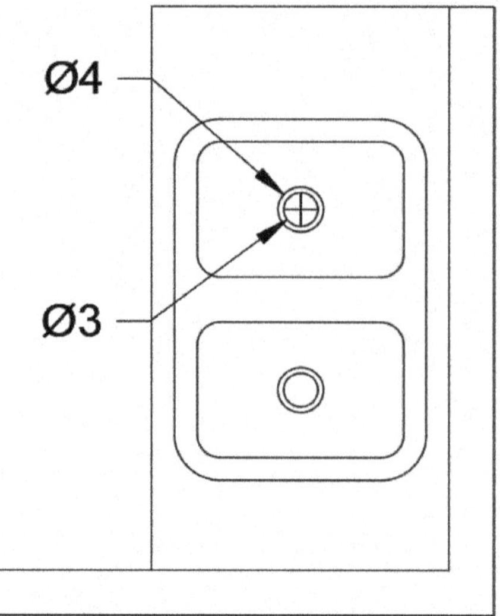

- Activate the **Circle** command and hover the pointer on the midpoints of the sink edges and move, as shown below.

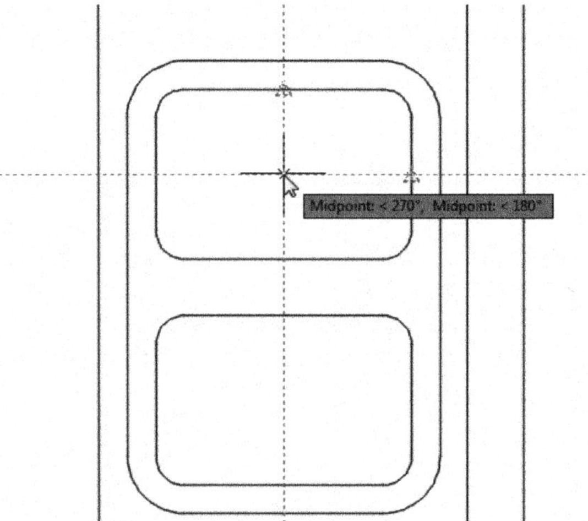

- Create the circles at the intersection points of the trace lines.

Creating Bathroom Fixtures

- Zoom into the bathroom area and create offset lines, as shown below.

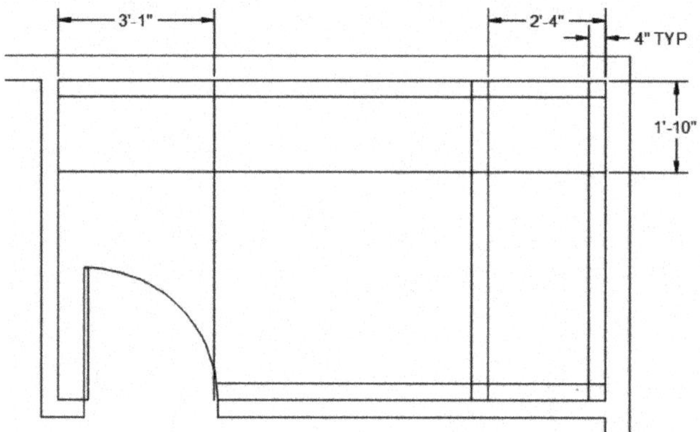

- Trim the unwanted elements, as shown below.

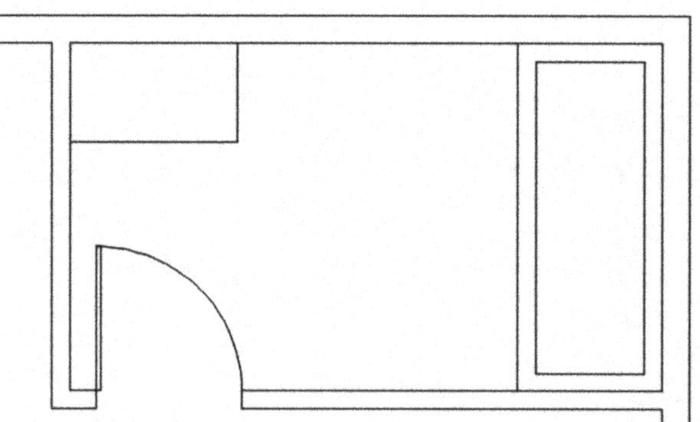

- Fillet the corners, as shown below. The fillet radius is 4.

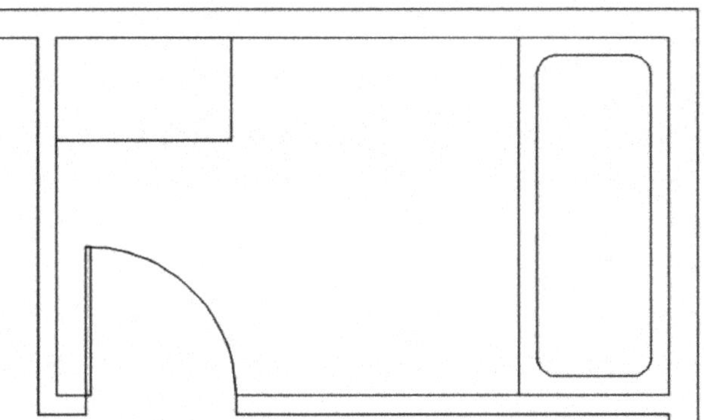

- On the ribbon, click **Home > Draw > Ellipse drop-down > Center**.

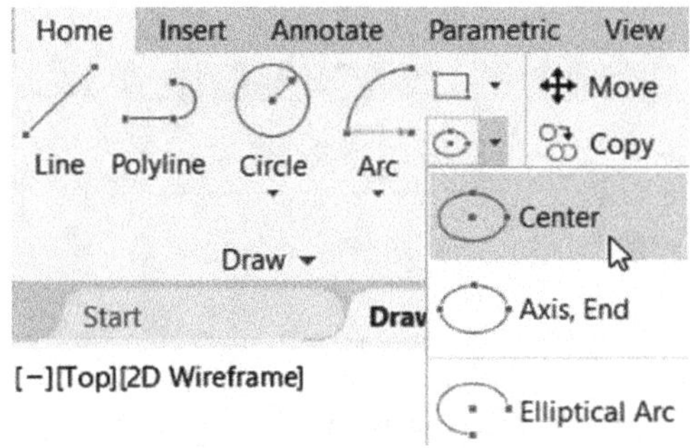

- Hover the pointer on the midpoints of the vertical and horizontal lines, as shown below.

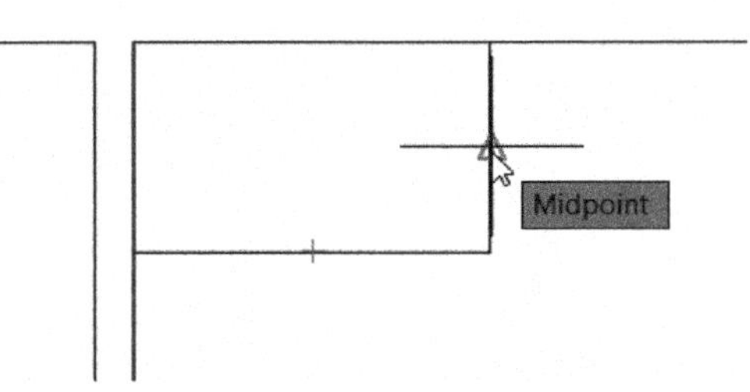

- Move the pointer and click at the intersection point of the trace lines.

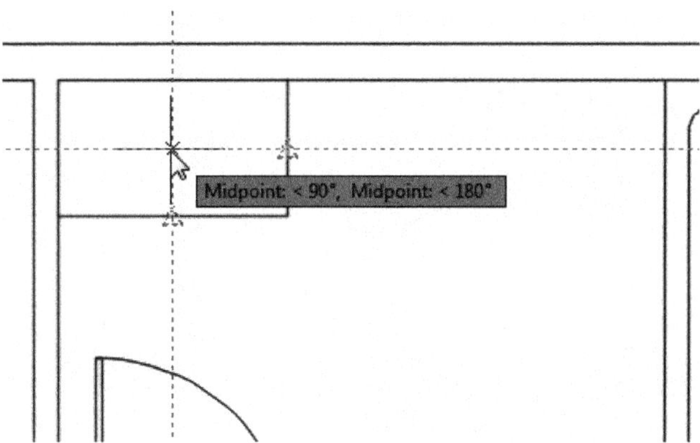

- Move the pointer toward the right and type in 10, and then press Enter. It defines the major radius of the ellipse.
- Move the pointer downward and type in 5, and then press Enter. It defines the minor radius of the ellipse.

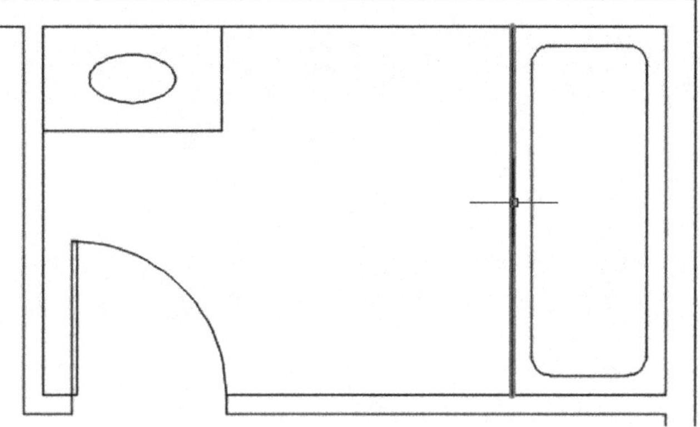

- Likewise, create another ellipse of 11 major radius and 7 minor radius.

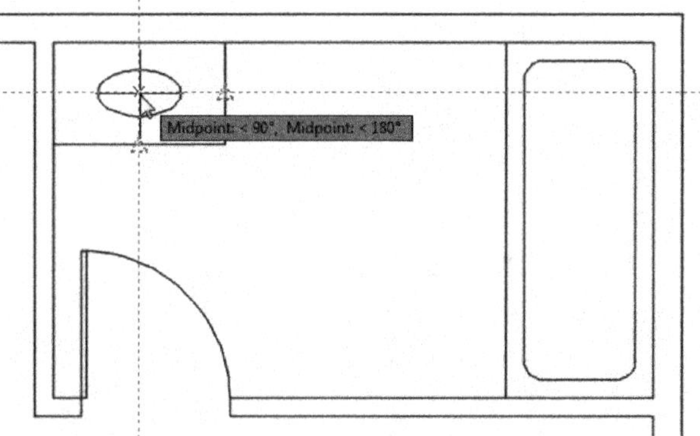

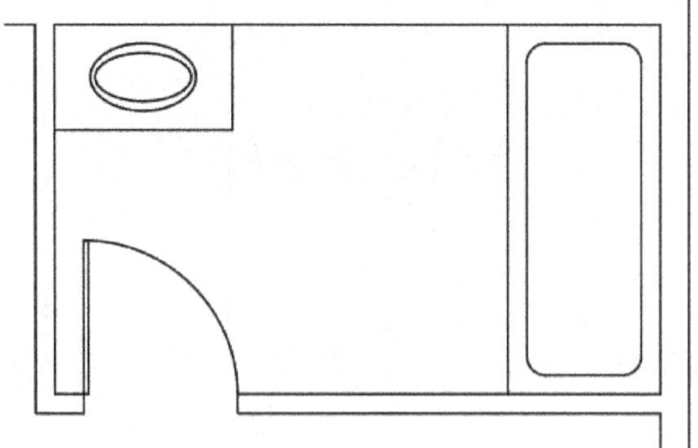

- Select the outer ellipse, and then click on the center point of the ellipse.
- Move the pointer up and type-in 1, and then press Enter. The outer ellipse moves up.

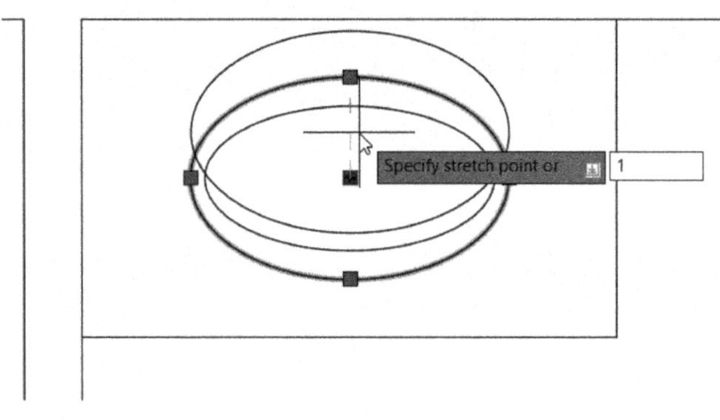

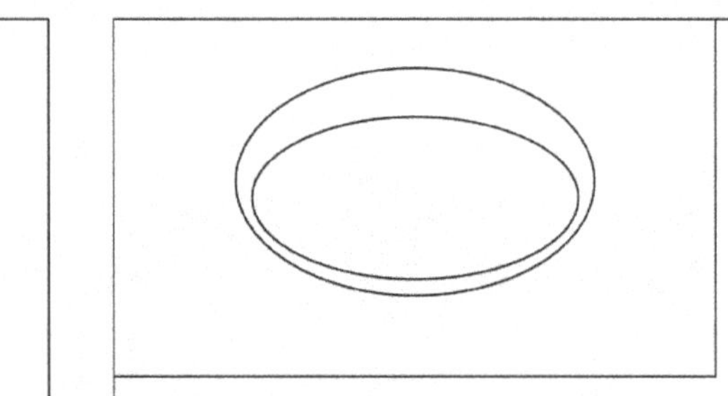

- Activate the **Rectangle** command and create a 22 x 9 rectangle, as shown below.

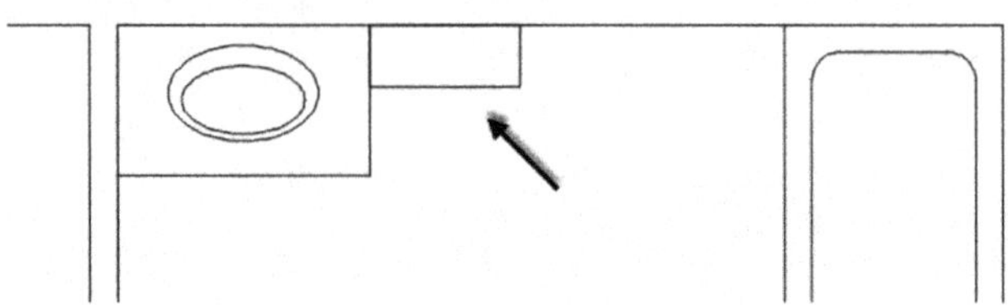

- Move the rectangle up to 19.5 rightwards and 1 downwards.

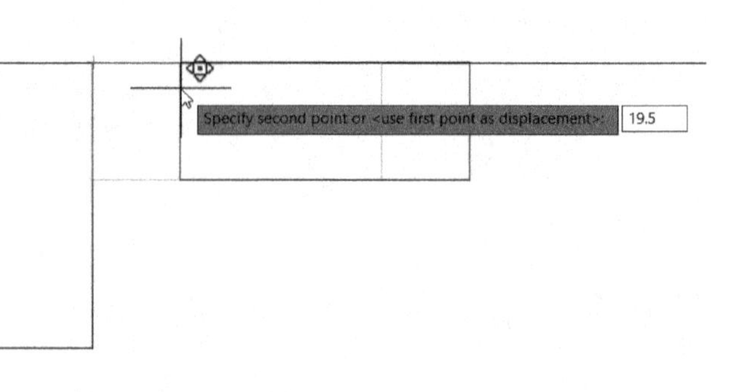

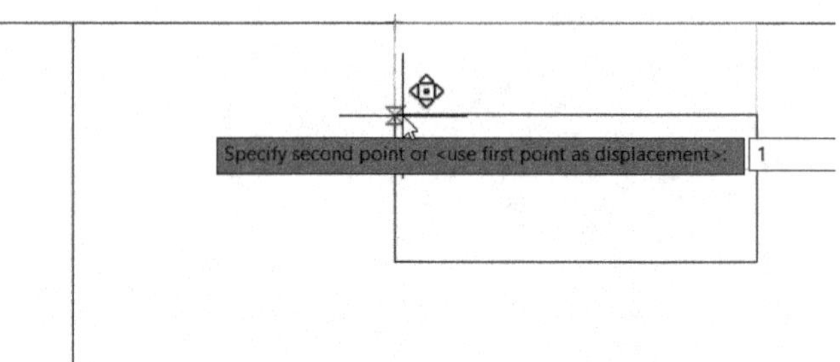

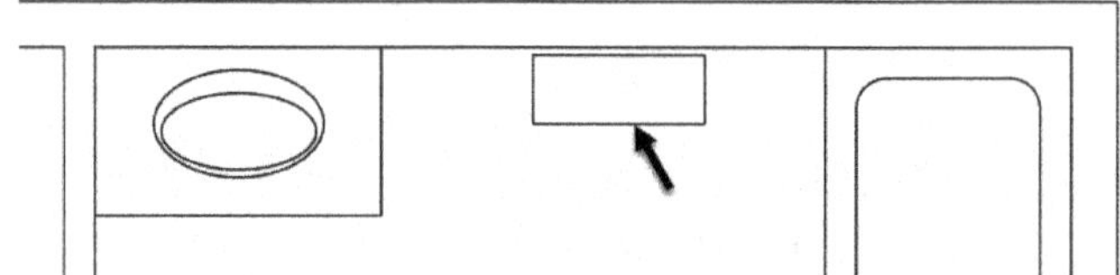

- On the ribbon, click **Home > Draw > Ellipse** drop-down **> Axis, End**.

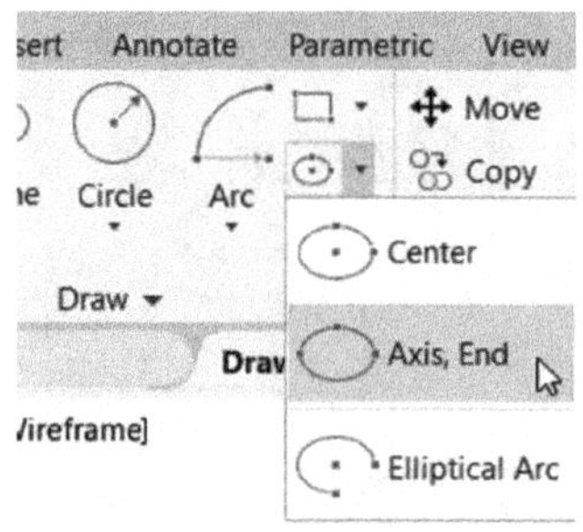

- Select the midpoint of the lower horizontal line of the rectangle.
- Move the pointer downward and type in 18, and then press Enter.
- Type-in 6 as the minor radius and press Enter.

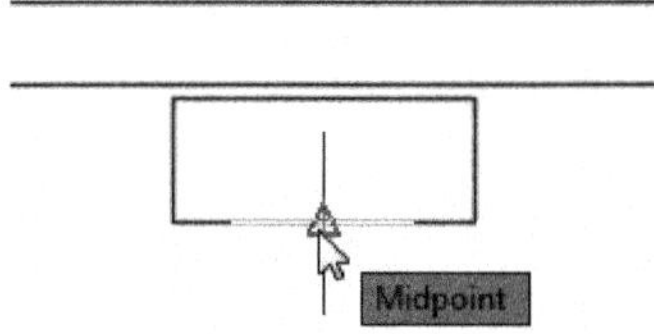

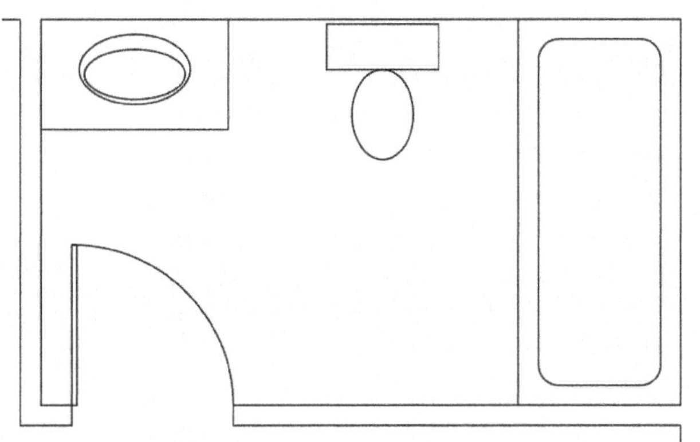

Adding Furniture using Blocks

- Type **DC** and press Enter; the **Design Center** palette appears.
- On the **Design Center** palette, click the **Home** button; the folder containing all the samples is opened.

- In the **Design Center** palette, expand the **Sample** folder and go to **en-us > Design Center > Home – Space Planner.dwg**.

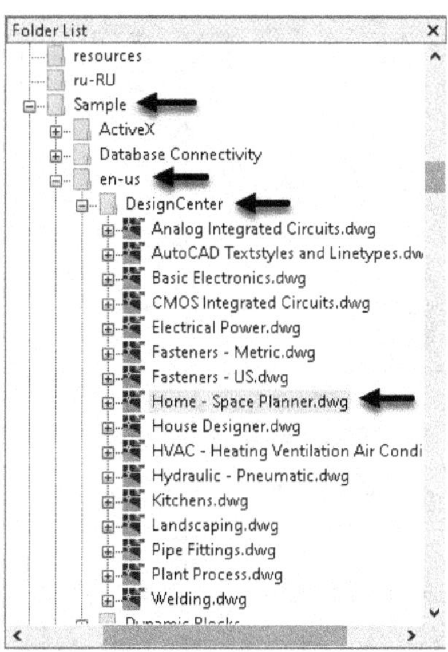

- Double-click the **Blocks** icon. It displays all the blocks available in the selected drawing file.

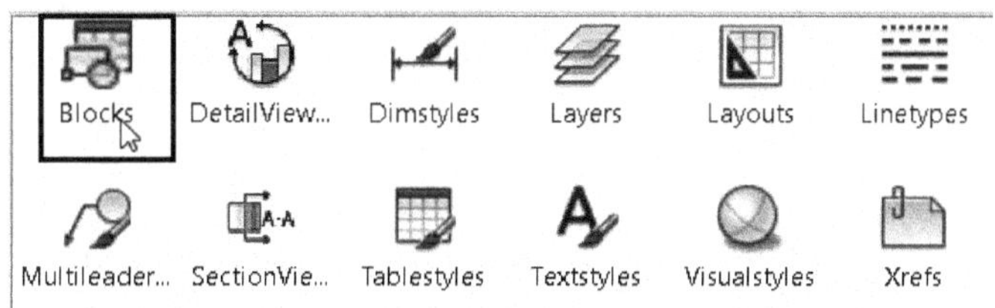

- Click and drag the highlighted blocks into the graphics window.

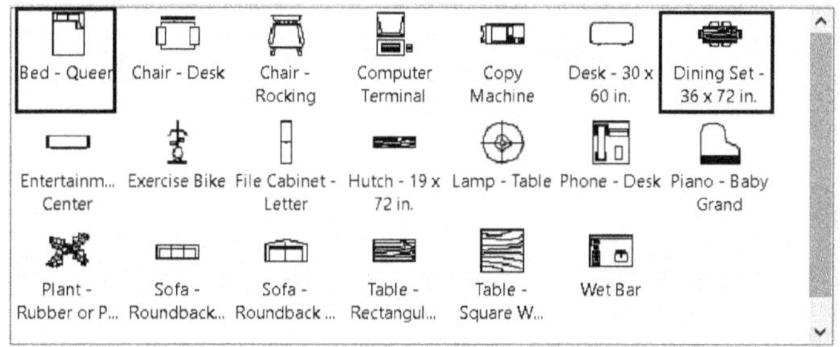

- Close the **Design Center** palette.
- Select the Dining set block, and then click on the point located at its center.
- Move the block and place it at the location shown below.

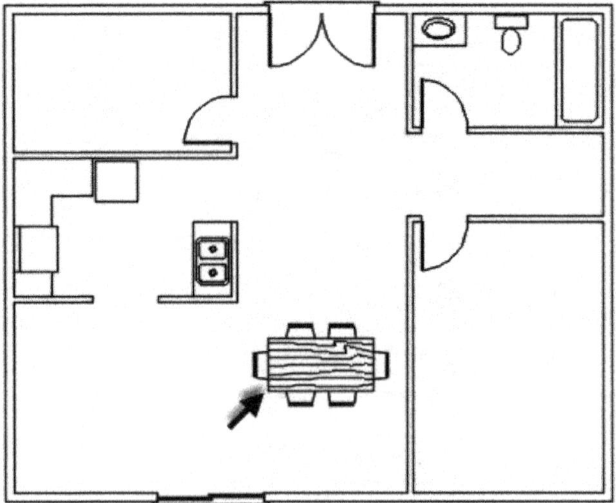

- Activate the **Rectangle** command and select the corner point of the bedroom, as shown.

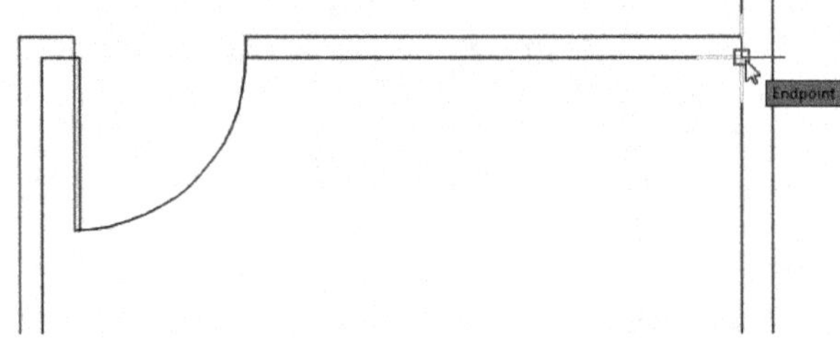

- Select the **Dimensions** option from the command line, and then specify **86** and **27.5** as the length and width of the rectangle, respectively.
- Move the pointer downward and click to create the rectangle.

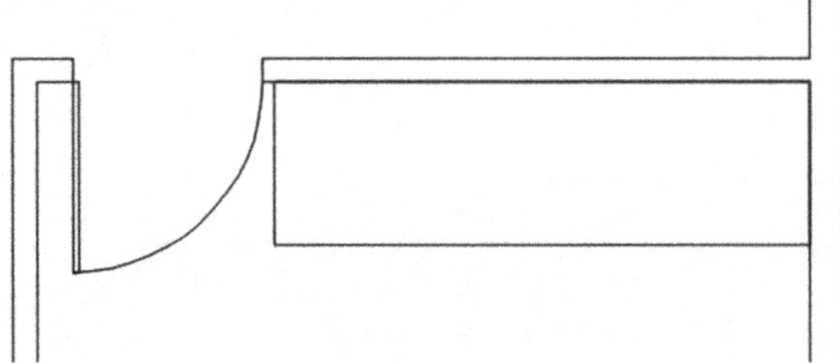

- Create another rectangle by selecting the corner points, as shown below.

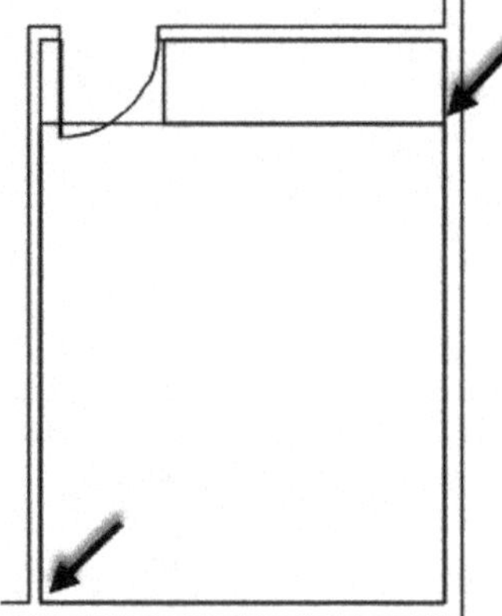

- Offset the rectangle by a distance of 47.5 inwards.
- Delete the original rectangle.

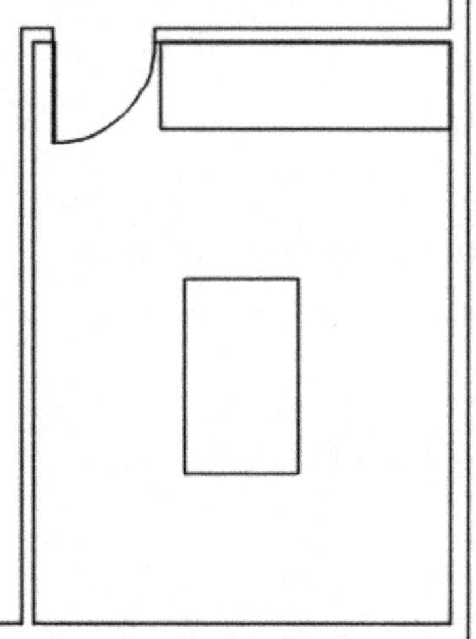

- Rotate the bed by **90** degrees.
- Activate the **Move** command and select the bed. Press Enter to accept the selection.
- Select the top left corner of the bed to define the base point.
- Select the top left corner of the offset rectangle to define the destination point.

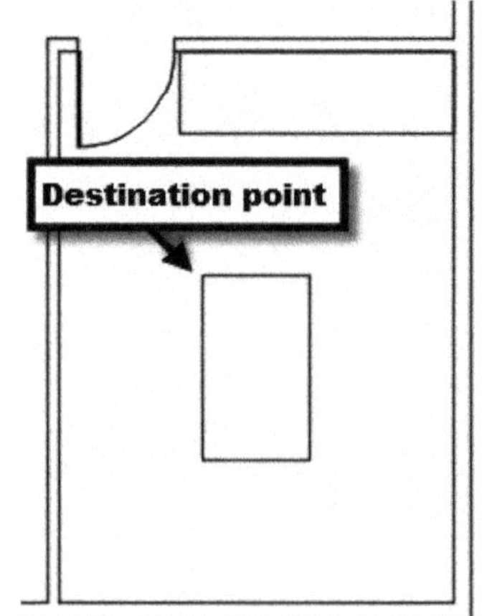

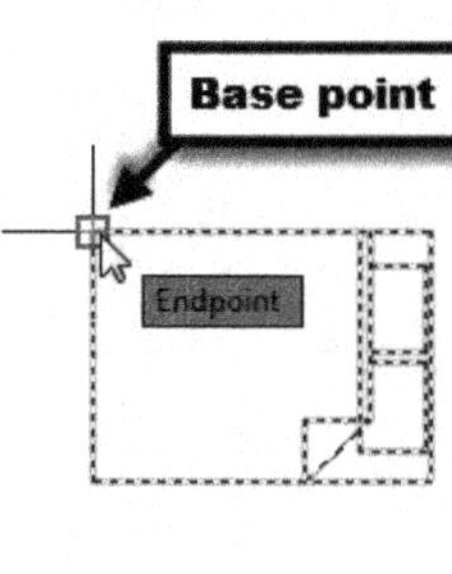

- Delete the offset rectangle.

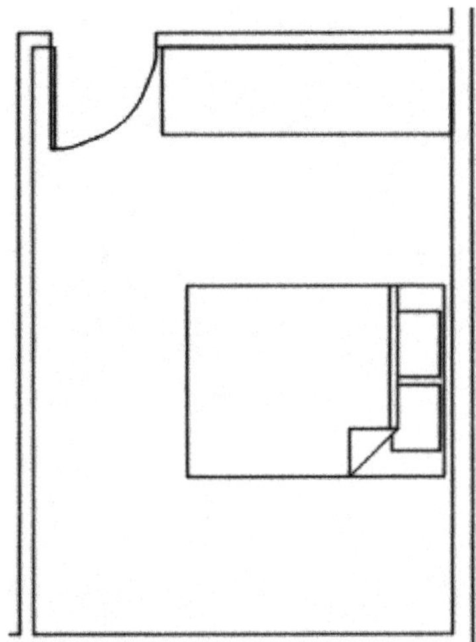

Adding Windows

- In the empty space, create the window using the **Line** command, as shown below.

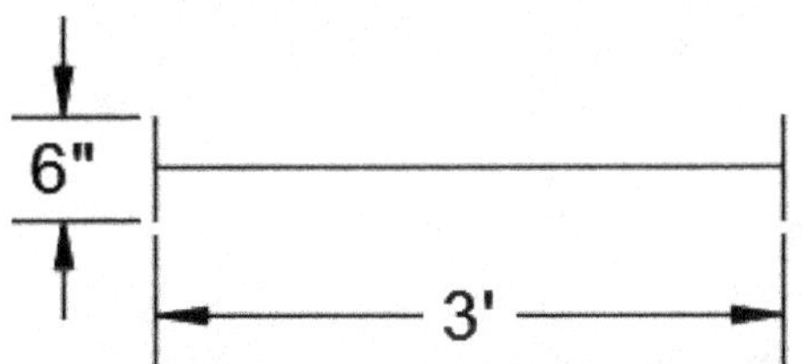

- On the ribbon, click **Insert > Block Definition > Create Block**.
- On the **Block Definition** dialog, type-in **Window** in the **Name** box.
- Click the **Select Objects** button and select all the elements of the window by dragging a selection window.
- Press **Enter**.
- Click the **Pick point** button and select the lower-left corner of the window.

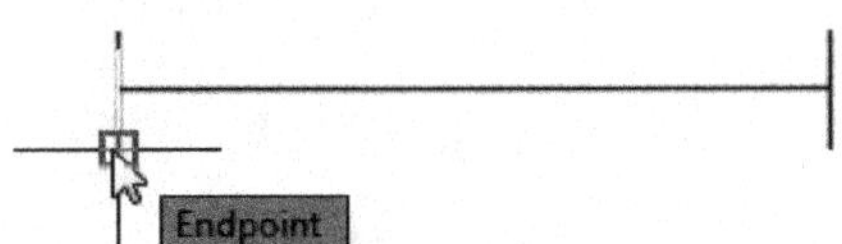

- On the dialog, check the **Open in block editor** option and click **OK**. It creates the block and opens it in the **Block Editor**.
- On the ribbon, click **Block Editor** tab > **Action Parameters** > **Parameters** drop-down > **Linear**.

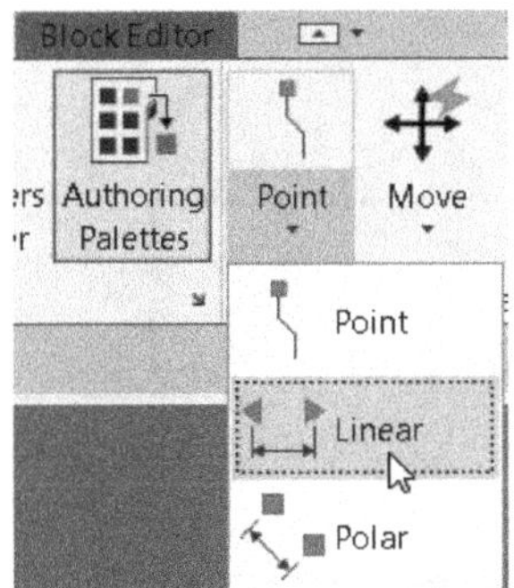

- Click the endpoints of the horizontal line.
- Move the pointer downward and click to define the parameter location.

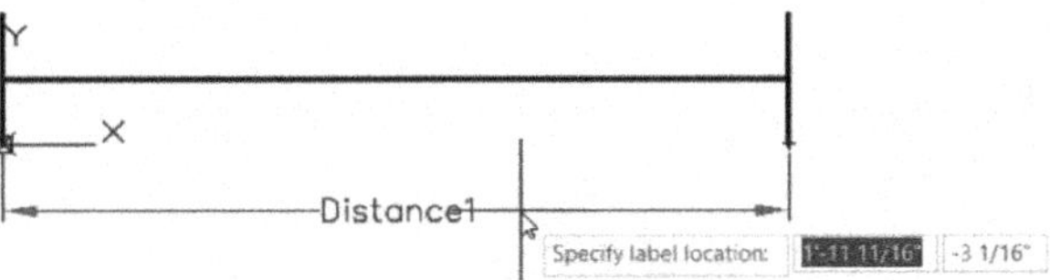

- Press Enter to specify 2 as the number of the grips to be displayed when you select the parameter.
- On the ribbon, click **Block Editor** tab > **Action Parameters** > **Actions** drop-down > **Stretch**.

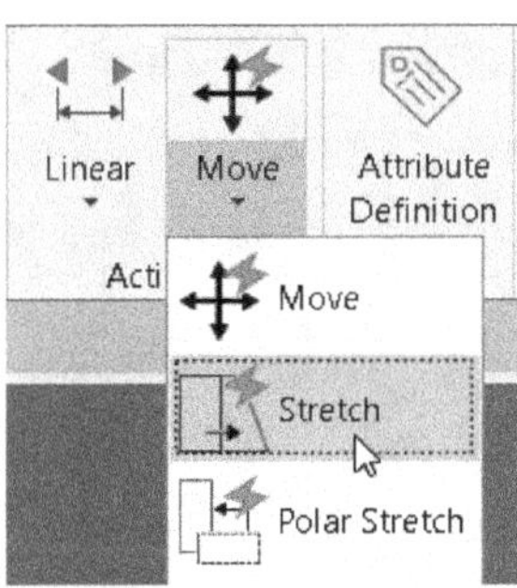

- Select the **Distance1** parameter.
- Select the right endpoint of the horizontal line. It defines the point that can be used to stretch the block.

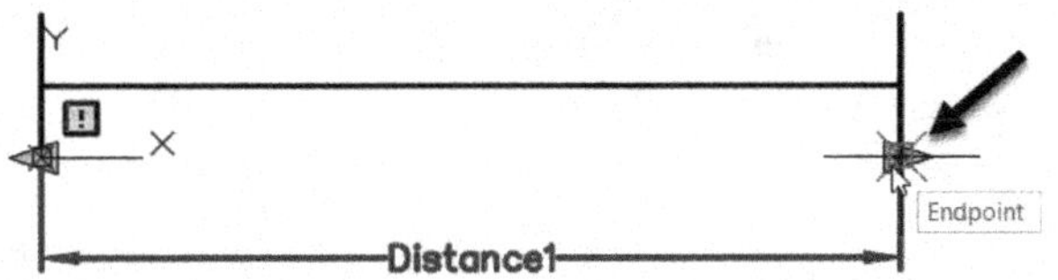

- Create a window around the selected endpoint.

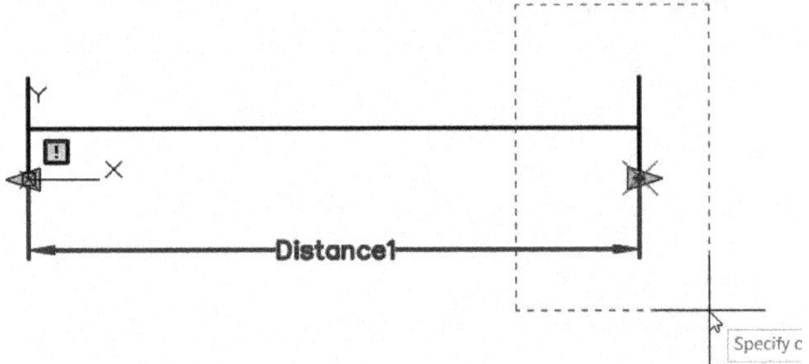

- Select the horizontal and right vertical lines, and then press Enter. It defines the elements that can be stretched.

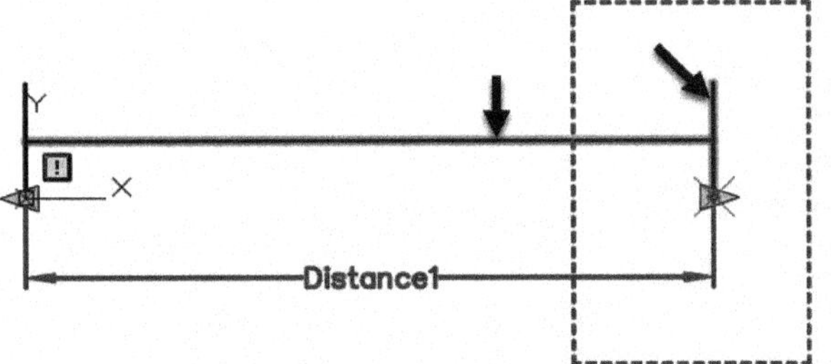

- On the **Block Editor** ribbon tab, click **Open/Save > Test Block**. The **Test Block Window** appears.
- Select the block and click the arrow grip. Drag the pointer to stretch the block.

- On the ribbon, click the **Close Test Block** button.
- Click the **Save Block** button on the **Open/Save** panel.
- Click the **Close Block Editor** button on the **Close** panel. It closes the **Block Editor** window. Now, you need to place the windows.
- On the ribbon, click **Insert > Block > Insert > Window**.

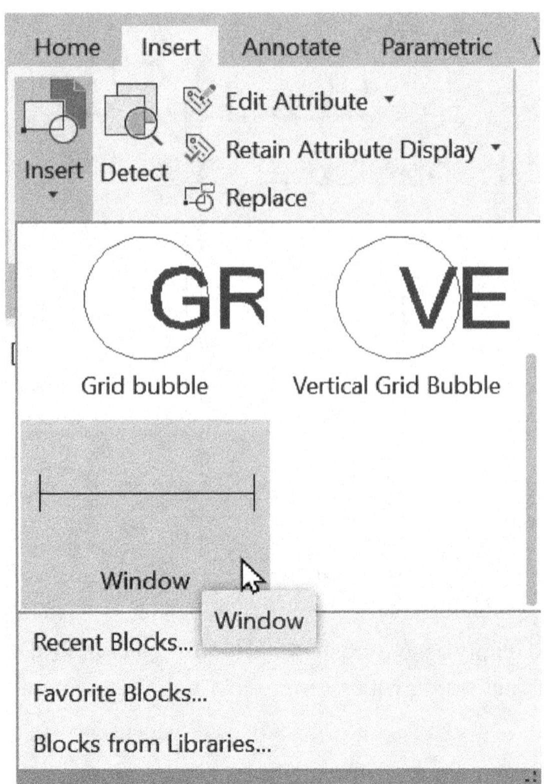

- Press and hold the Shift key and right click.
- Select **From**.
- Select the lower right corner of the bedroom.
- Move the pointer on the horizontal wall and type in 95, and then press Enter. The **Window** block will be placed at the specified location.

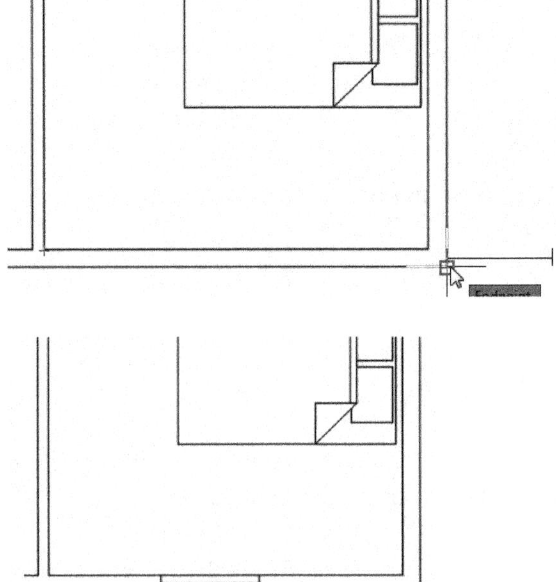

- Activate the **Dynamic Input** icon on the Status bar.
- Select the **Window** block and drag the arrow grip.
- Type-in **54** and press Enter. It changes the window size to **54**.

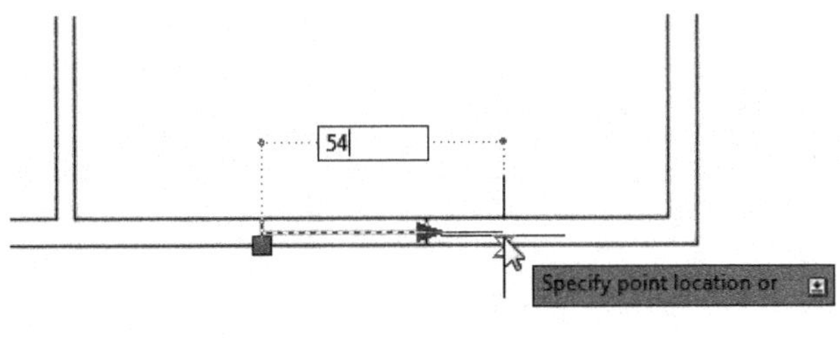

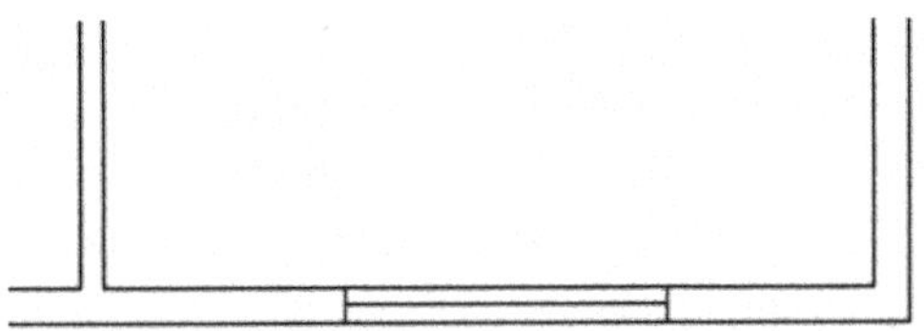

- On the ribbon, click **Insert > Block > Insert > Window**.
- Select the **Rotate** option from the command line.
- Type-in **90** and press Enter.
- Place the **Window** block on the kitchen wall, as shown below.

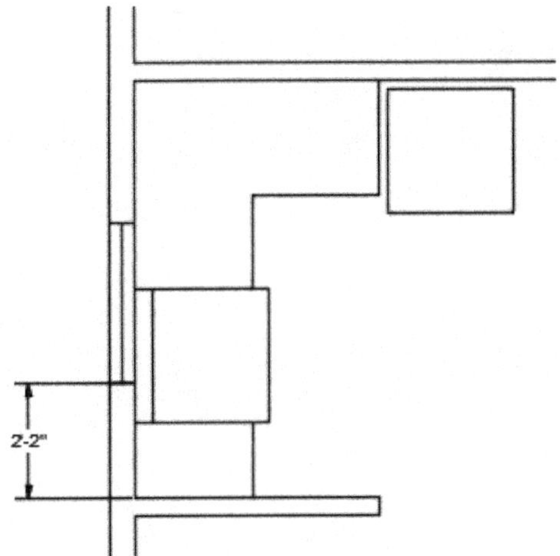

- Likewise, place the window blocks, as shown below.

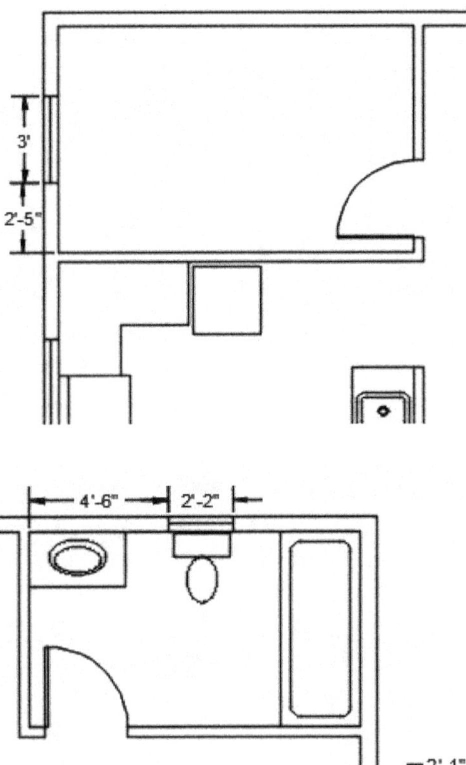

Arranging Objects of the drawing in Layers

- On the ribbon, click the **Home > Layers > Layer Properties**. It displays the Layer Properties Manager.
- On the **Layer Properties Manager** palette, click the **New Layer** button.

- Type **Wall** in the layer **Name** box and press Enter.
- Create another layer, and then type-in **Door** — press Enter.
  - Likewise, create other layers and define the layer properties, as shown below. Refer to Chapter 3 to learn more about layers.

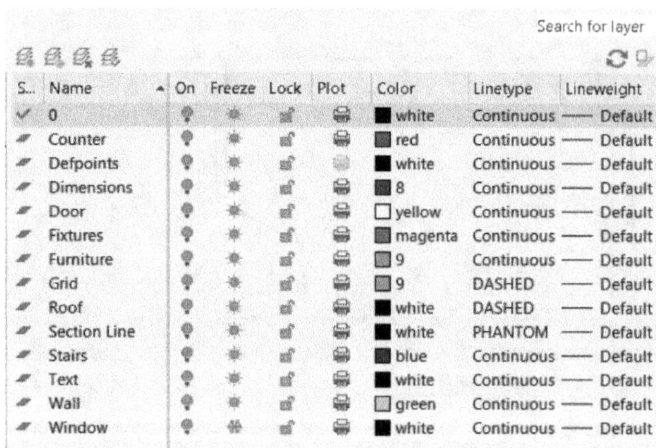

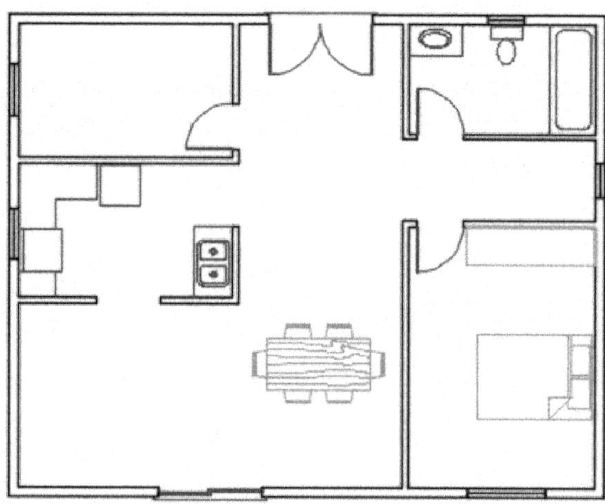

- Close the **Layer Properties Manager**.
- Select the Dining set, cupboard, and bed.
- On the ribbon, click **Home > Layers > Layer drop-down > Furniture**. The selected objects will be transferred to the Furniture layer.

- Open the **Layer Properties Manager** and click the bulb symbols associated with Door, Window, Fixtures, Furniture, and Counter layers. It will hide the corresponding layers.

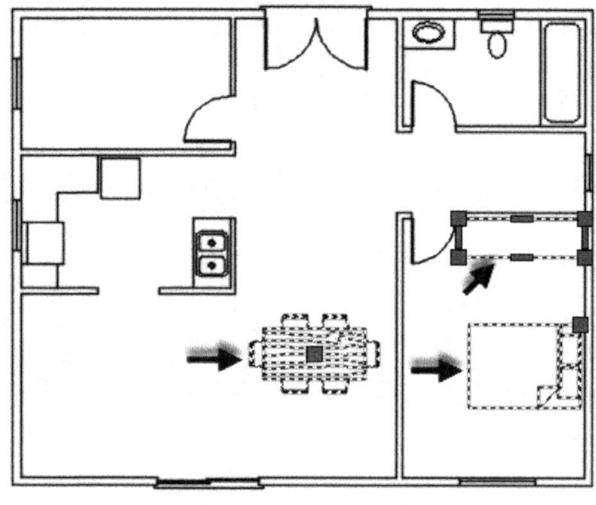

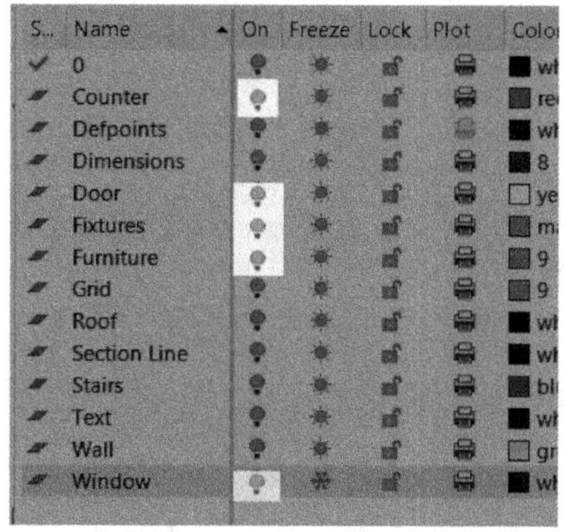

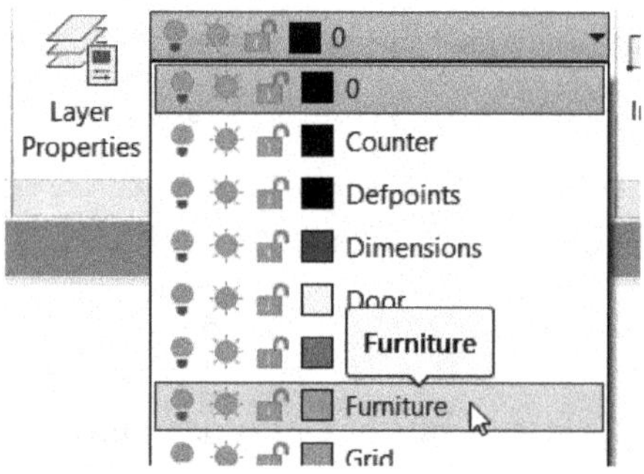

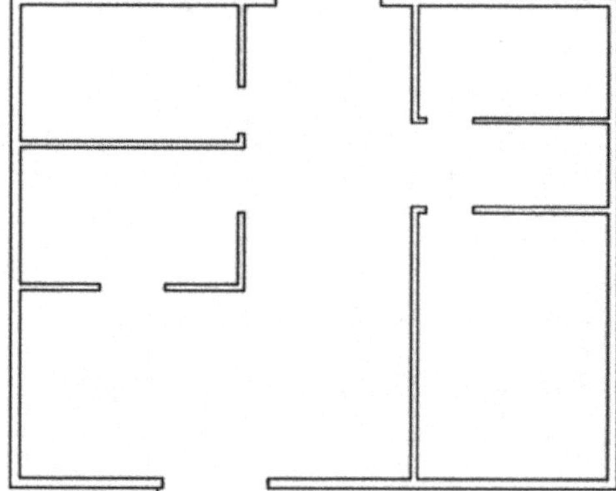

- Press Esc to deselect the selected objects.
- Likewise, transfer the other objects to their respective layers.

- Create a selection window and select all the walls.
- On the ribbon, click **Home > Layers > Layer drop-down > Wall**. All the walls will be transferred to the **Wall** layer.

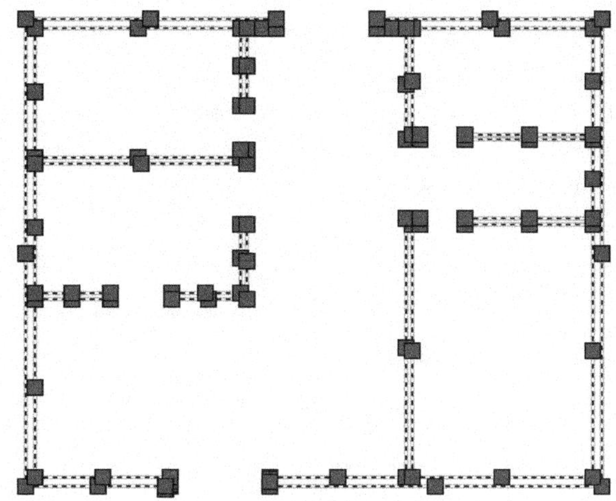

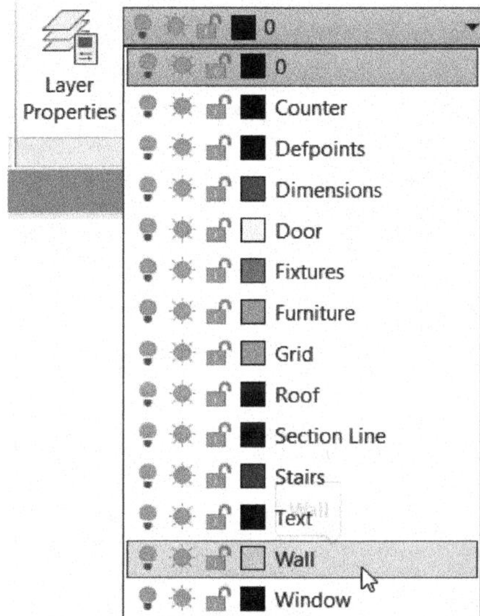

- Now, turn ON the hidden layers by clicking the bulb symbols.

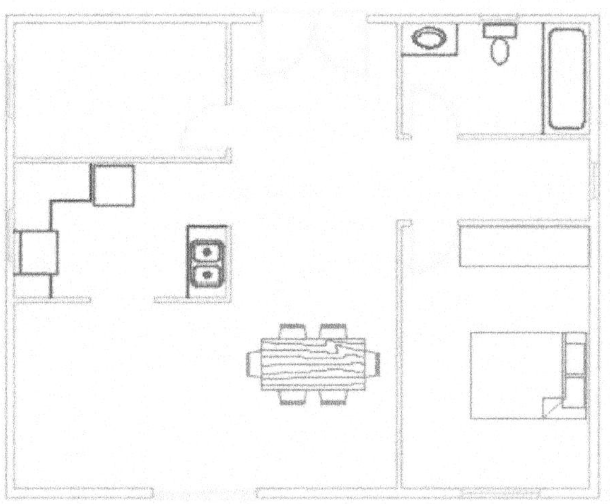

Creating Grid Lines

- On the ribbon, click **Home > Layers > Layer drop-down > Grid**. The Grid layer becomes active.

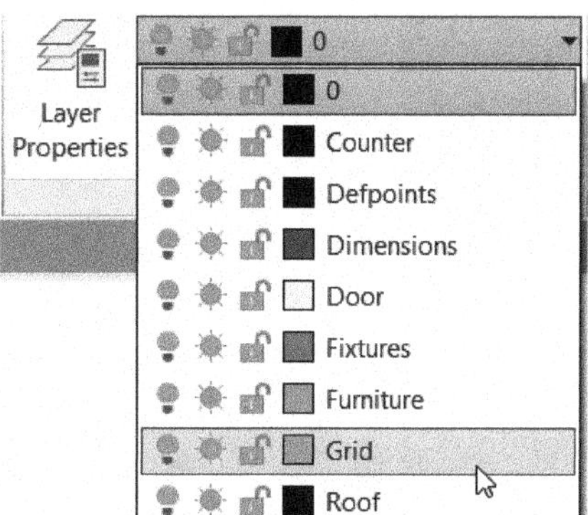

- Activate the **Line** command.
- Press and hold the Shift key and right-click, and then select the **Mid Between 2 Points** option.
- Select the endpoints of the wall, as shown below.

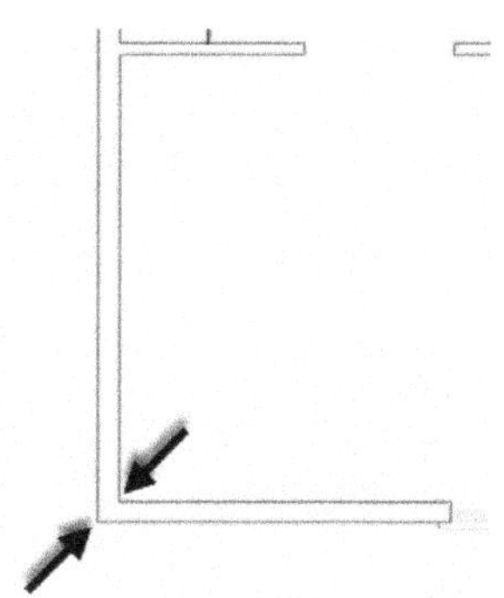

- Move the point upward and click to draw a vertical line of arbitrary length.

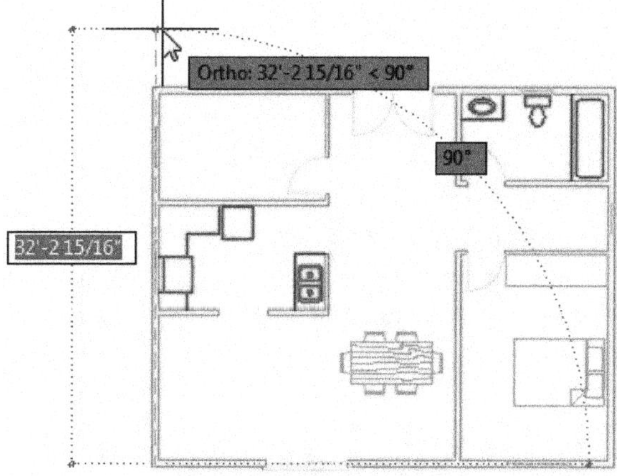

- Press Esc to deactivate the **Line** command.
- Select the line to display grips on it.

- Click the lower end grip and drag the pointer to increase the length of the line.
- Activate the **Offset** command and offset the grid line up to 406.
- Create other grid lines, as shown below.

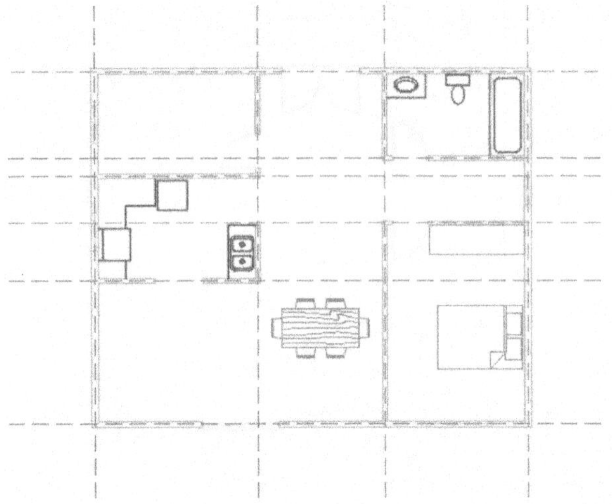

- Create a new layer called **Grid Bubbles** and make it current.

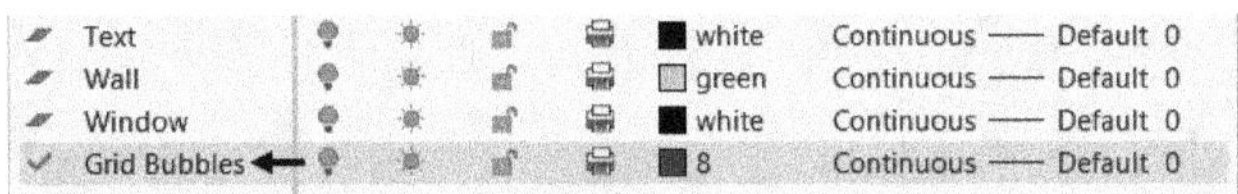

- Create a circle of 12 diameter.
- On the ribbon, click **Insert > Block Definition > Define Attributes**.

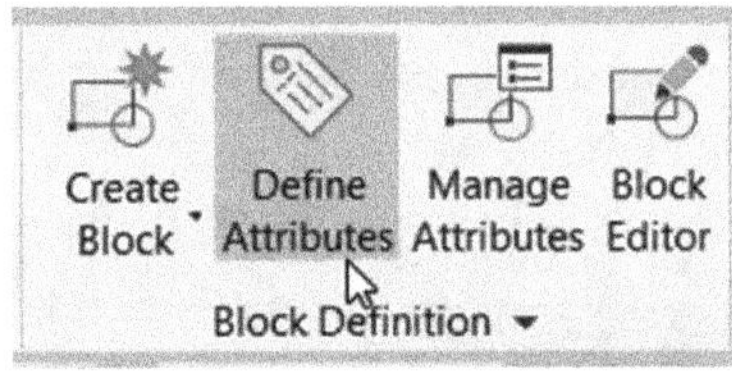

- On the **Attribute Definition** dialog, type-in GRIDBUBBLE in the **Tag** box and select **Justification > Middle center**.
- Type-in 6″ in the **Text height** box and click **OK**.
- Select the center point of the circle. The attribute text will be placed at its center.

GRIDBUBBLE

- On the ribbon, click **Insert > Block Definition >**

Create Block.

- Type-in Grid Bubble in the **Name** box and click the **Select objects** button.
- Draw a crossing window to select the circle and attribute. Press Enter to accept the selection.
- Click the **Pick point** icon under the **Base point** section.
- Select the lower quadrant point of the circle to define the base point of the block.

- Uncheck the **Open in block editor** option and click **OK**.
- On the ribbon, click **Insert > Block > Insert > Grid bubble**.

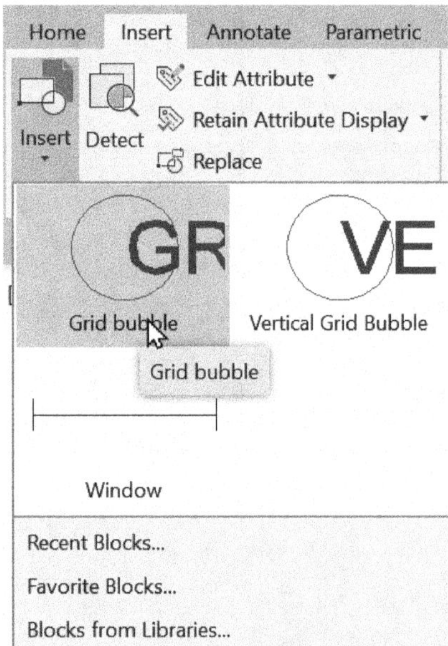

- Select the top endpoint of the first vertical grid line. The **Edit Attributes** dialog pops up.
- Type-in **A** in the GRIDBUBBLE box and click **OK**.

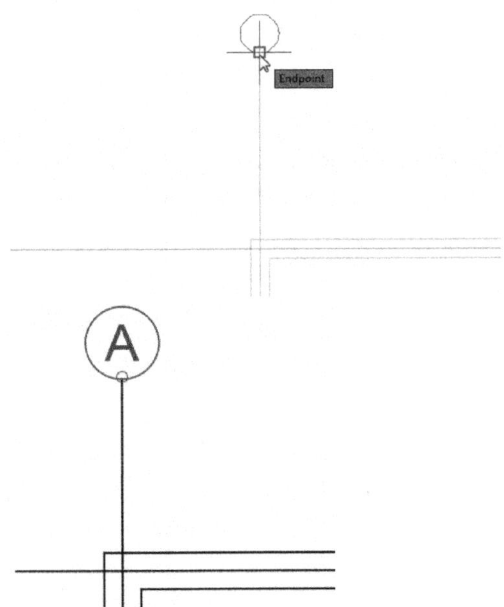

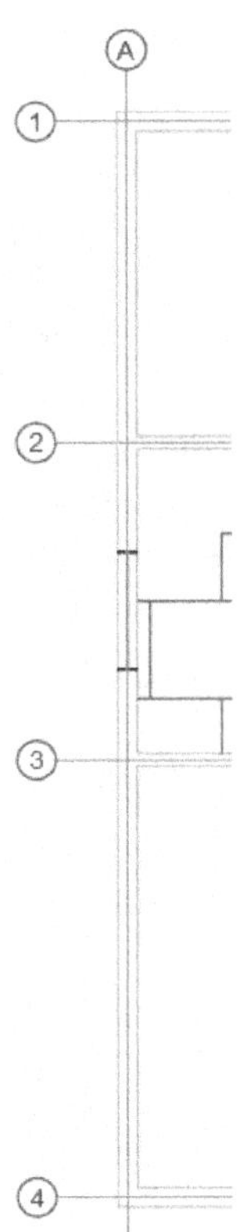

- Likewise, add other grid bubbles to the vertical grid lines.

- Create another block with the name Vertical Grid bubble. Make sure that you select the right quadrant point of the circle as the base point.

- Insert the vertical grid bubbles, as shown below.

Adding Dimensions

- On the ribbon, click **Home > Layers > Layer drop-down > Dimensions** to make it current.
- Type **D** in the command line and press Enter.
- On the **Dimension Style Manager** dialog, select the **Standard** dimension style and click the **New** button.
- Type-in Floor Plan in the **New Style Name** box and click **Continue**.
- Click the **Primary Units** tab and select **Unit format > Architectural**.
- Set **Precision** to **0'-01/16"**.
- Set **Fraction format** to **Horizontal**.
- Under the **Zero Suppression** section, uncheck the **0 inches** option.
- Click the **Symbols and Arrows** tab.
- Under the **Arrowheads** section, select **First > Architectural tick**. The second arrowhead is automatically changed to **Architectural tick**.
- Select **Leader > Closed Filled** and enter 1/4' in the **Arrow Size** box.
- Click the **Lines** tab and set **Extend beyond dim lines** and **Offset from origin** to 3".
- Click the **Text** tab and **Text height** to 6".
- In the **Text placement** section, set the following settings.

Vertical-Centered
Horizontal-Centered
View Direction-Left-to-Right

- In the **Text alignment** section, select the **Aligned with dimension line** option.
- Click the **Fit** tab and select **Either text or arrows (best fit)** option from the **Fit Options** section.
- In the **Text placement** section, select the **Over dimension line, without Leader** option.
- Click **OK** and click **Set Current** on the **Dimension Style Manager**. Click **Close**.
- On the ribbon, click **Annotate > Dimensions > Dimension**.
- Select the points on the vertical grid lines, as shown below.
- Move the pointer and click to locate the dimension.

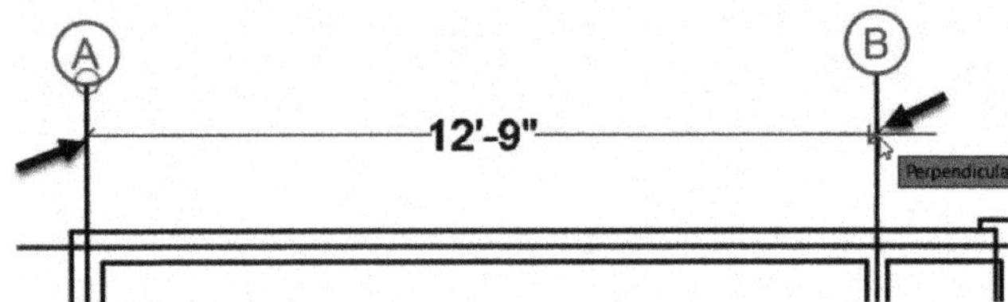

- On the ribbon, click **Annotate > Dimensions > Continue**. You will notice that a dimension is attached to the pointer
- Move the pointer and click on the next grid line.
- Likewise, move the pointer and click on the next grid line.

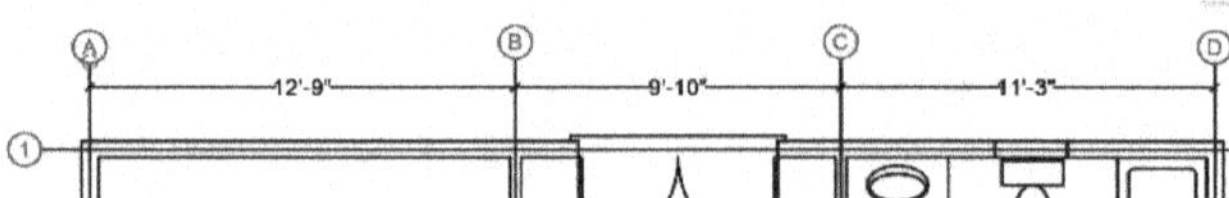

- Activate the **Dimension** command and create the overall horizontal dimension.

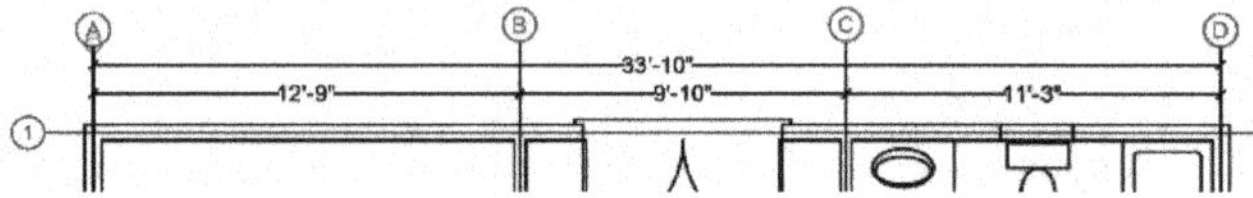

- Likewise, add vertical dimensions to the grid lines.

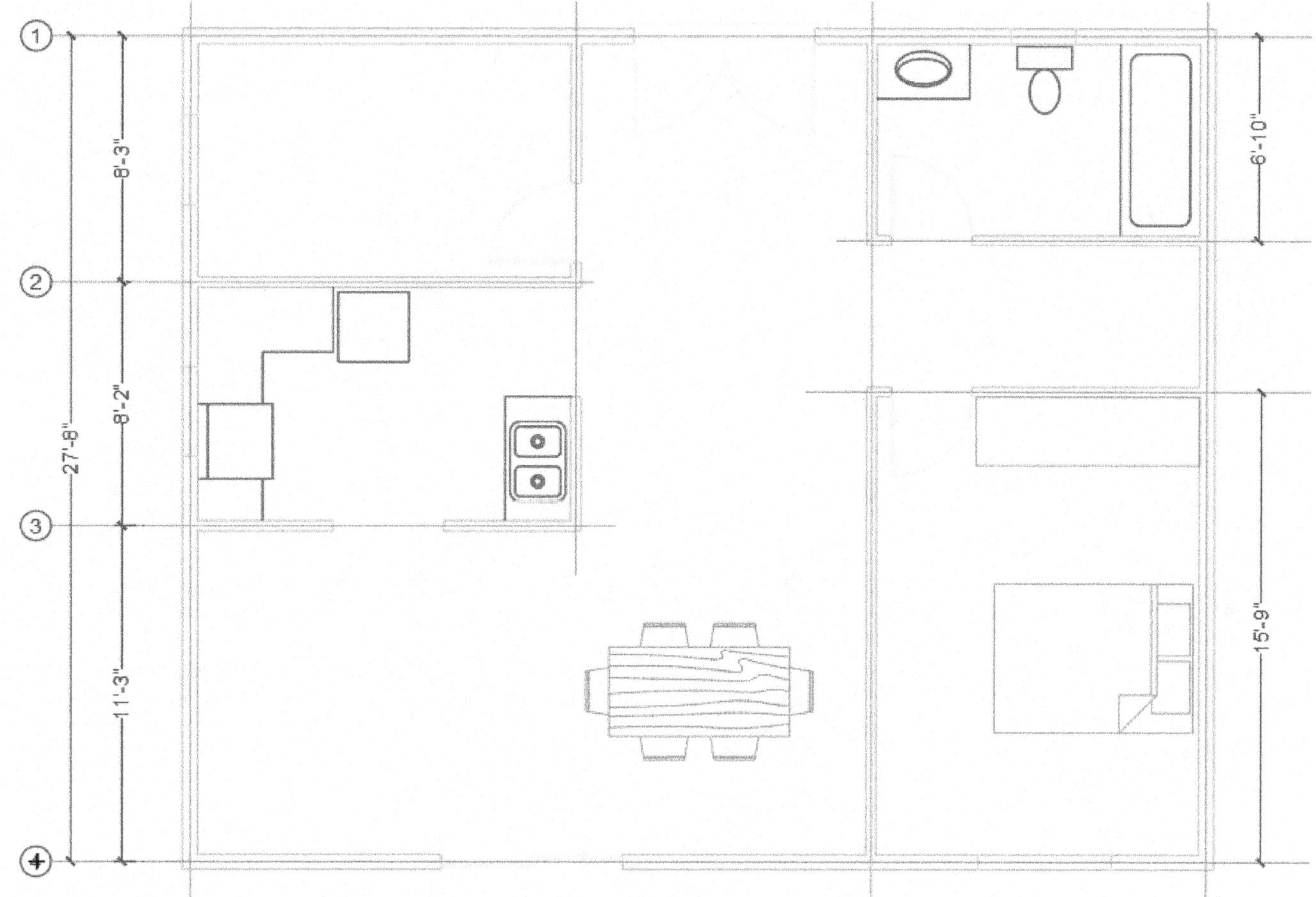

- Complete adding dimensions to the drawing, as shown below.

- On the ribbon, click **View > Palettes > Count**.

The **Count** palette appears. It displays the blocks available in the drawing and the count of each block.

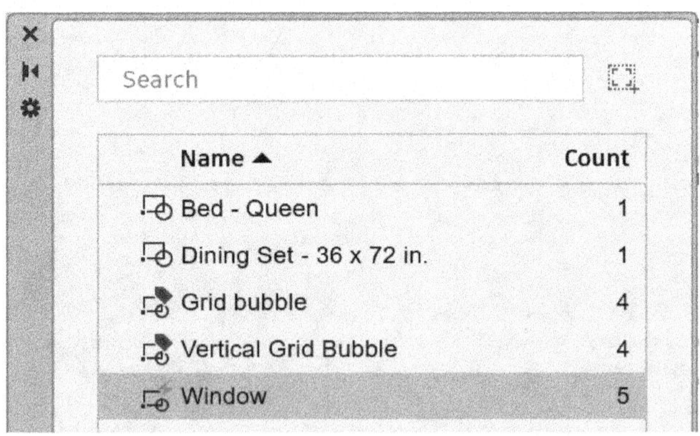

Name ▲	Count
Bed - Queen	1
Dining Set - 36 x 72 in.	1
Grid bubble	4
Vertical Grid Bubble	4
Window	5

- On the Count palette, click the **Count in a specified area** icon.

- Create a window by specifying the two corner points, as shown.

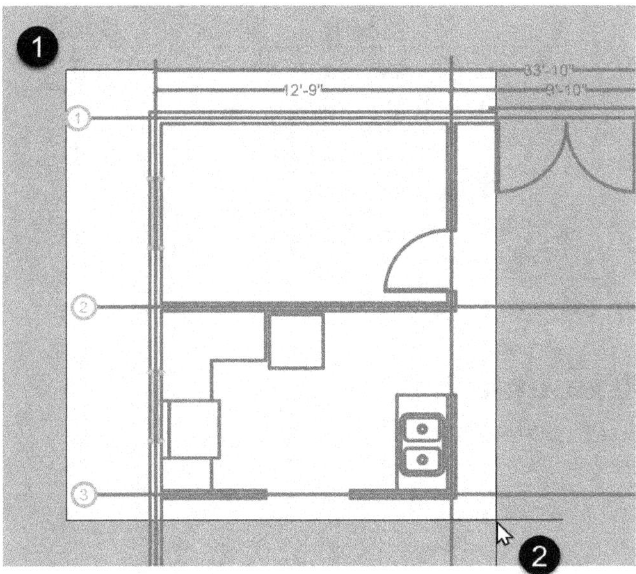

The blocks available in the specified region are displayed on the **Count** palette.

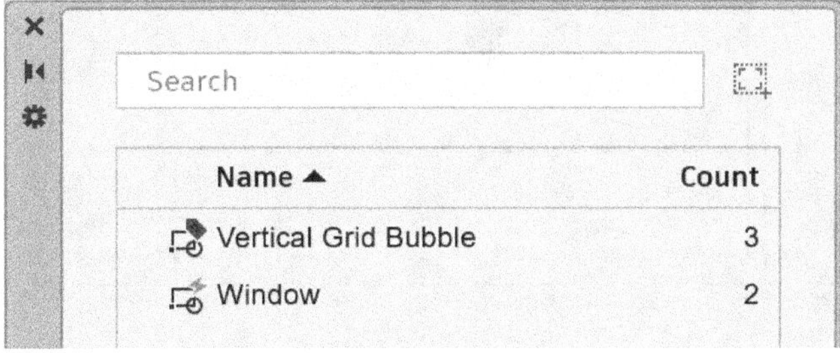

You can click the **Specify Area** icon on the Count toolbar and specify another area in the drawing.

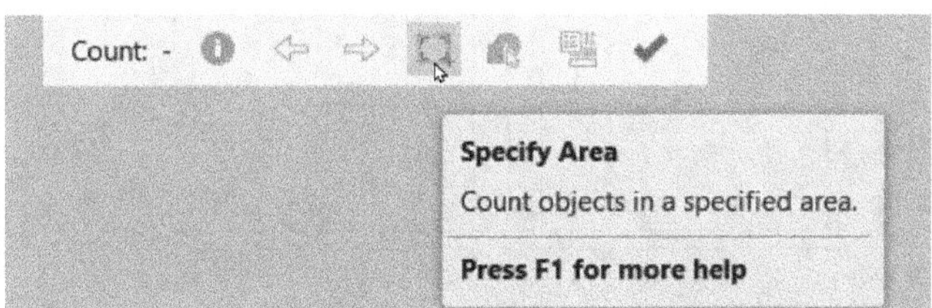

- Select the rectangular selection box and press DELETE.

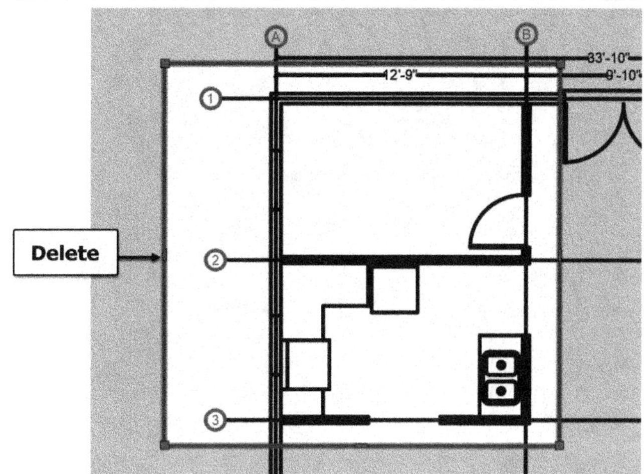

- Click the **Continue and count the entire model space** option on the **Count – Invalid Area** message box.
- On the **Count** palette, click the right mouse button on the **Window** block and select **Review Count Details**.

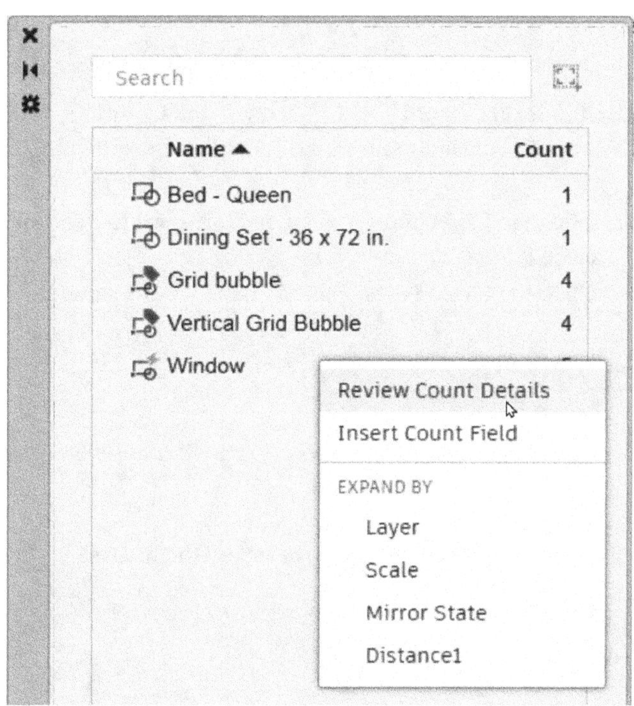

Use the arrows on the **Count** toolbar to zoom to the instances of the Window blocks.

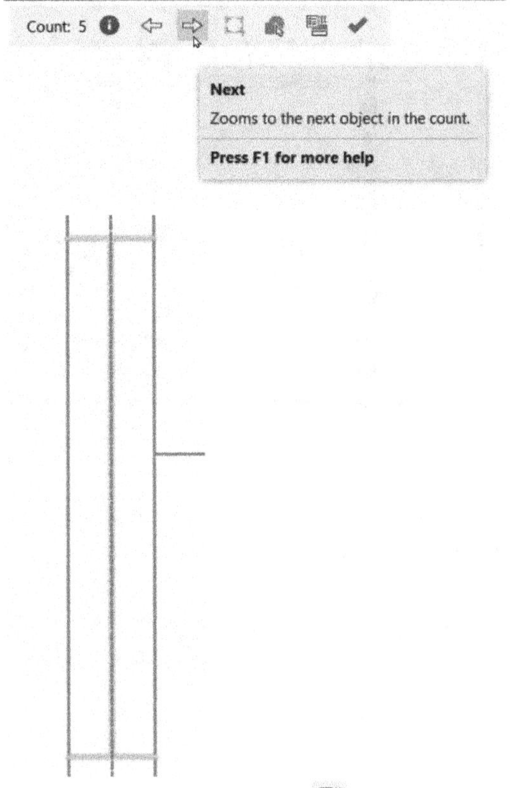

Use the **Insert Count Field** icon on the **Count** toolbar, if you want to insert the count into the drawing.

- Click the **End Count** icon on the **Count** toolbar to close it.
- Click the **Create table** button on the **Count** palette.

- Check the **Select all** box to select all the blocks.

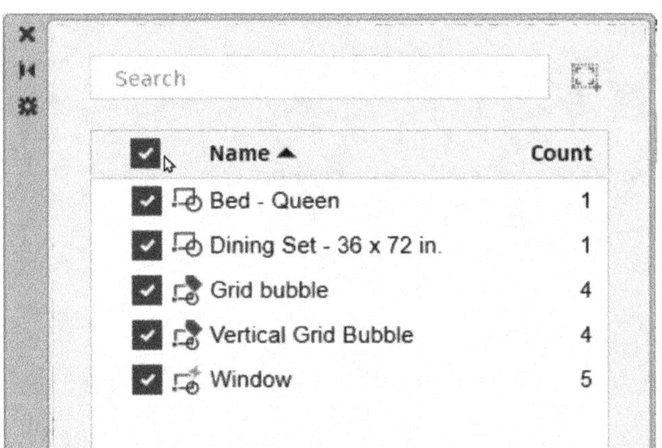

- Click the **Insert** button.

- Click in the graphics window to place the count table.

Item	Count
Window	5
Vertical Grid Bubble	4
Grid bubble	4
Dining Set - 36 x 72 in.	1
Bed - Queen	1

- Save and close the drawing.

Example 2

In this tutorial, you will draw stairs.

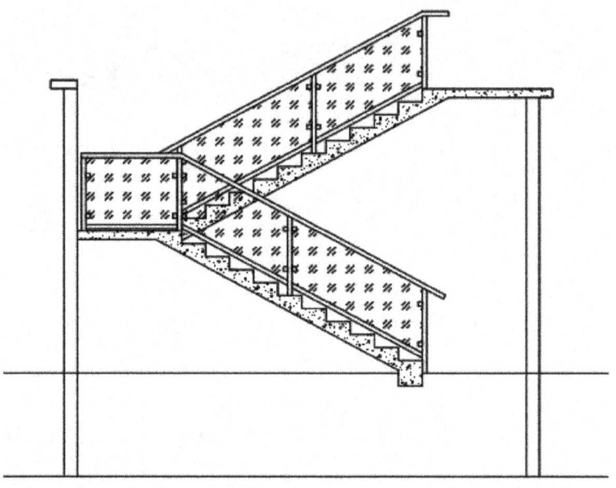

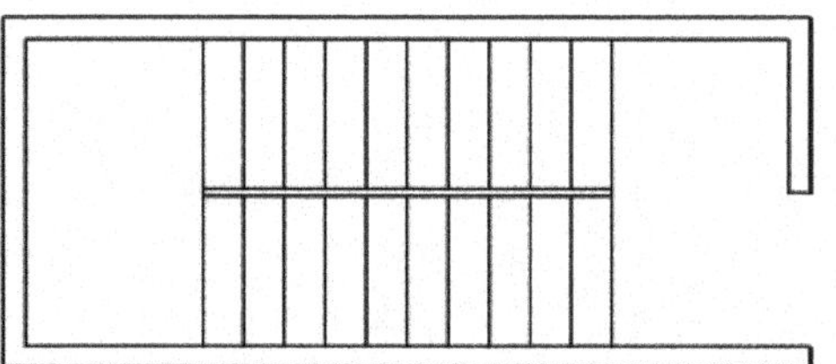

Staircase Nomenclature

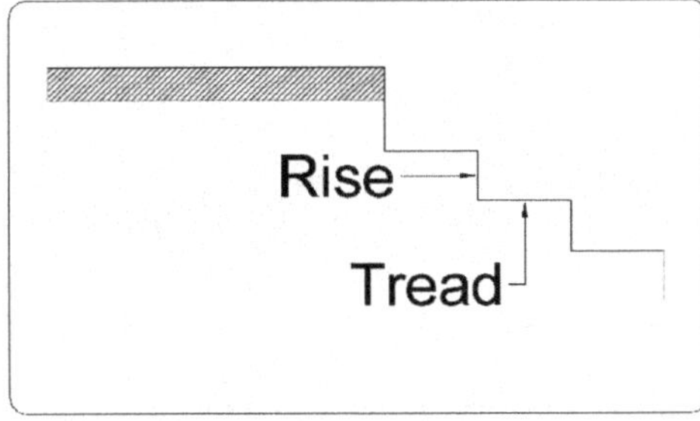

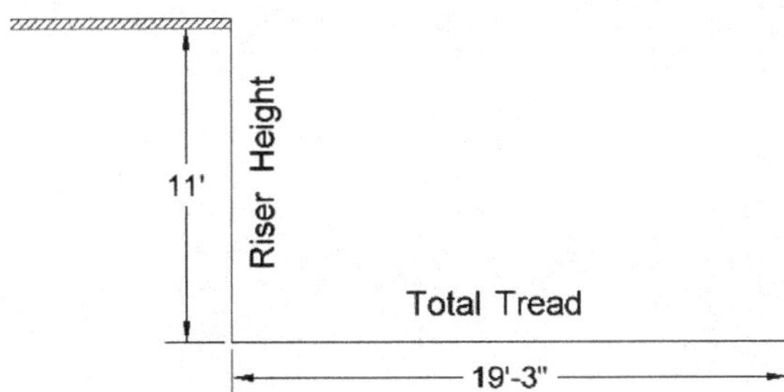

Creating the Stairs

- Start a new AutoCAD file using the **acad.dwt** template.

- Set the **Workspace** to **Drafting & Annotation**.

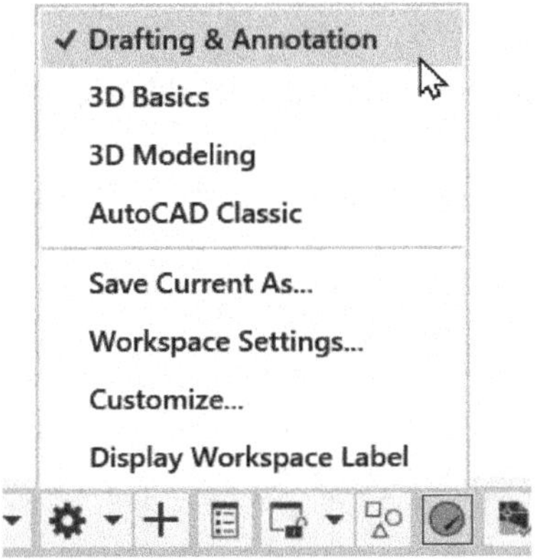

- Type **UN** in the command line and press Enter.
- On the **Drawing Units** dialog, select **Type > Architectural**.
- Select **Precision > 0-01/16**.
- Set the **Insertion Scale** to **Inches**, and click **OK**.
- Type LIMITS in the command line and press Enter.
- Press Enter to accept 0, 0 as the lower limit.
- Type 50', 40' in the command line, and press Enter. The program sets the upper limit of the drawing.
- Click the **Zoom** drop-down > **Zoom All** on the Navigation Bar.
- Turn OFF the grid.

- Click the **ORTHOMODE** icon on the Status bar.
- Click the **Polyline** tool on the **Draw** panel of the **Home** ribbon tab.
- Click to define the start point of the line.
- Move the pointer toward left.
- Type 17'8" and press ENTER.
- Move the pointer upward.
- Type 7' and press ENTER.
- Move the pointer toward the right.
- Type 17'2" and press ENTER.
- Move the pointer downward.
- Type 3'6" and press ENTER.
- Press Esc.

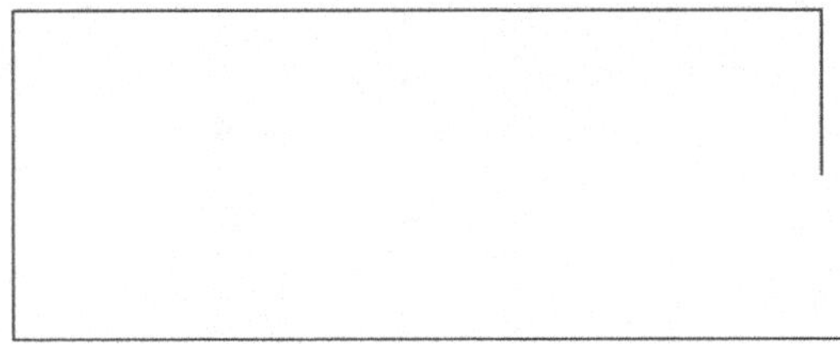

- Click the **Offset** icon on the **Modify** panel of the **Home** ribbon tab.
- Type 6" and press ENTER.
- Select the polyline.
- Move the pointer outward and click.

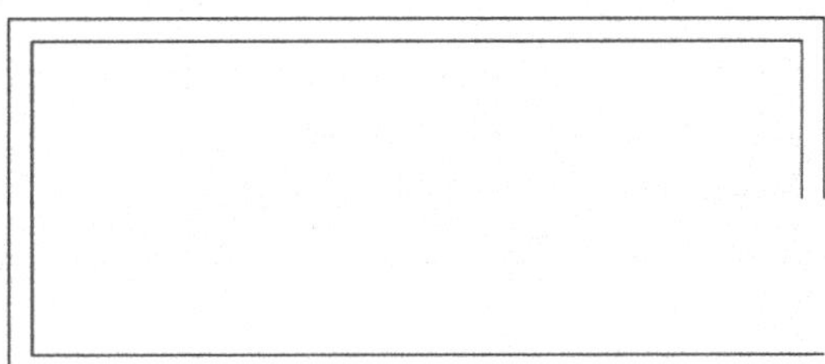

- Click the **Line** tool and close the open ends of the drawing, as shown.

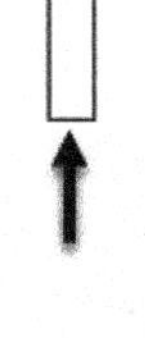

- Create a selection window across all the elements of the drawing.

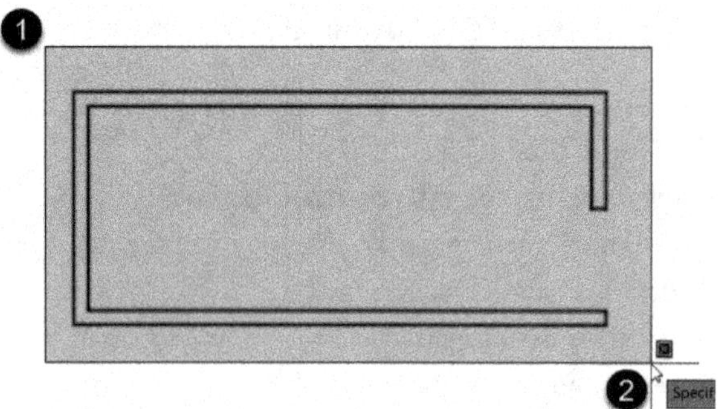

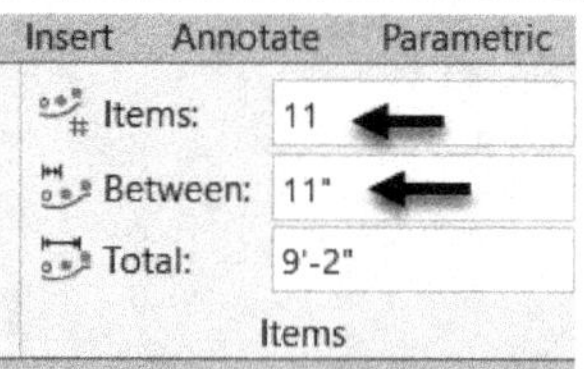

- Click the **Explode** icon on the **Modify** panel of the **Home** ribbon tab. The polylines are exploded into lines.
- Click the **Offset** icon on the **Modify** panel of the **Home** ribbon tab.
- Type 4' and press ENTER.
- Select the left vertical inner edge.
- Move the pointer toward right and click.

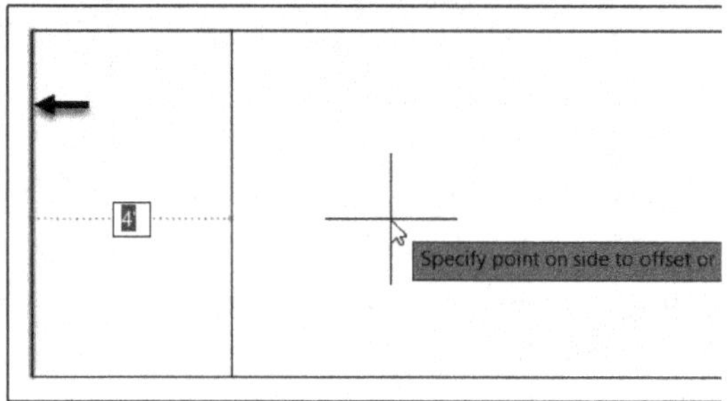

- Press ENTER.
- On the **Home** tab of the ribbon, click **Modify** panel > **Array** drop-down > **Path Array**.
- Select the offset line and press ENTER.
- Click on the inner horizontal line at the location, as shown.

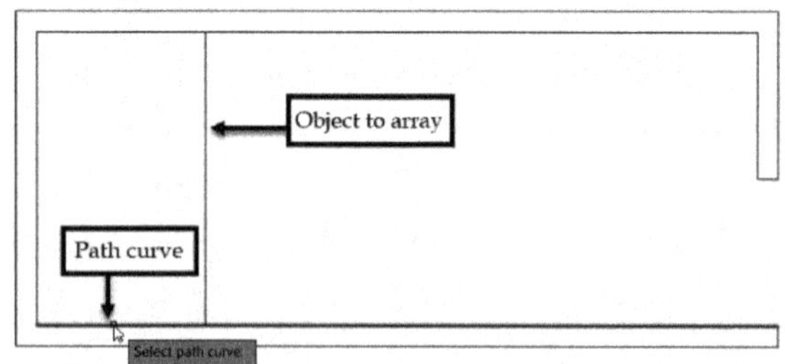

- On the **Array Creation** tab, click the **Items** icon on the **Items** panel.
- Type **11** in the **Items** and **Between** boxes, respectively.

- Deactivate the **Associative** icon on the **Properties** panel.
- Click the **Close Array** icon.

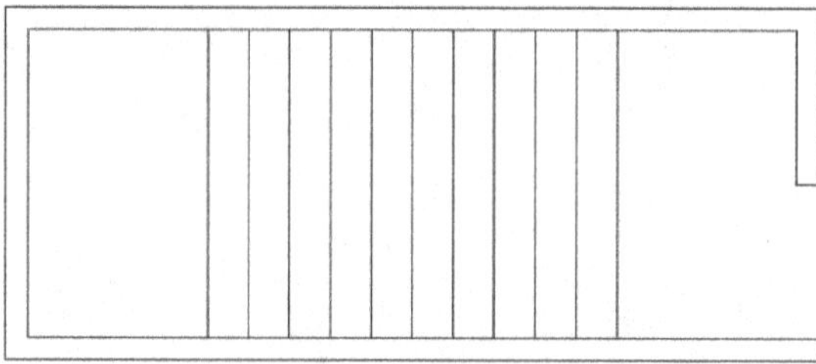

- Offset the inner horizontal lines by 3'5" distance in the inward direction.

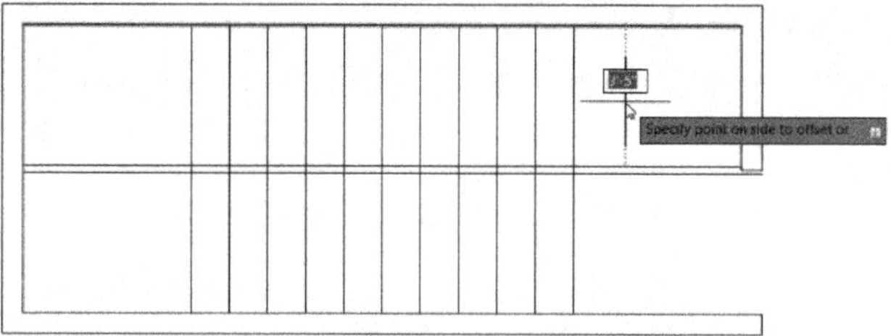

- On the **Home** tab of the ribbon, click **Modify** panel > **Trim/Extend** drop-down > **Trim**.
- Select the portions of the horizontal lines, as shown.

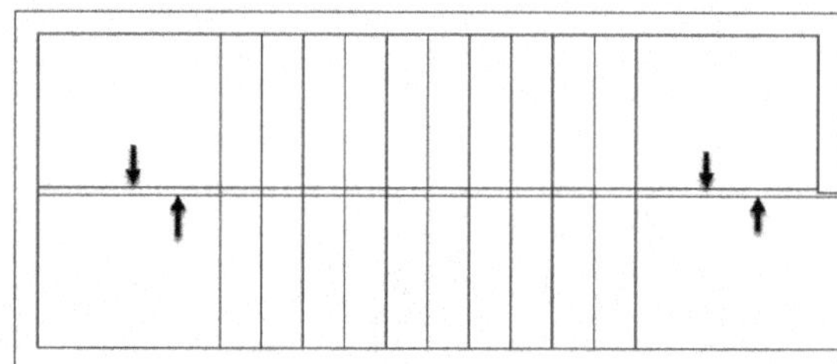

- Zoom-in to the center portion of the stairs.
- Click on the portions of the vertical lines, as shown.

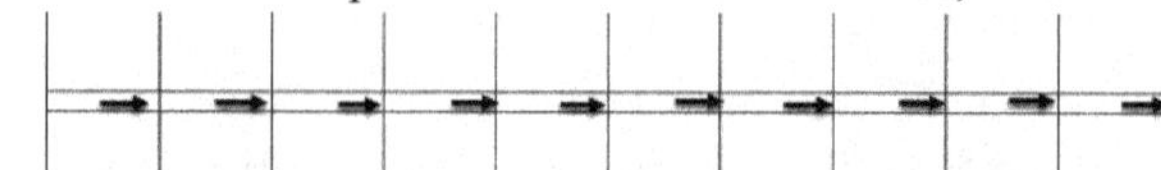

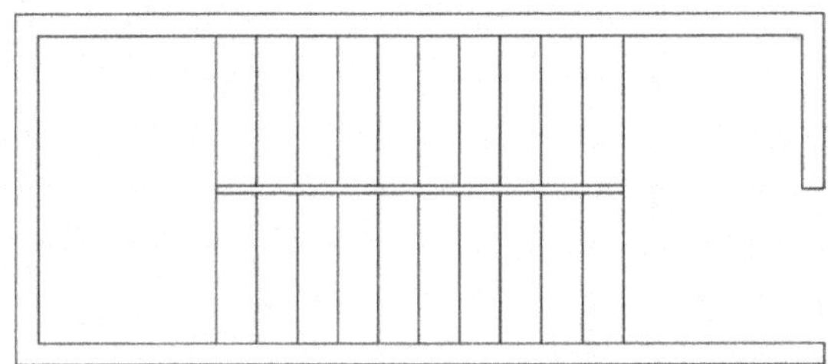

Creating the Section elevation of the Staircase

- Create a horizontal line above the staircase, as shown.

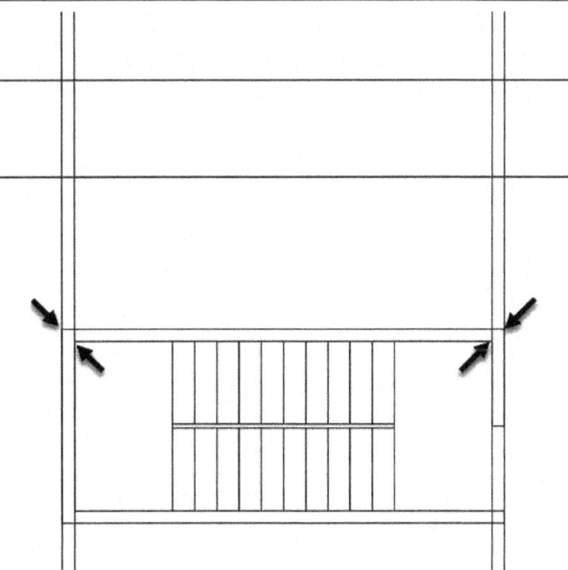

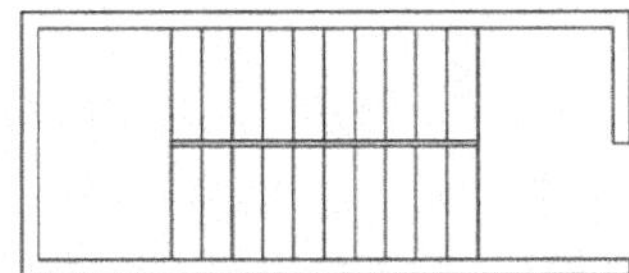

- Click the **Offset** icon on the **Modify** panel of the **Home** ribbon tab.
- Type 4' and press ENTER.
- Select the newly created horizontal line.
- Move the pointer upward and click.

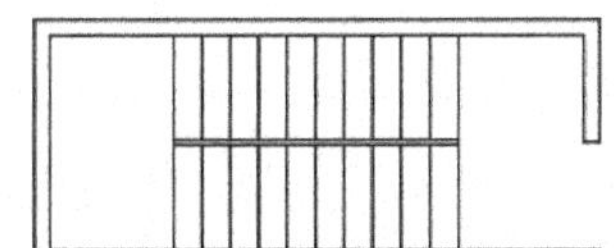

- On the **Home** tab of the ribbon, expand the **Draw** panel and click the **Construction line** icon.
- Select the **Ver** option from the command line.
- Select the corners of the drawing, as shown.

- Click the **Offset** icon on the **Modify** panel of the **Home** ribbon tab.
- Type 11' and press ENTER.
- Select the offset horizontal line.
- Move the pointer upward and click.

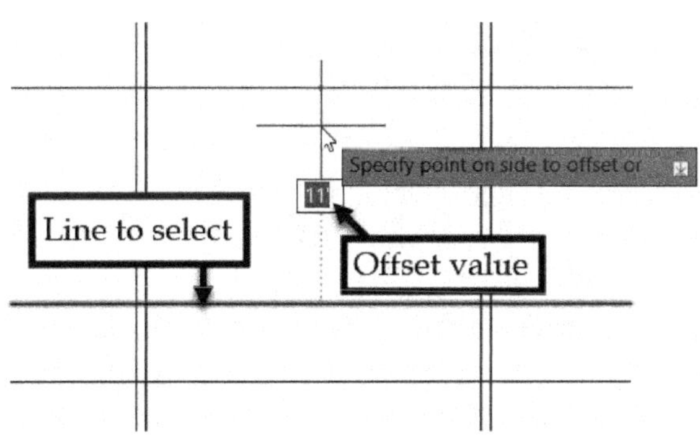

- Press ENTER twice to deactivate the **Offset** tool and then activate it again.
- Type 4" and press ENTER.
- Select the newly created offset line.
- Move the pointer upward and click.

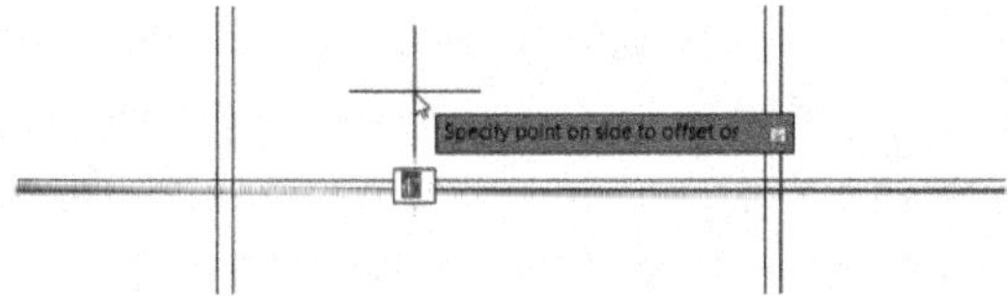

- On the **Home** tab of the ribbon, click **Modify** panel > **Trim/Extend** drop-down > **Trim**.

- Press and hold the left mouse button and drag the pointer across the portions of the construction lines, as shown.

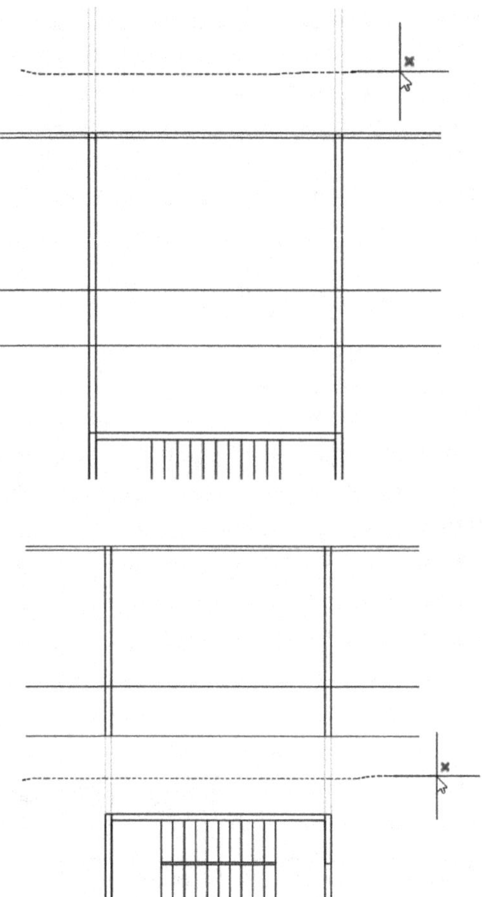

- Click the **Offset** ⊆ icon on the **Modify** panel of the **Home** ribbon tab.
- Type 6" and press ENTER.
- Offset the outer vertical lines on both sides.

- On the **Home** tab of the ribbon, click **Modify** panel > **Trim/Extend** drop-down > **Trim**.
- Trim the portions of the vertical and horizontal lines, as shown.

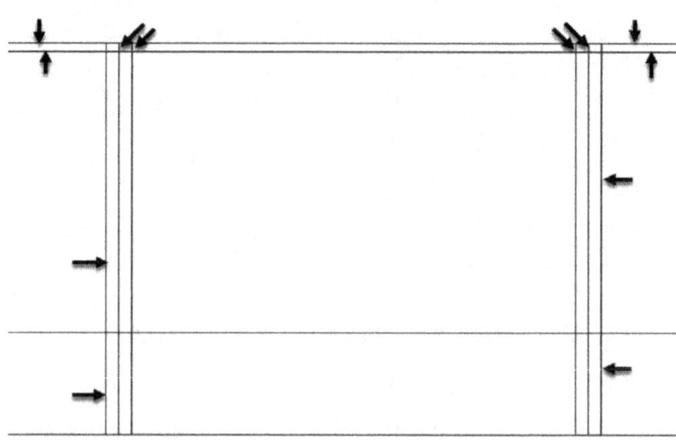

- On the **Home** tab of the ribbon, click **Modify** panel > **Trim/Extend** drop-down > **Extend**.
- Select the **Boundary edges** option from the command line.
- Select the lower horizontal edge of the roof, as shown.

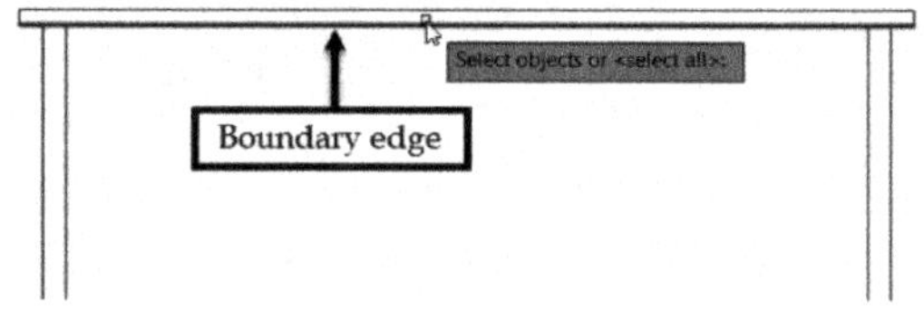

- Press ENTER.
- Press and hold the left mouse button.
- Drag the pointer across the staircase lines; the lines are extended up to the boundary edge.

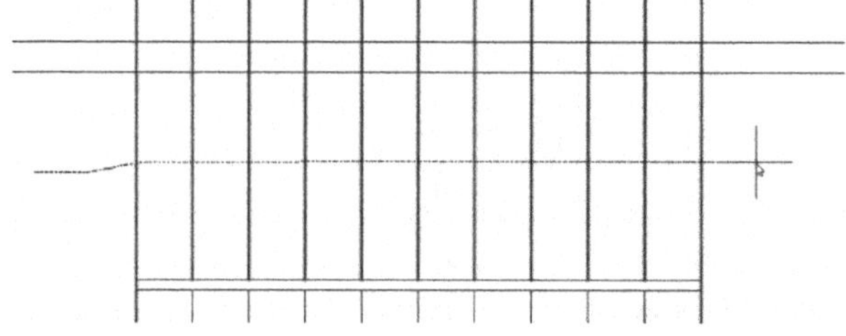

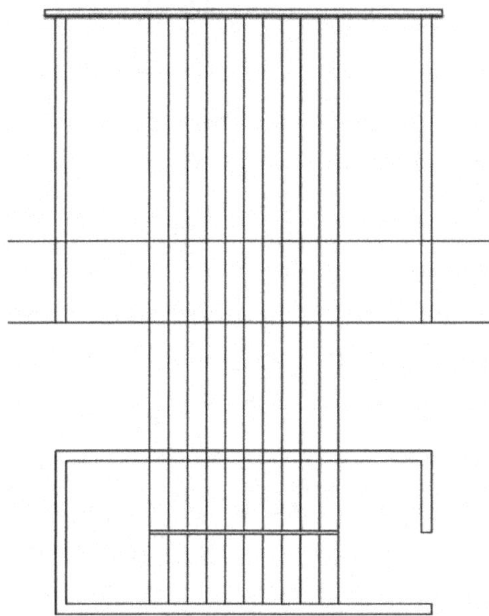

- On the **Home** tab of the ribbon, click **Modify** panel > **Trim/Extend** drop-down > **Trim**.
- Select the **cuTting edges** option from the command line.
- Select the horizontal lines, as shown.
- Press ENTER.

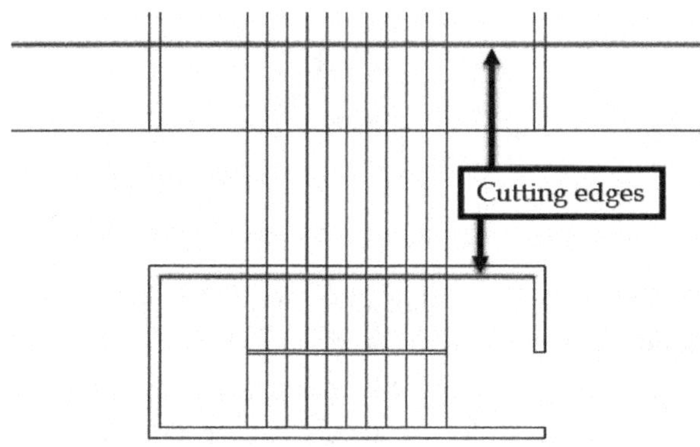

- Click and drag the pointer across the vertical lines, as shown.

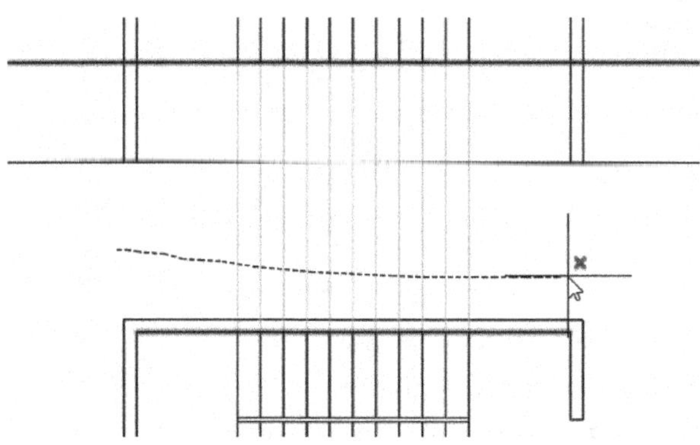

- On the **Home** tab of the ribbon, click **Draw** panel > **Polyline**.
- Select the first point of the polyline.
- Move the pointer upward.
- Type 6" and press ENTER.

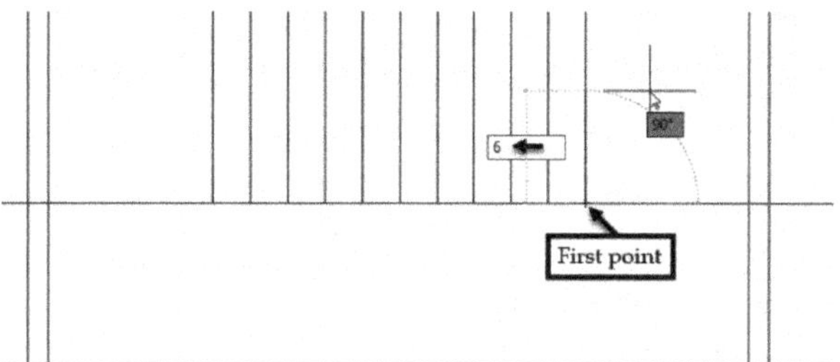

- Move the pointer toward left.
- Type 11" and press ENTER.
- Press Esc.

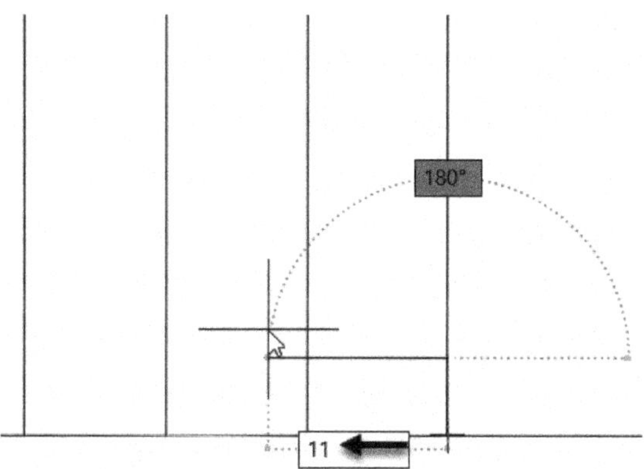

- Select the polyline and click the **Copy** icon on the **Modify** panel of the **Home** ribbon tab.
- Select the first point of the polyline as the base point.

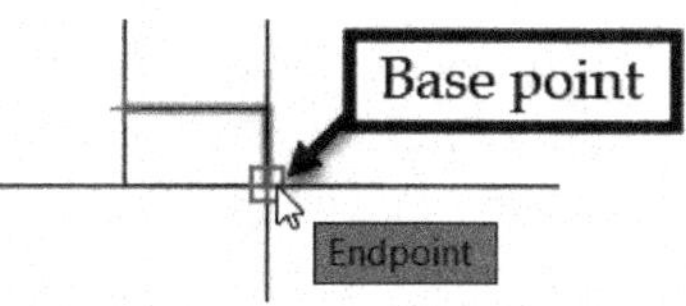

- Move the pointer upward and select the endpoint of the polyline. The polyline is copied.

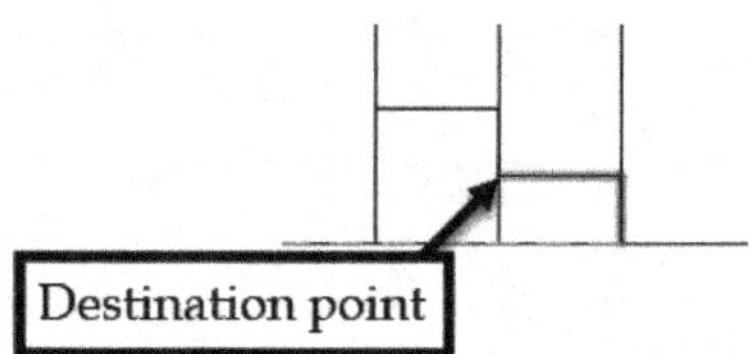

- Likewise, create copies of the polylines, as shown.

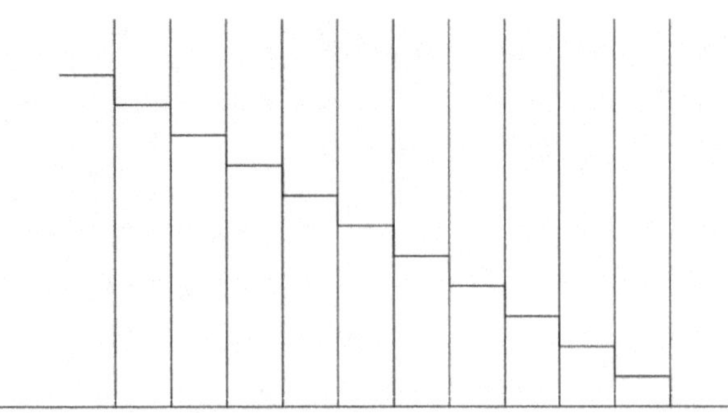

- Expand the **Modify** panel on the **Home** ribbon tab, and then click the **Join** icon.

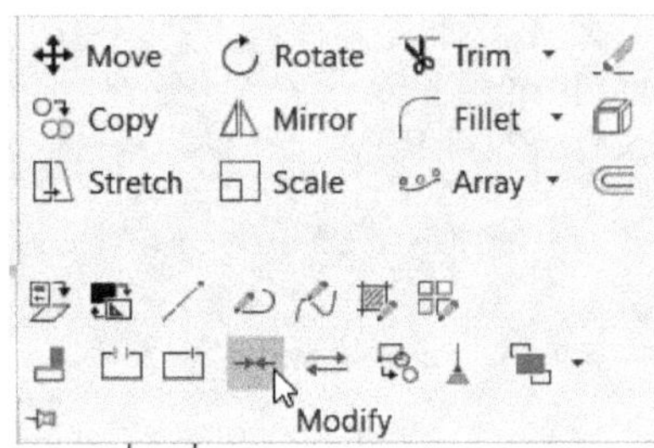

*The **Join** tool allows you to combine two of the same objects (for example, two collinear Lines) into one object (for example, one Line). You can also use Join to close an Arc to form a complete Circle or close an elliptical arc to form a complete Ellipse.*

Lines: The Lines to join must be collinear, but they can have gaps between them. To join lines, select the source object and then select the lines to join to the source. The lines you selected are joined to the source to form a single line.

Arcs: The Arc objects must lie on the same imaginary circle but can have gaps between them. The Close option converts the source arc into a Circle. To join arcs, select the source object and then select the arcs to join to the source or choose to close the arc. The arcs you selected are joined to the source to form a single arc or a circle.

Polylines: Objects to Join to Polylines can be Polylines, Lines, or Arcs. The objects cannot have gaps between them and must lie on the UCS XY plane or on a plane parallel to it. If Arcs and Lines are joined to the Polyline, they are converted to one Polyline.

Elliptical Arcs: The elliptical arcs must lie on the same ellipse shape but can have gaps between them. The Close

option closes the source elliptical arc into a complete Ellipse.

Splines: The Spline objects must lie in the same plane, and the end points to join must be connected.

- Select all the polylines and press ENTER. All the polylines are joined.

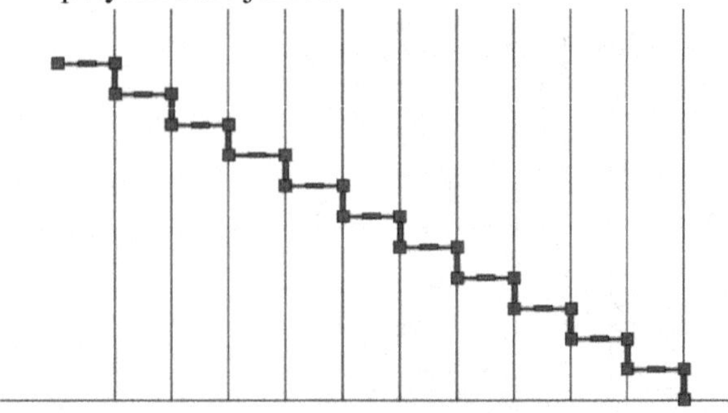

- On the **Home** tab of the ribbon, click **Modify** panel > **Trim/Extend** drop-down > **Extend**.
- Click on the end portion of the polyline to extend it up to the left vertical line.

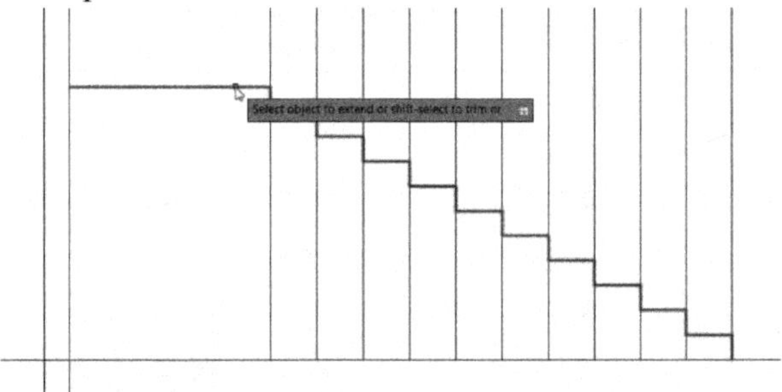

- Press Esc.
- Select the stairs and click the **Mirror** icon on the **Modify** panel of the **Home** ribbon tab.
- Specify the start point of the mirror line, as shown.
- Move the pointer toward the left and specify the endpoint of the mirror line, as shown.

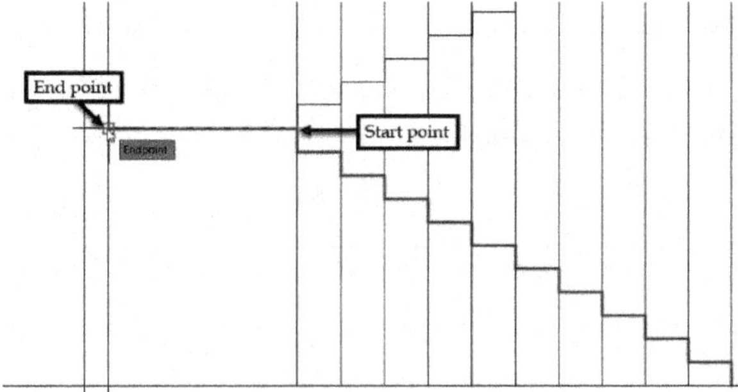

- Select **No** from the command line.
- Select the mirrored polyline.
- Click on the endpoint of the polyline.

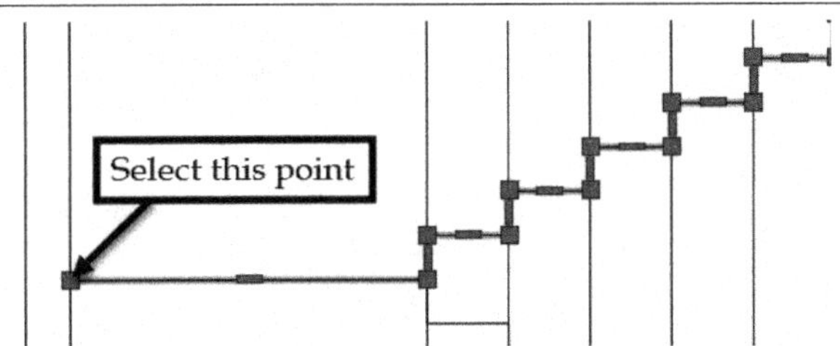

- Move the pointer toward the right and select the vertex point, as shown. The polyline is shortened.

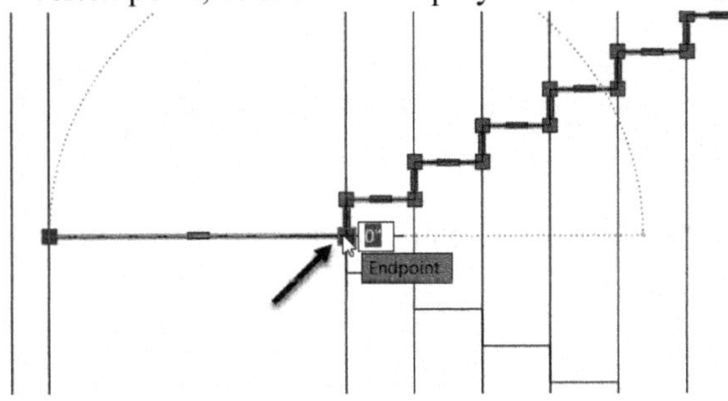

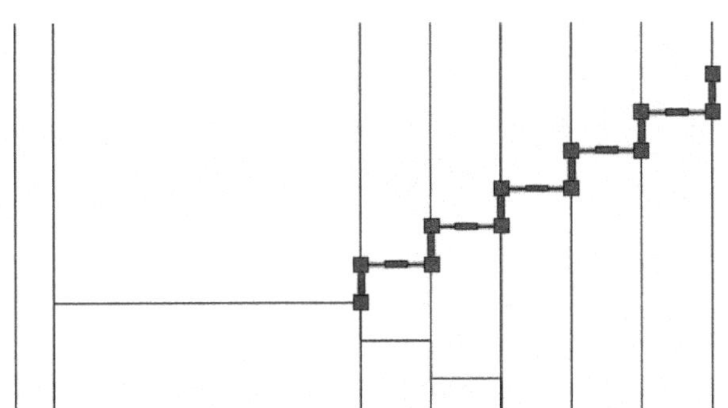

- Press Esc to deselect the mirrored polyline.
- Drag a selection window across the vertical lines from right to left, as shown.

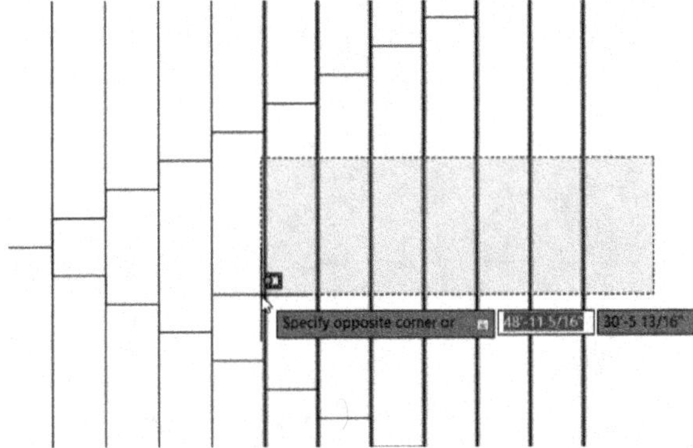

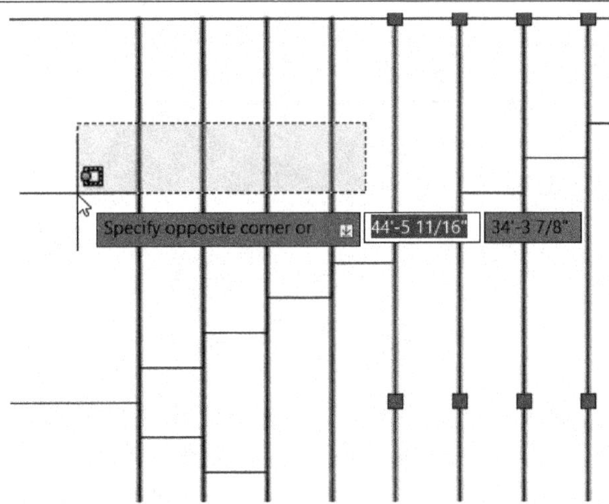

- Press Delete on your keyboard.
- On the **Home** tab of the ribbon, click **Draw** panel >**Line**.
- Select the corner points, as shown.

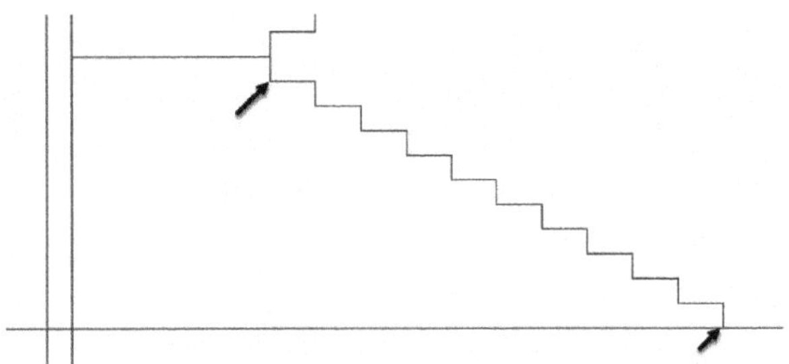

- Offset the newly created line by 4".

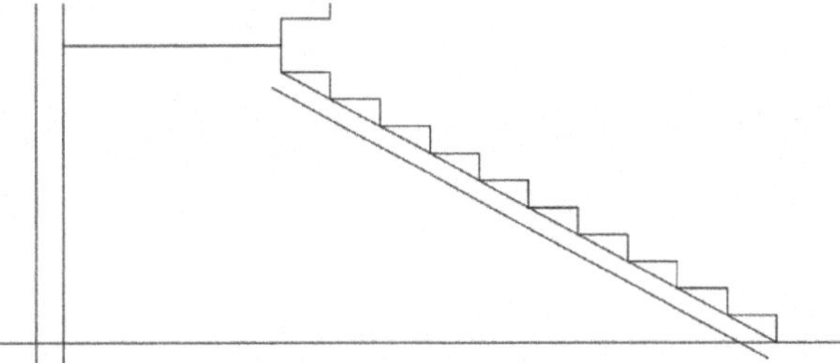

- On the **Home** tab of the ribbon, click **Draw** panel > **Line**.
- Press and hold the Shift key and right click.
- Select the **From** option from the **Object Snap** menu.
- Select the point, as shown.

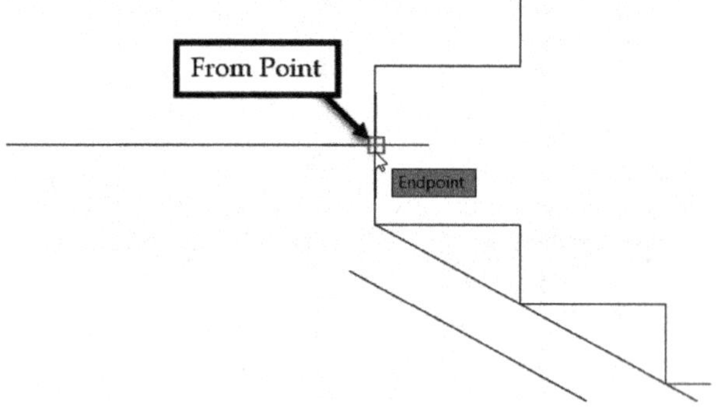

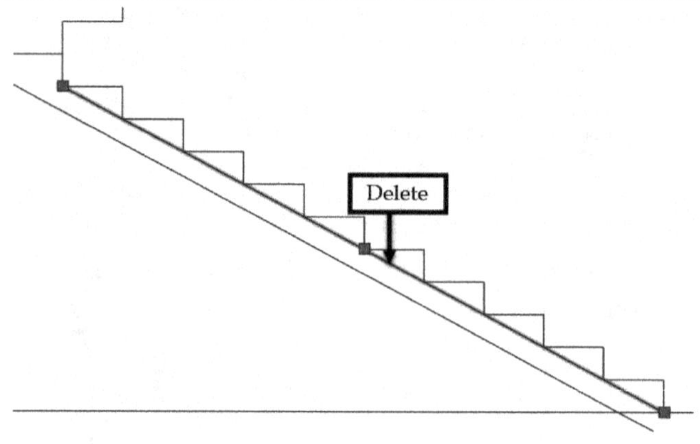

- Move the pointer downward and type 4".
- Press ENTER to specify the start point of the line.
- Move the pointer toward the left and click to create a horizontal line.

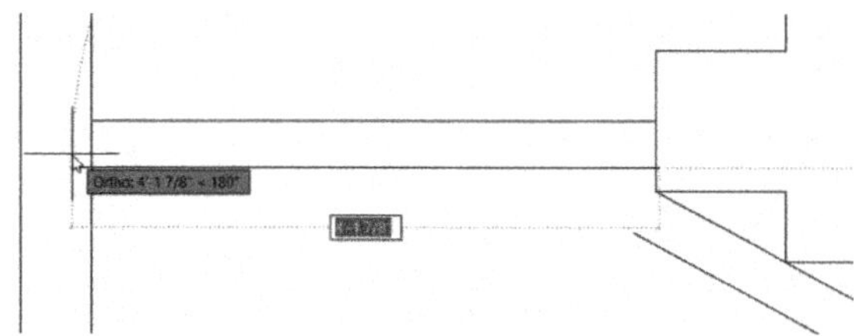

- Click the **Fillet** icon on the **Modify** panel.
- Select the horizontal and inclined lines, as shown.

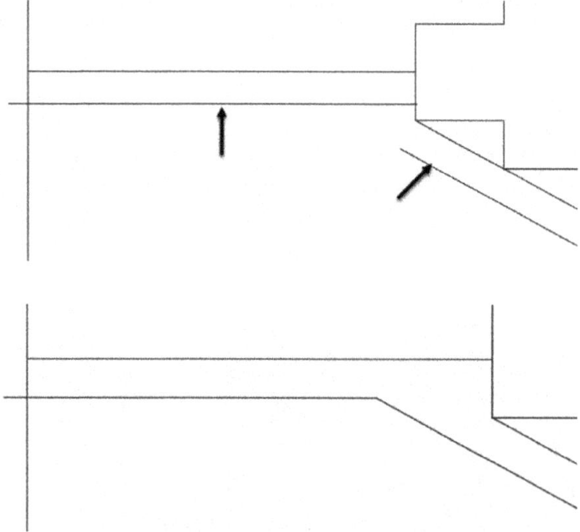

- Delete the inclined line, as shown.

- On the **Home** tab of the ribbon, click **Draw** panel > **Line**.
- Select the corner point of the stair, as shown.

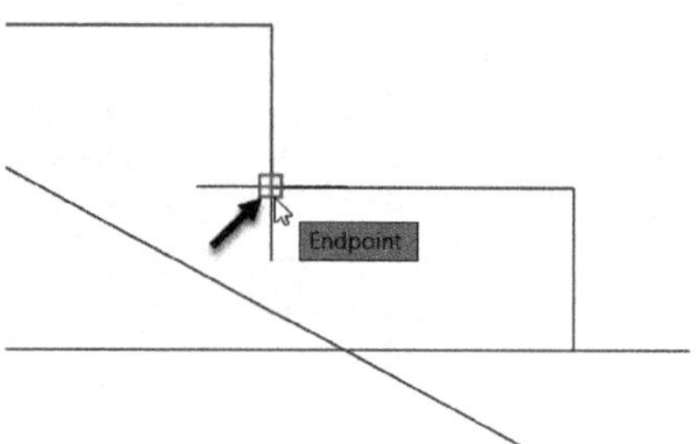

- Move the pointer downward.
- Type 1' and press ENTER.
- Move the pointer toward the right.
- Type 11" and press ENTER.
- Move the pointer upward.
- Type 6" and press ENTER.

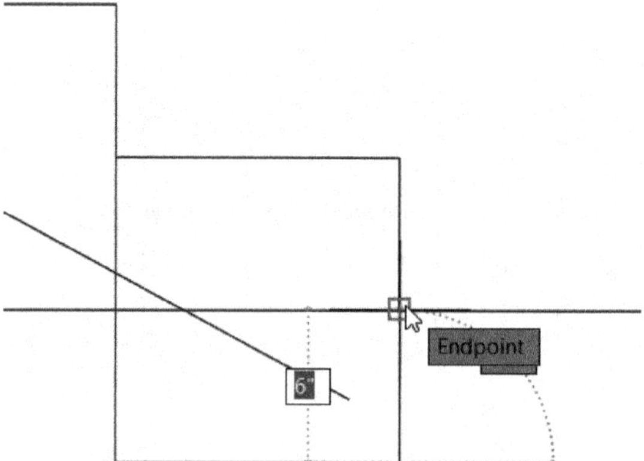

- On the **Home** tab of the ribbon, click **Modify** panel > **Trim/Extend** drop-down > **Trim**.
- Select the portions of the lines, as shown.

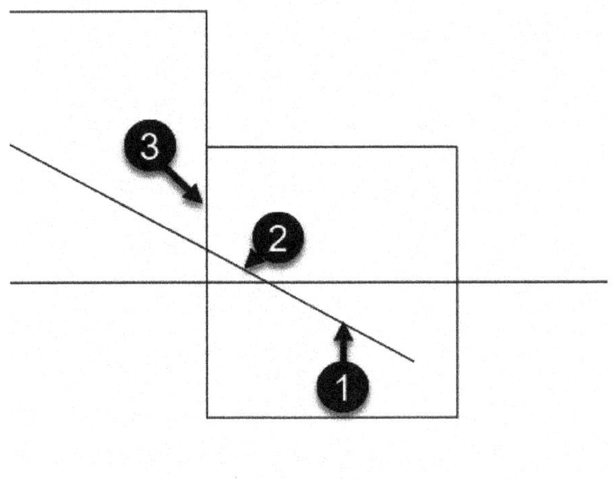

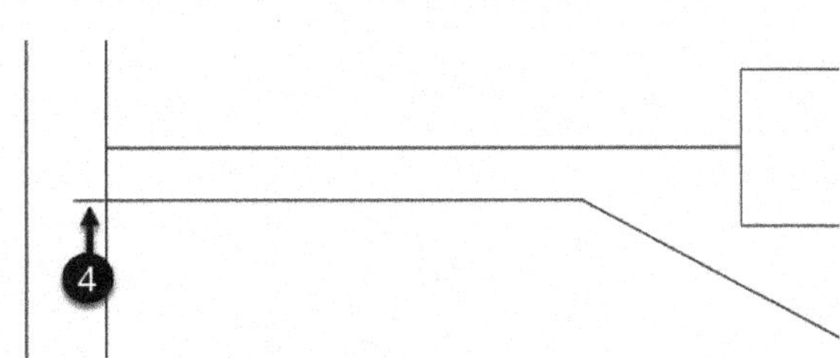

- On the **Home** tab of the ribbon, click **Draw** panel >**Line**.
- Select the corner points, as shown.

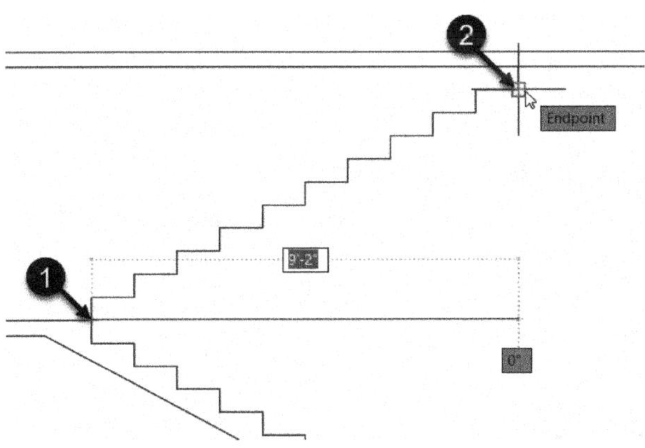

- Offset the newly created line by 4".

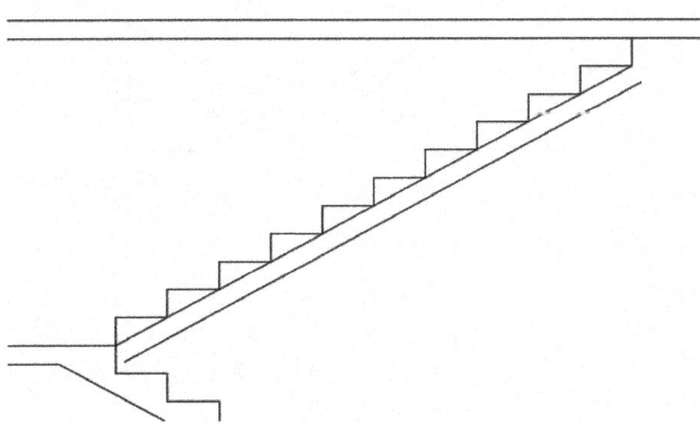

- On the **Home** tab of the ribbon, click **Modify** panel > **Trim/Extend** drop-down > **Extend**.
- Select the inclined line, as shown.

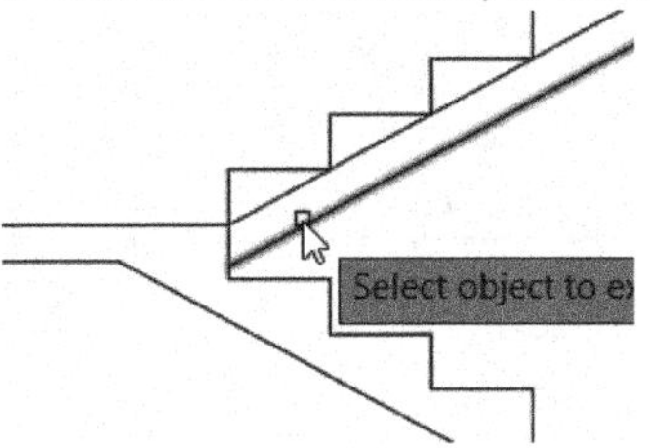

- Extend the inclined line up to the horizontal line, as shown.

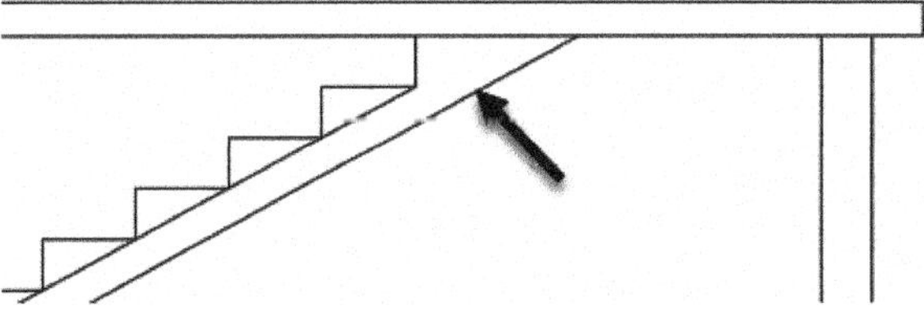

- Extend the vertical lines, as shown. Next, press Esc.

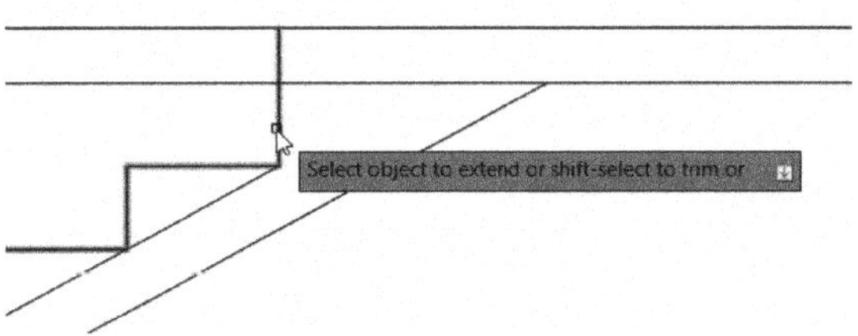

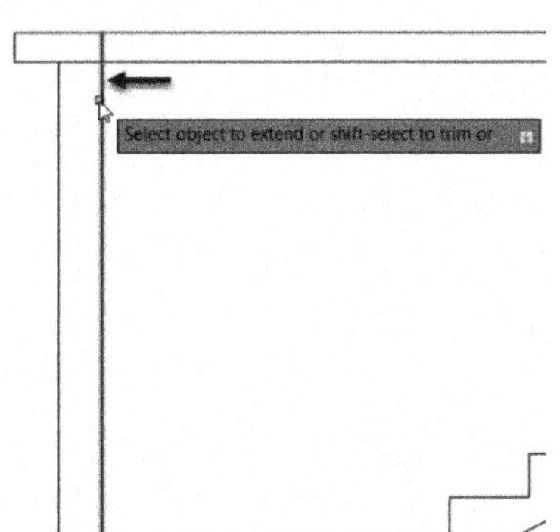

- Select the inclined line, as shown.

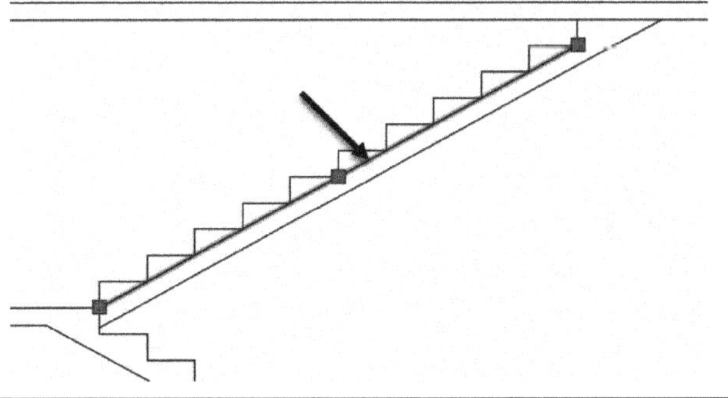

- Press Delete.
- On the **Home** tab of the ribbon, click **Modify** panel > **Trim/Extend** drop-down > **Trim**.
- Select the horizontal lines, as shown.

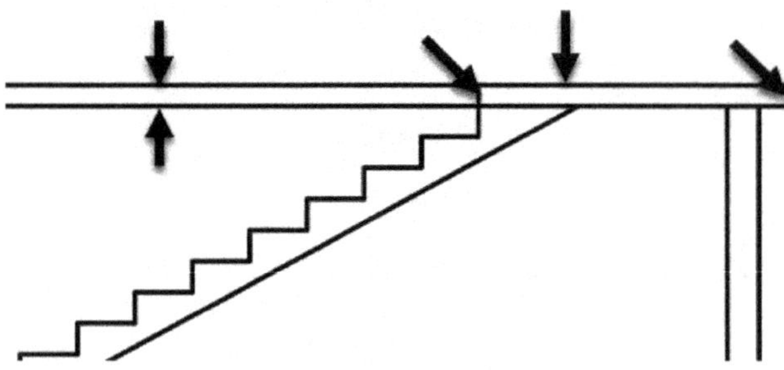

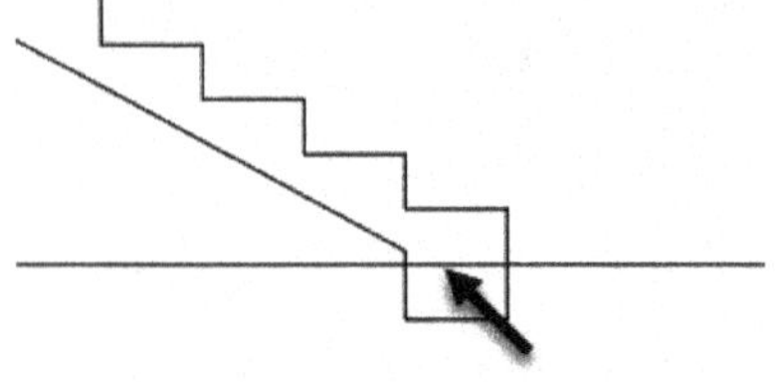

- Offset the horizontal line by 4" in the downward direction.

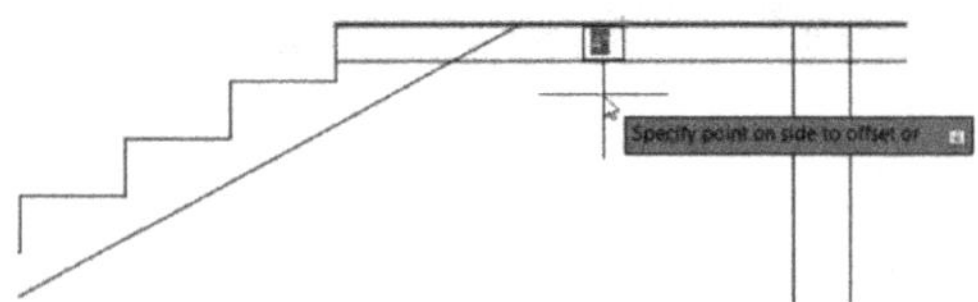

- Trim the elements, as shown.

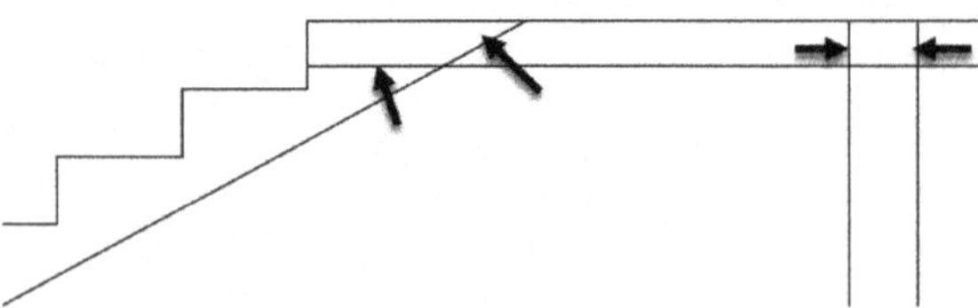

- Close the end of the offset line.

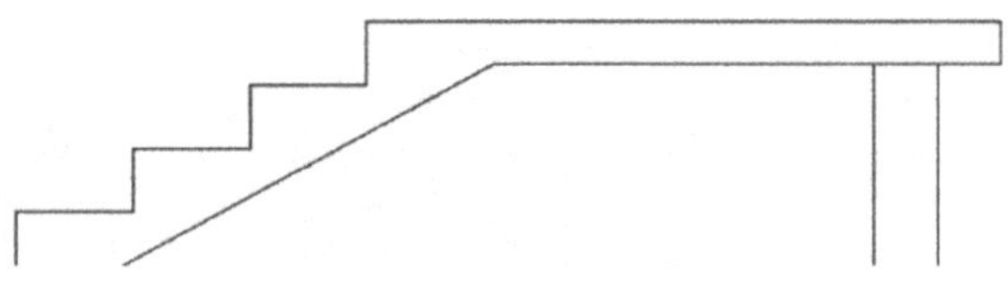

- On the **Home** tab of the ribbon, click **Draw** panel > **Hatch** drop-down > **Hatch**.
- On the **Hatch Creation** tab of the ribbon, expand the **Pattern** gallery, and select the **AR-CONC** pattern.

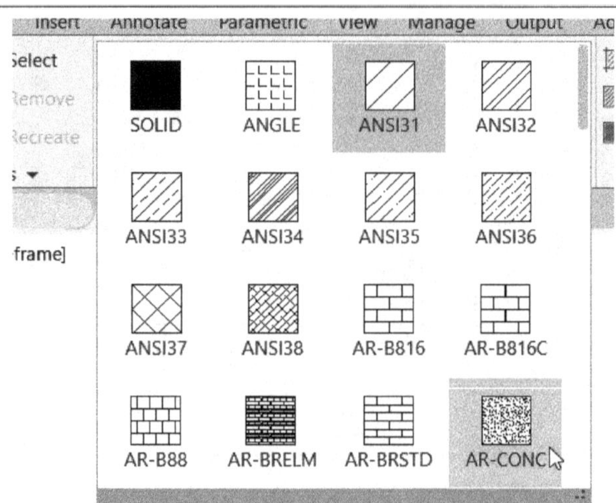

- Pick points in the areas, as shown.

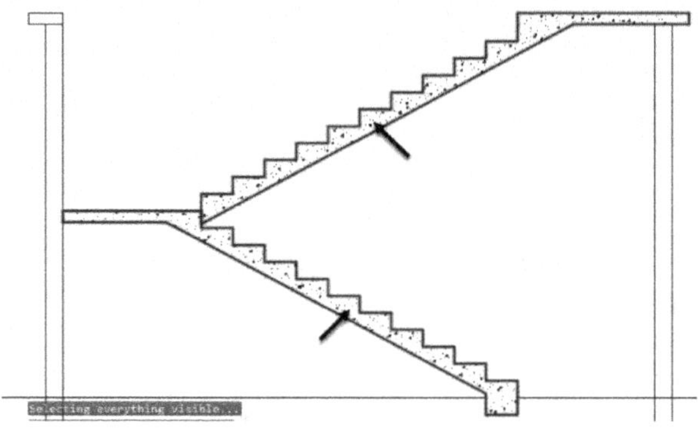

- Click the **Close Hatch Creation** icon on the ribbon.

Creating the Handrail

- On the **Home** tab of the ribbon, click **Draw** panel > **Line**.
- Create two vertical lines of 3' length each at the locations, as shown.

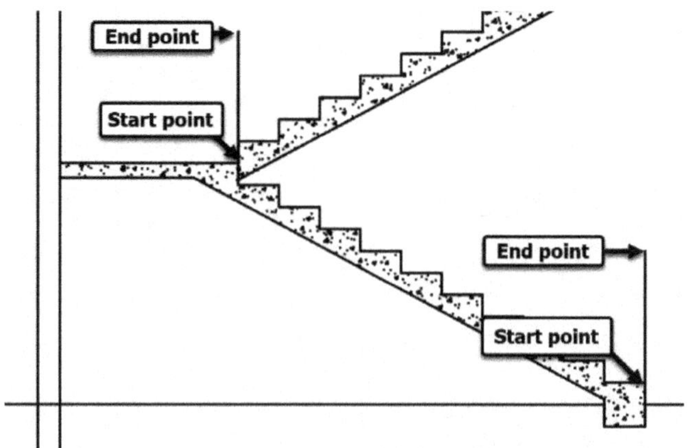

- Activate the **Line** tool and connect the endpoints of the two vertical lines, as shown.

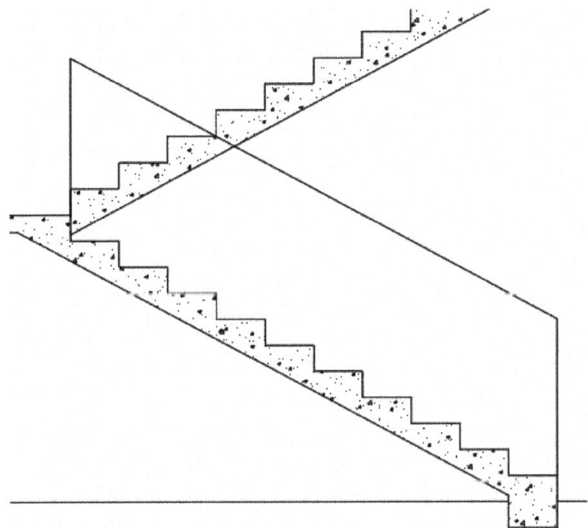

* On the **Home** tab of the ribbon, expand the **Modify** panel and click the **Lengthen** icon.

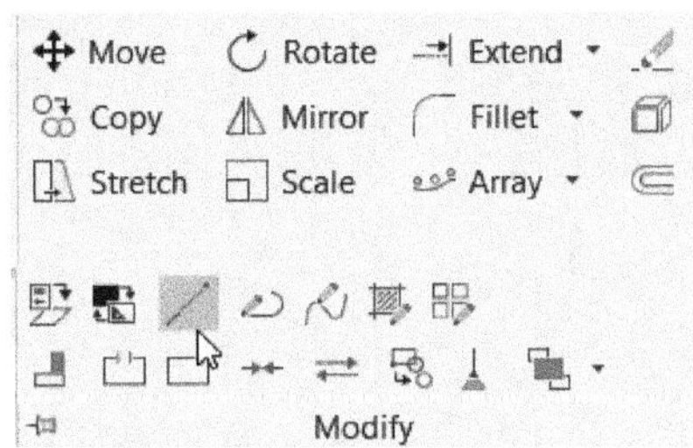

*The **Lengthen** tool enables you to modify the length of linear objects and included angle of arcs without requiring additional objects, unlike Trim and Extend. You can specify changes as a percentage, an increment, or as a final length or angle.*

* Select **DElta** from the command line. This option lets you change the current length of an object (including an arc) by any specified increment. Entering a positive value increases the length, while a negative value decreases it. The selected end of the object changes, while the other end remains fixed.

You can also select the other options from the command line. These options are discussed next:

Percent: *On selecting this option you change the length of the selected line by a percentage of the current total length. For arcs, the percentage equally affects the length and included angle. A value greater than 100 increases the current length, and a value less than 100 decreases it. Note that you cannot enter negative values.*

Total: *Select this option and specify a value for the new total length. Next, select the end of the object to change. The **Angle** option changes the total included angle of a selected arc.*

DYnamic: *Select this option and select the end of the object to change. Next, drag the pointer to change the length. You can use Object Snaps and Polar Tracking while dragging.*

* Type 12" and press ENTER.
* Click near the endpoint of the inclined line.

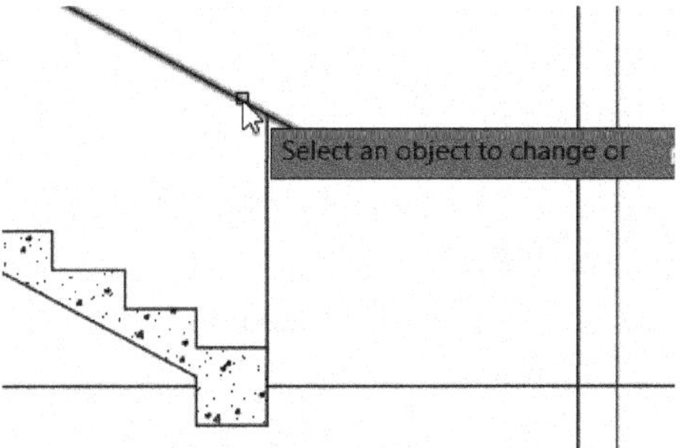

The inclined line is lengthened.

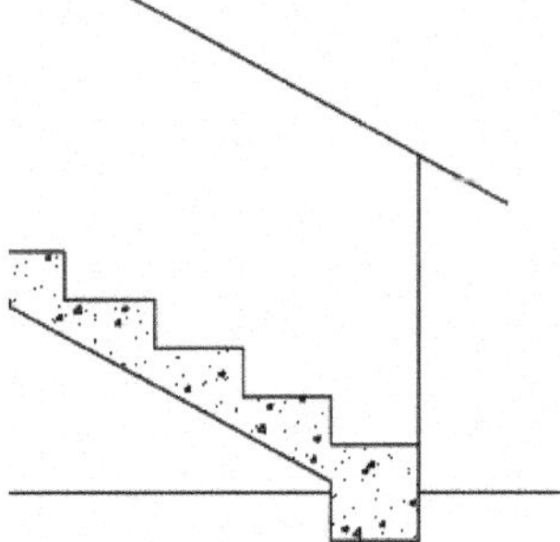

* Create a horizontal line, as shown.

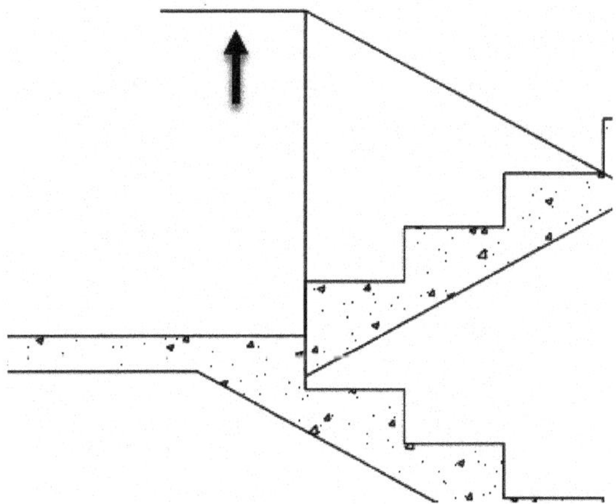

* Click the **Offset** icon on the **Modify** panel.
* Offset the newly created lines by 2" distance, as shown.

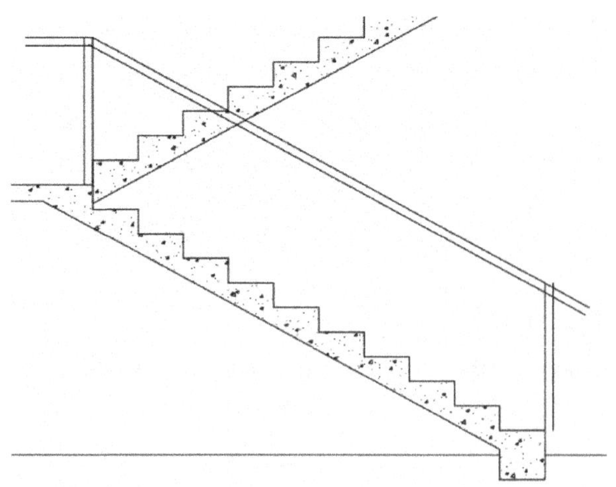

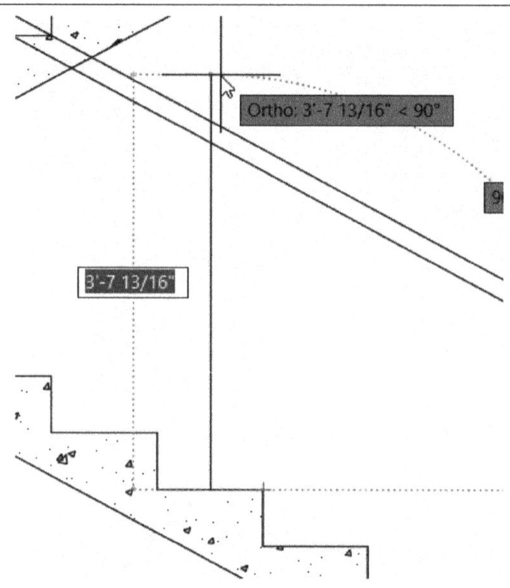

- On the **Home** tab of the ribbon, click **Modify** panel > **Trim/Extend** drop-down > **Extend**.
- Extend the two vertical lines up to the bottom horizontal edge, as shown.

- Click the **Offset** icon on the **Modify** panel.
- Offset the newly created line by 1" on both sides, as shown.
- Delete the middle line.

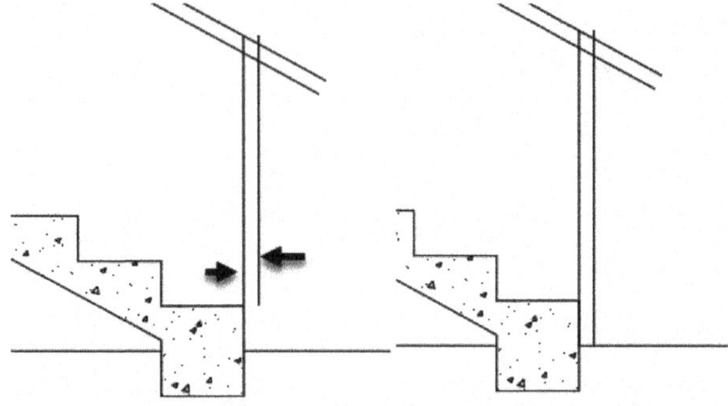

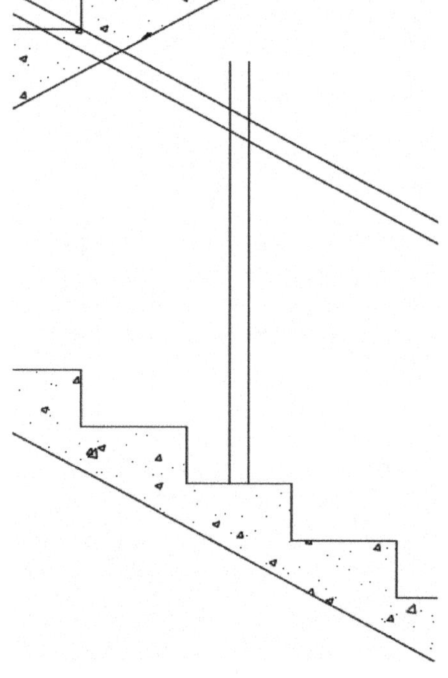

- Activate the **Line** tool.
- Zoom to the fifth step from the top.
- Press and hold the Shift key and right click.
- Select the **Mid between 2 Points** option.
- Select the two endpoints of the step; the start point of the line is specified at the midpoint.

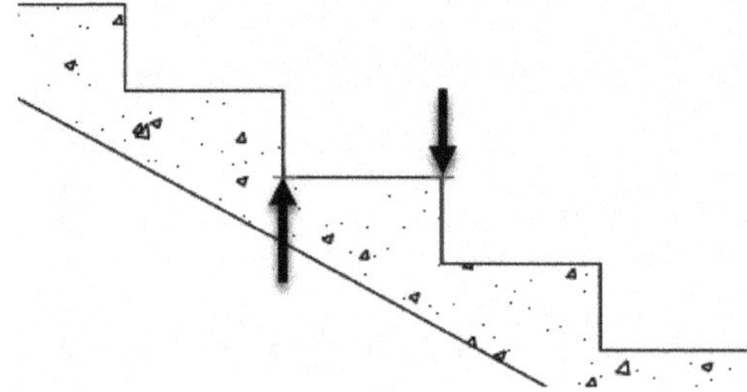

- Move the pointer upward and click.

- On the **Home** tab of the ribbon, click **Modify** panel > **Trim/Extend** drop-down > **Trim**.
- Select the **cuTting edges** option from the command line.
- Select the lower inclined and horizontal lines of the handrail.
- Press ENTER.

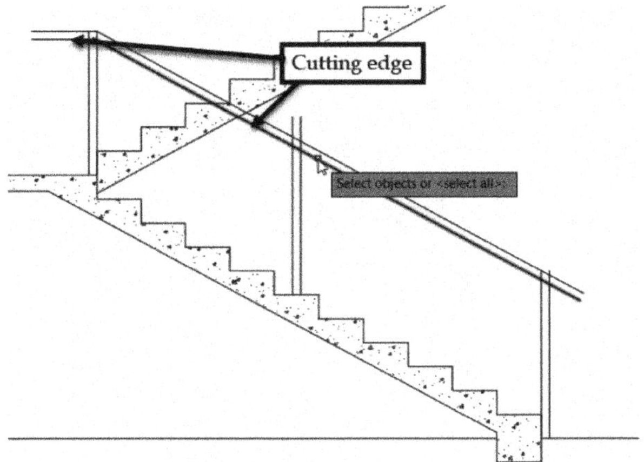

- Trim the portions of the vertical lines, as shown.

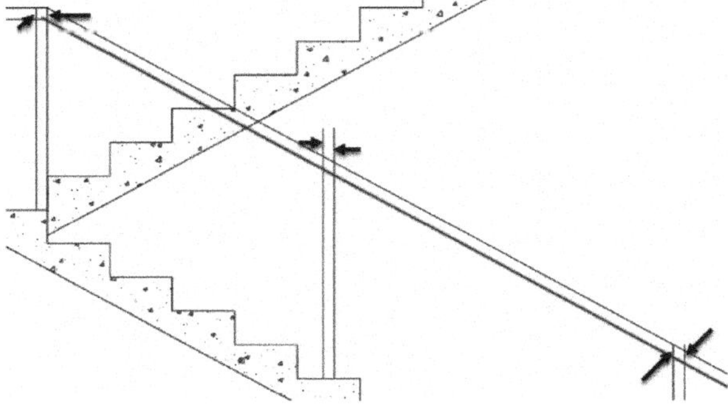

- On the **Home** tab of the ribbon, click **Modify** panel > **Trim/Extend** drop-down > **Trim**.
- Select the unwanted portions of the lines, as shown.

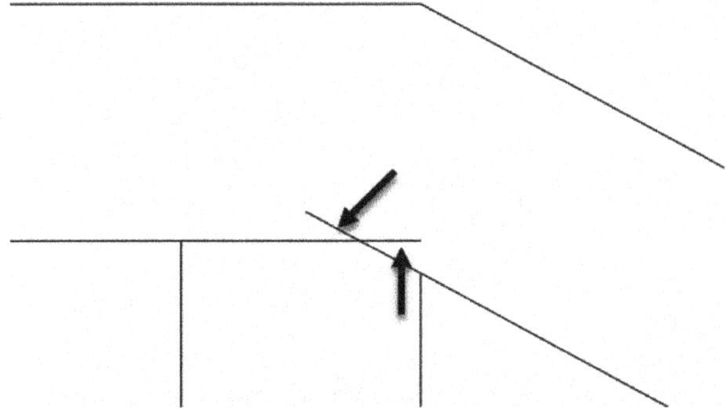

- On the **Home** tab of the ribbon, expand the **Modify** panel and click the **Break at Point** icon.

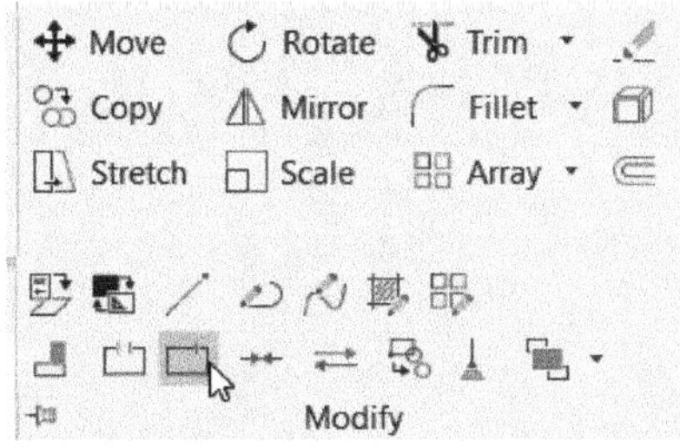

*The **Break at Point** tool allows you to create a break in an object at a specific point without leaving any space.*

- Select the vertical line, as shown.
- Press and hold the Shift key and right click.
- Select the **Midpoint** option.
- Select the midpoint of the vertical line, as shown. The vertical line is broken at the midpoint.

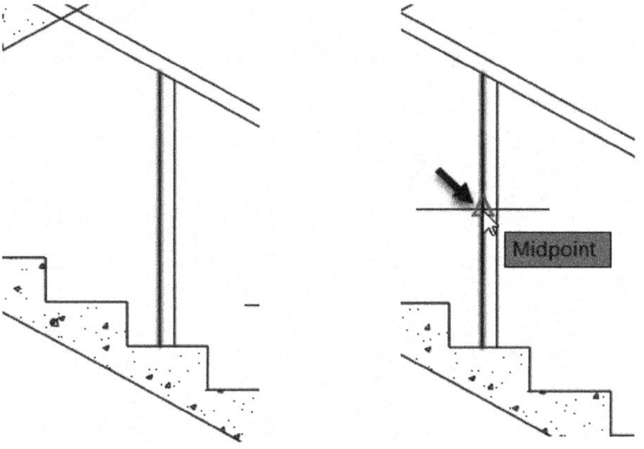

- Click the **Object Snap** drop-down on the status bar and select the **Midpoint** option.
- On the **Home** tab of the ribbon, click **Draw** panel > **Rectangle/Polygon** drop-down > **Rectangle**.
- Select the midpoint of the lower portion of the broken line, as shown.

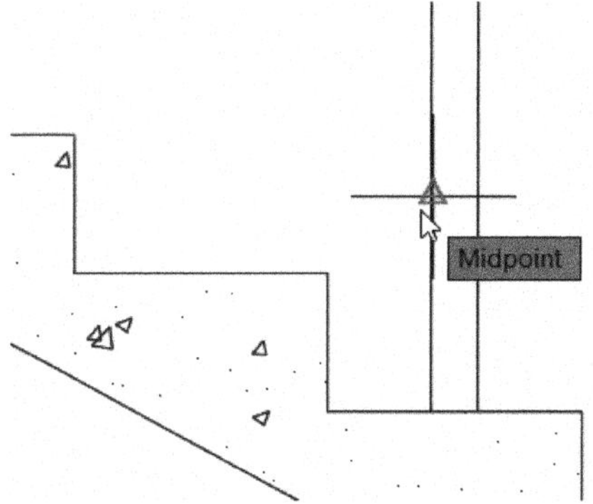

- Select the **Dimensions** option from the command line.
- Type 2 and press ENTER.
- Type 2 and press ENTER.
- Move the pointer upward and click.

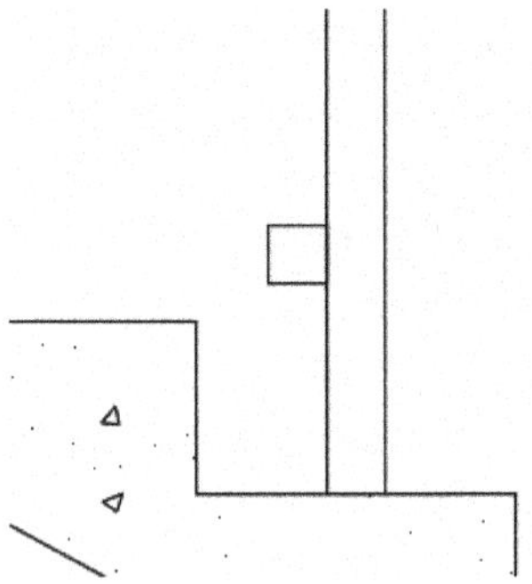

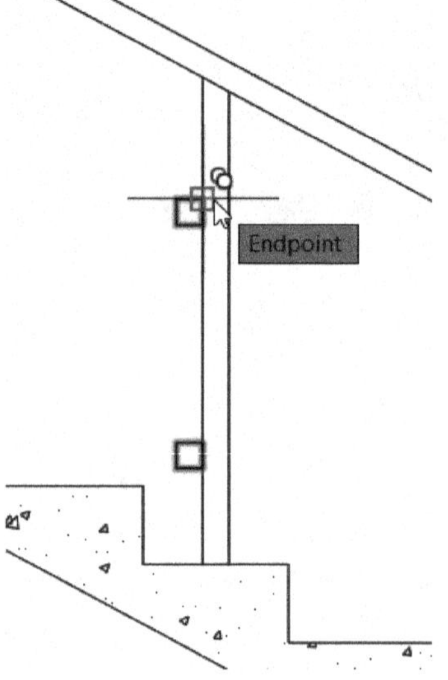

- Select the rectangle and click the **Copy** icon on the **Modify** panel.
- Select the top right corner point of the rectangle.
- Move the pointer upward.
- Select the midpoint of the upper portion of the broken line, as shown.

- Move the pointer toward the right.
- Type 4" and press ENTER.

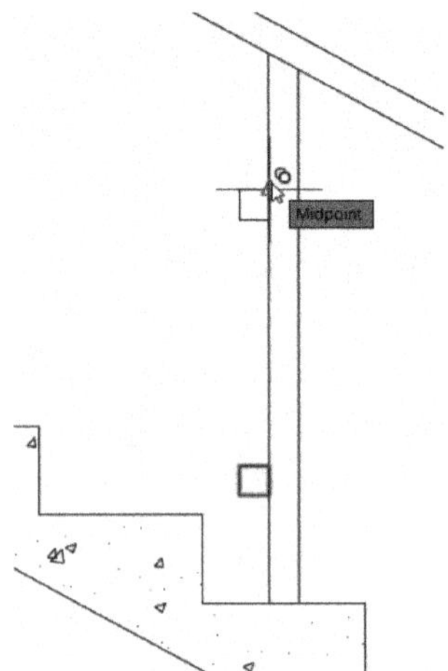

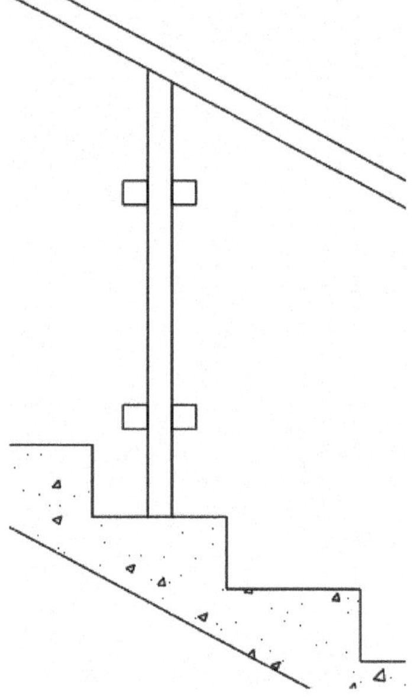

- Select the two rectangles and click the **Copy** icon on the **Modify** panel.
- Select the top right corner point of anyone of the rectangles.

- Press Esc.
- Select the four rectangles and click the **Copy** icon on the **Modify** panel.
- Select the midpoint of the right vertical line.

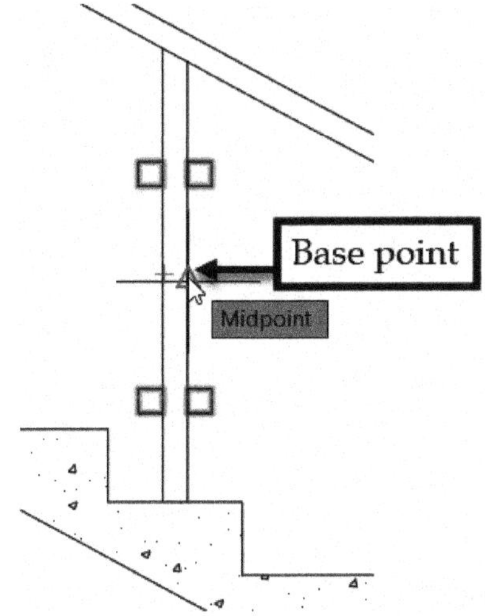

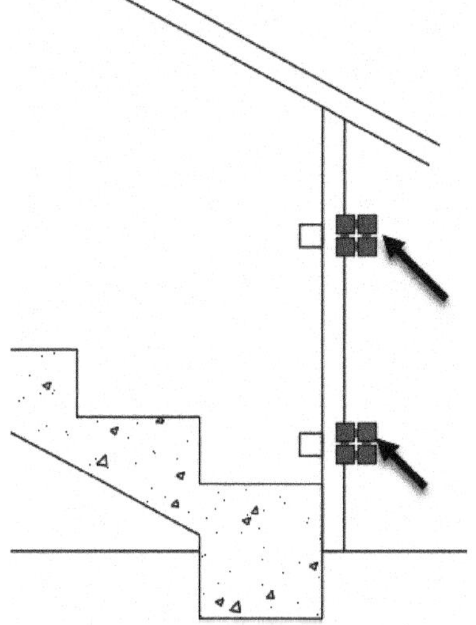

- Move the pointer toward right and select the midpoint of the vertical line, as shown.

- Select the vertical line and click the **Offset** icon on the **Modify** panel.
- Type 3'8" and press ENTER.
- Move the pointer toward the left and click.

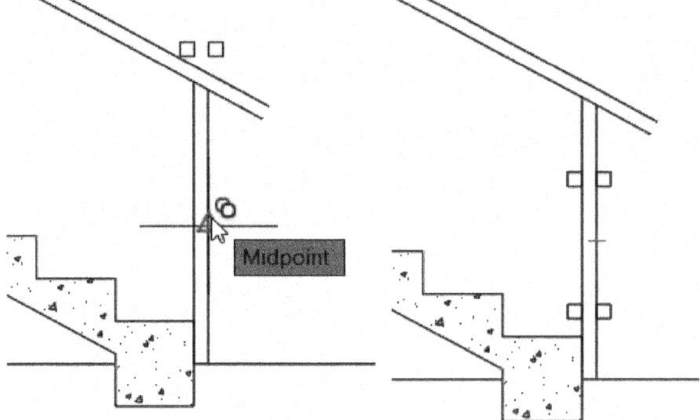

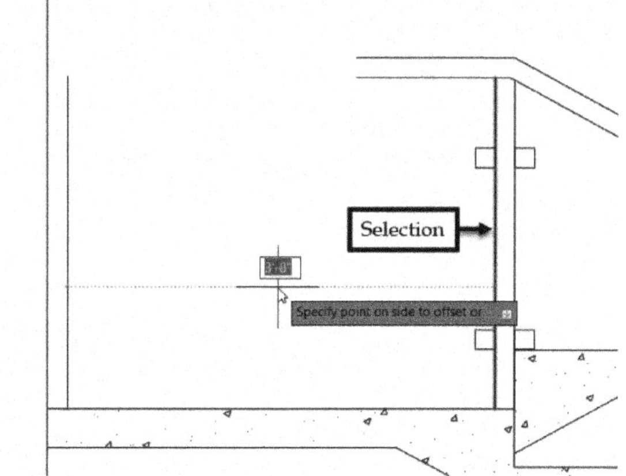

- Move the pointer toward the left and select the midpoint of the vertical line, as shown.

- Press ENTER twice.
- Type 2" and press ENTER.
- Select the newly offset line.
- Move the pointer toward right and click.

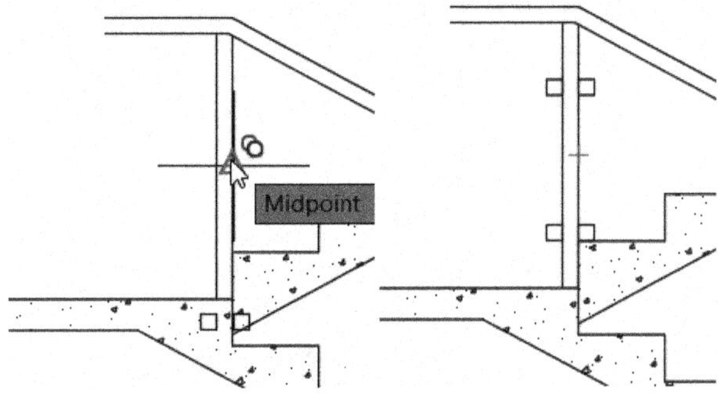

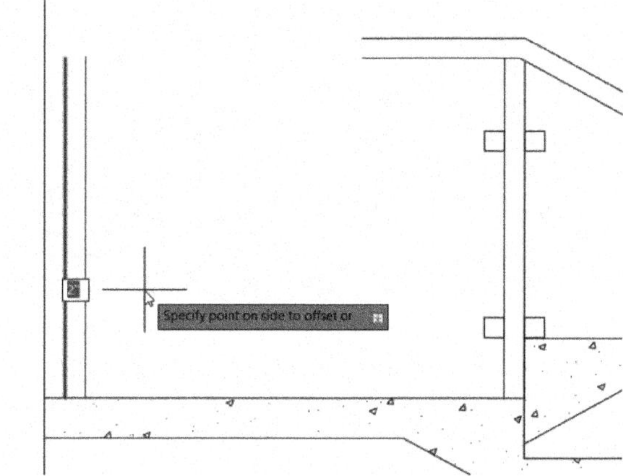

- Press ESC.
- Delete the two rectangles, as shown.

- Click the **Fillet** icon on the **Modify** panel.
- Select the left vertical and top horizontal line, as shown.

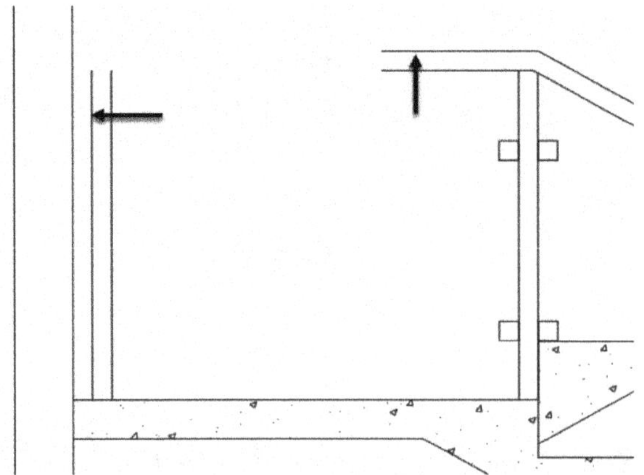

- On the **Home** tab of the ribbon, click **Modify** panel > **Trim/Extend** drop-down > **Extend**.
- Extend the horizontal line up to the vertical line.

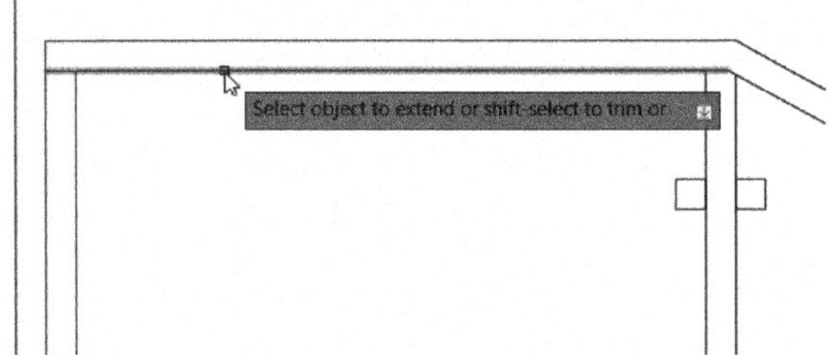

- Press Esc.
- Select the two rectangles and click the **Copy** icon on the **Modify** panel.
- Specify the base and destination points, as shown.

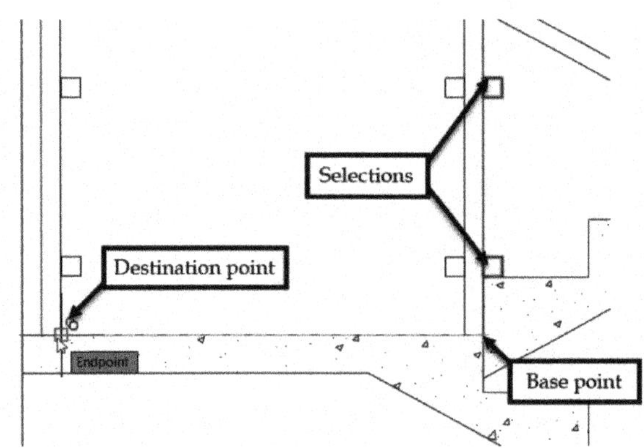

- Click the **Line** icon on the **Draw** panel.
- Select the corner points of the top and bottom steps, as shown.
- Press Esc.

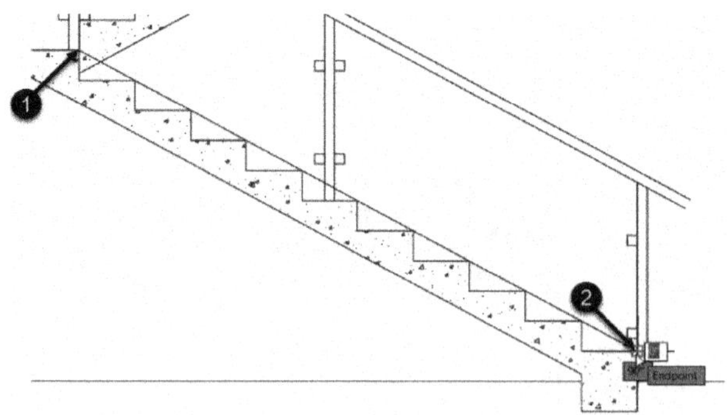

- Select the newly created line and click the **Offset** icon on the **Modify** panel.
- Type 1" and press ENTER.
- Move the pointer upward and click.

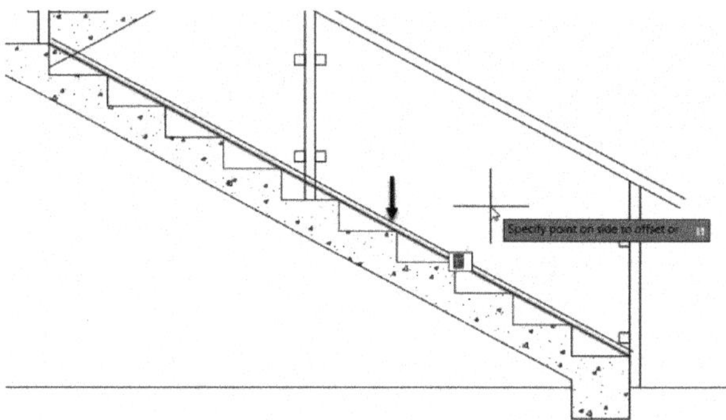

- Press ENTER twice.
- Type 2" and press ENTER.
- Select the newly offset line.
- Move the pointer upward and click.

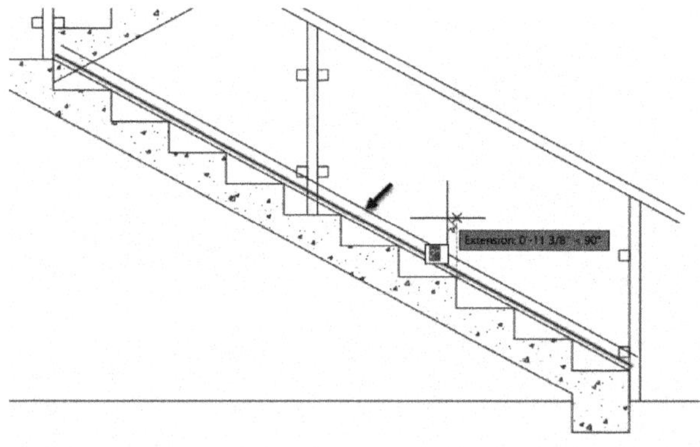

- On the **Home** tab of the ribbon, click **Modify** panel > **Trim/Extend** drop-down > **Trim**.
- Trim the intersecting portions of the lines, as shown.

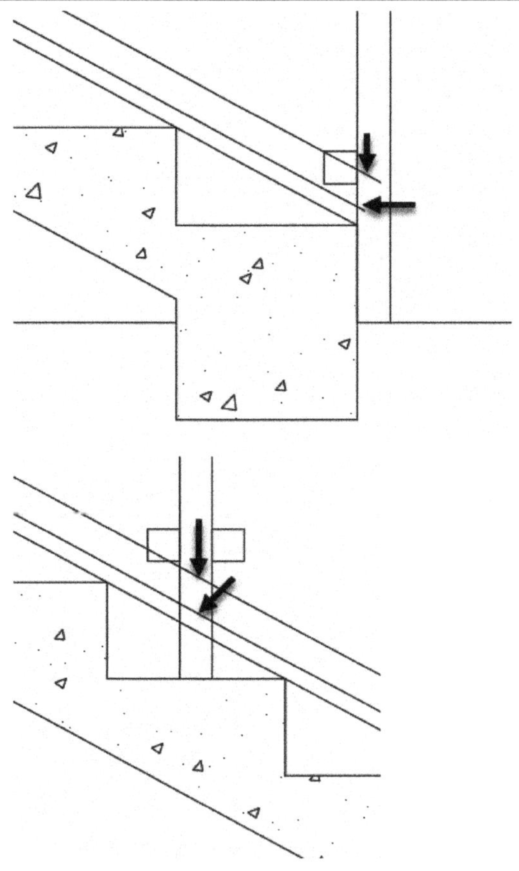

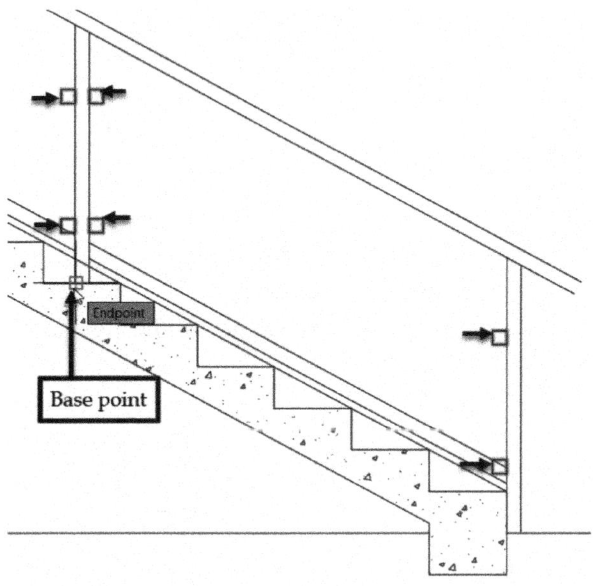

- Press Esc.
- Select the rectangles and click the **Move** icon on the **Modify** panel.
- Specify the base point, as shown.

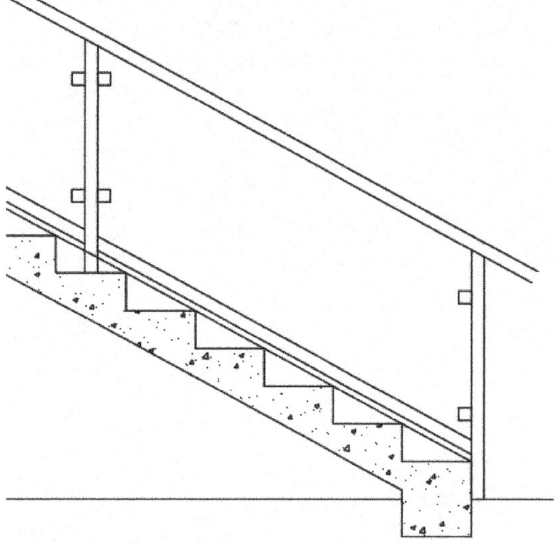

- Select the horizontal line, as shown.
- Click the **Offset** icon on the **Modify** panel.
- Type 33" and press ENTER.
- Move the pointer downward and click.

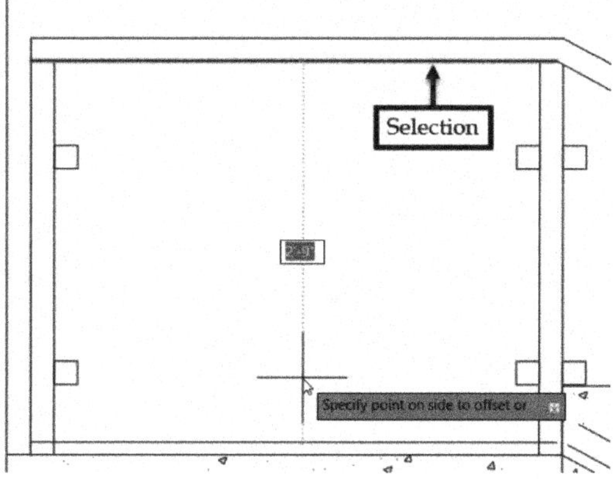

- Press ENTER twice.
- Type 2" and press ENTER.
- Select the newly offset line.
- Move the pointer upward and click.

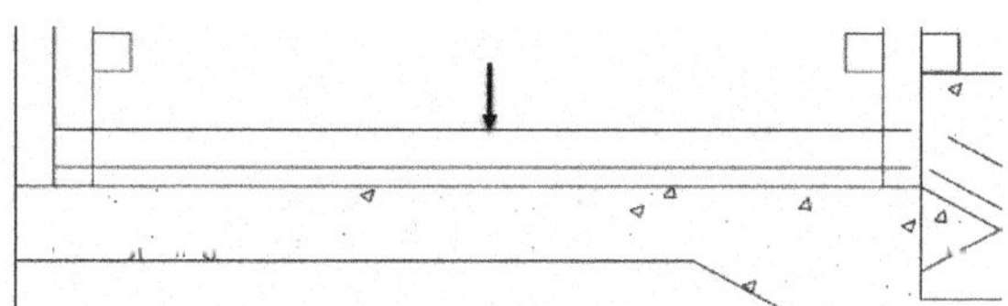

- Click the **Fillet** icon on the **Modify** panel.
- Select the horizontal and inclined lines, as shown.
- Press ENTER and select the horizontal and inclined lines, as shown.

- Move the pointer upward.
- Type 4" and press ENTER.

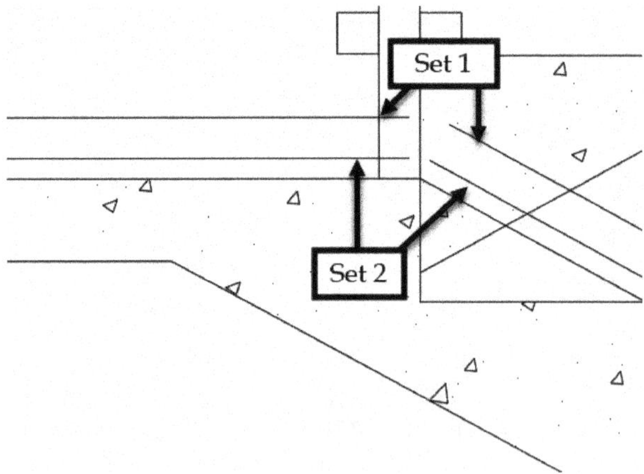

- Click the **Trim** icon on the **Modify** panel.
- Select the portions of the horizontal and inclined line, as shown.

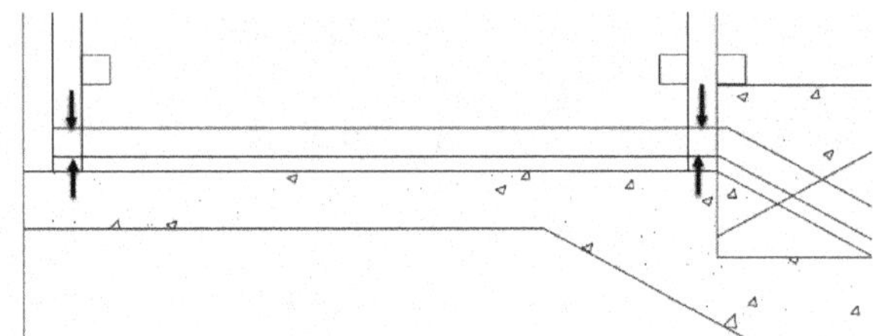

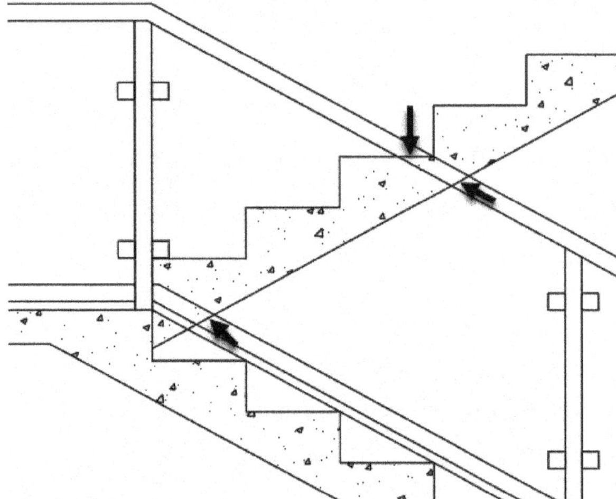

- Select the **eRase** option from the command line.
- Select the inclined line, as shown.
- Press ENTER.

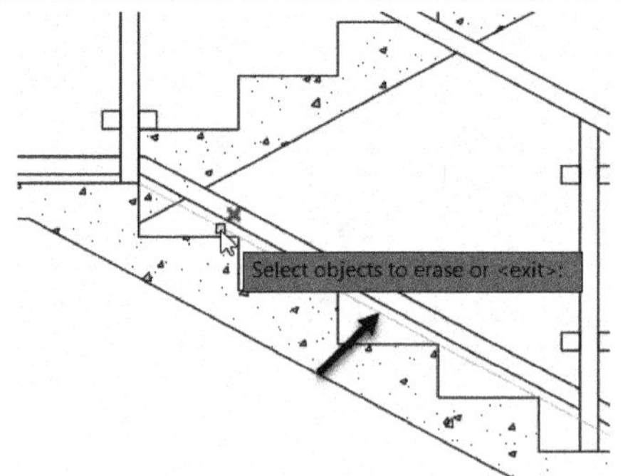

- Close the end of the offset lines using the **Line** tool.

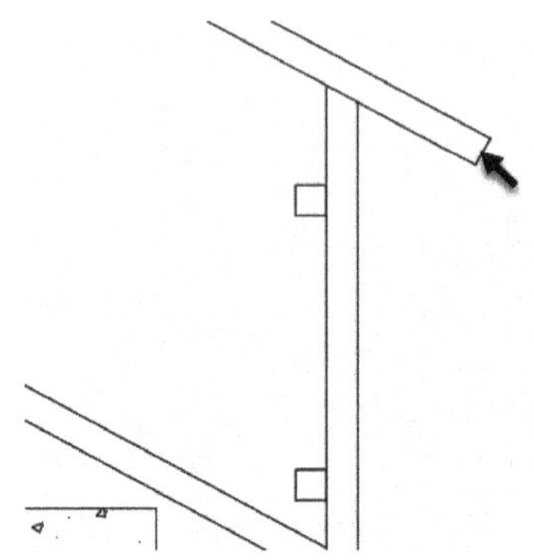

- Select the elements of the handrail.

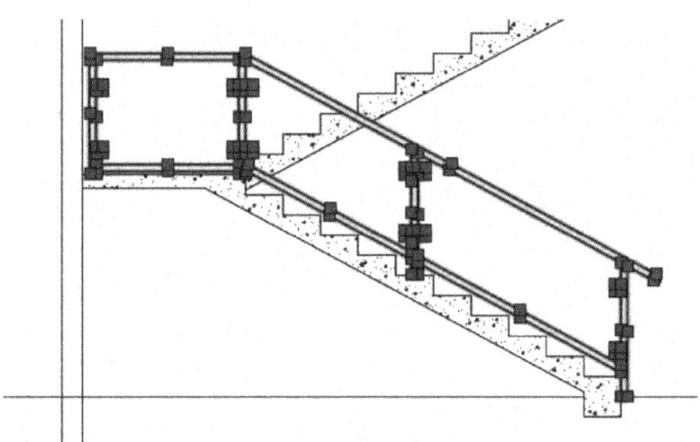

- Click the **Copy** icon on the **Modify** panel.
- Specify the base point, as shown.
- Move the pointer toward the right and click to create the copy.

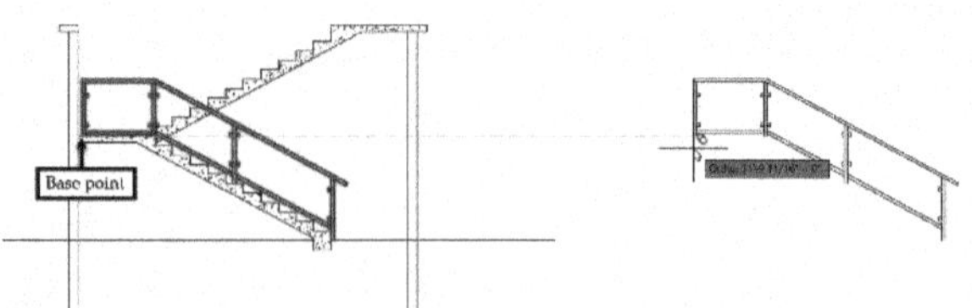

- Click the **Mirror** icon on the **Modify** panel.

- Create a selection window covering all the copied entities of the handrail.

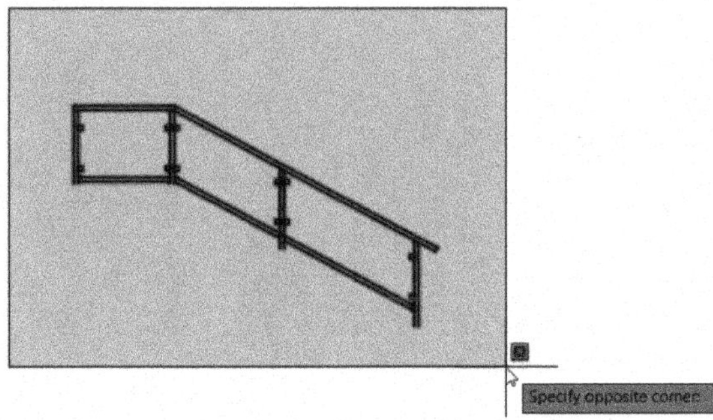

- Press ENTER.
- Select the base point, as shown.
- Move the pointer vertically upward and click.

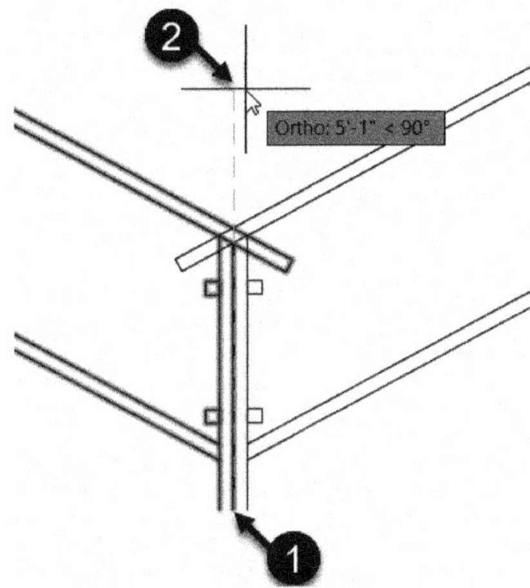

- Select **Yes** from the command line.
- Create a selection window across all the mirrored entities.
- Click the **Move** icon on the **Modify** panel.
- Specify the base point, as shown.

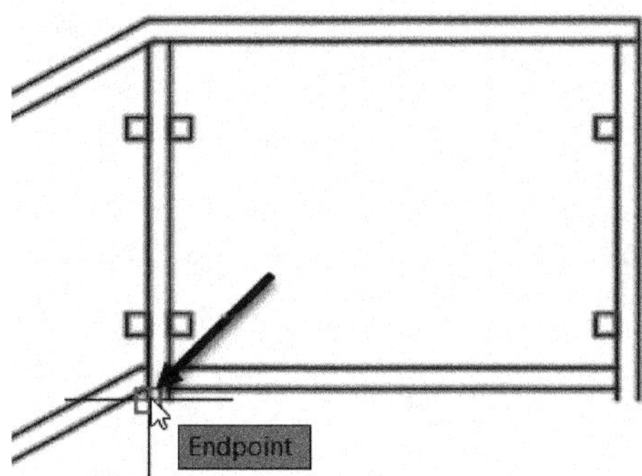

- Move the pointer toward the right and select the destination point.

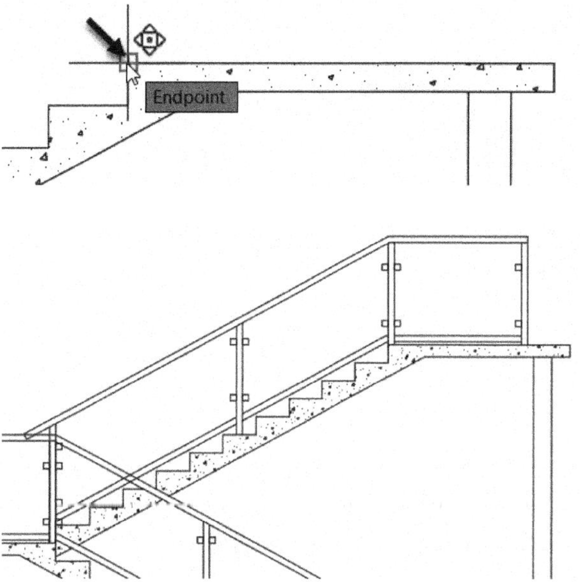

- Select the elements of the handrail, as shown.

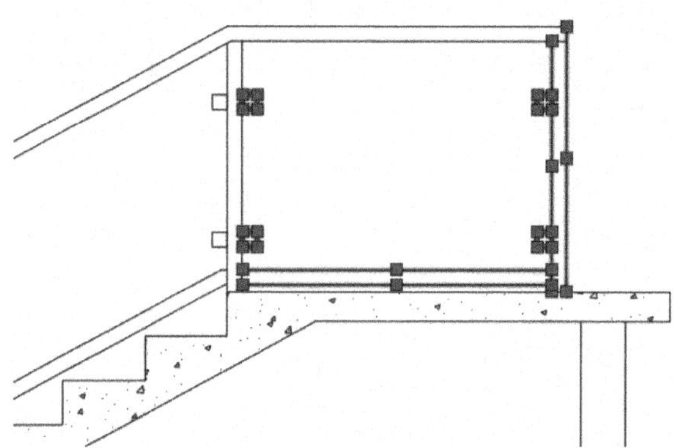

- Press Delete.
- Click the **Line** icon on the **Draw** panel.
- Press and hold the Shift key.
- Right click and select **From** from the **Object Snap** menu.
- Select the corner point of the handrail, as shown.

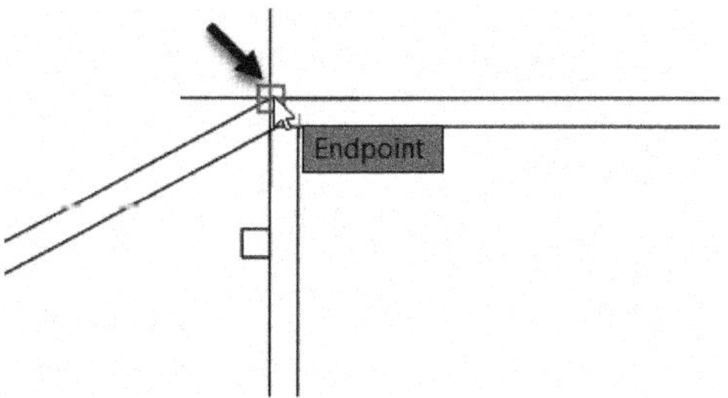

- Move the pointer along the horizontal line, as shown.

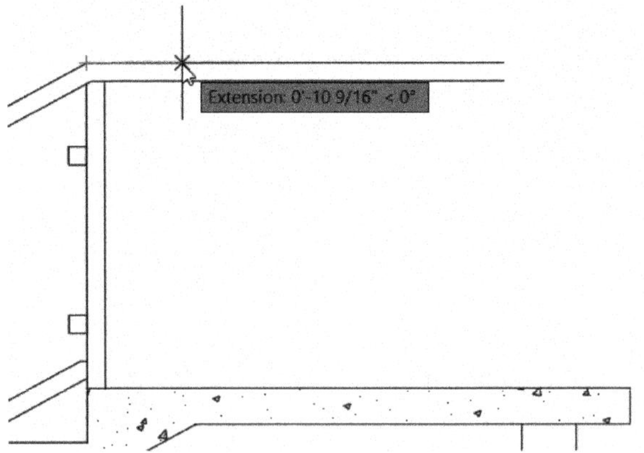

- Type 12 and press ENTER.
- Move the pointer downward and click.
- Click the **Trim** icon on the **Modify** panel.
- Trim the unwanted elements.

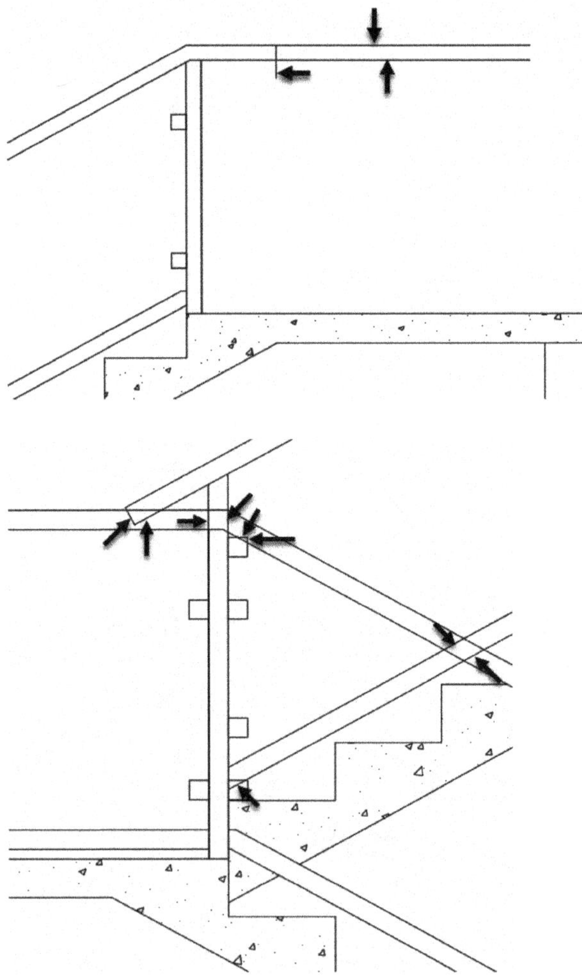

- On the **Home** tab of the ribbon, click **Draw** panel > **Hatch** drop-down > **Hatch**.

- On the **Hatch Creation** tab of the ribbon, expand the **Pattern** gallery, and select the **GOST-GLASS** pattern.

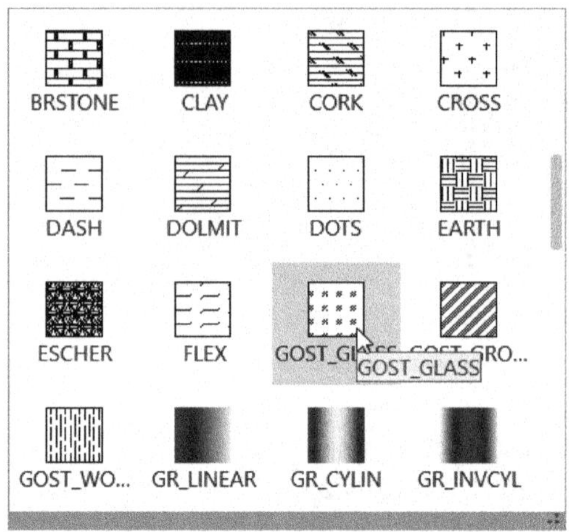

- Pick points in the areas, as shown.

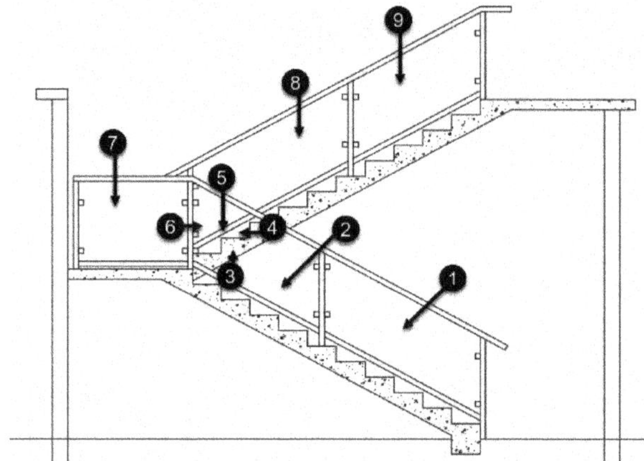

- Right click and select Enter.

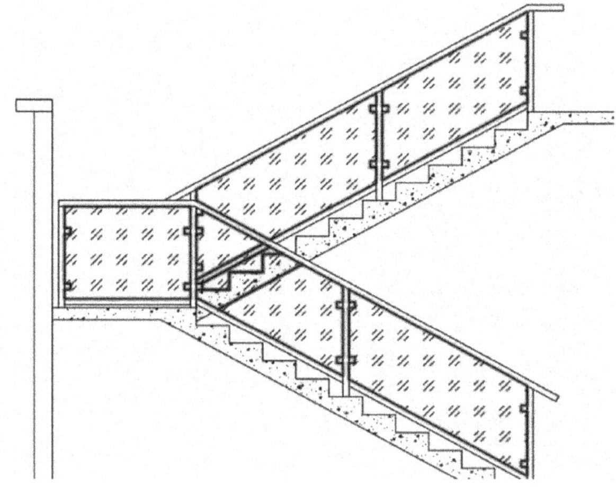

- Delete the construction lines, as shown.

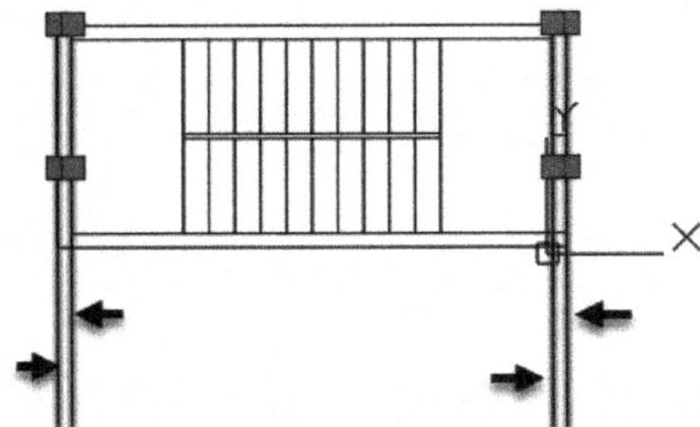

- Save and close the file.

Example 3

In this tutorial, you will create the elevation view using the floor plan.

- Download the Elevation_plan from the companion website and open it.
- Click the **Layer Properties** icon on the **Layers** panel of the **Home** ribbon tab.
- Click the **New Layer** icon on the Layer Properties Manager.
- Type Elevation as the layer name.
- Double-click on the Elevation layer.

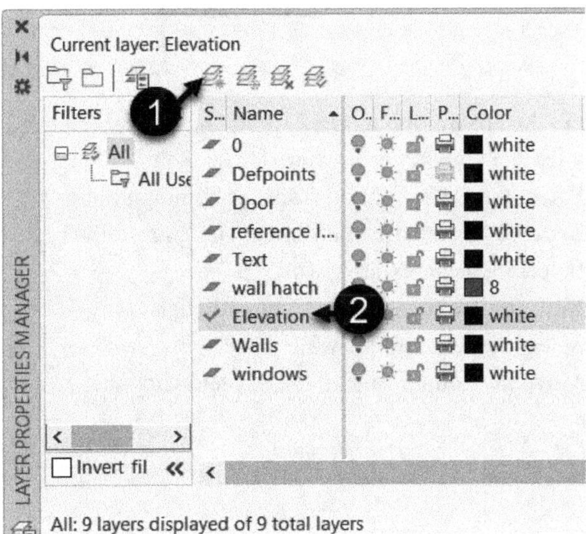

- Close the Layer Properties Manager.
- Draw a horizontal line above the floor plan, as shown.

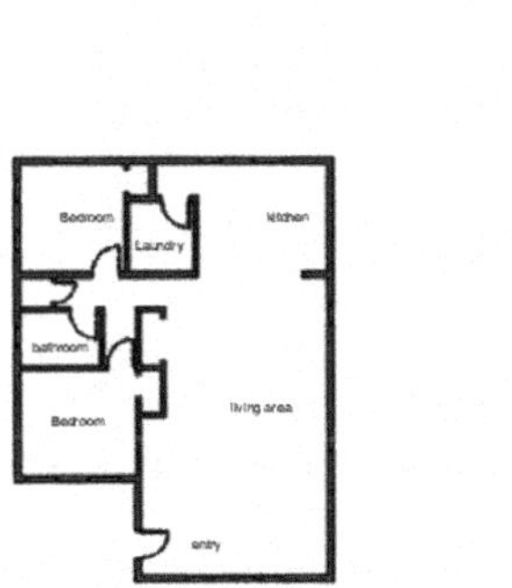

- On the **Home** ribbon tab, expand the **Draw** panel and click the **Ray** tool.

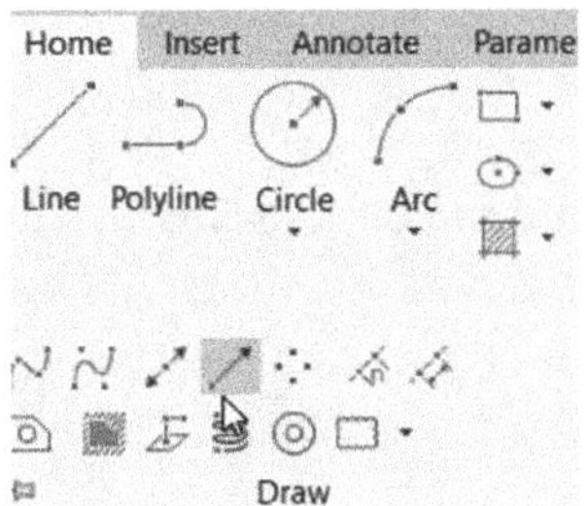

- Select the top-left corner of the floor plan.
- Move the pointer upward and click.

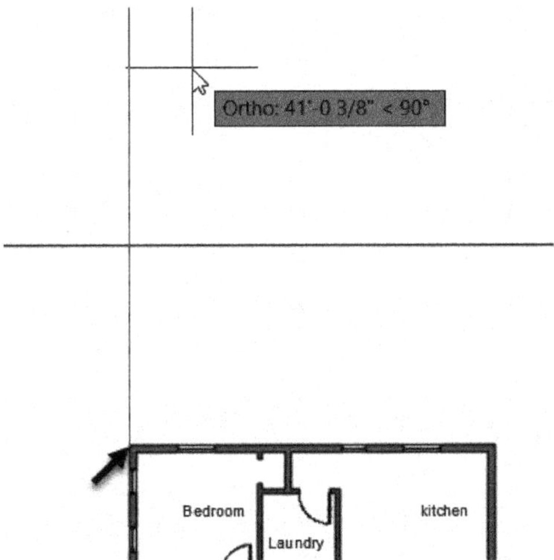

- Press ENTER twice.
- Select the top-right corner of the floor plan.
- Move the pointer upward and click.

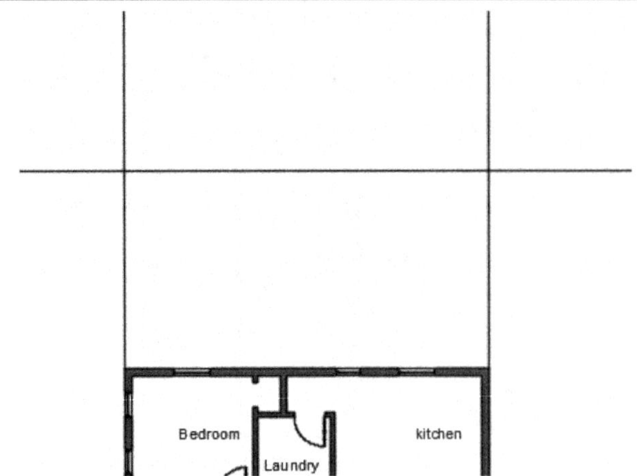

- Click the **Offset** tool on the **Modify** panel of the **Home** ribbon tab.
- Type 6" and press ENTER.
- Select the horizontal line.
- Move the pointer upward and click to create an offset line.

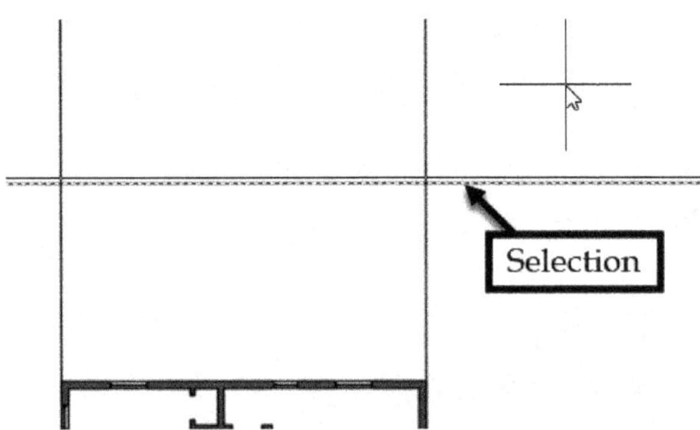

- Press ENTER twice.
- Type 9' as the offset distance. Next, press ENTER.
- Select the offset line created previously.
- Move the pointer upward and click.

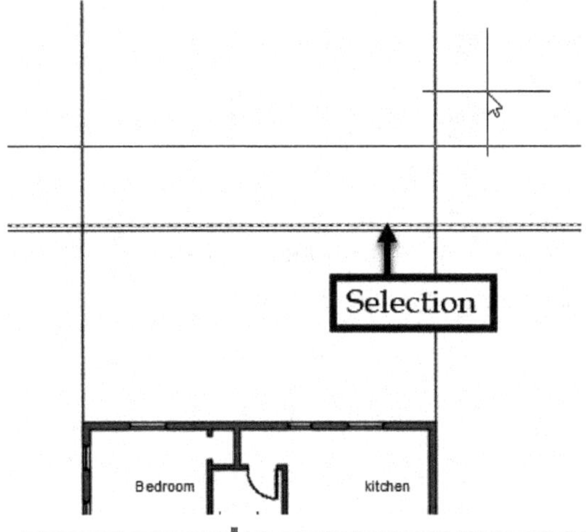

- Press ENTER twice.
- Type 10" as the offset distance. Next, press ENTER.
- Select the offset line created previously.
- Move the pointer upward and click.

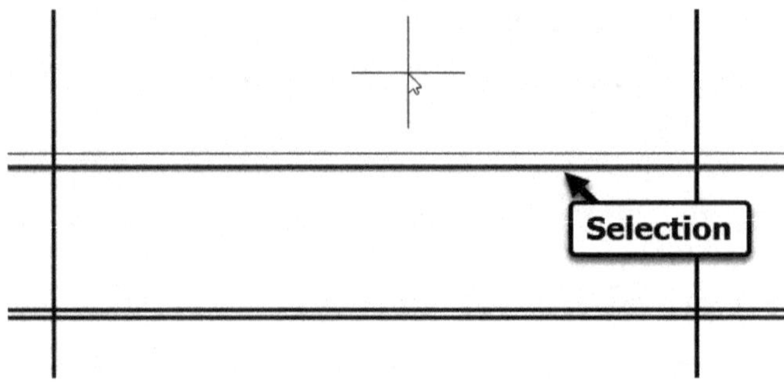

- Press ENTER twice.
- Type 6' as the offset distance. Next, press ENTER.
- Select the offset line created previously.
- Move the pointer upward and click.

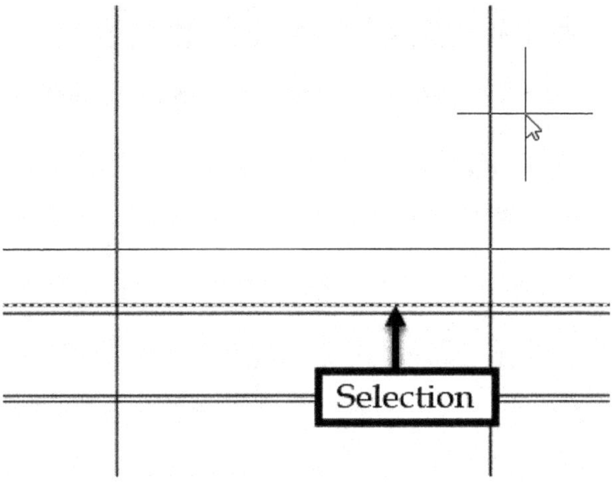

- On the **Home** ribbon tab, expand the **Draw** panel and click the **Construction Line** tool.
- Select the **Offset** option from the command line.
- Type 16" as the offset distance. Next, press ENTER.
- Select the right exterior wall.
- Move the pointer toward right and click.
- Select the left exterior wall.
- Move the pointer toward the left and click.

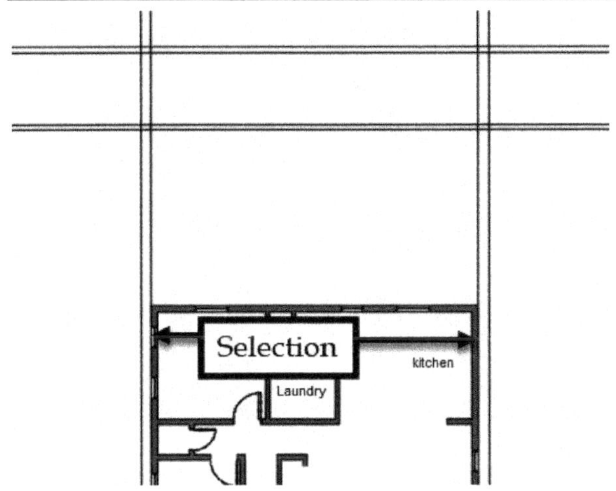

- Press ENTER twice.
- Select the **Ver** option from the command line.
- Select the corner point of the exterior wall, as shown.

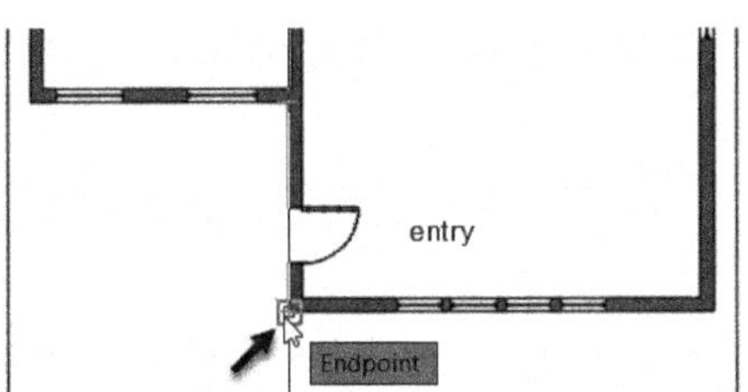

- Press ENTER twice.
- Select the **Offset** option from the command line.
- Type 16" as the offset distance. Next, press ENTER.
- Select the construction line created in the last step.
- Move the pointer toward the left and click.

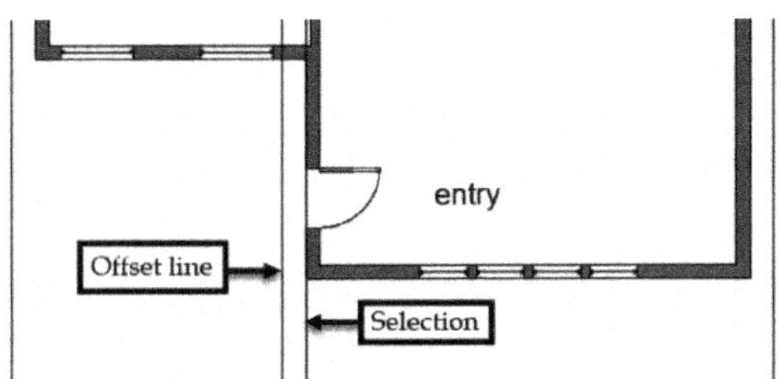

- On the **Home** ribbon tab, expand the **Modify** panel and click the **Break at Point** tool.

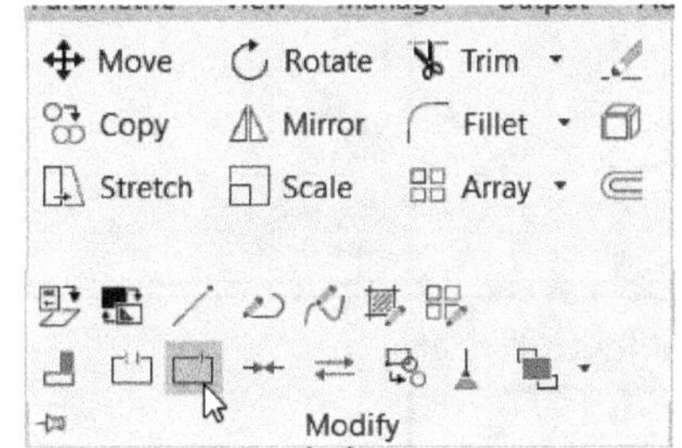

- Select the horizontal line, as shown.

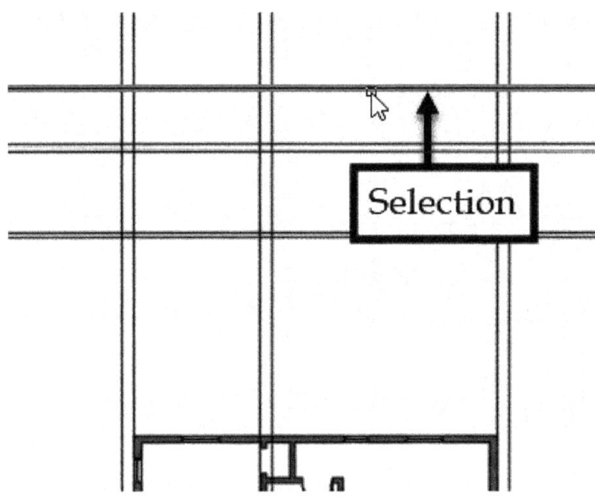

- Select the intersection point between the horizontal and vertical lines, as shown.

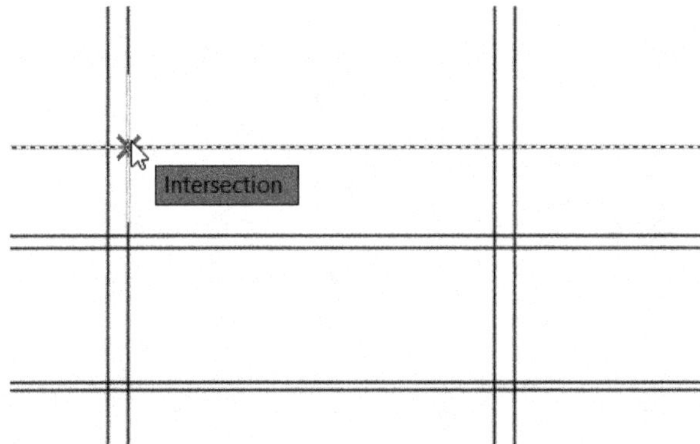

- Press ENTER to activate the **Break at Point** tool.
- Select the right portion of the broken line.
- Select the intersection point between the horizontal and vertical lines, as shown.

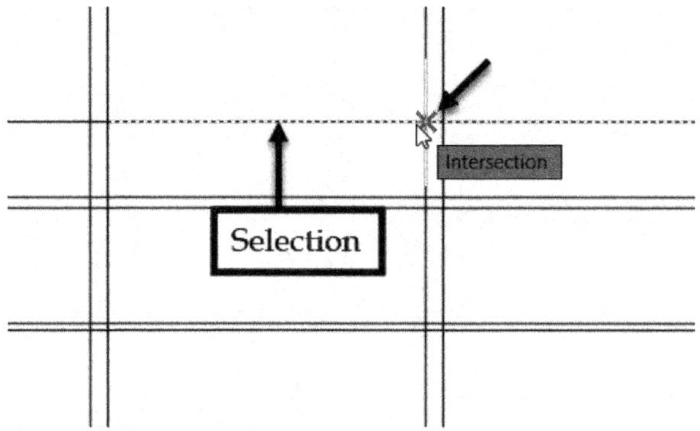

- Click the **Line** tool on the **Draw** panel of the **Home** ribbon tab.
- Select the midpoint of the broken line, as shown.

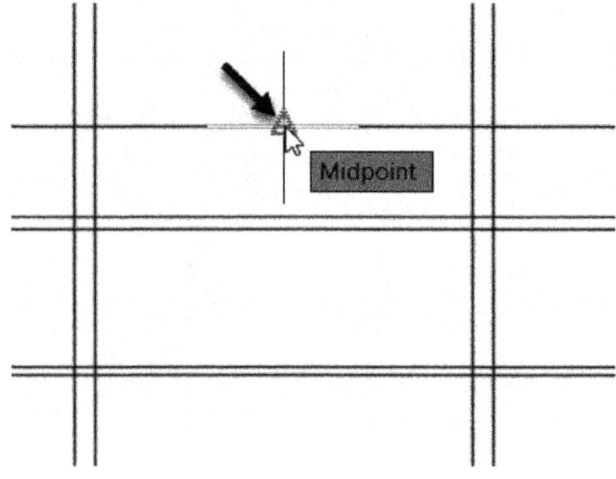

- Select the intersection point between the horizontal and vertical lines, as shown.

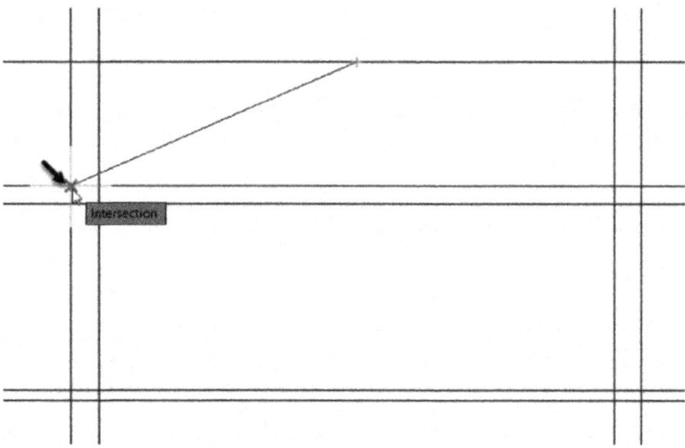

- Press ENTER twice.
- Select the start point of the line created in the last step.
- Select the intersection point between the horizontal and vertical lines, as shown.

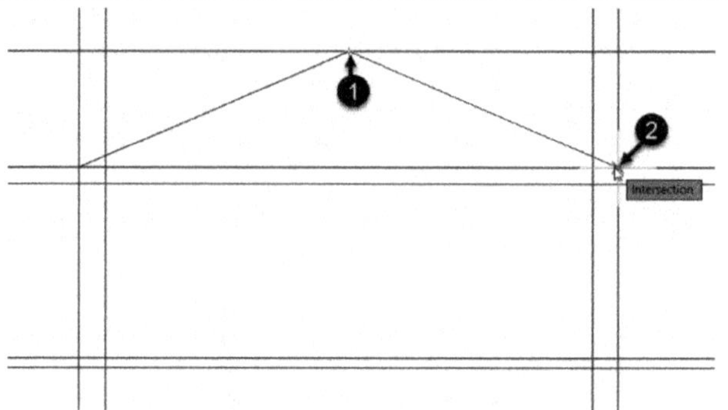

- Click the **Trim** tool on the **Modify** panel of the **Home** ribbon tab.
- Select the portions of the vertical lines, as shown.

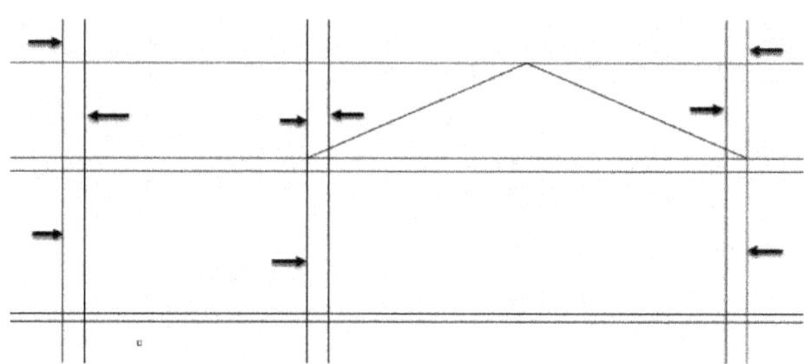

- Click and drag the mouse pointer across the vertical lines, as shown.

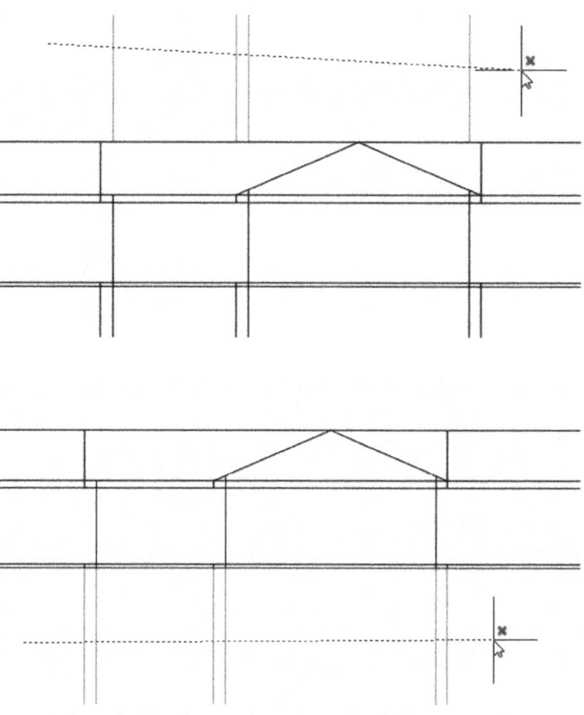

- Trim the horizontal and vertical lines, as shown.

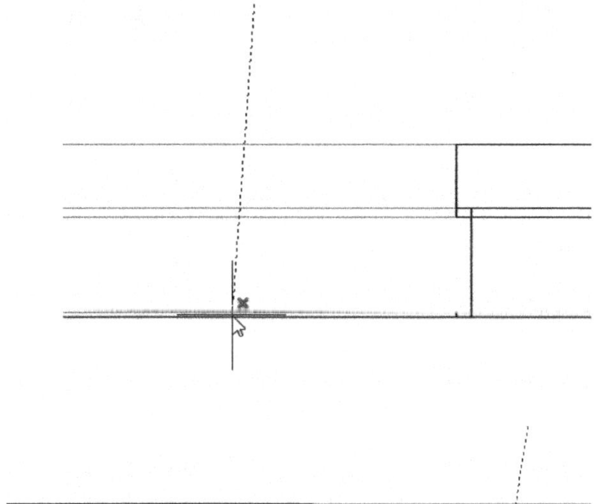

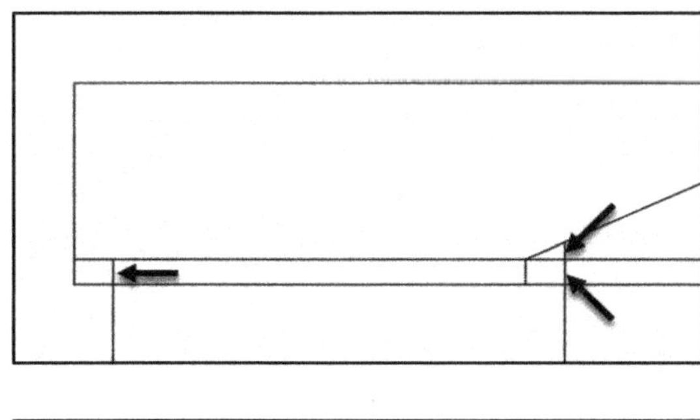

- Trim the small portions, as shown.

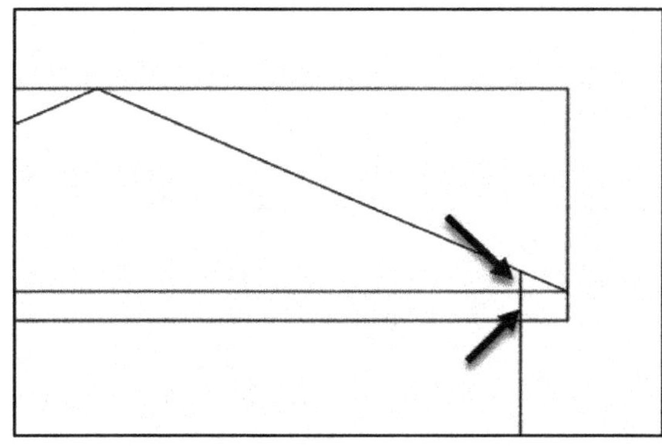

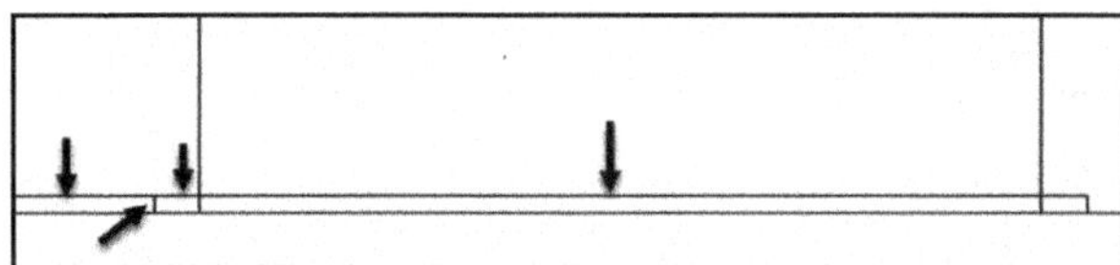

- Press Esc.
- Select the inclined line, as shown.

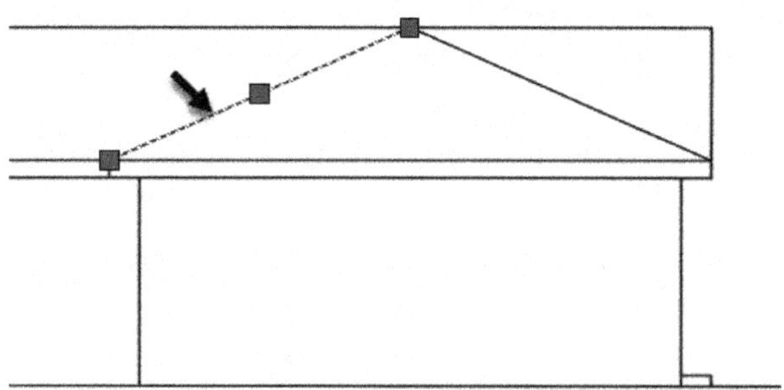

- Click the **Copy** tool on the **Modify** panel of the **Home** ribbon tab.
- Specify the base point, as shown.
- Move the pointer downward and select the intersection point, as shown.

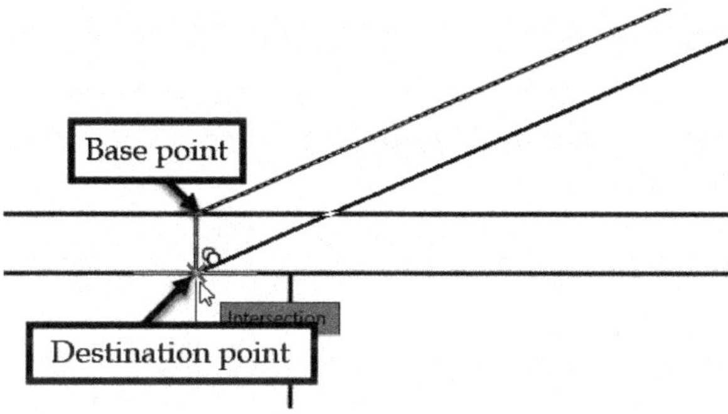

- Press Esc.
- Likewise, copy the other inclined line, as shown.

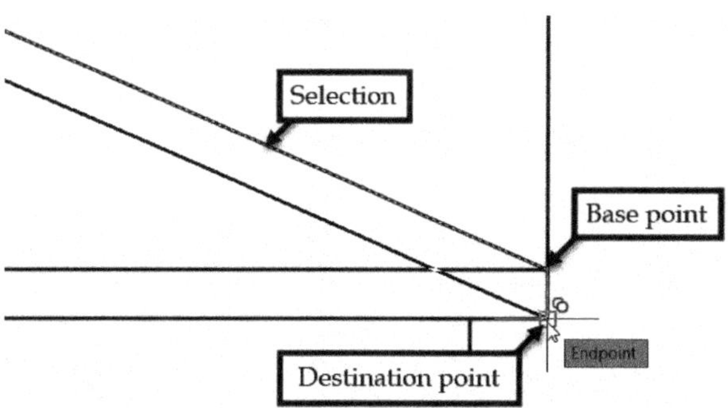

- Click the **Trim** tool on the **Modify** panel of the **Home** ribbon tab.
- Select the portions of the horizontal line, as shown.

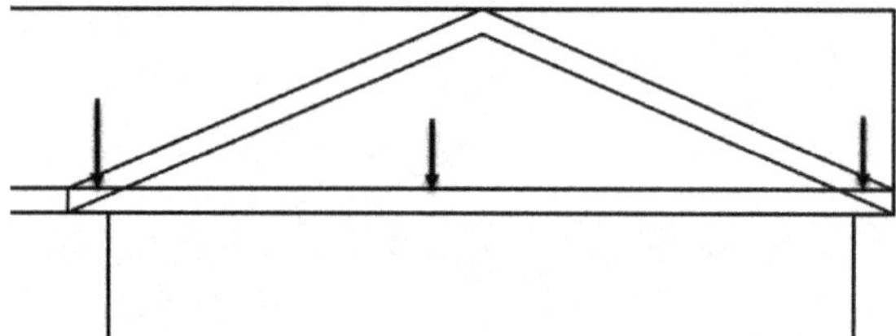

- On the **Home** ribbon tab, expand the **Modify** panel and click the **Break at Point** tool.
- Select the horizontal line, as shown.
- Select the intersection point, as shown.

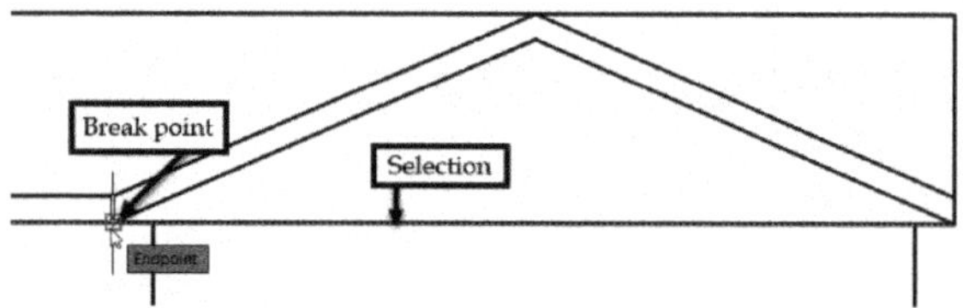

- On the **Home** ribbon tab, expand the **Modify** panel and click the **Break at Point** tool.
- Select the vertical line, as shown.
- Select the intersection point, as shown.

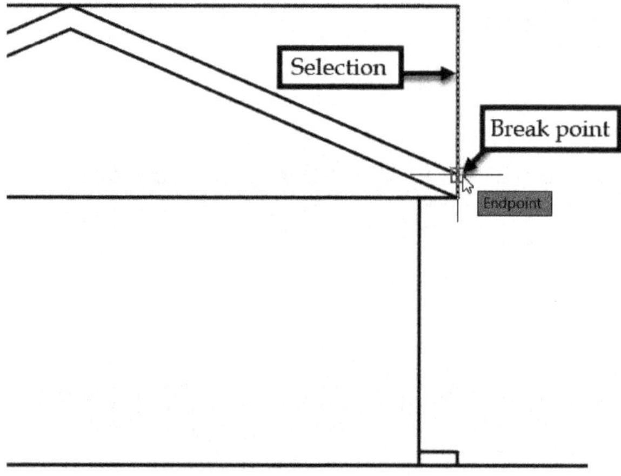

- On the **Home** ribbon tab, expand the **Modify** panel and click the **Break at Point** tool.
- Select the vertical line, as shown.
- Select the intersection point, as shown.

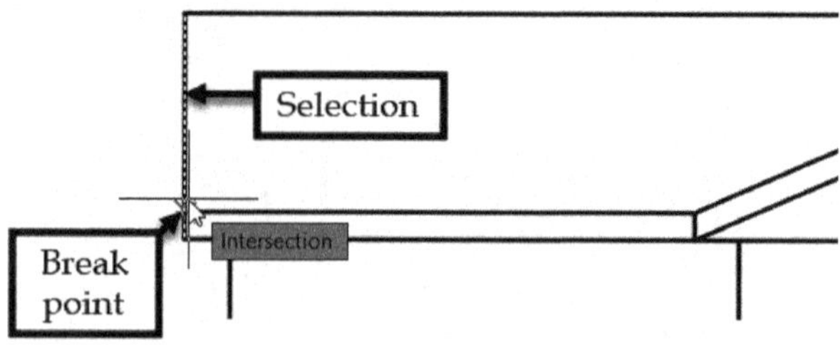

- Select the horizontal line, as shown.
- Press Delete.

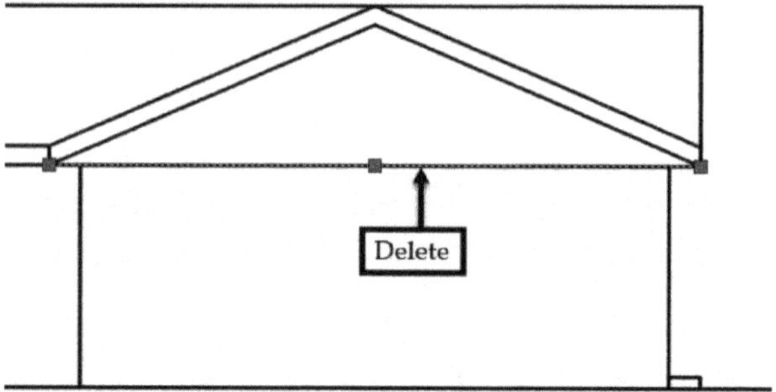

- Click the **Trim** drop-down > **Extend** on the **Modify** panel of the **Home** ribbon tab.
- Select the two vertical lines, as shown.

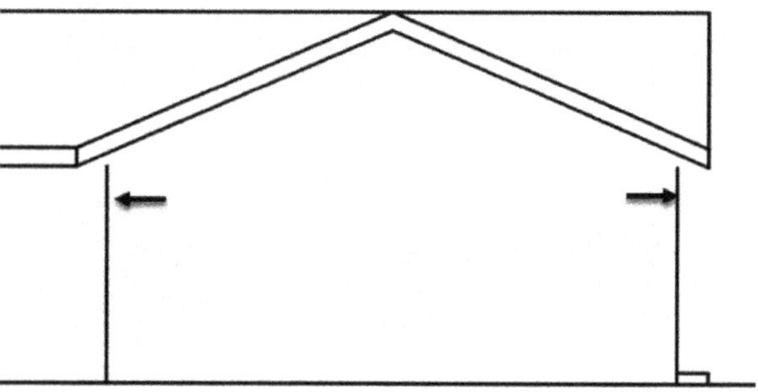

- Create a horizontal line connecting the endpoints of the two vertical lines.

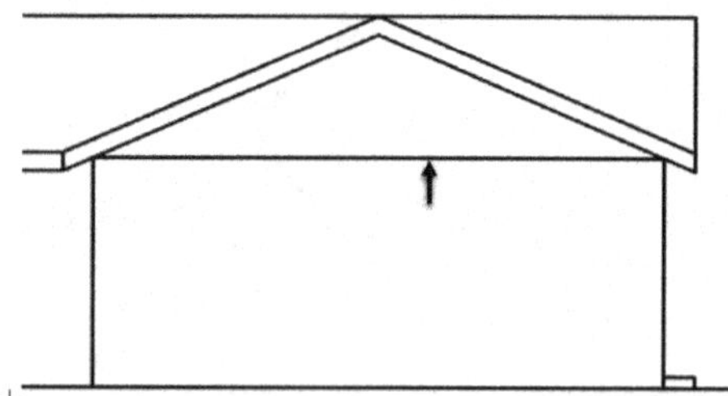

- Select the two construction lines, as shown.
- Press Delete.

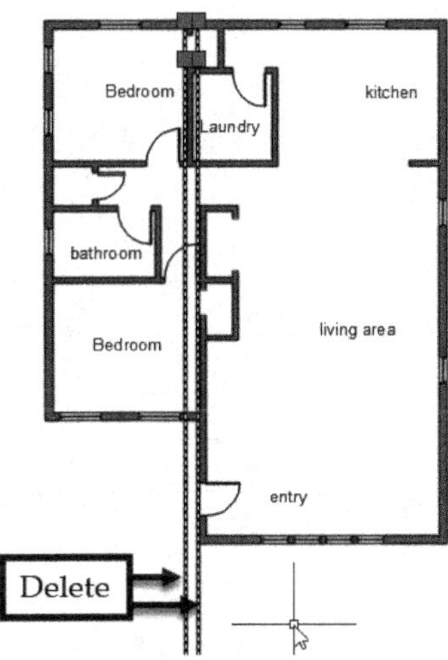

- On the **Home** ribbon tab, expand the **Draw** panel and click the **Construction Line** tool.
- Select the **Ver** option from the command line.
- Zoom to the lower portion of the floor plan and select the vertex points on the window, as shown.

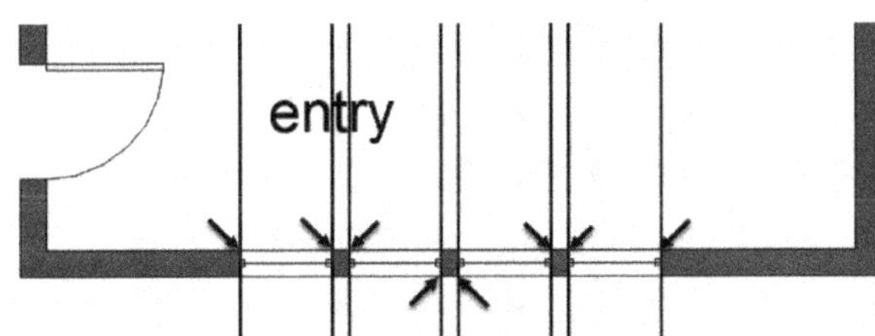

- Click the **Offset** tool on the **Modify** panel of the **Home** ribbon tab.
- Type 3' as the offset distance. Next, press ENTER.
- Select the horizontal line, as shown.
- Move the pointer upward and click.

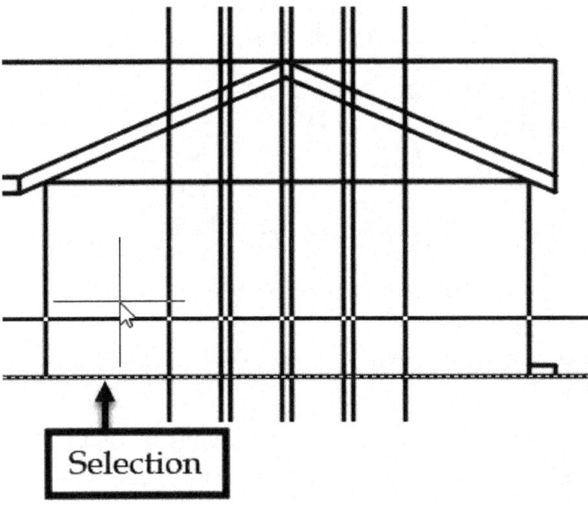

- Click the **Rectangle** tool on the **Draw** panel of the **Home** ribbon tab.
- Select the intersection point, as shown.

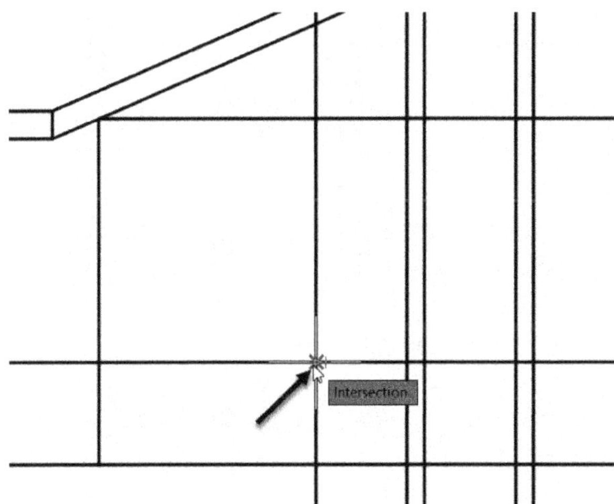

- Select the **Dimensions** option from the command line.
- Select the two intersection points, as shown.

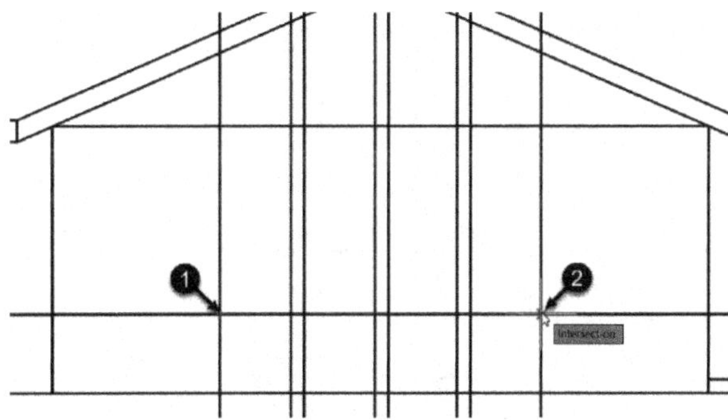

- Type 54 as the rectangle width and press ENTER.
- Move the pointer upward and click.

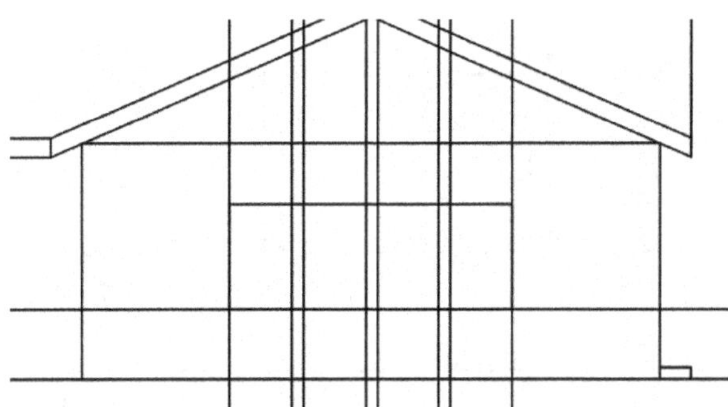

- Click the **Offset** tool on the **Modify** panel of the **Home** ribbon tab.
- Type 4" as the offset distance. Next, press ENTER.

- Select the rectangle.
- Move the pointer outward and click.

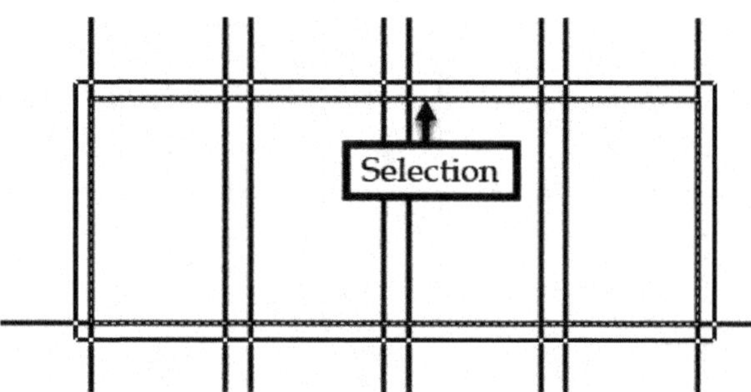

- Click the **Trim** tool on the **Modify** panel of the **Home** ribbon tab.
- Click and drag the pointer across the vertical lines, as shown.

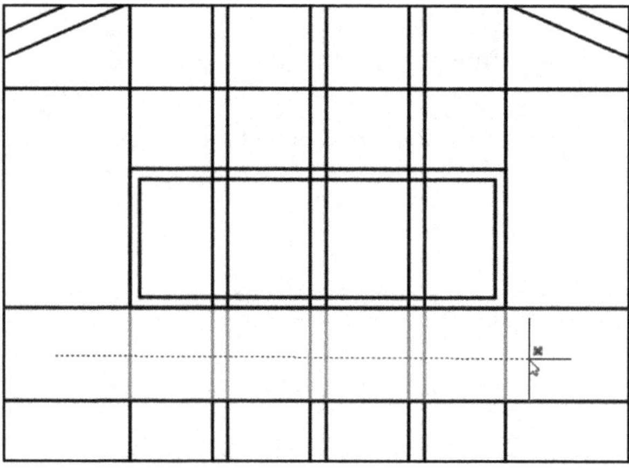

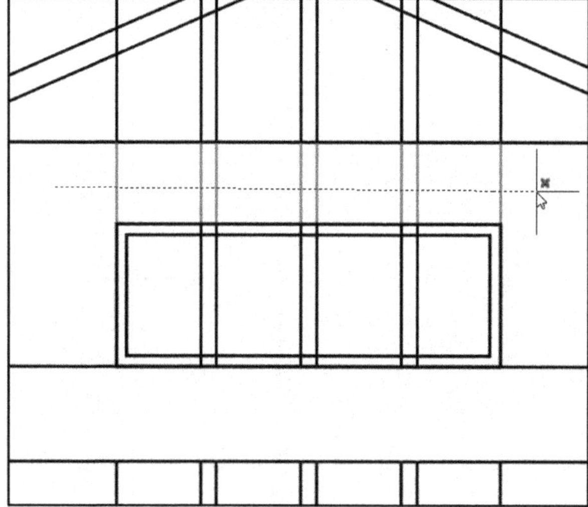

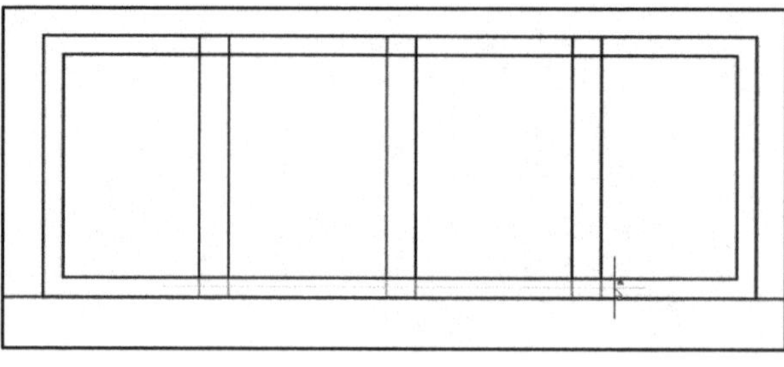

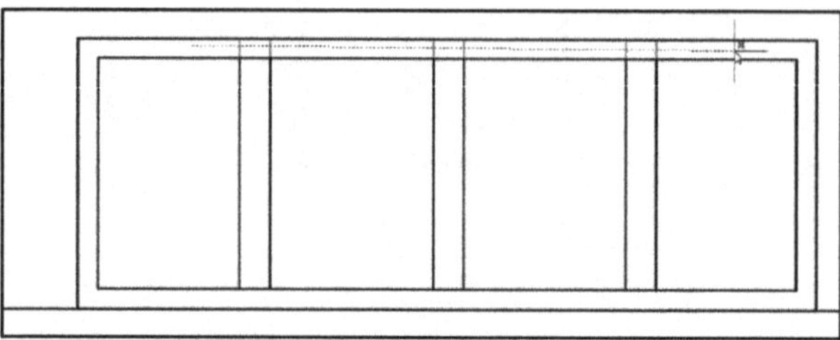

- Press ENTER.
- Select the vertical and horizontal construction lines, and then press Delete.

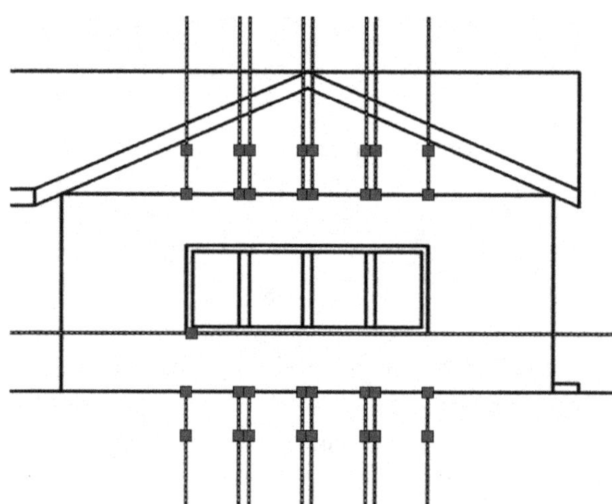

- Select the two rectangles and click the **Explode** tool on the **Modify** panel of the **Home** ribbon tab.

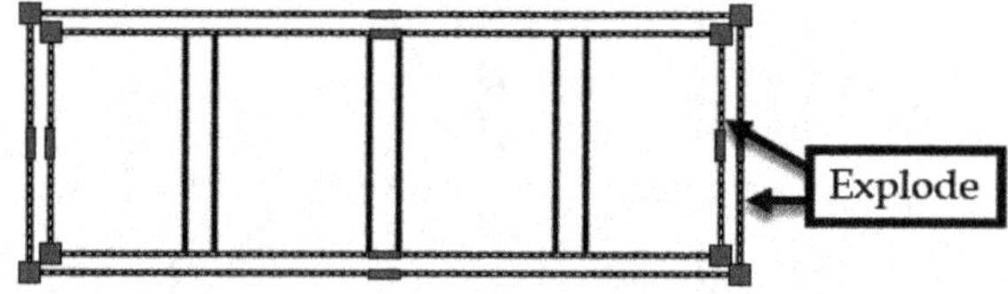

- Type **MLINE** in the command line and press ENTER.
- Select the **Justification** option from the command line.
- Select the **Zero** option from the command line.
- Select the **Scale** option from the command line.

- Type 0.25 and press ENTER.
- Press and hold the Shift key, and then right click.
- Select the **Mid between 2 Points** option.
- Select the two points, as shown.
- Move the pointer downward and click.

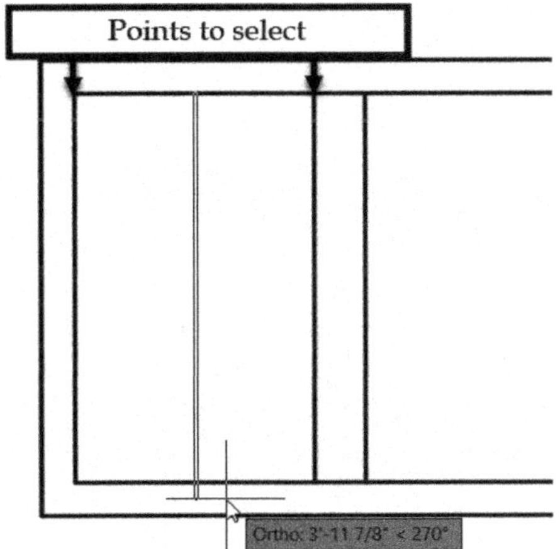

- Press ENTER twice.
- Select the midpoint of the vertical line, as shown.

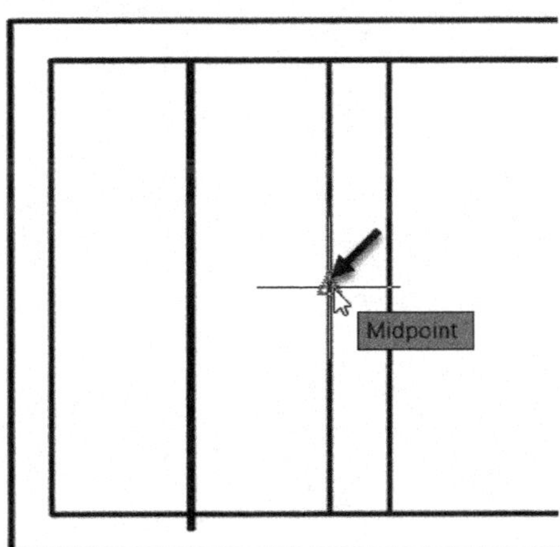

- Move the pointer toward the left and select the midpoint of the vertical line.

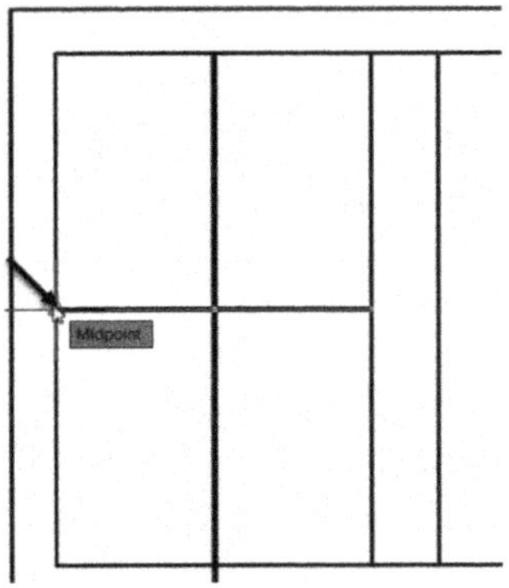

- Press Esc.
- Type **MLEDIT** in the command line and press ENTER.
- Click the **Open Cross** icon on **the Multilines Edit Tools** dialog.

- Select the two multilines; the open cross is created at the intersection of the two multilines.

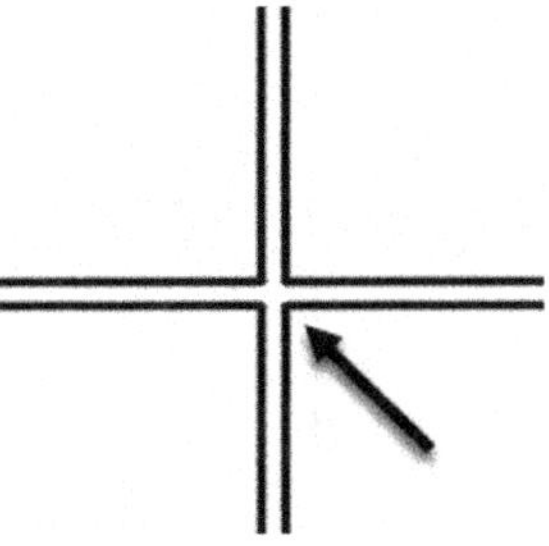

- Click the **Trim** tool on the **Modify** panel of the **Home** ribbon tab.
- Click and drag the pointer across the unwanted portions of the multilines, as shown.

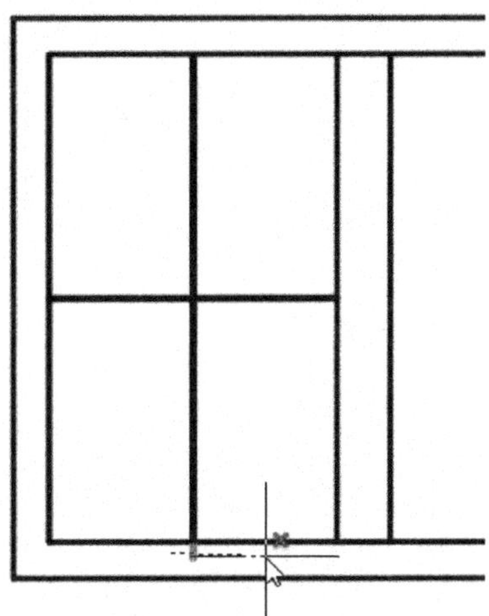

- Click the **Copy** tool on the **Modify** panel of the **Home** ribbon tab.
- Select the two multilines and press ENTER.
- Select the lower-left corner point.
- Move the pointer toward right and select the corner point, as shown.

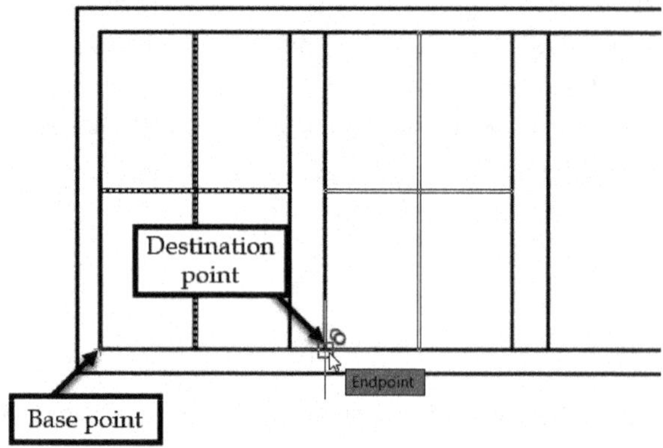

- Likewise, create two more copies of the multi-lines, as shown.

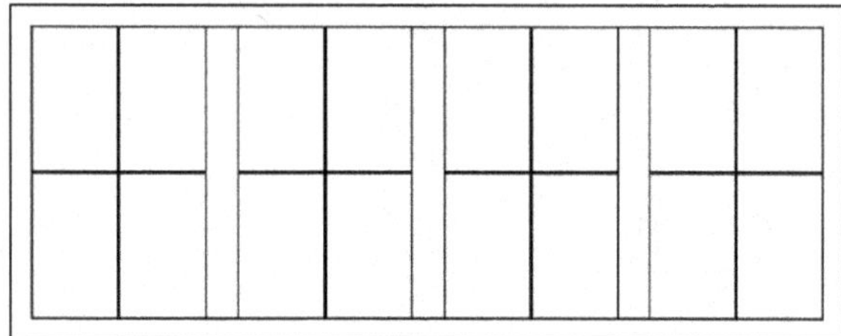

- Likewise, create two windows on the left side.

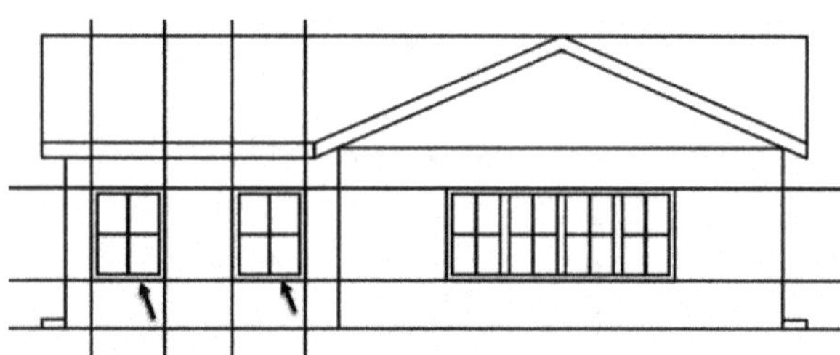

- Delete the construction lines.

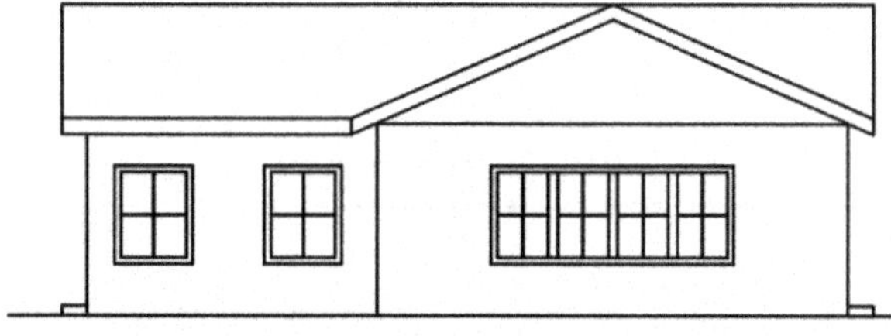

- Click the **Hatch** tool on the **Draw** panel of the **Home** ribbon tab.
- On the **Hatch Creation** tab, click **Pattern** panel > **Pattern** gallery > **AR-RSHKE**.

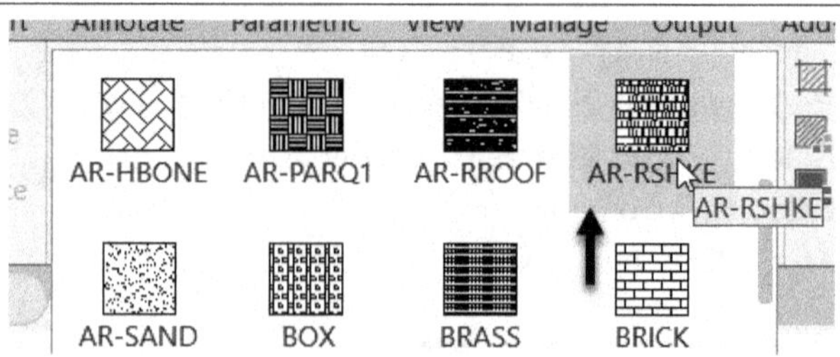

- Click in the regions, as shown.

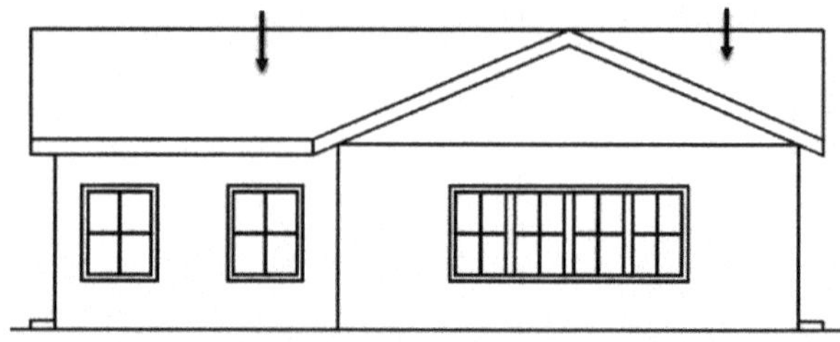

- Press ENTER twice.
- On the **Hatch Creation** tab, click **Pattern** panel > **Pattern** gallery > **AR-B816**.

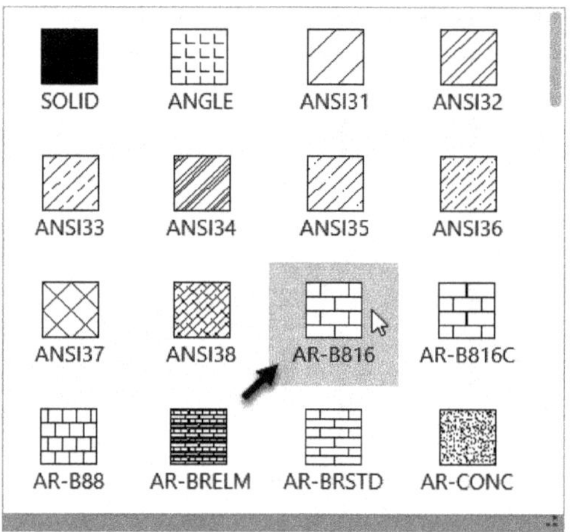

- Click in the regions, as shown.

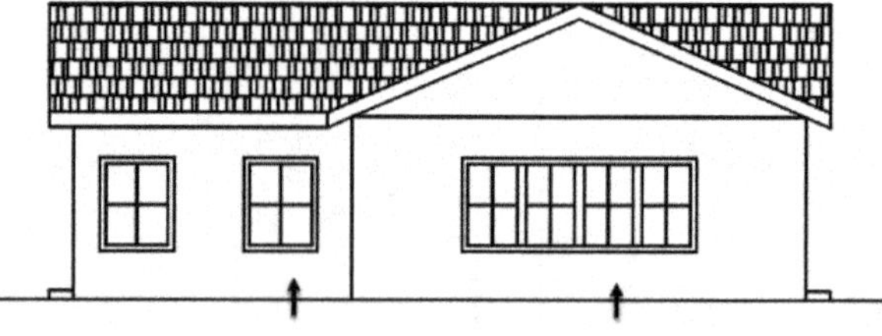

- Press ENTER twice.
- On the **Hatch Creation** tab, click **Pattern** panel > **Pattern** gallery > **ANSI31**.
- On the **Properties** panel, enter **135** and **50** in the **Angle** and **Scale** boxes, respectively.

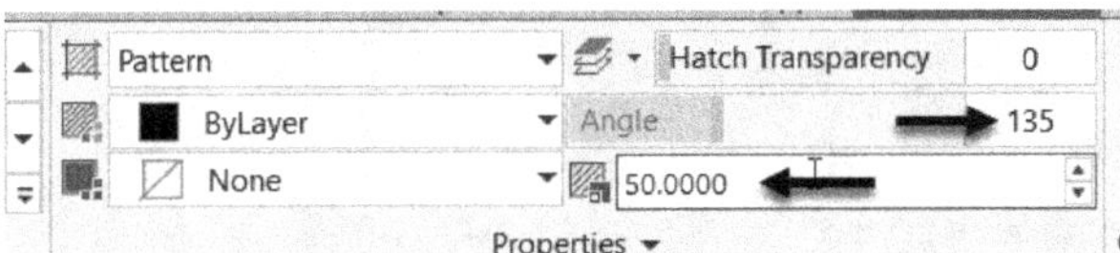

- Click in the region, as shown.

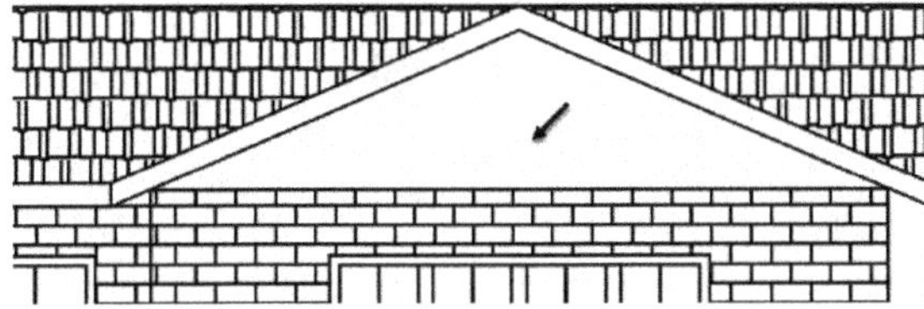

- Press ENTER.
- Save and close the file.

Example 4

In this tutorial, you will create the Roof plan using the floor plan.

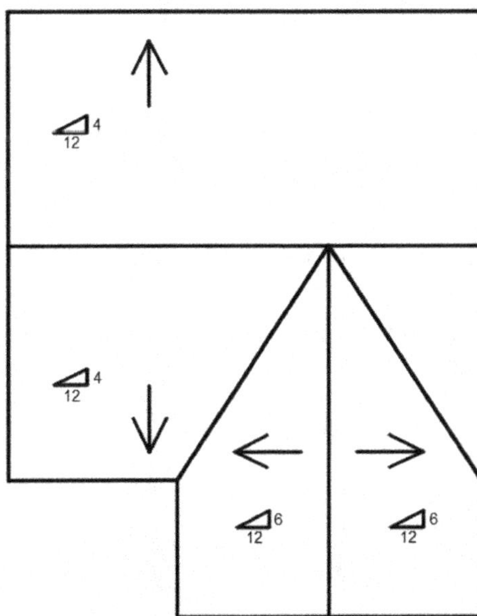

- Download the Floor_plan.dwg from the companion website.
- Start a new drawing using the acad.dwt template.
- Click the **Attach** tool on the **Reference** panel of the **Insert** ribbon tab.
- On the **Select Reference file** dialog, select **Drawing** from the **Files of type** drop-down.
- Go to the location of the Floor_plan.dwg file and double-click on it.

- Click **OK** on the **Attach External Reference** dialog.
- Click in the graphics window.
- Click **Zoom > Zoom All** on the Navigation Bar.
- Click the **Polyline** tool on the **Draw** panel of the **Home** ribbon tab.
- Select the corner points of the floor plan.

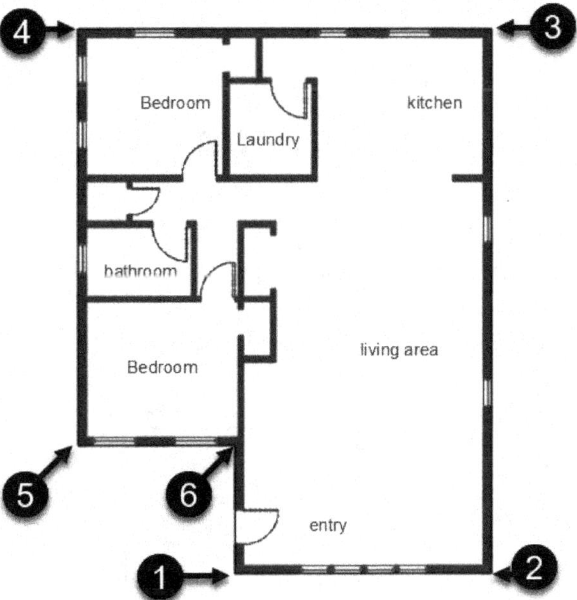

- Select the **Close** option from the command line.
- Click the **Offset** tool on the **Modify** panel of the **Home** ribbon tab.
- Type 16 and press ENTER.
- Select the newly created polyline.
- Move the pointer outward and click.

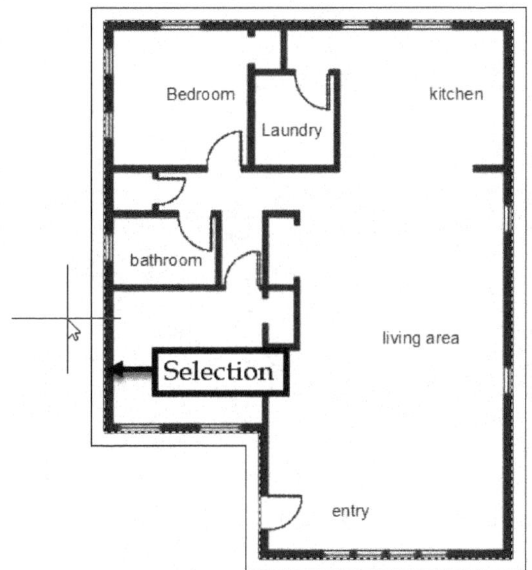

- Click the **Erase** tool on the **Modify** panel of the **Home** ribbon tab.

- Select the polyline used to create the offset.

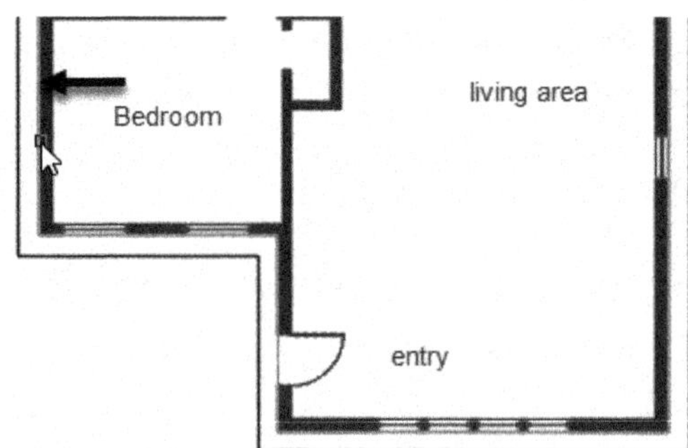

- Press ENTER.
- Click the **Line** tool on the **Draw** panel of the **Home** ribbon tab.
- Select the midpoint of the left vertical line.

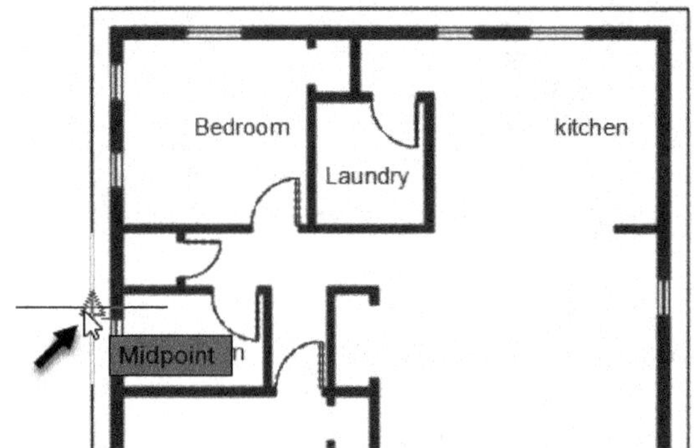

- Make sure the ORTHOMODE icon is active on the status bar.
- Move the pointer toward right and click.

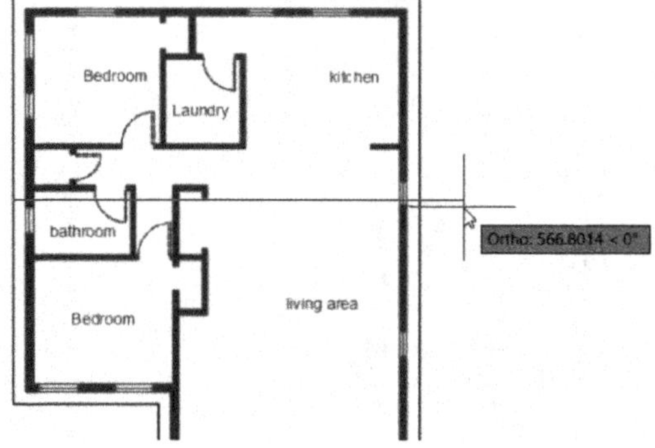

- Press ENTER twice.
- Select the midpoint of the lower horizontal line, as shown.

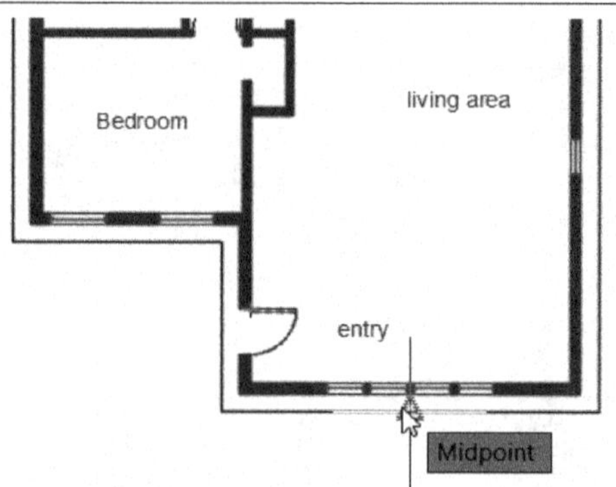

- Move the pointer upward and click.

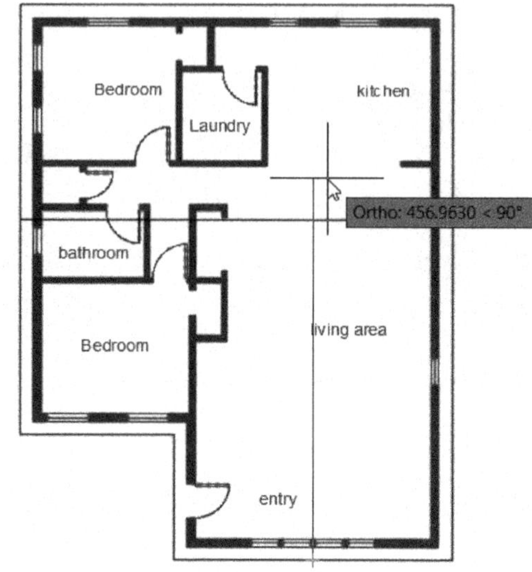

- Click the **Trim** tool on the **Modify** panel of the **Home** ribbon tab.
- Select the unwanted portions of the lines, as shown.

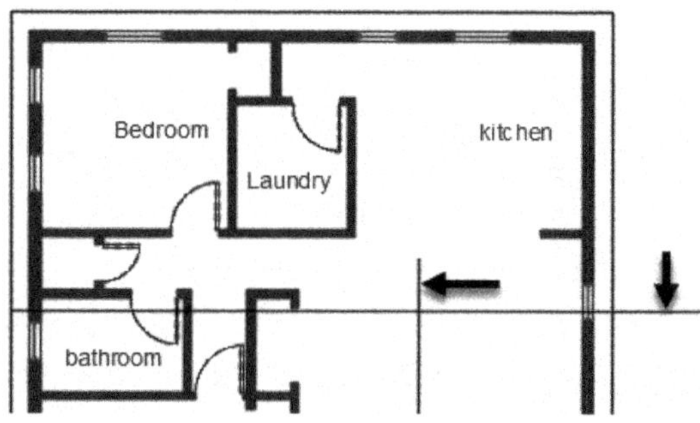

- Click the **Line** tool on the **Draw** panel of the **Home** ribbon tab.
- Select the corner point of the polyline.
- Select the intersection point of the vertical and horizontal lines.

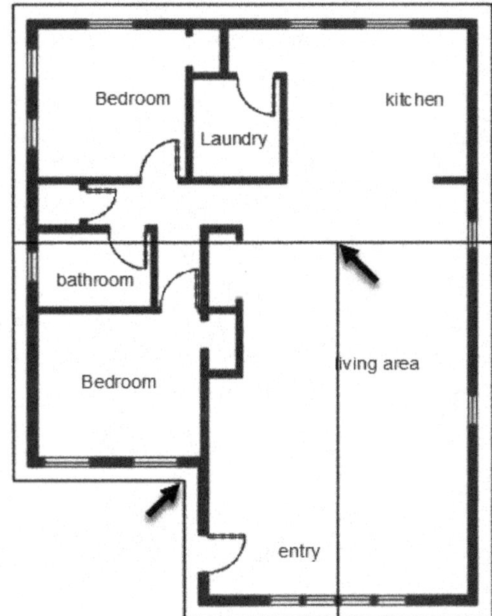

- Press Esc.
- Select the inclined line.
- Click the **Mirror** tool on the **Modify** panel of the **Home** ribbon tab.
- Select the endpoints of the vertical line.
- Select the **No** option from the command line.

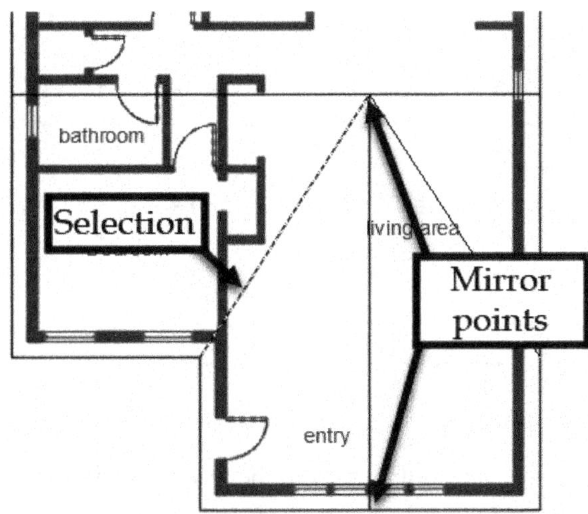

- Select the attachment.
- Click on the origin point of the attachment, and then move the pointer upward.

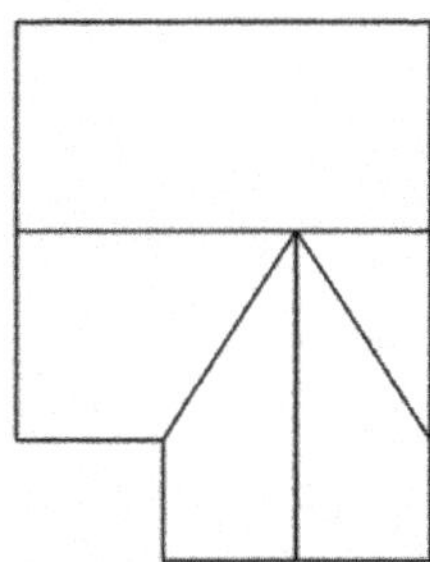

- Click the **Line** tool on the **Draw** panel of the **Home** ribbon tab.
- Click in the graphics window.
- Move the pointer toward the right.
- Type 36 and press ENTER.
- Move the pointer upward.
- Type 18 and press ENTER.

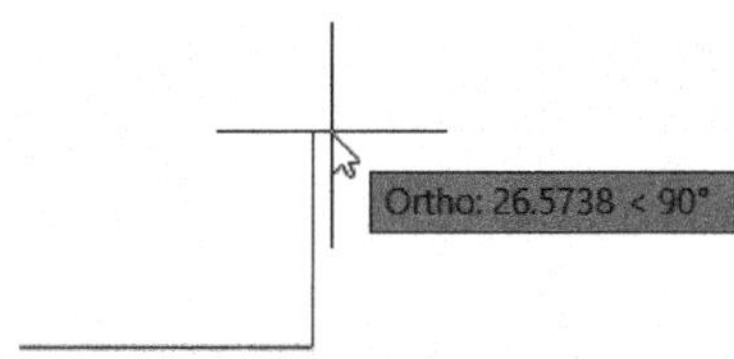

- Select the start point of the horizontal line.

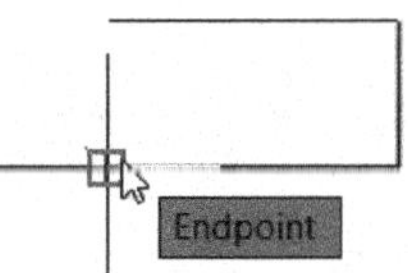

- Press ESC.

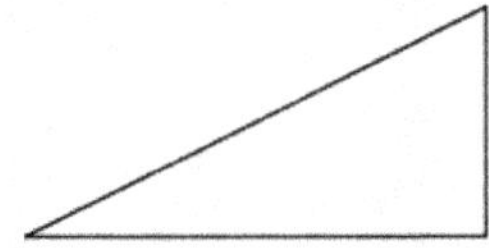

- Click the **Text** drop-down > **Single Line** on the **Annotation** panel of the **Home** ribbon tab.

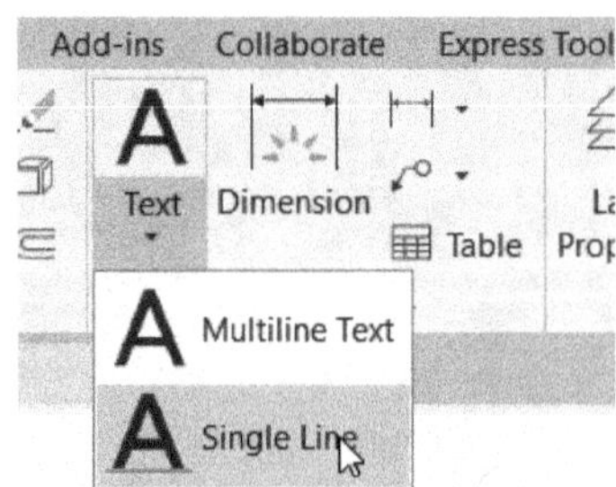

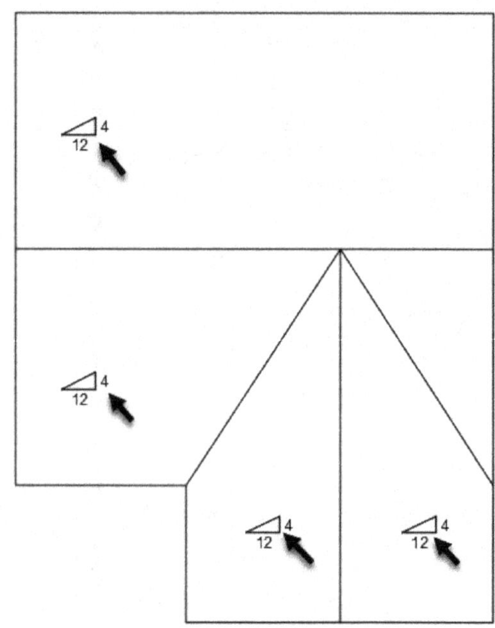

- Click in the graphics window.
- Type **12** as the text height. Next, press ENTER.
- Type 0 as the rotation angle, and then press ENTER.
- Type 4 and click in the graphics window.
- Type 12 and click in the graphics window.
- Press ESC.
- Position the texts at the locations, as shown.

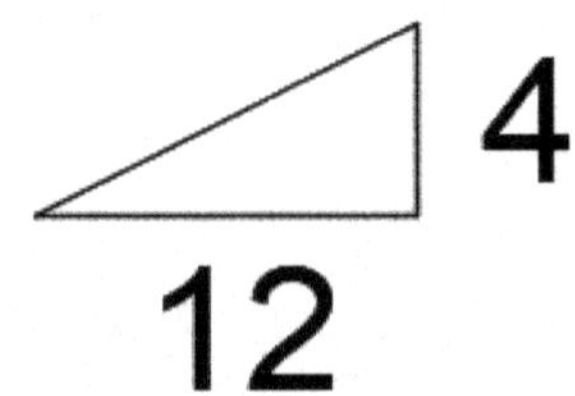

- Create a selection window across the triangle and the texts.
- Click the **Copy** tool on the **Modify** panel of the **Home** ribbon tab.
- Select the base point, as shown.

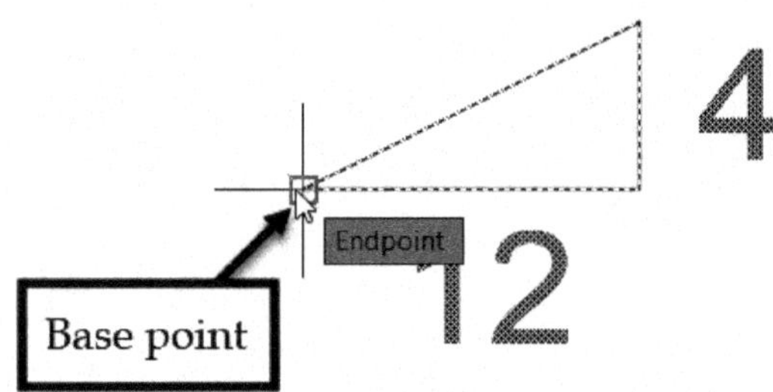

- Place the copies at the locations, as shown.

- Zoom the lower portion of the drawing.
- Double-click on 4.
- Type 6 and click in the graphics window.
- Likewise, change the text on the right side to 6.

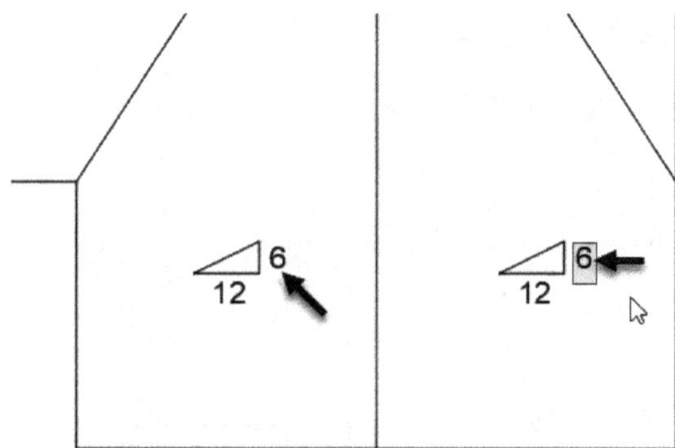

- Press ESC.
- Click the **Rectangle** tool on the **Draw** panel of the **Home** ribbon tab.
- Click at the location, as shown.
- Select the **Dimensions** option from the command line.
- Type 36 and press ENTER.
- Type 72 and press ENTER.
- Move the pointer downward and click.

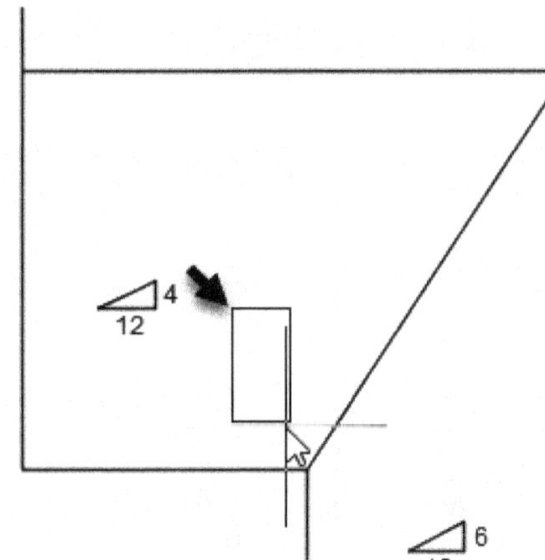

- Click the **Line** tool on the **Draw** panel of the **Home** ribbon tab.
- Select the midpoints of the horizontal edges of the rectangle.

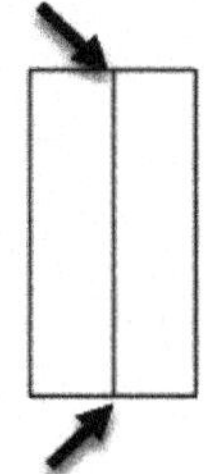

- Press ENTER twice.
- Select the midpoint of the left vertical edge of the rectangle.
- Select the lower endpoint of the vertical line.
- Select the midpoint of the right vertical edge of the rectangle.

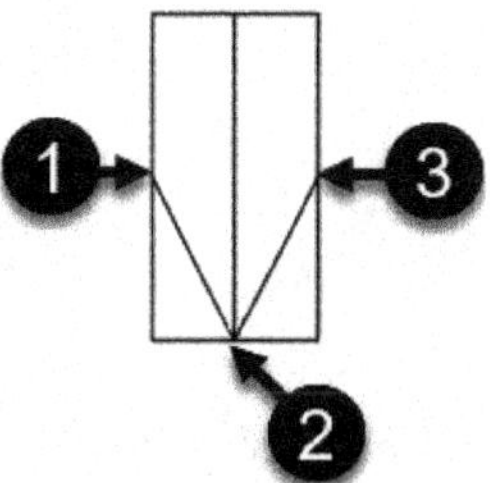

- Press ESC.
- Select the rectangle and press Delete.

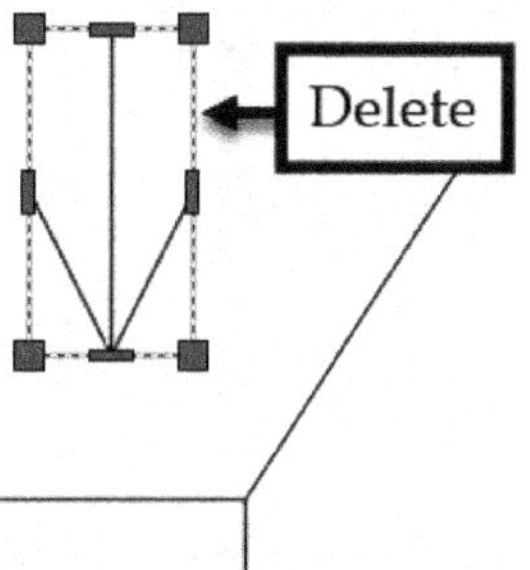

- Create a selection window across all the elements of the arrow.
- Click the **Mirror** tool on the **Modify** panel of the **Home** ribbon tab.
- Select the endpoints of the horizontal line to define the mirror line.

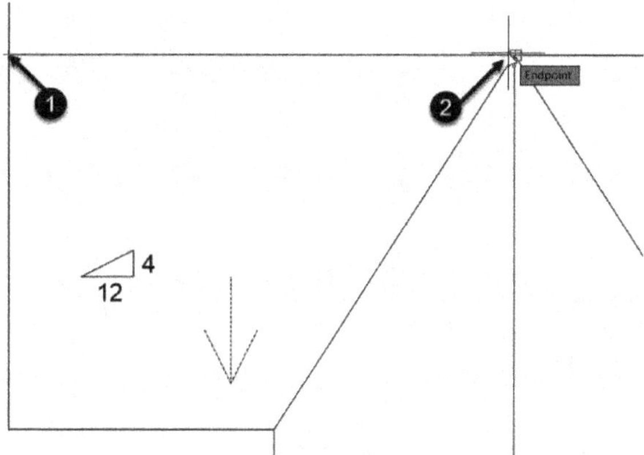

- Select **NO** from the command line.
- Create a selection window across all the elements of the arrow.
- Click the **Rotate** tool on the **Modify** panel of the **Home** ribbon tab.
- Select the base point, as shown.

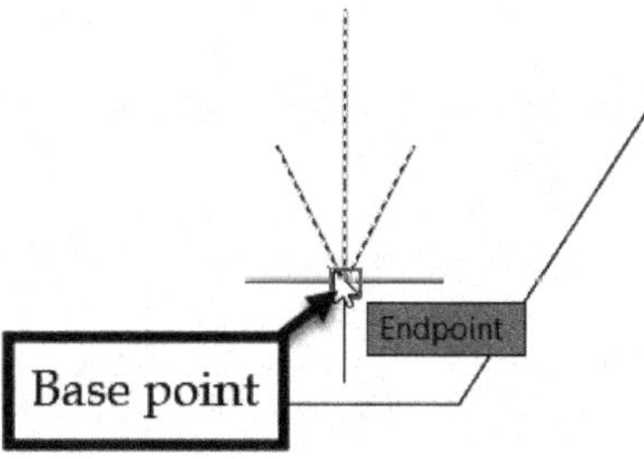

- Select the **Copy** option from the command line.
- Move the pointer vertically downward and click.

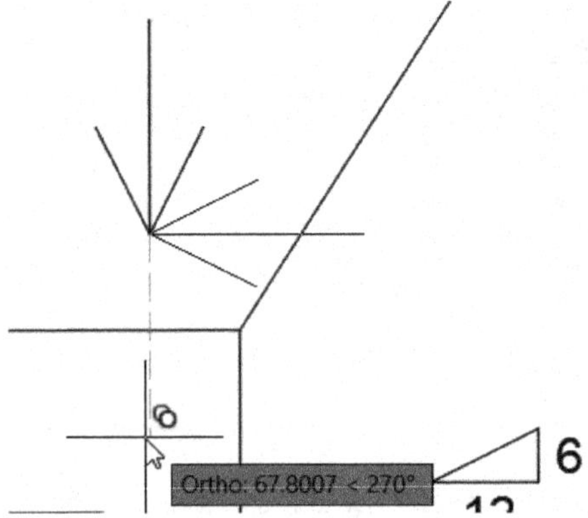

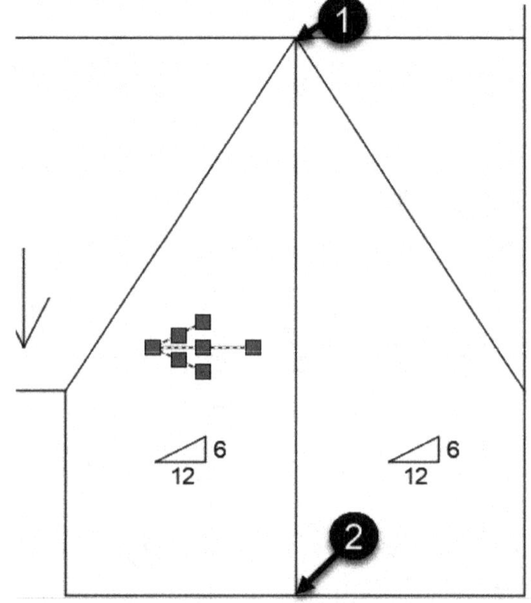

- Select the elements of the rotated arrow.
- Click the **Move** tool on the **Modify** panel of the **Home** ribbon tab.
- Select the base point, as shown.

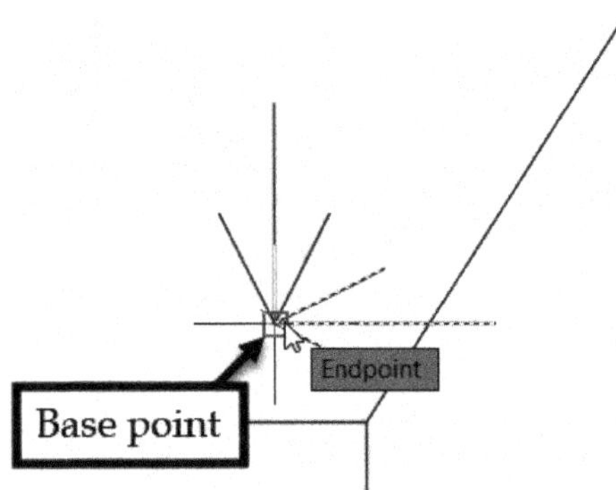

- Select **No** from the command line.
- Save and close the drawing file.

Example 5

In this tutorial, you will create the Roof and wall detail.

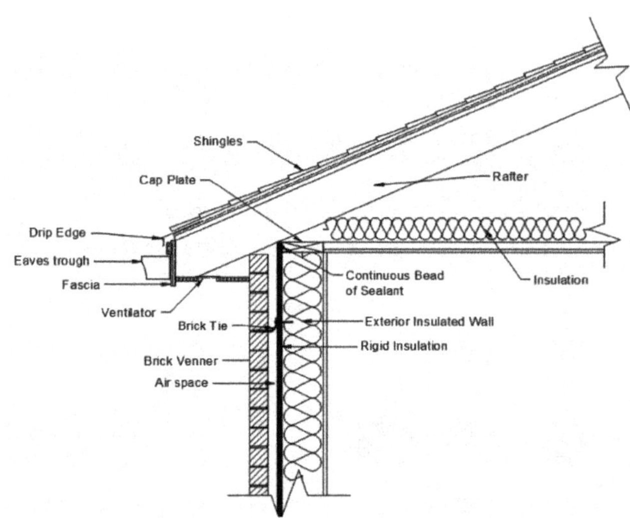

- Move the pointer toward right and click.

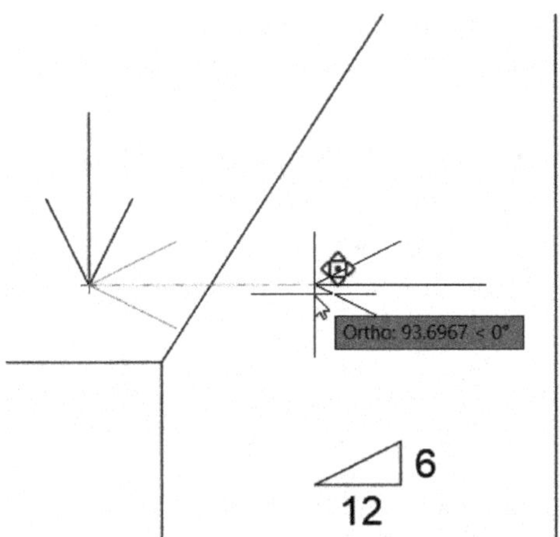

- Download the Roof_&_wall_detail.dwg file and open it.
- Click the **Layer Properties** tool on the **Layers** panel of the **Home** ribbon tab.
- Create a new layer and name it as Roof_wall_detail.
- Make the new layer are current.

- Select the elements of the arrow moved in the previous step.
- Click the **Mirror** tool on the **Modify** panel of the **Home** ribbon tab.
- Select the endpoints of the vertical line, as shown.

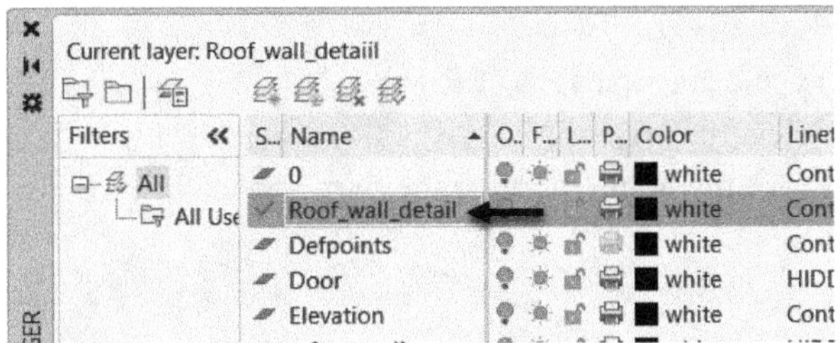

- Close the **Layer Properties Manager** palette.
- On the **Home** ribbon tab, expand the **Draw** panel and click the **Ray** tool.
- Create the projection lines from the elevation view, as shown.

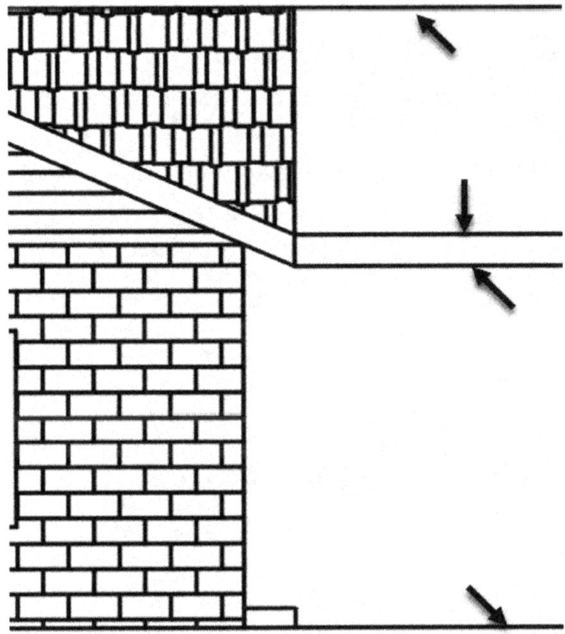

- Create a vertical line, as shown.

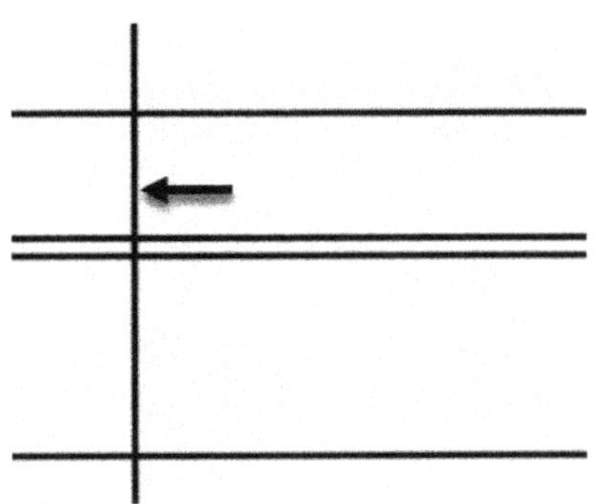

- Select the two inclined lines of the roof, as shown.
- Select the two vertical lines, as shown.

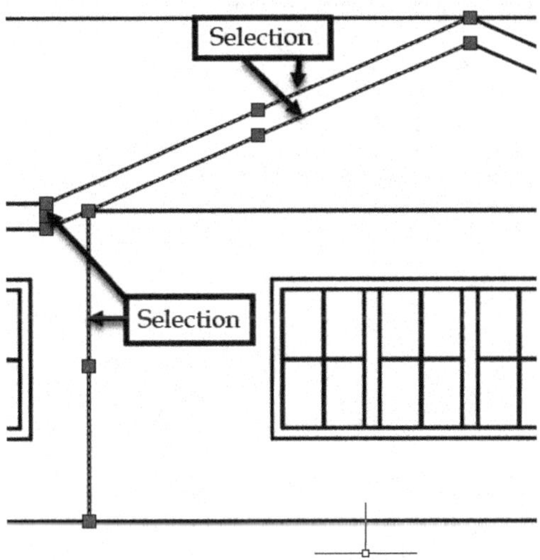

- Click the **Copy** tool on the **Modify** panel of the **Home** ribbon tab.
- Select the base point, as shown.

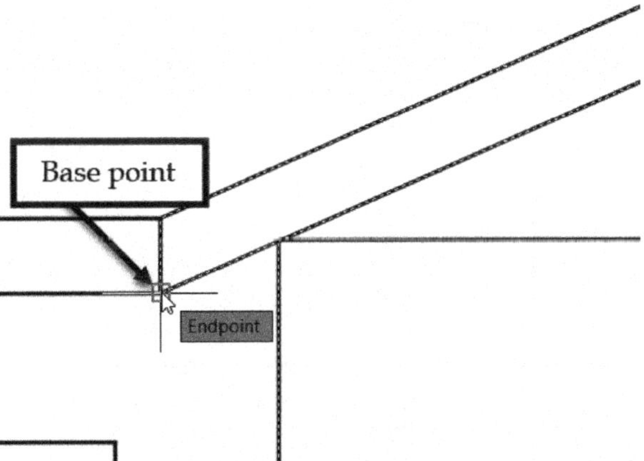

- Move the pointer toward right and select the intersection point, as shown.

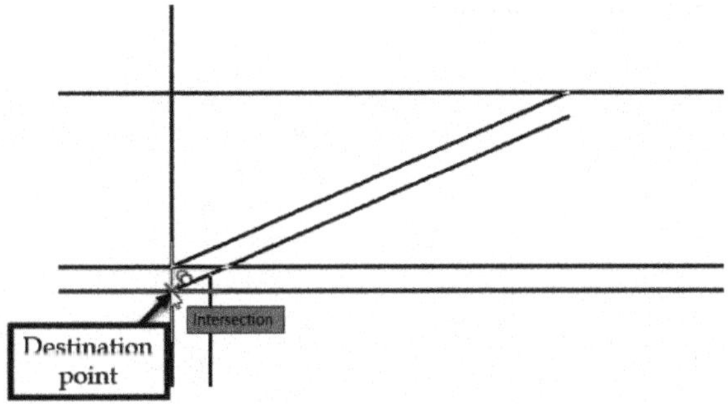

- Delete the reference lines, as shown.

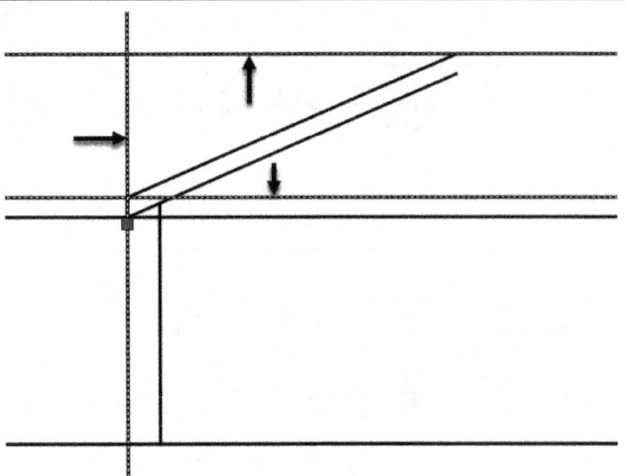

- Click the **Trim** tool on the **Modify** panel of the **Home** ribbon tab.
- Select the portion of the horizontal line, as shown.

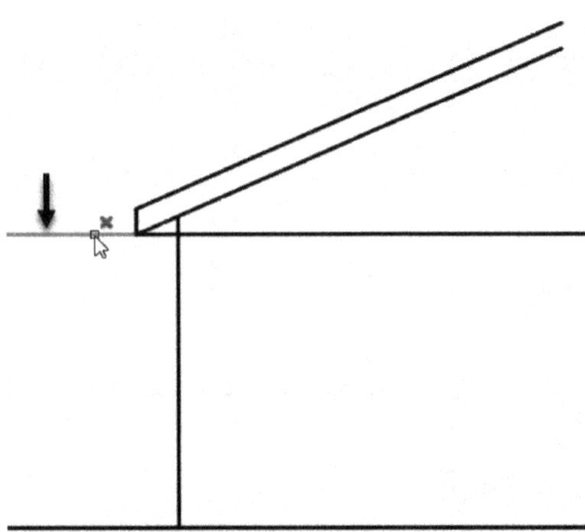

- Click the **Offset** tool on the **Modify** panel of the **Home** ribbon tab.
- Type 4 and press ENTER.
- Select the vertical line.
- Move the pointer toward right and click.

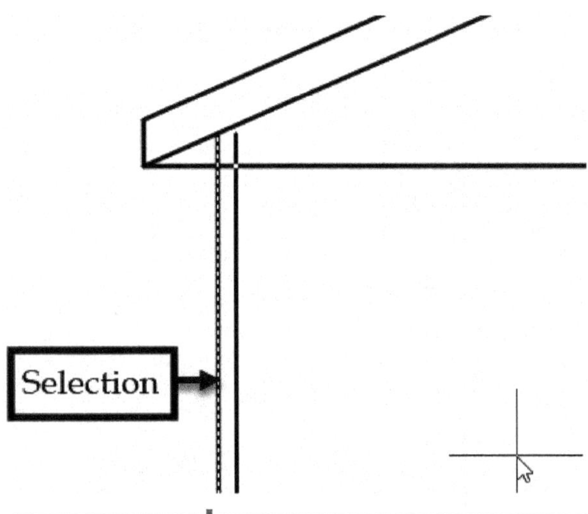

- Press ENTER twice.
- Type 2 and press ENTER.
- Select the offset line.
- Move the pointer toward the right and click.

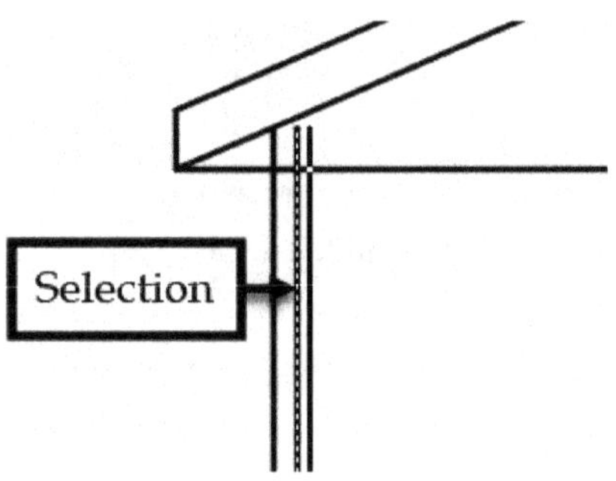

Creating the Brick Venner

- Click the **Rectangle** tool on the **Draw** panel of the **Home** ribbon tab.
- Specify the corner point, as shown.

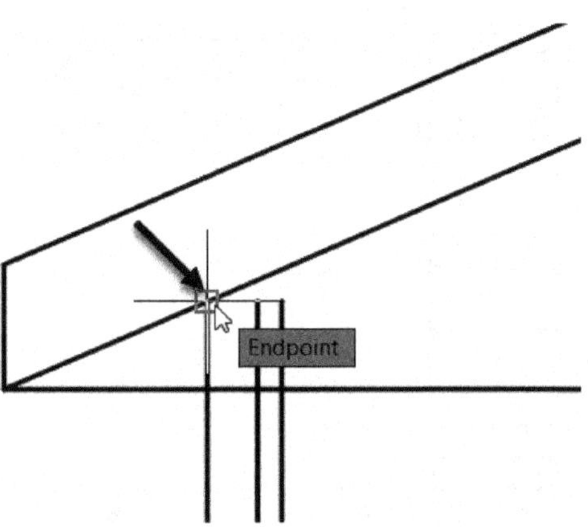

- Select the **Dimensions** option from the command line.
- Type 4 and press ENTER.
- Type 4 and press ENTER.
- Move the pointer downward and click.

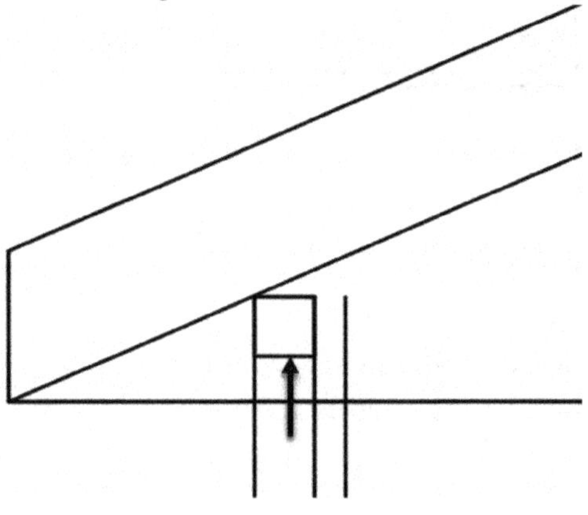

- Select the rectangle and click **Array** drop-down > **Path Array** on the **Modify** panel of the **Home** ribbon tab.

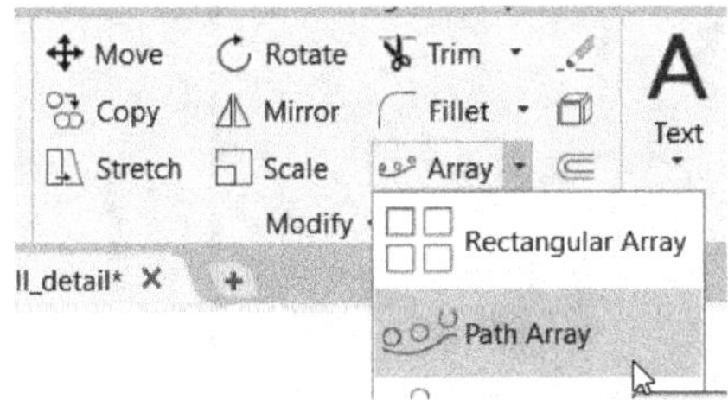

- Select the left vertical line to define the path.

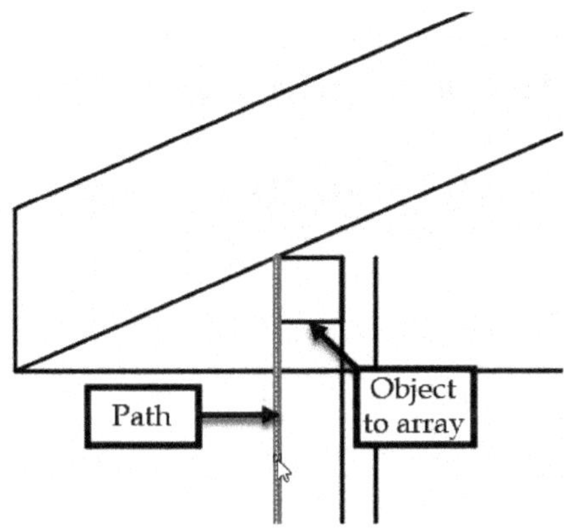

- Click the **Item Count** icon on the **Items** panel of the **Array Creation** ribbon tab.

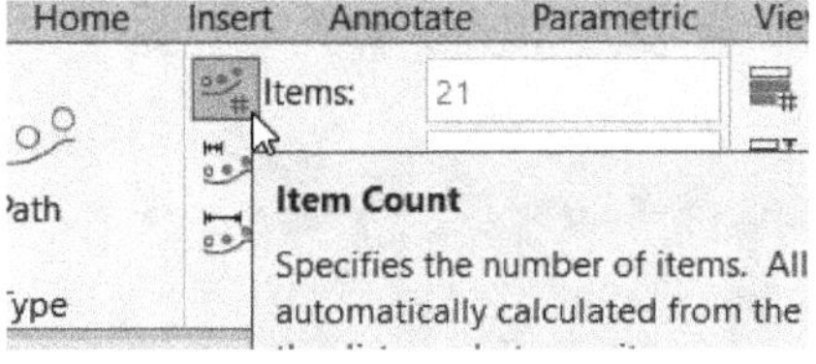

- Type **14** in the **Items** box.
- Type **4.25** in the **Between** box.

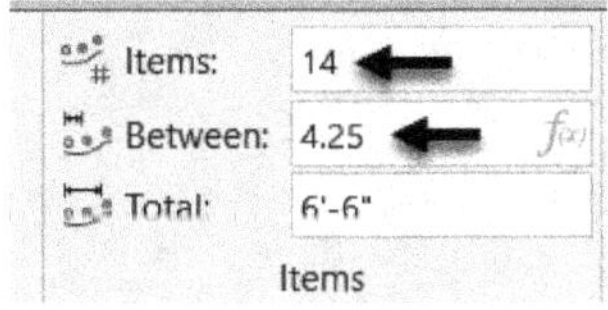

- Deactivate the **Associative** option on the **Properties** panel of the **Array Creation** ribbon tab.

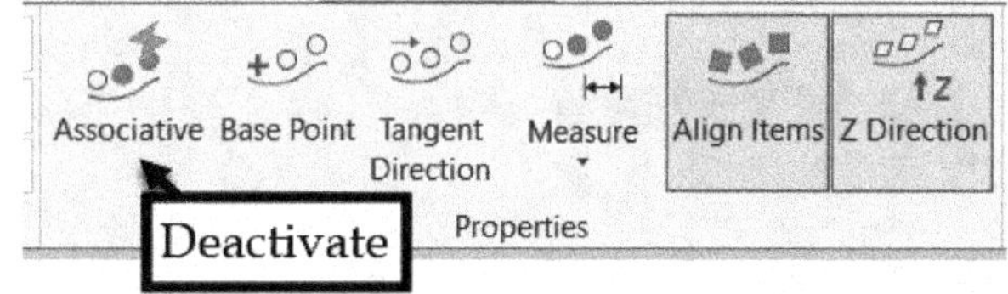

- Click **Close Array** on the ribbon.

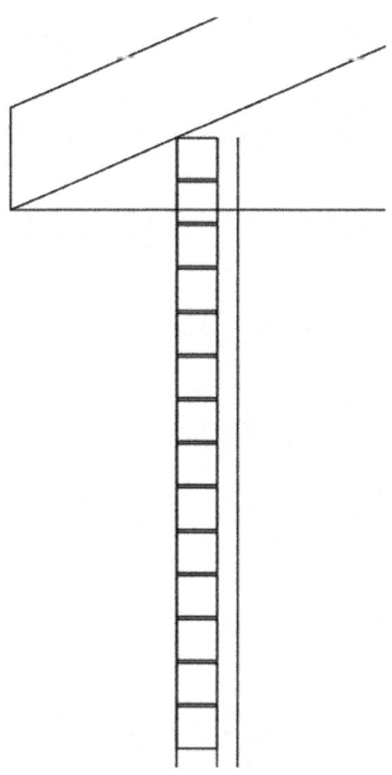

- Select anyone of the rectangles.

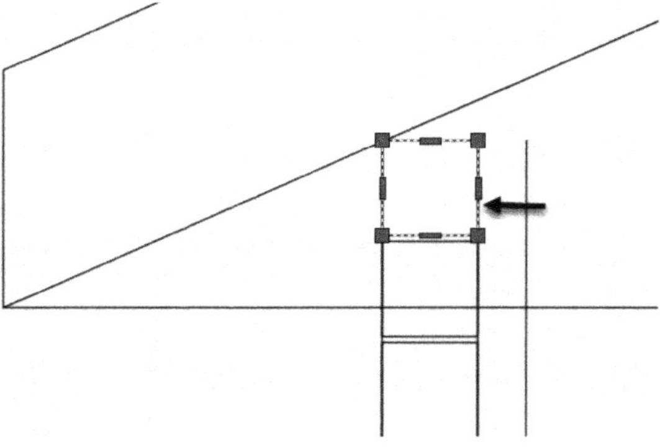

- Right click and select **Select Similar** from the shortcut menu.

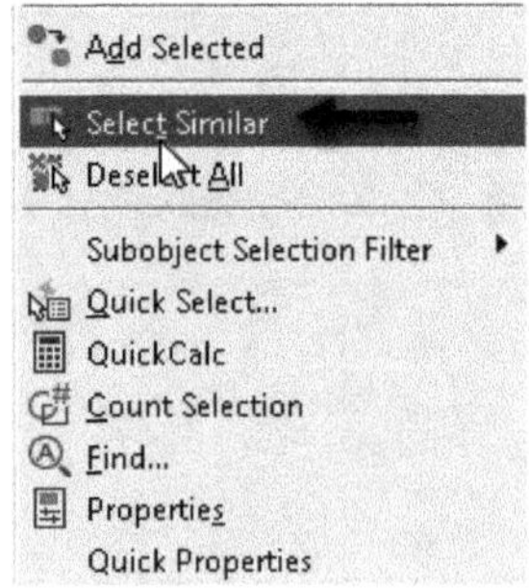

- Click the **Explode** tool on the **Modify** panel of the **Home** ribbon tab. All the rectangles are exploded into individual objects.
- Click the **Line** tool on the **Draw** panel of the **Home** ribbon tab.
- Zoom to the top portion of the drawing.
- Create a line by selecting the two points, as shown.

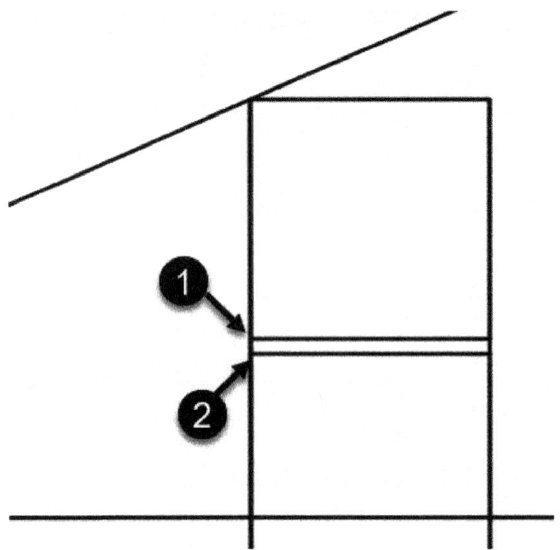

- Press ESC.
- Select the newly created line.
- Click the **Move** tool on the **Modify** panel of the **Home** ribbon tab.
- Select the top endpoint of the selected line.
- Move the pointer toward the right.

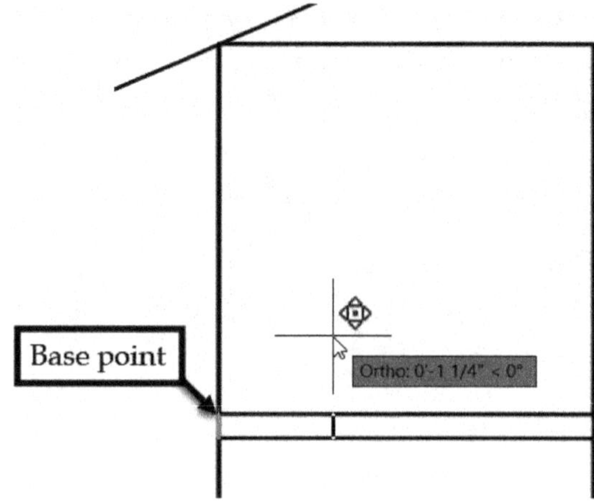

- Type 0.125, and press ENTER.
- Select the line moved in the last step.
- Click **Array** drop-down > **Rectangular Array** on the **Modify** panel of the **Home** ribbon tab.
- On the **Columns** panel, type **2** and **3.75** in the **Columns** and **Between** boxes, respectively.

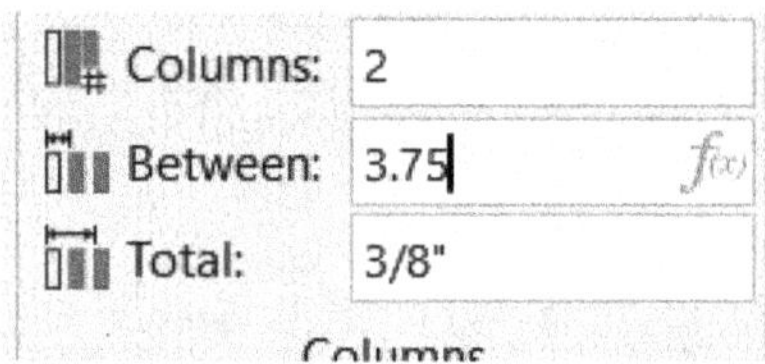

- On the **Rows** panel, type **13** and **-4.25** in the **Rows** and **Between** boxes, respectively.

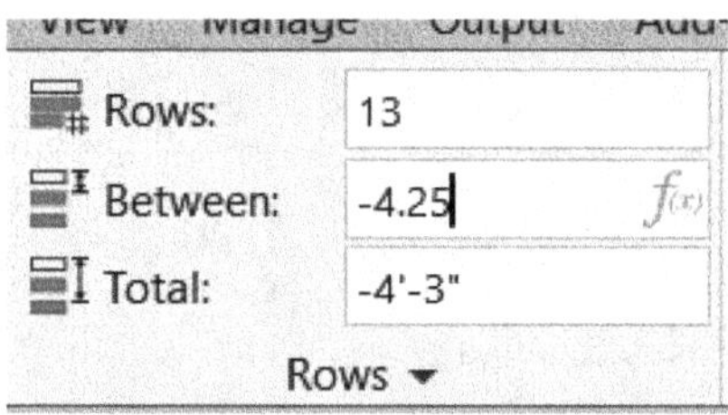

- Deactivate the **Associative** option.
- Click **Close Array** on the ribbon.
- Select the two vertical lines, as shown.

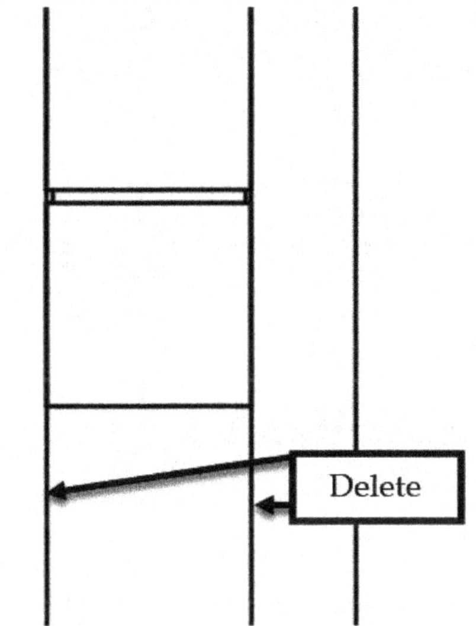

- Press Delete.

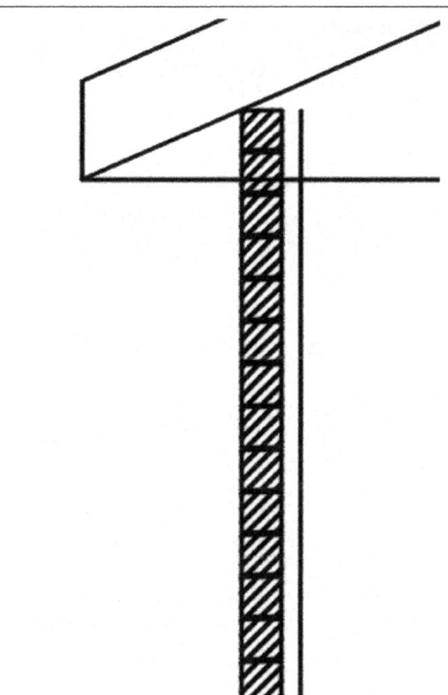

- Click **Close Hatch Creation** on the ribbon.

Creating the Brick Tie

- On the Navigation Bar, click **Zoom** drop-down > **Zoom Window**.
- Create a zoom window at the location, as shown.

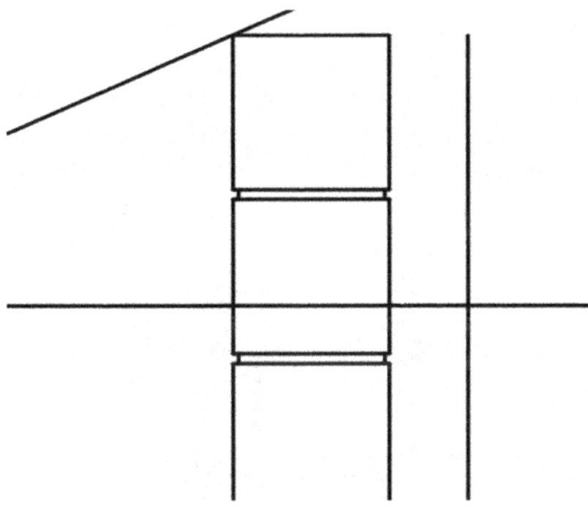

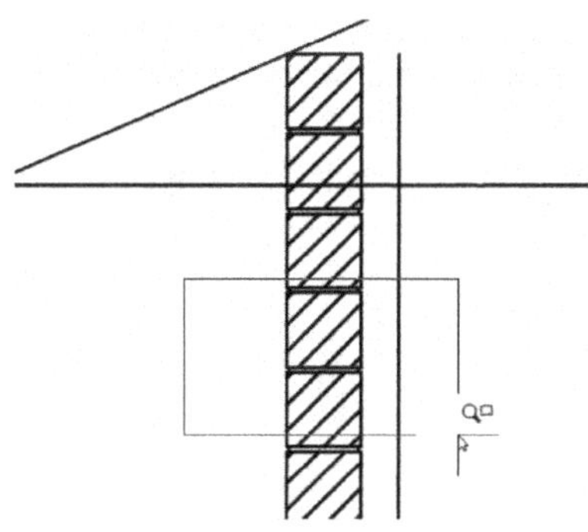

- Click the **Hatch** tool on the **Draw** panel of the **Home** ribbon tab.
- Click the **ANSI31** pattern on the **Pattern** panel.
- Type 8 in the **Hatch pattern Scale** box and press ENTER.

- Click the **Offset** tool on the **Modify** panel of the **Home** ribbon tab.
- Type 0.025, and press ENTER.
- Offset the two horizontal lines in the inward direction.

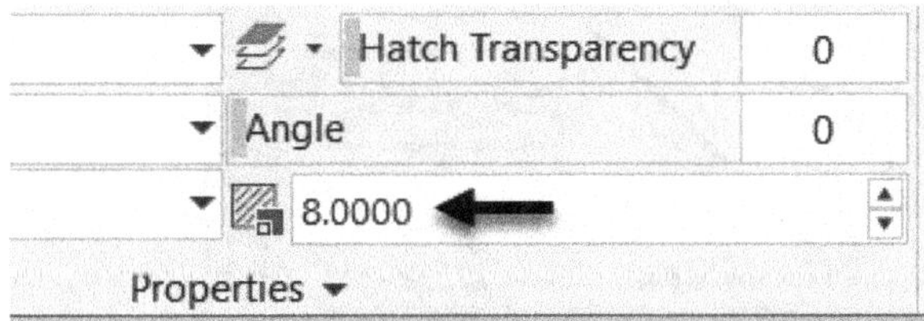

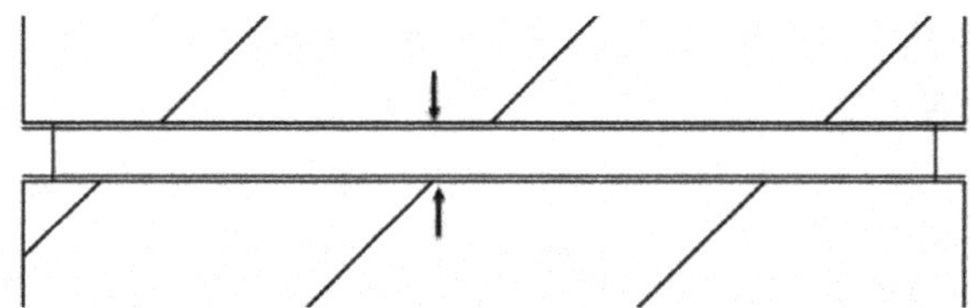

- Click in the regions, as shown.

- Press ENTER twice.

- Type 1 and press ENTER.
- Offset the left vertical line towards the right.

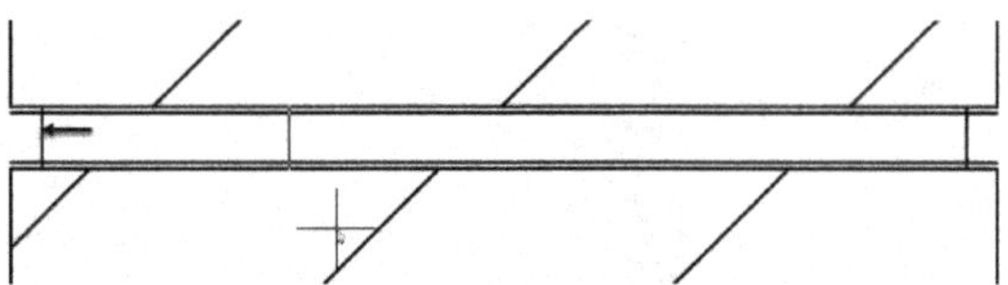

- Click the **Trim** tool on the **Modify** panel of the **Home** ribbon tab.
- Trim the portions of the lines, as shown.

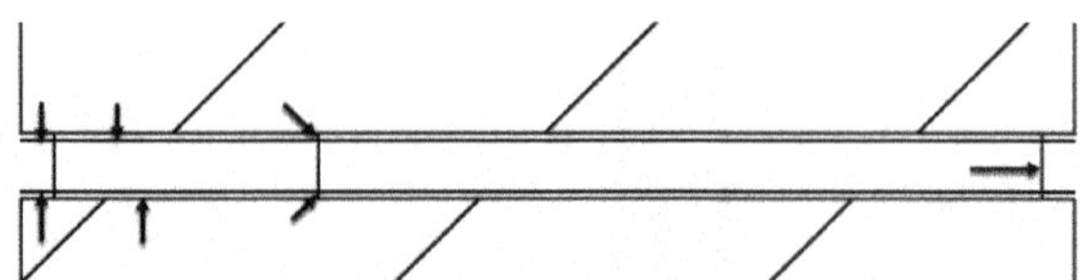

- Click the **Trim** drop-down > **Extend** on the **Modify** panel of the **Home** ribbon tab.
- Select the ends of the horizontal lines, as shown.

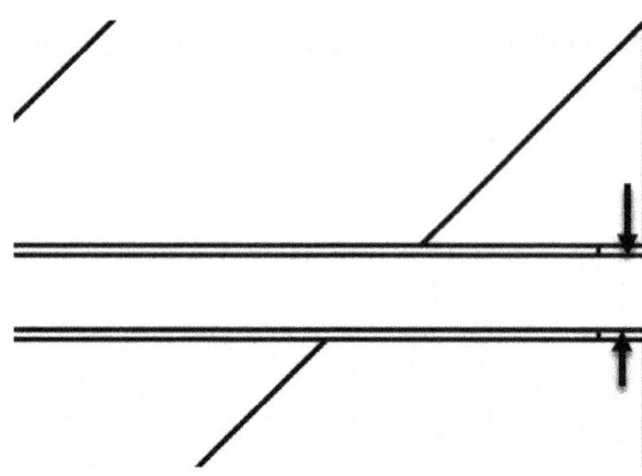

The horizontal lines are extended up to the right vertical line.

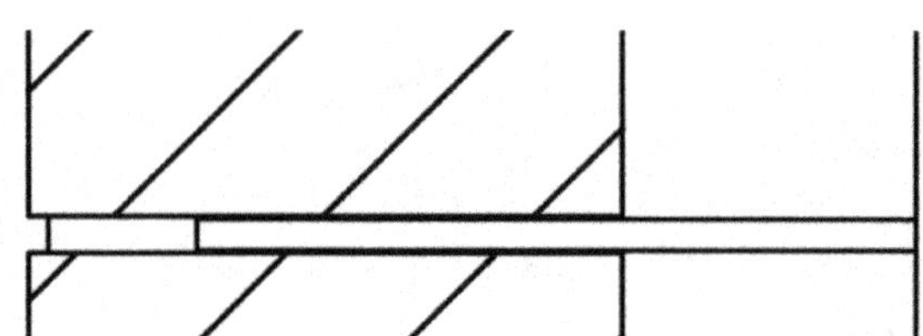

- Click the **Line** tool on the **Draw** panel of the **Home** ribbon tab.
- Select the endpoint of the lower horizontal line.
- Move the pointer vertically upward.
- Type 3 and press ENTER.
- Click the **Offset** tool on the **Modify** panel of the **Home** ribbon tab.

- Type 0.2 and press ENTER.
- Select the vertical line created in the last step.
- Move the pointer toward the left and click.

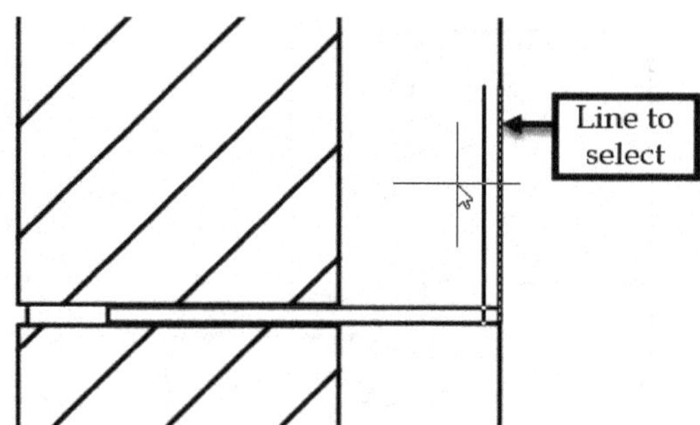

- Click the **Fillet** drop-down > **Chamfer** on the **Modify** panel of the **Home** ribbon tab.
- Select the **Angle** option from the command line.
- Type 1 as the chamfer length.
- Type 45 as the chamfer angle.
- Select horizontal and vertical lines, as shown.

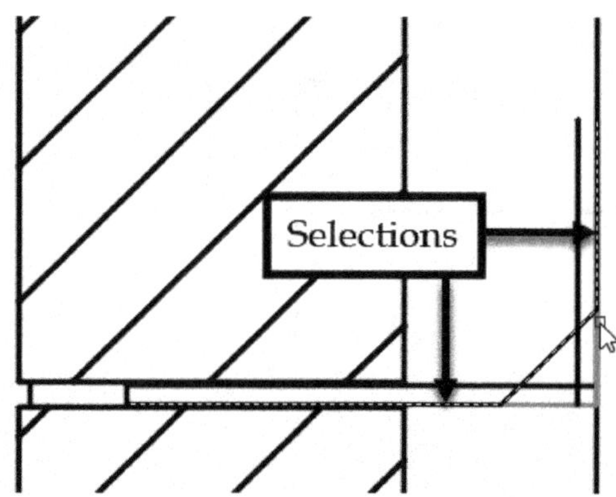

- Likewise, create another chamfer, as shown.

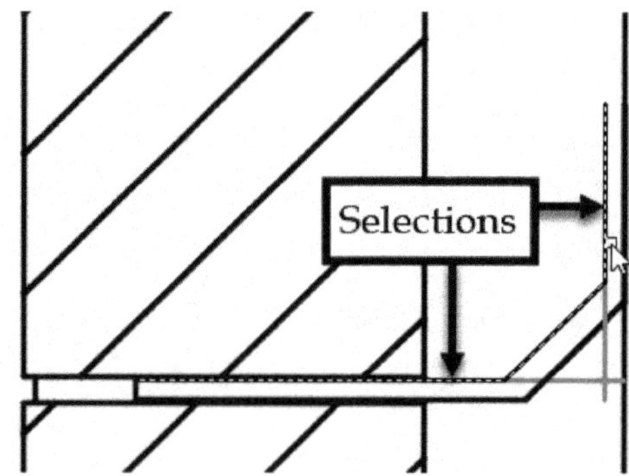

- Click the **Line** tool on the **Draw** panel of the **Home** ribbon tab.
- Cap the ends of the offset lines, as shown.

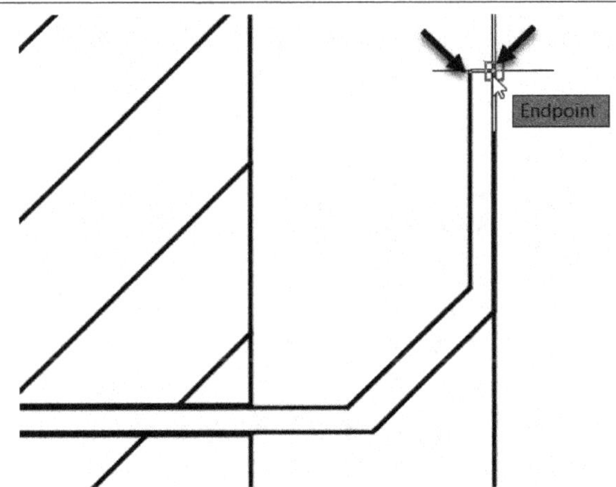

- Click the **Rectangle** tool on the **Draw** panel of the **Home** ribbon tab.
- Click in the graphic window.
- Select the **Dimensions** option from the command line.
- Type 0.2 and press ENTER.
- Type 0.5 and press ENTER.
- Click to create a rectangle.
- Select the rectangle and click the **Move** tool on the **Modify** panel of the **Home** ribbon tab.
- Select the midpoint of the right vertical edge of the rectangle.

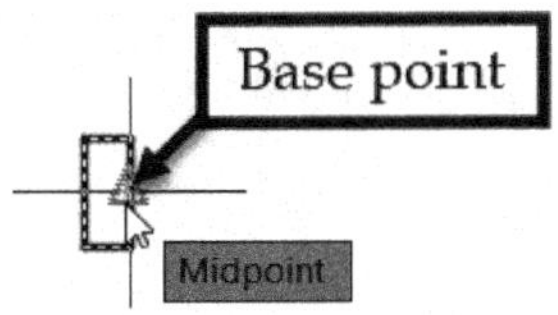

- Move the pointer and select the midpoint of the vertical line, as shown.

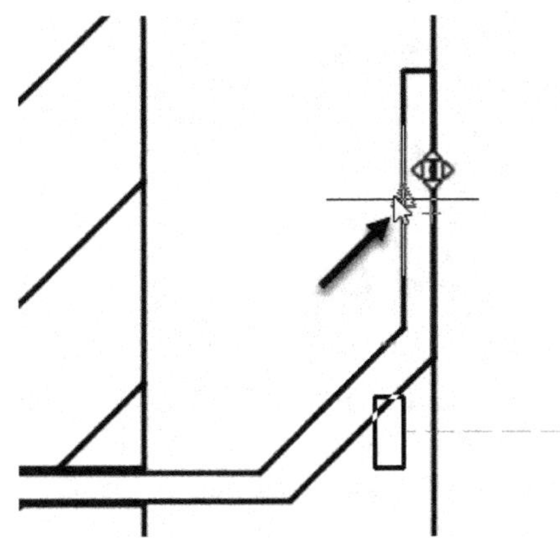

- Click the **Line** tool on the **Draw** panel of the **Home** ribbon tab.

- Select the midpoint of the right vertical edge of the rectangle.
- Move the pointer toward the right.

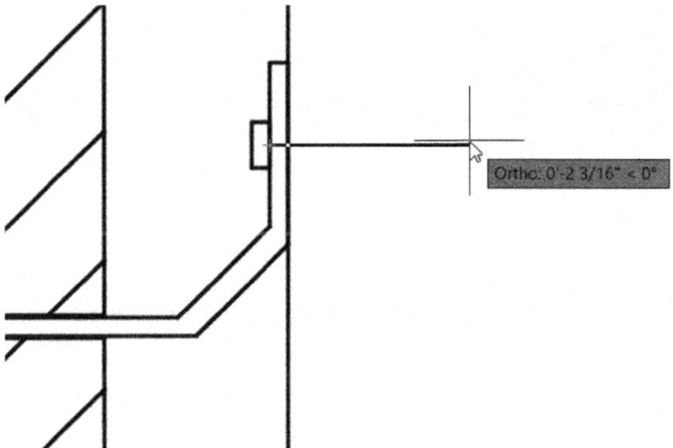

- Type 3.5 and press ENTER.
- Click the **Offset** tool on the **Modify** panel of the **Home** ribbon tab.
- Type 0.1 and press ENTER.
- Offset the newly created horizontal line on both sides.

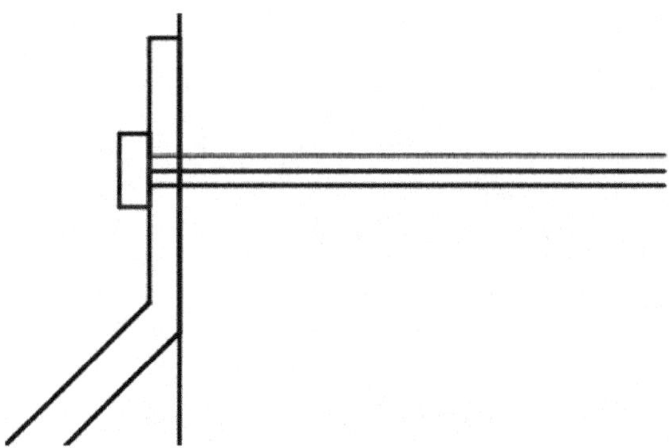

- Press ESC.
- Select the center line and press Delete.
- Click the **Arc** drop-down > **Start, End, Direction** on the **Draw** panel of the **Home** ribbon tab.
- Select the endpoints of the offset lines.
- Move the pointer toward right and click.

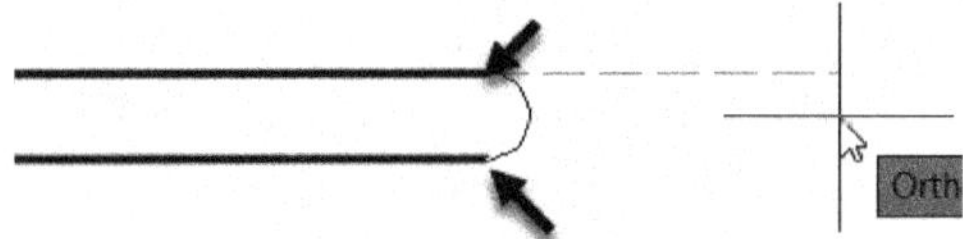

- Click the **Trim** tool on the **Modify** panel of the **Home** ribbon tab.
- Trim the portion of the vertical line, as shown.

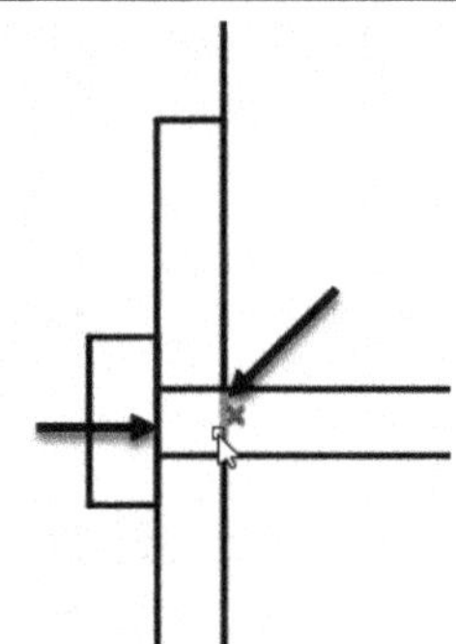

- Click the **Hatch** tool on the **Draw** panel of the **Home** ribbon tab.
- Click the **SOLID** pattern on the **Pattern** panel.

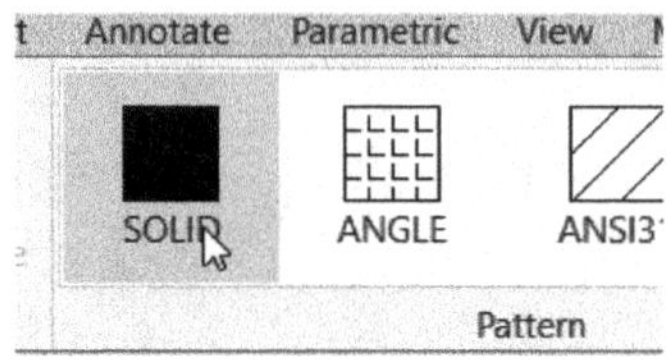

- Click in the regions, as shown.

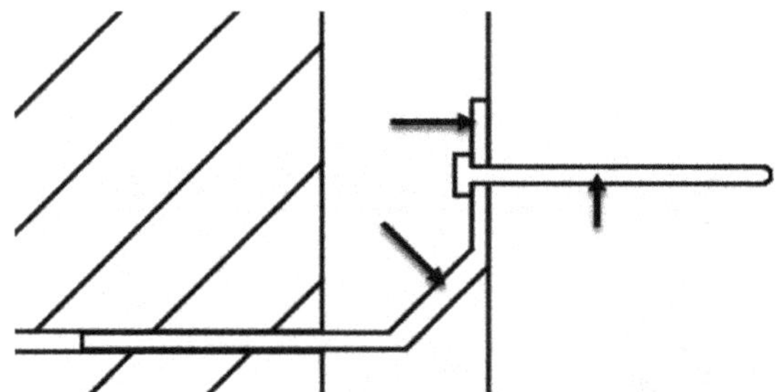

- Click **Close Hatch Creation** on the ribbon.

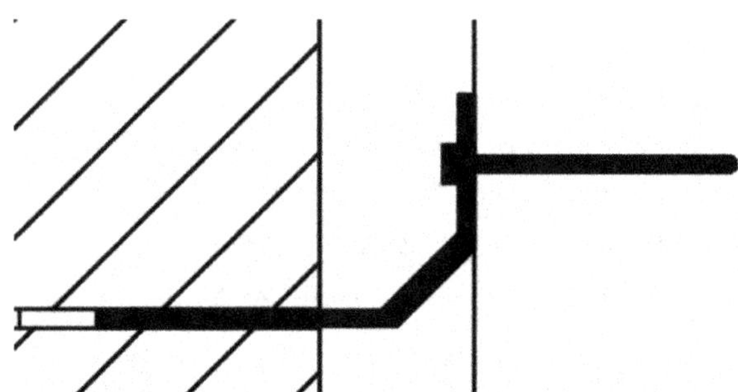

Creating the Insulation

- Click the **Offset** tool on the **Modify** panel of the **Home** ribbon tab.
- Type 1 and press ENTER.
- Select the vertical line, as shown.
- Move the pointer toward right and click.

- Likewise, offset the bottom vertical line.

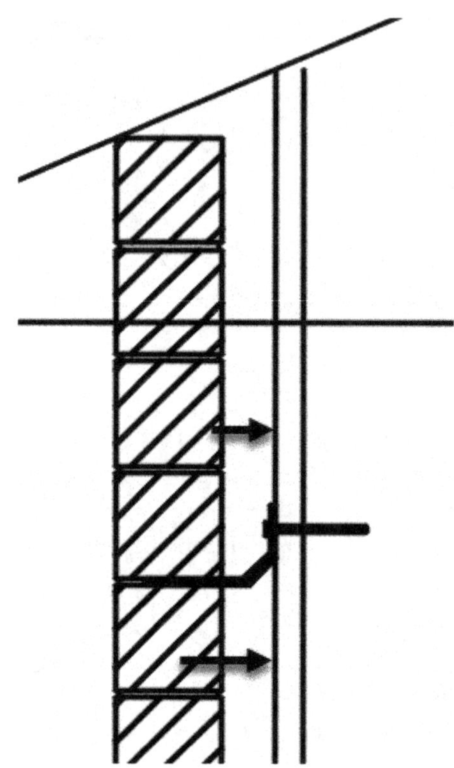

- Press ENTER twice.
- Type 9 and press ENTER.
- Select the offset line.
- Move the pointer toward right and click.

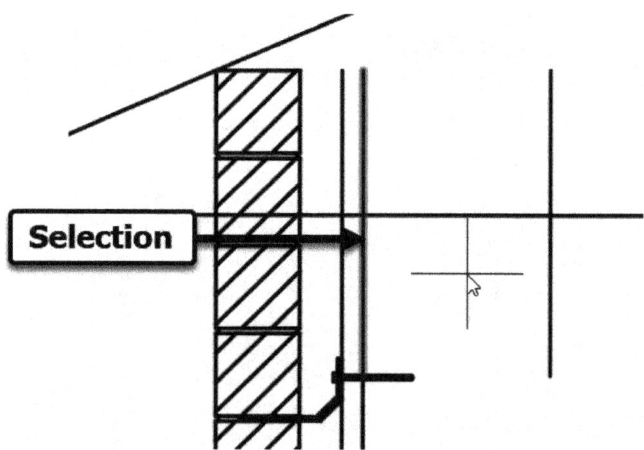

- Click the **Trim** drop-down > **Extend** on the **Modify** panel of the **Home** ribbon tab.
- Click on the lower portion of the newly offset line.

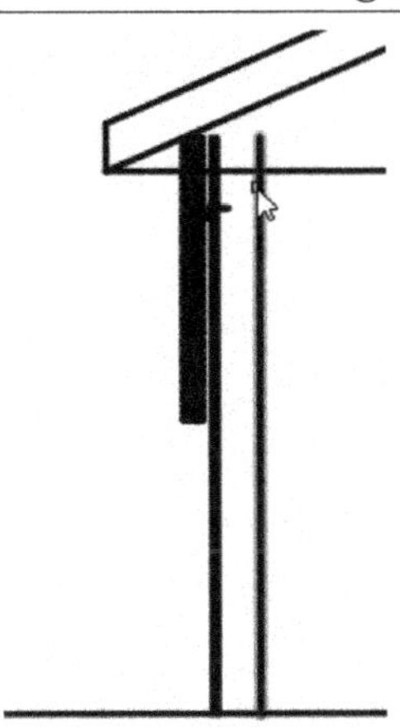

- Create the two horizontal lines, as shown.

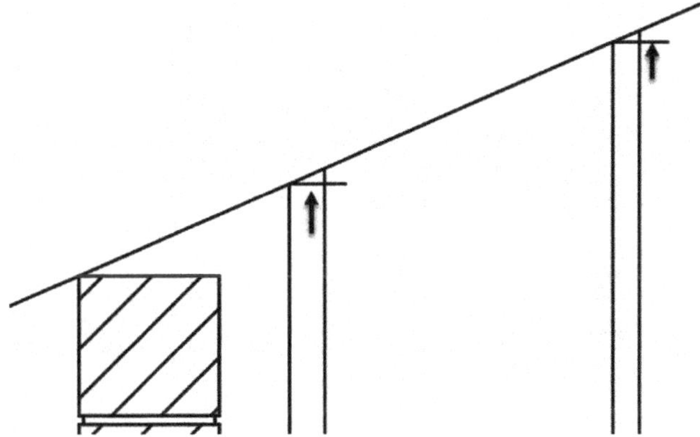

- Click the **Offset** tool on the **Modify** panel of the **Home** ribbon tab.
- Type 0.75 and press ENTER.
- Select the offset line.
- Move the pointer toward right and click.

- Trim the extending portions.

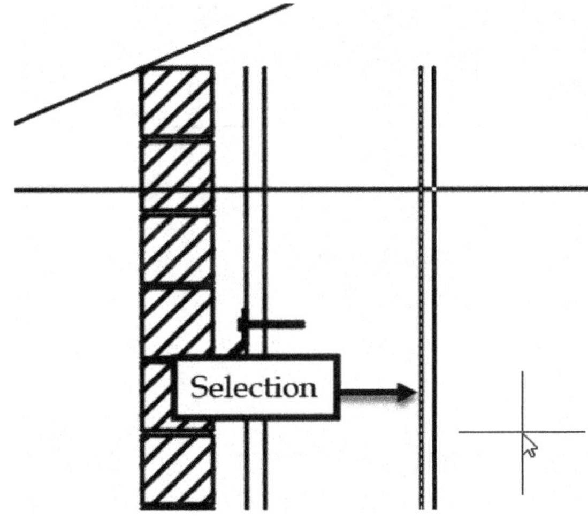

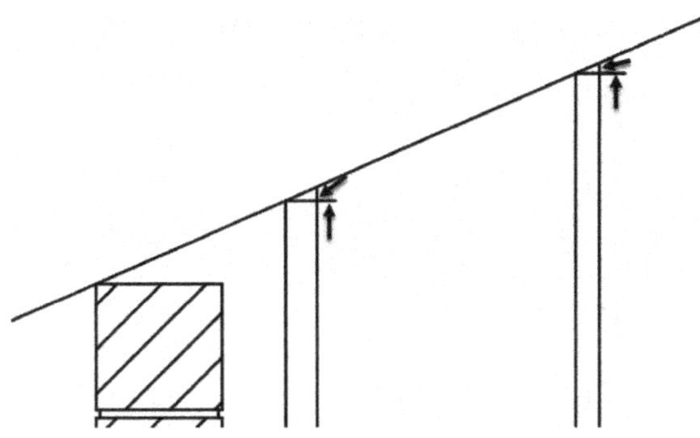

- Click the **Trim** drop-down > **Extend** on the **Modify** panel of the **Home** ribbon tab.
- Click and drag the pointer across the ends of the vertical lines, as shown.

- Click the **Rectangle** tool on the **Draw** panel of the **Home** ribbon tab.
- Select the corner point, as shown.

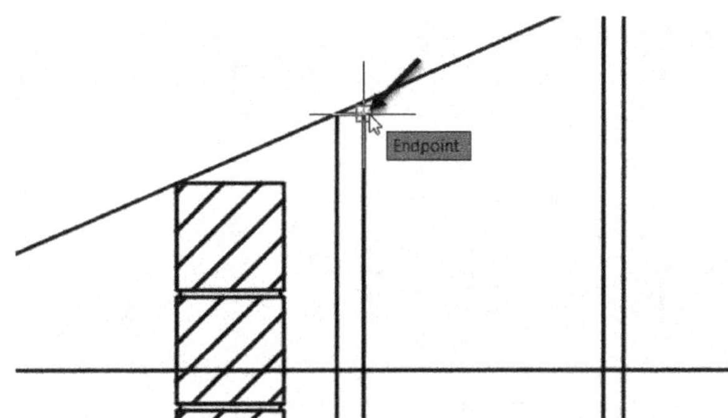

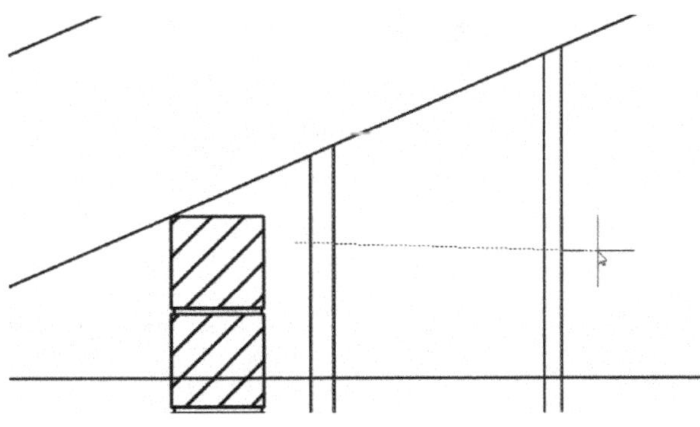

- Select the **Dimensions** option from the command line.
- Type 9 and press ENTER.
- Type 2.25 and press ENTER.
- Move the pointer downward and click.
- Click the **Line** tool on the **Draw** panel of the **Home** ribbon tab.
- Create the diagonal lines by selecting the corner points of the rectangle.

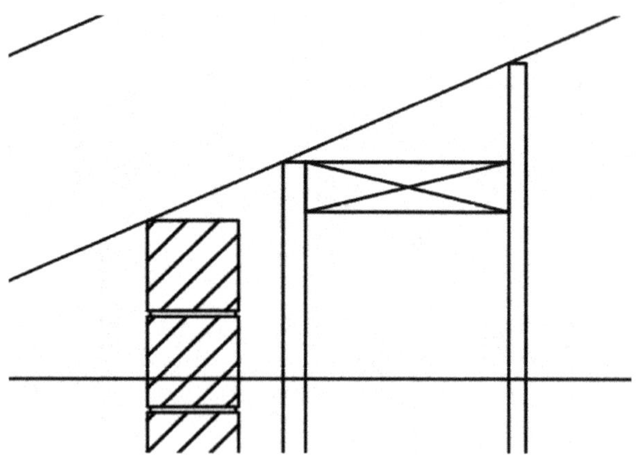

- Expand the **Draw** panel on the **Home** ribbon tab, and then click the **Donut** tool.

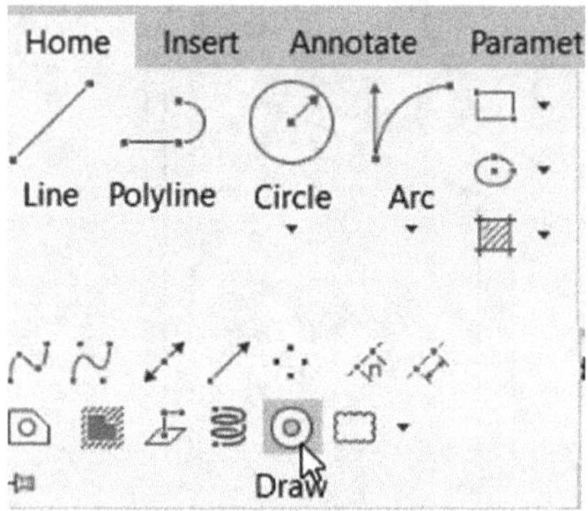

- Type 0 as the internal diameter, and then press ENTER.
- Type 1 as the external diameter, and then press ENTER.
- Select the midpoint of the left vertical edge of the rectangle.

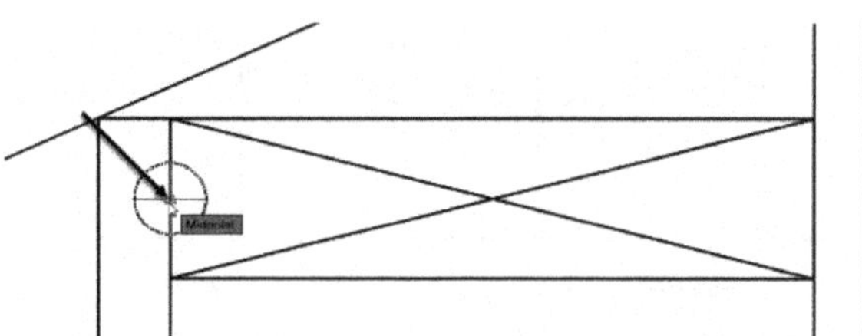

- Press Esc.
- Click the **Line** tool on the **Draw** panel of the **Home** ribbon tab.
- Create a horizontal line, as shown.

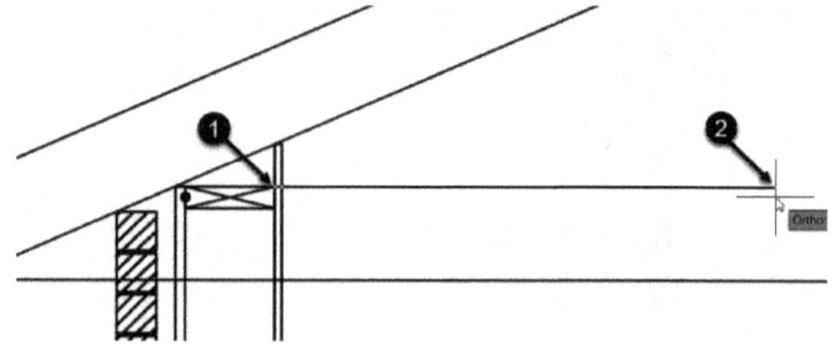

- Click the **Offset** tool on the **Modify** panel of the **Home** ribbon tab.
- Type 1.5 and press ENTER.
- Select the newly created line.
- Move the pointer downward and click.

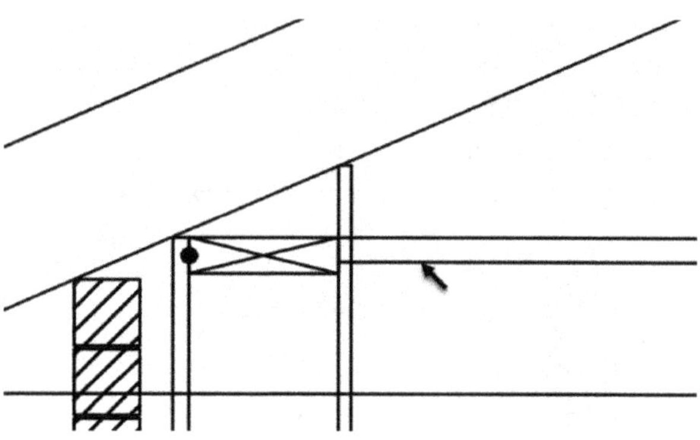

- Press ENTER twice.
- Type 0.75 and press ENTER.
- Select the offset line.
- Move the pointer downward and click.

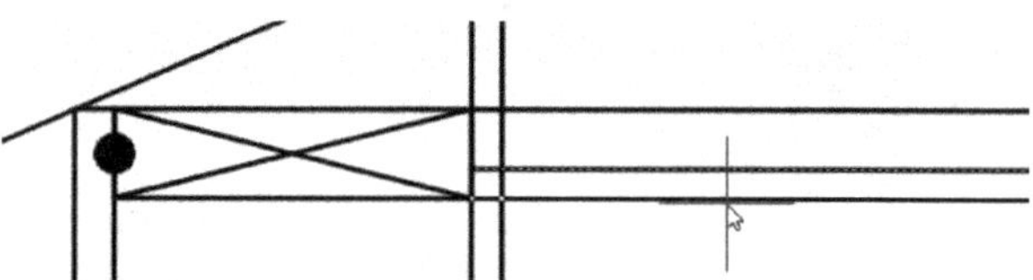

- Press ENTER.
- Click the **Trim** tool on the **Modify** panel of the **Home** ribbon tab.
- Trim the elements, as shown.

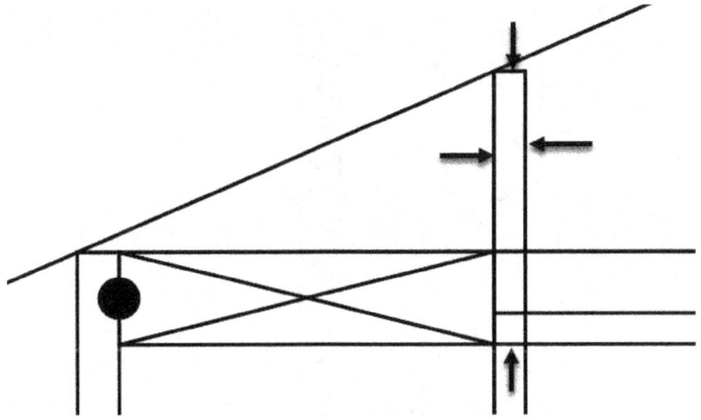

- Click the **Hatch** tool on the **Draw** panel of the **Home** ribbon tab.
- Click the **ANSI37** pattern on the **Pattern** panel.

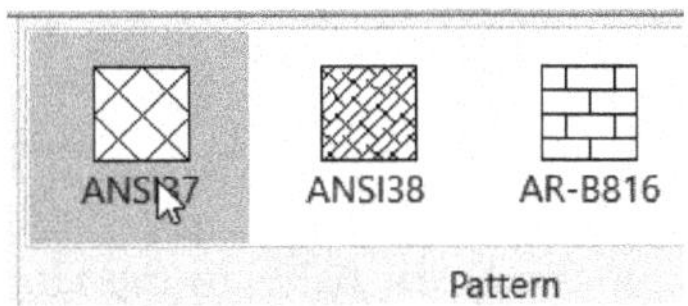

- Type **2** in the **Hatch Pattern Scale** box on the **Properties** panel.
- Type **45** in the **Angle** box.

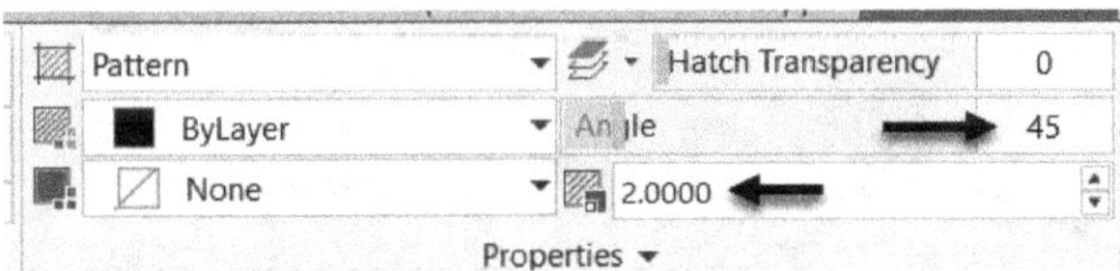

- Click in the regions, as shown.

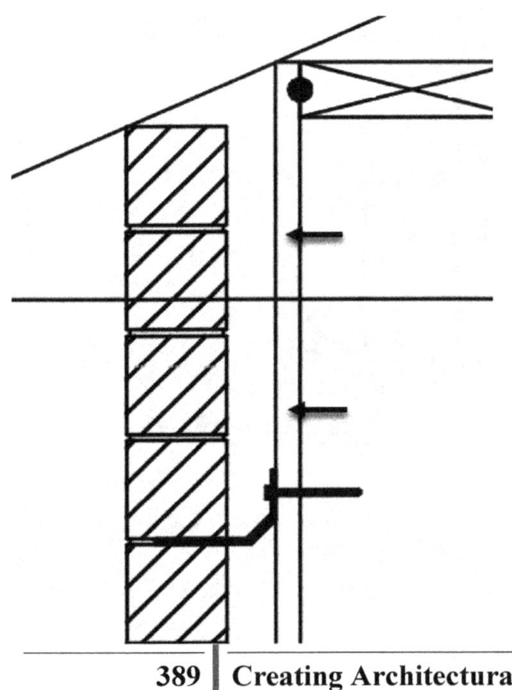

- Click in the area below the brick tie; the **Hatch – Boundary Definition Error** message box appears.

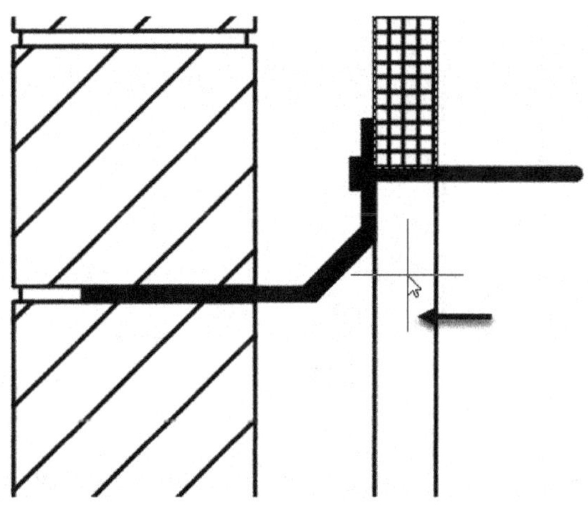

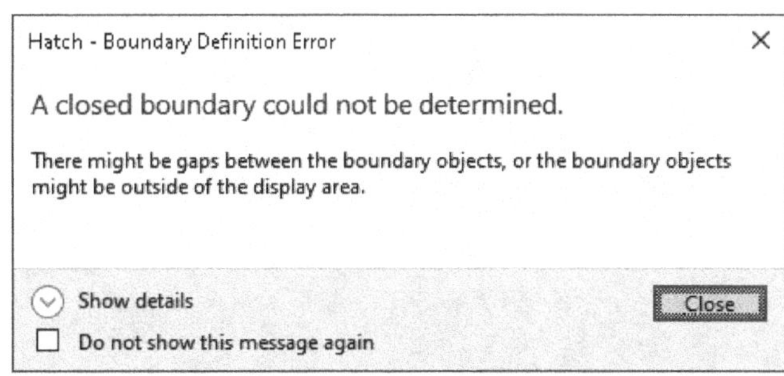

- Click **Close** on the message box.
- Click **Close Hatch Creation** on the ribbon.
- Click the **Line** tool on the **Draw** panel of the **Home** ribbon tab.
- Select the end points of the line, as shown.

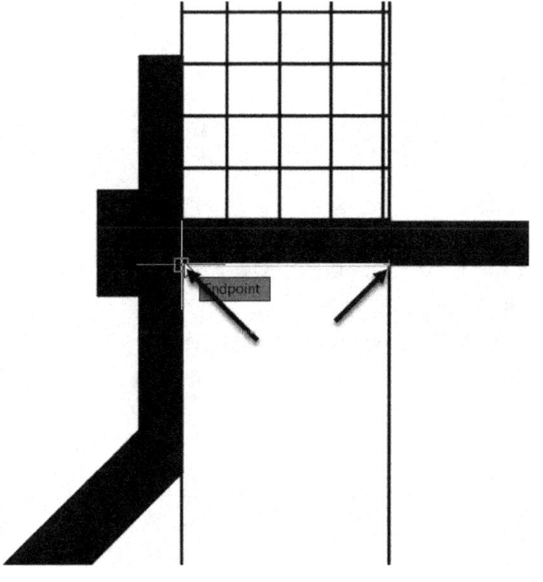

- Press ENTER twice.
- Zoom to the lower portion of the and select the lower endpoints of the vertical lines, as shown.

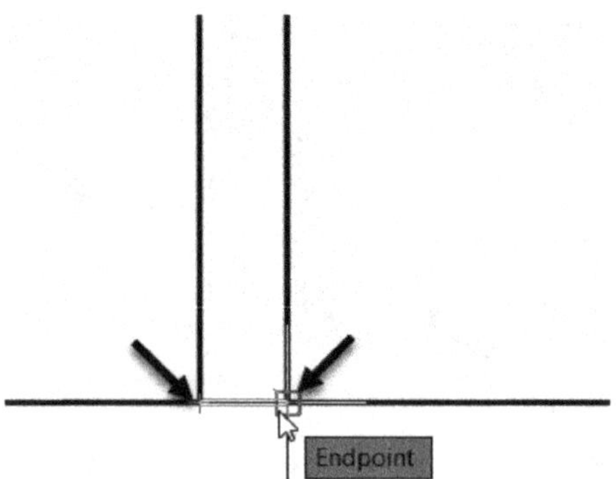

- Expand the **Draw** panel on the **Home** ribbon tab, and then click the **Region** tool.

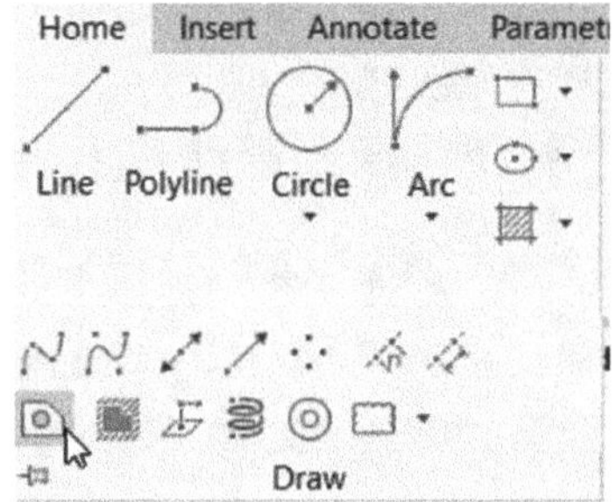

- Select the vertical and horizontal lines, as shown.

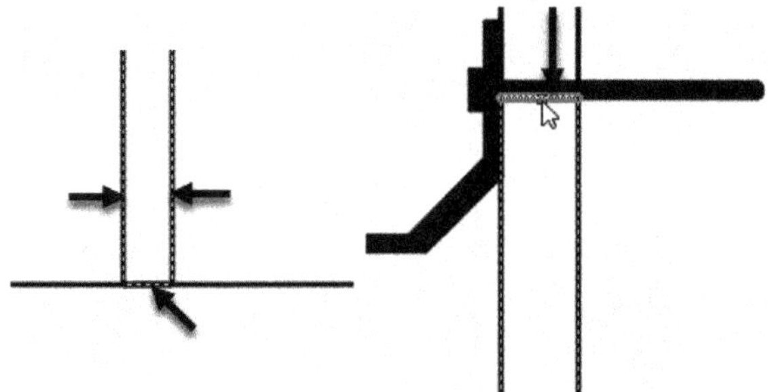

- Press ENTER.
- Click the **Hatch** tool on the **Draw** panel of the **Home** ribbon tab.
- Click in the area below the brick tie.
- Click **Close Hatch Creation** on the ribbon.

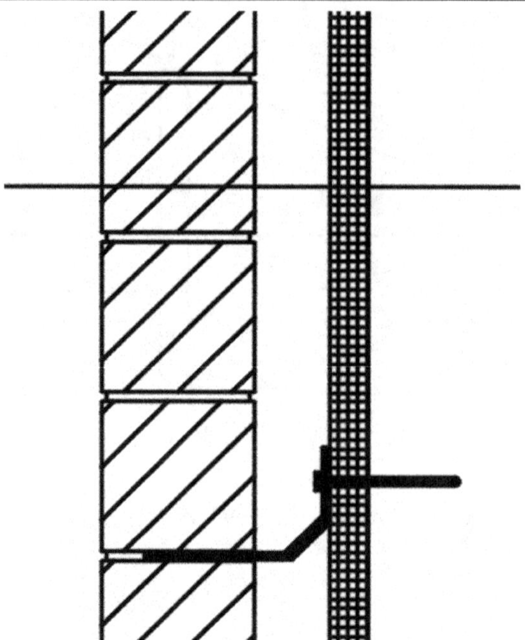

- Click the **Line** tool on the **Draw** panel of the **Home** ribbon tab.
- Select the midpoint of the horizontal line, as shown.
- Move the pointer downward and click.

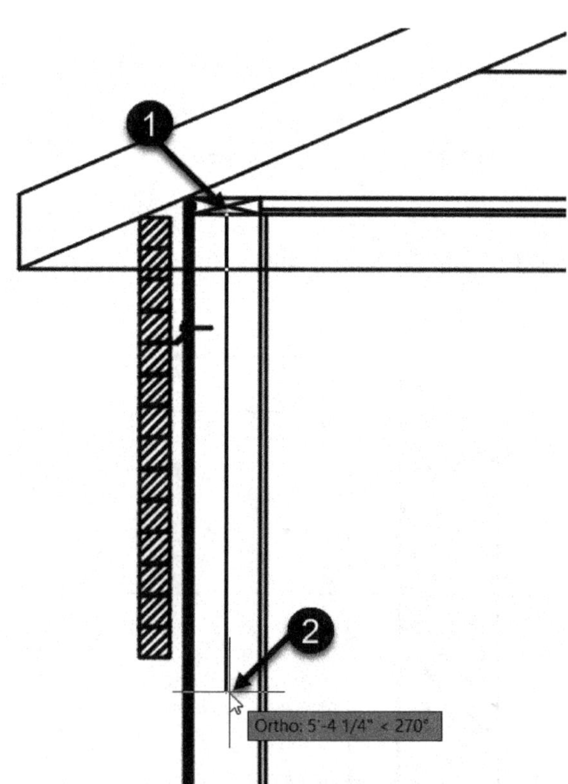

- Click the **Layer Properties** icon on the **Layers** panel of the **Home** ribbon tab.
- Click the **New Layer** icon on the Layer Properties Manager.

- Type **Insulation** as the layer name.
- Click in the **Linetype** column on the Layer Properties Manager.

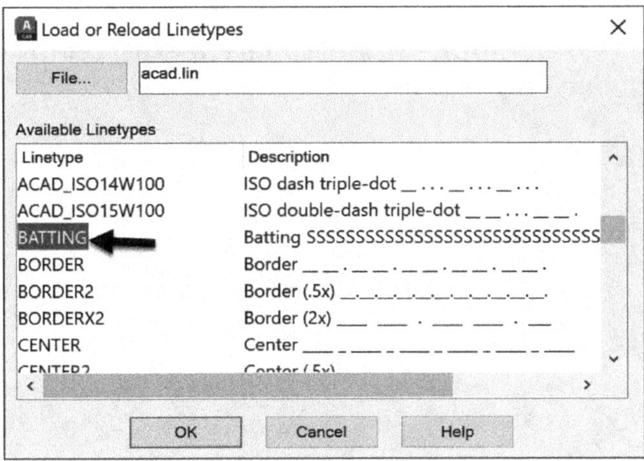

- Click the **Load** button on the **Select Linetype** dialog.
- Select the **BATTING** linetype from the linetype list.
- Click **OK**.

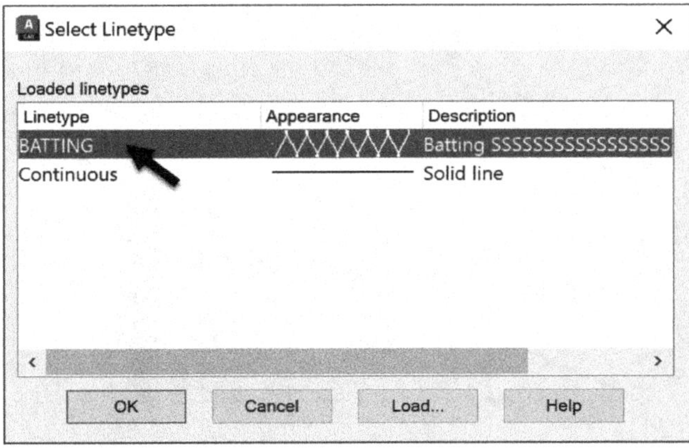

- Select the **BATTING** linetype from the **Select Linetype** dialog.

- Click **OK**.
- Select the newly created line.
- Select **Insulation** from the **Layer** drop-down on the **Layers** panel.

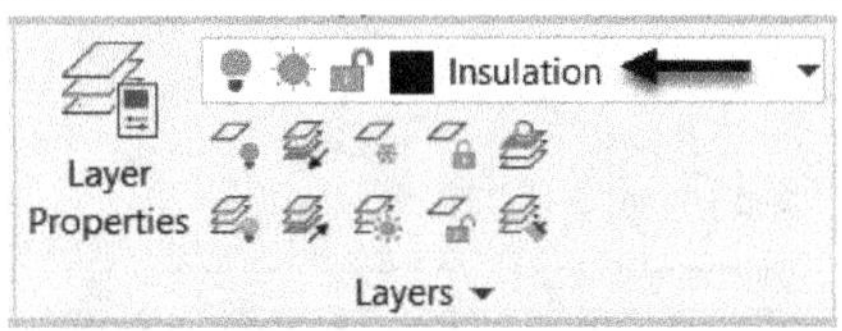

- Select the newly created line.
- Click the **Properties** icon on the **Properties** panel.

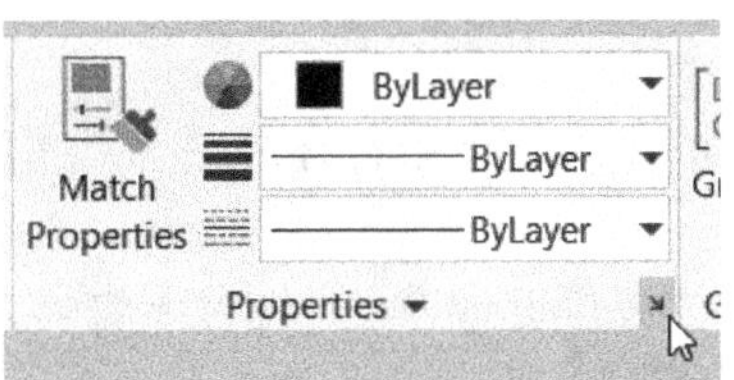

- Type 10 in the **Linetype Scale** box and press ENTER.

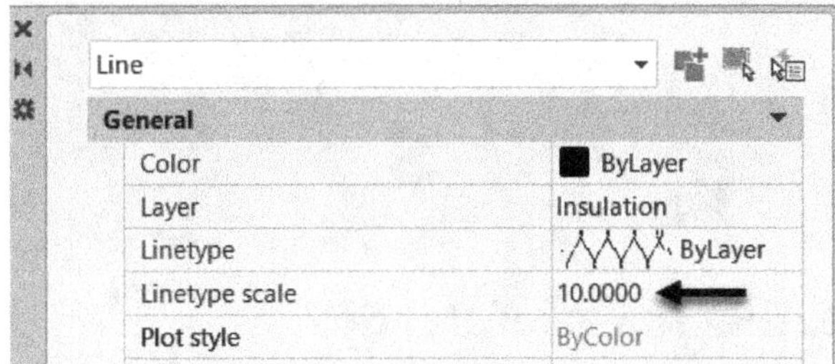

- Press ESC.

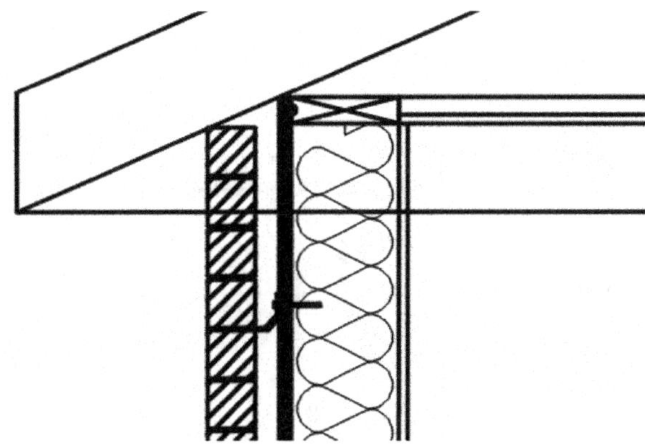

- Click the **Offset** tool on the **Modify** panel of the **Home** ribbon tab.
- Type 3 and press ENTER.
- Select the horizontal line, as shown.
- Move the pointer upward and click.

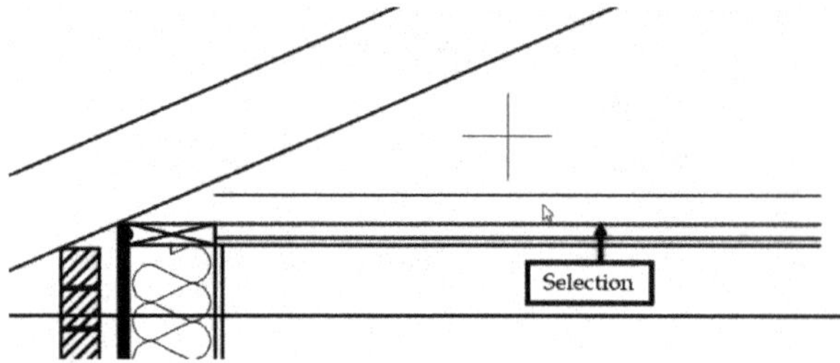

- Press ESC.
- Select the newly created line.
- Select **Insulation** from the **Layer** drop-down on the **Layers** panel.
- Click the **Properties** icon on the **Properties** panel.
- Type 6 in the **Linetype Scale** box and press ENTER.
- Press ESC.

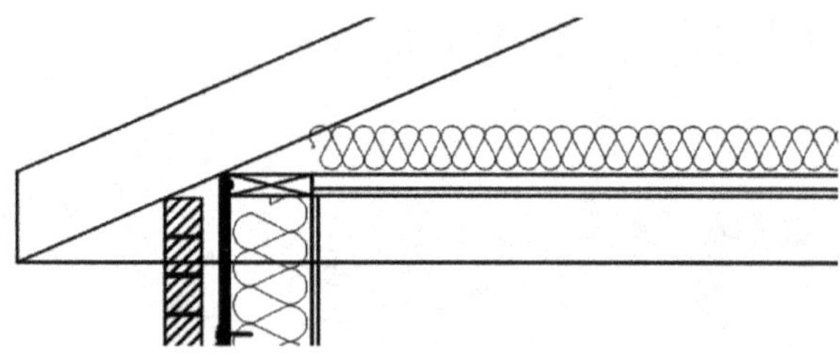

Creating the Roof Detail

- Offset the inclined line by 1".

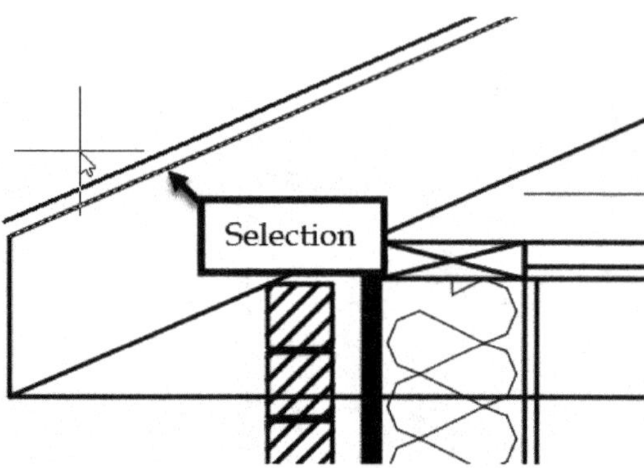

- Close the end of the offset lines.

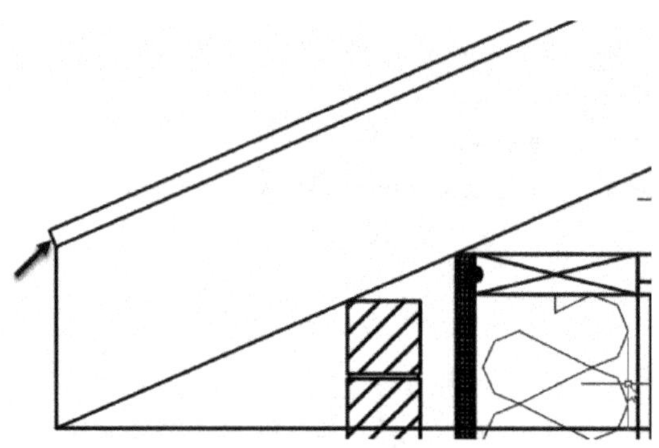

- Offset the new line by 0.5".

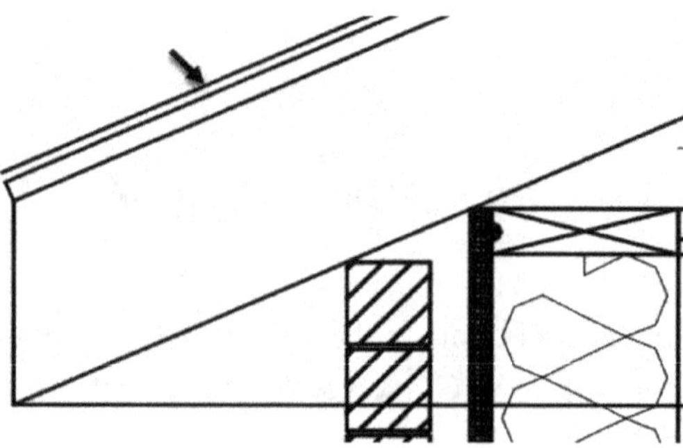

- Select the newly created offset line.
- Select HIDDENX2 from the **Linetype** drop-down on the **Properties** panel.

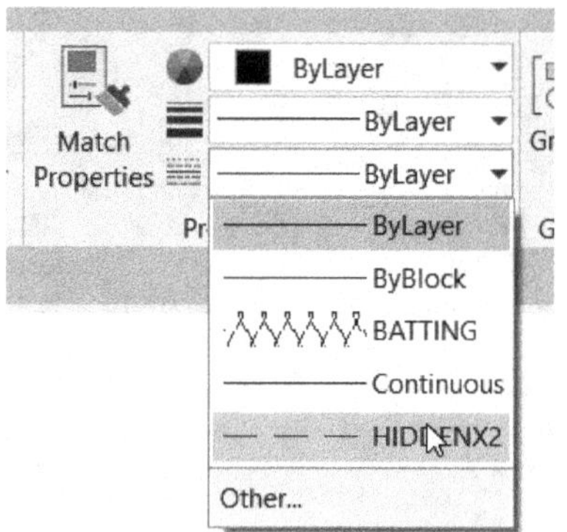

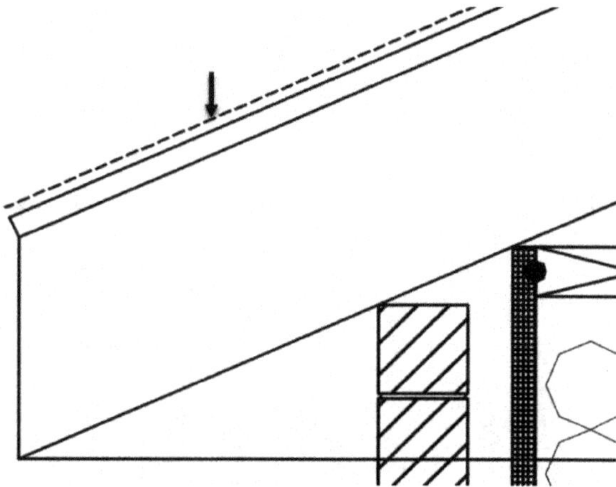

- Create another line with the offset distance of 0.75".

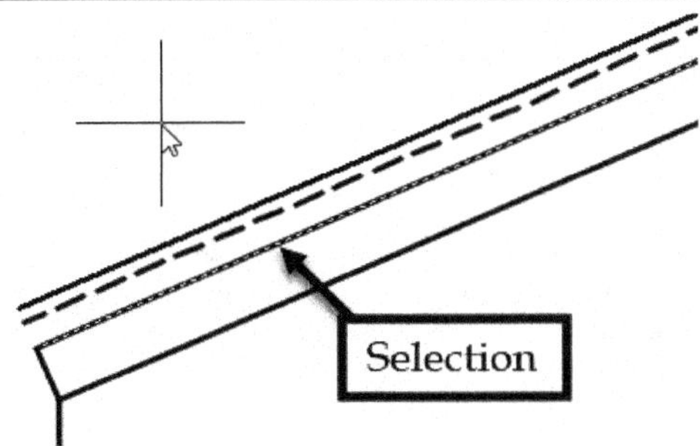

- Expand the **Modify** panel and click the **Lengthen** tool.
- Select the **DElta** option from the command line.
- Type 2.5 and press ENTER.
- Select the newly offset line.

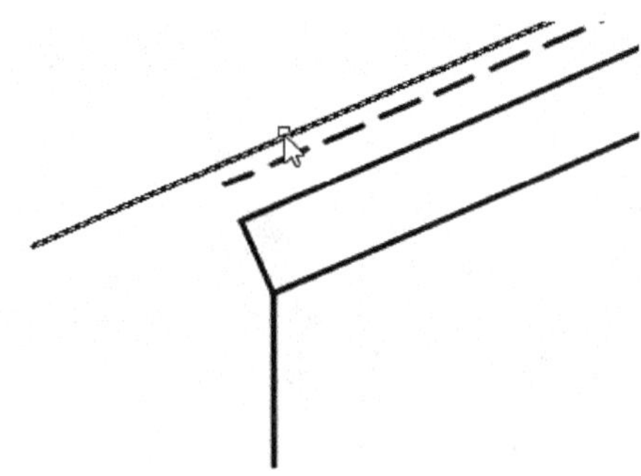

- Deactivate the ORTHOMODE icon on the status bar.
- Click the **Line** tool on the **Draw** panel of the **Home** ribbon tab.
- Select the endpoint of the inclined line, as shown.

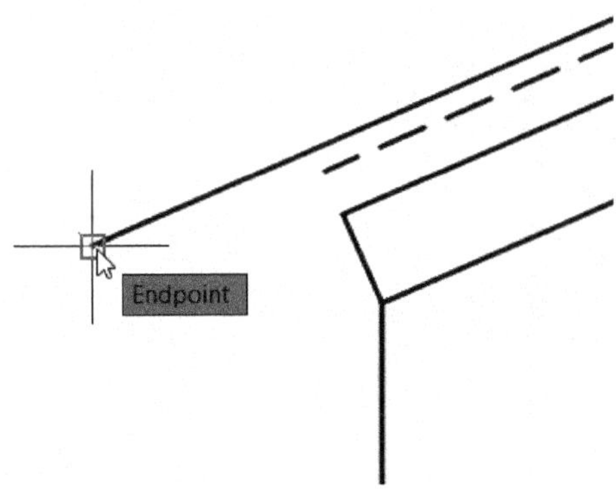

- Press and hold the SHIFT key, and then right click.
- Select the **Parallel** option from the shortcut menu.

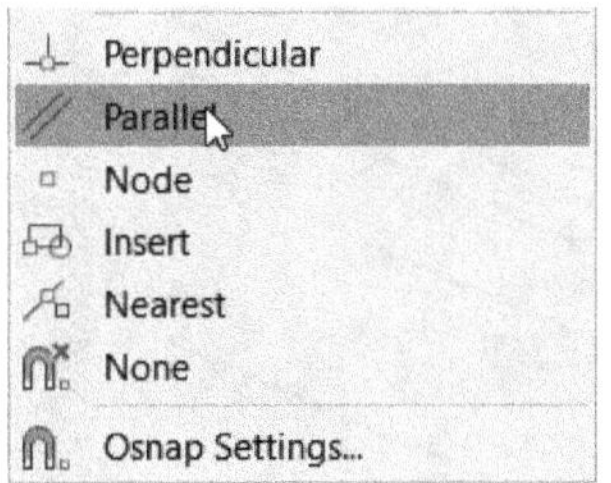

- Move the pointer and hover it on the inclined line, as shown.

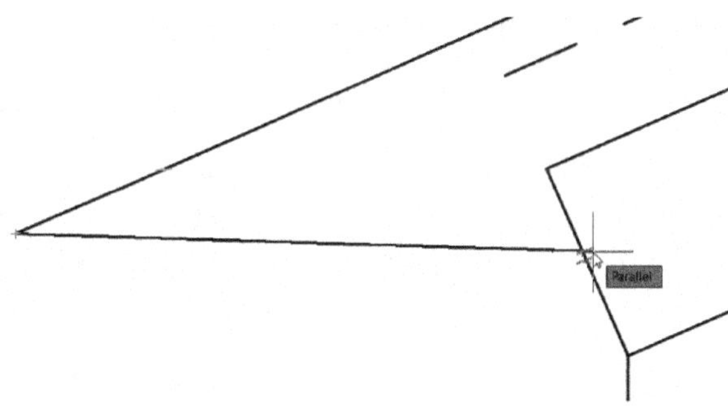

- Move the pointer inline to the start point of the line; a tracking line appears with a parallel symbol, as shown.

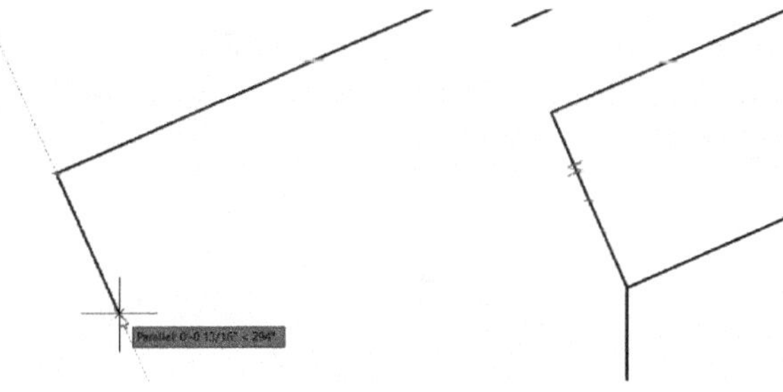

- Type 0.25 and press ENTER.
- Press and hold the SHIFT key, and then right click.
- Select the **Parallel** option from the shortcut menu.
- Move the pointer toward the right and hover the pointer on the endpoint of the hidden line; the tracking line appears from the endpoint.

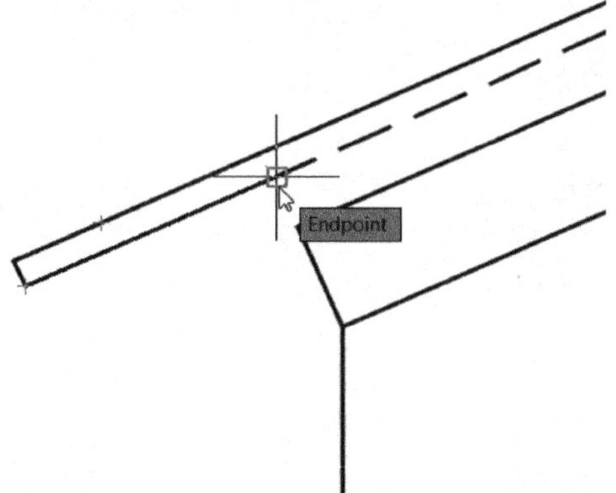

- Type 0.375, and press ENTER.

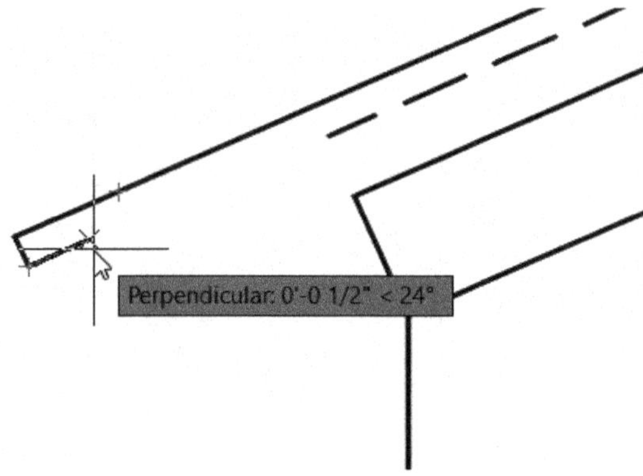

- Hover the pointer on the endpoint of the previous line and move the pointer downward; a tracking line appears from the endpoint.

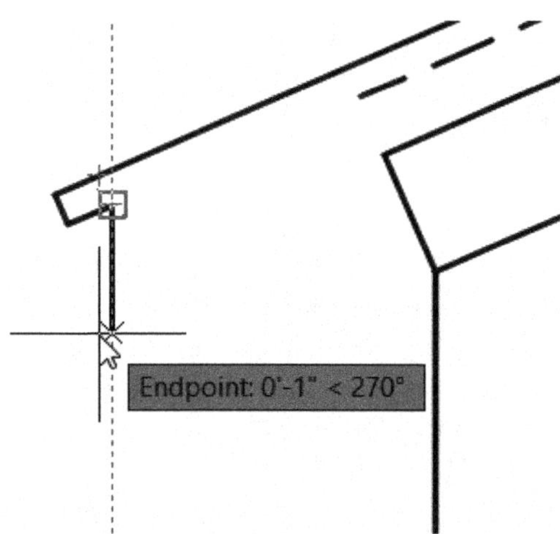

- Type 1.5 and press ENTER.
- Type @.375<225 in the command line and press ENTER.
- Press Esc.

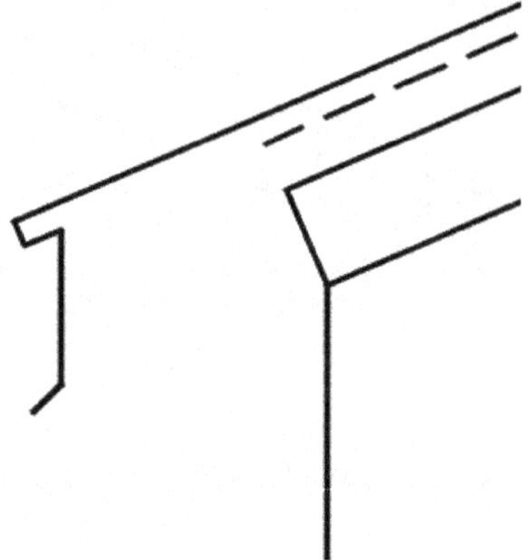

- On the **Draw** panel, click **Arc** drop-down > **Start, End, Direction**.
- Select the end points of the line, as shown.
- Press and hold the Ctrl key and select the endpoint, as shown.

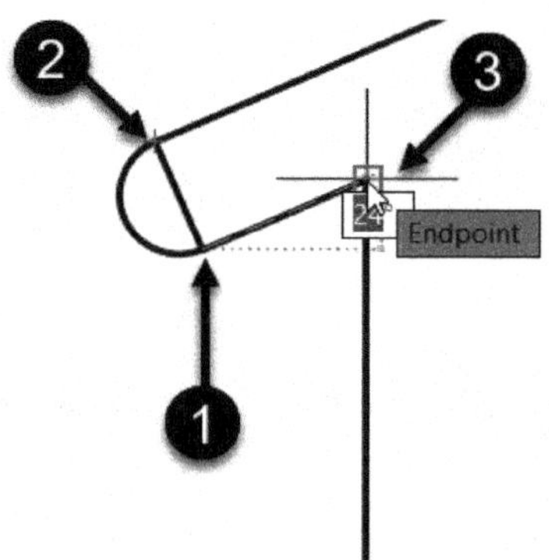

- Delete the line between the endpoints of the arc.

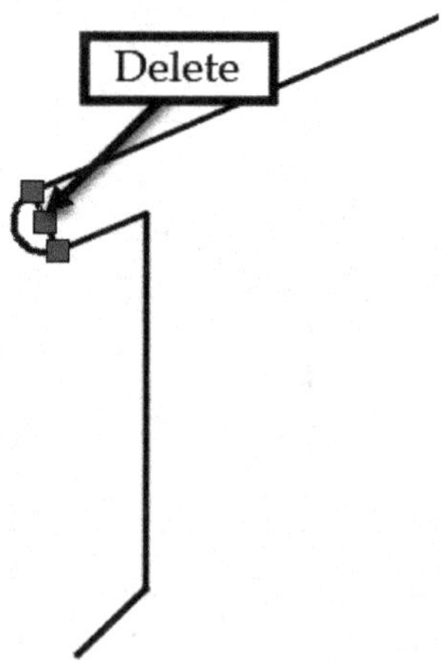

- Expand the **Modify** panel and click the **Break at point** tool.
- Select the inclined line.

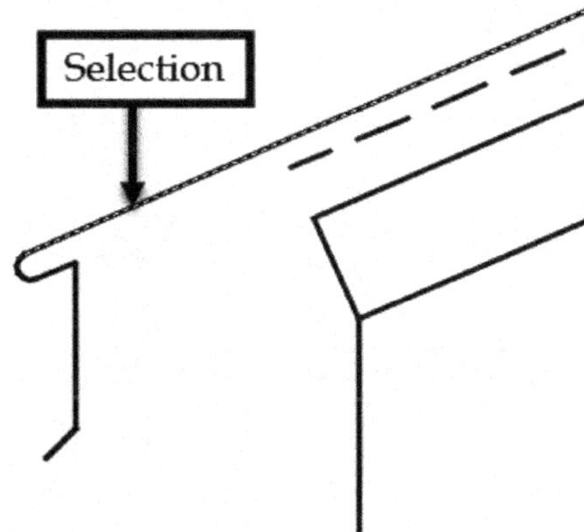

- Press and hold the SHIFT key, and then right click.
- Select the **From** option from the shortcut menu.
- Select the endpoint of the selected line.

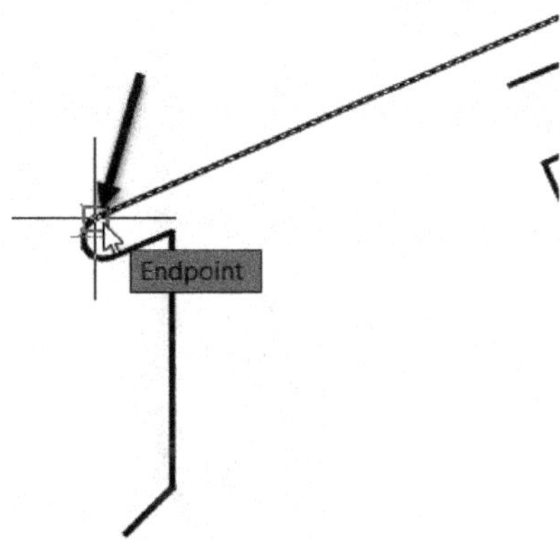

- Move the pointer on the selected line.
- Type 9 and press ENTER; the line is broken at the specified distance.
- Delete the right-side portion of the line.

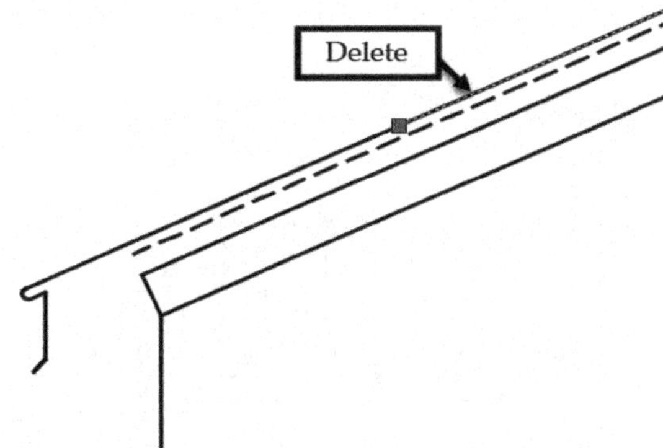

- Click the **Rectangle** tool on the **Draw** panel of the **Home** ribbon tab.
- Select the corner point, as shown.

- Select the **Dimensions** option from the command line.
- Type 1 and press ENTER.
- Type 10 and press ENTER.
- Move the pointer toward the left and click.

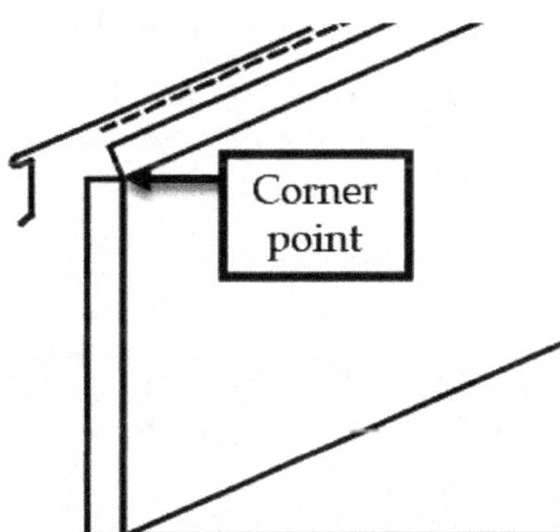

- Click the **Rectangle** tool on the **Draw** panel of the **Home** ribbon tab.
- Select the top-left corner of the rectangle, as shown.
- Select the **Dimensions** option from the command line.
- Type 1 and press ENTER.
- Type 2.5 and press ENTER.
- Move the pointer toward the left and click.

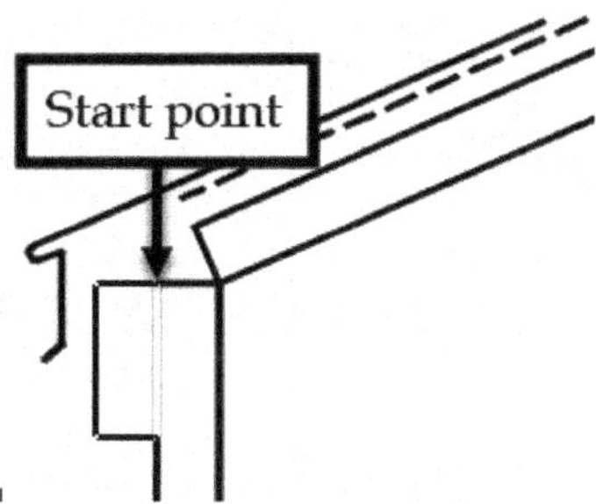

- Move the newly created rectangle downward by 0.5".

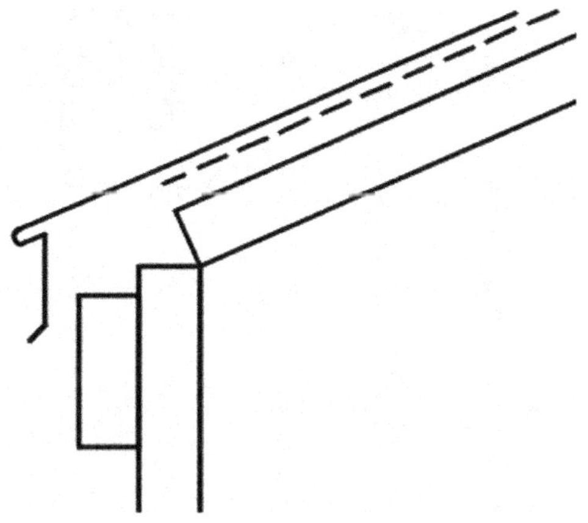

- Click the **Trim** tool on the **Modify** panel of the **Home** ribbon tab.
- Select the **cuTting edges** option from the command line.
- Select the vertical edge of the brick, as shown.
- Press ENTER.
- Click on the horizontal line on the right side.

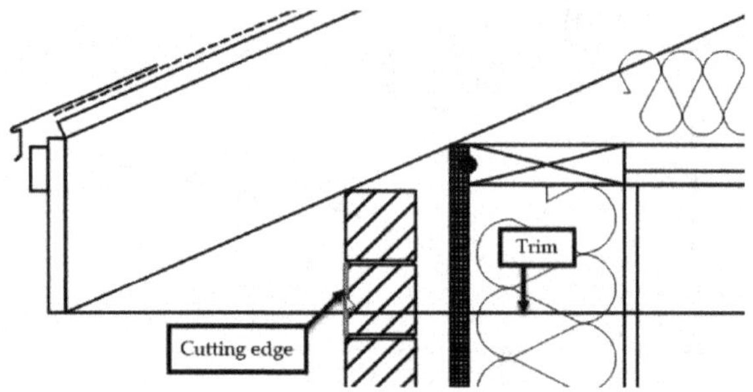

- Click the **Offset** tool on the **Modify** panel of the **Home** ribbon tab.
- Type 1 and press ENTER.
- Select the horizontal line trimmed in the last step.
- Move the pointer upward and click.

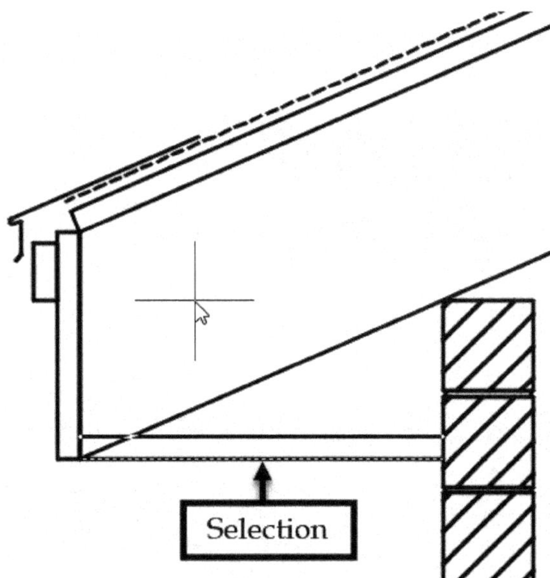

- Select the offset line.
- Move the pointer upward and click.

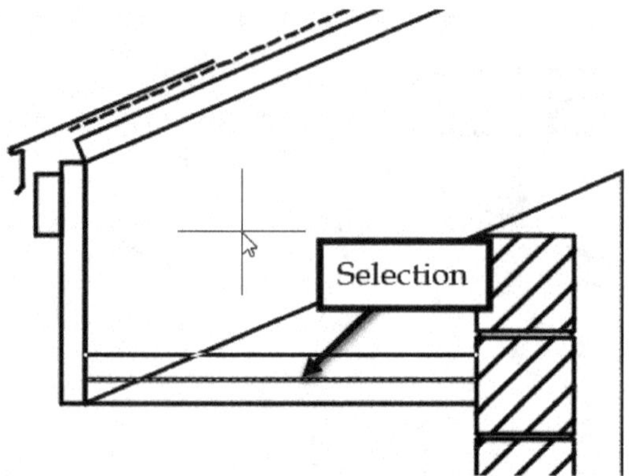

- Click the **Trim** tool on the **Modify** panel of the **Home** ribbon tab.
- Select the portions of the lines, as shown.

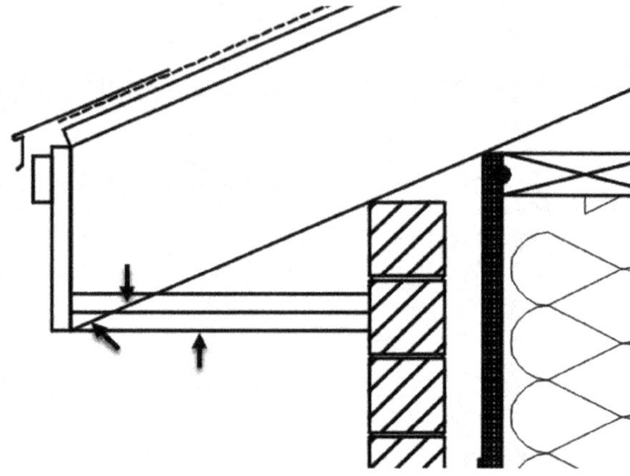

- Click the **Offset** tool on the **Modify** panel of the **Home** ribbon tab.
- Type 7 and press ENTER.
- Select the left vertical line of the veneer brick.
- Move the pointer toward the left and click.

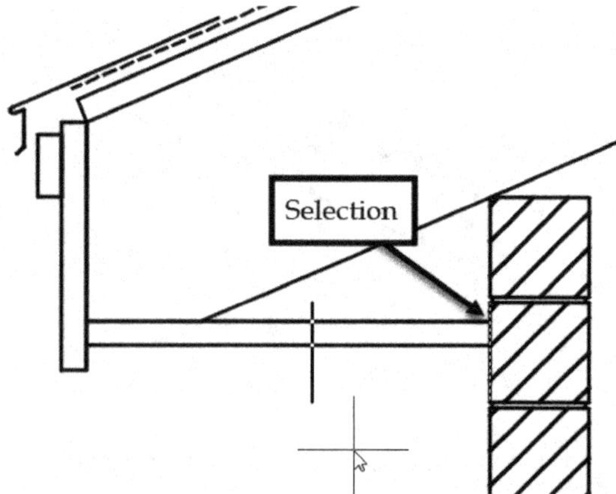

- Press ENTER twice.
- Type 4 and press ENTER.

- Select the offset line.
- Move the pointer toward the left and click.

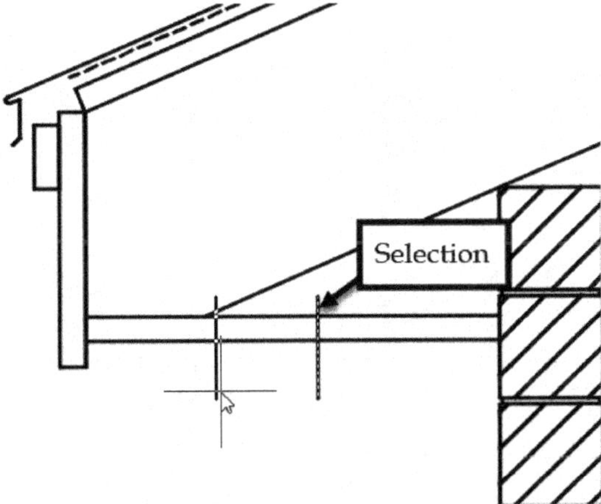

- Click the **Trim** tool on the **Modify** panel of the **Home** ribbon tab.
- Select the portions of the lines, as shown.

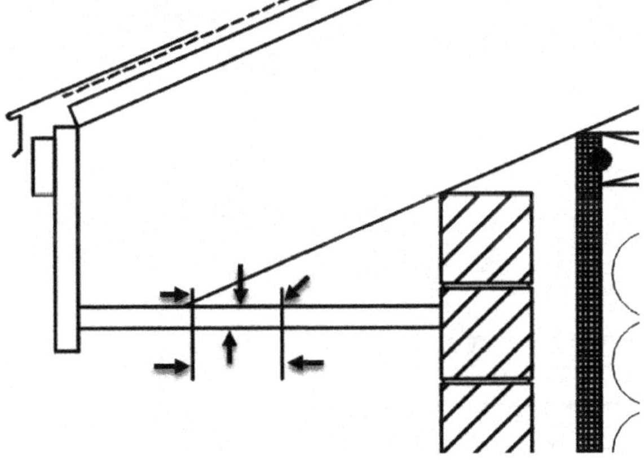

- Create a line by selecting the corner points of the opening, as shown.

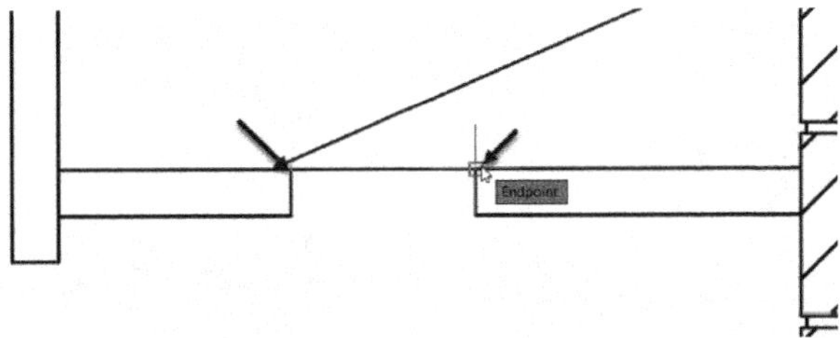

- Press ESC.
- Activate the ORTHOMODE icon on the status bar.
- Select the newly created line and click the **Scale** tool on the **Modify** panel of the **Home** ribbon tab.
- Select the midpoint.

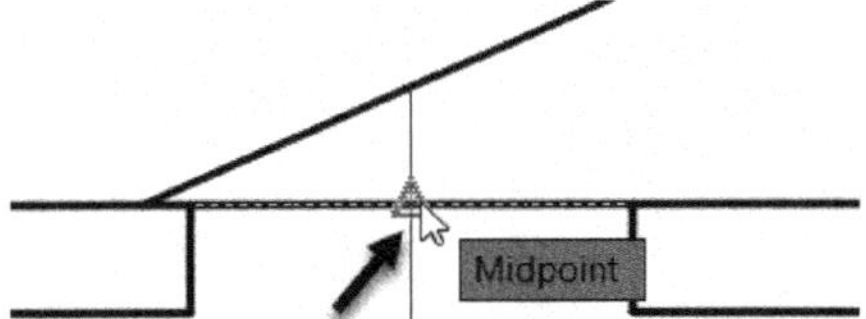

- Move the pointer vertically downward.
- Type 1.25 as the scale factor, and then press ENTER.
- Select the horizontal line and click on its midpoint grip.
- Move the pointer upward.

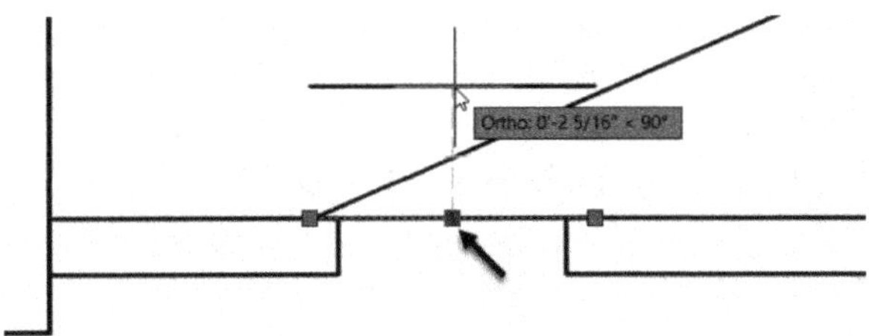

- Type 0.2 and press ENTER.
- Create an inclined line and pattern it, as shown.

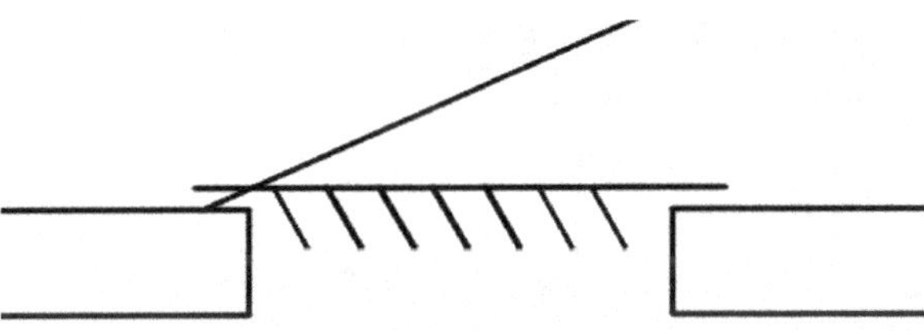

- On the **Home** tab of the ribbon, click **Draw** panel > **Hatch** drop-down > **Hatch**.
- On the **Hatch Creation** tab of the ribbon, expand the **Pattern** gallery, and select the **GOST_WOOD** pattern.

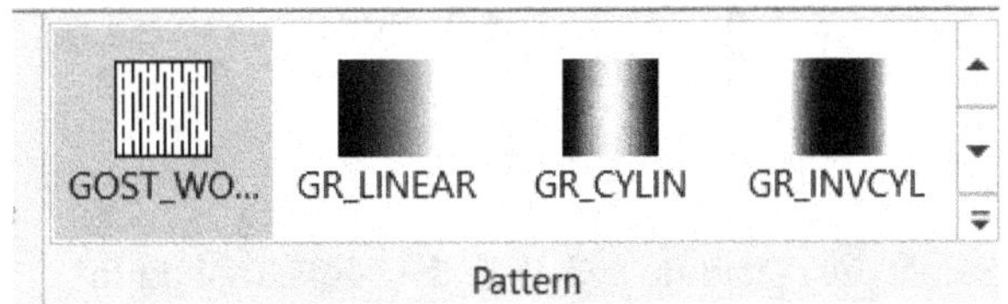

- Pick points in the areas, as shown.

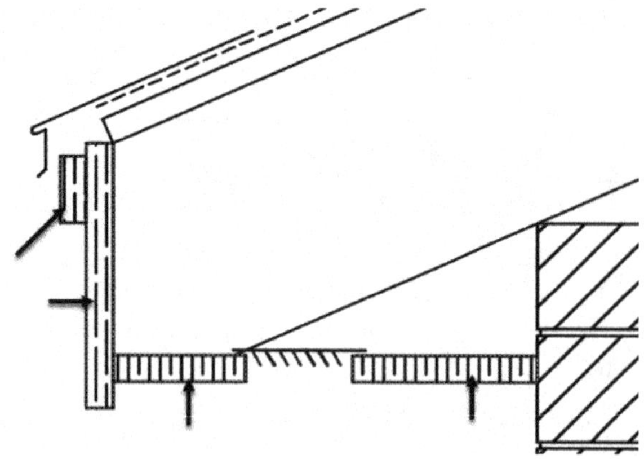

- Type 0.2 in the **Pattern Hatch Scale** box and press ENTER.
- Click the **Close Hatch Creation** icon on the ribbon.
- On the **Home** tab of the ribbon, click **Draw** panel > **Rectangle/Polygon** drop-down > **Rectangle**.
- Select the lower right corner of the rectangle, as shown.
- Select the **Dimensions** option from the command line.
- Type 6 and press ENTER.
- Type 5 and press ENTER.
- Move the pointer downward and click.

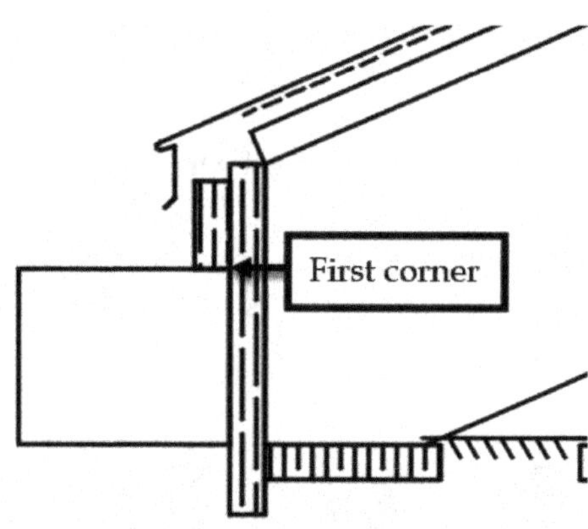

- Select the rectangle and click the **Move** tool on the **Modify** panel.
- Select the top right corner point of the rectangle.
- Move the pointer downward.
- Type 0.5 and press ENTER.
- Select the rectangle and click the **Move** tool on the **Modify** panel.
- Select the top right corner point of the rectangle.
- Move the pointer toward left.
- Type 0.25 and press ENTER.

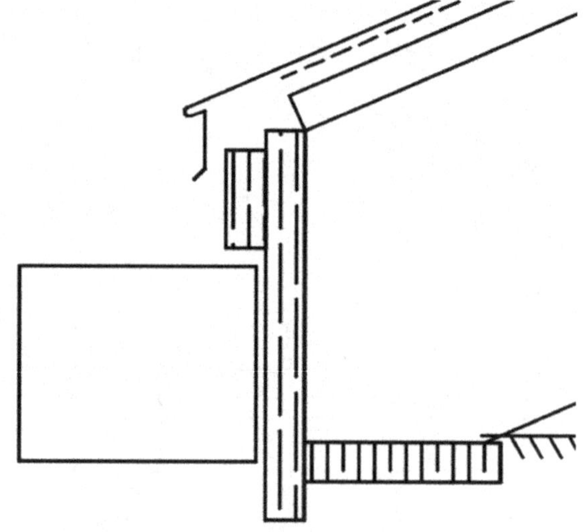

- Click **Circle** drop-down > **Center, Radius** on the **Draw** panel of the **Home** ribbon tab.
- Select the lower-left corner of the rectangle.
- Type 8 and press ENTER.

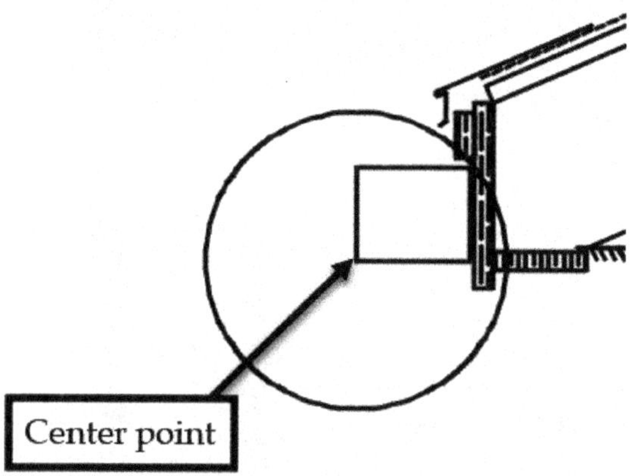

- Select the circle.
- Click on the centerpoint of the circle.
- Move the pointer toward left.
- Type 7 and press ENTER.

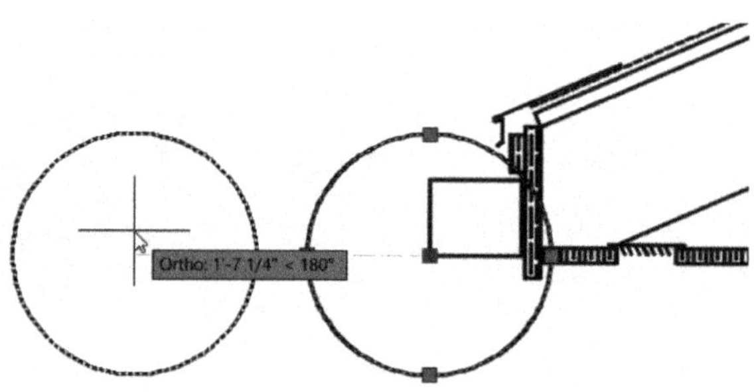

- Click the **Trim** tool on the **Modify** panel.
- Trim the edges of the circle and rectangle, as shown.

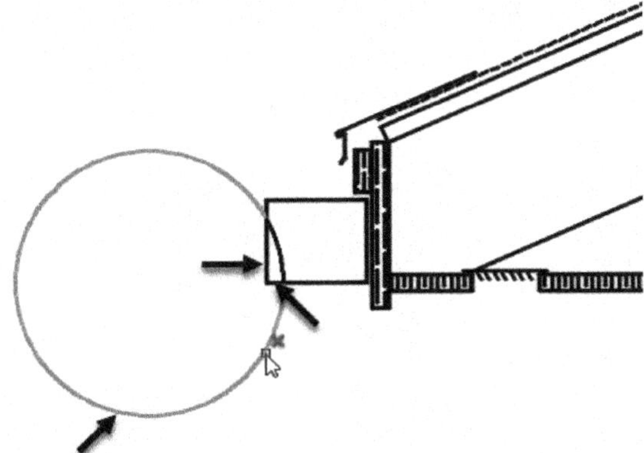

- Press ESC.
- Select the rectangle and click the **Explode** tool on the **Modify** panel.

- Press Esc.
- Click the **Offset** tool on the **Modify** panel.
- Type 1.25 and press ENTER.
- Select the offset line, as shown in the figure.
- Move the pointer upward and click.

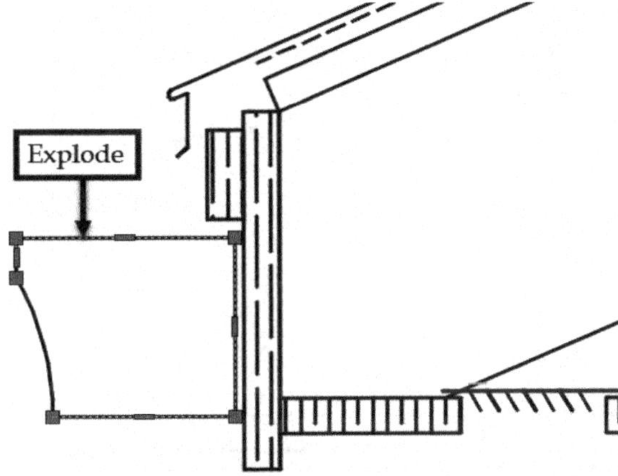

- Select the lines and arcs, as shown in the figure.

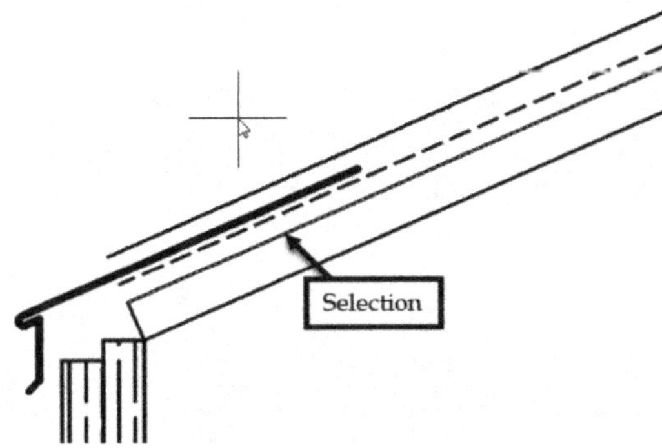

- Deactivate the ORTHOMODE icon on the Status bar.
- Click the **Line** tool on the **Draw** panel.
- Select the endpoint of the offset line.
- Press and hold the SHIFT key and right click.
- Select the **Parallel** option from the shortcut menu.
- Hover the pointer on the line, as shown.

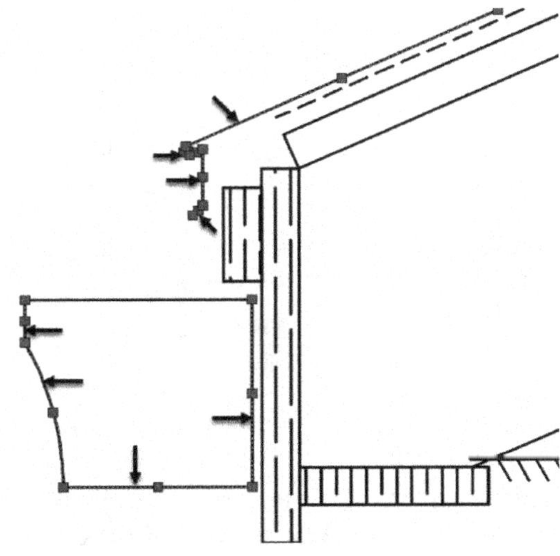

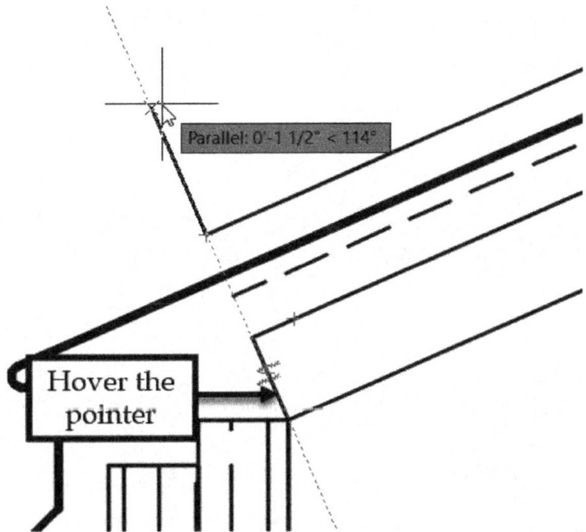

- On the **Home** ribbon tab, click the **Lineweight** drop-down on the **Properties** panel, and then select 0.70.

- Move the pointer along the tracking line.
- Type 2 and press ENTER.
- Type @7<20 and press ENTER.

- Press Esc.

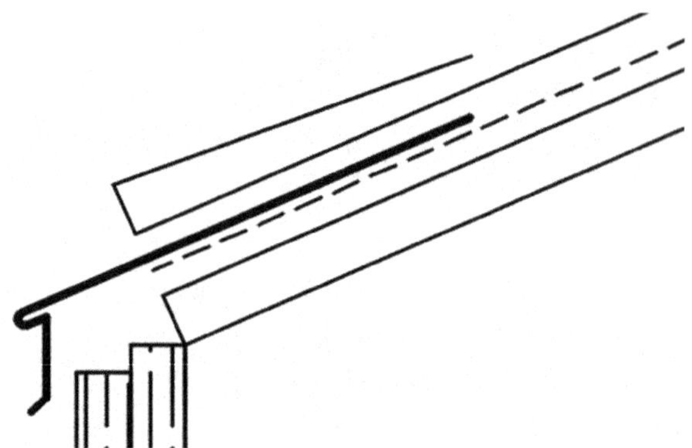

- Select the two newly created lines.
- Click the **Array** drop-down > **Path Array** tool on the **Modify** panel.
- Select the inclined line, as shown.

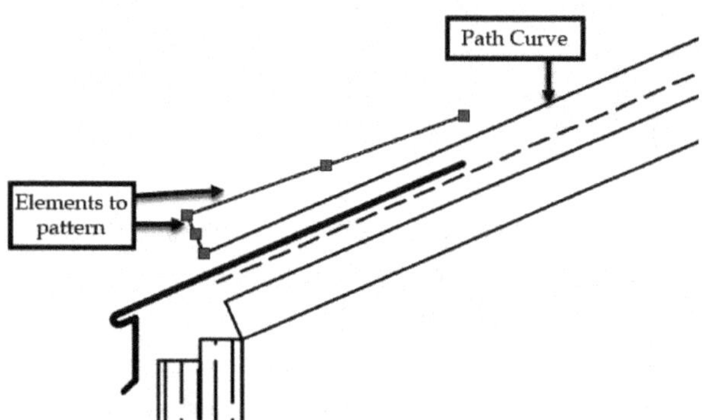

- Type 7 in the **Between** box on the **Items** panel.

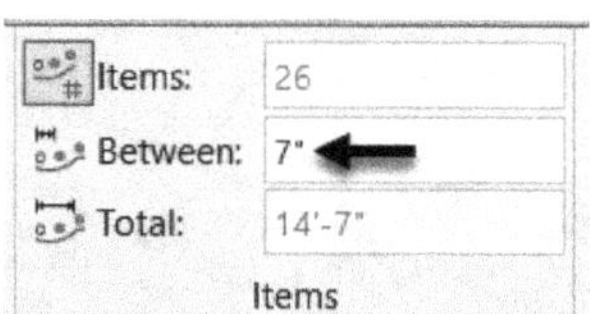

- Click **Close Array** on the ribbon.

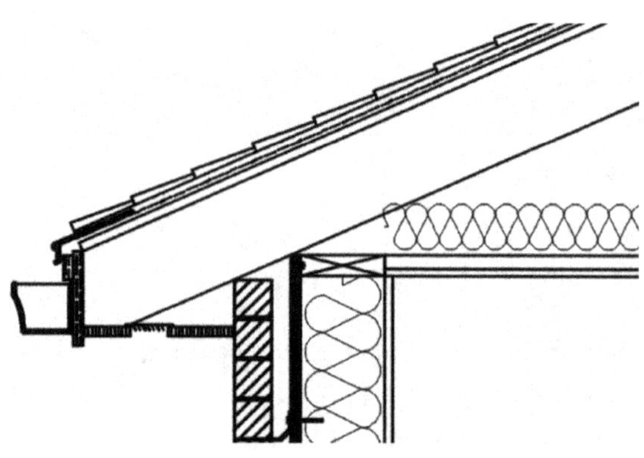

Adding Annotations

- On the **Home** ribbon tab, click **Leader** drop-down > **Leader** on the **Annotation** panel.

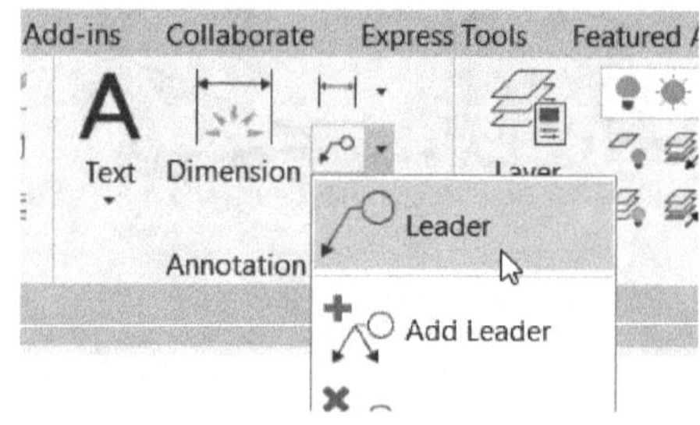

- Deactivate the **ORTHOMODE** icon on the status bar.
- Specify the start point of the leader on the insulation, as shown.
- Move the pointer diagonally toward the bottom right corner, and then click.
- Type **Insulation** and click in the graphics area.

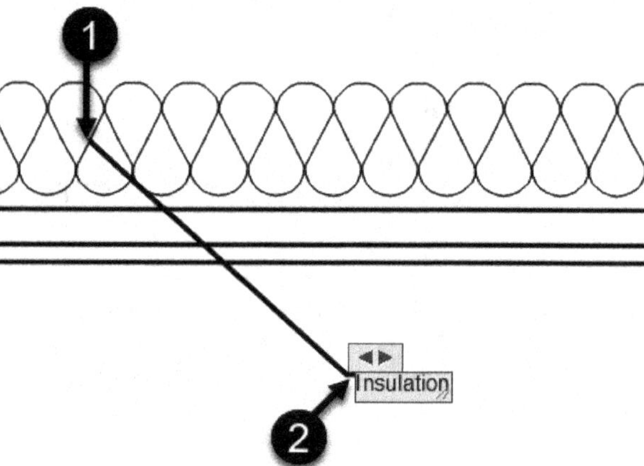

- Select the leader and click the **Properties** icon on the **Properties** panel of the **Home** ribbon tab.

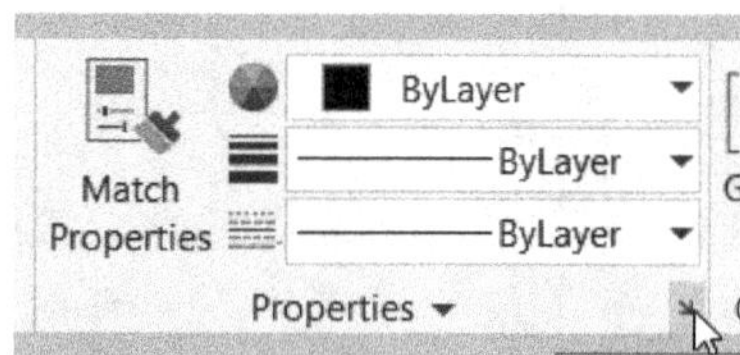

- On the **Properties** palette, scroll to the **Leaders** section and enter 2 in the **Arrowhead size** and **Landing distance** boxes, respectively.

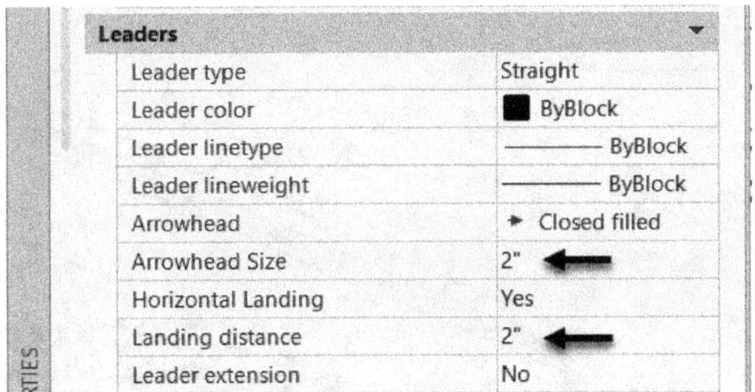

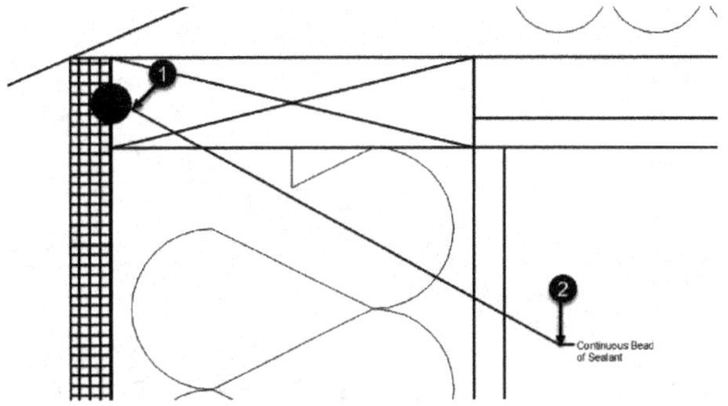

- Scroll to the **Text** section, and then enter **2** and **1** in the **Height** and **Landing gap** boxes, respectively.

- Click the **Match Properties** tool on the **Properties** panel.

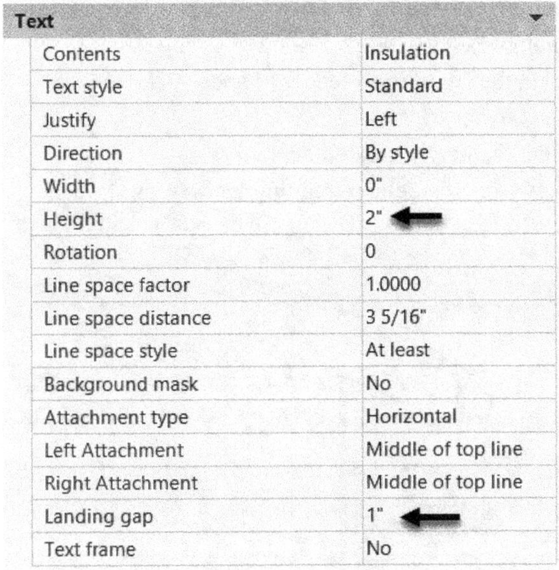

- Select the **Insulation** leader to specify the source object.

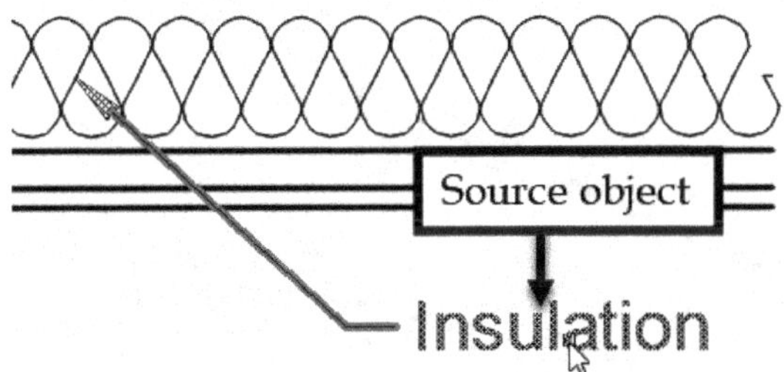

- Select the newly created leader; the properties of the source object are matched with the destination object.

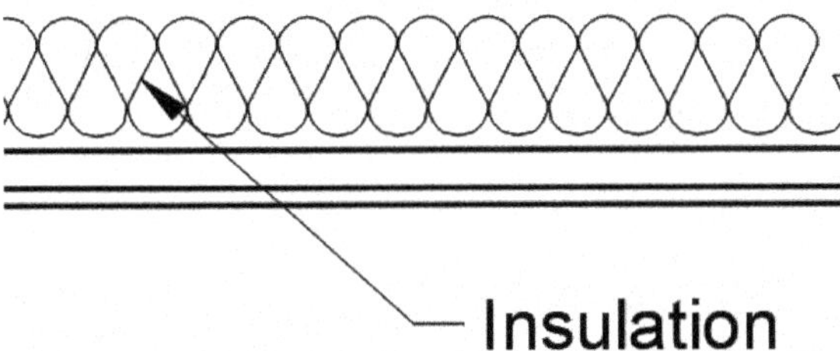

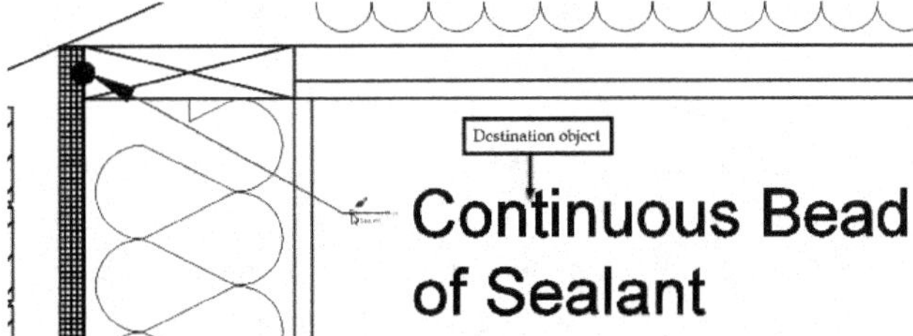

- On the **Home** ribbon tab, click **Leader** drop-down > **Leader** on the **Annotation** panel.
- Specify the start point of the leader on the donut, as shown.
- Move the pointer diagonally toward the bottom right corner, and then click.
- Type Continuous Bead of Sealant and click in the graphics area.

- On the ribbon, click **Annotate > Text > Multiline Text**.
- Click at the location, as shown.

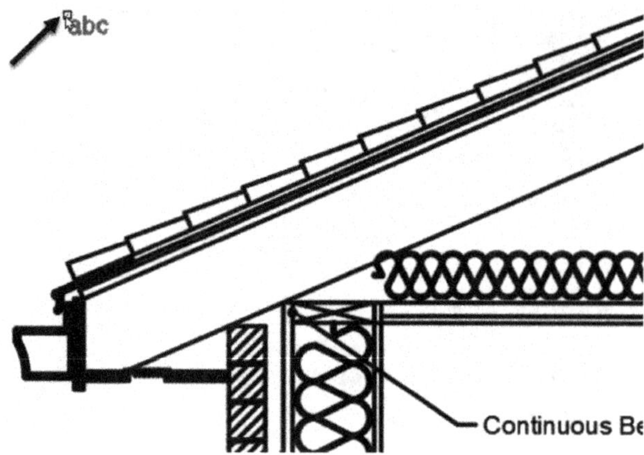

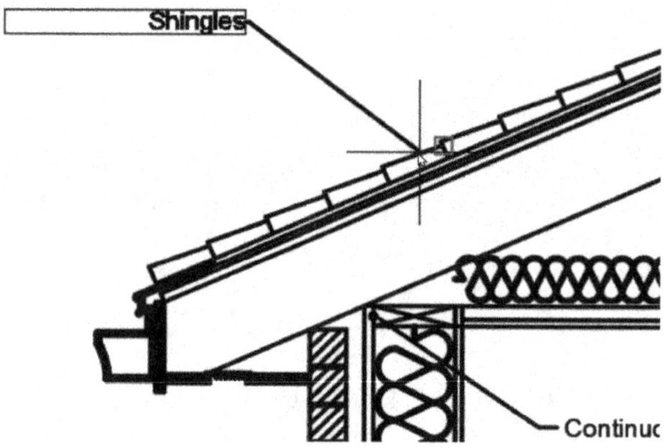

- Select the **Height** option from the command line.
- Type 2" and press ENTER.
- Specify the second corner of the text box, as shown.

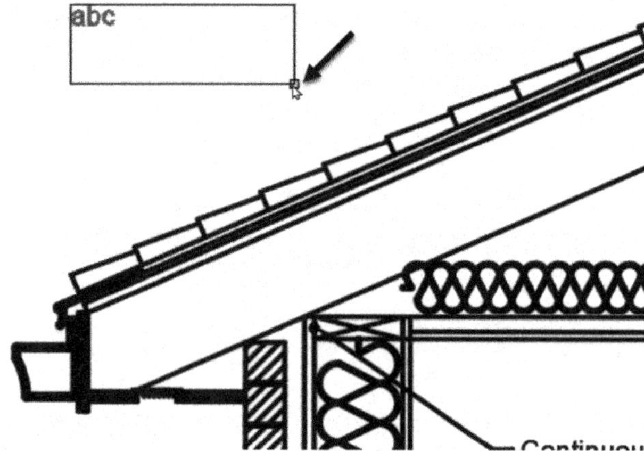

- Click the **Match Properties** tool on the **Properties** panel.
- Select the **Insulation** leader to specify the source object.
- Select the newly created leader.
- Likewise, create the remaining leaders, as shown.

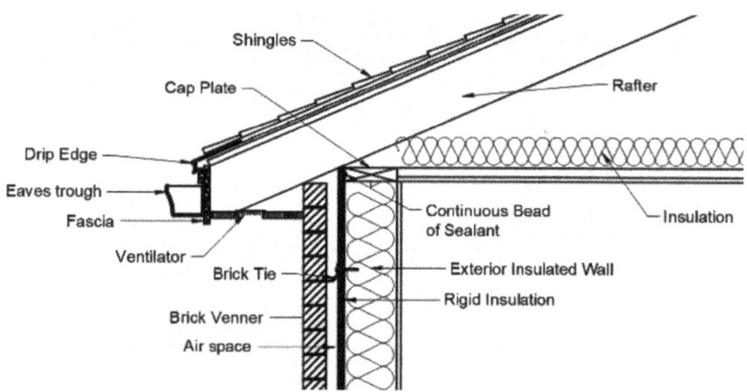

- Type **Shingles** and click in graphics window.
- On the ribbon, click **Annotate > Leaders > Multileader**.
- Select the **select Mtext** option from the command line.
- Select the multiline text from the graphics window.
- Select a point from anyone of the shingles.

- Activate the **ORTHOMODE** icon on the status bar.
- On the ribbon, click the **Express Tools** tab > **Draw > Break-line Symbol**.

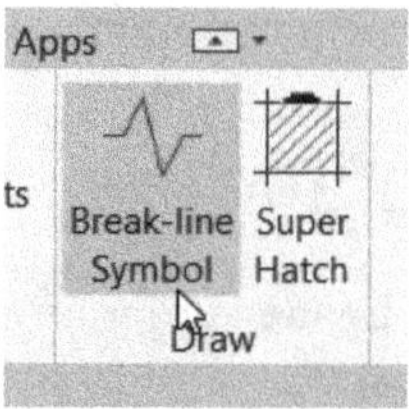

- Select the **Size** option from the command line.
- Type **8** and press ENTER.
- Zoom to the bottom portion and specify the start and endpoints of the break line.

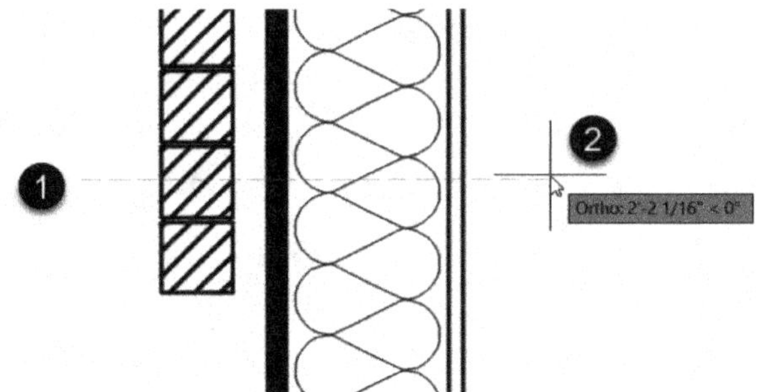

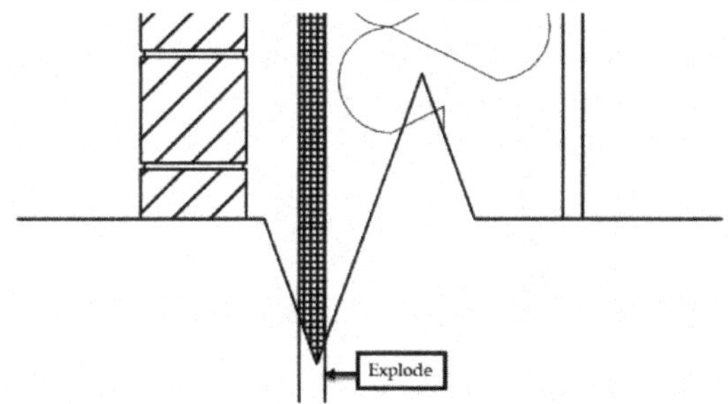

- Select the midpoint of the break line; the break line symbol is placed.

- Trim the vertical lines.

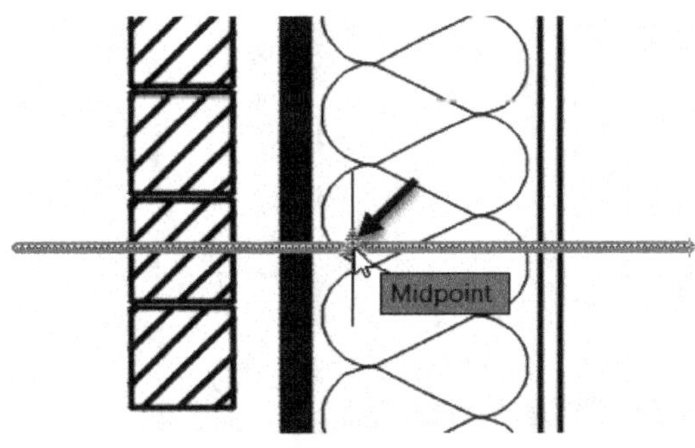

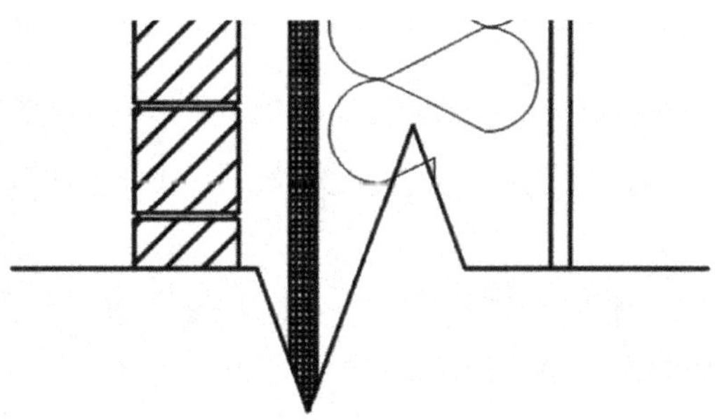

- On the **Home** ribbon tab, click **Trim** drop-down > **Trim** on the **Modify** panel.
- Select the **cuTting edges** option from the command line.
- Select the break line and press ENTER.

- Likewise, create the break lines and trim the elements, as shown.

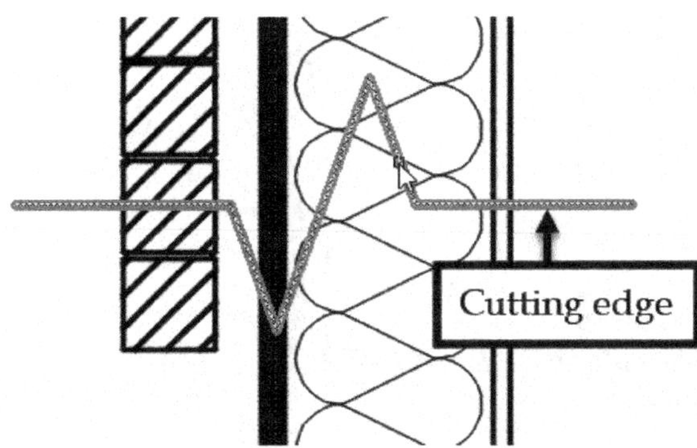

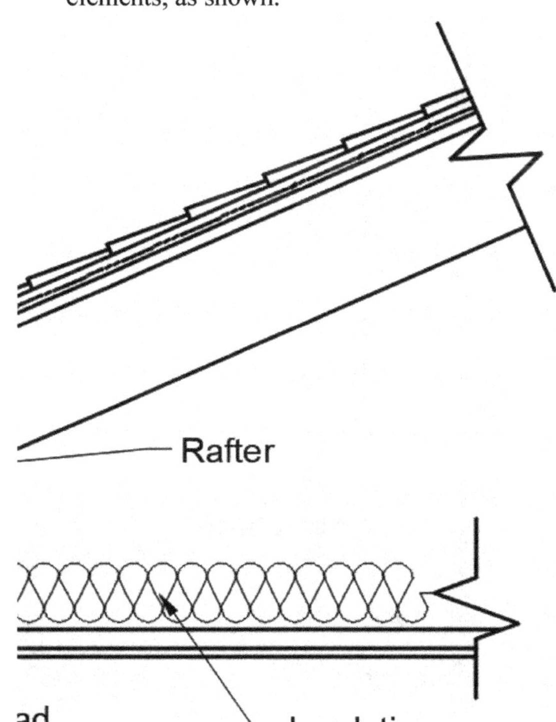

- Trim the elements on the bottom side of the drawing.
- Select the region below the break line and click the **Explode** tool on the **Modify** panel of the **Home** ribbon tab.

- Save and close the drawing file.

Exercise

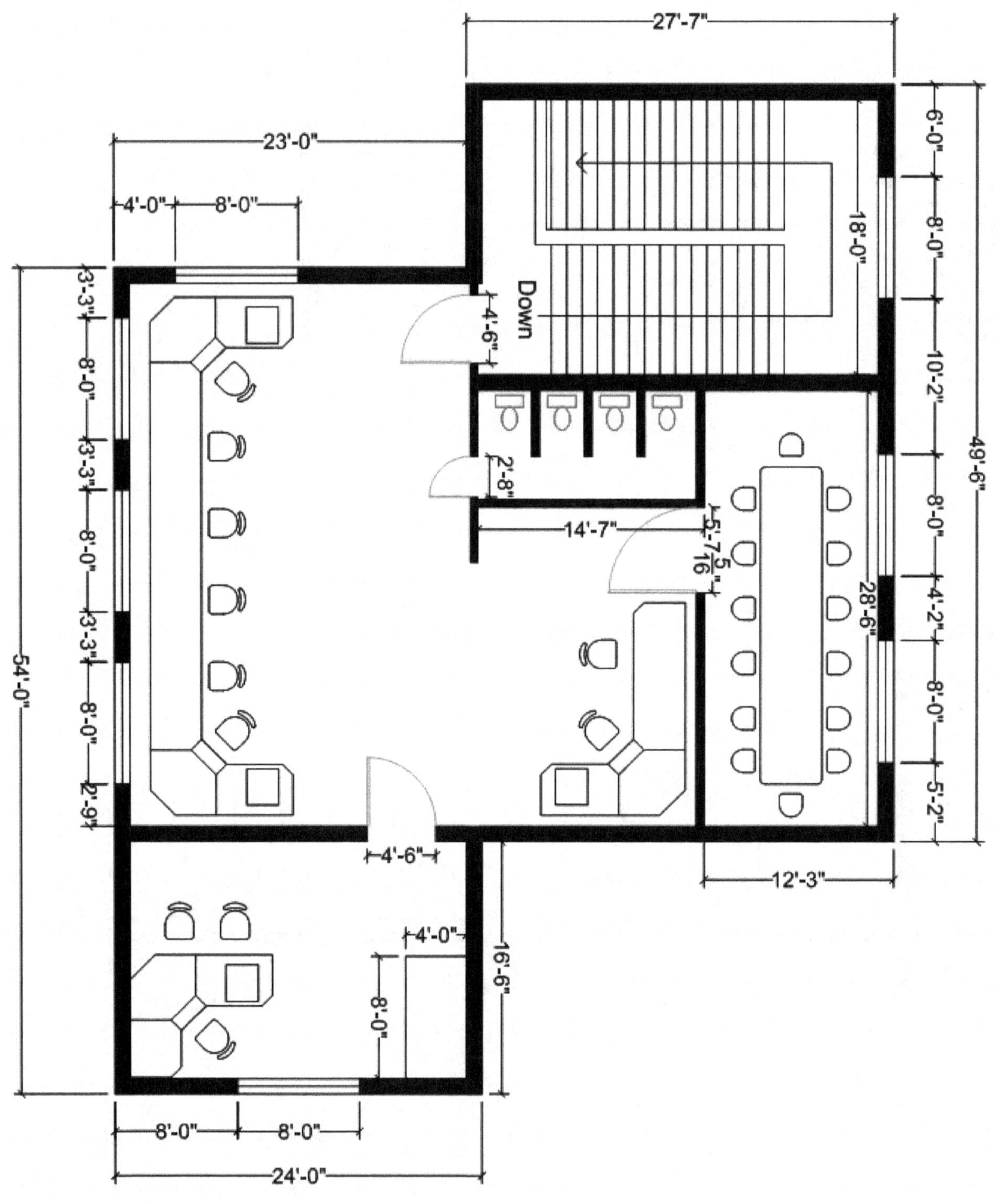

Index

www.ingramcontent.com/pod-product-compliance
Lightning Source LLC
LaVergne TN
LVHW080506200726
843507LV00008B/1042